T0224346

Lecture Notes in Computer Science　10175

Commenced Publication in 1973
Founding and Former Series Editors:
Gerhard Goos, Juris Hartmanis, and Jan van Leeuwen

More information about this series at http://www.springer.com/series/7410

Serge Fehr (Ed.)

Public-Key Cryptography – PKC 2017

20th IACR International Conference
on Practice and Theory in Public-Key Cryptography
Amsterdam, The Netherlands, March 28–31, 2017
Proceedings, Part II

 Springer

Editor
Serge Fehr
CWI
Amsterdam
The Netherlands

ISSN 0302-9743   ISSN 1611-3349 (electronic)
Lecture Notes in Computer Science
ISBN 978-3-662-54387-0   ISBN 978-3-662-54388-7 (eBook)
DOI 10.1007/978-3-662-54388-7

Library of Congress Control Number: 2017932641

LNCS Sublibrary: SL4 – Security and Cryptology

Printed on acid-free paper

This Springer imprint is published by Springer Nature
The registered company is Springer-Verlag GmbH Germany
The registered company address is: Heidelberger Platz 3, 14197 Berlin, Germany

Preface

The 20th IACR International Conference on Practice and Theory of Public-Key Cryptography (PKC 2017) was held March 28–31, 2017, in Amsterdam, The Netherlands. The conference is sponsored by the International Association for Cryptologic Research (IACR) and has an explicit focus on public-key cryptography.

These proceedings, consisting of two volumes, feature 36 papers; these were selected by the Program Committee from 160 qualified submissions. Each submission was reviewed independently by at least three reviewers, or four in the case of Program Committee member submissions. Following the initial reviewing phase, the submissions and their reviews were discussed over a period of one month, before final decisions were then made. During this discussion phase, the Program Committee made substantial use of a newer feature of the submission/review software, which allows direct yet anonymous communication between the Program Committee and the authors; I think this interaction proved very useful in resolving pending issues and questions.

The reviewing and selection process was an intensive and time-consuming task, and I thank the members of the Program Committee, along with the external reviewers, for all their hard work and their excellent job. I also want to acknowledge Shai Halevi for his awesome submission/review software, which tremendously simplifies the program chair's work, and I thank him for his 24/7 and always-prompt assistance.

The conference program also included two invited talks, one by Vipul Goyal on "Recent Advances in Non-Malleable Cryptography," and the other by Kenny Paterson on "The Evolution of Public Key Cryptography in SSL/TLS." I would like to thank the two invited speakers as well as all the other speakers for their contributions to the program.

I also want to thank all the authors who submitted papers; you made it very challenging for the Program Committee to decide on what should be "the best" submissions — which of course is very much a matter of taste and perspective. I know that having good papers rejected because of a tough competition, and because there is always some amount of randomness involved, is disappointing, but I am optimistic that these "unlucky" papers will find their place and get the deserved recognition.

Last but not least, I would like to thank Marc Stevens, the general chair, for setting up a great conference and ensuring a smooth running of the event, and Ronald Cramer for his advisory support and allowing me to tap into his experience.

January 2017   Serge Fehr

PKC 2017

The 20th International Conference on Practice and Theory of Public-Key Cryptography

Amsterdam, The Netherlands
March 28–31, 2017

Sponsored by the
International Association of Cryptologic Research

General Chair

Marc Stevens   CWI Amsterdam, The Netherlands

Program Chair

Serge Fehr   CWI Amsterdam, The Netherlands

Program Committee

Masayuki Abe   NTT Secure Platform Labs, Japan
Fabrice Benhamouda   IBM Research, USA
Nir Bitansky   MIT, USA
Zvika Brakerski   Weizmann Institute of Science, Israel
Nishanth Chandran   Microsoft Research, India
Dana Dachman-Soled   University of Maryland, USA
Nico Döttling   UC Berkeley, USA
Léo Ducas   CWI Amsterdam, The Netherlands
Sebastian Faust   Ruhr-University Bochum, Germany
Dario Fiore   IMDEA Software Institute, Spain
Pierre-Alain Fouque   Rennes 1 University, France
Georg Fuchsbauer   ENS, France
Sanjam Garg   UC Berkeley, USA
Jens Groth   University College London, UK
Carmit Hazay   Bar-Ilan University, Israel
Dennis Hofheinz   KIT, Germany
Tibor Jager   Paderborn University, Germany
Abhishek Jain   Johns Hopkins University, USA
Marcel Keller   University of Bristol, UK
Markulf Kohlweiss   Microsoft Research, UK
Vadim Lyubashevsky   IBM Research Zurich, Switzerland

Takahiro Matsuda	AIST, Japan
Adam O'Neill	Georgetown University, USA
Arpita Patra	Indian Institute of Science, India
Ludovic Perret	Sorbonnes University, UPMC/Inria/CNRS, France
Christophe Petit	University of Oxford, UK
Vanishree Rao	PARC, USA
Alessandra Scafuro	North Carolina State University, USA
Gil Segev	Hebrew University of Jerusalem, Israel
Fang Song	Portland State University, USA
Daniele Venturi	Sapienza University of Rome, Italy
Ivan Visconti	University of Salerno, Italy
Hoeteck Wee	ENS, France
Vassilis Zikas	Rensselaer Polytechnic Institute, USA

External Reviewers

Hamza Abusalah	Mahdi Cheraghchi	Kristina Hostakova
Shashank Agrawal	Céline Chevalier	Vincenzo Iovino
Tristan Allard	Seung Geol Choi	Malika Izabachène
Miguel Ambrona	Arka Rai Choudhary	Sune Jakobsen
Daniel Apon	Kai-Min Chung	Marc Joye
Diego F. Aranha	Aloni Cohen	Charanjit Jutla
Nuttapong Attrapadung	Sandro Coretti	Ali El Kaafarani
Christian Badertscher	Véronique Cortier	Bhavana Kanukurthi
Saikrishna Badrinarayanan	Anamaria Costache	Koray Karabina
Shi Bai	Geoffroy Couteau	Aniket Kate
Foteini Baldimtsi	Lisa Eckey	Dakshita Khurana
Marshall Ball	Antonio Faonio	Eike Kiltz
Carsten Baum	Luca di Feo	Taechan Kim
David Bernhard	Tore Kasper Frederiksen	Elena Kirshanova
Silvio Biagioni	Tommaso Gagliardoni	Fuyuki Kitagawa
Jean-Francois Biasse	Steven Galbraith	Yutaro Kiyomura
Olivier Blazy	David Galindo	Susumu Kiyoshima
Jonathan Bootle	Pierrick Gaudry	Lisa Kohl
Joppe Bos	Romain Gay	Ilan Komargodski
Cecilia Boschini	Marilyn George	Yashvanth Kondi
Florian Bourse	Essam Ghadafi	Venkata Koppula
Elette Boyle	Junqing Gong	Luke Kowalczyk
Chris Brzuska	Aurore Guillevic	Juliane Krämer
Angelo De Caro	Felix Günther	Mukul Kulkarni
Wouter Castryck	Ryo Hiromasa	Thijs Laarhoven
Dario Catalano	Mohammad Hajiabadi	Sebastian Lauer
Andrea Cerulli	Yoshikazu Hanatani	Moon Sung Lee
Pyrros Chaidos	Ethan Heilman	Tancrède Lepoint
Jie Chen	Justin Holmgren	Qinyi Li

Benoît Libert
Satyanarayana Lokam
Patrick Longa
Steve Lu
Yun Lu
Bernardo Magri
Mary Maller
Alex Malozemoff
Antonio Marcedone
Giorgia Azzurra Marson
Daniel Masny
Nicolas Meloni
Peihan Miao
Giacomo Micheli
Michele Minelli
Ameer Mohammed
Pratyay Mukherjee
Debdeep Mukhopadhyay
Patrick Märtens
Pierrick Méaux
Michael Naehrig
Gregory Neven
Anca Nitulescu
Luca Nizzardo
Ariel Nof
Koji Nuida
Maciej Obremski
Miyako Ohkubo
Cristina Onete
Michele Orrù
Daniel Page
Jiaxin Pan

Dimitris Papadopoulos
Sunoo Park
Anat Paskin-Cherniavsky
Alain Passelègue
Valerio Pastro
Cécile Pierrot
Rafael del Pino
Rachel Player
Oxana Poburinnaya
David Pointcheval
Antigoni Polychroniadou
Manoj Prabhakaran
Benjamin Pring
Srinivasan Raghuraman
Joost Renes
Răzvan Roşie
Dragos Rotaru
Tim Ruffing
Akshayaram Srinivasan
Yusuke Sakai
Kazuo Sakiyama
John M. Schanck
Benedikt Schmidt
Peter Scholl
Jacob Schuldt
Peter Schwabe
Sven Schäge
Ido Shahaf
Igor Shparlinski
Shashank Singh
Luisa Siniscalchi
Ben Smith

Douglas Stebila
Kim Taechan
Atsushi Takayasu
Vanessa Teague
Adrien Thillard
Aishwarya
  Thiruvengadam
Yan Bo Ti
Mehdi Tibouchi
Junichi Tomida
Daniel Tschudi
Dominique Unruh
Alexander Ushakov
Satyanarayana Vusirikala
Xiao Wang
Yohei Watanabe
Avi Weinstock
Mor Weiss
David Wu
Keita Xagawa
Shota Yamada
Takashi Yamakawa
Avishay Yanai
Eylon Yogev
Kazuki Yoneyama
Yang Yu
Mark Zhandry
Jean Karim Zinzindohoué
Michael Zohner

Contents – Part II

Real-World Schemes

Multiparty Computation

Primitives

Contents – Part I

Encryption with Access Control

Dual System Framework in Multilinear Settings and Applications to Fully Secure (Compact) ABE for Unbounded-Size Circuits

Nuttapong Attrapadung[⊠]

National Institute of Advanced Industrial Science and Technology (AIST), Tokyo, Japan
n.attrapadung@aist.go.jp

Abstract. We propose a new generic framework for constructing fully secure attribute based encryption (ABE) in *multilinear* settings. It is applicable in a generic manner to *any predicates*. Previous generic frameworks of this kind are given only in *bilinear* group settings, where applicable predicate classes are limited. Our framework provides an abstraction of dual system paradigms over composite-order graded multilinear encoding schemes in a black-box manner.

As applications, we propose new fully secure ABE systems for general predicates, namely, ABE for circuits. We obtain two schemes for each of key-policy (KP) and ciphertext-policy (CP) variants of ABE. All of our four fully secure schemes can deal with *unbounded-size* circuits, while enjoy *succinctness*, meaning that the key and ciphertext sizes are (less than or) proportional to corresponding circuit sizes. In the CP-ABE case, no scheme ever achieves such properties, even when considering selectively secure systems. Furthermore, our second KP-ABE achieves *constant-size ciphertexts*, whereas our second CP-ABE achieves *constant-size keys*. Previous ABE systems for circuits are either selectively secure (Gorbunov *et al.* STOC'13, Garg *et al.* Crypto'13, and subsequent works), or semi-adaptively secure (Brakerski and Vaikuntanathan Crypto'16), or fully-secure but not succinct and restricted to bounded-size circuits (Garg *et al.* ePrint 2014/622, and Garg *et al.* TCC'16-A).

Keywords: Attribute-based encryption · Full security · Multilinear maps · Dual system · Pair encodings · Circuits

1 Introduction

Attribute-based encryption (ABE), introduced by Sahai and Waters [44], is a new paradigm that generalizes traditional public key encryption. Instead of encrypting to a target recipient, a sender can specify in a more general way about who should be able to view the message. In ABE for predicate $R : \mathbb{X} \times \mathbb{Y} \to \{0,1\}$,

---

This paper subsumes [4]. The full version is available at [6].

© International Association for Cryptologic Research 2017
S. Fehr (Ed.): PKC 2017, Part II, LNCS 10175, pp. 3–35, 2017.
DOI: 10.1007/978-3-662-54388-7_1

a ciphertext encrypting message M is associated with a ciphertext attribute, say, $Y \in \mathbb{Y}$, while a secret key, issued by an authority, is associated with a key attribute, say, $X \in \mathbb{X}$, and the decryption will succeed if and only if $R(X, Y) = 1$. From an application point of view, it is instructive to consider one kind of attributes as *policies*, which are Boolean functions, and the other kind as inputs to functions. In this sense, there are two variants of ABE. In Key-Policy (KP) type [33], $\mathbb{X}$ is a set of Boolean functions, while $\mathbb{Y}$ is a set of inputs to functions, and we define $R(f, x) = f(x)$. In Ciphertext-Policy (CP) type [10], the roles of $\mathbb{X}$ and $\mathbb{Y}$ are swapped (that is, ciphertexts are associated with policies).

A central theme to ABE has been to expand the class of allowable boolean functions. Until recently, there were only ABE for simple classes such as boolean formulae [10,33,37,40] and inner product predicate [7,34,41]. Only recently, ABE systems that allow any unbounded polynomial-size circuits (but bounded-depth) were proposed independently by Garg et al. (GGHSW) [24] and Gorbunov et al. (GVW) [31]. The former is based on multi-linear maps (more precisely, graded encoding systems) [20,23], while the latter is based on the Learning-With-Error assumption. They proposed key-policy variants, and by using universal circuits, ciphertext-policy systems can also be obtained albeit for only bounded-size circuits. Subsequently, Garg et al. [28] proposed ABE for circuits based on witness encryption. Boneh et al. [13] (BGG+) proposed KP-ABE for circuits with short keys or short ciphertexts.

Full vs Selective Security. The standard security for ABE is *adaptive security*, or often called *full security*. However, previous ABE systems for circuits [13, 24,28,31] were proved only in a weaker model called *selective security*. Such a notion requires the adversary to announce a target ciphertext attribute Y^* upfront before seeing the public key, after then, he can ask for secret keys of X such that $R(X, Y^*) = 0$. Contrastingly, full security allows the adversary to adaptively ask for secret keys and choose a target in any order.

Complexity Leveraging. There is a trivial method to generically bootstrap selective security to full security called *complexity leveraging* [12]. In this approach, the security reduction would incur a loss factor $|\mathbb{Y}|$ (stemmed from the probability of guessing Y^* from the ciphertext attribute domain $\mathbb{Y}$). In KP-ABE for circuits that allows inputs of length n, we have $|\mathbb{Y}| = 2^n$, hence the loss factor is *exponential*. Although this loss can be compensated by increasing the security parameter by n, this is undesirable by two reasons. First, as a direct consequence, it makes the resulting scheme inefficient. Second, and perhaps more importantly, the resulting security reduction becomes "unfalsifiable" in the sense that even an attacker with probability 1 in attacking the scheme cannot be used to solve the underlying hard problem in sub-exponential time [16].

Fully Secure CP-ABE for Circuits. The situation for CP-ABE for unbounded-size circuits is even more devastating since the loss factor can be as large as *double exponential*, as the number of all Boolean functions with n inputs is 2^{2^n}. In this case, complexity leveraging cannot be used since we cannot compensate by increasing the security parameter by 2^n, which is exponential.

Moreover, even when we restrict to bounded-depth circuits, the loss factor can still be super-exponential or large exponential functions (in parameters such as depth ℓ).[1],[2]

Problem Statement. To this end, we consider the following problem:

> Problem 1: *Is it possible to construct fully secure KP-ABE and CP-ABE for circuits with polynomial reductions (in all parameters) to some non-interactive assumptions?*

Unbounded-size Circuits and Succinctness. It is desirable for new fully secure schemes to preserve functionalities and efficiency from previous selectively secure systems. For functionalities, the goal is ABE that allows *unbounded-size* circuits. For efficiency, we require *succinctness*: the size of a key (resp., a ciphertext) for circuit f is less than or proportional to the circuit size in KP-ABE (resp., CP-ABE). In KP-ABE case, we refine our question to:

> Problem 1': *Is it possible to construct fully secure KP-ABE that allows unbounded circuits (possibly bounded-depth) and/or admits succinctness (again, with polynomial reductions to non-interactive assumptions)?*

In CP-ABE case, however, all the available schemes [24,31] are for bounded-size circuits and do not admit succinctness, not to mention that they are selectively secure. This is due to the use of universal circuits [46]. We thus ask:

> Problem 2: *Is it possible to construct (even selectively secure) CP-ABE that allows unbounded-size circuits and/or admits succinctness?*

Short Ciphertexts and Short Keys. Finally, we focus on optimizing the size of a ciphertext (resp. a key) for an input string x in KP-ABE (resp. CP-ABE). We say that a scheme admits *constant-size* ciphertext (resp., key) if the size besides the description of x is constant in term of the length n of x. We ask:

> Problem 3: *Is it possible to construct fully-secure KP-ABE with constant-size ciphertexts, fully-secure CP-ABE with constant-size keys (again, for unbounded-size circuits and with polynomial reductions)?*

1.1   Our Contributions on ABE Instantiations

Our contribution is twofold: a generic framework and instantiations. We first introduce our results regarding instantiations, which are summarized as:

---

[1] We do not elaborate the exact number as it is quite tricky to count the number of all Boolean functions that can be computed by unbounded-size bounded-depth circuits.

[2] When we further restrict to bounded-size circuits, the loss factor is $2^{\mathrm{poly}(g_{max})}$, where g_{max} is the maximum circuit size. This is exactly the reduction loss for all the available fully secure CP-ABE via complexity leveraging (see Table 2).

Table 1. KP-ABE for circuits.

Schemes	$|$Cipher$|$[†]	$|$Key$|$[†]	Unbound $|$circuit$|$?	Tool	Security[‡]	Reduction	Assumptions[§]
GVW [31]	$O(n)$	$O(g)$	yes	LWE	full	$O(2^n)$	$2^{O(n^\epsilon)}$-hardness of LWE
					selective	$O(1)$	$2^{O(n^\epsilon)}$-hardness of LWE
GGHSW [24]	$O(n')$	$O(g)$	yes	ℓ-multmap	full	$O(2^n)$	param-ass. size $O(\ell)$
					selective	$O(1)$	param-ass. size $O(\ell)$
BGG+1 [13]	$O(n)$	$O(1)$	yes	LWE	full	$O(2^n)$	$2^{O(n^\epsilon)}$-hardness of LWE
					selective	$O(1)$	$2^{O(n^\epsilon)}$-hardness of LWE
BGG+2 [13]	$O(1)$	$O(n^2+g)$	yes	ℓ-multmap	full	$O(2^n)$	param-ass. size $O(\ell+n)$
					selective	$O(1)$	param-ass. size $O(\ell+n)$
GGHZ1,2 [26, 27]	$\mathsf{poly}(g_{max})$	$\mathsf{poly}(g_{max})$	no	$\mathsf{poly}(g_{max})$-multmap	full	$\mathsf{poly}(g_{max},\,q_{\mathrm{all}})$	param-ass. size $\mathsf{poly}(g_{max})$
BV [11]**	$O(n)$	$O(1)$	yes	LWE	semi-adapt	$O(1)$	subexp-hardness of LWE
Our KP1 (§4)	$O(n')$	$O(g)$	yes	3ℓ-multmap	full	$O(q_1)$	param-ass. size $O(\ell m^2)$
					semi-adapt	$O(1)$	param-ass. size $O(\ell)$
Our KP2 (§5)	$O(1)$	$O(n^2+g)$	yes	3ℓ-multmap	full	$O(q_1)$	param-ass. size $O(\ell m^2+n^2)$
					semi-adapt	$O(1)$	param-ass. size $O(\ell+n)$

Table 2. CP-ABE for circuits.

Schemes	$|$Cipher$|$[†]	$|$Key$|$[†]	Unbound $|$circuit$|$?	Tool	Security[‡]	Reduction	Assumptions[§]
GVW [31][¶]	$\mathsf{poly}(g_{max})$	$\mathsf{poly}(g_{max})$	no	LWE	full	$2^{\mathsf{poly}(g_{max})}$	$2^{O(n^\epsilon)}$-hardness of LWE
					selective	$O(1)$	$2^{O(n^\epsilon)}$-hardness of LWE
GGHSW [24][¶]	$\mathsf{poly}(g_{max})$	$\mathsf{poly}(g_{max})$	no	$\mathsf{poly}(g_{max})$-multmap	full	$2^{\mathsf{poly}(g_{max})}$	param-ass. size $\mathsf{poly}(g_{max})$
					selective	$O(1)$	param-ass. size $\mathsf{poly}(g_{max})$
BGG+1 [13][¶]	$\mathsf{poly}(g_{max})$	$O(1)$	no	LWE	full	$2^{\mathsf{poly}(g_{max})}$	$2^{O(n^\epsilon)}$-hardness of LWE
					selective	$O(1)$	$2^{O(n^\epsilon)}$-hardness of LWE
BGG+2 [13][¶]	$O(1)$	$\mathsf{poly}(n^2,g_{max})$	no	$\mathsf{poly}(g_{max})$-multmap	full	$2^{\mathsf{poly}(g_{max})}$	param-ass. size $\mathsf{poly}(g_{max})$
					selective	$O(1)$	param-ass. size $\mathsf{poly}(g_{max})$
GGHZ1,2 [26, 27]	$\mathsf{poly}(g_{max})$	$\mathsf{poly}(g_{max})$	no	$\mathsf{poly}(g_{max})$-multmap	full	$\mathsf{poly}(g_{max},\,q_{\mathrm{all}})$	param-ass. size $\mathsf{poly}(g_{max})$
Our CP1 (§6.2)	$O(g)$	$O(n')$	yes	3ℓ-multmap	full	$O(q_{\mathrm{all}})$	param-ass. size $O(\ell m^2)$
Our CP2 (§6.2)	$O(n^2+g)$	$O(1)$	yes	3ℓ-multmap	full	$O(q_{\mathrm{all}})$	param-ass. size $O(\ell m^2+n^2)$

* Notation for variables: n is the length of input to a circuit; $n'(\leq n)$ is the number of 1's in the input bit string to circuits; g is the size of a circuit (the number of gates including input nodes); g_{max} is the maximum bound for g (if bounded); m is the width of a circuit; ℓ is the bounded depth of circuits; q_1 is the number of pre-challenge key queries; q_{all} is the number of all key queries. ϵ is a parameter for LWE ($0 < \epsilon < 1/2$) [31].

** Only ABE of [11] achieves unbounded input length, $i.e.$, the input string length n is not a-priori bounded.

† Sizes ($|$Cipher$|$, $|$Key$|$) are shown in the number of "unit" elements naturally defined in the respective underlying tool. Let λ be the security parameter. For multi-linear maps, one unit element is a graded encoded element; for previous (now-broken) candidates [20, 22], the size of one unit is $\mathsf{poly}(\lambda, \kappa)$ bits, for κ-multilinear maps. For LWE, intuitively, one unit element is a matrix that defines a single instance of the LWE assumption; the size for one unit is $\mathsf{poly}(\lambda, \ell^{1/\epsilon})$ bits for the GVW [31] and the BGG+1 systems [13]. The overall ciphertext size is then $|$Cipher$||$unit$| + |Y|$, where $|Y|$ is the description size of ciphertext attribute (circuit f for CP, input string x for KP). Similarly, The overall key size is $|$Key$||$unit$| + |X|$. We provide overall sizes in Table 3,4.

‡ For each scheme satisfying two levels of security, we provide respective reduction/assumptions in each line.

§ All multi-linear map based schemes in the tables use "parameterized" assumptions (param-ass.). To be able to compare quantitatively, we write their complexities in terms of the assumption size. (Intuitively but not necessarily, the larger the size, the stronger the assumption is). All of these schemes use at most three assumptions, and the size in the table represents the largest one.

¶ These CP-ABE schemes were obtained by converting from KP-ABE via universal circuits. In doing so, one must fix g_{max}, $i.e.$, the resulting schemes are for bounded-size circuit. An (asymptotically) optimal universal circuit [46] has size $O(g_{max} \log g_{max})$ and depth $O(g_{max})$, hence related parameters can be given by $\mathsf{poly}(g_{max})$.

Table 3. KP-ABE for circuits (sizes given in more details).

Schemes	|Cipher| (no. of bits)	|Key| (no. of bits)
GVW [31]	$O(n)\mathsf{poly}(\lambda, \ell^{1/\epsilon})$	$O(g)\mathsf{poly}(\lambda, \ell^{1/\epsilon})$
GGHSW [24]	$O(n')\mathsf{poly}(\lambda, \ell) + n$	$O(g)\mathsf{poly}(\lambda, \ell)$
BGG+1,BV [13, 11]	$O(n)\mathsf{poly}(\lambda, \ell^{1/\epsilon})$	$\mathsf{poly}(\lambda, \ell^{1/\epsilon}) + |f|$
BGG+2 [13]	$\mathsf{poly}(\lambda, \ell) + n$	$O(n^2 + g)\mathsf{poly}(\lambda, \ell)$
GGHZ1,2 [26, 27]	$\mathsf{poly}(g_{max})\mathsf{poly}(\lambda, g_{max})$	$\mathsf{poly}(g_{max})\mathsf{poly}(\lambda, g_{max})$
Our KP1 (§4)	$O(n')\mathsf{poly}(\lambda, \ell) + n$	$O(g)\mathsf{poly}(\lambda, \ell)$
Our KP2 (§5)	$\mathsf{poly}(\lambda, \ell) + n$	$O(n^2 + g)\mathsf{poly}(\lambda, \ell)$

Table 4. CP-ABE for circuits (sizes given in more details).

Schemes	|Cipher| (no. of bits)	|Key| (no. of bits)
GVW [31]	$\mathsf{poly}(g_{max})\mathsf{poly}(\lambda, g_{max}^{1/\epsilon})$	$\mathsf{poly}(g_{max})\mathsf{poly}(\lambda, g_{max}^{1/\epsilon})$
GGHSW [24]	$\mathsf{poly}(g_{max})\mathsf{poly}(\lambda, g_{max})$	$\mathsf{poly}(g_{max})\mathsf{poly}(\lambda, g_{max})$
BGG+1 [13]	$\mathsf{poly}(g_{max})\mathsf{poly}(\lambda, g_{max}^{1/\epsilon})$	$\mathsf{poly}(\lambda, g_{max}^{1/\epsilon}) + n$
BGG+2 [13]	$\mathsf{poly}(\lambda, g_{max}) + |f|$	$\mathsf{poly}(g_{max})\mathsf{poly}(\lambda, g_{max})$
GGHZ1,2 [26, 27]	$\mathsf{poly}(g_{max})\mathsf{poly}(\lambda, g_{max})$	$\mathsf{poly}(g_{max})\mathsf{poly}(\lambda, g_{max})$
Our CP1 (§6.2)	$O(g)\mathsf{poly}(\lambda, \ell)$	$O(n')\mathsf{poly}(\lambda, \ell) + n$
Our CP2 (§6.2)	$O(n^2 + g)\mathsf{poly}(\lambda, \ell)$	$\mathsf{poly}(\lambda, \ell) + n$

Theorem 1. *(Instantiations, informally). There exist fully secure KP-ABE, CP-ABE for unbounded-size bounded-depth circuits with polynomial reductions to some non-interactive assumptions on composite-order 3ℓ-multilinear maps, where ℓ is the bounded depth. Constructively, we obtain 4 schemes:*

1. *fully secure KP-ABE admitting succinctness.*
2. *fully secure KP-ABE admitting succinctness and constant-size ciphertexts.*
3. *fully secure CP-ABE admitting succinctness.*
4. *fully secure CP-ABE admitting succinctness and constant-size keys.*

Our schemes affirmatively answer Problem 1, constructing fully secure ABE with polynomial reductions. (See below for independent works [26, 27] that also solve Problem 1.) Moreover, both of our KP-ABE schemes and both of our CP-ABE schemes are the first to affirmatively answer Problem 1′ and Problem 2, respectively. Finally, our second KP-ABE and our second CP-ABE provide the first positive answers to Problem 3.

We provide comparisons to the other schemes in the literature in Tables 1 and 2 (and with sizes provided in more details in Tables 3 and 4).

Comparisons. From Tables 1 and 2, we can see that our first and second (fully secure) KP-ABE schemes are comparable to the (selectively secure) KP-ABE of GGHSW [24] and BGG+2 [13] in both functionality (unbounded-size circuits) and efficiency (succinctness, constant-size ciphertext). On the other hand, both of our (fully secure) CP-ABE schemes perform much better than all the previous (selectively secure) schemes in both functionality (ours are the first to allow unbounded-size circuits) and efficiency (ours are the first to be succinct).

In independent[3] works, Garg *et al.* proposed fully-secure ABE [26] (and FE [27], see Sect. 1.4) for circuits, thus also answer Problem 1; however, their schemes are for bounded-size circuits and do not admit succinctness, due to their essential use of "fixed-once and for all" universal circuits. Moreover, as shown in Tables 1 and 2, our schemes require much less multi-linearity and admit tighter reductions.

---

[3] Our preliminary version [4] has been made available shortly after [26, 27].

On Assumptions. To prove security of our schemes, we introduce some new non-interactive assumptions (thus, they are falsifiable [39]). They somewhat extend the Multi-linear Decisional Diffie-Hellman Assumption (MDDH) [15,20, 23]. These assumptions are of "parameterized" type (or often called "q-type"), where the size of assumption grows depending on some parameters. Although they are not standard, we prove that they hold in the generic model. To compare these assumptions quantitatively, in Tables 1 and 2, we represent their complexities in terms of their assumption sizes. Intuitively, but not necessarily, the larger the size, the stronger the assumption is. We note that, in our schemes, the parameters for the assumptions depend only on the depth ℓ, width m, or input length n, of a circuit in one query (and not on the number of key queries). The reduction cost in our schemes is $O(q_1)$ where q_1 is the number of pre-challenge key queries.

Implementations. Unfortunately, currently there is no known secure multilinear map (see more later in Sect. 1.4). Hence, at present, our results can be considered as only theoretical black-box reductions from fully secure succinct ABE for unbounded circuits to (composite-order) multi-linear maps. Nevertheless, due to the nature of black-box usages, any future secure candidates can be used.

1.2   Our Contributions on New Framework

The main building block behind our ABE schemes is a new generic and modular framework, based on a new primitive called *multilinear pair encoding*. Our main result for framework can be summarized as:

Theorem 2. *(Framework, informally). Suppose that a (new) subgroup decision assumption in multilinear settings holds. A "doubly-selectively" secure multilinear pair encoding scheme for predicate R implies a fully secure ABE scheme for predicate R via a generic construction.*

Our Formalization. Our framework generalizes the recent framework by Attrapadung [3] (and Wee [51]), which works only in bilinear settings, to multi-linear settings. The framework of [3] provides an algebraic abstraction of *dual-system encryption* techniques, introduced by Waters [48] and utilized by many works [35–37,40,51], via a primitive called *pair encoding*. As seemingly inherent to bilinear settings, pair encoding of [3] is confined to only *linear* functions, so that the security proof under subgroup decision assumptions can be achieved. This prevents multiplication of variables in encodings since it would exactly destroy linearity. On the other hand, in generalizing to multi-linear settings, it is exactly the multiplication operation that we would like to enable. We resolve this conundrum by formalizing our multilinear version of pair encoding via a new notion we call *multilinear programs*, which allows both addition and multiplication. Our novelty then lies in identifying a subclass of multilinear programs that we call *associative programs* that will exactly admit the security proof under a subgroup decision assumption. Intuitively, associative programs allow us to compute the same encodings in two equivalent ways (hence the name, associative); one is used for the construction, and the other is used in simulation for the security proof.

"Doubly selective security" of pair encodings [3] can then be generalized to multi-linear settings in a natural manner. This consists of selective and co-selective notions for encodings, which mimic the definitions of selective and co-selective security of ABE. Selective notion refers to the situation where a cipher-text attribute is queried before a key attribute, while in co-selective notion, the order is reversed. This reflects one of the advantages of the framework: to achieve secure encodings in the selective notion, we can borrow algebraic techniques for selective security of ABE, which is much easier to achieve than full security.

Dual Conversion. Another advantage of the pair encoding framework is that it comes equipped with the powerful *dual conversion* [3,9]. For a predicate $R : \mathbb{X} \times \mathbb{Y} \to \{0,1\}$, its dual is defined by $\bar{R} : \mathbb{Y} \times \mathbb{X} \to \{0,1\}$ where $\bar{R}(Y,X) := R(X,Y)$. Hence KP-ABE and CP-ABE are dual to each other. Attrapadung and Yamada [9] described a generic conversion that converts (bilinear) pair encoding P for a predicate R to another scheme $\bar{P}$ for its dual while preserves doubly selective security and efficiency. More precisely, selective security of P implies co-selective security of $\bar{P}$ (and analogously in an alternating manner). We generalize to multilinear settings in this paper. This, for the first time, allows us to convert KP-ABE to CP-ABE for circuits without using universal circuits, which was the only known (and highly inefficient) method so far.

Perspective. Ananth *et al.* [2] recently proposed a generic conversion from selective to full security in functional encryption (FE) for sufficiently expressive classes. (More on this later in Sect. 1.4.) However, they left an open problem of constructing a similar selective-to-full conversion for ABE. The ABE case is a harder task since the starting primitive, *i.e.*, selectively secure ABE, is less powerful than selectively secure FE. Our framework provides a partial solution by starting with any doubly selectively secure pair encodings (rather than any selective ABE), and converting to fully secure ABE via Theorem 2.

Potential Applications. Although we demonstrate applications of our framework by considering circuits, we may try to use it for plausibly constructing ABE for "moderate" classes in the Chomsky hierarchy (*e.g.*, Pushdown Automata, Linear-bounded Automata) with the hope that it can be done under multilinear maps with much *lower multi-linearity* (*e.g.*, small constant), which itself might be easier to achieve than general-purpose multi-linear maps. Indeed, this is the case for ABE for Deterministic Finite Automata, where the sufficient multi-linearity is *2* (*i.e.*, bilinear) [3,49].

1.3 Our Techniques

Here, we highlight techniques for constructing new fully secure ABE for circuits. We first quickly note that the "information-theoretic variant" of dual system techniques [3,51] will not work for circuit predicate due to "backtracking attack" [24] (due to the multi-fanout property of circuits).

We thus seek for "doubly selectively" secure encoding for the circuit predicate, which exhibits the "computational variant" of dual system techniques [3,36]. Our blueprint starts with KP-ABE of GGHSW [24]. We immediately obtain selectively secure encoding by borrowing techniques for proving selective security of KP-ABE. The missing piece is then to prove the *co-selective* security for this encoding, or equivalently, the selective security of its *dual* encoding. Intuitively, we need new techniques to directly prove selective security of CP-ABE for circuits (without using universal circuits). One evidence that constructing selectively secure CP-ABE for circuits can be hard is that the Waters CP-ABE [47], which is for *Boolean formulae*, is proved under an already more complex (q-type) assumption than the KP-ABE counterpart [33], *à la* the Parallel BDHE [47].

Our goal is to generalize the selective proof of Waters' CP-ABE to the case of circuits. This poses two main issues. First, the output of a gate can be wired as an input to another gate (we call this a hierarchy issue). Second, and more essentially, the output of a gate (or a circuit input) can be wired as inputs to many gates (this is called multi-fanout). In the Waters CP-ABE, these two issues were not problematic since the scheme can be thought of using one big gate (multi-fan-in) that can express a linear secret-sharing scheme.

We solve these issues by designing a new assumption and a security proof that generalize "individual randomness" techniques similar to Waters [47], and Rouselakis and Waters [43] to work with circuits. The security proof works by "chaining" information on the paths from a given input gate to the output gate. One technical difficulty is that the number of chains can be exponential in the number of all gates (which would result in an exponential size assumption). We resolve this by giving out "decomposed" elements separately and letting the reduction multiply these terms on the fly to form the chains. In doing so, we carefully avoid enabling multiplication that results in a term that would trivially break the assumption. We note that our resulting assumption itself will not be tied to any particular circuit; it is only parameterized by the width, the input length, and the depth of the queried circuit.

Semi-adaptive Security Under Simpler Assumptions. For the purpose of basing our schemes under *simple* assumptions, we consider *semi-adaptive* security of ABE [19,45], which is an intermediate notion between selective and full security. We establish a *tight reduction* from semi-adaptive security of our generic construction to the selective security of pair encodings. Loosely speaking, this enables us to upgrade the KP-ABE of GGHSW [24] from selective to semi-adaptive security *for almost free*[4], since the selective security of our encodings relies on a similar (simple) assumption as that of GGHSW. See Tables 1 and 2.

1.4   Related Work

Multilinear Map Candidates. Our framework is based on multi-linear maps. More precisely, we use *composite-order asymmetric graded encoding* systems

---
[4] We although still need the subgroup decision assumption required for framework.

(in a black-box manner). Multi-linear graded encoding systems was first proposed by Garg et al. [23] and subsequently by Coron et al. [20] (CLT13). Gentry et al. [29] extended the CLT13 system to the composite-order setting. Unfortunately, these candidates (and their variants, notably CLT15 [22]) were later shown to be broken [17,18,21].[5] As an alternative approach, multilinear maps based on indistinguishability obfuscation (IO) are recently proposed in [1]. However, the current security proof of IO under a polynomial-size set of assumptions requires complexity leveraging and hence exponential loss in reduction [30]. Nevertheless, this sheds some light on possibility of multilinear maps in the future.

Fully Secure FE. Recently, Waters [50] and Ananth et al. [2] obtained fully-secure *functional encryption* (FE) for circuits. Waters provides a direct scheme based on IO [25,30], while Ananth et al. provide a generic conversion from selective to full security for FE in unconditional manner and one can then use selectively secure FE from [25,50], which is again based on IO. Due to an implicit exponential loss via IO, we do not elaborately include [2,50] in Tables 1 and 2.

As mentioned earlier, Garg et al. [27] obtained fully secure FE for circuits without obfuscation, hence also implies ABE with polynomial reduction. As in [26], it uses universal circuits, and thus can deal only with bounded-size circuits. Its asymptotic efficiency is also similar to [26] (*cf.* Tables 1 and 2), albeit with much larger polynomials. Moreover, it requires stronger multilinear maps with the so-called Extension functionality [27].

Semi-adaptive Secure ABE. Very recently, Brakerski and Vaikuntanathan [11] obtained semi-adaptively secure KP-ABE for circuits that also achieves a remarkable feature of unbounded input length. Also very recently, Goyal et al. [32] proposed a generic selective-to-*semi-adaptive* conversion for ABE.

2   Preliminaries

Predicate Family. We consider a predicate family $R = \{R_\Lambda\}_{\Lambda \in \mathbb{N}^c}$, for some constant $c \in \mathbb{N}$, where a relation $R_\Lambda : \mathbb{X}_\Lambda \times \mathbb{Y}_\Lambda \to \{0,1\}$ is a predicate function that maps a pair of key attribute in a space $\mathbb{X}_\Lambda$ and ciphertext attribute in a space $\mathbb{Y}_\Lambda$ to $\{0,1\}$. The family index $\Lambda = (n_1, n_2, \ldots)$ specifies the description of a predicate from the family, where we let n_1 be the security parameter $\lambda \in \mathbb{N}$.

ABE Syntax. An ABE scheme for predicate R consists of the following:

- Setup(1^Λ) $\to$ (PK, MSK): takes as input a a family index Λ (which includes the security parameter λ) of predicate family R, and outputs a master public key PK and a master secret key MSK.
- Encrypt($Y, M, $PK) $\to$ CT: takes as input a ciphertext attribute $Y \in \mathbb{Y}_\Lambda$, a message $M \in \mathcal{M}$ (the message space), and PK. It outputs a ciphertext CT.

---

[5] As a caveat, some schemes are plausibly secure in the setting where encodings of zero are not given out. However, in ABE, we will need them for our security proof.

- KeyGen$(X, \mathsf{MSK}, \mathsf{PK}) \to \mathsf{SK}$: takes as input a key attribute $X \in \mathbb{X}_\Lambda$ and the master key MSK. It outputs a secret key SK.
- Decrypt$(\mathsf{CT}, \mathsf{SK}) \to M$: given a ciphertext CT with its attribute Y and the decryption key SK with its attribute X, it outputs a message M or $\bot$.

Correctness. Consider all indexes Λ, all $M \in \mathcal{M}$, $X \in \mathbb{X}_\Lambda$, $Y \in \mathbb{Y}_\Lambda$ such that $R_\Lambda(X, Y) = 1$. If Encrypt$(Y, M, \mathsf{PK}) \to \mathsf{CT}$ and KeyGen$(X, \mathsf{MSK}, \mathsf{PK}) \to \mathsf{SK}$ where (PK, MSK) is generated from Setup(1^Λ), then Decrypt$(\mathsf{CT}, \mathsf{SK}) \to M$.

Security Notions for ABE. We use the standard definitions for full security and semi-adaptive security. Due to the lack of space, we refer to the full version. The advantages of $\mathcal{A}$ against the full and semi-adaptive security of the scheme ABE are denoted by $\mathsf{Adv}_{\mathcal{A}}^{\mathsf{ABE}}(\lambda), \mathsf{Adv}_{\mathcal{A}}^{\mathsf{semi},\mathsf{ABE}}(\lambda)$, respectively.

Circuit Notations. A circuit consists of six tuples $f = (\ell, n, \{m_i\}_{i \in [2,\ell]}, \mathsf{L}, \mathsf{R}, \mathsf{Type})$. We first note that it is wlog that we consider only *monotone* and *layered* circuits [24]. We let ℓ be the number of layers (the depth), n be the number of inputs, and m_i be the number of gates in the i-th layer for $i \in [2, \ell]$. Define $m := \max_{i \in [2,\ell]} m_i$, which represents the width. We also define $m_1 = n$. We define $\mathsf{Inputs} = \{w_{1,1}, \dots, w_{1,n}\}$, and for $i \in [2, \ell]$, $\mathsf{Gates}_i = \{w_{i,1}, \dots, w_{i,m_i}\}$. We let $\mathsf{Gates} = \bigcup_{i \in [2,n]} \mathsf{Gates}_i$, and let $\mathsf{Nodes} = \mathsf{Inputs} \cup \mathsf{Gates}$. Also denote $w_{\mathsf{top}} = w_{\ell,1}$ (the output gate). We define $\mathsf{Depth}(w_{i,j}) = i$ and $\mathsf{Num}(w_{i,j}) = j$. The two functions $\mathsf{L} : \mathsf{Gates} \to \mathsf{Gates} \setminus \{w_{\mathsf{top}}\}$ and $\mathsf{R} : \mathsf{Gates} \to \mathsf{Gates} \setminus \{w_{\mathsf{top}}\}$ identify the two input gates; that is, $\mathsf{L}(w_{i,j})$, $\mathsf{R}(w_{i,j})$ have outputs wired to $w_{i,j}$ as the first input (left input) and the second input (right input), respectively. We require that $\mathsf{Num}(\mathsf{L}(w_{i,j})) < \mathsf{Num}(\mathsf{R}(w_{i,j}))$. The function $\mathsf{Type} : \mathsf{Gates} \to \{\mathsf{OR}, \mathsf{AND}\}$ specifies the type of gate as either OR or AND. For $w \in \mathsf{Gates}$, we denote $f_w(x)$ to be the circuit evaluation of x at the output of w.

The predicate of KP-ABE for circuits is $R_{\lambda,n,\ell} : \mathbb{F}_{n,\ell} \times \{0,1\}^n \to \{0,1\}$ where $R(f, x) = f(x)$, where $\mathbb{F}_{n,\ell}$ is the set of all circuits with bounded input length n and bounded depth ℓ.

Composite-order Graded Encoding. We use the same syntax of (composite-order) graded encoding schemes as in [20,22,23]. Due to the lack of space, we postpone the full definition to the full version and only give a short description here. A composite-order asymmetric graded encoding scheme is parameterized by multi-linearity $\kappa \in \mathbb{N}$ and the number of subrings $\nu \in \mathbb{N}$. It allows us to encode a scalar a in a given ring $\mathcal{R} = \mathbb{Z}_{N_1} \times \cdots \times \mathbb{Z}_{N_\nu}$, together with an index, which is a set $S \subseteq [1, \kappa]$, to a corresponding encoding, which we denote it by $[a]_S$. Intuitively, it is hard to recover the original scalar from its encoding, yet we are still allowed to perform some arithmetic operations on encodings. More precisely, we are allowed to perform operations $+, -, \cdot$ on encodings as

$$[a]_S + [b]_S = [a + b]_S, \qquad [a]_{S_1} \cdot [b]_{S_2} = [a \cdot b]_{S_1 \cup S_2},$$

and $-[a]_S = [-a]_S$, for $a, b \in \mathcal{R}$, $S, S_1, S_2 \subseteq [1, \kappa]$ such that $S_1 \cap S_2 = \emptyset$.

We also give some notation, originally appeared in [26], when the encoded scalar is projected to only subring components. In our ABE scheme, we will use $\nu = 2$. We denote $[a]_S^1 := [a_1]_S$ where we set $a_1 \equiv a \pmod{N_1}$ and $a_1 \equiv 0 \pmod{N_2}$. $[a]_S^2$ is denoted similarly. Thus, $[a]_S^1$ and $[a]_S^2$ are independently distributed due to the Chinese Remainder Theorem. Also, we can decompose $[a]_S$ uniquely to $[a]_S = [a]_S^1 + [a]_S^2$. Moreover, we have orthogonality: $[a_1]_{S_1}^1 \cdot [a_2]_{S_2}^2 = [0]_{S_1 \cup S_2}$, for any $a_1, a_2 \in \mathcal{R}$ (and disjoint S_1, S_2). More importantly, we can establish some subgroup decision problems. We describe this in Sect. 3.4.

Our scheme will not require public encoding functionality of *any* element; instead, we only need public encoding procedures of *unknown random* elements (as is the case for previous candidates [20,22,23]). We denote it by $[a]_{\emptyset} \leftarrow \mathsf{Samp}(\mathsf{param})$, which gives us a level-$\emptyset$ encoding of an unknown random element $a \in \mathcal{R}$. To encode it to level S, we need an encoding of 1, namely, $[1]_S$, to compute $[a]_{\emptyset} \cdot [1]_S = [a]_S$.

We briefly describe procedures for graded encodings here. $\mathsf{InstGen}(1^\lambda, \kappa, \nu)$ outputs $(\mathsf{param}, \mathsf{esk}, \{N_i\}_i)$, where param is public parameter, esk is a secret encoding key, and the order $\{N_i\}_i$ of subrings. By using esk, one can encode any $a \in R$ to $[a]_S^V$ for any S, V. Extraction algorithm Ext takes param and a level-$[1, \kappa]$ encoding $[a]_{[1,\kappa]}$ as inputs, and outputs a string $K \in \{0, 1\}^\lambda$. We require that if $a \in_R \mathcal{R}$, then $K \in_R \{0, 1\}^\lambda$ ($\in_R$ means uniformly distributed). As in all previous candidates, encodings may be non-deterministic. In such a case, we have a re-randomization procedure, and we require that the extraction of two encodings of the same value will result in the same string.

3   Our Dual System Framework in Multilinear Settings

In this section, we describe our framework for constructing ABE for any given predicate R from a new primitive called *multilinear pair encoding scheme* (for predicate R). This primitive is defined using formal variables in polynomials. To capture a formal system of graded encoding, we introduce the following notion of *indexed polynomials*, which are basically formal polynomials with the index being sets, and their operations mimic those of graded encodings.

Definition 1 (Formal Variables and Polynomials). *A formal variable is a bit string, and distinct variables denote different strings. A fresh variable is any string that has not been assigned to another former variable. A formal polynomial is a polynomial with formal variables.*

Definition 2 (Indexed Polynomial). *An indexed polynomial p is defined as a pair of formal polynomial a with coefficients in $\mathbb{Z}$ and a set $S \subseteq [1, \kappa]$. We denote it as $p = (a)_S$. We define its formal operations $+, -, \cdot$ as*

$$(a_1)_S + (a_2)_S = (a_1 + a_2)_S, \qquad (a_1)_{S_1} \cdot (a_2)_{S_2} = (a_1 \cdot a_2)_{S_1 \cup S_2},$$

and $-(a)_S = (-a)_S$, for $S, S_1, S_2 \subseteq [1, \kappa]$ and $S_1 \cap S_2 = \emptyset$.

Definition 3 (Indexed Singleton). *An indexed singleton is an indexed polynomial of a single variable (degree-1 monomial of a variable with coefficient 1) or a constant. The former is also called indexed variable.*

We formalize algorithms that perform formal operations on indexed polynomials as *multilinear programs*. Below, we then capture a kind of multilinear programs, called *associative programs*, that will be useful for our framework. We will typically denote a vector of indexed polynomials using bold fonts.

Definition 4 (Multilinear Program). *A* multilinear program, *say* $\mathcal{P}$, *is a procedure that takes a vector of indexed polynomials, say* $\boldsymbol{x}$, *as an input, performs only formal operations on its elements, and outputs a vector of indexed polynomials, say* $\boldsymbol{v}$. *When a security parameter* λ *is considered, we require the number of formal operations to be polynomial in* λ.

Definition 5 (Associative Program). *We say that a multilinear program* $\mathcal{P}$ *is* associative *over an ordered pair of vectors* $(\boldsymbol{x}, \boldsymbol{w})$ *of indexed singletons if its input is a vector of indexed polynomials each of which is of the form*[6]

$$(x_i)_{\emptyset} \cdot (w_{j_1})_{T_{j_1}} \cdots (w_{j_k})_{T_{j_k}},$$

for some $(w_{j_1})_{T_{j_1}}, \ldots, (w_{j_k})_{T_{j_k}} \in \boldsymbol{w}$ *(for some* k*)*[7] *and some variable* x_i *such that there exists* $(x_i)_{S_i} \in \boldsymbol{x}$ *where* $T_{j_1} \cup \cdots \cup T_{j_k} = S_i$.

Using Associative Programs. The reason why we define associative programs is that we can identify the following associativity property:

$$(x_i)_{\emptyset} \cdot (w_{j_1})_{T_{j_1}} \cdots (w_{j_k})_{T_{j_k}} = (x_i)_{S_i} \cdot (w_{j_1})_{\emptyset} \cdots (w_{j_k})_{\emptyset} \tag{1}$$

(where $T_{j_1} \cup \cdots \cup T_{j_k} = S_i$). Intuitively, this property will allows us to have two ways of obtaining an equivalent element to be input to the program. Looking forward in our ABE context, one way will allow us to define ABE constructions and the other will allow us to simulate equivalent elements in the security proof. More precisely, we have a lemma below. Before that, we define two more notions.

A Useful Notation. We define the notation of *index-less projection* that maps a vector $\boldsymbol{a}$ of indexed polynomials to the same vector but with all indexes being $\emptyset$, denoted $\mathsf{V}_{\boldsymbol{a}}$. That is,

$$\boldsymbol{a} = \{(a_i)_{S_i} | i \in [1, k]\} \mapsto \mathsf{V}_{\boldsymbol{a}} := \{(a_i)_{\emptyset} | i \in [1, k]\}.$$

Extended Program. For a multilinear program $\mathcal{P}$ that is associative over $(\boldsymbol{x}, \boldsymbol{w})$, we define its *canonically extended multilinear program*, denoted as $\mathcal{E}_{\mathcal{P}}$, that takes $(\mathsf{V}_{\boldsymbol{x}}, \boldsymbol{w})$ as inputs, and does as follows. From $\mathsf{V}_{\boldsymbol{x}}$ and $\boldsymbol{w}$, $\mathcal{E}_{\mathcal{P}}$ computes each indexed polynomial $(x_i)_{\emptyset} \cdot (w_{j_1})_{T_{j_1}} \cdots (w_{j_k})_{T_{j_k}}$ that appears in the input set of $\mathcal{P}$ by formal multiplications. These thus comprise the whole input set to $\mathcal{P}$ and $\mathcal{E}_{\mathcal{P}}$ then finally computes $\mathcal{P}$ and outputs the result. We have the following:

Lemma 1 (Associativity). *For any vectors* $\boldsymbol{x}, \boldsymbol{w}$ *of indexed polynomials, for any multilinear program* $\mathcal{P}$ *that is associative over* $(\boldsymbol{x}, \boldsymbol{w})$, *we have*

$$\mathcal{E}_{\mathcal{P}}(\mathsf{V}_{\boldsymbol{x}}, \boldsymbol{w}) = \mathcal{E}_{\mathcal{P}}(\boldsymbol{x}, \mathsf{V}_{\boldsymbol{w}}).$$

---

[6] This form implies that all $T_{j_1}, \ldots, T_{j_k}$ are pairwise disjoint.

[7] Here, for a vector $\boldsymbol{x}$, the notation '$z \in \boldsymbol{x}$' means that z is an element in $\boldsymbol{x}$.

Proof. The left-hand side and the right-hand side programs compute each input to $\mathcal{P}$ in the form of left-hand side and right-hand side of Eq. (1), respectively, which are equal. From that point on, both compute the same program $\mathcal{P}$.   □

Applying Graded-encoding Schemes to Formal System. Let us fix a graded encoding scheme and use the bracket notation. For an indexed polynomial $p = (a)_S$, we denote its corresponding graded-encoded element as $[p] = [a]_S$, where we abuse the bracket notation. It also applies component-wise to vectors.

Let $\mathcal{P}$ be a multilinear program with an input size z and an output size z' (sizes are the length of vectors). We define a corresponding algorithm that takes a vector of z graded-encoded elements as an input and outputs a vector of z' graded-encoded elements. This algorithm has the same procedure as $\mathcal{P}$ but replaces each formal operation $+, -, \cdot$ on indexed polynomials to operation $+, -, \cdot$ on graded-encoded elements, resp. We thus abuse the notation and denote this algorithm also as $\mathcal{P}$. The following lemma will be useful in the proof.

Lemma 2 (Decomposability). *For any multilinear program $\mathcal{P}$, any input x, we have $\mathcal{P}([\boldsymbol{x}]) = \mathcal{P}([\boldsymbol{x}]^1) + \mathcal{P}([\boldsymbol{x}]^2)$.*

Proof. We decompose $[\boldsymbol{x}] = [\boldsymbol{x}]^1 + [\boldsymbol{x}]^2$. We claim that the decomposition will be preserved for each operation. For $+, -$, it is trivial. For multiplication we see that $([\boldsymbol{x}]_{S_1}^1 + [\boldsymbol{x}]_{S_1}^2)([\boldsymbol{x}']_{S_2}^1 + [\boldsymbol{x}']_{S_2}^2) = [\boldsymbol{x}]_{S_1}^1 \cdot [\boldsymbol{x}']_{S_2}^1 + [\boldsymbol{x}]_{S_1}^2 \cdot [\boldsymbol{x}']_{S_2}^2$, due to orthogonality. Hence, multiplication also preserves decomposition.   □

We also obtain the following two corollaries from Lemmas 1 and 2, resp., which will be used in the security proof. They hold for any vectors $\boldsymbol{x}, \boldsymbol{w}$ of indexed polynomials, and for any multilinear program $\mathcal{P}$ that is associative over $(\boldsymbol{x}, \boldsymbol{w})$.

Corollary 1. $\mathcal{E}_{\mathcal{P}}([\mathsf{V}_{\boldsymbol{x}}], [\boldsymbol{w}]^1) = \mathcal{E}_{\mathcal{P}}([\boldsymbol{x}]^1, [\mathsf{V}_{\boldsymbol{w}}]) = \mathcal{E}_{\mathcal{P}}([\boldsymbol{x}]^1, [\mathsf{V}_{\boldsymbol{w}}]^1).$

Proof. Since each input to $\mathcal{P}$ is of the form in Definition 5, when $[\boldsymbol{x}]$ is projected to $[\boldsymbol{x}]^1$, the input term to $\mathcal{P}$ is also projected due to orthogonality. Hence, we have the latter equality. The rest follows from Lemma 1.   □

Corollary 2. $\mathcal{E}_{\mathcal{P}}([\boldsymbol{x}], [\mathsf{V}_{\boldsymbol{w}}]) = \mathcal{E}_{\mathcal{P}}([\boldsymbol{x}]^1, [\mathsf{V}_{\boldsymbol{w}}]) + \mathcal{E}_{\mathcal{P}}([\boldsymbol{x}]^2, [\mathsf{V}_{\boldsymbol{w}}]).$

3.1 Multilinear Pair Encodings

Syntax. A multilinear pair encoding scheme for predicate family R consists of four deterministic polynomial-time algorithms as $\mathsf{P} = (\mathsf{Init}, \mathsf{EncK}, \mathsf{EncC}, \mathsf{Pair})$:[8]

---

[8] We define *syntax* in such a way that it does not refer to multilinear maps. We do this so that it can accommodate both perfect and computational flavor of *security* (the former *will not* refer to mult-maps while the latter *will*, cf. Sect. 3.2), similarly to [3,5].

- $\mathsf{Init}(\Lambda) \rightarrow (\kappa, \boldsymbol{h_c}, \boldsymbol{h_k}, n)$. It outputs a multi-linearity level κ, two vectors $\boldsymbol{h_c}, \boldsymbol{h_k}$ of indexed singletons, and an integer n specifying the number of all variables in $\boldsymbol{h_c}, \boldsymbol{h_k}$. We require that each singleton is h_i or 1, where $h_1, \ldots, h_n$ are variables. Let $\mathcal{S}_c, \mathcal{S}_k$ be the set of all indexes in $\boldsymbol{h_c}, \boldsymbol{h_k}$, respectively. Also let $S_c = \bigcup_{S \in \mathcal{S}_c} S$, $S_k = \bigcup_{S \in \mathcal{S}_k} S$. We require that $S_c \cap S_k = \emptyset$ and $S_c \cup S_k = [1, \kappa]$. Also we require $(1)_{S_k} \in \boldsymbol{h_k}$.[9]
- $\mathsf{EncK}(X, \boldsymbol{h_k}) \rightarrow (\boldsymbol{B}, \boldsymbol{r}, \mathcal{P}_X)$. The *Key Encoding algorithm* takes $X \in \mathbb{X}_\Lambda$ and $\boldsymbol{h_k}$ as inputs. It outputs two vectors $\boldsymbol{B}, \boldsymbol{r}$ of indexed polynomials, and a multilinear program $\mathcal{P}_X$. We require that $\boldsymbol{r} = ((r_1)_{S_1}, \ldots, (r_m)_{S_m})$, where $r_1, \ldots, r_m$ are fresh variables, for some $S_1, \ldots, S_m \subseteq S_k$ for some integer m. We require that

$$\mathcal{P}_X \text{ is associative over } (\boldsymbol{r}, \boldsymbol{h_k}) \qquad \text{and} \qquad \mathcal{E}_{\mathcal{P}_X}(\mathsf{V}_{\boldsymbol{r}}, \boldsymbol{h_k}) = \boldsymbol{B}.$$

We distinguish the first indexed polynomial in $\boldsymbol{B}$ and require it to have index S_k; we call it the *Master-key Masking term*[10] and denote it as $(K_0)_{S_k}$. Hence, $\boldsymbol{B} = ((K_0)_{S_k}, \boldsymbol{K})$.
- $\mathsf{EncC}(Y, \boldsymbol{h_c}) \rightarrow (\boldsymbol{C}, \boldsymbol{s}, \mathcal{P}_Y)$. The *Ciphertext Encoding algorithm* takes $Y \in \mathbb{Y}_\Lambda$ and $\boldsymbol{h_c}$ as inputs. It outputs two vectors $\boldsymbol{C}, \boldsymbol{s}$ of indexed polynomials, and a multilinear program $\mathcal{P}_Y$. We require that $\boldsymbol{s} = ((s_0)_{S_c}, (s_1)_{T_1}, \ldots, (s_w)_{T_w})$, where $s_0, s_1, \ldots, s_w$ are fresh variables, for some $T_1, \ldots, T_w \subseteq S_c$ for some integer w. We require that

$$\mathcal{P}_Y \text{ is associative over } (\boldsymbol{s}, \boldsymbol{h_c}) \qquad \text{and} \qquad \mathcal{E}_{\mathcal{P}_Y}(\mathsf{V}_{\boldsymbol{s}}, \boldsymbol{h_c}) = \boldsymbol{C}.$$

We distinguish the first indexed variable $(s_0)_{S_c}$ in $\boldsymbol{s}$ where we require it to have index S_c. Also, we require that $(s_0)_{S_c} \in \boldsymbol{C}$ and call it the *Base Randomness term*. (Wlog, we let it be the first indexed polynomial in $\boldsymbol{C}$).
- $\mathsf{Pair}(X, Y) \rightarrow \mathcal{P}_{X,Y}$. It outputs a description of multilinear program $\mathcal{P}_{X,Y}$.

Correctness. If $R(X, Y) = 1$ then $\mathcal{P}_{X,Y}(\boldsymbol{K}, \boldsymbol{C}) = (K_0 s_0)_{[1,\kappa]}$, for $\boldsymbol{K}, K_0, \boldsymbol{C}, s_0$ defined as above. In particular, $(K_0)_{S_k}$ and $(s_0)_{S_c}$ are the master-key masking term in $\boldsymbol{K}$ and the base randomness term in $\boldsymbol{C}$, respectively.

3.2   Security Definitions for Multilinear Pair Encoding

In this section, we formalize security notions for multilinear pair encoding. Looking forward, intuitively, they are formalized so as to provide indistinguishability between certain game switchings in the security proof for ABE. Nevertheless, it is simpler than the full security of ABE as the adversary will not obtain elements corresponding to public keys (graded-encoded $\boldsymbol{h_c}$ in our context).

---

[9] Or, $(1)_{S_k}$ is computable from $\boldsymbol{h_k}$. This is only for our purpose of dual conversion in Sect. 6.

[10] It will be used to mask the master-key in our generic scheme in Sect. 3.3, hence the name.

We formalize the computational security here, and postpone the information-theoretic one to the full version. It generalizes that of (bilinear) pair encoding in [3] (with a refinement regarding the number of queries in [9]). It consists of two sub-notions: *selective* and *co-selective master-key hiding* (SMH, CMH) in a graded encoding system G. We recall that G.Samp gives a level-$\emptyset$ encoding of random element. We use the same notation for a vector x of indexed polynomial: that is, $[V_x] \leftarrow \mathsf{Samp(param)}$ gives $[x_1]_\emptyset, \cdots, [x_k]_\emptyset \leftarrow \mathsf{Samp(param)}$.

Selective Master-key Hiding. Let $t_1, t_2 \in \mathbb{N}$. The (t_1, t_2)-SMH security is defined via the following game between the challenger $\mathcal{C}$ and the adversary $\mathcal{A}$ in the following order. For a definitional purpose, we fix $b \in \{0, 1\}$.

1 **Setup:** The challenger $\mathcal{C}$ setups the pair encoding $\mathsf{P.Init}(\Lambda) \to (\kappa, h_c, h_k, n)$, and setups the graded encoding $\mathsf{G.InstGen}(1^\lambda, \kappa, 2) \to (\mathsf{param}, \mathsf{esk}, N_1, N_2)$. $\mathcal{C}$ graded-encodes 1 for all indexes in $\mathcal{S}_c \cup \mathcal{S}_k$ to obtain $I := \{[1]_S^1, [1]_S^2\}_{S \in \mathcal{S}_c \cup \mathcal{S}_k}$. The input to $\mathcal{A}$ is (param, I). $\mathcal{C}$ further samples $[V_h], [\beta]_\emptyset \leftarrow \mathsf{Samp(param)}$ for using in the next phases. From b, define

$$\beta^\star := 0 \quad \text{if } b = 0 \qquad \text{and} \qquad \beta^\star := \beta \quad \text{if } b = 1.$$

2 **Ciphertext query phase:** $\mathcal{A}$ makes a query Y for graded-encoded EncC. $\mathcal{C}$ then runs $\mathsf{P.EncC}(Y, h_c) \to (C, s, \mathcal{P}_Y)$, samples $[V_s] \leftarrow \mathsf{Samp(param)}$, and returns $[C]^2$ to $\mathcal{A}$. At most t_1 ciphertext queries are allowed.

3 **Key query phase:** $\mathcal{A}$ makes a query X for graded-encoded EncK. We require that $R(X, Y) = 0$ for all queries Y in the previous phase. $\mathcal{C}$ runs $\mathsf{P.EncK}(X, h_k) \to (B, r, \mathcal{P}_X)$, samples $[V_r] \leftarrow \mathsf{Samp(param)}$. Parse $B = ((K_0)_{\mathcal{S}_k}, K)$ and returns

$$([\beta^\star]_{\mathcal{S}_k}^2 + [K_0]_{\mathcal{S}_k}^2, [K]^2)$$

to $\mathcal{A}$. At most t_2 key queries are allowed.

4 **Guess:** The adversary $\mathcal{A}$ outputs a guess $b' \in \{0, 1\}$.

Let $\mathsf{Exp}_b(\lambda)$ denote the output of the game. We define the advantage of $\mathcal{A}$ as $\mathsf{Adv}_{\mathcal{A}}^{(t_1, t_2)\text{-SMH(P)}}(\lambda) := |\Pr[\mathsf{Exp}_0(\lambda) = 1] - \Pr[\mathsf{Exp}_1(\lambda) = 1]|$. We say that P is (t_1, t_2)-SMH in G if the advantage is negligible for all polynomial time attackers $\mathcal{A}$. If t_i is not a-priori bounded, we denote $t_i = \mathsf{poly}$.

Remark 1. We note that, in the above game, $\mathcal{C}$ can compute the returned graded-encoded elements by using I and known level-$\emptyset$ graded-encoded variables, $[V_h]$, $[V_s], [V_r]$. Also note that, if graded encoding is noisy, $\mathcal{C}$ re-randomizes answers to have a certain noise level before returning back to $\mathcal{A}$.

Co-selective Master-key Hiding. The (t_1, t_2)-CMH security is defined in exactly the same manner as that of SMH except that we swap the order of the two query phases: we let the key query phase comes before the ciphertext query phase. Now, t_1, t_2 denotes the number of key and ciphertext queries, respectively. We note that an analogous restriction is required in the ciphertext query phase.

3.3   Our Generic ABE Construction for Any Predicate

Construction. From a multi-linear pair encoding scheme P for predicate R and a graded encoding system G, we construct an ABE scheme for R, denoted ABE(P, G), as follows. We let the message space be $\mathcal{M} = \{0,1\}^\lambda$.

- **Setup**$(1^\Lambda) \to$ (PK, MSK). Initialize P.Init$(\Lambda) \to (\kappa, \boldsymbol{h}_c, \boldsymbol{h}_k, n)$ and generate G.InstGen$(1^\lambda, \kappa, 2) \to$ (param, esk, N_1, N_2). For $i \in [1, n]$, sample $h_i \xleftarrow{\$} \mathcal{R}$. Sample $\alpha \xleftarrow{\$} \mathcal{R}$. It graded-encodes all elements in $\boldsymbol{h}_c, \boldsymbol{h}_k$, in $\mathbb{Z}_{N_1}$ components (by using the secret encoding key esk). Output:

$$PK = \left(\text{param}, [\,\boldsymbol{h}_c\,]^1, [\,\alpha\,]^1_{[1,\kappa]}\right), \qquad MSK = \left(\text{param}, [\,\boldsymbol{h}_k\,]^1, [\,\alpha\,]^{1,2}_{S_k}\right).$$

- **Encrypt**$(PK, Y, M) \to$ CT. Run P.EncC$(Y, \boldsymbol{h}_c) \to (\boldsymbol{C}, \boldsymbol{s}, \mathcal{P}_Y)$. Sample $[\,V_{\boldsymbol{s}}\,] \leftarrow$ Samp(param). Compute

$$[\,\boldsymbol{C}\,]^1 = \mathcal{E}_{\mathcal{P}_Y}([\,V_{\boldsymbol{s}}\,], [\,\boldsymbol{h}_c\,]^1).$$

It then computes $[\,\alpha s_0\,]^1_{[1,\kappa]} = [\,\alpha\,]^1_{[1,\kappa]} \cdot [\,s_0\,]_\emptyset$ and $C_0 =$ G.Ext(param, $[\,\alpha s_0\,]^1_{[1,\kappa]}) \oplus M$. Output CT $= ([\,\boldsymbol{C}\,]^1, C_0)$.

- **KeyGen**$(MSK, X) \to$ SK. Run P.EncK$(X, \boldsymbol{h}_k) \to ((K_0)_{S_k}, \boldsymbol{K}, \boldsymbol{r}, \mathcal{P}_X)$. Sample $[\,V_{\boldsymbol{r}}\,] \leftarrow$ Samp(param). Compute

$$([\,K_0\,]^1_{S_k}, [\,\boldsymbol{K}\,]^1) = \mathcal{E}_{\mathcal{P}_X}([\,V_{\boldsymbol{r}}\,], [\,\boldsymbol{h}_k\,]^1)$$

Output SK $= \left([\,\alpha\,]^{1,2}_{S_k} + [\,K_0\,]^1_{S_k}, [\,\boldsymbol{K}\,]^1\right)$.

- **Decrypt**$(SK, CT) \to M$. Assume $R(X, Y) = 1$. Parse $[\,s_0\,]^1_{S_c}$ from CT. Run P.Pair$(X, Y) \to \mathcal{P}_{X,Y}$. Compute $\mathcal{P}_{X,Y}([\,\boldsymbol{K}\,]^1, [\,\boldsymbol{C}\,]^1) \to [\,K_0 s_0\,]^1_{[1,\kappa]}$ and

$$([\,\alpha\,]^{1,2}_{S_k} + [\,K_0\,]^1_{S_k}) \cdot [\,s_0\,]^1_{S_c} - [\,K_0 s_0\,]^1_{[1,\kappa]} = [\,\alpha s_0\,]^1_{[1,\kappa]},$$

and obtain M as $C_0 \oplus$ G.Ext(param, $[\,\alpha s_0\,]^1_{[1,\kappa]})$.

Semi-functional Algorithms. In the security proof, we will use semi-functional algorithms defined below. In these, we will use hatted variables which are fresh variables (thus are independent from their non-hatted counterparts). For a vector $\boldsymbol{x}$ of indexed variables, let $\hat{\boldsymbol{x}}$ be a vector of indexed variables where we swap each variable in $\boldsymbol{x}$ with its hatted counterpart. In particular, this defines $\hat{\boldsymbol{h}}_c, \hat{\boldsymbol{h}}_k, \hat{\boldsymbol{s}}, \hat{\boldsymbol{r}}$.

- **SFSetup**$(1^\Lambda) \to$ (PK, MSK, $\widehat{PK}$, $\widehat{MSK}$). This is exactly the same as Setup albeit it additionally outputs $\widehat{PK}$, $\widehat{MSK}$ as follows. For $i \in [1, n]$, sample $\hat{h}_i \xleftarrow{\$} \mathcal{R}$. It graded-encodes all elements in $\hat{\boldsymbol{h}}_c, \hat{\boldsymbol{h}}_k$ projecting to subring $\mathbb{Z}_{N_2}$ and outputs:

$$\widehat{PK} = \left([\,\hat{\boldsymbol{h}}_c\,]^2, [\,\alpha\,]^2_{[1,\kappa]}\right), \qquad \widehat{MSK} = [\,\hat{\boldsymbol{h}}_k\,]^2,$$

It also outputs $[\,1\,]^2_{S_k}$ (for using as an input to SFKeyGen below).

- **SFEncrypt**$(\mathsf{PK}, Y, M, \widehat{\mathsf{PK}}) \rightarrow \mathsf{CT}$. First, proceed as $\mathsf{Encrypt}(\mathsf{PK}, Y, M)$ to obtain $[C]^1$ and $[\alpha s_0]^1_{[1,\kappa]}$. Sample $[\mathsf{V}_{\hat{s}}] \leftarrow \mathsf{Samp}(\mathsf{param})$. Compute

$$[\widehat{C}]^2 := \mathcal{E}_{\mathcal{P}_Y}\left([\mathsf{V}_{\hat{s}}], [\hat{h}_\mathsf{c}]^2\right).$$

Compute $[\alpha\hat{s}_0]^2_{[1,\kappa]} = [\alpha]^2_{[1,\kappa]} \cdot [\hat{s}_0]_\emptyset$, and $\widehat{C}_0 = \mathsf{G.Ext}(\mathsf{param}, [\alpha s_0]^1_{[1,\kappa]} + [\alpha\hat{s}_0]^2_{[1,\kappa]}) \oplus M$. Output $\mathsf{CT} = \left([C]^1 + [\widehat{C}]^2, \widehat{C}_0\right)$.

- **SFKeyGen**$(\mathsf{MSK}, X, \mathsf{type}, \mathsf{aux}) \rightarrow \mathsf{SK}$. aux is an auxiliary input. If $\mathsf{type} = 1$, let $\mathsf{aux} = \widehat{\mathsf{MSK}}$. If $\mathsf{type} = 2$, let $\mathsf{aux} = (\widehat{\mathsf{MSK}}, [1]^2_{S_\mathsf{k}}, [\beta]_\emptyset)$. If $\mathsf{type} = 3$, let $\mathsf{aux} = ([1]^2_{S_\mathsf{k}}, [\beta]_\emptyset)$. First, run $\mathsf{KeyGen}(\mathsf{MSK}, X) \rightarrow ([\alpha]^{1,2}_{S_\mathsf{k}} + [K_0]^1_{S_\mathsf{k}}, [K]^1)$. Sample $[\mathsf{V}_{\hat{r}}] \leftarrow \mathsf{Samp}(\mathsf{param})$. If $\mathsf{type} = 1$ or 2, compute

$$([\widehat{K_0}]^2_{S_\mathsf{k}}, [\widehat{K}]^2) := \mathcal{E}_{\mathcal{P}_X}\left([\mathsf{V}_{\hat{r}}], [\hat{h}_\mathsf{k}]^2\right).$$

For $\mathsf{type} = 2$ or 3, also compute $[\beta]^2_{S_\mathsf{k}} = [1]^2_{S_\mathsf{k}} \cdot [\beta]_\emptyset$. Output

$$\mathsf{SK} = \begin{cases} ([\alpha]^{1,2}_{S_\mathsf{k}} + [K_0]^1_{S_\mathsf{k}} \qquad\qquad + [\widehat{K_0}]^2_{S_\mathsf{k}}, \; [K]^1 + [\widehat{K}]^2) & \text{if } \mathsf{type} = 1 \\ ([\alpha]^{1,2}_{S_\mathsf{k}} + [K_0]^1_{S_\mathsf{k}} + [\beta]^2_{S_\mathsf{k}} + [\widehat{K_0}]^2_{S_\mathsf{k}}, \; [K]^1 + [\widehat{K}]^2) & \text{if } \mathsf{type} = 2 \\ ([\alpha]^{1,2}_{S_\mathsf{k}} + [K_0]^1_{S_\mathsf{k}} + [\beta]^2_{S_\mathsf{k}} \qquad\qquad, \; [K]^1 \qquad\qquad\quad) & \text{if } \mathsf{type} = 3 \end{cases}$$

3.4 Multilinear Subgroup Decision Assumption

We introduce a new subgroup decision assumption in multilinear settings. It generalizes the First and Second Subgroup Decision Assumptions in [3, 35, 37], which are defined in bilinear groups, to multilinear settings. We require the composite settings with only two subrings, instead of three as in [3, 35, 37, 51].

Definition 6 (MSD). *For $\kappa \in \mathbb{N}$, $U \subseteq [1, \kappa]$, we define the (κ, U)-Multilinear Subgroup Decision Assumption as follows. Let $\mathsf{InstGen}(1^\lambda, \kappa, 2) \rightarrow (\mathsf{param}, \mathsf{esk}, N_1, N_2)$. For $i \in U$, let $z_i \xleftarrow{s} \mathcal{R}$. Define $\bar{U} = [1, \kappa] \setminus U$. For $i \in \bar{U}$, let $a_i \xleftarrow{s} \mathcal{R}$. It states that the following distributions are computationally indistinguishable:*

$$\left(D, Z = \left\{[z_i]^1_{\{i\}}\right\}_{i \in U}\right) \qquad and \qquad \left(D, Z = \left\{[z_i]^{1,2}_{\{i\}}\right\}_{i \in U}\right),$$

where $D = \left(\mathsf{param}, I = \left\{[1]^1_{\{i\}}\right\}_{i \in [1,\kappa]}, A = \left\{[a_i]^{1,2}_{\{i\}}\right\}_{i \in \bar{U}}, B = [1]^2_{\bar{U}}\right).$

We are able to use only two subrings thanks to *asymmetric* settings. Intuitively, if we were to use symmetric ones, B, which has only the $\mathbb{Z}_{N_2}$ component, can be used to test Z by multiplying to it. (And hence to prevent it, a mask from another subgroup was needed). In asymmetric settings, we cannot multiply B with any element in Z since their indexes intersect.

Properties from MSD. We describe some properties from MSD that will be used in the security proof. We can write $Z_i := [z_i]^{1,2}_{\{i\}} = [z_{i,1}]^1_{\{i\}} + [z_{i,2}]^2_{\{i\}}$.

The problem can be restated as to distinguish whether $z_{i,2} = 0$ for all $i \in U$ or $z_{i,2} \in_R \mathcal{R}$ for all $i \in U$. For further use in the proofs, we denote the following. For $S \subseteq U$, we denote $Z_S := \prod_{i \in S} Z_i$ and $z_{S,j} := \prod_{i \in S} z_{i,j}$, for $j = 1, 2$. Hence, we have $Z_S = [z_{S,1}]_S^1 + [z_{S,2}]_S^2$ by orthogonality. Similarly, we write $A_i := [a_i]_{\{i\}}^{1,2} = [a_{i,1}]_{\{i\}}^1 + [a_{i,2}]_{\{i\}}^2$. For $S \subseteq \bar{U}$, $A_S := \prod_{i \in S} A_i$ and $a_{S,j} := \prod_{i \in S} a_{i,j}$, for $j = 1, 2$; hence, we have $A_S = [a_{S,1}]_S^1 + [a_{S,2}]_S^2$. We also note that from I, for any $S \subseteq [1, \kappa]$, we can compute $\prod_{i \in S} [1]_{\{i\}}^1 = [1]_S^1$.

3.5   Security for Our Generic Construction

Theorem 3. *Suppose that a pair encoding* P *for predicate* R *is* $(1,1)$-CMH *and* $(1, \text{poly})$-SMH *in* G. *Suppose the* MSD *Assumption holds in* G. *Then, our generic construction,* ABE(P, G), *for predicate* R *is fully secure. More precisely, for any PPT adversary* $\mathcal{A}$, *there exist PPT algorithms* $\mathcal{B}_1, \mathcal{B}_2, \mathcal{B}_3, \mathcal{B}_4$, *whose running times are the same as* $\mathcal{A}$ *plus some polynomial times, such that for any* λ,

$$\mathsf{Adv}_{\mathcal{A}}^{\mathsf{ABE(P,G)}}(\lambda) \leq \mathsf{Adv}_{\mathcal{B}_1}^{(\kappa, S_c)\text{-MSD}}(\lambda) + (2q_1 + 2)\mathsf{Adv}_{\mathcal{B}_2}^{(\kappa, S_k)\text{-MSD}}(\lambda)$$
$$+ q_1 \mathsf{Adv}_{\mathcal{B}_3}^{(1,1)\text{-CMH(P)}}(\lambda) + \mathsf{Adv}_{\mathcal{B}_4}^{(1,\text{poly})\text{-SMH(P)}}(\lambda),$$

where q_1 *is the number of queries in phase 1,* κ *is the multi-linearity level, and* $S_c, S_k \subseteq [1, \kappa]$ *are specified by the encoding scheme* P.

Proof. We use a sequence of games in the following order:

$$G_{\text{real}} \quad G_0 \quad G_{1,1} \qquad\quad G_{k-1,3} \;\; G_{k,1} \;\; G_{k,2} \;\; G_{k,3} \qquad\quad G_{q_1,3} \;\; G_{q_1+1} \;\; G_{q_1+2} \;\; G_{q_1+3} \;\; G_{\text{final}}$$

$$\underset{\text{MSD}}{\circ\!\!\rightarrow\!\!\circ\!\!\rightarrow\!\!\circ\!\!\rightarrow} \cdots \underset{\text{MSD CMH MSD}}{\rightarrow\!\!\circ\!\!\rightarrow\!\!\circ\!\!\rightarrow\!\!\circ\!\!\rightarrow\!\!\circ\!\!\rightarrow} \cdots \underset{\text{MSD SMH MSD =}}{\rightarrow\!\!\circ\!\!\rightarrow\!\!\circ\!\!\rightarrow\!\!\circ\!\!\rightarrow\!\!\circ\!\!\rightarrow\!\!\circ}$$

where each game is defined as follows.[11] G_{real} is the actual security game. Each of the following game is defined exactly as *its previous game* in the sequence except the specified modification as follows. For notational purpose, let $G_{0,3} := G_0$.

- G_0: We modify the challenge ciphertext to be semi-functional type.
- $G_{k,i}$ where $k \in [1, q_1]$, $i \in \{1, 2, 3\}$: We modify the k-th queried key to be semi-functional of type-i. We use fresh β for each key (for type $i = 2, 3$).
- G_{q_1+i} where $i \in \{1, 2, 3\}$: We modify all the keys in phase 2 to be semi-functional of type-i at once. We use the same β for all these keys (for type $i = 2, 3$).
- G_{final}: We modify the challenge to encrypt a random message.

In the final game, the advantage of $\mathcal{A}$ is trivially 0. We prove the indistinguishability between all these adjacent games. Due to the lack of space, we provide only two of these lemmata below and defer the rest to the full version. In these lemmata, we define $G_j \mathsf{Adv}_{\mathcal{A}}^{\mathsf{ABE(P,G)}}(\lambda)$ to be the advantage of $\mathcal{A}$ in the game G_j. Summing all the advantage differences from these lemmata, we obtain the advantage bound stated as in Theorem 3.   □

---

[11] More precise definitions of these games are given in the full version.

Proof Intuition. We describe some intuition for proofs of lemmata for game switching with key modifications. We consider two categories. (Ciphertext modification works similarly to the first category below).

For the game switching where β is not changed (normal to type-1 keys, type-2 to type-3 keys), the difference between the two games is exactly the key encodings in the $\mathbb{Z}_{N_2}$ component. We thus simulate the key randomness $[\, r\,]$ using Z from the MSD problem instance, where we have to distinguish whether Z has the $\mathbb{Z}_{N_2}$ component or not. The reduction would then compute $\mathcal{E}_{\mathcal{P}}([\, r\,], [\, \mathsf{V}_{h_k}\,])$, where $[\, \mathsf{V}_{h_k}\,]$ is sampled by the reduction and is used for generating other keys. But, due to *associativity* (Lemma 1), this is equal to $\mathcal{E}_{\mathcal{P}}([\, \mathsf{V}_r\,], [\, h_k\,])$, and due to *decomposability* (Lemma 2), we can deduce that it is exactly the form of normal or semi-functional key as per definition, depending on whether Z has the $\mathbb{Z}_{N_2}$ component or not. Hence, the reduction to MSD is established.

For the game switching where β is changed (type-1 to type-2 keys), the difference between the two games is exactly β. We can embed exactly the challenge from the CMH or SMH game, where we have to distinguish if $\beta^\star = 0$ or $\beta^\star$ is random. If the switched key is in phase 1, we use CMH, where the key query comes before the ciphertext query. If the switched key is in phase 2, we use SMH. The parameter $(1, \mathsf{poly})$ of SMH lets us switch all post-challenge keys at once.

We provide here the proofs for the game switching from $\mathsf{G}_{\mathsf{real}}$ to G_0 (changing normal to semi-functional ciphertext), and $\mathsf{G}_{k,1}$ to $\mathsf{G}_{k,2}$ (changing type-1 to type-2 semi-functional key).

Lemma 3 ($\mathsf{G}_{\mathsf{real}}$ to G_0). *For any adversary $\mathcal{A}$, there exists an algorithm $\mathcal{B}$ that breaks the (κ, S_c)-MSD Assumption with* $|\mathsf{G}_{\mathsf{real}}\mathsf{Adv}_{\mathcal{A}}^{\mathsf{ABE(P,G)}}(\lambda) - \mathsf{G}_0\mathsf{Adv}_{\mathcal{A}}^{\mathsf{ABE(P,G)}}(\lambda)|$
$\leq \mathsf{Adv}_{\mathcal{B}}^{(\kappa, S_c)\text{-}\mathsf{MSD}}(\lambda).$

Proof. As an instance of the (κ, S_c)-MSD Assumption, the algorithm $\mathcal{B}$ obtains an input $(D, \{Z_i\}_{i \in S_c})$ where $Z_i = [\, z_{i,1}\,]_{\{i\}}^1 + [\, z_{i,2}\,]_{\{i\}}^2$. $\mathcal{B}$'s task is to guess whether $z_{i,2} = 0$ or $z_{i,2} \in_R \mathcal{R}$ (both for all $i \in S_c$).

$\mathcal{B}$ simulates SFSetup as follows. First, $\mathcal{B}$ samples $[\, \tilde{\alpha}\,]_\emptyset \leftarrow \mathsf{Samp}(\mathsf{param})$ and sets $[\, \alpha\,]_{S_k}^{1,2} = [\, \tilde{\alpha}\,]_\emptyset \cdot A_{S_k}$ for MSK, and $[\, \alpha\,]_{[1,\kappa]}^1 = [\, \alpha\,]_{S_k}^{1,2} \cdot [\, 1\,]_{S_c}^1$ for PK.

For $i \in [1, n]$, $\mathcal{B}$ samples $[\, \tilde{h}_i\,]_\emptyset \leftarrow \mathsf{Samp}(\mathsf{param})$. For each indexed variable $(h_i)_S$ in h_c or h_k (for some S), $\mathcal{B}$ computes $[\, h_i\,]_S^1 = [\, \tilde{h}_i\,]_\emptyset \cdot [\, 1\,]_S^1$ (computable since $[\, 1\,]_S^1$ is available in I) and *implicitly* sets $[\, \hat{h}_i\,]_S^2 = [\, \tilde{h}_i\,]_\emptyset \cdot [\, 1\,]_S^2$ (unknown since $[\, 1\,]_S^2$ is not available). Hence we have $h_i = \tilde{h}_i \bmod N_1$ and $\hat{h}_i = \tilde{h}_i \bmod N_2$. Due to CRT, h_i and $\hat{h}_i$ distribute independently, as required by definition of SFSetup. This feature is called *parameter-hiding* [3,36]. All these terms completely define PK, MSK. PK is given to $\mathcal{A}$.

Phase 1,2. When $\mathcal{A}$ makes the j-th key query for $X^{(j)}$, $\mathcal{B}$ generates a key as usual: $\mathsf{SK}_j \leftarrow \mathsf{KeyGen}(\mathsf{MSK}, X^{(j)})$.

Challenge. The adversary $\mathcal{A}$ outputs messages $M_0, M_1 \in \{0,1\}^\lambda$ along with a target $Y^\star$. $\mathcal{B}$ chooses $\mathfrak{b} \xleftarrow{\$} \{0,1\}$. $\mathcal{B}$ runs $\mathsf{P.EncC}(Y^\star, h_c) \to (C, s, \mathcal{P}_{Y^\star})$. Let

$w = |s| - 1$. For $i \in [0, w]$, sample $[\tilde{s}_i]_\emptyset \leftarrow \mathsf{Samp}(\mathsf{param})$. Suppose that $s = ((s_0)_{S_c}, (s_1)_{T_1}, \ldots, (s_w)_{T_w})$. $\mathcal{B}$ then computes

$$[\bar{s}] := \Big([\tilde{s}_0]_\emptyset \cdot Z_{S_c}, [\tilde{s}_1]_\emptyset \cdot Z_{T_1}, \ldots, [\tilde{s}_w]_\emptyset \cdot Z_{T_w}\Big),$$

$$[\bar{C}] := \mathcal{E}_{\mathcal{P}_{Y^*}}\Big([\bar{s}], [\mathsf{V}_{\tilde{h}_c}]\Big),$$

$$\bar{C}_0 := \mathsf{G.Ext}\Big(\mathsf{param}, [\alpha]_{S_k}^{1,2} \cdot [\tilde{s}_0]_\emptyset \cdot Z_{S_c}\Big) \oplus M_\flat$$

where $Z_S = [z_{S,1}]_S^1 + [z_{S,2}]_S^2$ for $S \subseteq S_c$ is indeed derivable from the problem instance. (See at the end of Sect. 3.4 for the definition of Z_S). $\mathcal{B}$ sets $\mathsf{CT} = ([\bar{C}], \bar{C}_0)$. We claim that CT properly distributes as a normal or semi-functional ciphertext. To prove this, we observe that

$$[\bar{C}] = \mathcal{E}_{\mathcal{P}_{Y^*}}\Big([\bar{s}], [\mathsf{V}_{\tilde{h}_c}]\Big) = \mathcal{E}_{\mathcal{P}_{Y^*}}\Big([\bar{s}]^1, [\mathsf{V}_{\tilde{h}_c}]\Big) + \mathcal{E}_{\mathcal{P}_{Y^*}}\Big([\bar{s}]^2, [\mathsf{V}_{\tilde{h}_c}]\Big) \qquad (2)$$

$$= \mathcal{E}_{\mathcal{P}_{Y^*}}\Big([\mathsf{V}_s], [h_c]^1\Big) + \mathcal{E}_{\mathcal{P}_{Y^*}}\Big([\mathsf{V}_{\hat{s}}], [\hat{h}_c]^2\Big), \qquad (3)$$

where Eq. (2) is due to decomposability (via Corollary 1), while Eq. (3) is due to the associativity (via Corollary 2), where the variable $s_i, \hat{s}_i$ (for $i \in [0, w]$) in $s, \hat{s}$ are implicitly set as $s_i = \tilde{s}_i z_{T_i,1}$ and $\hat{s}_i = \tilde{s}_i z_{T_i,2}$, respectively. (Denote $T_0 = S_c$). In particular, $s_0 = \tilde{s}_0 z_{S_c,1}$ and $\hat{s}_0 = \tilde{s}_0 z_{S_c,2}$, hence in $\bar{C}_0$ we have $[\alpha]_{S_k}^{1,2} \cdot [\tilde{s}_0]_\emptyset \cdot Z_{S_c} = [\alpha s_0]_{[1,\kappa]}^1 + [\alpha \hat{s}_0]_{[1,\kappa]}^2$. Hence, if $z_{i,2} = 0$ for all $i \in S_c$, then CT is normal. Otherwise, $z_{i,2} \in_R \mathcal{R}$ for all $i \in S_c$, then CT is semi-functional.

Guess. The algorithm $\mathcal{B}$ has properly simulated $\mathsf{G}_{\mathrm{real}}$ if $z_{i,2} = 0$ for all $i \in S_c$, and G_0 if $z_{i,2} \in_R \mathcal{R}$ for all $i \in S_c$. Hence, $\mathcal{B}$ can use the output of $\mathcal{A}$ to break the (κ, S_c)-MSD Assumption. $\qquad \square$

Lemma 4 ($\mathsf{G}_{k,1}$ to $\mathsf{G}_{k,2}$). *For any adversary $\mathcal{A}$ against the $\mathsf{ABE(P, G)}$ scheme, there exists an algorithm $\mathcal{B}$ that breaks the $(1,1)$-CMH security of the pair encoding scheme P with $|\mathsf{G}_{k,1}\mathsf{Adv}_\mathcal{A}^{\mathsf{ABE(P,G)}}(\lambda) - \mathsf{G}_{k,2}\mathsf{Adv}_\mathcal{A}^{\mathsf{ABE(P,G)}}(\lambda)| \leq \mathsf{Adv}_\mathcal{B}^{(1,1)\text{-}\mathsf{CMH}}(\lambda)$.*

Proof In the CMH game, $\mathcal{B}$ is given param and $I = \big\{[1]_S^1, [1]_S^2\big\}_{S \in S_c \cup S_k}$ from its challenger. It simulates $\mathsf{G}_{k,1}$ or $\mathsf{G}_{k,2}$ for $\mathcal{A}$ as follows.

$\mathcal{B}$ simulates $\mathsf{SFSetup}$ as follows. It generates $\mathsf{PK}, \mathsf{MSK}$ as in the construction but using the given I instead. Namely, $\mathcal{B}$ runs $\mathsf{P.Init}(\Lambda) \rightarrow (\kappa, h_c, h_k, n)$. It samples $[\alpha]_\emptyset, [h_1]_\emptyset, \ldots, [h_n]_\emptyset \leftarrow \mathsf{Samp}(\mathsf{param})$. By using I, $\mathcal{B}$ can then obtain $[h_c]^1, [\alpha]_{[1,\kappa]}^1$ for PK, and $[h_k]^1, [\alpha]_{S_k}^{1,2}$ for MSK. It sends PK to $\mathcal{A}$. We remark that $[\hat{h}_c]^2, [\hat{h}_k]^2$ (as parts of $\widehat{\mathsf{PK}}, \widehat{\mathsf{MSK}}$) are not yet defined until the first query that requires using them, which is the k-th key query below.

Phase 1. When $\mathcal{A}$ makes the j-th key query for $X^{(j)}$, $\mathcal{B}$ does as follows.

(Case $j < k$). $\mathcal{B}$ samples $[\beta_j]_\emptyset \leftarrow \mathsf{Samp}(\mathsf{param})$, and computes a type-3 semi-functional key as $\mathsf{SK}_j \leftarrow \mathsf{SFKeyGen}(\mathsf{MSK}, X^{(j)}, 3, [1]_{S_k}^2, [\beta_j]_\emptyset)$.

(**Case** $j = k$). $\mathcal{B}$ generates a type-1 or type-2 semi-functional key as follows. $\mathcal{B}$ first obtains $\mathsf{KeyGen}\big(\mathsf{MSK}, X^{(k)}\big) \to \mathsf{SK} = \big([\,\alpha\,]_{S_k}^{1,2} + [\,K_0\,]_{S_k}^{1}, [\,K\,]^{1}\big)$. $\mathcal{B}$ then makes a key query for $X^{(k)}$ to its challenger in the CMH game and obtains

$$\widehat{\mathsf{SK}} = \big([\,\beta^\star\,]_{S_k}^{2} + [\,\widehat{K_0}\,]_{S_k}^{2}, [\,\widehat{K}\,]^{2}\big).$$

This is the challenge for $\mathcal{B}$ to guess if $\beta^\star = 0$ or $\beta^\star \in_R \mathcal{R}$. $\mathcal{B}$ then returns $\mathsf{SK} + \widehat{\mathsf{SK}}$ to $\mathcal{A}$. If $\beta^\star = 0$, then this is a type-1 semi-functional key. If $\beta^\star \in_R \mathcal{R}$, then it is of type-2. We note that this simulated key implicitly defines $[\,\hat{h}_c\,]^2, [\,\hat{h}_k\,]^2$.

(**Case** $j > k$). $\mathcal{B}$ generates a normal key as $\mathsf{SK}_j \leftarrow \mathsf{KeyGen}(\mathsf{MSK}, X^{(j)})$.

Challenge. The adversary $\mathcal{A}$ outputs messages $M_0, M_1 \in \{0,1\}^\lambda$ along with a target $Y^\star$ such that $R(X_j, Y^\star) = 0$ for all $j \in [1, q_1]$. $\mathcal{B}$ first obtains $[\,C\,]^1$ by running $\mathsf{Encrypt}(\mathsf{PK}, Y, M)$. $\mathcal{B}$ then makes a ciphertext query for $Y^\star$ to its challenger in the CMH game and receives back $[\,\widehat{C}\,]^2$. This query can be made since $R(X_k, Y^\star) = 0$. $\mathcal{B}$ parses $[\,s_0\,]_{S_c}^{1}$ from $[\,C\,]^1$, and $[\,\hat{s}_0\,]_{S_c}^{2}$ from $[\,\widehat{C}\,]^2$. $\mathcal{B}$ then chooses $\mathfrak{b} \xleftarrow{\$} \{0,1\}$ and computes $\widehat{C}_0 = \mathsf{G.Ext}(\mathsf{param}, [\,\alpha\,]_\emptyset \cdot [\,1\,]_{S_k}^{1} \cdot [\,s_0\,]_{S_c}^{1} + [\,\alpha\,]_\emptyset \cdot [\,1\,]_{S_k}^{2} \cdot [\,\hat{s}_0\,]_{S_c}^{2}) \oplus M_\mathfrak{b}$. $\mathcal{B}$ forms the challenge ciphertext as $\mathsf{CT} = \big([\,C\,]^1 + [\,\widehat{C}\,]^2, \widehat{C}_0\big)$, which is a properly distributed semi-functional ciphertext as required.

Phase 2. For each query in this phase, $\mathcal{B}$ generates a normal key as usual.

Guess. The algorithm $\mathcal{B}$ has properly simulated $\mathsf{G}_{k,1}$ if $\beta^\star = 0$, and $\mathsf{G}_{k,2}$ if $\beta^\star$ is random. Hence, $\mathcal{B}$ can use the output of $\mathcal{A}$ to guess $\beta^\star$. □

Variants of Security Theorems. We also obtain a theorem for the case of $(1, 1)$-SMH, instead of $(1, \mathsf{poly})$-SMH. This results in looser reduction. We defer their proofs to the full version, where we also provide some more variants.

Corollary 3 *Suppose that a pair encoding* P *for predicate* R *is* $(1, 1)$-CMH, $(1, 1)$-SMH *in* G. *Suppose that the* MSD *Assumption holds in* G. *Then,* $\mathsf{ABE}(\mathsf{P}, \mathsf{G})$ *is fully secure, with advantage bounded by*

$$\mathsf{Adv}_{\mathcal{A}}^{\mathsf{ABE}(\mathsf{P},\mathsf{G})}(\lambda) \le \mathsf{Adv}_{\mathcal{B}_1}^{(\kappa, S_c)\text{-}\mathsf{MSD}}(\lambda) + 2q_{\mathsf{all}}\mathsf{Adv}_{\mathcal{B}_2}^{(\kappa, S_k)\text{-}\mathsf{MSD}}(\lambda)$$
$$+ q_1\mathsf{Adv}_{\mathcal{B}_3}^{(1,1)\text{-}\mathsf{CMH(P)}}(\lambda) + q_2\mathsf{Adv}_{\mathcal{B}_4}^{(1,1)\text{-}\mathsf{SMH(P)}}(\lambda).$$

On the other hand, we can establish tight reduction from semi-adaptive security to $(1, \mathsf{poly})$-SMH as shown in the following corollary.

Corollary 4 *Suppose that a pair encoding* P *for predicate* R *is* $(1, \mathsf{poly})$-SMH *in* G. *Suppose that the* MSD *Assumption holds in* G. *Then,* $\mathsf{ABE}(\mathsf{P}, \mathsf{G})$ *is semi-adaptively secure, with advantage bounded by*

$$\mathsf{Adv}_{\mathcal{A}}^{\mathsf{semi},\mathsf{ABE}(\mathsf{P},\mathsf{G})}(\lambda) \le \mathsf{Adv}_{\mathcal{B}_1}^{(\kappa, S_c)\text{-}\mathsf{MSD}}(\lambda) + 2\mathsf{Adv}_{\mathcal{B}_2}^{(\kappa, S_k)\text{-}\mathsf{MSD}}(\lambda) + \mathsf{Adv}_{\mathcal{B}_3}^{(1,\mathsf{poly})\text{-}\mathsf{SMH(P)}}(\lambda).$$

4   Fully Secure KP-ABE for Circuits

We describe our first KP-ABE via multilinear pair encoding scheme P_{KPABE1}. It is based on the (selectively-secure) KP-ABE of GGHSW [24], albeit we require 3ℓ-multilinear maps, instead of $(\ell+1)$ as in [24]. More precisely, instead of using all singleton-set levels $\{1\}, \ldots, \{\ell+1\}$, we implement the scheme on encodings of levels in $\mathcal{S} := \{[1, \ell+1], [\ell+2, 2\ell+1], \{2\ell+2\}, \ldots, \{3\ell\}\}$. In the construction, each of the first two "bundled" levels will always be used as a whole bundle. We only decompose them in the simulation to accommodate the assumption in the proof. Another difference are some additional terms T_1, T_2, D_1, D_2, for the purpose of proving the $\mathsf{CMH}, \mathsf{SMH}$ security using randomizer techniques [3, 36].

Construction P_{KPABE1}.

- $\mathsf{Init}(\lambda, n, \ell) \to (\kappa, \boldsymbol{h}_{\mathsf{c}}, \boldsymbol{h}_{\mathsf{k}}, \bar{n})$. Set $\kappa = 3\ell$. Set $\bar{n} = n+2$ where we use variables $h_1, \ldots, h_n, \phi_1, \phi_2$. Let $\mathcal{S}' := \{[\ell+2, 2\ell+1], \{2\ell+2\}, \ldots, \{3\ell\}\}$. Define

$$\boldsymbol{h}_{\mathsf{c}} = \big((1)_{S_{\mathsf{c}}}, (h_1)_{S_{\mathsf{c}}} \ldots, (h_n)_{S_{\mathsf{c}}}, (\phi_1)_{S_{\mathsf{c}}}, (\phi_2)_{S_{\mathsf{c}}}\big),$$
$$\boldsymbol{h}_{\mathsf{k}} = \big(\{(1)_S\}_{S \in \mathcal{S}'}, (h_1)_{[\ell+2, 2\ell+1]} \ldots, (h_n)_{[\ell+2, 2\ell+1]}, (\phi_1)_{S_{\mathsf{k}}}, (\phi_2)_{S_{\mathsf{k}}}\big),$$

  where $S_{\mathsf{c}} = [1, \ell+1], S_{\mathsf{k}} = [\ell+2, 3\ell]$.
- $\mathsf{EncC}(\boldsymbol{h}_{\mathsf{c}}, x \in \{0,1\}^n) \to (\boldsymbol{C}, \boldsymbol{s}, \mathcal{P}_x).$[12] Let $A_x = \{j \in [1, n] | x_j = 1\}$. Output a ciphertext encoding $\boldsymbol{C} = \big(T_1, C, \{C_j\}_{j \in A_x}, T_2\big)$ where

$$T_1 = (t)_{[1, \ell+1]}, \quad C = (s)_{[1, \ell+1]}, \quad C_j = (h_j s)_{[1, \ell+1]}, \quad T_2 = (\phi_2 t + \phi_1 s)_{[1, \ell+1]}.$$

  The indexed variable vector is $\boldsymbol{s} = \big((t)_{[1, \ell+1]}, (s)_{[1, \ell+1]}\big)$. That is, the base randomness term is $(t)_{[1, \ell+1]}$.[13]
- $\mathsf{EncK}(\boldsymbol{h}_{\mathsf{k}}, f \in \mathbb{F}_{n,\ell}) \to \big((K_0)_{S_{\mathsf{k}}}, \boldsymbol{K}, \boldsymbol{r}, \mathcal{P}_f\big).$[12] Set the indexed variable vector:

$$\boldsymbol{r} = \Big((r)_{[\ell+2, 3\ell]}, \{(\alpha_w)_{[\ell+2, 2\ell+i_w]}\}_{w \in \mathsf{Nodes}}, \{(v_w)_{[\ell+2, 2\ell+1]}\}_{w \in \mathsf{Inputs}},$$
$$\{(\ell_w)_{\{2\ell+i_w\}}, (r_w)_{\{2\ell+i_w\}}\}_{w \in \mathsf{Gates}}\Big)$$

  where we denote $i_w := \mathsf{Depth}(w)$. Define

$$D_1 = (\phi_2 r)_{[\ell+2, 3\ell]}, \qquad D_2 = (r)_{[\ell+2, 3\ell]}, \qquad D_3 = (\phi_1 r - \alpha_{w_{\mathsf{top}}})_{[\ell+2, 3\ell]}.$$

  Define the key element $\boldsymbol{K}_w$ for each $w \in \mathsf{Nodes}$ as follows.
  1. For each input node $w \in \mathsf{Inputs}$ (*i.e.*, $\mathsf{Depth}(w) = 1$), let $j = \mathsf{Num}(w)$. Define $\boldsymbol{K}_w = (U_w, K_w)$ as

$$U_w = (v_w)_{[\ell+2, 2\ell+1]}, \qquad K_w = (\alpha_w + h_j v_w)_{[\ell+2, 2\ell+1]}.$$

---

[12] The multilinear programs $\mathcal{P}_x$ output from EncC and $\mathcal{P}_f$ output from EncK are straightforwardly deducible from the respective encodings.

[13] That is, we use variable t in place of s_0 of the generic construction.

2. For each gate $w \in$ Gates (*i.e.*, $\mathsf{Depth}(w) > 1$), define $L_w = (\ell_w)_{\{2\ell+i_w\}}$, $R_w = (r_w)_{\{2\ell+i_w\}}$, and do as follows.
   - If $\mathsf{Type}(w) = \mathsf{OR}$, then set $\boldsymbol{K}_w = (L_w, R_w, K_{w,1}, K_{w,2})$, where we let

$$K_{w,1} = (\alpha_w + \alpha_{\mathsf{L}(w)}\ell_w)_{[\ell+2, 2\ell+i_w]}, \quad K_{w,2} = (\alpha_w + \alpha_{\mathsf{R}(w)}r_w)_{[\ell+2, 2\ell+i_w]}.$$

   - If $\mathsf{Type}(w) = \mathsf{AND}$, then we set $\boldsymbol{K}_w = (L_w, R_w, K_w)$, where we let

$$K_w = (\alpha_w + \alpha_{\mathsf{L}(w)}\ell_w + \alpha_{\mathsf{R}(w)}r_w)_{[\ell+2, 2\ell+i_w]}.$$

   Output the key encoding as $((K_0)_{S_k}, \boldsymbol{K})$ where the master-key masking term is $(K_0)_{S_k} = D_1$ and the rest is $\boldsymbol{K} = (D_2, D_3, \{\boldsymbol{K}_w\}_{w \in \mathsf{Nodes}})$.

- **Pair** $(f, x) \to \mathcal{P}_{f,x}$. Assume $f(x) = 1$. We describe multilinear program $\mathcal{P}_{f,x}$ that takes $(\boldsymbol{C}, \boldsymbol{K})$ as an input, and outputs $(K_0 t)_{[1, 3\ell]}$. It computes at each node w such that $f_w(x) = 1$ in the bottom-up manner. It will derive $E_w := (\alpha_w s)_{[1, 2\ell+i]}$, where $i = \mathsf{Depth}(w)$. We show this by induction on i (1 to ℓ).

  1. For each input node $w \in \mathsf{Inputs} = [1, n]$ such that $f_w(x) = 1$, we have $x_w = 1$ and $j := \mathsf{Num}(w) \in A_x$. Compute

$$E_w = C \cdot K_w - C_j \cdot U_w = (\alpha_w s)_{[1, 2\ell+1]}.$$

  This effectively proves the base case of the induction.

  2. For each gate $w \in \mathsf{Gates}$ such that $f_w(x) = 1$, we have two cases.
     - If $\mathsf{Type}(w) = \mathsf{OR}$, then $f_{\mathsf{L}(w)}(x) = 1$ or $f_{\mathsf{R}(w)}(x) = 1$. Wlog, we can assume that $f_{\mathsf{L}(w)}(x) = 1$. Hence, $E_{\mathsf{L}(w)} = (\alpha_{\mathsf{L}(w)} s)_{[1, 2\ell+i-1]}$ by the induction hypothesis, as $\mathsf{Depth}(\mathsf{L}(w)) = i - 1$. Then, compute

$$E_w = C \cdot K_{w,1} - E_{\mathsf{L}(w)} \cdot L_w = (\alpha_w s)_{[1, 2\ell+i]}.$$

     - If $\mathsf{Type}(w) = \mathsf{AND}$, then $f_{\mathsf{L}(w)}(x) = 1$ and $f_{\mathsf{R}(w)}(x) = 1$. Hence, $E_{\mathsf{L}(w)} = (\alpha_{\mathsf{L}(w)} s)_{[1, 2\ell+i-1]}$, $E_{\mathsf{R}(w)} = (\alpha_{\mathsf{R}(w)} s)_{[1, 2\ell+i-1]}$, by the induction hypothesis. Then, compute

$$E_w = C \cdot K_w - (E_{\mathsf{L}(w)} \cdot L_w + E_{\mathsf{R}(w)} \cdot R_w) = (\alpha_w s)_{[1, 2\ell+i]}.$$

This concludes the induction. Finally, at the top gate w_{top}, where $\mathsf{Depth}(w_{\mathsf{top}}) = \ell$, we obtain $E_{w_{\mathsf{top}}} = (\alpha_{w_{\mathsf{top}}} s)_{[1, 3\ell]}$. Compute and obtain

$$T_2 \cdot D_2 - E_{w_{\mathsf{top}}} - C \cdot D_3 = (K_0 t)_{[1, 3\ell]},$$

as required.

Properties. We can see that the key encoding for circuit f contains (at most) $2n + 4g' + 3$ elements, where g' is the number of internal gates. Hence it admits succinctness (the size is $O(g)$, where $g = n + g'$ is the size of a circuit). The ciphertext encoding for x contains $|A_x| + 3 \leq n + 3$ elements. Moreover, it has no bound on circuit size and fan-out. We only require bounds on input length n and depth ℓ.

Assumptions. We describe two new assumptions, SMDDH1 and EMDDH1, which extend the regular Multi-linear DDH assumption (MDDH) [15,20,23] in asymmetric setting. (S, E is for Simple/Esoteric extension, resp.) For assumption X, we define the advantage $\mathsf{Adv}_{\mathcal{A}}^{\mathsf{X}}(\lambda) := |\Pr[\mathcal{A}(D, Z) = 1] - \Pr[\mathcal{A}(D, Z') = 1]|$, for adversary $\mathcal{A}$, where D, Z, Z' are specified in each assumption.

Definition 7 (ℓ-SMDDH1). *Let* $\mathsf{InstGen}(1^\lambda, 3\ell, 2) \rightarrow (\mathsf{param}, \mathsf{esk})$. *Sample* $\zeta, z, c_1, \ldots, c_{\ell+1}$, *from* $\mathcal{R}$. *The* ℓ-SMDDH1 *Assumption states that the following distributions are computationally indistinguishable:*

$$\left(D, Z = [c_1 \cdots c_{\ell+1} z]^2_{[\ell+2, 3\ell]}\right) \quad and \quad \left(D, Z' = [\zeta]^2_{[\ell+2, 3\ell]}\right),$$

where D *consists of:* param, $\left\{[1]^1_{\{i\}}, [1]^2_{\{i\}}\right\}_{i \in [1, 3\ell]}, [z]^2_{[1, \ell+1]}, [c_1 z]^2_{[\ell+2, 3\ell]},$

$$[c_1]^2_{[1, \ell+1]}, [c_1]^2_{[\ell+2, 2\ell+1]}, [c_1]^2_{\{2\ell+2\}}, \ldots, [c_1]^2_{\{3\ell\}},$$
$$[c_2]^2_{[\ell+2, 2\ell+1]}, [c_3]^2_{\{2\ell+2\}}, \ldots, [c_{\ell+1}]^2_{\{3\ell\}}.$$

SMDDH1 differs from MDDH (in asymmetric settings) in two aspects. First, the target element is in the level $[\ell + 2, 3\ell]$, instead of the whole, which is $[1, 3\ell]$. Second, it gives out one more element $[c_1 z]^2_{[\ell+2, 3\ell]}$. We can see that this would not help attacking since it cannot be multiplied with available $c_2, \ldots, c_\ell$ as they are all encoded in levels that are subsets of $[\ell + 2, 3\ell]$.

Definition 8 ((ℓ, m)-EMDDH1). *Let* $\mathsf{InstGen}(1^\lambda, 3\ell, 2) \rightarrow (\mathsf{param}, \mathsf{esk})$. *Sample* $b, z, v, c_1, \cdots, c_{\ell+1}, \mu_1, \cdots, \mu_\ell, \nu_1, \cdots, \nu_\ell, \omega_1, \cdots, \omega_\ell, \{a_{i,j}, d_{i,j}\}_{i \in [1, \ell], j \in [1, m]}$, *and* ζ *from* $\mathcal{R}$. *Denote* $\mu = \mu_1 \cdots \mu_\ell, \nu = \nu_1 \cdots \nu_\ell, \omega = \omega_1 \cdots \omega_\ell$. *The* ($\ell, m$)-EMDDH1 *Assumption states that the following distributions are computationally indistinguishable:*

$$\left(D, Z = [c_1 \cdots c_{\ell+1} b]^2_{[\ell+2, 3\ell]}\right) \quad and \quad \left(D, Z' = [\zeta]^2_{[\ell+2, 3\ell]}\right),$$

where D *consists of[14]:* param, $\left\{[1]^1_S, [1]^2_S\right\}_{S \in \mathsf{S}}, [\frac{z}{b}]^2_{[1, \ell+1]}, [v]^2_{[1, \ell+1]}, [v]^2_{[\ell+2, 3\ell]}, [vb]^2_{[\ell+2, 3\ell]}, [\frac{c_1 \cdots c_{\ell+1}}{v}]^2_{[\ell+2, 3\ell]}$, *and*

$$\forall_{e \in \{0, -1\}} \ [\mu_i a_{i,j}^e]^2_{\{i\}}, \qquad\qquad [\frac{z}{\mu}]^2_{\{\ell+1\}},$$

$$\forall_{e \in \{0, 1\}} \ [\nu_i a_{i,j}^e d_{i,j}]^2_{\{i\}}, \qquad\qquad [\frac{c_1}{\nu}]^2_{\{\ell+1\}},$$

$$\forall_{e \in \{0, -1\}} \ [\omega_i a_{i,j}^e]^2_{\{i\}}, \qquad\qquad [\frac{\omega_i}{\omega} z v \frac{1}{a_{i,j}}]^2_{\{i, \ell+1\}},$$

$$\forall_{(e, e') \in \mathsf{E}} \ [\frac{a_{i,j}^e}{a_{i,j'}^{e'}} d_{i,j}]^2_{\{i\}}, \qquad \forall_{(e, e') \in \mathsf{E}^\star} \ [z c_1 \frac{a_{i,j}^e}{a_{i,j'}^{e'}} d_{i,j}]^2_{\{i, \ell+1\}},$$

$$[\frac{c_2}{d_{1,j}}]^2_{[\ell+2, 2\ell+1]}, \qquad \forall_{i \in [2, \ell]} \ [\frac{c_{i+1}}{d_{i,j}}]^2_{\{2\ell+i\}},$$

---

[14] We refer the definition of S to the beginning of this section (Sect. 4).

$$\forall_{i\in[2,\ell]}\forall_{e\in\{0,1\}}\ [\,a_{i,j}^{e}d_{i,j}\,]_{\{\ell+1+i\}}^{2},$$

$$\forall_{e\in\{0,1\}}\ [\,c_1\cdots c_i a_{i,j}^{e}d_{i,j}\,]_{S_i}^{2}, \qquad \forall_{e\in\{0,1\}}\ [\,c_1\cdots c_{i+1}a_{i,j}^{e}\frac{d_{i,j}}{d_{i,j'}}\,]_{S_i}^{2},$$

where, unless stated above, subscripts range for all $i\in[1,\ell]$, $j,j'\in[1,m]$ *such that* $j'\neq j$. *Denote* $\mathsf{E}=\{(0,0),(0,1),(1,0),(1,1),(-1,0)\}$; $\mathsf{E}^{\star}=\mathsf{E}\setminus\{(0,0)\}$. *Denote* $S_1=\{\ell+2\}$ *and* $S_i=[\ell+2,\ell+1+i]\cup[2\ell+2,2\ell+i]$ *for* $i\geq2$.

Due to the lack of space, we defer the intuition, some remark, and its generic hardness for EMDDH1 to the full version. We provide some discussions regarding EMDDH1 as follows.

On Assumption Simplicity. To compare simplicity of assumptions *quantitatively*, we measure their sizes. The size of EMDDH1 is $O(\ell m^2)$. In bilinear groups, we already have the Expanded m-BDHE [49] assumption, or the one in [43], of which size is $O(m^2)$. The expansion factor of $O(\ell)$ in ours is somewhat natural since we extend to 3ℓ-linear maps. Indeed, the most basic assumption for ℓ-linear maps, namely, the normal ℓ-MDDH [15,20,23], already has size $\Omega(\ell)$.

Comparing to Uber Assumption. The Uber Assumptions in multilinear settings (Uber) are introduced in [38,42], for proving their IO schemes. Intuitively, Uber assumes the indistinguishability of (D,Z) and (D,Z') for *all non-trivial triples* of (D,Z,Z'). We compare EMDDH1 to Uber as they share this similar intuition. However, contrastingly to Uber, EMDDH1 requires only *one such specific triple*, parameterized by (ℓ,m). Our scheme could possibly be proved as well under Uber, so that new assumptions would not be needed. However, this would be undesirable since Uber is *not* efficiently falsifiable [42]; while, on the other hand, our assumptions are. In other words, we believe that it is important to come up with such a specific triple, even if it might look complex. Indeed, our novelty exactly lies in identifying such an explicit triple (D,Z,Z') defined for EMDDH1.

Security. We now state the security theorems for our encoding $\mathsf{P}_{\mathsf{KPABE1}}$. Their proofs are deferred to the full version. From these and Theorem 3, Corollary 4, we also obtain the full and semi-adaptive security of our first KP-ABE below.

Theorem 4. $\mathsf{P}_{\mathsf{KPABE1}}$ *is* $(1,1)$-*CMH under the* (ℓ,m)-*EMDDH1 assumption with tight reduction, where* ℓ,m *is the bounded depth and the width of queried circuit.*

Theorem 5. $\mathsf{P}_{\mathsf{KPABE1}}$ *is* $(1,\mathsf{poly})$-*SMH under the* ℓ-*SMDDH1 assumption with tight reduction, where* ℓ *is the bounded depth.*

Corollary 5. $\mathsf{ABE}(\mathsf{P}_{\mathsf{KPABE1}},\mathsf{G})$ *is fully secure under* EMDDH1, SMDDH1, MSD, *and semi-adaptively secure under* SMDDH1, MSD, *with advantage bounded by*

$$\mathsf{Adv}_{\mathcal{A}}^{\mathsf{ABE}(\mathsf{P}_{\mathsf{KPABE1}},\mathsf{G})}(\lambda)\leq\mathsf{Adv}_{\mathcal{B}_1}^{(\kappa,S_c)\text{-MSD}}(\lambda)+(2q_1+2)\mathsf{Adv}_{\mathcal{B}_2}^{(\kappa,S_k)\text{-MSD}}(\lambda)$$

$$+q_1\mathsf{Adv}_{\mathcal{B}_3}^{(\ell,m)\text{-EMDDH1}}(\lambda)+\mathsf{Adv}_{\mathcal{B}_4}^{\ell\text{-SMDDH1}}(\lambda),$$

$$\mathsf{Adv}_{\mathcal{A}}^{\mathsf{semi},\mathsf{ABE}(\mathsf{P}_{\mathsf{KPABE1}},\mathsf{G})}(\lambda)\leq\mathsf{Adv}_{\mathcal{B}_1'}^{(\kappa,S_c)\text{-MSD}}(\lambda)+2\mathsf{Adv}_{\mathcal{B}_2'}^{(\kappa,S_k)\text{-MSD}}(\lambda)+\mathsf{Adv}_{\mathcal{B}_3'}^{\ell\text{-SMDDH1}}(\lambda),$$

where $\kappa=3\ell$, $S_c=[1,\ell+1]$, $S_k=[\ell+2,3\ell]$.

5 Fully Secure KP-ABE with Short Ciphertext

We describe our KP-ABE for circuits with short ciphertexts. We use similar techniques from compact ABE for formulae of [3,8], which are also similar to [13, 19], for designing elements related to the input layer of circuits. The mechanism regarding internal gates of circuits are exactly the same as our first KP-ABE.

Construction P_{KPABE2}.

- $\mathsf{Init}(\lambda, n, \ell) \to (\kappa, \boldsymbol{h_c}, \boldsymbol{h_k}, \bar{n})$. Set $\kappa = 3\ell$. Set $\bar{n} = n+4$ where we use variables $h_0, h_1, \ldots, h_n, \phi_1, \phi_2, \phi_3$. Define $\boldsymbol{h_c}$ and $\boldsymbol{h_k}$ as in our first KP-ABE except that we have one additional term for each: $(\phi_3)_{[1,\ell+1]}$ in $\boldsymbol{h_c}$; $(\phi_3)_{[\ell+2,2\ell+1]}$ in $\boldsymbol{h_k}$.
- $\mathsf{EncC}(\boldsymbol{h_c}, x \in \{0,1\}^n) \to (\boldsymbol{C}, \boldsymbol{s}, \mathcal{P}_x)$. Let $A_x = \{j \in [1,n] | x_j = 1\}$. Output a ciphertext encoding $\boldsymbol{C} = (C, C_1, C_2, T_1, T_2)$ where

$$C = (s)_{[1,\ell+1]}, \quad C_1 = (\phi_3 s + (h_0 + \sum_{j \in A_x} h_j)u)_{[1,\ell+1]}, \quad C_2 = (u)_{[1,\ell+1]}$$

$$T_1 = (t)_{[1,\ell+1]}, \quad T_2 = (\phi_2 t + \phi_1 s)_{[1,\ell+1]}.$$

  The indexed variable vector is $\boldsymbol{s} = \Big((t)_{[1,\ell+1]}, (s)_{[1,\ell+1]}, (u)_{[1,\ell+1]}\Big)$.
- $\mathsf{EncK}(\boldsymbol{h_k}, f \in \mathbb{F}_{n,\ell}) \to ((K_0)_{S_k}, \boldsymbol{K}, \boldsymbol{r}, \mathcal{P}_f)$. All the elements are the same as our first KP-ABE except $\{\boldsymbol{K_w}\}_{w \in \mathsf{Inputs}}$. Let $j = \mathsf{Num}(w)$. We define $\boldsymbol{K_w} = (U_w, K_w, F_w, \{G_{w,i}\}_{i \in [1,n] \setminus \{j\}})$ as

$$U_w = (v_w)_{[\ell+2,2\ell+1]}, \qquad K_w = (\alpha_w + \phi_3 v_w)_{[\ell+2,2\ell+1]},$$
$$F_w = ((h_0 + h_j)v_w)_{[\ell+2,2\ell+1]}, \qquad G_{w,i} = (h_i v_w)_{[\ell+2,2\ell+1]}.$$

- $\mathsf{Pair}(f, x) \to \mathcal{P}_{f,x}$. Assume that $f(x) = 1$. We describe the multilinear program $\mathcal{P}_{f,x}$ that takes $(\boldsymbol{C}, \boldsymbol{K})$ as an input and outputs $(K_0 t)_{[1,3\ell]}$. It computes exactly as in our first KP-ABE except the computation regarding input nodes. For each input node $w \in \mathsf{Inputs} = [1,n]$ such that $f_w(x) = 1$, we have $x_w = 1$. Let $j = \mathsf{Num}(w)$. We have $j \in A_x$. We compute:

$$E_w = C \cdot K_w - C_1 \cdot U_w + C_2 \cdot F_w + C_2 \cdot \sum_{i \in A_x \setminus \{j\}} G_{w,i} = (\alpha_w s)_{[1,2\ell+1]}$$

  The rest of algorithm is defined as in P_{KPABE1}.

Properties. We can see that the ciphertext encoding for string x always contains 5 elements (hence constant-size relative to n). The key encoding for circuit f contains $n(n-1) + 4g' + 6$ elements, where g' is the number of internal gates.

Assumptions. We use new assumptions SMDDH2, EMDDH2, which are similar to SMDDH1, EMDDH1 respectively, albeit with some additional terms that will be used for simulating the new input layer. In particular, SMDDH2 consists of terms that are similar to the BDHE [14] and the Multi-linear BDHE [13] assumptions (the terms of the form $g, g^a, \ldots, g^{a^n}, g^{a^{n+2}}, \ldots, g^{a^{2n}}$), depicted in the last line of SMDDH2 below. Again, we prove their generic hardness in the full version.

Definition 9 $((\ell, n)$-SMDDH2$)$. *Let* $\mathsf{InstGen}(1^\lambda, 3\ell, 2) \to (\mathsf{param}, \mathsf{esk})$. *Sample* $\zeta, z, c_1, \ldots, c_{\ell+1}, b$ *from* $\mathcal{R}$. *Let* $S = [\ell+2, 2\ell+1]$. *The* (ℓ, n)-SMDDH2 *Assumption states that the following distributions are computationally indistinguishable:*

$$\left(D, Z = [c_1^{n+1}c_2 \cdots c_{\ell+1}b]_{[\ell+2,3\ell]}^2\right) \quad and \quad \left(D, Z' = [\zeta]_{[\ell+2,3\ell]}^2\right),$$

where D *consists of:* param, $\left\{[1]_{\{i\}}^1, [1]_{\{i\}}^2\right\}_{i \in [1,3\ell]}$, *and*

$$[z]_{[1,\ell+1]}^2, [\tfrac{z}{b}]_{[1,\ell+1]}^2, [c_1^{n+1}b]_{[\ell+2,3\ell]}^2,$$
$$[c_1^{n+1}]_{\{2\ell+2\}}^2, \ldots, [c_1^{n+1}]_{\{3\ell\}}^2,$$
$$[c_2]_{[\ell+2,2\ell+1]}^2, [c_3]_{\{2\ell+2\}}^2, \ldots, [c_{\ell+1}]_{\{3\ell\}}^2,$$
$$[c_1]_{[1,\ell+1]}^2, \ldots, [c_1^{n+1}]_{[1,\ell+1]}^2, [c_1]_S^2, \ldots, [c_1^{n+1}]_S^2$$
$$[c_1c_2]_S^2, \ldots, [c_1^nc_2]_S^2, [c_1^{n+2}c_2]_S^2, \ldots, [c_1^{2n+1}c_2]_S^2.$$

Definition 10 $((\ell, m, n)$-EMDDH2$)$. *The* (ℓ, m, n)-EMDDH2 *is defined in exactly the same manner as* (ℓ, m)-EMDDH1 *except that the given part* D *contains also additional elements as follows. The problem instance additionally samples* b_j *for* $j \in [1, n]$. *It augments* D *to also contain, for* $j, j' \in [1, n]$ *such that* $j \neq j'$,

$$[\mu_1 b_j]_{\{1\}}^2, [\nu_1 b_j^2]_{\{1\}}^2, [\tfrac{1}{b_j}]_{\{1\}}^2, [\tfrac{zc_1b_j}{b_{j'}^2}]_{\{1,\ell+1\}}^2,$$
$$[b_jc_2]_{[\ell+2,2\ell+1]}^2, [\tfrac{c_1}{b_j}]_{\{\ell+2\}}^2, [\tfrac{c_1}{b_j^2}]_{\{\ell+2\}}^2, [\tfrac{c_1c_2b_j}{b_{j'}}]_{\{\ell+2\}}^2, [\tfrac{c_1c_2b_j}{b_{j'}^2}]_{\{\ell+2\}}^2.$$

Security. We now state the security theorems for $\mathsf{P}_{\mathsf{KPABE2}}$. We prove them in the full version. The full/semi-adaptive security of the resulting ABE is also given below.

Theorem 6. $\mathsf{P}_{\mathsf{KPABE2}}$ *is* $(1,1)$-CMH *under the* (ℓ, m, n)-EMDDH2 *assumption with tight reduction, where* ℓ *is the bounded depth,* n *is the input length, and* m *is the width of the queried circuit.*

Theorem 7. $\mathsf{P}_{\mathsf{KPABE2}}$ *is* $(1, \mathsf{poly})$-SMH *under the* (ℓ, n)-SMDDH2 *assumption with tight reduction, where* ℓ *is the bounded depth and* n *is the input length.*

Corollary 6. $\mathsf{ABE}(\mathsf{P}_{\mathsf{KPABE2}}, \mathsf{G})$ *is fully secure under* EMDDH2, SMDDH2, MSD, *and semi-adaptively secure under* SMDDH2, MSD, *with advantage bounded by*

$$\mathsf{Adv}_{\mathcal{A}}^{\mathsf{ABE}(\mathsf{P}_{\mathsf{KPABE2}}, \mathsf{G})}(\lambda) \leq \mathsf{Adv}_{\mathcal{B}_1}^{(\kappa, S_c)\text{-MSD}}(\lambda) + (2q_1 + 2)\mathsf{Adv}_{\mathcal{B}_2}^{(\kappa, S_k)\text{-MSD}}(\lambda)$$
$$+ q_1\mathsf{Adv}_{\mathcal{B}_3}^{(\ell, m, n)\text{-EMDDH2}}(\lambda) + \mathsf{Adv}_{\mathcal{B}_4}^{(\ell, n)\text{-SMDDH2}}(\lambda),$$
$$\mathsf{Adv}_{\mathcal{A}}^{\mathsf{semi}, \mathsf{ABE}(\mathsf{P}_{\mathsf{KPABE2}}, \mathsf{G})}(\lambda) \leq \mathsf{Adv}_{\mathcal{B}_1'}^{(\kappa, S_c)\text{-MSD}}(\lambda) + 2\mathsf{Adv}_{\mathcal{B}_2'}^{(\kappa, S_k)\text{-MSD}}(\lambda) + \mathsf{Adv}_{\mathcal{B}_3'}^{(\ell, n)\text{-SMDDH2}}(\lambda),$$

where $\kappa = 3\ell$, $S_c = [1, \ell + 1], S_k = [\ell + 2, 3\ell]$.

6   Dual Conversion and CP-ABE

In this section, we provide a generic dual conversion for multilinear pair encoding. It uses essentially the same idea as the dual conversion for bilinear pair encoding of [9]. We then apply it to our KP-ABE and obtain CP-ABE for circuits.

6.1   Generic Dual Conversion

Given a multi-linear pair encoding scheme P for predicate R, we construct a scheme $\mathrm{CON}(\mathsf{P})$ for its dual predicate $\bar{R}$ as follows. We also denote $\overline{\mathsf{P}} = \mathrm{CON}(\mathsf{P})$.

- $\overline{\mathsf{P}}.\mathsf{Init}(\varLambda)$: Run $\mathsf{P}.\mathsf{Init}(\varLambda) \to (\kappa, \boldsymbol{h}_{\mathsf{c}}, \boldsymbol{h}_{\mathsf{k}}, n)$. Parse $S_{\mathsf{c}}, S_{\mathsf{k}}$ from $\boldsymbol{h}_{\mathsf{c}}, \boldsymbol{h}_{\mathsf{k}}$. Let

$$\bar{S}_{\mathsf{c}} := S_{\mathsf{k}}, \qquad \bar{S}_{\mathsf{k}} := S_{\mathsf{c}}, \qquad \overline{\boldsymbol{h}}_{\mathsf{c}} := (\boldsymbol{h}_{\mathsf{k}}, (\phi)_{\bar{S}_{\mathsf{c}}}), \qquad \overline{\boldsymbol{h}}_{\mathsf{k}} := (\boldsymbol{h}_{\mathsf{c}}, (\phi)_{\bar{S}_{\mathsf{k}}}),$$

where ϕ is a fresh variable. Output $(\kappa, \overline{\boldsymbol{h}}_{\mathsf{c}}, \overline{\boldsymbol{h}}_{\mathsf{k}}, n + 1)$.
- $\overline{\mathsf{P}}.\mathsf{EncK}(Y, \overline{\boldsymbol{h}}_{\mathsf{k}})$: Parse $\boldsymbol{h}_{\mathsf{c}}$ from $\overline{\boldsymbol{h}}_{\mathsf{k}}$. Run $\mathsf{P}.\mathsf{EncC}(Y, \boldsymbol{h}_{\mathsf{c}}) \to (\boldsymbol{C}, \boldsymbol{s}, \mathcal{P}_Y)$. Define

$$\bar{K}_0 := \phi s_0, \qquad \overline{\boldsymbol{K}} := \boldsymbol{C}, \qquad \bar{\boldsymbol{r}} := \boldsymbol{s}.$$

Define $\overline{\mathcal{P}}_Y$ exactly as $\mathcal{P}_Y$ (which outputs $\boldsymbol{C}$) but with an additional input $(\phi s_0)_{\bar{S}_{\mathsf{k}}}$, which is trivially wired to output $(\bar{K}_0)_{\bar{S}_{\mathsf{k}}}$. Output $((\bar{K}_0)_{\bar{S}_{\mathsf{k}}}, \overline{\boldsymbol{K}}, \bar{\boldsymbol{r}}, \overline{\mathcal{P}}_Y)$.
- $\overline{\mathsf{P}}.\mathsf{EncC}(X, \overline{\boldsymbol{h}}_{\mathsf{c}})$: Parse $\boldsymbol{h}_{\mathsf{k}}$ from $\overline{\boldsymbol{h}}_{\mathsf{c}}$. Run $\mathsf{P}.\mathsf{EncK}(X, \boldsymbol{h}_{\mathsf{k}}) \to ((K_0)_{S_{\mathsf{k}}}, \boldsymbol{K}, \boldsymbol{r}, \mathcal{P}_X)$. Define

$$\overline{\boldsymbol{C}} := \left((\bar{s}_0)_{\bar{S}_{\mathsf{c}}}, (\phi \bar{s}_0 + K_0)_{\bar{S}_{\mathsf{c}}}, \boldsymbol{K}\right), \qquad \bar{\boldsymbol{s}} := \left((\bar{s}_0)_{\bar{S}_{\mathsf{c}}}, \boldsymbol{r}\right).$$

where $\bar{s}_0$ is a fresh variable. Define $\overline{\mathcal{P}}_X$ exactly as $\mathcal{P}_X$ (which is a program that outputs $((K_0)_{S_{\mathsf{k}}}, \boldsymbol{K})$) but with additional inputs $(\bar{s}_0)_{\bar{S}_{\mathsf{c}}}, (\phi \bar{s}_0)_{\bar{S}_{\mathsf{c}}}$, which is used for the two new output elements in $\overline{\boldsymbol{C}}$. Output $(\overline{\boldsymbol{C}}, \bar{\boldsymbol{s}}, \overline{\mathcal{P}}_X)$.
- $\overline{\mathsf{P}}.\mathsf{Pair}(Y, X)$: Run $\mathsf{P}.\mathsf{Pair}(X, Y) \to \mathcal{P}_{X,Y}$. Define program $\overline{\mathcal{P}}_{Y,X}$ as:

$$\overline{\mathcal{P}}_{Y,X}(\overline{\boldsymbol{K}}, \overline{\boldsymbol{C}}) : \ \text{Output } (\phi \bar{s}_0 + K_0)_{\bar{S}_{\mathsf{c}}}(s_0)_{\bar{S}_{\mathsf{k}}} - \mathcal{P}_{X,Y}(\boldsymbol{K}, \boldsymbol{C}).$$

Note that $(\phi \bar{s}_0 + K_0)_{\bar{S}_{\mathsf{c}}}$ and $\boldsymbol{K}$ are parsed from $\overline{\boldsymbol{C}}$, while $(s_0)_{\bar{S}_{\mathsf{k}}}$ is parsed from the first element of $\overline{\boldsymbol{K}} = \boldsymbol{C}$. Outputs the description of $\overline{\mathcal{P}}_{Y,X}$.

Correctness. Assume $\bar{R}(Y, X) = 1$. Hence, $R(X, Y) = 1$. From the correctness of P, we have $\mathcal{P}_{X,Y}(\boldsymbol{K}, \boldsymbol{C}) = (K_0 s_0)_{[1,\kappa]}$. Hence

$$\begin{aligned}
\overline{\mathcal{P}}_{Y,X}(\overline{\boldsymbol{K}}, \overline{\boldsymbol{C}}) &= (\phi \bar{s}_0 + K_0)_{\bar{S}_{\mathsf{c}}}(s_0)_{\bar{S}_{\mathsf{k}}} - (K_0 s_0)_{[1,\kappa]} \\
&= (\phi \bar{s}_0)_{\bar{S}_{\mathsf{c}}}(s_0)_{\bar{S}_{\mathsf{k}}} = (\bar{s}_0)_{\bar{S}_{\mathsf{c}}}(\phi s_0)_{\bar{S}_{\mathsf{k}}} = (\bar{K}_0 \bar{s}_0)_{[1,\kappa]},
\end{aligned}$$

as required. We must also verify the associativity of $\overline{\mathcal{P}}_Y$ over $(\bar{\boldsymbol{r}}, \overline{\boldsymbol{h}}_{\mathsf{k}})$, and of $\overline{\mathcal{P}}_X$ over $(\bar{\boldsymbol{s}}, \overline{\boldsymbol{h}}_{\mathsf{c}})$. But these are straightforward due to the associativity of $\mathcal{P}_Y$ over $(\boldsymbol{s}, \boldsymbol{h}_{\mathsf{c}})$, and of $\mathcal{P}_X$ over $(\boldsymbol{r}, \boldsymbol{h}_{\mathsf{k}})$, and the new elements can be easily inspected, in particular, $(\bar{s}_0)_{\bar{S}_{\mathsf{c}}}(1)_{\emptyset} = (\bar{s}_0)_{\emptyset}(1)_{\bar{S}_{\mathsf{c}}}$, and we have $(1)_{\bar{S}_{\mathsf{c}}} \in \boldsymbol{h}_{\mathsf{k}}$.

The following lemma shows that the conversion preserves security (in an alternating manner). The proof is similar to [9], and is given in the full version.

Lemma 5. $(1, 1)$-CMH security of P implies $(1, 1)$-SMH security of $\overline{\mathsf{P}}$. Oppositely, $(1, 1)$-SMH security of P implies $(1, 1)$-CMH security of $\overline{\mathsf{P}}$.

6.2 Fully-Secure CP-ABE for Circuits

We obtain multi-linear pair encoding schemes for CP-ABE by applying the dual conversion to our two encoding schemes for KP-ABE. In particular, we obtain two schemes: $P_{CPABE1} := CON(P_{KPABE1})$ and $P_{CPABE2} := CON(P_{KPABE2})$. The efficiency is obtained by swapping the key encoding size and the ciphertext encoding size of the original KP-ABE schemes, plus one element for each encoding due to the conversion. Therefore, both resulting CP-ABE schemes admit succinctness, and the second CP-ABE achieves constant-size keys. The functionality is also preserved, hence they can deal with unbounded-size circuits.

From Lemma 5 and the security of P_{KPABE1} and P_{KPABE2} (Theorems 4, 5, 6 and 7), and the fact that $(1, poly)$-SMH trivially implies $(1, 1)$-SMH, we have the following corollaries. Recall that ℓ is the bounded depth, n is the input length, while m is the width of the queried circuit.

Corollary 7. P_{CPABE1} is $(1, 1)$-CMH under the ℓ-SMDDH1 assumption.

Corollary 8. P_{CPABE1} is $(1, 1)$-SMH under the (ℓ, m)-EMDDH1 assumption.

Corollary 9. P_{CPABE2} is $(1, 1)$-CMH under the (ℓ, n)-SMDDH2 assumption.

Corollary 10. P_{CPABE2} is $(1, 1)$-SMH under the (ℓ, m, n)-EMDDH2 assumption.

All the above corollaries admit tight reductions. From these and Corollary 3, we obtain fully secure CP-ABE schemes with $O(q_{all})$ reduction as follows.

Corollary 11. $ABE(P_{CPABE1}, G)$ is fully secure under EMDDH1, SMDDH1, MSD. $ABE(P_{CPABE2}, G)$ is fully secure under EMDDH2, SMDDH2, MSD. We have

$$\mathsf{Adv}_{\mathcal{A}}^{ABE(P_{CPABE1},G)}(\lambda) \leq \mathsf{Adv}_{\mathcal{B}_1}^{(\kappa,\bar{S}_c)\text{-MSD}}(\lambda) + 2q_{all}\mathsf{Adv}_{\mathcal{B}_2}^{(\kappa,\bar{S}_k)\text{-MSD}}(\lambda)$$
$$+ q_1\mathsf{Adv}_{\mathcal{B}_3}^{\ell\text{-SMDDH1}}(\lambda) + q_2\mathsf{Adv}_{\mathcal{B}_4}^{(\ell,m)\text{-EMDDH1}}(\lambda).$$
$$\mathsf{Adv}_{\mathcal{A}}^{ABE(P_{CPABE2},G)}(\lambda) \leq \mathsf{Adv}_{\mathcal{B}_1}^{(\kappa,\bar{S}_c)\text{-MSD}}(\lambda) + 2q_{all}\mathsf{Adv}_{\mathcal{B}_2}^{(\kappa,\bar{S}_k)\text{-MSD}}(\lambda)$$
$$+ q_1\mathsf{Adv}_{\mathcal{B}_3}^{(\ell,n)\text{-SMDDH2}}(\lambda) + q_2\mathsf{Adv}_{\mathcal{B}_4}^{(\ell,m,n)\text{-EMDDH2}}(\lambda).$$

Here, $\kappa = 3\ell$, $\bar{S}_c = [\ell + 2, 3\ell], \bar{S}_k = [1, \ell + 1]$.

References

1. Albrecht, M.R., Farshim, P., Hofheinz, D., Larraia, E., Paterson, K.G.: Multilinear maps from obfuscation. In: Kushilevitz, E., Malkin, T. (eds.) TCC 2016. LNCS, vol. 9562, pp. 446–473. Springer, Heidelberg (2016). doi:10.1007/978-3-662-49096-9_19
2. Ananth, P., Brakerski, Z., Segev, G., Vaikuntanathan, V.: From selective to adaptive security in functional encryption. In: Gennaro, R., Robshaw, M. (eds.) CRYPTO 2015. LNCS, vol. 9216, pp. 657–677. Springer, Heidelberg (2015). doi:10.1007/978-3-662-48000-7_32

3. Attrapadung, N.: Dual system encryption via doubly selective security: framework, fully secure functional encryption for regular languages, and more. In: Nguyen, P.Q., Oswald, E. (eds.) EUROCRYPT 2014. LNCS, vol. 8441, pp. 557–577. Springer, Heidelberg (2014). doi:10.1007/978-3-642-55220-5_31

4. Attrapadung N.: Fully secure and succinct attribute based encryption for circuits from multi-linear maps. Cryptology ePrint Archive: report 2014/772 (2014)

5. Attrapadung, N.: Dual system encryption framework in prime-order groups via computational pair encodings. In: Cheon, J.H., Takagi, T. (eds.) ASIACRYPT 2016. LNCS, vol. 10032, pp. 591–623. Springer, Heidelberg (2016). doi:10.1007/978-3-662-53890-6_20

6. Attrapadung, N.: Dual system framework in multilinear settings and applications to fully secure (compact) ABE for unbounded-size circuits. Cryptology ePrint Archive: report 2017/023 (2017). (The full version of this paper)

7. Attrapadung, N., Libert, B.: Functional encryption for inner product: achieving constant-size ciphertexts with adaptive security or support for negation. In: Nguyen, P.Q., Pointcheval, D. (eds.) PKC 2010. LNCS, vol. 6056, pp. 384–402. Springer, Heidelberg (2010). doi:10.1007/978-3-642-13013-7_23

8. Attrapadung, N., Libert, B., Panafieu, E.: Expressive key-policy attribute-based encryption with constant-size ciphertexts. In: Catalano, D., Fazio, N., Gennaro, R., Nicolosi, A. (eds.) PKC 2011. LNCS, vol. 6571, pp. 90–108. Springer, Heidelberg (2011). doi:10.1007/978-3-642-19379-8_6

9. Attrapadung, N., Yamada, S.: Duality in ABE: converting attribute based encryption for dual predicate and dual policy via computational encodings. In: Nyberg, K. (ed.) CT-RSA 2015. LNCS, vol. 9048, pp. 87–105. Springer, Heidelberg (2015). doi:10.1007/978-3-319-16715-2_5

10. Waters, B.: Ciphertext-policy attribute-based encryption: an expressive, efficient, and provably secure realization. In: Catalano, D., Fazio, N., Gennaro, R., Nicolosi, A. (eds.) PKC 2011. LNCS, vol. 6571, pp. 53–70. Springer, Heidelberg (2011). doi:10.1007/978-3-642-19379-8_4

11. Brakerski, Z., Vaikuntanathan, V.: Circuit-ABE from LWE: unbounded attributes and semi-adaptive security. In: Robshaw, M., Katz, J. (eds.) CRYPTO 2016. LNCS, vol. 9816, pp. 363–384. Springer, Heidelberg (2016). doi:10.1007/978-3-662-53015-3_13

12. Boneh, D., Boyen, X.: Efficient selective-ID secure identity-based encryption without random oracles. In: Cachin, C., Camenisch, J.L. (eds.) EUROCRYPT 2004. LNCS, vol. 3027, pp. 223–238. Springer, Heidelberg (2004). doi:10.1007/978-3-540-24676-3_14

13. Boneh, D., Gentry, C., Gorbunov, S., Halevi, S., Nikolaenko, V., Segev, G., Vaikuntanathan, V., Vinayagamurthy, D.: Fully key-homomorphic encryption, arithmetic circuit ABE and compact garbled circuits. In: Nguyen, P.Q., Oswald, E. (eds.) EUROCRYPT 2014. LNCS, vol. 8441, pp. 533–556. Springer, Heidelberg (2014). doi:10.1007/978-3-642-55220-5_30

14. Boneh, D., Gentry, C., Waters, B.: Collusion resistant broadcast encryption with short ciphertexts and private keys. In: Shoup, V. (ed.) CRYPTO 2005. LNCS, vol. 3621, pp. 258–275. Springer, Heidelberg (2005). doi:10.1007/11535218_16

15. Boneh, D., Silverberg, A.: Applications of multilinear forms to cryptography. Contemp. Math. **324**, 71–90 (2003)

16. Boyen, X. Fan, X., Shi, E.: Adaptively secure fully homomorphic signatures based on lattices. Cryptology ePrint Archive, report 2014/916 (2014)

17. Cheon, J.H., Han, K., Lee, C., Ryu, H., Stehlé, D.: Cryptanalysis of the multilinear map over the integers. In: Oswald, E., Fischlin, M. (eds.) EUROCRYPT 2015. LNCS, vol. 9056, pp. 3–12. Springer, Heidelberg (2015). doi:10.1007/978-3-662-46800-5_1

18. Cheon, J.H., Fouque, P.-A., Lee, C., Minaud, B., Ryu, H.: Cryptanalysis of the New CLT multilinear map over the integers. In: Fischlin, M., Coron, J.-S. (eds.) EUROCRYPT 2016. LNCS, vol. 9665, pp. 509–536. Springer, Heidelberg (2016). doi:10.1007/978-3-662-49890-3_20

19. Chen, J., Wee, H.: Semi-adaptive Attribute-Based Encryption and Improved Delegation for Boolean Formula. In: Abdalla, M., Prisco, R. (eds.) SCN 2014. LNCS, vol. 8642, pp. 277–297. Springer, Heidelberg (2014). doi:10.1007/978-3-319-10879-7_16

20. Coron, J.-S., Lepoint, T., Tibouchi, M.: Practical multilinear maps over the integers. In: Canetti, R., Garay, J.A. (eds.) CRYPTO 2013. LNCS, vol. 8042, pp. 476–493. Springer, Heidelberg (2013). doi:10.1007/978-3-642-40041-4_26

21. Coron, J.-S., et al.: Zeroizing without low-level zeroes: new MMAP attacks and their limitations. In: Gennaro, R., Robshaw, M. (eds.) CRYPTO 2015. LNCS, vol. 9215, pp. 247–266. Springer, Heidelberg (2015). doi:10.1007/978-3-662-47989-6_12

22. Coron, J.-S., Lepoint, T., Tibouchi, M.: New multilinear maps over the integers. In: Gennaro, R., Robshaw, M. (eds.) CRYPTO 2015. LNCS, vol. 9215, pp. 267–286. Springer, Heidelberg (2015). doi:10.1007/978-3-662-47989-6_13

23. Garg, S., Gentry, C., Halevi, S.: Candidate multilinear maps from ideal lattices. In: Johansson, T., Nguyen, P.Q. (eds.) EUROCRYPT 2013. LNCS, vol. 7881, pp. 1–17. Springer, Heidelberg (2013). doi:10.1007/978-3-642-38348-9_1

24. Garg, S., Gentry, C., Halevi, S., Sahai, A., Waters, B.: Attribute-based encryption for circuits from multilinear maps. In: Canetti, R., Garay, J.A. (eds.) CRYPTO 2013. LNCS, vol. 8043, pp. 479–499. Springer, Heidelberg (2013). doi:10.1007/978-3-642-40084-1_27

25. Garg, S., Gentry, C., Halevi, S., Raykova, M., Sahai, A., Waters, B.: Candidate indistinguishability obfuscation and functional encryption for all circuits. FOCS 2013, 40–49 (2013)

26. Garg, S., Gentry, C., Halevi, S., Zhandry, M.: Fully secure attribute based encryption from multilinear maps. Cryptology ePrint Archive: report 2014/622 (2014)

27. Garg, S., Gentry, C., Halevi, S., Zhandry, M.: Functional encryption without obfuscation. In: Kushilevitz, E., Malkin, T. (eds.) TCC 2016. LNCS, vol. 9563, pp. 480–511. Springer, Heidelberg (2016). doi:10.1007/978-3-662-49099-0_18

28. Garg, S., Gentry, C., Sahai, A., Waters, B.: Witness encryption and its applications. STOC 2013, 467–476 (2013)

29. Garg, S., Gentry, C., Halevi, S., Sahai, A., Waters, B.: Attribute-based encryption for circuits from multilinear maps. In: Canetti, R., Garay, J.A. (eds.) CRYPTO 2013. LNCS, vol. 8043, pp. 479–499. Springer, Heidelberg (2013). doi:10.1007/978-3-642-40084-1_27

30. Gentry, C., Lewko, A., Sahai, A., Waters, B.: Indistinguishability Obfuscation from the Multilinear Subgroup Elimination Assumption. In: FOCS 2015, pp. 151–170 (2015)

31. Gorbunov, S., Vaikuntanathan, V., Wee, H.: Attribute-based encryption for circuits. In: STOC, pp. 545–554 (2013)

32. Goyal, R., Koppula, V., Waters, B.: Semi-adaptive security and bundling functionalities made generic and easy. In: Hirt, M., Smith, A. (eds.) TCC 2016. LNCS, vol. 9986, pp. 361–388. Springer, Heidelberg (2016). doi:10.1007/978-3-662-53644-5_14

33. Goyal, V., Pandey, O., Sahai, A., Waters, B.: Attribute-based encryption for fine-grained access control of encrypted data. ACM CCS **2006**, 89–98 (2006)
34. Katz, J., Sahai, A., Waters, B.: Predicate encryption supporting disjunctions, polynomial equations, and inner products. In: Smart, N. (ed.) EUROCRYPT 2008. LNCS, vol. 4965, pp. 146–162. Springer, Heidelberg (2008). doi:10.1007/978-3-540-78967-3_9
35. Lewko, A., Waters, B.: New techniques for dual system encryption and fully secure HIBE with short ciphertexts. In: Micciancio, D. (ed.) TCC 2010. LNCS, vol. 5978, pp. 455–479. Springer, Heidelberg (2010). doi:10.1007/978-3-642-11799-2_27
36. Lewko, A., Waters, B.: New proof methods for attribute-based encryption: achieving full security through selective techniques. In: Safavi-Naini, R., Canetti, R. (eds.) CRYPTO 2012. LNCS, vol. 7417, pp. 180–198. Springer, Heidelberg (2012). doi:10.1007/978-3-642-32009-5_12
37. Lewko, A., Okamoto, T., Sahai, A., Takashima, K., Waters, B.: Fully secure functional encryption: attribute-based encryption and (hierarchical) inner product encryption. In: Gilbert, H. (ed.) EUROCRYPT 2010. LNCS, vol. 6110, pp. 62–91. Springer, Heidelberg (2010). doi:10.1007/978-3-642-13190-5_4
38. Lin, H.: Indistinguishability obfuscation from constant-degree graded encoding schemes. In: Fischlin, M., Coron, J.-S. (eds.) EUROCRYPT 2016. LNCS, vol. 9665, pp. 28–57. Springer, Heidelberg (2016). doi:10.1007/978-3-662-49890-3_2
39. Naor, M.: On cryptographic assumptions and challenges. In: Boneh, D. (ed.) CRYPTO 2003. LNCS, vol. 2729, pp. 96–109. Springer, Heidelberg (2003). doi:10.1007/978-3-540-45146-4_6
40. Okamoto, T., Takashima, K.: Fully secure functional encryption with general relations from the decisional linear assumption. In: Rabin, T. (ed.) CRYPTO 2010. LNCS, vol. 6223, pp. 191–208. Springer, Heidelberg (2010). doi:10.1007/978-3-642-14623-7_11
41. Okamoto, T., Takashima, K.: Adaptively attribute-hiding (hierarchical) inner product encryption. In: Pointcheval, D., Johansson, T. (eds.) EUROCRYPT 2012. LNCS, vol. 7237, pp. 591–608. Springer, Heidelberg (2012). doi:10.1007/978-3-642-29011-4_35
42. Pass, R., Seth, K., Telang, S.: Indistinguishability obfuscation from semantically-secure multilinear encodings. In: Garay, J.A., Gennaro, R. (eds.) CRYPTO 2014. LNCS, vol. 8616, pp. 500–517. Springer, Heidelberg (2014). doi:10.1007/978-3-662-44371-2_28. http://dblp.uni-trier.de/rec/bibtex1/conf/crypto/PassST14
43. Rouselakis, Y., Waters, B.: Practical constructions and new proof methods for large universe attribute-based encryption. In: ACM CCS 2013, pp. 463–474 (2013)
44. Sahai, A., Waters, B.: Fuzzy identity-based encryption. In: Cramer, R. (ed.) EUROCRYPT 2005. LNCS, vol. 3494, pp. 457–473. Springer, Heidelberg (2005). doi:10.1007/11426639_27
45. Takashima, K.: Expressive attribute-based encryption with constant-size ciphertexts from the decisional linear assumption. In: Abdalla, M., Prisco, R. (eds.) SCN 2014. LNCS, vol. 8642, pp. 298–317. Springer, Heidelberg (2014). doi:10.1007/978-3-319-10879-7_17
46. Valiant, L.G.: Universal circuits (preliminary report). In: STOC 1976, pp. 196–203 (1976)
47. Waters, B.: Ciphertext-policy attribute-based encryption: an expressive, efficient, and provably secure realization. In: Catalano, D., Fazio, N., Gennaro, R., Nicolosi, A. (eds.) PKC 2011. LNCS, vol. 6571, pp. 53–70. Springer, Heidelberg (2011). doi:10.1007/978-3-642-19379-8_4

48. Waters, B.: Dual system encryption: realizing fully secure IBE and HIBE under simple assumptions. In: Halevi, S. (ed.) CRYPTO 2009. LNCS, vol. 5677, pp. 619–636. Springer, Heidelberg (2009). doi:10.1007/978-3-642-03356-8_36

49. Waters, B.: Functional encryption for regular languages. In: Safavi-Naini, R., Canetti, R. (eds.) CRYPTO 2012. LNCS, vol. 7417, pp. 218–235. Springer, Heidelberg (2012). doi:10.1007/978-3-642-32009-5_14

50. Waters, B.: A punctured programming approach to adaptively secure functional encryption. In: Gennaro, R., Robshaw, M. (eds.) CRYPTO 2015. LNCS, vol. 9216, pp. 678–697. Springer, Heidelberg (2015). doi:10.1007/978-3-662-48000-7_33

51. Wee, H.: Dual system encryption via predicate encodings. In: Lindell, Y. (ed.) TCC 2014. LNCS, vol. 8349, pp. 616–637. Springer, Heidelberg (2014). doi:10.1007/978-3-642-54242-8_26

CCA-Secure Inner-Product Functional Encryption from Projective Hash Functions

Fabrice Benhamouda[1]([⊠]), Florian Bourse[2], and Helger Lipmaa[3]

[1] IBM Research, Yorktown Heights, NY, USA
fabrice.benhamouda@normalesup.org
[2] ENS, CNRS, INRIA, PSL Research University, Paris, France
[3] Institute of Computer Science, University of Tartu, Tartu, Estonia

Abstract. In an inner-product functional encryption scheme, the plaintexts are vectors and the owner of the secret key can delegate the ability to compute weighted sums of the coefficients of the plaintext of any ciphertext. Recently, many inner-product functional encryption schemes were proposed. However, none of the known schemes are secure against chosen ciphertext attacks (IND-FE-CCA).

We present a generic construction of IND-FE-CCA inner-product functional encryption from projective hash functions with homomorphic properties. We show concrete instantiations based on the DCR assumption, the DDH assumption, and more generally, any Matrix DDH assumption.

Keywords: DCR · DDH · Inner-product functional encryption · Projective hash functions · CCA-security

1 Introduction

Traditionally, encryption has been an all-or-nothing affair: either a recipient owns the secret key (and thus can decrypt) or she does not. Functional encryption [10,21,28,32] enables a much more fine-grained handling of encrypted data. Here, the owner of the master key can delegate partial secret keys to various recipients. In a functional encryption scheme for functionality $\mathcal{F}$, the knowledge of a secret key corresponding to some y enables one to decrypt an encryption of z to $\mathcal{F}(y, z)$. As such, functional encryption has many potential applications, and has spurred a long line of research.

A functional encryption scheme can be required to satisfy several different security requirements [10,28]. In the case of the *adaptive* IND-FE-CPA security [10,28], it must be difficult for an adversary to distinguish functional ciphertexts of any two plaintexts z_0 and z_1. This must hold even if the adversary is given an oracle access to the partial secret key generator, where the secret key queries must satisfy the condition that $\mathcal{F}(y, z_0) = \mathcal{F}(y, z_1)$ for each queried y. In the weaker *selective security* model, the adversary is required to choose z_0 and z_1 before seeing the public key and answers to any of the secret key queries. See [10,28] for discussion.

© International Association for Cryptologic Research 2017
S. Fehr (Ed.): PKC 2017, Part II, LNCS 10175, pp. 36–66, 2017.
DOI: 10.1007/978-3-662-54388-7_2

Constructing adaptively IND-FE-CPA secure functional encryption for arbitrary functionalities has been an elusive goal, achieved only recently under strong assumptions like the existence of indistinguishability obfuscation or multilinear maps [11,19,20,33]. However, achieving functional encryption for restricted classes of functionalities is often easier. One of the simplest type of functional encryption schemes is inner-product functional encryption (IPFE).

Inner-Product Functional Encryption. In an inner-product functional encryption scheme, one encrypts a possibly long vector $\vec{z}$, and a recipient who has a partial secret key $k_{\vec{y}}$ can obtain the inner product $\langle \vec{y}, \vec{z} \rangle$ of $\vec{y}$ and $\vec{z}$. Recently, Abdalla et al. [2] proposed the first IPFE schemes based on some of the most standard (and yet useful) cryptographic assumptions like the DDH and the LWE [31] assumptions. Unfortunately, their IPFE schemes are only selectively IND-FE-CPA secure. Subsequent work has reached better security notions while still relying on standard assumptions. In the secret key setting for example, function privacy has been achieved using bilinear maps [7,17], as well as a multi-input variant [4]. Adaptively IND-FE-CPA secure versions of the IPFE schemes of [2] were recently proposed by Agrawal et al. [5], together with a new scheme based on the DCR [29].

CCA Security. IND-CPA is a property every public-key encryption (PKE) scheme should have. It ensures that the plaintext is protected from any eavesdropping. However, it does not guarantee any security against active adversaries. The go-to security notion in this case is IND-CCA.[1] Informally, it states that a decryption oracle cannot help the adversary break the semantic security of the scheme, and it has been studied for years in the setting of PKE [12,30]. It has also been examined in the context of identity-based encryption [9,23] and attribute-based encryption [34], which are particular cases of functional encryption. It is thus natural to analyze it for inner-product functional encryption. In our setting of inner-product functional encryption, the decryption queries are as follows: the adversary chooses a ciphertext c and a vector $\vec{y}$ and gets back the decryption of c with $\mathrm{msk}_{\vec{y}}$, a freshly generated secret key for $\vec{y}$. Note that in this case, the decryption oracle is stronger than the partial key generation oracle because it doesn't have any requirement over its input $\vec{y}$, but on the other hand, the adversary doesn't get $\mathrm{msk}_{\vec{y}}$.

To the best of our knowledge, the only paper considering IND-FE-CCA security is [26]. In this paper, Nandi and Pandit construct IND-FE-CCA secure schemes from IND-FE-CPA secure ones with some properties that are verified by a lot of functional encryption schemes: key-policy or ciphertext-policy attribute-based encryption, and functional encryption for regular languages for example. However, this does not apply for inner-product functional encryption, so another technique is required.

In [27], Naor and Yung proposed a generic way of transforming an IND-CPA encryption scheme into an IND-CCA encryption scheme. While this transform

---

[1] In the current paper, CCA stands for CCA2.

could be adapted to functional encryption, it uses non-interactive zero-knowledge proofs, the constructions of which have strong requirements, such as bilinear groups or the random oracle model.

Our Contributions. In this paper, we propose a generic construction of IND-FE-CCA IPFE. This generic construction yields the first IND-FE-CCA IPFE schemes based on the DDH assumption, the DCR assumption, and any of the MDDH assumptions [18]. MDDH assumptions generalize the DDH assumption and might hold in settings where the DDH assumption cannot hold, as in symmetric bilinear groups.

Our generic construction is based on projective hash functions with homomorphic properties. Projective hash functions (PHFs) were introduced by Cramer and Shoup in [14], as a way to explain their efficient IND-CCA encryption scheme [12] and to extend it to other assumptions. Similarly to the generic IND-CCA encryption in [14], our IND-FE-CCA IPFE uses two PHFs and the second PHF enables to reject ciphertexts which are not well-formed.

If the second PHF is not used in the scheme, we get a generic IND-FE-CPA IPFE. We actually start by describing this generic IND-FE-CPA IPFE as a warm-up for our main contribution, a generic IND-FE-CCA IPFE.

Interestingly, when instantiated using the DDH assumption, this IND-FE-CPA scheme coincides exactly with the DDH-based IPFE of Agrawal et al. [5]. When instantiated using the DCR assumption, it corresponds to a variant of the DCR-based IPFE over $\mathbb{Z}$ of Agrawal et al. that has slightly worse parameters but avoids the use of discrete Gaussian distributions.

As a side contribution, we introduce a tag-based variant of functional encryption, where tags are associated to ciphertexts, together with a slightly weaker IND-TBFE-CCA (i.e., tag-based) security notion, in which the adversary is not allowed to query the decryption oracle with the tag of the challenge ciphertext. To simplify the description of our IND-FE-CCA IPFE scheme, we actually first construct an IND-TBE-CCA IPFE scheme. We then use an adapted version of the generic transformation from tag-based PKE to CCA secure PKE in [22]: the tag is the hash of a fresh verification key for a one-time signature scheme, used to sign the ciphertext. This one-time signature prevents malleability of the ciphertext.

Overview of Our Constructions. Our constructions are inspired from the Cramer-Shoup encryption scheme [14]. A Cramer-Shoup ciphertext consists of three parts: a random word $\mathfrak{b}$ in some NP language (e.g., $\mathfrak{b}$ is a DDH tuple), the message masked by a hash of $\mathfrak{b}$ for a (smooth) PHF, and another hash of $\mathfrak{b}$ for a (2-universal) PHF. The hash value of any PHF can be computed both by someone knowing a witness for $\mathfrak{b}$ together with the public key (called projection key), and by someone knowing the secret key (called hashing key). The second hash value is used to reject ill-formed ciphertexts. Without it, the scheme is IND-CPA.

To build an IND-FE-CPA IPFE for vectors of dimension ℓ, we mask each coordinate of the message with a different hash value of the same word $\mathfrak{b}$. If the PHF is homomorphic, a linear combination of the corresponding hashing keys will allow for the decryption of the same linear combination of the coordinates, which is the inner product of the message and the coefficients of the linear combination. In order to reach IND-FE-CCA security and reject ill-formed ciphertexts, we add ℓ independent hash values of $\mathfrak{b}$ for ℓ independent 2-universal homomorphic PHF. We could not naively use only one such hash, because then anyone knowing the unique hashing key would be able to fake the last part of the ciphertext.

Road Map. We first provide some general preliminaries and recall definitions related to PHFs and functional encryption in Sect. 2. In this section, we also define the concrete assumptions we are using: DDH, DCR, and MDDH. In Sect. 3, we formally define the properties of the PHF used in our generic IND-FE-CPA IPFE scheme, which is described in Sect. 4. We then move to the CCA setting. In Sect. 5, we define the properties of the second PHF used in our generic IND-FE-CCA IPFE scheme, which is described in Sect. 6.

2 Preliminaries

Let $\mathbb{Z}$ be the set of integers. If n is a positive integer, $\mathrm{spf}(n)$ is its smallest prime factor. If $S \subset \mathbb{Z}$ and $t \in \mathbb{Z}$, then let $S + t = \{s + t \ : \ s \in S\}$. If S is a finite set, then $|S|$ is its cardinal.

Let $\mathcal{R}$ be a commutative ring. We denote the set of d-dimensional column vectors over $\mathcal{R}$ by $\mathcal{R}^d$, the set of d-dimensional row vectors by $\mathcal{R}^{1 \times d}$, and the set of $\ell \times d$ matrices by $\mathcal{R}^{\ell \times d}$. Unless explicitly said otherwise, each vector is a column vector. We denote vectors by using either boldface lower-case letters or lower-case letters with an arrow over it as in $\boldsymbol{b}$ and $\vec{b}$. We denote matrices by using boldface upper-case letters like in $\boldsymbol{A}$. We have two possible notations for vectors, as we sometimes need to consider vectors of vectors $(\vec{\boldsymbol{b}})$ and vectors of matrices $(\vec{\boldsymbol{A}})$. The ith coefficient of a vector $\boldsymbol{b}$ or $\vec{b}$ is denoted by b_i, while the ith coefficient of a vector of vectors $\vec{\boldsymbol{b}}$ is a vector and is denoted by $\boldsymbol{b}_i$. The jth coefficient of this latter vector is $b_{i,j}$. The same convention is used with coefficients of matrices and coefficients of vectors of matrices.

Within this paper, κ is the security parameter. A function $f(\kappa)$ is *negligible*, if for any polynomial p, $f(\kappa) = O(1/p(\kappa))$.

If $\mathcal{A}$ is a randomized algorithm, then we denote by $\mathcal{A}(x)$ the output distribution of $\mathcal{A}$ on input x. If S is a finite set, we denote by $U(S)$ the uniform distribution. If D is a distribution, we denote by $x \leftarrow_r D$ the assignment of a fresh sample from D to the variable x. If D is a distribution over some set S and if D is clear from context, $x \leftarrow_r D$ is also denoted by $x \leftarrow_r S$. If S is a finite set on which we did not explicitly defined any distribution, $x \leftarrow_r S$ stands for $x \leftarrow_r U(S)$.

Statistical and Computational Indistinguishability. Let $(A_\kappa)_\kappa$ and $(B_\kappa)_\kappa$ be two ensembles of distributions over some set Ω and indexed by the security parameter κ. In the sequel the security parameter is often omitted for the sake of simplicity. Let $\mathcal{A}$ be an algorithm, called an adversary. The advantage of $\mathcal{A}$ in distinguishing $(A_\kappa)_\kappa$ and $(B_\kappa)_\kappa$ is defined by $\mathsf{Adv}_\mathcal{A}(\kappa) = |\Pr_{x \leftarrow_r A_\kappa}[\mathcal{A}(x) = 1] - \Pr_{x \leftarrow_r B_\kappa}[\mathcal{A}(x) = 1]|$.

The distributions A and B are *computationally indistinguishable* if for any (probabilistic) polynomial time $\mathcal{A}$, its advantage $\mathsf{Adv}_\mathcal{A}(\kappa)$ is negligible. They are *statistically indistinguishable* if this is true for any (not necessarily polynomial-time) $\mathcal{A}$. The statistical distance $\mathrm{SD}(A, B)$ of distributions A and B is the supremum of the advantage of all adversaries in distinguishing them. Equivalently, if A and B are defined over a finite or countable set Ω,

$$\mathrm{SD}(A, B) = \frac{1}{2} \sum_{y \in \Omega} |\Pr_{x \leftarrow_r A}[x = y] - \Pr_{x \leftarrow_r B}[x = y]|. \tag{1}$$

We will often implicitly use the following lemmas.

Lemma 1. *Let S_1 and S_2 be two finite sets. If $S_1 \subseteq S_2$, we have $\mathrm{SD}(U(S_1), U(S_2)) = 1 - |S_1|/|S_2|$. In particular, if $|S_2| = (1 + 1/t) \cdot |S_1|$ for some positive integer t, then $\mathrm{SD}(U(S_1), U(S_2)) = 1/(t + 1)$.*

Proof. $\mathrm{SD}(U(S_1), U(S_2)) = \frac{1}{2}(|S_2 \setminus S_1|/|S_2| + |S_1| \cdot (1/|S_1| - 1/|S_2|)) = 1 - |S_1|/|S_2|$. □

Lemma 2. *Let $S \subseteq \mathbb{Z}$ be an interval and t be an integer. Then $\mathrm{SD}(U(S), U(S + t)) = |t|/|S|$.*

Proof. In the sum in Eq. (1), exactly $2|t|$ terms are non-zero: the ones corresponding to y in $(S \setminus (S + t)) \cup ((S + t) \setminus S)$. And these terms are equal to $1/|S|$. □

Abelian Groups. We extensively use Abelian groups. In particular, in our concrete instantiations, we use prime-order cyclic groups over an elliptic curve or subgroups of the (multiplicative) group $\mathbb{Z}_N^*$, for some positive integer N. We denote the elements of such groups by using the Fraktur script like in $\mathfrak{g}$ or $\mathfrak{b}$. By extension, even in our generic constructions and definitions, we also use this font to indicate values which, in our concrete instantiations, are group elements in such group $\mathbb{G}$ or vectors of such elements. However, we are also considering other Abelian groups (e.g., the group $\mathcal{K}$ of hashing keys of a key-homomorphic PHF in Definition 6) that are not related to cryptographic assumptions and for which group elements are not denoted using the Fraktur script.

Except if explicitly stated otherwise, we use *additive notation* for all our Abelian groups, even when this is not usual (as in the case of subgroups of $\mathbb{Z}_N^*$).

Let $\mathbb{G}$ be an Abelian group. We recall that if $\mathfrak{g}$ is a group element of order M, then we have a canonical monomorphism $w \in \mathbb{Z}_M \mapsto w \cdot \mathfrak{g} \in \mathbb{G}$. If $\mathbb{G}$ is a multiplicative group, this monomorphism corresponds to exponentiation. Hence, we denote the inverse of this monomorphism by $\log_\mathfrak{g}$. That is, if $\mathfrak{b} = w \cdot \mathfrak{g}$, then $\log_\mathfrak{g} \mathfrak{b} = w$.

Furthermore, let $\mathcal{R}$ be $\mathcal{R} = \mathbb{Z}$ or $\mathcal{R} = \mathbb{Z}_M$ with M being such that the order of any group element in $\mathbb{G}$ divides M. Then $\mathbb{G}$ can be seen as a $\mathcal{R}$-module. This means that for any $w \in \mathcal{R}$ and $\mathfrak{g} \in \mathbb{G}$, $w \cdot \mathfrak{g}$ is well defined. Importantly, by using additive notation, we can use the standard "matrix-vector" notation without prior explanation.

Basic Number Theory. Let N be a positive integer. Let $\varphi(N)$ be the Euler totient function. For any integer a and an odd prime q, the Legendre symbol $\left(\frac{a}{q}\right)$ is defined as $\left(\frac{a}{q}\right) := 0$, if $a \equiv 0 \pmod{q}$, $\left(\frac{a}{q}\right) := +1$, if $a \not\equiv 0 \pmod{q}$ and for some integer y, $a \equiv y^2 \pmod{q}$, and $\left(\frac{a}{q}\right) := -1$, if $a \not\equiv 0 \pmod{q}$ and there is no such y. For any integer a and any positive odd integer N, the Jacobi symbol is defined as the product of the Legendre symbols corresponding to the prime factors of N, $\left(\frac{a}{N}\right) := \prod_{i=1}^{t} \left(\frac{a}{p_i}\right)^{\alpha_i}$, where $N = \prod_{i=1}^{t} p_i^{\alpha_i}$ for distinct primes p_i. Let $J_N = \{a \in \mathbb{Z}_N : \left(\frac{a}{N}\right) = 1\}$; clearly J_N is a subgroup of $\mathbb{Z}_N^*$. The Jacobi symbol can be computed in polynomial time, given only a and N [25, Algorithm 2.149].

2.1 Subset Membership Problems and Concrete Assumptions

Our framework uses *subset membership problems*, which were originally defined in [14]. Basically, a subset membership problem defines an NP language $\mathcal{L} \subset \mathcal{X}$, in which a random word in $\mathcal{L}$ is hard to distinguish from a random word in $\mathcal{X} \setminus \mathcal{L}$. In this paper, we consider a slight extension, where we instead require a random word in $\mathcal{L}$ to be hard to distinguish from a random word in a given set $\bar{\mathcal{L}} \subseteq \mathcal{X} \setminus \mathcal{L}$.

More formally, a subset membership problem **P** specifies an ensemble $(I_\kappa)_{\kappa \geq 0}$ of distributions. For every value of a security parameter $\kappa \geq 0$, I_κ is a probability distribution of instance descriptions. An instance description $\Lambda = \Lambda[\mathcal{X}, \mathcal{L}, \mathcal{W}, \varrho, \bar{\mathcal{L}}]$ specifies the following: (a) finite, non-empty sets $\mathcal{X}$, $\mathcal{L}$, $\mathcal{W}$, and $\bar{\mathcal{L}}$, such that $\mathcal{L}$ is a proper subset of $\mathcal{X}$ and $\bar{\mathcal{L}}$ is a non-empty subset of $\mathcal{X} \setminus \mathcal{L}$, (b) a binary relation $\varrho \subset \mathcal{X} \times \mathcal{W}$. For $\mathfrak{b} \in \mathcal{X}$ and $w \in \mathcal{W}$, we say that w is a witness for $\mathfrak{b}$ if $(\mathfrak{b}, w) \in \varrho$. We require that instance descriptions and elements of $\mathcal{X}$ and $\mathcal{W}$ can be uniquely encoded as bitstrings of length poly(κ).

A subset membership problem satisfies the following properties: (i) I_κ is efficiently samplable, which means that there exists a probabilistic polynomial time instance sampling algorithm that on input 1^κ samples an instance Λ according to the distribution I_κ; (ii) ϱ is efficiently samplable, which means that there exists a probabilistic polynomial time subset sampling algorithm that on input Λ outputs a random $\mathfrak{b} \in \mathcal{L}$ together with a witness $w \in \mathcal{W}$ for $\mathfrak{b}$; the distribution over ϱ implicitly defines a distribution over $\mathcal{L}$; (iii) $\bar{\mathcal{L}}$ is efficiently samplable; (iv) $\mathcal{X}$ is efficiently recognizable, which means that there exists a deterministic polynomial algorithm that on input (Λ, ζ) checks whether ζ is a valid binary encoding of an element of $\mathcal{X}$; (v) ϱ is efficiently recognizable; (vi) $(\mathcal{L}, \bar{\mathcal{L}})$-*indistinguishability:* a sample from $\mathcal{L}$ is computationally indistinguishable from a sample from $\bar{\mathcal{L}}$.

We do not require the distributions over ϱ, $\mathcal{L}$, and $\bar{\mathcal{L}}$ to be uniform. However, when we do not specify these distributions, we implicitly use the uniform distributions.

Let us now introduce the subset membership problems we use in our concrete instantiations. We name them according to the assumption under which we prove their $(\mathcal{L}, \bar{\mathcal{L}})$-indistinguishability property, namely DDH, MDDH, and DCR.

DDH-Based Subset Membership Problem. Let $\mathbb{G}$ be an additive cyclic group of prime order q, let $\mathcal{X} = \mathbb{G}^2$, let $\mathcal{L}$ be the subgroup of $\mathcal{X}$ generated by $\mathfrak{g} = (\mathfrak{g}_1, \mathfrak{g}_2)^\mathsf{T} \in \mathbb{G}^2$, where $\mathfrak{g}_i$ are random generators of $\mathbb{G}$, and let $\bar{\mathcal{L}} = \mathcal{X} \setminus \mathcal{L}$. A witness $w \in \mathcal{W} = \mathbb{Z}_q$ for $\mathfrak{b} \in \mathcal{L}$ is such that $\mathfrak{b} = w\mathfrak{g}$. In other words, we have $\mathcal{W} = \mathbb{Z}_q$ and $\varrho = \{(w \cdot \mathfrak{g}, w) : w \in \mathbb{Z}_q\}$. We set $\Lambda = (\mathbb{G}, \mathfrak{g})$.

This defines a subset membership problem, whose $(\mathcal{L}, \bar{\mathcal{L}})$-indistinguishability property is equivalent to the DDH assumption.

MDDH-Based Subset Membership Problem. For some interesting cryptographic cyclic groups, such as groups with a symmetric pairing, the DDH assumption does not hold. That is why weaker assumptions, such as the decisional linear assumption (DLIN [8]), have been considered. More recently, Escala et al. introduced the *Matrix Diffie-Hellman* (*MDDH*) assumption family [18] that generalizes DDH and its weaker variants like DLIN. Let us recall the MDDH assumption families in the context of subset membership problems.

Let $\mathbb{G}$ be a cyclic group of prime order q. Let $\mathcal{D}$ be a distribution of matrices in $\mathbb{G}^{t \times d}$ with $d < t$ being two positive integers. Let $\mathfrak{g} \leftarrow_r \mathcal{D}$. Let $\mathcal{X} = \mathbb{G}^t$. Let $\mathcal{L}$ be the subgroup of $\mathcal{X}$ generated by the columns of $\mathfrak{g}$ and let $\bar{\mathcal{L}} = \mathcal{X} \setminus \mathcal{L}$. A witness $\boldsymbol{w} \in \mathcal{W} = \mathbb{Z}_q^d$ for $\mathfrak{b} \in \mathcal{L}$ is such that $\mathfrak{b} = \mathfrak{g} \cdot \boldsymbol{w}$. In other words, we have $\mathcal{W} = \mathbb{Z}_q^d$ and $\varrho = \{(\mathfrak{g} \cdot \boldsymbol{w}, \boldsymbol{w}) : \boldsymbol{w} \in \mathbb{Z}_q^d\}$. We set $\Lambda = (\mathbb{G}, \mathfrak{g})$.

This defines a subset membership problem, whose $(\mathcal{L}, \bar{\mathcal{L}})$-indistinguishability property corresponds to the $\mathcal{D}$-MDDH assumption.

When $d = 1$, $t = 2$, and $\mathcal{D}$ is the uniform distribution over vectors of two generators of $\mathbb{G}$, then we get back the DDH-based subset membership problem.

DCR-Based Subset Membership Problem. Let $N = pq$ be a product of two λ-bit random safe primes $p = 2p' + 1$ and $q = 2q' + 1$, where p' and q' are also primes and where λ is a function of the security parameter κ. Let $N' = p'q'$. Let $s \geq 1$. Write $\mathbb{Z}_{N^{s+1}}^* \cong G_{N^s} \oplus G_{N'} \oplus G_2 \oplus T$, where $\cong$ denotes group isomorphism, $\oplus$ is the direct sum or Cartesian product, G_i are cyclic groups of order i, and T is the order-2 cyclic group generated by $-1 \bmod N^{s+1}$. Let $\mathbb{G} = \mathcal{X} = J_{N^{s+1}} \cong G_{N^s} \oplus G_{N'} \oplus T$. We recall that we use additive notation for $\mathbb{G}$. Let $\mathfrak{g}$ be a random generator of $\mathcal{L} \cong G_{N'}$, that is a subgroup of $\mathcal{X}$; $\mathfrak{g}$ can be thought of as a random $2N^s$-th residue. A witness $w \in \mathcal{W} = \mathbb{Z}$ for $\mathfrak{b} \in \mathcal{L}$ is such that $\mathfrak{b} = w \cdot \mathfrak{g}$. Finally, let $\mathfrak{g}_\perp$ be an arbitrary generator of the cyclic group G_{N^s} (for example $\mathfrak{g}_\perp = 1 + N \in \mathbb{Z}_{N^{s+1}}$, where $+$ here is the additive law of $\mathbb{Z}_{N^{s+1}}$) and let $\bar{\mathcal{L}} = \mathcal{L} + \mathfrak{g}_\perp$. We set $\Lambda = (N, s, \mathfrak{g}, \mathfrak{g}_\perp)$.

One cannot sample uniform witnesses as $\mathcal{W} = \mathbb{Z}$ is infinite. We cannot set $\mathcal{W} = \mathbb{Z}_{N'}$, as computing N' from $\Lambda = (N, s, \mathfrak{g})$ requires to factor N.

Instead, we sample witnesses uniformly from $S_N := \{0, \ldots, \lfloor N/4 \rfloor - 1\}$. Clearly, $\mathrm{SD}(U(\mathbb{Z}_{N'}), U(S_N)) = 1 - p'q'/(pq/4) = (2p' + 2q' + 1)/(pq) < 2(p+q)/(pq) < 4/\mathrm{spf}(N)$. From this distribution over $\mathcal{W}$, we can derive distributions over ϱ, $\mathcal{L}$, and $\bar{\mathcal{L}} = \mathcal{L} + \mathfrak{g}_\perp$. The two latter distributions are statistically close to uniform.

This setting defines a subset membership problem, whose $(\mathcal{L}, \bar{\mathcal{L}})$-indistinguishability property can be proven under the *Decisional Composite Residuosity* (DCR [29]) assumption. More precisely, we consider the DCR assumption for moduli that are product of safe primes; the DCR assumption then basically states that in the case $s = 1$, no probabilistic polynomial time adversary can distinguish between uniform elements of $\mathcal{L}$ and $\mathcal{X}$.[2] This is a classical variant of DCR, which is equivalent to the original DCR assumption [29], assuming that safe primes are sufficiently dense (see, e.g., [14]). We prove the following lemma in the full version following [15]:

Lemma 3. *Assuming the DCR assumption, the above subset membership problems is $(\mathcal{L}, \bar{\mathcal{L}})$-indistinguishable. More precisely, if there exists an adversary $\mathcal{A}$ that has advantage $\varepsilon_\mathcal{A}$ in breaking $(\mathcal{L}, \bar{\mathcal{L}})$-indistinguishability, then there exists an attacker $\mathcal{B}$ that runs in approximately the same time and that has advantage $\varepsilon_\mathcal{B}$ in breaking DCR, such that $\varepsilon_\mathcal{A} \leq 2s \cdot \varepsilon_\mathcal{B} + 8/\mathrm{spf}(N)$.*

2.2 Projective Hash Functions

In [14], Cramer and Shoup defined the influential notion of *projective hash functions* (PHFs) to construct IND-CPA and even IND-CCA secure public-key encryption schemes. In this section, we recall the definition of a PHF using the notation of [3].

Let **P** be a subset membership problem, specifying an ensemble $(I_\kappa)_\kappa$ of instance distributions. A *projective hash function* for **P** is a tuple $\mathsf{PHF} = (\mathsf{hashkg}, \mathsf{projkg}, \mathsf{hash}, \mathsf{projhash})$ of four probabilistic polynomial time algorithms:

- $\mathsf{hashkg}(\Lambda)$ generates a hashing key hk in some set $\mathcal{K}$ for the instance $\Lambda = \Lambda[\mathcal{X}, \mathcal{L}, \mathcal{W}, \varrho]$,
- $\mathsf{projkg}(\mathsf{hk})$ (deterministically) derives from the hashing key hk a projection key $\mathfrak{hp}$,
- $\mathsf{hash}(\mathsf{hk}, \mathfrak{b})$ (deterministically) computes the hash value $\mathfrak{H}$ (in some efficiently recognizable set Π) of $\mathfrak{b} \in \mathcal{X}$ under $\mathsf{hk} \in \mathcal{K}$,
- $\mathsf{projhash}(\mathfrak{hp}, \mathfrak{b}, w)$ (deterministically) computes the projected hash value $\mathfrak{pH}$ of $\mathfrak{b} \in \mathcal{L}$ using a witness $w \in \mathcal{W}$.

A PHF must be *complete*, in the following sense:

- For any instance Λ, for any $\mathfrak{b} \in \mathcal{X}$ and $w \in \mathcal{W}$, such that $(\mathfrak{b}, w) \in \varrho$, for any hashing key $\mathsf{hk} \in \mathcal{K}$, if $\mathfrak{hp} \leftarrow \mathsf{projkg}(\mathsf{hk})$, then

$$\mathsf{hash}(\mathsf{hk}, \mathfrak{b}) = \mathsf{projhash}(\mathfrak{hp}, \mathfrak{b}, w).$$

---

[2] The original assumption actually does not restrict the elements to be of Jacobi symbol 1, but doing this restriction yields an equivalent assumption, since we can multiply element of Jacobi symbol -1 by an arbitrary N^s-residue of Jacobi symbol -1.

The instance Λ is implicitly included in the hashing key hk and the projection key $\mathfrak{hp}$.

2.3   Functional Encryption

A *functionality* $\mathcal{F}$ defined over $(\mathcal{Y}, \mathcal{Z})$ is a function $\mathcal{Y} \times \mathcal{Z} \to \Sigma \cup \{\bot\}$, where $\mathcal{Y}$ is a key space, $\mathcal{Z}$ is a message space, and Σ is an output space that does not contain the special symbol $\bot$.

A *functional encryption scheme for functionality* $\mathcal{F}$ [10,28] is a tuple FE = (setup, keygen, enc, dec) of four probabilistic polynomial time algorithms:

setup$(1^\kappa, \ell)$: generates system parameters pp, and then returns a master secret and public key pair (msk, mpk), where both msk and mpk also contain pp,

keygen$_{\mathrm{msk}}(y \in \mathcal{Y})$: given a master secret key msk and a key (or a function) y, returns a partial secret key $\mathrm{msk}_y = (\mathrm{pp}, k_y, y)$,

enc$_{\mathrm{mpk}}(z \in \mathcal{Z})$: given a master public key mpk and a plaintext z, returns a ciphertext c,

dec$_{\mathrm{msk}_y}(c)$: returns $S \in \Sigma \cup \{\bot\}$.

Note that according to this definition, pp and y are always a part of msk_y, and thus k_y is basically "the rest of" msk_y. The public value ℓ contains some information about y and z that can be made public (e.g., their lengths).

FE must be *complete*, in the sense that if (y, z) is in the domain of $\mathcal{F}$, then for all (msk, mpk) $\leftarrow_r$ setup(1^κ), for all $\mathrm{msk}_y \leftarrow_r$ keygen$_{\mathrm{msk}}(y)$, and for all $c \leftarrow_r$ enc$_{\mathrm{mpk}}(z)$, it holds that dec$_{\mathrm{msk}_y}(c) = \mathcal{F}(y, z)$.

Definition 4 (IND-FE-CCA Security). *A functional encryption scheme* FE = (setup, keygen, enc, dec) *is IND-FE-CCA secure (or, secure against chosen ciphertext attacks) [26], if no probabilistic polynomial time adversary $\mathcal{A}$ has a non-negligible advantage in the following game:*

1. *The challenger sets* (msk, mpk) $\leftarrow_r$ setup$(1^\kappa, 1^\ell)$ *and sends* mpk *to* $\mathcal{A}$.
2. *$\mathcal{A}$ makes adaptive secret key and decryption queries to the challenger. At each secret key query, $\mathcal{A}$ chooses $y \in \mathcal{Y}$ and obtains $\mathrm{msk}_y = (\mathrm{pp}, k_y, y) \leftarrow_r$ keygen$_{\mathrm{msk}}(y)$. Let y_i be the ith queried secret key.*
   At each decryption query, $\mathcal{A}$ chooses a ciphertext c' and $y \in \mathcal{Y}$, then the challenger computes $\mathrm{msk}_y = (\mathrm{pp}, k_y, y) \leftarrow_r$ keygen$_{\mathrm{msk}}(y)$ and sends back dec$_{\mathrm{msk}_y}(c')$ to $\mathcal{A}$.
3. *$\mathcal{A}$ chooses $z_0 \neq z_1$ such that $\mathcal{F}(y_i, z_0) = \mathcal{F}(y_i, z_1)$ for all queried y_i. $\mathcal{A}$ sends z_0 and z_1 to the challenger. The challenger chooses $\beta \leftarrow_r \{0,1\}$, and sends $c \leftarrow_r$ enc$_{\mathrm{mpk}}(z_\beta)$ to $\mathcal{A}$.*
4. *$\mathcal{A}$ makes more secret key queries for keys $y_i \in \mathcal{Y}$, with the condition that $\mathcal{F}(y_i, z_0) = \mathcal{F}(y_i, z_1)$, and possibly some more decryption queries (c', y), with the condition that $c' \neq c$.*
   Let q_{dec} be the number of decryption queries made during the whole game, and let (c_j', y_j) be the jth decryption query.
5. *$\mathcal{A}$ outputs a bit $\beta_A \in \{0,1\}$ and wins if $\beta_A = \beta$.*

More precisely, the advantage of $\mathcal{A}$ is defined as

$$\mathsf{Adv}_{\mathsf{FE},\mathcal{A}}^{\mathsf{ind-fe-cca}}(\kappa) := 2 \cdot |\Pr[\beta_A = \beta] - 1/2|.$$

FE *is* IND-FE-CCA *secure, if* $\mathsf{Adv}_{\mathsf{FE},\mathcal{A}}^{\mathsf{ind-fe-cca}}$ *is negligible for all probabilistic polynomial time adversaries $\mathcal{A}$.*

FE is *IND-FE-CPA secure* (or, *adaptively secure against chosen plaintexts attacks*, [10,28]), if $\mathsf{Adv}_{\mathsf{FE},\mathcal{A}}^{\mathsf{ind-fe-cca}}$ is negligible for all probabilistic polynomial time adversaries $\mathcal{A}$ that make no decryption queries.

The selective IND-FE-CPA security satisfied by [2] has the further requirement that the challenge messages $\vec{z}_0$ and $\vec{z}_1$ have to be chosen before the adversary sees the public key mpk.

Definition 5 (Inner-Product Functional Encryption). *In the inner-product functional encryption [2],* $\mathsf{setup}(1^\kappa, \ell)$ *in particular chooses a ring $\mathcal{R}$ and two efficiently recognizable subsets $\mathcal{Y}$ and $\mathcal{Z}$ of $\mathcal{R}^\ell$, each y (resp., z) corresponds to some vector $\vec{y} \in \mathcal{Y} \subseteq \mathcal{R}^\ell$ (resp., $\vec{z} \in \mathcal{Z} \subseteq \mathcal{R}^\ell$), and $\mathcal{F}(\vec{y}, \vec{z}) := \langle \vec{y}, \vec{z} \rangle \in \mathcal{R}$.*

We insist on the fact that $\langle \vec{y}, \vec{z} \rangle$ is computed in $\mathcal{R}$.

3 FE-CPA-Friendly Projective Hash Function

In this section, we first present the properties we need on PHFs in order to build an IND-FE-CPA secure IPFE. Then we show some examples of standard PHFs satisfying them.

3.1 Key Homomorphism and Projection Key Homomorphism

For correctness of the IPFE we will need the following property.

Definition 6 (Key Homomorphism [6]). *A projective hash function* PHF = (hashkg, projkg, hash, projhash) *for a subset membership problem* **P** *is key-homomorphic, if it satisfies the following additional properties:*

1. *the set $\mathcal{K}$ of hashing keys and the set Π of hash values are additive Abelian groups, with polynomial time group operations;*
2. *for any instance Λ, and any word $\mathfrak{b} \in \mathcal{X}$, the function* $\mathsf{hk} \in \mathcal{K} \mapsto \mathsf{hash}(\mathsf{hk}, \mathfrak{b}) \in \Pi$ *is a group homomorphism, that is,* $\mathsf{hash}(\mathsf{hk}, \mathfrak{b}) + \mathsf{hash}(\mathsf{hk}', \mathfrak{b}) = \mathsf{hash}(\mathsf{hk} + \mathsf{hk}', \mathfrak{b})$, *for any* $\mathsf{hk}, \mathsf{hk}' \in \mathcal{K}$.

We do not require $\mathcal{K}$ to be finite. In the DCR construction, $\mathcal{K} = \mathbb{Z}$. However, we require that each group element of $\mathcal{K}$ and Π has a unique representation as a bit-string.

The next property, *projection key homomorphism*, is only required in Sect. 5.3 (for the CCA security). We will introduce it already here, since all our concrete examples from Sect. 3.5 coincidentally satisfy this property.

Definition 7 (Projection Key Homomorphism). *A projective hash function* PHF = (hashkg, projkg, hash, projhash) *for a subset membership problem* **P** *is* projection-key-homomorphic *if it satisfies the following additional properties:*

1. *the set* $\mathcal{K}$ *of hashing keys and the set* $\mathcal{K}_{hp}$ *of projection keys are additive Abelian groups, with polynomial time group operations;*
2. *for any instance* Λ, *the function* hk $\in \mathcal{K} \mapsto$ projkg(hk) $\in \mathcal{K}_{hp}$ *is a group homomorphism, that is,* projkg(hk + hk′) = projkg(hk) + projkg(hk′), *for any* hk, hk′ $\in \mathcal{K}$.

3.2   Strong Diversity

The second property we need for our PHFs is strong diversity. More precisely, we require that for each $\mathfrak{b}$ there exists a (not necessarily efficiently computable) hashing key $\mathsf{hk}_\perp(\mathfrak{b})$, such that hk and hk + $\mathsf{hk}_\perp(\mathfrak{b})$ result in the same projection key, while the hash value of $\mathfrak{b}$ under the key $\mathsf{hk}_\perp(\mathfrak{b})$ is equal to $\mathfrak{g}_\perp$, where $\mathfrak{g}_\perp$ is a fixed efficiently computable group element.

Definition 8 (Strong diversity). *A key-homomorphic projective hash function* PHF = (hashkg, projkg, hash, projhash) *for a subset membership problem* **P** *is* (hk$_\perp$, $\mathfrak{g}_\perp$, M$_\perp$)-*strongly diverse for a function* hk$_\perp$: $\bar{\mathcal{L}} \to \Pi$, *an element* $\mathfrak{g}_\perp$ *of* Π, *and a positive integer* M$_\perp$, *if the following properties are satisfied:*

1. $\mathfrak{g}_\perp$ *and* $M_\perp$ *can be efficiently computed from* Λ;
2. *the group element* $\mathfrak{g}_\perp$ *has order* $M_\perp$,
3. *for any hashing key* hk $\in \mathcal{K}$ *and any word* $\mathfrak{b} \in \bar{\mathcal{L}}$:

$$\mathsf{projkg}(\mathsf{hk} + \mathsf{hk}_\perp(\mathfrak{b})) = \mathsf{projkg}(\mathsf{hk}), \tag{2}$$

$$\mathsf{hash}(\mathsf{hk}_\perp(\mathfrak{b}), \mathfrak{b}) = \mathfrak{g}_\perp. \tag{3}$$

We do not require $\mathsf{hk}_\perp$ to be efficiently computable, as we are only using it to bound statistical distance.

In what follows, we will use the following straightforward lemma.

Lemma 9. *If a key-homomorphic PHF is also projection-key homomorphic, then Eq. (2) is true iff* projkg(hk$_\perp$($\mathfrak{b}$)) = 0.

Relation with Diverse Groups. Diverse groups were introduced in [14] as a way to construct PHFs. They can be seen as key-homomorphic projection-key-homomorphic strongly diverse PHFs with the two following differences: $\bar{\mathcal{L}} = \mathcal{X} \backslash \mathcal{L}$ (instead of $\bar{\mathcal{L}} \subseteq \mathcal{X} \backslash \mathcal{L}$), and for any hk $\in \mathcal{K}$ and any $\mathfrak{b} \in \bar{\mathcal{L}}$, it is only required that hash(hk + hk$_\perp$($\mathfrak{b}$), $\mathfrak{b}$) $\neq 0$ instead of hash(hk + hk$_\perp$($\mathfrak{b}$), $\mathfrak{b}$) = $\mathfrak{g}_\perp$. Nevertheless, all the diverse groups we currently know of are also strongly diverse for $\bar{\mathcal{L}} = \mathcal{X} \backslash \mathcal{L}$.

3.3 Translation Indistinguishability

We also require one last statistical property, translation indistinguishability. Informally it says that translating the hashing key of the PHF by a small multiple of $\mathsf{hk}_\perp(\mathfrak{b})$ cannot be detected with non-negligible probability. In the proof, we use this as a statistical argument to conclude after using the computational assumption.

Definition 10 (Translation indistinguishability). *A key-homomorphic projective hash function* $\mathsf{PHF} = (\mathsf{hashkg}, \mathsf{projkg}, \mathsf{hash}, \mathsf{projhash})$ *is* $(\mathsf{hk}_\perp, M_z, \varepsilon_{\mathsf{ti}})$-*translation-indistinguishable for a function* $\mathsf{hk}_\perp : \bar{\mathcal{L}} \to \Pi$, *a positive integer* M_z, *and* $\varepsilon_{\mathsf{ti}} \in [0, 1]$, *if for any integer* $z \in \{-M_z, \ldots, M_z\}$ *and for any* $\mathfrak{b} \in \bar{\mathcal{L}}$,

$$\mathsf{SD}(\mathsf{hashkg}(\Lambda), \mathsf{hashkg}(\Lambda) + z \cdot \mathsf{hk}_\perp(\mathfrak{b})) \leq \varepsilon_{\mathsf{ti}}.$$

Important Particular Case: Key Uniformity. For many key-homomorphic PHFs, like the above described ones based on DDH and MDDH, the output of hashkg is actually uniform over the group $\mathcal{K}$. In this case, the PHF is automatically $(\cdot, \cdot, 0)$-translation-indistinguishable. More formally, we have the following lemma.

Lemma 11. *Let* $\mathsf{PHF} = (\mathsf{hashkg}, \mathsf{projkg}, \mathsf{hash}, \mathsf{projhash})$ *be a key-homomorphic PHF such that the distribution of* $\mathsf{hashkg}(\Lambda)$ *is uniform over* $\mathcal{K}$. *Let* $\bar{\mathcal{L}}$ *be a nonempty subset of* $\mathcal{X}$, $\mathsf{hk}_\perp$ *be a function from* $\bar{\mathcal{L}}$ *to* Π *and* M_z *be a positive integer. Then* PHF *is* $(\bar{\mathcal{L}}, \mathsf{hk}_\perp, M_z, 0)$-*translation-indistinguishable.*

Proof. Both $\mathsf{hashkg}(\Lambda)$ and $\mathsf{hashkg}(\Lambda) + z \cdot \mathsf{hk}_\perp(\mathfrak{b})$ are uniform group elements in $\mathcal{K}$. □

3.4 FE-CPA Friendliness

In the following, we regroup all 3 properties we have defined under the FE-CPA friendliness property.

Definition 12 (FE-CPA Friendliness). *A projective hash function* $\mathsf{PHF} = (\mathsf{hashkg}, \mathsf{projkg}, \mathsf{hash}, \mathsf{projhash})$ *is* $(\mathsf{hk}_\perp, \mathfrak{g}_\perp, M_\perp, M_z, \varepsilon_{\mathsf{ti}})$-*FE-CPA-friendly for a function* $\mathsf{hk}_\perp$ *from* $\bar{\mathcal{L}}$ *to* Π', *an element* $\mathfrak{g}_\perp$ *of* Π, *and two positive integers* $M_\perp$ *and* M_z, *if it is key-homomorphic,* $(\mathsf{hk}_\perp, \mathfrak{g}_\perp, M_\perp)$-*strongly diverse, and* $(\mathsf{hk}_\perp, M_z, \varepsilon_{\mathsf{ti}})$-*translation-indistinguishable.*

3.5 Examples

In this section, we describe FE-CPA-friendly PHFs for the subset membership problems described in Sect. 2.1.

DDH. Let $\mathbb{G}$ be an additive cyclic group of prime order q, let $\mathcal{X} = \mathbb{G}^2$, let $\mathcal{L}$ be the subgroup of $\mathcal{X}$ generated by $\mathbf{g} = (\mathfrak{g}_1, \mathfrak{g}_2)^\mathsf{T} \in \mathbb{G}^2$, where $\mathfrak{g}_i$ are random generators of $\mathbb{G}$. A witness $w \in \mathcal{W} = \mathbb{Z}_q$ for $\mathfrak{b} \in \mathcal{L}$ is such that $\mathfrak{b} = w \cdot \mathbf{g}$. We set $\Lambda = (\mathbb{G}, \mathbf{g})$.

We recall the PHF of Cramer and Shoup [13, Sect. 8.1.1] defined as follows:

---

hashkg(Λ): output $\mathbf{hk} \leftarrow_r \mathbb{Z}_q^2 = \mathcal{K}$,
projkg($\mathbf{hk}$): output $\mathfrak{hp} \leftarrow \mathbf{hk}^\mathsf{T} \cdot \mathbf{g} \in \mathbb{G}$,
hash($\mathbf{hk}, \mathfrak{b}$): output $\mathfrak{H} \leftarrow \mathbf{hk}^\mathsf{T} \cdot \mathfrak{b} \in \mathbb{G} = \Pi$,
projhash($\mathfrak{hp}, \mathfrak{b}, w$): output $\mathfrak{pH} \leftarrow \mathfrak{hp} \cdot w \in \mathbb{G} = \Pi$.

Lemma 13. *Using above notation, let $\mathfrak{g}_\perp$ an arbitrary generator of $\mathbb{G}$, $M_\perp = q$, M_z be a positive integer, and $\varepsilon_{\mathsf{ti}} = 0$. For any $\mathfrak{b} \in \mathcal{X} \setminus \mathcal{L}$, let $\mathbf{hk}_\perp(\mathfrak{b})$ be defined as follows:*

$$\mathbf{hk}_\perp(\mathfrak{b}) = \frac{\log_{\mathfrak{g}_1} \mathfrak{g}_\perp}{\log_{\mathfrak{g}_1} \mathfrak{b}_1 \cdot \log_{\mathfrak{g}_1} \mathfrak{g}_2 - \log_{\mathfrak{g}_1} \mathfrak{b}_2} \cdot \begin{pmatrix} \log_{\mathfrak{g}_1} \mathfrak{g}_2 \\ -1 \end{pmatrix} \quad with \ \mathfrak{b} = \begin{pmatrix} \mathfrak{b}_1 \\ \mathfrak{b}_2 \end{pmatrix} \in \mathbb{G}^2.$$

Then, the PHF described above is $(\mathbf{hk}_\perp, \mathfrak{g}_\perp, M_\perp, M_z, \varepsilon_{\mathsf{ti}})$-FE-CPA-friendly.

Proof. We first remark that $\mathbf{hk}_\perp(\mathfrak{b})$ is well defined, as $\log_{\mathfrak{g}_1} \mathfrak{b}_1 \cdot \log_{\mathfrak{g}_1} \mathfrak{g}_2 \neq \log_{\mathfrak{g}_1} \mathfrak{b}_2$ since $\mathfrak{b} \notin \mathcal{L}$.

KEY HOMOMORPHISM is straightforward.

STRONG DIVERSITY. Since the space of projection keys is also a group and projkg is a group homomorphism, we can use Lemma 9. Hence, we just need to prove that $\mathsf{projkg}(\mathbf{hk}_\perp(\mathfrak{b})) = 0$ and $\mathsf{hash}(\mathbf{hk}_\perp(\mathfrak{b}), \mathfrak{b}) = \mathfrak{g}_\perp$. This follows from the following two facts:

$$\mathsf{projkg}(\mathbf{hk}_\perp(\mathfrak{b})) = \frac{\log_{\mathfrak{g}_1} \mathfrak{g}_\perp}{\log_{\mathfrak{g}_1} \mathfrak{b}_1 \cdot \log_{\mathfrak{g}_1} \mathfrak{g}_2 - \log_{\mathfrak{g}_1} \mathfrak{b}_2} \cdot \left(\log_{\mathfrak{g}_1} \mathfrak{g}_2 \quad -1 \right) \cdot \begin{pmatrix} \mathfrak{g}_1 \\ \mathfrak{g}_2 \end{pmatrix},$$

$$\mathsf{hash}(\mathbf{hk}_\perp(\mathfrak{b}), \mathfrak{b}) = \frac{\log_{\mathfrak{g}_1} \mathfrak{g}_\perp}{\log_{\mathfrak{g}_1} \mathfrak{b}_1 \cdot \log_{\mathfrak{g}_1} \mathfrak{g}_2 - \log_{\mathfrak{g}_1} \mathfrak{b}_2} \cdot \left(\log_{\mathfrak{g}_1} \mathfrak{g}_2 \quad -1 \right) \cdot \begin{pmatrix} \mathfrak{b}_1 \\ \mathfrak{b}_2 \end{pmatrix}.$$

TRANSLATION INDISTINGUISHABILITY follows from Lemma 11.   □

MDDH. Let $\Lambda = (\mathbb{G}, \mathbf{g})$ be defined as in the MDDH subsubsection of Sect. 2.1 on page 7. We recall that $\mathbf{g} \in \mathbb{G}^{t \times d}$, $\mathcal{X} = \mathbb{G}^t$, $\mathcal{L}$ is the subgroup generated by the columns of $\mathbf{g}$, and $\bar{\mathcal{L}} = \mathcal{X} \setminus \mathcal{L}$. A witness $w \in \mathcal{W} = \mathbb{Z}_q^d$ for $\mathfrak{b} \in \mathcal{L}$ is such that $\mathfrak{b} = \mathbf{g} \cdot w$.

We recall the PHF defined by Escala et al. in [18]:

---

hashkg(Λ): output $\mathbf{hk} \leftarrow_r \mathbb{Z}_q^t = \mathcal{K}$,
projkg($\mathbf{hk}$): output $\mathfrak{hp} \leftarrow \mathbf{g}^\mathsf{T} \cdot \mathbf{hk} \in \mathbb{G}^d$,
hash($\mathbf{hk}, \mathfrak{b}$): output $\mathfrak{H} \leftarrow \mathbf{hk}^\mathsf{T} \cdot \mathfrak{b} \in \mathbb{G} = \Pi$,
projhash($\mathfrak{hp}, \mathfrak{b}, w$): output $\mathfrak{pH} \leftarrow \mathfrak{hp}^\mathsf{T} \cdot w \in \mathbb{G} = \Pi$.

We can prove the following lemma similarly to Lemma 13:

Lemma 14. *Using above notation, let* $\mathfrak{g}_\perp$ *an arbitrary generator of* $\mathbb{G}$, $M_\perp = q$, M_z *be a positive integer, and* $\varepsilon_{ti} = 0$. *Let* $\mathsf{hk}_\perp(\mathfrak{b})$ *be an arbitrary vector satisfying* $\mathsf{hk}_\perp(\mathfrak{b})^\mathsf{T} \cdot \mathfrak{g} = 0$ *and* $\mathsf{hk}_\perp(\mathfrak{b})^\mathsf{T} \cdot \vec{\mathfrak{b}} = \mathfrak{g}_\perp$, *which exists as* $\vec{\mathfrak{b}}$ *is not in the span of the columns of* $\mathfrak{g}$. *Then, the PHF described above is* $(\mathsf{hk}_\perp, \mathfrak{g}_\perp, M_\perp, M_z, \varepsilon_{ti})$-*FE-CPA-friendly.*

DCR. Let $\Lambda = (N, s, \mathfrak{g}, \mathfrak{g}_\perp)$ be defined as in the DCR subsection of Sect. 2.1 on page 7. We have: $\mathbb{G} = \mathcal{X} = J_{N^{s+1}} \cong G_{N^s} \oplus G_{N'} \oplus T$, $\mathcal{L} = G_{N'}$, and $\bar{\mathcal{L}} = \mathcal{L} + \mathfrak{g}_\perp$. The element $\mathfrak{g}$ is a generator of $\mathcal{L}$, while $\mathfrak{g}_\perp$ is a generator of G_{N^s}. We recall that we use additive notation for the group $\mathbb{G}$.

We define the DCR-based PHF as follows:

$\mathsf{hashkg}(\Lambda)$: output $\mathsf{hk} \leftarrow_r \{0, \ldots, \lfloor MN^{s+1}/4 \rfloor\} =: \mathcal{K}^* \subseteq \mathbb{Z} =: \mathcal{K}$, where M is
  a positive integer and is a parameter of the scheme,
$\mathsf{projkg}(\mathsf{hk})$: output $\mathfrak{hp} \leftarrow \mathsf{hk} \cdot \mathfrak{g} \in \mathbb{G}$,
$\mathsf{hash}(\mathsf{hk}, \mathfrak{b})$: output $\mathfrak{H} \leftarrow \mathsf{hk} \cdot \mathfrak{b} \in \mathbb{G} =: \Pi$,
$\mathsf{projhash}(\mathfrak{hp}, \mathfrak{b}, w)$: output $\mathfrak{ph} \leftarrow \mathfrak{hp} \cdot w \in \mathbb{G} = \Pi$.

When $M = 2$, this PHF corresponds to the one of Cramer and Shoup in [14]. We insist on the fact that the set of hashing keys is $\mathcal{K} = \mathbb{Z}$ so that it is a group. However, hashkg only samples a hashing key from a finite subset $\mathcal{K}^*$ of $\mathcal{K}$.

Lemma 15. *Using above notation, let* $M_\perp = N^s$, M_z *be a positive integer, and* $\varepsilon_{ti} = M_z/M$. *Let* $\mathsf{hk}_\perp$ *be defined as follows:*

$$\mathsf{hk}_\perp(\mathfrak{b}) = N' \cdot (N'^{-1} \bmod N^s) \quad (< N'N^s < N^{s+1}/4).$$

Then, the PHF described above is $(\mathsf{hk}_\perp, \mathfrak{g}_\perp, M_\perp, M_z, \varepsilon_{ti})$-*FE-CPA-friendly.*

Key homomorphism and strong diversity are proven similarly as in the DDH case, while translation indistinguishability follows from Lemma 2. The complete proof is given in full version.

Interestingly, because of our choice of $\bar{\mathcal{L}}$, $\mathsf{hk}_\perp(\mathfrak{b})$ does not depend on $\mathfrak{b}$. Note also that for $M < M_z/\varepsilon_{ti}$, this PHF is still key-homomorphic and strongly diverse, but might lack the translation indistinguishability property that is necessary for our application.

4   IND-FE-CPA Inner-Product Functional Encryption

In this section, we first show a generic construction of an IND-FE-CPA secure inner-product functional encryption scheme from a FE-CPA-friendly projective hash function. Then, we show two concrete instantiations, based on the DDH and on the DCR assumptions.

4.1   Generic Construction

We now define our generic construction for IND-FE-CPA secure IPFEs. Intuitively, we use ℓ PHFs in parallel, that are combined during decryption in order to only reveal a linear combination of the hashes, which implies that it only reveals this same linear combination of the messages. This restriction is enforced by the key generation algorithm, which only outputs linear combinations of the hashing keys.

Construction. We suppose that we have a $(\mathsf{hk}_\perp, \mathfrak{g}_\perp, M_\perp, z, \varepsilon_{\mathsf{ti}})$-FE-CPA-friendly projective hash function $\mathsf{PHF} = (\mathsf{hashkg}, \mathsf{projkg}, \mathsf{hash}, \mathsf{projhash})$ for a subset membership problem $\mathbf{P}$. Let $\mathcal{R}$ be the ring $\mathbb{Z}$ or $\mathbb{Z}_{M_\perp}$, let ℓ be a positive integer parameter corresponding to the length of the message and key vectors, and let $\mathcal{Y}$ and $\mathcal{Z}$ two subsets of $\mathcal{R}^\ell$.[3] We always suppose ℓ to be polynomial in the security parameter κ.

We suppose that the following condition is satisfied.

Condition 1. *Using the above notation:*

1. *if $\mathcal{R} = \mathbb{Z}_{M_\perp}$, the order of any hashing key $\mathsf{hk} \in \mathcal{K}$ divides $M_\perp$;*
2. *$\mathcal{Y}$ and $\mathcal{Z}$ are efficiently recognizable subsets of $\mathcal{R}^\ell$;*
3. *for any $\vec{z} \in \mathcal{Z}$ and any i, $z_i \in \{-M_z, \dots, M_z\}$;*
4. *there exists a polynomial time algorithm (in the security parameter κ) that given as input $\mathfrak{c}_{\vec{y}} = \langle \vec{y}, \vec{z} \rangle \cdot \mathfrak{g}_\perp$ for $\vec{y} \in \mathcal{Y}$ and $\vec{z} \in \mathcal{Z}$, can compute $\log_{\mathfrak{g}_\perp} \mathfrak{c}_{\vec{y}} = \langle \vec{y}, \vec{z} \rangle$;*
5. *for any $\vec{y} \in \mathcal{Y}$ and $\vec{z} \in \mathcal{Z}$, $\langle \vec{y}, \vec{z} \rangle$ is the same over $\mathcal{R}$ and over $\mathbb{Z}_{M_\perp}$ (this condition is trivial when $\mathcal{R} = \mathbb{Z}_{M_\perp}$).*

The first subcondition implies that $\mathcal{K}$ is a $\mathcal{R}$-module, which implies that, for any $t \in \mathcal{R}$, $t \cdot \mathsf{hk}$ is well defined. The second subcondition enables keygen and enc to check in polynomial-time the validity of their arguments y and z respectively. The third subcondition is used in the proof to apply the $(\mathsf{hk}_\perp, M_z, \varepsilon_{\mathsf{ti}})$-translation indistinguishability property. The fourth subcondition ensures that decryption can be performed in polynomial time. The last subcondition is similar as the condition in the "over $\mathbb{Z}$ constructions in [5]. If $\mathcal{R} = \mathbb{Z}_{M_\perp}$, then—as in [5]— a simple way to guarantee that subconditions 3 and 5 hold is to assume that $|y_i|, |z_i| < (M_\perp/\ell)^{1/2}$ for each $\vec{y} \in \mathcal{Y}$, $\vec{z} \in \mathcal{Z}$, and $i \leq \ell$. The fourth subcondition can potential restrict the values $|y_i|$ and $|z_i|$ even more.

Our generic IND-FE-CPA IPFE scheme $\mathsf{FE}_{\mathsf{phf}}$ is depicted in Fig. 1.

Security. We define the following set:

$$\Delta\mathcal{Z} := \{\vec{z}_1 - \vec{z}_0 \ : \ \vec{z}_0, \vec{z}_1 \in \mathcal{Z}\}.$$

Its cardinality $|\Delta\mathcal{Z}|$ is at most $(4M_z - 1)^\ell$, as the cardinality of $\mathcal{Z}$ is at most $2M_z$.

We have the following security theorem.

---

[3] Formally, $\mathcal{Y}$ and $\mathcal{Z}$ are collections of subsets indexed by ℓ and Λ.

---

1. Let $\mathbf{P}$ be a subset membership problem. Let $\mathsf{PHF} = (\mathsf{hashkg}, \mathsf{projkg}, \mathsf{hash}, \mathsf{projhash})$ be a $(\mathsf{hk}_\perp, \mathfrak{g}_\perp, M_\perp, M_z, \varepsilon_{\mathsf{ti}})$-FE-CPA-friendly PHF. We assume that Cond. 1 is satisfied.

2. $\mathsf{setup}(1^\kappa, \ell)$: Sample $\Lambda \leftarrow_r I_\kappa$, and set $\mathsf{pp} \leftarrow (\kappa, \ell, \Lambda)$. Define $\vec{\mathsf{hk}} \in \mathcal{K}^\ell$ and $\vec{\mathfrak{hp}} \in \mathcal{K}^\ell_{\mathsf{hp}}$ by setting

$$\mathsf{hk}_i \leftarrow_r \mathsf{hashkg}(\Lambda), \qquad\qquad \mathfrak{hp}_i \leftarrow \mathsf{projkg}(\mathsf{hk}_i).$$

Set $\mathsf{msk} \leftarrow (\mathsf{pp}, \vec{\mathsf{hk}})$ and $\mathsf{mpk} \leftarrow (\mathsf{pp}, \vec{\mathfrak{hp}})$, and return $(\mathsf{msk}, \mathsf{mpk})$.

3. $\mathsf{keygen}_{\mathsf{msk}}(\vec{y} \in \mathcal{Y})$: Set $\mathsf{hk}_{\vec{y}} \leftarrow \langle \vec{y}, \vec{\mathsf{hk}} \rangle \in \mathcal{K}$, and return $\mathsf{msk}_{\vec{y}} \leftarrow (\mathsf{pp}, \mathsf{hk}_{\vec{y}}, \vec{y})$.

4. $\mathsf{enc}_{\mathsf{mpk}}(\vec{z} \in \mathcal{Z})$: Sample a random pair $(\mathfrak{b}, w) \in \varrho$. Define $\vec{\mathfrak{c}} \in \Pi^\ell$ by setting

$$\mathfrak{c}_i \leftarrow \mathsf{projhash}(\mathfrak{hp}_i, \mathfrak{b}, w) + z_i \cdot \mathfrak{g}_\perp.$$

Return $(\mathfrak{b}, \vec{\mathfrak{c}})$.

5. $\mathsf{dec}_{\mathsf{msk}_{\vec{y}}}(\mathfrak{b}, \vec{\mathfrak{c}})$: Check that $\mathfrak{b} \in \mathcal{X}$ and $\vec{\mathfrak{c}} \in \Pi^\ell$; return $\perp$ if any check fails. Set

$$\mathfrak{c}_{\vec{z}} \leftarrow \langle \vec{y}, \vec{\mathfrak{c}} \rangle - \mathsf{hash}(\mathsf{hk}_{\vec{y}}, \mathfrak{b}).$$

Return $\log_{\mathfrak{g}_\perp} \mathfrak{c}_{\vec{z}}$.

Fig. 1. Generic inner-product functional encryption $\mathsf{FE}_{\mathsf{phf}}$ scheme

Theorem 16. *Let $\mathbf{P}$ be a subset membership problem. Let $\mathsf{PHF} = (\mathsf{hashkg}, \mathsf{projkg}, \mathsf{hash}, \mathsf{projhash})$ be a $(\mathsf{hk}_\perp, \mathfrak{g}_\perp, M_\perp, M_z, \varepsilon_{\mathsf{ti}})$-FE-CPA-friendly projective hash function. We assume that Condition 1 is satisfied. Then the scheme $\mathsf{FE}_{\mathsf{phf}}$ depicted in Fig. 1 is complete and adaptively IND-FE-CPA secure.*

More precisely, if there exists an attacker $\mathcal{A} = \mathcal{A}_{\mathsf{FE}}$ that has advantage $\varepsilon_{\mathcal{A}}$ in breaking the IND-FE-CPA security of $\mathsf{FE}_{\mathsf{phf}}$, then there exists an attacker $\mathcal{B}$ that runs in approximately the same time and that has advantage $\varepsilon_{\mathcal{B}}$ in breaking the $(\mathcal{L}, \bar{\mathcal{L}})$-indistinguishability, such that

$$\varepsilon_{\mathcal{A}} \leq 2 \cdot \varepsilon_{\mathcal{B}} + \ell \cdot |\Delta \mathcal{Z}| \cdot \varepsilon_{\mathsf{ti}}.$$

The proof is provided in App. 16. As a quick overview, the proof is structured in two parts: first we use a computational assumption to show that sampling a word outside of the language for the challenge ciphertext is indistinguishable to the adversary. One this is done, the second part is a statistical argument claiming that the view of the adversary is then almost independent of the chosen bit β.

Remark 17. When $\varepsilon_{\mathsf{ti}} \neq 0$, there is an exponential loss in the security proof in the term $\ell |\Delta \mathcal{Z}| \varepsilon_{\mathsf{ti}}$. This term comes from the fact that at one point we guess the value of $\vec{z}_1 - \vec{z}_0$. This is not complexity leveraging, as the reduction loss is with regards to a statistical property. In particular, we do not need to rely on subexponential computational assumptions. Concretely, in our instantiations with DCR, we just need to take this security loss into account in the parameter

M defining the bound on the size of the hashing key (see Sects. 3.5 and 4.3). This approximately multiplies by $\log |\Delta \mathcal{Z}|$ the size of the secret keys which would be obtained if this security loss was not taken into account.

We also remark that if we used a selective security notion, where the adversary announces $\vec{z}_0$ and $\vec{z}_1$ before obtaining the public key, we would not lose the factor $|\Delta \mathcal{Z}|$. We could then use classical complexity leveraging to go from this selective notion to the adaptive one we are considering. But then, we would need to use sub-exponential $(\mathcal{L}, \bar{\mathcal{L}})$-indistinguishability (if ℓ is polynomial in the security parameter), and the size of the ciphertexts, of the secret and public keys, and of the public parameters (and not just of the secret keys) would be multiplied by $|\Delta \mathcal{Z}|$.

4.2   DDH-Based Instantiation

Let us instantiate the framework with the DDH-based PHF defined in Sect. 3.5 on page 13. We set $\mathcal{R} = \mathbb{Z}_q$ and $M_z = q$ (or any large enough integer). To satisfy Condition 1, we need to choose the efficiently recognizable subsets $\mathcal{Y}$ and $\mathcal{Z}$ of $\mathcal{R}^\ell$ so that the discrete logarithm of $\langle \vec{y}, \vec{z} \rangle \cdot \mathfrak{g}_\perp \in \mathbb{G}$ is efficient to compute, for any $\vec{y} \in \mathcal{Y}$ and $\vec{z} \in \mathcal{Z}$. We recall that there exist generic algorithms to compute the discrete logarithm of an element $t \cdot \mathfrak{g}_\perp$ in $O(\sqrt{|T|})$ group operations, when t is in an interval T; and in $O(T)$ group operations, when t is in an arbitrary subset of $T \subseteq \mathbb{Z}_q$.

The resulting construction $\mathsf{FE_{ddh}}$ coincides with the DDH-based scheme in [5]. An explicit description of $\mathsf{FE_{ddh}}$ is provided in full version. It can be easily extended to use any MDDH-based PHF defined in Sect. 3.5.

Applying Theorem 16, we immediately get the following security theorem.

Theorem 18. *Under the DDH assumption in $\mathbb{G}$, the scheme $\mathsf{FE_{ddh}}$ is complete and IND-FE-CPA.*

More precisely, if there exists an attacker $\mathcal{A} = \mathcal{A}_{\mathsf{FE}}$ that has advantage $\varepsilon_\mathcal{A}$ in breaking the IND-FE-CPA security of $\mathsf{FE_{ddh}}$, then there exists an attacker $\mathcal{B}$ that runs in approximately the same time and that has advantage $\varepsilon_\mathcal{B}$ in breaking the DDH assumption, such that $\varepsilon_\mathcal{A} \leq 2 \cdot \varepsilon_\mathcal{B}$.

It is worth noting that the term $\ell \cdot |\Delta \mathcal{Z}| \cdot \varepsilon_{\mathsf{ti}}$ has disappeared because of the key-uniformity.

4.3   DCR-Based Instantiation

Let us instantiate the framework with the DCR-based PHF defined in Sect. 3.5 on page 14. We set $\mathcal{R} = \mathbb{Z}$. Contrary the DDH-based instantiation, the discrete logarithm problem in the subgroup generated by $\mathfrak{g}_\perp$ is easy: given $t \cdot \mathfrak{g}_\perp$, we can always efficiently recover t. However, to satisfy Condition 1, we need to choose $\mathcal{Y}$ and $\mathcal{Z}$ so that for any $\vec{y} \in \mathcal{Y}$ and $\vec{z} \in \mathcal{Z}$, $\langle \vec{y}, \vec{z} \rangle$ is the same modulo $M_\perp = N^s$ and over the integers.

There are many ways to choose the parameters to satisfy this condition. We propose one possible way here.

Example 19 (Example of parameters for our DCR-based instantiation). Let M_y and M_z be positive integers such that $2M_yM_z + 1 \leq M_\perp = N^s$. We set:

$$\mathcal{Y} := \{\vec{y} \in \mathbb{Z}^\ell : \|\vec{y}\| \leq M_y\}, \qquad \mathcal{Z} := \{\vec{z} \in \mathbb{Z}^\ell : \|\vec{z}\| \leq M_z\},$$

$$M := \ell \cdot 2^\kappa \cdot M_z \cdot |\Delta\mathcal{Z}| \leq \ell \cdot 2^\kappa \cdot M_z \cdot (4 \cdot M_z)^\ell,$$

where $\|.\|$ denotes the Euclidean norm, so that $|\langle \vec{y}, \vec{z} \rangle| \leq M_yM_z$ (when the inner-product is over the integers). For the last inequality, we use the rough inequality $|\Delta\mathcal{Z}| \leq (4 \cdot M_z)^\ell$. $\qquad\qquad\qquad\qquad\qquad\qquad\qquad\qquad\qquad\qquad\qquad$ □

Then, we fix M_y and M_z so that $2M_yM_z + 1 \leq M_\perp$. And we choose M so that M_z/M is negligible.

The concrete DCR-based IPFE scheme $\mathsf{FE_{dcr}}$ is fully described in full version. $\mathsf{FE_{dcr}}$ is length-flexible in the same sense as the cryptosystems of [15, 16]. Namely, by fixing the parameter $s \in \mathbb{Z}^+$, one can obtain bigger or smaller sets M_z and M_y. Larger s however makes the scheme less efficient. Note that the sizes of our secret keys is slightly larger than those of [5], due to our security reduction; but we do not need to sample discrete Gaussian, as all the distributions we are using are uniform.

Applying Theorem 16 and Lemma 3, we immediately get the following security theorem.

Theorem 20. *Under the DCR assumption, the scheme $\mathsf{FE_{dcr}}$ is complete and IND-FE-CPA.*

More precisely, if there exists an attacker $\mathcal{A} = \mathcal{A}_{\mathsf{FE}}$ that has advantage $\varepsilon_\mathcal{A}$ in breaking the IND-FE-CPA security of $\mathsf{FE_{dcr}}$, then there exists an attacker $\mathcal{B}$ that runs in approximately the same time and that has advantage $\varepsilon_\mathcal{B}$ in breaking the DCR assumption, such that $\varepsilon_\mathcal{A} \leq 4s \cdot \varepsilon_\mathcal{B} + 16/\mathrm{spf}(N) + \ell \cdot |\Delta\mathcal{Z}| \cdot M_z/M$.

Using parameters from Example 19, we have the following security bound: $\varepsilon_\mathcal{A} \leq 4s \cdot \varepsilon_\mathcal{B} + 16/\mathrm{spf}(N) + 2^{-\kappa}$. Although there is an exponential loss in the security reduction of Theorem 16, we emphasize that there is no exponential loss using these parameters: the security loss is compensated by these well-chosen parameters. Most importantly, all the algorithms of the resulting scheme run in polynomial time (in the security parameter κ)[4] and the reduction to DCR is polynomial time. There is *no* complexity leveraging and we *do not* require subexponential assumption *nor* exponential-size keys or ciphertexts.

5   FE-CCA-Friendly Projective Hash Functions

In order to achieve IND-FE-CCA security, we will require another kind of PHFs: *tag-based projective hash functions* [1]. In this section, we first define this new tool, as well as the properties we need for our construction. Then we show tag-based PHFs satisfying these properties based on the same 3 examples as previously: DDH, MDDH and DCR.

---

[4] We recall that the length ℓ of the vectors is assumed to be polynomial in κ.

As both a FE-CPA-friendly PHF and a FE-CCA-friendly PHF are used in our constructions of IND-FE-CCA inner-product functional encryption scheme in Sect. 6, we distinguish the two PHFs by adding a dagger to all the symbols defining the latter PHF. Both PHFs will be used on the same subset membership problem **P**.

5.1   Tag-Based Projective Hash Function

A tag-based projective hash function [1] is defined as a PHF, except that $\mathsf{hash}^\dagger$ and $\mathsf{projhash}^\dagger$ take an additional input (in some efficiently recognizable set $\mathcal{T}$) called a tag τ. We suppose that we can efficiently uniquely encode any 2κ-bit string as a tag τ, as a tag is usually the output of a collision-resistant hash-function. In our constructions, $\mathcal{T}$ is $\mathbb{Z}_M$ for some large integer M.

Definition 21 (Tag-based Projective Hash Function [1]). *Let* **P** *be a subset membership problem, specifying an ensemble $(I_\ell)_{\ell \geq 0}$ of instance distributions. A tag-based projective hash function for* **P** *is a tuple* $\mathsf{PHF}^\dagger = (\mathsf{hashkg}^\dagger, \mathsf{projkg}^\dagger, \mathsf{hash}^\dagger, \mathsf{projhash}^\dagger)$ *of four probabilistic polynomial time algorithms:*

- $\mathsf{hashkg}^\dagger(\Lambda)$ *generates a hashing key $\mathsf{hk}^\dagger$ in some set $\mathcal{K}^\dagger$ for the instance $\Lambda = \Lambda[\mathcal{X}, \mathcal{L}, \mathcal{W}, \varrho]$,*
- $\mathsf{projkg}^\dagger(\mathsf{hk}^\dagger)$ *(deterministically) derives from the hashing key $\mathsf{hk}^\dagger$ a projection key $\mathfrak{hp}^\dagger$ from the set $\mathcal{K}_{\mathsf{hp}}$ of possible projection keys,*
- $\mathsf{hash}^\dagger(\mathsf{hk}^\dagger, \mathfrak{b}, \tau)$ *(deterministically) computes the hash value $\mathfrak{H}^\dagger$ (in some efficiently recognizable set Π), of $\mathfrak{b} \in \mathcal{X}$ under $\mathsf{hk}^\dagger \in \mathcal{K}^\dagger$, for the tag $\tau \in \mathcal{T}$,*
- $\mathsf{projhash}^\dagger(\mathfrak{hp}^\dagger, \mathfrak{b}, w, \tau)$ *(deterministically) computes the projected hash value $\mathfrak{pH}^\dagger$ of $\mathfrak{b} \in \mathcal{L}$ using a witness $w \in \mathcal{W}$, for the tag $\tau \in \mathcal{T}$.*

It has to satisfy the following correctness property:

- *For any instance Λ, for any $\mathfrak{b} \in \mathcal{X}$ and $w \in \mathcal{W}$, s.t. $(\mathfrak{b}, w) \in \varrho$, for any hashing key $\mathsf{hk}^\dagger \in \mathcal{K}^\dagger$, for any tag $\tau \in \mathcal{T}$, if $\mathfrak{hp}^\dagger \leftarrow \mathsf{projkg}^\dagger(\mathsf{hk}^\dagger)$, then:*

$$\mathsf{hash}^\dagger(\mathsf{hk}^\dagger, \mathfrak{b}, \tau) = \mathsf{projhash}^\dagger(\mathfrak{hp}^\dagger, \mathfrak{b}, w, \tau).$$

The notions of key homomorphism and projection key homomorphism can be adapted to tag-based PHFs in a straightforward way (key homomorphism has to hold for any tag $\tau \in \mathcal{T}$).

In the sequel, we sometimes omit the term "tag-based" when it is clear from context.

5.2   2-Universality

We now recall the notion of *2-universality*, first introduced by Cramer and Shoup in [14], in order to ensure non-malleability. This will not be directly required by the tag-based PHF we use in the construction, but by a slight modification on it that will be used during the proof. It will ensure that decryption queries made by the adversary do not leak too much information.

Definition 22 (2-universality). *A key-homomorphic tag-based projective hash function* $\mathsf{PHF}^\dagger = (\mathsf{hashkg}^\dagger, \mathsf{projkg}^\dagger, \mathsf{hash}^\dagger, \mathsf{projhash}^\dagger)$ *for a subset membership problem* $\mathbf{P}$ *is* $\varepsilon_{2u}^\dagger$*-2-universal if for any instance* Λ, *for any* $\mathfrak{b} \in \mathcal{X}$ *and* $\mathfrak{b}' \in \mathcal{X} \backslash \mathcal{L}$, *for any distinct tags* $\tau, \tau' \in \mathcal{T}$, *for any* $\mathfrak{hp}^\dagger \in \mathcal{K}_{\mathsf{hp}}$, *and for any* $\mathfrak{H}^\dagger \in \Pi$, $\tilde{\mathfrak{H}}^\dagger \in \Pi$:

$$\Pr_{\mathsf{hk}^\dagger} \left[\mathfrak{H}^\dagger = \mathsf{hash}^\dagger(\mathsf{hk}^\dagger, \mathfrak{b}, \tau) \ \wedge \ \mathfrak{H}'^\dagger = \mathsf{hash}^\dagger(\mathsf{hk}^\dagger, \mathfrak{b}', \tau') \ \wedge \ \mathfrak{hp}^\dagger = \mathsf{projkg}^\dagger(\mathsf{hk}^\dagger) \right]$$

$$\leq \varepsilon_{2u}^\dagger \cdot \Pr_{\mathsf{hk}^\dagger} \left[\mathfrak{H}^\dagger = \mathsf{hash}^\dagger(\mathsf{hk}^\dagger, \mathfrak{b}, \tau) \ \wedge \ \mathfrak{hp}^\dagger = \mathsf{projkg}^\dagger(\mathsf{hk}^\dagger) \right],$$

where probabilities are taken over $\mathsf{hk}^\dagger \leftarrow_r \mathsf{hashkg}^\dagger(\Lambda)$. *The PHF is* 2-universal *if it is* $\varepsilon_{2u}^\dagger(\kappa)$-*2-universal for some negligible function* $\varepsilon_{2u}^\dagger(\kappa)$.

In our generic construction, we will not require the PHF used in the construction to be 2-universal, but a variant of it where $\mathsf{hashkg}^\dagger$ is replaced by some other (not necessarily polynomial time) algorithm.

5.3   Universal Translation Indistinguishability

We also need one last statistical property to conclude the proof, as in the IND-FE-CPA case: *universal translation indistinguishability* . It is a strengthening of the previous translation indistinguishability in the sense that the algorithm defining the translation has to be the same for all words.

Definition 23 (Universal translation indistinguishability). *A key-homomorphic tag-based projective hash function* $\mathsf{PHF}^\dagger = (\mathsf{hashkg}^\dagger, \mathsf{projkg}^\dagger, \mathsf{hash}^\dagger, \mathsf{projhash}^\dagger)$ *is* $(\mathsf{hashkg}'^\dagger, M_z, \varepsilon_{\mathsf{uti}}^\dagger)$-*universally-translation-indistinguishable for a (not necessarily polynomial time) algorithm* $\mathsf{hashkg}'^\dagger$ *taking as input* Λ *and outputting a hashing key* $\mathsf{hk}^\dagger$ *in some set* $\mathcal{K}'^{*\dagger} \subseteq \mathcal{K}$, *and for a positive integer* M_z, *if for any integer* z *such that* $|z| \leq M_z$,

$$\mathsf{SD}(\mathsf{hashkg}^\dagger(\Lambda), \mathsf{hashkg}^\dagger(\Lambda) + z \cdot \mathsf{hashkg}'^\dagger(\Lambda)) \leq \varepsilon_{\mathsf{uti}}^\dagger.$$

Important Particular Case: Key Uniformity. For many key-homomorphic tag-based PHFs, the output of $\mathsf{hashkg}^\dagger$ is actually uniform over the group $\mathcal{K}^\dagger$. In this case, as for translation indistinguishability (Lemma 11), the PHF is automatically $(\mathsf{hashkg}'^\dagger, \cdot, 0)$-universally-translation-indistinguishable, for $\mathsf{hashkg}'^\dagger = \mathsf{hashkg}^\dagger$. More formally, we have the following lemma.

Lemma 24. *Let* $\mathsf{PHF}^\dagger = (\mathsf{hashkg}^\dagger, \mathsf{projkg}^\dagger, \mathsf{hash}^\dagger, \mathsf{projhash}^\dagger)$ *be a key-homomorphic tag-based PHF such that the distribution of* $\mathsf{hashkg}^\dagger(\Lambda)$ *is uniform over* $\mathcal{K}^\dagger$. *Let* M_z *be a positive integer. Then* PHF *is* $(\mathsf{hashkg}^\dagger, M_z, 0)$-*universally-translation-indistinguishable.*

Proof. Both $\mathsf{hashkg}^\dagger(\Lambda)$ and $\mathsf{hashkg}^\dagger(\Lambda) + z \cdot \mathsf{hashkg}^\dagger(\Lambda)$ are uniform group elements in $\mathcal{K}^\dagger$. □

5.4   FE-CCA Friendliness

In the following, we regroup the properties we need under the *FE-CCA friendliness* property. It is used as a shorthand for the sake of readability and regroups projection key homomorphism, universal translation indistinguishability, and 2-universality on a slight modification of the PHF.

Definition 25 (FE-CCA Friendliness). *A tag-based projective hash function* $\mathsf{PHF}^\dagger = (\mathsf{hashkg}^\dagger, \mathsf{projkg}^\dagger, \mathsf{hash}^\dagger, \mathsf{projhash}^\dagger)$ *is* $(\mathsf{hashkg'}^\dagger, \Sigma^\dagger, \varepsilon^\dagger_{2u}, M_z, \varepsilon^\dagger_{uti})$-*FE-CCA-friendly for a (not necessarily polynomial time) algorithm* $\mathsf{hashkg'}^\dagger$ *taking as input* Λ *and outputting a hashing key* $\mathsf{hk}^\dagger$ *in some set* $\mathcal{K}'^{*\dagger} \subseteq \mathcal{K}$, *and for a positive integer* M_z, *for a subset* $\Sigma^\dagger$ *of* $\mathbb{Z}$, *and for a positive integer* M_z, *if* $\mathsf{PHF}^\dagger$ *is key-homomorphic, projection-key-homomorphic,* $(\mathsf{hashkg'}^\dagger, M_z, \varepsilon^\dagger_{uti})$-*universally-translation-indistinguishable and if for any* $t \in \Sigma^\dagger$, *the PHF* $(t \cdot \mathsf{hashkg'}^\dagger, \mathsf{projkg}^\dagger, \mathsf{hash}^\dagger, \mathsf{projhash}^\dagger)$ *is* $\varepsilon^\dagger_{2u}$-*2-universal, where the algorithm* $t \cdot \mathsf{hashkg'}^\dagger$ *runs* $\mathsf{hashkg'}^\dagger$ *and multiplies the output by* t.

Important Particular Case: Key Uniformity. For many key-homomorphic PHFs, the output of $\mathsf{hashkg}^\dagger$ is actually uniform over the group $\mathcal{K}^\dagger$. In this case, we have the following lemma which proves FE-CCA friendliness from 2-universality.

Lemma 26. *Let* $\mathsf{PHF}^\dagger = (\mathsf{hashkg}^\dagger, \mathsf{projkg}^\dagger, \mathsf{hash}^\dagger, \mathsf{projhash}^\dagger)$ *be a* $\varepsilon^\dagger_{2u}$-*2-universal tag-based PHF such that the distribution of* $\mathsf{hashkg}^\dagger(\Lambda)$ *is uniform over* $\mathcal{K}^\dagger$. *Then for any* $t \in \mathbb{Z}$, $(t \cdot \mathsf{hashkg}^\dagger, \mathsf{projkg}^\dagger, \mathsf{hash}^\dagger, \mathsf{projhash}^\dagger)$ *is* $\varepsilon^\dagger_{2u}$-*2-universal.*

Proof. Since $\mathsf{hashkg}^\dagger(\Lambda)$ is uniformly distributed, $t \cdot \mathsf{hashkg}^\dagger(\Lambda)$ is as well, so both schemes are equal. □

5.5   Examples

2-universal tag-based PHFs can be constructed from diverse groups, as in [14]. All the constructions in [14] are key-homomorphic and projection-key-homomorphic. And for well-chosen parameters, they actually are FE-CCA-friendly. Let us now describe these FE-CCA-friendly constructions for our three usual example subset membership problems: DDH, MDDH, and DCRA.

DDH. Let $\mathbb{G}$ be a cyclic group of prime order q, let $\mathcal{X} = \mathbb{G}^2$, let $\mathcal{L}$ be the subgroup of $\mathcal{X}$ generated by $\mathbf{g} = (\mathfrak{g}_1, \mathfrak{g}_2)^\top \in \mathbb{G}^2$, where $\mathfrak{g}_i$ are random generators of $\mathbb{G}^*$. A witness $w \in \mathcal{W} = \mathbb{Z}_q$ for $\mathbf{b} \in \mathcal{L}$ is such that $\mathbf{b} = w \cdot \mathbf{g}$. We set $\Lambda = (\mathbb{G}, \mathbf{g})$.

We first recall the following 2-universal hash from [1]:

Tag set: $\mathcal{T} = \mathbb{Z}_q$,

$\mathsf{hashkg}^\dagger(\Lambda)$: output $\mathbf{hk}^\dagger \leftarrow_r \mathbb{Z}_q^4 =: \mathcal{K}$,

$\mathsf{projkg}^\dagger(\mathbf{hk}^\dagger)$: output $\mathfrak{hp}^\dagger \leftarrow \left(\begin{smallmatrix} \mathfrak{g} & 0 \\ 0 & \mathfrak{g} \end{smallmatrix}\right)^\mathsf{T} \cdot \mathbf{hk}^\dagger \in \mathbb{G}^2 =: \mathcal{K}_{\mathsf{hp}}$,

$\mathsf{hash}^\dagger(\mathbf{hk}^\dagger, \mathfrak{b}, \tau)$: output $\mathfrak{H}^\dagger \leftarrow \mathbf{hk}^{\dagger\mathsf{T}} \cdot \left(\begin{smallmatrix} \mathfrak{b} \\ \tau\cdot\mathfrak{b} \end{smallmatrix}\right) \in \mathbb{G} =: \Pi$;

$\mathsf{projhash}^\dagger(\mathfrak{hp}^\dagger, \mathfrak{b}, w, \tau)$: output $\mathfrak{pH}^\dagger \leftarrow \mathfrak{hp}^{\dagger\mathsf{T}} \cdot \left(\begin{smallmatrix} w \\ \tau\cdot w \end{smallmatrix}\right) \in \mathbb{G} = \Pi$.

We prove the following lemma in the full version.

Lemma 27. *Using above notation, let* $\mathsf{hashkg}'^\dagger = \mathsf{hashkg}^\dagger$, $\Sigma^\dagger = \mathbb{Z}_q$, $\varepsilon_{2u}^\dagger = 1/q$, M_z *be a positive integer, and* $\varepsilon_{uti}^\dagger = 0$. *Then, the PHF described above is a* $(\mathsf{hashkg}'^\dagger, \Sigma^\dagger, \varepsilon_{2u}^\dagger, M_z, \varepsilon_{uti}^\dagger)$-*FE-CCA-friendly.*

We use a slight extension of this PHF because we need an exponentially small security parameter $\varepsilon_{2u}^\dagger$, due our security reduction. The following PHF can be seen as repeating ν times the PHF of Lemma 27:

Tag set: $\mathcal{T} = \mathbb{Z}_q$,

$\mathsf{hashkg}^\dagger(\Lambda)$: output $\mathbf{hk}^\dagger \leftarrow_r \mathbb{Z}_q^{4\times\nu} =: \mathcal{K}$;

$\mathsf{projkg}^\dagger(\mathbf{hk}^\dagger)$: output $\mathfrak{hp}^\dagger \leftarrow \left(\begin{smallmatrix} \mathfrak{g} & 0 \\ 0 & \mathfrak{g} \end{smallmatrix}\right) \cdot \mathbf{hk}^\dagger \in \mathbb{G}^{2\times\nu} =: \mathcal{K}_{\mathsf{hp}}$;

$\mathsf{hash}^\dagger(\mathbf{hk}^\dagger, \mathfrak{b}, \tau)$: output $\mathfrak{H}^\dagger \leftarrow \mathbf{hk}^{\dagger\mathsf{T}} \cdot \left(\begin{smallmatrix} \mathfrak{b} \\ \tau\cdot\mathfrak{b} \end{smallmatrix}\right) \in \mathbb{G}^\nu =: \Pi$;

$\mathsf{projhash}^\dagger(\mathfrak{hp}^\dagger, \mathfrak{b}, w, \tau)$: output $\mathfrak{pH}^\dagger \leftarrow \left(\begin{smallmatrix} w \\ \tau\cdot w \end{smallmatrix}\right)^\mathsf{T} \cdot \mathfrak{hp}^\dagger \in \mathbb{G}^\nu = \Pi$.

We prove the following lemma in the full version.

Lemma 28. *Using above notation, let* $\mathsf{hashkg}'^\dagger = \mathsf{hashkg}^\dagger$, $\Sigma^\dagger = \mathbb{Z}_q$, $\varepsilon_{2u}^\dagger = 1/q^\nu$, M_z *be a positive integer, and* $\varepsilon_{uti}^\dagger = 0$. *Then, the PHF described above is a* $(\mathsf{hashkg}'^\dagger, \Sigma^\dagger, \varepsilon_{2u}^\dagger, M_z, \varepsilon_{ti})$-*FE-CCA-friendly.*

MDDH. The previous construction can be extended in a straightforward way to any MDDH-based subset membership problem in a straightforward way, similar to what is done for our FE-CPA-friendly construction in Sect. 3.5 in page 3.5.

DCR. Let $\Lambda = (N, s, \mathfrak{g}, \mathfrak{g}_\perp)$ be defined as in the DCR subsubsection of Sect. 2.1 on page 7. We have: $\mathbb{G} = \mathcal{X} = J_{N^{s+1}} \cong G_{N^s} \oplus G_{N'} \oplus T$, $\mathcal{L} = G_{N'}$, and $\bar{\mathcal{L}} = \mathcal{L} + \mathfrak{g}_\perp$. The element $\mathfrak{g}$ is a generator of $\mathcal{L}$, while $\mathfrak{g}_\perp$ is a generator of G_{N^s}. We recall that we use additive notation for the group $\mathbb{G}$.

We define a PHF as follows:

Tag set: $\mathcal{T} = \{0, \ldots, \lfloor N/2 \rfloor\} \subseteq \mathbb{Z}_{N'}$

$\mathsf{hashkg}^\dagger(\Lambda)$: output $\mathbf{hk}^\dagger \leftarrow_r \{0, \ldots, \lfloor \nu M^\dagger N^{s+1}/2 \rfloor\}^{2\times\nu} =: \mathcal{K}^* \subseteq \mathbb{Z}^{2\times\nu} =: \mathcal{K}$,

    where $M^\dagger$ is a positive integer and is a parameter of the scheme,

$\mathsf{projkg}^\dagger(\mathbf{hk}^\dagger)$: output $\mathfrak{hp}^\dagger \leftarrow \left(\begin{smallmatrix} \mathfrak{g} & 0 \\ 0 & \mathfrak{g} \end{smallmatrix}\right)^\mathsf{T} \cdot \mathbf{hk}^\dagger \in \mathbb{G}^{2\times\nu} =: \mathcal{K}_{\mathsf{hp}}$;

$\mathsf{hash}^\dagger(\mathbf{hk}^\dagger, \mathfrak{b}, \tau)$: output $\mathfrak{H}^\dagger \leftarrow \mathbf{hk}^{\dagger\mathsf{T}} \cdot \left(\begin{smallmatrix} \mathfrak{b} \\ \tau\cdot\mathfrak{b} \end{smallmatrix}\right) \in \mathbb{G}^\nu =: \Pi$;

$\mathsf{projhash}^\dagger(\mathfrak{hp}^\dagger, \mathfrak{b}, w, \tau)$: output $\mathfrak{pH}^\dagger \leftarrow \mathfrak{hp}^{\dagger\mathsf{T}} \cdot \left(\begin{smallmatrix} w \\ \tau\cdot w \end{smallmatrix}\right) \in \mathbb{G}^\nu = \Pi$.

We prove the following lemma in full version.

Lemma 29. *Using above notation, $\Sigma^\dagger = \{-N^s + 1, \ldots, N^s - 1\} \setminus \{0\}$, $\varepsilon_{2u}^\dagger = 1/2^\nu$, M_z be a positive integer, and $\varepsilon_{uti}^\dagger = M_z/M^\dagger$. Define in addition the following algorithm:*

$\mathsf{hashkg'}^\dagger(\Lambda)$: *output* $\mathsf{hk}^\dagger \leftarrow_r \mathbb{Z}_{N'N^s}^{2\times\nu} = \mathcal{K}^{*\dagger}$.

Then, the PHF described above is a $(\mathsf{hashkg'}^\dagger, \Sigma^\dagger, \varepsilon_{2u}^\dagger, M_z, \varepsilon_{uti}^\dagger)$-FE-CCA-friendly.

6 IND-FE-CCA Inner-Product Functional Encryption

In this section, we construct IND-FE-CCA inner-product functional encryption from FE-CPA-friendly PHFs and FE-CCA-friendly PHFs. For the sake of readability, we split our construction into two parts: we first show how to construct a CCA secure tag-based variant of inner-product functional encryption from PHFs with the right properties. Then we show how to construct a non tag-based functional encryption that reaches CCA security from the tag-based variant.

6.1 Tag-Based Functional Encryption

We now define tag-based functional encryption. It is an adaptation from the concept of tag-based encryption [24] to the context of functional encryption.

Definition 30. *A tag-based functional encryption scheme for functionality $\mathcal{F}$ is a tuple* $\mathsf{TBFE} = (\mathsf{setup}, \mathsf{keygen}, \mathsf{enc}, \mathsf{dec})$ *of four probabilistic polynomial time algorithms:*

$\mathsf{setup}(1^\kappa, \ell)$: *first generates system parameters* pp, *and then returns a master secret and public key pair* $(\mathsf{msk}, \mathsf{mpk})$, *where both* msk *and* mpk *also contain* pp,

$\mathsf{keygen}_{\mathsf{msk}}(y \in \mathcal{Y})$: *given a master secret key* msk *and* y, *returns a partial secret key* $\mathsf{msk}_y = (\mathsf{pp}, k_y, y)$,

$\mathsf{enc}_{\mathsf{mpk},\tau}(z \in \mathcal{Z})$: *given a master public key* mpk, *a tag* τ, *and a plaintext* z, *returns a ciphertext* c,

$\mathsf{dec}_{\mathsf{msk}_y,\tau}(c)$: *given a partial secret key* msk_y, *a tag* τ, *and a ciphertext* c, *returns* $S \in \Sigma \cup \{\bot\}$.

TBFE *must be* complete, *in the sense that if* (y, z) *is in the domain of* $\mathcal{F}$, *and* τ *is a tag, then for all* $(\mathsf{msk}, \mathsf{mpk}) \leftarrow \mathsf{setup}(1^\kappa)$, $\mathsf{msk}_y \leftarrow \mathsf{keygen}_{\mathsf{msk}}(y)$, *and* $c \leftarrow_r \mathsf{enc}_{\mathsf{mpk},\tau}(z; r)$, *it holds that* $\mathsf{dec}_{\mathsf{msk}_y,\tau}(c) = \mathcal{F}(y, z)$.

In the following definition, we have highlighted differences with the IND-FE-CCA definition, Definition 4.

Definition 31 (IND-TBFE-CCA Security). *A tag-based functional encryption scheme* $\mathsf{TBFE} = (\mathsf{setup}, \mathsf{keygen}, \mathsf{enc}, \mathsf{dec})$ *is IND-TBFE-CCA secure (or, secure against chosen ciphertext attacks), if no probabilistic polynomial time adversary $\mathcal{A}$ has a non-negligible advantage in the following game:*

1. *The challenger sets* $(\text{msk}, \text{mpk}) \leftarrow \text{setup}(1^{\kappa}, \ell)$ *and sends* mpk *to* $\mathcal{A}$.
2. $\mathcal{A}$ *makes adaptive secret key and decryption queries to the challenger. At each secret key query,* $\mathcal{A}$ *chooses* $y \in \mathcal{Y}$ *and obtains* $\text{msk}_y = (\text{pp}, k_y, y) \leftarrow \text{keygen}_{\text{msk}}(y)$. *At each decryption query,* $\mathcal{A}$ *chooses a ciphertext* c', *a tag* τ', *and* $y \in \mathcal{Y}$, *then the challenger computes* $\text{msk}_y = (\text{pp}, k_y, y) \leftarrow \text{keygen}_{\text{msk}}(y)$ *and sends back* $\text{dec}_{\text{msk}_y, \tau'}(c')$ *to* $\mathcal{A}$. *Let* y_i *be the ith queried secret key.*
3. $\mathcal{A}$ *chooses a tag* τ, *and* $z_0 \neq z_1$ *such that* $\mathcal{F}(y_i, z_0) = \mathcal{F}(y_i, z_1)$ *for all queried* y_i. *She sends* τ, z_0, *and* z_1 *to the challenger. The challenger chooses* $\beta \leftarrow_r \{0, 1\}$, *and sends* $c \leftarrow_r \text{enc}_{\text{mpk}, \tau}(z_{\beta})$ *to* $\mathcal{A}$.
4. $\mathcal{A}$ *makes more secret key queries for keys* $y_i \in \mathcal{Y}$, *with the condition that* $\mathcal{F}(y_i, z_0) = \mathcal{F}(y_i, z_1)$, *and decryption queries, with the condition that* $\tau' \neq \tau$. *Let* q_{dec} *be the number of decryption queries made during the whole game, and let* (y_j, τ'_j, c'_j) *be the jth decryption query.*
5. $\mathcal{A}$ *outputs a bit* $\beta_A \in \{0, 1\}$ *and wins if* $\beta_A = \beta$.

More precisely, the advantage of $\mathcal{A}$ *is defined as*

$$\text{Adv}^{\text{ind-tbfe-cca}}_{\text{TBFE}, \mathcal{A}}(\kappa) := 2 \cdot |\Pr[\beta_A = \beta] - 1/2|.$$

TBFE *is* secure against chosen ciphertext attacks (or, IND-TBFE-CCA secure), *if* $\text{Adv}^{\text{ind-tbfe-cca}}_{\text{TBFE}, \mathcal{A}}$ *is negligible for all probabilistic polynomial time adversaries* Adv.

6.2 Generic Construction

Intuition. The core idea of our construction is similar to the one used in the Cramer-Shoup encryption scheme [12,14]: adding a hash value (from a 2-universal PHF) to ensure that the word $\mathfrak{b}$ is in the language $\mathcal{L}$, to our generic IND-FE-CPA construction in Sect. 4.1. Then, at least information-theoretically, the values $\text{hash}(\text{hk}_i, \mathfrak{b})$ used to decrypt a ciphertext $(\mathfrak{b}, \vec{c})$ could be computed using only $\mathfrak{hp}_i$ and do not leak any information from hk_i. We can then conclude using the same ideas as in the IND-FE-CPA security proof of our generic construction.

However, this does not work directly, as checking a 2-universal hash value require to know the corresponding hashing key $\text{hk}^\dagger$, and knowing this hashing key enables to fake these hash values. In other words, with the naive scheme described previously, an attacker knowing a secret key for any $\vec{y}$ could then generate a ciphertext with $\mathfrak{b} \notin \mathcal{L}$, but a valid 2-universal hash values. This completely removes the usefulness of the 2-universal hash value.

Our new idea is the following: instead of using only one hash value, we use ℓ such values. The secret key $\text{msk}_{\vec{y}}$ only enables to check that a linear combination (with coefficient $\vec{y}$) of these hash values is valid. This uses the key homomorphism property. Knowing $\text{msk}_{\vec{y}}$ enables to generate hash values that would be accepted by the decryption oracle with $\vec{y}$, and knowing $\text{msk}_{\vec{y}}$ for multiple vectors $\vec{y}$ enables to generate hash values for any vector in the span of these $\vec{y}$. But intuitively, this is not really an issue, as if the attacker already knows $\text{msk}_{\vec{y}}$, calling the decryption oracle for $\vec{y}$ is of no use to him, as he could decrypt the given ciphertext himself. The proof however is more subtle and requires a careful design of hybrid games to deal with adaptivity and the fact that we are working over a ring and not a field. In particular, we cannot directly rely on the notion of span of vectors. Details can be found in the proof.

Construction. We suppose that we have a $(\mathsf{hk}_\perp, \mathfrak{g}_\perp, M_\perp, z, \varepsilon_{\mathsf{ti}})$-FE-CPA-friendly projective hash function $\mathsf{PHF} = (\mathsf{hashkg}, \mathsf{projkg}, \mathsf{hash}, \mathsf{projhash})$ and a $(\mathsf{hashkg}'^\dagger, \Sigma^\dagger, \varepsilon_{2\mathsf{u}}^\dagger, M_z, \varepsilon_{\mathsf{uti}}^\dagger)$-FE-CCA-friendly projective hash function $\mathsf{PHF}^\dagger = (\mathsf{hashkg}^\dagger, \mathsf{projkg}^\dagger, \mathsf{hash}^\dagger, \mathsf{projhash}^\dagger)$ for the subset membership problem $\mathbf{P}$. Let $\mathcal{R}$ be the ring $\mathbb{Z}$ or $\mathbb{Z}_{M_\perp}$, let ℓ be a positive integer parameter corresponding to the length of the message and key vectors, and let $\mathcal{Y}$ and $\mathcal{Z}$ be two subsets of $\mathcal{R}^\ell$. We always suppose ℓ to be polynomial in the security parameter κ. The scheme is depicted in Fig. 2.

We suppose that Condition 1 is satisfied, in addition to the following new condition.

---

1. Let $\mathbf{P}$ be a subset membership problem. Let $\mathsf{PHF} = (\mathsf{hashkg}, \mathsf{projkg}, \mathsf{hash}, \mathsf{projhash})$ be a $(\mathsf{hk}_\perp, \mathfrak{g}_\perp, M_\perp, M_z, \varepsilon_{\mathsf{ti}})$-FE-CPA-friendly PHF, and $\mathsf{PHF}^\dagger = (\mathsf{hashkg}^\dagger, \mathsf{projkg}^\dagger, \mathsf{hash}^\dagger, \mathsf{projhash}^\dagger)$ be a $(\mathsf{hashkg}'^\dagger, \Sigma^\dagger, \varepsilon_{2\mathsf{u}}^\dagger, M_z, \varepsilon_{\mathsf{uti}}^\dagger)$-FE-CCA-friendly tag-based PHF. We assume that Cond. 1 is satisfied.

2. $\mathsf{setup}(1^\kappa, \ell)$: Sample $\Lambda \leftarrow_r I_\kappa$, and set $\mathsf{pp} \leftarrow (\kappa, \ell, \Lambda)$. For $i = 1, \dots, \ell$, set

$$\mathsf{hk}_i \leftarrow_r \mathsf{hashkg}(\Lambda), \qquad\qquad \mathfrak{hp}_i \leftarrow \mathsf{projkg}(\mathsf{hk}_i),$$
$$\mathsf{hk}_i^\dagger \leftarrow_r \mathsf{hashkg}^\dagger(\Lambda), \qquad\qquad \mathfrak{hp}_i^\dagger \leftarrow \mathsf{projkg}^\dagger(\mathsf{hk}_i^\dagger),$$

Set $\mathsf{msk} \leftarrow (\mathsf{pp}, \vec{\mathsf{hk}}, \vec{\mathsf{hk}}^\dagger)$ and $\mathsf{mpk} \leftarrow (\mathsf{pp}, \vec{\mathfrak{hp}}, \vec{\mathfrak{hp}}^\dagger)$, and return $(\mathsf{msk}, \mathsf{mpk})$.

3. $\mathsf{keygen}_{\mathsf{msk}}(\vec{y} \in \mathcal{Y})$: Set $\mathsf{hk}_{\vec{y}} \leftarrow \langle \vec{y}, \vec{\mathsf{hk}} \rangle \in \mathcal{K}$ and $\mathsf{hk}_{\vec{y}}^\dagger \leftarrow_r \langle \vec{y}, \vec{\mathsf{hk}}^\dagger \rangle \in \mathcal{K}^\dagger$, and return $\mathsf{msk}_{\vec{y}} \leftarrow (\mathsf{pp}, \mathsf{hk}_{\vec{y}}, \mathsf{hk}_{\vec{y}}^\dagger, \vec{y})$.

4. $\mathsf{enc}_{\mathsf{mpk}, \tau}(\vec{z} \in \mathcal{Z})$: Sample a random pair $(\mathfrak{b}, w) \in \varrho$. For $i = 1, \dots, \ell$, set

$$\mathfrak{c}_i \leftarrow \mathsf{projhash}(\mathfrak{hp}_i, \mathfrak{b}, w) + z_i \cdot \mathfrak{g}_\perp, \qquad \mathfrak{c}_i^\dagger \leftarrow \mathsf{projhash}^\dagger(\mathfrak{hp}_i^\dagger, \mathfrak{b}, w, \tau).$$

Return $(\mathfrak{b}, \vec{\mathfrak{c}}, \vec{\mathfrak{c}}^\dagger)$.

5. $\mathsf{dec}_{\mathsf{msk}_{\vec{y}}, \tau}(\mathfrak{b}, \vec{\mathfrak{c}}, \vec{\mathfrak{c}}^\dagger)$: Check that $\mathfrak{b} \in \mathcal{X}$, and $\mathfrak{c}_i \in \Pi$ and $\langle \vec{y}, \vec{\mathfrak{c}}^\dagger \rangle = \mathsf{hash}^\dagger(\mathsf{hk}_{\vec{y}}^\dagger, \mathfrak{b}, \tau)$ for $i = 1, \dots, \ell$; return $\perp$ if any check fails. Set

$$\mathfrak{c}_{\vec{z}} \leftarrow \langle \vec{y}, \vec{\mathfrak{c}} \rangle - \mathsf{hash}(\mathsf{hk}_{\vec{y}}, \mathfrak{b}).$$

Return $\log_{\mathfrak{g}_\perp} \mathfrak{c}_{\vec{z}}$.

Fig. 2. Generic inner-product tag-based functional encryption $\mathsf{TBFE}_{\mathsf{phf}}$ from a FE-CPA-friendly PHF and a FE-CCA-friendly tag-based PHF

Condition 2. *Using the above notation:*

1. if $\mathcal{R} = \mathbb{Z}_{M_\perp}$, the order of any hashing key $\mathsf{hk} \in \mathcal{K}^\dagger$ divides $M_\perp$; and
2. for any $\vec{y} \in \mathcal{Y}$ and $\vec{z} \in \mathcal{Z}$, $\langle \vec{y}, \vec{z} \rangle \in \Sigma^\dagger \cup \{0\} \subseteq \mathcal{R}$.

Security. We have the following security theorem.

Theorem 32. *Let* **P** *be a subset membership problem. Let* PHF $=$ (hashkg, projkg, hash, projhash) *be a* $(\mathsf{hk}_\perp, \mathfrak{g}_\perp, M_\perp, M_z, \varepsilon_{\mathsf{ti}})$-*FE-CPA-friendly PHF.* $(\mathsf{hashkg}'^\dagger, \Sigma^\dagger, \varepsilon_{2\mathsf{u}}^\dagger, M_z, \varepsilon_{\mathsf{uti}}^\dagger)$-*FE-CCA-friendly projective hash function. Then the scheme* $\mathsf{TBFE}_{\mathrm{phf}}$ *is complete and IND-TBFE-CCA.*

More precisely, if there exists an adversary $\mathcal{A} = \mathcal{A}_{\mathsf{FE}}$ that has advantage $\varepsilon_{\mathcal{A}}$ in breaking the IND-TBFE-CCA security of $\mathsf{TBFE}_{\mathrm{phf}}$, *then there exists an attacker $\mathcal{B}$ that runs in approximately the same time and that has advantage $\varepsilon_{\mathcal{B}}$ in breaking the $(\mathcal{L}, \bar{\mathcal{L}})$-indistinguishability, such that*

$$\varepsilon_{\mathcal{A}} \leq 2 \cdot \varepsilon_{\mathcal{B}} + \ell \cdot |\Delta\mathcal{Z}| \cdot (\varepsilon_{\mathsf{ti}} + 2 \cdot \varepsilon_{\mathsf{uti}}^\dagger) + 2 \cdot q_{dec} \cdot |\Delta\mathcal{Z}| \cdot \varepsilon_{2\mathsf{u}}^\dagger,$$

where q_{dec} is the number of queries to the decryption oracle.

The proof is in the full version.

Remark 33. In addition to the exponential loss $\ell \cdot |\Delta\mathcal{Z}| \cdot (\varepsilon_{\mathsf{ti}} + 2 \cdot \varepsilon_{\mathsf{uti}}^\dagger)$ similar to the one for the generic IND-FE-CPA construction (Theorem 16), there is an addition exponential loss in the security proof in the term $2q_{\mathrm{dec}}|\Delta\mathcal{Z}|\varepsilon_{2\mathsf{u}}^\dagger$. We point out however that the resulting requirement that $|\Delta\mathcal{Z}|\varepsilon_{2\mathsf{u}}^\dagger$ is negligible in the security parameter can easily to achieve: given a $\varepsilon_{2\mathsf{u}}^\dagger$-2-universal PHF, we can get a $(\varepsilon_{2\mathsf{u}}^\dagger)^\nu$-2-universal PHF, by repeating it ν-times in parallel. This transformation preserves FE-CCA friendliness. Our examples in Sect. 5.5 actually already uses this trick. We emphasize that the resulting key and ciphertext sizes remain polynomial in the security parameter κ, and that we do not rely on complexity leveraging nor subexponential assumptions (see Remark 17 on page 16).

Furthermore, as for the IND-FE-CPA construction from translation-indistinguishable key-homomorphic PHF in Sect. 4.1, if we only consider a selective version of IND-TBFE-CCA where the adversary announces $\vec{z}_0$ and $\vec{z}_1$ before receiving the public key, then we would not have this factor $|\Delta\mathcal{Z}|$.

6.3 DDH-Based Instantiation

Let us instantiate the framework with the DDH-based FE-CPA-friendly PHF defined in Sect. 3.5 on page 13, and the DDH-based FE-CCA-friendly tag-based PHF defined in Sect. 5.5 on page 21. We set $\mathcal{R} = \mathbb{Z}_q$ and $M_z = q$ (or any large enough integer). As for the IND-FE-CPA scheme in Sect. 4.2, we need to choose the efficiently recognizable subsets $\mathcal{Y}$ and $\mathcal{Z}$ of $\mathcal{R}^\ell$ so that the discrete logarithm of $\langle \vec{y}, \vec{z} \rangle \cdot \mathfrak{g}_\perp \in \mathbb{G}$ is efficient to compute, for any $\vec{y} \in \mathcal{Y}$ and $\vec{z} \in \mathcal{Z}$ in order to satisfy Condition 2. The resulting construction $\mathsf{TBFE}_{\mathrm{ddh}}$ is depicted in Fig. 3 and can be easily extended to use any MDDH-based PHF defined in Sect. 5.5.

1. Let $\mathbb{G}$ be a cyclic group of prime order q, $\mathfrak{g}_\perp$ a generator of $\mathbb{G}$.
2. $\mathsf{setup}(1^\kappa, \ell)$: Choose $\mathbf{g} \leftarrow_r \mathbb{G}^2$. Set $\mathrm{pp} = (\kappa, \ell, \mathbf{g})$. For $i = 1, \dots, \ell$, set

$$\mathsf{hk}_i \leftarrow_r \mathbb{Z}_q^2, \qquad\qquad \mathfrak{hp}_i \leftarrow \mathsf{hk}_i^\mathsf{T} \cdot \mathbf{g} \in \mathbb{G},$$

$$\mathsf{hk}_i^\dagger \leftarrow_r \mathbb{Z}_q^{4 \times \nu}, \qquad\qquad \mathfrak{hp}_i^\dagger \leftarrow \left(\begin{smallmatrix} \mathbf{g} & 0 \\ 0 & \mathbf{g} \end{smallmatrix}\right)^\mathsf{T} \cdot \mathsf{hk}_i^\dagger \in \mathbb{G}^{2 \times n\nu}.$$

Set $\mathrm{msk} \leftarrow (\mathrm{pp}, \vec{\mathsf{hk}} \in \mathbb{Z}_q^\ell, \vec{\mathsf{hk}}^\dagger \in (\mathbb{Z}_q^{4\times\nu})^\ell)$ and $\mathrm{mpk} \leftarrow (\mathrm{pp}, \vec{\mathfrak{hp}} \in \mathbb{G}, \vec{\mathfrak{hp}}^\dagger \in (\mathbb{G}^{2\times\nu})^\ell)$. Return $(\mathrm{msk}, \mathrm{mpk})$.

3. $\mathsf{keygen}_{\mathrm{msk}}(\vec{y} \in \mathbb{Z}_q^\ell)$: Set $\mathsf{hk}_{\vec{y}} \leftarrow \langle \vec{y}, \vec{\mathsf{hk}} \rangle \in \mathbb{Z}_q^2$ and $\mathsf{hk}_{\vec{y}}^\dagger \leftarrow \langle \vec{y}, \vec{\mathsf{hk}}^\dagger \rangle \in \mathbb{Z}_q^{4 \times \nu}$. Return $\mathrm{msk}_{\vec{y}} \leftarrow (\mathrm{pp}, \mathsf{hk}_{\vec{y}}, \mathsf{hk}_{\vec{y}}^\dagger, \vec{y})$.

4. $\mathsf{enc}_{\mathrm{mpk}, \tau}(\vec{z} \in \mathbb{Z}_q^\ell)$: Pick $r \leftarrow_r \mathbb{Z}_q$ and set $\mathfrak{b} \leftarrow r \cdot \mathbf{g} \in \mathbb{G}^2$. For $i = 1, \dots, \ell$, set

$$\mathfrak{c}_i \leftarrow z_i \cdot \mathfrak{g}_\perp + r \cdot \mathfrak{hp}_i \in \mathbb{G}, \qquad\qquad \mathfrak{c}_i^\dagger \leftarrow \mathfrak{hp}_i^\dagger \cdot \left(\begin{smallmatrix} r \\ \tau \cdot r \end{smallmatrix}\right) \in \mathbb{G}^\nu.$$

Return $(\mathfrak{b}, \vec{\mathfrak{c}} \in \mathbb{G}^\ell, \vec{\mathfrak{c}}^\dagger \in (\mathbb{G}^\nu)^\ell)$.

5. $\mathsf{dec}_{\mathrm{msk}_{\vec{y}}, \tau}(\mathfrak{b}, \vec{\mathfrak{c}}, \vec{\mathfrak{c}}^\dagger)$: Check that $\langle \vec{y}, \vec{\mathfrak{c}}^\dagger \rangle = \mathsf{hk}_{\vec{y}}^{\dagger\mathsf{T}} \cdot \left(\begin{smallmatrix} \mathfrak{b} \\ \tau \cdot \mathfrak{b} \end{smallmatrix}\right)$; return $\perp$ if it fails. Set

$$\mathfrak{c}_{\vec{z}} \leftarrow \langle \vec{y}, \vec{\mathfrak{c}} \rangle - \mathsf{hk}_{\vec{y}}^\mathsf{T} \cdot \mathfrak{b} \in \mathbb{G}.$$

Return $\log_{\mathfrak{g}_\perp} \mathfrak{c}_{\vec{z}}$.

Fig. 3. DDH-based inner-product tag-based functional encryption $\mathsf{TBFE}_{\mathrm{ddh}}$

Applying Theorem 32, we immediately get the following security theorem.

Theorem 34. *Under the DDH assumption in $\mathbb{G}$, the scheme $\mathsf{TBFE}_{\mathrm{ddh}}$ depicted in Fig. 3 is complete and IND-TBFE-CCA.*

More precisely, if there exists an attacker $\mathcal{A} = \mathcal{A}_{\mathsf{TBFE}}$ that has advantage $\varepsilon_\mathcal{A}$ in breaking the IND-TBFE-CCA security of $\mathsf{TBFE}_{\mathrm{ddh}}$, then there exists an attacker $\mathcal{B}$ that runs in approximately the same time and that has advantage $\varepsilon_\mathcal{B}$ in breaking the DDH assumption, such that $\varepsilon_\mathcal{A} \leq 2 \cdot \varepsilon_\mathcal{B} + 2 \cdot q_{dec} \cdot q^{\ell-\nu}$.

In particular, setting $\nu = \ell + 1$, we have the following bound: $\varepsilon_\mathcal{A} \leq 2 \cdot \varepsilon_\mathcal{B} + 2 \cdot \frac{q_{dec}}{q}$.

6.4 DCR-Based Instantiations

Let us now instantiate the framework with the DCR-based FE-CPA-friendly PHF defined in Sect. 3.5 on page 14, and the DDH-based FE-CCA-friendly tag-based PHF defined in Sect. 5.5 on page 22. We use the same parameters as for the IND-FE-CPA scheme in Sect. 4.3. The resulting construction $\mathsf{TBFE}_{\mathrm{dcr}}$ is depicted in Fig. 4. We switch back to the multiplicative notation so that the scheme looks more familiar.

Applying Theorem 32 and Lemma 3, we immediately get the following security theorem.

1. Let $N = pq$ be a product of two λ-bit random safe primes. We suppose that Cond. 2 is satisfied. Let $u \leftarrow_r \mathbb{Z}_{N^{s+1}}^*$, $\mathfrak{g} \leftarrow u^{2N^s}$, and $\mathfrak{g}_\perp \leftarrow 1 + N$.

2. $\mathsf{setup}(1^\kappa, \ell)$: Set $\mathsf{pp} \leftarrow (\kappa, \ell, N, \mathfrak{g})$. For $i = 1, \dots, \ell$, $j = 1, 2$, and $k = 1, \dots, \nu$, set

$$\mathsf{hk}_i \leftarrow_r \{0, \dots, \lfloor MN^{s+1}/4 \rfloor\}, \qquad \mathfrak{hp}_i \leftarrow \mathfrak{g}^{\mathsf{hk}_i} \in \mathbb{G},$$

$$\mathsf{hk}_{k,i,j}^\dagger \leftarrow_r \{0, \dots, \lfloor \nu M^\dagger N^{s+1}/2 \rfloor\}, \qquad \mathfrak{hp}_{k,i,j}^\dagger \leftarrow \mathfrak{g}^{\mathsf{hk}_{k,i,j}^\dagger} \in \mathbb{G}.$$

   Set $\mathsf{msk} \leftarrow (\mathsf{pp}, \vec{\mathsf{hk}} \in \mathbb{Z}^\ell, \vec{\mathsf{hk}}^\dagger \in (\mathbb{Z}^{2\times\nu})^\ell)$ and $\mathsf{mpk} \leftarrow (\mathsf{pp}, \vec{\mathfrak{hp}} \in \mathbb{G}^\ell, \vec{\mathfrak{hp}}^\dagger \in (\mathbb{G}^{2\times\nu})^\ell)$. Return $(\mathsf{msk}, \mathsf{mpk})$.

3. $\mathsf{keygen}_{\mathsf{msk}}(\vec{y} \in \mathcal{Y})$: Set $\mathsf{hk}_{\vec{y}} \leftarrow \langle \vec{y}, \vec{\mathsf{hk}} \rangle$ over $\mathbb{Z}$ and $\mathbf{hk}_{\vec{y}}^\dagger \leftarrow \langle \vec{y}, \vec{\mathsf{hk}}^\dagger \rangle$ over $\mathbb{Z}^{2\times\nu}$. Return $\mathsf{msk}_{\vec{y}} \leftarrow (\mathsf{pp}, \mathsf{hk}_{\vec{y}}, \mathbf{hk}_{\vec{y}}^\dagger, \vec{y})$.

4. $\mathsf{enc}_{\mathsf{mpk},\tau}(\vec{z} \in \mathcal{Z})$: Sample $r \leftarrow_r \{0, \dots, \lfloor N/4 \rfloor\}$. Set $\mathfrak{b} \leftarrow \mathfrak{g}^r$. For $i = 1, \dots, \ell$ and $k = 1, \dots, \nu$, set

$$\mathfrak{c}_i \leftarrow (1 + N)^{z_i} \cdot \mathfrak{hp}_i^r \in \mathbb{Z}_{N^{s+1}}^*, \qquad \mathfrak{c}_{k,i}^\dagger = \mathfrak{g}^{r \cdot \mathfrak{hp}_{i,k,1}^\dagger + r \cdot \tau \cdot \mathfrak{hp}_{i,k,2}^\dagger} \in \mathbb{G}.$$

   Return $(\mathfrak{b}, \vec{\mathfrak{c}} \in \mathbb{G}^\ell, \vec{\mathfrak{c}}^\dagger \in (\mathbb{G}^\nu)^\ell)$.

5. $\mathsf{dec}_{\mathsf{msk}_{\vec{y}},\tau}(\mathfrak{b}, \vec{\mathfrak{c}}, \vec{\mathfrak{c}}^\dagger)$: Check that $\sum_{i=1}^\ell y_i \cdot \mathfrak{c}_{i,k}^\dagger = \mathfrak{b}^{\mathsf{hk}_{\vec{y},1,k}^\dagger + \tau \cdot \mathsf{hk}_{\vec{y},2,k}^\dagger}$ for $k = 1, \dots, \nu$; return $\perp$ if any check fails. Set $\mathfrak{c}_{\vec{z}} \leftarrow \prod_{i=1}^\ell \mathfrak{c}_i^{y_i} / \mathfrak{b}^{\mathsf{hk}_{\vec{y}}}$, and return $(\mathfrak{c}_{\vec{z}} - 1)/N \bmod N^s$.

Fig. 4. DCR-based inner-product tag-based functional encryption $\mathsf{TBFE}_{\mathsf{dcr}}$ over the integers (using multiplicative notation for elements of $\mathbb{G} = J_{N^{s+1}}^*$)

Theorem 35. *Under the DCR assumption, the scheme* $\mathsf{TBFE}_{\mathsf{dcr}}$ *depicted in Fig. 4 is complete and IND-TBFE-CCA.*

More precisely, if there exists an attacker $\mathcal{A} = \mathcal{A}_{\mathsf{TBFE}}$ *that has advantage* $\varepsilon_{\mathcal{A}}$ *in breaking the IND-TBFE-CCA security of* $\mathsf{TBFE}_{\mathsf{ddh}}$, *then there exists an attacker* $\mathcal{B}$ *that runs in approximately the same time and that has advantage* $\varepsilon_{\mathcal{B}}$ *in breaking the DCR assumption, such that* $\varepsilon_{\mathcal{A}} \leq 4s \cdot \varepsilon_{\mathcal{B}} + 16/\mathsf{spf}(N) + \ell \cdot |\Delta\mathcal{Z}| \cdot M_z \cdot (1/M + 2/M^\dagger) + 2 \cdot q_{dec} \cdot |\Delta\mathcal{Z}|/2^\nu$.

Using parameters from Example 19 and setting $M^\dagger = M$ and $\nu \geq \kappa + \log_2(2 \cdot q_{\mathsf{dec}} \cdot |\Delta\mathcal{Z}|) = O(\mathsf{poly}(\kappa))$, we have the following security bound: $\varepsilon_{\mathcal{A}} \leq 4s \cdot \varepsilon_{\mathcal{B}} + 16/\mathsf{spf}(N) + 4 \cdot 2^{-\kappa}$. Similarly to what happens in our DCR-based IND-FE-CPA instantiation in Sect. 4.3, although there is an exponential loss in the security reduction of Theorem 32, we emphasize that there is no exponential loss using these parameters: the security loss is compensated by these well-chosen parameters.

6.5 From Tag-Based Inner-Product Functional Encryption to CCA Security

In the full version, we show how to construct a CCA-secure inner-product functional encryption from the tag-based variant, a one-time signature, and a collision resistant hash function. The transformation is a straightforward application of the generic transformation that has been applied to PKE in [22]: the tag is the hash of a fresh verification key for the one-time signature scheme, used to sign the ciphertext. This prevents malleability.

Acknowledgments. We would like to thank David Pointcheval for useful discussions. This work was partially done while the first author was student at ENS, CNRS, INRIA, and PSL Research University, Paris, France. The first author was supported in part by the CFM Foundation and by the Defense Advanced Research Projects Agency (DARPA) and Army Research Office (ARO) under Contract No. W911NF-15-C-0236. The second author was supported by the European Research Council under the European Community's Seventh Framework Programme (FP7/2007-2013 Grant Agreement No. 339563 – CryptoCloud). This third author was supported by the European Union's Horizon 2020 research and innovation programme under grant agreement No. 653497 (project PANORAMIX), and by institutional research funding IUT2-1 of the Estonian Ministry of Education and Research.

References

1. Abdalla, M., Benhamouda, F., Pointcheval, D.: Disjunctions for hash proof systems: new constructions and applications. In: Oswald, E., Fischlin, M. (eds.) EUROCRYPT 2015. LNCS, vol. 9057, pp. 69–100. Springer, Heidelberg (2015). doi:10.1007/978-3-662-46803-6_3

2. Abdalla, M., Bourse, F., Caro, A., Pointcheval, D.: Simple functional encryption schemes for inner products. In: Katz, J. (ed.) PKC 2015. LNCS, vol. 9020, pp. 733–751. Springer, Heidelberg (2015). doi:10.1007/978-3-662-46447-2_33

3. Abdalla, M., Chevalier, C., Pointcheval, D.: Smooth projective hashing for conditionally extractable commitments. In: Halevi, S. (ed.) CRYPTO 2009. LNCS, vol. 5677, pp. 671–689. Springer, Heidelberg (2009). doi:10.1007/978-3-642-03356-8_39

4. Abdalla, M., Raykova, M., Wee, H.: Multi-input inner-product functional encryption from pairings. Cryptology ePrint Archive, Report 2016/425 (2016). http://eprint.iacr.org/

5. Agrawal, S., Libert, B., Stehlé, D.: Fully secure functional encryption for linear functions from standard assumptions. In: Robshaw, M., Katz, J. (eds.) CRYPTO 2016. LNCS, vol. 9816, pp. 333–362. Springer, Heidelberg (2016). doi:10.1007/978-3-662-53015-3_12

6. Benhamouda, F., Joye, M., Libert, B.: A new framework for privacy-preserving aggregation of time-series data. ACM Trans. Inf. Syst. Secur. **18**(3), 10 (2016)

7. Bishop, A., Jain, A., Kowalczyk, L.: Function-hiding inner product encryption. In: Iwata, T., Cheon, J.H. (eds.) ASIACRYPT 2015. LNCS, vol. 9452, pp. 470–491. Springer, Heidelberg (2015). doi:10.1007/978-3-662-48797-6_20

8. Boneh, D., Boyen, X., Shacham, H.: Short group signatures. In: Franklin, M. (ed.) CRYPTO 2004. LNCS, vol. 3152, pp. 41–55. Springer, Heidelberg (2004). doi:10.1007/978-3-540-28628-8_3

9. Boneh, D., Franklin, M.: Identity-based encryption from the Weil pairing. In: Kilian, J. (ed.) CRYPTO 2001. LNCS, vol. 2139, pp. 213–229. Springer, Heidelberg (2001). doi:10.1007/3-540-44647-8_13

10. Boneh, D., Sahai, A., Waters, B.: Functional encryption: definitions and challenges. In: Ishai, Y. (ed.) TCC 2011. LNCS, vol. 6597, pp. 253–273. Springer, Heidelberg (2011). doi:10.1007/978-3-642-19571-6_16

11. Boyle, E., Chung, K.-M., Pass, R.: On extractability obfuscation. In: Lindell, Y. (ed.) TCC 2014. LNCS, vol. 8349, pp. 52–73. Springer, Heidelberg (2014). doi:10.1007/978-3-642-54242-8_3

12. Cramer, R., Shoup, V.: A practical public key cryptosystem provably secure against adaptive chosen ciphertext attack. In: Krawczyk, H. (ed.) CRYPTO 1998. LNCS, vol. 1462, pp. 13–25. Springer, Heidelberg (1998). doi:10.1007/BFb0055717

13. Cramer, R., Shoup, V.: Universal hash proofs and a paradigm for adaptive chosen ciphertext secure public-key encryption. Cryptology ePrint Archive, Report 2001/085 (2001). Full version of [14]. http://eprint.iacr.org/2001/085

14. Cramer, R., Shoup, V.: Universal hash proofs and a paradigm for adaptive chosen ciphertext secure public-key encryption. In: Knudsen, L.R. (ed.) EUROCRYPT 2002. LNCS, vol. 2332, pp. 45–64. Springer, Heidelberg (2002). doi:10.1007/3-540-46035-7_4

15. Damgård, I., Jurik, M.: A generalisation, a simplification and some applications of Paillier's probabilistic public-key system. In: Kim, K.-C. (ed.) PKC 2001. LNCS, vol. 1992, pp. 119–136. Springer, Heidelberg (2001)

16. Damgård, I., Jurik, M.: A length-flexible threshold cryptosystem with applications. In: Safavi-Naini, R., Seberry, J. (eds.) ACISP 2003. LNCS, vol. 2727, pp. 350–364. Springer, Heidelberg (2003). doi:10.1007/3-540-45067-X_30

17. Datta, P., Dutta, R., Mukhopadhyay, S.: Functional encryption for inner product with full function privacy. In: Cheng, C.-M., Chung, K.-M., Persiano, G., Yang, B.-Y. (eds.) PKC 2016. LNCS, vol. 9614, pp. 164–195. Springer, Heidelberg (2016). doi:10.1007/978-3-662-49384-7_7

18. Escala, A., Herold, G., Kiltz, E., Ràfols, C., Villar, J.: An algebraic framework for Diffie-Hellman assumptions. In: Canetti, R., Garay, J.A. (eds.) CRYPTO 2013. LNCS, vol. 8043, pp. 129–147. Springer, Heidelberg (2013). doi:10.1007/978-3-642-40084-1_8

19. Garg, S., Gentry, C., Halevi, S., Raykova, M., Sahai, A., Waters, B.: Candidate indistinguishability obfuscation and functional encryption for all circuits. In: FOCS 2013, pp. 40–49 (2013)

20. Garg, S., Gentry, C., Halevi, S., Zhandry, M.: Functional encryption without obfuscation. In: Kushilevitz, E., Malkin, T. (eds.) TCC 2016. LNCS, vol. 9563, pp. 480–511. Springer, Heidelberg (2016). doi:10.1007/978-3-662-49099-0_18

21. Katz, J., Sahai, A., Waters, B.: Predicate encryption supporting disjunctions, polynomial equations, and inner products. In: Smart, N. (ed.) EUROCRYPT 2008. LNCS, vol. 4965, pp. 146–162. Springer, Heidelberg (2008). doi:10.1007/978-3-540-78967-3_9

22. Kiltz, E.: Chosen-ciphertext security from tag-based encryption. In: Halevi, S., Rabin, T. (eds.) TCC 2006. LNCS, vol. 3876, pp. 581–600. Springer, Heidelberg (2006). doi:10.1007/11681878_30

23. Kiltz, E., Vahlis, Y.: CCA2 secure IBE: standard model efficiency through authenticated symmetric encryption. In: Malkin, T. (ed.) CT-RSA 2008. LNCS, vol. 4964, pp. 221–238. Springer, Heidelberg (2008). doi:10.1007/978-3-540-79263-5_14

24. MacKenzie, P., Reiter, M.K., Yang, K.: Alternatives to non-malleability: definitions, constructions, and applications. In: Naor, M. (ed.) TCC 2004. LNCS, vol. 2951, pp. 171–190. Springer, Heidelberg (2004). doi:10.1007/978-3-540-24638-1_10

25. Menezes, A.J., Oorschot, P.C.V., Vanstone, S.A.: Handbook of Applied Cryptography. CRC Press, Boca Raton (1996)

26. Nandi, M., Pandit, T.: Generic conversions from CPA to CCA secure functional encryption. Cryptology ePrint Archive, Report 2015/457 (2015). http://eprint.iacr.org/2015/457

27. Naor, M., Yung, M.: Public-key cryptosystems provably secure against chosen ciphertext attacks. In: STOC 1990, pp. 427–437 (1990)

28. O'Neill, A.: Definitional issues in functional encryption. Technical report 2010/556, IACR (2010). http://eprint.iacr.org/2010/556. Accessed 18 Mar 2011

29. Paillier, P.: Public-key cryptosystems based on composite degree residuosity classes. In: Stern, J. (ed.) EUROCRYPT 1999. LNCS, vol. 1592, pp. 223–238. Springer, Heidelberg (1999). doi:10.1007/3-540-48910-X_16

30. Rackoff, C., Simon, D.R.: Non-interactive zero-knowledge proof of knowledge and chosen ciphertext attack. In: Feigenbaum, J. (ed.) CRYPTO 1991. LNCS, vol. 576, pp. 433–444. Springer, Heidelberg (1992). doi:10.1007/3-540-46766-1_35

31. Regev, O.: On lattices, learning with errors, random linear codes, and cryptography. In: STOC 2005, pp. 84–93 (2005)

32. Sahai, A., Waters, B.: Fuzzy identity-based encryption. In: Cramer, R. (ed.) EUROCRYPT 2005. LNCS, vol. 3494, pp. 457–473. Springer, Heidelberg (2005). doi:10.1007/11426639_27

33. Waters, B.: A punctured programming approach to adaptively secure functional encryption. In: Gennaro, R., Robshaw, M. (eds.) CRYPTO 2015. LNCS, vol. 9216, pp. 678–697. Springer, Heidelberg (2015). doi:10.1007/978-3-662-48000-7_33

34. Yamada, S., Attrapadung, N., Hanaoka, G., Kunihiro, N.: Generic constructions for chosen-ciphertext secure attribute based encryption. In: Catalano, D., Fazio, N., Gennaro, R., Nicolosi, A. (eds.) PKC 2011. LNCS, vol. 6571, pp. 71–89. Springer, Heidelberg (2011). doi:10.1007/978-3-642-19379-8_5

Bounded-Collusion Attribute-Based Encryption from Minimal Assumptions

Gene Itkis[1], Emily Shen[1], Mayank Varia[2], David Wilson[1], and Arkady Yerukhimovich[1(✉)]

[1] MIT Lincoln Laboratory, Lexington, MA, USA
{itkis,emily.shen,david.wilson,arkady}@ll.mit.edu
[2] Boston University, Boston, MA, USA
varia@bu.edu

Abstract. Attribute-based encryption (ABE) enables encryption of messages under access policies so that only users with attributes satisfying the policy can decrypt the ciphertext. In standard ABE, an arbitrary number of colluding users, each without an authorized attribute set, cannot decrypt the ciphertext. However, all existing ABE schemes rely on concrete cryptographic assumptions such as the hardness of certain problems over bilinear maps or integer lattices. Furthermore, it is known that ABE cannot be constructed from generic assumptions such as public-key encryption using black-box techniques.

In this work, we revisit the problem of constructing ABE that tolerates collusions of arbitrary but *a priori* bounded size. We present two ABE schemes secure against bounded collusions that require only semantically secure public-key encryption. Our schemes achieve significant improvement in the size of the public parameters, secret keys, and ciphertexts over the previous construction of bounded-collusion ABE from minimal assumptions by Gorbunov et al. (CRYPTO 2012). In fact, in our second scheme, the size of ABE secret keys does not grow at all with the collusion bound. As a building block, we introduce a multidimensional secret-sharing scheme that may be of independent interest. We also obtain bounded-collusion symmetric-key ABE (which requires the secret key for encryption) by replacing the public-key encryption with symmetric-key encryption, which can be built from the minimal assumption of one-way functions.

Keywords: Attribute-based encryption · Public-key encryption · Bounded collusion · Secret sharing

G. Itkis, E. Shen, D. Wilson and A. Yerukhimovich—This material is based upon work supported by the Assistant Secretary of Defense for Research and Engineering (ASDR&E) under Air Force Contract No. FA8721-05-C-0002. Any opinions, findings, conclusions or recommendations expressed in this material are those of the author(s) and do not necessarily reflect the views of the United States Government.

M. Varia—This material is based upon work supported by the National Science Foundation under Grant No. 1414119.

S. Fehr (Ed.): PKC 2017, Part II, LNCS 10175, pp. 67–87, 2017.
DOI: 10.1007/978-3-662-54388-7_3

1   Introduction

In traditional public-key encryption, data is encrypted for an individual user whose public key is known at the time of encryption, and only the target user is able to decrypt the resulting ciphertext. However, many applications require encryption with more expressive access control capabilities. For example, electronic medical records contain a wealth of sensitive patient information that should be accessible only to medical administrators (e.g., doctors, nurses, pharmacists, and researchers) whose credentials satisfy complex access policies based on their roles and relationships to the patient [2].

For these applications, straightforward encryption solutions are inadequate for two reasons. First, the ciphertext must be decryptable by potentially many users with distinct keys. The trivial solution of encrypting the data separately to each user results in long ciphertexts. A long line of work on broadcast encryption (e.g., [5, 11, 23]) aims to reduce the ciphertext size for this problem. Second, the identities of the authorized users may not be known to the encryptor; instead of encrypting to individual users we wish to encrypt to access policies so that only users whose credentials satisfy the policy can decrypt. The trivial solution of providing a separate key for each group of attributes results in long keys for the recipients of messages.

Attribute-based encryption (ABE), introduced by Sahai and Waters [26], addresses both of these issues. In ABE, each secret key corresponds to a predicate f, and each ciphertext corresponds to a message and an index ind. Decryption returns the message if and only if $f(\text{ind}) = 1$. Thus, ABE allows automatic enforcement of any access policy that can be expressed as the evaluation of $f(\text{ind})$. Two commonly considered special cases of ABE are ciphertext-policy ABE (CP-ABE) [4], where the secret key predicate is a set of attributes and the ciphertext index is an access policy over attributes, and key-policy ABE (KP-ABE) [18], where the roles of the index and the predicate are reversed.

Since the introduction of ABE, many constructions and related primitives have appeared in the literature (e.g., [4,12,16,18,22,24,28]). ABE has also been implemented in some applications, including the protection of electronic medical records [2]; we refer readers to [19, Sect. 3.2] for a longer overview of the history of ABE.

However, all known constructions of ABE rely on concrete assumptions such as the hardness of certain problems over bilinear maps or integer lattices rather than generic assumptions such as the existence of CPA-secure public-key encryption. In fact, it is known that, when using black-box techniques, the security of ABE cannot be based on such generic assumptions [6, 21].

The difficulty of building ABE from generic assumptions stems from its *collusion resistance* requirement, which states that two or more users, neither of whose attributes satisfy the policy embedded in a ciphertext, should not be able to decrypt the message using their joint key material. Intuitively, for CP-ABE this requires the secret key corresponding to a set of attributes to be "bound" together so that the contribution that each attribute makes to the key cannot be detached and re-purposed toward decrypting a message requiring a different combination of attributes. ABE typically requires security against *unbounded* collusion. That is, even if a very large and *a priori* unbounded number of users collude, they should fail to decrypt any ciphertexts that none of them can decrypt individually.

In this work, we consider a relaxation of the unbounded collusion requirement and instead consider schemes that are secure against an *a priori* bounded number of colluders. Positive results have recently been shown in constructing *bounded-collusion ABE* (BC-ABE) schemes assuming only the existence of public-key encryption [15, 25].[1] We stress that this relaxation does not limit the number of keys that may be issued, but rather only the number of colluders that the scheme can withstand.

Such generic constructions of ABE based on public-key encryption have several benefits. First, they can be instantiated from a number of standard cryptographic hardness assumptions. Second, by replacing CPA-secure public-key encryption with its symmetric-key counterpart, these schemes directly yield a construction of symmetric-key ABE schemes that require the secret key for encryption as well.[2] In particular, this implies that bounded-collusion symmetric-key ABE can be constructed from the minimal assumption of the existence of one-way functions. By contrast, constructions of ABE based on specific assumptions lack a clear transformation into symmetric-key ABE without still relying on "public-key" assumptions.

However, the only known constructions of BC-ABE from public-key encryption [15] require keys and ciphertexts that grow very quickly with the collusion bound (see Table 1). Thus, it remains worthwhile to reduce the key and ciphertext length in constructions of bounded-collusion ABE to understand what can be achieved using these minimal assumptions.

1.1 Our Results

In this paper we address exactly this problem, showing two different constructions of bounded-collusion ABE based only on the existence of public-key encryption, achieving shorter key sizes, public parameters, and ciphertexts. We adopt the two-step procedure taken by Gorbunov et al. [15]: first design an ABE scheme that is secure against an adversary with only a single key (which we call a *1-ABE scheme*), and then design a bootstrapping procedure that yields a BC-ABE scheme secure against a larger number of collusions q (which we call a *q-ABE scheme*). Indeed, we retain the 1-ABE scheme of [15], which can be instantiated based only on CPA-secure public-key encryption. Therefore, the focus of our work is to reduce the dependence on q in the construction of q-ABE from 1-ABE. Specifically, we show a construction satisfying the following theorem:

---

[1] These works actually build bounded-collusion functional encryption (FE), a stronger primitive that implies ABE. The bounded-collusion FE construction [15] actually requires an additional assumption of the existence of bounded-degree PRGs, but, as the authors show, this assumption is not needed for bounded-collusion ABE. For the purposes of this paper, we will only discuss the ABE constructions.

[2] Symmetric-key ABE is useful for applications such as publish-subscribe allowing a single publisher to disseminate information to subscribers based on their attributes or interests.

Theorem 1 (Informal). *Suppose there exists a public-key (resp., symmetric-key) 1-ABE scheme for a class of access policies. Then there exists a public-key (resp., symmetric-key) BC-ABE scheme for the same class of access policies tolerating collusions of size at most q with the following characteristics: public parameters consisting of $O(\frac{q^2}{\log q}\lambda)$ 1-ABE encryption keys, secret keys consisting of $O(\frac{1}{\log q}\lambda)$ 1-ABE keys, and ciphertexts consisting of $O(\frac{q^2}{\log q}\lambda)$ 1-ABE ciphertexts, where λ is the security parameter.*

We formalize and prove this theorem in Sect. 5. We then instantiate the 1-ABE scheme with the construction of Sahai and Seyalioglu [25] (subsequently improved to handle full, adaptive security by Gorbunov et al. [15]), which gives 1-ABE for the access policies expressed by arbitrary Boolean circuits from CPA-secure encryption. This immediately yields the following result:

Corollary 1. *If public-key (respectively, symmetric-key) encryption exists, then there exist public-key (resp., symmetric-key) ABE schemes for access policies expressed by boolean circuits tolerating collusion of size at most q. The sizes of the public parameters, secret keys, and ciphertexts in the resulting BC-ABE scheme come from two sources: (1) the use of CPA-secure encryption to construct 1-ABE (e.g., in [15,25]) and (2) the use of 1-ABE to construct q-ABE in Theorem 1. In particular, the only dependencies of these parameters on q come from Theorem 1, since any 1-ABE construction from CPA-secure encryption is clearly independent of q.*

1.2 Comparison to Prior Work

We construct two schemes in this paper: a basic scheme in Sect. 4 that is easier to analyze but whose bounds are slightly weaker than those in Theorem 1, and then an improved scheme that fully meets the theorem. This section and Table 1 compare the parameters of our schemes with two related works: Dodis et al.'s bounded-collusion identity-based encryption (IBE) scheme [10] and Gorbunov et al.'s bounded-collusion ABE scheme [15].

Our basic scheme has asymptotic dependence on q that is roughly comparable to the Dodis et al. [10] construction of bounded-collusion IBE, a weaker primitive than ABE, from public-key encryption, while avoiding the need for cover-free sets used by that construction. Specifically, our scheme has shorter secret keys but larger ciphertexts; the asymptotic size of the public parameters is the same in both constructions.

Our basic scheme is also a significant improvement over the bounded-collusion ABE scheme of [15], in which both the public parameters and the ciphertext grow as $O(q^4)$. Indeed, the secret key size in our basic scheme does not grow with the collusion bound. This is a significant improvement allowing us to keep secret key sizes short even when tolerating a high collusion bound. Also, the dependence on q of the ciphertext size of our basic scheme matches that of the best known constructions of bounded-collusion functional encryption (which implies ABE) from lattice assumptions [1].

Table 1. Comparison of bounded-collusion ABE schemes tolerating collusions of size at most q (note: DKXY only provides IBE). Sizes are given in terms of number of 1-ABE keys or 1-ABE ciphertexts. Here λ is a security parameter.

	DKXY [10]	GVW [15]	Basic scheme	Improved scheme
Public parameters	$O(q^2\lambda)$	$O(q^4\lambda)$	$O(q^2\lambda)$	$O\left(\frac{q^2}{\log q}\lambda\right)$
Secret keys	$O(q\lambda)$	$O(q^2\lambda)$	$O(\lambda)$	$O\left(\frac{1}{\log q}\lambda\right)$
Ciphertexts	$O(q\lambda)$	$O(q^4\lambda)$	$O(q^2\lambda)$	$O\left(\frac{q^2}{\log q}\lambda\right)$

Our improved scheme further reduces the size of public parameters, secret keys, and ciphertexts each by a factor of $\log q$. This leads to the somewhat counterintuitive property that the size of secret keys *decreases* as the collusion bound increases!

1.3 Our Techniques

Our main technique follows the same high-level approach taken by Gorbunov et al. [15]. Specifically, during setup, N key pairs for a 1-ABE scheme are generated. The secret keys become the master secret key of the BC-ABE scheme while the public keys become the public parameters. Then, every BC-ABE secret key consists of a subset of the secret keys. To encrypt a message m with an index ind, the message is first secret-shared and then each share is encrypted under ind using a different 1-ABE public key. To make this work, the subset of keys included in a BC-ABE secret key and the secret sharing are chosen in such a way that if $f(\text{ind}) = 1$ for the predicate f encoded in a secret key, then that key will allow the recovery of sufficiently many shares of m so decryption will succeed. However, any set of q keys not satisfying ind reveals no information about m. In particular, such a set of keys cannot be combined to recover the appropriate shares to reconstruct m.

In [15] this property is achieved by using a t-out-of-n secret sharing of the message and then partitioning the secret keys in such a way that sets of keys included in different BC-ABE secret keys have small pairwise intersections. Since at least t key intersections are needed to recover the message (each intersection allows the attacker to recover one share), this guarantees that a large number of keys is needed.

Our basic scheme improves on this technique by (1) using an n-out-of-n secret sharing of the message and encrypting each share under l independent 1-ABE keys and then (2) for each BC-ABE secret key giving 1 out of the l possible keys to recover each share to reduce the probability of key intersection. This requires an adversary to be able to reconstruct all of the n top level shares by getting enough intersections for each of them. We show that this approach allows us to reduce the size of the public parameters and the ABE secret keys while still guaranteeing resistance against q bounded-collusions with overwhelming probability.

Our improved scheme uses a *multi-dimensional secret-sharing* algorithm, which has the properties that (1) there exist small sets of shares that suffice to reconstruct the message and (2) such small sets of shares are rare, so for shares chosen at random a large number of shares is needed to reconstruct the message. By using multi-dimensional secret-sharing, the secret keys of our ABE scheme only need to include keys allowing decryption of such a small set of shares, whereas an adversary who only learns shares at random must recover a large number of shares in order to reconstruct the message. This allows us to further reduce the size of public parameters, keys, and ciphertexts by an additional logarithmic factor in the collusion bound q.

1.4 Paper Organization

The rest of the paper is organized as follows. In Sect. 2, we provide more details on related work. In Sect. 3, we give some necessary background and define bounded-collusion ABE. In Sect. 4, we present our basic construction. Then, in Sect. 5, we present our improved construction. Finally, in Sect. 6 we briefly discuss how to instantiate 1-ABE.

2 Related Work

Impossibility of Unbounded Collusion From Generic Assumptions.
Several prior works have aimed to understand the difficulty of building ABE and related primitives from generic assumptions such as CPA-secure encryption. Evidence that such constructions are unlikely was first given by Boneh et al. [6], who showed that there is no black-box construction of IBE from CPA-secure encryption or trapdoor permutations. This result was subsequently extended by Katz and Yerukhimovich [21], who also ruled out constructions of ABE for several classes of access policies. Finally, Goyal et al. [17] showed that for certain classes of access policies, ABE cannot be even constructed from the much stronger assumption that IBE exists. Note that the latter two works prove impossibility of *public-index predicate encryption*, a construct that is equivalent to ABE and that we will use in this paper as well (cf. Definition 3).

Bounded Collusion Constructions.
Our restriction to tolerating collusions of bounded size has been used before to build ABE and related primitives from (somewhat) standard assumptions. Early works [9,10] showed how to construct bounded-collusion identity-based encryption (IBE), a special case of ABE where the only formulas allowed are equalities over the set of attributes, from standard public-key encryption. Later, Goldwasser et al. [14] showed a more efficient construction of bounded-collusion IBE if the underlying encryption scheme satisfied a key-homomorphism property and had an associated hash-proof system. This latter requirement of hash-proof systems was subsequently removed by Tessaro and Wilson [27].

Going beyond IBE, Sahai and Seyalioglu [25] showed that standard public-key secure encryption can be used to achieve 1-query security for functional encryption, a powerful generalization of ABE. This construction was then leveraged and improved by Gorbunov et al. [15] to achieve bounded-collusion security for functional encryption under the assumption that a low-depth pseudorandom number generator exists. However, their construction can be used to realize bounded-collusion ABE without this latter assumption.

Additionally, the bounded-collusion relaxation has also been used for several constructions relying on stronger computational assumptions. For example, Goldwasser et al. [13] show how to build a 1-key succinct functional encryption scheme based on any fully-homomorphic encryption and attribute-based encryption for circuits, both of which can be realized from lattice assumptions. More recently, Agrawal and Rosen [1] showed how to build a bounded-collusion functional encryption scheme achieving online/offline encryption, allowing much of the encryption procedure to be precomputed before the message is known, from a specific lattice-based functional encryption scheme for inner product functions.

3 Definitions

In this section, we provide notation and definitions of the primitives we will use.

3.1 Preliminaries

For $n \in \mathbb{N}$, we let $[n]$ denote the set of integers $\{1, \ldots, n\}$. Let negl denote a negligible function. Let PPT denote the class of algorithms that run in probabilistic polynomial time. Additionally, we assume in this work that all sets are ordered.

We first define public- and symmetric-key encryption.

Definition 1 (Encryption scheme). *A public-key (respectively, symmetric-key) encryption scheme Σ for the message space $\mathcal{M}$ consist of three PPT algorithms* KeyGen, Enc, *and* Dec *defined as follows.*

- KeyGen(1^λ) *takes as input the unary representation of the security parameter λ and outputs the public and private keys* (pk, sk). *(For a symmetric-key encryption scheme,* pk *must be the empty string.)*
- Enc(ek, m) *takes as input an encryption key* ek *and a message $m \in \mathcal{M}$ and outputs a ciphertext* ct, *where* ek = pk *(resp.,* ek = sk*).*
- Dec(sk, ct) *takes as input the secret key* sk *and a ciphertext* ct *and outputs either a message $m \in \mathcal{M}$ or the distinguished symbol $\perp$.*

For correctness we require the following condition: for all λ and $m \in \mathcal{M}$, if we compute (pk, sk) $\leftarrow$ KeyGen(1^λ) *and* ct $\leftarrow$ Enc(ek, m), *then* Dec(sk, ct) = m.

We use a standard notion of security against chosen plaintext attacks defined in terms of a left-or-right oracle. For $b \in \{0, 1\}$, we define Enc$_b$(ek, m_0, m_1) = Enc(ek, m_b).

Definition 2 (CPA-security for encryption). *An encryption scheme* $\Sigma =$ (KeyGen, Enc, Dec) *is* CPA*-secure if for all valid* PPT *adversaries* $\mathcal{A}$,

$$| \Pr[\mathcal{A}^{\mathsf{Enc}_0(\mathsf{ek},\cdot,\cdot)}(1^\lambda, \mathsf{pk}) = 1] - \Pr[\mathcal{A}^{\mathsf{Enc}_1(\mathsf{ek},\cdot,\cdot)}(1^\lambda, \mathsf{pk}) = 1]| \leq \mathsf{negl}(\lambda),$$

where the probability is taken over the randomness of (pk, sk) $\leftarrow$ KeyGen(1^λ), Enc, *and* $\mathcal{A}$. *An adversary* $\mathcal{A}$ *is valid if* $|m_0| = |m_1|$ *for all* Enc_b *queries* (m_0, m_1).

3.2   Attribute-Based Encryption with Bounded-Collusion Security

We now define attribute-based encryption (ABE) (also called predicate encryption with public index). This definition encompasses both ciphertext-policy ABE and key-policy ABE.

Definition 3 (Attribute-based encryption scheme). *A public-key, (respectively, symmetric-key) attribute-based encryption scheme* Π *for a message space* $\mathcal{M}$, *an index space* $\mathcal{I}$, *and a predicate space* $\mathcal{F}$ *consists of four* PPT *algorithms* (Setup, KeyGen, Enc, Dec) *defined as follows.*

- Setup($1^\lambda, q$) *takes as input the unary representation of the security parameter* λ *and (optionally) a collusion bound* q, *and outputs the master public and secret keys* (MPK, MSK). *(For a symmetric-key attribute-based encryption scheme,* MPK *must be the empty string.)*
- KeyGen(MSK, f) *takes as input the master secret key* MSK *and a predicate* $f \in \mathcal{F}$, *and outputs a secret key* sk_f.
- Enc(EK, m, ind) *takes as input an encryption key* EK, *a message* $m \in \mathcal{M}$, *and an index* ind $\in \mathcal{I}$, *and outputs a ciphertext* ct, *where* EK = MPK *(resp.,* EK = MSK*).*
- Dec(sk_f, ct) *takes as input a secret key* sk_f *and a ciphertext* ct, *and outputs either a message* $m \in \mathcal{M}$ *or the distinguished symbol* $\perp$.

For correctness we require the following: for all λ, $q \in \mathbb{N}$, $m \in \mathcal{M}$, ind $\in \mathcal{I}$, *and* $f \in \mathcal{F}$ *such that* $f(\mathsf{ind}) = 1$, *if we compute* (MPK, MSK) $\leftarrow$ Setup($1^\lambda, q$), $\mathsf{sk}_f \leftarrow$ KeyGen(MSK, f), *and* ct $\leftarrow$ Enc(EK, m, ind), *then we require* Dec(sk_f, ct) = m.

We stress that in the above definition Setup takes the query bound q as a parameter; therefore, MPK and MSK may depend on q.

We now define bounded-collusion security for attribute-based encryption. Our definitions follow the functional encryption definitions of Brakerski and Segev [7]. We define security in terms of left-or-right indistinguishability. For $b \in \{0, 1\}$, we define $\mathsf{Enc}_b(\mathsf{EK}, (m_0, m_1), \mathsf{ind}) = \mathsf{Enc}(\mathsf{EK}, m_b, \mathsf{ind})$.

Definition 4 (q-query security for ABE). *An attribute-based encryption scheme* Π = (Setup, KeyGen, Enc, Dec) *is* q*-query secure if for all valid* PPT *adversaries* $\mathcal{A}$ *making at most* q *key queries,*

$$Adv_{\Pi,\mathcal{A},q}(\lambda) = | \Pr[\mathcal{A}^{\mathsf{KeyGen}(\mathsf{MSK},\cdot),\mathsf{Enc}_0(\mathsf{EK},\cdot,\cdot)}(1^\lambda, q, \mathsf{MPK}) = 1]$$
$$- \Pr[\mathcal{A}^{\mathsf{KeyGen}(\mathsf{MSK},\cdot),\mathsf{Enc}_1(\mathsf{EK},\cdot,\cdot)}(1^\lambda, q, \mathsf{MPK}) = 1]| \leq \mathsf{negl}(\lambda).$$

In the definition of advantage, the probabilities are taken over the randomness of (MPK, MSK) $\leftarrow$ Setup($1^\lambda, q$), KeyGen, Enc, *and* $\mathcal{A}$. *An adversary* $\mathcal{A}$ *is* valid *if for all* Enc$_b$ *queries* ((m_0, m_1), ind), $|m_0| = |m_1|$; *furthermore, if there exists any* KeyGen *query* f *such that* $f(\text{ind}) = 1$, *then* $m_0 = m_1$.

4   Basic BC-ABE Construction

We now present our basic bounded-collusion construction that builds a q-query secure attribute-based encryption scheme from a 1-query secure attribute-based encryption scheme.

For intuition, consider an encryption algorithm that encrypts the message with its associated index many times under independent instances of a 1-query attribute-based encryption scheme. Let the secret key for a predicate be generated as the secret key for that predicate for one of the 1-query schemes, chosen at random. Then an authorized user (a user with a predicate satisfied by the index) can decrypt the message using the 1-query scheme for which she has a key. If two unauthorized users collude, as long as their keys are from different instances of the 1-query ABE scheme, the 1-query security property suffices to ensure that they cannot learn anything about the message.

However, this simple parallel encryption approach does not scale well. If the total number of users exceeds the number of 1-query ABE instances, there will necessarily be two users with keys from the same instance, exceeding the collusion bound for that instance.

Instead, in our construction, we first additively secret-share the message, then perform parallel encryptions as described above on each additive share. Each user is given for each additive share a key from a random 1-query ABE instance. This approach allows us to make a combinatorial argument about the number of unauthorized colluders necessary to reconstruct the message with non-negligible probability.

Note, however, that unlike the message, the index is not secret shared and is included in each of the 1-query ABE ciphertexts. For this reason our construction cannot be used to achieve q-query security for the stronger primitive of predicate encryption with private index, even if the 1-query scheme has this stronger property. Specifically, the index will be revealed any time an adversary receives two keys for any of the component 1-query schemes, thus breaking index privacy.

4.1   Construction

Let 1-ABE be a 1-query secure attribute-based encryption scheme with message space $\mathcal{M}$, index space $\mathcal{I}$, and predicate space $\mathcal{F}$; we require that $\mathcal{M}$ have the property that the set of elements of each length form a finite group, so that we may perform additive secret sharing. Additionally, let ℓ and w be integers; we will explain later how to set these parameters based on the security parameter λ and the collusion bound q. We define the scheme q-ABE for message space $\mathcal{M}$,

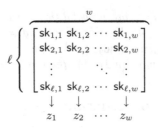

Fig. 1. Overview of our basic construction. A user with predicate $f \in \mathcal{F}$ receives w 1-ABE secret keys, one from each column, where $\mathsf{sk}_{i,j} \leftarrow$ 1-ABE.KeyGen($\mathsf{MSK}_{i,j}, f$). A ciphertext for a message m contains $\ell \cdot w$ 1-ABE ciphertexts, formed by using each of the ℓ keys in the jth column, individually, to encrypt secret share z_j, where $m = \sum_{j=1}^{w} z_j$. One key from each column is required for decryption.

index space $\mathcal{I}$, and predicate space $\mathcal{F}$ formally below; we also refer readers to Fig. 1 for an informal visual depiction.

Setup($1^\lambda, q$): For each row $i \in [\ell]$ and column $j \in [w]$, independently sample $(\mathsf{MPK}_{i,j}, \mathsf{MSK}_{i,j}) \leftarrow$ 1-ABE.Setup(1^λ). Output $\mathsf{MPK} = \{\mathsf{MPK}_{i,j}\}_{i \in [\ell], j \in [w]}$ and $\mathsf{MSK} = \{\mathsf{MSK}_{i,j}\}_{i \in [\ell], j \in [w]}$.

KeyGen($\mathsf{MSK}, f \in \mathcal{F}$): Choose one cell from each column uniformly at random; formally, choose a set $\{r_1, \ldots, r_w\} \stackrel{R}{\leftarrow} [\ell]^w$. Next, for each column $j \in [w]$, set $\mathsf{sk}_{r_j,j} \leftarrow$ 1-ABE.KeyGen($\mathsf{MSK}_{r_j,j}, f$). Output $\mathsf{sk}_f = \{r_j, \mathsf{sk}_{r_j,j}\}_{j \in [w]}$.

Enc($\mathsf{EK}, m \in \mathcal{M}, \mathsf{ind} \in \mathcal{I}$): Perform the following steps:
1. Perform a w-of-w secret sharing of m; formally, choose $z_1, \ldots, z_w \stackrel{R}{\leftarrow} \mathcal{M}$ uniformly such that $\sum_{j=1}^{w} z_j = m$. (Note that due to the finite group requirement described above, $|z_j| = |m|$ for all j.)
2. Compute the set of ciphertexts $\mathsf{ct}_{i,j} \leftarrow$ 1-ABE.Enc($\mathsf{EK}_{i,j}, z_j, \mathsf{ind}$) for each row $i \in [\ell]$ and column $j \in [w]$,
3. Output the concatenation of $\ell \cdot w$ ciphertexts $\mathsf{ct} = \{\mathsf{ct}_{i,j}\}_{i \in [\ell], j \in [w]}$.

Dec($\mathsf{sk}_f, \mathsf{ct}$): Perform the following steps:
1. Parse sk_f as $\{r_j, \mathsf{sk}_{r_j,j}\}_{j \in [w]}$ and parse ct as $\{\mathsf{ct}_{i,j}\}_{i \in [\ell], j \in [w]}$.
2. For each column $j \in [w]$, let $z_j \leftarrow$ 1-ABE.Dec($\mathsf{sk}_{r_j,j}, \mathsf{ct}_{r_j,j}$).
3. If any $z_j = \bot$, then output $\bot$. Otherwise, output $m = \sum_{j=1}^{w} z_j$.

Correctness. Suppose that a user receives a ciphertext $\mathsf{ct} = \mathsf{Enc}(\mathsf{EK}, m, \mathsf{ind})$ and she possesses a secret key $\mathsf{sk} \leftarrow \mathsf{KeyGen}(\mathsf{MSK}, f)$ for a predicate f such that $f(\mathsf{ind}) = 1$. For each column $j \in [w]$, the user possesses some secret key $\mathsf{sk}_{r_j,j}$; by the correctness of the underlying 1-ABE scheme, this key suffices to decrypt the message z_j contained in the ciphertext 1-ABE.Enc($\mathsf{EK}_{i,j}, z_j, \mathsf{ind}$). Finally, from all of the secret shares, the user may recover the original message $m = \sum_{j=1}^{w} z_j$.

As the scheme is written, repeated key queries would count as separate queries towards the bound q. In order to avoid this, the values $\{r_1, \ldots, r_w\}$ in KeyGen can be chosen pseudorandomly based on the predicate f so that the same key is issued for repeated key queries. This conversion is straightforward and we omit the details.

4.2 Setting the Parameters

The following combinatorial lemma provides a good setting of the parameters ℓ and w. We first define two probabilistic events about any set of up to q key queries made to the q-ABE scheme. Let Bad_j denote the event that there exists a row $i \in [\ell]$ such that the key query responses include two or more keys corresponding to $\mathsf{MSK}_{i,j}$. Additionally, let Bad denote the event that Bad_j occurs for all columns $j \in [w]$.

Lemma 1. *Let the* q-ABE *scheme be instantiated with* $\ell = q^2$ *and* $w = \lambda$, *and suppose at most* q KeyGen *queries are made. Then* $\Pr[\mathsf{Bad}] \leq \mathsf{negl}(\lambda)$.

Proof. Consider a single column $j \in [w]$. Note that each sk_f contains exactly one 1-ABE key $\mathsf{sk}_{r_j,j}$ for that value of j, where r_j is chosen randomly. Thus, the probability that q such values are all distinct is

$$1 \cdot \left(1 - \frac{1}{\ell}\right) \cdot \left(1 - \frac{2}{\ell}\right) \cdot \ldots \cdot \left(1 - \frac{q-1}{\ell}\right) \geq \left(1 - \frac{q-1}{\ell}\right)^q.$$

Thus, for a given column j, the event Bad_j holds with probability at most $(1 - (1 - \frac{q-1}{\ell})^q)$. The probability of Bad_j is independent for each j, so the probability that Bad_j holds for all w columns is at most $(1 - (1 - \frac{q-1}{\ell})^q)^w$. Letting $\ell = q^2$ and $w = \lambda$, we find that Bad occurs with probability at most

$$\left(1 - \left(1 - \frac{q-1}{q^2}\right)^q\right)^\lambda = \left(1 - \left(1 - \frac{1}{q} + \frac{1}{q^2}\right)^q\right)^\lambda < \left(1 - e^{-1}\right)^\lambda \leq \mathsf{negl}(\lambda),$$

where the first inequality follows from the fact that $(1 - \frac{1}{x} + \frac{1}{x^2})^x > 1/e$ for all $x > 0$.

Setting ℓ and w as indicated in Lemma 1, we arrive at the following performance characteristics for our q-ABE construction.

- MPK and MSK consist of $O(q^2\lambda)$ 1-ABE keys.
- The ciphertext size is $O(q^2\lambda)$ 1-ABE ciphertexts.
- Each decryption key has $O(\lambda)$ 1-ABE secret keys.

4.3 Security

We now prove that the q-ABE scheme defined in Sect. 4.1 is q-query secure if the underlying 1-ABE scheme is 1-query secure.

Theorem 2. *Let* 1-ABE *be any public-key (respectively, symmetric-key) ABE scheme that is 1-query secure. For any valid* PPT *ABE adversary* $\mathcal{A}$ *for the resulting public-key (resp., symmetric-key) scheme* q-ABE *making at most* q *key queries, there exists a valid* PPT *ABE adversary* $\mathcal{B}$ *for* 1-ABE *making at most* 1 *key query, with advantage* $Adv_{\text{1-ABE},\mathcal{B},1}(\lambda) \geq \frac{1}{q^2\lambda} Adv_{\text{q-ABE},\mathcal{A},q}(\lambda) - \mathsf{negl}(\lambda)$.

Proof. Let $\mathcal{A}$ be an adversary against our q-ABE construction that makes at most q key queries. We begin with the observation that the event Bad (and also all Bad_j events) depends only on the randomness tape of q-ABE.KeyGen (which chooses the random values r_j), and *not* on the values fed in as input. For the rest of this proof, we restrict KeyGen only to use randomness tapes that will not lead to the event Bad within the first q key oracle queries, so that in particular adversary $\mathcal{A}$ never causes the event Bad. Denote $\mathcal{A}$'s advantage in this modified security game as $\mathsf{Adv}'_{\mathsf{q\text{-}ABE},\mathcal{A},q}$. Since $\Pr[\mathsf{Bad}]$ is negligible by Lemma 1, our restriction causes at most negligible change to our distinguishing advantage by a standard reasoning up to failure argument:

$$\mathsf{Adv}'_{\mathsf{q\text{-}ABE},\mathcal{A},q}(\lambda) \geq \mathsf{Adv}_{\mathsf{q\text{-}ABE},\mathcal{A},q}(\lambda) - 2 \cdot \Pr[\mathsf{Bad}]. \tag{1}$$

Given some column $j^* \in [w]$, we consider a series of hybrid experiments $\mathcal{H}_0^{j^*}, \mathcal{H}_1^{j^*}, \ldots, \mathcal{H}_\ell^{j^*}$. Each experiment $\mathcal{H}_k^{j^*}$ is defined to use the same Setup and KeyGen as the modified q-ABE game, but it responds to Enc_b oracle queries $((m_0, m_1), \mathsf{ind})$ by forming the ciphertext in a special way:

Choose z_j uniformly at random for all $j \in [w], j \neq j^*$. Let $z_{j^*,0} = m_0 - \sum_{j \neq j^*} z_j$ and $z_{j^*,1} = m_1 - \sum_{j \neq j^*} z_j$.

- For $j \neq j^*$, for all i let $\mathsf{ct}_{i,j} \leftarrow \mathsf{1\text{-}ABE.Enc}(\mathsf{EK}_{i,j}, z_j, \mathsf{ind})$.
- For $i > k$, let $\mathsf{ct}_{i,j^*} \leftarrow \mathsf{1\text{-}ABE.Enc}(\mathsf{EK}_{i,j^*}, z_{j^*,0}, \mathsf{ind})$.
- For $i \leq k$, let $\mathsf{ct}_{i,j^*} \leftarrow \mathsf{1\text{-}ABE.Enc}(\mathsf{EK}_{i,j^*}, z_{j^*,1}, \mathsf{ind})$.

Finally, the modified Enc_b oracle outputs $\mathsf{ct} = \{\mathsf{ct}_{i,j}\}_{i \in [\ell], j \in [w]}$.

Note that for all j^*, $\mathcal{H}_0^{j^*}$ corresponds exactly to the modified ABE security game with the encryption oracle being Enc_0, and $\mathcal{H}_\ell^{j^*}$ corresponds exactly to the modified ABE security game with the encryption oracle being Enc_1. Let $\varepsilon = \mathsf{Adv}'_{\mathsf{q\text{-}ABE},\mathcal{A},q}(\lambda)$, and let p_k denote the probability that $\mathcal{A}$ outputs 1 in experiment $\mathcal{H}_k^{j^*}$. Then $\varepsilon = |p_\ell - p_0| \leq \sum_{k=1}^\ell |p_k - p_{k-1}|$, so there must exist some k such that $|p_k - p_{k-1}| \geq \varepsilon/\ell$.

We now construct an adversary $\mathcal{B}$ for 1-ABE that breaks 1-query security. $\mathcal{B}$ first samples $j^* \in [w]$ uniformly at random, and chooses row $i^* \in [\ell]$ such that $|p_{i^*} - p_{i^*-1}| \geq \varepsilon/\ell$ for the chosen j^*. $\mathcal{B}$ then plays its game and interacts with $\mathcal{A}$ as follows.

Setup. $\mathcal{B}$ sets MPK_{i^*,j^*} as the public key it receives from its 1-ABE game. For all i, j such that $i \neq i^*$ or $j \neq j^*$, $\mathcal{B}$ sets $(\mathsf{MPK}_{i,j}, \mathsf{MSK}_{i,j}) \leftarrow \mathsf{1\text{-}ABE.Setup}(1^\lambda)$.

Simulating the KeyGen oracle. When $\mathcal{A}$ makes a query to KeyGen for predicate f, $\mathcal{B}$ honestly runs q-ABE.KeyGen, with two exceptions. First, if the value r_{j^*} randomly chosen within q-ABE.KeyGen returns the value i^*, then $\mathcal{B}$ queries f to its 1-ABE KeyGen oracle and sets sk_{i^*,j^*} to be the result. Second, if the event Bad_{j^*} occurs, then $\mathcal{B}$ aborts execution of $\mathcal{A}$ and outputs a random guess in its game.

Simulating the Enc_b oracle. $\mathcal{B}$ responds to any encryption oracle query by $\mathcal{A}$ of the form $((m_0, m_1), \mathsf{ind})$ as follows. First, $\mathcal{B}$ chooses z_j uniformly at random for all $j \in [w], j \neq j^*$. Let $z_{j^*,0} = m_0 - \sum_{j \neq j^*} z_j$ and $z_{j^*,1} = m_1 - \sum_{j \neq j^*} z_j$. $\mathcal{B}$ constructs the oracle response as follows:

- For $j \neq j^*$, for all i let $\mathsf{ct}_{i,j} \leftarrow 1\text{-ABE.Enc}(\mathsf{EK}_{i,j}, z_j, \mathsf{ind})$.
- For $i > i^*$, let $\mathsf{ct}_{i,j^*} \leftarrow 1\text{-ABE.Enc}(\mathsf{EK}_{i,j^*}, z_{j^*,0}, \mathsf{ind})$.
- For $i < i^*$, let $\mathsf{ct}_{i,j^*} \leftarrow 1\text{-ABE.Enc}(\mathsf{EK}_{i,j^*}, z_{j^*,1}, \mathsf{ind})$.
- Query $((z_{j^*,0}, z_{j^*,1}), \mathsf{ind})$ to the Enc_b oracle of the 1-ABE game, and set ct_{i^*,j^*} to be the result.
  Output $\mathsf{ct} = \{\mathsf{ct}_{i,j}\}_{i \in [\ell], j \in [w]}$.

Guess. $\mathcal{B}$ outputs the same guess as $\mathcal{A}$.

We argue that since $\mathcal{A}$ is a valid ABE adversary, $\mathcal{B}$ is also a valid ABE adversary. Since $\mathcal{A}$ is valid, for all $((m_0, m_1), \mathsf{ind})$ queried to Enc_b and f queried to KeyGen, we have that $|m_0| = |m_1|$ and that if $f(\mathsf{ind}) = 1$, then $m_0 = m_1$. It follows that $\mathcal{B}$ is a valid ABE adversary: all shares are generated to be the same length as the secret-shared message, so $|z_{j^*,0}| = |z_{j^*,1}|$. The same f and ind are passed through to $\mathcal{B}$'s game, so if $f(\mathsf{ind}) = 1$ in $\mathcal{B}$'s queries, then $f(\mathsf{ind}) = 1$ in $\mathcal{A}$'s queries and $m_0 = m_1$, which means that the same shares are generated for the two messages, i.e., $z_{j^*,0} = z_{j^*,1}$. Furthermore, by construction, $\mathcal{B}$ queries its 1-ABE KeyGen oracle at most once.

Next, we return to the assumption from the beginning of this proof: by construction of the KeyGen oracle, the event Bad cannot occur for $\mathcal{A}$, i.e., there exists at least one column that is not bad. As a result, with probability at least $1/w$ the event Bad_{j^*} does not occur. Additionally, because the event Bad_{j^*} is independent of the specific calls made to KeyGen, it is equally likely to occur in experiments $\mathcal{H}_{i^*-1}^{j^*}$ and $\mathcal{H}_{i^*}^{j^*}$.

If the event Bad_{j^*} occurs, then $\mathcal{B}$ has no distinguishing advantage in its game by construction. Conversely, if the event Bad_{j^*} does not occur, then $\mathcal{B}$'s simulation of all oracles is faithful since $\mathcal{B}$ does not abort. Furthermore, when $b = 0$, $\mathcal{B}$ perfectly simulates $\mathcal{H}_{i^*-1}^{j^*}$, and when $b = 1$, $\mathcal{B}$ perfectly simulates $\mathcal{H}_{i^*}^{j^*}$. Putting everything together, we have

$$\mathsf{Adv}_{1\text{-ABE}, \mathcal{B}, 1}(\lambda) \geq \frac{1}{w} \cdot |p_{i^*} - p_{i^*-1}| \geq \frac{1}{\ell w} \mathsf{Adv}'_{\mathsf{q}\text{-ABE}, \mathcal{A}, q}(\lambda),$$

which, combined with inequality (1) and using the values of ℓ and w from Lemma 1, completes the proof.

5 Improved BC-ABE Construction

We can improve the asymptotic parameters of the above construction by performing another level of secret-sharing of each z_j. Instead of simply performing ℓ independent 1-ABE encryptions, we can reshare the z_j values once more, and then encrypt *those* shares using the 1-ABE scheme. If this new resharing were a simple linear scheme it would be equivalent to the first construction; instead, we will arrange these shares in a *multidimensional* structure.

This multidimensional secret-sharing will be created to satisfy the following two properties. First, there exist small sets of shares that are able to reconstruct.

Second, such sets of shares are rare, such that any party who only possesses the ability to obtain random shares will need to collect many shares to reconstruct.

When we use the multidimensional secret-sharing inside of our BC-ABE construction, the small sets of shares will correspond to the secret keys, yielding very short secret keys. Intuitively, security will be achieved by ensuring that the set of shares revealed when the adversary exceeds the collusion bound of the underlying 1-ABE schemes is effectively distributed randomly.

5.1   Multidimensional Secret-Sharing

In this section, we provide a multidimensional secret-sharing system. While we only use the scheme toward an improved BC-ABE construction, we codify it separately in this section because it may be of independent interest.

Definition 5 (Multidimensional secret-sharing). *Given a message y, we construct a multidimensional secret sharing scheme* $\mathsf{MultiSS}_{s,d}(y)$ *that outputs s^d shares $\sigma_{[1,1,\ldots,1]}, \ldots, \sigma_{[s,s,\ldots,s]}$ produced as follows.*

1. *Choose $s \cdot d$ "intermediate" shares $\rho_{1,1}, \ldots, \rho_{d,s}$ uniformly at random such that $\sum_{h\in[d], i\in[s]} \rho_{h,i} = y$. That is, the ρ's form a sd-of-sd secret sharing of y.*
2. *For each $\boldsymbol{v} \in [s]^d$, form the share $\sigma_{\boldsymbol{v}} = \sum_{i=1}^{d} \rho_{i,\boldsymbol{v}[i]}$.*

We can visualize the sharing in terms of a d-dimensional hypercube of side length s, where the shares $\sigma_{\boldsymbol{v}}$ are points whose coordinates are given by their subscript $\boldsymbol{v}$. Each value $\rho_{h,i}$ influences a $(d-1)$-dimensional *slice* of the hypercube—namely, it is a summand in the computation of the σ values whose h-th coordinate equals i. See Fig. 2 for a graphical representation of a three-dimensional secret-sharing scheme (i.e., $d = 3$).

We observe that a carefully-chosen set of s shares suffice to recover the original message y.

Definition 6. *Let $V = \{\boldsymbol{v}_1, \ldots, \boldsymbol{v}_{|V|}\}$ be a set containing vectors in $[s]^d$. We call this set* spanning *if it has the property that for each dimension $h \in [d]$, the list $(\boldsymbol{v}_1[h], \ldots, \boldsymbol{v}_{|V|}[h])$ contains all elements in $[s]$.*

If $|V| = s$, then we call this set minimally spanning. *In this case, the list $(\boldsymbol{v}_1[h], \ldots, \boldsymbol{v}_{|V|}[h])$ is a permutation of $[s]$.*

Lemma 2 (Correctness of $\mathsf{MultiSS}$). *Let $\{\sigma_{\boldsymbol{v}}\}_{\boldsymbol{v}\in[s]^d} \leftarrow \mathsf{MultiSS}_{s,d}(y)$ be a multidimensional secret-sharing of y, and let V be any minimally spanning set. Then, the message y may be recovered from the s shares $\{\sigma_{\boldsymbol{v}}\}_{\boldsymbol{v}\in V}$.*

Proof. The sum $\sum_{\boldsymbol{v}\in V} \sigma_{\boldsymbol{v}}$ includes each $\rho_{h,i}$ term exactly once, so it sums to y.

Security provided by a multidimensional secret-sharing of y is captured in the following lemma.

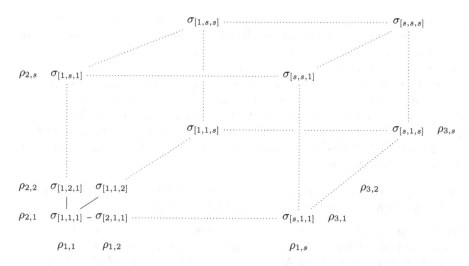

Fig. 2. Visualization of a three-dimensional secret-sharing scheme $\mathsf{MultiSS}_{s,3}(y)$. The input value y is additively secret-shared into $3s$ values $\rho_{1,1}, \ldots, \rho_{3,s}$. Each intermediate value ρ contributes to a 2-dimensional planar face of the 3-dimensional cube in which one of the dimensions is fixed to a given value (as specified by the indices to ρ). Concretely, we construct each of the s^3 shares as $\sigma_{[t,u,v]} = \rho_{1,t} + \rho_{2,u} + \rho_{3,v}$.

Lemma 3 (Security of MultiSS). *Let $\{\sigma_{\boldsymbol{v}}\}_{\boldsymbol{v} \in [s]^d} \leftarrow \mathsf{MultiSS}_{s,d}(y)$ be a multidimensional secret-sharing of y, and let $V^* \subseteq [s]^d$ be any set of vectors that is not spanning. Then, the set of shares $\{\sigma_{\boldsymbol{v}^*} : \boldsymbol{v}^* \in V^*\}$ information-theoretically reveals no information about y.*

Proof. Because $\boldsymbol{v}^*$ is not spanning, there exist a dimension $h \in [d]$ and value $i \in [s]$ such that $\boldsymbol{v}^*[h] \neq i$ for all vectors $\boldsymbol{v}^* \in V^*$. Thus, none of the shares $\{\sigma_{\boldsymbol{v}^*} : \boldsymbol{v}^* \in V^*\}$ depend on the "intermediate" share $\rho_{h,i}$, implying that $\{\sigma_{\boldsymbol{v}^*}\}$ reveals no information about y.

5.2 Construction

This construction uses similar ideas to the basic construction, with the addition of multidimensional secret-sharing. Essentially,

- The message m is additively secret-shared into $m = \sum_j z_j$, as before.
- Each of the shares z_j is multidimensionally secret-shared to form a series of s^d shares denoted by $\sigma_{\boldsymbol{v}}^j$ for $\boldsymbol{v} \in [s]^d$.
- Each $\sigma_{\boldsymbol{v}}^j$ share is encrypted using a 1-query ABE scheme in a black-box manner, producing a total of $s^d w$ resulting 1-ABE ciphertexts.

Users are given a set of keys that enable them to recover a specifically-crafted subset of the shares. If the predicate is satisfied by the index, that subset will be sufficient to reconstruct the original value at each stage of the sharing, ultimately recovering the message. On the other hand, the multidimensional sharing step ensures that a random subset of the shares will likely need to be very large in order to recover the message. We thus gain additional collusion resistance, since the locations where collisions occur are effectively random.

Formally, let 1-ABE be a 1-query ABE scheme whose message space $\mathcal{M}$ is a finite group represented additively; we again require that $\mathcal{M}$ have the property that the set of elements of each length form a finite group. Our improved q-query secure CP-ABE scheme q-ABE* is defined below; it uses $s^d w$ independent instances of the 1-ABE scheme, where $s(\lambda)$, $d(\lambda)$, and $w(\lambda)$ are parameters that are specified later in Sect. 5.3.

Setup($1^\lambda, q$): For $v \in [s]^d$ and $j \in [w]$, let $(\mathsf{MPK}_v^j, \mathsf{MSK}_v^j) \leftarrow$ 1-ABE.Setup(1^λ). Output $\mathsf{MPK} = \{\mathsf{MPK}_v^j\}_{v \in [s]^d, j \in [w]}$ and $\mathsf{MSK} = \{\mathsf{MSK}_v^j\}_{v \in [s]^d, j \in [w]}$.

KeyGen($\mathsf{MSK}, f \in \mathcal{F}$): For each $j \in [w]$, choose a set of d permutations of $[s]$ uniformly at random. Transpose them to produce a minimally spanning set of s vectors V^j. Sample a 1-ABE key $\mathsf{sk}_v^j \leftarrow$ 1-ABE.KeyGen(MSK_v^j, f) for each $j \in [w]$ and $v \in V^j$. Finally, output $\mathsf{sk}_f = \{V^j, \{\mathsf{sk}_v^j\}_{v \in V^j}\}_{j \in [w]}$.

Enc($\mathsf{EK}, m \in \mathcal{M}, \mathsf{ind} \in \mathcal{I}$): Perform the following steps:
1. Perform a w-of-w additive secret-sharing of m to get shares $z_1, \ldots, z_w$ such that $\sum_{j \in [w]} z_j = m$.
2. Multidimensionally secret-share each z_j with d dimensions and s values in each dimension to create s^d shares $\{\sigma_v^j\}_{v \in [s]^d} \leftarrow$ MultiSS$_{s,d}(z_j)$.
3. For each $v \in [s]^d$, $j \in [w]$, set $\mathsf{ct}_v^j \leftarrow$ 1-ABE.Enc($\mathsf{EK}_v^j, \sigma_v^j, \mathsf{ind}$).
4. Output $\mathsf{ct} = \{\mathsf{ct}_v^j\}_{v \in [s]^d, j \in [w]}$.

Dec($\mathsf{sk}_f, \mathsf{ct}$): Perform the following steps:
1. Parse sk_f as $\{V^j, \{\mathsf{sk}_v^j\}_{v \in V^j}\}_{j \in [w]}$ and parse ct as $\{\mathsf{ct}_v^j\}_{v \in [s]^d, j \in [w]}$.
2. For each $j \in [w]$ and each $v \in V^j$, let $\sigma_v^j \leftarrow$ 1-ABE.Dec($\mathsf{sk}_v^j, \mathsf{ct}_v^j$).
3. Output $m = \sum_{j \in [w], v \in V^j} \sigma_v^j$.

Correctness. Suppose that a user receives a ciphertext $\mathsf{ct} = \mathsf{Enc}(\mathsf{EK}, m, \mathsf{ind})$ and she possesses a secret key $\mathsf{sk} \leftarrow \mathsf{KeyGen}(\mathsf{MSK}, f)$ for a predicate f such that $f(\mathsf{ind}) = 1$. By the correctness of the underlying 1-ABE scheme, each 1-ABE.Dec in step 2 of q-ABE*.Dec successfully returns σ_v^j. For each $j \in [w]$, we may reconstruct $z_j = \sum_{v \in V^j} \sigma_v$ since KeyGen produces a minimally spanning set V^j (cf. Lemma 2), and the sum of all z_j's equals the original message m due to the w-of-w additive secret sharing.

5.3   Setting the Parameters

The combinatorial lemma in this section provides a good setting of the parameters s, d, and w. Recall that each key query yields 1-ABE keys for a minimally spanning set of vectors in each coordinate $j \in [w]$. Intuitively, we must choose s and d to be large enough that there are several minimally spanning sets, so that KeyGen rarely chooses the same vector twice. Specifically, the set of *replicated* vectors across q key queries must not be spanning.

Formally, fix some index $j \in [w]$ and consider $\mathcal{A}$'s ability to learn the jth secret share $z_j = \sum_{h \in [d], i \in [s]} \rho^j_{h,i}$. The adversary $\mathcal{A}$ makes up to q queries, each of which returns s keys sk^j_v for vectors v in a randomly-chosen minimally spanning set V^j (independent of the index queried). If $\mathcal{A}$ ever receives two keys for the same v, then we no longer have any security against σ_v, and therefore we assume the worst-case outcome that all of the shares $\rho^j_{h,i}$ with $v[h] = i$ have been compromised. Let $\bar{V}^j$ denote the set of all vectors that are returned in two or more key queries.

Let Good^j denote the event that there exists some $\rho^j_{h,i}$ that remains uncompromised after $\mathcal{A}$'s queries. Observe that this is precisely the event that $\bar{V}^j$ is not spanning! In this case, the additive secret sharing protects z_j and thus m as well. Finally, let Good denote the event that there exists some $j \in [w]$ for which Good^j holds.

Lemma 4. *Let s be any constant, and instantiate the q-ABE^* scheme with $d = \lceil 2 \log_s q + 1 \rceil$ and $w = \lceil \frac{\lambda}{d \cdot s} \rceil$. For any adversary $\mathcal{A}$ who makes at most q KeyGen queries, the event Good holds with overwhelming probability in λ.*

Proof. First, consider a fixed $h \in [d]$, $i \in [s]$, and $j \in [w]$. We consider $\mathcal{A}$'s ability to learn $\rho^j_{h,i}$. By construction, each of $\mathcal{A}$'s key queries yields exactly one 1-ABE key sk^j_v where v is randomly chosen subject to the constraint that $v[h] = i$. The probability that all of these vectors v are distinct (and thus $\rho^j_{h,i}$ is uncompromised) is therefore

$$1 \times \left(1 - \frac{1}{s^{d-1}}\right) \times \left(1 - \frac{2}{s^{d-1}}\right) \times \cdots \times \left(1 - \frac{q-1}{s^{d-1}}\right) \geq \left(1 - \frac{q-1}{s^{d-1}}\right)^q.$$

This probability holds independently for all $h \in [d]$, $i \in [s]$, and $j \in [w]$. Hence, $\Pr[\mathsf{Good}] \geq 1 - [1 - (1 - \frac{q-1}{s^{d-1}})^q]^{sdw}$.

Next, if we instantiate s, d, and w with the values provided in the lemma, we find that $1 - \Pr[\mathsf{Good}]$ is negligible:

$$\left[1 - \left(1 - \frac{q-1}{s^{d-1}}\right)^q\right]^{sdw} \leq \left[1 - \left(1 - \frac{q-1}{q^2}\right)^q\right]^{\lambda} < (1 - e^{-1})^{\lambda} = \mathsf{negl}(\lambda).$$

We list below the key and ciphertext lengths produced by our construction, when instantiated with the parameters specified in Lemma 4.

- The MPK and MSK consist of $s^d \cdot w = O(\frac{q^2 \lambda}{\log q})$ 1-ABE public keys.
- A secret key consists of $s \cdot w = O(\frac{\lambda}{\log q})$ 1-ABE keys.
- A single ciphertext consists of $s^d \cdot w = O(\frac{q^2 \lambda}{\log q})$ 1-ABE ciphertexts.

5.4 Security

We now prove that the q-ABE^* scheme defined above is q-query secure if the underlying 1-ABE scheme is 1-query secure.

Theorem 1 (Formal). *Let* 1-ABE *be any public-key (respectively, symmetric-key) ABE scheme that is 1-query secure. For any valid* PPT *adversary* $\mathcal{A}$ *for the resulting public-key (resp., symmetric-key)* q-ABE* *construction instantiated with the parameters given in Lemma 4, there exists a valid* PPT *adversary* $\mathcal{B}$ *for* 1-ABE *making at most 1 key query, with advantage* $Adv_{1\text{-}ABE,\mathcal{B},1}(\lambda) \geq \frac{1}{q^2\lambda}Adv_{q\text{-}ABE^*,\mathcal{A},q}(\lambda) - \mathsf{negl}(\lambda)$.

Proof (sketch). Here, we provide a high-level description of the reduction to the security of 1-ABE. The details mostly follow the same pattern as the proof of Theorem 2, so here we highlight the differences. Lemma 4 provides the reasoning up to failure argument analogous to that of Lemma 1.

Recall that in the proof of Theorem 2 we change a valid encryption of m_0 into a valid encryption of m_1 by changing one of the additive shares (z_j values) of the final message. Since this value is encrypted using the underlying 1-ABE scheme ℓ times, we perform this change via a sequence of hybrids. Our reduction decreases the advantage of the 1-ABE adversary by a factor of ℓ due to the selection of a hybrid step and a factor of w due to the selection of a secret share z_{j^*} to target.

In the q-ABE* construction, note that the message is effectively additively shared among sdw different values $\rho_{h,i}^j$. We can thus change an encryption of m_0 into an encryption of m_1 by changing a single one of the $\rho_{h,i}^j$ values. In this case, this value is a summand in s^{d-1} of the σ values that are encrypted using the underlying 1-ABE scheme (specifically, $\sigma_{\boldsymbol{v}}^j$ where $\boldsymbol{v}[h] = i$).

We thus require a hybrid step to change each of these encryptions to an encryption of a new value reflecting the changed $\rho_{h,i}^j$; the proof is otherwise the same. The advantage of the 1-ABE adversary decreases by a factor of s^{d-1} due to the selection of a hybrid step and a factor of sdw due to the selection of $\rho_{h,i}^j$; we omit the details. Thus, $Adv_{1\text{-}ABE,\mathcal{B},1}(\lambda) \geq \frac{1}{s^ddw}Adv_{q\text{-}ABE^*,\mathcal{A},q}^*(\lambda) - \mathsf{negl}(\lambda)$, and instantiating this formula with the parameters from Lemma 4 completes the proof.

6   Instantiating 1-ABE

Thus far, we have presented two schemes for transforming any 1-ABE scheme into a q-ABE scheme. To obtain a construction of bounded-collusion ABE from CPA-secure encryption, we need to instantiate 1-ABE from CPA-secure encryption. To do so, we can use the construction of Gorbunov et al. [15] and Sahai-Seyalioglu [25] for 1-query-secure functional encryption, restricting its functionality to that of attribute-based encryption.

In this section, we briefly sketch the resulting 1-ABE scheme. We assume that it has predicates describable using n bits, that is $\mathcal{F} \subseteq \{0,1\}^n$. Note that the 1-FE from Gorbunov et al. [15] and Sahai-Seyalioglu [25] uses randomized encodings [3,20], which can be instantiated using garbled circuits. For simplicity, we will use the language of garbled circuits in this section. Given a CPA-secure encryption scheme Σ, the 1-ABE scheme operates as follows.

Setup(1^λ): Generate $2n$ key pairs for the public-key encryption scheme Σ to get $(\mathsf{pk}_{i,0}, \mathsf{sk}_{i,0})$ and $(\mathsf{pk}_{i,1}, \mathsf{sk}_{i,1})$ for $i \in [n]$. Output MPK $\leftarrow \{\mathsf{pk}_{i,b}\}_{i\in[n],b\in\{0,1\}}$ and MSK $\leftarrow \{\mathsf{sk}_{i,b}\}_{i\in[n],b\in\{0,1\}}$

KeyGen(MSK, f): Let $f[i]$ denote the i-th bit of f for $i \in [n]$. Output $\mathsf{sk}_f \leftarrow \{\mathsf{sk}_{i,f[i]}\}_{i\in[n]}$.

Enc(MPK, M, ind): Let $U_{M,\mathsf{ind}}(f)$ be a universal circuit that takes a predicate $f \in \{0,1\}^n$ and outputs M if $f(\mathsf{ind}) = 1$ and 0 otherwise. Build a garbled circuit for $U_{M,\mathsf{ind}}$. Encrypt the two labels for each wire corresponding to the predicate f: for the i-th bit of f, encrypt the 0-label under $\mathsf{pk}_{i,0}$ and the 1-label under $\mathsf{pk}_{i,1}$. Output the garbled circuit and the encrypted wire labels.

Dec(sk_f, ct): Use sk_f to decrypt the wire labels corresponding to f. Evaluate the garbled circuit and output the result.

As Sahai and Seyalioglu [25] show, the above scheme achieves selective security for one query. Gorbunov et al. [15] show how to modify this scheme to achieve adaptive security by using a variant of non-committing encryption [8]. This increases the number of underlying PKE components of the public parameters, keys, and the label encryptions by a factor of $O(\lambda)$ due to having to encrypt λ-bit long messages.

Thus, for a predicate description of size n and using a universal circuit U, the 1-ABE scheme has the following parameters:

- The public parameters consist of $O(n\lambda)$ PKE public keys.
- Secret keys consist of $O(n\lambda)$ PKE secret keys.
- Ciphertexts consist of $O(|U|\lambda)$ bits for the garbled gates and $O(n\lambda)$ PKE ciphertexts for the encrypted wire labels.

Putting this construction together with the parameters of our improved transformation from any 1-ABE scheme to a q-ABE scheme, we arrive at the following result that crystallizes Corollary 1.

Corollary 2. *If public-key (respectively, symmetric-key) CPA-secure encryption exists, then there exists a public-key (resp., symmetric-key) q-query secure ABE scheme for predicates that are expressible using n bits and can be evaluated by a universal circuit U with the following characteristics: public parameters (resp., MSK) consisting of $O(\frac{q^2}{\log q}n\lambda^2)$ PKE public keys (resp., secret keys), secret keys consisting of $O(\frac{n}{\log q}\lambda^2)$ PKE secret keys, and ciphertexts consisting of $O(\frac{q^2}{\log q}|U|\lambda^2)$ bits plus $O(\frac{q^2}{\log q}n\lambda^2)$ PKE ciphertexts.*

Acknowledgments. We thank the anonymous reviewers for their helpful comments.

References

1. Agrawal, S., Rosen, A.: Online-offline functional encryption for bounded collusions. IACR Cryptology ePrint Archive, 2016:361 (2016)

2. Akinyele, J.A., Lehmann, C.U., Green, M.D., Pagano, M.W., Peterson, Z.N.J., Rubin, A.D.: Self-protecting electronic medical records using attribute-based encryption. Cryptology ePrint Archive, Report 2010/565 (2010). http://eprint.iacr.org/

3. Applebaum, B., Ishai, Y., Kushilevitz, E.: Computationally private randomizing polynomials and their applications. Comput. Complex. 15(2), 115–162 (2006)

4. Bethencourt, J., Sahai, A., Waters, B.: Ciphertext-policy attribute-based encryption. In: 2007 IEEE Symposium on Security and Privacy (S&P 2007), Oakland, California, USA, 20–23 May 2007, pp. 321–334 (2007)

5. Boneh, D., Gentry, C., Waters, B.: Collusion resistant broadcast encryption with short ciphertexts and private keys. In: Shoup, V. (ed.) CRYPTO 2005. LNCS, vol. 3621, pp. 258–275. Springer, Heidelberg (2005). doi:10.1007/11535218_16

6. Boneh, D., Papakonstantinou, P.A., Rackoff, C., Vahlis, Y., Waters, B.: On the impossibility of basing identity based encryption on trapdoor permutations. In: 49th Annual IEEE Symposium on Foundations of Computer Science, FOCS 2008, Philadelphia, PA, USA, 25–28 October 2008, pp. 283–292 (2008)

7. Brakerski, Z., Segev, G.: Function-private functional encryption in the private-key setting. In: Dodis, Y., Nielsen, J.B. (eds.) TCC 2015. LNCS, vol. 9015, pp. 306–324. Springer, Heidelberg (2015). doi:10.1007/978-3-662-46497-7_12

8. Canetti, R., Feige, U., Goldreich, O., Naor, M.: Adaptively secure multi-party computation. In: Proceedings of the Twenty-Eighth Annual ACM Symposium on the Theory of Computing, Philadelphia, Pennsylvania, USA, 22–24 May 1996, pp. 639–648 (1996)

9. Cramer, R., Hanaoka, G., Hofheinz, D., Imai, H., Kiltz, E., Pass, R., Shelat, A., Vaikuntanathan, V.: Bounded CCA2-secure encryption. In: Kurosawa, K. (ed.) ASIACRYPT 2007. LNCS, vol. 4833, pp. 502–518. Springer, Heidelberg (2007). doi:10.1007/978-3-540-76900-2_31

10. Dodis, Y., Katz, J., Xu, S., Yung, M.: Key-insulated public key cryptosystems. In: Knudsen, L.R. (ed.) EUROCRYPT 2002. LNCS, vol. 2332, pp. 65–82. Springer, Heidelberg (2002). doi:10.1007/3-540-46035-7_5

11. Fiat, A., Naor, M.: Broadcast encryption. In: Stinson, D.R. (ed.) CRYPTO 1993. LNCS, vol. 773, pp. 480–491. Springer, Heidelberg (1994). doi:10.1007/3-540-48329-2_40

12. Garg, S., Gentry, C., Halevi, S., Sahai, A., Waters, B.: Attribute-based encryption for circuits from multilinear maps. In: Canetti, R., Garay, J.A. (eds.) CRYPTO 2013. LNCS, vol. 8043, pp. 479–499. Springer, Heidelberg (2013). doi:10.1007/978-3-642-40084-1_27

13. Goldwasser, S., Kalai, Y.T., Popa, R.A., Vaikuntanathan, V., Zeldovich, N.: Reusable garbled circuits and succinct functional encryption. In: Symposium on Theory of Computing Conference, STOC 2013, Palo Alto, CA, USA, 1–4 June 2013, pp. 555–564 (2013)

14. Goldwasser, S., Lewko, A., Wilson, D.A.: Bounded-collusion IBE from key homomorphism. In: Cramer, R. (ed.) TCC 2012. LNCS, vol. 7194, pp. 564–581. Springer, Heidelberg (2012). doi:10.1007/978-3-642-28914-9_32

15. Gorbunov, S., Vaikuntanathan, V., Wee, H.: Functional encryption with bounded collusions via multi-party computation. In: Safavi-Naini, R., Canetti, R. (eds.) CRYPTO 2012. LNCS, vol. 7417, pp. 162–179. Springer, Heidelberg (2012). doi:10.1007/978-3-642-32009-5_11

16. Gorbunov, S., Vaikuntanathan, V., Wee, H.: Attribute-based encryption for circuits. In: Symposium on Theory of Computing Conference, STOC 2013, Palo Alto, CA, USA, 1–4 June 2013, pp. 545–554 (2013)

17. Goyal, V., Kumar, V., Lokam, S., Mahmoody, M.: On black-box reductions between predicate encryption schemes. In: Cramer, R. (ed.) TCC 2012. LNCS, vol. 7194, pp. 440–457. Springer, Heidelberg (2012). doi:10.1007/978-3-642-28914-9_25
18. Goyal, V., Pandey, O., Sahai, A., Waters, B.: Attribute-based encryption for fine-grained access control of encrypted data. In: Proceedings of the 13th ACM Conference on Computer and Communications Security, CCS 2006, Alexandria, VA, USA, 30 October–3 November 2006, pp. 89–98 (2006)
19. Hamlin, A., Schear, N., Shen, E., Varia, M., Yakoubov, S., Yerukhimovich, A.: Cryptography for big data security. In: Fei, H. (ed.) Big Data: Storage, Sharing, and Security (3S), pp. 241–288. CRC Press, Taylor & Francis Group, Boca Raton (2016). (Chapter 7)
20. Ishai, Y., Kushilevitz, E.: Randomizing polynomials: a new representation with applications to round-efficient secure computation. In: 41st Annual Symposium on Foundations of Computer Science, FOCS 2000, Redondo Beach, California, USA, 12–14 November 2000, pp. 294–304 (2000)
21. Katz, J., Yerukhimovich, A.: On black-box constructions of predicate encryption from trapdoor permutations. In: Matsui, M. (ed.) ASIACRYPT 2009. LNCS, vol. 5912, pp. 197–213. Springer, Heidelberg (2009). doi:10.1007/978-3-642-10366-7_12
22. Lewko, A., Okamoto, T., Sahai, A., Takashima, K., Waters, B.: Fully secure functional encryption: attribute-based encryption and (hierarchical) inner product encryption. In: Gilbert, H. (ed.) EUROCRYPT 2010. LNCS, vol. 6110, pp. 62–91. Springer, Heidelberg (2010). doi:10.1007/978-3-642-13190-5_4
23. Naor, D., Naor, M., Lotspiech, J.: Revocation and tracing schemes for stateless receivers. In: Kilian, J. (ed.) CRYPTO 2001. LNCS, vol. 2139, pp. 41–62. Springer, Heidelberg (2001). doi:10.1007/3-540-44647-8_3
24. Ostrovsky, R., Sahai, A., Waters, B.: Attribute-based encryption with non-monotonic access structures. In: Proceedings of the 2007 ACM Conference on Computer and Communications Security, CCS 2007, Alexandria, Virginia, USA, 28–31 October 2007, pp. 195–203 (2007)
25. Sahai, A., Seyalioglu, H.: Worry-free encryption: functional encryption with public keys. In: Proceedings of the 17th ACM Conference on Computer and Communications Security, CCS 2010, Chicago, Illinois, USA, 4–8 October 2010, pp. 463–472 (2010)
26. Sahai, A., Waters, B.: Fuzzy identity-based encryption. In: Cramer, R. (ed.) EUROCRYPT 2005. LNCS, vol. 3494, pp. 457–473. Springer, Heidelberg (2005). doi:10.1007/11426639_27
27. Tessaro, S., Wilson, D.A.: Bounded-collusion identity-based encryption from semantically-secure public-key encryption: generic constructions with short ciphertexts. In: Krawczyk, H. (ed.) PKC 2014. LNCS, vol. 8383, pp. 257–274. Springer, Heidelberg (2014). doi:10.1007/978-3-642-54631-0_15
28. Waters, B.: Ciphertext-policy attribute-based encryption: an expressive, efficient, and provably secure realization. In: Catalano, D., Fazio, N., Gennaro, R., Nicolosi, A. (eds.) PKC 2011. LNCS, vol. 6571, pp. 53–70. Springer, Heidelberg (2011). doi:10.1007/978-3-642-19379-8_4

Access Control Encryption for Equality, Comparison, and More

Georg Fuchsbauer[1]([✉]), Romain Gay[1], Lucas Kowalczyk[2], and Claudio Orlandi[3]

[1] ENS, CNRS, Inria and PSL Research University, Paris, France
{georg.fuchsbauer,romain.gay}@ens.fr
[2] Columbia University, New York, USA
luke@cs.columbia.edu
[3] Aarhus University, Aarhus, Denmark
orlandi@cs.au.dk

Abstract. Access Control Encryption (ACE) is a novel paradigm for encryption which allows to control not only what users in the system are allowed to *read* but also what they are allowed to *write*.

The original work of Damgård et al. [DHO16] introducing this notion left several open questions, in particular whether it is possible to construct ACE schemes with polylogarithmic complexity (in the number of possible identities in the system) from standard cryptographic assumptions.

In this work we answer the question in the affirmative by giving (efficient) constructions of ACE for an interesting class of predicates which includes equality, comparison, interval membership, and more.

We instantiate our constructions based both on standard pairing assumptions (SXDH) or more efficiently in the generic group model.

1 Introduction

Access Control Encryption (ACE) is a novel paradigm for encryption that was introduced by Damgård, Haagh and Orlandi [DHO16]. (A similar concept had previously been introduced in [IPV10].) The main difference between ACE and other advanced encryption primitives (such as *identity-based* [Sha84,BF01, Sak00], *attribute-based* [SW05] or *functional encryption* [BSW11]) is that while previous concepts for encryption prevent parties from *receiving* messages (or functions of these) that are not meant for them, ACE also prevents unauthorized parties from *sending* messages to others they are not allowed to communicate with.

In a nutshell, ACE considers a set of senders $\{S_i\}_{i \in \{0,1\}^n}$ and a set of receivers $\{R_j\}_{j \in \{0,1\}^n}$. An ACE scheme is parameterized by a predicate P and $P(i,j) = 1$ indicates that S_i is allowed to communicate with R_j while $P(i,j) = 0$ means that no communication should be possible. All communication is assumed to be routed through a special party, called the *sanitizer*, which is assumed to be *semi-honest*; in particular, the sanitizer will follow the protocol specification but might try to learn additional information by colluding with other parties in the system.

© International Association for Cryptologic Research 2017
S. Fehr (Ed.): PKC 2017, Part II, LNCS 10175, pp. 88–118, 2017.
DOI: 10.1007/978-3-662-54388-7_4

During the key distribution phase each sender S_i is given an encryption key ek_i while each receiver is given a decryption key dk_j. A sender can then create a ciphertext $c = \mathsf{Enc}(ek_i, m)$ which is sent to the sanitizer. The sanitizer need not know (nor does he learn) the message which is being transmitted nor the identity of the sender, but performs a simple sanitization of the ciphertext and broadcasts the output $c' = \mathsf{San}(pp, c)$ to all receivers. *Correctness* of the ACE scheme guarantees that if $P(i, j) = 1$ then $\mathsf{Dec}(dk_j, c) = m$ i.e., authorized receivers should be able to recover the message.

ACE also imposes two security requirements: the first, called the *no-read rule*, requires any set of unauthorized receivers (even colluding with the sanitizer) to be unable to learn any information from ciphertexts that they are not allowed to decrypt. The second (and more interesting) one is called the *no-write rule* and guarantees that no set of corrupt senders $\{S_i\}$ can transfer any information to any set of corrupt receivers $\{R_j\}$ under the condition that $P(i, j) = 0$ for each combination of sender-receiver pair.

In [DHO16] the authors present two ACE schemes which can implement any predicate $P : \{0, 1\}^n \times \{0, 1\}^n \rightarrow \{0, 1\}$. However, both constructions have severe limitations. The first construction can be instantiated under standard number-theoretic assumptions, such as the decisional Diffie-Hellman (DDH) assumption or the decisional composite residuosity (DCR) assumption underlying Paillier encryption. However, its complexity, e.g. in terms of key and ciphertext size, is exponential in n and can therefore only be used when the number of identities in a system is very small. The second construction, whose complexity is poly-nomial in n, relies on a special flavor of general-purpose functional encryption (defined in [DHO16]) that, to the best of our knowledge, can only be instanti-ated using indistinguishability obfuscation [GGH+13]; the scheme is therefore not practically useful at this time.

The authors of [DHO16] left as an open question whether it is possible to construct asymptotically efficient ACE schemes without obfuscation, even for limited classes of predicates. In this work we answer this question in the affirma-tive by showing asymptotically efficient constructions for interesting predicates such as equality, comparison, and interval membership, as summarized in Table 1 which are based on standard pairing assumptions (SXDH). (The construction can be instantiated even more efficiently in the generic group model, see Table 2 for the exact constants involved in the constructions).

Technical Overview of Our Contributions. Our first technical contribution is an ACE scheme for the equality predicate i.e.,

$$\mathsf{P_{eq}}(i, j) = 1 \Leftrightarrow i = j$$

The scheme can be instantiated using generic assumptions (see Sect. 3.2) and very efficiently using cryptographic pairings and in particular *structure-preserving signatures on equivalence classes* [HS14] (see Sect. 3.3). We show how to instantiate this construction based on standard pairing assumptions (SDXH) or more efficiently in the generic group model. See Table 2 for a detailed efficiency comparison.

Table 1. Comparison of the construction in this work and in [DHO16], for predicates $P : \{0,1\}^n \times \{0,1\}^n \to \{0,1\}$. The ciphertext size dominates the complexity in all three constructions, and is therefore used as a metric for comparison.

Construction	Predicate	Ciphertext size	Assumption
[DHO16, Sect. 3]	any	$O(2^n)$	DDH or DCR
[DHO16, Sect. 4]	any	$\mathsf{poly}(n)$	iO
This work	$\mathsf{P_{eq}, P_{comp}, \dots}$	$O(n)$	SXDH

We then show how to use the scheme for equality in a black-box way to implement ACE for a predicate defined in the following way. Let S and R be two efficient functions which map identities into sets of identities:

$$\mathsf{S}\colon \{0,1\}^n \to 2^{\{0,1\}^n} \text{ and } \mathsf{R}\colon \{0,1\}^n \to 2^{\{0,1\}^n}$$

under the constraint that $\max_{i,j}\{|\mathsf{S}(i)|, |\mathsf{R}(j)|\} = \mathsf{poly}(n)$. Then we can construct efficient ACE for the predicate defined by

$$\mathsf{P_{disj}}(i,j) = 1 \Leftrightarrow \mathsf{S}(i) \cap \mathsf{R}(j) \neq \emptyset.$$

We show that this class of predicates is quite rich (using results from [SBC+07, GMW15]) and includes useful predicates such as comparison (i..e, the predicate $\mathsf{P_{comp}}(i,j) = 1 \Leftrightarrow i \leq j$) and interval membership (i.e., the predicate $\mathsf{P_{range}}$ defined for all points $z \in [N]$ and intervals $I \subset [N]$ as $\mathsf{P_{range}}(z, I) = 1 \Leftrightarrow z \in I$).

In a nutshell, the composed ACE scheme works as follows: assuming an ACE for equality, sender i is given all the encryption keys corresponding to the identities contained in the set $\mathsf{S}(i)$ and receiver j is given all the decryption keys for identities contained in the set $\mathsf{R}(j)$. To encrypt a message, the sender encrypts it under all his encryption keys (padding to the size of the largest possible set). Now if the intersection of $\mathsf{S}(i)$ and $\mathsf{R}(j)$ is not empty, the receiver can decrypt at least one of the ciphertexts and therefore learn the message; the scheme thus satisfies *correctness*. Intuitively, the scheme also satisfies the *no-read* and *no-write* rule since $\mathsf{P_{disj}}(i,j) = 0 \Rightarrow \mathsf{S}(i) \cap \mathsf{R}(j) = \emptyset$, which allows us to use the security property of the underlying equality ACE scheme.

For correctness, the receiver must be able to tell when decryption of the underlying ACE succeeds. This can be achieved using standard techniques, e.g., by using a sparse message space. The trivial implementation of decryption, where the receiver tries all keys on all ciphertexts, would lead to a decryption complexity *quadratic* in the size of $\mathsf{R}(j)$. In Sect. 4 we overcome this shortcoming by defining the overall predicate with *disjunction of equalities* instead of *disjointness of sets*.

We note that the *linear construction* from [DHO16] might at first glance look similar to the one proposed here, with $\mathsf{R}(j) = \{j\}$ (each receiver is given a single key) and $\mathsf{S}(i) = \{j \mid P(i,j) = 1\}$ (each sender is given a key for every receiver she is allowed to talk to). Note however that the complexity of this construction is *inherently* exponential, due to the way that ciphertexts are constructed and sanitized: in the *linear construction* of [DHO16], ciphertexts contain one entry for *every possible receiver in the system* (senders encrypt the message using the keys of all the receivers they are allowed to talk to and add random ciphertexts for the other receivers), and the sanitization process treats each component of the ciphertext differently (i.e., the sanitizer sanitizes each component of the ciphertext using a receiver-dependent procedure). Our approach is to start with an ACE for equality with the property that the sanitizer's algorithm is oblivious of the identity of the sender/receiver.

Finally, we note that all constructions in [DHO16] require the sanitizer to store some *secret* information, the knowledge of which would allow the adversary to break the *no-write* rule. In contrast, for the schemes presented in this paper, the sanitizer does not need to store any secret information, thereby significantly reducing the chances for an adversary to break the security of the system. In particular, the adversary must perform an *active* corruption of the sanitizer in order to break the *no-write rule*.

2 Defining ACE

ACE Notation. An *access control encryption* (ACE)[1] scheme is defined by the following PPT algorithms:

Setup: Setup is a randomized algorithm that on input the security parameter κ and a policy $P\colon \{0,1\}^n \times \{0,1\}^n \to \{0,1\}$ outputs a master secret key *msk* and public parameters *pp* (which include the message space $\mathcal{M}$ and ciphertext spaces $\mathcal{C}, \mathcal{C}'$).

Key Generation: Gen is a deterministic algorithm[2] that on input the master secret key *msk*, a type $t \in \{\mathsf{sen}, \mathsf{rec}\}$ and an identity $i \in \{0,1\}^n$, outputs a key k. We use the following notation for the two kinds of keys in the system:
- $ek_i \leftarrow \mathsf{Gen}(msk, i, \mathsf{sen})$ and call it an *encryption key for* $i \in \{0,1\}^n$
- $dk_j \leftarrow \mathsf{Gen}(msk, j, \mathsf{rec})$ and call it a *decryption key for* $j \in \{0,1\}^n$

We remark that, as opposed to [DHO16], there is no need for a private *sanitizer key* in our schemes.

Encrypt: Enc is a randomized algorithm that, on input an encryption key ek_i and a message m, outputs a ciphertext c.

Sanitizer: San is a randomized algorithm that using the public parameters *pp* transforms an incoming ciphertext $c \in \mathcal{C}$ into a sanitized ciphertext $c' \in \mathcal{C}'$.

Decryption: Dec is a deterministic algorithm that recovers a message $m' \in \mathcal{M} \cup \{\bot\}$ from a ciphertext $c' \in \mathcal{C}'$ using a decryption key dk_j.

---

[1] This section is taken almost verbatim from [DHO16].

[2] This is without loss of generality, since we can always add a PRF key to *msk* and derive the randomness for Gen from the PRF and the identity of the party.

Definition 1 (Correctness). *For all* $m \in \mathcal{M}$, $i, j \in \{0, 1\}^n$ *with* $P(i, j) = 1$:

$$\Pr\left[\mathsf{Dec}\left(dk_j, \mathsf{San}\left(pp, \mathsf{Enc}\left(ek_i, m\right)\right)\right) \neq m\right] \leq \mathsf{negl}\left(\kappa\right)$$

with $(pp, msk) \leftarrow \mathsf{Setup}(1^\kappa, P)$, $ek_i \leftarrow \mathsf{Gen}(msk, i, \mathsf{sen})$, $dk_j \leftarrow \mathsf{Gen}(msk, j, \mathsf{rec})$, *and the probability is taken over the random coins of all algorithms.*

Complementary to correctness, we require that it is detectable when decryption does not succeed, formalized as follows.

Definition 2 (Detectability). *For all* $m \in \mathcal{M}$, $i, j \in \{0, 1\}^n$ *with* $P(i, j) = 0$:

$$\Pr\left[\mathsf{Dec}\left(dk_j, \mathsf{San}\left(pp, \mathsf{Enc}\left(ek_i, m\right)\right)\right) \neq \perp\right] \leq \mathsf{negl}\left(\kappa\right)$$

with $(pp, msk) \leftarrow \mathsf{Setup}(1^\kappa, P)$, $ek_i \leftarrow \mathsf{Gen}(msk, i, \mathsf{sen})$, $dk_j \leftarrow \mathsf{Gen}(msk, j, \mathsf{rec})$, *and the probability is taken over the random coins of all algorithms.*

Definition 3 (No-Read Rule). *Consider the following game between a challenger C and a stateful adversary A:*

No-Read Rule	
Game Definition	**Oracle Definition**
1. $(pp, msk) \leftarrow \mathsf{Setup}(1^\kappa, P)$;	$\mathcal{O}_G(j, t)$:
2. $(m_0, m_1, i_0, i_1) \leftarrow A^{\mathcal{O}_G(\cdot), \mathcal{O}_E(\cdot)}(pp)$;	1. Output $k \leftarrow \mathsf{Gen}(msk, j, t)$;
3. $b \leftarrow \{0, 1\}$;	
4. $c \leftarrow \mathsf{Enc}(\mathsf{Gen}(msk, i_b, \mathsf{sen}), m_b)$;	$\mathcal{O}_E(i, m)$:
5. $b' \leftarrow A^{\mathcal{O}_G(\cdot), \mathcal{O}_E(\cdot)}(c)$;	1. $ek_i \leftarrow \mathsf{Gen}(msk, i, \mathsf{sen})$;
	2. Output $c \leftarrow \mathsf{Enc}(ek_i, m)$;

We say that A wins the No-Read game if $b = b'$, $|m_0| = |m_1|$, $i_0, i_1 \in \{0, 1\}^n$ and for all queries q to $\mathcal{O}_G$ with $q = (j, \mathsf{rec})$ it holds that

$$P(i_0, j) = P(i_1, j) = 0.$$

We say an ACE scheme satisfies the No-Read *rule if for all PPT A*

$$\mathsf{adv}^A_{\mathsf{No\text{-}Read}}(ACE) = \Pr[A \text{ wins the No-Read game}] - \tfrac{1}{2} \leq \mathsf{negl}(\kappa).$$

Remark: The definition in [DHO16] requires $2 \cdot |\Pr[A \text{ wins the No-Read game}] - \frac{1}{2}| \leq \mathsf{negl}(\kappa)$, which is unachievable, since any A whose output satisfies $|m_0| \neq |m_1|$ has advantage $= 1$ (the same also applies to their version of Definition 4).

Our definition of the *no-read rule* is also weaker in that it does not guarantee anonymity of the sender against an adversary who can decrypt the ciphertext (in the context of attribute-based encryption a similar property is called *weak attribute hiding* [OT12]). However, none of the applications of ACE described in [DHO16] require this property.

Definition 4 (No-Write Rule). *Consider the following game between a challenger C and a stateful adversary A:*

No-Write Rule	
Game Definition	**Oracle Definition**
1. $(pp, msk) \leftarrow \mathsf{Setup}(1^\kappa, P)$; 2. $m' \leftarrow \mathcal{M}$; $b \leftarrow \{0,1\}$; 3. $(c_0, i') \leftarrow A^{\mathcal{O}_E(\cdot), \mathcal{O}_S(\cdot)}(pp)$; 4. $c_1 \leftarrow \mathsf{Enc}(\mathsf{Gen}(msk, i', \mathsf{sen}), m')$; 5. $b' \leftarrow A^{\mathcal{O}_E(\cdot), \mathcal{O}_R(\cdot)}(\mathsf{San}(pp, c_b))$;	$\mathcal{O}_S(j,t)$ and $\mathcal{O}_R(j,t)$: 1. Output $k \leftarrow \mathsf{Gen}(msk, j, t)$; $\mathcal{O}_E(i, m)$: 1. $ek_i \leftarrow \mathsf{Gen}(msk, i, \mathsf{sen})$; 2. Output $c \leftarrow \mathsf{San}(pp, \mathsf{Enc}(ek_i, m))$;

Let Q_S (resp. Q) be the set of all queries $q = (j, t)$ that A issues to $\mathcal{O}_S$ (resp. both $\mathcal{O}_S$ and $\mathcal{O}_R$). Let I_S be the set of all $i \in \{0,1\}^n$ such that $(i, \mathsf{sen}) \in Q_S$ and let J be the set of all $j \in \{0,1\}^n$ such that $(j, \mathsf{rec}) \in Q$. Then we say that A wins the No-Write game if $b' = b$ and all of the following hold:

1. $i' \in I_S \cup \{0\}$;
2. $\forall i \in I_S, j \in J, P(i, j) = 0$;
3. $\mathsf{San}(pp, c_0) \neq \perp$.

We say an ACE scheme satisfies the No-Write rule if for all PPT A

$$\mathsf{adv}^A_{\mathsf{No\text{-}Write}}(ACE) = \Pr[A \text{ wins the No-Write game}] - \tfrac{1}{2} \leq \mathsf{negl}(\kappa).$$

Remark: Note that the *no-write rule* as defined in [DHO16] does not require the third condition above, which essentially just requires the ciphertext output by the adversary to be *well-formed* relative to the public parameters pp (which crucially means that the adversary already *knows* if the ciphertext is well-formed or not). The constructions in [DHO16] deal with this by letting the sanitizer output a random encryption when running on an malformed ciphertext instead. We find the notion presented here to be more natural.

3   ACE for Equality

Here, we show two how to build an ACE for the *equality predicate* defined by $\mathsf{P_{eq}} \colon \{0,1\}^n \times \{0,1\}^n \to \{0,1\}$ and

$$\mathsf{P_{eq}}(x, y) = 1 \iff x = y.$$

We present two constructions, one based on generic assumptions and a second (more efficient) one based on cryptographic pairings.

3.1   Generic Construction Preliminaries

We start with reviewing the notation we will use for standard cryptographic building blocks and we refer to standard textbooks in cryptography (such as [Gol09,KL14]), for formal definitions of security. For real functions f and g, we write $f(\kappa) \approx g(\kappa)$ if $|f(\kappa) - g(\kappa)| \leq \mathsf{negl}(\kappa)$, where negl is a negligible function in κ.

Non-interactive Zero-Knowledge Proofs. Let L be a language and R a relation s.t. $x \in L$ if and only if there exists a witness w such that $(x, w) \in R$. A non-interactive proof system [BFM88] for a relation R is defined by the PPT algorithms (NIZK.Gen, NIZK.Prove, NIZK.Ver) with $crs \leftarrow$ NIZK.Gen$(1^\kappa, L)$, $\pi \leftarrow$ NIZK.Prove(crs, x, w) and NIZK.Ver$(crs, x, \pi) \in \{0, 1\}$. We require *correctness*, *(perfect) soundness, knowledge extraction*, and *zero-knowledge*.

Correctness. For all PPT adversaries A:

$$\Pr \left[\begin{array}{l} crs \leftarrow \text{NIZK.Gen}(1^\kappa, L); \\ (x, w) \leftarrow A(crs); \\ \pi \leftarrow \text{NIZK.Prove}(crs, x, w) \end{array} : \text{NIZK.Ver}(crs, x, \pi) = 1 \text{ if } (x, w) \in R \right] \approx 1.$$

Soundness. For all PPT adversaries A:

$$\Pr \left[\begin{array}{l} crs \leftarrow \text{NIZK.Gen}(1^\kappa, L); \\ (x, \pi) \leftarrow A(crs) \end{array} : \text{NIZK.Ver}(crs, x, \pi) = 0 \text{ if } x \notin L \right] \approx 1.$$

Knowledge Extraction. We say that a system (NIZK.Gen, NIZK.Prove, NIZK.Ver) has knowledge-extraction security if there exists a knowledge extractor, which is a pair of PPT algorithms (E_1, E_2) with the following two properties:

1. For all PPT adversaries A:

$$\Pr[crs \leftarrow \text{NIZK.Gen}(1^\kappa, L) : A(crs) = 1]$$
$$\approx \Pr[(crs, \tau) \leftarrow E_1(1^\kappa, L) : A(crs) = 1].$$

2. For all PPT adversaries A:

$$\Pr \left[\begin{array}{l} (crs, \tau) \leftarrow E_1(1^\kappa, L); \\ (x, \pi) \leftarrow A(crs); \\ w \leftarrow E_2(crs, \tau, x, \pi) \end{array} : \text{NIZK.Ver}(crs, x, \pi) = 0 \text{ or } (x, w) \in R \right] \approx 1.$$

Zero-Knowledge. We say that proof system (NIZK.Gen, NIZK.Prove, NIZK.Ver) has zero-knowledge security if there exists a simulator, which is a pair of PPT algorithms (S_1, S_2) with the following property: For all PPT adversaries A:

$$\Pr[crs \leftarrow \text{NIZK.Gen}(1^\kappa, L) : A^{\text{NIZK.Prove}(crs, \cdot, \cdot)}(crs) = 1]$$
$$\approx \Pr[(crs, \tau) \leftarrow S_1(1^\kappa, L) : A^{S'(crs, \tau, \cdot, \cdot)}(crs) = 1],$$

where $S'(crs, \tau, x, w) = S_2(crs, \tau, x)$ if $(x, w) \in R$ and outputs *failure* otherwise.

We speak of perfect correctness, perfect soundness, perfect knowledge extraction, and perfect zero-knowledge if for sufficiently large security parameters, and for all adversaries (unbounded, and not just PPT), we have equalities in the respective definitions.

Digital Signatures. A signature scheme is a tuple of PPT algorithms (Sig.Gen, Sig.Sig, Sig.Ver) with $(sk, vk) \leftarrow$ Sig.Gen(1^κ), $\sigma =$ Sig.Sig(sk, m), and

Sig.Ver$(vk, m, \sigma) \in \{0, 1\}$. We require *correctness* and *existential unforgeability under chosen-message attacks*. (Note that we defined the signature algorithm to be deterministic. Any randomized signature scheme can be de-randomized using a pseudorandom tape generated with a PRF on the message).

Anonymous and Weakly Sanitizable Public-Key Encryption. We use a public-key encryption (PKE) scheme which must satisfy *semantic security*, *anonymity*, and which must be *weakly sanitizable*. The syntax is as follows: $pp \leftarrow$ PKE.Par(1^κ) outputs public parameters, $(ek, dk) \leftarrow$ PKE.Gen(pp) outputs an encryption/decryption key pair, $c \leftarrow$ PKE.Enc(ek, m) outputs an encryption of m, $c' \leftarrow$ PKE.San(pp, c) outputs a sanitized version of c and $m' \leftarrow$ PKE.Dec(dk, c) decrypts ciphertext c.

Anonymity can be formalized as in [BBDP01] via a game where the adversary receives (pp, ek_0, ek_1), chooses a message m, receives $c \leftarrow$ PKE.Enc(ek_b, m) and must guess b.

In [DHO16] the notion of *sanitizable encryption* is introduced as a relaxation of *rerandomizable encryption*. Here we only require an even weaker property: we define an encryption scheme to be *weakly sanitizable* if the adversary cannot win a game where he is given (pp, ek), chooses $(m_0, r_0), (m_1, r_1)$, receives

$$c' = \text{PKE.San}(pp, \text{PKE.Enc}(ek, m_b; r_b); r')$$

with uniform randomness r' and must guess b.

The weakening lies in the fact that sanitizations only have to be computationally indistinguishable, whereas in the sanitizable PKE of [DHO16], sanitizations of encryptions of the same message must be statistically indistinguishable.

An Anonymous and Weakly Sanitizable Scheme. An encryption scheme that satisfies the above properties under the DDH assumption is the following simple variation of ElGamal [Gam85]. As for the original scheme, the parameters $pp = (\mathbb{G}, p, g)$ consist of the description of a DDH-hard group $\mathbb{G}$ of order p generated by g; the decryption key is a random element $dk \in \mathbb{Z}_p$ and the encryption key is defined as $ek = g^{dk}$. Encryption of a message $m \in \mathbb{G}$ is now defined as picking random $r \in \mathbb{Z}_p^*$ and $s \in \mathbb{Z}_p$ and defining a ciphertext as

$$\text{Enc}(ek, m; (r, s)) = (d_0, d_1, c_0, c_1) = (g^r, ek^r, g^s, ek^s \cdot m).$$

A ciphertext (d_0, d_1, c_0, c_1) is sanitized by first checking if $d_0 = 1$ or $d_1 = 1$, in which case the sanitizer outputs two random group elements; otherwise it picks a random $t \in \mathbb{Z}_p^*$ and returns $(d_0^t \cdot c_0, d_1^t \cdot c_1) = (g^{rt+s}, ek^{rt+s} \cdot m)$, which is (statistically close to) a fresh encryption of m.

This scheme can be made detectable (see Definition 2) using standard techniques, e.g. by choosing a sparse message space $\mathcal{M}'$, that is, with $\frac{|\mathcal{M}'|}{p} \leq \text{negl}(\kappa)$, where p is the order of $\mathbb{G}$. Decryption of a sanitized ciphertext $(d_0^t c_0, d_1^t c_1) = (g^{rt+s}, ek^{rt+s} \cdot m)$ with a different key $dk' \neq dk$ yields: $(g^{rt+s})^{-dk'} \cdot ek^{rt+s} \cdot m = (g^{dk-dk'})^{rt+s} \cdot m$, which is statistically close to a random element of $\mathbb{G}$. If $\frac{|\mathcal{M}'|}{p} \leq \text{negl}(\kappa)$, the probability that this element is in $\mathcal{M}'$ is negligible and so:

$$\Pr\left[\mathsf{Dec}\left(dk', \mathsf{San}\left(pp, \mathsf{Enc}\left(ek, m\right)\right)\right) \neq \bot\right] \leq \mathsf{negl}\left(\kappa\right),$$

meeting our definition for detectability.

Proposition 1. *The above encryption scheme is anonymous and weakly sanitizable.*

Proof. For anonymity, notice that we can define a hybrid anonymity game where the adversary is given an encryption of its message m under a new encryption key $e_x = g^x$ (where x is a random element of $\mathbb{Z}_p$) instead of ek_0 or ek_1 and move from the game that uses ek_0 to encrypt the challenge ciphertext to one that uses ek_x using DDH. Given a DDH challenge g, g^a, g^b, and g^{ab+x} where either $x = 0$ or x is a random element in $\mathbb{Z}_p$, one can play the game using $ek_0 = g^a$ and create the challenge ciphertext as $((g^b)^{\tilde{r}}, (g^{ab+x})^{\tilde{r}}, g^b, g^{ab+x} \cdot m)$. If $x = 0$, then this is distributed like the game that uses ek_0 (where $dk = a$, $r = b\tilde{r}$ and $s = b$). If x is a random element of $\mathbb{Z}_p$, then this is distributed like the game that uses ek_x. (Moving from ek_x to ek_1 follows symmetrically).

To see that the variant is weakly sanitizable, notice that we can similarly define a hybrid sanitizability game where the adversary is given two random group elements as its challenge sanitized ciphertext. In such a game, the challenge sanitized ciphertext is independent of b, so the adversary cannot achieve any advantage. We can move to this game using DDH. Given a DDH challenge g, g^a, g^b, and g^{ab+x} where either $x = 0$ or x is a random element in $\mathbb{Z}_p$, one can play the game using $ek = g^a$ and create the challenge sanitized ciphertext as $(g^b, g^{ab+x} \cdot m_b)$ (unless r_b causes d_0 or d_1 to be the identity, in which case it uses two random group elements). If $x = 0$, then this is distributed like the normal game (a sanitized ciphertext $(d_0^t \cdot c_0, d_1^t \cdot c_1) = (g^{rt+s}, ek^{rt+s} \cdot m_b)$ looks like an ElGamal encryption of m_b when $d_0 \neq 1$ and $d_1 \neq 1$). If x is a random element of $\mathbb{Z}_p$, then the challenge sanitized ciphertext is distributed as two random group elements. □

3.2 Generic Construction

Construction 1 (ACE for Equality – Generic). *We construct an ACE scheme* $\mathsf{ACE} = (\mathsf{Setup}, \mathsf{Gen}, \mathsf{Enc}, \mathsf{San}, \mathsf{Dec})$ *defined by the following algorithms:*

Setup: Compute $pp^{\mathsf{pke}} \leftarrow \mathsf{PKE.Par}(1^\kappa)$ and $(vk, sk) \leftarrow \mathsf{Sig.Gen}(1^\kappa)$.
Let L be the language defined by the following NP relation: for $x = (vk, c)$ and $w = (pk, \sigma, m, r)$, define $R(x, w) = 1$ iff

$$\mathsf{Sig.Ver}(vk, pk, \sigma) = 1 \ \wedge \ c = \mathsf{PKE.Enc}(pk, m; r).$$

Compute $crs \leftarrow \mathsf{NIZK.Gen}(1^\kappa, L)$. Pick a random PRF key K for a PRF F.
Output $pp = (pp^{\mathsf{pke}}, vk, crs)$ and $msk = (sk, K)$.

Key Generation: Given the master secret key msk and an identity i, the encryption and decryption keys are computed as follows: run

$$(pk, dk) \leftarrow \mathsf{PKE.Gen}(pp^{\mathsf{pke}}; F_K(i)) \text{ and } \sigma = \mathsf{Sig.Sig}(sk, pk)$$

and define

$$ek_i = (pk, \sigma) \quad \text{and} \quad dk_i = dk$$

Encryption: On input a message m and an encryption key $ek_i = (pk, \sigma)$ pick encryption randomness r, compute $c' = \mathsf{PKE.Enc}(pk, m; r)$, let $x = (vk, c')$, $w = (pk, \sigma, m, r)$ and compute $\pi \leftarrow \mathsf{NIZK.Prove}(crs, x, w)$. Output $c = (c', \pi)$.

Sanitizer: On input $pp = (pp^{\mathsf{pke}}, vk, crs)$ and a ciphertext $c = (c', \pi)$ the sanitizer outputs $\bot$ if $\mathsf{NIZK.Ver}(crs, x = (vk, c'), \pi) = 0$; otherwise it returns $c'' \leftarrow \mathsf{PKE.San}(pp, c')$.

Decryption: Given a ciphertext c' and a decryption key $dk_j = dk$ output

$$m' = \mathsf{PKE.Dec}(dk, c').$$

Theorem 1. *Construction 1 satisfies the No-Read Rule if the underlying PKE scheme satisfies semantic security and anonymity, if the proof system is zero-knowledge and the PRF is pseudorandom.*

Proof. We assume that A makes queries $\mathcal{O}_G(i_0, \mathsf{sen})$ and $\mathcal{O}_G(i_1, \mathsf{sen})$ (this is w.l.o.g., as any A can be transformed into such an adversary without affecting its winning probability). We define a hybrid game which guesses A's oracle queries that lead to the creation of the encryption keys of users i_0 and i_1. If the guess was wrong, the game outputs a random bit. (The differences to the original game are items 0. and 6. below.) Let $q_{\max}$ be an upper bound on the number of $\mathcal{O}_G(\cdot, \mathsf{sen})$ plus the number $\mathcal{O}_E$ queries that A makes during the game. (The keys could also be first created during an encryption query.) Since A is PPT, it is clear that $q_{\max}$ is polynomial in κ.

Hybrid Game for No-Read Rule	
Game Definition	**Oracle Definition**
0. $q_0, q_1 \leftarrow \{1, \ldots, q_{\max}\}$; $\hat{q} \leftarrow 1$ 1. $(pp, msk) \leftarrow \mathsf{Setup}(1^\kappa, P)$; 2. $(m_0, m_1, i_0, i_1) \leftarrow A^{\mathcal{O}_G(\cdot), \mathcal{O}_E(\cdot)}(pp)$; 3. $b \leftarrow \{0, 1\}$; 4. $c \leftarrow \mathsf{Enc}(\mathsf{Gen}(msk, i_b, \mathsf{sen}), m_b)$; 5. $b' \leftarrow A^{\mathcal{O}_G(\cdot), \mathcal{O}_E(\cdot)}(c)$; 6. If $Q[q_0] = i_0$ and $Q[q_1] = i_1$ $\quad$ Return b'; $\quad$ Else return $b' \leftarrow \{0, 1\}$;	$\mathcal{O}_G(j, t)$: 0. If $t = \mathsf{sen}$ and $\mathsf{Gen}(msk, j, \mathsf{sen})$ has $\quad$ not been called yet, then $\qquad Q[\hat{q}] = j$; $\hat{q} = \hat{q} + 1$; 1. Output $ek_j \leftarrow \mathsf{Gen}(msk, j, t)$; $\mathcal{O}_E(i, m)$: 0. If $t = \mathsf{sen}$ and $\mathsf{Gen}(msk, i, \mathsf{sen})$ has $\quad$ not been called yet, then $\qquad Q[\hat{q}] = i$; $\hat{q} = \hat{q} + 1$; 1. $\quad ek_i \leftarrow \mathsf{Gen}(msk, i, \mathsf{sen})$; 2. Output $c \leftarrow \mathsf{Enc}(ek_i, m)$;

Lemma 1. *An adversary that wins the no-read game with non-negligible advantage also wins the hybrid game with non-negligible advantage.*

Proof. Assume an adversary breaks the no-read rule, that is, there exists c s.t.

$$\mathsf{adv}^A_{\mathsf{No\text{-}Read}}(ACE) = \Pr[b' = b \text{ in the No-Read Game}] - \tfrac{1}{2} \geq \tfrac{1}{\kappa^c}$$

for infinitely many κ. Let E denote the event that in the hybrid game $Q[q_0] = i_0$ and $Q[q_1] = i_1$. Note that this event is independent of A's view; moreover, conditioned on E occurring, the hybrid game and the original No-Read-Rule game are equivalent; finally $\Pr[E] = q_{max}^{-2}$. We thus have

$$\mathsf{adv}_{\text{hybrid}}^A(ACE) = \Pr[b' = b \text{ in the hybrid game}] - \tfrac{1}{2}$$
$$= \Pr[b' = b \text{ in hybrid} \mid E] \cdot \Pr[E] + \Pr[b' = b \text{ in hybrid} \mid \neg E] \cdot \Pr[\neg E] - \tfrac{1}{2}$$
$$= \Pr[b' = b \text{ in No-Read} \mid E] \cdot \Pr[E] + \tfrac{1}{2} \cdot \Pr[\neg E] - \tfrac{1}{2}$$
$$= \Pr[b' = b \text{ in No-Read}] \cdot \tfrac{1}{q_{max}^2} + \tfrac{1}{2} \cdot (1 - \tfrac{1}{q_{max}^2}) - \tfrac{1}{2}$$
$$= \tfrac{1}{q_{max}^2} \cdot \mathsf{adv}_{\text{hybrid}}^A(ACE) \geq \tfrac{1}{q_{max}^2 \cdot \kappa^c}$$

for infinitely many κ. Thus, $\mathsf{adv}_{\text{hybrid}}^A(ACE)$ is not negligible in κ. $\qquad\square$

Assuming an arbitrary PPT A, we will now show that H_0, the hybrid above with b fixed to 0, is computationally indistinguishable from H_1 (b fixed to 1). By Lemma 1, A cannot have won the original game, thus proving the theorem. We define a sequence of hybrid games between H_0 and H_1 and show that each one is computationally indistinguishable from the previous one (i.e., the probability that the hybrid game returns 1 only changes negligibly).

Game $H_{b,1}$ (for $b \in \{0,1\}$) is defined as H_b, except we use a truly random function instead of F to generate all secret keys.
$H_{b,0} \approx_c H_{b,1}$ (which we use as shorthand for $\Pr[A \text{ wins } H_{b,0}] \approx \Pr[A \text{ wins } H_{b,1}]$): Indistinguishability follows from PRF security (as K is never revealed to A).

Game $H_{b,2}$ is the same as $H_{b,1}$, except crs, contained in pp, and π in the challenge ciphertext c are simulated.
$H_{b,1} \approx_c H_{b,2}$: Indistinguishability follows from the zero-knowledge property of the proof system.

Game $H_{0,3}$ is the same as $H_{0,2}$, except c is computed as encryption of m_1 (instead of m_0) under identity i_0's key.
$H_{0,2} \approx_c H_{0,3}$: Indistinguishability follows from semantic security of the encryption scheme: We construct a PPT reduction B that receives a challenge pk and simulates game $H_{0,2}$. When A makes the query that generates the q_0-th encryption key, B sets this key to pk. If A queries the corresponding decryption key, B aborts (outputting a random bit). When A outputs (m_0, m_1, i_0, i_1) and i_0 is not the identity corresponding to the q_0-th key, B aborts. Otherwise, B submits (m_0, m_1) as challenge to receive c from its challenger (which is either m_0 or m_1 encrypted under pk) and forwards c to A together with a simulated proof π. Reduction B perfectly simulates either $H_{0,2}$ or $H_{0,3}$, depending on its own challenge: if B guesses q_0 and q_1 correctly, it does not abort and otherwise it outputs a random bit anyway.
$H_{0,3} \approx_c H_{1,2}$: The two games differ in that m_1 is encrypted under i_0's key in $H_{0,3}$ and i_1's key in $H_{1,2}$. Indistinguishability follows from anonymity of the encryption scheme: We construct a PPT reduction B, which receives pk_0 and pk_1 and simulates $H_{1,2}$ for A, except that it sets the q_0th key to pk_0 and the q_1th key to pk_1. If A queries a corresponding decryption key or if in A's output (m_0, m_1, i_0, i_1), i_0 does not correspond to the q_0th key or i_1 does not

correspond to the q_1th key then B aborts. Otherwise, B submits m_1 as a challenge to receive c from its challenger (which is m_1 encrypted under pk_0 or pk_1), which it forwards to A together with a simulated proof π. Depending on its own challenge, B perfectly simulates either $H_{1,2}$ or $H_{1,3}$: if B guesses q_0 and q_1 correctly, it does not abort and otherwise it outputs a random bit anyway.

We have thus shown $H_0 \approx_c H_{0,1} \approx_c H_{0,2} \approx_c H_{0,3} \approx_c H_{1,2} \approx_c H_{1,1} \approx_c H_1$, which concludes the proof. $\qquad\square$

Theorem 2. *Construction 1 satisfies the No-Write Rule if the underlying PKE scheme is anonymous and weakly sanitizable, if the proof system is perfectly sound and has knowledge extraction security, the signature scheme is unforgeable and the PRF is pseudorandom.*

Proof. Let H_0 denote the No-Write-Rule game. W.l.o.g. we assume that A makes a query $\mathcal{O}_S(i', \mathsf{sen})$ and that $I_S \cap J = \emptyset$ (i.e., A satisfies the 2nd item in the winning condition in Definition 4). We start with defining two hybrid games whose indistinguishability from H_0 is immediate:

Game H_1 is defined as H_0, except we use a truly random function instead of F to generate all secret keys.

$H_0 \approx_c H_1$: Indistinguishability follows from PRF security.

Game H_2 is the same as H_1, except that crs is computed via the knowledge extractor: $(crs, \tau) \leftarrow E_1(1^\kappa, L)$ (where τ is the extraction trapdoor). When A outputs $c_0 = (c, \pi)$, we run the second part of the extractor: $w \leftarrow E_2(crs, \tau, x = (vk, c), \pi)$, where vk is contained in pp.

$H_1 \approx_c H_2$: Indistinguishability follows from the first property of knowledge extraction (i.e., a CRS output by E_1 is indistinguishable from one output by NIZK.Gen) of the proof system. (Running E_2 has no effect on the outcome of the game.)

Hybrid Game H_2 for No-Write Rule	
(Note that $\mathcal{O}_E$ need not compute the proof as it is discarded by San anyway.)	
Game Definition	**Oracle Definition**
1. $pp^{\mathsf{pke}} \leftarrow \mathsf{PKE.Par}(1^\kappa)$; $\quad (vk, sk) \leftarrow \mathsf{Sig.Gen}(1^\kappa)$; $\quad (crs, \tau) \leftarrow E_1(1^\kappa, L)$; $pp = (pp^{\mathsf{pke}}, vk, crs)$ 2. $m^* \leftarrow \mathcal{M}$; $b \leftarrow \{0,1\}$; 3. $((c, \pi), i') \leftarrow A^{\mathcal{O}_E(\cdot), \mathcal{O}_S(\cdot)}((pp^{\mathsf{pke}}, vk, crs))$; $\quad (pk, \sigma, m, r) \leftarrow E_2(crs, \tau, x = (vk, c), \pi)$; 4. $c_0 := (c, \pi)$; $c_1 \leftarrow \mathsf{Enc}(ek_{i'}, m^*)$; 5. $b' \leftarrow A^{\mathcal{O}_E(\cdot), \mathcal{O}_R(\cdot)}(\mathsf{San}(pp, c_b))$; 6. Return b';	$\mathcal{O}_S(j, t)$ and $\mathcal{O}_R(j, t)$: 1. If pk_j not yet defined, then $\quad (pk_j, dk_j) \leftarrow \mathsf{PKE.Gen}(pp^{\mathsf{pke}})$; $\quad \sigma_j = \mathsf{Sig.Sig}(sk, pk_j)$; If $t = \mathsf{rec}$ then return dk_j; Else return $ek_j = (pk_j, \sigma_j)$; $\mathcal{O}_E(i, m)$: 1. If pk_i not yet defined, then $\quad (pk_j, dk_j) \leftarrow \mathsf{PKE.Gen}(pp^{\mathsf{pke}})$; 2. $c' \leftarrow \mathsf{PKE.Enc}(pk, m)$; $\quad$ Return $c'' \leftarrow \mathsf{PKE.San}(pp, c')$;

For a particular run of game H_2 (which is determined by the coins used by the adversary and the challenger when running the probabilistic algorithms), we now differentiate four types. We let $w = (pk, \sigma, m, r)$ denote the output of E_2.

Type 1: A outputs $c_0 = (c, \pi)$ with $\mathsf{NIZK.Ver}(crs, (vk, c), \pi) = 0$ (where crs, vk come from the public parameters used in the game).

Type 2: A outputs $c_0 = (c, \pi)$ with $\mathsf{NIZK.Ver}(crs, (vk, c), \pi) = 1$ but $R((vk, c), w) = 0$, i.e. $\mathsf{Sig.Ver}(vk, pk, \sigma) \neq 1$ or $c \neq \mathsf{PKE.Enc}(pk, m; r)$.

Type 3: A outputs $c_0 = (c, \pi)$ with $\mathsf{NIZK.Ver}(crs, (vk, c), \pi) = 1$, we have

$$\mathsf{Sig.Ver}(vk, pk, \sigma) = 1 \ \wedge \ c = \mathsf{PKE.Enc}(pk, m; r) \tag{1}$$

and pk was *not* issued in an oracle query by $\mathcal{O}_S$.

Type 4 is defined as Type 3 except pk *was* issued in an oracle query by $\mathcal{O}_S$.

The 4 types are a partitioning of the coin space of the experiment, which we denote by $T_1, \ldots, T_4$. Let W_2 denote the event that A wins hybrid game H_2.

Lemma 2. $\Pr[W_2 \wedge T_1] = 0$.

Proof. T_1 means A outputs $c_0 = (c, \pi)$ with $\mathsf{NIZK.Ver}(crs, (vk.c), \pi) = 0$. In this case, the San procedure aborts, and by definition A loses the game.   □

Lemma 3. $\Pr[T_2] \approx 0$.

Proof. In case T_2 occurs A broke property 2 of knowledge-extraction security of the proof system: it output a valid proof π for statement $x = (vk, c)$ but the extractor E_2 failed to extract a witness w with $R(x, w) = 1$.   □

Lemma 4. $\Pr[T_3] \approx 0$.

Proof. T_3 implies that A output (c, π) from which E_2 extracted $w = (pk, \sigma, m, r)$ with $\mathsf{Sig.Ver}(vk, pk, \sigma) = 1$ and pk was not issued in an oracle query.

If T_3 occurred with non-negligible probability then we could construct a PPT adversary B that achieves the same advantage in the signature forging game as follows: B simulates H_2 for A, creating a crs with an extraction trapdoor τ and using its signature oracle to respond to *send key* queries, i.e., queries of the form $(\cdot, \mathsf{sen})$ to $\mathcal{O}_S$. When A outputs $c_0 = (c, \pi)$, B runs $(pk, \sigma, m, r) \leftarrow E_2(crs, \tau, (vk, c), \pi)$ and returns (pk, σ). If T_3 occurred then B did not query pk to its signing oracle, meaning B output a valid forgery. Assuming our signature scheme is unforgeable, this (and thus T_3) can only occur with negligible probability.   □

Lemma 5. $\left| \Pr[W_2 \mid T_4] - \frac{1}{2} \right| \approx 0$.

Proof. T_4 implies that A outputs $c_0 = (c, \pi)$ from which E_2 extracted $w = (pk, \sigma, m, r)$ with $c = \mathsf{PKE.Enc}(pk, m; r)$ and pk *was* issued in an oracle query by $\mathcal{O}_S$.

Similarly to the proof of Theorem 1, we first define a hybrid game which guesses A's oracle queries that lead to the creation of the encryption keys of users i' (from A's output (c_0, i')) and i (the identity corresponding to pk extracted by E_2). If the guess was wrong, the game outputs a random bit.

Let q_{max} be an upper bound on the number of $\mathcal{O}_S(\cdot, \text{sen})$ plus the number of $\mathcal{O}_E$ queries that A makes during the game. Since A is PPT, q_{max} is polynomial in κ. (The differences to the original game are items 0., 6., and 7. below.)

Hybrid Game H_3 for No-Write Rule	
Game Definition	**Oracle Definition**

0. $q, q' \leftarrow \{1, \ldots, q_{max}\}$; $\hat{q} \leftarrow 1$
 1. $pp^{\text{pke}} \leftarrow \text{PKE.Par}(1^\kappa)$;
   $(vk, sk) \leftarrow \text{Sig.Gen}(1^\kappa)$;
   $(crs, \tau) \leftarrow E_2(1^\kappa, L)$; $pp = (pp^{\text{pke}}, vk, crs)$
 2. $m^* \leftarrow \mathcal{M}$; $b \leftarrow \{0, 1\}$;
 3. $((c, \pi), i') \leftarrow A^{\mathcal{O}_E(\cdot), \mathcal{O}_S(\cdot)}((pp^{\text{pke}}, vk, crs))$;
   $(pk, \sigma, m, r) \leftarrow E_2(crs, \tau, x = (vk, c), \pi)$;
 4. $c_0 := (c, \pi)$; $c_1 \leftarrow \text{Enc}(ek_{i'}, m^*)$;
 5. $b' \leftarrow A^{\mathcal{O}_E(\cdot), \mathcal{O}_R(\cdot)}(\text{San}(pp, c_b))$;
 6. Let i be s.t. $pk = pk_i$
 7. If $Q[q] = i$ and $Q[q'] = i'$
   Return b';
   Else return $b' \leftarrow \{0, 1\}$;
	$\mathcal{O}_S(j, t)$ and $\mathcal{O}_R(j, t)$:
	 1. If pk_j not yet defined
	   $(pk_j, dk_j) \leftarrow \text{PKE.Gen}(pp^{\text{pke}})$;
	   $\sigma_j = \text{Sig.Sig}(sk, pk_j)$;
	   $Q[\hat{q}] = j$; $\hat{q} = \hat{q} + 1$;
	 If $t = \text{rec}$ then return dk_j;
	 Return $ek_j = (pk_j, \sigma_j)$;
	
	 $\mathcal{O}_E(i, m)$:
	 1. If pk_i not yet defined, then
	   $(pk_j, dk_j) \leftarrow \text{PKE.Gen}(pp^{\text{pke}})$;
	   $Q[\hat{q}] = i$; $\hat{q} = \hat{q} + 1$;
	 2. $c' \leftarrow \text{PKE.Enc}(pk, m)$;
	 Return $c'' \leftarrow \text{PKE.San}(pp^{\text{pke}}, c')$;

Following the argument from Lemma 1, we have that an adversary that wins H_2 with non-negligible advantage also wins H_3 (event which we denote by W_3) with non-negligible advantage. Thus,

$$\left| \Pr[W_3 \mid T_4] - \tfrac{1}{2} \right| \approx 0 \; \Rightarrow \; \left| \Pr[W_2 \mid T_4] - \tfrac{1}{2} \right| \approx 0. \tag{2}$$

Assuming an arbitrary PPT A we will now show that if T_4 occurs then $H_3^{(0)}$, the hybrid H_3 with b fixed to 0, is indistinguishable from $H_3^{(1)}$ (b fixed to 1). Thus $|\Pr[W_3 \mid T_4] - \tfrac{1}{2}| \approx 0$ and the lemma follows via (2).

To show indistinguishability of $H_3^{(0)}$ and $H_3^{(1)}$, we define an intermediate hybrid game H_4 and show that, conditioned on T_4, it is computationally indistinguishable from both $H_3^{(0)}$ and $H_3^{(1)}$ (i.e., the probability that the hybrid game returns 1 only changes negligibly).

In $H_3^{(0)}$, A is given the challenge ciphertext $c' \leftarrow \text{San}(pp, c_0)$. If T_4 occurs then (cf. (1)) the ciphertext contained in $c_0 = (c, \pi)$ satisfies $c = \text{PKE.Enc}(pk, m; r)$ (with pk, m and r extracted by E_2). Moreover, T_4 implies that π is valid and A thus receives $c' \leftarrow \text{PKE.San}(pp, \text{PKE.Enc}(pk, m; r))$.

Game H_4 is the same as $H_3^{(0)}$, except that we define the ciphertext given to A as $c' \leftarrow \text{PKE.San}(pp, \text{PKE.Enc}(pk, m^*, r^*))$ where m^*, r^* are random.

$\Pr[1 \leftarrow H_3^{(0)} \mid T_4] \approx \Pr[1 \leftarrow H_4 \mid T_4]$: Indistinguishability follows from sanitizing security of the encryption scheme: We construct a PPT reduction B that receives a challenge pk and simulates game $H_3^{(0)}$. When A makes the query that generates the q-th encryption key, B sets this key to pk. If A queries the corresponding decryption key, B aborts (outputting a random bit). Note that B will never abort if it guesses q and q' correctly, since a correct guess means that pk will be given out as a call to $\mathcal{O}(i, \mathsf{sen})$, and the security game then prohibits a request for the decryption key for i.

Upon receiving $(c_0 = (c, \pi), i')$ from A, B runs $(pk', \sigma, m_0, r_0) \leftarrow E_2(crs, \tau, (vk, c), \pi)$ (where T_4 implies that pk' was queried in an oracle call).

If $pk' \neq pk$ or $i' \neq Q[q']$ (B has not guessed q, q' correctly), then B aborts.

Otherwise B submits (m_0, r_0, m^*, r^*) for random m^*, r^* and receives a sanitized ciphertext c', which it gives to A. The received c' is a sanitization of either A's output c_0 (for which we have $c_0 = \mathsf{PKE.Enc}(pk, m_0; r_0)$) or of $\mathsf{PKE.Enc}(pk, m^*; r^*)$ (always assuming B's guesses were correct). B can answer *decryption key* oracle queries for all allowed queries.

Reduction B perfectly simulates either $H_3^{(0)}$ or H_4, depending on its own challenge: if B guesses q and q' correctly, it does not abort and otherwise it outputs a random bit anyway.

$\Pr[1 \leftarrow H_4 \,|\, T_4] \approx \Pr[1 \leftarrow H_3^{(1)} \,|\, T_4]$: Letting $((c, \pi), i')$ denote A's output, the two games differ in that m^* is encrypted under pk in H_4 (where pk is such that $c = \mathsf{PKE.Enc}(pk, m; r)$) and under i''s key in $H_3^{(1)}$. Indistinguishability follows from anonymity of the encryption scheme: We construct a PPT B, which receives pk_0 and pk_1, and simulates $H_3^{(1)}$ for A, except that it sets the q-th and the q'-th created keys to pk_0 and pk_1, respectively. (If $q = q'$ then it sets both to pk_0.) If A queries a corresponding decryption key, B aborts.

Upon receiving $(c_0 = (c, \pi), i')$ from A, B runs $(pk, \sigma, m, r) \leftarrow E_2(crs, \tau, (vk, c), \pi)$ and aborts if $pk \neq pk_0$ or if i' does not correspond to the q'th key (B's guess was wrong). If $q \neq q'$ then B submits a random m^* as a challenge to receive $\hat{c}$ from its challenger (which is m^* encrypted under pk_0 or pk_1); if $q = q'$ then B sets $\hat{c} = \mathsf{PKE.Enc}(pk_0, m^*, r^*)$. Next, B gives $c' \leftarrow \mathsf{PKE.San}(pp, \hat{c})$ to A.

Reduction B perfectly simulates either $H_3^{(1)}$ or H_4 (which are the same if $q = q'$), depending on its own challenge: if B guesses q and q' correctly, it does not abort and otherwise it outputs a random bit anyway.   □

The theorem now follows from Lemmas 2–5. Letting W_0 denote the event that A wins the No-Write game H_0, we have

$$\mathsf{adv}^A_{\mathsf{No\text{-}Write}}(ACE) = \Pr[W_0] - \tfrac{1}{2} \approx \Pr[W_2] - \tfrac{1}{2}$$

$$\leq \underbrace{\Pr[W_2 \wedge T_1]}_{\underset{=}{\text{Lemma 2}} 0} + \underbrace{\Pr[T_2]}_{\underset{\approx}{\text{Lemma 3}} 0} + \underbrace{\Pr[T_3]}_{\underset{\approx}{\text{Lemma 4}} 0} + \underbrace{\left(\Pr[W_2 \,|\, T_4] - \tfrac{1}{2}\right)}_{\underset{\approx}{\text{Lemma 5}} 0} \Pr[T_4] + \underbrace{\tfrac{1}{2}\Pr[T_4] - \tfrac{1}{2}}_{\leq 0}$$

$$\leq \mathsf{negl}.$$

□

Here we show how to instantiate the generic construction, based on the SXDH assumption (Corollary 1), or based on the generic group model (Corollary 2). Both instantiation use structure-preserving signatures (SPS) [AFG+10],

Groth-Sahai proofs [GS08] and the weakly sanitizable version of ElGamal encryption [Gam85] described in Sect. 3.3. In Corollary 1, we use the most efficient SPS scheme from SXDH, namely the one from [KPW15]. In Corollary 2, we use the most efficient SPS scheme with a security proof in the generic group model, which is [AGHO11]. The exact efficiency of the resulting ACE schemes are given in Table 2 on p. 23.

Corollary 1. *If the SXDH assumption holds, then by Theorems 1 and 2, Construction 1 instantiated with the signature scheme from [KPW15], Groth-Sahai proofs [GS08] and the weakly sanitizable version of ElGamal encryption [Gam85] from Sect. 3.3 satisfies the No-Read and No-Write rules.*

Corollary 2. *Theorems 1 and 2 imply that Construction 1 instantiated with the signature scheme from [AGHO11], Groth-Sahai proofs [GS08] and the weakly sanitizable version of ElGamal encryption [Gam85] satisfies the No-Read and No-Write rules in the generic group model.*

3.3 A More Efficient Construction from Pairings

Our next construction is based on ElGamal encryption, which is anonymous and re-randomizable; however, re-randomization of a ciphertext requires knowledge of its public key, so the sanitizer, who will randomize ciphertexts before passing them on, would be able to link ciphertexts to receivers.

Under a public key $pk = g^{sk}$, a message m is encrypted as $c_0 = g^r$, $c_1 = pk^r \cdot m$. In order to enable randomization without revealing the public key, the sender will *randomize* the public key as $d = (g^s, pk^s)$ for some random $s \neq 0$. Given c and d, the sanitizer now picks a random t and defines $c' := (c_0 \cdot d_0^t, c_1 \cdot d_1^t)$. Since $c' = (g^{r+st}, pk^{r+st} \cdot m)$ is an ElGamal encryption of m under pk, the receiver, who knows the corresponding secret key, can decrypt. On the other hand, t randomizes the ciphertext, thus to someone computationally bounded and not knowing sk, the pair looks random. This ensures anonymity towards the sanitizer and thus the no-read rule.

However, the no-write rule can easily be violated: a sender could send ciphertexts under any key and since the key is hidden, this would even be hard to detect. To enforce sending ciphertexts under legitimate keys, in the previous construction keys were signed; but without again resorting to proofs, it seems hard to verify that the key underlying the randomized key d was signed.

Fortunately, structure-preserving signatures on equivalence classes (SPS-EQ) [HS14] achieve precisely what is needed here, so the sketched construction goes through without including any proofs in the ciphertext. This primitives allows signing of pairs (d_0, d_1) of group elements and adapting such signatures to multiples of the message. In particular, given a signature σ on (d_0, d_1), anyone can adapt the signature to (d_0^s, d_1^s) for any s. On the other hand, unforgeability guarantees that these are the only transformations one can do. The signatures are thus valid on all messages from the equivalence class

$$[(d_0, d_1)]_{\mathcal{R}} := \{(m_0, m_1) \mid \exists s : m_0 = d_0^s \wedge m_1 = d_1^s\}.$$

Adaptivity of SPS-EQ requires that signatures that were adapted to a multiple of the original message are indistinguishable from a fresh signature on the multiple.

Enforcement of the no-read rule follows in a straightforward fashion from DDH (the tuple $(g^r, pk^r \cdot m, g^s, pk^s)$ is indistinguishable from random under DDH and an instance can be embedded by using the adaptivity property of SPS-EQ). Enforcement of the no-write rule is harder to prove and relies on unforgeability for SPS-EQ (which precludes the attack sketched above). The latter ensures that the values (d_0, d_1) sent by the adversary must be multiples of (g, pk_i) for some pk_i obtained from the key oracle.

The tricky part is that once the reduction embeds a DDH challenge, it cannot find out *which* public key was used, and so cannot simulate the game. We thus rely on the knowledge-of-exponent assumption which implies that for any adversary that is given (g, pk) and returns (g^s, pk^s) there exists an extractor that extracts s from the adversary. Now the reduction can guess which public key pk_i the adversary randomizes and *efficiently check* whether its guess was correct. If it is not the case, the reduction can abort and output a random bit. (If the reduction does not abort when its simulation is incorrect, we do not have any guarantees as to the adversary's behavior.)

Bilinear Groups. A bilinear-group generator BG.Gen is a PPT algorithm that takes input a security parameter 1^κ and outputs a description BG of a bilinear group $(p, \mathbb{G}_1, \mathbb{G}_2, \mathbb{G}_T, e, g, \hat{g})$, where p is a prime of length κ; $\mathbb{G}_1$, $\mathbb{G}_2$ and $\mathbb{G}_T$ are groups of order p; g generates $\mathbb{G}_1$, $\hat{g}$ generates $\mathbb{G}_2$ and $e \colon \mathbb{G}_1 \times \mathbb{G}_2 \to \mathbb{G}_T$ is a bilinear map that is non-degenerate, i.e. $e(g, \hat{g})$ generates $\mathbb{G}_T$.

We say that the DDH assumption holds in $\mathbb{G}_1$ for BG.Gen if no PPT adversary A, given $(p, \mathbb{G}_1, \mathbb{G}_2, \mathbb{G}_T, e, g, \hat{g}) \leftarrow$ BG.Gen(1^κ), and (S, T, U) with $s, t, u \leftarrow \mathbb{Z}_p^*$, $b \leftarrow \{0,1\}$ and $S = g^s$, $T = g^t$, $U = g^{(1-b)u+bst}$, can decide b with non-negligible advantage. It holds in $\mathbb{G}_2$ if the same is true when g is replaced by $\hat{g}$. We say that SXDH holds for BG.Gen if DDH holds in both $\mathbb{G}_1$ and $\mathbb{G}_2$.

SPS-EQ. A *structure-preserving signature scheme on equivalence classes* [HS14, FHS15] consists of the following PPT algorithms:

EQS.Gen, on input a bilinear group BG and a vector length $\ell > 1$ (in unary) outputs a key pair (sk, pk). EQS.Sig takes a secret key sk and a representative $M = (m_1, \ldots, m_\ell) \in (\mathbb{G}_1^*)^\ell$ of class $[M]_\mathcal{R}$ and outputs a signature σ for the equivalence class $[M]_\mathcal{R}$. EQS.Adp, on input a representative $M \in (\mathbb{G}_1^*)^\ell$, a signature σ for M, a scalar μ and a public key pk, returns an updated signature σ' for the new representative $M' = M^\mu := (m_1^\mu, \ldots, m_\ell^\mu)$. EQS.Ver takes a representative $M \in (\mathbb{G}_1^*)^\ell$, a signature σ and a public key pk and outputs 1 if σ is valid for M under pk and 0 otherwise. EQS.VfK checks if a secret key sk corresponds to a public key pk and if so returns 1 and 0 otherwise.

The scheme should satisfy correctness, existential unforgeability under chosen-message attacks (EUF-CMA) and perfect signature adaptation. Let $M \in \mathbb{G}_1^*$, $\mu \in \mathbb{Z}_p^*$, and (sk, pk) be output by EQS.Gen; σ by EQS.Sig(sk, M); and σ' by EQS.Adp(M, σ, μ, pk). Then the scheme is *correct* if EQS.VfK$(sk, pk) = 1$, EQS.Ver$(M, \sigma) = 1$ and EQS.Ver$(M^\mu, \sigma') = 1$.

Unforgeability is defined w.r.t. equivalence classes, i.e., a forgery must be on a message from an equivalence class for which the forger has not seen signatures.

Definition 5 (EUF-CMA). *Consider the following game for an adversary A:*

<table>
<tr><th colspan="2">EUF-CMA Game for SPS-EQ</th></tr>
<tr><th>Game Definition</th><th>Oracle Definition</th></tr>
<tr>
<td>

1. $BG \leftarrow \mathsf{BG.Gen}(1^\kappa)$;
2. $(sk, pk) \leftarrow \mathsf{EQS.Gen}(BG, 1^\ell)$;
3. $(M^*, \sigma^*) \leftarrow A^{\mathcal{O}(\cdot)}(pk)$;

</td>
<td>

$\mathcal{O}(M)$:
1. Return $\mathsf{EQS.Sig}(sk, M)$;

</td>
</tr>
</table>

Let Q be the set of all queries that A issues to $\mathcal{O}$. Then we say that A wins the EUF-CMA game if the following hold:

1. For all $M \in Q$: $[M^*]_{\mathcal{R}} \neq [M]_{\mathcal{R}}$;
2. $\mathsf{EQS.Ver}(M^*, \sigma^*, pk) = 1$

An SPS-EQ scheme is EUF-CMA *if for all $\ell > 1$ and all PPT algorithms A*

$$\mathsf{adv}^A_{\mathsf{EUF\text{-}CMA}}(SPS\text{-}EQ) = \Pr[A \text{ wins the } EUF\text{-}CMA \text{ game}] \leq \mathsf{negl}(\kappa).$$

The final property requires that signatures adapted by EQS.Adp are distributed like fresh signatures from EQS.Sig.

Definition 6 (Signature Adaptation). *An SPS-EQ scheme perfectly adapts signatures if for all tuples $\ell > 1$, (sk, pk, M, σ, μ) with*

$$\mathsf{EQS.VfK}(sk, pk) = 1 \qquad \mathsf{EQS.Ver}(M, \sigma, pk) = 1 \qquad M \in (\mathbb{G}_1^*)^\ell \qquad \mu \in \mathbb{Z}_p^*$$

$\mathsf{EQS.Adp}(M, \sigma, \mu, pk)$ *and* $\mathsf{EQS.Sig}(sk, M^\mu)$ *are identically distributed.*

The most efficient construction of SPS-EQ is the following from [FHS14]. It has perfect signature adaptation and satisfies EUF-CMA in the generic group model (GGM).

<table>
<tr><th colspan="2">SPS-EQ Construction from [FHS14]</th></tr>
<tr>
<td>

$\mathsf{EQS.Gen}(BG, 1^\ell)$:
  Choose $(x_i)_{i \in [\ell]} \leftarrow (\mathbb{Z}_p^*)^\ell$;
  $sk \leftarrow (x_i)_{i \in [\ell]}$; $pk \leftarrow (\hat{g}^{x_i})_{i \in [\ell]}$;
  Return (sk, pk);

$\mathsf{EQS.Sig}((x_i)_{i \in [\ell]}, M)$: //$M \in (\mathbb{G}_1^*)^\ell$;
  Choose $y \leftarrow \mathbb{Z}_p^*$;
  Return $\sigma = \left(\prod m_i^{x_i y}, g^{y^{-1}}, \hat{g}^{y^{-1}}\right)$;

$\mathsf{EQS.Adp}(pk, M, \sigma = (Z, Y, \hat{Y}), \mu)$: //$\mu \in \mathbb{Z}_p^*$
  if $\mathsf{EQS.Ver}(pk, M, \sigma) = 0$, return $\perp$;
  Choose $\psi \leftarrow \mathbb{Z}_p^*$;
  Return $\sigma' = (Z^{\psi\mu}, Y^{\psi^{-1}}, \hat{Y}^{\psi^{-1}})$;

</td>
<td>

$\mathsf{EQS.Ver}(pk, M, \sigma = (Z, Y, \hat{Y}))$
  Return 1 if all of the following hold:
  $Y \neq 1$;
  $\prod_{i \in [\ell]} e(M_i, \hat{X}_i) = e(Z, \hat{Y})$;
  $e(Y, \hat{g}) = e(g, \hat{Y})$;
  Else return 0;

$\mathsf{EQS.Ver}(sk = (x_i), pk = (\hat{X}_i))$:
  If for all $i \in [\ell] : \hat{X}_i = \hat{g}^{x_i}$;
    then return 1;
  Else return 0;

</td>
</tr>
</table>

KEA. The knowledge of exponent assumption [BP04] for a bilinear group generator BG.Gen states that for every PPT algorithm A, which given the output $(p, \mathbb{G}_1, \mathbb{G}_2, \mathbb{G}_T, e, g, \hat{g})$ of BG.Gen and a random $h \leftarrow \mathbb{G}_1$ as input outputs g^s, h^s for some s, there exists a PPT extractor which, when given the coins of A as input, extracts s with non-negligible probability. Note that KEA trivially holds in the GGM, and since for our most efficient construction we already work in the GGM to use SPS-EQ, this is not an extra assumption.

Construction 2 (ACE for Equality – Pairing). *We construct an ACE scheme* ACE = (Setup, Gen, Enc, San, Dec) *defined by the following algorithms:*

Setup: Given a bilinear group $BG = (p, \mathbb{G}_1, \mathbb{G}_2, \mathbb{G}_T, g, \hat{g}, e)$, run $(sk, vk) \leftarrow$ EQS.Gen(BG), pick a PRF key K and return $pp = (BG, vk)$ and $msk = (sk, K)$.
Key Generation: Define $dk_i = F_K(0||i)$ and $pk_i = g^{dk_i}$, and compute $\sigma_i =$ EQS.Sig$(sk, (g, pk_i); F_K(1||i))$; Return $ek_i = (pk_i, \sigma_i)$ and dk_i.
Encryption: On input a message m and an encryption key $ek_i = (pk_i, \sigma_i)$, pick randomness $r, s \leftarrow \mathbb{Z}_p^*$ and compute $\sigma' \leftarrow$ EQS.Adp$(vk, (g, pk_i), \sigma_i, s)$ and return
$$c_0 = g^r, \quad c_1 = pk_i^r \cdot m, \quad c_2 = g^s, \quad c_3 = pk_i^s, \quad \sigma'.$$
Sanitizer: If EQS.Ver$(vk, (c_2, c_3), \sigma') = 0$ then output $\bot$. Else choose a random t and return
$$c_0' = c_0 \cdot c_2^t, \quad c_1' = c_1 \cdot c_3^t.$$
Decryption: Return $m = c_1' \cdot (c_0')^{-dk_j}$.

Correctness follows by inspection, and detectability of the ACE follows from the detectability of the underlying PKE we use, namely ElGamal. We will now show that the scheme also satisfies the no-read and the no-write rule.

Theorem 3. *Construction 2 satisfies the No-Read Rule if the PRF is pseudorandom, the SPS-EQ scheme has perfect adaptivity and the DDH assumption holds in $\mathbb{G}_1$.*

Proof. Plugging Construction 2 into the security game yields the game in Fig. 1 (where we replaced PRF values by consistent random values). The proof is similar to that of Theorem 3 also proceeds by a series of hybrid games.

Game H: As the original game but at the beginning the challenger makes a random guess q from $\{1, \ldots, q_{max}\}$ where q_{max} is a bound on the number of $\mathcal{O}_G(\cdot, \mathsf{sen})$ queries plus the number of $\mathcal{O}_E(\cdot, \cdot)$ queries. Let $(j^*, \cdot)$ be the qth such query. If $j^* \neq i_b$, the challenger returns a random bit as the output of the game.
No-Write Game $\rightarrow H$: This results in a polynomial loss $\frac{1}{q_{max}}$ in the adversary's winning probability, shown analogously to Lemma 1. If the latter was non-negligible before, it is so afterwards.
Game $H_{b,1}$: As hybrid H with b fixed and the values of the PRF replaced with (consistent) random values.

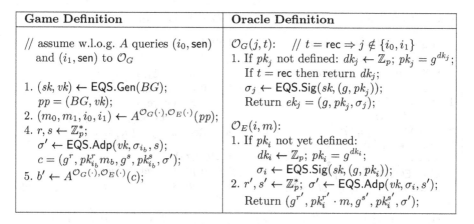

Game Definition	Oracle Definition
// assume w.l.o.g. A queries (i_0, sen) and (i_1, sen) to $\mathcal{O}_G$ 1. $(sk, vk) \leftarrow \mathsf{EQS.Gen}(BG)$; 　　$pp = (BG, vk)$; 2. $(m_0, m_1, i_0, i_1) \leftarrow A^{\mathcal{O}_G(\cdot), \mathcal{O}_E(\cdot)}(pp)$; 4. $r, s \leftarrow \mathbb{Z}_p^*$; 　　$\sigma' \leftarrow \mathsf{EQS.Adp}(vk, \sigma_{i_b}, s)$; 　　$c = (g^r, pk_{i_b}^r m_b, g^s, pk_{i_b}^s, \sigma')$; 5. $b' \leftarrow A^{\mathcal{O}_G(\cdot), \mathcal{O}_E(\cdot)}(c)$;	$\mathcal{O}_G(j, t)$:　　// $t = \mathsf{rec} \Rightarrow j \notin \{i_0, i_1\}$ 1. If pk_j not defined: $dk_j \leftarrow \mathbb{Z}_p$; $pk_j = g^{dk_j}$; 　　If $t = \mathsf{rec}$ then return dk_j; 　　$\sigma_j \leftarrow \mathsf{EQS.Sig}(sk, (g, pk_j))$; 　　Return $ek_j = (g, pk_j, \sigma_j)$; $\mathcal{O}_E(i, m)$: 1. If pk_i not yet defined: 　　$dk_i \leftarrow \mathbb{Z}_p$; $pk_i = g^{dk_i}$; 　　$\sigma_i \leftarrow \mathsf{EQS.Sig}(sk, (g, pk_i))$; 2. $r', s' \leftarrow \mathbb{Z}_p^*$; $\sigma' \leftarrow \mathsf{EQS.Adp}(vk, \sigma_i, s')$; 　　Return $(g^{r'}, pk_i^{r'} \cdot m, g^{s'}, pk_i^{s'}, \sigma')$;

Fig. 1. No-Read Rule for Construction 2 for fixed b and PRF outputs replaced by random

$H_b \approx_c H_{b,1}$: The games are indistinguishable by PRF security.

Game $H_{b,2}$: As $H_{b,1}$, but instead of running EQS.Adp, σ' is computed as a fresh signature on $(g^s, pk_{i_b}^s)$.

$H_{b,1} \approx_c H_{b,2}$: The two games are equally distributed by the *perfect signature-adaptation* property of SPS-EQ.

Game $H_{b,3}$: Defined as $H_{b,2}$, except c is replaced by $c = (g^r, pk_{i_b}^r m_b, g^s, pk_{i_b}^t, \sigma')$, that is, the 4th component is random.

$H_{b,2} \approx_c H_{b,3}$: Indistinguishable under DDH. Note that pk_{i_b} is known in advance (as i_b is guessed as j^*) and that dk_i is not revealed and s is not used anywhere else (since $H_{b,2}$). The reduction can thus replace the values $(g, pk_{i_b}, g^s, pk_{i_b}^s)$ with a DDH challenge.

Game $H_{b,4}$: Defined as $H_{b,3}$, except c is replaced by $c = (g^r, pk_{i_b}^u m_b, g^s, pk_{i_b}^t, \sigma')$, that is, the 2nd component is random.

$H_{b,3} \approx_c H_{b,4}$: Indistinguishable under DDH. The reduction replaces the values $(g, pk_{i_b}, g^r, pk_{i_b}^r)$ with a DDH challenge.

Since $H_{0,4} \equiv H_{1,4}$ (in both the adversary receives c which consists of 4 random group elements and a signature on the last 2), we showed that H_0 and H_1 are indistinguishable, which contradicts the assumption that A distinguishes them. $\qquad \square$

Theorem 4. *Construction 2 satisfies the No-Write Rule if the PRF is pseudorandom, the SPS-EQ scheme is unforgeable, and KEA and DDH hold in $\mathbb{G}_1$.*

Proof. As it is straightforward to prove indistinguishability to the original game, let us immediately assume that all calls to the PRF are replaced by (consistent) random values, which yields the game described in Fig. 2. (Note that in the definition of $\mathcal{O}_E$, we need not generate σ in Gen, as it is then discarded by San anyway.)

We first distinguish between two types of PPT adversaries:

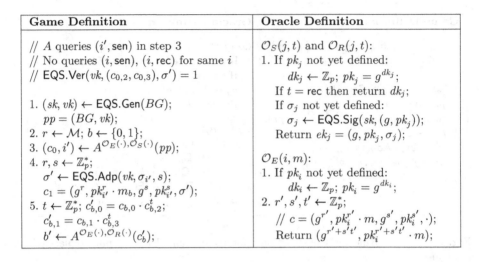

Game Definition	Oracle Definition
// A queries (i', sen) in step 3 // No queries (i, sen), (i, rec) for same i // $\mathsf{EQS.Ver}(vk, (c_{0,2}, c_{0,3}), \sigma') = 1$ 1. $(sk, vk) \leftarrow \mathsf{EQS.Gen}(BG)$; $\quad pp = (BG, vk)$; 2. $r \leftarrow \mathcal{M}$; $b \leftarrow \{0,1\}$; 3. $(c_0, i') \leftarrow A^{\mathcal{O}_E(\cdot), \mathcal{O}_S(\cdot)}(pp)$; 4. $r, s \leftarrow \mathbb{Z}_p^*$; $\quad \sigma' \leftarrow \mathsf{EQS.Adp}(vk, \sigma_{i'}, s)$; $\quad c_1 = (g^r, pk_{i'}^r \cdot m_b, g^s, pk_{i'}^s, \sigma')$; 5. $t \leftarrow \mathbb{Z}_p^*$; $c'_{b,0} = c_{b,0} \cdot c_{b,2}^t$; $\quad c'_{b,1} = c_{b,1} \cdot c_{b,3}^t$ $\quad b' \leftarrow A^{\mathcal{O}_E(\cdot), \mathcal{O}_R(\cdot)}(c'_b)$;	$\mathcal{O}_S(j, t)$ and $\mathcal{O}_R(j, t)$: 1. If pk_j not yet defined: $\quad dk_j \leftarrow \mathbb{Z}_p$; $pk_j = g^{dk_j}$; $\quad$ If $t = \mathsf{rec}$ then return dk_j; $\quad$ If σ_j not yet defined: $\qquad \sigma_j \leftarrow \mathsf{EQS.Sig}(sk, (g, pk_j))$; $\quad$ Return $ek_j = (g, pk_j, \sigma_j)$; $\mathcal{O}_E(i, m)$: 1. If pk_i not yet defined: $\quad dk_i \leftarrow \mathbb{Z}_p$; $pk_i = g^{dk_i}$; 2. $r', s', t' \leftarrow \mathbb{Z}_p^*$; $\quad$ // $c = (g^{r'}, pk_i^{r'} \cdot m, g^{s'}, pk_i^{s'}, \cdot)$; $\quad$ Return $(g^{r'+s't'}, pk_i^{r'+s't'} \cdot m)$;

Fig. 2. No-Write Rule for Construction 2 and PRF outputs replaced by random

Type 1 returns c_0, which contains an SPS-EQ forgery with non-negligible probability; that is, $(c_{0,2}, c_{0,3})$ is *not* a multiple of any (g, pk_i) where pk_i is the key obtained from oracle call $\mathcal{O}_G(i, \mathsf{sen})$.

Type 2 returns such a forgery with negligible probability only.

Breaking EUF-CMA of SPS-EQ can be reduced to Type 1 forgeries in a straightforward fashion: the PPT reduction B simulates the no-write game using the given vk and replacing all calls of $\mathsf{EQS.Sig}(sk, (g, pk_i))$ by queries to its signature oracle; when A outputs $c_0 = (c_{0,0}, c_{0,1}, c_{0,2}, c_{0,3}, \sigma_0)$ then B returns σ_0 as a forgery on $M = (c_{0,2}, c_{0,3})$. By assumption (Type 1), with non-negligible probability M is not a multiple of the messages (g, pk_i) queried to the signing oracle; B thus breaks EUF-CMA.

We now show how to use Type 2 adversaries to break DDH assuming KEA. Let $q_{\max}$ denote an upper bound on the number of A's queries $(\cdot, \mathsf{sen})$ to $\mathcal{O}_S$ and $\mathcal{O}_R$ plus the number of queries to $\mathcal{O}_E$.

We first construct a PPT algorithm B with input (g, h). B picks two uniform values $q_0, q_1 \leftarrow [q_{\max}]$ and simulates the no-write game for A, except for the following changes: when the q_0th key pk is created during an oracle query $(j_0, \cdot)$, B sets $pk_{j_0} = h$. Let j_1 be the index of the q_1th key created. If A later queries (j_0, rec) or (j_1, rec) to $\mathcal{O}_S$ or $\mathcal{O}_R$ then B aborts. When A outputs (c_0, i') then B stops and returns $(c_{0,2}, c_{0,3})$.

Let us analyze B's behavior: Since A is of Type 2, we know that with overwhelming (i.e. all except with negligible) probability, A outputs (c_0, i') with $(c_{0,2}, c_{0,c}) = (g^a, pk_j^a)$, for some a and j s.t. (j, sen) was queried to $\mathcal{O}_S$ or $\mathcal{O}_R$. Now with probability $\frac{1}{q_{\max}^2}$, we have $j = j_0$ and $i' = j_1$. This event is independent of A's view and if it occurs then B's simulation does not abort: by assumption A makes queries (j, sen) and (i', sen) and can therefore not make queries (j, rec) and (i', rec).

With probability at least $\frac{1}{q_{max}^2} - \text{negl}(\kappa)$, B thus returns (g^a, h^a) for some a. Assuming KEA there exists thus an extractor X that, given B's coins, outputs a.

We now consider the following hybrid H of the no-write-rule game: first choose $h \leftarrow \mathbb{G}_1$ and $j_0, j_1 \leftarrow [q_{max}]$ then run the game setting $pk_{j_1} = h$. On the same coins as used to run the game run X and let a be its output. If A's output (c_0, i') satisfies

$$(c_{0,2}, c_{0,3}) = (g^a, pk_{j_0}^a) \tag{3}$$

and $i' = j_1$ then return A's final output b'. Else return a random bit $b' \leftarrow \{0,1\}$

Since H, until the event that A outputs c_0 is defined as B, X's output a satisfies (3) with non-negligible probability, as shown above. The probability that hybrid game H outputs A's bit b' is thus non-negligible.

Further note that setting $h = pk_{j_0}$ is only a syntactical change, so H differs from the original game only in the event that the latter aborts (outputting a random bit). An analysis analogue to "$0 \rightarrow 1$" in the proof of Theorem 3 shows that if A wins the original game with non-negligible probability then it wins H with non-negligible probability.

Define H_β as H with b fixed to β. Our last step is now to show that under DDH A cannot distinguish H_0 from H_1, which contradicts A winning H and concludes the proof.

For this, we define another hybrid H'_β which modifies H_β in that c'_β is defined as $(c_{\beta,0} \cdot c_{\beta,2}^t, c_{\beta,1} \cdot U)$, where U is a uniform group element. Thus, c'_β is a uniformly random pair and so the game H'_β is independent of β. Therefore H'_0 is distributed as H'_1. What remains to show is that H_β is indistinguishable from H'_β.

We first show that H_0 is indistinguishable from H'_0. The games only differ when X returns a satisfying (3) (otherwise both output a random bit). In this case $h = pk_{j_0}$. Consider a DDH adversary D_0 that receives a challenge $(P, T = g^t, U)$ where either $U = P^t$ or U is random. D_0 simulates H_0 setting $h = P$ and associating the values t from the challenge and the game: it sets $c_{0,2}^t = T^a$ and $c_{0,3} = U^a$. If $U = P^t$ then D_0 simulates H_0; otherwise it simulates H'_0.

Finally, H'_1 is shown indistinguishable from H_1 by a similar reduction: on input a DDH challenge (P, T, U), D_1 simulates H_1, except that it sets $pk_{j_1} = P$ and $c_{1,2}^t = T^s$ and $c_{1,3} = U^s$. If $U = P^t$ then D_1 simulates H_1; otherwise it simulates H'_1. $\square$

Using Theorems 3 and 4 with the SPS-EQ from [FHS14], which has perfect signature adaptation and satisfies EUF-CMA in the generic group model (GGM), we obtain the following corollary. The concrete efficiency of the resulting scheme is given in Table 2.

Corollary 3. *In the generic group model, Construction 2 instantiated with the SPS-EQ from [FHS14] satisfies the No-Read and No-Write rules.*

3.4 Comparing the Two Constructions

In Table 2 we compare the efficiency and the assumptions required for our constructions. The most efficient way to instantiate the generic construction from

Sect. 3.2 is via structure-preserving signatures (SPS) [AFG+16], Groth-Sahai proofs [GS08] and the weakly sanitizable version of ElGamal encryption [Gam85] described in Sect. 3.3. The security of the latter two relies on the SXDH assumption. The most efficient SPS scheme from SXDH is the one from [KPW15] (signatures from $\mathbb{G}_1^6 \times \mathbb{G}_2$, public keys from $\mathbb{G}_2^7$). The most efficient SPS scheme with a security proof in the generic group model (GGM) is from [AGHO11] (signatures from $\mathbb{G}_1^2 \times \mathbb{G}_2$, public keys from $\mathbb{G}_1 \times \mathbb{G}_2^3$). See Corollaries 1 and 2. We also include Construction 2 from Sect. 3.3, which does not require zero-knowledge proofs, and which we proved secure in the GGM.

Table 2. Comparison of the constructions in Sects. 3.2 and 3.3. In all cases pp also includes the description of the group. A ciphertext produced by Enc is denoted by c while c' denotes a sanitized ciphertext, output of San.

Construction	pp	ek	dk	c	c'	Assumpt'n
Generic[·, ·]	$vk + crs$	$1\mathbb{G}_1 + sig$	$1\mathbb{Z}_p$	$4\mathbb{G}_1 + \pi$	$2\mathbb{G}_1$	
Generic[KPW15, GS12]	$4\mathbb{G}_1 + 11\mathbb{G}_2$	$7\mathbb{G}_1 + 1\mathbb{G}_2$	$1\mathbb{Z}_p$	$34\mathbb{G}_1 + 16\mathbb{G}_2$	$2\mathbb{G}_1$	SXDH
Generic[AGHO11, GS12]	$5\mathbb{G}_1 + 7\mathbb{G}_2$	$3\mathbb{G}_1 + 1\mathbb{G}_2$	$1\mathbb{Z}_p$	$20\mathbb{G}_1 + 14\mathbb{G}_2$	$2\mathbb{G}_1$	GGM
Construction 2 (Sect. 3.3)	$2\mathbb{G}_2$	$3\mathbb{G}_1 + 1\mathbb{G}_2$	$1\mathbb{Z}_p$	$6\mathbb{G}_1 + 1\mathbb{G}_2$	$2\mathbb{G}_1$	GGM

4   ACE for Disjunction of Equalities

In this section we show how to use the equality ACE scheme in a black-box way to implement more interesting predicates. Intuitively, as stated in the introduction, this is done by assigning sets of identities for the ACE scheme to each sender and receiver, in such a way that the intersection between the set $S(i)$ of identities given to sender i and the set $R(j)$ of identities given to receiver j is non-empty if and only if $P(i, j) = 1$. Note however that in this case a receiver, to be able to decrypt, would have to try each decryption key on each ciphertext, thus resulting in quadratic complexity. To avoid this, we compose our scheme using the following *disjunction of equalities* predicate instead: here each sender is assigned a *vector* of identities $\mathbf{x}$ and each receiver a vector of identities $\mathbf{y}$, and the predicate is defined as $\mathsf{P}_{\mathsf{or\text{-}eq}} : \mathcal{D}^\ell \times \mathcal{D}^\ell \to \{0, 1\}$, and

$$\mathsf{P}_{\mathsf{or\text{-}eq}}(\mathbf{x}, \mathbf{y}) = 1 \;\Leftrightarrow\; \bigvee_{i=1}^{\ell} (x_i = y_i).$$

We give a generic construction that relies on any ACE for equality, namely, for the predicate $\mathsf{P}_{\mathsf{eq}} : (\mathcal{D} \times [\ell]) \times (\mathcal{D} \times [\ell]) \to \{0, 1\}$, defined by

$$\mathsf{P}_{\mathsf{eq}}((x, i), (y, j)) = 1 \;\Leftrightarrow\; x = y \text{ and } i = j,$$

such as those of Sect. 3.[3]

---

[3] To use an ACE for predicate $\mathsf{P}_{\mathsf{eq}} : \{0, 1\}^n \times \{0, 1\}^n \to \{0, 1\}$, such as those in Sect. 3, one uses an injective hash function from $\mathcal{D} \times [\ell]$ to $\{0, 1\}^n$, which exists as long as $2^n \geq |\mathcal{D}| \cdot [\ell]$.

Construction 3 (ACE for Disjunction of Equality–Generic). *We construct an ACE scheme $\mathsf{ACE}_{\text{or-eq}}$ for $\mathsf{P}_{\text{or-eq}}$ from an ACE scheme $\mathsf{ACE}_{\text{eq}} = (\mathsf{Setup}_{\text{eq}}, \mathsf{Gen}_{\text{eq}}, \mathsf{Enc}_{\text{eq}}, \mathsf{San}_{\text{eq}}, \mathsf{Dec}_{\text{eq}})$ for P_{eq}. $\mathsf{ACE}_{\text{or-eq}}$ is defined by the following algorithms:*

Setup: Output $(pp, msk) \leftarrow \mathsf{Setup}_{\text{eq}}(1^\kappa)$.

Key Generation: Given the master secret key msk and vectors $\mathbf{x}, \mathbf{y} \in \mathcal{D}^\ell$, the encryption and decryption keys are computed as follows:

$$ek_{\mathbf{x}} = (ek_{(x_1,1)}, \ldots, ek_{(x_\ell,\ell)}) \text{ with } ek_{(x_i,i)} \leftarrow \mathsf{Gen}_{\text{eq}}(msk, (x_i, i), \mathsf{sen}) \text{ for } i \in [\ell];$$
$$dk_{\mathbf{y}} = (dk_{(y_1,1)}, \ldots, dk_{(y_\ell,\ell)}) \text{ with } dk_{(y_i,i)} \leftarrow \mathsf{Gen}_{\text{eq}}(msk, (y_i, i), \mathsf{rec}) \text{ for } i \in [\ell].$$

Encryption: On input a message m and an encryption key $ek_{\mathbf{x}} = (ek_{(x_1,1)}, \ldots, ek_{(x_\ell,\ell)})$ pick some independent randomness $r_1, \ldots, r_\ell$, compute

$$c_i = \mathsf{Enc}(ek_{(x_i,i)}, m; r_i),$$

for $i \in [\ell]$, and output $c = (c_1, \ldots, c_\ell)$.

Sanitizer: Given a ciphertext $c = (c_1, \ldots, c_\ell)$, apply San_{eq} component-wise.

Decryption: Given a ciphertext $c = (c_1, \ldots, c_\ell)$ and a decryption key $dk_{\mathbf{y}} = (dk_{(y_1,1)}, \ldots, dk_{(y_\ell,\ell)})$ for $\mathbf{y} \in \mathcal{D}^\ell$, compute $\mathsf{Dec}(dk_{(y_i,i)}, c_i)$ for $i \in [\ell]$. Let $m_i = \mathsf{Dec}(dk_{(y_i,i)}, c_i)$, then output the first $m_i \neq \perp$ or $\perp$ if there is no such successful decryption.

Remark: Note that the complexity of the composed scheme, including the decryption algorithm, is linear in ℓ.

Lemma 6 (Correctness and Detectability). *Construction 3 is correct, according to Definition 1.*

Proof. For all $i \in [\ell]$ and $x_i, y_i \in \mathcal{D}$ such that $x_i = y_i$,

$$\Pr[\mathsf{Dec}_{\text{eq}}(dk_{(y_i,i)}, \mathsf{San}_{\text{eq}}(\mathsf{Enc}_{\text{eq}}(ek_{(x_i,i)}, m))) = m] \geq 1 - \mathsf{negl}(\kappa),$$

by correctness of ACE_{eq}. Moreover, by detectability of ACE_{eq}, for all $x_i, y_i \in \mathcal{D}$ such that $x_i \neq y_i$, we have:

$$\Pr[\mathsf{Dec}_{\text{eq}}(dk_{(y_i,i)}, \mathsf{San}_{\text{eq}}(\mathsf{Enc}_{\text{eq}}(ek_{(x_i,i)}, m))) = \perp] \geq 1 - \mathsf{negl}(\kappa).$$

Therefore, by a union bound over the ℓ disjunctions, we obtain that for all $\mathbf{x}, \mathbf{y} \in \mathcal{D}^\ell$ such that $\mathsf{P}_{\text{or-eq}}(\mathbf{x}, \mathbf{y}) = 1$:

$$\Pr[\mathsf{Dec}(dk_{\mathbf{x}}, \mathsf{San}(pp, \mathsf{Enc}(ek_{\mathbf{x}}, m))) = m] \geq 1 - \mathsf{negl}(\kappa),$$

that is, $\mathsf{ACE}_{\text{or-eq}}$ is correct. A similar argument is used to show that $\mathsf{ACE}_{\text{or-eq}}$ is detectable. $\qquad\square$

Lemma 7 (No-Read-Rule). *If the underlying ACE_{eq} for P_{eq} satisfies the No-Read-Rule from Definition 3, then so does $\mathsf{ACE}_{\text{or-eq}}$ from Construction 3. In particular, for any PPT adversary A against the No-Read-Rule for $\mathsf{ACE}_{\text{or-eq}}$, there exists a PPT adversary B such that*

$$\mathsf{adv}^A_{\text{No-Read}}(\mathsf{ACE}_{\text{or-eq}}) \leq \ell \cdot \mathsf{adv}^B_{\text{No-Read}}(\mathsf{ACE}_{\text{eq}}).$$

Proof. We define $\ell+1$ hybrid games, where for all $i \in [\ell+1]$, Hybrid i is defined as in the table below.

Hybrid i	Oracle Definition
1. $(pp, msk) \leftarrow \mathsf{Setup}(1^\kappa, \mathsf{P_{or\text{-}eq}})$; 2. $(m_0, m_1, \mathbf{x}^{(0)}, \mathbf{x}^{(1)}) \leftarrow A^{\mathcal{O}_G(\cdot), \mathcal{O}_E(\cdot)}(pp)$; 3. For $j \leq i-1$: $c_j \leftarrow \mathsf{Enc_{eq}}(ek_{(x_j^{(1)}, j)}, m_1)$. For $j \geq i$: $c_j \leftarrow \mathsf{Enc_{eq}}(ek_{(x_j^{(0)}, j)}, m_0)$. 4. $b' \leftarrow A^{\mathcal{O}_G(\cdot), \mathcal{O}_E(\cdot)}(c_1, \ldots, c_\ell)$;	$\mathcal{O}_G(j, t)$: 1. Output $k \leftarrow \mathsf{Gen}(msk, j, t)$; $\mathcal{O}_E(i, m)$: 1. $ek_i \leftarrow \mathsf{Gen}(msk, i, \mathsf{sen})$; 2. Output $c \leftarrow \mathsf{Enc}(ek_i, m)$;

We say an adversary A wins hybrid i if it returns 1 and $|m_0| = |m_1|$, $\mathbf{x}^{(0)}$, $\mathbf{x}^{(1)} \in \mathcal{D}^\ell$, and for all queries q to $\mathcal{O}_G$ with $q = (\mathbf{y}, \mathsf{rec})$ it holds that

$$\mathsf{P_{or\text{-}eq}}(\mathbf{x}^{(0)}, \mathbf{y}) = \mathsf{P_{or\text{-}eq}}(\mathbf{x}^{(1)}, \mathbf{y}) = 0.$$

Note that for any PPT adversary A,

$$\mathsf{adv}^A_{\mathsf{No\text{-}Read}}(\mathsf{ACE_{or\text{-}eq}}) \leq \tfrac{1}{2} \, | \Pr[A \text{ wins Hybrid } \ell + 1] - \Pr[A \text{ wins Hybrid } 1]|.$$

For all $i \in [\ell]$, we build a PPT adversary B_i, such that:

$$| \Pr[A \text{ wins Hybrid } i + 1] - \Pr[A \text{ wins Hybrid } i]| \leq 2 \cdot \mathsf{adv}^{B_i}_{\mathsf{No\text{-}Read}}(\mathsf{ACE_{eq}}),$$

thereby proving the lemma. This comes from the facts that $\mathsf{ACE_{eq}}$ satisfies the No-Read Rule, and that for all $\mathbf{y} \in \mathcal{D}^\ell$, $\mathsf{P_{or\text{-}eq}}(\mathbf{x}^{(0)}, \mathbf{y}) = \mathsf{P_{or\text{-}eq}}(\mathbf{x}^{(1)}, \mathbf{y}) = 0$ implies $\mathsf{P_{eq}}((x_i^{(0)}, i), (y_j, j)) = \mathsf{P_{eq}}((x_i^{(1)}, i), (y_j, j)) = 0$ for all $i, j \in [\ell]$. $\square$

Lemma 8 (No-Write Rule). *If the underlying $\mathsf{ACE_{eq}}$ for $\mathsf{P_{eq}}$ satisfies the No-Write Rule from Definition 4 and the No-Read-Rule from Definition 3, then $\mathsf{ACE_{or\text{-}eq}}$ from Construction 3 satisfies the No-Write rule. In particular, for any PPT adversary A against the No-Write Rule for $\mathsf{ACE_{or\text{-}eq}}$, there exist PPT adversaries B_1 and B_2 such that*

$$\mathsf{adv}^A_{\mathsf{No\text{-}Write}}(\mathsf{ACE_{or\text{-}eq}}) \leq \ell \cdot \mathsf{adv}^{B_1}_{\mathsf{No\text{-}Write}}(\mathsf{ACE_{eq}}) + 2\ell \cdot \mathsf{adv}^{B_2}_{\mathsf{No\text{-}Read}}(\mathsf{ACE_{eq}}).$$

Proof. As for the No-Read rule, we use a hybrid argument; for $i \in [2\ell]$ Hybrid i is defined in the tables below, where $m_0 \in \mathcal{M}$ is an arbitrary, fixed message:

Hybrid i, for $i \in [\ell+1]$	Oracle Definition
1. $(pp, msk) \leftarrow \mathsf{Setup}(1^\kappa, \mathsf{P_{or\text{-}eq}})$; 2. $((c_1^{(0)}, \ldots, c_\ell^{(0)}), \mathbf{x}') \leftarrow A^{\mathcal{O}_E(\cdot), \mathcal{O}_S(\cdot)}(pp)$; 3. $(c_1^{(1)}, \ldots, c_\ell^{(1)}) \leftarrow \mathsf{Enc}(\mathsf{Gen}(msk, \mathbf{x}', \mathsf{sen}), m_0)$; 4. $b' \leftarrow A^{\mathcal{O}_E(\cdot), \mathcal{O}_R(\cdot)}(\mathsf{San}(pp, c_1^{(1)}, \ldots, c_i^{(1)}, c_{i+1}^{(0)}, \ldots, c_\ell^{(0)}))$;	$\mathcal{O}_S(j, t)$ and $\mathcal{O}_R(j, t)$: 1. Output $k \leftarrow \mathsf{Gen}(msk, j, t)$; $\mathcal{O}_E(i, m)$: 1. $ek_i \leftarrow \mathsf{Gen}(msk, i, \mathsf{sen})$; 2. Output $\mathsf{San}(pp, \mathsf{Enc}(ek_i, m))$;

Hybrid $\ell + i$, for $i \in [\ell+1]$	Oracle Definition
1. $(pp, msk) \leftarrow \mathsf{Setup}(1^\kappa, \mathsf{P_{or\text{-}eq}})$; 2. $m_1 \leftarrow \mathcal{M}$ 3. $((c_1^{(0)}, \ldots, c_\ell^{(0)}), \mathbf{x}') \leftarrow B^{\mathcal{O}_E(\cdot), \mathcal{O}_S(\cdot)}(pp)$; 4. $(c_1^{(1)}, \ldots, c_\ell^{(1)}) \leftarrow \mathsf{Enc}(\mathsf{Gen}(msk, \mathbf{x}', \mathsf{sen}), m_0)$; 4. $(c_1^{(2)}, \ldots, c_\ell^{(2)}) \leftarrow \mathsf{Enc}(\mathsf{Gen}(msk, \mathbf{x}', \mathsf{sen}), m_1)$; 5. $b' \leftarrow B^{\mathcal{O}_E(\cdot), \mathcal{O}_R(\cdot)}(\mathsf{San}(pp, c_1^{(2)}, \ldots, c_i^{(2)},$ $\qquad\qquad\qquad\qquad c_{i+1}^{(1)}, \ldots, c_\ell^{(1)}))$;	$\mathcal{O}_S(j, t)$ and $\mathcal{O}_R(j, t)$: 1. Output $k \leftarrow \mathsf{Gen}(msk, j, t)$; $\mathcal{O}_E(i, m)$: 1. $ek_i \leftarrow \mathsf{Gen}(msk, i, \mathsf{sen})$; 2. Output $\mathsf{San}(pp, \mathsf{Enc}(ek_i, m))$;

Let I_S and J be defined as in the No-Write Rule game from Definition 4. We say an adversary A wins Hybrid i, for $i \in [2\ell]$, if it returns 1 and all of the following hold:

1. $\mathbf{x}' \in I_S \cup \{0\}$;
2. $\forall \mathbf{x} \in I_S, \mathbf{y} \in J, \mathsf{P_{or\text{-}eq}}(\mathbf{x}, \mathbf{y}) = 0$.

We denote by ε_i the probability that A wins Hybrid i, for $i \in [2\ell]$. Note that for any PPT adversary A:

$$\mathsf{adv}^A_{\mathsf{No\text{-}Write}}(\mathsf{ACE_{or\text{-}eq}}) \le \tfrac{1}{2}|\varepsilon_{2\ell} - \varepsilon_1|.$$

The proof proceeds in two steps:

First Step: for all $i \in [\ell]$, we build PPT adversaries $B_{1.i}$ and $B_{2.i}$ such that $|\varepsilon_{i-1} - \varepsilon_i| \le 2 \cdot \mathsf{adv}^{B_{1.i}}_{\mathsf{No\text{-}Write}}(\mathsf{ACE_{eq}}) + 2 \cdot \mathsf{adv}^{B_{2.i}}_{\mathsf{No\text{-}Read}}(\mathsf{ACE_{eq}})$.

First, the No-Write Rule allows to switch the sanitized ciphertext in Hybrid $i-1$ from

$$\mathsf{San}(pp, c_1^{(1)}, \ldots, c_{i-1}^{(1)}, \boxed{c_i^{(0)}}, c_{i+1}^{(0)}, \ldots, c_\ell^{(0)}) \text{ to}$$

$$\mathsf{San}(pp, c_1^{(1)}, \ldots, c_{i-1}^{(1)}, \boxed{c_i^{(2)}}, c_{i+1}^{(0)}, \ldots, c_\ell^{(0)}),$$

where $c_i^{(2)} := \mathsf{Enc}(\mathsf{Gen}(msk, (x_i', i), \mathsf{sen}), m^*)$ and $m^* \leftarrow \mathcal{M}$.

Namely, adversary $B_{1.i}$ playing against the No-Write Rule for $\mathsf{P_{eq}}$, after receiving the public parameters pp, sends them to A and simulates all the queries to $\mathcal{O}_E(\cdot)$ and $\mathcal{O}_S(\cdot)$ in the straightforward way: using its own oracles $\mathcal{O}_E(\cdot)$ and $\mathcal{O}_S(\cdot)$ for $\mathsf{P_{eq}}$, coordinate-wise. Note that the restriction on A's queries, namely $\forall \mathbf{x} \in I_S, \mathbf{y} \in J, \mathsf{P_{or\text{-}eq}}(\mathbf{x}, \mathbf{y}) = 0$, implies that $\mathsf{P_{eq}}((x_i, i), (y_j, j)) = 0$ for all $i, j \in [\ell]$. Thus, $B_{1.i}$ can answer valid queries from A by valid queries to its own oracles.

Then, $B_{1.i}$ receives the challenge $((c_1^{(0)}, \ldots, c_\ell^{(0)}), \mathbf{x}')$ from A, and it sends $(c_i^{(0)}, (x_i', i))$ to the challenger for $\mathsf{P_{eq}}$, to receive ct_i^b where $b \leftarrow \{0, 1\}$, and

$$\mathsf{ct}_i^0 := \mathsf{San}(pp, c_i^{(0)}) \text{ and } \mathsf{ct}_i^1 := \mathsf{San}(pp, \mathsf{Enc}(\mathsf{Gen}(msk, (x_i', i), \mathsf{sen}), m^*))$$

for $m^* \leftarrow \mathcal{M}$. Since $B_{1.i}$ knows m_0 (here we crucially rely on the fact that m_0 is a fixed message, and not a random message as in the No-Write Rule experiment, since it would be unknown to $B_{1.i}$), it can compute

$$\mathsf{ct}_j := \mathsf{San}(pp, \mathsf{Enc}(\mathsf{Gen}(msk, (x'_j, j), \mathsf{sen}), m_0)) \text{ for } j < i,$$

using its $\mathcal{O}_E$ oracle on input $((x'_j, j), m_0)$. Finally, it sets $\mathsf{ct}_j := c_j^{(0)}$ for $j > i$, and sends the sanitized ciphertext $(\mathsf{ct}_1, \ldots, \mathsf{ct}_{i-1}, \mathsf{ct}_i^b, \mathsf{ct}_{i+1}, \ldots, \mathsf{ct}_\ell)$ to A, and keeps simulating the oracles $\mathcal{O}_E(\cdot)$ and $\mathcal{O}_R(\cdot)$ as before.

Then, because $\mathsf{ACE}_{\mathsf{eq}}$ satisfies the No-Read Rule, and because for all $\mathbf{y} \in J$, $\mathsf{P}_{\mathsf{or\text{-}eq}}(\mathbf{x}', \mathbf{y}) = 0$, which implies $\mathsf{P}_{\mathsf{eq}}((x'_i, i), (y_j, j)) = 0$ for all $i, j \in [\ell]$, we can switch a sanitized ciphertext from

$$\mathsf{San}(pp, c_1^{(1)}, \ldots, c_{i-1}^{(1)}, \boxed{c_i^{(2)}}, c_{i+1}^{(0)}, \ldots, c_\ell^{(0)}) \text{ to}$$

$$\mathsf{San}(pp, c_1^{(1)}, \ldots, c_{i-1}^{(1)}, \boxed{c_i^{(1)}}, c_{i+1}^{(0)}, \ldots, c_\ell^{(0)}),$$

where $c_i^{(1)} = \mathsf{Enc}(\mathsf{Gen}(msk, (x'_j, j), \mathsf{sen}), m_0)$, as in Hybrid i. Namely, adversary $B_{2.i}$ simulates pp, $\mathcal{O}_E(\cdot)$, $\mathcal{O}_S(\cdot)$, $\mathcal{O}_R(\cdot)$, and computes sanitized ciphertexts ct_j for $j > i$ as described previously for $B_{1.i}$. For the ciphertexts ct_j for $j < i$, $B_{2.i}$ uses its oracle $\mathcal{O}_E$, and then, applies San to obtain the sanitized ciphertexts. It can do so since applying San only requires to know pp. Then, $B_{2.i}$ sends $(m_0, m_1, (x'_i, i), (x'_i, i))$ to the No-Read Rule experiment, where $m_1 \leftarrow \mathcal{M}$, to get back $c \leftarrow \mathsf{Enc}(\mathsf{Gen}(msk, (x'_i, i)), m_b)$. It sets $\mathsf{ct}_i := \mathsf{San}(pp, c)$, and sends the sanitized $(\mathsf{ct}_1, \ldots, \mathsf{ct}_\ell)$ to A.

Second Step: we build a PPT adversary $B_{3.i}$ such that $|\varepsilon_{\ell+i-1} - \varepsilon_{\ell+i}| \leq 2 \cdot \mathsf{adv}_{\mathsf{No\text{-}Read}}^{B_{3.i}}(\mathsf{ACE}_{\mathsf{eq}})$.

We use the No-Read Rule as for the first step. Namely, $B_{3.i}$ simulates pp, $\mathcal{O}_E(\cdot)$, $\mathcal{O}_S(\cdot)$, $\mathcal{O}_R(\cdot)$ as descried previously for $B_{2.i}$. Then, $B_{3.i}$ ignores the challenge $((c_1^{(0)}, \ldots, c_\ell^{(0)}), \mathbf{x}')$ sent by A, samples $m_1 \leftarrow \mathcal{M}$, computes

$$ct_j := \mathsf{San}(pp, \mathsf{Enc}(\mathsf{Gen}(msk, (x'_j, j), \mathsf{sen}), m_1)) \text{ for } j < i,$$

$$ct_j := \mathsf{San}(pp, \mathsf{Enc}(\mathsf{Gen}(msk, (x'_j, j), \mathsf{sen}), m_0)) \text{ for } j > i,$$

thanks to its oracle $\mathcal{O}_E$. Then, $B_{3.i}$ sends $(m_0, m_1, (x'_i, i), (x'_i, i))$ to the No-Read Rule experiment, to get back $c \leftarrow \mathsf{Enc}(\mathsf{Gen}(msk, (x'_i, i)), m_b)$. It sets $\mathsf{ct}_i := \mathsf{San}(pp, c)$, and sends the sanitized ciphertext $(\mathsf{ct}_1, \ldots, \mathsf{ct}_\ell)$ to A. $\qquad\square$

5   Predicates in Disjunction of Equalities

We show how to reduce the predicate $\mathsf{P}_{\mathsf{range}}$ defined for all points $z \in [N]$ and intervals $I \subset [N]$ as:

$$\mathsf{P}_{\mathsf{range}}(z, I) = 1 \Leftrightarrow z \in I$$

to $\mathsf{P}_{\mathsf{or\text{-}eq}}$ described in Sect. 4. This requires writing intervals I and points z as vectors, using a standard tree structure [DVOS00].

Lemma 9 (Interval to Vector [DVOS00]). *There is an efficient PPT algorithm* IntVec, *that on input an interval* $I \subset [N]$ *outputs*

$$(w_1, w_2, \ldots, w_{2n}) \in \left(\{0,1\}^* \cup \{\bot\}\right)^{2n},$$

where $n := \lceil \log N \rceil$, *with the following properties:*

- *for each* $i = 1, \ldots, n$, *we have* $w_{2i-1}, w_{2i} \in \{0,1\}^i \cup \{\bot\}$;
- *for all* $z \in [N]$, *we have* $z \in I$ *iff one of* $w_1, \ldots, w_{2t}$ *is a prefix of* z.

Here, $\bot$ *is special symbol such that* $\bot \notin \bigcup_{i=1}^n \{0,1\}^i$.

For instance, IntVec$([010, 110]) = (\bot, \bot, 01, 10, 110, \bot)$.

Remark 1 (Hashing bit strings into $\mathcal{D}$). We want to use the ACE of Sect. 4, which requires finding an injective map from $\bigcup_{i=1}^n \{0,1\}^i \cup \{\bot\}$ into $\mathcal{D}$, where $n := \lceil \lceil \log N \rceil \rceil$. Such map exists as long as $|\mathcal{D}| \geq 2^{n+1} - 1$.

Now we give the description of algorithm PtVec, used to map points to vectors.

PtVec: On input $z \in [N]$, output $(v_1, \ldots, v_{2n})$, where

$$v_{2i-1} = v_{2i} := i\text{'th bit prefix of } z, \ i = 1, \ldots, n.$$

For instance, PtVec$(011) = (0, 0, 01, 01, 011, 011)$ (See Fig. 3).

Remark 2 (Duplicate Entries). Note that some strings appear more than once in the vector. This is necessary since the predicate is a function of both the *entries in the vector* and *their positions*.

Lemma 10. *For any point* $z \in [N]$ *and any interval* $I \subseteq [N]$,

$$z \in I \text{ iff } \mathsf{P}_{or\text{-}eq}(\mathsf{PtVec}(z), \mathsf{IntVec}(I)) = 1.$$

Lemma 10 follows readily from Lemma 9.

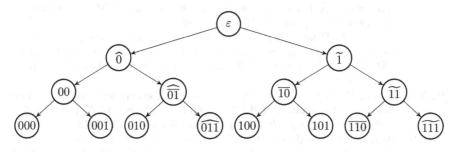

Fig. 3. Tree structure [DVOS00] for interval $[010, 110]$ (bar nodes), point 011 (hat nodes) and point 111 (tilde nodes). The common node 01 allows to decrypt for $011 \in [010, 110]$. No such node exists for $111 \notin [010, 110]$, which prevents decryption.

Acknowledgements. We would like to thank the reviewers of PKC'17 for their diligent proofreading and valuable remarks, helping us to improve the paper.

Fuchsbauer is supported in part by the French ANR ALAMBIC project (ANR-16-CE39-0006). Gay is supported by ERC Project aSCEND (639554).

Kowalczyk is supported in part by the Defense Advanced Research Project Agency (DARPA) and Army Research Office (ARO) under Contract #W911NF-15-C-0236; NSF grants #CNS-1445424, #CNS-1552932, and #CCF-1423306; an NSF Graduate Research Fellowship #DGE-16-44869; and ERC Project aSCEND (639554). Any opinions, findings, and conclusions or recommendations expressed are those of the authors and do not necessarily reflect the views of the Defense Advanced Research Projects Agency, Army Research Office, the National Science Foundation, or the U.S. Government.

Orlandi is supported by the Danish Council for Independent Research (grant id: 6108-00169) and COST Action IC1306.

References

[AFG+10] Abe, M., Fuchsbauer, G., Groth, J., Haralambiev, K., Ohkubo, M.: Structure-preserving signatures and commitments to group elements. In: Rabin, T. (ed.) CRYPTO 2010. LNCS, vol. 6223, pp. 209–236. Springer, Heidelberg (2010). doi:10.1007/978-3-642-14623-7_12

[AFG+16] Abe, M., Fuchsbauer, G., Groth, J., Haralambiev, K., Ohkubo, M.: Structure-preserving signatures and commitments to group elements. J. Cryptol. **29**(2), 363–421 (2016)

[AGHO11] Abe, M., Groth, J., Haralambiev, K., Ohkubo, M.: Optimal structure-preserving signatures in asymmetric bilinear groups. In: Rogaway, P. (ed.) CRYPTO 2011. LNCS, vol. 6841, pp. 649–666. Springer, Heidelberg (2011). doi:10.1007/978-3-642-22792-9_37

[BBDP01] Bellare, M., Boldyreva, A., Desai, A., Pointcheval, D.: Key-privacy in public-key encryption. In: Boyd, C. (ed.) ASIACRYPT 2001. LNCS, vol. 2248, pp. 566–582. Springer, Heidelberg (2001). doi:10.1007/3-540-45682-1_33

[BF01] Boneh, D., Franklin, M.: Identity-based encryption from the Weil pairing. In: Kilian, J. (ed.) CRYPTO 2001. LNCS, vol. 2139, pp. 213–229. Springer, Heidelberg (2001). doi:10.1007/3-540-44647-8_13

[BFM88] Blum, M., Feldman, P., Micali, S.: Non-interactive zero-knowledge and its applications (extended abstract). In: 20th Annual ACM Symposium on Theory of Computing, pp. 103–112 (1988)

[BP04] Bellare, M., Palacio, A.: The knowledge-of-exponent assumptions and 3-round zero-knowledge protocols. In: Franklin, M. (ed.) CRYPTO 2004. LNCS, vol. 3152, pp. 273–289. Springer, Heidelberg (2004). doi:10.1007/978-3-540-28628-8_17

[BSW11] Boneh, D., Sahai, A., Waters, B.: Functional encryption: definitions and challenges. In: Ishai, Y. (ed.) TCC 2011. LNCS, vol. 6597, pp. 253–273. Springer, Heidelberg (2011). doi:10.1007/978-3-642-19571-6_16

[DHO16] Damgård, I., Haagh, H., Orlandi, C.: Access control encryption: enforcing information flow with cryptography. In: Hirt, M., Smith, A. (eds.) TCC 2016. LNCS, vol. 9986, pp. 547–576. Springer, Heidelberg (2016). doi:10.1007/978-3-662-53644-5_21

[DVOS00] De Berg, M., Van Kreveld, M., Overmars, M., Schwarzkopf, O.C.: Computational Geometry. Springer, Heidelberg (2000)

[FHS14] Fuchsbauer, G., Hanser, C., Slamanig, D.: Structure-preserving signatures on equivalence classes and constant-size anonymous credentials. IACR Cryptology ePrint Archive, 2014:944 (2014)

[FHS15] Fuchsbauer, G., Hanser, C., Slamanig, D.: Practical round-optimal blind signatures in the standard model. In: Gennaro, R., Robshaw, M. (eds.) CRYPTO 2015. LNCS, vol. 9216, pp. 233–253. Springer, Heidelberg (2015). doi:10.1007/978-3-662-48000-7_12

[Gam85] El Gamal, T.: A public key cryptosystem and a signature scheme based on discrete logarithms. IEEE Trans. Inf. Theory **31**(4), 469–472 (1985)

[GGH+13] Garg, S., Gentry, C., Halevi, S., Raykova, M., Sahai, A., Waters, B.: Candidate indistinguishability obfuscation and functional encryption for all circuits. In: 54th Annual IEEE Symposium on Foundations of Computer Science, FOCS, pp. 40–49 (2013)

[GMW15] Gay, R., Méaux, P., Wee, H.: Predicate encryption for multi-dimensional range queries from lattices. In: Katz, J. (ed.) PKC 2015. LNCS, vol. 9020, pp. 752–776. Springer, Heidelberg (2015). doi:10.1007/978-3-662-46447-2_34

[Gol09] Goldreich, O.: Foundations of Cryptography: Volume 2, Basic Applications. Cambridge University Press, Cambridge (2009)

[GS08] Groth, J., Sahai, A.: Efficient non-interactive proof systems for bilinear groups. In: Smart, N. (ed.) EUROCRYPT 2008. LNCS, vol. 4965, pp. 415–432. Springer, Heidelberg (2008). doi:10.1007/978-3-540-78967-3_24

[GS12] Groth, J., Sahai, A.: Efficient non-interactive proof systems for bilinear groups. SIAM J. Comput. **41**(5), 1193–1232 (2012)

[HS14] Hanser, C., Slamanig, D.: Structure-preserving signatures on equivalence classes and their application to anonymous credentials. In: Sarkar, P., Iwata, T. (eds.) ASIACRYPT 2014. LNCS, vol. 8873, pp. 491–511. Springer, Heidelberg (2014). doi:10.1007/978-3-662-45611-8_26

[IPV10] Izabachène, M., Pointcheval, D., Vergnaud, D.: Mediated traceable anonymous encryption. In: Abdalla, M., Barreto, P.S.L.M. (eds.) LATINCRYPT 2010. LNCS, vol. 6212, pp. 40–60. Springer, Heidelberg (2010). doi:10.1007/978-3-642-14712-8_3

[KL14] Katz, J., Lindell, Y.: Introduction to Modern Cryptography. CRC Press, Boca Raton (2014)

[KPW15] Kiltz, E., Pan, J., Wee, H.: Structure-preserving signatures from standard assumptions, revisited. In: Gennaro, R., Robshaw, M. (eds.) CRYPTO 2015. LNCS, vol. 9216, pp. 275–295. Springer, Heidelberg (2015). doi:10.1007/978-3-662-48000-7_14

[OT12] Okamoto, T., Takashima, K.: Adaptively attribute-hiding (hierarchical) inner product encryption. In: Pointcheval, D., Johansson, T. (eds.) EUROCRYPT 2012. LNCS, vol. 7237, pp. 591–608. Springer, Heidelberg (2012). doi:10.1007/978-3-642-29011-4_35

[Sak00] Sakai, R.: Cryptosystems based on pairings. In: Symposium on Cryptography and Information Security 2000, SCIS 2000 (2000)

[SBC+07] Shi, E., Bethencourt, J., Chan, H.T.-H., Song, D.X., Perrig, A.: Multi-dimensional range query over encrypted data. In: 2007 IEEE Symposium on Security and Privacy (S&P 2007), 20–23 May 2007, Oakland, California, USA, pp. 350–364 (2007)

[Sha84] Shamir, A.: Identity-based cryptosystems and signature schemes. In: Blakley, G.R., Chaum, D. (eds.) CRYPTO 1984. LNCS, vol. 196, pp. 47–53. Springer, Heidelberg (1985). doi:10.1007/3-540-39568-7_5

[SW05] Sahai, A., Waters, B.: Fuzzy identity-based encryption. In: Cramer, R. (ed.) EUROCRYPT 2005. LNCS, vol. 3494, pp. 457–473. Springer, Heidelberg (2005). doi:10.1007/11426639_27

Special Signatures

Deterring Certificate Subversion: Efficient Double-Authentication-Preventing Signatures

Mihir Bellare[1], Bertram Poettering[2], and Douglas Stebila[3]([✉])

[1] Department of Computer Science and Engineering, University of California,
San Diego, 9500 Gilman Drive, La Jolla, CA 92093, USA
mihir@eng.ucsd.edu
http://cseweb.ucsd.edu/~mihir/

[2] Department of Mathematics, Ruhr University Bochum, Bochum, Germany
bertram.poettering@rub.de
http://www.crypto.rub.de/

[3] Department of Computing and Software, McMaster University,
Hamilton, ON, Canada
stebilad@mcmaster.ca
https://www.cas.mcmaster.ca/~stebilad/

Abstract. We present highly efficient double authentication preventing signatures (DAPS). In a DAPS, signing two messages with the same first part and differing second parts reveals the signing key. In the context of PKIs we suggest that CAs who use DAPS to create certificates have a court-convincing argument to deny big-brother requests to create rogue certificates, thus deterring certificate subversion. We give two general methods for obtaining DAPS. Both start from trapdoor identification schemes. We instantiate our transforms to obtain numerous specific DAPS that, in addition to being efficient, are proven with tight security reductions to standard assumptions. We implement our DAPS schemes to show that they are not only several orders of magnitude more efficient than prior DAPS but competitive with in-use signature schemes that lack the double authentication preventing property.

1 Introduction

DAPS. Double authentication preventing signature (DAPS) schemes were introduced by Poettering and Stebila (PS) [15]. In such a signature scheme, the message being signed is a pair $m = (a, p)$ consisting of an "address" a and a "payload" p. Let us say that messages $(a_1, p_1), (a_2, p_2)$ are *colliding* if $a_1 = a_2$ but $p_1 \neq p_2$. The double authentication prevention requirement is that there be an efficient extraction algorithm that given a public key PK and valid signatures σ_1, σ_2 on colliding messages $(a, p_1), (a, p_2)$, respectively, returns the secret signing key SK underlying PK. Additionally, the scheme must satisfy standard unforgeability under a chosen-message attack [10], but in light of the first property we must make the restriction that the address components of all messages signed in the attack are different.

© International Association for Cryptologic Research 2017
S. Fehr (Ed.): PKC 2017, Part II, LNCS 10175, pp. 121–151, 2017.
DOI: 10.1007/978-3-662-54388-7_5

WHY DAPS? PS [15] suggested that DAPS could deter *certificate subversion*. This is of particular interest now in light of the Snowden revelations. We know that the NSA obtains court orders to compel corporations into measures that compromise security. The case we consider here is that the corporation is a Certificate Authority (CA) and the court order asks it to produce a rogue certificate. Thus, the CA (eg. Comodo, Go Daddy, ...) has already issued a (legitimate) certificate $cert_1 = (\texttt{example.com}, pk_1, \sigma_1)$ for a server $\texttt{example.com}$. Here pk_1 is the public key of $\texttt{example.com}$ and σ_1 is the CA's signature on the pair $(\texttt{example.com}, pk_1)$, computed under the secret key SK of the CA. Big brother (this is what we will call the subverting adversary) is targeting clients communicating with $\texttt{example.com}$. It obtains a court order that requires the CA to issue another certificate—this is the rogue certificate—$cert_2 = (\texttt{example.com}, pk_2, \sigma_2)$ in the name of $\texttt{example.com}$, where now pk_2 is a public key supplied by big brother, so that the latter knows the corresponding secret key sk_2, and σ_2 is the CA's signature on the pair $(\texttt{example.com}, pk_2)$, again computed under the secret key SK of the CA. With this rogue certificate in hand, big brother could impersonate $\texttt{example.com}$ in a TLS session with a client, compromising security of $\texttt{example.com}$'s communications.

The CA wants to deny the order (complying with it only hurts its reputation and business) but, under normal conditions, has no argument to make to the court in support of such a denial. Using DAPS to create certificates, rather than ordinary signatures, gives the CA such an argument, namely that complying with the order (issuing the rogue certificate) would compromise not just the security of big brother's target clients communicating with $\texttt{example.com}$, but would compromise security much more broadly. Indeed, if big brother uses the rogue certificate with a client, it puts the rogue certificate in the client's hand. The legitimate certificate can be viewed as public. So the client has σ_1, σ_2. But these are valid signatures on the colliding messages $(\texttt{example.com}, pk_1)$, $(\texttt{example.com}, pk_2)$, respectively, which means that the client can extract the CA's signing key SK. This would lead to widespread insecurity. The court may be willing to allow big brother to compromise communications of clients with $\texttt{example.com}$, but it will *not* be willing to create a situation where the security of *all* TLS hosts with certificates from this CA is compromised. Ultimately this means the court would have strong incentives to deny big brother's request for a court order to issue a rogue certificate in the first place.

Further discussion of this application of DAPS may be found in [15,16] and also in the full version of this paper [2]. The latter includes comparisons with other approaches such as certificate transparency and public key pinning.

PRIOR DAPS SCHEMES. PS [15,16] give a factoring-based DAPS that we call PS. Its signature contains $n + 1$ elements in a group $\mathbb{Z}_N^*$, where n is the length of the output of a hash function and N is a (composite) modulus in the public key. With a 2048-bit modulus and 256-bit hash, a signature contains 257 group elements, for a length of 526,336 bits or 64.25 KiB. This is a factor 257 times longer than a 2048-bit RSA PKCS#1 signature. Signing and verifying times are also significantly greater than for RSA PKCS#1. Ruffing, Kate, and Schröder

[17, Appendix A] give a chameleon hash function (CHF) based DAPS that we call RKS and recall in the full version of this paper [2]. Instantiating it with DLP-based CHFs makes signing quite efficient, but signature sizes and verification times are about the same as in PS. The large signature sizes in particular of both PS and RKS inhibits their use in practice.

GOALS AND CONTRIBUTIONS. If we want DAPS to be a viable practical option, we need DAPS schemes that are competitive with current non-DAPS schemes on *all* cost parameters, meaning signature size, key size, signing time and verifying time. Furthermore, to not lose efficiency via inflated security parameters, we need to establish the unforgeability with tight security reductions. Finally, given the high damage that would be created by certificate forgery, we want these reductions to be to assumptions that are standard (factoring, RSA, ...) rather than new. This is what we deliver. We will give two general methods to build DAPS, and thence obtain many particular schemes that are efficient while having tight security reductions to standard algebraic assumptions in the random oracle model. We begin with some background on our main tool, identification schemes.

BACKGROUND. An identification scheme is a three-move protocol ID where the prover sends a *commitment* Y computed using private randomness y, the verifier sends a random *challenge* c, the prover returns a *response* z computed using y and its secret key isk, and the verifier computes a boolean decision from the conversation transcript $Y\|c\|z$ and public key ivk (see Fig. 2). Practical ID schemes are typically Sigma protocols, which means they satisfy honest-verifier zero-knowledge and special soundness. The latter says that from two accepting conversation transcripts with the same commitment but different challenges, one can extract the secret key. The identification scheme is *trapdoor* [3,12] if the prover can pick the commitment Y directly at random from the commitment space and compute the associated private randomness y using its secret key.

The classic way to get a signature scheme from an identification scheme is via the Fiat-Shamir transform [9], denoted **FS**. Here, a signature of a message m is a pair (Y, z) such that the transcript $Y\|c\|z$ is accepting for $c = H(Y\|m)$, where H is a random oracle. This signature scheme meets the standard unforgeability notion of [10] assuming the identification scheme is secure against impersonation under passive attack (IMP-PA) [1]. BPS [3] give several alternative transforms of (trapdoor) identification schemes to unforgeable signature schemes, the advantage over **FS** being that in some cases the reduction of unforgeability to the underlying algebraic assumption is tight. (That of **FS** is notoriously loose.) No prior transform yields DAPS. Our first transform, described next, is however an adaptation and extension of the **MdCmtCh** transform of [3].

DOUBLE-HASH TRANSFORM **H2**. The novel challenge in getting DAPS is to provide the double authentication prevention property. Our idea is to turn to identification schemes, and specifically to exploit their special soundness. Recall this says that from two accepting conversations with the same commitment and different challenges, one can extract the secret key. What we want now is to create identification-based signatures in such a way that signatures are accepting conversations and *signatures of messages with the same address have the same commitment, but if payloads differ then challenges differ*. This will allow us, from valid signatures of colliding messages, to obtain the secret key.

To ensure signatures of messages with the same address have the same commitment, we make the commitment a hash of the address. This, however, leaves us in general unable to complete the signing, because the prover in an identification scheme relies on having create the commitment Y in such a way that it knows some underlying private randomness y which is used crucially in the identification. To get around this, we use identification schemes that are trapdoor (see above), so y can be derived from the commitment given a secret key. To ensure unforgeability, we incorporate a fresh random seed into each signature.

In more detail, our first method to obtain DAPS from a trapdoor identification scheme is via a transform that we call the double-hash transform and denote **H2** (cf. Sect. 5.1). To sign a message $m = (a, p)$, the signer specifies the commitment as a hash $Y = \mathrm{H}_1(a)$ of the address, picks a random seed s of length sl (a typical seed length would be $\mathsf{sl} = 256$), obtains a challenge $c = \mathrm{H}_2(a\|p\|s)$, uses the trapdoor property of the identification scheme and the secret key to compute a response z, and returns (z, s) as the signature. Additionally the public key is enhanced so that recovery of the secret identification key allows recovery of the full DAPS secret key. Theorem 1 establishes the double-authentication prevention property via the special soundness property of the identification Sigma protocol, and is unconditional. Theorem 2 shows unforgeability of the DAPS in the ROM under two assumptions on the identification scheme: (1) CIMP-UU, a notion defined in [3] (which refers to security under <u>c</u>onstrained <u>imp</u>ersonation attacks, where in the successful impersonation the commitment was <u>un</u>chosen by the adversary and the challenge was also <u>un</u>chosen by the adversary), and (2) KR, security against key recovery. Specific identification schemes can be shown to meet both notions under standard assumptions [3], yielding DAPS from the same assumptions. If typical factoring or RSA based identification schemes are used, DAPS signatures have size $k + \mathsf{sl}$, where k is the bitlength of the modulus.

DOUBLE-ID TRANSFORM **ID2**. The signature size $k + \mathsf{sl}$ of **H2** when instantiated with RSA is more than the length k of a signature in RSA PKCS#1. We address this via a second transform of trapdoor identification schemes into DAPS that we call the double ID transform, denoted **ID2**. When instantiated with the same identification schemes as above, corresponding DAPS signatures have length $k+1$ bits, while maintaining (up to a small constant factor) the signing and verifying times of schemes obtained via **H2**.

The **ID2** transform has several novel features. It requires that the identification scheme supports multiple challenge lengths, specifically challenge lengths 1 and l (e.g., $l = 256$). To sign a message $m = (a, p)$, first we work with the single challenge-bit version of the identification scheme, computing for this a commitment $Y_1 = H_1(a)$, picking a random 1-bit challenge c_1, and letting z_1 be the response, computed using the trapdoor and secret key. Now a random bijection (a public bijection accessible, in both directions, via oracles) is applied to z_1 to get a commitment Y_2 for the l-bit challenge version of the identification scheme. A challenge for this is computed as $H_2(a, p)$, and then a response z_2 is produced. The signature is simply (c_1, z_2). Section 5.2 specifies the transform in detail and proves the DAP property and unforgeability, modeling the random bijection as ideal. Notably, the CIMP-UU assumption used for the **H2** transform needs to be replaced by the (slightly stronger) CIMP-UC notion [3] (in CIMP-UC, the challenge in the successful impersonation can be chosen by the adversary).

INSTANTIATIONS. We discuss three different instantiations of the above in Sect. 6. The RSA-based **GQ** identification scheme [11] is not trapdoor as usually written, but can be made so by including the decryption exponent in the secret key [3]. Applying **H2** and **ID2**, we get **H2**[GQ] and **ID2**[GQ]. The factoring-based **MR** identification scheme of Micali and Reyzin [12] is trapdoor, which we exploit (in the full version [2]) to get **H2**[MR]. For details see Fig. 15. (Both GQ and MR support multiple challenge lengths and meet the relevant security requirements.) Figure 1 shows the signing time, verifying time and signature size for these schemes. In a bit we will discuss implementation results that measure actual performance.

REDUCTION TIGHTNESS. Figure 1 says the signing time for **H2**[GQ] is $\mathcal{O}(lk^2 + k^3)$, but what this means in practice depends very much on the choice of k (the length of composite N). Roughly speaking, we can expect that doubling k leads to an 8-fold increase in runtime, so signing with $k = 2048$ is 8 times slower than with $k = 1024$. So we want to use the smallest k for which we have a desired level of security. Suppose this is approximately 128 bits. Many keylength recommendations match the difficulty of breaking a 128-bit symmetric cipher with the difficulty of factoring a 2048-bit modulus. But this does not generally mean it is safe to use **H2**[GQ] with $k = 2048$, because the reduction of unforgeability to RSA may not be tight: the Fiat-Shamir transform **FS** has a very

Scheme	Signing		Verifying		|sig|	(bits)
PS [15,16]	$\mathcal{O}(nk^3)$	516.58 ms	$\mathcal{O}(nk^3)$	161.84 ms	nk	528 384
RKS [17]	$\mathcal{O}(n^4)$	13.48 ms	$\mathcal{O}(n^4)$	5.99 ms	$2n^2$	131 072
H2[GQ]	$\mathcal{O}(lk^2 + k^3)$	0.88 ms	$\mathcal{O}(lk^2)$	0.41 ms	$k + \mathsf{sl}$	2 304
ID2[GQ]		1.80 ms		1.49 ms	$k + 1$	2 049
H2[MR]	$\mathcal{O}(k^3)$	1.27 ms	$\mathcal{O}(lk^2)$	0.37 ms	$k + \mathsf{sl}$	2 304

Fig. 1. DAPS efficiency. Performance indications for the DAPS obtained by our **H2** and **ID2** transforms applied to the GQ and MR trapdoor identification schemes. The first two rows show the prior scheme of PS [15,16] and the scheme of RKS [17], with n being the length of the output of a hash function, eg. $n = 256$. By k we denote the length of a composite modulus N in the public key, eg. $k = 2048$. The challenge length of GQ and MR is l, and sl is the seed length, eg. $l = \mathsf{sl} = 256$. The 4th column is the size of a signature in bits. Absolute runtimes and signature sizes are for $k = 2048$-bit moduli and $n = l = \mathsf{sl} = 256$-bit hashes/challenges/seeds; details appear in Sect. 6.

loose reduction, so when signatures are identification based, one should be extra suspicious. Remarkably, our reductions are tight, so we can indeed get 128 bits of security with $k = 2048$. This tightness has two steps or components. First, the reduction of unforgeability to the CIMP-UU/CIMP-UC and KR security of the identification scheme, as given by Theorems 2 and 4, is tight. Second, the reductions of CIMP-UU/CIMP-UC and KR to the underlying algebraic problem (here RSA or factoring) are also tight (cf. Lemma 1, adapting [3]).

IMPLEMENTATION. The efficiency measures of Fig. 1 are asymptotic, with hidden constants. Implementation is key to gauge and compare performance in practice. We implement our two GQ based schemes, **H2**[GQ] and **ID2**[GQ], as well as **H2**[MR]. For comparison we also implement the prior PS DAPS, and also compare with the existing implementation of RKS. Figure 16 shows the signing time, verifying time, signature size and key sizes for all schemes. **H2**[GQ] emerges as around 587 times faster than PS for signing and 394 times faster for verifying while also having signatures about 229 times shorter. Compared with the previous fastest and smallest DAPS, RKS, **H2**[GQ] is 15× faster for both signing and verifying, with signatures 56× shorter. **ID2**[GQ] is about a factor two slower than **H2**[GQ] but with signatures about 15% shorter. **H2**[MR] has the smallest public keys of our new DAPS schemes, with signing runtime about halfway between **H2**[GQ] and **ID2**[GQ]. The DAPS by RKS remains the one with the smallest public keys, (640 bits), but the schemes in this paper have public keys that are still quite reasonable (between 2048 and 6144 bits). As Fig. 16 shows, **H2**[GQ], **H2**[MR], and **ID2**[GQ] are close to RSA PKCS#1 in all parameters and runtimes (but with potentially improved security, considering our reductions to RSA and factoring are tight). This means that DAPS can replace the signatures currently used for certificates with minimal loss in performance.

NECESSITY OF OUR ASSUMPTION. Trapdoor identification schemes may seem a very particular assumption from which to obtain DAPS. However we show in the full version of this paper [2] that from *any* DAPS satisfying double authentication prevention and unforgeability, one can build a CIMP-UU and CIMP-UC secure trapdoor identification scheme. This shows that the assumption we make is effectively necessary for DAPS.

2 Preliminaries

NOTATION. By ε we denote the empty string. If X is a finite set, $x \leftarrow\!\!\!{}_\$\, X$ denotes selecting an element of X uniformly at random and $|X|$ denotes the size of X. We use $a_1\|a_2\|\cdots\|a_n$ as shorthand for $(a_1, a_2, \ldots, a_n)$, and by $a_1\|a_2\|\cdots\|a_n \leftarrow x$ we mean that x is parsed into its constituents. If A is an algorithm, $y \leftarrow A(x_1, \ldots; r)$ denotes running A on inputs $x_1, \ldots$ with random coins r and assigning the result to y, and $y \leftarrow\!\!\!{}_\$\, A(x_1, \ldots)$ means we pick r at random and let $y \leftarrow A(x_1, \ldots; r)$. By $[A(x_1, \ldots)]$ we denote the set of all y that have positive probability of being returned by $A(x_1, \ldots)$.

Our proofs use the code-based game playing framework of BR [5]. In these proofs, $\Pr[G]$ denotes the event that game G returns true. When we speak of running time of algorithms, we mean worst case. For adversaries playing games, this includes the running time of the adversary and that of the game, i.e., the time taken by game procedures to respond to oracle queries is included. Boolean flags (like bad) in games are assumed initialized to false.

In our constructions, we will need random oracles with different ranges. For example we may want one random oracle returning points in a group $\mathbb{Z}_N^*$ and another returning strings of some length l. To provide a single unified notation, following [3], we have the game procedure H take not just the input x but a description Rng of the set from which outputs are to be drawn at random. Thus $y \leftarrow \mathrm{H}(x, \mathbb{Z}_N^*)$ will return a random element of $\mathbb{Z}_N^*$, and so on.

Our **ID2** transform also relies on a random bijection. In the spirit of a random oracle, a random bijection is an idealized unkeyed public bijection to which algorithms and adversaries have access via two oracles, one for the forward direction and one for the backward direction. Cryptographic constructions that build on such objects include the Even-Mansour cipher and the SHA3 hash function. We denote by $\Pi^+(\cdot, \mathrm{Dom}, \mathrm{Rng})$ a bijection from Dom to Rng, and we denote its inverse with Π^{-1}. Once Dom and Rng are fixed, our results view $\Pi^{+1}(\cdot, \mathrm{Dom}, \mathrm{Rng})$ as being randomly sampled from the set of all bijections from Dom to Rng. We discuss instantiation of a random bijection in Sect. 6.

SIGNATURE SCHEMES. A signature scheme DS specifies the following. The signer runs key generation algorithm DS.Kg to get a verification key vk and a signing key sk. A signature of message m is generated via $\sigma \leftarrow_\$ \mathrm{DS.Sig}(vk, sk, m)$. Verification is done by $v \leftarrow \mathrm{DS.Vf}(vk, m, \sigma)$, which returns a boolean v. DS is correct if for all $(vk, sk) \in [\mathrm{DS.Kg}]$, all messages $m \in \{0,1\}^*$ and all signatures $\sigma \in [\mathrm{DS.Sig}(vk, sk, m)]$, we have $\mathrm{DS.Vf}(vk, m, \sigma) = \mathrm{true}$.

3 Identification Schemes

Identification schemes are our main tool. Here we give the necessary definitions and results.

IDENTIFICATION. An identification (ID) scheme ID is a three-move protocol between a prover and a verifier, as shown in Fig. 2. A novel feature of our formulation (which we exploit for the **ID2** transform) is that identification schemes support challenges of multiple lengths. Thus, associated to ID is a set $\mathrm{ID.clS} \subseteq \mathbb{N}$ of admissible challenge lengths. At setup time the prover runs key generation algorithm ID.Kg to generate a public *verification key* ivk, a private *identification key* isk, and a *trapdoor* itk. To execute a run of the identification scheme for a challenge length $\mathrm{cl} \in \mathrm{ID.clS}$, the prover runs $\mathrm{ID.Cmt}(ivk, \mathrm{cl})$ to generate a *commitment* Y and a private state y. The prover sends Y to the verifier, who samples a random *challenge* c of length cl and returns it to the prover. The prover computes its *response* $z \leftarrow \mathrm{ID.Rsp}(ivk, isk, c, y)$. The verifier checks the response by invoking $\mathrm{ID.Vf}(ivk, Y\|c\|z)$ which returns a boolean value. We require perfect correctness. For any ivk, cl we denote with $\mathrm{ID.CS}(ivk, \mathrm{cl})$ and $\mathrm{ID.RS}(ivk, \mathrm{cl})$ the space of commitments and responses, respectively.

Prover	Verifier
Input: ivk, isk, cl	Input: ivk, cl
$(Y, y) \leftarrow\!\!{\$}\ \mathsf{ID.Cmt}(ivk, \mathsf{cl})$ $\xrightarrow{\ Y\ }$	
	$\xleftarrow{\ c\ }$ $c \leftarrow\!\!{\$}\ \{0,1\}^{\mathsf{cl}}$
$z \leftarrow \mathsf{ID.Rsp}(ivk, isk, c, y)$ $\xrightarrow{\ z\ }$	$v \leftarrow \mathsf{ID.Vf}(ivk, Y\|c\|z)$

Game $\mathbf{G}^{\mathrm{ex}}_{\mathsf{ID}}(\mathcal{A})$	Game $\mathbf{G}^{\mathrm{zk}}_{\mathsf{ID},\mathsf{cl}}(\mathcal{A})$
$(ivk, isk, itk) \leftarrow\!\!{\$}\ \mathsf{ID.Kg}$	$(ivk, isk, itk) \leftarrow\!\!{\$}\ \mathsf{ID.Kg}$; $b \leftarrow\!\!{\$}\ \{0,1\}$
$(Y, c_1, z_1, c_2, z_2) \leftarrow\!\!{\$}\ \mathcal{A}(ivk, isk, itk)$	$(Y_1, y_1) \leftarrow\!\!{\$}\ \mathsf{ID.Cmt}(ivk, \mathsf{cl})$
$T_1 \leftarrow Y\|c_1\|z_1$; $T_2 \leftarrow Y\|c_2\|z_2$	$c_1 \leftarrow\!\!{\$}\ \{0,1\}^{\mathsf{cl}}$
$v_1 \leftarrow \mathsf{ID.Vf}(ivk, T_1)$; $v_2 \leftarrow \mathsf{ID.Vf}(ivk, T_2)$	$z_1 \leftarrow \mathsf{ID.Rsp}(ivk, isk, c_1, y_1)$
If $\neg v_1 \vee \neg v_2 \vee (\|c_1\| \neq \|c_2\|) \vee (c_1 = c_2)$:	$Y_0\|c_0\|z_0 \leftarrow\!\!{\$}\ \mathsf{ID.Sim}(ivk, \mathsf{cl})$
$\quad$ Return false	$b' \leftarrow\!\!{\$}\ \mathcal{A}(ivk, \mathsf{cl}, Y_b\|c_b\|z_b)$
$isk^* \leftarrow\!\!{\$}\ \mathsf{ID.Ex}(ivk, T_1, T_2)$	Return $(b = b')$
Return $(isk^* \neq isk)$	

Fig. 2. Top: Message flow of an identification scheme ID. **Bottom:** Games defining extractability and HVZK of an identification scheme ID.

In basic ID schemes, key generation only outputs ivk and isk. The inclusion of itk was given by [3] in their definition of trapdoor ID schemes. Following [3] (and extending to multiple challenge lengths) we say ID is trapdoor if it specifies an additional algorithm $\mathsf{ID.Cmt}^{-1}$ that can compute y from any Y using trapdoor itk. The property required of $\mathsf{ID.Cmt}^{-1}$ is that the following two distributions on (Y, y) are identical for any admissible challenge length cl: (1) Let $(ivk, isk, itk) \leftarrow\!\!{\$}\ \mathsf{ID.Kg}$; $(Y, y) \leftarrow\!\!{\$}\ \mathsf{ID.Cmt}(ivk, \mathsf{cl})$ and return (Y, y), and (2) Let $(ivk, isk, itk) \leftarrow\!\!{\$}\ \mathsf{ID.Kg}$; $Y \leftarrow\!\!{\$}\ \mathsf{ID.CS}(ivk, \mathsf{cl})$; $y \leftarrow\!\!{\$}\ \mathsf{ID.Cmt}^{-1}(ivk, itk, Y, \mathsf{cl})$ and return (Y, y).

FURTHER PROPERTIES. We give several further identification-related definitions we will use. First we extend honest-verifier zero-knowledge (HVZK) and extractability to identification schemes with variable challenge length.

HVZK of ID asks that there exists an algorithm $\mathsf{ID.Sim}$ (called the simulator) that given the verification key and challenge length, generates transcripts which have the same distribution as honest ones. Formally, if $\mathcal{A}$ is an adversary and $\mathsf{cl} \in \mathsf{ID.clS}$ is an admissible challenge length, let $\mathbf{Adv}^{\mathrm{zk}}_{\mathsf{ID},\mathsf{cl}}(\mathcal{A}) = 2\Pr[\mathbf{G}^{\mathrm{zk}}_{\mathsf{ID},\mathsf{cl}}(\mathcal{A})] - 1$ where the game is shown in Fig. 2. Then ID is HVZK if $\mathbf{Adv}^{\mathrm{zk}}_{\mathsf{ID},\mathsf{cl}}(\mathcal{A}) = 0$ for all (even computationally unbounded) adversaries $\mathcal{A}$ and all $\mathsf{cl} \in \mathsf{ID.clS}$.

Extractability of ID asks that there exists an algorithm $\mathsf{ID.Ex}$ (called the extractor) which from any two (valid) transcripts that have the same commitment but different same-length challenges can recover the secret key. Formally, if $\mathcal{A}$ is an adversary, let $\mathbf{Adv}^{\mathrm{ex}}_{\mathsf{ID}}(\mathcal{A}) = \Pr[\mathbf{G}^{\mathrm{ex}}_{\mathsf{ID}}(\mathcal{A})]$ where the game is shown in Fig. 2. Then ID is perfectly extractable if $\mathbf{Adv}^{\mathrm{ex}}_{\mathsf{ID}}(\mathcal{A}) = 0$ for all (even computationally unbounded) adversaries $\mathcal{A}$. Perfect extractability is sometimes called special soundness. We say that an identification scheme is a Sigma protocol [7] if it is both HVZK and perfectly extractable.

We define three further notions that are not standard, but sometimes needed and true of typical schemes (cf. Sect. 6). For instance, at times we require that ID includes a *key-verification algorithm* ID.KVf for which ID.KVf$(ivk, isk) = $ true iff $(ivk, isk, itk) \in$ [ID.Kg] for some itk. We say that ID is *commitment recovering* if ID.Vf verifies a transcript $Y\|c\|z$ by recovering Y from c, z and then comparing. More precisely, we require that there exist an efficient algorithm ID.Rsp^{-1} that takes a verification key, a challenge, and a response, and outputs a commitment, such that ID.Vf$(ivk, Y\|c\|z) = $ true iff $Y = $ ID.Rsp$^{-1}(ivk, c, z)$. Finally, ID is said to have *unique responses* if for any commitment Y and any challenge c there is precisely one response z such that we have ID.Vf$(ivk, Y\|c\|z) = $ true.

Game $\mathbf{G}_{\mathsf{ID}}^{\text{cimp-xy}}(\mathcal{P})$

$i \leftarrow 0 \,;\, j \leftarrow 0$

$(ivk, isk, itk) \leftarrow\!\!{\scriptstyle\$}\, $ID.Kg

$(k, z) \leftarrow\!\!{\scriptstyle\$}\, \mathcal{P}^{\text{TR,CH}}(ivk)$

If not $(1 \leq k \leq j)$:

$\quad$ Return false

$T \leftarrow \text{CT}_k \| z$

Return ID.Vf(ivk, T)

Game $\mathbf{G}_{\mathsf{ID}}^{\text{kr-pa}}(\mathcal{I})$

$i \leftarrow 0 \,;\, (ivk, isk, itk) \leftarrow\!\!{\scriptstyle\$}\, $ID.Kg

$isk^* \leftarrow\!\!{\scriptstyle\$}\, \mathcal{I}^{\text{TR}}(ivk)$

Return ID.KVf(ivk, isk^*)

TR(cl)

If not cl $\in$ ID.clS: Return $\perp$

$i \leftarrow i + 1 \,;\, \text{cl}_i \leftarrow \text{cl}$

$(Y_i, y_i) \leftarrow\!\!{\scriptstyle\$}\, $ID.Cmt$(ivk, \text{cl}_i)$

$c_i \leftarrow\!\!{\scriptstyle\$}\, \{0,1\}^{\text{cl}_i}$

$z_i \leftarrow$ ID.Rsp(ivk, isk, c_i, y_i)

$T_i \leftarrow Y_i \| c_i \| z_i$

Return T_i

CH(l)   // xy=uu

If not $(1 \leq l \leq i)$: Return $\perp$

$j \leftarrow j + 1 \,;\, c \leftarrow\!\!{\scriptstyle\$}\, \{0,1\}^{\text{cl}_l}$

$\text{CT}_j \leftarrow Y_l \| c \,;\,$ Return c

CH(l, c)   // xy=uc

If not $(1 \leq l \leq i)$: Return $\perp$

If $(c = c_l$ or $|c| \neq \text{cl}_l)$: Return $\perp$

$j \leftarrow j + 1$

$\text{CT}_j \leftarrow Y_l \| c \,;\,$ Return c

Fig. 3. Games defining security of identification scheme ID against constrained impersonation (CIMP-UU and CIMP-UC) and against key recovery under passive attack.

SECURITY OF IDENTIFICATION. A framework of notions of security under constrained impersonation was given in [3]. We reproduce and use their CIMP-UU and CIMP-UC notions but extend them to support multiple challenge lengths. The value of these notions as starting points is that they can be proven to be achieved by typical identification schemes with *tight* reductions to *standard* assumptions, following [3], which is not true of classical notions like IMP-PA (impersonation under passive attack [1]). The formalization relies on the games $\mathbf{G}_{\mathsf{ID}}^{\text{cimp-xy}}(\mathcal{P})$ of Fig. 3 associated to identification scheme ID and adversary $\mathcal{P}$, where xy $\in \{$uu, uc$\}$. The transcript oracle TR returns a fresh identification transcript $Y_i\|c_i\|z_i$ each time it is called, for a challenge length passed in by the adversary. This models a passive attack. In the xy = uu case, the adversary can call CH with the index l of an existing transcript $Y_l\|c_l\|z_l$ to indicate that it wants to be challenged to produce a response for a fresh challenge against the commitment Y_l. The index j records the session for future reference. In the xy = uc case, the adversary continues to call CH with the index l of an existing transcript, but this time provides its own challenge c, indicating it wants to be challenged to find a response. The game allows this only if the provided challenge is different from the one in the original transcript. The adversary can call TR and CH as many times as it wants, in any order. The adversary terminates by outputting the index k of a challenge session against which it hopes its response z will verify. Define the advantage via $\mathbf{Adv}_{\mathsf{ID}}^{\mathrm{cimp\text{-}xy}}(\mathcal{P}) = \Pr[\mathbf{G}_{\mathsf{ID}}^{\mathrm{cimp\text{-}xy}}(\mathcal{P})]$.

We also define a metric of security of the identification scheme against key recovery under passive attack. The formalization considers game $\mathbf{G}_{\mathsf{ID}}^{\mathrm{kr\text{-}pa}}(\mathcal{I})$ of Fig. 3 associated to identification scheme ID and kr adversary $\mathcal{I}$. The transcript oracle TR is as before. Adversary $\mathcal{I}$ aims to find a private key isk^* that is functionally equivalent to isk in the sense that $\mathsf{ID.KVf}(ivk, isk^*) = \mathsf{true}$. (In particular, it certainly succeeds if it recovers the private key isk.) We let $\mathbf{Adv}_{\mathsf{ID}}^{\mathrm{kr\text{-}pa}}(\mathcal{I})$ $= \Pr[\mathbf{G}_{\mathsf{ID}}^{\mathrm{kr\text{-}pa}}(\mathcal{I})]$ be the probability that it succeeds. The notion of KR security from [3,14] did not give the adversary a TR oracle (excluding even passive attacks) and required that for success it find the target key isk (rather than, as here, being allowed to get away with something functionally equivalent).

ACHIEVING THE NOTIONS. For typical identification schemes that are HVZK, security against key recovery under passive attack corresponds exactly to the standard assumption underlying the scheme, for example the one-wayness of RSA for GQ. The following says that under the assumption of security against key recovery under passive attack, we can establish both CIMP-UC and CIMP-UU for identification schemes that are extractable. In the second case, however, we require that the challenge-lengths used be large.

The identification schemes we will use to build DAPS are Sigma protocols, meaning perfectly extractable, and hence for these schemes $\mathbf{Adv}_{\mathsf{ID}}^{\mathrm{ex}}(\mathcal{A})$ below will be 0. We omit the proof as it uses standard arguments [3].

Lemma 1. *Let* ID *be an identification scheme. For any adversary* $\mathcal{P}$ *against* CIMP-UC *we construct a key recovery adversary* $\mathcal{I}$ *and extraction adversary* $\mathcal{A}$ *such that*
$$\mathbf{Adv}_{\mathsf{ID}}^{\mathrm{cimp\text{-}uc}}(\mathcal{P}) \le \mathbf{Adv}_{\mathsf{ID}}^{\mathrm{kr\text{-}pa}}(\mathcal{I}) + \mathbf{Adv}_{\mathsf{ID}}^{\mathrm{ex}}(\mathcal{A}).$$

Also for any adversary $\mathcal{P}$ *against* CIMP-UU *that makes* q_c *queries to its* CH *oracle, each with challenge length at least* cl, *we construct a key recovery adversary* $\mathcal{I}$ *such that*
$$\mathbf{Adv}_{\mathsf{ID}}^{\mathrm{cimp\text{-}uu}}(\mathcal{P}) \le \mathbf{Adv}_{\mathsf{ID}}^{\mathrm{kr\text{-}pa}}(\mathcal{I}) + \mathbf{Adv}_{\mathsf{ID}}^{\mathrm{ex}}(\mathcal{A}) + q_c \cdot 2^{-\mathrm{cl}}.$$

In both cases, the running times of $\mathcal{I}$ *and* $\mathcal{A}$ *are about that of* $\mathcal{P}$ *plus the time for one execution of* ID.Ex.

Above, CIMP-UU was established assuming long challenges. We note that this is necessary, meaning CIMP-UU does not hold for short challenges, such as one-bit ones. To see this, assume $\mathsf{cl} \in \mathsf{ID.clS}$ and $q \geq 1$ is a parameter. Consider the following attack (adversary) $\mathcal{P}$. It makes a single query $Y\|c\|z \leftarrow_\$ \mathrm{TR}(\mathsf{cl})$. Then for $i = 1, \ldots, q$ it queries $c_i \leftarrow_\$ \mathrm{CH}(1)$. If there is a k such that $c_k = c$ then it returns (k, z) and wins, else it returns $\perp$. We have

$$\mathbf{Adv}_{\mathsf{ID}}^{\mathrm{cimp\text{-}uu}}(\mathcal{P}) = 1 - \left(1 - \frac{1}{2^{\mathsf{cl}}}\right)^q \approx \frac{q}{2^{\mathsf{cl}}}.$$

Thus, roughly, the attack succeeds in time 2^{cl}, so if the latter is small, CIMP-UU security will not hold. Our **H2** transform will use long challenges and be able to rely only on CIMP-UU, but our **ID2** transform will require security on both long and short (1-bit) challenges, and thus will rely on CIMP-UC in addition to CIMP-UU. We note that given Lemma 1, we could use CIMP-UC throughout, but for the reductions it is simpler and more convenient to work with CIMP-UU when possible.

4   DAPS Definitions

Let DS be a signature scheme. When used as a DAPS [15,16], a message $m = (a, p)$ for DS is a pair consisting of an *address* a and a *payload* p. We require (1) the double authentication prevention (DAP) property and (2) a restricted form of unforgeability, as defined below.

Game $\mathbf{G}_{\mathsf{DS}}^{\mathrm{uf}}(\mathcal{A})$	Game $\mathbf{G}_{\mathsf{DS}}^{\mathrm{dap}}(\mathcal{A})$
$(vk, sk) \leftarrow_\$ \mathsf{DS.Kg}$	$(vk, sk) \leftarrow_\$ \mathsf{DS.Kg}$
$A, M \leftarrow \emptyset$	$(m_1, m_2, \sigma_1, \sigma_2) \leftarrow_\$ \mathcal{A}(vk, sk)$
$(m, \sigma) \leftarrow_\$ \mathcal{A}^{\mathrm{SIGN}}(vk)$	$v_1 \leftarrow \mathsf{DS.Vf}(vk, m_1, \sigma_1)$
$d \leftarrow \mathsf{DS.Vf}(vk, m, \sigma)$	$v_2 \leftarrow \mathsf{DS.Vf}(vk, m_2, \sigma_2)$
Return $(d \wedge (m \notin M))$	If $\neg v_1 \vee \neg v_2$: Return false
	$(a_1, p_1) \leftarrow m_1$; $(a_2, p_2) \leftarrow m_2$
$\underline{\mathrm{SIGN}(m)}$	If $a_1 \neq a_2 \vee p_1 = p_2$: Return false
$(a, p) \leftarrow m$	$sk^* \leftarrow_\$ \mathsf{DS.Ex}(vk, m_1, m_2, \sigma_1, \sigma_2)$
If $a \in A$: Return $\perp$	Return $(sk^* \neq sk)$
$A \leftarrow A \cup \{a\}$	
$M \leftarrow M \cup \{m\}$	
$\sigma \leftarrow_\$ \mathsf{DS.Sig}(vk, sk, m)$	
Return σ	

Fig. 4. Games defining unforgeability and the DAP property of signature scheme DS.

THE DAP PROPERTY. Call messages $m_1 = (a_1, p_1)$ and $m_2 = (a_2, p_2)$ *colliding* if $a_1 = a_2$ but $p_1 \neq p_2$. Double authentication prevention (DAP) [15,16] requires that possession of signatures on colliding messages allow anyone to extract the

signing key. It is captured formally by the advantage $\mathbf{Adv}_{\mathsf{DS}}^{\mathrm{dap}}(\mathcal{A}) = \Pr[\mathbf{G}_{\mathsf{DS}}^{\mathrm{dap}}(\mathcal{A})]$
associated to adversary $\mathcal{A}$, where game $\mathbf{G}_{\mathsf{DS}}^{\mathrm{dap}}(\mathcal{A})$ is in Fig. 4. The adversary
produces messages m_1, m_2 and signatures σ_1, σ_2, and an extraction algorithm
DS.Ex associated to the scheme then attempts to compute sk. The adversary
wins if the key sk^* produced by DS.Ex is different from sk yet extraction should
have succeeded, meaning the messages were colliding and their signatures were
valid. The adversary has sk as input to cover the fact that the signer is the
one attempting—due to coercion and subversion, but nonetheless—to produce
signatures on colliding messages. (And thus it does not need access to a SIGN
oracle.) We note that we are not saying it is hard to produce signatures on
colliding messages—it isn't, given sk—but rather that doing so will reveal sk. We
also stress that extraction is not required just for honestly-generated signatures,
but for *any*, even adversarially generated signatures that are valid, again because
the signer is the adversary here.

UNFORGEABILITY. Let $\mathbf{Adv}_{\mathsf{DS}}^{\mathrm{uf}}(\mathcal{A}) = \Pr[\mathbf{G}_{\mathsf{DS}}^{\mathrm{uf}}(\mathcal{A})]$ be the uf-advantage associated
to adversary $\mathcal{A}$, where game $\mathbf{G}_{\mathsf{DS}}^{\mathrm{uf}}(\mathcal{A})$ is in Fig. 4. This is the classical notion
of [10], except that addresses of the messages the signer signs must be all differ-
ent, as captured through the set A in the game. This is necessary because the
double authentication prevention requirement precludes security if the signer
releases signatures of two messages with the same address. In practice it means
that the signer must maintain a log of all messages it has signed and make sure
that it does not sign two messages with the same address. A CA is likely to
maintain such a log in any case so this is unlikely to be an extra burden.

DISCUSSION. Regarding the dap property, asking that the key sk^* returned by the
extractor DS.Ex be equal to sk may seem unnecessarily strong. It might suffice
if sk^* was "functionally equivalent" to sk, allowing computation of signatures
that could not be distinguished from real ones. Such a property is considered
in PS [16]. Formalizing it would require adding another security game based on
indistinguishability. As our schemes (as well as the ones from [15,16]) achieve
the simpler and stronger property we have defined, we adopt it in our definition.

The dap game chooses the keys vk, sk honestly. Allowing these to be adversarially chosen would result in a stronger requirement, also formalized in PS [15,16].
Our view is that our (weaker) requirement is appropriate for the application we
envision because the CA does not wish to create rogue certificates and has no
incentive to create keys allowing it, and the court order happens after the CA
and its keys are established, so that key establishment is honest.

5 Our ID to DAPS Transforms

We specify and analyze our two generic transformations, **H2** and **ID2**, of trapdoor identification schemes to DAPS. Both deliver efficient DAPS, signature
sizes being somewhat smaller in the second case.

5.1   The Double-Hash Transform

THE CONSTRUCTION. Let ID be a trapdoor identification scheme. Our **H2** (double hash) transform associates to it, a supported challenge length $cl \in ID.clS$, and a seed length $sl \in \mathbb{N}$, a DAPS $DS = \mathbf{H2}[ID, cl, sl]$. The algorithms of DS are defined in Fig. 5. We give some intuition on the design. In the signing algorithm, we specify the commitment Y as a hash of the address, i.e., messages with the same address result in transcripts with the same commitment. We then specify the challenge c as a hash of the message (i.e., address and payload) and a random seed. Signatures consist of the seed and the corresponding response. Concerning the extractability property, observe that the ID.Ex algorithm, when applied to colliding signature transcripts, reveals isk but not itk, whereas DAPS extraction needs to recover both, i.e., the full secret key $sk = (isk, itk)$. We resolve this by putting in the verification key a particular encryption, denoted ITK, of itk, under isk (we assume itk can be encoded in tl bits).

The scheme uses random oracles $H(\cdot, \{0,1\}^{tl})$, $H(\cdot, ID.CS(ivk, cl))$ and $H(\cdot, \{0,1\}^{cl})$. For simplicity it is assumed that the three range sets involved here are distinct, which makes the random oracles independent. If the range sets are not distinct, the scheme must be modified to use domain separation [4] in calling these oracles. This can be done simply by prefixing the query to the i-th oracle with i ($i = 1, 2, 3$ for our three oracles).

H2[ID, cl, sl].Kg^H

$(ivk, isk, itk) \leftarrow\!\!{\scriptstyle\$}\; ID.Kg$
$ITK \leftarrow itk \oplus H(isk, \{0,1\}^{tl})$
$vk \leftarrow (ivk, ITK)\,;\; sk \leftarrow (isk, itk)$
Return (vk, sk)

H2[ID, cl, sl].Ex^H$(vk, m_1, m_2, \sigma_1, \sigma_2)$

$(ivk, ITK) \leftarrow vk$
For $i = 1, 2$ do
$\quad (a_i, p_i) \leftarrow m_i\,;\; (z_i, s_i) \leftarrow \sigma_i$
$\quad Y_i \leftarrow H(a_i, ID.CS(ivk, cl))$
$\quad c_i \leftarrow H(a_i \| p_i \| s_i, \{0,1\}^{cl})$
$isk^* \leftarrow ID.Ex(ivk, Y_1 \| c_1 \| z_1, Y_2 \| c_2 \| z_2)$
$itk^* \leftarrow H(isk^*, \{0,1\}^{tl}) \oplus ITK$
$sk^* \leftarrow (isk^*, itk^*)\,;$ Return sk^*

H2[ID, cl, sl].Sig^H(vk, sk, m)

$(ivk, ITK) \leftarrow vk\,;\; (isk, itk) \leftarrow sk$
$(a, p) \leftarrow m\,;\; s \leftarrow\!\!{\scriptstyle\$}\; \{0,1\}^{sl}$
$Y \leftarrow H(a, ID.CS(ivk, cl))$
$y \leftarrow\!\!{\scriptstyle\$}\; ID.Cmt^{-1}(ivk, itk, Y, cl)$
$c \leftarrow H(a \| p \| s, \{0,1\}^{cl})$
$z \leftarrow ID.Rsp(ivk, isk, c, y)$
$\sigma \leftarrow (z, s)\,;$ Return σ

H2[ID, cl, sl].Vf^H(vk, m, σ)

$(ivk, ITK) \leftarrow vk\,;\; (a, p) \leftarrow m\,;\; (z, s) \leftarrow \sigma$
$Y \leftarrow H(a, ID.CS(ivk, cl))$
$c \leftarrow H(a \| p \| s, \{0,1\}^{cl})$
Return $ID.Vf(ivk, Y \| c \| z)$

Fig. 5. Our construction of a DAPS **H2**[ID, cl, sl] from a trapdoor identification scheme ID, a challenge length $cl \in ID.clS$, and a seed length $sl \in \mathbb{N}$.

DAP SECURITY OF OUR CONSTRUCTION. The following confirms that double authentication prevention is achieved. We model H as a random oracle.

Theorem 1. *Let DAPS* $\mathsf{DS} = \mathbf{H2}[\mathsf{ID}, \mathsf{cl}, \mathsf{sl}]$ *be obtained from trapdoor identification scheme* ID, *challenge length* cl, *and seed length* sl *as above. Let* $\mathcal{A}$ *be an adversary making* $q \geq 2$ *distinct* $\mathrm{H}(\cdot, \{0,1\}^{\mathsf{cl}})$ *queries. If* ID *has perfect extractability then*

$$\mathbf{Adv}_{\mathsf{DS}}^{\mathrm{dap}}(\mathcal{A}) \leq q(q-1)/2^{\mathsf{cl}+1}.$$

Proof (Theorem 1). In game $\mathbf{G}_{\mathsf{DS}}^{\mathrm{dap}}(\mathcal{A})$ of Fig. 4, consider the execution of the algorithm $\mathsf{DS.Ex}^{\mathrm{H}}$ of Fig. 5 on $vk, m_1, m_2, \sigma_2, \sigma_2$ where $(m_1, m_2, \sigma_1, \sigma_2) \leftarrow\!\!\$ $\mathcal{A}^{\mathrm{H}}(vk, sk)$. Let $Y_1 \| c_1 \| z_1, Y_2 \| c_2 \| z_2$ be the transcripts computed within. Assume σ_1, σ_2 are valid signatures of m_1, m_2, respectively, relative to $vk = (ivk, ITK)$. As per the verification algorithm $\mathsf{DS.Vf}^{\mathrm{H}}$ of Fig. 5 this means that the transcripts $Y_1 \| c_1 \| z_1, Y_2 \| c_2 \| z_2$ are valid under the ID scheme, meaning $\mathsf{ID.Vf}(ivk, Y_1 \| c_1 \| z_1) = \mathsf{ID.Vf}(ivk, Y_2 \| c_2 \| z_2) = \mathsf{true}$. If the messages $m_1 = (a_1, p_1)$ and $m_2 = (a_2, p_2)$ output by $\mathcal{A}$ are colliding then we also have $Y_1 = Y_2$. This is because $a_1 = a_2$ and verification ensures that $Y_1 = \mathrm{H}(a_1, \mathsf{ID.CS}(ivk, \mathsf{cl}))$ and $Y_2 = \mathrm{H}(a_2, \mathsf{ID.CS}(ivk, \mathsf{cl}))$. So if $c_1 \neq c_2$ then the extraction property of ID ensures that $isk^* = isk$. If so, we also can obtain $itk^* = itk$, so that the full secret key $sk = (isk, itk)$ is recovered. So $\mathbf{Adv}_{\mathsf{DS}}^{\mathrm{dap}}(\mathcal{A})$ is at most the probability that the challenges are equal even though the payloads are not. But the challenges are outputs of $\mathrm{H}(\cdot, \{0,1\}^{\mathsf{cl}})$, to which the game makes at most q queries. So the probability that these challenges collide is at most $q(q-1)/2^{\mathsf{cl}+1}$. $\square$

We note this proof does not essentially rely on H being a random oracle.

UNFORGEABILITY OF OUR CONSTRUCTION. The following shows that the restricted unforgeability of our DAPS tightly reduces to the cimp-uu plus kr security of the underlying ID scheme. As before we model H as a random oracle.

Theorem 2. *Let DAPS* $\mathsf{DS} = \mathbf{H2}[\mathsf{ID}, \mathsf{cl}, \mathsf{sl}]$ *be obtained from trapdoor identification scheme* ID, *challenge length* cl, *and seed length* sl *as in Fig. 5. Let* $\mathcal{A}$ *be a uf adversary against* DS *and suppose the number of queries that* $\mathcal{A}$ *makes to its* $\mathrm{H}(\cdot, \{0,1\}^{\mathsf{tl}})$, $\mathrm{H}(\cdot, \mathsf{ID.CS}(ivk, \mathsf{cl}))$, $\mathrm{H}(\cdot, \{0,1\}^{\mathsf{cl}})$, SIGN *oracles are, respectively,* q_1, q_2, q_3, q_s. *Then from* $\mathcal{A}$ *we can construct* cimp-uu *adversary* $\mathcal{P}$ *and* kr *adversary* $\mathcal{I}$ *such that*

$$\mathbf{Adv}_{\mathsf{DS}}^{\mathrm{uf}}(\mathcal{A}) \leq \mathbf{Adv}_{\mathsf{ID}}^{\mathrm{cimp\text{-}uu}}(\mathcal{P}) + \mathbf{Adv}_{\mathsf{ID}}^{\mathrm{kr\text{-}pa}}(\mathcal{I}) + \frac{q_s(2q_3 + q_s - 1)}{2^{\mathsf{sl}+1}}.$$

Adversaries $\mathcal{P}, \mathcal{I}$ *make* $q_2 + q_s + 1$ *queries to* TR. *Adversary* $\mathcal{P}$ *makes* q_3 *queries to* CH. *The running time of adversary* $\mathcal{P}$ *is about that of* $\mathcal{A}$. *The running time of adversary* $\mathcal{I}$ *is that of* $\mathcal{A}$ *plus the time for* q_1 *executions of* $\mathsf{ID.KVf}$.

Proof (Theorem 2). We assume that $\mathcal{A}$ avoids certain pointless behavior that would only cause it to lose. Thus, we assume that, in the messages it queries to SIGN, the addresses are all different. Also we assume it did not query to SIGN the message m in the forgery (m, σ) that it eventually outputs. The two together mean that the sets A, M in game $\mathbf{G}_{\mathsf{DS}}^{\mathrm{uf}}(\mathcal{A})$, and the code and checks associated

Game G_0/$\boxed{G_1}$

$(ivk, isk, itk) \leftarrow\!\!{}_\$ \ \mathsf{ID.Kg}$
$ITK \leftarrow itk \oplus H(isk, \{0,1\}^{tl})$
$vk \leftarrow (ivk, ITK)$
$(m, \sigma) \leftarrow\!\!{}_\$ \ \mathcal{A}^{\mathrm{SIGN}, H}(vk)$
Return $\mathsf{DS.Vf}^H(vk, m, \sigma)$

$H(x, \mathrm{Rng})$
If (not $HT[x, \mathrm{Rng}]$):
$\quad HT[x, \mathrm{Rng}] \leftarrow\!\!{}_\$ \ \mathrm{Rng}$
Return $HT[x, \mathrm{Rng}]$

$\mathrm{SIGN}(m)$

$(a, p) \leftarrow m$; $s \leftarrow\!\!{}_\$ \ \{0,1\}^{sl}$
$Y \leftarrow H(a, \mathsf{ID.CS}(ivk, cl))$
$y \leftarrow\!\!{}_\$ \ \mathsf{ID.Cmt}^{-1}(ivk, itk, Y, cl)$
If (not $HT[a\|p\|s, \{0,1\}^{cl}]$):
$\quad HT[a\|p\|s, \{0,1\}^{cl}] \leftarrow\!\!{}_\$ \ \{0,1\}^{cl}$
Else
$\quad \text{bad} \leftarrow \text{true}$
$\quad \boxed{HT[a\|p\|s, \{0,1\}^{cl}] \leftarrow\!\!{}_\$ \ \{0,1\}^{cl}}$
$c \leftarrow HT[a\|p\|s, \{0,1\}^{cl}]$
$z \leftarrow \mathsf{ID.Rsp}(ivk, isk, c, y)$
$\sigma \leftarrow (z, s)$; Return σ

Game $\boxed{G_2}$/G_3

$(ivk, isk, itk) \leftarrow\!\!{}_\$ \ \mathsf{ID.Kg}$
$ITK \leftarrow\!\!{}_\$ \ \{0,1\}^{tl}$
$vk \leftarrow (ivk, ITK)$
$(m, \sigma) \leftarrow\!\!{}_\$ \ \mathcal{A}^{\mathrm{SIGN}, H}(vk)$
Return $\mathsf{DS.Vf}^H(vk, m, \sigma)$

$H(x, \mathrm{Rng})$
If (not $HT[x, \mathrm{Rng}]$):
$\quad HT[x, \mathrm{Rng}] \leftarrow\!\!{}_\$ \ \mathrm{Rng}$
$\quad$ If $((\mathrm{Rng} = \{0,1\}^{tl}) \wedge (x = isk))$:
$\quad\quad \text{bad} \leftarrow \text{true}$; $\boxed{HT[x, \mathrm{Rng}] \leftarrow ITK \oplus itk}$
Return $HT[x, \mathrm{Rng}]$

$\mathrm{SIGN}(m)$

$(a, p) \leftarrow m$; $s \leftarrow\!\!{}_\$ \ \{0,1\}^{sl}$
$Y \leftarrow H(a, \mathsf{ID.CS}(ivk, cl))$
$y \leftarrow\!\!{}_\$ \ \mathsf{ID.Cmt}^{-1}(ivk, itk, Y, cl)$
$c \leftarrow\!\!{}_\$ \ \{0,1\}^{cl}$
$HT[a\|p\|s, \{0,1\}^{cl}] \leftarrow c$
$z \leftarrow \mathsf{ID.Rsp}(ivk, isk, c, y)$
$\sigma \leftarrow (z, s)$; Return σ

Fig. 6. Games for proof of Theorem 2. Games G_1, G_2 include the boxed code and games G_0, G_3 do not.

with them, are redundant and can be removed. We will work with this simplified form of the game, that we call G_0.

Identical-until-bad games G_0, G_1 of Fig. 6 move us to allow picking a random seed in responding to a SIGN query, regardless of whether the corresponding hash table entry was defined or not. We have

$$\mathbf{Adv}_{DS}^{uf}(\mathcal{A}) = \Pr[G_0] = \Pr[G_1] + \Pr[G_0] - \Pr[G_1]$$
$$\leq \Pr[G_1] + \Pr[G_0 \text{ sets bad}],$$

where the inequality is by the Fundamental Lemma of Game Playing of [5]. The random choice of s made by procedure SIGN ensures

$$\Pr[G_0 \text{ sets bad}] \leq \sum_{i=0}^{q_s-1} \frac{q_3 + i}{2^{sl}} = \frac{q_s(2q_3 + q_s - 1)}{2^{sl+1}}.$$

Now we need to bound $\Pr[G_1]$. We start by considering whether the ciphertext $ITK = itk \oplus H(isk, \{0,1\}^{tl})$ helps $\mathcal{A}$ over and above access to SIGN. Consider the games G_2, G_3 of Fig. 6. They pick ITK directly at random rather than as prescribed in the scheme. However, via the boxed code that it contains, game G_2 compensates, replying to $H(\cdot, \{0,1\}^{tl})$ queries in such a way that $ITK = itk \oplus H(isk, \{0,1\}^{tl})$. Thus G_2 is equivalent to G_1. Game G_3 omits the boxed code, but the games are identical-until-bad. So we have

$$\Pr[G_1] = \Pr[G_2] = \Pr[G_3] + \Pr[G_2] - \Pr[G_3]$$
$$\leq \Pr[G_3] + \Pr[G_3 \text{ sets bad}], \qquad (1)$$

where again the inequality is by the Fundamental Lemma of Game Playing of [5]. Now we have two tasks, namely to bound $\Pr[G_3]$ and to bound $\Pr[G_3 \text{ sets bad}]$. The first corresponds to showing $\mathcal{A}$ cannot forge if ciphertext ITK is random, and the second corresponds to showing that changing the ciphertext to random makes little difference. The first relies on the cimp-uu security of ID, the second on its kr security.

To bound $\Pr[G_3]$, consider game G_4 of Fig. 7. It moves us towards using cimp-uu by generating conversation transcripts $Y_i \| c_i \| z_i$ and having SIGN use these. We have

$$\Pr[G_3] = \Pr[G_4].$$

We build cimp-uu adversary $\mathcal{P}$ so that

$$\Pr[G_4] \leq \mathbf{Adv}_{\mathsf{ID}}^{\text{cimp-uu}}(\mathcal{P}).$$

The construction of $\mathcal{P}$ is described in detail in Fig. 8. The idea is as follows. Adversary $\mathcal{P}$ uses its transcript oracle TR to generate the transcripts that G_4 generates directly. It can then simulate $\mathcal{A}$'s SIGN oracle as per game G_4. Simulation of $H(\cdot, \text{Rng})$ is done directly as in the game for $\text{Rng} = \{0,1\}^{tl}$ and $\text{Rng} = \mathsf{ID.CS}(ivk, cl)$. When a query x is made to $H(\cdot, \{0,1\}^{cl})$, adversary $\mathcal{P}$ parses x as $a \| p \| s$, sends the index of the corresponding TR query to its challenge oracle CH to get back a challenge, and returns this challenge as the response to the oracle query. Finally when $\mathcal{A}$ produces a forgery, the response in the corresponding signature is output as an impersonation that is successful as long as the forgery was valid.

To bound $\Pr[G_3 \text{ sets bad}]$, consider game G_5 of Fig. 7. It answers SIGN queries just like G_4, and the only modification in answering H queries is to keep track of queries to $H(\cdot, \{0,1\}^{tl})$ in the set T. The game ignores the forgery, returning true if isk was queried to $H(\cdot, \{0,1\}^{tl})$. We have

$$\Pr[G_3 \text{ sets bad}] = \Pr[G_5].$$

We build $\mathcal{I}$ so that

$$\Pr[G_5] \leq \mathbf{Adv}_{\mathsf{ID}}^{\text{kr-pa}}(\mathcal{I}).$$

The idea is simple, namely that if the adversary queries isk to $H(\cdot, \{0,1\}^{tl})$ then we can obtain isk by watching the oracle queries of $\mathcal{A}$. The difficulty is that, to run $\mathcal{A}$, one first has to simulate answers to SIGN queries using transcripts, and it is to enable this that we moved to G_5. Again the game was crafted to make the construction of adversary $\mathcal{I}$ quite direct. The construction is described in detail

---

Game G_4

$(ivk, isk, itk) \leftarrow\!\!\text{\$}\ \text{ID.Kg}$
$ITK \leftarrow\!\!\text{\$}\ \{0,1\}^{\text{tl}}$
$vk \leftarrow (ivk, ITK)$
For $i = 1, \ldots, q_2 + q_s + 1$ do
$\quad (Y_i, y_i) \leftarrow\!\!\text{\$}\ \text{ID.Cmt}(ivk, \text{cl})$
$\quad c_i \leftarrow\!\!\text{\$}\ \{0,1\}^{\text{cl}}$
$\quad z_i \leftarrow \text{ID.Rsp}(ivk, isk, c_i, y_i)$
$i_2 \leftarrow 0$
$(m, \sigma) \leftarrow\!\!\text{\$}\ \mathcal{A}^{\text{SIGN,H}}(vk)$
$(a, p) \leftarrow m$; $(z, s) \leftarrow \sigma$
$Y \leftarrow \text{H}(a, \text{ID.CS}(ivk, \text{cl}))$
$c \leftarrow \text{H}(a \| p \| s, \{0,1\}^{\text{cl}})$
Return $\text{ID.Vf}(ivk, Y \| c \| z)$

Game G_5

$(ivk, isk, itk) \leftarrow\!\!\text{\$}\ \text{ID.Kg}$
$ITK \leftarrow\!\!\text{\$}\ \{0,1\}^{\text{tl}}$
$vk \leftarrow (ivk, ITK)$
For $i = 1, \ldots, q_2 + q_s + 1$ do
$\quad (Y_i, y_i) \leftarrow\!\!\text{\$}\ \text{ID.Cmt}(ivk, \text{cl})$
$\quad c_i \leftarrow\!\!\text{\$}\ \{0,1\}^{\text{cl}}$
$\quad z_i \leftarrow \text{ID.Rsp}(ivk, isk, c_i, y_i)$
$i_2 \leftarrow 0$; $T \leftarrow \emptyset$
$(m, \sigma) \leftarrow\!\!\text{\$}\ \mathcal{A}^{\text{SIGN,H}}(vk)$
Return $(isk \in T)$

$\text{SIGN}(m)$ $/\!/ \ G_4, G_5$

$(a, p) \leftarrow m$; $s \leftarrow\!\!\text{\$}\ \{0,1\}^{\text{sl}}$
$Y \leftarrow \text{H}(a, \text{ID.CS}(ivk, \text{cl}))$
$i \leftarrow \text{Ind}_2(a)$
$\text{HT}[a \| p \| s, \{0,1\}^{\text{cl}}] \leftarrow c_i$
$\sigma \leftarrow (z_i, s)$; Return σ

$\text{H}(x, \text{Rng})$ $/\!/ \ G_4$
If (not $\text{HT}[x, \text{Rng}]$):
$\quad \text{HT}[x, \text{Rng}] \leftarrow\!\!\text{\$}\ \text{Rng}$
$\quad$ If ($\text{Rng} = \{0,1\}^{\text{cl}}$):
$\qquad \text{HT}[x, \text{Rng}] \leftarrow\!\!\text{\$}\ \{0,1\}^{\text{cl}}$
$\quad$ If ($\text{Rng} = \text{ID.CS}(ivk, \text{cl})$):
$\qquad i_2 \leftarrow i_2 + 1$; $\text{HT}[x, \text{Rng}] \leftarrow Y_{i_2}$; $\text{Ind}_2(x) \leftarrow i_2$
Return $\text{HT}[x, \text{Rng}]$

$\text{H}(x, \text{Rng})$ $/\!/ \ G_5$
If (not $\text{HT}[x, \text{Rng}]$):
$\quad \text{HT}[x, \text{Rng}] \leftarrow\!\!\text{\$}\ \text{Rng}$
$\quad$ If ($\text{Rng} = \{0,1\}^{\text{tl}}$):
$\qquad T \leftarrow T \cup \{x\}$
$\quad$ If ($\text{Rng} = \text{ID.CS}(ivk, \text{cl})$):
$\qquad i_2 \leftarrow i_2 + 1$; $\text{HT}[x, \text{Rng}] \leftarrow Y_{i_2}$; $\text{Ind}_2(x) \leftarrow i_2$
Return $\text{HT}[x, \text{Rng}]$

Fig. 7. More games for the proof of Theorem 2.

in Fig. 8. The simulation of the SIGN oracle is as before. The simulation of H is more direct, following game G_5 rather than invoking the CH oracle. When $\mathcal{A}$ returns its forgery, the set T contains candidates for the identification secret key isk. Adversary $\mathcal{I}$ now verifies each candidate using the key-verification algorithm of the identification scheme, returning a successful candidate if one exists. □

5.2 The Double-ID Transform

Our **ID2** transform roughly maintains signing and verifying time compared to **H2** but signatures are shorter, consisting of an ID response plus one bit. Since the verifier can try both possibilities for this bit, if one is willing to double the verification time, even this bit is expendable.

THE CONSTRUCTION. Our construction assumes two main ingredients: The first is a trapdoor identification scheme ID that is commitment recovering, has unique responses, and simultaneously supports challenge lengths 1 and cl $\gg 1$. For the choice of cl we further assume $|\text{ID.RS}(ivk, 1)| = |\text{ID.CS}(ivk, \text{cl})|$ for all ivk, i.e.,

---

Adversary $\mathcal{P}^{\mathrm{TR},\mathrm{CH}}(ivk)$

$ITK \leftarrow_\$ \{0,1\}^{\mathrm{tl}}$
$vk \leftarrow (ivk, ITK)$
For $i = 1, \ldots, q_2 + q_s + 1$ do
$\quad (Y_i, c_i, z_i) \leftarrow_\$ \mathrm{TR}(\mathsf{cl})$
$i_2 \leftarrow 0$; $j \leftarrow 0$
$(m, \sigma) \leftarrow_\$ \mathcal{A}^{\mathrm{SIGN},\mathrm{H}}(vk)$
$(a, p) \leftarrow m$; $(z, s) \leftarrow \sigma$
$Y \leftarrow \mathrm{H}(a, \mathsf{ID.CS}(ivk, \mathsf{cl}))$
$c \leftarrow \mathrm{H}(a\|p\|s, \{0,1\}^{\mathrm{cl}})$
$k \leftarrow \mathrm{Ind}_3(a\|p\|s)$
Return (k, z)

Adversary $\mathcal{I}^{\mathrm{TR}}(ivk)$

$ITK \leftarrow_\$ \{0,1\}^{\mathrm{tl}}$
$vk \leftarrow (ivk, ITK)$
For $i = 1, \ldots, q_2 + q_s + 1$ do
$\quad (Y_i, c_i, z_i) \leftarrow_\$ \mathrm{TR}(\mathsf{cl})$
$i_2 \leftarrow 0$; $T \leftarrow \emptyset$; $j \leftarrow 0$
$(m, \sigma) \leftarrow_\$ \mathcal{A}^{\mathrm{SIGN},\mathrm{H}}(vk)$
For all $x \in T$ do
$\quad$ If $\mathsf{ID.KVf}(ivk, x)$:
$\quad\quad$ Return x
Return $\bot$

$\mathrm{SIGN}(m)$ // $\mathcal{P}, \mathcal{I}$

$(a, p) \leftarrow m$; $s \leftarrow_\$ \{0,1\}^{\mathrm{sl}}$
$Y \leftarrow \mathrm{H}(a, \mathsf{ID.CS}(ivk, \mathsf{cl}))$
$i \leftarrow \mathrm{Ind}_2(a)$
$HT[a\|p\|s, \{0,1\}^{\mathrm{cl}}] \leftarrow c_i$
$\sigma \leftarrow (z_i, s)$; Return σ

$\mathrm{H}(x, \mathrm{Rng})$ // $\mathcal{P}$

If (not $HT[x, \mathrm{Rng}]$):
$\quad HT[x, \mathrm{Rng}] \leftarrow_\$ \mathrm{Rng}$
$\quad$ If $(\mathrm{Rng} = \{0,1\}^{\mathrm{cl}})$:
$\quad\quad a\|p\|s \leftarrow x$; $Y \leftarrow \mathrm{H}(a, \mathsf{ID.CS}(ivk, \mathsf{cl}))$
$\quad\quad l \leftarrow \mathrm{Ind}_2(a)$; $j \leftarrow j + 1$; $c \leftarrow_\$ \mathrm{CH}(l)$
$\quad\quad \mathrm{Ind}_3(x) \leftarrow j$; $HT[x, \mathrm{Rng}] \leftarrow c$
$\quad$ If $(\mathrm{Rng} = \mathsf{ID.CS}(ivk, \mathsf{cl}))$:
$\quad\quad i_2 \leftarrow i_2 + 1$; $HT[x, \mathrm{Rng}] \leftarrow Y_{i_2}$; $\mathrm{Ind}_2(x) \leftarrow i_2$
Return $HT[x, \mathrm{Rng}]$

$\mathrm{H}(x, \mathrm{Rng})$ // $\mathcal{I}$

If (not $HT[x, \mathrm{Rng}]$):
$\quad$ If $(\mathrm{Rng} = \{0,1\}^{\mathrm{tl}})$: $T \leftarrow T \cup \{x\}$
$\quad$ If $(\mathrm{Rng} = \mathsf{ID.CS}(ivk, \mathsf{cl}))$:
$\quad\quad i_2 \leftarrow i_2 + 1$; $HT[x, \mathrm{Rng}] \leftarrow Y_{i_2}$; $\mathrm{Ind}_2(x) \leftarrow i_2$
Return $HT[x, \mathrm{Rng}]$

Fig. 8. Adversaries for proof of Theorem 2.

the response space for 1-bit challenges has the same cardinality as the commitment space for cl-bit challenges. The second component is a random bijection Π (cf. Sect. 2) between sets $\mathsf{ID.RS}(ivk, 1)$ and $\mathsf{ID.CS}(ivk, \mathsf{cl})$, i.e., oracle Π^{+1} implements a random mapping from $\mathsf{ID.RS}(ivk, 1)$ to $\mathsf{ID.CS}(ivk, \mathsf{cl})$ and oracle Π^{-1} implements its inverse. In Sect. 6 we discuss trapdoor ID schemes that fulfill these requirements and show how random bijections with the required domain and range can be obtained.

The details of the **ID2** transform are specified in Fig. 9. We write $\mathrm{H}_1(\cdot)$ shorthand for $\mathrm{H}(\cdot, \mathsf{ID.CS}(ivk, 1))$, and $\mathrm{H}_2(\cdot, \cdot)$ shorthand for $\mathrm{H}((\cdot, \cdot), \{0,1\}^{\mathrm{cl}})$. As in Sect. 5.1 we assume these random oracles are independent. Key generation is as in **H2**. Signing works as follows: First a commitment $Y_1 \leftarrow \mathrm{H}_1(a)$ is derived from the address using a random oracle that maps to the commitment space $\mathsf{ID.CS}(ivk, 1)$, then a random 1-bit challenge c_1 is picked and the corresponding response z_1 of the ID scheme computed. Using bijection Π^{+1}, response z_1 is mapped to a commitment $Y_2 \in \mathsf{ID.CS}(ivk, \mathsf{cl})$. A corresponding cl-bit challenge is derived from the address and the payload per $c_2 \leftarrow \mathrm{H}_2(a, p)$. The DAPS signature consists of the response z_2 corresponding to Y_2 and c_2, together with the one-bit challenge c_1. Signatures are verified using the commitment recovery algorithm $\mathsf{ID.Rsp}^{-1}$ to recover Y_2 from z_2, computing $z_1 \leftarrow \Pi^{-1}(Y_2)$, recovering Y_1

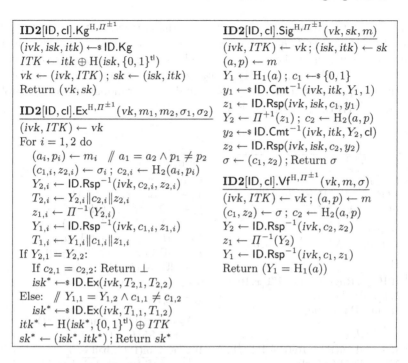

Fig. 9. Our construction of a DAPS **ID2**[ID, cl] from a trapdoor identification scheme ID, where $\{1, cl\} \subseteq$ ID.clS.

from c_1 and z_1 (again using the commitment recovery algorithm), and comparing with $H_1(a)$. Extraction algorithm DS.Ex works in the obvious way.

DAP SECURITY. The **ID2** construction achieves double authentication prevention, as the following result confirms. The proof relies on the extractability property of the ID scheme twice: once for each challenge length. We model H as a random oracle as usual. Nothing is assumed of Π other than it being a bijection.

Theorem 3. *Let DAPS* DS = **ID2**[ID, cl] *be obtained from trapdoor identification scheme* ID *and challenge length* cl *as above. Let* $\mathcal{A}$ *be an adversary making at most* q *queries to the* $H_2(\cdot) = H(\cdot, \{0, 1\}^{cl})$ *oracle. If* ID *has unique responses and perfect extractability, then* $\mathbf{Adv}_{DS}^{dap}(\mathcal{A}) \leq q(q-1)/2^{cl+1}$.

Proof (Theorem 3). Assume, in experiment $\mathbf{G}_{DS}^{dap}(\mathcal{A})$, that the adversary outputs message-signature pairs (m_1, σ_1) and (m_2, σ_2) such that for $i \in \{1, 2\}$ we have DS.Vf(vk, m_i, σ_i) = true. The latter implies for $m_i = (a_i, p_i)$ and $\sigma_i = (c_{1,i}, z_{2,i})$ that for recoverable values $z_{1,i}, Y_{2,i}$ and the corresponding transcripts $T_{1,i} = H_1(a_i)\|c_{1,i}\|z_{1,i}$ and $T_{2,i} = Y_{2,i}\|H_2(a_i, p_i)\|z_{2,i}$ we have ID.Vf$(ivk, T_{1,i})$ = ID.Vf$(ivk, T_{2,i})$ = true and $Y_{2,i} = \Pi^{+1}(z_{1,i})$. Assume $a_1 = a_2$ and $p_1 \neq p_2$. We have either $c_{1,1} \neq c_{1,2}$ or $c_{1,1} = c_{1,2}$. In the former case, the two transcripts $T_{1,1}, T_{1,2}$ have the same commitment but different challenges.

This allows us to extract the secret key via the extractability property of ID; further, by decrypting ITK we can recover itk, as required. Consider thus the case $c_{1,1} = c_{1,2}$ which implies $z_{1,1} = z_{1,2}$ and $Y_{2,1} = Y_{2,2}$ by the unique response property of ID. If $H_2(a_1, p_1) \neq H_2(a_2, p_2)$ we can extract isk, itk from the two transcripts $T_{2,1}, T_{2,2}$ as above. As $p_1 \neq p_2$ and H is a random oracle, the probability for $H_2(a_1, p_1) = H_2(a_2, p_2)$ is $q(q-1)/2^{cl+1}$. $\qquad\square$

Game $\boxed{G_0}$ / G_1	$\text{SIGN}(m)$
$(ivk, isk, itk) \leftarrow\!\!\text{\$ } \text{ID.Kg}$	$(a, p) \leftarrow m$
$ITK \leftarrow itk \oplus H(isk, \{0,1\}^{tl})$	$Y_1 \leftarrow H_1(a)$; $c_1 \leftarrow\!\!\text{\$ } \{0,1\}$
$vk \leftarrow (ivk, ITK)$	$y_1 \leftarrow\!\!\text{\$ } \text{ID.Cmt}^{-1}(ivk, itk, Y_1, 1)$
$(m, \sigma) \leftarrow\!\!\text{\$ } \mathcal{A}^{\text{SIGN},H,\Pi^{\pm 1}}(vk)$	$z_1 \leftarrow \text{ID.Rsp}(ivk, isk, c_1, y_1)$
Return $\text{DS.Vf}^{H,\Pi^{\pm 1}}(vk, m, \sigma)$	$Y_2 \leftarrow \Pi^{+1}(z_1)$; $c_2 \leftarrow H_2(a, p)$
$H(x, \text{Rng})$	$y_2 \leftarrow\!\!\text{\$ } \text{ID.Cmt}^{-1}(ivk, itk, Y_2, \text{cl})$
If $HT[x, \text{Rng}]$: Return $HT[x, \text{Rng}]$	$z_2 \leftarrow \text{ID.Rsp}(ivk, isk, c_2, y_2)$
$HT[x, \text{Rng}] \leftarrow\!\!\text{\$ } \text{Rng}$	$\sigma \leftarrow (c_1, z_2)$; Return σ
Return $HT[x, \text{Rng}]$	$\Pi^{-1}(Y_2)$
	If $Y_2 \in \text{rng}(PT)$: Return $PT^{-1}(Y_2)$
$\Pi^{+1}(z_1)$	$z_1 \leftarrow\!\!\text{\$ } \text{ID.RS}(ivk, 1)$
If $z_1 \in \text{dom}(PT)$: Return $PT^{+1}(z_1)$	If $z_1 \in \text{dom}(PT)$: bad $\leftarrow 1$
$Y_2 \leftarrow\!\!\text{\$ } \text{ID.CS}(ivk, \text{cl})$	$\boxed{z_1 \leftarrow\!\!\text{\$ } \text{ID.RS}(ivk, 1) \setminus \text{dom}(PT)}$
If $Y_2 \in \text{rng}(PT)$: bad $\leftarrow 1$	$PT \leftarrow PT \cup \{(z_1, Y_2)\}$
$\boxed{Y_2 \leftarrow\!\!\text{\$ } \text{ID.CS}(ivk, \text{cl}) \setminus \text{rng}(PT)}$	Return $PT^{-1}(Y_2)$
$PT \leftarrow PT \cup \{(z_1, Y_2)\}$	
Return $PT^{+1}(z_1)$	

Fig. 10. Games G_0, G_1 for proof of Theorem 4. Game G_0 includes the boxed code and game G_1 does not.

UNFORGEABILITY. The following establishes that if the ID scheme offers cimp-uc and kr security, then **ID2** transforms it into an unforgeable DAPS. Here we model H as a random oracle and Π as a public random bijection.

Theorem 4. *Let DAPS* DS = ID2[ID, cl] *be obtained from trapdoor identification scheme* ID *as in Fig. 9. Let* $N = \min |\text{ID.CS}(ivk, \text{cl})|$ *where the minimum is over all* $(ivk, isk, itk) \in [\text{ID.Kg}]$. *Let* $\mathcal{A}$ *be a* uf *adversary against* DS *and suppose the number of queries that* $\mathcal{A}$ *makes to its* $H(\cdot, \{0,1\}^{tl})$, $H(\cdot, \text{ID.CS}(ivk, 1))$, $H(\cdot, \{0,1\}^{cl})$, $\Pi^{\pm 1}$, SIGN *oracles are, respectively,* q_1, q_2, q_3, q_4, q_s. *Then from* $\mathcal{A}$ *we can construct* dap *adversary* $\mathcal{A}'$, kr *adversary* $\mathcal{I}$ *and* cimp-uc *adversaries* $\mathcal{P}_1, \mathcal{P}_2$ *such that*

$$\mathbf{Adv}_{\text{DS}}^{\text{uf}}(\mathcal{A}) \leq \mathbf{Adv}_{\text{DS}}^{\text{dap}}(\mathcal{A}') + \mathbf{Adv}_{\text{ID}}^{\text{kr-pa}}(\mathcal{I})$$

$$+ 2\mathbf{Adv}_{\text{ID}}^{\text{cimp-uc}}(\mathcal{P}_1) + 2\mathbf{Adv}_{\text{ID}}^{\text{cimp-uc}}(\mathcal{P}_2) + \frac{(q_4 + q_s)^2}{2N}.$$

Adversaries $\mathcal{I}, \mathcal{P}_1, \mathcal{P}_2$ make $q_2+q_3+q_4+q_s$ queries to TR, and adversaries $\mathcal{P}_1, \mathcal{P}_2$ make one query to CH. Beyond that, the running time of $\mathcal{A}', \mathcal{P}_1, \mathcal{P}_2$ is about that of $\mathcal{A}$, and the running time of $\mathcal{I}$ is that of $\mathcal{A}$ plus the time for q_1 executions of ID.KVf.

Game G_2	$\text{SIGN}(m)$
$(ivk, isk, itk) \leftarrow\!\!{\$}\ \text{ID.Kg}$	$(a, p) \leftarrow m$
$ITK \leftarrow\!\!{\$}\ \{0,1\}^{tl}$; $vk \leftarrow (ivk, ITK)$	If $\exists z \in \text{dom}(\text{PT})$ s.t.
$(m, \sigma) \leftarrow\!\!{\$}\ \mathcal{A}^{\text{SIGN}, \text{H}, \Pi^{\pm 1}}(vk)$	$\quad$ ID.Vf$(ivk, Y_1[a]\|0\|z)$ or
Return DS.Vf$^{\text{H}, \Pi^{\pm 1}}(vk, m, \sigma)$	$\quad$ ID.Vf$(ivk, Y_1[a]\|1\|z)$: $\text{bad}_2 \leftarrow 1$
	If $z_1[a] \in \text{dom}(\text{PT})$:
$\text{H}(x, \text{Rng})$	$\quad Y_2 \leftarrow \text{PT}^{+1}(z_1[a])$; $c_2 \leftarrow \text{H}_2(a, p)$
If $\text{HT}[x, \text{Rng}]$: Return $\text{HT}[x, \text{Rng}]$	$\quad y_2 \leftarrow\!\!{\$}\ \text{ID.Cmt}^{-1}(ivk, itk, Y_2, \text{cl})$
$\text{HT}[x, \text{Rng}] \leftarrow\!\!{\$}\ \text{Rng}$	$\quad z_2 \leftarrow \text{ID.Rsp}(ivk, isk, c_2, y_2)$
If $\text{Rng} = \{0,1\}^{tl}$:	Else:
$\quad$ If ID.KVf(ivk, x): $\text{bad}_1 \leftarrow 1$	$\quad Y_2 \leftarrow Y_2[a, p]$; $z_2 \leftarrow z_2[a, p]$
$\quad$ If $x = isk$: $\text{HT}[x, \text{Rng}] \leftarrow ITK \oplus itk$	$\quad \text{PT} \leftarrow \text{PT} \cup \{(z_1[a], Y_2)\}$
If $\text{Rng} = \text{ID.CS}(ivk, 1)$:	$\sigma \leftarrow (c_1[a], z_2)$; Return σ
$\quad Y_1[x]\|c_1[x]\|z_1[x] \leftarrow\!\!{\$}\ \text{TRANSC}(1)$	
$\quad \text{HT}[x, \text{Rng}] \leftarrow Y_1[x]$	$\Pi^{+1}(z_1)$
If $\text{Rng} = \{0,1\}^{cl}$:	If $z_1 \in \text{dom}(\text{PT})$: Return $\text{PT}^{+1}(z_1)$
$\quad Y_2[x]\|c_2[x]\|z_2[x] \leftarrow\!\!{\$}\ \text{TRANSC}(\text{cl})$	$Y_2[z_1]\|c_2[z_1]\|z_2[z_1] \leftarrow\!\!{\$}\ \text{TRANSC}(\text{cl})$
$\quad \text{HT}[x, \text{Rng}] \leftarrow c_2[x]$	$\text{PT} \leftarrow \text{PT} \cup \{(z_1, Y_2[z_1])\}$
Return $\text{HT}[x, \text{Rng}]$	Return $\text{PT}^{+1}(z_1)$
Algorithm $\text{TRANSC}(\text{cl})$	$\Pi^{-1}(Y_2)$
$(Y, y) \leftarrow\!\!{\$}\ \text{ID.Cmt}(ivk, \text{cl})$	If $Y_2 \in \text{rng}(\text{PT})$: Return $\text{PT}^{-1}(Y_2)$
$c \leftarrow\!\!{\$}\ \{0,1\}^{cl}$	$z_1 \leftarrow\!\!{\$}\ \text{ID.RS}(ivk, 1)$
$z \leftarrow \text{ID.Rsp}(ivk, isk, c, y)$	$\text{PT} \leftarrow \text{PT} \cup \{(z_1, Y_2)\}$
Return $Y\|c\|z$	Return $\text{PT}^{-1}(Y_2)$

Fig. 11. Game G_2 for proof of Theorem 4.

Proof (Theorem 4). In the proof, we handle queries to the random bijection Π (with oracles Π^{+1} and Π^{-1}) via lazy sampling and track input-output pairs using a table PT. Notation-wise we consider $\text{PT} \subseteq \text{ID.RS}(ivk, 1) \times \text{ID.CS}(ivk, \text{cl})$ a binary relation to which a mapping of the form $\Pi^{+1}(\alpha) = \beta$ or, equivalently, $\Pi^{-1}(\beta) = \alpha$ can be added by assigning $\text{PT} \leftarrow \text{PT} \cup \{(\alpha, \beta)\}$. We use functional expressions for table look-up, e.g., whenever $(\alpha, \beta) \in \text{PT}$ we write $\text{PT}^{+1}(\alpha) = \beta$ and $\text{PT}^{-1}(\beta) = \alpha$. We annotate the domain of PT with $\text{dom}(\text{PT}) = \{\alpha : (\alpha, \beta) \in \text{PT} \text{ for some } \beta\}$, and its range with $\text{rng}(\text{PT}) = \{\beta : (\alpha, \beta) \in \text{PT} \text{ for some } \alpha\}$.

Without loss of generality we assume from $\mathcal{A}$ the following behavior: (a) if $\mathcal{A}$ outputs a forgery attempt (m, σ) then σ was not returned by SIGN on input m; (b) $\mathcal{A}$ does not query SIGN twice on the same address; (c) for all messages $m = (a, p)$, $\mathcal{A}$ always queries $\text{H}_1(a)$ before $\text{H}_2(a, p)$; further, $\mathcal{A}$ always queries

$H_2(a, p)$ before querying $\text{SIGN}(m)$; (d) before outputting a forgery attempt, $\mathcal{A}$ makes all random oracle and random bijection queries required by the verification algorithm to verify the signature. We further may assume that $\mathcal{A}$ does not forge on an address a for which it queried a signature before: Otherwise, by DAP security, the adversary could extract the secret key and forge also on a fresh address; this is accounted for by the $\mathbf{Adv}_{\text{DS}}^{\text{dap}}(\mathcal{A}')$ term in the theorem statement. The correspondingly simplified form of the $\mathbf{G}_{\text{DS}}^{\text{uf}}(\mathcal{A})$ game is given as G_0 in Fig. 10. (Note that queries to Π^{+1} and Π^{-1} are expected to be answered with elements drawn uniformly at random from $\text{ID.CS}(ivk, \text{cl}) \setminus \text{rng}(\text{PT})$ and $\text{ID.RS}(ivk, 1) \setminus \text{dom}(\text{PT})$, respectively, and that our implementation does precisely this, though in an initially surprising form).

Observe that in G_0 the flag bad is set when resampling is required in the processing of Π^{+1} and Π^{-1}. The probability that this happens is at most $(0 + 1 + \ldots + (q_4 + q_s - 1))/N$, where N is the minimum cardinality of the commitment space for challenge length cl, as defined in the theorem statement. We define game G_1 like G_0 but with the resampling steps in the Π^{+1} and Π^{-1} oracles removed. We obtain

$$\Pr[\text{G}_0] = \Pr[\text{G}_1] + \frac{(q_4 + q_s)^2 - (q_4 + q_s)}{2N}.$$

Consider next game G_2 from Fig. 11. It is obtained from G_1 by applying the following rewriting steps. First, instead of computing ITK by evaluating $itk \oplus \text{H}(isk, \{0, 1\}^{\text{tl}})$ it picks ITK at random and programs random oracle H such that relation $ITK = itk \oplus \text{H}(isk, \{0, 1\}^{\text{tl}})$ is maintained. Second, the way random oracle queries of the form $\text{H}(x, \text{ID.CS}(ivk, 1))$ and $\text{H}(x, \{0, 1\}^{\text{cl}})$ are processed is changed: Now, the internal TRANSC algorithm is invoked to produce full identification transcripts for the corresponding challenge length; the H oracle outputs one component of these transcripts and keeps the other components for itself. Also the implementation of Π^{+1} is modified to use the TRANSC algorithm.

Concerning the SIGN oracle, observe that G_1 samples challenge c_1 and derives corresponding y_1 and z_1 values by itself. In G_2, as we assume that $\text{H}_1(a)$ is always queried before $\text{SIGN}(a, p)$, and as the $\text{H}_1(a)$ implementation now internally prepares a full transcript, the c_1, y_1, z_1 values from this transcript generation can be used within the SIGN oracle. That is, we replace the first invocations of ID.Cmt^{-1} and ID.Rsp in SIGN of G_1 by the assignments $Y_1 \leftarrow Y_1[a]$, $y_1 \leftarrow y_1[a]$, $c_1 \leftarrow c_1[a]$, and $z_1 \leftarrow z_1[a]$ in G_2. (Note that this works only because we also assume that SIGN is not queried more than once on the same address.) Consider next the assignment $Y_2 \leftarrow \Pi^{+1}(z_1)$ of SIGN in G_1 (which now would be annotated $Y_2 \leftarrow \Pi^{+1}(z_1[a])$) and the fact that Y_2 is completed by SIGN to a transcript with challenge $c_2[a, p]$. In the evaluation of $\Pi^{+1}(z_1)$, two cases can be distinguished: either the query is 'old', i.e., $z_1 \in \text{dom}(\text{PT})$, in which case SIGN proceeds its computations using the stored commitment $Y_2 = \text{PT}^{+1}(z_1)$, or the query is 'fresh', i.e., $z_1 \notin \text{dom}(\text{PT})$, in which case a new value Y_2 is sampled from $\text{ID.CS}(ivk, \text{cl})$. In both cases SIGN completes Y_2 to a full transcript with challenge $H_2(a, p) = c_2[a, p]$. As we assume that each $\text{SIGN}(a, p)$ query is preceded by a $H_2(a, p)$ query, and the latter internally generates a full transcript with challenge $c_2[a, p]$, similarly to what we did for the values Y_1, y_1, c_1, z_1 above, in the case of a 'fresh' $\Pi^{+1}(z_1)$ query game G_2 sets $Y_2 \leftarrow Y_2[a,p]$, $y_2 \leftarrow y_2[a,p]$, $c_2 \leftarrow c_2[a,p]$, and $z_2 \leftarrow z_2[a,p]$. The two described cases correspond with the two branches of the second If-statement in SIGN of Fig. 11.

The remaining changes between G_1 and G_2 concern the two added flags bad_1 and bad_2 and can be ignored for now. Thus all changes between games G_1 and G_2 are pure rewriting, so we obtain

$$\Pr[G_1] = \Pr[G_2].$$

Consider next in more detail the flags bad_1 and bad_2 that appear in game G_2. The former is set whenever a value is queried to $H(\cdot, \{0,1\}^{\mathsf{tl}})$ that is a valid secret identification key for verification key ivk, and the latter is set when SIGN is queried on some address a and the domain of PT contains an element that is a valid response for commitment $Y_1[a]$ and one of the two possible challenges $c_1 \in \{0,1\}$. Observe that any use of itk in H is preceded by setting $\mathsf{bad}_1 \leftarrow 1$, and that any execution of the first branch of the second If-statement of SIGN in G_2 is preceded by setting $\mathsf{bad}_2 \leftarrow 1$.

We'd like to proceed the proof by bounding the probabilities $\Pr[G_2 \text{ sets } \mathsf{bad}_1]$ and $\Pr[G_2 \text{ sets } \mathsf{bad}_2]$ (based on the hardness of key recovery and cimp-uc impersonation, respectively). However, the following technical problem arises: While in the two corresponding reductions we would be able to simulate the TRANSC algorithm with the TR oracle, when aiming at bounding the probability of $\mathsf{bad}_1 \leftarrow 1$ it would be unclear how to simulate the SIGN oracle (that uses isk and itk in the first If-branch), and when aiming at bounding the probability of $\mathsf{bad}_2 \leftarrow 1$ it would be unclear how to simulate the H oracle (that uses itk in the $\mathsf{Rng} = \{0,1\}^{\mathsf{tl}}$ branch). We help ourselves by defining the following three complementary events: (a) neither bad_1 nor bad_2 is set, (b) bad_1 is set before bad_2 (this includes the case that bad_2 is not set at all), and (c) bad_2 is set before bad_1 (this includes the case that bad_1 is not set at all). In Fig. 12 we construct a kr adversary $\mathcal{I}$ and a cimp-uc adversary $\mathcal{P}_1$ from $\mathcal{A}$ such that

$$\Pr[G_2 \text{ sets } \mathsf{bad}_1 \text{ first}] = \mathbf{Adv}_{\mathsf{ID}}^{\mathrm{kr\text{-}pa}}(\mathcal{I})$$

and

$$\Pr[G_2 \text{ sets } \mathsf{bad}_2 \text{ first}] = 2\mathbf{Adv}_{\mathsf{ID}}^{\mathrm{cimp\text{-}uc}}(\mathcal{P}_1).$$

The strategy for constructing the adversaries is clear: We derive $\mathcal{I}$ from G_2 by stripping off all code that is only executed after bad_2 is set, and we construct $\mathcal{P}_1$ by removing all code only executed after bad_1 is set. The $\mathcal{P}_1$-related code in SIGN deserves further explanation. The reduction obtained commitment $Y_1[a]$ via H from the TR oracle of the cimp-uc game, together with challenge $c_1[a]$ and response $z_1[a]$. As at the time the bad_2 flag is set in G_2 no information on $c_1[a]$ was used in the game or exposed to the adversary, for the challenge c^* for which $\mathsf{ID.Vf}(ivk, Y_1[a]\|c^*\|z) = \mathsf{true}$ we have that $c^* \neq c_1[a]$ with probability $1/2$. The reduction thus tries to break cimp-uc security with challenge $1 - c_1[a]$ and response z. Whenever this challenge is admissible (i.e., with probability $1/2$), the response is correct. That is, $\mathcal{P}_1$ is successful with breaking impersonation with half the probability of $\mathcal{A}$ having flag bad_2 be set first.

In Fig. 13 we define game G_3 which behaves exactly like G_2 until either bad_1 or bad_2 is set. Thus we have

$$\Pr[G_2 \text{ sets neither } \mathsf{bad}_1 \text{ nor } \mathsf{bad}_2] = \Pr[G_3].$$

In G_3 we expand the DS.Vf algorithm, i.e., the steps where the forgery attempt of $\mathcal{A}$ is verified. If signature $\sigma = (c_1, z_2)$ is identified as valid, the game sets flag bad to 1 if $c_1 \neq c_1[a]$, i.e., if the challenge c_1 included in the signature does not coincide with the one simulated in the H oracle for address a. Using the assumption that $\mathcal{A}$ does not forge on addresses a for which it posed a $\text{SIGN}(a, \cdot)$ query, observe that the game did not release any information on $c_1[a]$, so by an information theoretic argument, $c_1 \neq c_1[a]$ and thus $\mathsf{bad} \leftarrow 1$ with probability $1/2$.

In Fig. 13 we construct a cimp-uc adversary $\mathcal{P}_2$ from $\mathcal{A}$ that is successful whenever bad is set in game G_3. We obtain

$$\Pr[G_3] = 2\mathbf{Adv}_{\mathsf{ID}}^{\text{cimp-uc}}(\mathcal{P}_2).$$

Taken together, the established bounds imply the theorem statement.   □

Adversary $\mathcal{I}^{\text{TR}}(ivk)$	Adversary $\mathcal{P}_1^{\text{TR,CH}}(ivk)$
$ITK \leftarrow\!\!\text{s } \{0,1\}^{\text{tl}}$; $vk \leftarrow (ivk, ITK)$	$ITK \leftarrow\!\!\text{s } \{0,1\}^{\text{tl}}$; $vk \leftarrow (ivk, ITK)$
$(m, \sigma) \leftarrow\!\!\text{s } \mathcal{A}^{\text{SIGN,H},\Pi^{\pm 1}}(vk)$	$(m, \sigma) \leftarrow\!\!\text{s } \mathcal{A}^{\text{SIGN,H},\Pi^{\pm 1}}(vk)$
Output $\perp$ and stop	Output $\perp$ and stop

$\text{H}(x, \text{Rng})$	$\text{SIGN}(m)$	
If $HT[x, \text{Rng}]$: Return $HT[x, \text{Rng}]$	$(a, p) \leftarrow m$	
$HT[x, \text{Rng}] \leftarrow\!\!\text{s Rng}$	If $\exists z \in \text{dom}(\text{PT})$ s.t.	// only $\mathcal{P}_1$
If $\text{Rng} = \{0,1\}^{\text{tl}}$: // only $\mathcal{I}$	$\text{ID.Vf}(ivk, Y_1[a]\|0\|z)$ or	// only $\mathcal{P}_1$
If $\text{ID.KVf}(ivk, x)$: // only $\mathcal{I}$	$\text{ID.Vf}(ivk, Y_1[a]\|1\|z)$:	// only $\mathcal{P}_1$
Output x and stop // only $\mathcal{I}$	$\text{CH}(\#Y_1[a], 1 - c_1[a])$	// only $\mathcal{P}_1$
If $\text{Rng} = \text{ID.CS}(ivk, 1)$:	Output $(1, z)$ and stop	// only $\mathcal{P}_1$
as in G_2	$Y_2 \leftarrow Y_2[a, p]$; $z_2 \leftarrow z_2[a, p]$	
If $\text{Rng} = \{0,1\}^{\text{cl}}$:	$\text{PT} \leftarrow \text{PT} \cup \{(z_1[a], Y_2)\}$	
as in G_2	$\sigma \leftarrow (c_1[a], z_2)$; Return σ	
Return $HT[x, \text{Rng}]$		
Algorithm $\text{TRANSC}(cl)$	$\Pi^{+1}(z_1)/\Pi^{-1}(Y_2)$	
$Y\|c\|z \leftarrow\!\!\text{s TR}(cl)$	as in G_2	
Return $Y\|c\|z$		

Fig. 12. Adversaries for proof of Theorem 4. The oracles and the TRANSC implementation are shared by both adversaries. In SIGN, we write $\#Y_1[a]$ for the number of the TR query in which the value of $Y_1[a]$ was established.

Game G_3

$(ivk, isk, itk) \leftarrow_{\$} \text{ID.Kg}$
$ITK \leftarrow_{\$} \{0,1\}^{tl}$; $vk \leftarrow (ivk, ITK)$
$(m, \sigma) \leftarrow_{\$} \mathcal{A}^{\text{SIGN},\text{H},\Pi^{\pm 1}}(vk)$
$(a, p) \leftarrow m$; $(c_1, z_2) \leftarrow \sigma$
$Y_2 \leftarrow \text{ID.Rsp}^{-1}(ivk, c_2[a, p], z_2)$
$z_1 \leftarrow \Pi^{-1}(Y_2)$
$Y_1 \leftarrow \text{ID.Rsp}^{-1}(ivk, c_1, z_1)$
If $Y_1 \neq Y_1[a]$: Return false
If $c_1 \neq c_1[a]$: bad $\leftarrow 1$
Return true

$\text{SIGN}(m)$

$(a, p) \leftarrow m$
If $\exists z \in \text{dom}(PT)$ s.t.
  $\text{ID.Vf}(ivk, Y_1[a]\|0\|z)$ or
  $\text{ID.Vf}(ivk, Y_1[a]\|1\|z)$: $\text{bad}_2 \leftarrow 1$
$PT \leftarrow PT \cup \{(z_1[a], Y_2[a, p])\}$
$\sigma \leftarrow (c_1[a], z_2[a, p])$; Return σ

$H(x, \text{Rng})$

If $HT[x, \text{Rng}]$: Return $HT[x, \text{Rng}]$
$HT[x, \text{Rng}] \leftarrow_{\$} \text{Rng}$
If $\text{Rng} = \{0,1\}^{tl}$:
  If $\text{ID.KVf}(ivk, x)$: $\text{bad}_1 \leftarrow 1$
If $\text{Rng} = \text{ID.CS}(ivk, 1)$:
  $Y_1[x]\|c_1[x]\|z_1[x] \leftarrow_{\$} \text{TRANSC}(1)$
  $HT[x, \text{Rng}] \leftarrow Y_1[x]$
If $\text{Rng} = \{0,1\}^{cl}$:
  $Y_2[x]\|c_2[x]\|z_2[x] \leftarrow_{\$} \text{TRANSC}(cl)$
  $HT[x, \text{Rng}] \leftarrow c_2[x]$
Return $HT[x, \text{Rng}]$

$\Pi^{+1}(z_1)/\Pi^{-1}(Y_2)$
as in G_2

Algorithm $\text{TRANSC}(cl)$
as in G_2

Adversary $\mathcal{P}_2^{\text{TR},\text{CH}}(ivk)$

$ITK \leftarrow_{\$} \{0,1\}^{tl}$; $vk \leftarrow (ivk, ITK)$
$(m, \sigma) \leftarrow_{\$} \mathcal{A}^{\text{SIGN},\text{H},\Pi^{\pm 1}}(vk)$
$(a, p) \leftarrow m$; $(c_1, z_2) \leftarrow \sigma$
$Y_2 \leftarrow \text{ID.Rsp}^{-1}(ivk, c_2[a, p], z_2)$
$z_1 \leftarrow \Pi^{-1}(Y_2)$
$Y_1 \leftarrow \text{ID.Rsp}^{-1}(ivk, c_1, z_1)$
If $Y_1 \neq Y_1[a]$: Return $\perp$
If $c_1 \neq c_1[a]$:
  $\text{CH}(\#Y_1[a], c_1)$
  Output $(1, z_1)$ and stop
Return $\perp$

Algorithm $\text{TRANSC}(cl)$
$Y\|c\|z \leftarrow_{\$} \text{TR}(cl)$
Return $Y\|c\|z$

$\text{SIGN}(m)$

$(a, p) \leftarrow m$
$PT \leftarrow PT \cup \{(z_1[a], Y_2[a, p])\}$
$\sigma \leftarrow (c_1[a], z_2[a, p])$; Return σ

$H(x, \text{Rng})$

If $HT[x, \text{Rng}]$: Return $HT[x, \text{Rng}]$
$HT[x, \text{Rng}] \leftarrow_{\$} \text{Rng}$
If $\text{Rng} = \text{ID.CS}(ivk, 1)$:
  as in G_3
If $\text{Rng} = \{0,1\}^{cl}$:
  as in G_3
Return $HT[x, \text{Rng}]$

$\Pi^{+1}(z_1)/\Pi^{-1}(Y_2)$
as in G_3

Fig. 13. Top: game G_3 for proof of Theorem 4. **Bottom:** one more adversary for proof of Theorem 4. We write $\#Y_1[a]$ for the number of the TR query in which the value of $Y_1[a]$ was established.

GQ.Kg	Prover	Verifier
$(N, p, q, e, d) \leftarrow_\$ \mathsf{RSA}$	Input: $(N, e, X), x, \mathsf{cl}$	Input: $(N, e, X), \mathsf{cl}$
$x \leftarrow_\$ \mathbb{Z}_N^*$	$y \leftarrow_\$ \mathbb{Z}_N^*$	
$X \leftarrow x^e \bmod N$	$Y \leftarrow y^e \bmod N$ $\xrightarrow{\quad Y \quad}$ $c \leftarrow_\$ \{0,1\}^{\mathsf{cl}}$	
Return	$\xleftarrow{\quad c \quad}$	
$((N, e, X), x, d)$	$z \leftarrow yx^c \bmod N$ $\xrightarrow{\quad z \quad}$ $v \leftarrow (z^e \equiv YX^c \pmod{N})$	

GQ.Ex$((N,e,X), Y_1, c_1, z_1, Y_2, c_2, z_2)$	GQ.Cmt$^{-1}((N,e,X), d, Y, \mathsf{cl})$
If $z_1^e \not\equiv Y_1 X^{c_1} \vee z_2^e \not\equiv Y_2 X^{c_2}$: Return $\perp$	$y \leftarrow Y^d \bmod N$
If $Y_1 \neq Y_2 \vee \lvert c_1 \rvert \neq \lvert c_2 \rvert \vee c_1 = c_2$: Return $\perp$	Return y
$z \leftarrow z_1 z_2^{-1} \bmod N$	....
$c \leftarrow c_1 - c_2 \quad /\!/ \text{ w.l.o.g. } c > 0$	Game OW$_{\mathsf{RSA}}^{\mathcal{A}}$
$(a, b) \leftarrow \mathrm{egcd}(e, c)$	$(N, p, q, e, d) \leftarrow_\$ \mathsf{RSA}$
$x \leftarrow X^a z^b \bmod N$	$x \leftarrow_\$ \mathbb{Z}_N^* \; ; \; X \leftarrow x^e \bmod N$
Return x	$x' \leftarrow_\$ \mathcal{A}(N, e, X)$
	Return $(x' = x)$

Fig. 14. Trapdoor identification scheme GQ associated to RSA generator RSA and game defining the RSA one-wayness.

6 Instantiation and Implementation

We illustrate how to instantiate our **H2** and **ID2** transforms, using the GQ identification scheme as example, to obtain **H2**[GQ] and **ID2**[GQ]. Similar instantiations and implementations are possible with many other trapdoor identification schemes. For instance, see the full version of this paper [2] for instantiations based on claw-free permutations [10] or the MR identification scheme by Micali and Reyzin [12]. We implement **H2**[GQ], **ID2**[GQ], and **H2**[MR] to get performance data.

6.1 GQ-Based Schemes

GQ. An RSA generator for modulus length k is an algorithm RSA that returns a tuple (N, p, q, e, d) where p, q are distinct odd primes, $N = pq$ is the modulus in the range $2^{k-1} < N < 2^k$, encryption and decryption exponents e, d are in $\mathbb{Z}_{\varphi(N)}^*$, and $ed \equiv 1 \pmod{\varphi(N)}$. The assumption is one-wayness, formalized by defining the ow-advantage of an adversary $\mathcal{A}$ against RSA by $\mathbf{Adv}_{\mathsf{RSA}}^{\mathrm{ow}}(\mathcal{A}) = \Pr[\mathrm{OW}_{\mathsf{RSA}}^{\mathcal{A}}]$ where the game is in Fig. 14. Let L be a parameter and RSA be such that $\gcd(e, c) = 1$ for all $0 < c < 2^L$. (For instance, RSA may select encryption exponent e as an $L+1$ bit prime number.) If egcd denotes the extended gcd algorithm that given relatively-prime inputs e, c returns a, b such that $ea + cb = 1$, the GQ identification scheme associated to RSA is shown in Fig. 14. Any challenge length up to L is admissible, i.e., ID.clS $\subseteq \{1, \ldots, L\}$, and for all cl $\in$ ID.clS the commitment and response space is ID.CS$(ivk, \mathsf{cl}) =$ ID.RS$(ivk, \mathsf{cl}) = \mathbb{Z}_N^*$. Extraction works because of identity $X^a z^b = x^{ea} x^{(c_1 - c_2)b} = x$. Algorithm GQ.Cmt^{-1}

shows that the scheme is trapdoor; that it also is commitment recovering and has unique responses follows from inspection of the $z^e = YX^c$ condition of the verification algorithm. Finally, it is a standard result, and in particular follows from Lemma 1, that KR, CIMP-UU, CIMP-UC security of GQ tightly reduce to the one-wayness of RSA (note the CIMP-UU case requires a restriction on the deployed challenge lengths).

H2[GQ]. Figure 15 shows the algorithms of the **H2[GQ]** DAPS scheme derived by applying our **H2** transform to the GQ identification scheme of Fig. 14. To estimate security for a given modulus length k we use Theorems 1 and 2, and the reductions between CIMP-UU and KR security of GQ and the one-wayness of RSA from Lemma 1. The reductions are tight and so we need to estimate the advantage of an adversary against the one-wayness of RSA. We do this under the assumption that the NFS is the best factoring method. Thus, our implementation uses a 2048-bit modulus and 256-bit hashes and seeds. See below and Fig. 16 for implementation and performance information.

ID2[GQ]. Figure 15 also shows the algorithms of the DAPS scheme derived by applying the **ID2** transform to GQ. Reductions continue to be tight so instantiation and implementation choices are as for **H2[GQ]**. Concerning the random permutation Π on $\mathbb{Z}_N^*$ that the scheme requires, it effectively suffices to construct one that maps $\mathbb{Z}_N$ to $\mathbb{Z}_N$, and we propose one way to instantiate it in the following.

A random permutation Π on $\mathbb{Z}_N$ can be constructed from a random permutation Γ on $\{0,1\}^k$, where $2^{k-1} < N < 2^k$, by cycle walking [6,13]: if x is the input, let $c \leftarrow \Gamma(x)$; if $c \in \mathbb{Z}_N$, return c; else recurse on c; the inverse is analogous. A Feistel network can be used to construct a random permutation Γ on $\{0,1\}^{2n}$ from a set of public random functions $F_1, \ldots, F_r$ on $\{0,1\}^n$. In other words, for input $x_0 \| x_1 \in \{0,1\}^{2n}$, return $x_r \| x_{r+1}$ where $x_{i+1} = x_{i-1} \oplus F_i(x_i)$. Dai and Steinberger [8] give an indifferentiability result for 8 rounds, under the assumption that the F_i are independent public random functions. We construct F_i on $\{0,1\}^n$ as $F_i(x) = H(i\|1\|x)\| \ldots \|H(i\|\ell\|x)$ using $H = $ SHA-256, where $\ell = n/256$ (assuming for simplicity n is a multiple of 256), and the inputs to SHA-256 are encoded to the same length to avoid length extension attacks that make Merkle–Damgård constructions differentiable from a random oracle. Our implementation uses $r = 20$ rounds of the Feistel network as a safety margin for good indifferentiability and to avoid the non-tightness of the result [8] for $r = 8$.

6.2   Implementation and Performance

IMPLEMENTATION. We implemented **H2[GQ]**, **H2[MR]**, and **ID2[GQ]** (see [2] for the specification of MR). For comparison purposes we also implemented the original PS. Our implementation is in C[1], using OpenSSL's BIGNUM library for number theoretic operations. We also compared with OpenSSL's implementation

---

[1] The source code can be downloaded from https://github.com/dstebila/daps.

H2[GQ].Kg^H

$((N, e, X), x, d) \leftarrow_\$ \mathsf{GQ.Kg}$; $ITK \leftarrow d \oplus \mathrm{H}(x, \{0,1\}^k)$
Return $((N, e, X, ITK), (x, d))$

H2[GQ].Sig^H$((N, e, X, ITK), (x, d), m)$

$(a, p) \leftarrow m$; $s \leftarrow_\$ \{0,1\}^{\mathsf{sl}}$; $Y \leftarrow \mathrm{H}(a, \mathbb{Z}_N^*)$; $y \leftarrow Y^d \bmod N$
$c \leftarrow \mathrm{H}(a\|p\|s, \{0,1\}^{\mathsf{cl}})$; $z \leftarrow yx^c \bmod N$; $\sigma \leftarrow (z, s)$; Return σ

H2[GQ].Vf^H$((N, e, X, ITK), m, \sigma)$

$(a, p) \leftarrow m$; $(z, s) \leftarrow \sigma$; $Y \leftarrow \mathrm{H}(a, \mathbb{Z}_N^*)$; $c \leftarrow \mathrm{H}(a\|p\|s, \{0,1\}^{\mathsf{cl}})$
Return $(z^e \equiv YX^c \pmod{N})$

H2[GQ].Ex^H$((N, e, X, ITK), m_1, m_2, \sigma_1, \sigma_2)$

For $i = 1, 2$ do
$\quad (a_i, p_i) \leftarrow m_i$; $(z_i, s_i) \leftarrow \sigma_i$
$\quad Y_i \leftarrow \mathrm{H}(a_i, \mathbb{Z}_N^*)$; $c_i \leftarrow \mathrm{H}(a_i\|p_i\|s_i, \{0,1\}^{\mathsf{cl}})$
$x \leftarrow \mathsf{GQ.Ex}((N, e, X), Y_1, c_1, z_1, Y_2, c_2, z_2)$
$d \leftarrow \mathrm{H}(x, \{0,1\}^k) \oplus ITK$; Return (x, d)

ID2[GQ].Kg$^{H, \Pi^{\pm 1}}$

$((N, e, X), x, d) \leftarrow_\$ \mathsf{GQ.Kg}$; $ITK \leftarrow d \oplus \mathrm{H}(x, \{0,1\}^k)$
Return $((N, e, X, ITK), (x, d))$

ID2[GQ].Sig$^{H, \Pi^{\pm 1}}$$((N, e, X, ITK), (x, d), m)$

$(a, p) \leftarrow m$; $Y_1 \leftarrow \mathrm{H}(a, \mathbb{Z}_N^*)$; $c_1 \leftarrow_\$ \{0,1\}$; $y_1 \leftarrow Y_1^d \bmod N$
$z_1 \leftarrow y_1 x^{c_1} \bmod N$; $Y_2 \leftarrow \Pi^{+1}(z_1)$; $y_2 \leftarrow_\$ Y_2^d \bmod N$
$c_2 \leftarrow \mathrm{H}(a\|p, \{0,1\}^{\mathsf{cl}})$; $z_2 \leftarrow y_2 x^{c_2} \bmod N$
$\sigma \leftarrow (c_1, z_2)$; Return σ

ID2[GQ].Vf$^{H, \Pi^{\pm 1}}$$((N, e, X, ITK), m, \sigma)$

$(a, p) \leftarrow m$; $(c_1, z_2) \leftarrow \sigma$; $c_2 \leftarrow \mathrm{H}(a\|p, \{0,1\}^{\mathsf{cl}})$
$Y_2 \leftarrow (z_2)^e X^{-c_2}$; $z_1 \leftarrow \Pi^{-1}(Y_2)$; $Y_1 \leftarrow (z_1)^e X^{-c_1}$
Return $(Y_1 = \mathrm{H}(a, \mathbb{Z}_N^*))$

ID2[GQ].Ex$^{H, \Pi^{\pm 1}}$$((N, e, X, ITK), m_1, m_2, \sigma_1, \sigma_2)$

For $i = 1, 2$ do
$\quad (a_i, p_i) \leftarrow m_i$; $(c_{1,i}, z_{2,i}) \leftarrow \sigma_i$; $c_{2,i} \leftarrow \mathrm{H}(a_i\|p_i, \{0,1\}^{\mathsf{cl}})$
$\quad Y_{2,i} \leftarrow (z_{2,i})^e X^{-c_{2,i}}$; $z_{1,i} \leftarrow \Pi^{-1}(Y_{2,i})$
$\quad Y_{1,i} \leftarrow (z_{1,i})^e X^{-c_{1,i}}$
If $Y_{2,1} = Y_{2,2}$: $x \leftarrow \mathsf{GQ.Ex}((N, e, X), Y_{2,1}, c_{2,1}, z_{2,1}, Y_{2,2}, c_{2,2}, z_{2,2})$
Else: $x \leftarrow \mathsf{GQ.Ex}((N, e, X), Y_{1,1}, c_{1,1}, z_{1,1}, Y_{1,2}, c_{1,2}, z_{1,2})$
$d \leftarrow \mathrm{H}(x, \{0,1\}^k) \oplus ITK$; Return (x, d)

Fig. 15. DAPS schemes **H2**[GQ, cl, sl] and **ID2**[GQ, cl] derived via our transforms from ID scheme GQ.

Scheme	Operation count		Runtime (ms)		Size (bits)	
	sign	verify	sign	verify	pub.	sig.
PS [16]	$n\exp_k^k$	$n\exp_k^k$	$516.58_{\pm15.3}$	$161.84_{\pm7.96}$	2 048	528 384
RKS [17]	$2\lambda\,\mathrm{grp\,exp}$	$2\lambda\,\mathrm{grp\,dbl\,exp}$	13.48	5.99	640	131 072
H2[GQ] (Fig. 15)	$2\exp_{k/2}^{k/2}+\exp_k^l$	$\exp_k^l$	$0.88_{\pm0.04}$	$0.41_{\pm0.02}$	6 144	2 304
ID2[GQ] (Fig. 15)	$4\exp_{k/2}^{k/2}+2\exp_k^l$	$3\exp_k^l$	$1.80_{\pm0.14}$	$1.49_{\pm0.26}$	6 144	2 049
H2[MR] [2]	$2\exp_{k/2}^{k/2}+\exp_k^l$	$1.5l\,\mathrm{mul}_k$	$1.27_{\pm0.16}$	$0.37_{\pm0.01}$	2 048	2 304
RSA PKCS#1v1.5	$2\exp_{k/2}^{k/2}$	$\exp_k^{|e|}$	$0.53_{\pm0.08}$	$0.02_{\pm0.00}$	2 048	2 048

Fig. 16. Operation count, average runtime, and public key/signature sizes of DAPS schemes and RSA signatures. By $\exp_m^x$ we denote the cost of computing a modular exponentiation with modulus of bitlength m and exponent of bitlength x. All concrete values are for the $\lambda = 128$-bit security level: timing and size values for RSA and factoring based schemes are based on $k = 2048$-bit moduli and $n = l = 2\lambda = 256$-bit hash values, and for the RKS scheme we assume a group with $2\lambda = 256$-bit element representation, hash values of the same length, and a binary tree. See also [2].

of standard RSA PKCS#1v1.5 signatures currently used by CAs for creating certificates. We use the Chinese remainder theorem to speed-up secret key operations whenever possible. For GQ, we use encryption exponent $e = \mathrm{nextprime}(2^{cl})$; for RSA public key encryption we use OpenSSL's default public key exponent, $e = 65537$. We compared against the RKS DAPS implementation.

PERFORMANCE. We measured timings of our implementations on an Intel Core i7 (6700K "Skylake") with 4 cores each running at 4.0 GHz. The tests were run on a single core with TurboBoost and hyper-threading disabled. Software was compiled for the x86_64 architecture with -O3 optimizations using llvm 8.0.0 (clang 800.0.38). The OpenSSL version used was v1.0.2j. We use RKS' implementation of their DAPS, which relies on a different library for the secp256k1 elliptic curve. Table 16 shows mean runtimes in milliseconds (with standard deviations) and key sizes using 2048-bit modulii and 256-bit hashes. For DAPS schemes, address is 15 bytes and payload is 33 bytes; for RSA PKCS#1v1.5, message is 48 bytes. Times reported are an average over 30 s. The table omits runtimes for key generation as this is a one-time operation.

Compared with the existing PS, our H2[GQ], ID2[GQ], and H2[MR] schemes are several orders of magnitude faster for both signing and verification. When using 2048-bit modulii, H2[GQ] signatures can be generated 587× and verified 394× faster, and ID2[GQ] signatures can be generated 287× and verified 108× faster; moreover our signatures are 229× and 257× shorter, respectively, compared with PS, and ours are nearly the same size as RSA PKCS#1v1.5 signatures. Compared with the previous fastest and smallest DAPS, RKS, H2[GQ] signatures can be generated and verified 15× faster; ID2[GQ] generated 7× and verified 4× faster; and H2[MR] generated 10× and verified 16× faster. H2[GQ] and H2[MR] signatures are 56× shorter compared with RKS; H2[GQ] and **ID2**[GQ] public keys are 9.6× larger, though still under 1 KiB total, and **H2**[MR] keys are only 3.2× larger than RKS.

Signing times for our schemes are competitive with RSA PKCS#1v1.5: using **H2**[GQ], **ID2**[GQ], or **H2**[MR] for signatures in digital certificates would incur little computational or size overhead relative to currently used signatures.

Acknowledgments. We thank the authors of [17] for helpful comments about their scheme. MB was supported by NSF grants CNS-1228890 and CNS-1526801, a gift from Microsoft corporation and ERC Project ERCC (FP7/615074). BP was supported by ERC Project ERCC (FP7/615074). DS was supported in part by Australian Research Council (ARC) Discovery Project grant DP130104304 and Natural Sciences and Engineering Research Council of Canada (NSERC) Discovery grant RGPIN-2016-05146 and an NSERC Discovery Accelerator Supplement.

References

1. Abdalla, M., An, J.H., Bellare, M., Namprempre, C.: From identification to signatures via the Fiat-Shamir transform: minimizing assumptions for security and forward-security. In: Knudsen, L.R. (ed.) EUROCRYPT 2002. LNCS, vol. 2332, pp. 418–433. Springer, Heidelberg (2002). doi:10.1007/3-540-46035-7_28

2. Bellare, M., Poettering, B., Stebila, D.: Deterring certificate subversion: efficient double-authentication-preventing signatures. Cryptology ePrint Archive, Report 2016/1016 (2016). http://eprint.iacr.org/2016/1016

3. Bellare, M., Poettering, B., Stebila, D.: From identification to signatures, tightly: a framework and generic transforms. In: Cheon, J.H., Takagi, T. (eds.) ASIACRYPT 2016. LNCS, vol. 10032, pp. 435–464. Springer, Heidelberg (2016). doi:10.1007/978-3-662-53890-6_15

4. Bellare, M., Rogaway, P.: Random oracles are practical: a paradigm for designing efficient protocols. In: Ashby, V. (ed.) ACM CCS 1993, pp. 62–73. ACM Press, November 1993. doi:10.1145/168588.168596

5. Bellare, M., Rogaway, P.: The security of triple encryption and a framework for code-based game-playing proofs. In: Vaudenay, S. (ed.) EUROCRYPT 2006. LNCS, vol. 4004, pp. 409–426. Springer, Heidelberg (2006). doi:10.1007/11761679_25

6. Black, J., Rogaway, P.: Ciphers with arbitrary finite domains. In: Preneel, B. (ed.) CT-RSA 2002. LNCS, vol. 2271, pp. 114–130. Springer, Heidelberg (2002). doi:10.1007/3-540-45760-7_9

7. Cramer, R.: Modular design of secure, yet practical protocls. Ph.D. thesis, University of Amsterdam (1996)

8. Dai, Y., Steinberger, J.: Indifferentiability of 8-round Feistel networks. In: Robshaw, M., Katz, J. (eds.) CRYPTO 2016. LNCS, vol. 9814, pp. 95–120. Springer, Heidelberg (2016). doi:10.1007/978-3-662-53018-4_4

9. Fiat, A., Shamir, A.: How to prove yourself: practical solutions to identification and signature problems. In: Odlyzko, A.M. (ed.) CRYPTO 1986. LNCS, vol. 263, pp. 186–194. Springer, Heidelberg (1987). doi:10.1007/3-540-47721-7_12

10. Goldwasser, S., Micali, S., Rivest, R.L.: A digital signature scheme secure against adaptive chosen-message attacks. SIAM J. Comput. **17**(2), 281–308 (1988). doi:10.1137/0217017

11. Guillou, L.C., Quisquater, J.-J.: A "paradoxical" indentity-based signature scheme resulting from zero-knowledge. In: Goldwasser, S. (ed.) CRYPTO 1988. LNCS, vol. 403, pp. 216–231. Springer, Heidelberg (1990). doi:10.1007/0-387-34799-2_16
12. Micali, S., Reyzin, L.: Improving the exact security of digital signature schemes. J. Cryptol. 15(1), 1–18 (2002). doi:10.1007/s00145-001-0005-8
13. Miracle, S., Yilek, S.: Reverse cycle walking and its applications. In: Cheon, J.H., Takagi, T. (eds.) ASIACRYPT 2016. LNCS, vol. 10031, pp. 679–700. Springer, Heidelberg (2016). doi:10.1007/978-3-662-53887-6_25
14. Ohta, K., Okamoto, T.: On concrete security treatment of signatures derived from identification. In: Krawczyk, H. (ed.) CRYPTO 1998. LNCS, vol. 1462, pp. 354–369. Springer, Heidelberg (1998). doi:10.1007/BFb0055741
15. Poettering, B., Stebila, D.: Double-authentication-preventing signatures. In: Kutyłowski, M., Vaidya, J. (eds.) ESORICS 2014. LNCS, vol. 8712, pp. 436–453. Springer, Heidelberg (2014). doi:10.1007/978-3-319-11203-9_25
16. Poettering, B., Stebila, D.: Double-authentication-preventing signatures. Int. J. Inf. Secur. (2015). doi:10.1007/s10207-015-0307-8
17. Ruffing, T., Kate, A., Schröder, D.: Liar, liar, coins on fire!: penalizing equivocation by loss of bitcoins. In: Ray, I., Li, N., Kruegel, C. (eds.) ACM CCS 15, pp. 219–230. ACM Press, October 2015. doi:10.1145/2810103.2813686

Chameleon-Hashes with Ephemeral Trapdoors
And Applications to Invisible Sanitizable Signatures

Jan Camenisch[1]([✉]), David Derler[2], Stephan Krenn[3], Henrich C. Pöhls[4],
Kai Samelin[1,5], and Daniel Slamanig[2]

[1] IBM Research – Zurich, Rüschlikon, Switzerland
{jca,ksa}@zurich.ibm.com
[2] IAIK, Graz University of Technology, Graz, Austria
{david.derler,daniel.slamanig}@tugraz.at
[3] AIT Austrian Institute of Technology GmbH, Vienna, Austria
stephan.krenn@ait.ac.at
[4] ISL & Chair of IT-Security, University of Passau, Passau, Germany
hp@sec.uni-passau.de
[5] TU Darmstadt, Darmstadt, Germany

Abstract. A chameleon-hash function is a hash function that involves a trapdoor the knowledge of which allows one to find arbitrary collisions in the domain of the function. In this paper, we introduce the notion of *chameleon-hash functions with ephemeral trapdoors*. Such hash functions feature additional, i.e., ephemeral, trapdoors which are chosen by the party computing a hash value. The holder of the main trapdoor is then unable to find a second pre-image of a hash value unless also provided with the ephemeral trapdoor used to compute the hash value. We present a formal security model for this new primitive as well as provably secure instantiations. The first instantiation is a generic black-box construction from any secure chameleon-hash function. We further provide three direct constructions based on standard assumptions. Our new primitive has some appealing use-cases, including a solution to the long-standing open problem of *invisible* sanitizable signatures, which we also present.

1 Introduction

Chameleon-hash functions, also called trapdoor-hash functions, are hash functions that feature a trapdoor that allows one to find arbitrary collisions in the domain of the functions. However, chameleon-hash functions are collision resistant as long as the corresponding trapdoor (or secret key) is not known. More precisely, a party who is privy of the trapdoor is able to find arbitrary collisions in the domain of the function. Example instantiations include trapdoor-commitment, and equivocal commitment schemes.

The full version of this paper is available as IACR Cryptology ePrint Archive Report 2017/011. J. Camenisch and K. Samelin were supported by the EU ERC PERCY, grant agreement n°32131. D. Derler, S. Krenn, H.C. Pöhls and D. Slamanig were supported by EU H2020 project PRISMACLOUD, grant agreement n°644962.

S. Fehr (Ed.): PKC 2017, Part II, LNCS 10175, pp. 152–182, 2017.
DOI: 10.1007/978-3-662-54388-7_6

One prominent application of this primitive are chameleon signatures [47]. Here, the intended recipient—who knows the trapdoor—of a signature σ for a message m can equivocate it to another message m' of his choice. This, in turn, means that a signature σ cannot be used to convince any other party of the authenticity of m, as the intended recipient could have "signed" arbitrary messages on its own. Many other applications appear in the literature, some of which we discuss in the related work section. However, all current constructions are "all-or-nothing" in that a party who computes a hash with respect to some public key cannot prevent the trapdoor holder from finding collisions. This can be too limiting for some use-cases.

Contribution. We introduce a new primitive dubbed chameleon-hash functions with ephemeral trapdoors. In a nutshell, this primitive requires that a collision in the hash function can be computed only when two secrets are known, i.e., the main trapdoor, and an ephemeral one. The main trapdoor is the secret key corresponding to the chameleon-hash function public key, while the second, ephemeral, trapdoor is generated by the party computing the hash value. The latter party can then decide whether the holder of the long-term secret key shall be able to equivocate the hash by providing or withholding the second trapdoor information. We present a formal security model for this new primitive. Furthermore, we present stronger definitions for existing chameleon-hash functions not considered before, including the new notion of uniqueness, and show how to construct chameleon-hash functions being secure in this stronger model. These new notions may also be useful in other scenarios.

Additionally, we provide four provably secure constructions for chameleon-hash functions with ephemeral trapdoors. The first is bootstrapped, while the three direct constructions are built on RSA-like and the DL assumption. Our new primitive has some interesting applications, including the first provably secure instantiation of *invisible* sanitizable signatures, which we also present. Additional applications of our new primitive may include revocable signatures [43], but also simulatable equivocable commitments [34]. However, in contrast to equivocable commitments, we want that parties can actually equivocate, not only a simulator. Therefore, we chose to call this primitive a chameleon-hash function rather than a commitment. Note, the primitive is different from "double-trapdoor chameleon-hash functions" [13, 25, 49], where knowing one out of two secrets is enough to produce collisions.

Related Work and State-of-the-Art. Chameleon-hash functions were introduced by Krawczyk and Rabin [47], and are based on some first ideas given by Brassard et al. [12]. Later, they have been ported to the identity-based setting (ID-based chameleon-hash functions), where the holder of a master secret key can extract new secret keys for each identity [6,8,26,57,60]. These were mainly used to tackle the key-exposure problem [7,47]. Key exposure means that seeing a single collision in the hash allows to find further collisions by extracting the corresponding trapdoor. This problem was then directly solved by the introduction of "key-exposure free" chameleon-hash functions [7,36,37,57], which prohibit extracting the (master) secret key. This allows for the partial re-use of generated key material. Brzuska et al. then proposed a formal framework for tag-based chameleon-hashes secure under random-tagging attacks, i.e., random identities [15].

Beside this "plain" usage of the aforementioned primitive, chameleon-hash functions also proved useful in other areas such as on/offline signatures [27,32, 58], (tightly) secure signature schemes [11,44,52], but also sanitizable signature schemes [4,15,41] and identity-based encryption schemes [61]. Moreover they are useful in context of trapdoor-commitments, direct anonymous attestation, Σ-protocols, and distributed hashing [3,9,12,34].

Additional related work is discussed when presenting the application of our new primitive.

2   Preliminaries

Let us give our notation, the required assumptions, building blocks, and the extended framework for chameleon-hashes (without ephemeral trapdoors) first.

Notation. $\lambda \in \mathbb{N}$ denotes our security parameter. All algorithms implicitly take 1^λ as an additional input. We write $a \leftarrow A(x)$ if a is assigned the output of algorithm A with input x. An algorithm is efficient if it runs in probabilistic polynomial time (ppt) in the length of its input. For the remainder of this paper, all algorithms are ppt if not explicitly mentioned otherwise. Most algorithms may return a special error symbol $\perp \notin \{0,1\}^*$, denoting an exception. If S is a set, we write $a \leftarrow S$ to denote that a is chosen uniformly at random from S. For a message $m = (m[1], m[2], \ldots, m[\ell])$, we call $m[i]$ a block, while $\ell \in \mathbb{N}$ denotes the number of blocks in a message m. For a list we require that we have an injective, and efficiently reversible encoding, mapping the list to $\{0,1\}^*$. In the definitions we speak of a general message space $\mathcal{M}$ to be as generic as possible. For our instantiations, however, we let the message space $\mathcal{M}$ be $\{0,1\}^*$ to reduce unhelpful boilerplate notation. A function $\nu : \mathbb{N} \to \mathbb{R}_{\geq 0}$ is negligible, if it vanishes faster than every inverse polynomial, i.e., $\forall k \in \mathbb{N}, \exists n_0 \in \mathbb{N}$ such that $\nu(n) \leq n^{-k}, \forall n > n_0$. For certain security properties we require that values only have one canonical representation, e.g., a "4" is not the same as a "04", even if written as elements of $\mathbb{N}$ for brevity. Finally, for a group G we use G^* to denote $G \setminus \{1_G\}$.

2.1   Assumptions

Discrete Logarithm Assumption. Let $(G, g, q) \leftarrow \mathsf{GGen}(1^\lambda)$ be a group generator for a multiplicatively written group G of prime-order q with $\log_2 q = \lambda$, generated by g, i.e., $\langle g \rangle = G$. The discrete-logarithm problem (DLP) associated to GGen is to find x when given G, g, q, and g^x with $x \leftarrow \mathbb{Z}_q$. The DL assumption now states that the DLP is hard, i.e., that for every ppt adversary $\mathcal{A}$, there exists a negligible function ν such that:

$$\Pr[(G, g, q) \leftarrow \mathsf{GGen}(1^\lambda), x \leftarrow \mathbb{Z}_q, x' \leftarrow \mathcal{A}(G, g, q, g^x) : x = x'] \leq \nu(\lambda).$$

We sometimes sample from $\mathbb{Z}_q^*$ instead of $\mathbb{Z}_q$. This changes the view of an adversary only negligibly, and is thus not made explicit.

2.2 Building Blocks

Collision-Resistant Hash Function Families. A family $\{\mathcal{H}_{\mathcal{R}}^k\}_{k \in \mathcal{K}}$ of hash-functions $\mathcal{H}_{\mathcal{R}}^k : \{0,1\}^* \to \mathcal{R}$ indexed by key $k \in \mathcal{K}$ is collision-resistant if for any ppt adversary $\mathcal{A}$ there exists a negligible function ν such that:

$$\Pr[k \leftarrow \mathcal{K}, (v, v') \leftarrow \mathcal{A}(k) : \mathcal{H}_{\mathcal{R}}^k(v) = \mathcal{H}_{\mathcal{R}}^k(v') \wedge v \neq v'] \leq \nu(\lambda).$$

Public-Key Encryption Schemes. Public-key encryption allows to encrypt a message m using a given public key pk so that the resulting ciphertext can be decrypted using the corresponding secret key sk. More formally:

Definition 1 (Public-Key Encryption Schemes). *A public-key encryption scheme Π is a triple* $(\mathsf{KGen}_{enc}, \mathsf{Enc}, \mathsf{Dec})$ *of ppt algorithms such that:*

KGen_{enc}. *The algorithm* KGen_{enc} *on input security parameter λ outputs the private and public keys of the scheme:* $(\mathsf{sk}_{enc}, \mathsf{pk}_{enc}) \leftarrow \mathsf{KGen}_{enc}(1^\lambda)$.
Enc. *The algorithm* Enc *gets as input the public key* pk_{enc}, *and the message $m \in \mathcal{M}$ and outputs a ciphertext c:* $c \leftarrow \mathsf{Enc}(\mathsf{pk}_{enc}, m)$.
Dec. *The algorithm* Dec *on input a private key* sk_{enc} *and a ciphertext c outputs a message $m \in \mathcal{M} \cup \{\bot\}$:* $m \leftarrow \mathsf{Dec}(\mathsf{sk}_{enc}, c)$.

Definition 2 (Secure Public-Key Encryption Schemes). *We call a public-key encryption scheme Π IND-T secure, if it is correct, and IND-T-secure with $T \in \{CPA, CCA2\}$.*

The formal security definitions are given in the full version of this paper.

Non-interactive Proof Systems. Let L be an **NP**-language with associated witness relation R, i.e., $L = \{x \mid \exists w : R(x, w) = 1\}$. Throughout this paper, we use the Camenisch-Stadler notation [20] to express the statements proven in non-interactive, simulation-sound extractable, zero-knowledge (as defined below). In particular, we write $\pi \leftarrow \mathrm{NIZKPoK}\{(w) : R(x, w) = 1\}$ to denote the computation of a non-interactive, simulation-sound extractable, zero-knowledge proof, where all values not in the parentheses are assumed to be public. For example, let L be defined by the following **NP**-relation for a group $(G, g, q) \leftarrow \mathsf{GGen}(1^\lambda)$:

$$((g, h, y, z), (a, b)) \in R \iff y = g^a \wedge z = g^b h^a.$$

Then, we write $\pi \leftarrow \text{NIZKPoK}\{(a,b) : y = g^a \wedge z = g^b h^a\}$ to denote the corresponding proof of knowledge of witness $(a,b) \in \mathbb{Z}_q^2$ with respect to the statement $(g,h,y,z) \in G^4$. Additionally, we use $\{\texttt{false}, \texttt{true}\} \leftarrow \text{Verify}(x,\pi)$ to denote the corresponding verification algorithm and $\text{crs} \leftarrow \text{Gen}(1^\lambda)$ to denote the crs generation algorithm. We do not make the crs explicit and, for proof systems where a crs is required, we assume it to be an implicit input to all algorithms.

Definition 3. *We call a NIZKPoK secure, if it is complete, simulation-sound extractable, and zero-knowledge.*

The corresponding definitions can be found in the full version of this paper.

Chameleon-Hashes. Let us formally define a "standard" chameleon-hash. The framework is based upon the work done by Ateniese et al. and Brzuska et al. [5, 15], but adapted to fit our notation. Additionally, we provide some extended security definitions.

Definition 4. *A chameleon-hash* CH *consists of five algorithms* (CParGen, CKGen, CHash, CHashCheck, Adapt), *such that:*

CParGen. *The algorithm* CParGen *on input security parameter* λ *outputs public parameters of the scheme:* $\text{pp}_{ch} \leftarrow \text{CParGen}(1^\lambda)$. *For brevity, we assume that* pp_{ch} *is implicit input to all other algorithms.*

CKGen. *The algorithm* CKGen *given the public parameters* pp_{ch} *outputs the private and public keys of the scheme:* $(\text{sk}_{ch}, \text{pk}_{ch}) \leftarrow \text{CKGen}(\text{pp}_{ch})$.

CHash. *The algorithm* CHash *gets as input the public key* pk_{ch}, *and a message* m *to hash. It outputs a hash* h, *and some randomness* r: $(h,r) \leftarrow \text{CHash}(\text{pk}_{ch}, m)$.[1]

CHashCheck. *The deterministic algorithm* CHashCheck *gets as input the public key* pk_{ch}, *a message* m, *randomness* r, *and a hash* h. *It outputs a decision* $d \in \{\texttt{false}, \texttt{true}\}$ *indicating whether the hash* h *is valid:* $d \leftarrow \text{CHashCheck}(\text{pk}_{ch}, m, r, h)$.

Adapt. *The algorithm* Adapt *on input of secret key* sk_{ch}, *the old message* m, *the old randomness* r, *hash* h, *and a new message* m' *outputs new randomness* r': $r' \leftarrow \text{Adapt}(\text{sk}_{ch}, m, m', r, h)$.

Correctness. For a CH we require the correctness property to hold. In particular, we require that for all $\lambda \in \mathbb{N}$, for all $\text{pp}_{ch} \leftarrow \text{CParGen}(1^\lambda)$, for all $(\text{sk}_{ch}, \text{pk}_{ch}) \leftarrow \text{CKGen}(\text{pp}_{ch})$, for all $m \in \mathcal{M}$, for all $(h,r) \leftarrow \text{CHash}(\text{pk}_{ch}, m)$, for all $m' \in \mathcal{M}$, we have for all for all $r' \leftarrow \text{Adapt}(\text{sk}_{ch}, m, m', r, h)$, that $\texttt{true} = \text{CHashCheck}(\text{pk}_{ch}, m, r, h) = \text{CHashCheck}(\text{pk}_{ch}, m', r', h)$. This definition captures perfect correctness. The randomness is drawn by CHash, and not outside. This was done to capture "private-coin" constructions [5].

Indistinguishability. Indistinguishability requires that the randomnesses r does not reveal if it was obtained through CHash or Adapt. The messages are chosen

---

[1] The randomness r is also sometimes called "check value" [5].

by the adversary. We relax the perfect indistinguishability definition of Brzuska et al. [15] to a computational version, which is enough for most use-cases, including ours.

Experiment $\mathsf{Indistinguishability}_{\mathcal{A}}^{\mathsf{CH}}(\lambda)$
  $\mathsf{pp}_{\mathsf{ch}} \leftarrow \mathsf{CParGen}(1^{\lambda})$
  $(\mathsf{sk}_{\mathsf{ch}}, \mathsf{pk}_{\mathsf{ch}}) \leftarrow \mathsf{CKGen}(\mathsf{pp}_{\mathsf{ch}})$
  $b \leftarrow \{0,1\}$
  $a \leftarrow \mathcal{A}^{\mathsf{HashOrAdapt}(\mathsf{sk}_{\mathsf{ch}},\cdot,\cdot,\cdot,b),\mathsf{Adapt}(\mathsf{sk}_{\mathsf{ch}},\cdot,\cdot,\cdot,\cdot)}(\mathsf{pk}_{\mathsf{ch}})$
    where oracle HashOrAdapt on input $\mathsf{sk}_{\mathsf{ch}}, m, m', b$:
      $(h, r) \leftarrow \mathsf{CHash}(\mathsf{pk}_{\mathsf{ch}}, m')$
      $(h', r') \leftarrow \mathsf{CHash}(\mathsf{pk}_{\mathsf{ch}}, m)$
      $r'' \leftarrow \mathsf{Adapt}(\mathsf{sk}_{\mathsf{ch}}, m, m', r', h')$
      If $r = \bot \vee r'' = \bot$, return $\bot$
      if $b = 0$:
        return (h, r)
      if $b = 1$:
        return (h', r'')
  return 1, if $a = b$
  return 0

Fig. 1. Indistinguishability

Note that we need to return $\bot$ in the HashOrAdapt oracle, as the adversary may try to enter a message $m \notin \mathcal{M}$, even if $\mathcal{M} = \{0,1\}^*$, which makes the algorithm output $\bot$. If we would not do this, the adversary could trivially decide indistinguishability. For similar reasons these checks are also included in other definitions.

Definition 5 (Indistinguishability). *A chameleon-hash* CH *is indistinguishable, if for any efficient adversary* $\mathcal{A}$ *there exists a negligible function* ν *such that* $\left| \Pr[\mathsf{Indistinguishability}_{\mathcal{A}}^{\mathsf{CH}}(\lambda) = 1] - \frac{1}{2} \right| \leq \nu(\lambda)$. *The corresponding experiment is depicted in Fig. 1.*

Collision Resistance. Collision resistance says, that even if an adversary has access to an adapt oracle, it cannot find any collisions for messages other than the ones queried to the adapt oracle. Note, this is an even stronger definition than key-exposure freeness [7]: key-exposure freeness only requires that one cannot find a collision for some new "tag", i.e., for some auxiliary value for which the adversary has never seen a collision.

Definition 6 (Collision-Resistance). *A chameleon-hash* CH *is collision-resistant, if for any efficient adversary* $\mathcal{A}$ *there exists a negligible function* ν *such that* $\Pr[\mathsf{CollRes}_{\mathcal{A}}^{\mathsf{CH}}(1^{\lambda}) = 1] \leq \nu(\lambda)$. *The corresponding experiment is depicted in Fig. 2.*

Uniqueness. Uniqueness requires that it is hard to come up with two different randomness values for the same message m^* such that the hashes are equal, for the same adversarially chosen pk^*.

Experiment $\mathsf{CollRes}_{\mathcal{A}}^{\mathsf{CH}}(\lambda)$
  $\mathsf{pp_{ch}} \leftarrow \mathsf{CParGen}(1^\lambda)$
  $(\mathsf{sk_{ch}}, \mathsf{pk_{ch}}) \leftarrow \mathsf{CKGen}(\mathsf{pp_{ch}})$
  $\mathcal{Q} \leftarrow \emptyset$
  $(m^*, r^*, m'^*, r'^*, h^*) \leftarrow \mathcal{A}^{\mathsf{Adapt}'(\mathsf{sk_{ch}}, \cdot, \cdot, \cdot, \cdot)}(\mathsf{pk_{ch}})$
    where oracle Adapt' on input $\mathsf{sk_{ch}}, m, m', r, h$:
      Return $\perp$, if $\mathsf{CHashCheck}(\mathsf{pk_{ch}}, m, r, h) \neq \mathbf{true}$
      $r' \leftarrow \mathsf{Adapt}(\mathsf{sk_{ch}}, m, m', r, h)$
      If $r' = \perp$, return $\perp$
      $\mathcal{Q} \leftarrow \mathcal{Q} \cup \{m, m'\}$
      return r'
  return 1, if $\mathsf{CHashCheck}(\mathsf{pk_{ch}}, m^*, r^*, h^*) = \mathsf{CHashCheck}(\mathsf{pk_{ch}}, m'^*, r'^*, h^*) = \mathbf{true} \wedge$
    $m'^* \notin \mathcal{Q} \wedge m^* \neq m'^*$
  return 0

Fig. 2. Collision resistance

Experiment $\mathsf{Uniqueness}_{\mathcal{A}}^{\mathsf{CH}}(\lambda)$
  $\mathsf{pp_{ch}} \leftarrow \mathsf{CParGen}(1^\lambda)$
  $(\mathsf{pk}^*, m^*, r^*, r'^*, h^*) \leftarrow \mathcal{A}(\mathsf{pp_{ch}})$
  return 1, if $\mathsf{CHashCheck}(\mathsf{pk}^*, m^*, r^*, h^*) = \mathsf{CHashCheck}(\mathsf{pk}^*, m^*, r'^*, h^*) = \mathbf{true}$
    $\wedge\; r^* \neq r'^*$
  return 0

Fig. 3. Uniqueness

Definition 7 (Uniqueness). *A chameleon-hash* CH *is unique, if for any efficient adversary* $\mathcal{A}$ *there exists a negligible function* ν *such that* $\Pr[\mathsf{Uniqueness}_{\mathcal{A}}^{\mathsf{CH}}$ $(1^\lambda) = 1] \leq \nu(\lambda)$. *The corresponding experiment is depicted in Fig. 3.*

Definition 8 (Secure Chameleon-Hashes). *We call a chameleon-hash* CH *secure, if it is correct, indistinguishable, and collision-resistant.*

We do not consider uniqueness as a fundamental security property, as it depends on the concrete use-case whether this notion is required.

In the full version of this paper, we show how to construct a unique chameleon-hash satisfying our strong notions, based on the ideas by Brzuska et al. [15].

3   Chameleon-Hashes with Ephemeral Trapdoors

As already mentioned, a chameleon-hash with ephemeral trapdoor (CHET) allows to prevent the holder of the trapdoor $\mathsf{sk_{ch}}$ from finding collisions, as long as no additional ephemeral trapdoor etd is known. This additional ephemeral trapdoor is chosen freshly for each new hash, and providing, or withholding, this trapdoor thus allows to decide upon each hash computation if finding a collision is possible for the holder of the long-term trapdoor. Hence, we need to introduce a new framework given next, which is also accompanied by suitable security definitions.

Definition 9 (Chameleon-Hashes with Ephemeral Trapdoors). *A chameleon-hash with ephemeral trapdoors* CHET *is a tuple of five algorithms* (CParGen, CKGen, CHash, CHashCheck, Adapt), *such that:*

CParGen. *The algorithm* CParGen *on input security parameter* λ *outputs the public parameters:* $pp_{ch} \leftarrow$ CParGen(1^λ). *For simplicity, we assume that* pp_{ch} *is an implicit input to all other algorithms.*

CKGen. *The algorithm* CKGen *given the public parameters* pp_{ch} *outputs the long-term private and public keys of the scheme:* $(sk_{ch}, pk_{ch}) \leftarrow$ CKGen(pp_{ch}).

CHash. *The algorithm* CHash *gets as input the public key* pk_{ch}, *and a message* m *to hash. It outputs a hash* h, *randomness* r, *and the trapdoor information:* $(h, r, etd) \leftarrow$ CHash(pk_{ch}, m).

CHashCheck. *The deterministic algorithm* CHashCheck *gets as input the public key* pk_{ch}, *a message* m, *a hash* h, *and randomness* r. *It outputs a decision bit* $d \in \{$false, true$\}$, *indicating whether the given hash is correct:* $d \leftarrow$ CHashCheck(pk_{ch}, m, r', h).

Adapt. *The algorithm* Adapt *gets as input* sk_{ch}, *the old message* m, *the old randomness* r, *the new message* m', *the hash* h, *and the trapdoor information* etd *and outputs new randomness* r': $r' \leftarrow$ Adapt($sk_{ch}, m, m', r, h, etd$).

Correctness. For each CHET we require the correctness properties to hold. In particular, we require that for all security parameters $\lambda \in \mathbb{N}$, for all $pp_{ch} \leftarrow$ CParGen(1^λ), for all $(sk_{ch}, pk_{ch}) \leftarrow$ CKGen(pp_{ch}), for all $m \in \mathcal{M}$, for all $(h, r, etd) \leftarrow$ CHash(pk_{ch}, m), we have CHashCheck(pk_{ch}, m, r, h) = true, and additionally for all $m' \in \mathcal{M}$, for all $r' \leftarrow$ Adapt($sk_{ch}, m, m', r, h, etd$), we have CHashCheck($pk_{ch}, m', r', h$) = true. This definition captures perfect correctness. We also require some security guarantees, which we introduce next.

Indistinguishability. Indistinguishability requires that the randomnesses r does not reveal if it was obtained through CHash or Adapt. In other words, an outsider cannot decide whether a message is the original one or not.

Definition 10 (Indistinguishability). *A chameleon-hash with ephemeral trapdoor* CHET *is indistinguishable, if for any efficient adversary* $\mathcal{A}$ *there exists a negligible function* ν *such that* $\left| \Pr[\text{Indistinguishability}_{\mathcal{A}}^{\text{CHET}}(\lambda) = 1] - \frac{1}{2} \right| \leq \nu(\lambda)$. *The corresponding experiment is depicted in Fig. 4.*

Public Collision Resistance. Public collision resistance requires that, even if an adversary has access to an Adapt oracle, it cannot find any collisions by itself. Clearly, the collision must be fresh, i.e., must not be produced using the Adapt oracle.

Definition 11 (Public Collision-Resistance). *A chameleon-hash with ephemeral trapdoor* CHET *is publicly collision-resistant, if for any efficient adversary* $\mathcal{A}$ *there exists a negligible function* ν *such that* $\Pr[\text{PublicCollRes}_{\mathcal{A}}^{\text{CHET}}(1^\lambda) = 1] \leq \nu(\lambda)$. *The corresponding experiment is depicted in Fig. 5.*

Experiment Indistinguishability$_{\mathcal{A}}^{\mathsf{CHET}}(\lambda)$

    $\mathsf{pp}_{\mathsf{ch}} \leftarrow \mathsf{CParGen}(1^{\lambda})$

    $(\mathsf{sk}_{\mathsf{ch}}, \mathsf{pk}_{\mathsf{ch}}) \leftarrow \mathsf{CKGen}(\mathsf{pp}_{\mathsf{ch}})$

    $b \leftarrow \{0, 1\}$

    $a \leftarrow \mathcal{A}^{\mathsf{HashOrAdapt}(\mathsf{sk}_{\mathsf{ch}}, \cdot, \cdot, b), \mathsf{Adapt}(\mathsf{sk}_{\mathsf{ch}}, \cdot, \cdot, \cdot, \cdot, \cdot)}(\mathsf{pk}_{\mathsf{ch}})$

        where oracle HashOrAdapt on input $\mathsf{sk}_{\mathsf{ch}}, m, m', b$:

            let $(h, r, \mathsf{etd}) \leftarrow \mathsf{CHash}(\mathsf{pk}_{\mathsf{ch}}, m')$

            let $(h', r', \mathsf{etd}') \leftarrow \mathsf{CHash}(\mathsf{pk}_{\mathsf{ch}}, m)$

            let $r'' \leftarrow \mathsf{Adapt}(\mathsf{sk}_{\mathsf{ch}}, m, m', r', h', \mathsf{etd}')$

            if $r'' = \bot \vee r' = \bot$, return $\bot$

            if $b = 0$:

                return (h, r, etd)

            if $b = 1$:

                return (h', r'', etd')

    return 1, if $a = b$

    return 0

Fig. 4. Indistinguishability

Experiment PublicCollRes$_{\mathcal{A}}^{\mathsf{CHET}}(\lambda)$

    $\mathsf{pp}_{\mathsf{ch}} \leftarrow \mathsf{CParGen}(1^{\lambda})$

    $(\mathsf{sk}_{\mathsf{ch}}, \mathsf{pk}_{\mathsf{ch}}) \leftarrow \mathsf{CKGen}(\mathsf{pp}_{\mathsf{ch}})$

    $\mathcal{Q} \leftarrow \emptyset$

    $(m^*, r^*, m'^*, r'^*, h^*) \leftarrow \mathcal{A}^{\mathsf{Adapt}'(\mathsf{sk}_{\mathsf{ch}}, \cdot, \cdot, \cdot, \cdot, \cdot)}(\mathsf{pk}_{\mathsf{ch}})$

        where oracle Adapt' on input $\mathsf{sk}_{\mathsf{ch}}, m, m', r, \mathsf{etd}, h$:

            return $\bot$, if $\mathsf{CHashCheck}(\mathsf{pk}_{\mathsf{ch}}, m, r, h) = \mathtt{false}$

            $r' \leftarrow \mathsf{Adapt}(\mathsf{sk}_{\mathsf{ch}}, m, m', r, h, \mathsf{etd})$

            If $r' = \bot$, return $\bot$

            $\mathcal{Q} \leftarrow \mathcal{Q} \cup \{m, m'\}$

            return r'

    return 1, if $\mathsf{CHashCheck}(\mathsf{pk}_{\mathsf{ch}}, m^*, r^*, h^*) = \mathtt{true} \wedge$

    $\mathsf{CHashCheck}(\mathsf{pk}_{\mathsf{ch}}, m'^*, r'^*, h^*) = \mathtt{true} \wedge$

    $m'^* \notin \mathcal{Q} \wedge m^* \neq m'^*$

    return 0

Fig. 5. Public collision-resistance

Private Collision-Resistance. Private collision resistance requires that even the holder of the secret key $\mathsf{sk}_{\mathsf{ch}}$ cannot find collisions as long as etd is unknown. This is formalized by a honest hashing oracle which does not return etd. Hence, $\mathcal{A}$'s goal is to return an actual collision on a non-adversarially generated hash h, for which it does not know etd.

Definition 12 (Private Collision-Resistance). *A chameleon-hash with ephemeral trapdoor* CHET *is privately collision-resistant, if for any efficient adversary* $\mathcal{A}$ *there exists a negligible function* ν *such that* $\Pr[\mathsf{PrivateCollRes}_{\mathcal{A}}^{\mathsf{CHET}} (1^{\lambda}) = 1] \leq \nu(\lambda)$. *The corresponding experiment is depicted in Fig. 6.*

Uniqueness. Uniqueness requires that it is hard to come up with two different randomness values for the same message m^* and hash value h^*, where pk^* is adversarially chosen.

Experiment PrivateCollRes$_{\mathcal{A}}^{\mathsf{CHET}}(\lambda)$
  $\mathsf{pp}_{\mathsf{ch}} \leftarrow \mathsf{CParGen}(1^{\lambda})$
  $\mathcal{Q} \leftarrow \emptyset$
  $(\mathsf{pk}^*, \mathsf{state}) \leftarrow \mathcal{A}(\mathsf{pp}_{\mathsf{ch}})$
  $(m^*, r^*, m'^*, r'^*, h^*) \leftarrow \mathcal{A}^{\mathsf{CHash}'(\mathsf{pk}^*, \cdot)}(\mathsf{state})$
    where oracle CHash' on input pk^*, m:
      $(h, r, \mathsf{etd}) \leftarrow \mathsf{CHash}(\mathsf{pk}^*, m)$
      If $h = \perp$, return $\perp$
      $\mathcal{Q} \leftarrow \mathcal{Q} \cup \{(h, m)\}$
      return (h, r)
  return 1, if $\mathsf{CHashCheck}(\mathsf{pk}^*, m^*, r^*, h^*) = \mathbf{true} \wedge$
    $\mathsf{CHashCheck}(\mathsf{pk}^*, m'^*, r'^*, h^*) = \mathbf{true} \wedge$
    $(h^*, m^*) \notin \mathcal{Q} \wedge (h^*, \cdot) \in \mathcal{Q}$
  return 0

Fig. 6. Private collision-resistance

Experiment Uniqueness$_{\mathcal{A}}^{\mathsf{CHET}}(\lambda)$
  $\mathsf{pp}_{\mathsf{ch}} \leftarrow \mathsf{CParGen}(1^{\lambda})$
  $(\mathsf{pk}^*, m^*, r^*, r'^*, h^*) \leftarrow \mathcal{A}(\mathsf{pp}_{\mathsf{ch}})$
  return 1, if $\mathsf{CHashCheck}(\mathsf{pk}^*, m^*, r^*, h^*) = \mathsf{CHashCheck}(\mathsf{pk}^*, m^*, r'^*, h^*) = \mathbf{true} \wedge$
    $r^* \neq r'^*$
  return 0

Fig. 7. Uniqueness

Definition 13 (Uniqueness). *A chameleon-hash with ephemeral trapdoor* CHET *is unique, if for any efficient adversary $\mathcal{A}$ there exists a negligible function ν such that* $\Pr[\mathsf{Uniqueness}_{\mathcal{A}}^{\mathsf{CHET}}(1^{\lambda}) = 1] \leq \nu(\lambda)$. *The corresponding experiment is depicted in Fig. 7.*

Definition 14 (Secure Chameleon-Hashes with Ephemeral Trapdoors). *We call a chameleon-hash with ephemeral trapdoor* CHET *secure, if it is correct, indistinguishable, publicly collision-resistant, and privately collision-resistant.*

Note, we do not require that a secure CHET is unique, as it depends on the use-case whether this strong security notion is required.

4   Constructions

Regarding constructions of CHET schemes, we first ask the natural question whether CHETs can be built from existing primitives in a black-box way. Interestingly, we can show how to elegantly "bootstrap" a CHET scheme in a black-box fashion from *any* existing secure (and unique) chameleon-hash. Since, however, a secure chameleon-hash does not exist to date, we show how to construct it in based on the ideas by Brzuska et al. [15]. If one does not require uniqueness, one can, e.g., resort to the recent scheme given by Ateniese et al. [5].

We then proceed in presenting three direct constructions, two based on the DL assumption, and one based on an RSA-like assumption. While the DL-based constructions are not unique, the construction from RSA-like assumptions even achieves uniqueness. We however note that this strong security notion is not required in all use-cases. For example, in our application scenario (cf. Sect. 5), the CHETs do not need to be unique.

4.1   Black-Box Construction: Bootstrapping

We now present a black-box construction from any existing chameleon-hash. Namely, we show how one can achieve our desired goals by combining two instances of a secure chameleon-hash CH.

Construction 1 (Bootstrapped Construction). *We omit obvious checks for brevity. Let* CHET *be defined as:*

CParGen. *The algorithm* CParGen *does the following:*
  1. Return $\mathsf{pp}_{\mathsf{ch}} \leftarrow \mathsf{CH.CParGen}(1^\lambda)$.
CKGen. *The algorithm* CKGen *generates the key pair in the following way:*
  1. Return $(\mathsf{sk}_{\mathsf{ch}}^1, \mathsf{pk}_{\mathsf{ch}}^1) \leftarrow \mathsf{CH.CKGen}(\mathsf{pp}_{\mathsf{ch}})$.
CHash. *To hash a message* m, *w.r.t. public key* $\mathsf{pk}_{\mathsf{ch}}^1$ *do:*
  1. Let $(\mathsf{sk}_{\mathsf{ch}}^2, \mathsf{pk}_{\mathsf{ch}}^2) \leftarrow \mathsf{CH.CKGen}(\mathsf{pp}_{\mathsf{ch}})$.
  2. Let $(h_1, r_1) \leftarrow \mathsf{CH.CHash}(\mathsf{pk}_{\mathsf{ch}}^1, m)$.
  3. Let $(h_2, r_2) \leftarrow \mathsf{CH.CHash}(\mathsf{pk}_{\mathsf{ch}}^2, m)$.
  4. Return $((h_1, h_2, \mathsf{pk}_{\mathsf{ch}}^2), (r_1, r_2), \mathsf{sk}_{\mathsf{ch}}^2)$.
CHashCheck. *To check whether a given hash* $h = (h_1, h_2, \mathsf{pk}_{\mathsf{ch}}^2)$ *is valid on input* $\mathsf{pk}_{\mathsf{ch}} = \mathsf{pk}_{\mathsf{ch}}^1$, m, $r = (r_1, r_2)$, *do:*
  1. Let $b_1 \leftarrow \mathsf{CH.CHashCheck}(\mathsf{pk}_{\mathsf{ch}}^1, m, r_1, h_1)$.
  2. Let $b_2 \leftarrow \mathsf{CH.CHashCheck}(\mathsf{pk}_{\mathsf{ch}}^2, m, r_2, h_2)$.
  3. If $b_1 = \mathtt{false} \vee b_2 = \mathtt{false}$, *return* $\mathtt{false}$.
  4. Return $\mathtt{true}$.
Adapt. *To find a collision w.r.t.* m, m', *randomness* $r = (r_1, r_2)$, *hash* $h = (h_1, h_2, \mathsf{pk}_{\mathsf{ch}}^2)$, $\mathsf{etd} = \mathsf{sk}_{\mathsf{ch}}^2$, *and* $\mathsf{sk}_{\mathsf{ch}} = \mathsf{sk}_{\mathsf{ch}}^1$ *do:*
  1. If $\mathtt{false} = \mathsf{CHashCheck}(\mathsf{pk}_{\mathsf{ch}}, m, r, h)$, *return* $\bot$.
  2. Compute $r_1' \leftarrow \mathsf{CH.Adapt}(\mathsf{sk}_{\mathsf{ch}}^1, m, m', r_1, h_1)$.
  3. Compute $r_2' \leftarrow \mathsf{CH.Adapt}(\mathsf{sk}_{\mathsf{ch}}^2, m, m', r_2, h_2)$.
  4. Return (r_1', r_2').

The proof of the following theorem can be found in the full version of this paper.

Theorem 1. *If* CH *is secure and unique, then the chameleon-hash with ephemeral trapdoors* CHET *in Construction 1 is secure, and unique.*

This construction is easy to understand and only uses standard primitives. The question is now, if we can also directly construct CHET, which we answer to the affirmative subsequently.

4.2 A First Direct Construction

We now present a direct construction in groups where the DLP is hard using some ideas related to Pedersen commitments [53]. In a nutshell, the long-term secret is the discrete logarithm x between two elements g and h (i.e., $g^x = h$) of the long-term public key, while the ephemeral trapdoor is the randomness of the "commitment". To prohibit that a seen collision allows to extract the long-term secret key x, both trapdoors are hidden in a NIZKPoK. To make the "commitment" equivocable, it is then again randomized. To avoid that the holder of $\mathsf{sk_{ch}}$ needs to store state, the randomness is encrypted to a public key of a IND-CCA2 secure encryption scheme contained in $\mathsf{pk_{ch}}$. Security then directly follows from the DL assumption, IND-CCA2, the collision-resistance of the used hash function, and the extractability property of the NIZKPoK system. For brevity we assume that the **NP**-languages involved in the NIZKPoKs are implicitly defined by the scheme. Note, this construction is not unique.

Construction 2 (CHET in Known-Order Groups). *Let* $\{\mathcal{H}_{\mathbb{Z}_q^*}^k\}_{k \in \mathcal{K}}$ *denote a family of collision-resistant hash functions* $\mathcal{H}_{\mathbb{Z}_q^*}^k : \{0,1\}^* \to \mathbb{Z}_q^*$ *indexed by a key* $k \in \mathcal{K}$ *and let* CHET *be as follows:*

CParGen. *The algorithm* CParGen *generates the public parameters in the following way:*
  1. *Let* $(G, g, p) \leftarrow \mathsf{GGen}(1^\lambda)$.
  2. *Let* $k \leftarrow \mathcal{K}$ *for the hash function.*
  3. *Let* $\mathsf{crs} \leftarrow \mathsf{Gen}(1^\lambda)$.[2]
  4. *Return* $((G, g, q), k, \mathsf{crs})$.
CKGen. *The algorithm* CKGen *generates the key pair in the following way:*
  1. *Draw random* $x \leftarrow \mathbb{Z}_q^*$. *Set* $h \leftarrow g^x$.
  2. *Generate* $\pi_{\mathsf{pk}} \leftarrow \mathrm{NIZKPoK}\{(x) : h = g^x\}$.
  3. *Let* $(\mathsf{sk_{enc}}, \mathsf{pk_{enc}}) \leftarrow \Pi.\mathsf{KGen_{enc}}(1^\lambda)$.
  4. *Return* $((x, \mathsf{sk_{enc}}), (h, \pi_{\mathsf{pk}}, \mathsf{pk_{enc}}))$.
CHash. *To hash* m *w.r.t.* $\mathsf{pk_{ch}} = (h, \pi_{\mathsf{pk}}, \mathsf{pk_{enc}})$ *do:*
  1. *Return* $\bot$, *if* $h \notin G^*$.
  2. *If* π_{pk} *is not valid, return* $\bot$.
  3. *Draw random* $r \leftarrow \mathbb{Z}_q^*$.
  4. *Draw random* $\mathsf{etd} \leftarrow \mathbb{Z}_q^*$.
  5. *Let* $h' \leftarrow g^{\mathsf{etd}}$.
  6. *Generate* $\pi_t \leftarrow \mathrm{NIZKPoK}\{(\mathsf{etd}) : h' = g^{\mathsf{etd}}\}$.
  7. *Encrypt* r, *i.e., let* $C \leftarrow \Pi.\mathsf{Enc}(\mathsf{pk_{enc}}, r)$.
  8. *Let* $a \leftarrow \mathcal{H}_{\mathbb{Z}_q^*}^k(m)$.
  9. *Let* $p \leftarrow h^r$.
  10. *Generate* $\pi_p \leftarrow \mathrm{NIZKPoK}\{(r) : p = h^r\}$.
  11. *Let* $b \leftarrow ph'^a$.
  12. *Return* $((b, h', \pi_t), (p, C, \pi_p), \mathsf{etd})$.

---

[2] Actually we need one crs per language, but we do not make this explicit here.

CHashCheck. *To check whether a given hash* (b, h', π_t) *is valid on input* $\mathsf{pk_{ch}} = (h, \pi_{pk}, \mathsf{pk_{enc}}), m, r = (p, C, \pi_p), do:$
  1. *Return* false, *if* $p \notin G^* \vee h' \notin G^*.$
  2. *If either* $\pi_p, \pi_t,$ *or* π_{pk} *are not valid, return* $\perp.$
  3. *Let* $a \leftarrow \mathcal{H}^k_{\mathbb{Z}_q^*}(m).$
  4. *Return* true, *if* $b = ph'^a.$
  5. *Return* false.

Adapt. *To find a collision w.r.t.* $m, m', (b, h', \pi_t),$ *randomness* $(p, C, \pi_p),$ *and trapdoor information* etd, *and* $\mathsf{sk_{ch}} = (x, \mathsf{sk_{enc}})$ *do:*
  1. *If* false $= $ CHashCheck$(\mathsf{pk_{ch}}, m, (p, C, \pi_p), (b, h', \pi_t)),$ *return* $\perp.$
  2. *Decrypt* $C,$ *i.e.,* $r \leftarrow \Pi.\mathsf{Dec}(\mathsf{sk_{enc}}, C).$ *If* $r = \perp,$ *return* $\perp.$
  3. *If* $h' \neq g^{\mathsf{etd}},$ *return* $\perp.$
  4. *Let* $a \leftarrow \mathcal{H}^k_{\mathbb{Z}_q^*}(m).$
  5. *Let* $a' \leftarrow \mathcal{H}^k_{\mathbb{Z}_q^*}(m').$
  6. *If* $p \neq g^{xr},$ *return* $\perp.$
  7. *If* $a = a',$ *return* $(p, C, \pi_p).$
  8. *Let* $r' \leftarrow \frac{rx + a \cdot \mathsf{etd} - a' \cdot \mathsf{etd}}{x}.$
  9. *Let* $p' \leftarrow h^{r'}.$
  10. *Encrypt* $r',$ *i.e., let* $C' \leftarrow \Pi.\mathsf{Enc}(\mathsf{pk_{enc}}, r').$
  11. *Generate* $\pi'_p \leftarrow \mathsf{NIZKPoK}\{(r') : p' = h^{r'}\}.$
  12. *Return* $(p', C', \pi'_p).$

Some of the checks can already be done in advance, e.g., at a PKI, which only generates certificates, if the restrictions on each public key are fulfilled.

The proof of the following Theorem is given in the full version of this paper.

Theorem 2. *If the DL assumption in* G *holds,* $\mathcal{H}^k_{\mathbb{Z}_{|G|}^*}$ *is collision-resistant,* Π *is IND-CCA2 secure, and* NIZKPoK *is secure, then the chameleon-hash with ephemeral trapdoors* CHET *in Construction 2 is secure.*

Two further constructions, one based on the DL assumption in gap-groups, and one based on RSA-like assumptions (in the random oracle model, which is also unique), are given in the full version of this paper.

5   Application: Invisible Sanitizable Signatures

Informally, security of digital signatures requires that a signature σ on a message m becomes invalid as soon as a single bit of m is altered [40]. However, there are many real-life use-cases in which a subsequent change to signed data by a semi-trusted party without invalidating the signature is desired. As a simplified example, consider a patient record which is signed by a medical doctor. The accountant, which charges the insurance company, only requires knowledge of the treatments and the patient's insurance number. This protects the patient's privacy. In this constellation, having the data re-signed by the M.D. whenever subsets of the record need to be forwarded to some party induces too much overhead to be practical in real scenarios or may even be impossible due to availability constraints.

Sanitizable signature schemes (SSS) [4] address these shortcomings. They allow the signer to determine which blocks $m[i]$ of a given message $m = (m[1], m[2], \ldots, m[i], \ldots, m[\ell])$ are admissible. Any such admissible block can be changed to a different bitstring $m[i]' \in \{0, 1\}^*$, where $i \in \{1, 2, \ldots, \ell\}$, by a semi-trusted party named the sanitizer. This party is identified by a private/public key pair and the sanitization process described before requires the private key. In a nutshell, sanitization of a message m results in an altered message $m' = (m[1]', m[2]', \ldots, m[i]', \ldots, m[\ell]')$, where $m[i] = m[i]'$ for every non-admissible block, and also a signature σ', which verifies under the original public key. Thus, authenticity of the message is still ensured. In the prior example, for the server storing the data it is possible to already black-out the sensitive parts of a signed document without any additional communication with the M.D. and in particular without access to the signing key of the M.D.

Real-world applications of SSSs include the already mentioned privacy-preserving handling of patient data, secure routing, privacy-preserving document disclosure, credentials, and blank signatures [4,17–19,24,30,42].

Our Contribution. We introduce the notion of *invisible* SSSs. This strong privacy notion requires that a third party not holding any secret keys cannot decide whether a specific block is admissible, i.e., can be sanitized. This has already been discussed by Ateniese et al. [4] in the first work on sanitizable signatures, but they neither provide a formal framework nor a provably secure construction. However, we identify some use-cases where such a notion is important, and we close this gap by introducing a new framework for SSSs, along with an extended security model. Moreover, we propose a construction being provably secure in our framework. Our construction paradigm is based on IND-CPA secure encryption schemes, standard, yet unique, chameleon-hashes, and strongly unforgeable signature schemes. These can be considered standard tools nowadays. We pair those with a chameleon-hash with ephemeral trapdoors.

Motivation. At PKC '09, Brzuska et al. formalized the most common security model of SSSs [15]. For our work, the most important property they are addressing is "weak transparency". It means that although a third party sees which blocks of a message are admissible, it cannot decide whether some block has already been sanitized by a sanitizer. More precisely, their formalization explicitly requires that the third party is always able to decide whether a given block in a message is admissible. However, as this may invade privacy, having a construction which hides this additional information is useful as well. To address this problem the notion of "strong transparency" has been informally proposed in the original work by Ateniese et al. [4].

Examples. To make the usefulness of such a stronger privacy property more visible, consider the following two application scenarios.

In the first scenario, we consider that a document is the output of a workflow that requires several—potentially heavy—computations to become ready. We assume that the output of each workflow step could be produced by one party alone, but could also be outsourced. However, if the party decides to outsource the production of certain parts of the document it wants the potential involvement of other parties to stay hidden, e.g., the potential and actual outsourcing might be considered a trade secret. In order to regain some control that all tasks are done only by authorized subordinates, the document—containing template parts—is signed with a sanitizable signature. Such an approach, i.e., to use SSS for workflow control, was proposed in [29].

The second one is motivated by an ongoing legal debate in Germany.[3] Consider a school class where a pupil suffers from dyslexia[4] and thus can apply for additional help to compensate the illness. One way to compensate this is to consider spelling mistakes less when giving grades. Assume that only the school's principal shall decide to what extent a certain grade shall be improved. Of course, this shall only be possible for pupils who are actually handicapped. For the pupil with dyslexia, e.g., known to the teacher of the class in question, the grade is marked as sanitizable by the principal. The legal debate in Germany is about an outsider, e.g., future employer, who should not be able to decide that grades had the potential to be altered and of course also not see for which pupils the grades have been altered to preserve their privacy. To achieve this, standard sanitizable signature schemes are clearly not enough, as they do not guarantee that an outsider cannot derive which blocks are potentially sanitizable, i.e., which pupil is actually handicapped. We offer a solution to this problem, where an outsider cannot decide which block is admissible, i.e., can be altered.

State-of-the-Art. SSSs have been introduced by Ateniese et al. [4]. Brzuska et al. formalized most of the current security properties [15]. These have been later extended for (strong) unlinkability [17,19,35] and non-interactive public accountability [18,19]. Some properties discussed by Brzuska et al. [15] have then been refined by Gong et al. [41]. Namely, they also consider the admissible blocks in the security games, while still requiring that these are visible to everyone. Recently, Krenn et al. further refined the security properties to also account for the signatures, not only the message [48].[5] We use the aforementioned results as our starting point for the extended definitions.

Also, several extensions such as limiting the sanitizer to signer-chosen values [21,31,46,56], trapdoor SSSs (which allow to add new sanitizers after signature generation by the signer) [23,59], multi-sanitizer and -signer environments for SSSs [16,19,22], and sanitization of signed and encrypted data [33] have been

---

[3] See for example the ruling from the German Federal Administrative Court (BVerwG) 29.07.2015, Az.: 6 C 33.14, 6 C 35.14.

[4] A disorder involving difficulty in learning to read or interpret words, letters and other symbols.

[5] We want to stress that Krenn et al. [48] also introduce "strong transparency", which is not related to the definition given by Ateniese et al. [4].

considered. SSSs have also been used as a tool to make other primitives accountable [55], and to build other primitives [10,51]. Also, SSSs and data-structures being more complex than lists have been considered [56]. Our results carry over to the aforementioned extended settings with only minor additional adjustments. Implementations of SSSs have also been presented [18,19,50,54].

Of course, computing on signed messages is a broad field. We can therefore only give a small overview. Decent and comprehensive overviews of other related primitives, however, have already been published [2,14,28,38,39].

5.1 Additional Building Blocks

We assume that the reader is familiar with digital signatures, PRGs, and PRFs, and only introduce the notation used in the following. A PRF consists of a key generation algorithm $\mathsf{KGen}_{\mathsf{prf}}$ and an evaluation algorithm $\mathsf{Eval}_{\mathsf{prf}}$; similarly, a PRG consists of an evaluation algorithm $\mathsf{Eval}_{\mathsf{prg}}$. Finally, a digital signature scheme $\varSigma$ consists of a key generation algorithm $\mathsf{KGen}_{\mathsf{sig}}$, a signing algorithm Sign, and a verification algorithm Verify. The formal definition and security notions are given in the full version of this paper.

5.2 Our Framework for Sanitizable Signature Schemes

Subsequently, we introduce our framework for SSSs. Our definitions are based on existing work [15,18,19,41,48]. However, due to our goals, we need to modify the current framework to account for the fact that the admissible blocks are only visible to the sanitizer. We do not consider "non-interactive public accountability" [18,19,45], which allows a third party to decide which party is accountable, as transparency is mutually exclusive to this property, but is very easy to achieve, e.g., by signing the sanitizable signature again [18].

Before we present the formal definition, we settle some notation. The variable ADM contains the set of indices of the modifiable blocks, as well as the number ℓ of blocks in a message m. We write $\mathrm{ADM}(m) = \mathtt{true}$, if ADM is valid w.r.t. m, i.e., ADM contains the correct ℓ and all indices are in m. For example, let $\mathrm{ADM} = (\{1, 2, 4\}, 4)$. Then, m must contain four blocks, while all but the third will be admissible. If we write $m_i \in \mathrm{ADM}$, we mean that m_i is admissible. MOD is a set containing pairs $(i, m[i]')$ for those blocks that shall be modified, meaning that $m[i]$ is replaced with $m[i]'$. We write $\mathrm{MOD}(\mathrm{ADM}) = \mathtt{true}$, if MOD is valid w.r.t. ADM, meaning that the indices to be modified are contained in ADM. To allow a compact presentation of our construction we write $\widetilde{X}_{n,m}$ with $n \leq m$ for the vector $(X_n, X_{n+1}, X_{n+2}, \ldots, X_{m-1}, X_m)$.

Definition 15. (Sanitizable Signatures). *A sanitizable signature scheme* SSS *consists of eight ppt algorithms* (SSSParGen, $\mathsf{KGen}_{\mathsf{sig}}$, $\mathsf{KGen}_{\mathsf{san}}$, Sign, Sanit, Verify, Proof, Judge) *such that*

SSSParGen. *The algorithm* SSSParGen, *on input security parameter* λ, *generates the public parameters:* $\mathsf{pp}_{\mathsf{sss}} \leftarrow \mathsf{SSSParGen}(1^\lambda)$. *We assume that* $\mathsf{pp}_{\mathsf{sss}}$ *is implicitly input to all other algorithms.*

KGen$_{sig}$. *The algorithm* KGen$_{sig}$ *takes the public parameters* pp$_{sss}$ *and returns the signer's private key and the corresponding public key:* (pk$_{sig}$, sk$_{sig}$) ← KGen$_{sig}$(pp$_{sss}$).

KGen$_{san}$. *The algorithm* KGen$_{san}$ *takes the public parameters* pp$_{sss}$ *and returns the sanitizer's private key and the corresponding public key:* (pk$_{san}$, sk$_{san}$) ← KGen$_{san}$(pp$_{sss}$).

Sign. *The algorithm* Sign *takes as input a message* m, sk$_{sig}$, pk$_{san}$, *as well as a description* ADM *of the admissible blocks. If* ADM(m) = false, *this algorithm returns* ⊥. *It outputs a signature* σ ← Sign(m, sk$_{sig}$, pk$_{san}$, ADM).

Sanit. *The algorithm* Sanit *takes a message* m, *modification instruction* MOD, *a signature* σ, pk$_{sig}$, *and* sk$_{san}$. *It outputs* m' *together with* σ': (m', σ') ← Sanit(m, MOD, σ, pk$_{sig}$, sk$_{san}$) *where* m' ← MOD(m) *is message* m *modified according to the modification instruction* MOD.

Verify. *The algorithm* Verify *takes as input the signature* σ *for a message* m *w.r.t. the public keys* pk$_{sig}$ *and* pk$_{san}$ *and outputs a decision* d ∈ {true, false}: d ← Verify(m, σ, pk$_{sig}$, pk$_{san}$).

Proof. *The algorithm* Proof *takes as input* sk$_{sig}$, *a message* m, *a signature* σ, *a set of polynomially many additional message/signature pairs* {(m$_i$, σ$_i$)} *and* pk$_{san}$. *It outputs a string* π ∈ {0, 1}* *which can be used by the* Judge *to decide which party is accountable given a message/signature pair* (m, σ): π ← Proof(sk$_{sig}$, m, σ, {(m$_i$, σ$_i$) | i ∈ ℕ}, pk$_{san}$).

Judge. *The algorithm* Judge *takes as input a message* m, *a signature* σ, pk$_{sig}$, pk$_{san}$, *as well as a proof* π. *Note, this means that once a proof* π *is generated, the accountable party can be derived by anyone for that message/signature pair* (m, σ). *It outputs a decision* d ∈ {Sig, San}, *indicating whether the message/signature pair has been created by the signer, or the sanitizer:* d ← Judge(m, σ, pk$_{sig}$, pk$_{san}$, π).

Correctness of Sanitizable Signature Schemes. We require the usual correctness requirements to hold. In a nutshell, every signed and sanitized message/signature pair should verify, while a honestly generated proof on a honestly generated message/signature pair should point to the correct accountable party. We refer to [15] for a formal definition, which straightforwardly extends to our framework.

5.3   Security of Sanitizable Signature Schemes

Next, we introduce our security model, where our definitions already incorporate newer insights [15, 19, 41, 48]. In particular, we mostly consider the "strong" definitions by Krenn et al. [48] as the new state-of-the-art. Due to our goals, we also see the data-structure corresponding to the admissible blocks, i.e., ADM, as an asset which needs protection, which addresses the work done by Gong et al. [41]. All formal definitions can be found in the full version of this paper.

Unforgeability. No one should be able to generate any new signature not seen before without having access to any private keys.

Immutability. Sanitizers must only be able to perform allowed modifications. In particular, a sanitizer must not be able to modify non-admissible blocks.

Privacy. Similar to semantic security for encryption schemes, privacy captures the inability of an attacker to derive any knowledge about sanitized parts.

Transparency. An attacker cannot tell whether a specific message/signature pair has been sanitized or not.

Accountability. For signer-accountability, a signer should not be able to accuse a sanitizer if the sanitizer is actually not responsible for a given message, and vice versa for sanitizer-accountability.

5.4   Invisibility of SSSs

Next, we introduce the new property of invisibility. Basically, invisibility requires that an outsider cannot decide which blocks of a given message are admissible. With $ADM_0 \cap ADM_1$, we denote the intersection of the admissible blocks, ignoring the length of the messages.

In a nutshell, the adversary can query an LoRADM oracle which either makes ADM_0 or ADM_1 admissible in the final signature. Of course, the adversary has to be restricted to $ADM_0 \cap ADM_1$ for sanitization requests for signatures originating from those created by LoRADM and their derivatives to avoid trivial attacks. The sign oracle can be simulated by querying the LoRADM oracle with $ADM_0 = ADM_1$. We stress that our invisibility definition is very strong, as it also takes the signatures into account, much like the definitions given by Krenn et al. [48]. One can easily alter our definition to only account for the messages in question, e.g., if one wants to avoid strongly unforgeable signatures, or even allow re-randomizable signatures. An adjustment is straightforward.

Definition 16. (Invisibility). *An SSS is invisible, if for any efficient adversary $\mathcal{A}$ there exists a negligible function ν such that $\left| \Pr[\mathsf{Invisibility}_{\mathcal{A}}^{SSS}(\lambda) = 1] - \frac{1}{2} \right| \leq \nu(\lambda)$, where the corresponding experiment is defined in Fig. 8.*

It is obvious that invisibility is not implied by any other property. In a nutshell, taking any secure SSS, it is sufficient to non-malleably append ADM to each block $m[i]$ to prevent invisibility. Clearly, all other properties of such a construction are still preserved.

Definition 17. (Secure SSS). *We call an SSS secure, if it is correct, private, unforgeable, immutable, sanitizer-accountable, signer-accountable, and invisible.*

We do neither consider non-interactive public accountability nor unlinkability nor transparency as essential security requirements, as it depends on the concrete use-case whether these properties are required.

5.5   Construction

We now introduce our construction and use the construction paradigm of Ateniese et al. [4], enriching it with several ideas of prior work [15,41,50]. The

Experiment $\text{Invisibility}_{\mathcal{A}}^{\text{SSS}}(\lambda)$
  $\text{pp}_{\text{sss}} \leftarrow \text{SSSParGen}(1^\lambda)$
  $(\text{pk}_{\text{sig}}, \text{sk}_{\text{sig}}) \leftarrow \text{KGen}_{\text{sig}}(\text{pp}_{\text{sss}})$
  $(\text{pk}_{\text{san}}, \text{pk}_{\text{san}}) \leftarrow \text{KGen}_{\text{san}}(\text{pp}_{\text{sss}})$
  $b \leftarrow \{0, 1\}$
  $\mathcal{Q} \leftarrow \emptyset$
  $a \leftarrow \mathcal{A}^{\text{Sanit}'(\cdot,\cdot,\cdot,\cdot,\text{sk}_{\text{san}}),\text{Proof}(\text{sk}_{\text{sig}},\cdot,\cdot,\cdot,\cdot),\text{LoRADM}(\cdot,\cdot,\cdot,\text{sk}_{\text{sig}},b)}(\text{pk}_{\text{sig}}, \text{pk}_{\text{san}})$
     where oracle LoRADM on input of $m, \text{ADM}_0, \text{ADM}_1, \text{sk}_{\text{sig}}, b$:
       return $\bot$, if $\text{ADM}_0(m) \neq \text{ADM}_1(m)$
       let $\sigma \leftarrow \text{Sign}(m, \text{sk}_{\text{sig}}, \text{pk}_{\text{san}}, \text{ADM}_b)$
       let $\mathcal{Q} \leftarrow \mathcal{Q} \cup \{(m, \sigma, \text{ADM}_0 \cap \text{ADM}_1)\}$
       return σ
     where oracle Sanit' on input of $m, \text{MOD}, \sigma, \text{pk}'_{\text{sig}}, \text{sk}_{\text{san}}$:
       return $\bot$, if $\text{pk}'_{\text{sig}} \neq \text{pk}_{\text{sig}} \vee \not\exists (m, \sigma, \text{ADM}) \in \mathcal{Q} : \text{MOD}(\text{ADM}) = \textbf{true}$
       let $(m', \sigma') \leftarrow \text{Sanit}(m, \text{MOD}, \sigma, \text{pk}'_{\text{sig}}, \text{sk}_{\text{san}})$
       if $\text{pk}'_{\text{sig}} = \text{pk}_{\text{sig}} \wedge \exists (m, \sigma, \text{ADM}') \in \mathcal{Q} : \text{MOD}(\text{ADM}') = \textbf{true}$,
         let $\mathcal{Q} \leftarrow \mathcal{Q} \cup \{(m', \sigma', \text{ADM}')\}$
       return (m', σ')
  return 1, if $a = b$
  return 0

Fig. 8. Invisibility

main idea is to hash each block using a chameleon-hash with ephemeral trapdoors, and then sign the hashes. The main trick we introduce to limit the sanitizer is that only those etd_i are given to the sanitizer, for which the respective block $m[i]$ should be sanitizable. To hide whether a given block is sanitizable, each etd_i is encrypted; a sanitizable block contains the real etd_i, while a nonadmissible block encrypts a 0, where 0 is assumed to be an invalid etd. For simplicity, we require that the IND-CPA secure encryption scheme Π allows that each possible etd, as well as 0, is in the message space $\mathcal{M}$ of Π, which can be achieved using standard embedding and padding techniques, or using KEM/DEM combinations [1]. To achieve accountability, we generate additional "tags" for a "standard" chameleon-hash (which binds everything together) in a special way, namely we use PRFs and PRGs, which borrows ideas from the construction given by Brzuska et al. [15].

Construction 3. (Secure and Transparent SSS). *The secure and transparent SSS construction is as follows:*

SSSParGen. *To generate the public parameters, do the following steps:*
  1. Let $\text{pp}_{\text{ch}} \leftarrow \text{CHET.CParGen}(1^\lambda)$.
  2. Let $\text{pp}'_{\text{ch}} \leftarrow \text{CH.CParGen}(1^\lambda)$.
  3. Return $\text{pp}_{\text{sss}} = (\text{pp}_{\text{ch}}, \text{pp}'_{\text{ch}})$.
KGen$_{\text{sig}}$. *To generate the key pair for the signer, do the following steps:*
  1. Let $(\text{pk}_s, \text{sk}_s) \leftarrow \Sigma.\text{KGen}_{\text{sig}}(1^\lambda)$.
  2. Pick a key for a PRF, i.e., $\kappa \leftarrow \text{PRF.KGen}_{\text{prf}}(1^\lambda)$.
  3. Return $(\text{pk}_s, (\kappa, \text{sk}_s))$.

$\mathsf{KGen}_{\mathsf{san}}$. *To generate the key pair for the sanitizer, do the following steps:*
1. *Let* $(\mathsf{pk}_{\mathsf{ch}}, \mathsf{sk}_{\mathsf{ch}}) \leftarrow \mathsf{CHET.CKGen}(\mathsf{pp}_{\mathsf{ch}})$.
2. *Let* $(\mathsf{pk}'_{\mathsf{ch}}, \mathsf{sk}'_{\mathsf{ch}}) \leftarrow \mathsf{CH.CKGen}(\mathsf{pp}'_{\mathsf{ch}})$.
3. *Let* $(\mathsf{pk}_{\mathsf{enc}}, \mathsf{sk}_{\mathsf{enc}}) \leftarrow \Pi.\mathsf{KGen}_{\mathsf{enc}}(1^\lambda)$.
4. *Return* $((\mathsf{pk}_{\mathsf{ch}}, \mathsf{pk}'_{\mathsf{ch}}, \mathsf{pk}_{\mathsf{enc}}), (\mathsf{sk}_{\mathsf{ch}}, \mathsf{sk}'_{\mathsf{ch}}, \mathsf{sk}_{\mathsf{enc}}))$.

Sign. *To generate a signature* σ, *on input of* $m = (m[1], m[2], \ldots, m[\ell])$, $\mathsf{sk}_{\mathsf{sig}} = (\kappa, \mathsf{sk}_{\mathsf{s}})$, $\mathsf{pk}_{\mathsf{san}} = (\mathsf{pk}_{\mathsf{ch}}, \mathsf{pk}'_{\mathsf{ch}}, \mathsf{pk}_{\mathsf{enc}})$, *and* ADM *do the following steps:*
1. *If* $\mathrm{ADM}(m) \neq \mathtt{true}$, *return* $\bot$.
2. *Draw* $x_0 \leftarrow \{0,1\}^\lambda$.
3. *Let* $x'_0 \leftarrow \mathsf{PRF.Eval}_{\mathsf{prf}}(\kappa, x_0)$.
4. *Let* $\tau \leftarrow \mathsf{PRG.Eval}_{\mathsf{prg}}(x'_0)$.
5. *For each* $i \in \{1, 2, \ldots, \ell\}$ *do:*
   (a) *Set* $(h_i, r_i, \mathsf{etd}_i) \leftarrow \mathsf{CHET.CHash}(\mathsf{pk}_{\mathsf{ch}}, (i, m[i], \mathsf{pk}_{\mathsf{sig}}))$.
   (b) *If block* i *is not admissible, let* $\mathsf{etd}_i \leftarrow 0$.
   (c) *Compute* $c_i \leftarrow \Pi.\mathsf{Enc}(\mathsf{pk}_{\mathsf{enc}}, \mathsf{etd}_i)$.
6. *Set* $(h_0, r_0) \leftarrow \mathsf{CH.CHash}(\mathsf{pk}'_{\mathsf{ch}}, (0, m, \tau, \ell, \widetilde{h}_{1,\ell}, \widetilde{c}_{1,\ell}, \widetilde{r}_{1,\ell}, \mathsf{pk}_{\mathsf{sig}}))$.
7. *Set* $\sigma' \leftarrow \Sigma.\mathsf{Sign}(\mathsf{sk}_{\mathsf{s}}, (x_0, \widetilde{h}_{0,\ell}, \widetilde{c}_{1,\ell}, \mathsf{pk}_{\mathsf{san}}, \mathsf{pk}_{\mathsf{sig}}, \ell))$.
8. *Return* $\sigma = (\sigma', x_0, \widetilde{r}_{0,\ell}, \tau, \widetilde{c}_{1,\ell}, \widetilde{h}_{0,\ell})$.

Verify. *To verify a signature* $\sigma = (\sigma', x_0, \widetilde{r}_{0,\ell}, \tau, \widetilde{c}_{1,\ell}, \mathsf{etd}_0, \widetilde{h}_{0,\ell})$, *on input of* $m = (m[1], m[2], \ldots, m[\ell])$, *w.r.t. to* $\mathsf{pk}_{\mathsf{sig}} = \mathsf{pk}_{\mathsf{s}}$ *and* $\mathsf{pk}_{\mathsf{san}} = (\mathsf{pk}_{\mathsf{ch}}, \mathsf{pk}'_{\mathsf{ch}}, \mathsf{pk}_{\mathsf{enc}})$, *do:*
1. *For each* $i \in \{1, 2, \ldots, \ell\}$ *do:*
   (a) *Set* $b_i \leftarrow \mathsf{CHET.CHashCheck}(\mathsf{pk}_{\mathsf{ch}}, (i, m[i], \mathsf{pk}_{\mathsf{sig}}), r_i, h_i)$. *If any* $b_i = \mathtt{false}$, *return* $\mathtt{false}$.
2. *Let* $b_0 \leftarrow \mathsf{CH.CHashCheck}(\mathsf{pk}'_{\mathsf{ch}}, (0, m, \tau, \ell, \widetilde{h}_{1,\ell}, \widetilde{c}_{1,\ell}, \widetilde{r}_{1,\ell}, \mathsf{pk}_{\mathsf{sig}}), r_0, h_0)$.
3. *If* $b_0 = \mathtt{false}$, *return* $\mathtt{false}$.
4. *Return* $d \leftarrow \Sigma.\mathsf{Verify}(\mathsf{pk}_{\mathsf{s}}, (x_0, \widetilde{h}_{0,\ell}, \widetilde{c}_{1,\ell}, \mathsf{pk}_{\mathsf{san}}, \mathsf{pk}_{\mathsf{sig}}, \ell), \sigma')$.

Sanit. *To sanitize a signature* $\sigma = (\sigma', x_0, \widetilde{r}_{0,\ell}, \tau, \widetilde{c}_{1,\ell}, \widetilde{h}_{0,\ell})$, *on input of* $m = (m[1], m[2], \ldots, m[\ell])$, *w.r.t. to* $\mathsf{pk}_{\mathsf{sig}} = \mathsf{pk}_{\mathsf{s}}$, $\mathsf{sk}_{\mathsf{san}} = (\mathsf{sk}_{\mathsf{ch}}, \mathsf{sk}'_{\mathsf{ch}}, \mathsf{sk}_{\mathsf{enc}})$, *and* MOD *do:*
1. *Verify the signature, i.e., run* $d \leftarrow \mathsf{SSS.Verify}(m, \sigma, \mathsf{pk}_{\mathsf{sig}}, \mathsf{pk}_{\mathsf{san}})$. *If* $d = \mathtt{false}$, *return* $\bot$.
2. *Decrypt each* c_i *for* $i \in \{1, 2, \ldots, \ell\}$, *i.e., let* $\mathsf{etd}_i \leftarrow \Pi.\mathsf{Dec}(\mathsf{sk}_{\mathsf{enc}}, c_i)$. *If any decryption fails, return* $\bot$.
3. *For each index* $i \in \mathrm{MOD}$ *check that* $\mathsf{etd}_i \neq 0$. *If not, return* $\bot$.
4. *For each block* $m[i]' \in \mathrm{MOD}$ *do:*
   (a) *Let* $r'_i \leftarrow \mathsf{CHET.Adapt}(\mathsf{sk}_{\mathsf{ch}}, (i, m[i], \mathsf{pk}_{\mathsf{sig}}), (i, m[i]', \mathsf{pk}_{\mathsf{sig}}), r_i, \mathsf{etd}_i)$.
   (b) *If* $r'_i = \bot$, *return* $\bot$.
5. *For each block* $m[i]' \notin \mathrm{MOD}$ *do:*
   (a) *Let* $r'_i \leftarrow r_i$.
6. *Let* $m' \leftarrow \mathrm{MOD}(m)$.
7. *Draw* $\tau' \leftarrow \{0,1\}^{2\lambda}$.
8. *Let* $r'_0 \leftarrow \mathsf{CH.Adapt}(\mathsf{sk}'_{\mathsf{ch}}, (0, m, \tau, \ell, \widetilde{h}_{1,\ell}, \widetilde{c}_{1,\ell}, \widetilde{r}_{1,\ell}, \mathsf{pk}_{\mathsf{sig}}), (0, m', \tau', \ell, \widetilde{h}_{1,\ell}, \widetilde{c}_{1,\ell}, \widetilde{r}'_{1,\ell}, \mathsf{pk}_{\mathsf{sig}}), r_0, h_0)$.
9. *Return* $(m', (\sigma', x_0, \widetilde{r}'_{0,\ell}, \tau', \widetilde{c}_{1,\ell}, \widetilde{h}_{0,\ell}))$.

Proof. *To create a proof* π, *on input of* $m = (m[1], m[2], \ldots, m[\ell])$, *a signature* σ, *w.r.t. to* $\mathsf{pk_{san}}$ *and* $\mathsf{sk_{sig}}$, *and* $\{(m_i, \sigma_i) \mid i \in \mathbb{N}\}$ *do:*

1. *Return* $\perp$, *if* false = SSS.Verify($m, \sigma, \mathsf{pk_{sig}}, \mathsf{pk_{san}}$).
2. *Verify each signature in the list, i.e., run* $d_i \leftarrow$ SSS.Verify($m_i, \sigma_i, \mathsf{pk_{sig}}, \mathsf{pk_{san}}$). *If for any* $d_i =$ false, *return* $\perp$.
3. *Go through the list of* (m_i, σ_i) *and find a (non-trivial) colliding tuple of the chameleon-hash with* (m, σ), *i.e.,* $h_0 = h'_0$, *where also* true = CH.CHashCheck($\mathsf{pk'_{ch}}, (0, m, \tau, \ell, \tilde{h}_{1,\ell}, \tilde{c}_{1,\ell}, \tilde{r}_{1,\ell}, \mathsf{pk_{sig}}), r_0, h_0$), *and* true = CH.CHashCheck($\mathsf{pk'_{ch}}, (0, m', \tau', \ell, \tilde{h'}_{1,\ell}, \tilde{c'}_{1,\ell}, \tilde{r'}_{1,\ell}, \mathsf{pk_{sig}}), r'_0, h'_0$) *for some different tag* τ' *or message* m'. *Let this signature/message pair be* $(\sigma', m') \in \{(m_i, \sigma_i) \mid i \in \mathbb{N}\}$.
4. *Return* $\pi = ((\sigma', m'), \mathsf{PRF.Eval_{prf}}(\kappa, x_0))$, *where* x_0 *is contained in* (σ, m).

Judge. *To find the accountable party on input of* $m = (m[1], m[2], \ldots, m[\ell])$, *a valid signature* σ, *w.r.t. to* $\mathsf{pk_{san}}, \mathsf{pk_{sig}}$, *and a proof* π *do:*

1. *Check if* π *is of the form* $((\sigma', m'), v)$ *with* $v \in \{0,1\}^\lambda$. *If not, return* Sig.
2. *Also return* $\perp$, *if* false = SSS.Verify($m', \sigma', \mathsf{pk_{sig}}, \mathsf{pk_{san}}$), *or* false = SSS.Verify($m, \sigma, \mathsf{pk_{sig}}, \mathsf{pk_{san}}$).
3. *Let* $\tau'' \leftarrow$ PRG.Eval$_{\mathsf{prg}}(v)$.
4. *If* $\tau' \neq \tau''$, *return* Sig.
5. *If we have* $h_0 = h'_0$, true = CH.CHashCheck($\mathsf{pk_{ch}}, (0, m, \tau, \ell, \tilde{h}_{1,\ell}, \tilde{c}_{1,\ell}, \mathsf{pk_{sig}}), r_0, \mathsf{pk_{sig}}, h_0$) = CH.CHashCheck($\mathsf{pk'_{ch}}, (0, m', \tau', \ell', \tilde{h'}_{1,\ell'}, \tilde{c'}_{1,\ell'}, \mathsf{pk_{sig}}), r'_0, \mathsf{pk_{sig}}, h'_0$), $\tilde{c}_{1,\ell} = \tilde{c'}_{1,\ell'}$, $x_0 = x'_0$, $\ell = \ell'$, *and* $\tilde{h}_{0,\ell} = \tilde{h'}_{0,\ell'}$, *return* San.
6. *Return* Sig.

Theorem 3. *If* Π *is IND-CPA secure,* Σ, PRF, PRG, CHET *are secure,* CH *is secure and unique, Construction 3 is a secure and transparent* SSS.

Note, CHET is not required to be unique. We prove each property on its own.

Proof. Correctness follows by inspection.

Unforgeability. To prove that our scheme is unforgeable, we use a sequence of games:

Game 0: The original unforgeability game.

Game 1: As Game 0, but we abort if the adversary outputs a forgery (m^*, σ^*) with $\sigma^* = (\sigma'^*, x_0^*, \tilde{r}_{0,\ell^*}^*, \tilde{\tau}^*, \tilde{c}_{1,\ell^*}^*, \tilde{h}_{0,\ell^*}^*)$, where $(\sigma'^*, (x_0, \tilde{h}_{0,\ell}, \tilde{c}_{1,\ell}, \mathsf{pk_{san}}, \mathsf{pk_{sig}}, \ell))$ was never obtained from the sign or sanitizing oracle. Let this event be E_1.

Transition - Game 0 $\rightarrow$ Game 1: Clearly, if $(\sigma'^*, (x_0, \tilde{h}_{0,\ell}, \tilde{c}_{1,\ell}, \mathsf{pk_{san}}, \mathsf{pk_{sig}}, \ell))$ was never obtained by the challenger, this tuple breaks the strong unforgeability of the underlying signature scheme. The reduction works as follows. We obtain a challenge public key pk_c from a strong unforgeability challenger and embed it as $\mathsf{pk_{sig}}$. For every required "inner" signature σ', we use the signing oracle provided by the challenger. Now, whenever E_1 happens, we can output σ'^* together with the message protected by σ'^* as a forgery to the challenger. That is, E_1 happens with exactly the same probability as a forgery. Further, both games proceed identically, unless E_1 happens. Taking everything together yields $|\Pr[S_0] - \Pr[S_1]| \leq \nu_{\mathsf{unf\text{-}cma}}(\lambda)$.

Game 2: Among others, we now have established that the adversary can no longer win by modifying $\mathsf{pk}_{\mathsf{sig}}$, and $\mathsf{pk}_{\mathsf{san}}$. We proceed as in Game 1, but abort if the adversary outputs a forgery (m^*, σ^*), where message m^* or any of the other values protected by the outer chameleon-hash were never returned by the signer or the sanitizer oracle. Let this event be E_2.

Transition - Game 1 → Game 2: The probability of the abort event E_2 to happen is exactly the probability of the adversary breaking collision freeness for the outer chameleon-hash. Namely, we already established that the adversary cannot tamper with the inner signature and therefore the hash value h_0^* must be from a previous oracle query. Now, assume that we obtain $\mathsf{pk}'_{\mathsf{ch}}$ from a collision freeness challenger. If E_2 happens, there must be a previous oracle query with associated values $(0, m, \tau, \ell, \tilde{h}_{1,\ell}, \tilde{c}_{1,\ell}, \tilde{r}_{1,\ell}, \mathsf{pk}_{\mathsf{sig}})$ and r_0 so that h_0^* is a valid hash with respect to some those values and r_0. Further, we also have that $(0, m, \tau, \ell, \tilde{h}_{1,\ell}, \tilde{c}_{1,\ell}, \tilde{r}_{1,\ell}, \mathsf{pk}_{\mathsf{sig}}) \neq (0, m^*, \tau^*, \ell^*, \tilde{h}^*_{1,\ell^*}, \tilde{c}^*_{1,\ell^*}, \tilde{r}^*_{1,\ell^*}, \mathsf{pk}_{\mathsf{sig}})$, and can thus output $((0, m^*, \tau^*, \ell^*, \tilde{h}^*_{1,\ell^*}, \tilde{c}^*_{1,\ell^*}, \tilde{r}^*_{1,\ell^*}, \mathsf{pk}_{\mathsf{sig}}), r_0^*, (0, m, \tau, \ell, \tilde{h}_{1,\ell}, \tilde{c}_{1,\ell}, \tilde{r}_{1,\ell}, \mathsf{pk}_{\mathsf{sig}}), r_0, h_0^*)$ as the collision. Thus, the probability that E_2 happens is exactly the probability of a collision for the chameleon-hash. Both games proceed identically, unless E_2 happens. $|\Pr[S_1] - \Pr[S_2]| \leq \nu_{\mathsf{ch\text{-}coll\text{-}res}}(\lambda)$ follows.

Game 3: As Game 2, but we abort if the adversary outputs a forgery where only the randomness r_0 changed, i.e., we have previously generated a signature with respect to r_0 so that $r_0 \neq r_0^*$. Let this be event E_3.

Transition - Game 2 → Game 3: If the abort event E_3 happens, the adversary breaks uniqueness of the chameleon-hash. In particular we have values $(0, m^*, \tau^*, \ell^*, \tilde{h}^*_{1,\ell^*}, \tilde{c}^*_{1,\ell^*}, \tilde{r}^*_{1,\ell^*}, \mathsf{pk}_{\mathsf{sig}})$ in the forgery which also correspond to some previous query, but r_0 from the previous query is different from r_0^*. Obtaining $\mathsf{pp}'_{\mathsf{ch}}$ from a uniqueness challenger thus shows that E_3 happens with exactly the same probability as the adversary breaks uniqueness of the chameleon hash. Thus, we have that $|\Pr[S_2] - \Pr[S_3]| \leq \nu_{\mathsf{ch\text{-}unique}}(\lambda)$.

In the last game, the adversary can no longer win the unforgeability game; this game is computationally indistinguishable from the original game, which concludes the proof.

Immutability. We prove immutability using a sequence of games.

Game 0: The immutability game.

Game 1: As Game 0, but we abort if the adversary outputs a forgery (m^*, σ^*) with $\sigma^* = (\sigma'^*, x_0^*, \tilde{r}^*_{0,\ell^*}, \tilde{\tau}^*, \tilde{c}^*_{1,\ell^*}, \tilde{h}^*_{0,\ell^*})$ where $(\sigma'^*, (x_0, \tilde{h}_{0,\ell}, \tilde{c}_{1,\ell}, \mathsf{pk}_{\mathsf{san}}, \mathsf{pk}_{\mathsf{sig}}, \ell))$ was never obtained from the sign oracle.

Transition - Game 0 → Game 1: Let us use E_1 to refer to the abort event. Clearly, if $(\sigma'^*, (x_0, \tilde{h}_{0,\ell}, \tilde{c}_{1,\ell}, \mathsf{pk}_{\mathsf{san}}, \mathsf{pk}_{\mathsf{sig}}, \ell))$ was never obtained by the challenger, this tuple breaks the strong unforgeability of the underlying signature scheme. The reduction works as follows. We obtain a challenge public key pk_c from a strong unforgeability challenger and embed it as $\mathsf{pk}_{\mathsf{sig}}$. For every required "inner" signature σ', we use the signing oracle provided by the challenger.

Now, whenever E_1 happens, we can output σ'^* together with the message protected by σ'^* as a forgery to the challenger. That is, E_1 happens with exactly the same probability as a forgery of the underlying signature scheme. Further, both games proceed identically, unless E_1 happens. Taking everything together yields $|\Pr[S_0] - \Pr[S_1]| \leq \nu_{\text{unf-cma}}(\lambda)$.

Game 2: As Game 1, but the challenger aborts, if the message m^* is not derivable from any returned signature. Note, we already know that tampering with the signatures is not possible, and thus pk_{sig}, and pk_{san}, are fixed. The same is true for deleting or appending blocks, as ℓ is signed in every case. Let this event be denoted E_2.

Transition - Game 1 $\rightarrow$ Game 2: Now assume that E_2 is non-negligible. We can then construct an adversary $\mathcal{B}$ which breaks the private collision-resistance of the underlying chameleon-hash with ephemeral trapdoors. Let the signature returned be $\sigma^* = (\sigma'^*, x_0^*, \widetilde{r}_{0,\ell^*}^*, \widetilde{\tau}^*, \widetilde{c}_{1,\ell^*}^*, \widetilde{h}_{0,\ell^*}^*)$, while $\mathcal{A}$'s public key is pk^*. Due to prior game hops, we know that $\mathcal{A}$ cannot tamper with the "inner" signatures. Thus, there must exists another signature $\sigma = (\sigma'^*, x_0^*, \widetilde{r}'_{0,\ell^*}^*, \widetilde{\tau}'^*, \widetilde{c}_{1,\ell^*}^*, \widetilde{h}_{0,\ell^*}^*)$ returned by the signing oracle. This, however, also implies that there must exists an index $i \in \{1, 2, \ldots, \ell^*\}$, for which we have $\text{CHET.CHashCheck}(\text{pk}_{\text{ch}}, (i, m^*[i], \text{pk}_{\text{sig}}), r_i^*, h_i^*) = \text{CHET.CHashCheck}$ $(\text{pk}_{\text{ch}}, (i, m'^*[i], \text{pk}_{\text{sig}}), r_i'^*, h_i^*) = \text{true}$, where $m^*[i] \neq m'^*[i]$ by assumption. $\mathcal{B}$ proceeds as follows. Let q_h be the number of "inner hashes" created. Draw an index $i \leftarrow \{1, 2, \ldots, q_h\}$. For a query $i \neq j$, proceed as in the algorithms. If $i = j$, however, $\mathcal{B}$ returns the current public key pk_c for the chameleon-hash with ephemeral trapdoors. This key is contained in pk_{san}^*. $\mathcal{B}$ then receives back control, and queries its CHash oracle with $(i, m[i], \text{pk}_{\text{sig}})$, where i is the current index of the message m to be signed. Then, if $((i, m^*[i], \text{pk}_{\text{sig}}), r_i^*, (i, m'^*[i], \text{pk}_{\text{sig}}), r_i'^*, h_i^*)$ is the collision w.r.t. pk_c, it can directly return it. $|\Pr[S_1] - \Pr[S_2]| \leq q_h \nu_{\text{priv-coll}}(\lambda)$ follows, as $\mathcal{B}$ has to guess where the collision will take place.

As each hop changes the view of the adversary only negligibly, immutability is proven, as the adversary has no other way to break immutability in Game 2.

Privacy. We prove privacy; we use a sequence of games.

Game 0: The original privacy game.

Game 1: As Game 0, but we abort if the adversary queries a verifying message-signature pair (m^*, σ^*) which was never returned by the signer or the sanitizer oracle, and queries it to the sanitization or proof generation oracle.

Transition - Game 0 $\rightarrow$ Game 1: Let us use E_1 to refer to the abort event. Clearly, whenever the adversary queries such a new pair, we can output it to break the unforgeability of our scheme, as this tuple is fresh. However, we have already proven that this can only happen with negligible probability. $|\Pr[S_0] - \Pr[S_1]| \leq \nu_{\text{sss-unf}}(\lambda)$ follows.

Game 2: As Game 1, but instead of hashing the blocks $(i, m_b[i], \text{pk}_{\text{sig}})$ for the inner chameleon-hashes using CHash, and then Adapt to $(i, m[i], \text{pk}_{\text{sig}})$, we directly apply CHash to $(i, m[i], \text{pk}_{\text{sig}})$.

Transition - Game 1 → Game 2: Assume that the adversary can distinguish this hop. We can then construct an $\mathcal{B}$ which wins the indistinguishability game. $\mathcal{B}$ receives pk_c as it's own challenge, $\mathcal{B}$ embeds pk_c as pk_{ch}, and proceeds honestly with the exception that it uses the HashOrAdapt oracle to generate the inner hashes. Then, whatever $\mathcal{A}$ outputs, is also output by $\mathcal{B}$. $|\Pr[S_1] - \Pr[S_2]| \leq \nu_{\mathsf{chet\text{-}ind}}(\lambda)$ follows.

Game 3: As Game 2, but instead of adapting $(0, m, \tau, \ell, \widetilde{h}_{1,\ell}, \widetilde{c}_{1,\ell}, \widetilde{r}_{1,\ell}, \mathsf{pk}_{sig})$ to the new values, directly use CHash.

Transition - Game 2 → Game 3: Assume that the adversary can distinguish this hop. We can then construct an $\mathcal{B}$ which wins the indistinguishability game. $\mathcal{B}$ receives pk'_c as it's own challenge, $\mathcal{B}$ embeds pk'_c as pk'_{ch}, and proceeds honestly with the exception that it uses the HashOrAdapt oracle to generate the outer hashes. Then, whatever $\mathcal{A}$ outputs, is also output by $\mathcal{B}$. $|\Pr[S_2] - \Pr[S_3]| \leq \nu_{\mathsf{ch\text{-}ind}}(\lambda)$ follows.

Clearly, we are now independent of the bit b. As each hop changes the view of the adversary only negligibly, privacy is proven.

Transparency. We prove transparency by showing that the distributions of sanitized and fresh signatures are indistinguishable. Note, the adversary is not allowed to query Proof for values generated by Sanit/Sign.

Game 0: The original transparency game, where $b = 0$.

Game 1: As Game 0, but we abort if the adversary queries a valid message-signature pair (m^*, σ^*) which was never returned by any of the calls to the sanitization or signature generation oracle. Let us use E_1 to refer to the abort event.

Transition - Game 0 → Game 1: Clearly, whenever the adversary queries such a new pair, we can output it to break the unforgeability of our scheme, as this tuple is fresh. A reduction is straightforward. Thus, we have $|\Pr[S_0] - \Pr[S_1]| \leq \nu_{\mathsf{sss\text{-}unf}}(\lambda)$.

Game 2: As Game 1, but instead of computing $x'_0 \leftarrow \mathsf{PRF.Eval}_{prf}(\lambda, x_0)$, we set $x'_0 \leftarrow \{0,1\}^\lambda$ within every call to Sign in the Sanit/Sign oracle.

Transition - Game 1 → Game 2: A distinguisher between these two games straightfowardly yields a distinguisher for the PRF. Thus, we have $|\Pr[S_1] - \Pr[S_2]| \leq \nu_{\mathsf{ind\text{-}prf}}(\lambda)$.

Game 3: As Game 2, but instead of computing $\tau \leftarrow \mathsf{PRG.Eval}_{prg}(x'_0)$, we set $\tau \leftarrow \{0,1\}^{2\lambda}$ for every call to Sign within the Sanit/Sign oracle.

Transition - Game 2 → Game 3: A distinguisher between these two games yields a distinguisher for the PRG using a standard hybrid argument. Thus, we have $|\Pr[S_2] - \Pr[S_3]| \leq q_s \nu_{\mathsf{ind\text{-}prg}}(\lambda)$, where q_s is the number of calls to the PRG.

Game 4: As Game 3, but we abort if a tag τ was drawn twice. Let this event be E_4.

Transition - Game 3 → Game 4: As the tags τ are drawn completely random, event E_4 only happens with probability $\frac{q_t^2}{2^{2\lambda}}$, where q_t is the number of drawn tags. $|\Pr[S_3] - \Pr[S_4]| \leq \frac{q_t^2}{2^{2\lambda}}$ follows.

Game 5: As Game 4, but instead of hash and then adapting the inner chameleon-hashes, directly hash $(i, m[i], \mathsf{pk}_{\mathsf{sig}})$.

Transition - Game 4 $\rightarrow$ Game 5: Assume that the adversary can distinguish this hop. We can then construct an $\mathcal{B}$ which wins the indistinguishability game. In particular, the reduction works as follows. $\mathcal{B}$ receives pk_c as it's own challenge, $\mathcal{B}$ embeds pk_c as $\mathsf{pk}_{\mathsf{ch}}$, and proceeds honestly except that it uses the HashOrAdapt oracle to generate the inner hashes. Then, whatever $\mathcal{A}$ outputs, is also output by $\mathcal{B}$. $|\Pr[S_4] - \Pr[S_5]| \leq \nu_{\mathsf{ind\text{-}chet}}(\lambda)$ follows.

Game 6: As Game 5, but instead of hashing and then adapting the outer hash, we directly hash the message, i.e., $(0, m, \tau, \ell, \tilde{h}_{1,\ell}, \tilde{c}_{1,\ell}, \tilde{r}_{1,\ell}, \mathsf{pk}_{\mathsf{sig}})$.

Transition - Game 5 $\rightarrow$ Game 6: Assume that the adversary can distinguish this hop. We can then construct an $\mathcal{B}$ which wins the indistinguishability game. In particular, the reduction works as follows. $\mathcal{B}$ receives pk'_c as it's own challenge, embeds pk'_c as $\mathsf{pk}'_{\mathsf{ch}}$, and proceeds honestly with the exception that it uses the HashOrAdapt oracle to generate the outer hashes. Then, whatever $\mathcal{A}$ outputs, is also output by $\mathcal{B}$. $|\Pr[S_5] - \Pr[S_6]| \leq \nu_{\mathsf{ind\text{-}ch}}(\lambda)$ follows.

We are now in the case $b = 1$, while each hop changes the view of the adversary only negligibly. This concludes the proof.

Signer-Accountability. We prove that our construction is signer-accountable by a sequence of games.

Game 0: The original signer-accountability game.

Game 1: As Game 0, but we abort if the sanitization oracle draws a tag τ' which is in the range of the PRG. Let this event be E_1.

Transition - Game 0 $\rightarrow$ Game 1: This hop is indistinguishable by a standard statistical argument: at most 2^λ values lie in the range of the PRG. $|\Pr[S_0] - \Pr[S_1]| \leq \frac{q_s 2^\lambda}{2^{2\lambda}} = \frac{q_s}{2^\lambda}$ follows, where q_s is the number of sanitizing requests. Note, this also means, that there exists no valid pre-image x_0.

Game 2: As Game 1, but we now abort, if a tag was drawn twice by the sanitization oracles. Let this event be E_2.

Transition - Game 1 $\rightarrow$ Game 2: As the tags are drawn uniformly from $\{0,1\}^{2\lambda}$, this case only happens with negligible probability. $|\Pr[S_1] - \Pr[S_2]| \leq \frac{q_s^2}{2^{2\lambda}}$ follows, where q_s is the number of sanitization oracle queries.

Game 3: As Game 2, but we now abort, if the adversary was able to find $(\mathsf{pk}^*, \pi^*, m^*, \sigma^*)$ for some message m^* with a τ^* which was never returned by the sanitization oracle. Let this event be E_3.

Transition - Game 2 $\rightarrow$ Game 3: In the previous games we have already established that the sanitizer oracle will never return a signature with respect to a tag τ in the range of the PRG. Thus, if event E_3 happens, we know by the condition checked in step 4 of Judge that at least one of the tags (either τ^* in σ^*, or τ^π in π^*) was chosen by the adversary, which, in further consequence, implies a collision for CH. Namely, assume that E_3 happens with non-negligible probability. Then we embed the challenge public key pk_c in $\mathsf{pk}'_{\mathsf{ch}}$, and use the provided adaption oracle to simulate the sanitizer oracle. If

E_3 happens we can output $((0, m^*, \tau^*, \ell^*, \widetilde{h}^*_{1,\ell^*}, \widetilde{c}^*_{1,\ell^*}, \widetilde{r}^*_{1,\ell^*}, \mathsf{pk}^*), r^*_0, (0, m'^*, \tau'^*,$ $\ell^*, \widetilde{h}^*_{1,\ell^*}, \widetilde{c}_{1,\ell}, \widetilde{r}^*_{1,\ell^*}, \mathsf{pk}^*), r'^*_0, h^*_0)$, as a valid collision. These values can simply be compiled using π^*, m^*, and σ^*. $|\Pr[S_2] - \Pr[S_3]| \leq \nu_{\mathsf{ch\text{-}coll\text{-}res}}(\lambda)$ follows.

Game 4: As Game 3, but we now abort, if the adversary was able to find $(\mathsf{pk}^*, \pi^*, m^*, \sigma^*)$ for a new message m^* which was never returned by the sanitization oracle. Let this event be E_4.

Transition - Game 3 → Game 4: Assume that E_4 happens with non-negligible probability. In the previous games we have already established that the only remaining possibility for the adversary is to re-use tags τ^*, τ^π corresponding to some query/response to the sanitizer oracle. Then, m^* must be fresh, as it was never returned by the sanitization oracle by assumption. Thus, $((0, m^*, \tau^*, \ell^*, \widetilde{h}^*_{1,\ell^*}, \widetilde{c}^*_{1,\ell^*}, \widetilde{r}^*_{1,\ell^*}, \mathsf{pk}^*), r^*_0, (0, m'^*, \tau'^*, \ell^*, \widetilde{h}^*_{1,\ell^*}, \widetilde{c}_{1,\ell},$ $\widetilde{r}^*_{1,\ell^*}, \mathsf{pk}^*), r'^*_0, h^*_0)$, is a valid collision. These values can simply be compiled using π^*, m^*, and σ^*. $|\Pr[S_3] - \Pr[S_4]| \leq \nu_{\mathsf{ch\text{-}coll\text{-}res}}(\lambda)$ follows.

In the last game the adversary can no longer win; each hop only changes the view negligibly. This concludes the proof.

Sanitizer-Accountability. We prove that our construction is sanitizer-accountable by a sequence of games.

Game 0: The original sanitizer-accountability definition.

Game 1: As Game 0, but we abort if the adversary outputs a forgery $(m^*, \sigma^*,$ $\mathsf{pk}^*)$ with $\sigma^* = (\sigma'^*, x^*_0, \widetilde{r}^*_{0,\ell^*}, \widetilde{\tau}^*, \widetilde{c}^*_{1,\ell^*}, \widetilde{h}^*_{0,\ell^*})$ where $(\sigma'^*, (x_0, \widetilde{h}_{0,\ell}, \widetilde{c}_{1,\ell}, \mathsf{pk}^*,$ $\mathsf{pk}_{\mathsf{sig}}, \ell))$ was never obtained from the signing oracle.

Transition - Game 0 → Game 1: Let us use E_1 to refer to the abort event. Clearly, if $(\sigma'^*, (x_0, \widetilde{h}_{0,\ell}, \widetilde{c}_{1,\ell}, \mathsf{pk}^*, \mathsf{pk}_{\mathsf{sig}}, \ell))$ was never obtained by the challenger, this tuple breaks the strong unforgeability of the underlying signature scheme. The reduction works as follows. We obtain a challenge public key pk_c from a strong unforgeability challenger and embed it as $\mathsf{pk}_{\mathsf{sig}}$. For every required "inner" signature σ', we use the signing oracle provided by the challenger. Now, whenever E_1 happens, we can output σ'^* together with the message protected by σ'^* as a forgery to the challenger. That is, E_1 happens with exactly the same probability as a forgery. Further, both games proceed identically, unless E_1 happens. Taking everything together yields $|\Pr[S_0] - \Pr[S_1]| \leq \nu_{\mathsf{unf\text{-}cma}}(\lambda)$.

Game 2: As Game 1, but we abort if the adversary outputs a forgery where only the randomness r_0 changed, i.e., we have previously generated a signature with respect to r_0 so that $r_0 \neq r^*_0$. Let this event be E_2.

Transition - Game 1 → Game 2: If the abort event E_2 happens, the adversary breaks uniqueness of the chameleon-hash. In particular we have values $(0,$ $m^*, \tau^*, \ell^*, \widetilde{h}^*_{1,\ell^*}, \widetilde{c}^*_{1,\ell^*}, \widetilde{r}^*_{1,\ell^*}, \mathsf{pk}_{\mathsf{sig}})$ in the forgery which also correspond to some previous query, but r_0 from the previous query is different from r^*_0. Obtaining $\mathsf{pp}'_{\mathsf{ch}}$ from a uniqueness challenger thus shows that E_2 happens with exactly the same probability as the adversary breaks uniqueness of the chameleon hash and we have that $|\Pr[S_1] - \Pr[S_2]| \leq \nu_{\mathsf{ch\text{-}unique}}(\lambda)$.

In Game 2 the forgery is different from any query/answer tuple obtained using Sign by definition. Due to the previous hops, the only remaining possibility is a collision in the outer chameleon-hash, i.e., for $h_0^* = h_0'^*$ we have CH.CHashCheck($\mathsf{pk}'^*, (0, m^*, \tau^*, \ell^*, \tilde{h}_{1,\ell^*}^*, \tilde{c}_{1,\ell^*}^*, \tilde{r}_{1,\ell^*}^*, \mathsf{pk}_{\mathsf{sig}}), r_0^*, h_0^*) = $ CH.CHashCheck($\mathsf{pk}'^*, (0, m'^*, \tau'^*, \ell'^*, \tilde{h}_{1,\ell'^*}'^*, \tilde{c}_{1,\ell'^*}'^*, \tilde{r}_{1,\ell'^*}'^*, \mathsf{pk}_{\mathsf{sig}}), r_0'^*, h_0'^*) = $ true. In this case the Judge algorithm returns San and $\Pr[S_2] = 0$ which concludes the proof.

Invisibility. We prove that our construction is invisible by a sequence of games. The idea is to show that we can simulate the view of the adversary without giving out any useful information at all.

Game 0: The original invisibility game, i.e., the challenger runs the experiment as defined.

Game 1: As Game 0, but we abort if the adversary queries a valid message-signature pair (m^*, σ^*) which was never returned by the signer or the sanitizer oracle to the sanitization or proof generation oracle.

Transition - Game 0 → Game 1: Let us use E_1 to refer to the abort event. Clearly, whenever the adversary outputs such a new pair, we can output it to break unforgeability of our scheme, as this tuple is fresh. However, we have already proven that this can only happen with negligible probability. $|\Pr[S_0] - \Pr[S_1]| \leq \nu_{\mathsf{sss\text{-}unf}}(\lambda)$ follows.

Game 2: As Game 1, but we internally keep all etd_i.

Transition - Game 1 → Game 2: This is only a conceptual change. $|\Pr[S_1] - \Pr[S_2]| = 0$ follows.

Game 3: As Game 2, but we encrypt only zeroes instead of the real etd_i in LoRADM independent of whether block are admissible or not. Note, the challenger still knows all etd_i, and can thus still sanitize correctly.

Transition - Game 2 → Game 3: A standard reduction, using hybrids, shows that this hop is indistinguishable by the IND-CPA security of the encryption scheme used. $|\Pr[S_2] - \Pr[S_3]| \leq q_h \nu_{\mathsf{ind\text{-}cpa}}(\lambda)$ follows, where q_h is the number of generated ciphertexts by LoRADM.[6]

At this point, the distribution is independent of the LoRADM oracle. Note, the sanitization, and proof oracles, can be still be simulated without any restrictions, as each etd_i is known to the challenger. Thus, the view the adversary receives is now completely independent of the bit b used in the invisibility definition. As each hop only changes the view of the adversary negligibly, our construction is thus proven to be invisible. □

Acknowledgements. We are grateful to the anonymous reviewers of PKC 2017 for providing valuable comments and suggestions that helped to significantly improve the presentation of the paper.

---

[6] We note that IND-CPA security of the encryption scheme Π is sufficient, as the abort in Game 1 ensures that the adversary can only submit queries with respect to ciphertexts which were previously generated in the reduction, i.e., where we can simply look up the respective values etd_i instead of decryption.

References

1. Abe, M., Gennaro, R., Kurosawa, K.: Tag-kem/dem: a new framework for hybrid encryption. J. cryptology **21**(1), 97–130 (2008)
2. Ahn, J.H., Boneh, D., Camenisch, J., Hohenberger, S., Shelat, A., Waters, B.: Computing on authenticated data. In: Cramer, R. (ed.) TCC 2012. LNCS, vol. 7194, pp. 1–20. Springer, Heidelberg (2012). doi:10.1007/978-3-642-28914-9_1
3. Alsouri, S., Dagdelen, Ö., Katzenbeisser, S.: Group-based attestation: enhancing privacy and management in remote attestation. In: Acquisti, A., Smith, S.W., Sadeghi, A.-R. (eds.) Trust 2010. LNCS, vol. 6101, pp. 63–77. Springer, Heidelberg (2010). doi:10.1007/978-3-642-13869-0_5
4. Ateniese, G., Chou, D.H., Medeiros, B., Tsudik, G.: Sanitizable signatures. In: Vimercati, S.C., Syverson, P., Gollmann, D. (eds.) ESORICS 2005. LNCS, vol. 3679, pp. 159–177. Springer, Heidelberg (2005). doi:10.1007/11555827_10
5. Ateniese, G., Magri, B., Venturi, D., Andrade, E.R.: Redactable blockchain - or - rewriting history in bitcoin and friends. IACR Cryptology ePrint Archive, 757 (2016)
6. Ateniese, G., Medeiros, B.: Identity-based chameleon hash and applications. In: Juels, A. (ed.) FC 2004. LNCS, vol. 3110, pp. 164–180. Springer, Heidelberg (2004). doi:10.1007/978-3-540-27809-2_19
7. Ateniese, G., Medeiros, B.: On the key exposure problem in Chameleon hashes. In: Blundo, C., Cimato, S. (eds.) SCN 2004. LNCS, vol. 3352, pp. 165–179. Springer, Heidelberg (2005). doi:10.1007/978-3-540-30598-9_12
8. Bao, F., Deng, R.H., Ding, X., Lai, J., Zhao, Y.: Hierarchical identity-based chameleon hash and its applications. In: Lopez, J., Tsudik, G. (eds.) ACNS 2011. LNCS, vol. 6715, pp. 201–219. Springer, Heidelberg (2011). doi:10.1007/978-3-642-21554-4_12
9. Bellare, M., Ristov, T.: A characterization of chameleon hash functions and new, efficient designs. J. Cryptology **27**(4), 799–823 (2014)
10. Bilzhause, A., Huber, M., Pöhls, H.C., Samelin, K.: Cryptographically Enforced Four-Eyes Principle. In: ARES, pp. 760–767 (2016)
11. Blazy, O., Kakvi, S.A., Kiltz, E., Pan, J.: Tightly-secure signatures from Chameleon hash functions. In: Katz, J. (ed.) PKC 2015. LNCS, vol. 9020, pp. 256–279. Springer, Heidelberg (2015). doi:10.1007/978-3-662-46447-2_12
12. Brassard, G., Chaum, D., Crépeau, C.: Minimum disclosure proofs of knowledge. J. Comput. Syst. Sci. **37**(2), 156–189 (1988)
13. Bresson, E., Catalano, D., Gennaro, R.: Improved on-line/off-line threshold signatures. In: Okamoto, T., Wang, X. (eds.) PKC 2007. LNCS, vol. 4450, pp. 217–232. Springer, Heidelberg (2007). doi:10.1007/978-3-540-71677-8_15
14. Brzuska, C., Busch, H., Dagdelen, O., Fischlin, M., Franz, M., Katzenbeisser, S., Manulis, M., Onete, C., Peter, A., Poettering, B., Schröder, D.: Redactable signatures for tree-structured data: definitions and constructions. In: Zhou, J., Yung, M. (eds.) ACNS 2010. LNCS, vol. 6123, pp. 87–104. Springer, Heidelberg (2010). doi:10.1007/978-3-642-13708-2_6
15. Brzuska, C., Fischlin, M., Freudenreich, T., Lehmann, A., Page, M., Schelbert, J., Schröder, D., Volk, F.: Security of sanitizable signatures revisited. In: Jarecki, S., Tsudik, G. (eds.) PKC 2009. LNCS, vol. 5443, pp. 317–336. Springer, Heidelberg (2009). doi:10.1007/978-3-642-00468-1_18
16. Brzuska, C., Fischlin, M., Lehmann, A., Schröder, D.: Sanitizable signatures: How to partially delegate control for authenticated data. In: BIOSIG, pp. 117–128 (2009)

17. Brzuska, C., Fischlin, M., Lehmann, A., Schröder, D.: Unlinkability of sanitizable signatures. In: Nguyen, P.Q., Pointcheval, D. (eds.) PKC 2010. LNCS, vol. 6056, pp. 444–461. Springer, Heidelberg (2010). doi:10.1007/978-3-642-13013-7_26

18. Brzuska, C., Pöhls, H.C., Samelin, K.: Non-interactive public accountability for sanitizable signatures. In: Capitani di Vimercati, S., Mitchell, C. (eds.) EuroPKI 2012. LNCS, vol. 7868, pp. 178–193. Springer, Heidelberg (2013). doi:10.1007/978-3-642-40012-4_12

19. Brzuska, C., Pöhls, H.C., Samelin, K.: Efficient and perfectly unlinkable sanitizable signatures without group signatures. In: Katsikas, S., Agudo, I. (eds.) EuroPKI 2013. LNCS, vol. 8341, pp. 12–30. Springer, Heidelberg (2014). doi:10.1007/978-3-642-53997-8_2

20. Camenisch, J., Stadler, M.: Efficient group signature schemes for large groups. In: Kaliski, B.S. (ed.) CRYPTO 1997. LNCS, vol. 1294, pp. 410–424. Springer, Heidelberg (1997). doi:10.1007/BFb0052252

21. Canard, S., Jambert, A.: On extended sanitizable signature schemes. In: Pieprzyk, J. (ed.) CT-RSA 2010. LNCS, vol. 5985, pp. 179–194. Springer, Heidelberg (2010). doi:10.1007/978-3-642-11925-5_13

22. Canard, S., Jambert, A., Lescuyer, R.: Sanitizable signatures with several signers and sanitizers. In: Mitrokotsa, A., Vaudenay, S. (eds.) AFRICACRYPT 2012. LNCS, vol. 7374, pp. 35–52. Springer, Heidelberg (2012). doi:10.1007/978-3-642-31410-0_3

23. Canard, S., Laguillaumie, F., Milhau, M.: *Trapdoor* sanitizable signatures and their application to content protection. In: Bellovin, S.M., Gennaro, R., Keromytis, A., Yung, M. (eds.) ACNS 2008. LNCS, vol. 5037, pp. 258–276. Springer, Heidelberg (2008). doi:10.1007/978-3-540-68914-0_16

24. Canard, S., Lescuyer, R.: Protecting privacy by sanitizing personal data: a new approach to anonymous credentials. In: ASIACCS, pp. 381–392 (2013)

25. Catalano, D., Raimondo, M., Fiore, D., Gennaro, R.: Off-line/on-line signatures: theoretical aspects and experimental results. In: Cramer, R. (ed.) PKC 2008. LNCS, vol. 4939, pp. 101–120. Springer, Heidelberg (2008). doi:10.1007/978-3-540-78440-1_7

26. Chen, X., Tian, H., Zhang, F., Ding, Y.: Comments and improvements on key-exposure free Chameleon hashing based on factoring. In: Lai, X., Yung, M., Lin, D. (eds.) Inscrypt 2010. LNCS, vol. 6584, pp. 415–426. Springer, Heidelberg (2011). doi:10.1007/978-3-642-21518-6_29

27. Chen, X., Zhang, F., Susilo, W., Mu, Y.: Efficient generic on-line/off-line signatures without key exposure. In: Katz, J., Yung, M. (eds.) ACNS 2007. LNCS, vol. 4521, pp. 18–30. Springer, Heidelberg (2007). doi:10.1007/978-3-540-72738-5_2

28. Demirel, D., Derler, D., Hanser, C., Pöhls, H.C., Slamanig, D., Traverso, G.: PRIS-MACLOUD D4.4: overview of functional and malleable signature schemes. Technical report, H2020 Prismacloud (2015). www.prismacloud.eu

29. Derler, D., Hanser, C., Pöhls, H.C., Slamanig, D.: Towards authenticity and privacy preserving accountable workflows. In: Aspinall, D., Camenisch, J., Hansen, M., Fischer-Hübner, S., Raab, C. (eds.) Privacy and Identity 2015. IAICT, vol. 476, pp. 170–186. Springer, Heidelberg (2016). doi:10.1007/978-3-319-41763-9_12

30. Derler, D., Hanser, C., Slamanig, D.: Blank digital signatures: optimization and practical experiences. In: Camenisch, J., Fischer-Hübner, S., Hansen, M. (eds.) Privacy and Identity 2014. IAICT, vol. 457, pp. 201–215. Springer, Heidelberg (2015). doi:10.1007/978-3-319-18621-4_14

31. Derler, D., Slamanig, D.: Rethinking privacy for extended sanitizable signatures and a black-box construction of strongly private schemes. In: Au, M.-H., Miyaji, A. (eds.) ProvSec 2015. LNCS, vol. 9451, pp. 455–474. Springer, Heidelberg (2015). doi:10.1007/978-3-319-26059-4_25
32. Even, S., Goldreich, O., Micali, S.: On-line/off-line digital signatures. J. Cryptology 9(1), 35–67 (1996)
33. Fehr, V., Fischlin, M.: Sanitizable signcryption: Sanitization over encrypted data (full version). IACR Cryptology ePrint Archive, report 2015/765 (2015)
34. Fischlin, M.: Trapdoor commitment schemes and their applications. Ph.D. thesis, University of Frankfurt (2001)
35. Fleischhacker, N., Krupp, J., Malavolta, G., Schneider, J., Schröder, D., Simkin, M.: Efficient unlinkable sanitizable signatures from signatures with re-randomizable keys. In: Cheng, C.-M., Chung, K.-M., Persiano, G., Yang, B.-Y. (eds.) PKC 2016. LNCS, vol. 9614, pp. 301–330. Springer, Heidelberg (2016). doi:10.1007/978-3-662-49384-7_12
36. Gao, W., Li, F., Wang, X.: Chameleon hash without key exposure based on Schnorr signature. Comput. Stand. Interfaces 31(2), 282–285 (2009)
37. Gao, W., Wang, X., Xie, D.: Chameleon hashes without key exposure based on factoring. J. Comput. Sci. Technol. 22(1), 109–113 (2007)
38. Ghosh, E., Goodrich, M.T., Ohrimenko, O., Tamassia, R.: Fully-dynamic verifiable zero-knowledge order queries for network data. ePrint 2015, 283 (2015)
39. Ghosh, E., Ohrimenko, O., Tamassia, R.: Zero-knowledge authenticated order queries and order statistics on a list. In: Malkin, T., Kolesnikov, V., Lewko, A.B., Polychronakis, M. (eds.) ACNS 2015. LNCS, vol. 9092, pp. 149–171. Springer, Heidelberg (2015). doi:10.1007/978-3-319-28166-7_8
40. Goldwasser, S., Micali, S., Rivest, R.L.: A digital signature scheme secure against adaptive chosen-message attacks. SIAM J. Comput. 17, 281–308 (1988)
41. Gong, J., Qian, H., Zhou, Y.: Fully-secure and practical sanitizable signatures. In: Lai, X., Yung, M., Lin, D. (eds.) Inscrypt 2010. LNCS, vol. 6584, pp. 300–317. Springer, Heidelberg (2011). doi:10.1007/978-3-642-21518-6_21
42. Hanser, C., Slamanig, D.: Blank digital signatures. In: ASIACCS, pp. 95–106 (2013)
43. Hanzlik, L., Kutyłowski, M., Yung, M.: Hard invalidation of electronic signatures. In: Lopez, J., Wu, Y. (eds.) ISPEC 2015. LNCS, vol. 9065, pp. 421–436. Springer, Heidelberg (2015). doi:10.1007/978-3-319-17533-1_29
44. Hohenberger, S., Waters, B.: Short and stateless signatures from the RSA assumption. In: Halevi, S. (ed.) CRYPTO 2009. LNCS, vol. 5677, pp. 654–670. Springer, Heidelberg (2009). doi:10.1007/978-3-642-03356-8_38
45. Höhne, F., Pöhls, H.C., Samelin, K.: Rechtsfolgen editierbarer signaturen. Datenschutz und Datensicherheit 36(7), 485–491 (2012)
46. Klonowski, M., Lauks, A.: Extended sanitizable signatures. In: Rhee, M.S., Lee, B. (eds.) ICISC 2006. LNCS, vol. 4296, pp. 343–355. Springer, Heidelberg (2006). doi:10.1007/11927587_28
47. Krawczyk, H., Rabin, T.: Chameleon Hashing and Signatures. In: NDSS, pp. 143–154 (2000)
48. Krenn, S., Samelin, K., Sommer, D.: Stronger security for sanitizable signatures. In: Garcia-Alfaro, J., Navarro-Arribas, G., Aldini, A., Martinelli, F., Suri, N. (eds.) DPM/QASA 2015. LNCS, vol. 9481, pp. 100–117. Springer, Heidelberg (2016). doi:10.1007/978-3-319-29883-2_7

49. Lai, R.W.F., Zhang, T., Chow, S.S.M., Schröder, D.: Efficient sanitizable signatures without random oracles. In: Askoxylakis, I., Ioannidis, S., Katsikas, S., Meadows, C. (eds.) ESORICS 2016. LNCS, vol. 9878, pp. 363–380. Springer, Heidelberg (2016). doi:10.1007/978-3-319-45744-4_18

50. de Meer, H., Pöhls, H.C., Posegga, J., Samelin, K.: Scope of security properties of sanitizable signatures revisited. In: ARES, pp. 188–197 (2013)

51. Meer, H., Pöhls, H.C., Posegga, J., Samelin, K.: On the relation between redactable and sanitizable signature schemes. In: Jürjens, J., Piessens, F., Bielova, N. (eds.) ESSoS 2014. LNCS, vol. 8364, pp. 113–130. Springer, Heidelberg (2014). doi:10.1007/978-3-319-04897-0_8

52. Mohassel, P.: One-time signatures and chameleon hash functions. In: Biryukov, A., Gong, G., Stinson, D.R. (eds.) SAC 2010. LNCS, vol. 6544, pp. 302–319. Springer, Heidelberg (2011). doi:10.1007/978-3-642-19574-7_21

53. Pedersen, T.P.: Non-interactive and information-theoretic secure verifiable secret sharing. In: Feigenbaum, J. (ed.) CRYPTO 1991. LNCS, vol. 576, pp. 129–140. Springer, Heidelberg (1992). doi:10.1007/3-540-46766-1_9

54. Pöhls, H.C., Peters, S., Samelin, K., Posegga, J., Meer, H.: Malleable signatures for resource constrained platforms. In: Cavallaro, L., Gollmann, D. (eds.) WISTP 2013. LNCS, vol. 7886, pp. 18–33. Springer, Heidelberg (2013). doi:10.1007/978-3-642-38530-8_2

55. Pöhls, H.C., Samelin, K.: Accountable redactable signatures. In: ARES, pp. 60–69 (2015)

56. Pöhls, H.C., Samelin, K., Posegga, J.: Sanitizable signatures in XML signature — performance, mixing properties, and revisiting the property of transparency. In: Lopez, J., Tsudik, G. (eds.) ACNS 2011. LNCS, vol. 6715, pp. 166–182. Springer, Heidelberg (2011). doi:10.1007/978-3-642-21554-4_10

57. Ren, Q., Mu, Y., Susilo, W.: Mitigating Phishing by a new id-based Chameleon hash without key exposure. In: AusCERT, pp. 1–13 (2007)

58. Shamir, A., Tauman, Y.: Improved online/offline signature schemes. In: Kilian, J. (ed.) CRYPTO 2001. LNCS, vol. 2139, pp. 355–367. Springer, Heidelberg (2001). doi:10.1007/3-540-44647-8_21

59. Yum, D.H., Seo, J.W., Lee, P.J.: Trapdoor sanitizable signatures made easy. In: Zhou, J., Yung, M. (eds.) ACNS 2010. LNCS, vol. 6123, pp. 53–68. Springer, Heidelberg (2010). doi:10.1007/978-3-642-13708-2_4

60. Zhang, F., Safavi-naini, R., Susilo, W.: Id-based Chameleon hashes from bilinear pairings. IACR Cryptology ePrint Archive 2003, 208 (2003)

61. Zhang, R.: Tweaking TBE/IBE to PKE transforms with Chameleon hash functions. In: Katz, J., Yung, M. (eds.) ACNS 2007. LNCS, vol. 4521, pp. 323–339. Springer, Heidelberg (2007). doi:10.1007/978-3-540-72738-5_21

Improved Structure Preserving Signatures Under Standard Bilinear Assumptions

Charanjit S. Jutla[1][(⊠)] and Arnab Roy[2]

[1] IBM T.J. Watson Research Center, Yorktown Heights, NY, USA
csjutla@us.ibm.com
[2] Fujitsu Laboratories of America, Sunnyvale, CA, USA
aroy@us.fujitsu.com

Abstract. We show that the recent structure-preserving signature (SPS) scheme of Kiltz et al. [CRYPTO 2015], provably secure under the standard bilinear pairings group assumption SXDH, can be improved to have one less group element and one less pairing product equation in the signature verification step. Our improved SPS scheme only requires six group elements (five in one group, and one in the other), and two pairing product equations for verification. The number of pairing product equations is optimal, as it matches a known lower bound of Abe et al. [CRYPTO 2011]. The number of group elements in the signature also approaches the known lower bound of four for SXDH assumption. Further, while the earlier scheme had a security reduction which incurred a security loss that is quadratic in number of queries Q, our novel security reduction incurs only a $Q \log Q$ factor loss in security.

Structure-preserving signatures are used pervasively in group signatures, group encryptions, blind signatures, proxy signatures and many other anonymous credential applications. Our work directly leads to improvements in these schemes. Moreover, the improvements are usually of a higher multiplicative factor order, as these constructions use Groth-Sahai NIZK proofs for zero-knowledge verification of pairing-product equations.

We also give our construction under the more general and standard $\mathcal{D}_k$-MDDH (Matrix-DDH) assumption. The signature size in our scheme is $3k+2$ elements in one group, and one element in the other. The number of pairing product equations required for verification is only $2k$, whereas the earlier schemes required at least $2k + 1$ equations.

Keywords: Structure preserving signatures · Bilinear pairings · SXDH · Matrix-DDH · Groth-Sahai · Cramer-Shoup · QA-NIZK

1 Introduction

The notion of *structure-preserving signatures* (SPS) was introduced in [AFG+10] so that such signatures are compatible with the bilinear-pairings based efficient non-interactive zero-knowledge (NIZK) proofs of Groth and Sahai [GS08]. The

S. Fehr (Ed.): PKC 2017, Part II, LNCS 10175, pp. 183–209, 2017.
DOI: 10.1007/978-3-662-54388-7_7

messages, signatures, and verification keys are required to be elements of groups that support efficient bilinear-pairings (*bilinear groups*), and the signature verification consists of just evaluating one or more bilinear-pairing product equations. With the structure of the signature preserved, one can then build many interesting cryptographic primitives and protocols that require (hiding) commitments to such messages and signatures and yet retain the ability to prove properties about these using Groth-Sahai NIZK proofs (GS-NIZK proofs). To list a few, SPS have been used to build blind signatures [AO09, AFG+10], group signatures [AHO10], traceable signatures [ACHO11], group encryption [CLY09], and delegatable credential systems [Fuc11].

The first SPS was introduced by Groth in 2006 even before GS-NIZK proofs were introduced [Gro06]. In the same work Groth also introduced NIZK proofs for algebraic equations over bilinear groups, but since this construction was rather inefficient, it was best viewed as a feasibility study. A variation of the Camenisch-Lysyanskaya signature scheme [CL04] was shown to be an SPS secure against random message attacks [GH08]. Cathalo et al. [CLY09] and Fuchsbauer [Fuc09] gave schemes which are efficient when signing a single group element, but their signature size increases linearly in the size of the message. In [AHO10], the authors presented the first constant-size SPS consisting of seven group elements, provable under a non-interactive but dynamic q-type assumption. In [AGHO11], the authors show a three group element SPS scheme provable in the generic asymmetric pairings group model. Interestingly, they also showed that any SPS scheme in asymmetric bilinear groups must require at least three group elements and two pairing product verification equations. They also gave a four group element SPS scheme under a non-interactive but dynamic q-type assumption. In [AGO11], the authors show that any SPS scheme proven secure by a black-box reduction of the standard SXDH assumption in asymmetric bilinear groups must have four group elements.

Recently, Kiltz et al. [KPW15] and Libert et al. [LPY15] gave efficient SPS schemes under standard bilinear assumptions such as SXDH (Symmetric eXternal Diffie-Hellman assumption) or MDDH (Matrix-DDH assumption). While the latter scheme required ten group elements, the former was even shorter requiring only seven group elements (under SXDH). However, both schemes required three pairing product equations for signature verification, which is sub-optimal. Moreover, the security proofs given for both schemes incurred a quadratic (in the number of signature queries) loss in security.

1.1　Our Contributions

In this work, we show that the scheme of Kiltz et al. [KPW15] can be modified to have a signature size of only six group elements. More importantly, the number of pairing product equations required for signature verification is reduced to two, which is optimal by the lower bound of [AGHO11]. Further, we give a security proof that only has a $Q \log Q$ security loss in reduction from standard SXDH or MDDH assumptions.

The ramifications of these improvements are many-fold. First, note that since SPS are used along with commitments, encryptions and GS-NIZK proofs, this can lead to a multiplicative factor improvement in the final cryptographic application. For example, every group element in the SPS that needs a Groth-Sahai commitment leads to a factor two blowup. A CCA2-encryption such as the Cramer-Shoup encryption [CS02] could lead to a factor four or five blowup. Each pairing product equation can lead to up to eight extra group elements in GS-NIZK proofs (under SXDH assumption), and indeed the type of extra pairing product equation in [KPW15] does take eight extra group elements (four in each of the two asymmetric bilinear groups).

Using the methodology of [AHO10, AFG+10], [LPY15] build a dynamic group signature scheme with signature size of 30 group elements in $\mathbb{G}_1$, 14 group elements in $\mathbb{G}_2$ and an integer tag. The improvements presented in this work are directly applicable and should lead to a reduction of at least ten group elements in the size of the signature. Similar improvements are expected in blind signature schemes and other anonymous credentials based schemes.

We also give constructions and security proofs under the more general k-MDDH (matrix-DDH) assumption. Our results and comparison with previous work is summarized in Table 1.

As for the improved security reduction, [KPW15] show that if an adaptive chosen-message attack adversary makes at most Q signature queries, then its success probability of forging a signature on a new message is bounded from above by (roughly)

$$Q^2 \cdot \mathrm{ADV}_{\mathrm{DDH}} + Q^2/q$$

where q is the order of the cyclic groups, and $\mathrm{ADV}_{\mathrm{DDH}}$ is the maximum advantage an efficient adversary has in a (decisional Diffie-Hellman) DDH-challenge game in either of the asymmetric bilinear groups. In this work, we show that the success probability of forging a signature is at most (roughly)

$$Q \cdot \log Q \cdot \mathrm{ADV}_{\mathrm{DDH}} + Q^2/q$$

Since, by Pollard's Rho method [Pol78], $\mathrm{ADV}_{\mathrm{DDH}}$ is at least $1/\sqrt{q}$, the first term in both of the above success probabilities is dominant. Thus, for the same security guarantee, and for large number of signatures (which should be expected for group signatures and other such anonymous credential applications), the earlier schemes would require almost twice the number of bits in representation of the group elements.

1.2   Our Techniques

The underlying idea in the SPS schemes of both [KPW15] and [LPY15], and our scheme is to hide a secret using a CCA2 encryption scheme, and in particular the Cramer-Shoup encryption [CS02], and prove in zero-knowledge that the signer knows the secret encrypted in the ciphertext. This methodology of building signature schemes was already described in [CCS09] (also, see a refinement

Table 1. Comparison with existing unbounded security SPS schemes with table adapted from [KPW15]. (n_1, n_2) denotes n_1 $\mathbb{G}_1$ elements and n_2 $\mathbb{G}_2$ elements. The table gives message, signature and public key sizes and finally the number of pairing product equations needed for verification. $RE(\mathcal{D}_k)$ is the number of group elements needed for representing a sample from $\mathcal{D}_k$; $\overline{RE}(\mathcal{D}_k)$ is the same for all but the last row of a sample. For k-Linear assumption these are $k + 1$ and k respectively.

	Assumption	$|m|$	$|\sigma|$	$|pk|$	#PPEs
[AGHO11]	Interactive (Generic)	(n_1, n_2)	$(2, 1)$	$n_1 + n_2 + 2$	2
[AGHO11]	Non-interactive (Generic)	(n_1, n_2)	$(3, 3)$	$n_1 + n_2 + 2$	2
[AGHO11]	Non-Interactive (Generic)	$(n_1, 0)$	$(3, 1)$	$n_1 + 2$	2
[ACD+12]	SXDH, XDLIN	$(n_1, 0)$	$(7, 4)$	$20 + n_1$	4
[ACD+12]	SXDH, XDLIN	(n_1, n_2)	$(8, 6)$	$22 + n_1 + n_2$	5
[ADK+13]	2-Lin ($\mathbb{G}_1 = \mathbb{G}_2$)	n	14	$22 + n$	7
[AFG+10]	q-SFP	$(n_1, 0)$	$(5, 2)$	$13 + n_1$	2
[LPY15]	SXDH, XDLIN	$(n_1, 0)$	$(9, 1)$	$2n_1 + 21$	5
[KPW15]	$\mathcal{D}_k$ − MDDH	(n_1, n_2)	$(4k + 3, k + 2)$	$(n_1 + n_2 + 3k + 3)k + 2RE(\mathcal{D}_k)$	$3k + 1$
[KPW15]	$\mathcal{D}_k$ − MDDH	$(n_1, 0)$	$(3k + 3, 1)$	$(n_1 + 2k + 3)k + RE(\mathcal{D}_k)$	$2k + 1$
This paper	$\mathcal{D}_k$ − MDDH	$(n_1, 0)$	$(3k + 2, 1)$	$(n_1 + 2k + 3)k + \overline{RE}(\mathcal{D}_k)$	$2k$

of this method in [JR13]). However, as is well-known, the Cramer-Shoup encryption scheme requires exponentiation with a tag which is computed from other elements in the ciphertext in a 1-1 fashion. This enforces the tag to be different if the ciphertext is changed in any way. However, this clearly is not structure-preserving, as the 1-1 mapping is required to map from the group elements to another group $\mathbb{Z}_q$, where q is the order of the bilinear groups.

In [KPW15] and [LPY15], the tag is instead chosen afresh at random (i.e., independent of other elements in the ciphertext), and its representation in the bilinear group is given as part of the signature. The tag is also used in the aforementioned exponentiation (in fact, more than one), and simple bilinear tests can check that these values are consistent. To get a better understanding, we now give some specific details. Let k be the secret of the signer. To create the signature, it generates a Cramer-Shoup encryption, by picking r at random, and setting

$$\rho = g_1^r, \hat{\rho} = (g_1^b)^r, \gamma = g_1^k \cdot (g_1^d)^r \cdot (g_1^e)^{t \cdot r}$$

where t is the tag, and g_1^b, g_1^d, g_1^e are part of the public key. In SPS, since t is chosen afresh, the signer also gives $\psi = g_1^{t \cdot r}$ and $\tau = g_2^t$. Note that τ is in group

$\mathbb{G}_2$, whereas all other elements are in group $\mathbb{G}_2$. The consistency of ρ, ψ and τ is easily checked by a bilinear pairing product equation, i.e., $\mathsf{e}(\rho, \tau) = \mathsf{e}(\psi, g_2)$.

If one were to follow the methodology of [CCS09], the signer also gives a NIZK proof π that $\rho, \hat{\rho}, \psi$ and γ are consistent with the public key, and some public information about k. However, with the quasi-adaptive computationally-sound NIZK proofs (QA-NIZK) of [JR13], one can give a QA-NIZK proof that these elements are in an affine span of the underlying linear subspace language, with the verifier CRS independent of the affine component (i.e. g_1^k).

The scheme in [KPW15] (also [LPY15]) also gives an additional element $\hat{\psi} = (g_1^b)^{t \cdot r}$, and the signature verification requires another consistency check, i.e. $\mathsf{e}(\hat{\rho}, \tau) = \mathsf{e}(\hat{\psi}, g_2)$. The main reason for this additional verification is that [KPW15] does not follow the above methodology for the security proof, and instead uses a core computational lemma which was used to give an unbounded-simulation sound QA-NIZK scheme [KW15]. As mentioned earlier, it suffices to use a (non simulation-sound) NIZK as long as one uses a CCA2 encryption like Cramer-Shoup (which in itself is just a one-time simulation-sound method). Now, readers familiar with Cramer-Shoup encryption will recall that the main idea there is the ability for the simulator to use an alternate decryption. However, in signature schemes, as opposed to Cramer-Shoup encryption, there is no real decryption, but just a verification of the signature using private trapdoor keys. This can also be done efficiently using the bilinear pairing available, and this is the reason why a single additional test of the relationship between ψ, ρ and τ suffices. More details can be found in Sect. 3.1.

1.3 Recursive Complexity-Leveraging for Improved Security Reduction

For improving the security reduction, we first note that [KPW15] requires a complexity-leveraging technique, because the simulator of the challenger in the SPS security game must guess a query index (the one for which the adversary may use the same tag), and then try to simulate signatures only for indices other than this guess. However, since the adversary is adaptive, this guess is only correct with probability $1/Q$, where Q is the maximum number of queries the adversary makes.

We follow a recursive approach, where the simulator goes through Q hybrid games. In the first $Q/2$ hybrid games, the simulator guesses a set Z of size $Q/2$, and then simulates queries outside this set. Now, the simulator's correct guess probability that the adversary's tag will match a tag in query from set Z is much higher, i.e., $1/2$. From the $Q/2$-th hybrid onwards, we show that the simulator can switch to another sequence of hybrid games, where now the simulator guesses a set Z of size $Q/4$, and so forth inductively. The penalty in the security reduction in this switch is only a factor of two. Note that we are paying a penalty of factor 2^m for only the last $Q/2^{m-1}$ hybrids, and this leads to a reduction with only a $Q \log Q$ security loss. We expect our novel complexity-leveraging technique to be more widely applicable, and of independent interest.

2   Preliminaries

We will consider cyclic groups $\mathbb{G}_1, \mathbb{G}_2$ and $\mathbb{G}_T$ of prime order q, with an efficient bilinear map $e : \mathbb{G}_1 \times \mathbb{G}_2 \to \mathbb{G}_T$. Group elements $\mathbf{g}_1$ and $\mathbf{g}_2$ will typically denote generators of the group $\mathbb{G}_1$ and $\mathbb{G}_2$ respectively. Following [EHK+13], we will use the notations $[a]_1, [a]_2$ and $[a]_T$ to denote $a\mathbf{g}_1, a\mathbf{g}_2$, and $a \cdot e(\mathbf{g}_1, \mathbf{g}_2)$ respectively and use additive notations for group operations. When talking about a general group $\mathbb{G}$ with generator $\mathbf{g}$, we will just use the notation $[a]$ to denote $a\mathbf{g}$. The notation generalizes to vectors and matrices in a natural component-wise way.

For two vector or matrices A and B, we will denote the product $A^\top B$ as $A \cdot B$. The pairing product $e([A]_1, [B]_2)$ evaluates to the matrix product $[AB]_T$ in the target group with pairing as multiplication and target group operation as addition.

We recall the *Matrix Decisional Diffie-Hellman* or MDDH assumptions from [EHK+13]. A matrix distribution $\mathcal{D}_{l,k}$, where $l > k$, is defined to be an efficiently samplable distribution on $\mathbb{Z}_q^{l \times k}$ which is full-ranked with overwhelming probability. The $\mathcal{D}_{l,k}$-*MDDH assumption* in group $\mathbb{G}$ states that with samples $\mathbf{A} \leftarrow \mathcal{D}_{l,k}, \mathbf{s} \leftarrow \mathbb{Z}_q^k$ and $\mathbf{s}' \leftarrow \mathbb{Z}_q^l$, the tuple $([\mathbf{A}], [\mathbf{As}])$ is computationally indistinguishable from $([\mathbf{A}], [\mathbf{s}'])$. A matrix distribution $\mathcal{D}_{k+1,k}$ is simply denoted by $\mathcal{D}_k$.

2.1   Quasi-Adaptive NIZK Proofs

A witness relation is a binary relation on pairs of inputs, the first called a word and the second called a witness. Each witness relation R defines a corresponding language L which is the set of all words x for which there exists a witness w, such that $R(x, w)$ holds.

We will consider Quasi-Adaptive NIZK proofs [JR13] for a probability distribution $\mathcal{D}$ on a collection of (witness-) relations $\mathcal{R} = \{R_\rho\}$ (with corresponding languages L_ρ). Recall that in a quasi-adaptive NIZK, the CRS can be set after the language parameter has been chosen according to $\mathcal{D}$. Please refer to [JR13] for detailed definitions.

For our SPS construction we will also need a property called true-simulation-soundness and an extension of QA-NIZKs called strong split-CRS QA-NIZK. We also recall the definitions of these concepts below.

Definition 1 (QA-NIZK [JR13]). *We call a tuple of efficient algorithms* (pargen, crsgen, prover, ver) *a quasi-adaptive non-interactive zero-knowledge (QA-NIZK) proof system for witness-relations* $\mathcal{R}_\lambda = \{R_\rho\}$ *with parameters sampled from a distribution* $\mathcal{D}$ *over associated parameter language* $\mathcal{L}_{par}$, *if there exist simulators* crssim *and* sim *such that for all non-uniform PPT adversaries* $\mathcal{A}_1, \mathcal{A}_2, \mathcal{A}_3$, *we have (in all of the following probabilistic experiments, the experiment starts by setting* λ *as* $\lambda \leftarrow \text{pargen}(1^m)$, *and choosing* ρ *as* $\rho \leftarrow \mathcal{D}_\lambda$):

Quasi-Adaptive Completeness:

$$\Pr \left[\begin{array}{l} \mathsf{CRS} \leftarrow \mathsf{crsgen}(\lambda, \rho) \\ (x, w) \leftarrow \mathcal{A}_1(\mathsf{CRS}, \rho) \\ \pi \leftarrow \mathsf{prover}(\mathsf{CRS}, x, w) \end{array} : \begin{array}{c} \mathsf{ver}(\mathsf{CRS}, x, \pi) = 1 \text{ if} \\ R_\rho(x, w) \end{array} \right] = 1$$

Quasi-Adaptive Soundness:

$$\Pr\left[\begin{array}{l} \mathsf{CRS} \leftarrow \mathsf{crsgen}(\lambda, \rho) \\ (x, \pi) \leftarrow \mathcal{A}_2(\mathsf{CRS}, \rho) \end{array} : \begin{array}{l} x \notin L_\rho \text{ and} \\ \mathsf{ver}(\mathsf{CRS}, x, \pi) = 1] \end{array}\right] \approx 0$$

Quasi-Adaptive Zero-Knowledge:

$$\Pr\left[\mathsf{CRS} \leftarrow \mathsf{crsgen}(\lambda, \rho) : \mathcal{A}_3^{\mathsf{prover}(\mathsf{CRS},\cdot,\cdot)}(\mathsf{CRS}, \rho) = 1\right]$$

$$\approx$$

$$\Pr\left[(\mathsf{CRS}, \mathsf{trap}) \leftarrow \mathsf{crssim}(\lambda, \rho) : \mathcal{A}_3^{\mathsf{sim}^*(\mathsf{CRS},\mathsf{trap},\cdot,\cdot)}(\mathsf{CRS}, \rho) = 1\right],$$

where $\mathsf{sim}^*(\mathsf{CRS}, \mathsf{trap}, x, w) = \mathsf{sim}(\mathsf{CRS}, \mathsf{trap}, x)$ *for* $(x, w) \in R_\rho$ *and both oracles (i.e.* prover *and* sim*) output failure if* $(x, w) \notin R_\rho$.

Definition 2 (True-Simulation-Sound [Har11]). *A QA-NIZK is called* **true-simulation-sound** *if the verifier is sound even when an adaptive adversary has access to simulated proofs on language members. More precisely, for all PPT* $\mathcal{A}$,

$$\Pr\left[\begin{array}{l} (\mathsf{CRS}, \mathsf{trap}) \leftarrow \mathsf{crssim}(\lambda, \rho) \\ (x, \pi) \leftarrow \mathcal{A}^{\mathsf{sim}(\mathsf{CRS},\mathsf{trap},\cdot,\cdot)}(\mathsf{CRS}, \rho) \end{array} : \begin{array}{l} x \notin L_\rho \text{ and} \\ \mathsf{ver}(\mathsf{CRS}, x, \pi) = 1 \end{array}\right] \approx 0,$$

where the experiment aborts if the oracle is called with some $x \notin L_\rho$.

Definition 3 (Strong Split-CRS QA-NIZK [JR13]). *We call a tuple of efficient algorithms* $(\mathsf{pargen}, \mathsf{crsgen}_v, \mathsf{crsgen}_p, \mathsf{prover}, \mathsf{ver})$ *a* **strong split-CRS QA-NIZK** *proof system for an ensemble of distributions* $\{\mathcal{D}_\lambda\}$ *on collection of witness-relations* $\mathcal{R}_\lambda = \{R_\rho\}$ *with associated parameter language* $\mathcal{L}_{par}$ *if there exists probabilistic polynomial time simulators* $(\mathsf{crssim}_v, \mathsf{crssim}_p, \mathsf{sim})$, *such that for all non-uniform PPT adversaries* $\mathcal{A}_1, \mathcal{A}_2, \mathcal{A}_3$, *and* $\lambda \leftarrow \mathsf{pargen}(1^m)$, *we have:*

Quasi-Adaptive Completeness:

$$\Pr\left[\begin{array}{l} (\mathsf{CRS}_v, st) \leftarrow \mathsf{crsgen}_v(\lambda), \ \rho \leftarrow \mathcal{D}_\lambda \\ \mathsf{CRS}_p \leftarrow \mathsf{crsgen}_p(\lambda, \rho, st) \\ (x, w) \leftarrow \mathcal{A}_1(\lambda, \mathsf{CRS}_v, \mathsf{CRS}_p, \rho) \\ \pi \leftarrow \mathsf{prover}(\mathsf{CRS}_p, x, w) \end{array} : \begin{array}{l} \mathsf{ver}(\mathsf{CRS}_v, x, \pi) = 1 \text{ if} \\ R_\rho(x, w) \end{array}\right] = 1$$

Quasi-Adaptive Soundness:

$$\Pr\left[\begin{array}{l} (\mathsf{CRS}_v, st) \leftarrow \mathsf{crsgen}_v(\lambda), \ \rho \leftarrow \mathcal{D}_\lambda \\ \mathsf{CRS}_p \leftarrow \mathsf{crsgen}_p(\lambda, \rho, st) \\ (x, \pi) \leftarrow \mathcal{A}_2(\lambda, \mathsf{CRS}_v, \mathsf{CRS}_p, \rho) \end{array} : \begin{array}{l} \mathsf{ver}(\mathsf{CRS}_v, x, \pi) = 1 \text{ and} \\ \text{not } (\exists w : R_\rho(x, w)) \end{array}\right] \approx 0$$

Quasi-Adaptive Zero-Knowledge:

$$\Pr\left[\begin{array}{l} (\mathsf{CRS}_v, st) \leftarrow \mathsf{crsgen}_v(\lambda) \\ \rho \leftarrow \mathcal{D}_\lambda \\ \mathsf{CRS}_p \leftarrow \mathsf{crsgen}_p(\lambda, \rho, st) \end{array} : \mathcal{A}_3^{\mathsf{prover}(\mathsf{CRS}_p,\cdot,\cdot)}(\lambda, \mathsf{CRS}_v, \mathsf{CRS}_p, \rho) = 1\right]$$

$$\approx$$

$$\Pr\left[\begin{array}{l} (\mathsf{CRS}_v, \mathsf{trap}, st) \leftarrow \mathsf{crssim}_v(\lambda) \\ \rho \leftarrow \mathcal{D}_\lambda \\ \mathsf{CRS}_p \leftarrow \mathsf{crssim}_p(\lambda, \rho, st) \end{array} : \mathcal{A}_3^{\mathsf{sim}^*(\mathsf{trap},\cdot,\cdot)}(\lambda, \mathsf{CRS}_v, \mathsf{CRS}_p, \rho) = 1\right],$$

where $\mathsf{sim}^*(\mathsf{trap}, x, w) = \mathsf{sim}(\mathsf{trap}, x)$ *for* $(x, w) \in R_\rho$ *and both oracles (i.e.* prover *and* sim^*) *output failure if* $(x, w) \notin R_\rho$.

2.2 Strong Split-CRS QA-NIZK for Affine Languages

We now describe a strong split-CRS QA-NIZK ($\mathsf{pargen}, \mathsf{crsgen}_v, \mathsf{crsgen}_p, \mathsf{prover}$, ver) for affine linear subspace languages $\{L_{[\mathbf{M}]_1, [\mathbf{a}]_1}\}$, consisting of words of the form $[\mathbf{Mx} + \mathbf{a}]_1$, with parameters sampled from a robust and efficiently witness-samplable distribution $\mathcal{D}$ over the associated parameter language $\mathcal{L}_{par}$ and with soundness under a $\mathcal{D}_k$-MDDH assumption. Robustness means that the top square matrix of $\mathbf{M}$ is full-ranked with overwhelming probability. The construction is essentially the one of [JR13] adapted to the framework of [KW15].

Algorithm crsgen_v: The algorithm crsgen_v samples a matrix $\mathbf{K} \leftarrow \mathbb{Z}_q^{n \times k}$, a vector $\mathbf{k} \leftarrow \mathbb{Z}_q^k$ and a matrix $\mathbf{A}^{(k+1) \times k}$ from the MDDH distribution $\mathcal{D}_k$. Let $\bar{\mathbf{A}}$ be the top $k \times k$ square matrix of $\mathbf{A}$. Then it computes:

$$\mathsf{CRS}_v := \left([\mathbf{C}_0]_2^{n \times k} = [\mathbf{K}\bar{\mathbf{A}}]_2, \quad [\mathbf{C}_1]_2^{1 \times k} = [\mathbf{k} \cdot \bar{\mathbf{A}}]_2, \quad [\bar{\mathbf{A}}]_2^{k \times k} \right)$$

and state $st = (\mathbf{K}, \mathbf{k})$.

Algorithm crsgen_p: Let $\rho = ([\mathbf{M}]_1^{n \times t}, [\mathbf{a}]_1^{n \times 1})$ be the language parameter supplied to crsgen_p and $st = (\mathbf{K}, \mathbf{k})$ be the state transmitted by crsgen_v. Then it computes:

$$\mathsf{CRS}_p := \left([\mathbf{P}_0]_1^{t \times k} = [\mathbf{M}^\top \mathbf{K}]_1, \quad [\mathbf{P}_1]_1^{1 \times k} = [\mathbf{a} \cdot \mathbf{K} + \mathbf{k}^\top]_1 \right)$$

Prover prover: Given candidate $\mathbf{y} = [\mathbf{Mx} + \mathbf{a}]_1$ with witness vector $\mathbf{x}^{t \times 1}$, the prover generates the following proof consisting of k elements in $\mathbb{G}_1$:

$$\boldsymbol{\pi} := \mathbf{x} \cdot [\mathbf{P}_0]_1 + [\mathbf{P}_1]_1$$

Verifier ver: Given candidate $\mathbf{y}$, and proof $\boldsymbol{\pi}$, compute:

$$\mathsf{e}(\mathbf{y}^\top, [\mathbf{C}_0]_2) + \mathsf{e}([1]_1, [\mathbf{C}_1]_2) \stackrel{?}{=} \mathsf{e}(\boldsymbol{\pi}, [\bar{\mathbf{A}}]_2)$$

Simulators $\mathsf{crssim}_v, \mathsf{crssim}_p$ **and** sim: The algorithms crssim_v and crssim_p are identical to crsgen_v and crsgen_p respectively, except that crsgen_v also outputs trap $:= (\mathbf{K}, [\mathbf{k}]_1)$. The proof simulator sim takes candidate $\mathbf{y}$ and trapdoor $(\mathbf{K}, [\mathbf{k}]_1)$ and outputs:

$$\boldsymbol{\pi} := \mathbf{y} \cdot \mathbf{K} + [\mathbf{k}^\top]_1$$

Theorem 1. *The above algorithms* ($\mathsf{pargen}, \mathsf{crsgen}_v, \mathsf{crsgen}_p, \mathsf{prover}, \mathsf{ver}$) *constitute a true-simulation-sound strong split-CRS QA-NIZK proof system for affine languages* $\{L_{[\mathbf{M}]_1, [\mathbf{a}]_1}\}$ *with parameters* $([\mathbf{M}]_1, [\mathbf{a}]_1)$ *sampled from a robust and efficiently witness-samplable distribution* $\mathcal{D}$ *over the associated parameter language* $\mathcal{L}_{par}$, *given any group generation algorithm for which the* $\mathcal{D}_k$-MDDH *assumption holds for group* $\mathbb{G}_2$.

2.3 Projective Hash Proof System

For a language L, let X be a superset of L and let $H = (H_k)_{k \in K}$ be a collection of (hash) functions indexed by K with domain X and range another set Π. The hash function family is generalized to a notion of *projective hash function family* if there is a set S of projection keys, and a projection map $\alpha : K \to S$, and further the action of H_k on subset L of X is completely determined by the projection key $\alpha(k)$. Finally, the projective hash function family is defined to be ϵ-**universal₂** if for all $s \in S$, $x, x^* \in X$, and $\pi, \pi^* \in \Pi$ with $x \notin L \cup \{x^*\}$, the following holds:

$$\Pr[H_k(x) = \pi \mid H_k(x^*) = \pi^* \wedge \alpha(k) = s] \leq \epsilon.$$

A projective hash function family is called ϵ-**smooth** if for all $x \in X \setminus L$, the statistical difference between the following two distributions is ϵ: sample k uniformly from K and π' uniformly from Π; the first distribution is given by the pair $(\alpha(k), H_k(x))$ and the second by the pair $(\alpha(k), \pi')$. For languages defined by a witness-relation R, the projective hash proof family constitutes a *projective hash proof system* (PHPS) if α, H_k, and another *public evaluation function* $\hat{H}$ that computes H_k on $x \in L$, given a witness of x and *only* the projection key $\alpha(k)$, are all efficiently computable. An efficient algorithm for sampling the key $k \in K$ is also assumed.

The above notions can also incorporate labels. In an *extended PHPS*, the hash functions take an additional input called *label*. The public evaluation algorithm also takes this label. All the above notions are now required to hold for each possible value of label. The extended PHPS is now defined to be ϵ-**universal₂** is for all $s \in S$, $x, x^* \in X$, all labels 1 and 1^*, and $\pi, \pi^* \in \Pi$ with $x \notin L$ and $(x, 1) \neq (x^*, 1^*)$, the following holds:

$$\Pr[H_k(x, 1) = \pi \mid H_k(x^*, 1^*) = \pi^* \wedge \alpha(k) = s] \leq \epsilon.$$

Since we are interested in distributions of languages, we extend the above definition to distribution of languages. So consider a parametrized class of languages $\{L_\rho\}_\rho$ with the parameters coming from an associated parameter language $\mathcal{L}_{\text{par}}$. Assume that all the languages in this collection are subsets of X. Let H as above be a collection of hash functions from X to Π. We say that the hash family is a projective hash family if for all L_ρ, the action of H_k on L_ρ is determined by $\alpha(k)$. Similarly, the hash family is ϵ-universal₂ (ϵ-smooth) for $\{L_\rho\}_\rho$ if for all languages L_ρ the ϵ-universal₂ (resp. ϵ-smooth) property holds.

2.4 Structure-Preserving Signatures

Definition 4 (Structure-preserving signature). *A structure-preserving signature scheme SPS is defined as a triple of probabilistic polynomial time (PPT) algorithms* $SPS = (\mathsf{Gen}, \mathsf{Sign}, \mathsf{Verify})$:

- *The probabilistic key generation algorithm* $\mathsf{Gen}(par)$ *returns the public/secret key* (pk, sk)*, where* $pk \in \mathbb{G}^{n_{pk}}$ *for some* $n_{pk} \in poly(\lambda)$*. We assume that* pk *implicitly defines a message space* $M := \mathbb{G}^n$ *for some* $n \in poly(\lambda)$*.*

- *The probabilistic signing algorithm* $\mathsf{Sign}(sk, [m])$ *returns a signature* $\sigma \in \mathbb{G}^{n_\sigma}$ *for* $n_\sigma \in poly(\lambda)$.
- *The deterministic verification algorithm* $\mathsf{Verify}(pk, [m], \sigma)$ *only consists of pairing product equations and returns 1 (accept) or 0 (reject).*

Perfect correctness holds if for all $(pk, sk) \leftarrow \mathsf{Gen}(par)$ *and all messages* $[m] \in M$ *and all* $\sigma \leftarrow \mathsf{Sign}(sk, [m])$ *we have* $\mathsf{Verify}(pk, [m], \sigma) = 1$.

Definition 5 (Unforgeability against chosen message attack). *To an adversary A and scheme SPS we associate the advantage function:*

$$\mathrm{ADV}_{SPS}^{CMA}(A) := \Pr \left[\begin{matrix} (pk, sk) \leftarrow \mathsf{Gen}(par) \\ ([m^*], \sigma^*) \leftarrow A^{SignO(\cdot)}(pk) \end{matrix} : \begin{matrix} [m^*] \notin Q_{msg} \text{ and} \\ \mathsf{Verify}(pk, [m^*], \sigma^*) = 1 \end{matrix} \right]$$

where $SignO([m])$ *runs* $\sigma \leftarrow \mathsf{Sign}(sk, [m])$, *adds the vector* $[m]$ *to* Q_{msg} *(initialized with* $\emptyset$*) and returns* σ *to A. An SPS is said to be (unbounded) CMA-secure if for all PPT adversaries A,* $\mathrm{ADV}_{SPS}^{CMA}(A)$ *is negligible.*

3   SPS Construction

Our SPS construction for a general $\mathcal{D}_k$-MDDH assumption is given in Fig. 1. We also give the instantiation of this SPS for the Symmetric eXternal Diffie-Hellman Assumption (SXDH) assumption in Fig. 2. The construction assumes groups $\mathbb{G}_1$ and $\mathbb{G}_2$ and a target group $\mathbb{G}_T$ with an efficient bilinear pairing e from $\mathbb{G}_1 \times \mathbb{G}_2$ to $\mathbb{G}_T$.

3.1   Security of the SPS Scheme

In this section we state and prove the security of the scheme SPS_{MDDH} described in Fig. 1. The proof is similar to the proof of CCA2 secure encryption scheme of Cramer and Shoup [CS02], where tag-based universal$_2$ projective hash proofs were introduced. The main difference is that the tag in structure preserving signatures (SPS) cannot be generated by hashing some of the group elements. The tag is therefore generated randomly and independently in SPS. The adversary may then try to forge a signature by setting the tag to be the same as the tag in one of the signatures it obtained earlier, and choosing other elements in the forged signature by modifying and combining elements of various signatures it obtained. In contrast, in Cramer-Shoup encryption, any change in other group elements of a ciphertext forces the tag to be different from all earlier ciphertext tags. To circumvent this problem in SPS, the tag t is provided as both $[t]_2$ and $[tr]_1$, where $[r]_1$ is randomness introduced as part of the signature. The validity of this relation can be checked publicly and efficiently using asymmetric bilinear pairing. Intuitively, this disallows the adversary to modify and combine elements from various signatures. It is now forced to modify at most one signature, while keeping the tag the same as in that signature. However, an affine secret component $[k_0]_1$ in the SPS signature, which is issued encrypted under an CCA2 encryption scheme and verified using a publicly verifiable QA-NIZK for affine languages, then disallows even this kind of forgery.

Gen $(q, \mathbb{G}_1, \mathbb{G}_2, \mathbb{G}_T, \mathsf{e}, [1]_1, [1]_2, n, \mathcal{D}_k)$:

Let $\mathcal{D}$ be a distribution on $(\tilde{\mathbf{M}}, \tilde{\mathbf{a}})$ defined as follows :

Sample $\mathbf{B}^{(k+1) \times k} \leftarrow \mathcal{D}_k$ and $(k_0, \; \mathbf{k}, \; \mathbf{d}, \; \mathbf{e}) \leftarrow \mathbb{Z}_q \times \mathbb{Z}_q^n \times \mathbb{Z}_q^k \times \mathbb{Z}_q^k$.

Let $\tilde{\mathbf{M}} := \left(\begin{array}{c|c|c} \mathbf{I}^{n \times n} & \mathbf{0}^{n \times k} & \mathbf{0}^{n \times k} \\ \hline \mathbf{0}^{(k+1) \times n} & \mathbf{B} & \mathbf{0}^{(k+1) \times k} \\ \hline \mathbf{0}^{k \times n} & \mathbf{0}^{k \times k} & \overline{\mathbf{B}} \\ \hline \mathbf{k}^\top & \mathbf{d} \cdot \overline{\mathbf{B}} & \mathbf{e} \cdot \overline{\mathbf{B}} \end{array} \right) \in \mathbb{Z}_q^{(n+2k+2) \times (n+2k)}$

and $\tilde{\mathbf{a}} := \begin{pmatrix} \mathbf{0}^{(n+2k+1) \times 1} \\ k_0 \end{pmatrix} \in \mathbb{Z}_q^{n+2k+2}$.

Let Π be a strong split-CRS QA-NIZK for

$$L_{\tilde{\mathbf{M}}, \tilde{\mathbf{a}}} = \{ [\tilde{\mathbf{M}} \mathbf{x} + \tilde{\mathbf{a}}]_1 \mid \mathbf{x} \in \mathbb{Z}_q^{n+2k} \}, \text{ with } (\tilde{\mathbf{M}}, \tilde{\mathbf{a}}) \leftarrow \mathcal{D}$$

which is true-simulation-sound under the $\mathcal{D}_k$-MDDH assumption in $\mathbb{G}_2$.

Sample $(\mathsf{CRS}_v, \mathsf{trap}, st) \leftarrow \Pi.\mathsf{crssim}_v$ and $(\mathbf{M}, \mathbf{a}) \leftarrow \mathcal{D}$
Let $pk := \mathsf{CRS}_v$ and $sk := (\mathbf{M}, \; \mathbf{a}, \; \mathsf{trap})$
Return (pk, sk)

Sign $(sk = (\mathbf{M}, \mathbf{a}, \mathsf{trap}), \; \boldsymbol{\mu} \in \mathbb{G}_1^n)$:

Sample $\mathbf{r} \leftarrow \mathbb{Z}_q^k$ and $\text{TAG} \leftarrow \mathbb{Z}_q$

Let $(\boldsymbol{\mu}, \boldsymbol{\rho}, \hat{\rho}, \boldsymbol{\psi}, \gamma) := \mathbf{M} \begin{pmatrix} \boldsymbol{\mu} \\ [\mathbf{r}]_1 \\ [\text{TAG} \cdot \mathbf{r}]_1 \end{pmatrix} + [\mathbf{a}]_1 \; \in \mathbb{G}_1^n \times \mathbb{G}_1^k \times \mathbb{G}_1 \times \mathbb{G}_1^k \times \mathbb{G}_1$

Let $\boldsymbol{\pi} := \Pi.\mathsf{sim}(\mathsf{trap}, (\boldsymbol{\mu}, \boldsymbol{\rho}, \hat{\rho}, \boldsymbol{\psi}, \gamma))$ and $\tau := [\text{TAG}]_2$
Return $(\boldsymbol{\rho}, \hat{\rho}, \boldsymbol{\psi}, \gamma, \tau, \boldsymbol{\pi}) \in \mathbb{G}_1^k \times \mathbb{G}_1 \times \mathbb{G}_1^k \times \mathbb{G}_1 \times \mathbb{G}_2 \times \mathbb{G}_1^k$

Verify $(pk = \mathsf{CRS}_v, \; \boldsymbol{\mu}, \; \sigma = (\boldsymbol{\rho}, \hat{\rho}, \boldsymbol{\psi}, \gamma, \tau, \boldsymbol{\pi}))$:

Return $\Pi.\mathsf{ver}(\mathsf{CRS}_v, (\boldsymbol{\mu}, \boldsymbol{\rho}, \hat{\rho}, \boldsymbol{\psi}, \gamma), \boldsymbol{\pi})$ and $\mathsf{e}(\boldsymbol{\rho}, \tau) \stackrel{?}{=} \mathsf{e}(\boldsymbol{\psi}, [1]_2)$

Fig. 1. Structure Preserving Signature SPS_{MDDH}

Theorem 2. *For any efficient adversary* $\mathcal{A}$, *which makes at most* Q *signature queries before attempting a forgery, its probability of success in the EUF-CMA game against the scheme* SPS_{MDDH} *is at most*

$$\mathsf{ADV}_\Pi^{TSS} + Q^2 \cdot \left(\mathsf{ADV}_{\mathcal{D}_k - \text{MDDH}} + \frac{3}{2q} \right) + \frac{Q}{q} + \frac{1}{q}$$

Gen $(q, \mathbb{G}_1, \mathbb{G}_2, \mathbb{G}_T, \mathsf{e}, [1]_1, [1]_2, n)$: Sample b, k_0, d and e uniformly from $\mathbb{Z}_q$ and **k** uniformly from $\mathbb{Z}_q^n$. Define the language L of tuples $(\boldsymbol{\mu}, \rho, \hat{\rho}, \psi, \gamma) \in \mathbb{G}^{n+4}$, such that there exists $(\mathbf{m}, r, r') \in \mathbb{Z}_q^{n+2}$, such that:

$$\boldsymbol{\mu} = [\mathbf{m}]_1, \ \rho = [r]_1, \ \hat{\rho} = [br]_1, \ \psi = [r']_1, \ \gamma = [k_0 + \mathbf{k} \cdot \mathbf{m} + dr + er']_1$$

Let Π be a strong split-CRS QA-NIZK for the affine language L, which is true-simulation-sound under the DDH assumption in $\mathbb{G}_2$. Let the simulation CRS generator $\Pi.\mathsf{crssim}_v$ output $(\mathsf{CRS}_v, \mathsf{trap}, st)$. Set $pk := \mathsf{CRS}_v$ and $sk := (b, k_0, \mathbf{k}, d, e, \mathsf{trap})$, and return (pk, sk).

Sign $(sk = (b, k_0, \mathbf{k}, d, e, \mathsf{trap}), \ \boldsymbol{\mu} \in \mathbb{G}_1^n)$: Sample r and TAG uniformly from $\mathbb{Z}_q$. Let:

$$\rho = [r]_1, \ \hat{\rho} = [br]_1, \ \psi = [\text{TAG} \cdot r]_1, \ \gamma = \mathbf{k} \cdot \boldsymbol{\mu} + [k_0 + dr + \text{TAG} \cdot er]_1$$

Let $\pi := \Pi.\mathsf{sim}(\mathsf{trap}, (\boldsymbol{\mu}, \rho, \hat{\rho}, \psi, \gamma))$ and $\tau := [\text{TAG}]_2$. Return:

$$\sigma := (\rho, \hat{\rho}, \psi, \gamma, \tau, \pi) \in \mathbb{G}_1^4 \times \mathbb{G}_2 \times \mathbb{G}_1.$$

Verify $(pk = \mathsf{CRS}_v, \ \boldsymbol{\mu}, \ \sigma = (\rho, \hat{\rho}, \psi, \gamma, \tau, \pi))$: Return the boolean:

$$\Pi.\mathsf{ver}(\mathsf{CRS}_v, (\boldsymbol{\mu}, \rho, \hat{\rho}, \psi, \gamma), \pi) \text{ and } \mathsf{e}(\rho, \tau) \stackrel{?}{=} \mathsf{e}(\psi, [1]_2).$$

Fig. 2. Structure Preserving Signature SPS_{SXDH}

Proof. We go through a sequence of Games $\mathbf{G_0}$ to $\mathbf{G_6}$ which are described below and summarized in Fig. 3. In the following, $\mathrm{Prob}_i[X]$ will denote probability of predicate X holding in probability space defined in game $\mathbf{G_i}$.

Game $\mathbf{G_0}$: Given setup parameters $(q, \mathbb{G}_1, \mathbb{G}_2, \mathbb{G}_T, \mathsf{e}, [1]_1, [1]_2, n, \mathcal{D}_k)$, the challenger $\mathcal{C}$ initializes a list $\mathcal{M}$ to empty, generates $(\mathsf{CRS}_v, \mathsf{trap}, st) \leftarrow \Pi.\mathsf{crssim}_v$, and then samples $\mathbf{B}^{(k+1) \times k} \leftarrow \mathcal{D}_k$ and $(k_0, \mathbf{k}, \mathbf{d}, \mathbf{e}) \leftarrow \mathbb{Z}_q \times \mathbb{Z}_q^n \times \mathbb{Z}_q^k \times \mathbb{Z}_q^k$.

Then it sends the setup parameters and CRS_v to adversary $\mathcal{A}$ as public key. For $i \in [1..Q]$, $\mathcal{A}$ adaptively requests signature on $\boldsymbol{\mu}_i (\in \mathbb{G}_1^n)$. The challenger $\mathcal{C}$ generates signature σ_i by first sampling $(\mathbf{r}, \text{TAG}) \leftarrow \mathbb{Z}_q^k \times \mathbb{Z}_q$, and then setting:

$$\sigma_i := \begin{pmatrix} \boldsymbol{\rho} = [\overline{\mathbf{B}}\mathbf{r}]_1, \ \hat{\rho} = [\underline{\mathbf{B}}\mathbf{r}]_1, \ \boldsymbol{\psi} = \text{TAG} \, [\overline{\mathbf{B}}\mathbf{r}]_1, \\ \gamma = \mathbf{k} \cdot \boldsymbol{\mu}_i + [k_0]_1 + \mathbf{d} \cdot \boldsymbol{\rho} + \mathbf{e} \cdot \boldsymbol{\psi}, \ \tau = [\text{TAG}]_2, \\ \boldsymbol{\pi} = \Pi.\mathsf{sim}(\mathsf{trap}, (\boldsymbol{\mu}_i, \boldsymbol{\rho}, \hat{\rho}, \boldsymbol{\psi}, \gamma)) \end{pmatrix}$$

It then sends σ_i to $\mathcal{A}$, and adds $\boldsymbol{\mu}_i$ to the list $\mathcal{M}$. After it obtains Q signatures, $\mathcal{A}$ responds with a message $\boldsymbol{\mu}^*$ and a claimed signature on it σ^*. Adversary wins if $\boldsymbol{\mu}^* \notin \mathcal{M}$ and $(\boldsymbol{\mu}^*, \sigma^*)$ passes verify. Define:

$$\boxed{\text{WIN}_0 \stackrel{\triangle}{=} (\boldsymbol{\mu}^* \notin \mathcal{M}) \text{ and } (\mathsf{verify}(\mathsf{CRS}_v, \boldsymbol{\mu}^*, \sigma^*) = 1)}$$

$$
\begin{aligned}
&\mathsf{Gen}() : \ \cdots \ \text{Sample } \mathbf{B}^{(k+1)\times k} \leftarrow \mathcal{D}_k \\
&\qquad\quad \text{Let } \mathbf{t} = (\underline{\mathbf{B}}\, \overline{\mathbf{B}}^{-1})^{\top} \in \mathbb{Z}_q^k
\end{aligned}
$$

Games 0-3   Sample $(\mathbf{d},\ \mathbf{e}) \leftarrow \mathbb{Z}_q^k \times \mathbb{Z}_q^k$

Games 4-6   Sample $(\mathbf{d}_1,\ d_2,\ \mathbf{e}_1,\ e_2) \leftarrow \mathbb{Z}_q^k \times \mathbb{Z}_q \times \mathbb{Z}_q^k \times \mathbb{Z}_q \ \cdots$

$$
\mathsf{Sign}(sk,\ \boldsymbol{\mu}_j \in \mathbb{G}_1^n) :
$$
$$
\text{Sample } (\boldsymbol{\rho},\ \theta,\ \phi) \leftarrow \mathbb{G}_1^k \times \mathbb{G}_1 \times \mathbb{G}_1
$$

Game 0   Sample $\mathrm{TAG} \leftarrow \mathbb{Z}_q$

Games 1-6   Sample $\mathrm{TAG} \leftarrow \mathbb{Z}_q \setminus \{\mathrm{TAG}_l\}_{l<j}$

         Let $\boldsymbol{\psi} := \mathrm{TAG}\ \boldsymbol{\rho}$

         Let $(\hat{\rho}, \gamma) :=$

Game 0-3 $\left(\mathbf{t}\cdot\boldsymbol{\rho},\ \mathbf{k}\cdot\boldsymbol{\mu}_y + [k_0]_1 + \mathbf{d}\cdot\boldsymbol{\rho} + \mathrm{TAG}\ \mathbf{e}\cdot\boldsymbol{\rho}\right)$

Game 4-5 $\left(\mathbf{t}\cdot\boldsymbol{\rho},\ \mathbf{k}\cdot\boldsymbol{\mu}_y + [k_0]_1 + (\mathbf{d}_1 + d_2\mathbf{t})\cdot\boldsymbol{\rho} + \mathrm{TAG}\ (\mathbf{e}_1 + e_2\mathbf{t})\cdot\boldsymbol{\rho}\right)$

Game 6 $(\theta,\ \phi)$

         Let $\boldsymbol{\pi} := \Pi.\mathsf{sim}(\mathsf{trap},\ (\boldsymbol{\mu}_j, \boldsymbol{\rho}, \hat{\rho}, \boldsymbol{\psi}, \gamma))$ and $\tau := [\mathrm{TAG}]_2$

         Return $(\boldsymbol{\rho}, \hat{\rho}, \boldsymbol{\psi}, \gamma, \tau, \boldsymbol{\pi})$

WIN $\triangleq$ $(\boldsymbol{\mu}^* \notin \mathcal{M})$ and $\Pi.\mathsf{ver}(\mathsf{CRS}_v, (\boldsymbol{\mu}^*, \boldsymbol{\rho}^*, \hat{\rho}^*, \boldsymbol{\psi}^*, \gamma^*), \boldsymbol{\pi}^*)$ and $\mathsf{e}(\boldsymbol{\rho}^*, \tau^*) \overset{?}{=} \mathsf{e}(\boldsymbol{\psi}^*, [1]_2)$

Games 2-6   and $\sigma^* = (\boldsymbol{\rho}^*, \hat{\rho}^*, \boldsymbol{\psi}^*, \gamma^*, \tau^*, \boldsymbol{\pi}^*)$:

Game 2 $\gamma^* \overset{?}{=} \mathbf{k}\cdot\boldsymbol{\mu}^* + [k_0]_1 + \mathbf{d}\cdot\boldsymbol{\rho}^* + \mathbf{e}\cdot\boldsymbol{\psi}^*$

Game 3 $\mathsf{e}(\gamma^*, [1]_2) \overset{?}{=} \mathsf{e}(\mathbf{k}\cdot\boldsymbol{\mu}^* + [k_0]_1 + \mathbf{d}\cdot\boldsymbol{\rho}^*, [1]_2) + \mathsf{e}(\mathbf{e}\cdot\boldsymbol{\rho}^*, \tau^*)$

Games 4-6 $\mathsf{e}(\gamma^*, [1]_2) \overset{?}{=} \mathsf{e}(\mathbf{k}\cdot\boldsymbol{\mu}^* + [k_0]_1 + \mathbf{d}_1\cdot\boldsymbol{\rho}^* + d_2\hat{\rho}^*, [1]_2) + \mathsf{e}(\mathbf{e}_1\cdot\boldsymbol{\rho}^* + e_2\hat{\rho}^*, \tau^*)$

Games 0-4   and $\hat{\rho}^* \overset{?}{=} \mathbf{t}\cdot\boldsymbol{\rho}^*$

Fig. 3. G Games and winning conditions

This game exactly replicates the real construction to the adversary. So the adversary's advantage in $\mathbf{G_0}$ is the EUF-CMA advantage we seek to bound.

Game $\mathbf{G_1}$: The challenge-response in this game is the same as Game $\mathbf{G_0}$ except that in each signature the value TAG is chosen randomly but distinctly from all the earlier TAG's. The winning condition remains the same, i.e. WIN_0.

The statistical difference between the view of the adversary in $\mathbf{G_0}$ and $\mathbf{G_1}$ is the probability of collision in the choice of TAG for the Q signature queries in $\mathbf{G_0}$, which is at most $Q^2/(2 \cdot q)$.

Game $\mathbf{G_2}$: The challenge-response in this game is the same as $\mathbf{G_1}$. The winning condition is now defined as

$$\mathsf{WIN}_2 \overset{\triangle}{=} \mathsf{WIN}_0 \text{ and } (\sigma^* = (\rho^*, \hat{\rho}^*, \psi^*, \gamma^*, \tau^*, \pi^*)) \text{ s.t.}$$
$$(\gamma^* = \mathbf{k} \cdot \boldsymbol{\mu}^* + [k_0]_1 + \mathbf{d} \cdot \rho^* + \mathbf{e} \cdot \psi^*)$$
$$\text{and } ((\rho^*, \hat{\rho}^*) \in Span([\mathbf{B}]_1))$$

The difference in advantages of the adversary is upper bounded by the unbounded true-simulation-soundness of Π:

$$|\mathrm{Prob}_2[\mathsf{WIN}_2] - \mathrm{Prob}_1[\mathsf{WIN}_1]| \leq \mathrm{ADV}_\Pi^{TSS} \tag{1}$$

Game $\mathbf{G_3}$: The challenge-response in this game is the same as $\mathbf{G_2}$. The winning condition is now defined as

$$\mathsf{WIN}_3 \overset{\triangle}{=} \mathsf{WIN}_0 \text{ and } (\sigma^* = (\rho^*, \hat{\rho}^*, \psi^*, \gamma^*, \tau^*, \pi^*)) \text{ s.t.}$$
$$(\mathsf{e}(\gamma^*, [1]_2) = \mathsf{e}(\mathbf{k} \cdot \boldsymbol{\mu}^* + [k_0]_1 + \mathbf{d} \cdot \rho^*, [1]_2) + \mathsf{e}(\mathbf{e} \cdot \rho^*, \tau^*))$$
$$\text{and } ((\rho^*, \hat{\rho}^*) \in Span([\mathbf{B}]_1))$$

Note that the predicate WIN_3 is efficiently computable by the challenger $\mathcal{C}$ as it generated $\mathbf{B}$ as part of the language parameters $(\mathbf{M}, \mathbf{a})$. As WIN_0 implies $\mathsf{e}(\psi^*, [1]_2) = \mathsf{e}(\rho^*, \tau^*)$, the winning condition is unchanged from the previous game and thus, $\mathrm{Prob}_2[\mathsf{WIN}_2]$ is the same as $\mathrm{Prob}_3[\mathsf{WIN}_3]$.

Game $\mathbf{G_4}$: Define $\mathbf{t}^{k \times 1} \overset{\triangle}{=} (\underline{\mathbf{B}} \, \overline{\mathbf{B}}^{-1})^\top$. Since $\mathbf{B}$ is overwhelmingly a full ranked matrix, we observe that ρ can be just sampled uniformly randomly from $\mathbb{Z}_q^k$ and $\hat{\rho}$ can be set to $\mathbf{t} \cdot \rho$ in the signature generation algorithm. Also in the winning condition $(\rho^*, \hat{\rho}^*) \in Span([\mathbf{B}]_1)$ can be equivalently written as $\hat{\rho}^* \overset{?}{=} \mathbf{t} \cdot \rho^*$, with no other constraints on ρ^*.

In Game $\mathbf{G_4}$, the challenger $\mathcal{C}$ picks $(\mathbf{d}_1, \mathbf{d}_2, \mathbf{e}_1, \mathbf{e}_2)$ at random from $\mathbb{Z}_q^{2k+2}$, and sets $\mathbf{d} = \mathbf{d}_1 + \mathbf{d}_2 \mathbf{t}$ and $\mathbf{e} = \mathbf{e}_1 + \mathbf{e}_2 \mathbf{t}$ (i.e., instead of directly picking $\mathbf{d}$ and $\mathbf{e}$ at random while defining $\mathcal{L}_{par}$). This has no statistical change in the view of the adversary.

The winning condition is now defined and computed as:

$$\mathsf{WIN}_4 \overset{\triangle}{=} \mathsf{WIN}_0 \text{ and } (\sigma^* = (\rho^*, \hat{\rho}^*, \psi^*, \gamma^*, \tau^*, \pi^*)) \text{ s.t.}$$
$$(\mathsf{e}(\gamma^*, [1]_2) = \mathsf{e}(\mathbf{k} \cdot \boldsymbol{\mu}^* + [k_0]_1 + \mathbf{d}_1 \cdot \rho^* + \mathbf{d}_2 \hat{\rho}^*, [1]_2)$$
$$+ \mathsf{e}(\mathbf{e}_1 \cdot \rho^* + \mathbf{e}_2 \hat{\rho}^*, \tau^*))$$
$$\text{and } (\hat{\rho}^* \overset{?}{=} \mathbf{t} \cdot \rho^*)$$

Since $\hat{\rho}^* = \mathbf{t} \cdot \rho^*$, it directly follows that $(\mathbf{d}_1 + \mathbf{d}_2 \mathbf{t}) \cdot \rho^*$ is the same as $(\mathbf{d}_1 \cdot \rho^* + \mathbf{d}_2 \hat{\rho}^*)$, and $(\mathbf{e}_1 + \mathbf{e}_2 \mathbf{t}) \cdot \rho^*$ is the same as $(\mathbf{e}_1 \cdot \rho^* + \mathbf{e}_2 \hat{\rho}^*)$. Therefore $\mathsf{WIN}_4 \equiv \mathsf{WIN}_3$.

Game G_5: In this game, we define WIN_5 to be the same as WIN_4, except that it does not have the conjunct $\hat{\rho}^* \overset{?}{=} \mathbf{t} \cdot \boldsymbol{\rho}$.

$$\mathsf{WIN}_5 \overset{\triangle}{=} \mathsf{WIN}_0 \text{ and } (\sigma^* = (\boldsymbol{\rho}^*, \hat{\rho}^*, \boldsymbol{\psi}^*, \gamma^*, \tau^*, \boldsymbol{\pi}^*)) \text{ s.t.}$$
$$(\mathsf{e}(\gamma^*, [1]_2) = \mathsf{e}(\mathbf{k} \cdot \boldsymbol{\mu}^* + [k_0]_1 + \mathbf{d}_1 \cdot \boldsymbol{\rho}^* + d_2\hat{\rho}^*, [1]_2)$$
$$+ \mathsf{e}(\mathbf{e}_1 \cdot \boldsymbol{\rho}^* + e_2\hat{\rho}^*, \tau^*))$$

We now prove that:

$$|\mathrm{Prob}_5[\mathsf{WIN}_5] - \mathrm{Prob}_4[\mathsf{WIN}_4]| \leq 1/q \tag{2}$$

Firstly, note that the probability spaces in G_4 and G_5 are identical. We will now show that an adversary $\mathcal{A}$ in Game G_4 has probability at most $1/q$ of forcing WIN_5 while not satisfying WIN_4, i.e., forcing WIN_5 and $\hat{\rho}^* \neq \mathbf{t} \cdot \boldsymbol{\rho}^*$.

The claim is an easy consequence of private hash on a non-$Span([\mathbf{B}]_1)$ word being random and independent of the public (projection) hash key [CS02]. Here, the public hash key is $[\mathbf{d}_1 + d_2\mathbf{t}]_1$, with private hash key $(\mathbf{d}_1, d_2)$ (see Sect. 2.3). The public hash key is given to the adversary as part of all the signatures issued to the adversary. In particular it is used in computing γ component of the signature. The QA-NIZK proof is simulated, and the QA-NIZK simulator trapdoors do not use $(\mathbf{d}_1, d_2)$. Further, $(\mathbf{d}_1, d_2)$ are not used anywhere else, including CRS_v.

If $(\boldsymbol{\rho}^*, \hat{\rho}^*) \notin Span([\mathbf{B}]_1)$, then the right side of the pairing equation in WIN_5 includes an additive component $\mathsf{e}(\mathbf{d}_1 \cdot \boldsymbol{\rho}^* + d_2\hat{\rho}^*, [1]_2)$, which is the same as $\mathsf{e}(P, [1]_2)$ where P is the private hash of $(\boldsymbol{\rho}^*, \hat{\rho}^*)$ using keys $(\mathbf{d}_1, d_2)$. Since, all other additive terms on the right hand side of the pairing equation are independent of this hash proof system, and the adversary $\mathcal{A}$ also supplies γ^*, the probability of $\mathsf{e}(\gamma^*, [1]_2)$ equaling the right hand side is at most $1/q$. This finishes the proof of the claim.

Game G_6: In this game the challenger generates all signatures σ_i with $\hat{\rho}_i$ and γ_i set to uniformly and independently chosen random values. The computation of ρ, ψ, τ and π and the winning condition remain the same as in G_5.

We now claim that the difference between the advantage of the adversary in Game G_6 and Q times the advantage of the adversary in Game G_5 is negligible in Lemma 1 below, which is proved later:

Lemma 1.

$$|\mathrm{Prob}_5[\mathsf{WIN}_5] - Q \cdot \mathrm{Prob}_6[\mathsf{WIN}_6]| \leq Q^2 \left(\mathrm{ADV}_{\mathcal{D}_k - \mathrm{MDDH}} + \frac{1}{q} \right)$$

Now, in Game G_6, all the signatures on the Q adversarial queries are generated without using k_0. Since k_0 is also not part of the public key (which includes CRS_v), the probability of adversary satisfying WIN_6 is $1/q$. Thus, probability of WIN_6 holding in Game G_6 is at most $1/q$:

$$\mathrm{Prob}_6[\mathsf{WIN}_6] \leq 1/q$$

Thus the proof of Lemma 1 will conclude the proof, which we proceed to do next.

Proof (of Lemma 1). To prove this lemma we consider several hybrid Games $\mathbf{G_{5,i}}$, for $i \in [0..Q]$, where $\mathbf{G_{5,0}}$ will turn out to be the same as $\mathbf{G_5}$, and $\mathbf{G_{5,Q}}$ will turn out to be the same as $\mathbf{G_6}$. The hybrid Games $\mathbf{G_{5,i}}$ for $i \in [0..Q]$ are defined as follows.

Game $\mathbf{G_{5,i}}$: The game differs from $\mathbf{G_5}$ as follows: After it has generated the public key and sent it to $\mathcal{A}$ just as in $\mathbf{G_5}$, the challenger now picks a random index z from $[1..Q]$. If $i < Q$, it picks i distinct indices randomly from $[1..Q] \setminus \{z\}$. Call this set of indices as S (note S is empty in Game $\mathbf{G_{5,0}}$). If $i = Q$, let S be the full set $[1..Q]$. While generating a signature on a query with index $j \in S$, the challenger generates the signature as in Game $\mathbf{G_6}$ (i.e. random γ_i and $\hat{\rho}_i$ terms), and for a query with index outside S it generates the signature as in Game $\mathbf{G_5}$. The winning predicate for the adversary remains the same, i.e., WIN$_5$. As the winning condition will remain the same till the end of proof, we just define WIN $\equiv$ WIN$_5$. The game is described in Fig. 4.

Gen() : $\cdots$

      Sample $z \leftarrow [1..Q]$ and $S \leftarrow 2^{[1..Q] \setminus \{z\}}$, such that $|S| = i$

Sign(sk, $\boldsymbol{\mu}_j \in \mathbb{G}_1^n$) :

      Sample $(\boldsymbol{\rho}, \theta, \phi, \text{TAG}) \leftarrow \mathbb{G}_1^k \times \mathbb{G}_1 \times \mathbb{G}_1 \times (\mathbb{Z}_q \setminus \{\text{TAG}_l\}_{l < j})$

      Let $\psi := \text{TAG} \, \boldsymbol{\rho}$

      If $(j \notin S)$ let $(\hat{\rho}, \gamma) :=$

          $(\mathbf{t} \cdot \boldsymbol{\rho}, \; \mathbf{k} \cdot \boldsymbol{\mu}_j + [k_0]_1 + (\mathbf{d}_1 + d_2\mathbf{t}) \cdot \boldsymbol{\rho} + \text{TAG} \, (\mathbf{e}_1 + e_2\mathbf{t}) \cdot \boldsymbol{\rho})$

      Else if $(j \in S)$ let $(\hat{\rho}, \gamma) :=$

          $(\theta, \; \phi)$

      Let $\pi := \Pi.\text{sim}(\text{trap}, \; (\boldsymbol{\mu}_j, \boldsymbol{\rho}, \hat{\rho}, \psi, \gamma))$ and $\tau := [\text{TAG}]_2$

      Return $(\boldsymbol{\rho}, \hat{\rho}, \psi, \gamma, \tau, \pi)$

WIN $\triangleq$ WIN$_0$ and $\sigma^* = (\boldsymbol{\rho}^*, \hat{\rho}^*, \psi^*, \gamma^*, \tau^*, \pi^*)$:

      $e(\gamma^*, [1]_2) \stackrel{?}{=} e(\mathbf{k} \cdot \boldsymbol{\mu}^* + [k_0]_1 + \mathbf{d}_1 \cdot \boldsymbol{\rho}^* + d_2\hat{\rho}^*, [1]_2) + e(\mathbf{e}_1 \cdot \boldsymbol{\rho}^* + e_2\hat{\rho}^*, \tau^*)$

Fig. 4. Games $\mathbf{G_{5,i}}$

Note that in Game $\mathbf{G_{5,0}}$, the probability of adversary winning, i.e. WIN holding is the same as in Game $\mathbf{G_5}$, since the set S is empty, and hence z might as well not be chosen.

To prove the requisite probability relations between the different games, consider the following predicate GOOD, defined at the end of each game. We will denote the components of the j-th signature σ_j by using subscript j.

$$\boxed{\mathsf{GOOD} \triangleq \forall j \in [1..Q] \setminus \{z\} : (\mathrm{TAG}^* \neq \mathrm{TAG}_j)}$$

Lemma 2.
$$\mathrm{Prob}_{5,0}[\mathsf{WIN}] \leq Q \cdot \mathrm{Prob}_{5,0}[\mathsf{WIN} \ \mathbf{and} \ \mathsf{GOOD}]$$

Lemma 3. *For $i \in [1..Q-1]$,*
$$\left| \begin{array}{l} \mathrm{Prob}_{5,i-1}[\mathsf{WIN} \ \mathbf{and} \ \mathsf{GOOD}] \\ -\mathrm{Prob}_{5,i}[\mathsf{WIN} \ \mathbf{and} \ \mathsf{GOOD}] \end{array} \right| \leq \mathrm{ADV}_{\mathcal{D}_k\text{-MDDH}} + 1/q$$

Lemma 4.
$$|\mathrm{Prob}_{5,Q-1}[\mathsf{WIN}] - \mathrm{Prob}_{5,Q}[\mathsf{WIN}]| \leq \mathrm{ADV}_{\mathcal{D}_k\text{-MDDH}} + 1/q$$

Fig. 5. Lemmas

Given the definitions of Games $\mathbf{G_{5,i}}$ and GOOD above, we now prove the lemma via the three lemmas given in Fig. 5. Chaining Lemma 3 sequentially $(Q-1)$ times, it follows that

$$\left| \begin{array}{l} \mathrm{Prob}_{5,0}[\mathsf{WIN} \ \mathbf{and} \ \mathsf{GOOD}]- \\ \mathrm{Prob}_{5,Q-1}[\mathsf{WIN} \ \mathbf{and} \ \mathsf{GOOD}\,] \end{array} \right| \leq (Q-1) \cdot (\mathrm{ADV}_{\mathcal{D}_k-\text{MDDH}} + 1/q)$$

Now noting that $\mathrm{Prob}_{5,Q-1}[\mathsf{WIN} \ \mathbf{and} \ \mathsf{GOOD}\,] \leq \mathrm{Prob}_{5,Q-1}[\mathsf{WIN}]$ and using Lemma 4, we get:

$$\left| \begin{array}{l} \mathrm{Prob}_{5,0}[\mathsf{WIN} \ \mathbf{and} \ \mathsf{GOOD}] \\ - \ \mathrm{Prob}_{5,Q}[\mathsf{WIN}] \end{array} \right| \leq Q \cdot (\mathrm{ADV}_{\mathcal{D}_k-\text{MDDH}} + 1/q)$$

Now, using Lemma 2, we finally establish Lemma 1:

$$|\mathrm{Prob}_{5,0}[\mathsf{WIN}] - Q \cdot \mathrm{Prob}_{5,Q}[\mathsf{WIN}]| \leq Q^2 \left(\mathrm{ADV}_{\mathcal{D}_k-\text{MDDH}} + \frac{1}{q} \right)$$

We proceed to prove Lemmas 2, 3 and 4 now.

Proof (of Lemma 2). We equivalently show that:

$$\mathrm{Prob}_{5,0}[\overline{\mathsf{GOOD}} \mid \mathsf{WIN}] \leq (1 - 1/Q)$$

First note that in Game $\mathbf{G_{5,0}}$, the value z can be chosen after the adversary has supplied its forged signature. Now, observe that:

$$\text{Prob}_{5,0}[\overline{\text{GOOD}} \mid \text{WIN}] \leq \text{Prob}_{5,0}[\text{TAG}^* \neq \text{TAG}_z \mid \text{WIN and } \exists j : \text{TAG}^* = \text{TAG}_j]$$

Since z is chosen after the adversary has replied with the forgery and given TAG^* equals some TAG_j, the probability of $z = j$ is at least $1/Q$ (regardless of WIN holding or not), and thus the probability of TAG^* equaling TAG_z is at least $1/Q$.

Discussion of Lemmas 3 and 4. From a formal proof perspective, one goes through many hybrid games, where in each subsequent hybrid Game $\mathbf{G_{5,i}}$, the signature of one more element is simulated without using the affine component $[k_0]_1$. However, as is well known from proofs of Cramer-Shoup encryption, this can only be done as long as the forgery uses a different tag from the signature being simulated. Thus, the simulator instead guesses an index z, and picks the additional signature to be simulated from a query index different from z. This is always possible, as long as the simulator is in hybrid game $\mathbf{G_{5,i}}$, with $i < Q-1$. If the simulator's guess turns out to be wrong, the adversary is declared outright winner. However, this gives the adversary only a Q factor advantage over its success in an MDDH challenge game.

The other main difference from Cramer-Shoup encryption is that there is no real decryption, but just a verification of the signature using private trapdoor keys. This can also be done efficiently using the bilinear pairing available, and this is the reason why a single additional test of the relationship between $[t]_2$, $[\mathbf{tr}]_1$ and $[\mathbf{r}]_1$ suffices.

The proof of Lemma 4, which handles the case $i = Q - 1$ is similar to (and easier than) proof of Lemma 3 except that in game $\mathbf{G_{5,Q-1}}$, all but one signatures are simulated without keys k_0 and $\mathbf{k}$. This makes the analysis similar to that of a one-time signature scheme.

Proof (of Lemma 3). We will consider three hybrid games which are summarized in Fig. 6. Game $\mathbf{H_0}$ will be the same as game $\mathbf{G_{5,i-1}}$, and $\mathbf{H_2}$ the same as $\mathbf{G_{5,i}}$.

Game $\mathbf{H_0}$: The challenger picks yet another index y at random from $[1..Q] \setminus (\{z\} \cup S)$, and issues the signature on the y-th query in the same way as for other indices *not in* S. The idea is that in these sequence of games we will convert the signature generation on the y-th index to be same as for those indices *in* S. This will effectively expand the set S by one element and thus enable us to transition from Game $\mathbf{G_{5,i-1}}$ to $\mathbf{G_{5,i}}$, as long as $i \leq Q - 1$. Games $\mathbf{H_0}$ and $\mathbf{G_{5,i-1}}$ are semantically equivalent.

Game $\mathbf{H_1}$: In Game $\mathbf{H_1}$, the challenger issues the signature on the y-th query as follows: it picks $\boldsymbol{\rho}_y$, θ and TAG_y at random. It sets $\hat{\rho}_y = \theta$, $\psi_y = \text{TAG}_y \, \boldsymbol{\rho}_y$, $\tau_y = [\text{TAG}_y]_2$ and $\gamma_y = \mathbf{k} \cdot \boldsymbol{\mu}_y + [k_0]_1 + (\mathbf{d}_1 \cdot \boldsymbol{\rho}_y + d_2 \hat{\rho}_y) + \text{TAG}_y \, (\mathbf{e}_1 \cdot \boldsymbol{\rho}_y + e_2 \hat{\rho}_y)$. It computes a QA-NIZK $\boldsymbol{\pi}_y$, on the tuple $(\boldsymbol{\mu}_j, \boldsymbol{\rho}_y, \hat{\rho}_y, \psi_y, \gamma_y)$ using the QA-NIZK simulator crssim, just as in all previous games. It outputs as signature σ_y the tuple $(\boldsymbol{\rho}_y, \hat{\rho}_y, \psi_y, \gamma_y, \tau_y, \boldsymbol{\pi}_y)$. Rest of the game and the winning condition is the same as $\mathbf{H_0}$. We now prove that:

$$\left| \begin{array}{l} \text{Prob}_{H_0}[\text{WIN and GOOD}] - \\ \text{Prob}_{H_1}[\text{WIN and GOOD}] \end{array} \right| < \text{ADV}_{\mathcal{D}_k-\text{MDDH}} \tag{3}$$

Gen() : $\cdots$

        Sample $z \leftarrow [1..Q]$ and $S \leftarrow 2^{[1..Q]\setminus\{z\}}$, such that $|S| = i$

        Sample $y \leftarrow [1..Q] \setminus (\{z\} \cup S)$

Sign(sk, $\boldsymbol{\mu}_j \in \mathbb{G}_1^n$) :

        Sample $(\boldsymbol{\rho},\ \theta,\ \phi,\ \text{TAG}) \leftarrow \mathbb{G}_1^k \times \mathbb{G}_1 \times \mathbb{G}_1 \times (\mathbb{Z}_q \setminus \{\text{TAG}_l\}_{l<j})$

        Let $\boldsymbol{\psi} := \text{TAG } \boldsymbol{\rho}$

        If $(j \notin S \cup \{y\})$ let $(\hat{\rho}, \gamma) :=$

          $\big(\mathbf{t} \cdot \boldsymbol{\rho},\ \mathbf{k} \cdot \boldsymbol{\mu}_j + [k_0]_1 + (\mathbf{d}_1 + d_2\mathbf{t}) \cdot \boldsymbol{\rho} + \text{TAG } (\mathbf{e}_1 + e_2\mathbf{t}) \cdot \boldsymbol{\rho}\big)$

        Else if $(j \in S)$ let $(\hat{\rho}, \gamma) :=$

          $(\theta,\ \phi)$

        Else if $(j = y)$ let $(\hat{\rho}, \gamma) :=$

Game 0 $\big(\mathbf{t} \cdot \boldsymbol{\rho},\ \mathbf{k} \cdot \boldsymbol{\mu}_y + [k_0]_1 + (\mathbf{d}_1 + d_2\mathbf{t}) \cdot \boldsymbol{\rho} + \text{TAG } (\mathbf{e}_1 + e_2\mathbf{t}) \cdot \boldsymbol{\rho}\big)$

Game 1 $\big(\theta,\ \mathbf{k} \cdot \boldsymbol{\mu}_y + [k_0]_1 + (\mathbf{d}_1 \cdot \boldsymbol{\rho} + d_2\theta) + \text{TAG } (\mathbf{e}_1 \cdot \boldsymbol{\rho} + e_2\theta))\big)$

Game 2 $(\theta,\ \phi)$

        Let $\boldsymbol{\pi} := \Pi.\text{sim}(\text{trap},\ (\boldsymbol{\mu}_j, \boldsymbol{\rho}, \hat{\rho}, \boldsymbol{\psi}, \gamma))$ and $\tau := [\text{TAG}]_2$

        Return $(\boldsymbol{\rho}, \hat{\rho}, \boldsymbol{\psi}, \gamma, \tau, \boldsymbol{\pi})$

WIN $\overset{\triangle}{=}$ WIN$_0$ and $\sigma^* = (\boldsymbol{\rho}^*, \hat{\rho}^*, \boldsymbol{\psi}^*, \gamma^*, \tau^*, \boldsymbol{\pi}^*)$:

        $\mathsf{e}(\gamma^*, [1]_2) \overset{?}{=} \mathsf{e}(\mathbf{k} \cdot \boldsymbol{\mu}^* + [k_0]_1 + \mathbf{d}_1 \cdot \boldsymbol{\rho}^* + d_2\hat{\rho}^*, [1]_2) + \mathsf{e}(\mathbf{e}_1 \cdot \boldsymbol{\rho}^* + e_2\hat{\rho}^*, \tau^*)$

Fig. 6. H Games and winning condition

Let $\mathcal{A}$ be any efficient adversary playing against $\mathcal{C}$ in either game $\mathbf{H_0}$ or $\mathbf{H_1}$. Using $\mathcal{A}$ and the challenger $\mathcal{C}$ we will build another adversary $\mathcal{A}'$ that plays against a $\mathcal{D}_k-\text{MDDH}$ challenger. So, suppose the MDDH challenger issues either a real tuple $([\mathbf{B}]_1, \boldsymbol{\zeta} = [\mathbf{B}\mathbf{r}]_1)$ or a fake tuple $([\mathbf{B}]_1, \boldsymbol{\zeta} = [\mathbf{r}']_1 \in \mathbb{G}_1^{k+1})$, with $\mathbf{B} \leftarrow \mathcal{D}_k$ and $(\mathbf{r},\ \mathbf{r}') \leftarrow \mathbb{Z}_q^k \times \mathbb{Z}_q^{k+1}$. In the first case, we will say that $\mathcal{A}'$ is in the MDDHREAL game and in the latter case, we will say that $\mathcal{A}'$ is in the MDDHFAKE game. $\mathcal{A}'$ uses $[\mathbf{B}]_1$ to simulate $\mathcal{C}$ in building the language parameters $\mathcal{L}_{\text{par}}$ by choosing all other random values on its own. It then simulates $\mathcal{C}$ for the rest of the game $\mathbf{H_0}/\mathbf{H_1}$, including interaction with $\mathcal{A}$, till the point of issuing the y-th signature. For the y-th signature, $\mathcal{A}'$ sets $(\boldsymbol{\rho}_y, \hat{\rho}_y) := \boldsymbol{\zeta}$, and picks TAG$_y$ at random, and sets $\boldsymbol{\psi}_y = \text{TAG}_y\ \boldsymbol{\rho}_y$. The values τ_y and γ_y and $\boldsymbol{\pi}_y$ can then be computed from values already obtained.

After $\mathcal{A}'$ issues this signature to $\mathcal{A}$, adversary $\mathcal{A}'$ continues the simulation of $\mathcal{C}$, along with its interaction with $\mathcal{A}$ till the computation and output of winning condition. $\mathcal{A}'$ outputs 1 iff WIN **and** GOOD. Now, note that if $\mathcal{A}'$ is in the MDDHREAL game, then the view of the adversary $\mathcal{A}$ is identical to its view in $\mathbf{H_0}$. And, if $\mathcal{A}'$ is in the MDDHFAKE game, then the view of the adversary $\mathcal{A}$ is identical to its view in $\mathbf{H_1}$. Thus:

$$\mathrm{Prob}[\mathcal{A}'(\mathrm{MDDHREAL}) = 1] = \mathrm{Prob}_{H_0}[\text{WIN } \textbf{and } \textsf{GOOD}]$$

$$\mathrm{Prob}[\mathcal{A}'(\mathrm{MDDHFAKE}) = 1] = \mathrm{Prob}_{H_1}[\text{WIN } \textbf{and } \textsf{GOOD}].$$

That completes the proof of the claim, as the maximum advantage any efficient adversary has in winning an MDDH-challenge game is $\mathrm{ADV}_{\mathcal{D}_k-\mathrm{MDDH}}$.

Game $\mathbf{H_2}$: In Game $\mathbf{H_2}$, in the computation of the signature on y-th query, the value γ_y is just sampled independently randomly from $\mathbb{Z}_q$. The winning condition remains WIN. We now prove that the view of the adversary in Games $\mathbf{H_2}$ and $\mathbf{H_1}$ is statistically indistinguishable. More precisely,

$$|\mathrm{Prob}_{H_2}[\text{WIN } \textbf{and } \textsf{GOOD}] - \mathrm{Prob}_{H_1}[\text{WIN } \textbf{and } \textsf{GOOD}]| \leq 1/q$$

The claim is a consequence of private hash on a non-$Span([\mathbf{B}]_1)$ word being random and independent of the public universal$_2$ projection hash key [CS02]. Here, the public universal$_2$ projection hash key is the pair $[\mathbf{d}_1 + d_2\mathbf{t}]_1$ and $[\mathbf{e}_1 + e_2\mathbf{t}]_1$, with private universal$_2$ hash key $(\mathbf{d}_1, d_2, \mathbf{e}_1, e_2)$. The public hash key is given to the adversary as part of all the signatures issued to the adversary, with the exception of the signature issued by $\mathcal{C}$ on query index y. In the y-th query, the challenger discloses to the adversary one private hash on a non-$Span([\mathbf{B}]_1)$ word. In particular $\boldsymbol{\gamma}_y$ includes as an additive term $(\mathbf{d}_1 \cdot \boldsymbol{\rho}_y + d_2\hat{\rho}_y) + \mathrm{TAG}_y (\mathbf{e}_1 \cdot \boldsymbol{\rho}_y + e_2\hat{\rho}_y)$, which is exactly the private universal$_2$ hash on $(\boldsymbol{\rho}_y, \hat{\rho}_y)$ using tag t_y. Now note that GOOD and $z \neq y$ implies $\mathrm{TAG}^* \neq \mathrm{TAG}_y$, as y was chosen distinct from z. Thus, TAG^* is different from TAG_y used in the one private hash given to the adversary on a non-$Span([\mathbf{B}]_1)$ word.

Recall that the QA-NIZK proof is simulated, and the QA-NIZK simulator trapdoors do not use $(\mathbf{d}_1, d_2, \mathbf{e}_1, e_2)$. Further, $(\mathbf{d}_1, d_2, \mathbf{e}_1, e_2)$ are not used anywhere else, including CRS_v.

Thus the additive term $(\mathbf{d}_1 \cdot \boldsymbol{\rho}_y + d_2\hat{\rho}_y) + \mathrm{TAG}_y (\mathbf{e}_1 \cdot \boldsymbol{\rho}_y + e_2\hat{\rho}_y)$ in γ_y (in Game $\mathbf{H_1}$) completely hides $([k_0]_1 + \mathbf{k} \cdot \boldsymbol{\mu}_y)$. Thus, γ_y can just as well be sampled independently randomly. This is the same as Game $\mathbf{H_2}$, and that proves the claim.

Thus, collecting all the inequalities, between consecutive games from $\mathbf{H_0}$ to $\mathbf{H_2}$, it follows that:

$$\left| \begin{array}{l} \mathrm{Prob}_{5,i-1}[\text{WIN } \textbf{and } \textsf{GOOD}] \\ -\mathrm{Prob}_{5,i}[\text{WIN } \textbf{and } \textsf{GOOD}] \end{array} \right| \leq \mathrm{ADV}_{\mathcal{D}_k-\mathrm{MDDH}} + 1/q$$

Proof (of Lemma 4). The proof of this lemma is similar to proof of Lemma 3, except that the predicate GOOD here is just defined to be true. The proof of

Lemma 3 goes through all the hybrid games with predicate GOOD defined as true, except for the proof of

$$|\text{Prob}_{H_2}[\text{WIN and GOOD}] - \text{Prob}_{H_1}[\text{WIN and GOOD}]| \leq 1/q.$$

This proof for Lemma 3 required the fact that GOOD implies that $\text{TAG}^* \neq \text{TAG}_y$, where y was the query index being simulated with a fake MDDH tuple. Since, here we have defined GOOD to be true, there is no such restriction on TAG^*.

In case $\text{TAG}^* \neq \text{TAG}_y$, the proof continues to hold as before. If $\text{TAG}^* = \text{TAG}_y$, we note that since we are in various hybrids of initial game $\mathbf{H_0} = \mathbf{G_{5,Q-1}}$, no signature generated by $\mathcal{C}$ (other than the y-th signature) uses k_0 or $\mathbf{k}$. The trapdoors k_0 and $\mathbf{k}$ are also not used in generation of public key. Thus, the only information available to $\mathcal{A}$ about k_0 and $\mathbf{k}$ is through the y-th signature simulation, which includes $\mathbf{k} \cdot \boldsymbol{\mu}_y + [k_0]_1$ as an additive term. Thus, for WIN to hold, $\mathcal{A}$ must produce $\gamma^* - (\mathbf{d_1} \cdot \boldsymbol{\rho}^* + d_2 \hat{\rho}^*) - \text{TAG}^* (\mathbf{e_1} \cdot \boldsymbol{\rho}^* + e_2 \hat{\rho}^*)$ equal to $\mathbf{k} \cdot \boldsymbol{\mu}^* + [k_0]_1$. By simple linear algebra, this latter quantity is random, even given $\mathbf{k} \cdot \boldsymbol{\mu}_y + [k_0]_1$, for $\boldsymbol{\mu}^* \neq \boldsymbol{\mu}_y$.

This linear algebra fact is most conveniently seen by the following information-theoretic argument: Let $\alpha \overset{\triangle}{=} \mathbf{k} \cdot \boldsymbol{\mu}_y + [k_0]_1$ and $\beta \overset{\triangle}{=} \mathbf{k} \cdot \boldsymbol{\mu}^* + [k_0]_1$. Now sample $(\mathbf{k}, \ k') \leftarrow \mathbb{Z}_q^n \times \mathbb{Z}_q$, and then set $[k_0]_1 := [k']_1 - \mathbf{k} \cdot \boldsymbol{\mu}_y$. Then we have $\alpha = [k']_1$ and $\beta = [k']_1 + \mathbf{k} \cdot (\boldsymbol{\mu}^* - \boldsymbol{\mu}_y)$. Thus α is uniformly random and independent of $\mathbf{k}$, while β has an independent uniformly random distribution due to the additional term $\mathbf{k} \cdot (\boldsymbol{\mu}^* - \boldsymbol{\mu}_y)$, where $\mathbf{k}$ is uniformly random and $(\boldsymbol{\mu}^* - \boldsymbol{\mu}_y)$ is non-zero.

3.2   Improved Security Reduction for the SPS Scheme

Theorem 3. *For any efficient adversary $\mathcal{A}$, which makes at most Q signature queries before attempting a forgery, its probability of success in the EUF-CMA game against the SPS scheme is at most*

$$\text{ADV}_{\Pi}^{TSS} + Q \cdot (2 + \log Q) \cdot \left(\text{ADV}_{\mathcal{D}_k - \text{MDDH}} + \frac{1}{q}\right) + \frac{Q^2}{2q} + \frac{1}{q}$$

Proof. In the proof of this theorem and related lemmas, without loss of generality, we will assume that the number of signature queries Q made by the adversary is a power of two. This can cause at most a factor of two difference in the success probability of the adversary.

The Games $\mathbf{G_0}$ to $\mathbf{G_6}$ are same as in proof of Theorem 2. However, we now obtain a better upper bound on the probability of event WIN holding in Game $\mathbf{G_5}$, as opposed to the bound obtained in Lemma 1.

Lemma 5.

$$\text{Prob}_5[\text{WIN}] \leq Q \cdot (2 + \log Q) \cdot (\text{ADV}_{\mathcal{D}_k - \text{MDDH}} + 1/q)$$

Gen() :   · · ·

Game $\mathbf{G_{5,Q-2^{l}-u}}$ Sample $Z \leftarrow 2^{[1..Q]}$, such that $|Z| = 2^l$

Game $\mathbf{G'_{5,Q-2^{l}}}$ Sample $Z \leftarrow 2^{[1..Q]}$, such that $|Z| = 2^l/2$

Sample $S \leftarrow 2^{[1..Q]\setminus Z}$, such that $|S| = i$

Sign(sk, $\boldsymbol{\mu}_j \in \mathbb{G}_1^n$) :

Sample $(\boldsymbol{\rho}, \theta, \phi, \text{TAG}) \leftarrow \mathbb{G}_1^k \times \mathbb{G}_1 \times \mathbb{G}_1 \times (\mathbb{Z}_q \setminus \{\text{TAG}_l\}_{l<j})$

Let $\psi := \text{TAG} \, \boldsymbol{\rho}$

If $(j \notin S)$ let $(\hat{\rho}, \gamma) :=$

$\quad \left(\mathbf{t} \cdot \boldsymbol{\rho}, \; \mathbf{k} \cdot \boldsymbol{\mu}_j + [k_0]_1 + (\mathbf{d}_1 + \mathbf{d}_2\mathbf{t}) \cdot \boldsymbol{\rho} + \text{TAG} \, (\mathbf{e}_1 + \mathbf{e}_2\mathbf{t}) \cdot \boldsymbol{\rho}\right)$

Else if $(j \in S)$ let $(\hat{\rho}, \gamma) :=$

$\quad (\theta, \; \phi)$

Let $\boldsymbol{\pi} := \Pi.\text{sim}(\text{trap}, \; (\boldsymbol{\mu}_j, \boldsymbol{\rho}, \hat{\rho}, \psi, \gamma))$ and $\tau := [\text{TAG}]_2$

Return $(\boldsymbol{\rho}, \hat{\rho}, \psi, \gamma, \tau, \boldsymbol{\pi})$

WIN $\stackrel{\triangle}{=}$ WIN$_0$ and $\sigma^* = (\boldsymbol{\rho}^*, \hat{\rho}^*, \psi^*, \gamma^*, \tau^*, \boldsymbol{\pi}^*)$:

$e(\gamma^*, [1]_2) \stackrel{?}{=} e(\mathbf{k} \cdot \boldsymbol{\mu}^* + [k_0]_1 + \mathbf{d}_1 \cdot \boldsymbol{\rho}^* + d_2\hat{\rho}^*, [1]_2)$

$\quad + e(\mathbf{e}_1 \cdot \boldsymbol{\rho}^* + e_2\hat{\rho}^*, \tau^*)$

Fig. 7. Modified Games $\mathbf{G_{5,i}}$. Above, $\log Q \leq l \leq 0$ and $0 \leq u \leq 2^l - 1$.

Proof. Again, to prove this lemma we consider several hybrid Games $\mathbf{G_{5,i}}$, for $i \in [0..Q]$, where $\mathbf{G_{5,0}}$ will turn out to be same as $\mathbf{G_5}$, and $\mathbf{G_{5,Q}}$ will turn out to be same as $\mathbf{G_6}$. The hybrid Games $\mathbf{G_{5,i}}$ are defined slightly differently in this proof as compared to the proof of Lemma 1. These are summarized in Fig. 7 and explained below.

Game $\mathbf{G_{5,i}}$: For $0 \leq i < Q$, the game differs from $\mathbf{G_5}$ as follows: After it has generated the public key and sent it to $\mathcal{A}$ just as in $\mathbf{G_5}$, the challenger now picks a random set Z of size $2^{\lfloor \log(Q-i) \rfloor}$ of distinct indices from $[1..Q]$. It then picks i distinct indices randomly from $[1..Q] \setminus Z$. Call this set of indices as S (note that S is empty in Game $\mathbf{G_{5,0}}$). If $i = Q$, let S be the full set $[1..Q]$. While generating signatures on a query with index $j \in S$, the challenger generates the signature as in Game $\mathbf{G_6}$ (i.e., samples γ and $\hat{\rho}$ uniformly randomly), and for all other queries it generates the signature as in Game $\mathbf{G_5}$. The winning predicate for the adversary remains the same, i.e., WIN.

Note that for hybrid Game $\mathbf{G_{5,i}}$, such that $(Q - i)$ is a power of two, the union of disjoint sets S and Z is the complete set of indices $[1..Q]$. However, in the next hybrid Game $\mathbf{G_{5,i+1}}$, the set Z is cut by half in size, so that there is a choice to pick S from $[1..Q] \setminus Z$. Thus, to relate such a hybrid Game $\mathbf{G_{5,i}}$ (i.e. when $Q - i$ is a power of two) to the next hybrid Game $\mathbf{G_{5,i+1}}$, we introduce an intermediate Game $\mathbf{G'_{5,i}}$.

For i, define Game $\mathbf{G'_{5,i}}$ to be similar to Game $\mathbf{G_{5,i}}$ except that the set of random and distinct indices Z is chosen to be of size 2^{l-1}. For S, we choose i distinct indices from $[1..Q] \setminus Z$, as before. The rest of the game and the winning condition remains the same.

For each hybrid Game $\mathbf{G_{5,i}}$ or $\mathbf{G'_{5,i}}$, define the following predicate

$$\mathsf{GOOD} \triangleq \forall j \in [1..Q] \setminus Z : (\tau^* \neq \tau_j)$$

In Lemma 6 below, we show that for $i = Q - 2^l$, the probability of WIN and GOOD holding in Game $\mathbf{G_{5,i}}$ is at most two times the probability of WIN and GOOD holding in Game $\mathbf{G'_{5,i}}$. Note that, for $i = 0$ the predicate GOOD is equivalent to true, as Z is the complete set. Thus, this implies that the probability of WIN holding in Game $\mathbf{G_5}$ is at most two times the probability of WIN and GOOD holding in Game $\mathbf{G'_{5,0}}$.

Using Lemmas 6 and 7 below, we now prove the recurrence relation that for $l \in [2.. \log Q]$:

$$\mathrm{Prob}_{\mathbf{G'_{5,Q-2^l}}}[\mathsf{WIN \ and \ GOOD}] \leq 2^{l-1} \cdot (\mathrm{ADV}_{\mathcal{D}_k - \mathrm{MDDH}} + 1/q) +$$
$$2 \cdot \mathrm{Prob}_{\mathbf{G'_{5,Q-2^{l-1}}}}[\mathsf{WIN \ and \ GOOD}]$$

Also, as a base case we have (from Lemma 7),

$$\mathrm{Prob}_{\mathbf{G'_{5,Q-2}}}[\mathsf{WIN \ and \ GOOD}] \leq 2 \cdot (\mathrm{ADV}_{\mathcal{D}_k - \mathrm{MDDH}} + 1/q) +$$
$$\mathrm{Prob}_{\mathbf{G_{5,Q}}}[\mathsf{WIN \ and \ GOOD}]$$

However, in the proof of Lemma 1, we established that in the last hybrid Game $\mathbf{G_{5,Q}}$, the probability of WIN is at most $1/q$. Thus,

$$\mathrm{Prob}_{\mathbf{G'_{5,Q-2}}}[\mathsf{WIN \ and \ GOOD}] \leq 2 \cdot \mathrm{ADV}_{\mathcal{D}_k - \mathrm{MDDH}} + 3/q$$

Thus, by maintaining the induction hypothesis, for every $l \in [1.. \log Q]$:

$$\mathrm{Prob}_{\mathbf{G'_{5,Q-2^l}}}[\mathsf{WIN \ and \ GOOD}] \leq (2^{l-1}l + 2^l) \cdot (\mathrm{ADV}_{\mathcal{D}_k - \mathrm{MDDH}} + 1/q)$$

we get by induction that

$$\mathrm{Prob}_{\mathbf{G'_{5,0}}}[\mathsf{WIN \ and \ GOOD}] \leq \left(\frac{Q}{2} \cdot \log Q + Q\right) \cdot (\mathrm{ADV}_{\mathcal{D}_k - \mathrm{MDDH}} + 1/q)$$

Lemma 6. *For $i \in [0..Q-1]$, and $i = Q - 2^l$,*

$$\mathrm{Prob}_{\mathbf{G_{5,i}}}[\mathsf{WIN} \text{ and } \mathsf{GOOD}] \leq 2 \cdot \mathrm{Prob}_{\mathbf{G'_{5,i}}}[\mathsf{WIN} \text{ and } \mathsf{GOOD}]$$

Proof. For i, $0 \leq i < Q$, such that $(Q-i)$ a power of two, note that the Game $\mathbf{G_{5,i}}$ can be defined by first picking a set S of i distinct and random indices from $[1..Q]$, and then setting $Z = [1..Q] \setminus S$. Similarly, the Game $\mathbf{G'_{5,i}}$ can be defined by first picking a set S of i distinct indices, and then picking a set Z' of $(Q-i)/2$ distinct and random indices from $Z = [1..Q] \setminus S$. This set can be picked after the adversary has replied with its claimed forgery. In other words, the probability of WIN and GOOD holding in $\mathbf{G'_{5,i}}$ is same as probability of WIN and GOOD' holding in $\mathbf{G_{5,i}}$ where GOOD' is defined as

$$\mathsf{GOOD'} \overset{\triangle}{=} \forall j \in [1..Q] \setminus Z' : (\tau^* \neq \tau_j)$$

Letting DIST stand for the predicate $\forall j \in [1..Q] : (\tau^* \neq \tau_j)$, it follows that GOOD' and GOOD and ¬DIST is equivalent to GOOD' and ¬DIST. Thus,

$$\Pr[\mathsf{GOOD'} \mid \neg\mathsf{DIST} \text{ and } \mathsf{WIN}] = \Pr[\mathsf{GOOD'} \mid \mathsf{GOOD} \text{ and } \neg\mathsf{DIST} \text{ and } \mathsf{WIN}]$$
$$\cdot \Pr[\mathsf{GOOD} \mid \neg\mathsf{DIST} \text{ and } \mathsf{WIN}]$$

Now, $\Pr[\mathsf{GOOD'} \mid \mathsf{GOOD} \text{ and } \neg\mathsf{DIST} \text{ and } \mathsf{WIN}]$ is exactly $1/2$. Thus, noting that GOOD is equivalent to $\mathsf{DIST} \vee (\mathsf{GOOD} \text{ and } \neg\mathsf{DIST})$, and GOOD' is equivalent to $\mathsf{DIST} \vee (\mathsf{GOOD'} \text{ and } \neg\mathsf{DIST})$, it follows that

$$\Pr[\mathsf{GOOD} \mid \mathsf{WIN}] = \Pr[\mathsf{DIST} \mid \mathsf{WIN}]$$
$$+ \Pr[\mathsf{GOOD} \mid \neg\mathsf{DIST} \text{ and } \mathsf{WIN}] \cdot \Pr[\neg\mathsf{DIST} \mid \mathsf{WIN}] \quad (4)$$

$$\Pr[\mathsf{GOOD'} \mid \mathsf{WIN}] = \Pr[\mathsf{DIST} \mid \mathsf{WIN}]$$
$$+ \frac{1}{2}\Pr[\mathsf{GOOD} \mid \neg\mathsf{DIST} \text{ and } \mathsf{WIN}] \cdot \Pr[\neg\mathsf{DIST} \mid \mathsf{WIN}] \quad (5)$$

Now, this implies $\Pr[\mathsf{GOOD} \mid \mathsf{WIN}] \leq 2 \cdot \Pr[\mathsf{GOOD'} \mid \mathsf{WIN}]$, because otherwise we obtain a contradiction that $\Pr[\mathsf{DIST} \mid \mathsf{WIN}] < 0$. Thus,

$$\Pr[\mathsf{WIN} \text{ and } \mathsf{GOOD}] \leq 2 \cdot \Pr[\mathsf{WIN} \text{ and } \mathsf{GOOD'}]$$

Lemma 7. *For $i \in [1..Q]$, if $(Q-i+1)$ is a power of two and $i \neq Q$, then*

$$\left| \begin{matrix} \mathrm{Prob}_{\mathbf{G'_{5,i-1}}}[\mathsf{WIN} \text{ and } \mathsf{GOOD}] \\ -\mathrm{Prob}_{\mathbf{G_{5,i}}}[\mathsf{WIN} \text{ and } \mathsf{GOOD}] \end{matrix} \right| \leq \mathrm{ADV}_{\mathcal{D}_k-\mathrm{MDDH}} + 1/q$$

Otherwise (i.e., if $(Q-i+1)$ is not a power of two or $i = Q$),

$$\left| \begin{matrix} \mathrm{Prob}_{\mathbf{G_{5,i-1}}}[\mathsf{WIN} \text{ and } \mathsf{GOOD}] \\ -\mathrm{Prob}_{\mathbf{G_{5,i}}}[\mathsf{WIN} \text{ and } \mathsf{GOOD}] \end{matrix} \right| \leq \mathrm{ADV}_{\mathcal{D}_k-\mathrm{MDDH}} + 1/q$$

The proof of Lemma 7 is same as that for the proof of Lemma 3 (except for i equal to Q, when it is same as proof of Lemma 4). The only difference is in the proof of

$$|\mathrm{Prob}_{\mathbf{H_2}}[\mathsf{WIN} \text{ and } \mathsf{GOOD}] - \mathrm{Prob}_{\mathbf{H_1}}[\mathsf{WIN} \text{ and } \mathsf{GOOD}]| \leq 1/q$$

where we now argue that GOOD and $y \notin Z$ implies $t^* \neq t_y$.

Alternate Improved Reduction. The above reduction makes discrete 'big jumps' when $Q-i$ is a power of two and a series of smooth 'short jumps' in between these big jumps. Instead, we can smoothen the entire jump sequence by shortening the set Z by 1 at every i while going from a primed game to an unprimed game. In an unprimed game, Z and S will partition the set $[1..Q]$, while in a primed game there will be $Q - i$ choices for Z'. This will result in the following modifications of Lemmas 6 and 7 :

Lemma 8. *For $i \in [0..Q - 2]$,*

$$\mathrm{Prob}_{\mathbf{G_{5,i}}}[\mathsf{WIN} \text{ and } \mathsf{GOOD}] \leq \frac{Q - i}{Q - i - 1} \cdot \mathrm{Prob}_{\mathbf{G'_{5,i}}}[\mathsf{WIN} \text{ and } \mathsf{GOOD}]$$

Lemma 9. *For $i \in [1..Q - 1]$,*

$$\left| \begin{array}{l} \mathrm{Prob}_{\mathbf{G'_{5,i-1}}}[\mathsf{WIN} \text{ and } \mathsf{GOOD}] \\ -\mathrm{Prob}_{\mathbf{G_{5,i}}}[\mathsf{WIN} \text{ and } \mathsf{GOOD}] \end{array} \right| \leq \mathrm{ADV}_{\mathcal{D}_k-\mathrm{MDDH}} + 1/q$$

and

$$\left| \begin{array}{l} \mathrm{Prob}_{\mathbf{G_{5,Q-1}}}[\mathsf{WIN} \text{ and } \mathsf{GOOD}] \\ -\mathrm{Prob}_{\mathbf{G_{5,Q}}}[\mathsf{WIN} \text{ and } \mathsf{GOOD}] \end{array} \right| \leq \mathrm{ADV}_{\mathcal{D}_k-\mathrm{MDDH}} + 1/q$$

However, this still results in a $Q \log Q$ loss in security.

Acknowledgments. The authors would like to thank the anonymous referees for helpful comments and filling a couple of gaps in the submission.

References

[ACD+12] Abe, M., Chase, M., David, B., Kohlweiss, M., Nishimaki, R., Ohkubo, M.: Constant-size structure-preserving signatures: generic constructions and simple assumptions. In: Wang, X., Sako, K. (eds.) ASIACRYPT 2012. LNCS, vol. 7658, pp. 4–24. Springer, Heidelberg (2012). doi:10.1007/978-3-642-34961-4_3

[ACHO11] Abe, M., Chow, S.S.M., Haralambiev, K., Ohkubo, M.: Double-trapdoor anonymous tags for traceable signatures. In: Lopez, J., Tsudik, G. (eds.) ACNS 2011. LNCS, vol. 6715, pp. 183–200. Springer, Heidelberg (2011). doi:10.1007/978-3-642-21554-4_11

[ADK+13] Abe, M., David, B., Kohlweiss, M., Nishimaki, R., Ohkubo, M.: Tagged one-time signatures: tight security and optimal tag size. In: Kurosawa, K., Hanaoka, G. (eds.) PKC 2013. LNCS, vol. 7778, pp. 312–331. Springer, Heidelberg (2013). doi:10.1007/978-3-642-36362-7_20

[AFG+10] Abe, M., Fuchsbauer, G., Groth, J., Haralambiev, K., Ohkubo, M.: Structure-preserving signatures and commitments to group elements. In: Rabin, T. (ed.) CRYPTO 2010. LNCS, vol. 6223, pp. 209–236. Springer, Heidelberg (2010). doi:10.1007/978-3-642-14623-7_12

[AGHO11] Abe, M., Groth, J., Haralambiev, K., Ohkubo, M.: Optimal structure-preserving signatures in asymmetric bilinear groups. In: Rogaway, P. (ed.) CRYPTO 2011. LNCS, vol. 6841, pp. 649–666. Springer, Heidelberg (2011). doi:10.1007/978-3-642-22792-9_37

[AGO11] Abe, M., Groth, J., Ohkubo, M.: Separating short structure-preserving signatures from non-interactive assumptions. In: Lee, D.H., Wang, X. (eds.) ASIACRYPT 2011. LNCS, vol. 7073, pp. 628–646. Springer, Heidelberg (2011). doi:10.1007/978-3-642-25385-0_34

[AHO10] Abe, M., Haralambiev, K., Ohkubo, M.: Signing on elements in bilinear groups for modular protocol design. IACR Cryptology ePrint Archive, p. 133 (2010)

[AO09] Abe, M., Ohkubo, M.: A framework for universally composable non-committing blind signatures. In: Matsui, M. (ed.) ASIACRYPT 2009. LNCS, vol. 5912, pp. 435–450. Springer, Heidelberg (2009). doi:10.1007/978-3-642-10366-7_26

[CCS09] Camenisch, J., Chandran, N., Shoup, V.: A public key encryption scheme secure against key dependent chosen plaintext and adaptive chosen ciphertext attacks. In: Joux, A. (ed.) EUROCRYPT 2009. LNCS, vol. 5479, pp. 351–368. Springer, Heidelberg (2009). doi:10.1007/978-3-642-01001-9_20

[CL04] Camenisch, J., Lysyanskaya, A.: Signature schemes and anonymous credentials from bilinear maps. In: Franklin, M. (ed.) CRYPTO 2004. LNCS, vol. 3152, pp. 56–72. Springer, Heidelberg (2004). doi:10.1007/978-3-540-28628-8_4

[CLY09] Cathalo, J., Libert, B., Yung, M.: Group encryption: non-interactive realization in the standard model. In: Matsui, M. (ed.) ASIACRYPT 2009. LNCS, vol. 5912, pp. 179–196. Springer, Heidelberg (2009). doi:10.1007/978-3-642-10366-7_11

[CS02] Cramer, R., Shoup, V.: Universal hash proofs and a paradigm for adaptive chosen ciphertext secure public-key encryption. In: Knudsen, L.R. (ed.) EUROCRYPT 2002. LNCS, vol. 2332, pp. 45–64. Springer, Heidelberg (2002). doi:10.1007/3-540-46035-7_4

[EHK+13] Escala, A., Herold, G., Kiltz, E., Ràfols, C., Villar, J.: An algebraic framework for diffie-hellman assumptions. In: Canetti, R., Garay, J.A. (eds.) CRYPTO 2013. LNCS, vol. 8043, pp. 129–147. Springer, Heidelberg (2013). doi:10.1007/978-3-642-40084-1_8

[Fuc11] Fuchsbauer, G.: Commuting signatures and verifiable encryption. In: Paterson, K.G. (ed.) EUROCRYPT 2011. LNCS, vol. 6632, pp. 224–245. Springer, Heidelberg (2011). doi:10.1007/978-3-642-20465-4_14

[Fuc09] Fuchsbauer, G.: Automorphic signatures in bilinear groups and an application to round-optimal blind signatures. IACR Cryptology ePrint Archive, p. 320 (2009)

[GH08] Green, M., Hohenberger, S.: Universally composable adaptive oblivious transfer. In: Pieprzyk, J. (ed.) ASIACRYPT 2008. LNCS, vol. 5350, pp. 179–197. Springer, Heidelberg (2008). doi:10.1007/978-3-540-89255-7_12

[Gro06] Groth, J.: Simulation-sound NIZK proofs for a practical language and constant size group signatures. In: Lai, X., Chen, K. (eds.) ASIACRYPT 2006. LNCS, vol. 4284, pp. 444–459. Springer, Heidelberg (2006). doi:10.1007/11935230_29

[GS08] Groth, J., Sahai, A.: Efficient non-interactive proof systems for bilinear groups. In: Smart, N. (ed.) EUROCRYPT 2008. LNCS, vol. 4965, pp. 415–432. Springer, Heidelberg (2008). doi:10.1007/978-3-540-78967-3_24

[Har11] Haralambiev, K.: Efficient cryptographic primitives for non-interactive zero-knowledge proofs and applications. Ph.D. dissertation (2011)

[JR13]   Jutla, C.S., Roy, A.: Shorter quasi-adaptive NIZK proofs for linear subspaces. In: Sako, K., Sarkar, P. (eds.) ASIACRYPT 2013. LNCS, vol. 8269, pp. 1–20. Springer, Heidelberg (2013). doi:10.1007/978-3-642-42033-7_1

[KPW15] Kiltz, E., Pan, J., Wee, H.: Structure-preserving signatures from standard assumptions, revisited. In: Gennaro, R., Robshaw, M. (eds.) CRYPTO 2015. LNCS, vol. 9216, pp. 275–295. Springer, Heidelberg (2015). doi:10.1007/978-3-662-48000-7_14

[KW15]   Kiltz, E., Wee, H.: Quasi-adaptive NIZK for linear subspaces revisited. In: Oswald, E., Fischlin, M. (eds.) EUROCRYPT 2015. LNCS, vol. 9057, pp. 101–128. Springer, Heidelberg (2015). doi:10.1007/978-3-662-46803-6_4

[LPY15] Libert, B., Peters, T., Yung, M.: Short group signatures via structure-preserving signatures: standard model security from simple assumptions. In: Gennaro, R., Robshaw, M. (eds.) CRYPTO 2015. LNCS, vol. 9216, pp. 296–316. Springer, Heidelberg (2015). doi:10.1007/978-3-662-48000-7_15

[Pol78] Pollard, J.M.: Monte carlo methods for index computation (mod p). Math. Comp. **32**, 918–924 (1978)

Fully Homomorphic Encryption

Chosen-Ciphertext Secure Fully Homomorphic Encryption

Ran Canetti[1,3], Srinivasan Raghuraman[2], Silas Richelson[1,2(✉)],
and Vinod Vaikuntanathan[2]

[1] Boston University, Boston, USA
silas.richelson@gmail.com
[2] MIT, Cambridge, USA
[3] Tel-Aviv University & CPIIS, Tel Aviv, Israel

Abstract. We give three fully homomoprhic encryption (FHE) schemes
that are secure against non-adaptive chosen ciphertext attacks (CCA1).
For the first two, we extend the generic transformation of Boneh, Canetti,
Halevi and Katz to turn any multi-key identity-based FHE scheme into
a CCA1-secure FHE scheme. We then show two instantiations of multi-
key identity-based FHE: One from LWE in the random oracle model, and
one from sub-exponentially secure indistinguishability obfuscation. Both
constructions are compact with respect to the function evaluated homomorphically but not compact with respect to the number of ciphertext
involved in the homomorphic evaluation. The third scheme uses succinct
non-interactive arguments of knowledge (SNARKs) and is fully compact.

1 Introduction

Fully homomorphic encryption (FHE) [RAD78, Gen09, BV11] is a powerful cryptographic primitive that allows anyone to compute on encrypted data without
decrypting it, and without knowledge of the secret key. The basic security property considered for FHE is semantic security [GM84], also known as security
against chosen plaintext attacks (CPA), where it is required that an adversary
that has access to the public parameters cannot distinguish between ciphertexts
that result from encrypting two adversarially chosen plaintexts. This should hold
even though the public parameters allow for encrypting messages and for homomorphic evaluation of ciphertexts.

However, CPA security provides only a weak guarantee in settings where
ciphertexts can be generated maliciously. Indeed, it is easy to come up (either
intentionally or unintentionally) with CPA-secure encryption schemes where one

Research supported in part by DARPA and the U.S. Army Office under contract
number W911NF-15-C-0226 and W911NF-15-C-0236, NSF CAREER Award CNS-
1350619, NSF Grant CNS-1413964 (MACS: A Modular Approach to Computer Security, Israel Science Foundation grant, Alfred P. Sloan Research Fellowship, Microsoft
Faculty Fellowship, NEC Corporation, a Steven and Renee Finn Career Development
Chair from MIT, and a SIMONS Investigator Award Agreement Dated 6-5-12.

S. Fehr (Ed.): PKC 2017, Part II, LNCS 10175, pp. 213–240, 2017.
DOI: 10.1007/978-3-662-54388-7_8

can maliciously generate ciphertexts that completely compromise the security of the scheme. The same holds, of course, for CPA-secure FHE schemes, So, for instance, a client that sends a ciphertext $c = Enc(x)$ along with a function f to a server, expecting to obtain a ciphertext $c' = HomEval(f, c)$ that decrypts to $f(x)$, may instead receive a maliciously formed ciphertext c'' such that $Dec(c'')$ will output the secret decryption key which allows the server to fully recover x. This is so even when using CPA-secure FHE, and even when x is much larger than both the decryption key and c''. Such attacks can indeed be taken care of by adding verifiability mechanisms "at the protocol level" on top of plain CPA-secure FHE schemes. However, can we have FHE scheme that guarantee, in of themselves, security against malformed ciphertexts?

The golden standard of security for encryption schemes against malformed ciphertetxts is security against chosen ciphertext attacks, also called CCA security (see, e.g., [NY90, RS91, DDN91, CS98, Sah99] and more) which requires that semantic security holds even when the adversary gets to ask for decryption queries. CCA security comes in two flavors: the non-adaptive flavor, called CCA1 or lunchtime attack, where the adversary is limited to ask decryption queries before she receives the challenge ciphertext, and the adaptive, or CCA2 version, where she can continue asking decryption queries even after she receives the challenge ciphertext (as long as the decryption queries are different from the challenge ciphertext itself).

CCA2 security prevents any meaningful modification of a given ciphertext, and so appears to be in direct contradiction with homomorphism (althought some works do manage to reconcile the two notions in a meaningful way, see e.g. [CKN03, BSW12]). However, CCA1 security, which does consider security in face of malformed ciphertexts, but only ones that were generated before the challenge ciphertext is given, does not appear to be in contratiction for homomorphism. Indeed, the Cramer-Shoup-lite [CS98] scheme is both CCA1-secure and *additively* homomorphic. Still, several works [LMSV10, ZPS12, DGM15] show CCA1 attacks against (leveled) FHE schemes.[1] Moreover, the key paradigm for constructing unleveled FHE schemes goes through Gentry's bootstrapping theorem [Gen09], wherein one publishes a circular encryption of the secret key as part of the public evaluation key, an approach that by its very definition falls to a CCA1 attack.

Loftus et al. [LMSV10] give a *leveled* CCA1-secure FHE scheme under a highly non-standard "lattice-based knowledge assumption". This state of affairs leads us to ask:

Can we construct CCA1-secure fully homomorphic encryption schemes under better-understood computational assumptions? Can they be unleveled? Can they be compact?

---

[1] A leveled FHE scheme is one that permits evaluation of circuits of a-priori bounded polynomial depth on encrypted data. In contrast, a pure FHE scheme is one that permits evaluation of circuits of any depth.

1.1   Our Results and Techniques

We answer the above question positively.

CCA1-Secure FHE from Multi-key Identity-Based FHE. Our starting point is the work of Boneh et al. [BCHK07] who showed that any (semantically secure) identity-based encryption scheme can be used to construct a chosen-ciphertext-secure encryption scheme. An encryption of a message m in their (CCA1) construction is simply an ID-based encryption of m *under a randomly chosen identity*. Namely, the public key of the scheme is the IBE master public key, and the encryptor chooses a fresh random id every time, and outputs IBE.Enc(mpk, id, m). In a nutshell, CCA1-security of the scheme follows from the fact that an ID-based encryption under an identity id* is secure even given the secret keys for all identities id $\neq$ id*.

A natural idea to get a CCA1 *fully homomorphic* encryption scheme is to start with an Id-based *fully homomorphic* encryption scheme. This runs into a difficulty since in an FHE scheme, one has to be able to homomorphically evaluate ciphertexts that come from different sources (encryptors) but all encrypted to the same person (i.e., encrypted under the same public key). When we use the [BCHK07] transformation, this translates to being able to compute on IBE ciphertexts that all use the same master public key, but different identities. This leads us to our first connection: we define the notion of a multi-key Id-based FHE (IBFHE) scheme, and show that being able to construct one directly gives us a CCA1-secure FHE scheme.

This immediately gives two constructions of leveled CCA1 FHE based on two prior constructions of leveled multi-key IBFHE. The first is a generic construction from leveled multi-key FHE and IBE due to Brakerski, Cash, Tsabary and Wee [BCTW16]. Their scheme is very simple: to encrypt, draw a key pair and encrypt using the multi-key FHE; also encrypt the secret key using IBE. The second construction is based on LWE in the random oracle model, due to Clear and McGoldrick [CM15]. See Sect. 3 for our adaptation of the proof of [BCHK07], and more information on these transformations.

Obfuscation Construction. Recently, [CLTV15] showed how to use indistinguishability obfuscation to build homomorphism into an encryption scheme by publishing an obfuscation of a program which decrypts a pair of ciphertexts, evaluates and re-encrypts. Crucial to the proof of security is the ability to switch the underlying encryption scheme to lossy mode so that the output of the program which behaves honestly is statistically close to the output of the program which ignores the inputs and outputs an encryption of 0. We use this same idea, though in our setting things are more complex as we need to have the program continue to output valid encryptions for all identities except for the challenge. This is our main construction and is presented in Sect. 4.

A Note on Compactness. Compactness in FHE requires that the complexity of decryption (and thus ciphertext size) does not grow too much with the complexity of the function being evaluated. This prevents trivial schemes where the evaluator simply sends the circuit to be evaluated to the decryptor who decrypts and then evaluates the circuit. The ciphertexts in all of the above mentioned schemes grow with the number of inputs to the circuit to be evaluated, but not with the complexity of the circuit. We refer to such schemes as compact w.r.t. circuit complexity and we stress that this is *less ideal* than true compactness. The generic construction inherently is only compact w.r.t. circuit size (even if the underlying multi-key FHE is truly compact). The LWE and IO based constructions are also only compact w.r.t. circuit complexity, though it is not clear that this is inherent. Obtaining a truly compact CCA1 FHE would represent progress in either case, and would be particularly important for the LWE scheme as this would improve other constructions which have used the multi-key FHE scheme of [CM15]. We note that in many use cases multiple inputs to the FHE can be "batched together" and encrypted with the same key in order to keep ciphertext growth small.

CCA1 FHE from Knowledge Assumptions. Naor and Yung [NY90] show how to go from CPA encryption to CCA1 encryption using non-interactive zero-knowledge proofs (NIZKs). The CCA1 ciphertext is simply a (pair of) CPA ciphertexts along with a NIZK proving correctness. We adopt this approach to the FHE setting. We replace the NIZK with a zero-knowledge succinct non-interactive argument of knowledge (zkSNARK) to preserve compactness since otherwise the proof length would grow with the circuit being evaluated. This construction is described in Sect. 5.

Another Approach to CCA1 FHE. In the appendix, we present a different approach to constructing CCA1-secure FHE through what we call a linear-algebraic encryption scheme, a variant of a single-key-secure functional encryption scheme for linear functions. Although this approach currently only works to obtain additive homomorphism, we present it in the appendix as a potential approach to obtain alternative constructions of CCA1-secure FHE.

2   CCA-Secure Fully Homomorphic Encryption

Definition 1. Let $\mathcal{M}$, be a message space. A *CCA1-secure fully homomorphic encryption scheme* (CCA1 FHE) is a tuple of polynomial time algorithms (Gen, Enc, Dec, Eval), defined as follows, which satisfy the *correctness*, *compactness* and *security* properties below.

- $\underline{\mathsf{Gen}(1^\lambda)}$: a randomized algorithm which outputs a public key, secret key pair (pk, sk).
- $\underline{\mathsf{Enc}(\mu, \mathsf{pk})}$: a randomized algorithm which outputs a ciphertext ct.
- $\underline{\mathsf{Dec}(\mathsf{ct}, \mathsf{sk})}$: an algorithm which outputs a message $\mu \in \mathcal{M}$.
- $\underline{\mathsf{Eval}(\{\mathsf{ct}_i\}, \mathcal{C})}$: an algorithm which takes a collection of ciphertexts $\{\mathsf{ct}_i\}$ and a circuit to be evaluated $\mathcal{C}$ and outputs an evaluated ciphertext $\mathsf{ct}_{\mathsf{eval}}$.

Correctness: For any $\mu \in \mathcal{M}$, and whp over $(\mathsf{pk}, \mathsf{sk}) \leftarrow \mathsf{Gen}(1^\lambda)$,

$$\Pr\Big[\mathsf{Dec}\big(\mathsf{Enc}(\mu, \mathsf{pk}), \mathsf{sk}\big) = \mu\Big] = 1 - \mathsf{negl}.$$

Homomorphic Correctness: For any $\{\mu_i\} \in \mathcal{M}^{\mathsf{poly}(\lambda)}$, polynomially sized circuit $\mathcal{C}$, and whp over $(\mathsf{pk}, \mathsf{sk}) \leftarrow \mathsf{Gen}(1^\lambda)$, $\mathsf{ct}_i \leftarrow \mathsf{Enc}(\mu_i, \mathsf{pk})$,

$$\Pr\Big[\mathsf{Dec}\big(\mathsf{Eval}(\{\mathsf{ct}_i\}, \mathcal{C}), \mathsf{sk}\big) = \mathcal{C}(\{\mu_i\})\Big] = 1 - \mathsf{negl}.$$

Compactness: There exists a polynomial $\mathsf{poly}(\cdot)$ st $|\mathsf{ct}_{\mathsf{eval}}| \leq \mathsf{poly}(\lambda)$ for all $\mathsf{ct}_{\mathsf{eval}} \leftarrow \mathsf{Eval}(\{\mathsf{ct}_i\}, \mathcal{C})$. In particular, $\mathsf{poly}(\cdot)$ is independent of the size, depth or number of inputs to $\mathcal{C}$.

CCA1 Security: For any PPT adversary $\mathcal{A}$, its chance of winning the following game against a challenger $\mathcal{C}$ is at most $1/2 + \mathsf{negl}$.

1. $\mathcal{C}$ draws $(\mathsf{pk}, \mathsf{sk}) \leftarrow \mathsf{Gen}(1^\lambda)$ and sends pk to $\mathcal{A}$.
2. For $\alpha = 1, \ldots, \mathsf{poly}$:
   - $\mathcal{A}$ sends ct_α to $\mathcal{C}$;
   - $\mathcal{C}$ computes $\mu_\alpha = \mathsf{Dec}(\mathsf{ct}_\alpha, \mathsf{sk})$ and returns μ_α to $\mathcal{A}$.
3. $\mathcal{A}$ sends $\mu_0, \mu_1 \in \mathcal{M}$ to $\mathcal{C}$.
4. $\mathcal{C}$ draws $\mathsf{ct}^* \leftarrow \mathsf{Enc}(\mu_{\mathsf{bit}}, \mathsf{pk})$ for a random bit $\in \{0, 1\}$ and sends ct^* to $\mathcal{A}$.
5. $\mathcal{A}$ outputs $\mathsf{guess} \in \{0, 1\}$ and wins if $\mathsf{guess} = \mathsf{bit}$.

Remark. The query ciphertexts ct_α above are chosen by the adversary and can be base ciphertexts, evaluated ciphertexts, or may be altogether malformed.

Remark. We say that a CCA1 FHE scheme is *leveled* if there exists a polynomial $\ell = \ell(\lambda)$ such that homomorphic correctness only holds when $\mathcal{C}$ has depth at most ℓ. Also, we say that a CCA1 FHE is *compact wrt circuit complexity* if a weaker compactness condition holds which allows $|\mathsf{ct}_{\mathsf{eval}}|$ to grow with the number of inputs to $\mathcal{C}$, but demands that it remain independent of the size and depth of $\mathcal{C}$.

Remark. In general, evaluated ciphertexts are allowed to have a slightly different form from fresh ciphertexts, in which case evaluated ciphertexts are decrypted with a separate decryption algorithm $\mathsf{EvalDec}$. For notational simplicity, we refrain from explicitly specifying $\mathsf{EvalDec}$. For all the schemes in this paper, evaluated decryption is the same as ordinary decryption except for minor differences.

3 Multi-key Identity-Based FHE to CCA1 FHE

In this section, we define the notion of multi-key identity-based FHE (IBFHE), and show that it implies CCA1-secure FHE. The transformation preserves the homomorphic (*i.e.*, leveled or full) and compactness properties of the multi-key IBFHE scheme. By applying this transformation on prior multi-key IBFHE schemes we obtain two constructions of CCA1 FHE. Neither construction is fully compact as in each construction, the evaluated ciphertext size grows with the number of inputs to the circuit. They are however compact wrt circuit complexity as evaluated ciphertext sizes are independent of the size or depth of the circuit being evaluated. In Sect. 3.3 we apply our transformation to a recent construction of [BCTW16] to obtain CCA1 FHE from any multi-key FHE and IBE. In Sect. 3.4 we apply our transformation to the construction of [CM15] to obtain leveled CCA1 FHE based on sub-exponential LWE in the random oracle model.

We point out that in both of these constructions, the ciphertext size grows only with the number of batches of inputs to be evaluated. In settings where the total number of users is small and the input to the circuits are known all at once, this growth can be easily controlled.

3.1 Multi-key IBFHE

Definition 2. Let $\mathcal{M}, \mathcal{ID}$ be message and identity spaces. A *multi-key identity-based fully homomorphic encryption* scheme is a tuple of polynomial time algorithms $(\mathsf{Setup}, \mathsf{Extract}, \mathsf{Enc}, \mathsf{Dec}, \mathsf{Eval})$, defined as follows, which satisfy the *correctness* and *security* properties below.

- $\underline{\mathsf{Setup}(1^\lambda)}$: outputs the master key pair $(\mathsf{mpk}, \mathsf{msk})$.
- $\underline{\mathsf{Extract}(\mathsf{id}, \mathsf{msk})}$: outputs a secret key $\mathsf{sk_{id}}$ for the identity id.
- $\underline{\mathsf{Enc}(\mu, \mathsf{id}, \mathsf{mpk})}$: encrypts message μ to identity id, outputting $(\mathsf{ct_{id}}, \mathsf{id})$.
- $\underline{\mathsf{Dec}(\mathsf{ct_{id}}, \mathsf{id}, \mathsf{sk_{id}})}$: decrypts $\mathsf{ct_{id}}$ using $\mathsf{sk_{id}}$, outputting μ.
- $\underline{\mathsf{Eval}(\{(\mathsf{ct}_i, \mathsf{id}_i)\}, \mathcal{C})}$: takes a family of ciphertexts and a circuit and outputs $(\mathsf{ct_{eval}}, \mathsf{id_{eval}})$.

Correctness: For any $\mu \in \mathcal{M}$, $\mathsf{id} \in \mathcal{ID}$, and whp over $(\mathsf{mpk}, \mathsf{msk}) \leftarrow \mathsf{Setup}(1^\lambda)$, $\mathsf{sk_{id}} \leftarrow \mathsf{Extract}(\mathsf{id}, \mathsf{msk})$,

$$\Pr\Big[\mathsf{Dec}\big(\mathsf{Enc}(\mu, \mathsf{id}, \mathsf{mpk}), \mathsf{sk_{id}}\big) = \mu\Big] = 1 - \mathsf{negl}.$$

Homomorphic Correctness: For any $\{\mu_i\} \in \mathcal{M}^{\mathsf{poly}(\lambda)}$, $\{\mathsf{id}_i\} \in \mathcal{ID}^{\mathsf{poly}(\lambda)}$, circuit $\mathcal{C}$, and with high probability over $(\mathsf{mpk}, \mathsf{msk}) \leftarrow \mathsf{Setup}(1^\lambda)$, $\mathsf{sk}_i \leftarrow \mathsf{Extract}(\mathsf{id}_i, \mathsf{msk})$, $\mathsf{ct}_i \leftarrow \mathsf{Enc}(\mu_i, \mathsf{id}_i, \mathsf{mpk})$,

$$\Pr\Big[\mathsf{Dec}\big(\mathsf{Eval}(\{(\mathsf{ct}_i, \mathsf{id}_i)\}, \mathcal{C}), \mathsf{sk_{eval}}\big) = \mathcal{C}(\{\mu_i\})\Big] = 1 - \mathsf{negl},$$

where $\mathsf{sk_{eval}} \leftarrow \mathsf{Extract}(\mathsf{id_{eval}}, \mathsf{msk})$.

Compactness: There exists a polynomial $\mathsf{poly}(\cdot)$ st $|\mathsf{id_{eval}}|, |\mathsf{ct_{eval}}| \leq \mathsf{poly}(\lambda)$ for all evaluated $(\mathsf{id_{eval}}, \mathsf{ct_{eval}}) \leftarrow \mathsf{Eval}(\{\mathsf{id}_i, \mathsf{ct}_i\}, \mathcal{C})$. In particular, $\mathsf{poly}(\cdot)$ is independent of the size, depth or number of inputs to $\mathcal{C}$.

Selective Security for Random Identities: For any PPT adversary $\mathcal{A}$, its chance of winning the following game against a challenger $\mathcal{C}$ is at most $1/2 + \mathsf{negl}$.

1. $\mathcal{C}$ draws $\text{id}^* \leftarrow \mathcal{ID}$ and $(\text{mpk}, \text{msk}) \leftarrow \text{Setup}(1^\lambda)$ and sends mpk to $\mathcal{A}$.
2. For $\alpha = 1, \ldots, \text{poly}$:
   - $\mathcal{A}$ sends id_α to $\mathcal{C}$;
   - if $\text{id}_\alpha = \text{id}^*$, the game ends and $\mathcal{A}$ loses; if $\text{id}_\alpha = \text{id}_\beta$ for $\beta < \alpha$, $\mathcal{C}$ returns sk_β; otherwise $\mathcal{C}$ draws $\text{sk}_\alpha \leftarrow \text{Extract}(\text{id}_\alpha, \text{msk})$, sends sk_α to $\mathcal{A}$ and stores $(\text{id}_\alpha, \text{sk}_\alpha)$.
3. $\mathcal{A}$ sends $\mu_0, \mu_1 \in \mathcal{M}$ to $\mathcal{C}$.
4. $\mathcal{C}$ draws $\text{ct}^* \leftarrow \text{Enc}(\mu_b, \text{id}^*, \text{mpk})$ for a random $b \in \{0,1\}$ and sends ct^* to $\mathcal{A}$.
5. $\mathcal{A}$ outputs $b' \in \{0,1\}$ and wins if $b' = b$.

Remark. A stronger version of security allows $\mathcal{A}$ to specify the identity id^* he wishes to attack after seeing mpk and the sk_α. Additionally, we could allow $\mathcal{A}$ to ask another round of identity queries after receiving the challenge ciphertext (provided he does not ask id^*). We use the above notion as it is sufficient for CCA1 FHE.

Remark. As with CCA1 FHE, we consider relaxations of the above definition where homomorphic correctness is only required to hold for circuits whose depth is at most some polynomial $\ell = \ell(\lambda)$. We call such schemes *leveled*. Similarly, we consider relaxations of compactness where $|\text{id}_{\text{eval}}|$ and $|\text{ct}_{\text{eval}}|$ may grow polynomially with the number of inputs to $\mathcal{C}$, but remain otherwise independent of the complexity of $\mathcal{C}$.

3.2 CCA1 FHE from Multi-key IBFHE

Let $\mathcal{E}$ be a multi-key IBFHE scheme. Our CCA1 FHE scheme is as follows.

- $\text{Gen}(1^\lambda)$: Output $(\text{pk}, \text{sk}) = (\text{mpk}, \text{msk}) \leftarrow \mathcal{E}.\text{Setup}(1^\lambda)$.
- $\text{Enc}(\mu, \text{pk})$: Draw $\text{id} \leftarrow \mathcal{ID}$ and $\text{ct}_{\text{id}} \leftarrow \mathcal{E}.\text{Enc}(\mu, \text{id}, \text{mpk})$. Output $\text{ct} = (\text{ct}_{\text{id}}, \text{id})$.
- $\text{Dec}(\text{ct}, \text{sk})$: Parse $\text{ct} = (\mathcal{E}.\text{ct}, \text{id})$. Draw $\text{sk}_{\text{id}} \leftarrow \mathcal{E}.\text{Extract}(\text{id}, \text{msk})$, output $\mu \leftarrow \mathcal{E}.\text{Dec}(\text{ct}_{\text{id}}, \text{id}, \text{sk}_{\text{id}})$.
- $\text{Eval}(\{\text{ct}_i\}, \mathcal{C})$: Parse $\text{ct}_i = (\mathcal{E}.\text{ct}_i, \text{id}_i)$, output $\text{ct}_{\text{eval}} = (\mathcal{E}.\text{ct}_{\text{eval}}, \text{id}_{\text{eval}}) \leftarrow \mathcal{E}.\text{Eval}(\{(\mathcal{E}.\text{ct}_i, \text{id}_i)\}, \mathcal{C})$.

Lemma 1. *The above scheme is a CCA1-secure FHE scheme.*

Proof. Correctness and homomorphic correctness follow immediately from the same properties of $\mathcal{E}$. CCA1 security follows from the security of $\mathcal{E}$ via the proof from [BCHK07]. We sketch this proof for completeness. The idea is to use an adversary $\mathcal{A}$ who wins the CCA1 game to construct $\mathcal{B}$ who wins the selective IBE security game against a challenger $\mathcal{C}$. This $\mathcal{B}$ receives mpk which he forwards to $\mathcal{A}$. Each time $\mathcal{A}$ asks a ciphertext query ct_α, $\mathcal{B}$ asks $\mathcal{C}$ for secret keys for the identity in ct_α so he can decrypt them for $\mathcal{A}$. As id^* is random, the chance that some $\text{id}_\alpha = \text{id}^*$ is negligible. When $\mathcal{A}$ sends (μ_0, μ_1), $\mathcal{B}$ forwards it to $\mathcal{C}$ and receives ct^*. $\mathcal{B}$ sends $(\text{id}^*, \text{ct}^*)$ to $\mathcal{A}$, and forwards $\mathcal{A}$'s guess to $\mathcal{C}$. $\mathcal{B}$ wins the IBE security game if and only if $\mathcal{A}$ wins the CCA1 game.

3.3   Generic Instantiation of Multi-key IBFHE

In a recent work, Brakerski et al. [BCTW16] give a generic construction of a multi-key, attribute-based fully homomorphic encryption scheme from a multi-key FHE and an ABE scheme. Their scheme is very simple: to encrypt, draw a key pair and encrypt using the multi-key FHE; also encrypt the secret key using ABE. Their transformation applies in our setting as well to give a generic construction of multi-key IBFHE from multi-key FHE and IBE. The scheme is only compact wrt circuit complexity. We omit the definitions of multi-key FHE and IBE as they are analogous to our definition of multi-key IBFHE with proper relaxations. We refer the reader to [MW16, GPV08] for definitions of these primitives.

<u>BuildingBlocks</u>: Let (MK.Gen, MK.Enc, MK.Dec, MK.Eval) be a multi-key FHE scheme, and let (IBE.Setup, IBE.Extract, IBE.Enc, IBE.Dec) be an IBE scheme.

<u>Setup(1^λ)</u>: Draw and output (mpk, msk) $\leftarrow$ IBE.Setup.

<u>Extract(id, msk)</u>: Draw and output $\mathsf{sk_{id}} \leftarrow$ IBE.Extract(id, msk).

<u>Enc(μ, id, mpk)</u>: Draw (pk, sk) $\leftarrow$ MK.Gen(1^λ), $\mathsf{ct_1} \leftarrow$ MK.Enc(μ, pk) and $\mathsf{ct_2} \leftarrow$ IBE.Enc(sk, id, mpk). Output (id, $\mathsf{ct_{id}}$) where $\mathsf{ct_{id}} = (\mathsf{ct_1}, \mathsf{ct_2})$.

<u>Dec($\mathsf{ct_{id}}$, id, $\mathsf{sk_{id}}$)</u>: Parse $\mathsf{ct_{id}} = (\mathsf{ct_1}, \mathsf{ct_2})$. Compute sk = IBE.Dec($\mathsf{ct_2}$, id, $\mathsf{sk_{id}}$), output MK.Dec($\mathsf{ct_1}$, sk).

<u>Eval($\{(\mathsf{id}_i, \mathsf{ct}_i)\}, \mathcal{C}$)</u>: Set $\mathsf{id_{eval}} = \{\mathsf{id}_i\}$. Parse $\mathsf{ct}_i = (\mathsf{ct}_{i,1}, \mathsf{ct}_{i,2})$. Draw multi-key evaluation $\mathsf{ct_{eval,1}} \leftarrow$ MK.Eval($\{\mathsf{ct}_{i,1}\}, \mathcal{C}$), and set $\mathsf{ct_{eval,2}} = \{\mathsf{ct}_{i,2}\}$. Set $\mathsf{ct_{eval}} = (\mathsf{ct_{eval,1}}, \mathsf{ct_{eval,2}})$ and output ($\mathsf{ct_{eval}}$, $\mathsf{id_{eval}}$).

Lemma 2. *If* MK *and* IBE *are multi-key FHE and IBE schemes, respectively and* MK *is compact wrt circuit complexity, then the above scheme is a multi-key IBFHE scheme which is compact wrt circuit complexity.*

Remark. The second component of the evaluated ciphertext $\mathsf{ct_{eval}}$ is the concatenation of the encryptions of all of the secret keys from the MK ciphertexts. Therefore, the above multi-key IBFHE scheme is only compact wrt circuit complexity even if MK is fully compact. Moreover, if MK is a leveled multi-key FHE scheme then the resulting scheme is also leveled.

Remark. In the above scheme, evaluated identities are collections of identities: $\mathsf{id_{eval}} = \{\mathsf{id}_i\}$. We define Extract to work on such inputs: Extract($\mathsf{id_{eval}}$, msk) = $\{\mathsf{sk}_i\}$ where $\mathsf{sk}_i \leftarrow$ Extract(id_i, msk).

Proof. (Proof Sketch). Correctness follows immediately from correctness of MK and IBE. Security follows from security of IBE to change the IBE portion of the challenge ciphertext to an encryption of 0 instead of sk and then the security of MK to say that $\mathcal{A}$ cannot distinguish encryptions of μ_0 from μ_1.

Combining Lemma 2 with Lemma 1 we get the following.

Theorem 1. If there exists a multi-key FHE scheme which is compact wrt circuit complexity and an IBE scheme with selective security for random identities then there is a CCA1 FHE scheme which is compact wrt circuit complexity. If the multi-key FHE scheme is leveled, then the resulting CCA1 FHE scheme is also.

3.4 Multi-key IBFHE from LWE and ROs

Clear and McGoldrick [CM15] construct multi-key IBFHE (under the name "multi-identity IBFHE") from learning with errors in the random oracle model. Like the generic construction above, their scheme is only compact wrt circuit complexity, as their evaluated ciphertexts grow in size with the number of inputs to the circuit. However, unlike the generic construction, their ciphertext growth is dominated by the ciphertext growth in the multi-key FHE. In other words, the failure of their scheme to be fully compact is due only to the failure of current multi-key FHE scheme to be fully compact. Combining the main theorem of [CM15] with Lemma 1 we get the following.

Theorem 2. Assuming sub-exponential LWE, there is a leveled CCA1 FHE scheme in the random oracle model which is compact wrt circuit complexity. The size of the evaluated ciphertexts in the scheme is $S \cdot \mathsf{poly}(\lambda, \log |\mathcal{C}|, \ell$ where S is the number of inputs to $\mathcal{C}$, the circuit being evaluated, and $\ell \geq \mathrm{Depth}(\mathcal{C})$ is the maximum allowable depth for which homomorphic correctness still holds.

4   Instantiation from IO and Lossy Encryption

In this section, we construct a multi-key IBFHE from a sub-exponentially secure indistinguishability obfuscation (IO) and sub-exponentially secure lossy encryption. The latter primitive can be instantiated from standard assumptions, e.g., the decisional Diffie-Hellman (DDH) assumption. The multi-key IBFHE scheme in this section is fully compact and unleveled. The following lemma combined with Lemma 1 gives compact, non-leveled CCA1 FHE.

Lemma 3. *Assuming sub-exponential IO and sub-exponential hardness of DDH, there is a compact, non-leveled multi-key IBFHE scheme.*

In order to prove Lemma 3, we abstract an intermediate notion of encryption that we call tag-puncturable encryption. We then show that a tag-puncturable encryption scheme, together with IO, implies a multi-key IBFHE scheme, and finish up with showing a construction of tag-puncturable encryption from IO and additively homomorphic lossy encryption.

4.1   Tag-Puncturable Encryption

Definition 3. Let $\mathcal{M}, \mathcal{TAG}$ be message and tag spaces where $\mathcal{M}$ is an abelian group. Let $\mathsf{BAD} : \mathcal{TAG} \to \{U : U \subset \mathcal{TAG}\}$ be such that $|\mathsf{BAD}(\mathsf{tag})| \leq \mathsf{B}_{\max}$

for some parameter B_{max}. Let $\varepsilon > 0$. A $(BAD, B_{max}, \varepsilon)$–*tag-puncturable, additively homomorphic encryption scheme* is a tuple $(Gen, Punc.Gen, Enc, Dec, Add)$ of polytime algorithms, defined as follows, which satisfy the properties below.

- $Gen(1^\lambda)$: outputs the key pair (pk, sk).
- $Punc.Gen(tag^*)$: outputs the keys $(pk, sk, pk_{tag^*}, sk_{tag^*})$.
- $Enc(\mu, tag, pk)$: encrypts μ to tag, outputting ciphertext ct_{tag}.
- $Dec(ct_{tag}, tag, sk)$: outputs message μ.
- $Add(\{ct_i\}, tag)$: outputs a homomorphically evaluated ciphertext ct_{add}.

Correctness: For any $\mu \in \mathcal{M}$, $tag \in \mathcal{TAG}$, and whp over $(pk, sk) \leftarrow Gen(1^\lambda)$,

$$\Pr\Big[Dec\big(Enc(\mu, tag, pk), tag, sk\big) = \mu\Big] = 1.$$

Homomorphic Correctness: For any $\{\mu_i\} \in \mathcal{M}^k$, $tag \in \mathcal{TAG}$, and whp over $(pk, sk) \leftarrow Gen(1^\lambda)$, and $ct_i \leftarrow Enc(\mu_i, tag, pk)$,

$$\Pr\Big[Dec\big(Add(\{ct_i\}, tag), tag, sk\big) = \mu_1 + \cdots + \mu_k\Big] = 1.$$

Key Indistinguishability: This property comes in two parts. First, for any $tag^* \in \mathcal{TAG}$, $\{(pk, sk) : (pk, sk, pk_{tag^*}, sk_{tag^*}) \leftarrow Punc.Gen(tag^*)\}$ is distributed identically to $Gen(1^\lambda)$.

Secondly, for all PPT $\mathcal{A}$,

$$\Big|\Pr_{Punc.Gen(tag^*)}\big(\mathcal{A}(pk, sk_{tag^*}) = 1\big) - \Pr_{Punc.Gen(tag^*)}\big(\mathcal{A}(pk_{tag^*}, sk_{tag^*}) = 1\big)\Big| \leq \varepsilon.$$

(We remark that an alternate exposition could completely do away with Gen and simply refer to $Punc.Gen$ for both the "real" public keys and punctured ones. We choose to keep Gen around for familiarity.)

Punctured Key Utility: For every $tag^* \in \mathcal{TAG}$, and with high probability over $(pk, sk, pk_{tag^*}, sk_{tag^*}) \leftarrow Punc.Gen(tag^*)$, we have:

- **Lossiness with Bad Keys:** For all $tag \in BAD_{tag^*}$, and $\mu_0, \mu_1 \in \mathcal{M}$,

$$Enc(\mu_0, tag, pk_{tag^*}) \approx_s Enc(\mu_1, tag, pk_{tag^*}).$$

- **Correctness with Good Keys:** For all $tag \notin BAD_{tag^*}$, and $\mu \in \mathcal{M}$,

$$Dec\big(Enc(\mu, tag, pk_{tag^*}), tag, sk_{tag^*}\big) = \mu.$$

4.2   Multi-key IBFHE from Tag-Puncturable Encryption

The key ideas in this construction here borrow from recent works Canetti et al. [CLTV15] and Dodis et al. [DHRW16].

- **Parameters:** $L_{max} = \lambda^{\omega(1)}$ is an upper bound on the number of levels, $\varepsilon > 0$ such that $\varepsilon \cdot L_{max} = negl$; let $\mathcal{E}$ be a (L_{max}, ε)–tag-puncturable additively homomorphic encryption scheme with tag space $\mathcal{E}.\mathcal{TAG} = \mathcal{ID} \times [L_{max}]$, and for any $tag^* = (id^*, L^*) \in \mathcal{E}.\mathcal{TAG}$, define the bad set $BAD_{tag^*} = \{(id^*, L) : L \geq L^*\}$. Let the message space of $\mathcal{E}$ be $\mathcal{E}.\mathcal{TAG} \times \mathcal{M}$ where $\mathcal{M}$ is the message space of our multi-key IBFHE. Assume $\mathcal{M}$ is a ring. Also assume that the homomorphism of $\mathcal{E}$ is only over the second coordinate of the message. Let $pi\mathcal{O}$ be an ϵ-secure PIO scheme.

- **Setup(1^λ):** Draw $(pk, sk) \leftarrow \mathcal{E}.Gen(1^\lambda)$. Also, let $P_{eval}[pk, sk]$ and $P_{comb}[pk, sk]$ be the following probabilistic programs:
  - (pk, sk) is hardwired into both; both take inputs $(tag, ct), (tag', ct') \in \mathcal{E}.\mathcal{TAG} \times \mathcal{E}.\mathcal{CT}$;
  - both compute $(id, L, \mu) = \mathcal{E}.Dec(ct, tag, sk)$ and $(id', L', \mu') = \mathcal{E}.Dec(ct', tag', sk)$, if either decryption is not of this form, or if $tag \neq (id, L)$ or $tag' \neq (id', L')$, or if either of L or L' is $\geq L_{max}$, output $\bot$;
  - now the programs differ:
    $\underline{P_{eval}[pk, sk]}$: let $\eta, \eta' \in \mathcal{M}$ be random st $\eta + \eta' = \mu \cdot \mu'$, draw

    $$ct_{out} \leftarrow \mathcal{E}.Enc((id, L+1, \eta), tag, pk) \text{ and } ct'_{out} \leftarrow \mathcal{E}.Enc((id', L'+1, \eta'), tag', pk);$$

    output $((id, L+1, ct_{out}), (id', L'+1, ct'_{out}))$; $\mathcal{E}$-encryptions to tags $(id, L+1), (id', L'+1)$, respectively.
    $\underline{P_{comb}[pk, sk]}$: let $id_{out} = id \oplus id'$, $L_{out} = \max\{L, L'\} + 1$ and $tag_{out} = (id_{out}, L_{out})$. Draw $ct_{out} \leftarrow \mathcal{E}.Enc((id_{out}, L_{out}, \mu + \mu'), tag_{out}, pk)$; output (tag_{out}, ct_{out}).

  Let $\mathcal{O}_{eval}[pk, sk] = pi\mathcal{O}(P_{eval}[pk, sk])$ and $\mathcal{O}_{comb}[pk, sk] = pi\mathcal{O}(P_{comb}[pk, sk])$. Set $msk = sk$ and $mpk = (pk, \mathcal{O}_{eval}[pk, sk], \mathcal{O}_{comb}[pk, sk])$.

- **Extract(id, msk):** Parse $msk = sk$. Let $P_{dec}[id, sk]$ be the deterministic program:
  - id and sk are hardwired, take input $ct \in \mathcal{E}.\mathcal{CT}$;
  - compute $(id, L, \mu) = \mathcal{E}.Dec(ct, id, sk)$, if the decryption is not of this form, or if $L > L_{max}$, output $\bot$; otherwise output μ.

  Let $\mathcal{O}_{dec}[id, sk] = i\mathcal{O}(P_{dec}[id, sk])$. Output $sk_{id} = \mathcal{O}_{dec}[id, sk]$.

- **Enc(μ, id, mpk):** Parse $mpk = (pk, \mathcal{O}_{eval}[pk, sk], \mathcal{O}_{comb}[pk, sk])$, set $tag = (id, 0)$, $msg = (id, 0, \mu)$; draw $ct_{id} \leftarrow \mathcal{E}.Enc(msg, tag, pk)$, and output (ct_{id}, id).

- **Dec(ct_{id}, id, sk_{id}):** Parse $sk_{id} = \mathcal{O}_{dec}[id, sk]$, output $\mu = \mathcal{O}_{dec}[id, sk](ct_{id})$.

- **Eval$((ct_1, id_1), \ldots, (ct_t, id_t), \mathcal{C}, mpk)$:** Parse $mpk = (pk, \mathcal{O}_{eval}, \mathcal{O}_{comb})$ and write $\mathcal{C}$ as an algebraic circuit, organized so that each layer consists either entirely of addition gates or entirely of multiplication gates.

  1. **Evaluate $\mathcal{C}$ a la GMW:** For $i, j = 1, \ldots, t$, define ciphertext ct_j^i by $ct_i^i = ct_i$ and $ct_j^i \leftarrow \mathcal{E}.Enc((id_j, 0, 0), (id_j, 0), pk)$ for $i \neq j$. This defines a set of ciphertexts $\{ct_j^i\}_j$ for each input wire i, where for each j, ct_j^i is an $\mathcal{E}$–ciphertext to $tag_{j,0} = (id_j, 0)$. Consider a gate of $\mathcal{C}$ with input wires (u, v) and output wire w. Assume by induction that we have ciphertext families $\{ct_j^u\}_j$ and $\{ct_j^v\}_j$, where ct_j^u and ct_j^v are $\mathcal{E}$–ciphertexts for $tag_{j,L} = (id_j, L)$, we describe how to construct $\{ct_j^w\}_j$.

- **Addition Gate:** Set $\mathsf{ct}_j^w = \mathcal{E}.\mathsf{Add}(\mathsf{ct}_j^u, \mathsf{ct}_j^v, \mathsf{tag}_{j,\mathsf{L}})$, so ct_j^w is an $\mathcal{E}$-ciphertext to $\mathsf{tag}_{j,\mathsf{L}}$.
- **Multiplication Gate:** For $i, j = 1, \dots, t$, draw

$$\left(\mathsf{id}_i, \mathsf{L}+1, \mathsf{CT}_{i,j}^u\right), \left(\mathsf{id}_j, \mathsf{L}+1, \mathsf{CT}_{j,i}^v\right) \leftarrow \mathcal{O}_{\mathsf{eval}}\left((\mathsf{id}_i, \mathsf{L}, \mathsf{ct}_i^u), (\mathsf{id}_j, \mathsf{L}, \mathsf{ct}_j^v)\right).$$

  Note that $\mathsf{CT}_{j,i}^u$ and $\mathsf{CT}_{i,j}^v$ are both $\mathcal{E}$-ciphertexts to $\mathsf{tag}_{j,\mathsf{L}+1}$. Set

$$\mathsf{ct}_j^w = \mathcal{E}.\mathsf{Add}\left(\{\mathsf{CT}_{j,i}^u\}_i, \{\mathsf{CT}_{i,j}^v\}_i, \mathsf{tag}_{j,\mathsf{L}+1}\right).$$

  After all gates of $\mathcal{C}$ have been computed as above we have $(\mathsf{id}_1, \dots, \mathsf{id}_t, \mathsf{ct}_1^{\mathsf{out}}, \dots, \mathsf{ct}_t^{\mathsf{out}})$ where $\{\mathsf{ct}_j^{\mathsf{out}}\}_j$ is the ciphertext family for the output wire of $\mathcal{C}$. Note $\mathsf{ct}_j^{\mathsf{out}}$ is an $\mathcal{E}$-ciphertext to $\mathsf{tag}_{j,\mathsf{L}_{\mathsf{depth}}}$ where $\mathsf{L}_{\mathsf{depth}}$ is the multiplicative depth of $\mathcal{C}$.

2. **Combine output ciphertexts:** Initialize $\mathsf{tag}_{\mathsf{eval}} = (\mathsf{id}_1, \mathsf{L}_{\mathsf{depth}})$ and $\mathsf{ct}_{\mathsf{eval}} = \mathsf{ct}_1^{\mathsf{out}}$. For $j = 2, \dots, t$:
   - draw $(\mathsf{tag}_{\mathsf{eval}}, \mathsf{ct}_{\mathsf{eval}}) \leftarrow \mathcal{O}_{\mathsf{comb}}\left((\mathsf{tag}_{\mathsf{eval}}, \mathsf{ct}_{\mathsf{eval}}), (\mathsf{tag}_{j,\mathsf{L}_{\mathsf{depth}}}, \mathsf{ct}_j^{\mathsf{out}})\right)$;
   - parse $\mathsf{tag}_{\mathsf{eval}} = (\mathsf{id}_{\mathsf{eval}}, \mathsf{L}_{\mathsf{eval}})$; output $(\mathsf{ct}_{\mathsf{eval}}, \mathsf{id}_{\mathsf{eval}})$. Note $\mathsf{ct}_{\mathsf{eval}}$ is an $\mathcal{E}$-ciphertext to $\mathsf{tag}_{\mathsf{eval}}$, where $\mathsf{id}_{\mathsf{eval}} = \bigoplus_i \mathsf{id}_i$, and $\mathsf{L}_{\mathsf{eval}} = \mathsf{L}_{\mathsf{depth}} + t - 1 \ll \mathsf{L}_{\mathsf{max}}$.

Lemma 4. *The above scheme is a multi-key identity-based FHE assuming the existence of sub-exponential iO and that $\mathcal{E}$ is a $(\mathsf{L}_{\mathsf{max}}, \varepsilon)$-tag-puncturable additively homomorphic encryption scheme.*

4.3   Proof of Lemma 4

Correctness: This follows from the correctness of $\mathcal{E}$ and iO. For any $\mu \in \{0, 1\}$, $\mathsf{id} \in \mathcal{ID}$, whp over $(\mathsf{pk}, \mathsf{sk}) \leftarrow \mathcal{E}.\mathsf{Gen}(1^\lambda)$, and $\mathsf{ct} \leftarrow \mathcal{E}.\mathsf{Enc}((\mathsf{id}, 0, \mu), (\mathsf{id}, 0), \mathsf{pk})$, $\mathcal{E}.\mathsf{Dec}(\mathsf{ct}, (\mathsf{id}, 0), \mathsf{sk}) = (\mathsf{id}, 0, \mu)$, and so $\mathcal{O}_{\mathsf{dec}}[\mathsf{id}, \mathsf{sk}](\mathsf{ct}) = \mu$.

Homomorphic Correctness: For any $\{\mu_i\} \in \mathcal{M}^t$, $\{\mathsf{id}_i\} \in \mathcal{ID}^t$, circuit $\mathcal{C}$, we show that for any wire w at (multiplicative) level L, the ciphertexts $\{\mathsf{ct}_j^w\}_j$ satisfy $\mu^w = \sum_j \mathcal{E}.\mathsf{Dec}(\mathsf{ct}_j^w, \mathsf{tag}_{j,\mathsf{L}}, \mathsf{sk})$. Homomorphic correctness then follows from correctness of piO. This equality holds for the input wires by construction. Assume it is true for $\{\mathsf{ct}_j^u\}$ and $\{\mathsf{ct}_j^v\}$, the ciphertexts for wires u and v which are the input wires to a gate of $\mathcal{C}$ with output wire w. If the gate is addition then we have

$$\sum_j \mathcal{E}.\mathsf{Dec}(\mathsf{ct}_j^w, \mathsf{tag}_{j,\mathsf{L}}, \mathsf{sk}) = \sum_j \mathcal{E}.\mathsf{Dec}(\mathcal{E}.\mathsf{Add}(\mathsf{ct}_j^u, \mathsf{ct}_j^v, \mathsf{tag}_{j,\mathsf{L}}), \mathsf{tag}_{j,\mathsf{L}}, \mathsf{sk}))$$

$$= \sum_j \mu_j^u + \mu_j^v = \mu^u + \mu^v = \mu^w.$$

If the gate is multiplication then we have

$$\sum_j \mathcal{E}.\mathsf{Dec}(\mathsf{ct}_j^w, \mathsf{tag}_{j,\mathsf{L}}, \mathsf{sk}) = \sum_j \mathcal{E}.\mathsf{Dec}(\mathcal{E}.\mathsf{Add}(\{\mathsf{CT}_{j,i}^u\}_i, \{\mathsf{CT}_{i,j}^v\}_i, \mathsf{tag}_{j,\mathsf{L}+1}), \mathsf{tag}_{j,\mathsf{L}+1}, \mathsf{sk})$$

$$= \sum_{i,j} \eta_{i,j}^u + \eta_{i,j}^v = \sum_{i,j} \mu_i^u \cdot \mu_j^v = \mu^u \cdot \mu^v = \mu^w.$$

Security: We show that for any PPT $\mathcal{A}$, its chance of winning the selective IBE security game for random identities is at most $1/2 + \mathsf{negl}$. We use a hybrid argument.

Hybrid H_0: The IBE security game.

1. $\mathcal{C}$ draws $\mathsf{id}^* \leftarrow \mathcal{E}.\mathcal{ID}$ and $(\mathsf{pk}, \mathsf{sk}) \leftarrow \mathcal{E}.\mathsf{Gen}(1^\lambda)$, computes the obfuscated programs $\mathcal{O}_{\mathsf{eval}}[\mathsf{pk}, \mathsf{sk}]$, $\mathcal{O}_{\mathsf{comb}}[\mathsf{pk}, \mathsf{sk}]$ and sends $\big(\mathsf{pk}, \mathcal{O}_{\mathsf{eval}}[\mathsf{pk}, \mathsf{sk}], \mathcal{O}_{\mathsf{comb}}[\mathsf{pk}, \mathsf{sk}]\big)$ to $\mathcal{A}$.
2. For $\alpha = 1, \ldots, \mathsf{poly}(\lambda)$:
   - $\mathcal{A}$ sends id_α to $\mathcal{C}$;
   - if $\mathsf{id}_\alpha = \mathsf{id}^*$, the game ends $\mathcal{A}$ loses; if $\mathsf{id}_\alpha = \mathsf{id}_\beta$ for $\beta < \alpha$, $\mathcal{C}$ sends sk_β;
   - otherwise, $\mathcal{C}$ sends $\mathsf{sk}_\alpha = \mathcal{O}_{\mathsf{dec}}[\mathsf{id}_\alpha, \mathsf{sk}]$ to $\mathcal{A}$, and records $(\mathsf{id}_\alpha, \mathsf{sk}_\alpha)$.
3. $\mathcal{A}$ sends $\mu_0, \mu_1 \in \mathcal{M}$ to $\mathcal{C}$.
4. $\mathcal{C}$ chooses $\mathsf{bit} \leftarrow \{0,1\}$, $\mathsf{ct}^* \leftarrow \mathcal{E}.\mathsf{Enc}\big((\mathsf{id}^*, 0, \mu_{\mathsf{bit}}), (\mathsf{id}^*, 0), \mathsf{pk}\big)$, and sends ct^* to $\mathcal{A}$.
5. $\mathcal{A}$ outputs $\mathsf{guess} \in \{0,1\}$ and wins if $\mathsf{guess} = \mathsf{bit}$.

Hybrid H_1: This is the same as H_0 except that $\mathcal{C}$ draws $(\mathsf{pk}, \mathsf{sk}, \mathsf{pk}_{\mathsf{tag}^*}, \mathsf{sk}_{\mathsf{tag}^*}) \leftarrow \mathcal{E}.\mathsf{Punc}.\mathsf{Gen}(\mathsf{tag}^*)$, in step 1, where $\mathsf{tag}^* = (\mathsf{id}^*, \mathsf{L}_{\mathsf{max}})$. $\mathcal{C}$ still sends pk in step 1 and uses sk in all obfuscations. The following claim holds because $(\mathsf{pk}, \mathsf{sk})$ output by $\mathcal{E}.\mathsf{Punc}.\mathsf{Gen}(\mathsf{tag}^*)$ are distributed identically to $\mathcal{E}.\mathsf{Gen}(1^\lambda)$, by key indistinguishability of $\mathcal{E}$.

Claim 1. For any (unbounded) $\mathcal{A}$, $\Pr\big(\mathcal{A} \text{ wins } \mathsf{H}_0\big) = \Pr\big(\mathcal{A} \text{ wins } \mathsf{H}_1\big)$.

Hybrid H_2: This is the same as H_1 except that $\mathcal{C}$ now uses $\mathsf{sk}_{\mathsf{tag}^*}$, $\mathsf{tag}^* = (\mathsf{id}^*, \mathsf{L}_{\mathsf{max}})$ in all obfuscations instead of sk. Note that $P_{\mathsf{eval}}[\mathsf{pk}, \mathsf{sk}]$ (resp. $P_{\mathsf{comb}}[\mathsf{pk}, \mathsf{sk}]$) is functionally equivalent to $P_{\mathsf{eval}}[\mathsf{pk}, \mathsf{sk}_{\mathsf{tag}^*}]$ (resp. $P_{\mathsf{comb}}[\mathsf{pk}, \mathsf{sk}_{\mathsf{tag}^*}]$), as $\mathsf{BAD}_{\mathsf{tag}^*} = \{(\mathsf{id}^*, \mathsf{L}_{\mathsf{max}})\}$ and neither program ever decrypts at level $\mathsf{L}_{\mathsf{max}}$. Moreover, since $\mathcal{A}$ does not query $\mathsf{id}_\alpha = \mathsf{id}^*$ whp, $P_{\mathsf{dec}}[\mathsf{id}_\alpha, \mathsf{sk}]$ is functionally equivalent to $P_{\mathsf{dec}}[\mathsf{id}_\alpha, \mathsf{sk}_{\mathsf{tag}^*}]$. The claim follows from the security of $i\mathcal{O}$.

Claim 2. For any PPT $\mathcal{A}$, $\big|\Pr\big(\mathcal{A} \text{ wins } \mathsf{H}_1\big) - \Pr\big(\mathcal{A} \text{ wins } \mathsf{H}_2\big)\big| = \mathsf{negl}$.

Hybrid H_3: This is the same as H_2 except that $\mathcal{C}$ uses $\mathsf{sk}_{\mathsf{tag}^*}$ where $\mathsf{tag}^* = (\mathsf{id}^*, 0)$ in all obfuscations instead of $(\mathsf{id}^*, \mathsf{L}_{\mathsf{max}})$. The following claim is more involved than the others, requiring a few sub-hybrids. We prove it below.

Claim 3. For any PPT $\mathcal{A}$, $\big|\Pr\big(\mathcal{A} \text{ wins } \mathsf{H}_2\big) - \Pr\big(\mathcal{A} \text{ wins } \mathsf{H}_3\big)\big| = \mathsf{negl}$.

Hybrid H_4: This is the same as H_3 except that $\mathcal{C}$ uses $(\mathsf{pk}_{\mathsf{tag}^*}, \mathsf{sk}_{\mathsf{tag}^*})$ where $\mathsf{tag}^* = (\mathsf{id}^*, 0)$, instead of $(\mathsf{pk}, \mathsf{sk}_{\mathsf{tag}^*})$. Indistinguishability follows from key-indistinguishability of $\mathcal{E}$. As $\mathsf{pk}_{\mathsf{tag}^*}$ is lossy, even an unbounded adversary cannot have noticeable advantage in this hybrid's game. This completes our proof of security.

Claim 4. For any PPT $\mathcal{A}$, $\left|\Pr\big(\mathcal{A} \ wins \ H_3\big) - \Pr\big(\mathcal{A} \ wins \ H_4\big)\right| = \mathsf{negl}$.

Claim 5. For any (unbounded) $\mathcal{A}$, $\Pr\big(\mathcal{A} \ wins \ H_4\big) \leq 1/2 + \mathsf{negl}$.

Proof (Proof of Claim 3). Recall we must argue that H_2 and H_3 are indistinguishable, where the only difference is that $\mathcal{C}$ uses $(\mathsf{pk}, \mathsf{sk}_{\mathsf{tag}^*})$ where in H_2, $\mathsf{tag}^* = (\mathsf{id}^*, \mathsf{L}_{\mathsf{max}})$ and in H_3, $\mathsf{tag}^* = (\mathsf{id}^*, 0)$. Let $H_{3,i}$ be the game where $\mathcal{C}$ uses $\mathsf{tag}^* = (\mathsf{id}^*, i)$, so that $H_{3,0} = H_3$ and $H_{3,\mathsf{L}_{\mathsf{max}}} = H_2$. We prove that $\left|\Pr\big(\mathcal{A} \ wins \ H_{3,i}\big) - \Pr\big(\mathcal{A} \ wins \ H_{3,i-1}\big)\right| \leq 4\varepsilon$ for each $i = 1, \ldots, \mathsf{L}_{\mathsf{max}}$, from which it follows that $\left|\Pr\big(\mathcal{A} \ wins \ H_2\big) - \Pr\big(\mathcal{A} \ wins \ H_3\big)\right| \leq 4\varepsilon \cdot \mathsf{L}_{\mathsf{max}} = \mathsf{negl}$.

Let $G_0 = H_{3,i}$ and let G_1 be the same as G_0 except that $\mathcal{C}$ uses $(\mathsf{pk}_{\mathsf{tag}^*}, \mathsf{sk}_{\mathsf{tag}^*})$ in the obfuscations $\mathcal{O}_{\mathsf{eval}}$ and $\mathcal{O}_{\mathsf{comb}}$ instead of $(\mathsf{pk}, \mathsf{sk}_{\mathsf{tag}^*})$. The key-indistinguishability of $\mathcal{E}$ implies that for all PPT $\mathcal{A}$, $\left|\Pr\big(\mathcal{A} \ wins \ G_0\big) - \Pr\big(\mathcal{A} \ wins \ G_1\big)\right| \leq \varepsilon$.

Let G_2 be the same as G_1 except we change $\mathsf{P}_{\mathsf{eval}}$ and $\mathsf{P}_{\mathsf{comb}}$ so that instead of outputting an encryption of an evaluated value under the tag (id^*, j) for $j \geq i$, they just output encryptions of 0. As $\mathsf{pk}_{(\mathsf{id}^*, j)}$ is lossy, the output distributions of $\mathsf{P}_{\mathsf{eval}}$ and $\mathsf{P}_{\mathsf{comb}}$ in G_2 are statistically close to those in G_1. The security of $\mathsf{pi}\mathcal{O}$ ensures that for all PPT $\mathcal{A}$, $\left|\Pr\big(\mathcal{A} \ wins \ G_1\big) - \Pr\big(\mathcal{A} \ wins \ G_2\big)\right| \leq \varepsilon$.

Let G_3 be the same as G_2 except that $\mathcal{C}$ uses $(\mathsf{pk}, \mathsf{sk}_{\mathsf{tag}^*})$ where $\mathsf{tag}^* = (\mathsf{id}^*, i)$ instead of $(\mathsf{pk}_{\mathsf{tag}^*}, \mathsf{sk}_{\mathsf{tag}^*})$, but $\mathsf{P}_{\mathsf{eval}}$ and $\mathsf{P}_{\mathsf{comb}}$ still encrypt 0 instead of valid messages to tags (id^*, j) with $j \geq i$. The key-indistinguishability of $\mathcal{E}$ again gives $\left|\Pr\big(\mathcal{A} \ wins \ G_2\big) - \Pr\big(\mathcal{A} \ wins \ G_3\big)\right| \leq \varepsilon$ for all PPT $\mathcal{A}$.

Finally, let G_4 be the same as G_3 except that $\mathcal{C}$ uses $(\mathsf{pk}, \mathsf{sk}_{\mathsf{tag}^*})$ where $\mathsf{tag}^* = (\mathsf{id}^*, i-1)$ instead of (id^*, i). Since neither obfuscation ever decrypts ciphertexts with tag (id^*, i), program functionality does not change. Security of $\mathsf{pi}\mathcal{O}$ gives $\left|\Pr\big(\mathcal{A} \ wins \ G_3\big) - \Pr\big(\mathcal{A} \ wins \ G_4\big)\right| \leq \varepsilon$ for all PPT $\mathcal{A}$. $G_4 = H_{3,i-1}$ so the result follows.

4.4 Statistical Trapdoor Encryption

In order to instantiate our tag-puncturable encryption used in the previous section, we start from a statistical trapdoor encryption scheme, defined below. This was also the starting point for the $\mathsf{pi}\mathcal{O}$–based construction of FHE from [CLTV15], who note that any lossy encryption scheme implies statistical trapdoor encryption. Our construction also has the property that if the statistical trapdoor scheme is additively homomorphic then so will be the resulting tag-puncturable scheme. We can therefore use a DDH-based additively homomorphic, lossy encryption scheme as our starting point.

Definition 4. An ε–*statistical trapdoor encryption scheme* is a tuple of polytime algorithms $\big(\mathsf{Gen}, \mathsf{Enc}, \mathsf{Dec}, \mathsf{tGen}\big)$ such that $\big(\mathsf{Gen}, \mathsf{Enc}, \mathsf{Dec}\big)$ is a semantically secure encryption scheme and additionally $\mathsf{tGen}(1^\lambda)$ outputs a trapdoor public key pk^* such that

- for any $\mu_0, \mu_1 \in \mathcal{M}$ and whp over $\mathsf{pk}^* \leftarrow \mathsf{tGen}(1^\lambda)$,

$$\{\mathsf{Enc}(\mu_0, \mathsf{pk}^*)\} \approx_s \{\mathsf{Enc}(\mu_1, \mathsf{pk}^*)\};$$

- for all PPT $\mathcal{A}$,

$$\left| \Pr_{\mathsf{Gen}(1^\lambda)}\big(\mathcal{A}(\mathsf{pk}) = 1\big) - \Pr_{\mathsf{tGen}(1^\lambda)}\big(\mathcal{A}(\mathsf{pk}^*) = 1\big) \right| \leq \varepsilon.$$

4.5   From Statistical Trapdoor Encryption to Tag-Puncturable Encryption

- Setup: Let $\mathcal{E}$ be a statistical trapdoor encryption scheme. Let piO be a piO scheme and $\mathcal{F}$ be a puncturable PRF.
- $\mathsf{Gen}(1^\lambda)$: Sample a PRF key K and set $\mathsf{sk} = K$. Let $\mathsf{P_{gen}}[K]$ be the probabilistic program:
  - K is hardwired, take input $\mathsf{tag} \in \mathcal{TAG}$;
  - computes $(\mathsf{pk_{tag}}, \mathsf{sk_{tag}}) = \mathcal{E}.\mathsf{Gen}(1^\lambda; \mathcal{F}_K(\mathsf{tag}))$;
  - outputs $\mathsf{pk_{tag}}$.
  Set $\mathsf{pk} = \mathsf{piO}\big(P_{\mathsf{gen}}[K]\big) = \mathcal{O}_{\mathsf{gen}}[K]$. Output $(\mathsf{pk}, \mathsf{sk})$.
- $\mathsf{Enc}\big(\mu, \mathsf{tag}, \mathsf{pk}\big)$: Parse $\mathsf{pk} = \mathcal{O}_{\mathsf{gen}}$. Compute $\mathsf{pk_{tag}} = \mathcal{O}_{\mathsf{gen}}(\mathsf{tag})$ and output $\mathsf{ct_{tag}} \leftarrow \mathcal{E}.\mathsf{Enc}(\mu, \mathsf{pk_{tag}})$.
- $\mathsf{Dec}\big(\mathsf{ct_{tag}}, \mathsf{tag}, \mathsf{sk}\big)$: Compute $(\mathsf{pk_{tag}}, \mathsf{sk_{tag}}) = \mathcal{E}.\mathsf{Gen}\big(1^\lambda; \mathcal{F}_K(\mathsf{tag})\big)$, output $\mu = \mathcal{E}.\mathsf{Dec}(\mathsf{ct_{tag}}, \mathsf{sk_{tag}})$.
- $\mathsf{Punc.Gen}\big(\mathsf{tag}^*\big)$: Sample a PRF key K set $\mathsf{sk} = K$, and $\mathsf{pk} = \mathcal{O}_{\mathsf{gen}}[K] = \mathsf{piO}\big(P_{\mathsf{gen}}[K]\big)$, as in Gen. Additionally, let K_{tag^*} be K punctured at all $\mathsf{tag} \in \mathsf{BAD_{tag^*}}$ and set $\mathsf{sk_{tag^*}} = K_{\mathsf{tag}^*}$. Finally, let $\mathsf{P^*_{gen}}[K_{\mathsf{tag}^*}]$ be the probabilistic program:
  - K_{tag^*} is hardwired, take input $\mathsf{tag} \in \mathcal{TAG}$;
  - if $\mathsf{tag} \notin \mathsf{BAD_{tag^*}}$, compute $(\mathsf{pk_{tag}}, \mathsf{sk_{tag}}) = \mathcal{E}.\mathsf{Gen}\big(1^\lambda; \mathcal{F}_{K_{\mathsf{tag}^*}}(\mathsf{tag})\big)$;
  - if $\mathsf{tag} \in \mathsf{BAD_{tag^*}}$, sample $\mathsf{pk}^* \leftarrow \mathcal{E}.\mathsf{tGen}(1^\lambda)$
  - output either $\mathsf{pk_{tag}}$ in the first case, or pk^* in the second.
  Output the data $(\mathsf{pk}, \mathsf{sk}, \mathsf{pk_{tag^*}}, \mathsf{sk_{tag^*}}) = (\mathcal{O}_{\mathsf{gen}}, K, \mathcal{O}^*_{\mathsf{gen}}, K_{\mathsf{tag}^*})$ where $\mathcal{O}^*_{\mathsf{gen}} = \mathsf{piO}\big(P^*_{\mathsf{gen}}[K_{\mathsf{tag}^*}]\big)$.

Lemma 5. *The above scheme is a tag-puncturable encryption scheme assuming that $\mathcal{E}$ is an ε-statistical trapdoor encryption scheme and that sub-exponential iO exists.*

Proof. Correctness follows immediately from correctness of $\mathcal{E}$ and piO. The above scheme clearly satisfies the required punctured key utility properties as $\mathsf{Enc}(\mu, \mathsf{tag}, \mathsf{pk_{tag^*}})$ is lossy if and only if $\mathsf{tag} \in \mathsf{BAD_{tag^*}}$ and piO is correct. We now prove key-indistinguishability through a hybrid argument.

Hybrid H_0: This is the distribution $(\mathsf{pk}, \mathsf{sk}_{\mathsf{tag}^*})$ where $(\mathsf{pk}, \mathsf{sk}, \mathsf{pk}_{\mathsf{tag}^*}, \mathsf{sk}_{\mathsf{tag}^*}) \leftarrow$ Punc.Gen(tag^*).

Hybrid H_1: This is the distribution $(\mathsf{pk}', \mathsf{sk}_{\mathsf{tag}^*})$ where $\mathsf{pk}' = \mathsf{piO}(\mathsf{P}'_{\mathsf{gen}}[K_{\mathsf{tag}^*}])$ and $\mathsf{P}'_{\mathsf{gen}}[K_{\mathsf{tag}^*}]$ be the probabilistic program:

- K_{tag^*} is hardwired, take input $\mathsf{tag} \in \mathcal{TAG}$;
- if $\mathsf{tag} \notin \mathsf{BAD}_{\mathsf{tag}^*}$, compute $(\mathsf{pk}_{\mathsf{tag}}, \mathsf{sk}_{\mathsf{tag}}) = \mathcal{E}.\mathsf{Gen}\big(1^\lambda; \mathcal{F}_{K_{\mathsf{tag}^*}}(\mathsf{tag})\big)$;
- if $\mathsf{tag} \in \mathsf{BAD}_{\mathsf{tag}^*}$, sample $(\mathsf{pk}_{\mathsf{tag}}, \mathsf{sk}_{\mathsf{tag}}) = \mathcal{E}.\mathsf{Gen}\big(1^\lambda; r\big)$ where r is sampled at random
- output $\mathsf{pk}_{\mathsf{tag}}$.

The following claim holds because from the security of the puncturable PRF, even in the presence of the punctured key $K_{\mathsf{tag}^*} = \mathsf{sk}_{\mathsf{tag}^*}$, the output distributions of the programs $\mathsf{P}_{\mathsf{gen}}[K]$ and $\mathsf{P}'_{\mathsf{gen}}[K_{\mathsf{tag}^*}]$ are close, and hence, the security of piO implies that the obfuscations of the programs are also indistinguishable even given the punctured key.

Claim 6. For any PPT $\mathcal{A}$, $\big| \Pr\big(\mathcal{A} \text{ wins } H_0\big) - \Pr\big(\mathcal{A} \text{ wins } H_1\big) \big| = \mathsf{negl}$.

Hybrid H_2: This is the distribution $(\mathsf{pk}_{\mathsf{tag}^*}, \mathsf{sk}_{\mathsf{tag}^*})$ where $(\mathsf{pk}, \mathsf{sk}, \mathsf{pk}_{\mathsf{tag}^*}, \mathsf{sk}_{\mathsf{tag}^*}) \leftarrow$ Punc.Gen(tag^*).

The following claim holds because from the key-indistinguishability of $\mathcal{E}$, the output distributions of the programs $\mathsf{P}'_{\mathsf{gen}}[K]$ and $\mathsf{P}^*_{\mathsf{gen}}[K_{\mathsf{tag}^*}]$ are close (the constrained key is not relevant here and hence security holds even in its presence), and hence, the security of piO implies that the obfuscations of the programs are also indistinguishable (even given the punctured key).

Claim 7. For any PPT $\mathcal{A}$, $\big| \Pr\big(\mathcal{A} \text{ wins } H_1\big) - \Pr\big(\mathcal{A} \text{ wins } H_2\big) \big| = \mathsf{negl}$.

This completes the proof of key-indistinguishability.

5   CCA1 FHE from Knowledge Assumptions

Naor and Yung [NY90] show how to go from CPA encryption to CCA1 encryption using non-interactive zero-knowledge proofs (NIZKs). The CCA1 ciphertext is simply a (pair of) CPA ciphertexts along with a NIZK proving correctness. In this section we adopt this approach to the FHE setting. Applying this transformation directly results in a non-compact CCA1 FHE scheme even if the underlying CPA FHE scheme is compact as the proof length grows with the complexity of the circuit being evaluated. Thus we replace the NIZK with a zero-knowledge succinct non-interactive argument of knowledge (zkSNARK) to preserve compactness (argument of knowledge will be important in our proof of security). The zkSNARKs we use in our scheme are defined in [BCCT13, BCC+14] and constructed from knowledge assumptions. In Sect. 5.1 we formally define the zkSNARK primitive we will use, and in Sect. 5.2 we give our scheme based on them.

5.1 Zero-Knowledge SNARKs

Definition 5. Let L be a language in NP. A *zero-knowledge succinct non-interactive argument of knowledge* (zkSNARK) for L is a tuple of algorithms (Setup, Gen, Prove, Verify), defined as follows, which satisfy the correctness, succinctness, proof of knowledge, and zero-knowledge properties below.

- Setup(1^λ): is executed by a trusted third party and outputs crs $\in \{0,1\}^{\mathsf{poly}(\lambda)}$.
- Gen(1^λ): is executed by the verifier and outputs a reference string $\sigma \in \{0,1\}^{\mathsf{poly}(\lambda)}$.
- Prove$((\mathsf{crs},\sigma); x; w)$: is executed by the prover and outputs a proof π certifying $(x,w) \in L$.
- Verify$((\mathsf{crs},\sigma); x; \pi)$: is executed by the verifier and outputs 1 or 0 according to whether V accepts or rejects P's proof.

Correctness: If $(x,w) \in L$ then for any $(\mathsf{crs},\sigma) \leftarrow \mathsf{Setup}(1^\lambda) \times \mathsf{Gen}(1^\lambda)$,

$$\Pr\left[\mathsf{Verify}\big((\mathsf{crs},\sigma); x; \mathsf{Prove}((\mathsf{crs},\sigma); x; w)\big) = 1\right] = 1.$$

Succinctness: The length of the proof π output by Prove and the running time of Verify are bounded by $p(\lambda + |x|)$ where $p(\cdot)$ is a polynomial which does not depend on the language L.

Proof of Knowledge: For all PPT cheating provers Prove* who output (x,π) on input (crs,σ), there exists a PPT extractor $\mathsf{E}_{\mathsf{Prove}^*}$ such that with high probability over $(\mathsf{crs},\sigma) \leftarrow \mathsf{Setup}(1^\lambda) \times \mathsf{Gen}(1^\lambda)$,

$$\Pr\left[\mathsf{Verify}\big((\mathsf{crs},\sigma); \mathsf{Prove}^*(\mathsf{crs},\sigma)\big) = 1 \ \& \ \mathsf{E}_{\mathsf{Prove}^*}(\mathsf{crs},\sigma) = (x,w) \notin L\right] = \mathsf{negl}.$$

Zero Knowledge: For all PPT cheating verifiers Verify* who output an adversarial reference string σ^*, there exists a simulator S such that for all PPT distinguishers D, and all $(x,w) \in L$,

$$\left| \Pr_{\pi \leftarrow \mathsf{Prove}(\mathsf{crs},\sigma^*,x,w)}\Big[\mathsf{D}(\pi) = 1 \Big] - \Pr_{\pi \leftarrow \mathsf{S}(\mathsf{Verify}^*,\mathsf{crs},x)}\Big[\mathsf{D}(\pi) = 1 \Big] \right| = \mathsf{negl}.$$

Remark. The zkSNARKs defined above are *publicly verifiable*; one could (and often does) consider a weaker *designated verifier* variant, where Gen(1^λ) outputs (σ, τ) where σ is a public reference string as above and τ is a private verification tag, known only to the verifier. Our use of publicly verifiable zkSNARKS is for convenience; our construction could be made to work using designated verifier zkSNARKs using techniques of [BCCT12]. zkSNARKS can be constructed from a variety of non-standard assumptions including knowledge assumptions and extractable CRHF [BCCT12, BCCT13, BCC+14].

5.2 The Scheme

BuildingBlocks: Let $(G_{fhe}, E_{fhe}, D_{fhe}, Ev_{fhe})$ be an FHE scheme, and let $(S_{snark}, G_{snark}, P_{snark}, V_{snark})$ be a zkSNARK.

$Gen(1^\lambda)$: Draw $(pk_0, sk_0), (pk_1, sk_1) \leftarrow G_{fhe}(1^\lambda)$, and $(crs, \sigma) \leftarrow S_{snark}(1^\lambda) \times G_{snark}(1^\lambda)$. Output $(pk, sk) = ((pk_0, pk_1, crs, \sigma), (sk_0, sk_1))$.

$Enc(\mu, pk)$: For $\alpha = 0, 1$, draw $\omega_\alpha \leftarrow \$$ and set $ct^\alpha = E_{fhe}(\mu, pk_\alpha; \omega_\alpha)$ for $\alpha = 0, 1$. Also draw $\pi \leftarrow P_{snark}((crs, \sigma); (ct^0, ct^1); (\mu, \omega_0, \omega_1))$, a proof for the statement:

$$\text{``}\exists (\mu, \omega_0, \omega_1) \text{ st } ct^\alpha = E_{fhe}(\mu, pk_\alpha; \omega_\alpha) \text{ for } \alpha = 0, 1.\text{''}$$

Output $ct = (ct^0, ct^1, \pi)$.

$Dec(ct, sk)$: Parse $ct = (ct^0, ct^1, \pi)$, and $sk = (sk_0, sk_1)$. If $V_{snark}((crs, \sigma); (ct^0, ct^1); \pi) = 1$, output $D_{fhe}(ct^0, sk_0)$, otherwise output $\perp$.

$Eval(\{ct_i\}, C)$: Parse $ct_i = (ct_i^0, ct_i^1, \pi_i)$. For $\alpha = 0, 1$, draw $\omega_\alpha' \leftarrow \$$ set $ct_{eval}^\alpha = Ev_{fhe}(\{ct_i^\alpha\}, C; \omega_\alpha')$. Also draw $\pi_{eval} \leftarrow P_{snark}((crs, \sigma); (ct_{eval}^0, ct_{eval}^1); (\{ct_i^0\}, \{ct_i^1\}, \{\pi_i\}, C, \omega_0', \omega_1'))$, a proof for:

$$\exists (\{ct_i^0\}, \{ct_i^1\}, \{\pi_i\}, C, \omega_0', \omega_1') \text{ st both } \begin{array}{l} 1.\ ct_{eval}^\alpha = Ev_{fhe}(\{ct_i^\alpha\}, C, ; \omega_\alpha') \text{ for } \alpha = 0, 1; \\ 2.\ V_{snark}((crs, \sigma); (ct_i^0, ct_i^1); \pi_i) = 1 \ \forall \ i. \end{array}$$

Output $ct_{eval} = (ct_{eval}^0, ct_{eval}^1, \pi_{eval})$.

Theorem 3. If $(G_{fhe}, E_{fhe}, D_{fhe}, Ev_{fhe})$ is an FHE scheme, and $(S_{snark}, G_{snark}, P_{snark}, V_{snark})$ is a zkSNARK then the above scheme is CCA1 FHE.

Proof (Proof Sketch). We use essentially the same hybrid argument as [NY90]. *Hybrid*H_0^0: The CCA1 security game where C chooses $bit = 0$.

1. C draws $(pk_0, sk_0), (pk_1, sk_1) \leftarrow G_{fhe}(1^\lambda)$ and $(crs, \sigma) \leftarrow S_{snark}(1^\lambda) \times G_{snark}(1^\lambda)$, and sends $pk = (pk_0, pk_1, crs, \sigma)$ to A, and holds $sk = (sk_0, sk_1)$ for later use.
2. For $\beta = 1, \ldots, poly(\lambda)$:
   - A sends $ct_\beta = (ct_\beta^0, ct_\beta^1, \pi_\beta)$ to C.
   - C returns $Dec(ct_\beta, sk)$ to A. This involves checking $V_{snark}((crs, \sigma); (ct_\beta^0, ct_\beta^1); \pi_\beta) = 1$, and outputting $D_{fhe}(ct_\beta^0, sk_0)$.
3. A chooses $(\mu_0, \mu_1) \leftarrow M$ and sends (μ_0, μ_1) to C.
4. C draws $\omega_\alpha \leftarrow \$$ and sets $ct^\alpha = E_{fhe}(\mu_0, pk_\alpha; \omega_\alpha)$ for $\alpha = 0, 1$. Furthermore, C draws a certificate $\pi \leftarrow P_{snark}((crs, \sigma); (ct^0, ct^1); (\mu_0, \omega_0, \omega_1))$, sets $ct^* = (ct^0, ct^1, \pi)$ and sends ct^* to A.
5. A outputs $guess \in \{0, 1\}$ and wins if $guess = 0$.

Hybrid H_1^0: This is the same as H_0^0 except for the way A's queries are answered. Each time A sends $(ct_\beta^0, ct_\beta^1, \pi_\beta)$, C verifies π_β as usual: if $V_{snark}((crs, \sigma); (ct_\beta^0, ct_\beta^1); \pi_\beta) = 0$, C returns $\perp$. However, in addition, C computes $\mu_\beta^\alpha = D_{fhe}(ct_\beta^\alpha, sk_\alpha)$ for $\alpha = 0, 1$ and checks that $\mu_\beta^0 = \mu_\beta^1$. If not, C aborts and A wins the game. Otherwise, C returns μ_β^0 as usual.

Claim 8. For any PPT $\mathcal{A}$, $\left|\Pr\left(\mathcal{A} \text{ wins } \mathsf{H}_0^0\right) - \Pr\left(\mathcal{A} \text{ wins } \mathsf{H}_1^0\right)\right| = \mathsf{negl}$.

Proof (Proof Sketch). This follows immediately from the proof of knowledge of the zkSNARK.

Hybrid H_2^0: This is the same as H_1^0 except that $\mathcal{C}$ simulates the proof π in the challenge ciphertext. Specifically, $\mathcal{C}$ produces ct^* by drawing $\mathsf{ct}^\alpha \leftarrow \mathsf{E}_{\mathsf{fhe}}(\mu_{\mathsf{bit}}, \mathsf{pk}_\alpha)$ as usual, but draws $\pi \leftarrow \mathsf{S}\left(\mathcal{A}, (\mathsf{crs}, \sigma), (\mathsf{ct}^0, \mathsf{ct}^1)\right)$ instead of from $\mathsf{P}_{\mathsf{snark}}(\cdot)$ as in H_1.

Claim 9. For any PPT $\mathcal{A}$, $\left|\Pr\left(\mathcal{A} \text{ wins } \mathsf{H}_1^0\right) - \Pr\left(\mathcal{A} \text{ wins } \mathsf{H}_2^0\right)\right| = \mathsf{negl}$.

Proof (Proof Sketch). This follows immediately from the zero knowledge of the zkSNARK.

Hybrid $\mathsf{H}_2^{0,1}$: This is the same as H_2^0 except for the way $\mathcal{C}$ produces ct^*. This time, $\mathcal{C}$ draws ciphertexts $\mathsf{ct}^\alpha \leftarrow \mathsf{E}_{\mathsf{fhe}}(\mu_\alpha, \mathsf{pk}_\alpha)$ for $\alpha = 0, 1$ as well as a simulated π, and sends $\mathsf{ct}^* = (\mathsf{ct}^0, \mathsf{ct}^1, \pi)$.

Claim 10. For any PPT $\mathcal{A}$, $\left|\Pr\left(\mathcal{A} \text{ wins } \mathsf{H}_2^0\right) - \Pr\left(\mathcal{A} \text{ wins } \mathsf{H}_2^{0,1}\right)\right| = \mathsf{negl}$.

Proof (Proof Sketch). This follows immediately from the semantic security of the underlying FHE scheme.

Hybrid $\mathsf{H}_3^{0,1}$: This is the same as $\mathsf{H}_2^{0,1}$ except that now $\mathcal{C}$ answers ciphertext queries by sending μ_β^1 instead of μ_β^0. This game is identical to $\mathsf{H}_2^{0,1}$ because of the equality check performed during decryption.

Claim 11. For any (unbounded) $\mathcal{A}$, $\Pr\left(\mathcal{A} \text{ wins } \mathsf{H}_2^{0,1}\right) = \Pr\left(\mathcal{A} \text{ wins } \mathsf{H}_3^{0,1}\right)$.

Hybrid $\mathsf{H}_3^{1,1}$: This is the same as $\mathsf{H}_3^{0,1}$ except for the way $\mathcal{C}$ produces ct^*. Now, $\mathcal{C}$ draws $\mathsf{ct}^\alpha \leftarrow \mathsf{E}_{\mathsf{fhe}}(\mu_1, \mathsf{pk}_\alpha)$ for $\alpha = 0, 1$ and simulates π as usual. $\mathcal{C}$ sends $\mathsf{ct}^* = (\mathsf{ct}^0, \mathsf{ct}^1, \pi)$.

Claim 12. For any PPT $\mathcal{A}$, $\left|\Pr\left(\mathcal{A} \text{ wins } \mathsf{H}_3^{0,1}\right) - \Pr\left(\mathcal{A} \text{ wins } \mathsf{H}_3^{1,1}\right)\right| = \mathsf{negl}$.

Proof (Proof Sketch). This follows immediately from the semantic security of the underlying FHE scheme.

Hybrid H_2^1: This is the same as $\mathsf{H}_3^{1,1}$ except that $\mathcal{C}$ answers ciphertext queries by sending μ_β^0 again instead of μ_β^1. This game is identical to $\mathsf{H}_3^{1,1}$ because of the equality check performed during decryption.

Claim 13. For any (unbounded) $\mathcal{A}$, $\Pr\left(\mathcal{A} \text{ wins } \mathsf{H}_2^1\right) = \Pr\left(\mathcal{A} \text{ wins } \mathsf{H}_3^{1,1}\right)$.

We now complete the argument by going from H_2^1 to H_0^1 in reverse just as we went from H_0^0 to H_2^0. The next claim follows, and completes the proof of Theorem 3.

Claim 14. For any PPT $\mathcal{A}$, $\left|\Pr\left(\mathcal{A} \text{ wins } \mathsf{H}_0^0\right) - \Pr\left(\mathcal{A} \text{ wins } \mathsf{H}_0^1\right)\right| = \mathsf{negl}$.

A   Linear Algebraic Encryption

In this section we define *linear algebraic encryption*, LAE, as an intermediate type of encryption with which to instantiate CCA. Roughly speaking, a LAE scheme is an encryption scheme whose plaintext space $\mathcal{M}$ is a finite field, and which supports $\mathcal{M}$–linear operations on ciphertexts. If one encrypts $\mathbf{v} \in \mathcal{M}^k$, coordinate by coordinate obtaining ciphertexts $\{ct_i\}_{i=1,\dots,k}$, then for any linear map $\varphi : \mathcal{M}^k \to \mathcal{M}^\ell$, one can compute evaluated ciphertexts $\{ct'_j\}_{j=1,\dots,\ell} \leftarrow \mathsf{Eval}(\{ct_i\}, \varphi)$ which decrypt, using evaluated secret keys $\{sk'_j\} \leftarrow \mathsf{KeyEval}(\{sk_i\}, \varphi)$, to $\varphi(\mathbf{v}) \in \mathcal{M}^\ell$. Syntactically, this puts LAE very close to functional encryption for linear circuits; the correctness and security properties are essentially the same. LAE, however, also requires soundness. Specifically, it must be that evaluating ciphertexts and decrypting is the same as decrypting and evaluating plaintexts *even for adversarially chosen ciphertexts*. This will be crucial to obtain CCA security. We now define LAE formally.

Definition 6 (Linear Algebraic Encryption). Let $\mathcal{M}$, $\mathcal{CT}$, $\mathcal{PK}$, and $\mathcal{SK}$ represent the message, ciphertext, public key, and secret key spaces of the scheme, respectively; let $\mathcal{M}$ be a finite field. A *linear algebraic encryption scheme* is a tuple $(\mathsf{Gen}, \mathsf{Enc}, \mathsf{Dec}, \mathsf{CTEval}, \mathsf{SKEval}, \mathsf{EvalDec})$ of polytime algorithms, defined as follows, which satisfy the *correctness*, *soundness* and *security* properties below.

- $\underline{\mathsf{Gen}(1^\lambda, 1^k)}$: takes security parameter λ, $k \in \mathbb{Z}$ and outputs $(\{pk_i\}, \{sk_i\}) \in \mathcal{PK}^k \times \mathcal{SK}^k$. The algorithms below all also take $(1^\lambda, 1^k)$ as implied inputs.
- $\underline{\mathsf{Enc}(\{msg_i\}, \{pk_i\})}$: is a randomized algorithm which takes $(\{msg_i\}, \{pk_i\}) \in \mathcal{M}^k \times \mathcal{PK}^k$ and outputs ciphertexts $\{ct_i\} \in \mathcal{CT}^k$.
- $\underline{\mathsf{Dec}(\{ct_i\}, \{sk_i\})}$: takes $(\{ct_i\}, \{sk_i\}) \in \mathcal{CT}^k \times \mathcal{SK}^k$ and outputs $\{msg_i\} \in \mathcal{M}^k$.
- $\underline{\mathsf{CTEval}(\{ct_i\}, \varphi)}$: takes $\{ct_i\} \in \mathcal{CT}^k$, linear map $\varphi : \mathcal{M}^k \to \mathcal{M}^\ell$ and outputs $\{ct'_j\} \in \mathcal{CT}^\ell$.
- $\underline{\mathsf{SKEval}(\{sk_i\}, \varphi)}$: takes $\{sk_i\} \in \mathcal{SK}^k$, a linear map $\varphi : \mathcal{M}^k \to \mathcal{M}^\ell$ and outputs $\{sk'_j\} \in \mathcal{SK}^\ell$.
- $\underline{\mathsf{EvalDec}(\{ct'_j\}, \{sk'_j\})}$: takes $(\{ct'_j\}, \{sk'_j\}) \in \mathcal{CT}^\ell \times \mathcal{SK}^\ell$ and outputs $\{msg'_j\} \in \mathcal{M}^\ell$.

Correctness: For any $\{msg_i\} \in \mathcal{M}^k$, and whp over $(\{pk_i\}, \{sk_i\}) \xleftarrow{\$} \mathsf{Gen}(1^\lambda, 1^k)$,

$$\Pr\left[\mathsf{Dec}\big(\mathsf{Enc}(\{msg_i\}, \{pk_i\}), \{sk_i\}\big) = \{msg_i\}\right] = 1 - \mathsf{negl}.$$

Soundness: For any $\varphi : \mathcal{M}^k \to \mathcal{M}^\ell$ and whp over $(\{pk_i\}, \{sk_i\}) \xleftarrow{\$} \mathsf{Gen}(1^\lambda, 1^k)$, for any (potentially malformed) ciphertexts $\{ct_i\} \in \mathcal{CT}^k$, the following distributions are statistically close:

- draw $\{\mathsf{msg}_i\} \leftarrow \mathsf{Dec}(\{\mathsf{ct}_i\}, \{\mathsf{sk}_i\})$, output $\varphi(\{\mathsf{msg}_i\})$;
- draw $\{\mathsf{ct}'_j\} \leftarrow \mathsf{CTEval}(\{\mathsf{ct}_i\}, \varphi)$, $\{\mathsf{sk}'_j\} \leftarrow \mathsf{SKEval}(\{\mathsf{sk}_i\}, \varphi)$, output $\mathsf{EvalDec}(\{\mathsf{ct}'_j\}, \{\mathsf{sk}'_j\})$.

Security: For any PPT adversary $\mathcal{A}$, its chance of winning the following game against a challenger $\mathcal{C}$ is at most $1/2 + \mathsf{negl}$.

1. $\mathcal{A}$ sends (k, ℓ, φ) to $\mathcal{C}$ where $k = \mathsf{poly}(\lambda)$, $\ell < k$ and $\varphi : \mathcal{M}^k \to \mathcal{M}^\ell$ is a linear map.
2. $\mathcal{C}$ draws $(\{\mathsf{pk}_i\}, \{\mathsf{sk}_i\}) \overset{\$}{\leftarrow} \mathsf{Gen}(1^\lambda, 1^k)$, $\{\mathsf{sk}'_j\} \leftarrow \mathsf{SKEval}(\{\mathsf{sk}_i\}, \varphi)$, and sends $(\{\mathsf{pk}_i\}, \{\mathsf{sk}'_j\})$ to $\mathcal{A}$.
3. $\mathcal{A}$ chooses $\{\mathsf{msg}_i^0\}, \{\mathsf{msg}_i^1\} \in \mathcal{M}^k$ st $\varphi(\{\mathsf{msg}_i^0\}) = \varphi(\{\mathsf{msg}_i^1\})$, and sends $(\{\mathsf{msg}_i^0\}, \{\mathsf{msg}_i^1\})$ to $\mathcal{C}$. $\mathcal{C}$ draws $b \leftarrow \{0, 1\}$, $\{\mathsf{ct}_i^*\} \leftarrow \mathsf{Enc}(\{\mathsf{msg}_i^b\}, \{\mathsf{pk}_i\})$ and sends $\{\mathsf{ct}_i^*\}$ to $\mathcal{A}$.
4. $\mathcal{A}$ sends a bit $b' \in \{0, 1\}$ to $\mathcal{C}$ and wins if $b = b'$.

Remark 1. If a LAE scheme is such that every tuple in $\mathcal{CT}^k$ is a valid encryption of some message vector in $\mathcal{M}^k$, then perfect correctness implies soundness.

Remark 2. It is possible to define versions of the above security game where $\mathcal{A}$ gets to choose φ after receiving $\{\mathsf{pk}_i\}$, or in an adaptive, coordinate-by-coordinate fashion. We use the above simple version as it is already sufficient for CCA2 encryption.

A.1   Adding Homomorphism

Definition 7 (Additively Homomorphic LAE). Let LAE be a LAE scheme. We say that LAE is *additively homomorphic* if there exists a PPT algorithm Add which satisfies the properties below. Let $m, m' \in \mathcal{M}$ be arbitrary and $(\mathsf{pk}, \mathsf{sk}) \leftarrow \mathsf{Gen}(1^\lambda)$.

- $\mathsf{Add}(\mathsf{ct}, \mathsf{ct}')$: Given $\mathsf{ct} = \mathsf{Enc}(m, \mathsf{pk})$ and $\mathsf{ct}' = \mathsf{Enc}(m', \mathsf{pk})$, output $\mathsf{ct} + \mathsf{ct}'$ which satisfies $\mathsf{Dec}(\mathsf{ct} + \mathsf{ct}', \mathsf{sk}) = m + m'$.

Remark. Though the definition of homomorphic LAE only requires homomorphic additions on single ciphertexts, it extends coordinate-wise to give homomorphic addition on ciphertext vectors. We also have soundness.

Claim 15 (Homomorphic Soundness). For any (possibly malformed) ciphertexts $\mathsf{ct}, \mathsf{ct}' \in \mathcal{CT}^k$ and whp over $(\mathsf{pk}, \mathsf{sk}) \leftarrow \mathsf{Gen}(1^\lambda, 1^k)$ we have that for any linear $\varphi : \mathbb{Z}_q^k \to \mathbb{Z}_q^\ell$, if $\mathsf{sk}_\varphi = \mathsf{SKEval}(\mathsf{sk}, \varphi)$ then

$$\mathsf{EvalDec}\big(\mathsf{CTEval}(\mathsf{ct} + \mathsf{ct}', \varphi), \mathsf{sk}_\varphi\big) = \mathsf{EvalDec}\big(\mathsf{CTEval}(\mathsf{ct}, \varphi), \mathsf{sk}_\varphi\big)$$
$$+ \mathsf{EvalDec}\big(\mathsf{CTEval}(\mathsf{ct}', \varphi), \mathsf{sk}_\varphi\big).$$

Proof Let $\mathbf{v} = \mathsf{EvalDec}\big(\mathsf{CTEval}(\mathsf{ct}, \varphi), \mathsf{sk}_\varphi\big)$ and $\mathbf{v}' = \mathsf{EvalDec}\big(\mathsf{CTEval}(\mathsf{ct}', \varphi), \mathsf{sk}_\varphi\big)$. We have

$$\mathsf{EvalDec}\big(\mathsf{CTEval}(\mathsf{ct} + \mathsf{ct}', \varphi), \mathsf{sk}_\varphi\big) = \varphi\big(\mathsf{Dec}(\mathsf{ct} + \mathsf{ct}', \mathsf{sk})\big)$$
$$= \varphi\big(\mathsf{Dec}(\mathsf{ct}, \mathsf{sk})\big) + \varphi\big(\mathsf{Dec}(\mathsf{ct}', \mathsf{sk})\big) = \mathbf{v} + \mathbf{v}',$$

using soundness of LAE, additive homomorphism and linearity of φ.

A.2   Additively Homomorphic CCA1 Encryption from LAE

– <u>Setup:</u> Let LAE, be an additively homomorphic LAE scheme with message space $\mathcal{M} = \mathbb{Z}_q$ for a large prime $q = \lambda^{\omega(1)}$.
– <u>Gen(1^λ):</u> Draw $\big(\{\mathsf{pk}_i\}, \{\mathsf{sk}_i\}\big)_{i=1,\ldots,5} \leftarrow \mathsf{LAE.Gen}(1^\lambda, 1^5)$. Output $(\mathsf{pk}, \mathsf{sk}) = \big(\{\mathsf{pk}_i\}, \{\mathsf{sk}_i\}\big)$.
– <u>Enc(m, pk):</u> Choose random $r, s \leftarrow \mathbb{Z}_q$, and compute ciphertexts $\{\mathsf{ct}_i\} \leftarrow \mathsf{LAE.Enc}\big(\mathbf{v}, \{\mathsf{pk}_i\}\big)$, where $\mathbf{v} = (m - r - s, r, s, 0, 0) \in \mathbb{Z}_q^5$. Output $\mathsf{ct} = \{\mathsf{ct}_i\}$.
– <u>Add$(\mathsf{ct}, \mathsf{ct}')$:</u> Given $\mathsf{ct} = \{\mathsf{ct}_i\}$ and $\mathsf{ct}' = \{\mathsf{ct}'_i\}$, output $\mathsf{ct} + \mathsf{ct}' = \{\mathsf{ct}_i + \mathsf{ct}'_i\}$ where $+$ denotes the ciphertext addition of LAE.
– <u>Dec$(\mathsf{ct}, \mathsf{sk})$:</u> Parse $\mathsf{ct} = \{\mathsf{ct}_i\}$. Compute $\mathbf{v} = \mathsf{LAE.Dec}\big(\{\mathsf{ct}_i\}, \{\mathsf{sk}_i\}\big) \in \mathbb{Z}^5$. If $v_4 = v_5 = 0$, output $v_1 + v_2 + v_3$, otherwise output $\bot$.

Theorem 4. *The above scheme is an additively homomorphic CCA1 encryption scheme.*

Correctness and homomorphic correctness follow immediately from the same properties of LAE. To prove security, we use a hybrid argument.

Hybrid $\mathsf{H}_0^{\mathsf{bit}}$*: The CCA1 Game*

1. $\mathcal{C}$ draws $\big(\{\mathsf{pk}_i\}, \{\mathsf{sk}_i\}\big) \leftarrow \mathsf{LAE.Gen}(1^\lambda, 1^5)$ and sends $\{\mathsf{pk}_i\}$ to $\mathcal{A}$.
2. For $\alpha = 1, \ldots, \mathsf{poly}(\lambda)$:
   – $\mathcal{A}$ sends a ciphertext ct_α to $\mathcal{C}$;
   – $\mathcal{C}$ computes $\mathbf{v}_\alpha = \mathsf{LAE.Dec}(\mathsf{ct}_\alpha, \{\mathsf{sk}_i\})$, checks that $v_{\alpha,4} = v_{\alpha,5} = 0$, if not $\mathcal{C}$ returns $\bot$; if so sends $v_{\alpha,1} + v_{\alpha,2} + v_{\alpha,3}$ to $\mathcal{A}$.
3. $\mathcal{A}$ sends two messages $m_0, m_1 \in \mathbb{Z}_q$ to $\mathcal{C}$.
4. $\mathcal{C}$ sets $m^* = m_{\mathsf{bit}}$, draws $\mathsf{ct}^* \leftarrow \mathsf{Enc}\big(m^*, \{\mathsf{pk}_i\}\big)$ and returns ct^* to $\mathcal{A}$.
5. $\mathcal{A}$ outputs $\mathsf{guess} \in \{0, 1\}$ and wins if $\mathsf{guess} = \mathsf{bit}$.

Hybrid $\mathsf{H}_1^{\mathsf{bit}}$*:* This is the same as $\mathsf{H}_0^{\mathsf{bit}}$ except for the way $\mathcal{C}$ answers ciphertexts ct_α. In step 1, in addition to $\big(\{\mathsf{pk}_i\}, \{\mathsf{sk}_i\}\big) \leftarrow \mathsf{LAE.Gen}(1^\lambda, 1^5)$ $\mathcal{C}$ chooses random linear $\varphi : \mathbb{Z}_q^5 \rightarrow \mathbb{Z}_q$ such that $\varphi(H) = 0$ where $H = \{\mathbf{v} \in \mathbb{Z}_q^5 : v_4 = v_5 = 0\}$. Also, let $\varphi_{\mathsf{eval}} : \mathbb{Z}_q^5 \rightarrow \mathbb{Z}_q$ be a random linear map of the form $\varphi_{\mathsf{eval}}(\mathbf{v}) = v_1 + v_2 + v_3 + av_4 + bv_5$ for random $a, b \in \mathbb{Z}_q$. $\mathcal{C}$ computes $\mathbf{v}_\alpha = \mathsf{LAE.Dec}(\mathsf{ct}_\alpha, \{\mathsf{sk}_i\})$, as usual. If $\varphi(\mathbf{v}_\alpha) = 0$, $\mathcal{C}$ returns $\varphi_{\mathsf{eval}}(\mathbf{v}_\alpha)$, otherwise $\bot$.

Claim 16. For any (computationally unbounded) adversary $\mathcal{A}$ and bit $\in \{0,1\}$,

$$\left| \Pr\left(\mathcal{A} \ wins \ \mathsf{H}_1^{\mathsf{bit}} \right) - \Pr\left(\mathcal{A} \ wins \ \mathsf{H}_0^{\mathsf{bit}} \right) \right| = \mathsf{negl}(\lambda).$$

Proof (Proof Sketch). Note $\mathsf{H}_1^{\mathsf{bit}}$ is identical to $\mathsf{H}_0^{\mathsf{bit}}$ except that in $\mathsf{H}_0^{\mathsf{bit}}$, $\mathcal{C}$ checks that $\mathbf{v}_\alpha \in H$, while in $\mathsf{H}_1^{\mathsf{bit}}$, $\mathcal{C}$ checks that $\varphi(\mathbf{v}_\alpha) = 0$. As $\varphi : \mathbb{Z}_q^5 \to \mathbb{Z}_q$ is random such that $\varphi(H) = 0$, for any $\mathbf{v}_\alpha \notin H$, $\Pr_\varphi[\varphi(\mathbf{v}_\alpha) = 0] = 1/q = \mathsf{negl}(\lambda)$. Claim 16 follows from the union bound over the polynomially many query ciphertexts.

Hybrid $\mathsf{H}_2^{\mathsf{bit}}$: This is the same as $\mathsf{H}_1^{\mathsf{bit}}$ except that instead of computing decryptions honestly $\mathbf{v}_\alpha = \mathsf{LAE.Dec}(\mathsf{ct}_\alpha, \{\mathsf{sk}_i\})$ and checking $\varphi(\mathbf{v}_\alpha) = 0$, $\mathcal{C}$ computes $\mathsf{ct}' = \mathsf{LAE.CTEval}(\{\mathsf{ct}_i\}, (\varphi, \varphi_{\mathsf{eval}}))$, and evaluated decryption $(v, w) = \mathsf{LAE.EvalDec}(\mathsf{ct}', \mathsf{sk}')$, where $\mathsf{sk}' = \mathsf{LAE.SKEval}(\{\mathsf{sk}_i\}, (\varphi, \varphi_{\mathsf{eval}}))$, and $(\varphi, \varphi_{\mathsf{eval}}) : \mathbb{Z}_q^5 \to \mathbb{Z}_q^2$ is the linear map $\mathbf{v} \mapsto (\varphi(\mathbf{v}), \varphi_{\mathsf{eval}}(\mathbf{v}))$. If $v = 0$ $\mathcal{C}$ returns w, otherwise $\perp$. The claim follows immediately from the soundness of LAE.

Claim 17. For any (computationally unbounded) adversary $\mathcal{A}$ and bit $\in \{0,1\}$,

$$\left| \Pr\left(\mathcal{A} \ wins \ \mathsf{H}_2^{\mathsf{bit}} \right) - \Pr\left(\mathcal{A} \ wins \ \mathsf{H}_1^{\mathsf{bit}} \right) \right| = \mathsf{negl}(\lambda).$$

Hybrid $\mathsf{H}_3^{\mathsf{bit}}$: This is the same as $\mathsf{H}_2^{\mathsf{bit}}$ except for the way the challenge ciphertext is produced. Upon receiving (m_0, m_1) from $\mathcal{A}$, $\mathcal{C}$ chooses a random $\mathbf{v}^* \in \mathbb{Z}_q^5$ such that $v_1^* + v_2^* + v_3^* = m_{\mathsf{bit}}$ and $\varphi(\mathbf{v}^*) = 0$. $\mathcal{C}$ draws $\mathsf{ct}^* \leftarrow \mathsf{LAE.Enc}(\mathbf{v}^*, \{\mathsf{pk}_i\})$, and sends ct^* to $\mathcal{A}$.

Claim 18. For any PPT $\mathcal{A}$ and bit $\in \{0,1\}$, $\left| \Pr\left(\mathcal{A} \ wins \ \mathsf{H}_2^{\mathsf{bit}} \right) - \Pr\left(\mathcal{A} \ wins \ \mathsf{H}_3^{\mathsf{bit}} \right) \right| = \mathsf{negl}(\lambda)$.

Proof (Proof Sketch.). Let $\mathcal{A}$ be a PPT adversary who distinguishes between $\mathsf{H}_2^{\mathsf{bit}}$ and $\mathsf{H}_3^{\mathsf{bit}}$ with noticeable advantage, we construct $\mathcal{B}$ who breaks the security of the LAE scheme. $\mathcal{B}$ chooses φ as above and sends $(\varphi, \varphi_{\mathsf{eval}})$ to $\mathcal{C}$ and receives $\{\mathsf{pk}_i\}, \mathsf{sk}'$ from $\mathcal{C}$, and forwards $\{\mathsf{pk}_i\}$ to $\mathcal{A}$. Every time $\mathcal{A}$ asks a query ct_α, $\mathcal{B}$ uses sk' to decrypt the evaluated ciphertext like in both games. Upon receiving (m_0, m_1) from $\mathcal{A}$, $\mathcal{B}$ chooses $\mathbf{v}_0, \mathbf{v}_1$ such that $\varphi_{\mathsf{eval}}(\mathbf{v}_0) = \varphi_{\mathsf{eval}}(\mathbf{v}_1) = m_{\mathsf{bit}}$, $\mathbf{v}_0 \in H$ and $\mathbf{v}_1$ is otherwise random such that $\varphi(\mathbf{v}_1) = 0$. $\mathcal{B}$ sends $(\mathbf{v}_0, \mathbf{v}_1)$ to $\mathcal{C}$ and receives ct^*, which he forwards to $\mathcal{A}$. $\mathcal{B}$ forwards $\mathcal{A}$'s guess back to $\mathcal{C}$. It is clear that $\mathcal{B}$ wins if and only if $\mathcal{A}$ guesses correctly between $\mathsf{H}_2^{\mathsf{bit}}$ or $\mathsf{H}_3^{\mathsf{bit}}$.

Claim 19. For any $\mathcal{A}$, $\Pr\left(\mathcal{A} \ wins \ \mathsf{H}_3^0 \right) = \Pr\left(\mathcal{A} \ wins \ \mathsf{H}_3^1 \right)$.

Proof (Proof Sketch). Consider the random process specified by $m \in \mathbb{Z}_q$: (1) choose random $\varphi : \mathbb{Z}_q^5 \to \mathbb{Z}_q$ such that $\varphi(H) = 0$ and $a, b \leftarrow \mathbb{Z}_q$, defining $\varphi_{\mathsf{eval}} : \mathbb{Z}_q^5 \to \mathbb{Z}_q$ (2) choose and output random $\mathbf{v} \in \mathbb{Z}_q^5$ such that $\varphi(\mathbf{v}) = 0$ and $\varphi_{\mathsf{eval}}(\mathbf{v}) = m$. The randomness of φ and φ_{eval} ensures that the output of this process is identically distributed for all $m \in \mathbb{Z}_q$, so H_3^0 and H_3^1 are identical.

B   Instantiating Homomorphic LAE from DDH

In this section, we describe instantiations of linear algebraic encryption schemes from the Decisional Diffie-Hellman (DDH) assumption. The idea is to use El-Gamal encryption under different public keys but using the same randomness in order to enable the linear homomorphism we need. We describe the scheme below. The system is designed for small message spaces such as $\mathcal{M} = \{0, 1\}$.

- $\mathsf{Gen}(1^\lambda, 1^k)$ takes security parameter λ, $k \in \mathbb{Z}$. It chooses a group $\mathbb{G}$ of order q, where q is a prime of length $\mathsf{poly}(\lambda)$, along with a generator g of $\mathbb{G}$. Next, it samples k random values $\alpha_i \overset{\$}{\leftarrow} \mathbb{Z}_q$, $i \in [k]$. Finally, it sets and outputs $\mathsf{pk} = (\mathbb{G}, g, q, \{\mathsf{pk}_i\})$ and $\mathsf{sk} = (\{\mathsf{sk}_i\})$, where $\mathsf{sk}_i = \alpha_i$ and $\mathsf{pk}_i = g^{\alpha_i}$.
- $\mathsf{Enc}(\{\mathsf{msg}_i\}, \mathsf{pk})$ is a randomized algorithm which takes k messages msg_i, $i \in [k]$ and the public key pk. It first chooses a random value $r \overset{\$}{\leftarrow} \mathbb{Z}_q$. It outputs $\mathsf{ct} = (g^r, \{\mathsf{ct}_i\})$ where $\mathsf{ct}_i = \mathsf{pk}_i^r g^{\mathsf{msg}_i}$.
- $\mathsf{Dec}(\mathsf{ct}, \mathsf{sk})$ takes a ciphertext $\mathsf{ct} = (g^r, \{\mathsf{ct}_i\})$ and the secret key sk and outputs $\{\mathsf{msg}_i\}$ where for each $i \in [k]$,

$$\mathsf{msg}_i = \mathrm{dLog}_g\left(\frac{\mathsf{ct}_i}{(g^r)^{\mathsf{sk}_i}}\right)$$

where $\mathrm{dLog}_g(\cdot)$ denotes computing the discrete logarithm with respect to g.
- $\mathsf{CTEval}(\{\mathsf{ct}_i\}, \varphi)$ takes a ciphertext $\mathsf{ct} = (g^r, \{\mathsf{ct}_i\})$ and linear map $\varphi : \mathcal{M}^k \to \mathcal{M}^\ell$. Let $\varphi^\times$ denote the map which replaces addition in φ with multiplication and multiplication in φ with exponentiation. More formally, suppose

$$\varphi(x) = \left\{\sum_{i \in [k]} \varphi_{i,j} x_i\right\}_{j \in [\ell]}$$

Define

$$\varphi^\times(x) = \left\{\prod_{i \in [k]} x_i^{\varphi_{i,j}}\right\}_{j \in [\ell]}$$

The algorithm outputs $\mathsf{ct}' = g^r, \{\mathsf{ct}_j'\}_{j \in [\ell]} = \varphi^\times(\{\mathsf{ct}_i\})$.
- $\mathsf{KeyEval}(\{\mathsf{sk}_i\}, \varphi)$ takes the secret key sk, a linear map $\varphi : \mathcal{M}^k \to \mathcal{M}^\ell$ and outputs $\mathsf{sk}' = \{\mathsf{sk}_j'\}_{j \in [\ell]} = \varphi(\mathsf{sk})$.
- $\mathsf{EvalDec}(\mathsf{ct}', \mathsf{sk}')$ takes an evaluated ciphertext $\mathsf{ct}' = g^r, \{\mathsf{ct}_j'\}$ and an evaluated secret key $\mathsf{sk}' = \{\mathsf{sk}_j'\}$ outputs $\{\mathsf{msg}_j'\}$ where for each $j \in [\ell]$,

$$\mathsf{msg}_j' = \mathrm{dLog}_g\left(\frac{\mathsf{ct}_j'}{(g^r)^{\mathsf{sk}_j'}}\right)$$

where $\mathrm{dLog}_g(\cdot)$ denotes computing the discrete logarithm with respect to g.

Correctness and Soundness. The scheme is perfectly correct and sound. For any $\{\mathsf{msg}_i\} \in \mathcal{M}^k$ and $(\mathsf{pk}, \mathsf{sk}) \xleftarrow{\$} \mathsf{Gen}(1^\lambda, 1^k)$,

$$
\begin{aligned}
\mathsf{Dec}\big(\mathsf{Enc}(\{\mathsf{msg}_i\}, \{\mathsf{pk}_i\}), \{\mathsf{sk}_i\}\big) &= \left\{ \mathrm{dLog}_g \left(\frac{\mathsf{ct}_i}{(g^r)^{\mathsf{sk}_i}} \right) \right\} \\
&= \left\{ \mathrm{dLog}_g \left(\frac{\mathsf{pk}_i^r \, g^{\mathsf{msg}_i}}{(g^{\mathsf{sk}_i})^r} \right) \right\} \\
&= \left\{ \mathrm{dLog}_g \left(g^{\mathsf{msg}_i} \right) \right\} \\
&= \{\mathsf{msg}_i\}
\end{aligned}
$$

For any $\varphi : \mathcal{M}^k \to \mathcal{M}^\ell$, $(\mathsf{pk}, \mathsf{sk}) \xleftarrow{\$} \mathsf{Gen}(1^\lambda, 1^k)$ and any (potentially malformed) ciphertexts ct,

$$
\begin{aligned}
\varphi\big(\mathsf{Dec}(\{\mathsf{ct}_i\}, \{\mathsf{sk}_i\})\big) &= \left\{ \sum_{i \in [k]} \varphi_{i,j} \mathrm{dLog}_g \left(\frac{\mathsf{ct}_i}{(g^r)^{\mathsf{sk}_i}} \right) \right\}_{j \in [\ell]} \\
&= \left\{ \mathrm{dLog}_g \left(\prod_{i \in [k]} \left[\frac{\mathsf{ct}_i}{(g^r)^{\mathsf{sk}_i}} \right]^{\varphi_{i,j}} \right) \right\}_{j \in [\ell]} \\
&= \left\{ \mathrm{dLog}_g \left(\left[\frac{\prod_{i \in [k]} \mathsf{ct}_i^{\varphi_{i,j}}}{g^{r \sum_{i \in [k]} \varphi_{i,j} \mathsf{sk}_i}} \right] \right) \right\}_{j \in [\ell]} \\
&= \left\{ \mathrm{dLog}_g \left(\frac{\mathsf{ct}_j'}{(g^r)^{\mathsf{sk}_j'}} \right) \right\}_{j \in [\ell]} \\
&= \mathsf{EvalDec}\big(\mathsf{Eval}(\mathsf{ct}, \varphi), \mathsf{KeyEval}(\mathsf{sk}, \varphi)\big)
\end{aligned}
$$

Security. Security of the scheme is based on the security of the El-Gamal cryptosystem and hence the Decisional Diffie-Hellman (DDH) assumption. We prove here security for the case that $k = 2$ and $\ell = 1$ and note that the proof inductively generalizes for larger k and ℓ.

Suppose there exists a PPT adversary $\mathcal{A}$ who can break the security of the LA encryption scheme with $k = 2$ and $\ell = 1$. We now construct a PPT adversary $\mathcal{B}$ who breaks the semantic security of the El-Gamal encryption scheme with the same advantage. Since we know that under the DDH assumption, the latter advantage is negligible, so is the former.

$\mathcal{B}$ runs using $\mathcal{A}$ as follows. Let $\mathcal{C}$ denote the challenger of the El-Gamal encryption scheme. $\mathcal{A}$ sends $(k = 2, \ell = 1, \varphi)$ to $\mathcal{B}$ where $\varphi : \mathcal{M}^k \to \mathcal{M}^\ell$ is a linear map. Let $\varphi = [\varphi_1, \varphi_2]$. $\mathcal{B}$ also receives the public key $\mathsf{pk}_{\mathsf{EG}} = (\mathbb{G}, g, q, h_1)$ from $\mathcal{C}$, where $h = g^{\alpha_1}$ for some $\alpha_1 \in \mathbb{Z}_q$ unknown to $\mathcal{B}$. $\mathcal{B}$ then samples a random $\alpha \xleftarrow{\$} \mathbb{Z}_q$ and computes

$$h_2 = \left(\frac{g^\alpha}{h_1^{\phi_1}}\right)^{\varphi_2^{-1}}$$

Note that this implicitly sets $h_2 = g^{\alpha_2}$, where $\phi([\alpha_1, \alpha_2]^T) = \alpha$. $\mathcal{B}$ sets $\mathsf{pk} = (\mathbb{G}, g, q, \{\mathsf{pk}_i\})$ and $\mathsf{sk}' = \alpha$, where $\mathsf{pk}_i = h_i$, and sends $(\mathsf{pk}, \mathsf{sk}')$ to $\mathcal{A}$. $\mathcal{A}$ chooses $\{\mathsf{msg}_i^0\}, \{\mathsf{msg}_i^1\} \in \mathcal{M}^k$ such that $\varphi(\{\mathsf{msg}_i^0\}) = \varphi(\{\mathsf{msg}_i^1\}) = M$ (say), and sends $(\{\mathsf{msg}_i^0\}, \{\mathsf{msg}_i^1\})$ to $\mathcal{B}$. $\mathcal{B}$ forwards the messages $(\mathsf{msg}_1^0, \mathsf{msg}_1^1)$ to $\mathcal{C}$. $\mathcal{C}$ draws $b \leftarrow \{0,1\}$, $r \xleftarrow{\$} \mathbb{Z}_q$ and computes $\mathsf{ct}_{\mathsf{EG}} = (g^r, \mathsf{ct}_1^* = h_1^r g^{\mathsf{msg}_1^b})$ and sends $\mathsf{ct}_{\mathsf{EG}}$ to $\mathcal{B}$. $\mathcal{B}$ constructs ct_2^* as follows. We have that

$$\varphi_1 \mathsf{msg}_1^0 + \varphi_2 \mathsf{msg}_2^0 = \varphi_1 \mathsf{msg}_1^1 + \varphi_2 \mathsf{msg}_2^1 = M$$

$\mathcal{B}$ computes

$$\mathsf{ct}_2^* = \left(\frac{(g^r)^\alpha \cdot g^M}{(\mathsf{ct}_1^*)^{\phi_1}}\right)^{\varphi_2^{-1}}$$

Note that this implicitly sets $\mathsf{ct}_2^* = h_2^r g^{\mathsf{msg}_2^b}$. $\mathcal{B}$ then sends $\mathsf{ct}^* = (g^r, \{\mathsf{ct}_i^*\})$ to $\mathcal{A}$. $\mathcal{A}$ sends a bit $b' \in \{0,1\}$ to $\mathcal{B}$ which $\mathcal{B}$ forwards to $\mathcal{C}$. Note that the implicit bit chosen by $\mathcal{B}$ in the game against $\mathcal{A}$ is b and hence $\mathcal{B}$ succeeds with the same probability as $\mathcal{A}$. This completes the proof.

References

[BCC+14] Bitansky, N., Canetti, R., Chiesa, A., Goldwasser, S., Lin, H., Rubinstein, A., Tromer, E.: The hunting of the SNARK. IACR Cryptology ePrint, Archive 2014:580 (2014)

[BCCT12] Bitansky, N., Canetti, R., Chiesa, A., Tromer, E.: From extractable collision resistance to succinct non-interactive arguments of knowledge, and back again. In: Goldwasser [Gol12], pp. 326–349

[BCCT13] Bitansky, N., Canetti, R., Chiesa, A., Tromer, E.: Recursive composition and bootstrapping for SNARKS and proof-carrying data. In: Symposium on Theory of Computing Conference, STOC 2013, Palo Alto, CA, USA, pp. 111–120, June 1–4 2013 (2013)

[BCHK07] Boneh, D., Canetti, R., Halevi, S., Katz, J.: Chosen-ciphertext security from identity-based encryption. SIAM J. Comput. 36(5), 1301–1328 (2007)

[BCTW16] Brakerski, Z., Cash, D., Tsabary, R., Wee, H.: Targeted homomorphic attribute based encryption. Manuscript (2016)

[BSW12] Boneh, D., Segev, G., Waters, B.: Targeted malleability: homomorphic encryption for restricted computations. In: Goldwasser [Gol12], pp. 350–366

[BV11] Brakerski, Z., Vaikuntanathan, V.: Efficient fully homomorphic encryption from (standard) LWE. In: Ostrovsky, R. (ed.) FOCS, pp. 97–106. Piscataway, IEEE (2011). Invited to SIAM Journal on Computing

[CKN03] Canetti, R., Krawczyk, H., Nielsen, J.B.: Relaxing chosen-ciphertext security. In: Boneh, D. (ed.) CRYPTO 2003. LNCS, vol. 2729, pp. 565–582. Springer, Heidelberg (2003). doi:10.1007/978-3-540-45146-4_33

[CLTV15] Canetti, R., Lin, H., Tessaro, S., Vaikuntanathan, V.: Obfuscation of probabilistic circuits and applications. In: Dodis, Y., Nielsen, J.B. (eds.) TCC
2015. LNCS, vol. 9015, pp. 468–497. Springer, Heidelberg (2015). doi:10.
1007/978-3-662-46497-7_19

[CM15] Clear, M., McGoldrick, C.: Multi-identity and multi-key leveled FHE from
learning with errors. In: Gennaro, R., Robshaw, M. (eds.) CRYPTO 2015.
LNCS, vol. 9216, pp. 630–656. Springer, Heidelberg (2015). doi:10.1007/
978-3-662-48000-7_31

[CS98] Cramer, R., Shoup, V.: A practical public key cryptosystem provably
secure against adaptive chosen ciphertext attack. In: Krawczyk, H. (ed.)
CRYPTO 1998. LNCS, vol. 1462, pp. 13–25. Springer, Heidelberg (1998).
doi:10.1007/BFb0055717

[DDN91] Dolev, D., Dwork, C., Naor, M.: Non-malleable cryptography (extended
abstract). In: Koutsougeras, C., Vitter, J.S. (eds.) Proceedings of the 23rd
Annual ACM Symposium on Theory of Computing, pp. 542–552. ACM,
New York (1991)

[DGM15] Dahab, R., Galbraith, S., Morais, E.: Adaptive key recovery attacks
on NTRU-based somewhat homomorphic encryption schemes. In:
Lehmann, A., Wolf, S. (eds.) ICITS 2015. LNCS, vol. 9063, pp. 283–296.
Springer, Heidelberg (2015). doi:10.1007/978-3-319-17470-9_17

[DHRW16] Dodis, Y., Halevi, S., Rothblum, R.D., Wichs, D.: Spooky encryption and
its applications. IACR Cryptology ePrint Archive 2016:272 (2016)

[Gen09] Gentry, C.: Fully homomorphic encryption using ideal lattices. In: STOC,
pp. 169–178 (2009)

[GM84] Goldwasser, S., Micali, S.: Probabilistic encryption. J. Comput. Syst. Sci.
28(2), 270–299 (1984)

[Gol12] Goldwasser, S. (ed.): Innovations in Theoretical Computer Science 2012,
Cambridge, MA, USA, 8–10 January 2012. ACM (2012)

[GPV08] Gentry, C., Peikert, C., Vaikuntanathan, V.: Trapdoors for hard lattices
and new cryptographic constructions. In: Proceedings of the 40th Annual
ACM Symposium on Theory of Computing, Victoria, British Columbia,
Canada, pp. 197–206, 17–20 May 2008

[LMSV10] Loftus, J., May, A., Smart, N.P., Vercauteren, F.: On CCA-secure fully
homomorphic encryption. IACR Cryptology ePrint Archive 2010:560
(2010)

[MW16] Mukherjee, P., Wichs, D.: Two round multiparty computation via multi-
key FHE. In: Fischlin, M., Coron, J.-S. (eds.) EUROCRYPT 2016.
LNCS, vol. 9666, pp. 735–763. Springer, Heidelberg (2016). doi:10.1007/
978-3-662-49896-5_26

[NY90] Naor, M., Yung, M.: Public-key cryptosystems provably secure against chosen ciphertext attacks. In: Ortiz, H., (ed.) Proceedings of the 22nd Annual
ACM Symposium on Theory of Computing, Baltimore, Maryland, USA,
13–17 May 1990, pp. 427–437. ACM (1990)

[RAD78] Rivest, R., Adleman, L. Dertouzos, M.: On data banks and privacy homomorphisms. In: Foundations of Secure Computation, pp. 169–177. Academic Press (1978)

[RS91] Rackoff, C., Simon, D.R.: Non-interactive zero-knowledge proof of knowledge and chosen ciphertext attack. In: Feigenbaum, J. (ed.) CRYPTO 1991.
LNCS, vol. 576, pp. 433–444. Springer, Heidelberg (1992). doi:10.1007/
3-540-46766-1_35

[Sah99] Sahai, A.: Non-malleable non-interactive zero knowledge and adaptive chosen-ciphertext security. In: 40th Annual Symposium on Foundations of Computer Science, FOCS 1999, New York, NY, USA, 17–18 October 1999, pp. 543–553. IEEE Computer Society (1999)

[ZPS12] Zhang, Z., Plantard, T., Susilo, W.: On the CCA-1 security of somewhat homomorphic encryption over the integers. In: Ryan, M.D., Smyth, B., Wang, G. (eds.) ISPEC 2012. LNCS, vol. 7232, pp. 353–368. Springer, Heidelberg (2012). doi:10.1007/978-3-642-29101-2_24

Circuit-Private Multi-key FHE

Wutichai Chongchitmate[1(✉)] and Rafail Ostrovsky[1,2]

[1] Department of Computer Science, University of California,
Los Angeles, CA, USA
{wutichai,rafail}@cs.ucla.edu
[2] Department of Mathematics, University of California,
Los Angeles, CA, USA

Abstract. Multi-key fully homomorphic encryption (MFHE) schemes allow polynomially many users without trusted setup assumptions to send their data (encrypted under different FHE keys chosen by users independently of each other) to an honest-but-curious server that can compute the output of an arbitrary polynomial-time computable function on this joint data and issue it back to all participating users for decryption. One of the main open problems left in MFHE was dealing with malicious users without trusted setup assumptions. We show how this can be done, generalizing previous results of circuit-private FHE. Just like standard circuit-private FHE, our security model shows that even if both ciphertexts and public keys of individual users are not well-formed, no information is revealed regarding the server computation—other than that gained from the output on some well-formed inputs of all users. MFHE schemes have direct applications to server-assisted multiparty computation (MPC), called *on-the-fly* MPC, introduced by López-Alt et al. (STOC '12), where the number of users is not known in advance. In this setting, a poly-time server wants to evaluate a circuit C on data uploaded by multiple clients and encrypted under different keys. Circuit privacy requires that users' work is independent of $|C|$ held by the server, while each client learns nothing about C other than its output. We present a framework for transforming MFHE schemes with no circuit privacy into maliciously circuit-private schemes. We then construct 3-round on-the-fly MPC with circuit privacy against malicious clients in the plain model.

Keywords: Multi-key · Fully homomorphic encryption · Computing on encrypted data · Malicious setting · Server-assisted MPC

R. Ostrovsky—Research supported in part by NSF grant 1619348, US-Israel BSF grant 2012366, by DARPA Safeware program, OKAWA Foundation Research Award, IBM Faculty Research Award, Xerox Faculty Research Award, B. John Garrick Foundation Award, Teradata Research Award, and Lockheed-Martin Corporation Research Award. The views expressed are those of the authors and do not reflect position of the Department of Defense or the U.S. Government.

S. Fehr (Ed.): PKC 2017, Part II, LNCS 10175, pp. 241–270, 2017.
DOI: 10.1007/978-3-662-54388-7_9

1 Introduction

The multi-key fully homomorphic encryption scheme (MFHE), introduced by López-Alt et al. [17], allows homomorphic computation on inputs encrypted with different public keys. They construct a MFHE under the ring learning with errors (RLWE) assumption, the decisional small polynomial ratio (DSPR) assumption, and circular security of a multi-key homomorphic encryption scheme $\mathcal{E}_{SH}$ based on a variant of NTRU homomorphic encryption. In this paper we construct a MFHE scheme that satisfies circuit privacy in the malicious setting, where public keys and ciphertexts are not guaranteed to be well-formed. We also present a framework for transforming multi-key homomorphic encryption schemes without circuit privacy or fully homomorphic property into maliciously circuit-private MFHE. We then demonstrate an instantiation of this framework using a modified scheme based on MFHE in [17] without adding further assumptions.

As in [21], we only consider the plain model. In the common reference string (CRS) model, the malicious case can be reduced to the semi-honest case by adding non-interactive zero-knowledge (NIZK) arguments that public key and ciphertext pairs are well-formed. Though, even in this case, difficulties can arise, as the security needs to hold when the pairs are in the support of honestly generated ones, but with different distributions—as discussed in [11].

In [17], the MFHE scheme is used to construct *on-the-fly* multiparty computation (MPC), which can perform arbitrary, dynamically chosen computation on arbitrary sets of users chosen on-the-fly. This construction allows each *client* user to encrypt data without knowing the identity or the number of other clients in the system. The *server* can select any subsets of clients, and perform an arbitrary function on the encrypted data without further input from the selected clients (and without learning clients' inputs). The encrypted result is then broadcast to the clients who cooperate in the retrieval of the output using (short) MPC protocol. Thus, most computation is done by the server while the decryption phase is independent of both the function computed and the total number of parties in the system. The resulting protocol is a five-round on-the-fly MPC secure against *semi-malicious* users [3], which follows the protocol but chooses random coins from an arbitrary distribution. The protocol can be strengthened against malicious adversaries in the CRS model using NIZK arguments without an increase in the number of rounds.

In this paper we construct a three-round on-the-fly MPC with circuit privacy against malicious users in the plain model. Specifically, all players send their inputs to the server, which performs the computation and sends the results back to all users, who then decrypt the result in one round. Since there is no way to enforce which function the server will compute, we assume that the server is honest but curious. As with our MFHE, the circuit privacy is guaranteed against unbounded malicious adversaries corrupting any number of clients. We also note that a variant of circuit privacy can be achieved in [17] construction by allowing the server to participate in the decryption phase MPC described above with its encrypted result as an input. However, our construction allows the server to minimize its interaction with the clients to only two rounds (i.e., one message from client to server and one broadcast back to client). After the server sends its output back to the clients, the clients communicate with one another in only one additional round in order to decrypt the output. Since we use multi-key homomorphic encryption from [17] as the base of our construction, we also require the number of key pairs or users to be known is advance as in their protocol.

To summarize, our main theorems are as follows:

Theorem 1 *(informal). Assuming that there exists a privately expandable multi-key homomorphic encryption scheme, then there exists a maliciously circuit-private multi-key fully homomorphic encryption scheme.*

Theorem 2 *(informal). Assuming RLWE and DSPR assumptions, and circular security of $\mathcal{E}_{SH}$, there exists a maliciously circuit-private multi-key fully homomorphic encryption scheme.*

Theorem 3 *(informal). Assuming the preconditions of Theorems 1 or 2 hold, there exists a three-round on-the-fly MPC protocol where each client $i \in [U]$ in the system holds x_i, and the server chooses a circuit C with $N < U$ inputs and a subset $V \subseteq [U]$ with $|V| = N$. Only the clients in V learn $C(\{x_i\}_{i \in V})$ (but nothing else, not even $|C|$), and the server learns nothing about $\{x_i\}_{i \in [U]}$.*

1. *The privacy guarantee for clients is indistinguishability-based computational privacy against malicious adversaries corrupting $t < N$ clients and honest-but-curious servers.*
2. *The privacy guarantee for the server is based on unbounded simulation (against possibly unbounded clients).*

We note that condition 2 is incomparable with standard simulation framework as it requires stronger (i.e., information-theoretic) guarantees, but also unbounded simulation. As discussed in [21], this is unavoidable, even for single maliciously circuit-private FHE.

1.1 Previous Work

Multi-key FHE. As stated above, [17] introduces the concept of MFHE and constructs this scheme based on a variant of the NTRU encryption scheme under the RLWE and DSPR assumptions. The work of [7] gives an alternate construction based on [12], the FHE scheme under the LWE assumption. While their construction only relies on standard assumption such as LWE, it requires an additional set up step, equivalent to the CRS model. A recent work of [20] simplifies the construction of [7], and adds a threshold decryption protocol which is used to construct two-round MPC in the CRS model.

Circuit Privacy in FHE. In the semi-honest setting, where public keys and ciphertexts are supported by properly generated pairs, circuit privacy has been considered in [10,25], with the latter using Yao's garbled circuit. The generalization in [11] combines two HE schemes—one compact fully homomorphic and the other semi-honestly circuit-private—into compact semi-honestly circuit-private FHE.

The malicious setting has been addressed in the context of oblivious transfer (OT) [1,13]. The work of [15] constructs maliciously circuit-private HE for a class of depth-bounded branching programs by iteration from leaves of a branching program.

Finally, the work of [21] devises a framework for transforming single-key FHE schemes with no circuit privacy into maliciously circuit-private ones. They use techniques akin to Gentry's bootstrapping [10] and semi-honestly circuit-private HE constructions [1,11] combining FHE schemes with maliciously circuit-private HE schemes.

One-Round OT. Several definitions of OT security have been suggested—such as a general framework for defining two-party computation [5]. The work of [1] proposes a definition for one-round (2 messages) OT using unbounded simulation, which implies information theoretic security for sender, and demonstrates a construction based on the DDH assumption. In [15], Ishai and Paskin construct a one-round OT with perfect sender privacy based on the DJ homomorphic encryption scheme [8] in the semi-honest setting.

On-the-Fly MPC. In standard MPC protocols, the computational and communication complexities of each party depend on the circuit being computed. Thus, it is difficult to construct on-the-fly MPC, where only the server performs most of the computation, while the clients compute very little and do so independent of the circuit. This idea is explored in the work of [14,16]. However, the complexity of clients in the former protocol is still proportional to the size of the circuit, while the latter is only for a small class of functions.

A line of work uses single-key FHE schemes [3,10] by running a short MPC protocol to compute a joint public key and secretly shared corresponding secret key. However, this approach does not capture the dynamic and non-interactive properties of on-the-fly MPC. As mentioned above, López-Alt et al. [17] constructed on-the-fly MPC from multi-key FHE. However, their version is only secure against semi-malicious adversaries unless additional trusted setup assumptions are made.

Circuit Privacy in MPC. Private function evaluation (PFE) is a special case of MPC, where one party holds a function or circuit as an input. PFE follows immediately from MPC by evaluating a universal circuit and taking a circuit one wants to compute as an input. However, the known universal circuits have high complexity, namely, $\mathcal{O}(g^5)$ for arithmetic circuits [23] and $\mathcal{O}(g \log g)$ for Boolean circuits [24] for the class of circuits with at most g gates. This approach also does not hide the size of the circuits evaluated. Previous work [18,19] has constructed more efficient implementation of PFEs, even against an active adversary [19].

Comparison of MPC Protocols from MFHE. The following table illustrates the comparison between our results and other MPC protocols constructed from MFHE. Note that their securities are in different models, and thus are not directly comparable (Table 1).

Table 1. Comparison of MPC protocols from MFHE

Construction	Round	Adversary	Setup	Server-assisted	Circuit privacy
[17]	5	Semi-honest	No	Yes	No
[17]	5	Malicious	Yes	Yes	No
[20]	2	Malicious	Yes	No	No
This work	3	Malicious	No	Yes	Yes

1.2 Our Techniques

We now give an overview of our main construction of circuit-private MFHE in three steps:

Step 1. The first step is to define the main new ingredient of our construction, the *privately expandable* multi-key homomorphic encryption scheme. It is a multi-key HE together with efficient algorithms Expand such that, given a list of public keys and an encryption with respect to one of the keys, the output is a homomorphic encryption that does not depend on which key it was previously encrypted with. We note that in a standard construction of MFHE, a ciphertext may reveal which key is used to encrypt it. This information may persist even after homomorphic evaluation, thus revealing the structure of the evaluating program. Our new property allows the scheme to hide the source of the encryption used at each node of the branching program from an adversary, therefore hiding the branching program itself when combined with the technique in [15].

We show how to construct a privately expandable multi-key HE scheme from the multi-key somewhat homomorphic encryption scheme defined in [17]. The main idea is as follows: first, we re-randomize a given ciphertext to be statistically indistinguishable from a fresh ciphertext using algebraic properties of the scheme. We then show how to add encryptions of zero with respect to each of the other keys, and show how to homomorphically decrypt the result to get a "low-level" ciphertext. In fact, we note that our techniques are applicable to other known multi-key FHE schemes as well, such as in [20] to obtain a privately expandable multi-key FHE.

Step 2. The next step is to construct maliciously circuit-private multi-key HE for a class of depth-bounded branching programs. A (deterministic binary) branching program is represented by a directed acyclic graph whose nonterminal nodes with outdegree 2 are labeled with indices in $[n]$, while terminal nodes with outdegree 0 and edges are labeled with 0 or 1. An input $x \in \{0,1\}^n$ naturally induces a unique path from a distinguished initial node to a terminal node, whose label determines $P(x)$. Any logspace or NC function can be computed by polynomial size branching programs. We inductively compute a ciphertext for each node from terminal nodes upward. Given a ciphertext of each bit of $x \in \{0,1\}^n$, encrypted with different public keys, we expand the ciphertexts to hide public keys it was originally encrypted with. We use private expandability to homomorphically compute ciphertext at each node with a key-hiding ciphertext indistinguishable from a fresh one. Thus, each ciphertext reveals nothing about the path leading to its corresponding node along the branching program, including which bit each node uses to decide its path. Therefore, the output, which is the ciphertext corresponding to the root, contains no information about the program.

The protocol above is secure against semi-honest adversaries. We then show how to modify the protocol to achieve security against malicious adversaries. We use single-key malicious circuit-private FHE and a modified validation circuit from [21], generalizing their techniques. The server (homomorphically) verifies that public keys and ciphertexts received are well-formed. This guarantees that each corrupted party uses proper public key and ciphertext, independent of other parties. Since we can verify before expanding the ciphertexts, we can use single-key FHE instead of multi-key.

Step 3. In this step we finally combine the protocol from the previous step with compact MFHE with no circuit privacy to get maliciously circuit-private MFHE. We modify the framework in [21] and obtain a framework for multi-key HE. To evaluate a given circuit, we first use MFHE with no circuit privacy to evaluate. Then we homomorphically decrypt the output using maliciously circuit-private HE that can evaluate the decryption function. Then we homomorphically decrypt to the original compact MFHE output, and only return it if public keys and ciphertexts are well-formed. This can be checked homomorphically similarly to the previous step. Using MFHE from [17] for instantiation, we get a maliciously circuit-private MFHE scheme based on RLWE and DSPR assumptions.

Application. Finally, we construct an on-the-fly MPC with circuit privacy from the result of the last step. Unlike [17], we consider the plain model with no setup assumptions and malicious adversaries corrupting an arbitrary number of clients. Along the way, we also construct a one-round 1-out-of-2 OT that is secure against malicious receivers with information theoretic security by augmenting a known construction that is only secure against semi-honest receivers with circuit-private FHE. Finally, by using a garbling scheme and our OT protocol, we can reduce the number of rounds from the construction in [17] to three rounds, which is optimal even against semi-honest adversaries in the plain model. The idea of the third round is as follows: Instead of having the clients run an MPC protocol to decrypt the output, the server constructs a collection of garbled circuits that decrypts the output for each user. The clients create an OT query for each bit of their secret keys and send it to the server along with the ciphertext in the first round. The server then answers those queries with corresponding garbled input for the garbled circuit. Finally, each client decrypts and broadcasts their garbled inputs to all other clients to compute the final output from the garbled circuits by each client.

The security of our protocol is based on unbounded simulation for the server, which is necessary for circuit privacy as discussed in [15,21]. We note that it is impossible to obtain ideal functionality definition due to the impossibility of any computationally bounded simulators extracting the input in one round (without trusted setup assumptions). Instead, we show the security for honest clients based on indistinguishability of the view of the malicious adversaries corrupting clients and the view of the honest-but-curious server.

2 Background

2.1 Notation

For positive integer $n \in \mathbb{N}$, let $[n] = \{1, \ldots, n\}$. For a string $x \in \{0,1\}^*$, let $|x|$ denote its length. Let $\oplus$ denote bitwise XOR operation or bitwise addition modulo 2. For a distribution A, let $x \leftarrow A$ denote x is chosen according to a distribution A. For a finite set S, let $x \leftarrow S$ denote x is chosen uniformly from the set S. Let λ denote the security parameter. A function $f : \mathbb{N} \to \mathbb{R}^+$ is *negligible* if for every constant $c > 0$, there exists $\lambda_0 \in \mathbb{N}$ such that $f(\lambda) \leq \lambda^{-c}$ for all $\lambda \geq \lambda_0$. Algorithms may be randomized unless stated otherwise. A PPT algorithm runs in probabilistic polynomial-time; otherwise, it is unbounded. For an algorithm A, let $y \leftarrow A(x; r)$ denote running A on input x with random coins r. If r is chosen uniformly at random, we denote $y \leftarrow A(x)$. For two distributions X, Y, $X \simeq^s Y$ means X and Y are statistically closed, i.e. $\Delta(X, Y)$ is negligible. For two distributions X, Y, $X \simeq^c Y$ means X and Y are computationally indistinguishable, i.e. for any PPT algorithm D, $|\Pr[D(X) = 1] - \Pr[D(Y) = 1]|$ is negligible.

Setup vs. Plain Model. We say a protocol is in the *setup model* or the *common reference string (CRS) model* if every party has access to a common random string r that was ideally drawn from some publicly known distribution prior to the beginning of the protocol. Without such setup, we say a protocol is in the *plain model*.

Malicious vs. Honest-but-Curious Party. We say a party participating in a protocol is *honest-but-curious* if it follows the protocol, but may perform additional computation to learn more information than it should. We say a party is *(fully) malicious* if it deviates from the protocol arbitrarily.

Representation Models. In order to use a function or a program as an input of our algorithm, we consider a function represented by a string representation C. The correspondence between a program C and a function f it represents must be universally interpreted by an underlying representation model U. Formally, a *representation model* $U : \{0,1\}^* \times \{0,1\}^* \to \{0,1\}^*$ is a PPT algorithm that takes a input (C, x) and returns $f(x)$ for a function f represented by C. If (C, x) is syntactically malformed, we let $U(C, x) = 0$ for completeness. We let $|C|$ denote the size of program C as a string representation as opposed to the number of gates as a Boolean circuit.

2.2   Multi-key Homomorphic Encryption

We use the definition similar to the one defined in [17] with some modifications from [20,21]. We fix the order of public keys in Eval and secret keys in Dec, and allow the number of keys to be different from input size of the circuit. This definition better suits our definition of circuit privacy that we will define in the next section.

Definition 1 (Multi-key (Leveled) (U, C)-Homomorphic Encryption). *Let C be a class of circuits. A multi-key (leveled) (U, C)-homomorphic scheme $\mathcal{E} = (\mathsf{KeyGen}, \mathsf{Enc}, \mathsf{Eval}, \mathsf{Dec})$ is described as follows:*

- *$(pk, sk) \leftarrow \mathsf{KeyGen}(1^\lambda, 1^d)$: Given a security parameter λ (and the circuit depth d), outputs a public key pk and a secret key sk.*
- *$c \leftarrow \mathsf{Enc}(pk, \mu)$: Given a public key pk and a message μ, outputs a ciphertext c.*
- *$\hat{c} \leftarrow \mathsf{Eval}(C, (pk_1, \ldots, pk_N), (I_1, c_1), \ldots, (I_n, c_n))$: Given a (description of) a Boolean circuit C (of depth $\leq d$) along with a sequence of N public keys and n couples (I_i, c_i), each comprising of an index $I_i \in [N]$ and a ciphertext c_i, outputs an evaluated ciphertext $\hat{c}$.*
- *$b := \mathsf{Dec}(sk_1, \ldots, sk_N, \hat{c})$: Given a sequence of N secret keys $sk_1, \ldots, sk_N$ and a ciphertext $\hat{c}$, outputs a bit b.*

has the following properties:

- ***Semantic security:*** *$(\mathsf{KeyGen}, \mathsf{Enc})$ satisfies IND-CPA semantic security.*
- ***Correctness:*** *Let $(pk_i, sk_i) \leftarrow \mathsf{KeyGen}(1^\lambda, 1^d)$ for $i = 1, \ldots, N$. Let $x = x_1 \ldots x_n \in \{0, 1\}^n$ and $C \in C$ be a Boolean circuit of depth $\leq d$, $C : \{0, 1\}^n \rightarrow \{0, 1\}$. For $i = 1, \ldots, n$, let $c_i \leftarrow \mathsf{Enc}(pk_{I_i}, x_i)$ for some $I_i \in [N]$. Let $\hat{c} \leftarrow \mathsf{Eval}(C, (pk_1, \ldots, pk_N), (I_1, c_1), \ldots, (I_n, c_n))$. Then*

$$\mathsf{Dec}(sk_1, \ldots, sk_N, \hat{c}) = U(C, (x_1, \ldots, x_n)).$$

$\mathcal{E}$ *is compact if there exists a polynomial p such that $|\hat{c}| \leq p(\lambda, d, N)$ independent of C and n. If a scheme is multi-key (U, C)-homomorphic for the class C of all circuits (of depth $\leq d$), we call it a multi-key (leveled) fully homomorphic (MFHE). A scheme $\mathcal{E}$ is somewhat homomorphic if it is leveled (U, C)-homomorphic for $d \leq d_{\max}(\lambda, N)$. A scheme $\mathcal{E}$ is multi-hop if an output of Eval can be used as an input as long as the sum of the depths of circuits evaluated does not exceed d.*

2.3   López-Alt, Tromer and Vaikuntanathan's Multi-key FHE Scheme

In [17], López-Alt et al. construct a multi-key compact leveled fully homomorphic encryption scheme. They first construct a multi-key leveled somewhat HE scheme $\mathcal{E}_{SH}$, then apply Gentry's bootstrapping [10]. The security of the scheme is based on the ring learning with error (RLWE) assumption, the decisional small polynomial ratio (DSPR) assumption, and the weak circular security of $\mathcal{E}_{SH}$.

Let $q = q(\lambda)$ be an odd prime integer. Let the ring $R = \mathbb{Z}[x]/\langle \phi \rangle$ for polynomial $\phi \in \mathbb{Z}[x]$ of degree $m = m(\lambda)$ and $R_q = R/qR$. Let χ be the B-bounded truncated discrete Gaussian distribution over R for $B = B(\lambda)$.

Definition 2 (Ring Learning With Error (RLWE) Assumption [4]). *The* (decisional) ring learning with error assumption $RLWE_{\phi,q,\chi}$ *states that for any* $l = \mathsf{poly}(\lambda)$,

$$\{(a_i, a_i \cdot s + e_i)\}_{i \in [l]} \simeq^c \{(a_i, u_i)\}_{i \in [l]}$$

where $s, e_i \leftarrow \chi$ *and* a_i, u_i *are sampled uniformly at random over* R_q.

Definition 3 (Decisional Small Polynomial Ratio (DSPR) Assumption [17]). *The* decisional small polynomial ration assumption $DSPR_{\phi,q,\chi}$ *says that it is hard to distinguish the following two distributions:*

- *a polynomial* $h := [2gf^{-1}]_q$, *where* $f', g \leftarrow \chi$ *such that* $f := 2f'+1$ *is invertible over* R_q *and* f^{-1} *is the inverse of* f *in* R_q.
- *a polynomial* u *sampled uniformly at random over* R_q.

We describe the multi-key leveled somewhat HE scheme here as follows.

$\mathsf{KeyGen}_{SH}(1^\lambda, 1^d)$:

1. For $i = 0, 1, \ldots, d$,
   (a) Sample $\tilde{f}^i, g^i \leftarrow \chi$ and compute $f^i := 2\tilde{f}^i + 1$. If f^i is not invertible in R_q, resample $\tilde{f}^i$.
   (b) Let $(f^i)^{-1}$ be the inverse of f^i in R_q.
   (c) Let $h_i := [2g^i(f^i)^{-1}]_{q_i} \in R_{q_i}$.
   (d) For $i \geq 1$, sample $\boldsymbol{s}^i_\gamma, \boldsymbol{e}^i_\gamma, \boldsymbol{s}^i_\zeta, \boldsymbol{e}^i_\zeta \leftarrow \chi^{\lceil \log q_i \rceil}$.
   (e) Let $\gamma^i := \left[h^i \boldsymbol{s}^i_\gamma + 2\boldsymbol{e}^i_\gamma + \mathsf{Pow}(f^{i-1}) \right]_{q_i} \in R_{q_i}^{\lceil \log q_i \rceil}$
       and $\zeta^i := \left[h^i \boldsymbol{s}^i_\zeta + 2\boldsymbol{e}^i_\zeta + \mathsf{Pow}\left((f^{i-1})^2\right) \right]_{q_i} \in R_{q_i}^{\lceil \log q_i \rceil}$.
2. Output $pk = (h^0, \gamma^1, \ldots, \gamma^d, \zeta^1, \ldots, \zeta^d)$ and $sk = f^d \in R_{q_d}$.

$\mathsf{Enc}_{SH}(pk, \mu)$:

1. Parse $pk = h$. Sample $s, e \leftarrow \chi$.
2. Output $c = [hs + 2e + \mu]_{q_0} \in R_{q_0}$.

$\mathsf{Eval}_{SH}(C, (pk_1, \ldots, pk_N), (I_1, c_1), \ldots, (I_n, c_n))$:

1. For $i \in [N]$, parse $pk_i = (h_i, \gamma^1_i, \ldots, \gamma^d_i, \zeta^1_i, \ldots, \zeta^d_i)$
2. Given two ciphertexts $c, c' \in R_{q_i}$ associated with subsets of the public keys K, K', respectively. Let $c_0 = [c + c'] \in R_{q_i}$ and $K \cup K' = \{pk_{i_1}, \ldots, pk_{i_t}\}$. For $j = 1, \ldots, t$, compute

$$c_j = \left[\langle \mathsf{Bit}(c_{j-1}), \gamma^i_{i_j} \rangle \right]_{q_i} \in R_{q_i}$$

Then let c_{add} be the integral vector closest to $(q_{i+1}/q_i) \cdot c_t$ such that $c_{add} = c_t \pmod{2}$. Output $c_{add} \in R_{q_{i+1}}$ and the associated subset $K \cup K'$.

3. Given two ciphertexts $c, c' \in R_{q_i}$ associated with subsets of the public keys K, K', respectively. Let $c_0 = [c \cdot c'] \in R_{q_i}$ and $K \cup K' = \{pk_{i_1}, \ldots, pk_{i_t}\}$. For $j = 1, \ldots, t$,
   (a) If $pk_{i_j} \in K \cap K'$, compute

   $$c_j = \left[\langle \text{Bit}(c_{j-1}), \zeta_{i_j}^i \rangle \right]_{q_i} \in R_{q_i}$$

   (b) Otherwise, compute

   $$c_j = \left[\langle \text{Bit}(c_{j-1}), \gamma_{i_j}^i \rangle \right]_{q_i} \in R_{q_i}$$

   Then let c_{mult} be the integral vector closest to $(q_{i+1}/q_i) \cdot c_t$ such that $c_{mult} = c_t \pmod 2$. Output $c_{mult} \in R_{q_{i+1}}$ and the associated subset $K \cup K'$.

$\text{Dec}_{SH}(sk_1, \ldots, sk_N, c)$:

1. For $i \in [N]$, parse $sk_i = f_i$.
2. Let $\mu_0 = [f_1 \ldots f_N \cdot c]_{q_d} \in R_{q_d}$.
3. Output $\mu' = \mu_0 \pmod 2$.

Remarks

1. In [17], a different notation for $\text{Eval}_{SH}(C, (pk_1, \ldots, pk_N), (I_1, c_1), \ldots, (I_n, c_n))$ is used, namely, $\text{Eval}_{SH}(C, (pk_1, c_1), \ldots, (pk_n, c_n))$. These two notations are equivalent when $N = n$ and $I_j = j$ for $j = 1, \ldots, n$. For brevity, we also use this notation under such conditions.
2. We also denote the evaluation on intermediate ciphertexts $\tilde{c}_1, \ldots, \tilde{c}_n$ associated with nonempty subsets of public keys $K_1, \ldots, K_n$, respectively, by $\text{Eval}_{SH}(C, (K_1, \tilde{c}_1), \ldots, (K_n, \tilde{c}_n))$.

Theorem 4 [17]. *Assuming the DSPR and RLWE assumptions, and that the scheme $\mathcal{E}_{SH} = (\text{KeyGen}_{SH}, \text{Enc}_{SH}, \text{Eval}_{SH}, \text{Dec}_{SH})$ described above is weakly circular secure, then there exists a multi-key compact leveled fully homomorphic encryption scheme for N keys for any $N \in \mathbb{N}$, obtained by bootstrapping $\mathcal{E}_{SH}$.*

2.4   Circuit-Private Homomorphic Scheme

We describe the circuit privacy of single-key homomorphic encryption defined in [15,21]. In the next section we will define our multi-key variant based on this definition.

Definition 4. *Let $\mathcal{E} = (\text{KeyGen}, \text{Enc}, \text{Eval}, \text{Dec})$ denote a $(U, \mathcal{C})$-homomorphic encryption scheme. We say $\mathcal{E}$ is (maliciously) circuit-private if there exist unbounded algorithms $\text{Sim}(1^\lambda, pk^*, c_1^*, \ldots, c_n^*, b)$ and deterministic $\text{Ext}(1^\lambda, pk^*, c^*)$ such that for all λ, pk^*, $c_1^*, \ldots, c_n^*$, and all programs $C : \{0,1\}^n \to \{0,1\} \in (U, \mathcal{C})$, the following holds:*

- *for* $i = 1, \ldots, n$, $x_i^* := \mathsf{Ext}(1^\lambda, pk^*, c_i^*)$
- $\mathsf{Sim}(1^\lambda, pk^*, c_1^*, \ldots, c_n^*, U(C, x_1^*, \ldots, x_n^*)) \simeq^s \mathsf{Eval}(1^\lambda, C, pk^*, c_1^*, \ldots, c_n^*)$

We say the scheme is semi-honestly circuit-private *if the above holds only for* well-formed $pk^* = pk$, $c_i^* = c_i$, *i.e.* $(pk, sk) \leftarrow \mathsf{KeyGen}(1^\lambda)$ *and* $c_i \leftarrow \mathsf{Enc}(pk, x_i)$ *for some* $x_i \in \{0, 1\}$, $i = 1, \ldots, n$.

Theorem 5 [21]. *Assume an FHE scheme with decryption circuits in* NC^1 *exists. There exists a maliciously circuit-private single-key fully homomorphic encryption scheme.*

2.5 Branching Program

Definition 5. *A* (binary) branching program P *over* $x = (x_1, \ldots, x_n)$ *is a tuple* $(G = (V, E), v_0, T, \psi_V, \psi_E)$ *such that*

- *G is a connected directed acyclic graph. Let $\Gamma(v)$ denote the set of children of $v \in V$.*
- *v_0 is an initial node of indegree 0.*
- *$T \subseteq V$ is a set of terminal nodes of outdegree 0. Any node in $V \setminus T$ has outdegree 2.*
- *$\psi_V : V \to [n] \cup \{0, 1\}$ is a node labeling function with $\psi_V(v) \in \{0, 1\}$ for $v \in T$, and $\psi_V(v) \in [n]$ for $v \in V \setminus T$.*
- *$\psi_E : E \to \{0, 1\}$ is an edge labeling function, such that outgoing edges from each vertex is labeled by different values.*

The height *of* $v \in V$, *denoted* $height(v)$, *is the length of the longest path from* v *to a node in* T. *The* length *of* P *is the height of* v_0.

On input x, $P(x)$ *is defined by following the path induced by* x *from* v_0 *to a node* $v_l \in T$, *where an edge* (v, v') *is in the path if* $x_{\psi_V(v)} \in \psi_E(v, v')$. *By the last property, such* v' *is unique. Then* $P(x) = \psi_V(v_l)$. *Similarly, we also define* $P_v(x)$ *by following that path from any node* $v \in V$ *instead of* v_0.

Definition 6. *A layered branching program of length* l *is a branching program* $P = (G = (V, E), v_0, T, \psi_V, \psi_E)$ *such that for any* $e = (v, v') \in E$, $height(v) = height(v') + 1$.

Every path from an initial node to a terminal node in a layered branching program has the same length. Every branching program can be efficiently transformed into a layered branching program of the same length [22]. For simplicity, we assume all branching programs are layered.

3 Privately Expandable Multi-key Homomorphic Encryption

In this section we will define the properties of multi-key homomorphic encryption which are required for the construction of multi-key circuit private HE for branching programs discussed in the next section. Informally, private expandability allows masking of a ciphertext encrypted under a public key using other public keys in order to hide the key it was originally encrypted with. We then show how to modify the multi-key HE from [17] to achieve such property. We note that the multi-key HE from [20] can be modified to have this property in a similar way.[1] However, since it only works in the setup model, we cannot get a meaningful result in circuit privacy.

3.1 Private Expandability

We define an "expanded" ciphertext as one that associates with all public keys to be used in the evaluation algorithm. This notion is also used in [20]. However, expanded ciphertexts in [20] do not hide the original public key it is encrypted with. In both our construction and the one in [20], an expanded ciphertext can be thought of as a single-key homomorphic encryption ciphertext that can be decrypted with some function of all secret keys. In our case, it is the product of all secret keys; in the [20] case, it is the appending of all secret keys.

Definition 7. *A multi-key HE scheme* $(\mathsf{KeyGen}, \mathsf{Enc}, \mathsf{Eval}, \mathsf{Dec})$ *is privately expandable if there exist polynomial time algorithms* $\mathsf{Expand}, \widetilde{\mathsf{Eval}}, \widetilde{\mathsf{Dec}}$ *such that, for* $i = 1, \ldots, N$, $(pk_i, sk_i) \leftarrow \mathsf{KeyGen}(1^\lambda)$,

– *Let* $c \leftarrow \mathsf{Enc}(pk_i, \mu)$. *Then for any* $j \in [N]$,

$$\tilde{c} := \mathsf{Expand}(pk_1, \ldots, pk_N, i, c) \simeq^s \mathsf{Expand}(pk_1, \ldots, pk_N, j, \mathsf{Enc}(pk_j, \mu))$$

and $\widetilde{\mathsf{Dec}}(sk_1, \ldots, sk_N, \tilde{c}) = \mu$
– *if for* $i = 1, \ldots, N$, $\widetilde{\mathsf{Dec}}(sk_1, \ldots, sk_N, \tilde{c}_i) = b_i$, *then*

$$\widetilde{\mathsf{Dec}}(sk_1, \ldots, sk_N, \widetilde{\mathsf{Eval}}(P, pk_1, \ldots, pk_N, \tilde{c}_1, \ldots, \tilde{c}_l)) = P(b_1, \ldots, b_l).$$

We sometimes replace Eval and Dec with $\widetilde{\mathsf{Eval}}$ and $\widetilde{\mathsf{Dec}}$, respectively, and denote $(\mathsf{KeyGen}, \mathsf{Enc}, \mathsf{Expand}, \mathsf{Eval}, \mathsf{Dec})$ a privately expandable HE scheme if Expand, Eval and Dec satisfy the above conditions.

3.2 Privately Expandable Multi-key HE Based on LTV Encryption Scheme

In [17], Lopez et al. constructed a multi-key FHE scheme with security based on ring learning with error assumption (RLWE) and decisional small polynomial ration assumption (DSPR) by further assuming circular security. We will show that we can modify the scheme to be privately expandable by constructing $\mathsf{Expand}, \widetilde{\mathsf{Eval}}, \widetilde{\mathsf{Dec}}$ without additional assumption.

Let $\mathcal{E}_{SH} = (\mathsf{KeyGen}_{SH}, \mathsf{Enc}_{SH}, \mathsf{Eval}_{SH}, \mathsf{Dec}_{SH})$ be the multi-key somewhat homomorphic scheme given in [17] defined in the previous section.

---

[1] See the full version [6] of this paper for details.

A ciphertext of $\mathcal{E}_{SH}$ is a polynomial in $R_q = \mathbb{Z}_q[x]/(x^n + 1)$ which can be represented by a vector in $\mathbb{Z}_q^n$. In this scheme, N must be known in advance. We choose $n = N^{1/\epsilon'}$, $q = 2^{n^\epsilon}$ for some $\epsilon' < \epsilon$. Thus, $q = 2^{N^\delta}$ for $\delta > 1$. We need to use a bootstrappable somewhat homomorphic version instead of a bootstrapped FHE as we need its multi-hop property while we only need to evaluate low depth circuits. Let $t \in \mathbb{N}$ and $\mathcal{U}_t$ be a discrete uniform distribution on $\{0, \ldots, t\}$, which can be sampled in time $O(\log t)$. We define

$\widetilde{\mathsf{Expand}}^t (pk_1, \ldots, pk_N, i, c)$:

1. For each $j \in \{1, \ldots, N\}$
   - Parse $pk_j = h_j$.
   - Let $s_j, e_j \leftarrow \mathcal{U}_t^n$.
   - Let $c_j = h_j s_j + 2 e_j$
2. Output $\hat{c} = c + \sum\limits_{j=1}^{N} c_j$.

The following lemma is a variant of the smudging lemma in [3]:

Lemma 1. *Let $a_1, a_2 \in \mathbb{Z}^n$ be B-bounded. Then $\Delta(a_1+b, a_2+b) \leq 4nB/t$ where $b \leftarrow \mathcal{U}_t^n$. If t is superpolynomial in λ, then they are statistically indistinguishable.*

Proof. Let $c_1, c_2 \in \mathbb{Z}$ be corresponding entries in a_1 and a_2, respectively. Then $|c_1 - c_2| \leq 2B$. Thus, $\Delta(c_1 + \mathcal{U}_t, c_2 + \mathcal{U}_t) \leq 4B/t$. Therefore, $\Delta(a_1 + b, a_2 + b) \leq 4nB/t$. Since n and B are polynomial in λ, $\Delta(a_1 + b, a_2 + b)$ is negligible for superpolynomial t. $\qquad\square$

We apply the above lemma to get the following result.

Lemma 2. *Let $(pk_k, sk_k) \leftarrow \mathsf{KeyGen}_{SH}(1^\lambda, 1^d)$ for $k = 1, \ldots, N$. For $i \in [N]$, let $c \leftarrow \mathsf{Enc}_{SH}(pk_i, \mu)$. Let $t \leq \frac{1}{18}(\frac{q}{N(nB)^N})$. Then*

$$\hat{c} := \widetilde{\mathsf{Expand}}^t (pk_1, \ldots, pk_N, i, c) \simeq^s \widetilde{\mathsf{Expand}}^t (pk_1, \ldots, pk_N, j, \mathsf{Enc}_{SH}(pk_j, \mu))$$

for any $j \in [N]$, and $\mathsf{Dec}_{SH}(sk_1, \ldots, sk_N, \hat{c}) = \mu$.

Proof. Suppose t is superpolynomial. Then for any $s, e \leftarrow \chi$ and $s_i, e_i \leftarrow \mathcal{U}_t^n$, $[s + s_i] \simeq^s [s_i]$ and $[e + e_i] \simeq^s [e_i]$ by Lemma 1. Thus, for $c = h_i s + 2e + m$, we have $[c + (h_i s_i + 2 e_i)] \simeq^s [m + (h_i s_i + e_i)]$. Then

$$\widetilde{\mathsf{Expand}}^t (pk_1, \ldots, pk_N, i, c) \simeq^s [m + \sum_{k \in [N]} (h_k s_k + 2 e_k)].$$

By the same reason,

$$\widetilde{\mathsf{Expand}}^t (pk_1, \ldots, pk_N, j, \mathsf{Enc}_\mathcal{E}(pk_j, \mu)) \simeq^s [m + \sum_{k \in [N]} (h_k s_k + 2 e_k)].$$

Therefore, they are statistically indistinguishable.

Now let $\hat{c} = m + \sum_{j\in[N]}(h_j s_j + 2e_j)$ where s_j, e_j bounded by t. For each $j \in [N]$, $f_j(h_j s_j + 2e_j) = 2(g_j s_j + f_j e_j)$ is bounded by $E := 2nBt + 2nB(2t+1) = 2nB(3t+1) \leq 8nBt$. Then for $f = f_1 \ldots f_N$,

$$f\hat{c} = fm + \sum_{j\in[N]} \left(\prod_{k\in[N]\setminus\{j\}} f_k \right) f_j(h_j s_j + 2e_j)$$

is bounded by $(nB)^N + N(nB)^{N-1}E \leq 9N(nB)^N t$, which can be decrypted if it is less than $q/2$. Thus, for $t \leq \frac{1}{18}(\frac{q}{N(nB)^N})$, the correctness follows from that of LTV scheme. Note that as $q = 2^{N^\delta} = (2^{N^{\delta-1}})^N$, t is still superpolynomial in N and thus λ. $\square$

Lemma 3 (implied from [17]). *For any $C > 0$, for sufficiently large $\lambda, N = N(\lambda) \in \mathbb{N}$, there exists a multi-key somewhat homomorphic encryption scheme for N keys and circuits of depth $d \geq Cd_{\mathsf{Dec}}$ where d_{Dec} is the depth of its decryption circuit.*

The depth of circuits that can be evaluated is important here because the construction in the next section will require that the scheme can perform evaluation twice.

Now let t satisfy the above condition. Let $d_0 = d_{\mathsf{Dec}}$ and $d \geq 3d_0 + 2$. We define a scheme $\mathcal{F} = (\mathsf{KeyGen}_\mathcal{F}, \mathsf{Enc}_\mathcal{F}, \mathsf{Expand}_\mathcal{F}, \mathsf{Eval}_\mathcal{F}, \mathsf{Dec}_\mathcal{F})$ as follows:

$\mathsf{KeyGen}_\mathcal{F}(1^\lambda, 1^d)$:

1. Let $(pk_0, sk_0) \leftarrow \mathsf{KeyGen}_{SH}(1^\lambda, 1^{d_0})$ and $(pk_\mathcal{E}, sk_\mathcal{E}) \leftarrow \mathsf{KeyGen}_{SH}(1^\lambda, 1^{d+d_0})$
2. Let $f_{sk} = \mathsf{Enc}_{SH}(pk_\mathcal{E}, sk_0)$
3. Output $pk = (pk_0, pk_\mathcal{E}, f_{sk})$ and $sk = sk_\mathcal{E}$.

$\mathsf{Enc}_\mathcal{F}(pk, \mu)$:

1. Parse $pk = (pk_0, pk_\mathcal{E}, f_{sk})$.
2. Output $\mathsf{Enc}_{SH}(pk_0, \mu)$.

$\mathsf{Expand}_\mathcal{F}(pk_1, \ldots, pk_N, i, c)$:

1. Parse $pk_j = (pk_{0,j}, pk_{\mathcal{E},j}, f_{sk,j})$.
2. Let $\hat{c} = \overbrace{\mathsf{Expand}}^{t} (pk_{0,1}, \ldots, pk_{0,N}, i, c)$
3. Output $\tilde{c} = \mathsf{Eval}_{SH}(\mathsf{Dec}_{SH}(\cdot, \hat{c}), (pk_{\mathcal{E},1}, f_{sk,1}), \ldots, (pk_{\mathcal{E},N}, f_{sk,N}))$.

$\mathsf{Eval}_\mathcal{F}(P, pk_1, \ldots, pk_N, \tilde{c}_1, \ldots, \tilde{c}_n)$:

1. Parse $pk_j = (pk_{0,j}, pk_{\mathcal{E},j}, f_{sk,j})$.
2. Let $K = \{pk_1, \ldots, pk_N\}$
3. Output $\tilde{c} = \mathsf{Eval}_{SH}(P, (K, \tilde{c}_1), \ldots, (K, \tilde{c}_n))$.

$\mathsf{Dec}_{\mathcal{F}}(sk_1, \ldots, sk_N, \tilde{c})$:

1. Parse $sk_j = sk_{\mathcal{E},j}$.
2. Output $\mu' = \mathsf{Dec}_{SH}(sk_{\mathcal{E},1}, \ldots, sk_{\mathcal{E},N}, \tilde{c})$.

Note that $\mathsf{Dec}_{\mathcal{F}}$ has the same size as Dec_{SH}.

Lemma 4. *The scheme* $\mathcal{F} = (\mathsf{KeyGen}_{\mathcal{F}}, \mathsf{Enc}_{\mathcal{F}}, \mathsf{Expand}_{\mathcal{F}}, \mathsf{Eval}_{\mathcal{F}}, \mathsf{Dec}_{\mathcal{F}})$ *above is a privately expandable multi-key compact somewhat homomorphic scheme that can evaluate circuits up to a depth of* $2d_0 + 2$.

Proof. The security and compactness of $\mathcal{F}$ follows directly from that of $\mathcal{E}$. By Lemma 2, for $c = \mathsf{Enc}_{\mathcal{F}}(pk_i, \mu)$, $\tilde{c} = \mathsf{Expand}_{\mathcal{F}}(pk_1, \ldots, pk_N, i, c)$ is a level-d_0 encryption of μ associated with $K = \{pk_{\mathcal{E},1}, \ldots, pk_{\mathcal{E},N}\}$ under scheme $\mathcal{E}$. Thus, the correctness of evaluation and decryption of $\mathcal{F}$ follows from that of $\mathcal{E}$.

Also, by Lemma 2, $\hat{c} \simeq^s \overset{t}{\overbrace{\mathsf{Expand}}}(pk_1, \ldots, pk_N, j, \mathsf{Enc}_{\mathcal{E}}(pk_j, \mu))$. Then the result of homomorphically decrypting both sides gives $\tilde{c} \simeq^s \mathsf{Expand}_{\mathcal{F}}(pk_1, \ldots, pk_N, j, \mathsf{Enc}(pk_j, \mu))$. Since each $f_{sk,j}$ are level 1 encryption under $\mathcal{E}$, the output of $\mathsf{Expand}_{\mathcal{F}}$ is of level d_0. Thus, we can further evaluate circuits up to depth $2d_0 + 2$ as required. $\qquad\square$

Remarks

1. Recent results of Albrecht et al. [2] give a sub-exponential (in λ) attack on DSPR assumption when q is super-polynomial, which is required in [17].
2. Since our protocol is also based on $\mathcal{E}_{SH}$ with super-polynomial q, security parameter and other variables involved need to be chosen carefully to remain secure under such attack.
3. Another possible solution is to use the recent technique in [9] to construct a privately expandable scheme without adding superpolynomial-size errors to the ciphertexts. However, careful application of this technique is required in order to guarantee that the resulting scheme is both privately expandable and correctly decryptable. We leave this as an open problem.

4 Circuit-Private Multi-key HE for Branching Programs

We first define the multi-key version of circuit privacy given in the previous section.

Definition 8. *Let* $\mathcal{E} = (\mathsf{KeyGen}, \mathsf{Enc}, \mathsf{Eval}, \mathsf{Dec})$ *denote a multi-key* $(U, \mathcal{C})$*-homomorphic encryption scheme. We say* $\mathcal{E}$ *is* (*maliciously*) *circuit-private if there exist unbounded algorithms* $\mathsf{Sim}(1^{\lambda}, (pk_1^*, c_1^*), \ldots, (pk_n^*, c_n^*), b)$ *and deterministic* $\mathsf{Ext}(1^{\lambda}, pk^*, c^*)$ *such that for all* λ, $pk_1^*, \ldots, pk_N^*$, $I_1, \ldots, I_n$, $c_1^*, \ldots, c_n^*$, *and all programs* $C : \{0,1\}^n \to \{0,1\} \in (U, \mathcal{C})$, *the following holds:*

- for $i = 1, \ldots, n$, $x_i^* := \mathsf{Ext}(1^\lambda, pk_{I_i}^*, c_i^*)$
- $\mathsf{Sim}(1^\lambda, (pk_1^*, \ldots, pk_N^*), (I_1, c_1^*), \ldots, (I_n, c_n^*), U(C, x_1^*, \ldots, x_n^*))$
  $\cong^s \mathsf{Eval}(1^\lambda, C, (pk_1^*, \ldots, pk_N^*), (I_1, c_1^*), \ldots, (I_n, c_n^*))$

We say the scheme is semi-honestly circuit-private *if the above holds only for well-formed* $pk_{I_i}^* = pk_{I_i}$, $c_i^* = c_i$ *pairs, i.e.* $(pk_{I_i}, sk_{I_i}) \leftarrow \mathsf{KeyGen}(1^\lambda)$ *and* $c_i \leftarrow \mathsf{Enc}(pk_{I_i}, x_i)$.

In this section we construct a circuit-private multi-key HE for a class $\mathcal{C}$ of (depth bound) branching programs. As discussed above, the difficulty in the multi-key setting is that each decision one makes while traversing a branching program is dependent on its corresponding input bit, which in turn is dependent on which public key it is encrypted with. Using such encryption may reveal bit positions of the path it takes to reach a terminal node. Using a privately expandable multi-key HE scheme (previous section) solves this problem. Another implication of private expandability is that we can generate a fresh expanded encryption of bit b that is indistinguishable from an expanded encryption of any given encryption of b. This allows us to construct a simulator for circuit privacy, given an output bit.

We first give a construction that is secure against semi-honest adversaries where each pair of public key and ciphertext is correctly generated. The intuition behind this construction is as follows: given a branching program P, we assign to each node of P a ciphertext that multi-key decrypt to an output computed with that node as a root. Thus, the ciphertext assigned to the actual root will decrypt to the actual output. In order to construct such a ciphertext (called *label* below), we privately expand the input corresponding to a position given by ψ_V of that node in order to hide the position. We then homomorphically construct a ciphertext encrypting each bit of its child that is specified by the encrypted input (without knowing the input bit). Note that this result will be an encryption of an encryption of the output. Finally, we homomorphically decrypt it twice using HE evaluation. We show that, in this case, the output can be simulated knowing the public keys, ciphertext, and the output; it is thus independent of the program being evaluated.

We then show that we can augment this construction to handle malicious public key and ciphertext pairs using a single-key circuit-private FHE since the evaluated output does not depend on the branching program, unlike in the general case.

4.1 Semi-honest Model

Let $\mathcal{F} = (\mathsf{KeyGen}_\mathcal{F}, \mathsf{Enc}_\mathcal{F}, \mathsf{Expand}_\mathcal{F}, \mathsf{Eval}_\mathcal{F}, \mathsf{Dec}_\mathcal{F})$ be a privately expandable multi-hop multi-key compact somewhat homomorphic scheme that can evaluate circuit up to depth $2d_0 + 2$ where d_0 is the depth of $\mathsf{Dec}_\mathcal{F}$. Let l be the length of branching programs, and let $p(\lambda, l)$ be a polynomial to be specified later. Let $\mathsf{Dec}_\mathcal{F}^2(sk_1, \ldots, sk_N, c) = \mathsf{Dec}_\mathcal{F}(sk_1, \ldots, sk_N, \mathsf{Dec}_\mathcal{F}(sk_1, \ldots, sk_N, c))$. We describe $\mathcal{E}_S = (\mathsf{KeyGen}_S, \mathsf{Enc}_S, \mathsf{Eval}_S, \mathsf{Dec}_S)$ together with Expand and $\widehat{\mathsf{Enc}}$, an expanded encryption under a random public key. Note that $[1]$ is an encryption of 1 with no randomness.

$\mathsf{KeyGen}_S(1^\lambda, 1^l)$:

1. Let $d = p(\lambda, l)$.
2. Let $(pk_\mathcal{F}, sk_\mathcal{F}) \leftarrow \mathsf{KeyGen}_\mathcal{F}(1^\lambda, 1^d)$.
3. Output $pk = (pk_\mathcal{F}, f_{sk} := \mathsf{Enc}_\mathcal{F}(pk_\mathcal{F}, sk_\mathcal{F}))$ and $sk = sk_\mathcal{F}$.

$\mathsf{Enc}_S(pk, \mu)$:

1. Parse $pk = (pk_\mathcal{F}, f_{sk})$
2. Let $c_\alpha \leftarrow \mathsf{Enc}_\mathcal{F}(pk_\mathcal{F}, \mu)$
3. Output c

$\mathsf{Expand}(pk_1, \ldots, pk_N, i, c)$:

1. For $j = 1, \ldots, N$, parse $pk_j = (pk_{\mathcal{F},j}, f_{sk,j})$.
2. Let $c_\alpha = c$ and $c_\gamma = [1] - c$
3. Compute $\tilde{c}_\alpha = \mathsf{Expand}_\mathcal{F}(pk_{\mathcal{F},1}, \ldots, pk_{\mathcal{F},N}, i, c_\alpha)$
   and $\tilde{c}_\gamma = \mathsf{Expand}_\mathcal{F}(pk_{\mathcal{F},1}, \ldots, pk_{\mathcal{F},N}, i, c_\gamma)$
4. Output $\tilde{c} = (\tilde{c}_\alpha, \tilde{c}_\gamma)$.

$\widetilde{\mathsf{Enc}}(pk_1, \ldots, pk_N, \mu)$:

1. Let $i \leftarrow [N]$ and compute $c \leftarrow \mathsf{Enc}(pk_i, \mu)$.
2. Output $\tilde{c} = \mathsf{Expand}(pk_1, \ldots, pk_N, i, c)$.

$\mathsf{Eval}_S(P, (pk_1, \ldots, pk_N), (I_1, c_1), \ldots, (I_n, c_n))$

1. Let $P = (G = (V, E), v_0, T, \psi_V, \psi_E)$.
2. For $j = 1, \ldots, N$, parse $pk_j = (pk_{\mathcal{F},j}, f_{sk,j})$.
   Let $\tilde{f}_{sk,j} = \mathsf{Expand}_\mathcal{F}(pk_{\mathcal{F},1}, \ldots, pk_{\mathcal{F},N}, j, f_{sk,j})$
3. For $i = 1, \ldots, n$, Let $(\tilde{c}_{\alpha,i}, \tilde{c}_{\gamma,i}) = \mathsf{Expand}(pk_1, \ldots, pk_N, i, c_i)$.
4. For each $v \in T$, let $label(v) := \psi_V(v)$.
5. For each $v \in V \setminus T$ with both children labeled, let $h := height(v)$, $i := \psi_V(v)$
   (a) For $t = 1, \ldots, s = |label(u_0)|$ where $\Gamma(v) = \{u_0, u_1\}$, $\psi_E(v, u_0) = 0$,
       $\psi_E(v, u_1) = 1$
       i. Let $r_0 = label(u_0)[t]$ and $r_1 = label(u_1)[t]$.
       ii. Let $z_1, z_2 \leftarrow \widetilde{\mathsf{Enc}}(pk_1, \ldots, pk_N, 0)$
       iii. Consider 4 cases:
           A. if $r_0 = r_1 = 0$, $a_t := z_1 + z_2$
           B. if $r_0 = 0; r_1 = 1$, $a_t := \tilde{c}_{\alpha,i} + z_1$
           C. if $r_0 = 1; r_1 = 0$, $a_t := \tilde{c}_{\gamma,i} + z_1$
           D. if $r_0 = r_1 = 1$, $a_t := \tilde{c}_{\alpha,i} + \tilde{c}_{\gamma,i}$
   (b) $a_v = a_1 \ldots a_s$; if $h = 1$, $label(v) \leftarrow a_v$
   (c) otherwise, $label(v) \leftarrow \mathsf{Eval}_\mathcal{F}(\mathsf{Dec}^2_\mathcal{F}, pk_{\mathcal{F},1}, \ldots, pk_{\mathcal{F},N}, \tilde{f}_{sk,1}, \ldots, \tilde{f}_{sk,N}, a_v)$
6. Output $\tilde{c} = label(root)$

$\mathsf{Dec}_S(sk_1, \ldots, sk_N, \hat{c})$:

1. Parse $sk_i = sk_{\mathcal{F},i}$.
2. Output $\mu' := \mathsf{Dec}_\mathcal{F}(sk_{\mathcal{F},1}, \ldots, sk_{\mathcal{F},N}, \hat{c})$

4.2   Correctness and Security Against Semi-honest Adversaries

The correctness is a direct result of the following lemma:

Lemma 5. *Let* $x = x_1 \ldots x_n$. *For* $i = 1, \ldots, N$, $(pk_i, sk_i) \leftarrow \mathsf{KeyGen}(1^\lambda, 1^l)$. *For* $i = 1, \ldots, n$, $c_i = \mathsf{Enc}(pk_{I_i}, x_i)$ *for some* $I_i \in [N]$. *Then for any branching program* $P = (G = (V, E), v_0, T, \psi_V, \psi_E)$ *and for each* $v \in V \setminus T$ *with* $i = \psi_V(v)$,

1. $\mathsf{Dec}_{\mathcal{F}}(sk_{\mathcal{F},1}, \ldots, sk_{\mathcal{F},N}, a_v) = label(u_{x_i})$;
2. $\mathsf{Dec}_{\mathcal{F}}(sk_{\mathcal{F},1}, \ldots, sk_{\mathcal{F},N}, label(v)) = P_v(x)$;
3. $\mathsf{Dec}_S(sk_1, \ldots, sk_N, \hat{c}) = P(x)$.

Proof. Let $\Gamma(v) = \{u_0, u_1\}$. For each $t \in [s]$, consider the value $\mu = x_i$ that $\tilde{c}_{\alpha,i}$ encrypts. If $\mu = 0$, we get a sum of two encryptions of 0 in the first two cases, and a sum of an encryption of 1 and an encryption of 0 in the last two cases. If $\mu = 1$, we get a sum of two encryptions of 0 in the first case and third case, and a sum of an encryption of 1 and an encryption of 0 in the second case and the last case. All of which are correct with respect to r_0, r_1. Thus, $\mathsf{Dec}_{\mathcal{F}}(sk_{\mathcal{F},1}, \ldots, sk_{\mathcal{F},N}, a_v) = label(u_{x_i})$.

For v with $height(v) = 1$, we have $label(v) = a_v$. Thus, $\mathsf{Dec}_{\mathcal{F}}(sk_{\mathcal{F},1}, \ldots, sk_{\mathcal{F},N}, label(v)) = label(u_{x_i}) = P_v(x)$ as $u_{x_i} \in T$. Now assume that $height(v) > 1$. Since $label(v) \leftarrow \mathsf{Eval}_{\mathcal{F}}(\mathsf{Dec}_{\mathcal{F}}^2, \tilde{f}_{sk,1}, \ldots, \tilde{f}_{sk,N}, a_v)$, inductively, by part 1, we have $\mathsf{Dec}_{\mathcal{F}}(sk_{\mathcal{F},1}, \ldots, sk_{\mathcal{F},N}, label(v)) = \mathsf{Dec}_{\mathcal{F}}^2(sk_{\mathcal{F},1}, \ldots, sk_{\mathcal{F},N}, a_v) = \mathsf{Dec}_{\mathcal{F}}(sk_{\mathcal{F},1}, \ldots, sk_{\mathcal{F},N}, label(u_{x_i})) = P_v(x)$.

Applying part 2 to the case $v = v_0$, we get

$$\mathsf{Dec}_S(sk_1, \ldots, sk_N, \hat{c}) = \mathsf{Dec}_{\mathcal{F}}(sk_{\mathcal{F},1}, \ldots, sk_{\mathcal{F},N}, label(v_0)) = P_{v_0}(x) = P(x).$$

□

Now we prove circuit privacy against semi-honest adversaries, i.e., when each public key and ciphertext pair is generated correctly.

Lemma 6. *Assuming* $\mathcal{F}$ *is privately expandable HE scheme with circular security. Then the scheme* $\mathcal{E}_S$ *is a semi-honestly circuit-private HE scheme for branching programs.*

Proof. We construct a simulator Sim_S as follows:

$\mathsf{Sim}_S(1^\lambda, 1^l, (pk_1, \ldots, pk_N), (I_1, c_1), \ldots, (I_n, c_n), b)$:

1. For $i = 1, \ldots, N$, parse $pk_i = (pk_{\mathcal{F},i}, f_{sk,i})$.
2. Let $out_0 = b$.
3. For $h = 1, \ldots, l$,
    (a) For $t = 1, \ldots, s = \lfloor out_{h-1} \rfloor$, we construct $out_h[t]$ as follows:
        i. Let $y_0, y_2 \leftarrow \widetilde{\mathsf{Enc}}(pk_1, \ldots, pk_N, 0)$ and $y_1 \leftarrow \widetilde{\mathsf{Enc}}(pk_1, \ldots, pk_N, 1)$.
        ii. Consider 2 cases:
            A. If $out_{h-1}[t] = 0$, $out_h[t] := y_0 + y_2$.
            B. If $out_{h-1}[t] = 1$, $out_h[t] := y_1 + y_2$.

(b) If $h \geq 2$, replace out_h with $\mathsf{Eval}_{\mathcal{F}}(\mathsf{Dec}_{\mathcal{F}}^2, pk_{\mathcal{F},1}, \ldots, pk_{\mathcal{F},N}, \tilde{f}_{sk,1}, \ldots,$
$\tilde{f}_{sk,N}, out_h)$

4. Output $out = out_l$

Let $P = (G = (V, E), v_r, T, \psi_V, \psi_E)$. For $h = 1, \ldots, l$, let $v^h \in V$ be the vertex at height h along the path indicated by x. We have $b = U(P, x_1^*, \ldots, x_n^*) = \psi_V(v^0)$ and $v^l = v_0$. The result follows from the following claim when $h = l$:

Claim. For $h = 0, \ldots, l$, $out_h \simeq^s label(v^h)$.

Proof. Clearly, $out_0 = label(v^0) = U(P, x_1, \ldots, x_n) = b$. Suppose $out_{h-1} = label(v^{h-1})$. Let $i = \psi_V(v^h)$. For each bit $b = out_{h-1}[t]$, if $b = 0$, we have $out_h[t] = y_0 + y_2$ and

$$a_t = \begin{cases} z_1 + z_2 \text{ or } \tilde{c}_{\alpha,i} + z_1 & \text{if } x_i = \psi_E(v^h, v^{h-1}) = 0; \\ \tilde{c}_{\gamma,i} + z_1 & \text{if } x_i = \psi_E(v^h, v^{h-1}) = 1 \end{cases}$$

Clearly, z_1 and y_0 have the same distribution as both are $\widetilde{\mathsf{Enc}}(pk_1, \ldots, pk_N, 0)$. By private expandability, $\tilde{c}_{\alpha,i}$, $\tilde{c}_{\gamma,i}$ are statistically indistinguishable from y_2 when $x_i = \psi_E(v^h, v^{h-1}) = 0$ and $x_i = \psi_E(v^h, v^{h-1}) = 1$, respectively. We have $a_t \simeq^s out_h[t]$. Similarly, if $b = 1$, we have $out_h[t] = y_1 + y_2$ and

$$a_t = \begin{cases} \tilde{c}_{\gamma,i} + z_1 & \text{if } x_i = \psi_E(v^h, v^{h-1}) = 0; \\ \tilde{c}_{\alpha,i} + z_1 \text{ or } \tilde{c}_{\alpha,i} + \tilde{c}_{\gamma,i} & \text{if } x_i = \psi_E(v^h, v^{h-1}) = 1 \end{cases}$$

By private expandability, $\tilde{c}_{\gamma,i}$, $\tilde{c}_{\alpha,i}$ are statistically indistinguishable from y_1 when $x_i = \psi_E(v^h, v^{h-1}) = 0$ and $x_i = \psi_E(v^h, v^{h-1}) = 1$, respectively, while $\tilde{c}_{\gamma,i}$ is statistically indistinguishable from y_2 and z_1 when $x_i = \psi_E(v^h, v^{h-1}) = 1$. Again, we have $a_t \simeq^s out_h[t]$. Now average over the choice of $out_{h-1} \simeq^s label(v_{h-1})$, we have $a_t \simeq^s out_h$, and the result follows by applying $\mathsf{Eval}_{\mathcal{F}}(\mathsf{Dec}_{\mathcal{F}}^2, \tilde{f}_{sk,1}, \ldots, \tilde{f}_{sk,N}, \cdot)$ to both. $\square$

We have $\mathsf{Sim}_S((pk_1, \ldots, pk_N), (I_1, c_1), \ldots, (I_n, c_n), b) \simeq^s \mathsf{Eval}_S(P, (pk_1, \ldots, pk_N), (I_1, c_1), \ldots, (I_n, c_n))$. $\square$

4.3 Handling Malicious Inputs

Once we have an evaluation algorithm that can hide a branching program when public keys and ciphertexts are well-formed, we then consider the case when they are not properly generated. We use a single-key FHE with circuit privacy in Theorem 5 (such as one constructed in [21]) to homomorphically check the validity of each multi-key public key and ciphertext pair. If the check fails, we "mask" the output using a random string. The simulator can be constructed using the extractor guaranteed by the circuit privacy of single-key FHE to extract random coins and verify directly. If the check fails, it returns a random string with the same distribution as the masked output.

Let $\mathcal{P}$ be a circuit-private single-key FHE. We a define a circuit verifying each public key and corresponding ciphertexts:

$$\mathsf{Validate}_{\lambda,d,n}(pk, sk, r_k, (c_1, r_1), \ldots, (c_n, r_n), out) = \begin{cases} out & \text{if } (pk, sk) \leftarrow \mathsf{KeyGen}_{\mathcal{F}}(r_k) \\ & \text{and for each } i \in [n], \\ & c_i = \mathsf{Enc}_{\mathcal{F}}(pk, \mu_i; r_i) \\ & \text{for some } \mu_i \in \{0,1\}; \\ 0 & \text{otherwise} \end{cases}$$

We add a random string $S \in \{0,1\}^s$, where $s = s(\lambda, d) = |label(root)|$, to the output of Eval and return an encryption of S only if the verification passes. The original output can be computed if S can be recovered; otherwise, it is uniformly distributed. We define

$$v_j = \mathsf{Eval}_{\mathcal{P}}(\mathsf{Validate}(pk_j, \cdot, \cdot, \{(c_i, \cdot)\}_{I_i=j}, S_j), pk_{\mathcal{P},j}, p_{sk,j}, p_{kr,j}, \{p_{re,i}\}_{I_i=j})$$

where $p_{kr,j} = \mathsf{Enc}_{\mathcal{P}}(pk_{\mathcal{P},j}, r_{k,j})$, $p_{sk,j} = \mathsf{Enc}_{\mathcal{P}}(pk_{\mathcal{P},j}, sk_j)$ and $p_{re,i} = \mathsf{Enc}_{\mathcal{P}}(pk_{\mathcal{P},i}, r_{e,i})$, all of which are included in the new public key pk or the new ciphertext c. We also include $sk_{\mathcal{P}}$ in the new secret key sk. Finally, the new Eval returns $(label(root) \oplus (S_1 \oplus \ldots \oplus S_N), v_1, \ldots, v_N)$.

We describe $\mathcal{E}_M = (\mathsf{KeyGen}_M, \mathsf{Enc}_M, \mathsf{Eval}_M, \mathsf{Dec}_M)$ using the above Expand and $\widetilde{\mathsf{Enc}}$.

$\mathsf{KeyGen}_M(1^\lambda, 1^l)$:

1. Let $d = p(\lambda, l)$.
2. Let $(pk_{\mathcal{F}}, sk_{\mathcal{F}}) \leftarrow \mathsf{KeyGen}_{\mathcal{F}}(1^\lambda, 1^d; r_k)$.
3. Let $(pk_{\mathcal{P}}, sk_{\mathcal{P}}) \leftarrow \mathsf{KeyGen}_{\mathcal{P}}(1^\lambda)$.
4. Compute $f_{sk} := \mathsf{Enc}_{\mathcal{F}}(pk_{\mathcal{F}}, sk_{\mathcal{F}}; r_e)$, $p_{kr} := \mathsf{Enc}_{\mathcal{P}}(pk_{\mathcal{P}}, r_k)$ and $p_{sk} = \mathsf{Enc}_{\mathcal{P}}(pk_{\mathcal{P}}, sk_{\mathcal{F}})$.
5. Output $pk = (pk_{\mathcal{F}}, f_{sk}, p_{kr}, p_{sk})$ and $sk = (sk_{\mathcal{F}}, sk_{\mathcal{P}})$.

$\mathsf{Enc}_M(pk, \mu)$:

1. Parse $pk = (pk_{\mathcal{F}}, f_{sk}, pk_{\mathcal{P}}, p_{kr}, p_{sk})$.
2. Let $c_{\mathcal{F}} \leftarrow \mathsf{Enc}_{\mathcal{F}}(pk_{\mathcal{F}}, \mu; r_e)$
3. Compute $p_{re} = \mathsf{Enc}_{\mathcal{P}}(pk_{\mathcal{P}}, r_e)$
4. Output $c = (c_{\mathcal{F}}, p_{re})$.

$\mathsf{Eval}_M(P, (pk_1, \ldots, pk_N), (I_1, c_1), \ldots, (I_n, c_n))$

1. Let $P = (G = (V, E), v_0, T, \psi_V, \psi_E)$.
2. For $j = 1, \ldots, N$,
   (a) Parse $pk_j = (pk_{\mathcal{F},j}, f_{sk,j}, pk_{\mathcal{P},j}, p_{kr,j}, p_{sk,j})$.
   (b) Let $S_j \leftarrow \{0,1\}^s$ and $v_j = \mathsf{Eval}_{\mathcal{P}}(\mathsf{Validate}(pk_j, \cdot, \cdot, \{(c_i, \cdot)\}_{I_i=j}, S_j), pk_{\mathcal{P},j}, p_{sk,j}, p_{kr,j}, \{p_{re,i}\}_{I_i=j})$.
   (c) Let $\tilde{f}_{sk,j} = \mathsf{Expand}_{\mathcal{F}}(pk_{\mathcal{F},1}, \ldots, pk_{\mathcal{F},N}, j, f_{sk,j})$
3. For $i = 1, \ldots, n$,

(a) Parse $c_i = (c_{\mathcal{F},i}, p_{re,i})$.
(b) Let $(\tilde{c}_{\alpha,i}, \tilde{c}_{\gamma,i}) = \mathsf{Expand}(pk_1, \ldots, pk_N, i, c_{\mathcal{F},i})$.
4. For each $v \in T$, let $label(v) := \psi_V(v)$.
5. For each $v \in V \setminus T$ with both children labeled, let $h := height(v)$, $i := \psi_V(v)$
  (a) For $t = 1, \ldots, s = |label(u_0)|$ where $\Gamma(v) = \{u_0, u_1\}$, $\psi_E(v, u_0) = 0$,
    $\psi_E(v, u_1) = 1$
    i. Let $r_0 = label(u_0)[t]$ and $r_1 = label(u_1)[t]$.
    ii. Let $z_1, z_2 \leftarrow \widetilde{\mathsf{Enc}}(pk_1, \ldots, pk_N, 0)$
    iii. Consider 4 cases:
      A. if $r_0 = r_1 = 0$, $a_t := z_1 + z_2$
      B. if $r_0 = 0; r_1 = 1$, $a_t := \tilde{c}_{\alpha,i} + z_1$
      C. if $r_0 = 1; r_1 = 0$, $a_t := \tilde{c}_{\gamma,i} + z_1$
      D. if $r_0 = r_1 = 1$, $a_t := \tilde{c}_{\alpha,i} + \tilde{c}_{\gamma,i}$
  (b) $a_v = a_1 \ldots a_s$; if $h = 1$, $label(v) \leftarrow a_v$
  (c) otherwise, $label(v) \leftarrow \mathsf{Eval}_{\mathcal{F}}(\mathsf{Dec}_{\mathcal{F}}^2, pk_{\mathcal{F},1}, \ldots, pk_{\mathcal{F},N}, \tilde{f}_{sk,1}, \ldots, \tilde{f}_{sk,N}, a_v)$
6. Output $\hat{c} = (label(root) \oplus (S_1 \oplus \ldots \oplus S_N), v_1, \ldots, v_N)$

$\mathsf{Dec}_M(sk_1, \ldots, sk_N, \hat{c})$

1. Parse $\hat{c} = (\tilde{c}, v_{k,1}, \ldots, v_{k,N})$.
2. For $j = 1, \ldots, N$,
  (a) Parse $sk_j = (sk_{\mathcal{F},j}, sk_{\mathcal{P},j})$.
  (b) Let $S_j = \mathsf{Dec}_{\mathcal{P}}(sk_{\mathcal{P},j}, v_{k,j})$.
3. Let $\tilde{c}' = \tilde{c} \oplus (S_1 \oplus \ldots \oplus S_N)$
4. Output $\mu' := \mathsf{Dec}_{\mathcal{F}}(sk_{\mathcal{F},1}, \ldots, sk_{\mathcal{F},N}, \tilde{c}')$

4.4 Security Against Malicious Adversaries

We now prove that the above construction is secure against malicious adversaries as defined in Definition 8 by constructing a pair of algorithms Ext_M and Sim_M.

Theorem 6. *Assume $\mathcal{F}$ is a privately expandable multi-key HE scheme with circular security and $\mathcal{P}$ is maliciously circuit-private FHE. Then the above construction is a maliciously circuit-private HE scheme for the branching program.*

Proof. Let $\mathsf{Ext}_{\mathcal{P}}$ and $\mathsf{Sim}_{\mathcal{P}}$ be as defined in Definition 4. We construct Ext_M and Sim_M as follows:

$\mathsf{Ext}_M(1^\lambda, 1^l, pk^*, c^*)$:

1. Parse $pk^* = (pk_{\mathcal{F}}^*, f_{sk}^*, pk_{\mathcal{P}}^*, p_{kr}^*, p_{sk}^*)$. If it is malformed, output 0.
2. Let $r_e^* = \mathsf{Ext}_{\mathcal{P}}(pk_{\mathcal{P}}^*, p_{re}^*)$ and $sk_{\mathcal{F}}^* = \mathsf{Ext}_{\mathcal{P}}(pk_{\mathcal{P}}^*, p_{sk}^*)$.
3. If $(pk_{\mathcal{F}}^*, sk_{\mathcal{F}}^*) \neq \mathsf{KeyGen}_{\mathcal{F}}(1^\lambda, 1^d; r_e^*)$, return 0.
4. If $c^* = \mathsf{Enc}_{\mathcal{F}}(pk_{\mathcal{F}}^*, \mu; r_e^*)$ for some $\mu \in \{0,1\}$, output μ.
5. Otherwise, output 0.

$\mathsf{Sim}_M(1^\lambda, 1^l, (pk_1^*, \ldots, pk_N^*), (I_1, c_1^*), \ldots, (I_n, c_n^*), b)$:

1. For $i = 1, \ldots, n$,
   (a) Parse $c_i^* = (c_{\mathcal{F},i}^*, p_{re,i}^*)$.
   (b) Let $\tilde{c}_i^* = \mathsf{Expand}(pk_1^*, \ldots, pk_N^*, i, c_i^*)$.
2. For $j = 1, \ldots, N$,
   (a) Parse $pk_j^* = (pk_{\mathcal{F},j}^*, f_{sk,j}^*, pk_{\mathcal{P},j}^*, p_{kr,j}^*, p_{sk,j}^*)$.
   (b) Do the same test as in Ext for pk_j^* and $\{c_i^*\}_{I_i=j}$. If any of the test fails, let $v_{k,j} = \mathsf{Sim}_{\mathcal{P}}(pk_{\mathcal{P},j}^*, p_{sk,j}^*, p_{kr,j}^*, \{p_{re,i}^*\}_{I_i=j}, 0)$.
   (c) Otherwise, let $S_j \leftarrow \{0,1\}^s$ and $v_j = \mathsf{Sim}_{\mathcal{P}}(pk_{\mathcal{P},j}^*, p_{sk,j}^*, p_{kr,j}^*, \{p_{re,i}^*\}_{I_i=j}, S_j)$.
   (d) Let $\tilde{f}_{sk,j}^* = \mathsf{Expand}_{\mathcal{F}}(pk_{\mathcal{F},1}^*, \ldots, pk_{\mathcal{F},N}^*, j, f_{sk,j}^*)$
3. If any of the tests above fail, let out be a random string of length s and skip to the last step.
4. Otherwise, let $out_0 = b$.
5. For $h = 1, \ldots, l$,
   (a) For $t = 1, \ldots, s = |out_{h-1}|$, we construct $out_h[t]$ as follows:
      i. Let $y_0, y_2 \leftarrow \widetilde{\mathsf{Enc}}(pk_1, \ldots, pk_N, 0)$ and $y_1 \leftarrow \widetilde{\mathsf{Enc}}(pk_1, \ldots, pk_N, 1)$.
      ii. Consider 2 cases:
         A. If $out_{h-1}[t] = 0$, $out_h[t] := y_0 + y_2$.
         B. If $out_{h-1}[t] = 1$, $out_h[t] := y_1 + y_2$.
   (b) If $h \geq 2$, replace out_h with $\mathsf{Eval}_{\mathcal{F}}(\mathsf{Dec}_{\mathcal{F}}^2, pk_{\mathcal{F},1}^*, \ldots, pk_{\mathcal{F},N}^*, \tilde{f}_{sk,1}^*, \ldots, \tilde{f}_{sk,N}^*, out_h)$
6. Output $out = (out_l \oplus (S_1 \oplus \ldots \oplus S_N), v_{k,1}, \ldots, v_{k,N})$

We show that they satisfy the Definition 8.

Assume there exists $j \in [N]$ such that $\mathsf{Validate}(pk_{\mathcal{F},j}^*, sk_{\mathcal{F},j}^*, r_{k,j}^*, \{(c_i^*, r_{e,i}^*)\}_{I_i=j}, S_j) = 0$ for $sk_{\mathcal{F},j}^* = \mathsf{Ext}_{\mathcal{P}}(1^\lambda, pk_{\mathcal{P},j}^*, p_{sk,j}^*)$, $r_{k,j}^* = \mathsf{Ext}_{\mathcal{P}}(1^\lambda, pk_{\mathcal{P},j}^*, p_{kr,j}^*)$ and $r_{e,i}^* = \mathsf{Ext}_{\mathcal{P}}(1^\lambda, pk_{\mathcal{P},j}^*, p_{re,i}^*)$ for $I_i = j$. Then by circuit privacy of $\mathcal{P}$, v_i is statistically indistinguishable from $\mathsf{Sim}_{\mathcal{P}}(1^\lambda, pk_{\mathcal{P},j}^*, p_{sk,j}^*, p_{kr,j}^*, \{p_{re,i}^*\}_{I_i=j}, 0)$ independent from S_j. Thus, out has the same distribution as a random string of length s in both Eval and Sim_M.

Now suppose that all $\mathsf{Validate}$'s are not zero, then $pk_{\mathcal{F},i}^*$ and $c_{\mathcal{F},i}^*$ are generated correctly. Since out_l is computed the same way as in Sim_M, the result follows from Lemma 6. $\square$

Combining the above result with Lemma 4 results in the following theorem:

Theorem 7. *Let $\mathcal{F}$ be a privately expandable multi-hop multi-key compact somewhat homomorphic encryption scheme that can evaluate a circuit up to depth $2d + 2$ where d is the depth of $\mathsf{Dec}_{\mathcal{F}}$. Then the scheme described above is a maliciously circuit-private multi-key HE scheme for branching programs.*

Corollary 1. *Assuming RLWE and DSPR assumptions, and circular security for $\mathcal{E}_{SH}$, there exists a maliciously circuit-private multi-key HE scheme for branching programs.*

5   Circuit-Private Multi-key FHE

In this section we devise a framework turning a compact MFHE scheme and a circuit-private multi-key HE scheme into a circuit-private MFHE. This is a multi-key variant of the framework in [21]. As we discussed earlier, it is difficult to turn a single-key circuit-private HE scheme and a MFHE scheme into a circuit-private MFHE in the plain model. When both homomorphic encryption schemes are multi-key, each pair of public key and secret key can be generated together, thus allowing homomorphic decryption between two schemes. We use MFHE evaluation to evaluate a given circuit. We then switch to the circuit-private scheme to verify the input. Finally, we switch it back to the original scheme for compactness. Unlike the single-key case, we cannot verify all public keys and ciphertexts at once as it would lead to a larger verification circuit. We rely on the fully homomorphic property of the former to combine the result.

Let $\mathcal{F} = (\mathsf{KeyGen}_{\mathcal{F}}, \mathsf{Enc}_{\mathcal{F}}, \mathsf{Eval}_{\mathcal{F}}, \mathsf{Dec}_{\mathcal{F}})$ be a leveled compact multi-key FHE scheme and $\mathcal{P} = (\mathsf{KeyGen}_{\mathcal{P}}, \mathsf{Enc}_{\mathcal{P}}, \mathsf{Eval}_{\mathcal{P}}, \mathsf{Dec}_{\mathcal{P}})$ be a leveled multi-key circuit-private homomorphic scheme. Define the following programs:

$$\mathsf{KValidate}^{\lambda,d}_{pk_{\mathcal{F}},out}(sk_{\mathcal{F}}, r_{\mathcal{F}K}) = \begin{cases} out & \text{if } (pk_{\mathcal{F}}, sk_{\mathcal{F}}) = \mathsf{KeyGen}_{\mathcal{F}}(1^{\lambda}, 1^d; r_{\mathcal{F}K}) \\ 0 & \text{otherwise.} \end{cases}$$

$$\mathsf{CValidate}^{\lambda,d}_{pk_{\mathcal{F}},c_{\mathcal{F}},out}(r_{\mathcal{F}E}) = \begin{cases} out & \text{if } c_{\mathcal{F}} = \mathsf{Enc}_{\mathcal{F}}(pk_{\mathcal{F}}, b_i; r_{\mathcal{F}E}) \text{ for some } b_i \in \{0,1\} \\ 0 & \text{otherwise.} \end{cases}$$

$$\mathsf{CombineDec}(sk_{\mathcal{P},1}, \ldots, sk_{\mathcal{P},N}, c_1, \ldots, c_{N+n}) = \begin{cases} m & \text{if } \mathsf{Dec}_{\mathcal{P}}(sk_{\mathcal{P},1}, \ldots, sk_{\mathcal{P},N}, c_i) = m \\ & \text{for } \forall i = 1, \ldots, N+n \\ 0 & \text{otherwise.} \end{cases}$$

5.1   Construction

$\mathsf{KeyGen}(1^{\lambda}, 1^d)$:

1. Let $(pk_{\mathcal{F}}, sk_{\mathcal{F}}) = \mathsf{KeyGen}_{\mathcal{F}}(1^{\lambda}, 1^d; r_{\mathcal{F}K})$ and $(pk_{\mathcal{P}}, sk_{\mathcal{P}}) \leftarrow \mathsf{KeyGen}_{\mathcal{P}}(1^{\lambda}, 1^{d_0})$ where d_0 is the maximum between the depth of $\mathsf{KValidate}^{\lambda,d}_{pk_{\mathcal{F}},out}$, $\mathsf{CValidate}^{\lambda,d}_{pk_{\mathcal{F}},c_{\mathcal{F}},out}$ and $\mathsf{Dec}_{\mathcal{F}}$.
2. Let $p_{sk_{\mathcal{F}}} = \mathsf{Enc}_{\mathcal{P}}(pk_{\mathcal{P}}, sk_{\mathcal{F}})$, $p_{r_{\mathcal{F}K}} = \mathsf{Enc}_{\mathcal{P}}(pk_{\mathcal{P}}, r_{\mathcal{F}K})$ and $f_{sk_{\mathcal{P}}} = \mathsf{Enc}_{\mathcal{F}}(pk_{\mathcal{F}}, sk_{\mathcal{P}})$.
3. Output $pk = (pk_{\mathcal{P}}, pk_{\mathcal{F}}, p_{sk_{\mathcal{F}}}, p_{r_{\mathcal{F}K}}, f_{sk_{\mathcal{P}}})$, $sk = sk_{\mathcal{F}}$.

$\mathsf{Enc}(pk, \mu)$:

1. Parse $pk = (pk_{\mathcal{P}}, pk_{\mathcal{F}}, p_{sk_{\mathcal{F}}}, p_{r_{\mathcal{F}K}}, f_{sk_{\mathcal{P}}})$.
2. Let $c_{\mathcal{F}} = \mathsf{Enc}_{\mathcal{F}}(pk_{\mathcal{F}}, \mu; r_{\mathcal{F}E})$ and $p_{r_{\mathcal{F}E}} \leftarrow \mathsf{Enc}_{\mathcal{P}}(pk_{\mathcal{P}}, r_{\mathcal{F}E})$.
3. Output $c = (c_{\mathcal{F}}, p_{r_{\mathcal{F}E}})$.

$\mathsf{Eval}(C, (pk_1, \ldots, pk_N), (I_1, c_1), \ldots, (I_n, c_n))$

1. For $i = 1, \ldots, N$, parse $pk_i = (pk_{\mathcal{P},i}, pk_{\mathcal{F},i}, p_{sk_{\mathcal{F}},i}, p_{r_{\mathcal{F}K},i}, f_{sk_{\mathcal{P}},i})$.
2. For $i = 1, \ldots, n$, parse $c_i = (c_{\mathcal{F},i}, p_{r_{\mathcal{F}E},i})$.

3. If C is syntactically malformed, does not match n, or pk_i or c_i has incorrect size, replace C with a program returning 0.
4. Let $out_{\mathcal{F}} = \mathsf{Eval}_{\mathcal{F}}(C, (pk_{\mathcal{F},1}, \ldots, pk_{\mathcal{F},N}), (I_1, c_{\mathcal{F},1}), \ldots, (I_n, c_{\mathcal{F},n}))$.
5. Let $out_{\mathcal{P}} = \mathsf{Eval}_{\mathcal{P}}(\mathsf{Dec}_{\mathcal{F}}(\cdot, out_{\mathcal{F}}), (pk_{\mathcal{P},1}, \ldots, pk_{\mathcal{P},N}), (1, p_{sk_{\mathcal{F}},1}), \ldots, (N, p_{sk_{\mathcal{F}},N}))$.
6. For $i = 1, \ldots, N$, let
$$out_{K,i} = \mathsf{Eval}_{\mathcal{P}}(\mathsf{KValidate}^{\lambda,d}_{pk_{\mathcal{F}},i,out_{\mathcal{P}}}, (pk_{\mathcal{P},1}, \ldots, pk_{\mathcal{P},N}), (i, p_{sk_{\mathcal{F}},i}), (i, p_{r_{\mathcal{F}K},i})).$$
7. For $i = 1, \ldots, n$, let
$$out_{C,i} = \mathsf{Eval}_{\mathcal{P}}(\mathsf{CValidate}^{\lambda,d}_{pk_{\mathcal{F}},i,c_{\mathcal{F},i},out_{\mathcal{P}}}, (pk_{\mathcal{P},1}, \ldots, pk_{\mathcal{P},N}), (i, p_{r_{\mathcal{F}E},i})).$$
8. Output $\hat{c} = \mathsf{Eval}_{\mathcal{F}}(\mathsf{Dec}_{\mathcal{P}}(\cdot, \mathsf{CombineDec}(\cdot, out_{K,1}, \ldots, out_{K,N}, out_{C,1}, \ldots, out_{C,n})), (pk_{\mathcal{F},1}, \ldots, pk_{\mathcal{F},N}), (1, f_{sk_{\mathcal{P}},1}), \ldots, (N, f_{sk_{\mathcal{P}},N}))$.

$\mathsf{Dec}(sk_1, \ldots, sk_N, \hat{c})$

1. For $i = 1, \ldots, N$, parse $sk_i = sk_{\mathcal{F},i}$.
2. Output $y = \mathsf{Dec}_{\mathcal{F}}(sk_{\mathcal{F},1}, \ldots, sk_{\mathcal{F},N}, \hat{c})$.

We now prove that this construction gives a leveled compact circuit-private MFHE.

Theorem 8. *Assume a compact leveled MFHE scheme $\mathcal{F}$ and a leveled $(U, \mathcal{C}_{\mathcal{F}})$-homomorphic circuit-private multi-key HE scheme $\mathcal{P}$ exist., where $\mathcal{C}_{\mathcal{F}}$ includes $\mathsf{Dec}_{\mathcal{F}}(\cdot, out_{\mathcal{F}})$, $\mathsf{KValidate}^{\lambda,d}_{pk_{\mathcal{F}},out_{\mathcal{P}}}$ and $\mathsf{CValidate}^{\lambda,d}_{pk_{\mathcal{F}},c_{\mathcal{F}},out_{\mathcal{P}}}$ for all $\lambda, d, pk_{\mathcal{F}}, c_{\mathcal{F}}, out_{\mathcal{P}}, out_{\mathcal{F}}$. The resulting scheme in the above construction is a leveled compact circuit-private MFHE.*

We refer to the full version of this paper for the proof.

5.2 Instantiation

Finally, if we instantiate the result of Theorem 8 by our construction in Theorem 7, we get the following results:

Corollary 2. *Assume there exists a privately expandable multi-hop multi-key compact somewhat homomorphic encryption scheme that can evaluate circuits up to depth $2d+2$ where d is the depth of its decryption circuit. Then there exists a maliciously circuit-private multi-key fully homomorphic encryption scheme.*

Corollary 3. *Assuming RLWE and DSPR assumptions, and circular security for $\mathcal{E}_{SH}$, there exists a maliciously circuit-private multi-key fully homomorphic encryption scheme.*

6   Three-Round On-the-Fly MPC with Circuit Privacy

In this section we consider one application of the circuit-private MFHE scheme—on-the-fly MPC protocol. In this setting, a large number of clients P_i uploaded their encrypted inputs to a server or a cloud, denoted by S. The server selects an N-input function F on a subset of clients' input, and performs the computation without further information. Afterward, the server and the clients whose inputs are chosen run the rest of the protocol. At the end of an on-the-fly MPC protocol, only those clients learn the output while the server and other parties learn nothing. Furthermore, the communication complexity and the running time of clients should be independent of the function F. As in standard MPC, the input of each client should not be revealed to any other parties, including the server. In addition, we require circuit privacy for the server. Clients should not learn anything about the function other than its output. We give the formal definition of on-the-fly MPC protocol from [20] as follows:

Definition 9. *Let C be a class of functions with at most U inputs. An* on-the-fly *multi-party computation protocol Π for C is a protocol between $P_1, \ldots, P_U, S$ where P_i is given x_i as input, for $i \in [U]$, and S is given an ordered subset $V \subseteq [U]$ of size N and a function F on N inputs. At the end of the protocol, each party P_i for $i \in V$ outputs $F(\{x_i\}_{i \in V})$ while P_i for $i \notin V$ and S output $\bot$. The protocol consists of two phases:*

- **Offline phase** *is performed before F, V is chosen. All parties participate in this phase.*
- **Online phase** *starts after F, V is chosen. Only S and P_i for $i \in V$ participate in this phase, and ignore all messages from P_i, $i \notin V$.*

We require that the communication complexity of the protocol and the computation time of $P_1, \ldots, P_U$ be independent of (the complexity of) the function F. Furthermore, the computation time of P_i for $i \notin V$ is independent of the output size of F.

We then define the security and circuit privacy of on-the-fly MPC protocol in the plain model against malicious adversaries.

Definition 10. *An adversary $\mathcal{A}$ corrupting a party receives all messages directed to the corrupted party and controls the messages that it sends. Since the server ignores messages from parties outside V, we assume w.l.o.g. that an adversary only corrupts computing parties, i.e., parties in V.*

Let $\mathsf{View}_{\Pi,S}(F, V, \boldsymbol{x})$ denote the collection of messages the server S receives in an execution of protocol Π on a subset $V \subseteq [U]$ with $|V| = N$, an N-input function $F \in C$ and input vector $\boldsymbol{x}$. Let $\mathsf{View}_{\Pi,\mathcal{A}}(F, V, \boldsymbol{x})$ denote the joint collection of messages $\mathcal{A}$ receives through corrupted parties in an execution of protocol Π on V, F and $\boldsymbol{x}$.

An on-the-fly multi-party computation protocol Π for C is secure *if*

- *for every adversary $\mathcal{A}$ corrupting parties $\{P_i\}_{i \in T}$ with $|T| = t < N$, for all $V \subseteq [U]$ with $|V| = N$, for all N-input function $F \in C$ and for all input vectors $\boldsymbol{x}, \boldsymbol{x}'$ such that $x_i = x_i'$ for any $i \in T$,*

$$[\mathsf{View}_{\Pi,\mathcal{A}}(F, V, \boldsymbol{x}) | y = F(\{x_i\}_{i \in V})] \simeq^c [\mathsf{View}_{\Pi,\mathcal{A}}(F, V, \boldsymbol{x}') | y = F(\{x_i'\}_{i \in V})].$$

- *for every server S, for all $V \subseteq [U]$ with $|V| = N$, for all N-input function $F \in \mathcal{C}$ and for all input vectors $\boldsymbol{x}, \boldsymbol{x}'$,*

$$[\text{View}_{\Pi,S}(F, V, \boldsymbol{x}) | y = F(\{x_i\}_{i \in V})] \simeq^c [\text{View}_{\Pi,S}(F, V, \boldsymbol{x}') | y = F(\{x_i'\}_{i \in V})].$$

Let the ideal world protocol be where the computation of F is performed through a trusted functionality $\mathcal{F}$. Each party P_i sends their input x_i to $\mathcal{F}$, the server sends F and V to $\mathcal{F}$, which performs the computation and sends the output $F(\{x_i\}_{i \in V})$ to each P_i, $i \in V$. Let $\text{IDEAL}_{\mathcal{F},S}(F, V, x)$ denote the joint output of the ideal-world adversary S, parties $P_1, \ldots, P_U$ and the server S. Let $\text{REAL}_{\Pi,\mathcal{A}}(F, V, x)$ denote the joint output of the real-world adversary S, parties $P_1, \ldots, P_U$ and the server S.

The protocol Π has (malicious) circuit privacy if for every malicious (and possibly unbounded) adversary $\mathcal{A}$ corrupting any number of clients, there exists an unbounded simulator S with black-box access to $\mathcal{A}$ such that for all $V \subseteq [U]$ with $|V| = N$, for all N-input function $F \in \mathcal{C}$ and for all input vectors x, $\text{IDEAL}_{\mathcal{F},S}(F, V, x) \simeq^s \text{REAL}_{\Pi,\mathcal{A}}(F, V, x)$.

Adding circuit privacy to an on-the-fly MPC protocol via circuit-private MFHE scheme has two implications beyond the definition state above. First, it automatically strengthen the protocol against malicious adversaries without using setup. This is because the evaluated output only depends on the output and encrypted input even against malformed public keys and ciphertexts. On the other hand, it implies that the clients do not know the function being evaluated, which in turn makes it difficult, if even possible, to verify against a malicious server. Therefore, we assume that the server is only honest-but-curious, that it follows the protocol, but may try to learn clients' input data.

Naturally, the MFHE scheme leads to server-assisted MPC by having each client generate keys, and encrypt its inputs and uploads to the server. The server then runs an evaluation algorithm on the encrypted inputs. However, in order to decrypt the evaluated output, one needs to have all secret keys. One solution, as in [17], is to run another MPC protocol with each client's secret key as input to decrypt. However, this results in multiple rounds in the plain model. In order to solve this problem, we use a projective garbling scheme.

After the server runs the evaluation algorithm, it creates a garbled circuit of MFHE decryption with secret keys as input. In order to create a garbled input, the server cannot give e to the clients as it will allow the clients to generate multiple garbled inputs, thus rendering the security meaningless. We solve this problem by using a 1-out-of-2 oblivious transfer (OT). In order to minimize the round complexity of our MPC protocol, we consider an OT protocol that runs in one round. However, the standard one-round 1-out-of-2 OT protocols known are only secure against semi-honest receivers.

We refer to the full version of this paper for the formal definitions of the garbling scheme and OT, and the construction of a one-round 1-out-of-2 OT protocol that is secure against malicious receivers from maliciously circuit-private single-key FHE.

Theorem 9. *Assuming a circuit-private single-key FHE, there exists a one-round 1-out-of-2 oblivious transfer protocol that is secure against malicious receivers.*

6.1 Construction

Let $\mathcal{E}$ = (KeyGen, Enc, Eval, Dec) be a (leveled) compact maliciously circuit-private MFHE scheme with secret key length $s = s(\lambda)$ and using $r = r(\lambda)$ random bits for key generation. For simplicity, we assume that each client's input is 1 bit. The protocol can be easily generalized to the case where each client holds many bits of input. Compactness of the MFHE implies that the evaluated output do not depend on the size of the input. Thus, the rest of our protocol stays the same. Let $(G_{\mathsf{OT}}, Q_{\mathsf{OT}}, A_{\mathsf{OT}}, D_{\mathsf{OT}})$ be a one-round 1-out-of-2 OT protocol. Let (GarbCircuit, GarbEval) be a projective gabling scheme. Let U be the set of indices of all clients in the system. We describe an on-the-fly MPC protocol $\Pi_N(V, F, x)$ as follows:

On-the-Fly MPC Protocol

Step 1: For $i \in [U]$, client P_i generates a key pair $(pk_i, sk_i) = \mathsf{KeyGen}(1^\lambda; r_i)$ and encrypts his input $c_i \leftarrow \mathsf{Enc}(pk_i, x_i)$. For each $j = 0, \ldots, s + r - 1$, P_i also generates $(pk_{\mathsf{OT},i}^j, sk_{\mathsf{OT},i}^j) \leftarrow G_{\mathsf{OT}}(1^\lambda)$. It computes bitwise $q_i^j = Q_{\mathsf{OT}}(pk_{\mathsf{OT},i}^j, sk_i[j])$ for $j = 0, \ldots, s - 1$, and $q_i^{s+j} = Q_{\mathsf{OT}}(pk_{\mathsf{OT},i}^j, r_i[j])$ for $j = 0, \ldots, r - 1$. It then sends $(pk_i, c_i, pk_{\mathsf{OT},i}, \overrightarrow{q}_i)$ to the server S.

The server S then selects a circuit C representing the function F on inputs $\{x_i\}_{i \in V}$ for a subset $V \subseteq U$ such that $|V| = N$. We may assume w.l.o.g. that $V = [N]$.

Step 2: The server S computes $c = \mathsf{Eval}(C, pk_1, \ldots, pk_N, c_1, \ldots, c_N)$. S computes a garbled circuit $(G, e) = \mathsf{GarbCircuit}(1^\lambda, g_{c,pk_1,\ldots,pk_N})$ where

$$g_{c,pk_1,\ldots,pk_N}((sk_1, r_1), \ldots, (sk_N, r_N)) = \begin{cases} \mathsf{Dec}(sk_1, \ldots, sk_N, c) \text{ if } (pk_i, sk_i) = \\ \qquad \mathsf{KeyGen}(1^\lambda; r_i) \\ \qquad \text{for all } i \in [N]; \\ \bot \qquad \text{otherwise} \end{cases}$$

and $e = (X_0^0, X_0^1, \ldots, X_{N(r+s)-1}^0, X_{N(r+s)-1}^1)$. For each $i \in [N]$ and $j = 0, \ldots, r + s - 1$, it computes $a_i^j = A_{\mathsf{OT}}(pk_{\mathsf{OT},i}, q_i^j, X_{i(r+s)+j}^0, X_{i(r+s)+j}^1)$. It sends $(G, a_i^0, \ldots, a_i^{r+s-1})$ (and V) to P_i for each $i \in V$.

Step 3: For $i \in V$, client P_i computes its garbled input $X_{i(r+s)+j} = D_{\mathsf{OT}}(sk_{OT,i}, a_i^j)$ for $j = 0, \ldots, r + s - 1$ and broadcasts to other $P_{i'} \in V$. Each client computes $y = \mathsf{GarbEval}(G, X_0, \ldots, X_{N(r+s)-1})$.

Remarks

1. The upper bound on the number of clients whose inputs are used in a computation must be known in advance. This requirement is inherited from the multi-key homomorphic encryption scheme in [17] that we use to construct our MFHE. It is also the case for the on-the-fly MPC construction in [17].
2. Private channel (from the server) between clients is required to prevent the server learning clients' secret keys. This requirement can be done by the honest-but-curious server passing public keys of all parties in V along with its messages in step 2. The public key of P_i can be used to encrypt a garbled input from P_j to P_i.
3. We require circular security between MFHE and OT schemes. This can be done without additional assumptions by using OT constructed from the same circuit-private homomorphic scheme in Sect. 4.

Theorem 10. *Let $\mathcal{E} = (\mathsf{KeyGen}, \mathsf{Enc}, \mathsf{Eval}, \mathsf{Dec})$ be a leveled compact MFHE scheme. Let $\mathsf{OT} = (G_{\mathsf{OT}}, Q_{\mathsf{OT}}, A_{\mathsf{OT}}, D_{\mathsf{OT}})$ be an OT protocol. Let $\mathsf{Gb} = (GarbCir\text{-}cuit, GarbEval)$ be a projective garbling scheme. If $\mathcal{E}$ is maliciously circuit-private, OT is secure against malicious receivers, and Gb is a secure garbling scheme, then the protocol Π_N is a 3-round secure on-the-fly MPC protocol with circuit privacy.*

We refer to the full version of this paper for the proof.

7   Conclusion and Open Questions

We have shown that we can construct circuit-private MFHE from the existing multi-key HE and single-key circuit-private FHE. We also use it to construct an on-the-fly MPC with circuit privacy against malicious clients in the plain model. However, our construction inherits the same assumption as the construction of MFHE of López-Alt et al., including DSPR and RLWE. So, the main open question is:

Is it possible to construct a multi-key homomorphic encryption (with circuit privacy) under standard assumptions such as LWE in the plain model?

Since our technique only relies on properties that exist in many single-key constructions, we expect that we can apply it to other multi-key HE as well. Moreover, circuit privacy for on-the-fly MPC requires some degree of trust toward a server party. Our construction assumes the server to be honest-but-curious. We would like to capture a wider range of unintended behavior of the server while still achieving circuit privacy. So, another open question is:

Is there a better model for on-the-fly MPC with circuit privacy?

References

1. Aiello, B., Ishai, Y., Reingold, O.: Priced oblivious transfer: how to sell digital goods. In: Pfitzmann, B. (ed.) EUROCRYPT 2001. LNCS, vol. 2045, pp. 119–135. Springer, Heidelberg (2001). doi:10.1007/3-540-44987-6_8
2. Albrecht, M., Bai, S., Ducas, L.: A subfield lattice attack on overstretched NTRU assumptions: cryptanalysis of some FHE and graded encoding schemes. Technical report, Cryptology ePrint Archive, Report 2016/127 (2016)
3. Asharov, G., Jain, A., López-Alt, A., Tromer, E., Vaikuntanathan, V., Wichs, D.: Multiparty computation with low communication, computation and interaction via threshold FHE. In: Pointcheval, D., Johansson, T. (eds.) EUROCRYPT 2012. LNCS, vol. 7237, pp. 483–501. Springer, Heidelberg (2012). doi:10.1007/978-3-642-29011-4_29
4. Brakerski, Z., Vaikuntanathan, V.: Fully homomorphic encryption from ring-LWE and security for key dependent messages. In: Rogaway, P. (ed.) CRYPTO 2011. LNCS, vol. 6841, pp. 505–524. Springer, Heidelberg (2011). doi:10.1007/978-3-642-22792-9_29
5. Canetti, R.: Security and composition of multiparty cryptographic protocols. J. Cryptol. **13**(1), 143–202 (2000)
6. Chongchitmate, W., Ostrovsky, R.: Circuit-private multi-key FHE. Cryptology ePrint Archive, Report 2017/010 (2017). http://eprint.iacr.org/
7. Clear, M., McGoldrick, C.: Multi-identity and multi-key leveled FHE from learning with errors. In: Gennaro, R., Robshaw, M. (eds.) CRYPTO 2015. LNCS, vol. 9216, pp. 630–656. Springer, Heidelberg (2015). doi:10.1007/978-3-662-48000-7_31
8. Damgård, I., Jurik, M.: A generalisation, a simplification and some applications of Paillier's probabilistic public-key system. In: Kim, K. (ed.) PKC 2001. LNCS, vol. 1992, pp. 119–136. Springer, London (2001). doi:10.1007/3-540-44586-2_9. http://dl.acm.org/citation.cfm?id=648118.746742
9. Ducas, L., Stehlé, D.: Sanitization of FHE ciphertexts. In: Fischlin, M., Coron, J.-S. (eds.) EUROCRYPT 2016. LNCS, vol. 9665, pp. 294–310. Springer, Heidelberg (2016). doi:10.1007/978-3-662-49890-3_12
10. Gentry, C.: A fully homomorphic encryption scheme. Ph.D. thesis, Stanford University (2009)
11. Gentry, C., Halevi, S., Vaikuntanathan, V.: i-Hop homomorphic encryption and rerandomizable Yao circuits. In: Rabin, T. (ed.) CRYPTO 2010. LNCS, vol. 6223, pp. 155–172. Springer, Heidelberg (2010). doi:10.1007/978-3-642-14623-7_9
12. Gentry, C., Sahai, A., Waters, B.: Homomorphic encryption from learning with errors: conceptually-simpler, asymptotically-faster, attribute-based. In: Canetti, R., Garay, J.A. (eds.) CRYPTO 2013. LNCS, vol. 8042, pp. 75–92. Springer, Heidelberg (2013). doi:10.1007/978-3-642-40041-4_5
13. Halevi, S., Kalai, Y.T.: Smooth projective hashing and two-message oblivious transfer. J. Cryptol. **25**(1), 158–193 (2012)
14. Halevi, S., Lindell, Y., Pinkas, B.: Secure computation on the web: computing without simultaneous interaction. In: Rogaway, P. (ed.) CRYPTO 2011. LNCS, vol. 6841, pp. 132–150. Springer, Heidelberg (2011). doi:10.1007/978-3-642-22792-9_8. http://dl.acm.org/citation.cfm?id=2033036.2033047
15. Ishai, Y., Paskin, A.: Evaluating branching programs on encrypted data. In: Vadhan, S.P. (ed.) TCC 2007. LNCS, vol. 4392, pp. 575–594. Springer, Heidelberg (2007). doi:10.1007/978-3-540-70936-7_31. http://dl.acm.org/citation.cfm?id=1760749.1760790

16. Kamara, S., Mohassel, P., Raykova, M.: Outsourcing multi-party computation. IACR Cryptology ePrint Archive 2011, 272 (2011)

17. López-Alt, A., Tromer, E., Vaikuntanathan, V.: On-the-fly multiparty computation on the cloud via multikey fully homomorphic encryption. In: Proceedings of 44th Annual ACM Symposium on Theory of Computing, STOC 2012, NY, USA, pp. 1219–1234 (2012). http://doi.acm.org/10.1145/2213977.2214086

18. Mohassel, P., Sadeghian, S.: How to hide circuits in MPC an efficient framework for private function evaluation. In: Johansson, T., Nguyen, P.Q. (eds.) EUROCRYPT 2013. LNCS, vol. 7881, pp. 557–574. Springer, Heidelberg (2013). doi:10.1007/978-3-642-38348-9_33

19. Mohassel, P., Sadeghian, S., Smart, N.P.: Actively secure private function evaluation. In: Sarkar, P., Iwata, T. (eds.) ASIACRYPT 2014. LNCS, vol. 8874, pp. 486–505. Springer, Heidelberg (2014). doi:10.1007/978-3-662-45608-8_26

20. Mukherjee, P., Wichs, D.: Two round mutliparty computation via multi-key FHE. Cryptology ePrint Archive, Report 2015/345 (2015). http://eprint.iacr.org/

21. Ostrovsky, R., Paskin-Cherniavsky, A., Paskin-Cherniavsky, B.: Maliciously circuit-private FHE. In: Garay, J.A., Gennaro, R. (eds.) CRYPTO 2014. LNCS, vol. 8616, pp. 536–553. Springer, Heidelberg (2014). doi:10.1007/978-3-662-44371-2_30

22. Pippenger, N.: On simultaneous resource bounds. In: Proceedings of 20th Annual Symposium on Foundations of Computer Science, SFCS 1979, pp. 307–311 (1979). http://dx.doi.org/10.1109/SFCS.1979.29

23. Raz, R.: Elusive functions and lower bounds for arithmetic circuits. In: Proceedings of 40th Annual ACM Symposium on Theory of Computing, STOC 2008, NY, USA, pp. 711–720 (2008). http://doi.acm.org/10.1145/1374376.1374479

24. Valiant, L.G.: Universal circuits (preliminary report). In: Proceedings of 8th Annual ACM Symposium on Theory of Computing, STOC 1976, NY, USA, pp. 196–203 (1976). http://doi.acm.org/10.1145/800113.803649

25. Dijk, M., Gentry, C., Halevi, S., Vaikuntanathan, V.: Fully homomorphic encryption over the integers. In: Gilbert, H. (ed.) EUROCRYPT 2010. LNCS, vol. 6110, pp. 24–43. Springer, Heidelberg (2010). doi:10.1007/978-3-642-13190-5_2

FHE over the Integers: Decomposed and Batched in the Post-Quantum Regime

Daniel Benarroch[1], Zvika Brakerski[1(✉)], and Tancrède Lepoint[2]

[1] Weizmann Institute of Science, Rehovot, Israel
zvika.brakerski@weizmann.ac.il
[2] SRI International, New York, USA

Abstract. Fully homomorphic encryption over the integers (FHE-OI) is currently the only alternative to lattice-based FHE. FHE-OI includes a family of schemes whose security is based on the hardness of different variants of the approximate greatest common divisor (AGCD) problem. A lot of effort was made to port techniques from second generation lattice-based FHE (using tensoring) to FHE-OI. Gentry, Sahai and Waters (Crypto 13) showed that third generation techniques (which were later formalized using the "gadget matrix") can also be ported. However, the majority of these works was based on the noise-free variant of AGCD which is potentially weaker than the general one. In particular, the noise-free variant relies on the hardness of factoring and is thus vulnerable to quantum attacks.

In this work, we propose a comprehensive study of applying third generation FHE techniques to the regime of FHE-OI. We present and analyze a third generation FHE-OI based on decisional AGCD without the noise-free assumption. We proceed to showing a batch version of our scheme where each ciphertext can encode a vector of messages and operations are performed coordinate-wise. We use a similar AGCD variant to Cheon et al. (Eurocrypt 13) who suggested the batch approach for second generation FHE, but we do not require the noise-free component or a subset sum assumption. However, like Cheon et al., we do require circular security for our scheme, even for bounded homomorphism. Lastly, we discuss some of the obstacles towards efficient implementation of our schemes and discuss a number of possible optimizations.

1 Introduction

In homomorphic encryption (HE), it is possible to transform a ciphertext $\mathsf{Enc}(x)$ into $\mathsf{Enc}(f(x))$ for some class of functions in a public manner, i.e. without any secret information and without compromising the security of the encrypted message. Rivest et al. [27] proposed the notion of fully homomorphic encryption

D. Benarroch—Supported by the Israel Science Foundation (Grant No. 468/14).

Z. Brakerski—Supported by the Israel Science Foundation (Grant No. 468/14), the Alon Young Faculty Fellowship and Binational Science Foundation (Grant No. 712307).

© International Association for Cryptologic Research 2017
S. Fehr (Ed.): PKC 2017, Part II, LNCS 10175, pp. 271–301, 2017.
DOI: 10.1007/978-3-662-54388-7_10

(FHE) where the scheme is homomorphic w.r.t any efficiently computable f. This will allow to outsource computation to third parties without compromising security. In an exciting breakthrough, Gentry [19] presented the first candidate FHE scheme that was based on ideal lattices. Very shortly afterwards, van Dijk et al. [30] proposed a scheme with a similar structure to Gentry's but one that was based on a different hardness assumption, namely the hardness of the approximate greatest common divisor problem (AGCD) [22]. In AGCD, the attacker's goal is to find a hidden prime p given arbitrarily (polynomially) many samples of random "near multiples" of p, i.e. samples of the form $qp + r$ where q is chosen randomly from an appropriate domain, and $r \ll p$ is random noise. In the AGCD schemes, the basic elements are integers rather than lattice vectors, and the scheme was referred to as FHE over the integers (henceforth FHE-OI).

Lattice based FHE developed and new schemes with better security and efficiency guarantees emerged [2,4–6] in the lattice domain; this is sometimes called second generation FHE. A sequence of works on FHE-OI showed that many of these techniques can be applied in that regime as well, resulting in schemes with comparable efficiency to the lattice setting [9,14–16]. In particular, Cheon et al. [9] showed how to encrypt a vector of messages in a single ciphertext, similarly to the [3,4,29] SIMD approach. In the batch setting, when performing a homomorphic operation, the operation is performed in parallel on all coordinates of the respective message vectors. This allows to increase the throughput of the scheme while preventing the ciphertext size from growing too much. This was later improved by Coron et al. [14] who presented a "scale invariant" version of the batch scheme, again showing that the scale invariance notion from [2] can be applied in the FHE-OI setting.

These last two works [9,14], however, deviate from the original formulation of the AGCD assumption in a number of aspects: (i) In order to allow batched ciphertexts, they change p from being prime to being a product of primes, so as to allow encoding of multiple messages using the Chinese Remainder Theorem. Furthermore, they required a circular secure variant of the assumption, where indistinguishability holds even for elements of the form $qp + r + m$ where m depends on the factors of p. We discuss circular security further when we talk about our batch scheme below. (ii) Rather than just assuming that finding p is hard, they assume that the samples $qp + r$ are indistinguishable from uniform samples over some domain. This is now known as *decisional* AGCD. (iii) Only in [9]: They require that the problem remains hard even if a single multiple of p without noise is known, i.e. some $x_0 = q_0 p$. This is known as the noise free variant. However, they show that if this element is given, then there is a reduction from the original AGCD problem to the new decisional batch AGCD. (iv) They make an additional subset sum assumption.

Gentry et al. [20] proposed a new family of techniques for lattice based FHE, sometimes referred to as third generation FHE. They showed how to decrease the size of the public parameters and the asymptotic complexity of performing a single homomorphic multiplication. It was later shown that this approach can be used to weaken the hardness assumption of the scheme and achieve better parameters [1,7] and even for implementations [11,17,23]. It was observed in [20] that their techniques can be applied also to FHE-OI in the noise free variant. Subset sum was no longer required, but a batched scheme was not introduced. It is important to mention that third generation FHE is lacking in terms of information rate. Whereas in second generation FHE, a (post-evaluation) ciphertext of length ℓ can encrypt $\Omega(\ell)$ bits of information, in third generation scheme only $o(\ell)$ bits are possible while maintaining full homomorphism.

Although having a noise free element simplifies the schemes, its impact on security is unclear. On one hand, it allows to reduce from the hardness of the search AGCD all the way to batch decision. On the other hand, it gives the adversary additional information that might be harmful for security. One setting where this additional information is *known* to be harmful is for *post-quantum* security. In post quantum security, we are interested in schemes that can be run on standard classical computers, but which are secure even against adversaries that have a quantum computer. This corresponds to a situation where the majority of the population cannot afford a quantum computer, but big organizations or governments can, and the simple user would still like to maintain security even against these quantum capabilities. Since factoring can be solved using a quantum computer [28], noise free AGCD is *not* post quantum secure. On the other hand, Cheon and Stehlé [10] showed that (non batched) decisional AGCD without the noise free element is at least as hard as the learning with errors (LWE) problem, which is widely regarded as post quantumly secure. We note that even though a similar statement for the batch variant is not known, the [10] result increases our confidence in its post quantum security.

1.1 Our Results

We construct third generation FHE-OI schemes, with and without batching capabilities, based on decisional AGCD (without a noise free element). More accurately, we construct *leveled* FHE: a parameterized homomorphic encryption scheme, such that for any polynomial depth bound $d = \text{poly}(\lambda)$ there is a proper setting of parameters such that the scheme can evaluate all depth d circuits. Leveled FHE schemes can be converted to plain FHE using Gentry's bootstrapping principle [19], albeit at the cost of making an additional hardness assumption (the circular security of the scheme). Since the use of bootstrapping is identical to previous schemes in the literature, we leave it out of this paper and focus on constructing the leveled schemes.

Our first scheme is non-batched, i.e. each ciphertext encrypts a single bit message, and is based on decisional AGCD. This scheme is similar to the [20] proposed construction, but we do away with the noise free element. This scheme is presented in Sect. 3. Our second scheme is batched and is based on batched decisional AGCD in addition to a circular security assumption (similarly to [9,14] as mentioned above). This scheme is presented in Sect. 4. Known attacks against the batched AGCD problem work less well than for the classical AGCD problem: this problem can potentially offer a higher degree of security (cf. [18]).

Both schemes enjoy the same *noise propagation* features as the LWE scheme of [1,7,20]: In all known FHE candidates, the limitation on the homomorphism depth stems from noise accumulation. Upon encryption, ciphertexts contain a certain amount of noise (appropriately defined), and performing homomorphic operations increases the noise. For correct decryption, the noise has to be below a predefined threshold, hence the limitation on the number of operations. In our scheme, the noise grows by a poly(λ) factor with every multiplication or logical NAND operation (the exact polynomial depends on the choice of parameters). Furthermore, the noise growth is asymmetric as in [20], i.e. only the noise of one of the two operands grows by a polynomial factor, and the noise of the other does not grow at all. This means that we can apply similar optimizations such as the ones in [1,7].

Finally, in Sect. 5, we discuss a number of possible optimizations. We show that using the subset sum assumption we can reduce the public key size, using techniques inspired by Coron et al. [15]. We show that at the last steps of the homomorphic evaluation, we do not have to pay the full cost of multiplication. We then show that instead of binary decomposition of the ciphertext, which is a major ingredient in [20] (and even earlier in [5]), one can use decomposition over a larger index, specifically roughly polynomial in the security parameter. This will reduce the ciphertext size and the evaluation complexity, but will increase the noise growth. Lastly we discuss the limitations in choosing the actual parameters for future implementation.

1.2   Our Techniques

Let p be a secret prime sampled from the appropriate distribution, and consider a sequence of samples of the form $x_i = q_i p + r_i$, where q_i is again sampled uniformly across some properly defined domain, and r_i is chosen uniformly across a "small" domain so that $|r_i| \ll p$. The decisional AGCD assumption is that the x_i's are computationally indistinguishable from a uniform element modulo a known parameter $N \approx q_{max} p$ (in fact, the parameters are chosen so that first N is selected and then the distribution q_i's is chosen so that the maximum is approximately equal to N/p). Consider adding a few of the x_i's together, for example taking two such samples, x_1, x_2 and letting $y = x_1 + x_2$. Then $y = (q_1 + q_2)p + (r_1 + r_2)$, and it has a similar structure to the original x's. However, not exactly: First of all, the noise $r_1 + r_2$ is bigger than the original r. Secondly, and as it turns out more importantly, now y might be bigger than the modulus N. Looking ahead, this will translate to ciphertext size growth during homomorphic evaluation, a side effect that we need to prevent. Note that the first intuition of taking the result modulo N does not help here. While the ciphertext size will be reduced, the structure might be lost as well since $y \pmod N = y - kN$ for some integer k. The solution, as presented already in [30], is to consider the first sample $x_0 = q_0 p + r_0$ as the modulus. Since we know that y cannot be much larger than N (since it is just the sum of a small number, say 2, of x_i's), this means that k is not so large, and therefore $y \pmod{x_0} = y - kx_0 = (q_1 + q_2 - kq_0)p + (r_1 + r_2 - kr_0)$ both lies in the right domain, which we will now define to be integers modulo x_0, and has the right structure. We note that the aforementioned error free variant is simply taking $r_0 = 0$ which simplifies many of the computations ahead since there will not be an r_0 contribution to the noise term.

A Modified Distribution. The situation here is more challenging than [30], though. For security purposes we would like to argue that x_i (mod x_0) is indistinguishable from a uniform element modulo x_0. However, this is actually not true since x_i and x_0 are of similar magnitudes and therefore small elements have a higher probability of appearing in x_i (mod x_0). We therefore consider the *conditional* probability distribution of x_i conditioned on $x_i < x_0$. This distribution is indeed indistinguishable from uniform modulo x_0. We will therefore use *rejection sampling* to sample the x_i's: we will sample according to the AGCD distribution, and if we are above x_0, we will discard the sample and repeat. This will result in a distribution of x_i that both has the structure that we desire and is indistinguishable from uniform modulo x_0. The only remaining problem is that perhaps we get x_0 that is so small that we will reject too often thus increasing the computational complexity of generating the x_i's. There are a number of ways to avoid this problem, we chose to just apply rejection sampling to the choice of x_0 itself and condition on it being larger than $N/2$, which implies that x_i will be rejected with probability at most $1/2$. We note that if x_0 was error free, this process would not be needed since x_i (mod x_0) would have been distributed exactly like a fresh AGCD sample with q uniformly modulo q_{max}. The formal analysis of this process appears in Lemma 2.3.

Our Basic Scheme. Now that we have our building blocks, we can construct a GSW-style homomorphic encryption scheme (as formulated by [1]). Consider the operation of taking a number c modulo x_0 and decomposing it into its binary representation, which is a binary column vector of dimension $\lceil \log x_0 \rceil$. We denote this operation by $\mathbf{G}^{-1}(c)$ (for reasons that will become clear later), if $\mathbf{c}$ is a row vector, then $\mathbf{G}^{-1}(\mathbf{c})$ is a binary matrix. The complement of this operation is linear, i.e. there is a vector $\mathbf{g}$ s.t. $\mathbf{g} \cdot \mathbf{G}^{-1}(\mathbf{c}) = \mathbf{c}$ (mod x_0) for all $\mathbf{c}$. Therefore, we can devise a scheme where in order to encrypt a bit m, we produce a ciphertext which is a row vector of the form $\mathbf{c} = m\mathbf{g} + \mathbf{q}p + \mathbf{r}$, but which is still computationally indistinguishable from a uniform vector over $\mathbb{Z}_{x_0}$. Such a ciphertext can be generated using standard methods from a public key containing a sequence of x_i's: in a nutshell, a random subset sum of the x_i's will preserve the structure and produce a "fresh" x_i, although with somewhat larger noise, which is indistinguishable from uniform even given the public key due to the leftover hash lemma. One has to take special care when reducing modulo x_0 that the additional kr_0 term does not become too large. Such a ciphertext can be decrypted by first multiplying by $\mathbf{G}^{-1}(p/2)$, and then reducing modulo p, which results in $mp/2 + \mathbf{r}\mathbf{G}^{-1}(p/2)$. Since $\mathbf{G}^{-1}(\cdot)$ always output a binary vector, then if $\mathbf{r}$ is short enough then $\mathbf{r}\mathbf{G}^{-1}(p/2)$ is only slightly longer. So long as the norm of $\mathbf{r}\mathbf{G}^{-1}(p/2)$ is smaller than $p/4$, we will decrypt the correct bit. Homomorphic evaluation is performed as in [1] by computing

$c_1 G^{-1}(c_2)$ (mod x_0) which results in a ciphertext of the form $c = m_1 m_2 g + q'p + (r_1 G^{-1}(c_2) + m_1 r_2 + k r_0)$. Thus we have a noise growth very similar to GSW style encryption, but with an additional term that depends on r_0 are comes from taking the result modulo x_0. We therefore need to take into account in our analysis a bound on the modulus k so that we can bound the noise growth. Note that if x_0 had been noise free, this complication does not arise. See Sect. 3 for the full details, parameters and analysis.

A Batched Variant. The previous scheme only allows to encode a single bit in a ciphertext vector. This is of course a significant efficiency constraint. We show how to encode multiple bits in a single ciphertext vector using the Chinese Remainder Theorem (CRT), inspired by previous works such as [9]. We will now consider a batched AGCD distribution with samples of the form $x_i = q_i \pi + r_i$, where π is now a composite $\pi = \prod_{i \in [\ell]} p_i$, and the noise r_i is defined as the number modulo π s.t. $|r_i$ (mod $p_j)| \ll p_j$. Namely, r_i is not a short element by itself, but rather its CRT coefficients with respect to the p_j's are short. The batched AGCD hardness assumption again asserts that these samples are indistinguishable from random modulo some known N. We will use our modified distribution defined above to again generate x_0 and a distribution over x_i s.t. x_i (mod x_0) has the right form and is indistinguishable from uniform. Now consider a ciphertext of the form $c = mg + q\pi + r$, except now m itself is not a bit, but rather its CRT representation is a sequence of bits. Namely, m (mod $p_j) = m_j$ for some bit m_j. Decryption can be performed in analogous way to the basic scheme, multiplying by $G^{-1}(p_j)$ and reducing modulo p_j will allow to recover m_j. Similarly homomorphic operations are performed in the exact same manner as before, since e.g. multiplying two "CRT containers" m, m' will result in element-wise multiplication in each slot corresponding to a factor p_j.

This still leaves open the question of how to generate ciphertexts with the aforementioned structure. It is not a problem to encrypt zero by generating $c' = q\pi + r$ as above. In the basic scheme this was enough since we could just take $mg + c'$ (mod x_0) and get our ciphertext. Here, we cannot even generate, given the sequence of m_j, the CRT representation m without using secret information (that is, the factorization of π). We solve this problem by considering a set of messages that span the message space, and placing their encryptions as a part of the public key. Specifically, consider m_j^* s.t. $m_j^* = 0$ (mod $p_{j'}$) if $j \neq j'$ and $m_j^* = 1$ (mod p_j) and let $c_j^* = m_j^* g + q_j^* \pi + r_j^*$. The c_ℓ^* vectors can be generated during the key generation process using the factorization of π. Now, in order to encrypt a sequence of bits $\{m_j\}_j$, we take $\sum_j m_j c_j^* + c'$ (mod x_0), where c' is a freshly generated zero encryption as defined above. One can verify that this will indeed encrypt the right message.

We were able to solve the functionality problem, but we can no longer base security on batch AGCD, since in order to generate the public key we can no longer use the x_i alone without additional private information. Unfortunately, we do not know how to resolve this problem and we make the explicit assumption that the batch AGCD remains hard even when the c_j^* vectors are published as a part of the public key. In order to increase our confidence in the validity of this additional assumption, we show that it can be stated as assuming *circular security* for a different scheme which is CPA secure. A circular secure encryption scheme is one that can securely encrypt functions of its own secret key. This notion has been entangled in the FHE literature due to the batching technique which requires circular security in order to transform from leveled FHE to unbounded FHE. It is commonly believed that "normal" encryption schemes should be circular secure unless they are intentionally weakened. Clearly this vague definition does not provide a strong guarantee and there are ongoing attempts to come up with more natural schemes that are not circular secure. Yet, by showing that the security of our scheme relates to the circular security of a CPA secure scheme (which is in turn secure under batch AGCD), we can at least deduce that breaking our scheme will imply a surprising result in the study of encryption. We note that a similar assumption was made in previous works [9,14] but without an explicit proof of the relation to circular security. Formally, we consider the very encryption scheme which takes $m \in \mathbb{Z}$ (or some restriction thereof) and encrypts it as $\mathbf{c} = m\mathbf{g} + \mathbf{c}'$ (mod x_0), where $\mathbf{c}'$ is as above. We do not provide a decryption algorithm since we do not require functionality for this scheme, only security, but we consider the secret key to be the factorization of π. This scheme can be shown to be CPA secure under batch AGCD on one hand, and on the other our m_j^* can be written as a function of the secret key of this scheme. Therefore if this auxiliary scheme is circular secure for any function of the secret key, then our scheme is CPA secure.

For the formal statement and analysis of this scheme, see Sect. 4.

Optimizations Towards Practicality. In Sect. 5 we analyze parameters and suggested optimizations towards implementation of our schemes. Let us only mention here that one of the serious constraints appears to be the length of the ciphertext which now becomes a $\log(x_0)$ dimensional vector. We find that this can be mitigated by considering a $\mathbf{G}^{-1}(\cdot)$ function that does not perform binary decomposition but rather decomposes relative to a larger radix B. This will have a negative effect on the noise growth, but will decrease the ciphertext size to $\log(x_0)/\log(B)$ which might enhance performance substantially. This optimization was considered in the lattice setting as well, but we believe that it will be much more effective in our setting.

2   Preliminaries

We denote the parameters of our encryption schemes by Greek letters ($\eta, \rho, \gamma, \tau, \lambda$, etc.), where λ is always the security parameter. Scalars are denoted by lowercase Latin characters (p, q, x, y, r, etc.), whereas vectors are denoted by lowercase bold English letters ($\mathbf{x}, \mathbf{y}, \mathbf{r}, \mathbf{q}$, etc.). Finally matrices are denoted by uppercase English letters. For any integer, z, or any vector of integers $\mathbf{z}$, we denote by $[z]_p$ or $[\mathbf{z}]_p$ the value in $(-p/2, p/2]$ which is the remainder of z or of each coordinate of $\mathbf{z}$ when divided by p. For a vector $\mathbf{z}$, we denote the norm $\|\mathbf{z}\|$ to be the infinity norm of the vector, or the size of the maximum entry,

$\|\mathbf{z}\| := \|\mathbf{z}\|_\infty = \max_{z_i \text{ in } \mathbf{z}} |z_i|$. All logarithms mentioned in this paper are base two, unless stated otherwise. We note that for all $\mathbf{a}, \mathbf{b} \in \mathbb{Z}^n$ it holds that

$$\|[\mathbf{a} \pm \mathbf{b}]_p\| \leq \|[\mathbf{a}]_p\| + \|[\mathbf{b}]_p\|. \tag{1}$$

Computational Indistinguishability. Distribution ensembles $\{D_{0,\lambda}\}_\lambda$, $\{D_{1,\lambda}\}_\lambda$ are *computationally indistinguishable* if for every polynomial time algorithm $\mathcal{A}$ it holds that $\left|\Pr[\mathcal{A}^{D_{0,\lambda}}(1^\lambda) = 1] - \Pr[\mathcal{A}^{D_{1,\lambda}}(1^\lambda)] = 1\right| \leq negl(\lambda)$, where the oracle $D_{b,\lambda}$ is one that returns a fresh sample from $D_{b,\lambda}$ on every call.

Bit Decomposition. For some $n \in \mathbb{Z}$, define the gadget vector, $\mathbf{g} = (1, 2, 4, \dots, 2^n)$ and the gadget function $\mathbf{g}^{-1} \colon \mathbb{Z} \cap [0, 2^{n+1}) \to \{0,1\}^{n+1}$ to be the function that computes the $(n+1)$-th bit decomposition of any integer. For some integer, z, the function is defined as $\mathbf{g}^{-1}(z)^T = \mathbf{v}^T = (v_0, v_1, \dots, v_n)$ where $v_i \in \{0,1\}$ such that $z = \langle \mathbf{g}, \mathbf{v} \rangle$. By extension we define the augmented gadget function $\mathbf{G}^{-1} \colon (\mathbb{Z} \cap [0, 2^{n+1}))^k \to \{0,1\}^{(n+1)\times k}$ to be the function that computes the $(n+1)$-th bit decomposition of every integer in a vector, $\mathbf{z}$, of dimension k, and arranges them as vector columns of an $(n+1) \times k$ binary matrix which we denote $\mathbf{G}^{-1}(\mathbf{z})$. Hence, $\mathbf{g} \cdot \mathbf{G}^{-1}(\mathbf{z}) = \mathbf{z}$.

CRT Representation. We recall the Chinese Remainder Theorem over the integers, which we use during the construction of the batch version of the scheme.

Definition 2.1. *Given k pair-wise co-prime integers $\mathbf{p} = (p_1, \dots, p_k)$, let $\pi = \prod_{i=1}^k p_i$. For k integers $m_i \in \mathbb{Z}_{p_i}$, we define the CRT representation of $\mathbf{m} = (m_1, \dots, m_k)$ with respect to $\mathbf{p}$, to be the unique field element $m \in \mathbb{Z}_\pi$ such that $[m]_{p_i} = m_i$; we write $m = CRT_{p_1,\dots,p_k}(m_1, \dots, m_k)$ and recall that given $\mathbf{p}$ and $\mathbf{m}$, $CRT_\mathbf{p}(\mathbf{m})$ is an efficiently computable ring isomorphism from $\prod \mathbb{Z}_{p_i}$ to $\mathbb{Z}_\pi$.*

Leftover Hash Lemma. A family $\mathcal{H}$ of hash functions from X to Y, both finite sets, is said to be 2-universal if for all distinct $x, x' \in X$, $Pr_{h \leftarrow \mathcal{H}}[h(x) = h(x')] = 1/|Y|$. A distribution D is ε-uniform if its statistical distance from the uniform distribution is at most ε, where the statistical distance between two distributions D_1, D_2 over a finite domain X is $\frac{1}{2} \sum_{x \in X} |D_1(x) - D_2(x)|$.

Lemma 2.1 (Simplified Leftover Hash Lemma (LHL) [21]). *Let $\mathcal{H}$ be a family of 2-universal hash functions from X to Y. Suppose that $h \leftarrow \mathcal{H}$ and $x \leftarrow X$ are chosen uniformly and independently. Then, $(h, h(x))$ is $\frac{1}{2}\sqrt{|Y|/|X|}$-uniform over $\mathcal{H} \times Y$.*

We present the following version of the LHL, specifically adapted to our scheme.

Lemma 2.2. *Set $\mathbf{x} = (x_1, \dots, x_m) \leftarrow \mathbb{Z}_M^m$ uniformly and independently, set $\mathbf{S} \leftarrow \{0,1\}^{m \times n}$ for some n; and let $\mathbf{y} = \mathbf{x} \cdot \mathbf{S} \pmod{M}$. Then $(\mathbf{x}, \mathbf{y})$ is $1/2\sqrt{M/2^m}$-uniform over $\mathbb{Z}_M^{m+n}$.*

Proof. Consider the following hash function family $\mathcal{H} \subseteq \{0,1\}^{m \times n} \to \mathbb{Z}_M^n$. Each function $h \in \mathcal{H}$ is parametrized by the coordinates of $\mathbf{x} \in \mathbb{Z}_M^m$. Now, given any $\mathbf{S} \in \{0,1\}^{m \times n}$, we define $h(\mathbf{S}) = \mathbf{x} \cdot \mathbf{S} \pmod{M} \in \mathbb{Z}_M^n$. We have that the function family is 2-universal. Therefore by Lemma 2.1, $(h, h(\mathbf{S}))$ is $1/2\sqrt{M/2^m}$-uniform over $\mathbb{Z}_M^{m+n}$. $\qquad \square$

2.1 Homomorphic Encryption

A homomorphic (public-key) encryption scheme $\mathsf{HE} = (\mathsf{HE.Setup}, \mathsf{HE.Keygen}, \mathsf{HE.Enc}, \mathsf{HE.Dec}, \mathsf{HE.Eval})$ with message space $\mathcal{M}$ is a 4-tuple of PPT algorithms as follows (λ is the security parameter):

- **Key generation** $(\mathsf{pk}, \mathsf{sk}) \leftarrow \mathsf{HE.Keygen}(1^\lambda)$: Outputs a public encryption key pk and a secret decryption key sk.
- **Encryption** $c \leftarrow \mathsf{HE.Enc}(\mathsf{pk}, \mu)$: Using the public key pk, encrypts a message $\mu \in \mathcal{M}$ into a ciphertext c.
- **Decryption** $\mu \leftarrow \mathsf{HE.Dec}(\mathsf{sk}, c)$: Using the secret key sk, decrypts a ciphertext c to recover the message $\mu \in \mathcal{M}$.
- **Homomorphic evaluation** $\widehat{c} \leftarrow \mathsf{HE.Eval}(C, (c_1, \ldots, c_\ell), \mathsf{pk})$: Using the public key pk, applies a circuit $C \colon \mathcal{M}^\ell \to \mathcal{M}$ to $c_1, \ldots, c_\ell$, and outputs a ciphertext $\widehat{c}$.

A homomorphic encryption scheme is said to be secure if it is semantically secure. It is (perfectly) correct w.r.t a class of circuits $\mathcal{C}$, if for any efficiently computable circuit $C \in \mathcal{C}$ and any set of inputs $\mu_1, \ldots, \mu_\ell$, letting $(\mathsf{pk}, \mathsf{sk}) \leftarrow \mathsf{HE.Keygen}(1^\lambda)$ and $c_i \leftarrow \mathsf{HE.Enc}(\mathsf{pk}, \mu_i)$, it holds that $\mathsf{HE.Dec}(\mathsf{sk}, \mathsf{HE.Eval}(C, (c_1, \ldots, c_\ell), \mathsf{pk})) = C(\mu_1, \ldots, \mu_\ell)$. The scheme is compact if the decryption circuit's size only depends on λ. The scheme is leveled fully homomorphic if for every $L = \mathrm{poly}(\lambda)$ it can be instantiated so that it can evaluate all depth L circuits.

2.2 Approximate GCD (AGCD)

Variants of the Approximate GCD problem have been used for homomorphic encryption in a number of previous works [9,10,14–16,20,30]. In this work, we consider the decisional noisy variant, both in the standalone and batch regimes (definitions follow). We also show that the decisional noisy variant implies the hardness of "size-bounded" decisional AGCD which had been defined and used implicitly in the noise-free setting but to our knowledge not in the noisy setting.

We start by defining the distribution that underlies the AGCD problem. Essentially, this is a distribution over "near multiples" of a hidden parameter p, followed by a definition of the (standalone) AGCD problem.

Definition 2.2. *The distribution $\mathcal{D}_{\gamma,\rho}(p)$, parameterized by integers γ, ρ and a η-bit prime p, is supported over γ-bit integers and defined as follows.*

$$\mathcal{D}_{\gamma,\rho}(p) = \{sample \ q \leftarrow \mathbb{Z} \cap [0, 2^\gamma/p), r \leftarrow \mathbb{Z} \cap (-2^\rho, 2^\rho) : Output \ x = p \cdot q + r\} \tag{2}$$

Definition 2.3 $((\rho, \eta, \gamma)$-AGCD [9,30]). *The (ρ, η, γ)-AGCD problem is to find p given oracle access to $\mathcal{D}_{\gamma,\rho}(p)$, where p is a random η-bit prime. The decisional AGCD problem is to distinguish between $\mathcal{D}_{\gamma,\rho}(p)$ and the uniform distribution on $[0, 2^\gamma) \cap \mathbb{Z}$, given oracle access to both distributions.*

We note that these definitions are valid even if p is a non-prime odd integer, and our results carry over to this case as well.

The batched version is defined similarly, except with multiple p's. We start by defining a noise distribution via CRT representation, followed by the batch AGCD problem definition.

Definition 2.4. *Let $p_1, \ldots, p_l$ be η-bit primes. We define the following distribution:*

$$\Phi_\rho(p_1, \ldots, p_l) = \{r = CRT_{p_1,\ldots,p_l}(r_1, \ldots, r_l) | r_i \leftarrow \mathbb{Z} \cap (-2^\rho, 2^\rho)\}. \quad (3)$$

Definition 2.5 $((\rho, \eta, \Gamma)$-l-AGCD). *Let ρ, η, Γ, l be parameters instantiated as a function of the security parameter. Let $p_1, \ldots, p_l$ be random η-bit sized primes and define $\pi = \prod_{i=1}^{l} p_i$. Given oracle access to the distribution*

$$\mathcal{X}_{\rho,\Gamma}(p_1, \ldots, p_l) = \{q\pi + r | r \leftarrow \Phi_\rho(p_1, \ldots, p_l), q \leftarrow \mathbb{Z} \cap [0, 2^\Gamma/\pi)\},$$

output at least one of $p_1, \ldots, p_l$. The decisional version is to distinguish between $\mathcal{X}_{\rho,\Gamma}(p_1, \ldots, p_l)$ and the uniform distribution on $\mathbb{Z} \cap [0, 2^\Gamma)$.

We note that for $l = 1$ we get exactly the non-batched version, so this is a strict generalization.

Size Bounded AGCD. The distribution $\mathcal{D}_{\gamma,\rho}(p)$ defined above (and respectively $\mathcal{X}_{\rho,\Gamma}(p_1, \ldots, p_l)$ in the batch variant) produces elements of varying length. For functionality purposes, we would like to perform arithmetics with a single modulus x_0 in our scheme, and this modulus must itself be $\approx q_0 p$ (and respectively for the batch version). In some previous works [9,13–16,24], this was done by defining the modulus as a special noise free element $x_0 = q_0 p$. However, this could potentially weaken security and in particular makes the scheme vulnerable to quantum attacks (since factoring x_0 reveals p). Sampling x_0 from the distribution $\mathcal{D}_{\gamma,\rho}(p)$ itself was proposed already in [14,30], the former work only in the context of search AGCD, and the latter with an ad-hoc (unmentioned) circular security assumption. Recall that the standalone AGCD is a special case of the batched version, and therefore it is sufficient to take care of the latter.

We start by defining truncated versions of distributions, i.e. a distribution conditioned on some external condition.

Definition 2.6. *Let X be a distribution supported over $\mathbb{Z}$ and let $k \in \mathbb{Z}$. The distribution $X^{(\leq k)}$ is the distribution X conditioned on $X \leq k$. If $\Pr[X \leq k] = 0$ then $X^{(\leq k)}$ is undefined. Analogously we can define $X^{(\geq k)}$.*

Via rejection sampling it is easy to see that if X is efficiently sampleable and $\Pr[X \leq k]$ is noticeable then $X^{(\leq k)}$ is efficiently sampleable up to negligible statistical distance.

Lemma 2.3. *Let $(\rho, \eta, \gamma), l$ be as in the l-AGCD problem. For any polynomial t, we define the following distributions.*

- *The distribution $\vec{\mathcal{X}}_t = (x_0, x_1, \ldots, x_t)$ where $x_0 \leftarrow \mathcal{X}_{\rho, \Gamma}(p_1, \ldots, p_l)^{(\geq 2^{\Gamma}/2)}$ and for $i > 0$, $x_i \leftarrow \mathcal{X}_{\rho, \Gamma}(p_1, \ldots, p_l)^{(\leq x_0)}$.*
- *The distribution $\vec{\mathcal{U}}_t = (u_0, u_1, \ldots, u_t)$ where u_0 is uniform over $[2^{\Gamma}/2, 2^{\Gamma}) \cap \mathbb{Z}$ and for $i > 0$, u_i is uniform over $[0, u_0) \cap \mathbb{Z}$.*

It holds that under the (ρ, η, Γ)-l-AGCD assumption, both distributions are efficiently sampleable, up to negligible statistical distance, and computationally indistinguishable for any polynomial t.

Proof. Let U be the uniform distribution over $[0, 2^{\Gamma}) \cap \mathbb{Z}$. Then an equivalent formulation for $\vec{\mathcal{U}}_t$ is to set $u_0 \leftarrow U^{(\geq 2^{\Gamma}/2)}$ and for $i > 0$, $u_i \leftarrow U^{(\leq u_0)}$. In this formulation, $\vec{\mathcal{U}}_t$ is efficiently sampleable given oracle access to U and using rejection sampling, since for u_0 the rejection probability is at most $1/2$ and since $u_0 \geq 2^{\Gamma}/2$, the same holds for the rest of the u_i's. Note that in expectation only a constant number of samples of U is required to sample each u_i.

Replacing U with $\mathcal{X}_{\rho, \Gamma}(p_1, \ldots, p_l)$ implies the distribution $\vec{\mathcal{X}}_t$. Since U and $\mathcal{X}_{\rho, \Gamma}(p_1, \ldots, p_l)$ are computationally indistinguishable under (ρ, η, Γ)-l-AGCD, it implies that applying the same rejection sampler but with $\mathcal{X}_{\rho, \Gamma}(p_1, \ldots, p_l)$ samples instead of U samples will efficiently sample from $\vec{\mathcal{X}}_t$ and furthermore that the resulting distribution is indistinguishable from $\vec{\mathcal{U}}_t$.   □

3   Our Basic Scheme

In this section we will describe the full construction of our decomposed homomorphic encryption scheme, we will analyze it for correctness and efficiency and finally prove its underlying security.

3.1   Construction

We recall that for a specific η-bit odd integer p, we use the distribution from Definition 2.2 over γ-bit integers.

HE.Keygen(1^{λ}): We generate the public parameters $params = \{\gamma, \rho, \eta, \tau\}$ according to the security parameter λ and the parameter constraints in Sect. 3.3. Sample uniformly an η-bit integer p. Using Eq. (2) and via rejection sampling first sample an integer $x_0 \leftarrow (\mathcal{D}_{\gamma, \rho}(p))^{(\geq 2^{\gamma-1})}$ and then τ integers $\{x_i\}_{1 \leq i \leq \tau} \leftarrow (\mathcal{D}_{\gamma, \rho}(p))^{(\leq x_0)}$, such that $(x_0, x_1, \ldots, x_{\tau}) \leftarrow \vec{\mathcal{X}}_{\tau}$, as in Definition 2.6. We write $\mathbf{x} = (x_1, \ldots, x_{\tau})$, we let $pk = (params, \mathbf{x}, x_0)$ and $sk = p$.

HE.Enc(pk, m): We randomly sample a matrix $\mathbf{S} \leftarrow \{0,1\}^{\tau \times \gamma}$ and we compute

$$\mathbf{c} = [m \cdot \mathbf{g} + \mathbf{xS}]_{x_0}$$

which is a vector of dimension $\gamma = \lceil \log x_0 \rceil$.

HE.Eval$(pk, \mathcal{C}, \mathbf{c}_1, \ldots \mathbf{c}_t)$: Given t ciphertexts and a binary circuit $\mathcal{C}$ with t input bits, compute all the operations in the circuit over the integers and output the resulting integer modulo x_0. For pairwise ciphertexts, we compute the operations HE.Mult$(\mathbf{c}_1, \mathbf{c}_2)$ and HE.Nand$(\mathbf{c}_1, \mathbf{c}_2)$ in the following manner.

$$\begin{aligned} \mathbf{c}_{mult} &= \text{HE.Mult}(\mathbf{c}_1, \mathbf{c}_2) \\ &= [\mathbf{c}_1 \mathbf{G}^{-1}(\mathbf{c}_2)]_{x_0}. \end{aligned} \quad (4)$$

We similarly define the homomorphic NAND operation.

$$\begin{aligned} \mathbf{c}_{nand} &= \text{HE.Nand}(\mathbf{c}_1, \mathbf{c}_2) \\ &= [\mathbf{g} - \mathbf{c}_1 \mathbf{G}^{-1}(\mathbf{c}_2)]_{x_0}. \end{aligned}$$

Furthermore, our scheme allows for addition gates, HE.Add, only in the case when it is known that *at most one* of the plaintext messages is 1. In this case we perform the addition, between two ciphertexts, in the following way

$$\begin{aligned} \mathbf{c}_{add} &= \text{HE.Add}(\mathbf{c}_1, \mathbf{c}_2) \\ &= [\mathbf{c}_1 + \mathbf{c}_2]_{x_0}. \end{aligned}$$

HE.Dec$(sk, \mathbf{c})$: We have that $sk = p$. Hence, as mentioned earlier, this procedure simply computes $f = \mathbf{c} \cdot \mathbf{g}^{-1}(p/2) \pmod{p}$ and outputs the following

$$m \leftarrow \begin{cases} 1 & \text{if } |f| \geq p/4 \\ 0 & \text{if } |f| < p/4 \end{cases}.$$

3.2   Correctness and Noise Analysis

In this section we prove the correctness of our scheme and at the same time make a parallel analysis of the size of the noise component in the different relevant algorithms. Finally we present the optimal parameters as a function of the circuit depth.

Theorem 3.1. *For a Boolean circuit, $\mathcal{C}$, of depth d, for $(sk, pk) \leftarrow$ HE.Keygen(1^λ) and $\mathbf{c} \leftarrow$ HE.Eval$(\mathcal{C}, \mathbf{c}_1, \ldots, \mathbf{c}_t)$ such that $\mathbf{c}_i = $ HE.Enc(pk, m_i), where $m_i \in \{0, 1\}$. We have that*

$$\text{HE.Dec}(sk, \mathbf{c}) = \mathcal{C}(m_1, \ldots, m_t).$$

Remark 3.1. We note that we did not present the most general description of the boolean circuit to be evaluated. We mention a circuit of depth d, without considering the different effect of NAND and ADD gates. Our description assumes only NAND gates in the circuit. If we had a circuit with ADD gates, then its depth could be larger since the ADD gates contribute less to the growth of the noise of the ciphertext, as we will see below.

After the encryption procedure, HE.Enc, the resulting ciphertext is a vector of dimension $\lceil \log x_0 \rceil = \gamma$ with each entry being an integer in $[-x_0/2, x_0/2)$. We now formally define the noise component of a ciphertext and analyze the size.

Definition 3.1 (Noise Component HE). *For any ciphertext* $\mathbf{c}$, *we define its noise component to be* $\mathbf{r}_{m,p}(\mathbf{c}) = [\mathbf{c} - m\mathbf{g}]_p$ *and define its size to be the norm* $r_{m,p}(\mathbf{c}) = \|\mathbf{r}_{m,p}(\mathbf{c})\|$. *Note that we consider* $\mathbf{r}_{m,p}(\mathbf{c})$ *over* $\mathbb{Z}$ *and not over* $\mathbb{Z}_p$.

In the following lemma we first give an upper bound on the size of the noise of a fresh ciphertext and then an upper bound on the noise growth during the evaluation function for the multiplication, nand and addition functions.

Lemma 3.1 (Noise Size). *Let* $(pk, sk) \leftarrow$ HE.Keygen(1^λ). *Let* $\mathbf{c}_1, \mathbf{c}_2$ *be two ciphertexts, respectively encrypting messages* $m_1, m_2 \in \{0, 1\}$, *we define*

$$B = \max\{r_{m_1,p}(\mathbf{c}_1), r_{m_2,p}(\mathbf{c}_2)\}.$$

The following holds

1. *Given a fresh encryption* $\mathbf{c} =$ HE.Enc(pk, m), *the noise component,* $\mathbf{r}_{m,p}(\mathbf{c})$ *has norm* $r_{m,p}(\mathbf{c}) \leq \tau 2^{\rho+1}$.
2. *For* $\mathbf{c}_{mult} =$ HE.Mult$(\mathbf{c}_1, \mathbf{c}_2)$ *and* $\mathbf{c}_{nand} =$ HE.Nand$(\mathbf{c}_1, \mathbf{c}_2)$, *we have that* $r_{m_{mult},p}(\mathbf{c}_{mult}) = r_{m_{nand},p}(\mathbf{c}_{nand}) \leq (2\gamma + 1)B$, *where* $m_{mult} = m_1 m_2$ *and* $m_{nand} = 1 - m_1 m_2$.
3. *For* $\mathbf{c}_{add} =$ HE.Add$(\mathbf{c}_1, \mathbf{c}_2)$, *we have that* $r_{m_{add},p}(\mathbf{c}_{add}) \leq 2B + 2^{\rho+1}$, *where* $m_{add} = m_1 + m_2$.

Proof. 1. Let $pk = (x_0, \mathbf{x}) = (r_0 + q_0 \cdot p, \mathbf{r} + \mathbf{q} \cdot p)$. Given

$$\mathbf{c} = [m\mathbf{g} + \mathbf{x}\mathbf{S}]_{x_0}$$
$$= m\mathbf{g} + \mathbf{r}\mathbf{S} + \mathbf{q}\mathbf{S} \cdot p + \mathbf{k}x_0$$

the noise component is $\mathbf{r}_{m,p}(\mathbf{c}) = \mathbf{r}\mathbf{S} + \mathbf{k}r_0$, where $\mathbf{k}$ is the multiple of $x_0 = r_0 + q_0 \cdot p$ that is added after the mod x_0 operation on the ciphertext. The first term comes from the matrix operation with the public key vector, $\mathbf{x}\mathbf{S} = \mathbf{q}\mathbf{S}p + \mathbf{r}\mathbf{S}$, and has size $\|\mathbf{r}\mathbf{S}\| \leq \tau 2^\rho$. The second term derives from the mod x_0 operation on the ciphertext. Since the ciphertext cannot grow by more than $\tau \cdot x_0$ in each coordinate, then we have that $\|\mathbf{k}\| \leq \tau$, such that $\|\mathbf{k}r_0\| \leq \tau 2^\rho$. Thus the claim follows and $r_{m,p}(\mathbf{c}) \leq \tau 2^{\rho+1}$.

2. Let $\mathbf{c}_1, \mathbf{c}_2, B$ and $\mathbf{c}_{mult}$ be as in the statement of the lemma. Then we have

$$\|\mathbf{r}_{m_{mult},p}(\mathbf{c}_{mult})\| = \|[\mathbf{c}_{mult} - m_{mult}\mathbf{g}]_p\|$$
$$= \|[[\mathbf{c}_1 \cdot \mathbf{G}^{-1}(\mathbf{c}_2)]_{x_0} - m_{mult}\mathbf{g}]_p\|$$
$$= \|[\mathbf{c}_1 \cdot \mathbf{G}^{-1}(\mathbf{c}_2) + \mathbf{k}_{mult}x_0 - m_{mult}\mathbf{g}]_p\|$$
$$\leq \|[\mathbf{c}_1 \cdot \mathbf{G}^{-1}(\mathbf{c}_2) - m_{mult}\mathbf{g}]_p\| + \|[\mathbf{k}_{mult}x_0]_p\|,$$

where the last inequality comes from Eq. (1). Now $\|\mathbf{k}_{mult}\| \leq \gamma$ and $[x_0]_p = r_0$,[1] hence

$$
\begin{aligned}
\|\mathbf{r}_{m_{mult},p}(\mathbf{c}_{mult})\| &\leq \|[\mathbf{c}_1 \cdot \mathbf{G}^{-1}(\mathbf{c}_2) - m_{mult}\mathbf{g}]_p\| + \gamma \cdot 2^\rho \\
&\leq \|[m_1\mathbf{c}_2 + (\mathbf{c}_1 - m_1\mathbf{g})\mathbf{G}^{-1}(\mathbf{c}_2) - m_{mult}\mathbf{g}]_p\| + \gamma \cdot 2^\rho \\
&\leq \|[m_1 m_2 \mathbf{g} + m_1(\mathbf{c}_2 - m_2\mathbf{g}) + (\mathbf{c}_1 - m_1\mathbf{g})\mathbf{G}^{-1}(\mathbf{c}_2) - m_{mult}\mathbf{g}]_p\| + \gamma \cdot 2^\rho \\
&\leq \|m_1[\mathbf{c}_2 - m_2\mathbf{g}]_p\| + \|[\mathbf{c}_1 - m_1\mathbf{g}]_p\| \cdot \|\mathbf{G}^{-1}(\mathbf{c}_2)\| + \gamma \cdot 2^\rho \\
&\leq r_{m_2,p}(\mathbf{c}_2) + r_{m_1,p}(\mathbf{c}_1)\gamma + \gamma \cdot 2^\rho \\
&\leq B + B\gamma + \gamma \cdot 2^\rho
\end{aligned}
$$

since $m_{mult} = m_1 m_2$ by definition. Since $r_0 \leq 2^\rho \leq B$, we get

$$
\begin{aligned}
r_{m_{mult},p}(\mathbf{c}_{mult}) &\leq B + \gamma B + \gamma 2^\rho \\
&\leq (2\gamma + 1)B,
\end{aligned}
$$

which is exactly what we need. Analogously, the NAND operation causes the same increase in the size of the noise. This proves the statement.

3. Let $\mathbf{c}_1, \mathbf{c}_2, B$ and $\mathbf{c}_{add}$ be as in the statement of the lemma. Then we have

$$
\begin{aligned}
\|\mathbf{r}_{m_{add},p}(\mathbf{c}_{add})\| &= \|[\mathbf{c}_{add} - m_{add}\mathbf{g}]_p\| \\
&= \|[[\mathbf{c}_1 + \mathbf{c}_2]_{x_0} - m_1\mathbf{g} - m_2\mathbf{g}]_p\| \\
&= \|[\mathbf{c}_1 - m_1\mathbf{g} + \mathbf{c}_2 - m_2\mathbf{g} - \mathbf{k}_{add}x_0]_p\| \\
&\leq \|[\mathbf{c}_1 - m_1\mathbf{g}]_p\| + \|[\mathbf{c}_2 - m_2\mathbf{g}]_p\| + \|[\mathbf{k}_{add}x_0]_p\| \\
&\leq \|\mathbf{r}_{m_1,p}(\mathbf{c}_1)\| + \|\mathbf{r}_{m_2,p}(\mathbf{c}_2)\| + \|\mathbf{k}_{add}r_0\| \\
&\leq r_{m_1,p}(\mathbf{c}_1) + r_{m_2,p}(\mathbf{c}_2) + 2^{\rho+1}
\end{aligned}
$$

since in this case $\|\mathbf{c}_1 + \mathbf{c}_2\| \leq 2x_0$, thus $\|\mathbf{k}_{add}\| \leq 2$. This proves the statement.
$\square$

Generalizing the statement in 2, let us assume that we want to compute a circuit of depth d on ciphertexts whose noise components are bounded by B. The output ciphertext, $\mathbf{c}_d$, an encryption of m_d, will have a noise component with norm $r_{m_d,p}(\mathbf{c}_d) \leq (2\gamma + 1)^d B$. We now prove decryption correctness.

Lemma 3.2 (Correctness Homomorphic Decryption). *For any vector* $\mathbf{c} \in \mathbb{Z}_{x_0}^\gamma$ *and any* $m \in \mathbb{Z}_2$, *if* $r_{m,p}(\mathbf{c}) < p/(4\gamma)$ *then* $\mathsf{HE.Dec}(sk, \mathbf{c}) = m$.

---

[1] In order to upper bound $\mathbf{k}_{mult}$ we know that $\|\mathbf{c}_1 \cdot \mathbf{G}^{-1}(\mathbf{c}_2)\| \leq \|\mathbf{c}_1\| \cdot \gamma \leq x_0/2 \cdot \gamma$ since $\mathbf{c}_1 \in [-x_0/2, x_0/2)$. Thus for each coordinate $1 \leq i \leq l$ of $\mathbf{c}_{mult}$ we have that

$$
\begin{aligned}
-x_0/2 &\leq [(\mathbf{c}_1 \cdot \mathbf{G}^{-1}(\mathbf{c}_2))[i]]_{x_0} \\
&= (\mathbf{c}_1 \cdot \mathbf{G}^{-1}(\mathbf{c}_2))[i] - k_{mult}[i]x_0 \leq x_0/2. \quad (5)
\end{aligned}
$$

Hence, on the one hand we have $-x_0/2 \leq (\mathbf{c}_1 \cdot \mathbf{G}^{-1}(\mathbf{c}_2))[i] - k_{mult}[i]x_0$, which gives $k_{mult}[i] \leq (\gamma + 1)/2$. On the other hand we have that $(\mathbf{c}_1 \cdot \mathbf{G}^{-1}(\mathbf{c}_2))[i] - k_{mult}[i]x_0 \leq x_0/2$, which gives $(\gamma - 1)/2 < k_{mult}[i]$. Thus we conclude that $\|\mathbf{k}_{mult}\| \leq \gamma$.

Proof. Assume that for a ciphertext $\mathbf{c} \in \mathbb{Z}_{x_0}^{\gamma}$ we have $r_{m,p}(\mathbf{c}) < p/(4\gamma)$, then during decryption, we have that

$$
\begin{aligned}
f &= \mathbf{c} \cdot \mathbf{g}^{-1}(p/2) \pmod{p} \\
&= m\mathbf{g}\mathbf{g}^{-1}(p/2) + \mathbf{r}_{m,p}(\mathbf{c})\mathbf{g}^{-1}(p/2) \\
&\leq m(p/2) + \gamma \mathbf{r}_{m,p}(\mathbf{c}),
\end{aligned}
$$

where by assumption $\gamma \|\mathbf{r}_{m,p}(\mathbf{c})\| < p/4$. So by the decryption algorithm, if $|f| \leq m(p/2) + \gamma r_{m,p}(\mathbf{c}) < p/4$ then it necessarily means that $m = 0$. Whereas if instead $|f| \leq m(p/2) + \gamma r_{m,p}(\mathbf{c})$ and $|f| > p/4$ then it must be the case that $m = 1$, or else $\gamma r_{m,p}(\mathbf{c}) > p/4$. Hence in any case we get $\mathsf{HE.Dec}(sk, \mathbf{c}) = m$, which implies decryption correctness. $\qquad\square$

As mentioned earlier, one of the most important features of homomorphic operations is the size of the noise component, which must be somewhat controlled and, in our scheme, must be at all times less than $p/(4\gamma)$ in order for the ciphertext to decrypt correctly. This can give us mathematically an upper bound on the number of operations that we can perform, relative to some given parameters. Indeed, we can show the relationship between $\eta - \rho$ and the depth of the evaluation circuit d. Given that our scheme is not initially fully homomorphic, but only leveled-homomorphic, we must be able to compute $\eta - \rho$ given the circuit depth, d. This is proved in the next lemma.

Lemma 3.3. *Given a circuit of depth d and the parameters (τ, γ), correctness of the HE scheme implies that the following inequality is satisfied.*

$$
\eta - \rho > (d+1)\log\gamma + \log\tau + \mathcal{O}(1). \tag{6}
$$

Proof. Let us assume that the given circuit is of depth d, then in the worst-case scenario, a single ciphertext will undergo at most d multiplications with co-factor of the same noise level. Hence we know that if $\mathbf{c}_d$ is the output of the circuit, then $\|\mathbf{r}_{m_d,p}(\mathbf{c}_d)\| \leq (2\gamma+1)^d B$ by Lemma 3.1. We also know by Lemma 3.2 that the following inequality must hold for decryption correctness

$$
\|\mathbf{r}_{m_d,p}(\mathbf{c}_d)\| < p/(4\gamma) < 2^{\eta}/(4\gamma)
$$

and we can get a bound for $\eta - \rho$. More specifically we have that $\log B < (\eta - 2) - d\log(2\gamma + 1) - \log\gamma$. If we assume that B is the size of the noise of the input ciphertexts, which are fresh out of the encryption procedure, then $B = \tau 2^{\rho+1}$ by Lemma 3.1 and

$$
\begin{aligned}
&(\eta - 2) - d\log(2\gamma + 1) - \log\gamma > \log B \\
\Rightarrow\ &(\eta - 2) - d\log(2\gamma + 1) - \log\gamma - \log\tau > \rho + 1 \\
\Rightarrow\ &\qquad\qquad\qquad\qquad \eta - \rho > (d+1)\log\gamma + \log\tau + \mathcal{O}(1)
\end{aligned}
$$

as required. $\qquad\square$

Remark 3.2. Note that if instead, we are given the parameters, $\{\rho, \eta, \tau, \gamma\}$, one can derive d, an upper bound for the depth of the circuit, by rearranging Eq. (6) as follows

$$d < \frac{(\eta - 2) - (\rho + 1)\log \tau}{\log(2\gamma + 1)}.$$

3.3 Parameters

We present the constraints on the parameters needed in order for the HE scheme to be correct and secure against known attacks. Let d be the depth of the circuit used to evaluate the data and let λ be the security parameter.

- ρ is the bit-length of the noise components r_i's of the public key elements x_i's; $\rho = \omega(\lambda)$, to protect against brute-force attacks on the noise [8,13,16];
- η is the bit-length of the secret key p; $\eta = \Omega(\rho + (d+1)\log\gamma + \log\tau)$ in order to have correctness of the evaluation circuit (Lemma 3.3);
- γ is the bit-length of the elements of the public key, the x_i's; $\gamma \geq \Omega(\frac{\lambda}{\log\lambda}(\eta - \rho)^2)$ and $\gamma > \eta^2$, to thwart different lattice reduction attacks on the AGCD as studied in [10,18] such as the orthogonal lattice attacks [26,30], the simultaneous Diophantine approximation attack [25,30] and the multivariate polynomial approach in [12,22].
- τ is the number of x_i's in the public key; $\tau = \gamma + \Omega(\lambda)$, which is derived from the constraints given by the Leftover Hash Lemma in Sect. 2, needed in the security proof below. We note that the constraint requires that $1/2\sqrt{x_0/2^\tau}$ be negligible, where $\gamma = \lceil \log x_0 \rceil$.

3.4 Semantic Security

To prove the security of this scheme, we cannot use the same techniques as in DGHV because the use of the gadget vector causes the message to be encrypted in a higher bit, and thus the LSB predictor procedure used in [30] fails to output the correct bit. For this reason, we reduce the security of this scheme to the *decisional* AGCD problem instead. Hence, simply stated, we prove that our scheme is CPA secure under the *decisional* AGCD assumption.

Theorem 3.2. *The above* HE *scheme is CPA secure under the* (ρ, η, γ)*-decisional AGCD assumption.*

Proof. For $pk = (params, \mathbf{x}, x_0) \leftarrow$ HE.Keygen(1^λ) and $\mathbf{c}_b = $ HE.Enc(pk, b), where $b \leftarrow \{0,1\}$, $pk' = (params, \mathbf{u}, u_0)$ where $u_0 \leftarrow ([0, 2^\gamma) \cap \mathbb{Z})^{(\geq 2^{\gamma-1})}$ and $\mathbf{u} \leftarrow \mathcal{U}([0, u_0) \cap \mathbb{Z})^\tau$, we prove that $(pk, \mathbf{c}_b)$ and $(pk', \mathbf{v})$, where $\mathbf{v} \leftarrow \mathbb{Z}_{u_0}^\gamma$, are computationally indistinguishable. In other words, for every polynomial time algorithm $\mathcal{A}$, $\left|\Pr[\mathcal{A}(1^\lambda, pk, \mathbf{c}_b) = 1] - \Pr[\mathcal{A}(1^\lambda, pk', \mathbf{v}) = 1]\right| = negl(\lambda)$. In order to do this we will use a three step hybrid argument and use Lemmas 2.2 and 2.3, for $l = 1$, to show indistinguishability between each hybrid. For simplicity we use the notation in Lemma 2.3, where we sample from the distributions $\vec{\mathcal{X}}_\tau = (x_0, x_1, \ldots, x_\tau)$ and $\vec{\mathcal{U}}_\tau = (u_0, u_1, \ldots, u_\tau)$.

Hybrid 0: We define the distribution $(pk, \mathbf{c}_b)$ in the following way, let $pk = (params, \mathbf{x}, x_0) \leftarrow \mathsf{HE.Keygen}(1^\lambda)$, such that $(x_0, x_1, \ldots, x_\tau) \leftarrow \vec{\mathcal{X}}_\tau$, and let $\mathbf{c}_b = \mathsf{HE.Enc}(pk, b) = [b\mathbf{g} + \mathbf{xS}]_{x_0}$ for $b \leftarrow \{0, 1\}$. In this case, $(pk, \mathbf{c}_b)$ is distributed exactly as in our HE scheme.

Hybrid 1: We define the distribution $(pk, \mathbf{c}_b)$ as follows, let $pk = (params, \mathbf{u}, u_0)$, such that $(u_0, u_1, \ldots, u_\tau) \leftarrow \vec{\mathcal{U}}_\tau$, and let $\mathbf{c}_b = \mathsf{HE.Enc}(pk, b) = [b\mathbf{g} + \mathbf{uS}]_{u_0}$. Now, by Lemma 2.3 we know that $(pk, \mathbf{c}_b)_{H_0}$ and $(pk, \mathbf{c}_b)_{H_1}$ are computationally indistinguishable because $\vec{\mathcal{X}}_\tau$ and $\vec{\mathcal{U}}_\tau$ are indistinguishable by the lemma. Hence we have

$$\left| \Pr_{H_0}[\mathcal{A}(1^\lambda, pk, \mathbf{c}_b) = 1] - \Pr_{H_1}[\mathcal{A}(1^\lambda, pk, \mathbf{c}_b) = 1] \right| \leq negl(\lambda).$$

Hybrid 2: In this hybrid we define the distribution $(pk, \mathbf{c}_b)$ as follows. Again, let $pk = (params, \mathbf{u}, u_0)$, where $(u_0, u_1, \ldots, u_\tau) \leftarrow \vec{\mathcal{U}}_\tau$, and let $\mathbf{c}_b = [b\mathbf{g} + \mathbf{v}]_{u_0}$, where $\mathbf{v} \leftarrow \mathbb{Z}_{u_0}^\gamma$ is completely random. By the LHL in Lemma 2.2, the statistical distance between $(u_0, \mathbf{u}, \mathbf{uS})$ and $(u_0, \mathbf{u}, \mathbf{v})$ is upper bounded by $\frac{1}{2}\sqrt{u_0/2^\tau} = negl(\lambda)$. Finally, we know that $\mathbf{c}_b \equiv \mathbf{v}$, hence the probability of success for $\mathcal{A}$ in this hybrid is exactly $1/2$ since $\mathbf{v}$ is completely random. So we have that

$$\left| \Pr_{H_1}[\mathcal{A}(1^\lambda, pk, \mathbf{c}_b) = 1] - \Pr_{H_2}[\mathcal{A}(1^\lambda, pk, \mathbf{c}_b) = 1] \right| \leq \frac{1}{2}\sqrt{u_0/2^\tau}.$$

Thus we conclude that

$$\left| \Pr_{H_0}[\mathcal{A}(1^\lambda, pk, \mathbf{c}_b) = 1] - \Pr_{H_2}[\mathcal{A}(1^\lambda, pk, \mathbf{v}) = 1] \right|$$
$$\leq negl(\lambda) + \frac{1}{2}\sqrt{u_0/2^\tau}$$
$$= negl(\lambda)$$

as desired. □

4   Batch Generalization Construction

In this section we present a batched version of our scheme, called BHE, which uses the CRT representation to encrypt several messages at a time.

4.1   Overview

In this section we generalize our construction to allow for encryption of several messages at the same time. Given the messages $\mathbf{m} = (m_1, \ldots, m_l)$ where $m_i \in \{0, 1\}$ we want to pack these $l \in \mathbb{Z}$ messages into a single ciphertext. For this we will use the Chinese Remainder Theorem (CRT). It follows from the CRT and from modular arithmetic that homomorphic multiplication, i.e. MULT, and hence the NAND operation, will apply in parallel and component-wise. Let us look at the general idea first. We sample l primes of η-bit length $p_1, \ldots, p_l$ and define $\pi = \prod_{i=1}^{l} p_i$. Given $x_0 \in \mathbb{Z} \cap [0, 2^\Gamma)$ from the public key, the ciphertext has the following structure:

$$\mathbf{c} = [m\mathbf{g} + \mathbf{r} + \mathbf{q}\pi]_{x_0}$$

where we have that $m = \mathrm{CRT}_{p_1,\ldots,p_l}(m_1, \ldots, m_l)$ for $\mathbf{r} = (r_0, \ldots, r_n)$ such that $r_i = \mathrm{CRT}_{p_1,\ldots,p_l}(r_{i,1}, \ldots, r_{i,l})$ for $r_{i,j} \leftarrow \mathbb{Z} \cap (-2^\rho, 2^\rho)$ and finally $\mathbf{q} = (q_1, \ldots, q_n)$ such that $q_i \leftarrow \mathbb{Z} \cap [0, 2^\Gamma/\pi)$.

This packing method still allows for homomorphic multiplication, in the same way as for the single message construction,

$$\mathbf{c}_3 = \mathsf{BHE.Mult}(\mathbf{c}_1, \mathbf{c}_2)$$
$$= [\mathbf{c}_1 \mathbf{G}^{-1}(\mathbf{c}_2)]_{x_0}.$$

Finally, decryption happens in a very similar way, we compute $f_i = \mathbf{c}\mathbf{g}^{-1}(p_i/2) \mod p_i$ for all $1 \leq i \leq l$. Then for each f_i if $|f_i| \geq p_i/4$ output $m_i = 1$, otherwise $m_i = 0$.

4.2   The Batch Construction

$\mathsf{BHE.Keygen}(1^\lambda)$: We first generate the parameters $params = \{\Gamma, \rho, \eta, \tau, l\}$ according to the security parameter λ and correctness as explained in Sect. 4.4 below. Then we sample l η-bit primes $p_1, \ldots, p_l$ and let $\pi = \prod_{i=1}^{l} p_i$. We define $\pi_i = \frac{\pi}{p_i}$ and we let $y_i = CRT_{p_1,\ldots,p_l}(0, \ldots, 1, \ldots, 0) = \pi_i(\pi_i^{-1} \mod p_i) \mod \pi$ where only the i-th coordinate is non-zero. We will post encryptions of the y_i as a part of the public key so as to allow public encryption.

We sample $(x_0, x_1, \ldots, x_\tau) \leftarrow \vec{\mathcal{X}}_\tau$, where $\vec{\mathcal{X}}_\tau$ is as defined in Lemma 2.3.

We denote $\mathbf{x} = (x_1, \ldots, x_\tau)$, $\mathbf{r} = (r_1, \ldots, r_\tau)$ and $\mathbf{q} = (q_1, \ldots, q_\tau)$. Thus by sampling l matrices $\mathbf{W}_i \leftarrow \{0,1\}^{\tau \times (\Gamma+1)}$, the ciphertexts of the y_i's look like

$$\mathbf{y}_i = [y_i \mathbf{g} + \mathbf{x}\mathbf{W}_i]_{x_0}$$
$$= [y_i \mathbf{g} + \mathbf{r}_i + \mathbf{q}_i\pi]_{x_0} \qquad (7)$$

where $\mathbf{r}_i = \mathbf{r}\mathbf{W}_i$ and $\mathbf{q}_i = \mathbf{q}\mathbf{W}_i$. We set $\mathbf{Y} = (\mathbf{y}_1 \ldots \mathbf{y}_l)$. The public key is defined as $pk = (params, x_0, \mathbf{x}, \mathbf{Y})$ and the secret key as $sk = (p_1, \ldots, p_l)$.

$\mathsf{BHE.Enc}(pk, m_1, \ldots, m_l)$: For $m_i \in \{0,1\}$, sample a matrix $\mathbf{S} \leftarrow \{0,1\}^{\tau \times \Gamma}$. Then we encrypt the messages $\mathbf{m} = (m_1, \ldots, m_l)$ as follows:

$$\mathbf{c} = [\mathbf{m}\mathbf{Y} + \mathbf{x}\mathbf{S}]_{x_0}.$$

$\mathsf{BHE.Eval}(pk, \mathcal{C}, \mathbf{c}_1, \ldots \mathbf{c}_t)$: For any boolean circuit $\mathcal{C}$ we can homomorphically compute the operations $\mathsf{BHE.Mult}$ and $\mathsf{BHE.Nand}$ in an almost identical manner as in the non batch version. The former is computed as follows

$$\mathbf{c}_{mult} = \mathsf{BHE.Mult}(\mathbf{c}_1, \mathbf{c}_2)$$
$$= [\mathbf{c}_1 \mathbf{G}^{-1}(\mathbf{c}_2)]_{x_0}$$

and the latter as

$$\mathbf{c}_{nand} = \mathsf{BHE.Nand}(\mathbf{c}_1, \mathbf{c}_2)$$
$$= [\mathbf{g} - \mathbf{c}_1 \mathbf{G}^{-1}(\mathbf{c}_2)]_{x_0}.$$

$\mathsf{BHE.Dec}(sk, \mathbf{c})$: Given $\mathbf{c}$ we simply compute for each $i = 1, \ldots, l$, $f_i = \mathbf{c} \cdot \mathbf{g}^{-1}(p_i/2) \bmod p_i$. So for each f_i if $|f_i| \geq p/4$ then $m_i = 1$, otherwise $m_i = 0$.

4.3   Correctness and Noise Analysis

The goal of this section is again to prove the correctness of our scheme.

Theorem 4.1. *For a Boolean circuit of depth d, $\mathcal{C}$, for $(sk, pk) \leftarrow \mathsf{BHE.Keygen}(1^\lambda)$ and $\mathbf{c} \leftarrow \mathsf{BHE.Eval}(\mathcal{C}, \mathbf{c}_1, \ldots, \mathbf{c}_t)$ such that $\mathbf{c}_i = \mathsf{BHE.Enc}(pk, \mathbf{m}_i)$, where $\mathbf{m}_i \in \{0, 1\}^l$. We have that*

$$\mathsf{BHE.Dec}(sk, \mathbf{c}) = \mathcal{C}(\mathbf{m}_1, \ldots, \mathbf{m}_t).$$

Remark 3.1 also applies in this case.

We want to make an analysis of the noise components similar to the one in Sect. 3.2. We will start by defining the noise component of the ciphertext for the batched version of the scheme and then we will prove decryption correctness and show how the size behaves in this batch version of the scheme. We first note that after encryption, $\mathsf{BHE.Enc}(pk, \mathbf{m})$, the resulting ciphertext $\mathbf{c}$ is a vector of dimension $\lceil \log x_0 \rceil = \Gamma$ with each entry being an integer in $[-x_0/2, x_0/2)$.

Definition 4.1 (Batch Noise Component). *For any ciphertext $\mathbf{c}$, we define its noise components to be $\mathbf{r}_{m,p_i}(\mathbf{c}) = [\mathbf{c} - m\mathbf{g}]_{p_i}$ for any $i = 1, \ldots, l$. Therefore its size is the norm $r_{m,p_i}(\mathbf{c}) = \|\mathbf{r}_{m,p_i}(\mathbf{c})\|$. Here $m = CRT_{p_1, \ldots, p_l}(m_1, \ldots, m_l)$. We will further define the overall noise component of a ciphertext $\mathbf{c}$ to be $r_{m,\pi}(\mathbf{c}) = \max_{0 \leq i \leq l} r_{m,p_i}(\mathbf{c})$. We consider $\mathbf{r}_{m,p_i}(\mathbf{c})$ over $\mathbb{Z}$ and not over $\mathbb{Z}_{p_i}$.*

Lemma 4.1. *Given a vector $\mathbf{m} \in \{0, 1\}^l$ and a public key $pk = (params, \mathbf{x}, \mathbf{Y}, x_0)$, the ciphertext is of the form $\mathbf{c} = \mathsf{BHE.Enc}(pk, \mathbf{m}) = [CRT_{p_1, \ldots, p_l}(m_1\mathbf{g} + \mathbf{r}_1, \ldots, m_l\mathbf{g} + \mathbf{r}_l) + q \cdot \pi]_{x_0}$.*

Proof. The encryption procedure computes

$$\mathsf{BHE.Enc}(pk, \mathbf{m}) = [\mathbf{mY} + \mathbf{xS}]_{x_0}$$

$$= [\sum_{i=1}^{l}(m_i y_i \mathbf{g} + m_i \mathbf{r} \mathbf{W}_i + m_i q \mathbf{W}_i \pi) + \mathbf{xS}]_{x_0}$$

$$= [CRT_{p_1, \ldots, p_l}(m_1\mathbf{g}, \ldots, m_l\mathbf{g}) + \sum_{i=1}^{l}(m_i \mathbf{r} \mathbf{W}_i + m_i q \mathbf{W}_i \cdot \pi) + \mathbf{xS}]_{x_0},$$

where the last steps is obtained by the linear nature of the CRT representation, which allows for scalar multiplications and point-wise additions. Since $\mathbf{x} = \mathbf{r} + \mathbf{q} \cdot \pi$, we have that for each p_i

$$\sum_{i=1}^{l} (m_i \mathbf{r} \mathbf{W}_i) + \sum_{i=1}^{l} (m_i \mathbf{q} \mathbf{W}_i \cdot \pi) + \mathbf{r} \mathbf{S} + \mathbf{q} \mathbf{S} \cdot \pi$$

$$= \sum_{i=1}^{l} m_i \sum_{j=1}^{\tau} \mathbf{r}_j \cdot \mathbf{w}_{j,i} + \sum_{j=1}^{\tau} \mathbf{r}_j \cdot \mathbf{s}_j \pmod{p_i}$$

$$= \hat{\mathbf{r}}_i$$

where $\mathbf{x} = \mathbf{r}_j \pmod{p_i}$ are vectors whose coordinates are in $\Phi_\rho(p_1, \ldots, p_l)$, as in Eq. (3). So by combining the two we get that $\mathbf{c} = m_i \mathbf{g} + \hat{\mathbf{r}}_i \pmod{p_i}$ and hence

$$\mathbf{c} = \mathsf{BHE.Enc}(pk, \mathbf{m}) = [CRT_{p_1,\ldots,p_l}(m_1 \mathbf{g} + \mathbf{r}_1, \ldots, m_l \mathbf{g} + \mathbf{r}_l) + q \cdot \pi]_{x_0} \quad (8)$$

as required.   □

In the following lemma we first give an upper bound on the size of the noise of a fresh ciphertext in the batch scheme and then an upper bound on the noise growth during the evaluation function for the multiplication, nand and addition functions.

Lemma 4.2 (Batch Noise Size). *Let* $(pk, sk) \leftarrow \mathsf{BHE.Keygen}(1^\lambda)$. *For any two ciphertexts* $\mathbf{c}_1, \mathbf{c}_2 \in \mathbb{Z}_{x_0}^\Gamma$, *encrypting messages* $\mathbf{m}_1, \mathbf{m}_2 \in \{0,1\}^l$, *we define* $B = \max\{r_{m_1,\pi}(\mathbf{c}_1), r_{m_2,\pi}(\mathbf{c}_2)\}$. *The following holds*

1. *Given a fresh encryption* $\mathbf{c} = \mathsf{BHE.Enc}(pk, \mathbf{m})$, *the noise component,* $\mathbf{r}_{m,\pi}(\mathbf{c})$ *has norm* $r_{m,\pi}(\mathbf{c}) \leq (l+2)\tau 2^\rho$.
2. *For* $\mathbf{c}_{mult} = \mathsf{BHE.Mult}(\mathbf{c}_1, \mathbf{c}_2)$ *and* $\mathbf{c}_{nand} = \mathsf{BHE.Nand}(\mathbf{c}_1, \mathbf{c}_2)$, *we have that* $r_{m_{mult},\pi}(\mathbf{c}_{mult}) = r_{m_{nand},\pi}(\mathbf{c}_{nand}) \leq (2\Gamma + 1)B$, *where* $m_{mult} = m_1 m_2$ *and* $m_{nand} = 1 - m_1 m_2$.
3. *For* $\mathbf{c}_{add} = \mathsf{BHE.Add}(\mathbf{c}_1, \mathbf{c}_2)$, *we have that* $r_{m_{add},\pi}(\mathbf{c}_{add}) \leq 2B + 2^{\rho+1}$, *where* $m_{add} = m_1 + m_2$.

Proof. 1. Let $pk = (x_0, \mathbf{x}) = (r_0 + q_0 \cdot \pi, \mathbf{r} + \mathbf{q} \cdot \pi)$. From Eq. (8) we know that

$$\mathbf{c} = [m\mathbf{g} + \hat{\mathbf{r}} + \hat{\mathbf{q}} \cdot \pi]_{x_0}$$

$$= m\mathbf{g} + \hat{\mathbf{r}} + \hat{\mathbf{q}} \cdot \pi + \mathbf{k} x_0$$

where $\hat{\mathbf{r}} = \sum_{i=1}^{l}(m_i \mathbf{r} \mathbf{W}_i) + \mathbf{r} \mathbf{S}$ and $\hat{\mathbf{q}} = \sum_{i=1}^{l}(m_i \mathbf{q} \mathbf{W}_i) + \mathbf{q} \mathbf{S}$. Thus the noise component is $\mathbf{r}_{m,\pi}(\mathbf{c}) = (\sum_{i=1}^{l} m_i \mathbf{r} \mathbf{W}_i) + \mathbf{r} \mathbf{S} + r_0 \mathbf{k}$, where $\mathbf{k}$ is the multiple of x_0 that is added after the mod x_0 operation on the ciphertext. As we have seen in Lemma 4.1 the first term, $(\sum_{i=1}^{l} m_i \mathbf{r} \mathbf{W}_i)$, comes from the matrix operation $\mathbf{m} \mathbf{Y}$ such that $\| \sum_{i=1}^{l} m_i \mathbf{r} \mathbf{W}_i \| \leq l\tau 2^\rho$; the second term of the noise above comes from the matrix operation with the public key vector, $\mathbf{x} \mathbf{S} = \mathbf{q} \mathbf{S} p + \mathbf{r} \mathbf{S}$, with size $\| \mathbf{r} \mathbf{S} \| \leq \tau 2^\rho$. Finally, the last term derives from the mod x_0 operation on the ciphertext. We have that $\|\mathbf{k}\| \leq \tau$, such that $\|r_0\mathbf{k}\| \leq \tau 2^\rho$. The claim follows since

$$r_{m,\pi}(\mathbf{c}) \leq l\tau 2^\rho + \tau 2^\rho + \tau 2^\rho = (l+2)\tau 2^\rho \tag{9}$$

as required.

2. Let $\mathbf{c}_1, \mathbf{c}_2, B$ and $\mathbf{c}_{mult}$ be as in the statement of the lemma. Then we have

$$\|\mathbf{r}_{m_{mult},\pi}(\mathbf{c}_{mult})\| = \max_{i=1}^{l}(\|[\mathbf{c}_{mult} - m_{mult}\mathbf{g}]_{p_i}\|)$$

$$= \max_{i=1}^{l}(\|[[\mathbf{c}_1\mathbf{G}^{-1}(\mathbf{c}_2)]_{x_0} - m_{mult}\mathbf{g}]_{p_i}\|)$$

$$= \max_{i=1}^{l}(\|[\mathbf{c}_1\mathbf{G}^{-1}(\mathbf{c}_2) + \mathbf{k}_{mult}x_0 - m_{mult}\mathbf{g}]_{p_i}\|)$$

$$= \max_{i=1}^{l}(\|[m_1\mathbf{c}_2 + (\mathbf{c}_1 - m_1\mathbf{g})\mathbf{G}^{-1}(\mathbf{c}_2) + \mathbf{k}_{mult}x_0 - m_{mult}\mathbf{g}]_{p_i}\|)$$

$$= \max_{i=1}^{l}(\|[m_1m_2\mathbf{g} + m_1(\mathbf{c}_2 - m_2\mathbf{g}) + (\mathbf{c}_1 - m_1\mathbf{g})\mathbf{G}^{-1}(\mathbf{c}_2)$$

$$+ \mathbf{k}_{mult}x_0 - m_{mult}\mathbf{g}]_{p_i}\|)$$

$$\leq \max_{i=1}^{l}(\|m_{1,i}[\mathbf{c}_2 - m_2\mathbf{g}]_{p_i}\| + \|[\mathbf{c}_1 - m_1\mathbf{g}]_{p_i}\| \cdot \Gamma + \|[\mathbf{k}_{mult}x_0]_{p_i}\|)$$

$$\leq \max_{i=1}^{l}(r_{m_2,p_i}(\mathbf{c}_2) + r_{m_1,p_i}(\mathbf{c}_1) \cdot \Gamma + \|\mathbf{k}_{mult}r_{0,i}\|)$$

$$\leq r_{m_2,\pi}(\mathbf{c}_2) + r_{m_1,\pi}(\mathbf{c}_1) \cdot \Gamma + \|\mathbf{k}_{mult}2^\rho\|$$

$$\leq B + B\Gamma + \|\mathbf{k}_{mult}\|2^\rho,$$

where $m_{j,i}$ is the i-th coordinate of $\mathbf{m}_j$ and $r_{0,i} = [r_0]_p \leq 2^\rho$ such that $x_0 = r_0 + q_0 \cdot \pi$ and $r_0 \leftarrow \Phi_\rho(p_1,\ldots,p_l)$. In order to upper bound $\|\mathbf{k}_{mult}\|$ we use a method analogous to the one in Lemma 3.1 as described with Eq. (5) to conclude that $\|\mathbf{k}_{mult}\| \leq \Gamma$. Hence we get that

$$r_{m_{mult},\pi}(\mathbf{c}_{mult}) \leq B + \Gamma B + \Gamma 2^\rho$$
$$\leq (2\Gamma + 1)B,$$

which is exactly what we need. Analogously, the NAND operation causes the same increase in the size of the noise. This proves the statement.

3. Let $\mathbf{c}_1, \mathbf{c}_2, B$ and $\mathbf{c}_{add}$ be as in the statement of the lemma. Then we have

$$\|\mathbf{r}_{m_{add},\pi}(\mathbf{c}_{add})\| = \max_{i=1}^{l}(\|[\mathbf{c}_{add} - m_{add}\mathbf{g}]_{p_i}\|$$

$$= \max_{i=1}^{l}(\|[\mathbf{c}_1 - m_1\mathbf{g} + \mathbf{c}_2 - m_2\mathbf{g} + \mathbf{k}_{add}x_0]_{p_i}\|)$$

$$\leq \max_{i=1}^{l}(\|[\mathbf{c}_1 - m_1\mathbf{g}]_{p_i}\| + \|[\mathbf{c}_2 - m_2\mathbf{g}]_{p_i}\| + \|[\mathbf{k}_{add}x_0]_{p_i}\|)$$

$$\leq \max_{i=1}^{l}(\|\mathbf{r}_{m_1,p_i}(\mathbf{c}_1)\| + \|\mathbf{r}_{m_2,p_i}(\mathbf{c}_2)\| + \|\mathbf{k}_{mult}r_{0,i}\|)$$

$$\leq r_{m_1,\pi}(\mathbf{c}_1) + r_{m_2,\pi}(\mathbf{c}_2) + 2^{\rho+1}$$

since we have that $\|\mathbf{c}_1 + \mathbf{c}_2\| \leq 2x_0$, thus $\|\mathbf{k}_{add}\| \leq 2$. As before we have that $r_{0,i} = [r_0]_p \leq 2^\rho$ such that $x_0 = r_0 + q_0 \cdot \pi$ and $r_0 \leftarrow \Phi_\rho(p_1, \ldots, p_l)$. This proves the statement. $\square$

Generalizing the statement in 2, let us assume that we want to compute a circuit of depth d on ciphertexts whose noise components are bounded by B. The output ciphertext, $\mathbf{c}_d$, an encryption of m_d, will have a noise component with norm $r_{m_d,\pi}(\mathbf{c}_d) \leq (2\Gamma + 1)^d B$. We now prove decryption correctness.

Lemma 4.3 (Correctness Homomorphic Decryption BHE). *For any vector* $\mathbf{c} \in \mathbb{Z}_{x_0}^\Gamma$ *encrypting some messages* $m_1, \ldots, m_l \in \mathbb{Z}_2$ *under our scheme, such that* $m = CRT_{p_1,\ldots,p_l}(m_1, \ldots, m_l)$, *we have that if* $r_{m,p_i}(\mathbf{c}) < p_i/(4\Gamma)$ *for all* $i = 1, \ldots, l$ *then* HE.Dec$(\mathbf{c}) = (m_1, \ldots, m_l)$.

Proof. Assume that for a ciphertext $\mathbf{c} \in \mathbb{Z}_{x_0}^\Gamma$ we have $r_{m,p_i}(\mathbf{c}) < p/(4\Gamma)$, then during decryption, we have that

$$f_i = \mathbf{c} \cdot \mathbf{g}^{-1}(p_i/2) \pmod{p_i}$$
$$= m\mathbf{g}\mathbf{g}^{-1}(p_i/2) + \mathbf{r}_{m,\pi}(\mathbf{c})\mathbf{g}^{-1}(p_i/2) \pmod{p_i}$$
$$\leq m_i(p_i/2) + \Gamma r_{m,p_i}(\mathbf{c})$$

where by assumption $\Gamma\|\mathbf{r}_{m,p_i}(\mathbf{c})\| < p_i/4$ for all $1 \leq i \leq l$. So by the decryption algorithm, if $|f_i| \leq m_i(p_i/2) + \Gamma r_{m,p_i}(\mathbf{c}) < p_i/4$ then it necessarily means that $m_i = 0$. Whereas if instead $|f_i| \leq m_i(p_i/2) + \Gamma r_{m,p_i}(\mathbf{c})$ and $|f| > p_i/4$ then it must be the case that $m_i = 1$, or else $\Gamma r_{m,p_i}(\mathbf{c}) > p_i/4$. Hence in any case we get that BHE.Dec$(sk, \mathbf{c}) = (m_1, \ldots, m_l)$, which implies decryption correctness. $\square$

4.4   Parameters

Our BHE scheme uses the same parameters as the HE scheme except for

Γ is the bit-length of the elements of the public key, the x_i's, we change the symbol for convenience;
l is both the number of messages in the batch and the number of primes in the secret key;

In the batched version of the decomposed scheme, some of the parameters differ since we are now including several primes in the secret key. The following are the constraints on the parameters needed in order for the BHE scheme to be correct and secure against known attacks. Let d be the depth of the circuit used to evaluate the data.

– $\rho = \omega(\lambda)$, to protect against brute-force attacks on the noise [8,13,16];
– $\eta = \Omega(\rho + (d + 1)\log \Gamma + \log \tau + \log l)$ in order to have correctness of the evaluation circuit (Lemma 4.2);
– $\Gamma \geq \Omega(\frac{\lambda}{\log \lambda}(\eta - \rho)^2)$ and $\Gamma > \eta^2$, to thwart different lattice reduction attacks on the AGCD as studied in [10,12,18,22,25,26,30].

– $\tau = \Gamma + \Omega(\lambda)$, which is derived from the constraints given by the Leftover Hash Lemma in Sect. 2, needed in the security proof in Sect. 4.5.

Remark 4.1. The previous constraints are similar to those of Sect. 3.3 (with η depending additionally on $\log l$) and comes from the fact that there is no known attack on the (ρ, η, Γ)-l-AGCD (Definition 2.5) that exploits the CRT structure [18, Sect. 2.1]: the best known attack is to attack the AGCD on a single prime $p \in \{p_1, \ldots, p_l\}$. Thus, Γ has to be set larger than η^2. Informally, this shows that for the same parameters (Γ, η) as in Sect. 3, one can encrypt close to $l = \eta$ bits without increasing the ciphertext size while still maintaining correctness. (Note that the public key contains l additional ciphertexts compared to the scheme of Sect. 3.)

4.5 Security

In this section we would like to prove, similar to the non-batched version of the scheme, the semantic security. Unfortunately, the assumption in Definition 2.5 is not enough to ensure the security of the batched version of the scheme as it does not assure security when an encryption of key dependent messages is published, needed to compute the CRT representation of a batch of messages during the encryption procedure.

One way to go is to assume that even in spite of the new elements in the public key, the vector $\mathbf{x}$ is still indistinguishable from uniform. This would allow us to apply the same proof strategy as in the previous section. However, to increase our confidence in the validity of this assumption, we show that one can view it as assuming *circular security* for a different auxiliary scheme, one that we can actually prove secure under Definition 2.5. Furthermore, since our auxiliary scheme is only used in the proof of security, we do not even require that it is properly decryptable, only that it is CPA secure (we proved correctness for our actual scheme).

In what follows we introduce our auxiliary encoding scheme, AHE, which encrypts large messages, instead of the CRT representation of a batch of bits. We show that this scheme can be extended to the BHE. We prove that AHE is secure under the decisional batch AGCD assumption (Definition 2.5) and finally show that by adding the circular security assumption to AHE, we can make the BHE scheme secure.

Auxiliary HE Scheme. As explained above, we only require key generation and encryption for this scheme.

AHE.Keygen(1^λ): We first generate the parameters $params = \{\Gamma, \rho, \eta, \tau, l, k\}$ according to the security parameter λ and correctness. Then we sample l η-bit primes $p_1, \ldots, p_l$ and we define $\pi = \prod_{i=1}^{l} p_i$, as above. After this, using the distribution in Definition 2.4 and rejection sampling, we first sample an integer $x_0 \leftarrow (\mathcal{X}_{\rho,\Gamma}(p_1, \ldots, p_l))^{(\geq 2^{\Gamma-1})}$ and then τ integers $\{x_i\}_{1 \leq i \leq \tau} \leftarrow (\mathcal{X}_{\rho,\Gamma}(p_1, \ldots, p_l))^{(\leq x_0)}$, such that $(x_0, x_1, \ldots, x_\tau) \leftarrow \vec{\mathcal{X}}_\tau$, as in Lemma 2.3. We write $\mathbf{x} = (x_1, \ldots, x_\tau)$, $\mathbf{r} = (r_1, \ldots, r_\tau)$ and $\mathbf{q} = (q_1, \ldots, q_\tau)$. We let the message space be $\mathbb{Z}_k$ for some $k \leq \pi$, the public key $pk = (params, x_0, \mathbf{x})$ and the secret key $sk = (p_1, \ldots, p_l)$.

AHE.Enc(pk, m): For a message $m \in \mathbb{Z}_k$, we sample a matrix $\mathbf{S} \leftarrow \{0,1\}^{\tau \times \Gamma}$ and we compute

$$\mathbf{c} = [m\mathbf{g} + \mathbf{x}\mathbf{S}]_{x_0} \tag{10}$$

where again, $\mathbf{c}$ is a vector of dimension $\Gamma = \lceil \log x_0 \rceil$.

Remark 4.2. Given a message $m \in \mathbb{Z}_\pi$, the ciphertext generated by the AHE.Enc is decryptable in a similar way to BHE, where the secret key is the prime factorization of π. This only works in the case that $m = CRT_{p_1, \ldots, p_l}(m_1, \ldots, m_l)$.

Security of AHE. We start by proving a lemma that will be useful in proving both of the next two theorems. Simply said we prove that the structure $\mathbf{x}\mathbf{S}$ mod x_0, where $\mathbf{x}$ are AGCD samples, is computationally indistinguishable from uniform. This will help us avoid redundancy in the proofs of security of AHE and BHE since this structure is present in both of the encryption algorithms.

Lemma 4.4. *Let $(x_0, x_1, \ldots, x_\tau) \leftarrow \vec{\mathcal{X}}_\tau$ and $(u_0, u_1, \ldots, u_\tau) \leftarrow \vec{\mathcal{U}}_\tau$ as in Lemma 2.3, where $\mathbf{x} = (x_1, \ldots, x_\tau)$ and $\mathbf{u} = (u_1, \ldots, u_\tau)$. Then for $\mathbf{v} \leftarrow \mathbb{Z}_{u_0}^\Gamma$ and $\mathbf{S} \leftarrow \{0,1\}^{\tau \times \Gamma}$, the distribution $(\mathbf{x}, x_0, [\mathbf{x}\mathbf{S}]_{x_0})$ is computationally indistinguishable from the distribution $(\mathbf{u}, u_0, \mathbf{v})$.*

Proof. For convenience we write $pk = (\mathbf{x}, x_0)$ and $pk' = (\mathbf{u}, u_0)$. On the one hand, we know by Lemma 2.3 that pk and pk' are indistinguishable, so it follows that $(pk, [\mathbf{x}\mathbf{S}]_{x_0})$ is indistinguishable from $(pk', [\mathbf{u}\mathbf{S}]_{u_0})$ where $\mathbf{S} \leftarrow \{0,1\}^{\tau \times \Gamma}$. On the other hand, we have by the LHL from Lemma 2.2 that the statistical distance between $(pk', [\mathbf{u}\mathbf{S}]_{u_0})$ and $(pk', \mathbf{v})$ for $\mathbf{v} \leftarrow \mathbb{Z}_{u_0}^\Gamma$ is upper bounded by $\frac{1}{2}\sqrt{u_0/2^\tau} = negl(\lambda)$. Hence by transitivity, $(pk, [\mathbf{x}\mathbf{S}]_{x_0})$ is indistinguishable from $(pk', \mathbf{v})$ for $\mathbf{v} \leftarrow \mathbb{Z}_{u_0}^\Gamma$.

In other words, for every polynomial time algorithm $\mathcal{A}$, we have that

$$\left| \Pr[\mathcal{A}(1^\lambda, \mathbf{x}, x_0, [\mathbf{x}\mathbf{S}]_{x_0}) = 1] - \Pr[\mathcal{A}(1^\lambda, \mathbf{u}, u_0, \mathbf{v}) = 1] \right| \leq negl(\lambda).$$

$\square$

Theorem 4.2. *The above AHE scheme is CPA secure under the $(\rho, \eta, \Gamma) - l$-decisional AGCD assumption.*

Proof. For $pk = (params, \mathbf{x}, x_0) \leftarrow$ AHE.Keygen(1^λ) and $\mathbf{c} =$ AHE.Enc(pk, b), where $b \in \mathbb{Z}_k$ is chosen by the adversary, $pk' = (params, \mathbf{u}, u_0)$, as in Lemma 4.4, we prove that $(pk, \mathbf{c})$ and $(pk', \mathbf{v})$, where $\mathbf{v} \leftarrow \mathbb{Z}_{u_0}^\Gamma$, are computationally indistinguishable.

In order to do this we will use a two step hybrid argument and use Lemma 4.4 to show indistinguishability between the hybrids. Each hybrid is an interactive exchange between a challenger, $\mathcal{C}$, and a polynomial time adversary, $\mathcal{A}$.

Hybrid 0: The adversary, $\mathcal{A}$, gets $pk_{H_0} = pk$ from the challenger and then chooses a message $b \in \mathbb{Z}_k$, which he sends back to the challenger. In turn, $\mathcal{C}$ computes $\mathbf{c} = \text{AHE.Enc}(pk, b) = [b\mathbf{g} + \mathbf{xS}]_{x_0}$, which is then sent to the adversary. In this case, $(pk, \mathbf{c})$ is distributed exactly as in the AHE scheme.

Hybrid 1: The adversary, $\mathcal{A}$, gets $pk_{H_1} = pk'$ from the challenger and then chooses a message $b \in \mathbb{Z}_k$, which he sends back to the challenger. In turn, $\mathcal{C}$ computes $\mathbf{c} = [b\mathbf{g} + \mathbf{v}]_{u_0}$, which is then sent to the adversary. Now, by Lemma 4.4 we know that $(pk, \mathbf{c})_{H_0}$ and $(pk, \mathbf{c})_{H_1}$ are computationally indistinguishable because $(pk, [\mathbf{xS}]_{x_0})$ is indistinguishable from $(pk', [\mathbf{uS}]_{u_0})$. Finally, we know that $\mathbf{c} \equiv \mathbf{v}$, hence the probability of success for $\mathcal{A}$ in this hybrid is exactly $1/2$ since $\mathbf{v}$ is completely random.

In other words, for every polynomial time algorithm $\mathcal{A}$,

$$\left| \Pr[\mathcal{A}(1^\lambda, pk, \mathbf{c}) = 1] - \Pr[\mathcal{A}(1^\lambda, pk', \mathbf{v}) = 1] \right| = negl(\lambda).$$

$\square$

Security of BHE. As mentioned earlier, in order to prove security of BHE we must prove first that it is an extension of the AHE scheme under specific conditions, mainly we have the following definition.

Definition 4.2. *Let $\mathcal{E}(\mathcal{M}_\mathcal{E}, \mathcal{C}_\mathcal{E})$ be a public encoding scheme with message space $\mathcal{M}_\mathcal{E}$ and ciphertext space $\mathcal{C}_\mathcal{E}$. We say that $\mathcal{E}'(\mathcal{M}_{\mathcal{E}'}, \mathcal{C}_{\mathcal{E}'})$ is an extension by ciphertext of $\mathcal{E}$ if for some integer n there exists $\mathbf{c}_1, \ldots, \mathbf{c}_n$ and function $f : \mathcal{C}_\mathcal{E}^n \times \mathcal{M}_{\mathcal{E}'} \leftarrow \mathcal{C}_{\mathcal{E}'}$ such that for all $m \in \mathcal{M}_{\mathcal{E}'}$, $\mathcal{E}'.\text{Enc}(pk_{\mathcal{E}'}, m) = f(\mathbf{c}_1, \ldots, \mathbf{c}_n, m)$. Furthermore, $\mathcal{E}'$ is a public encryption scheme if decryption is correct.*

Lemma 4.5. *The BHE public encryption scheme is an extension by ciphertext of the AHE scheme.*

Proof. Let $(pk, sk) \leftarrow \text{AHE}$ and let $f : (\mathbb{Z}_{x_0}^\Gamma)^l \times \{0, 1\}^l \leftarrow \mathbb{Z}_{x_0}^\Gamma$ be the function

$$f(\mathbf{c}_1, \ldots, \mathbf{c}_l, \mathbf{m}) = [\mathbf{mC} + \mathbf{xS}]_{x_0}$$

where $\mathbf{S} \leftarrow \{0, 1\}^{\tau \times \Gamma}$ and $\mathbf{C} = (\mathbf{c}_1 \ldots \mathbf{c}_l)$. Now in order to obtain exactly the BHE scheme we must specify the ciphertexts used, which in this case are $\mathbf{c}_i = \text{AHE.Enc}(pk, y_i)$ where $y_i = CRT_{p_1, \ldots, p_l}(0, \ldots, 0, 1, 0, \ldots, 0) = \pi_i(\pi_i^{-1} \bmod p_i)$. This can be done as long as the AHE encryptions are done privately in the key generation process and we let $pk_{\text{BHE}} = (pk, \mathbf{C})$ for $\mathbf{C} = (\mathbf{c}_1 \ldots \mathbf{c}_l)$ and we let $sk_{\text{BHE}} = sk$. Correctness of BHE follows by the previous section. $\square$

We now connect the circular security of AHE with the CPA security of BHE secure. We start by defining the flavor of circular security we require. Note that this definition applies to encoding schemes (that do not have decryption) and not just to encryption schemes.

Definition 4.3. *A public key encoding scheme* (Keygen, Enc) *is weakly circular secure, if for any polynomial sequence of functions f_i from the secret key space to the message space, it holds that* $(\mathsf{pk}, \{\mathsf{Enc}_{\mathsf{pk}}(f_i(\mathsf{sk}))\}_i)$ *is computationally indistinguishable from* $(\mathsf{pk}, \{\mathsf{Enc}_{\mathsf{pk}}(0)\}_i)$.

The security of BHE follows by applying the circularity of AHE to account for the key dependent information in $\mathbf{Y}$ and then applying the standard security argument. Hence we show that

Theorem 4.3. *If* AHE *is circular secure and the* $(\rho, \eta, \Gamma)-l-AGCD$ *assumption holds, then* BHE *is CPA secure.*

Proof. Let us assume that AHE is circular secure, where we write $\mathcal{S}$ for the secret key space and $\mathcal{M}$ for the message space. We then let the sequence of functions, $f_i : \mathcal{S} \to \mathcal{M}$, be the following

$$f_i(p_1, \ldots, p_l) = CRT_{p_1, \ldots, p_l}(0, \ldots, 1, \ldots, 0).$$

We prove that for all polynomial time adversaries $\mathcal{B}$, the probability of distinguishing in the BHE scheme between an encryption of any message in $\{0,1\}^l$, $\mathbf{c}_1$, and a uniform vector is $negl(\lambda)$.

We proceed to prove this by using a hybrid argument. In each of the hybrids, some form of a CPA game is played between a challenger $\mathcal{A}$ and an adversary $\mathcal{B}$. Let $(pk, sk) \leftarrow \mathsf{AHE.Keygen}(1^\lambda)$ and let $\mathbf{c}_b$ be the BHE ciphertext that $\mathcal{B}$ receives during the game after choosing the message $\mathbf{m}_b \in \{0,1\}^l$. We have that $pk = (params, \mathbf{x}, x_0)$ where $(\mathbf{x}, x_0) = (x_0, \ldots, x_\tau) \leftarrow \vec{\mathcal{X}}_\tau$ and we let $(\mathbf{u}, u_0) = (u_0, u_1, \ldots, u_\tau) \leftarrow \vec{\mathcal{U}}_\tau$ as in Lemma 2.3.

Hybrid 0: In this Hybrid, the challenger $\mathcal{A}$ generates AHE encryptions of functions of the secret key, $\mathbf{c}_i = \mathsf{AHE.Enc}(pk, m_i)$, where $m_i = f_i(p_1, \ldots, p_l)$. Then $\mathcal{A}$ generates the BHE public key $pk' = (pk, \mathbf{Y})$, where $\mathbf{Y} = (\mathbf{c}_1 \ldots \mathbf{c}_l)$ and sends pk' to $\mathcal{B}$. By Lemma 4.5, we have that pk' is distributed exactly as the public key in BHE.Keygen. The BHE-CPA game is then played and $\mathcal{B}$ has some probability of success.

Hybrid 1: In this Hybrid, the challenger $\mathcal{A}$ generates AHE encryptions of zero, $\mathbf{c}_i = \mathsf{AHE.Enc}(pk, m_i)$, where $m_i = 0$. Then $\mathcal{A}$ generates the public key $pk' = (pk, \mathbf{Y})$, where $\mathbf{Y} = (\mathbf{c}_1 \ldots \mathbf{c}_l)$ and sends pk' to $\mathcal{B}$. The BHE-CPA game is then played and we claim that the probability of success for $\mathcal{B}$ is negligibly close to the probability of success for $\mathcal{B}$ in Hybrid 0. Otherwise it would imply that $\mathcal{B}$ can distinguish the AHE encryptions of key dependent messages from encryptions of zero, contradicting the circular security assumption. Thus we have that

$$\left| \Pr_{H_0}[\mathcal{B}(1^\lambda, pk', \mathbf{c}_b) = 1] - \Pr_{H_1}[\mathcal{B}(1^\lambda, pk', \mathbf{c}_b) = 1] \right| = negl(\lambda).$$

Hybrid 2: In this Hybrid, the challenger $\mathcal{A}$ generates AHE encryptions of zero, $\mathbf{c}_i = \mathsf{AHE.Enc}(pk, m_i)$, where $m_i = 0$. Then $\mathcal{A}$ generates the public key $pk' = (params, \mathbf{u}, u_0, \mathbf{Y})$, where $\mathbf{Y} = (\mathbf{c}_1 \ldots \mathbf{c}_l)$ and sends pk' to $\mathcal{B}$. Here $\mathcal{A}$ does not send $\mathcal{B}$ some encryption of a message or of zero, like in the CPA game, instead it sends the vector $\mathbf{c}_b = [m_b \mathbf{Y} + \mathbf{v}]_{u_0}$ where $\mathbf{v} \leftarrow \mathbb{Z}_{u_0}^{\Gamma}$. By Lemma 4.4 we know that $(pk', \mathbf{c}_b)_{H_1}$ is indistinguishable from $(pk', \mathbf{c}_b)_{H_2}$, which implies that $\mathcal{B}$ has probability of success that is negligibly close to that of Hybrid 1, hence

$$\left| \Pr_{H_1}[\mathcal{B}(1^\lambda, pk', \mathbf{c}_b) = 1] - \Pr_{H_2}[\mathcal{B}(1^\lambda, pk', \mathbf{c}_b) = 1] \right| = negl(\lambda).$$

Furthermore, we know that $\mathbf{c}_b \equiv \mathbf{v}$ and since $\mathbf{v}$ is completely random, the probability of success of $\mathcal{B}$ is exactly $1/2$. Thus, by transitivity, we have that

$$\left| \Pr_{H_0}[\mathcal{B}(1^\lambda, pk', \mathbf{c}_b) = 1] - \Pr_{H_2}[\mathcal{B}(1^\lambda, pk', \mathbf{v}) = 1] \right| = negl(\lambda).$$

Hence we have showed that if the AHE scheme is circular secure, then there does not exist an adversary that has non-negligible advantage in a CPA game in the BHE scheme. $\square$

5   Towards Practicality

In this section, we suggest some optimizations to improve the asymptotic and concrete parameters of our schemes, and discuss the obstacles towards efficient implementation thereof (some benchmarks are provided in the full version of this paper). Overcoming these limitations and obtaining a scheme as efficient as the lattice-based variants [11,17,23] remains a challenging open problem. In this section, for simplicity we focus on the scheme of Sect. 3 (our optimizations are easily generalizable to the batch variant of Sect. 4).

5.1   Reducing the Public-Key Size

To satisfy the constraints on the parameters of Sect. 3 for a depth-d circuit, we can take

$$\rho = 2\lambda, \eta = \tilde{\mathcal{O}}(\lambda + d), \gamma = \tilde{\mathcal{O}}(\lambda^2 + d^2) \text{ and } \tau = \tilde{\mathcal{O}}(\lambda^2 + d^2).$$

This gives a public key of size $\tilde{\mathcal{O}}(\lambda^6 + d^6)$. To reduce the size of the public key, we can use the technique suggested in [15] to use a subset-sum with words rather than bits. In particular, to encrypt a message $m \in \{0, 1\}$ as in Eq. (3), we sample a random matrix $\mathbf{S} \in [0, \beta)^{\tau \times \gamma}$ instead of a binary matrix. We have the following corollary of Lemma 2.1.

Corollary 5.1. *Let $\beta \geq 2$. Set $\mathbf{x} = (x_1, \ldots, x_m) \leftarrow \mathbb{Z}_M^m$ uniformly and independently, set $\mathbf{S} \leftarrow [0, \beta)^{m \times n}$ for some n; and let $\mathbf{y} = \mathbf{x} \cdot \mathbf{S} \pmod{M}$. Then $(\mathbf{x}, \mathbf{y})$ is $1/2\sqrt{M/2^{\log_2 \beta \cdot m}}$-uniform over $\mathbb{Z}_M^{m+n}$.*

Proof. Let us consider the hash function family $\mathcal{H}$ from $[0, 2^\beta)^m$ to $\mathbb{Z}_M^n$. Each member $h \in \mathcal{H}$ is parametrized by the element $(x_1, \ldots, x_m) \in \mathbb{Z}_M^n$. Given $\mathbf{S} \in [0, \beta)^{m \times n}$, we define $h(\mathbf{S}) = \mathbf{x} \cdot \mathbf{S}$. The family $\mathcal{H}$ is a 2-universal family of hash functions, and by Lemma 2.1 we get the desired result. $\qquad\square$

In the proof of security (**case 2**) instead of concluding that the statistical distance between $(\mathbf{x}, \mathbf{xS})$ and $(\mathbf{x}, \mathbf{u})$ where $\mathbf{u} \leftarrow \mathcal{U}([0, 2^\gamma)) \cap \mathbb{Z}$ is bounded by $\frac{1}{2}\sqrt{x_0/2^\tau}$, we get that it is bounded by $\frac{1}{2}\sqrt{x_0/2^{\log_2 \beta \cdot \tau}}$. Also in Lemma 3.1, the noise of a fresh encryption $\mathbf{c}$ of m now has norm

$$r_{m,p}(\mathbf{c}) \le \tau\beta \cdot 2^{\rho+1}.$$

Eventually, this gives the following new parameter constraints:

$$\log\beta \cdot \tau \ge \gamma + \mathcal{O}(\lambda), \qquad \eta - \rho > (d+1)\log\gamma + \log\tau + \log\beta + \mathcal{O}(1),$$

and by taking $\log\beta = \tilde{\mathcal{O}}(\lambda + d)$, we reduce the public key size to $\tilde{\mathcal{O}}(\lambda^5 + d^5)$.

5.2   Evaluating Partial Gates

Let us recall that the decryption procedure first computes

$$f = \mathbf{c} \cdot \mathbf{g}^{-1}(p/2) \pmod{p},$$

and outputs $m = 1$ if $|f| \ge p/4$ and $m = 0$ otherwise. Now, since $p/2 \le 2^{\eta-1}$, we have that

$$\mathbf{g}^{-1}(p/2) = (P_0, P_1, \ldots, P_{\eta-1}, 0, \ldots, 0),$$

where $P_0, \ldots, P_{\eta-1} \in \{0, 1\}$. In particular, this shows that only the first η coefficients of $\mathbf{c}$ are useful during the decryption procedure (the other coefficients are required for correctness when homomorphically processing the MULT and NAND gates; see Sect. 3.2). Therefore, when evaluating a circuit, one can only compute the η first coefficients of the outputs of the last MULT and NAND gates, and all the subsequent homomorphic additions; this reduces the computation cost by a multiplicative factor $\approx \gamma/\eta$.

5.3   Trade-Off on the Multiplication Complexity and the Ciphertext Size

Recall that the homomorphic multiplication (Eq. (4)) of two ciphertexts $\mathbf{c}_1$ and $\mathbf{c}_2$ is given by:

$$\mathbf{c}_{mult} = \mathbf{c}_1 \cdot \mathbf{G}^{-1}(\mathbf{c}_2) \bmod x_0.$$

In particular, computing $\mathbf{c}_{mult}$ requires to compute γ times (for each coefficient) about $\gamma/2$ modular additions of γ-bit numbers, i.e. a computational complexity of $\mathcal{O}(\gamma^2 \log(\gamma))$.

Now, assume that instead of using the gadget $\mathbf{g} = (1, 2, \ldots, 2^\gamma)$, we use the gadget

$$\mathbf{g}_\omega = (1, \omega, \ldots, \omega^{\gamma_\omega}),$$

where $\omega \geq 2$ and $\gamma'_\omega = \lceil \gamma' / \log_2 \omega \rceil$ assuming that we now work with γ'-bit integers; i.e. we perform a word decomposition instead of a bit decomposition (taking $\gamma' \geq \gamma$ to get the same homomorphic functionality). Then, computing c_{mult} requires to compute γ'_ω times (for each coefficient) γ'_ω modular multiplications between an element of $\mathbb{Z}_{\gamma'}$ and of $\mathbb{Z}_\omega$; i.e. an approximate complexity of $\mathcal{O}(\gamma'^2_\omega \log(\gamma') \log(\omega))$ (via a schoolbook multiplication).

Now, if one works with $\omega \geq 2$, the noise bounds have to be revisited. In particular, for any two ciphertexts c_1, c_2, where $B = \max\{r_{m_1,p}(c_1), r_{m_2,p}(c_2)\}$, then

$$r_{m_{mult},p}(c_{mult}) = r_{m_{nand},p}(c_{nand}) \leq (2\gamma'_\omega \omega + 1)B,$$

and the decryption condition of a ciphertext c of a message m becomes

$$r_{m,p}(c) < p/(4\gamma'_\omega \omega).$$

We have the following new parameter constraint:

$$\eta - \rho > (d+1)(\log \gamma'_\omega + \log \omega) + \log \tau + \log \beta + \mathcal{O}(1).$$

By taking $\log \omega = \tilde{\mathcal{O}}(\lambda)$, we obtain the same asymptotic complexities a before, but concrete complexities will differ. We will see in Sect. 5.4 how this trade-off (increasing ω also increases γ') impacts concrete parameters.

5.4 Limitations

In order to choose concrete parameters, we use the analyses of the concrete attacks against the AGCD problem from [8,10,15,16,18,30]. In particular, we deduce from [8,16] that ρ should be conservatively set to 2λ, and from [10,18] that the best lattice attacks require to work in dimension $t \geq (\gamma - \rho)/(\eta - \rho)$.

In [10], the AGCD based scheme is also a leveled homomorphic encryption scheme and its parameters can be set significantly smaller than previous works [9, 14–16]: indeed, $\eta - \rho$ can be selected to be small, and so can γ as long as (say) $800 \geq (\gamma - \rho)/(\eta - \rho)$. In the regular scheme of Sect. 3, we also have that $\eta - \rho$ is small, and hence that γ can be small. Unfortunately, our ciphertexts are γ time larger than the ciphertexts in [9], and the complexity of the homomorphic multiplication is at least quadratic in γ. In practice, for (say) $\lambda = 80, \rho = 160$ and $\eta = 172$ (which would only allow for one homomorphic multiplication), then $\gamma \approx 12000$, and the homomorphic multiplication would consist of about 10^9 modular additions, which takes several seconds on a modern CPU. Using the optimization of Sect. 5.3, one can reduce the homomorphic multiplication complexity at first; e.g. when $\omega = 2^{32}$ and $\gamma \approx 75000$, performing an homomorphic multiplication costs now $0.43 \cdot 10^9$ schoolbook modular multiplications between 32-bit words and 75000-bit integers (which still takes several seconds on a modern CPU). Unfortunately, as the gap between η and ρ widens, γ has to be significantly increased so that the AGCD problem remains hard. As ω increases, the number of unit operations increases again, and the unit operations becomes more and more costly (namely, modular multiplication between $\log \omega$-bit integers and γ-bit integers). It follows from our experiments that the size of the ciphertext is a bottleneck to make our schemes practical; a back of the hand computation shows that they are about two order of magnitude slower than their competitors [11,23]. We leave as a challenging open problem to improve the efficiency of this scheme. Note however that our batch variant can encrypt up to γ/η plaintexts in parallel for roughly the same computational cost (cf. Remark 4.1), which decreases the computational cost per bit of plaintext.

References

1. Alperin-Sheriff, J., Peikert, C.: Faster bootstrapping with polynomial error. In: Garay, J.A., Gennaro, R. (eds.) CRYPTO 2014. LNCS, vol. 8616, pp. 297–314. Springer, Heidelberg (2014). doi:10.1007/978-3-662-44371-2_17
2. Brakerski, Z.: Fully homomorphic encryption without modulus switching from classical GapSVP. In: Safavi-Naini, R., Canetti, R. (eds.) CRYPTO 2012. LNCS, vol. 7417, pp. 868–886. Springer, Heidelberg (2012). doi:10.1007/978-3-642-32009-5_50
3. Brakerski, Z., Gentry, C., Halevi, S.: Packed ciphertexts in LWE-based homomorphic encryption. In: Kurosawa, K., Hanaoka, G. (eds.) PKC 2013. LNCS, vol. 7778, pp. 1–13. Springer, Heidelberg (2013). doi:10.1007/978-3-642-36362-7_1
4. Brakerski, Z., Gentry, C., Vaikuntanathan, V.: (Leveled) fully homomorphic encryption without bootstrapping. In: ITCS, pp. 309–325. ACM (2012)
5. Brakerski, Z., Vaikuntanathan, V.: Efficient fully homomorphic encryption from (standard) LWE. In: FOCS, pp. 97–106. IEEE Computer Society (2011). Full version in https://eprint.iacr.org/2011/344.pdf
6. Brakerski, Z., Vaikuntanathan, V.: Fully homomorphic encryption from ring-LWE and security for key dependent messages. In: Rogaway, P. (ed.) CRYPTO 2011. LNCS, vol. 6841, pp. 505–524. Springer, Heidelberg (2011). doi:10.1007/978-3-642-22792-9_29
7. Brakerski, Z., Vaikuntanathan, V.: Lattice-based FHE as secure as PKE. In: ITCS, pp. 1–12. ACM (2014)
8. Chen, Y., Nguyen, P.Q.: Faster algorithms for approximate common divisors: breaking fully-homomorphic-encryption challenges over the integers. In: Pointcheval, D., Johansson, T. (eds.) EUROCRYPT 2012. LNCS, vol. 7237, pp. 502–519. Springer, Heidelberg (2012). doi:10.1007/978-3-642-29011-4_30
9. Cheon, J.H., Coron, J.-S., Kim, J., Lee, M.S., Lepoint, T., Tibouchi, M., Yun, A.: Batch fully homomorphic encryption over the integers. In: Johansson, T., Nguyen, P.Q. (eds.) EUROCRYPT 2013. LNCS, vol. 7881, pp. 315–335. Springer, Heidelberg (2013). doi:10.1007/978-3-642-38348-9_20
10. Cheon, J.H., Stehlé, D.: Fully homomophic encryption over the integers revisited. In: Oswald, E., Fischlin, M. (eds.) EUROCRYPT 2015. LNCS, vol. 9056, pp. 513–536. Springer, Heidelberg (2015). doi:10.1007/978-3-662-46800-5_20
11. Chillotti, I., Gama, N., Georgieva, M., Izabachène, M.: Faster fully homomorphic encryption: bootstrapping in less than 0.1 seconds. In: Cheon, J.H., Takagi, T. (eds.) ASIACRYPT 2016. LNCS, vol. 10031, pp. 3–33. Springer, Heidelberg (2016). doi:10.1007/978-3-662-53887-6_1
12. Cohn, H., Heninger, N.: Approximate common divisors via lattices. The Open Book Series, vol. 1, no. 1, pp. 271–293 (2013)

13. Coron, J.-S., Lepoint, T., Tibouchi, M.: Batch fully homomorphic encryption over the integers. IACR Cryptology ePrint Archive, 2013:36 (2013)

14. Coron, J.-S., Lepoint, T., Tibouchi, M.: Scale-invariant fully homomorphic encryption over the integers. In: Krawczyk, H. (ed.) PKC 2014. LNCS, vol. 8383, pp. 311–328. Springer, Heidelberg (2014). doi:10.1007/978-3-642-54631-0_18

15. Coron, J.-S., Mandal, A., Naccache, D., Tibouchi, M.: Fully homomorphic encryption over the integers with shorter public keys. In: Rogaway, P. (ed.) CRYPTO 2011. LNCS, vol. 6841, pp. 487–504. Springer, Heidelberg (2011). doi:10.1007/978-3-642-22792-9_28

16. Coron, J.-S., Naccache, D., Tibouchi, M.: Public key compression and modulus switching for fully homomorphic encryption over the integers. In: Pointcheval, D., Johansson, T. (eds.) EUROCRYPT 2012. LNCS, vol. 7237, pp. 446–464. Springer, Heidelberg (2012). doi:10.1007/978-3-642-29011-4_27

17. Ducas, L., Micciancio, D.: FHEW: bootstrapping homomorphic encryption in less than a second. In: Oswald, E., Fischlin, M. (eds.) EUROCRYPT 2015. LNCS, vol. 9056, pp. 617–640. Springer, Heidelberg (2015). doi:10.1007/978-3-662-46800-5_24

18. Galbraith, S.D., Gebregiyorgis, S.W., Murphy, S.: Algorithms for the approximate common divisor problem. IACR Cryptology ePrint Archive, 2016:215 (2016)

19. Gentry, C.: Fully homomorphic encryption using ideal lattices. In: STOC, pp. 169–178. ACM (2009)

20. Gentry, C., Sahai, A., Waters, B.: Homomorphic encryption from learning with errors: conceptually-simpler, asymptotically-faster, attribute-based. In: Canetti, R., Garay, J.A. (eds.) CRYPTO 2013. LNCS, vol. 8042, pp. 75–92. Springer, Heidelberg (2013). doi:10.1007/978-3-642-40041-4_5

21. Håstad, J., Impagliazzo, R., Levin, L.A., Luby, M.: A pseudorandom generator from any one-way function. SIAM J. Comput. 28(4), 1364–1396 (1999)

22. Howgrave-Graham, N.: Approximate integer common divisors. In: Silverman, J.H. (ed.) CaLC 2001. LNCS, vol. 2146, pp. 51–66. Springer, Heidelberg (2001). doi:10.1007/3-540-44670-2_6

23. Alhassan Khedr, P., Gulak, G., Vaikuntanathan, V.: SHIELD: scalable homomorphic implementation of encrypted data-classifiers. IEEE Trans. Comput. 65(9), 2848–2858 (2016)

24. Kim, J., Lee, M.S., Yun, A., Cheon, J.H.: CRT-based fully homomorphic encryption over the integers. IACR Cryptology ePrint Archive, 2013:57 (2013)

25. Lagarias, J.C.: The computational complexity of simultaneous diophantine approximation problems. SIAM J. Comput. 14(1), 196–209 (1985)

26. Nguyen, P.Q., Stern, J.: The two faces of lattices in cryptology. In: Silverman, J.H. (ed.) CaLC 2001. LNCS, vol. 2146, pp. 146–180. Springer, Heidelberg (2001). doi:10.1007/3-540-44670-2_12

27. Rivest, R., Adleman, L., Dertouzos, M.: On data banks and privacy homomorphisms. In: Foundations of Secure Computation, pp. 169–177. Academic Press (1978)

28. Shor, P.W.: Algorithms for quantum computation: discrete logarithms and factoring. In: FOCS, pp. 124–134. IEEE Computer Society (1994)

29. Smart, N.P., Vercauteren, F.: Fully homomorphic SIMD operations. Des. Codes Cryptogr. 71(1), 57–81 (2014)

30. Dijk, M., Gentry, C., Halevi, S., Vaikuntanathan, V.: Fully homomorphic encryption over the integers. In: Gilbert, H. (ed.) EUROCRYPT 2010. LNCS, vol. 6110, pp. 24–43. Springer, Heidelberg (2010). doi:10.1007/978-3-642-13190-5_2

Real-World Schemes

Ceremonies for End-to-End Verifiable Elections

Aggelos Kiayias[1]($\boxtimes$), Thomas Zacharias[1], and Bingsheng Zhang[2]

[1] University of Edinburgh, Edinburgh, UK
{akiayias,tzachari}@inf.ed.ac.uk
[2] Security Lancaster Research Centre, Lancaster University, Lancaster, UK
b.zhang2@lancaster.ac.uk

Abstract. State-of-the-art e-voting systems rely on voters to perform certain actions to ensure that the election authorities are not manipulating the election result. This so-called "end-to-end (E2E) verifiability" is the hallmark of current e-voting protocols; nevertheless, thorough analysis of current systems is still far from being complete.

In this work, we initiate the study of e-voting protocols as *ceremonies*. A ceremony, as introduced by Ellison [23], is an extension of the notion of a protocol that includes human participants as separate nodes of the system that should be taken into account when performing the security analysis. that centers on the two properties of end-to-end verifiability and voter privacy and allows the consideration of arbitrary behavioural distributions for the human participants.

We then analyse the Helios system as an e-voting ceremony. Security in the e-voting ceremony model requires the specification of a class of human behaviours with respect to which the security properties can be preserved. We show how end-to-end verifiability and voter privacy are sensitive to human behaviour in the protocol by characterizing the set of behaviours under which the security can be preserved and also showing explicit scenarios where it fails.

We then provide experimental evaluation with human subjects from two different sources where people used Helios: the elections of the International Association for Cryptologic Research (IACR) and a poll of senior year computer science students. We report on the auditing behaviour of the participants as we measured it and we discuss the effects on the level of certainty that can be given by each of the two electorates.

The outcome of our analysis is a negative one: the auditing behaviour of people (including cryptographers) is not sufficient to ensure the correctness of the tally with good probability in either case studied. The same holds true even for simulated data that capture the case of relatively well trained participants while, finally, the security of the ceremony can be shown but under the assumption of essentially ideally behaving human subjects. We note that while our results are stated for Helios, they automatically transfer to various other e-voting systems that, as Helios, rely on client-side encryption to encode the voter's choice.

A. Kiayias, T. Zacharias, B. Zhang—This research was partly supported by ERC project #259152 (CODAMODA), Horizon 2020 project #653497 (PANORAMIX), and project FINER, Greek Secretariat of Research and Technology, funded under action ARISTEIA 1.

S. Fehr (Ed.): PKC 2017, Part II, LNCS 10175, pp. 305–334, 2017.
DOI: 10.1007/978-3-662-54388-7_11

1   Introduction

A ceremony, introduced by Ellison [23], extends the notion of a security protocol to include "human nodes" in the protocol specification together with regular computer nodes. Human nodes, are computationally limited and error-prone; they are able to interact with computer nodes via a user interface (UI) as well as communicate with each other via direct communication lines. In this model, computer nodes can be thought of as stateful and probabilistic interactive Turing machines, while human nodes, even though they are stateful, they are limited in terms of computational power and their behaviour can only be considered as a random variable following some arbitrary probability distribution over a set of "admissible behaviours" that are dictated by the UI's they are provided with. Designing and analyzing the security of ceremonies has proven to be valuable for problems that non-trivially rely on human node interaction to ensure their security properties, such as key provisioning and web authentication, see e.g., [10,23,31,44].

In this work, we initiate the study of secure *E-voting ceremonies*. An e-voting ceremony is a protocol between computer and human nodes that aims to assist a subset of the humans (the voters) to cast a ballot for a specified election race. We argue that viewing e-voting as a ceremony (i.e., a protocol with human and computer nodes) captures the security intricacies of the e-voting problem much more effectively than standard protocol based modelling as it was done so far. The reason for this, is that the properties of an election system, most importantly verifiability, rely on human participant behaviour in a highly non-trivial manner. The ability of human nodes to compromise overall security due to their negligence is well known in e-voting system design (cf. [29]) and it is high time that cryptographic models extend to incorporate formally the human participants.

The capability to perform auditing is widely accepted as the most important characteristic for modern e-voting systems. However, even widely deployed[1] systems such as Helios [1] that are touted to be verifiable via auditing still provide only unquantified guarantees of verifiability. The main reason for this is that the correctness of the election result when the election authorities are adversarial is impossible to verify unless the humans that participate in the protocol follow a suitable behaviour. This means that the voters, beyond the ballot-casting procedure, are supposed to carry out additional steps that many may find to be counterintuitive, see e.g., [43] for more discussion of this issue. This potentially leads to the defective execution of the appropriate steps that are to be carried out for verifiability to be supported and hence the verifiability of the election may collapse. Recent studies have shown that voters have rather limited participation and interest to perform the verification steps (e.g., [22] reports about 23 out of a sample of 747 people performed a verifiability check in a deployed end-to-end (E2E) verifiable system). Given that the auditing performed by the

---

[1] The web-site of the project reports that more than 100,000 votes have been cast with the system.

voters is critical for the integrity of the election result as a whole, it is imperative to determine the class of distributions of behaviours that are able to detect (significant) misbehaviour of the election authorities. Once this class is characterised then one may then try to influence participants to approximate the behaviour by training them.

Traditionally (cf. [11,12,14,28,42,45]), election verifiability was considered at the "individual level" (i.e., a single voter is able to verify her vote intent is properly included in the tally) and the "universal level" (i.e., the election transcript appears to be properly formed). No voter behavioural characteristics were taken into account in the security analysis and the protocols were deemed "end-to-end verifiable" as long as they satisfied merely these two features[2]. The work of [37–39] showed that individual verifiability and universal verifiability, even if combined, can still fail to guarantee that the election tally is correct. To mend the concept of verifiability, a "holistic" notion of global verifiability was introduced. Nevertheless, such global verifiability is unattainable without any assumption on human behaviour. Indeed, [39] establishes the verifiability of the Helios system by assuming that voters perform an unbounded number of independent coin flips — an assumption which should be at best considered of theoretical interest, since no voter using the Helios system (or any e-voting system for that matter) should be expected to actually perform ballot-casting via the employment of independent coin flips.

Beyond verifiability, an e-voting system is supposed to also satisfy privacy and other desired properties such as receipt-freeness/coercion resistance. These properties interact with verifiability in various important ways: First, without privacy it is substantially easier to achieve verifiability (this is due to the fact that verification of the recording of one's vote can be done in relatively straight-forward manner assuming a public "bulletin-board" [4]). Second, receipt-freeness combined with verifiability suggests that the receipt obtained by the voter from ballot-casting can be delegated to a third-party without fear of coercion or privacy leakage. Given these reasons, a proper analysis of an e-voting system should also include the analysis of at least these properties. The fact that privacy will be entrusted to a set of "trustees" that are human participants in the e-voting system, points again to the importance of the ceremony approach for the case of privacy.

Our Results. Our results are as follows.

■ We initiate the study of e-voting ceremonies, i.e., e-voting protocols that involve computer and human nodes, and enable the human participant voters to cast privately their ballots and calculate their tally. In an execution of an e-voting ceremony, human nodes follow a certain behaviour which is sampled according to some distribution over all possible admissible behaviours. No specific assumptions can be made about how human nodes behave and thus the distribution of each human node is a parameter of the security analysis. It follows that the

---

[2] A notable departure from this restriction is [48], nevertheless no formal security analysis is performed for the verifiability of this system.

security properties of e-voting ceremonies are conditional on vectors of probability distributions of human behaviours. Such vectors are specified over sets of
suitably defined deterministic finite state machines with output (transducers[3])
that determine all possible ways that each human participant may interact with
the UI's of the computer nodes that are available to them.

■ Extending the work of [34,39], we provide a threat model for (end-to-end)
verifiability for e-voting ceremonies. Our threat model has the following characteristics: (i) it provides a holistic approach to argue about end-to-end verifiability
by casting the property as an "attack game" played between the adversary and a
challenger. (ii) it provides an explicit final goal the adversary wants to achieve by
introducing a metric over all possible election outcomes and stating an explicit
amount of deviation that the adversary wants to achieve in this metric space.
(iii) the adversary is successful provided that the election tally appears to be
correct even though it deviates from the true tally according to the stated metric while the number of complaining voters in any failed ballot-casting processes
is below a threshold (a ballot-casting process may fail because of adversarial
interference). (iv) the resources of the adversary include the complete control of
all trustees, election authorities, all voter PC's as well as a subset of the voters themselves. Regarding privacy, we extend the work of [8,34], by providing a
threat model for privacy and passive coercion resistance in the sense of [2] for
e-voting ceremonies.

■ We cast Helios as an e-voting ceremony: voters and trustees are the human
participants of the protocol that are supposed to handle credentials and receipts
as well as generate and validate ciphertexts. During ballot-casting, voters perform the Benaloh challenge process [5] and are free to choose to cast their ballot.
Voters may further choose to audit their ballot in the bulletin board if they wish
to. Trustees are supposed to execute deterministic steps in order to perform the
public-key generation during the setup stage of the election and are able to verify
their public-key in the bulletin board if they wish. The set of admissible behaviours for voters include any number of Benaloh challenges followed by casting
the ciphertext and choosing whether to audit it in the bulletin board.

■ We analyse the Helios e-voting ceremony with respect to the threat-model
for privacy and passive coercion and end-to-end verifiability. The behaviours
of voters are an explicit component of the security analysis. Specifically, for
end-to-end verifiability, we characterise the space of admissible behaviours that
enable the verifiability of the election result and we prove an infeasibility and a
feasibility result:

1. It is *infeasible* to detect a large deviation in the published tally of the election
   even if a high number of voters audit it, if (i) there is some i^* that the average
   voter will perform exactly i^* Benaloh audits with high enough probability
   compared to the tolerance level of complaints, or (ii) there is a set of indices

---

[3] We opt to use a finite state machine for voters in order to emphasise that voters do
not perform complex calculations. Nevertheless, our model readily generalises if one
is willing to assume that voters can perform more complex tasks.

$\mathcal{J}^*$ that if the average voter performs $j \in \mathcal{J}^*$ Benaloh audits, this can be used as a predictor for not auditing the bulletin board; (see Theorem 1 for the precise formulation of the infeasibility result).

2. It is *feasible* to detect a deviation in the tally if a suitable number of voters audit the election, provided that (i) for all i the probability that the adversary performs exactly i Benaloh audits is sufficiently small, and (ii) if the number j of Benaloh audits can be used as a predictor of not auditing the bulletin board, then it holds that the likelihood of j Benaloh audits is sufficiently small; (see Theorem 2 for the precise formulation of the feasibility result).

Regarding privacy, we show that assuming the trustees audit with sufficiently high probability the correct posting of the public-key information, Helios maintains privacy under the assumption that the underlying public-key encryption scheme is IND-CPA.

■ We provide an experimental evaluation from two different sources of human data where people used Helios. We report on the auditing behaviour of the participants as we measured it and we discuss the effects on the level of certainty that can be given in each of the two elections. The message from our evaluation is a negative one: The behaviour profile of people is not such that it can provide sufficient certainty on the correctness of the election result. For instance, as we show from the data collected from the elections of the directors of the International Association for Cryptologic Research (IACR), for elections in the order of hundreds (500) more than 3% of the votes could be overturned with significant probability of no detection (25%), cf. Fig. 2. Based on public data on recent election results of the IACR the votes for elected candidates were sufficiently close to candidates that lost in the election and consequently, the results could have been overturned with significant probability without being detected, cf. Table 3. Our results are similarly negative in the second case study. Given our negative results for actual human data, we turn to simulated results for investigating the case when the voters are supposedly well trained with respect to election guidelines. Even for a voter behaviour distribution with supposedly relatively well trained voters our simulated experiment show that the validity of the election result is sustained with rather low confidence.

We note that even though we focused on Helios in this work, our results (including our threat-model analysis for ceremonies and associated security theorems) immediately apply to a number of other e-voting systems. Such systems (that have been identified as single-pass systems in [8]) include [18–20,32,47].

Related Work

Ceremony Study. In 2008, protocol 'ceremony' was introduced by Ellison [23] to expand a security protocol with out-of-band channels and the human users. Subsequently, Karlof et al. [30] formalised the 'conditioned-safe ceremony' notion, that encompasses forcing functions, defence in depth, and human tendencies. They then evaluated an e-mail web authentication ceremony with 200 participants. Later, the strengths and weaknesses of the 'ceremony' notion were examined by Radke et al. [44] in the context of HTTPS, EMV and Opera

Mini protocols/ceremonies. In 2013, Carlos *et al.* [9,40] claimed that even though Dolev-Yao's threat model can represent the most powerful attacker in a ceremony, the attacker in this model is not realistic in certain scenarios, especially those related to human peers. They then proposed a threat model that can be adjusted according to each ceremony and consequently adapt the model and the ceremony analysis to realistic scenarios. In 2014, Hatunic-Webster *et al.* [26] proposed an Anti-Phishing Authentication Ceremony Framework for investigating phishing attacks in authentication ceremonies, which builds on the human-in-the-loop security framework of communication processing. Bella and Coles-Kemp [3] introduced a layered analysis of security ceremonies. Their work focuses on the human-computer interaction layer, which features a socio-technical protocol between a user "persona" and a computer interface. As a more related work, in 2015, Johansen and Jøsang [27] proposed a formal probabilistic model for verifying a security ceremony. In their work, the human agent interaction with the user interface are modelled as a non-deterministic process.

E-Voting Modelling. Conventionally, the verifiability and privacy of an e-voting system is modelled and analysed separately. In terms of the verifiability, individual verifiability [11] and universal verifiability [28,45] was introduced about 20 years ago. End-to-end verifiability in the sense of cast-as-intended, recorded-as-cast, tallied-as-recorded was introduced by [12,42] in 2004. The term of End-to-end verifiability/integrity also appeared in [16]. Later, Küsters *et al.* [37] formally proposed symbolic and computational definitions of verifiability. The verifiability of Helios was studied in both symbolic model [36] and computational model [46]. [38] showed that individual verifiability and universal verifiability are not sufficient to guarantee the "global" verifiability of an e-voting system and In [39], they introduced clash attacks, which break the verifiability of some variants of Helios. In terms of privacy, computational privacy was introduced by Benaloh and Fischer [15], while receipt-freeness has been first studied by Benaloh and Tuinstra [6]. Formal definitions for privacy and receipt-freeness have been proposed in the context of applied pi calculus [21] and the universal composability model [25,41]. In [38], the level of privacy of an e-voting system is measured w.r.t. to the observation power the adversary has in a protocol run. In [7], Bernhard *et al.* proposed a game-based notion of ballot privacy and study the privacy of Helios. Their definition was extended by Bernhard *et al.* [8] by allowing the adversary to statically corrupt election authorities. Both these definitions, although they imply a strong indistinguishability property, do not consider receipt-freeness.

Roadmap. The rest of the paper is organised as follows. In Sect. 2, we introduce the entities, the syntax and the security framework of an e-voting ceremony. In Sect. 3, we describe the Helios e-voting ceremony according to our syntax. In Sect. 4, we analyse the E2E verifiability of Helios ceremony. Namely, we prove (I) an infeasibility and (II) a feasibility result under specific classes of voter behaviours, and we comment on the logical tightness of the two classes. In Sect. 5, we prove the voter privacy/passive coercion resistance of the Helios ceremony. In Sect. 6, we present evaluations of our results for the E2E verifiability of Helios ceremony. Our evaluations are based on actual human data obtained by elections using Helios as well as simulated data for various sets of parameters. Finally, in the concluding Sect. 7, where we recall the objectives, methodology, analysis and results of this paper and discuss future work.

2   E-Voting Ceremonies

A ceremony [23] is an extension of a network protocol that involves human nodes along side computer nodes. Computer nodes will be modeled in a standard way while we will model humans as probability distributions over a support set of simple finite state machines. We base our framework for ceremonies on the e-voting system modeling from [34] suitably extending it to our setting.

2.1   The Entities of the E-Voting Ceremony

An e-voting ceremony $\mathcal{VC}$ is associated with three parameters set to be polynomial in the security parameter λ; the number of voters n, the number of options m and the number of trustees k. We use the notation $\mathcal{O} = \{\mathsf{opt}_1, ..., \mathsf{opt}_m\}$ for the set of options, $\mathcal{V} = \{V_1, ..., V_n\}$ for the set of voters and $\mathcal{T} = \{T_1, ..., T_k\}$ for the set of trustees. The allowed ways to vote is determined by the collection of subsets $\mathcal{U} \subseteq 2^{\mathcal{O}}$ an the option selection $\mathcal{U}_\ell$ of voter V_ℓ is an element in $\mathcal{U}$.

Let $\mathcal{U}^*$ be the set of vectors of option selections of arbitrary length. Let f be the *election evaluation function* from $\mathcal{U}^*$ to the set $\mathbb{Z}_+^m$ so that $f(\mathcal{U}_1, ..., \mathcal{U}_n)$ is equal to an m-vector whose i-th location is equal to the number of times opt_j was chosen in the option selections $\mathcal{U}_1, ..., \mathcal{U}_n$.

The interaction among the entities involved in an e-voting ceremony is depicted in Fig. 1. The said entities comprise:

■ *The human nodes* are the trustees $T_1, ..., T_k$, the voters $V_1, ..., V_n$ and the *credential distributor* (CD). The latter additional entity is responsible for issuing the credentials generated at the setup phase to the voters. Note that in practice, the CD may be an organization of more than one human nodes executing another ceremony but we do not model this as part of the e-voting ceremony. Here we make the simplifying choice of modeling CD as a single human node (that is able to identify voters using an external identification mechanism operating among humans).

■ *The computer nodes* are the voting supporting devices (VSDs), the trustee supporting devices (TSDs), the auditing supporting devices (ASDs), the election authority (EA), and the bulletin board (BB).

Modelling Human Nodes. We model each human node as a collection of simple finite state machines that can communicate with computer nodes (via a user interface) as well as with each other via direct communication. Specifically, we consider a – potentially infinite – collection of *transducers*, i.e. finite state machines with an input and an output tape, that is additionally equipped with a communication tape.

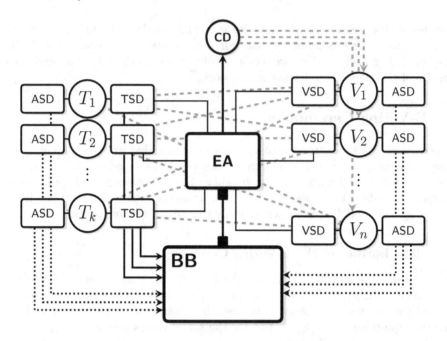

Fig. 1. The entities and the channels active in an e-voting ceremony. The human nodes and the computer nodes used are shown as circles and rectangles respectively. Each voter or trustee human node, interacts with two computer nodes (supporting devices) while the CD human node interacts with the EA. The dotted lines denote read-only access on the BB. The dotted lines denote read-only access on the BB. The grey dashed lines denote channels between human nodes.

We restrict the size of each voter transducer to depend only on the number of options m. Note that this has the implication that the voter transducer *cannot be used to perform cryptographic operations*, which require polynomial number of steps in λ. Transducers may interact with computer nodes, (supporting devices) and use them to produce ciphertexts and transmit them to other computer nodes. The transducers interact with each other via *human level communication channels* (depicted as dashed gray lines in Fig. 1), where the exchanged messages are readable by humans (e.g. credentials, PINs, or short message texts but not cryptographic data).

Transducer collections corresponding to voter nodes, trustee nodes and the CD will be denoted as the sets $\mathcal{M}^V$, $\mathcal{M}^T$, and $\mathcal{M}^{CD}$ respectively. We assume that all sets $\mathcal{M}^V, \mathcal{M}^T$ and $\mathcal{M}^{CD}$ are polynomial time samplable, i.e., one can produce the description of a transducer from the set in polynomial-time and they have an efficient membership test.

2.2   Syntax and Semantics

In order to express the threat model for the e-voting ceremony, we need to formally describe the syntax and semantics of the procedures executed by the ceremony. We think of an e-voting ceremony $\mathcal{VC}$ as a quintuple of algorithms and ceremonies denoted by $\langle \mathbf{Setup}, \mathbf{Cast}, \mathbf{Tally}, \mathbf{Result}, \mathbf{Verify} \rangle$ together with the sets of transducers $\mathcal{M}^V, \mathcal{M}^T$ and $\mathcal{M}^{CD}$ that express the human node operations; these are specified as follows:

The **Setup**$(1^\lambda, \mathcal{O}, \mathcal{V}, \mathcal{U}, \mathcal{T})$ *Ceremony*: The setup phase is a ceremony executed by the EA, the BB, the transducers $M_{i_1}, \ldots, M_{i_n} \in \mathcal{M}^V$ that determine the behaviour of voter $V_1, \ldots, V_n$ respectively, a transducer $M^{CD} \in \mathcal{M}^{CD}$ describing the behaviour of CD, the transducers $M_i^T \in \mathcal{M}^T$, $i = 1, \ldots, k$ describing the behaviour of the trustees $T_1, \ldots T_k$ respectively and their TSDs. The ceremony generates $\mathcal{VC}$'s public parameters info (which include $\mathcal{O}, \mathcal{V}, \mathcal{U}$) and the voter credentials $\mathsf{cr}_1, \ldots, \mathsf{cr}_n$. After the ceremony execution, each TSD has a private state st_i, each trustee T_i obtains a secret $\overline{s}_i$ and the CD obtains the credentials $\mathsf{cr}_1, \ldots, \mathsf{cr}_n$. In addition, the EA posts an election transcript τ initialised as info on BB. At the end of the **Setup**, the CD will provide $\mathsf{cr}_1, \ldots, \mathsf{cr}_n$ to the voters $V_1, \ldots, V_n$.

The **Cast** *Ceremony*: The voting phase is a ceremony executed by the EA, the BB, a transducer $M_{i_\ell} \in \mathcal{M}^V$ that determines the behaviour of voter V_ℓ and her supporting devices $\mathsf{VSD}_\ell, \mathsf{ASD}_\ell$. V_ℓ executes the **Cast** ceremony according to the behaviour M_{i_ℓ} as follows: M_{i_ℓ} has input $(\mathsf{cr}_\ell, \mathcal{U}_\ell)$, where cr_ℓ is the voter's credential and $\mathcal{U}_\ell$ represents the option selection of V_ℓ. All communication between the voter V_ℓ and EA (resp. BB) happens via VSD_ℓ (resp. ASD_ℓ), where BB has input τ. Upon successful termination, M_{i_ℓ}'s output tape contains the individual audit information audit_ℓ returned by VSD_ℓ. If the termination is not successful, M_{i_ℓ}'s output tape possibly contains a special symbol 'Complain', indicating that voter V_ℓ has decided to complain about the incorrect execution of the election procedure. In any case of termination (successful or not), M_{i_ℓ}'s output tape may contain a special symbol 'Audit', indicating that V_ℓ has taken the decision to use her individual audit information audit_ℓ to perform verification at the end of the election; in this case, the individual audit information audit_ℓ will be provided as input to the ASD of V_ℓ. At the end of the ceremony, EA updates its state and BB updates the public transcript τ as necessary.

The **Tally** *Ceremony*: After voting period ends, the tally phase is a ceremony executed by the EA, the BB and the trustees $M_i^T \in \mathcal{M}^T$, $i = 1, \ldots, k$ as well as their TSDs. Namely, the EA provides each trustee with the set of cast votes $\mathsf{V}_{\mathsf{tally}}$. Then, the trustees collectively compute the election result and upon successful termination and update the public transcript τ in the BB either directly or via the EA.

The **Result**(τ) *Algorithm*: The election result can be computed from any party by parsing the election transcript.

The **Verify**(τ, audit) *Algorithm*: The verification algorithm outputs a value in $\{0, 1\}$, where audit is a voter's individual audit information obtained after the voter's engagement in the **Cast** protocol.

The definition of correctness of an honest execution of $\mathcal{VC}$ is straightforward and is provided in the full version of this paper [33, Definition 1].

2.3 Threat Model for E2E Verifiability

In order to define the threat model for E2E verifiability we need first to determine the adversarial objective. Intuitively, the objective of the adversary is to manipulate the election result without raising suspicion amongst the participating voters. To express this formally, we have to introduce a suitable notation; given that option selections are elements of a set of m choices, we may encode them as m-bit strings, where the bit in the i-th position is 1 if and only if option P_i is selected. Further, we may aggregate the election results as the list with the number of votes each option has received, thus the output of the **Result** algorithm is a vector in $\mathbb{Z}_+^m$. In this case, a result is feasible if and only if the sum of any of its coordinates is no greater than the number of voters.

Vote Extractor. Borrowing from [34], in order to express the threat model for E2E verifiability properly, we will ask for a *vote extractor* algorithm $\mathcal{E}$ (not necessarily efficient, e.g., not running in polynomial-time) that receives as input the election transcript τ and the set of individual audit information $\{\alpha_\ell\}_{\ell \in \mathcal{V}_{\mathsf{succ}}}$, where by $\mathcal{V}_{\mathsf{succ}}$, we denote the set of honest voters that voted successfully. Given such input, $\mathcal{E}$ will attempt to compute $n - |\mathcal{V}_{\mathsf{succ}}|$ vectors $\langle \mathcal{U}_\ell \rangle_{V_\ell \in \mathcal{V} \setminus \mathcal{V}_{\mathsf{succ}}}$ in $\{0,1\}^m$ which correspond to all the voters outside of $\mathcal{V}_{\mathsf{succ}}$ and can be either a option selection, if the voter has voted adversarially or a zero vector, if the voter has not voted successfully. In case $\mathcal{E}$ is incapable of presenting such selection, the symbol $\perp$ will be returned instead. The purpose of the algorithm $\mathcal{E}$ is to express the requirement that the election transcript τ that is posted by the EA in the BB at the end of the procedure contains (in potentially encoded form) a set of well-formed actual votes. Using this notion of extractor, we are capable to express the "actual" result encoded in an election transcript despite the fact that the adversary controls some voters. Note when the extractor $\mathcal{E}$ fails it means that τ is meaningless as an election transcript and thus unverifiable.

Election Result Deviation. Next, we want to define a measure of *deviation* from the actual election result, as such deviation is the objective of the adversary in an E2E verifiability attack. This will complete the requirements for expressing the adversarial objective in the E2E attack game. To achieve this, it is natural to equip the space of results with a *metric*. We use the metric derived by the 1-norm, $\| \cdot \|_1$ scaled to half, i.e., $\mathrm{d}_1 : \mathbb{Z}_+^m \times \mathbb{Z}_+^m \longrightarrow \mathbb{R}$ and $\mathrm{d}_1(R, R') = \frac{1}{2} \cdot \sum_{i=1}^m |R_i - R_i'|$, where R_i, R_i' is the i-th coordinate of R, R' respectively. Intuitively, moving δ votes from one option to another translates to a distance $\mathrm{d}_1(R, R')$ of exactly δ.

The E2E Verifiability Game. Let $\mathcal{D} = \langle \mathbf{D}_1, \ldots, \mathbf{D}_n, \mathbf{D}_1^T, \ldots, \mathbf{D}_k^T, \mathbf{D}^{\mathsf{CD}} \rangle$ be a vector of distributions that consists of the distributions $\mathbf{D}_1, \ldots, \mathbf{D}_n$ over the collection of voter transducers $\mathcal{M}^V$, the distributions $\mathbf{D}_1^T, \ldots, \mathbf{D}_k^T$ over the collection of trustee transducers $\mathcal{M}^T$ and the distribution $\mathbf{D}^{\mathsf{CD}}$ over the collection of CD transducers $\mathcal{M}^{\mathsf{CD}}$. We define the E2E verifiability Ceremony game $G_{\mathrm{E2E}}^{\mathcal{A}, \mathcal{E}, \mathcal{D}, \delta, \theta, \phi}$ between the adversary $\mathcal{A}$ and a challenger $\mathcal{C}$ w.r.t. $\mathcal{D}$ and the vote extractor $\mathcal{E}$ which takes as input the security parameter λ, the number of voters n, the number of options m, and the number of trustees k and is parameterised by (i) the deviation amount, δ, (according to the metric $d_1(\cdot, \cdot)$) that the adversary wants to achieve, (ii) the number of honest voters, θ, that terminate the **Cast** ceremony successfully and (iii) the number of honest voters, ϕ, that submit a complaint in case of unsuccessful termination during the **Cast** ceremony.

Throughout the game, the adversary fully controls the election by corrupting the EA and all the trustees $\mathcal{T} = \{T_1, \ldots T_k\}$, while the CD remains honest during the setup phase. In addition, it corrupts all the voters VSDs and manages the **Cast** ceremony executions. For each voter V_ℓ, the adversary may choose to corrupt V_ℓ or to allow the challenger to play on her behalf. Note that the challenger retains the control of the ASD[4] for honest voters and samples for each honest voter a transducer from the corresponding distribution. If a voter V_ℓ is uncorrupted, the adversary provides the option selection that V_ℓ should use in the **Cast** ceremony; the challenger samples a transducer $M_{i_\ell} \xleftarrow{\mathbf{D}_\ell} \mathcal{M}^V$ from voter transducer distribution $\mathbf{D}_\ell$ and then executes the **Cast** ceremony according to M_{i_ℓ}'s description to vote the given option selection and decide whether to audit the election result at the end. The adversary finally posts the election transcript in the BB. The adversary will win the game provided that there are at least θ of honest voters that terminate the ballot-casting successfully and at most ϕ complaining honest voters, but the deviation of the tally is bigger than δ w.r.t. d_1 or the extractor fails to produce the option election of the dishonest voters. The attack game is specified in detail in Fig. 2.

Definition 1. *Let $\epsilon \in [0, 1]$ and $n, m, k, \delta, \theta, \phi \in \mathbb{N}$ with $\theta, \phi \leq n$. The e-voting ceremony $\mathcal{VC}$ w.r.t. the election function f achieves E2E verifiability with error ϵ, transducer distribution vector $\mathcal{D}$, a number of at least θ honest successful voters, at most ϕ honest complaining voters and tally deviation at most d if there exists a (not necessarily polynomial-time) vote extractor $\mathcal{E}$ such that for every PPT adversary $\mathcal{A}$:*

$$\Pr[G_{\text{E2E}}^{\mathcal{A}, \mathcal{E}, \mathcal{D}, \delta, \theta, \phi}(1^\lambda, n, m, k) = 1] \leq \epsilon.$$

Remark 1 (Universal voter distribution). In some e-voting systems, the voters can be uniquely identified during the **Cast** ceremonies, e.g. the voter's real ID is used. Hence, the adversary is able to identify each voter V_ℓ and learn its profile expressed by $\mathbf{D}_\ell$. Then, the adversary may choose the best attack strategy depending on $\mathbf{D}_\ell$. Nevertheless, in case the credentials are randomly and anonymously assigned to the voters by the CD, the adversary will not be able to profile voters given his view in the ballot-casting ceremony (recall that in the E2E game the CD remains honest). Therefore, it is possible to unify the distributions to a *universal voter* distribution, denoted as $\mathbf{D}$, which reflects the profile of the "average voter." Specifically, in this case, we will have $\mathbf{D}_1 = \cdots = \mathbf{D}_n = \mathbf{D}$.

---

[4] In the voting phase client-side encryption systems like Helios [1], the voters' ASDs must be live for potential ballot auditing.

E2E Verifiability Ceremony Game $G_{\text{E2E}}^{\mathcal{A},\mathcal{E},\mathcal{D},\delta,\theta,\phi}(1^\lambda, n, m, k)$

- The adversary $\mathcal{A}$ chooses a list of options $\mathcal{O} = \{\mathsf{opt}_1, ..., \mathsf{opt}_m\}$, a set of voters $\mathcal{V} = \{V_1, ..., V_n\}$, a set of trustees $\mathcal{T} = \{T_1, ... T_k\}$ and the set of allowed option selections $\mathcal{U}$. It provides Ch with the sets $\mathcal{O}, \mathcal{V}, \mathcal{T}, \mathcal{U}$. Throughout the game, the challenger $\mathcal{C}$ plays the role of the BB.

- $\mathcal{C}$ and $\mathcal{A}$ engage in the **Setup** ceremony on input $(1^\lambda, \mathcal{O}, \mathcal{V}, \mathcal{U}, \mathcal{T})$ with $\mathcal{A}$ playing the role of EA and all trustees and their associated TSDs while $\mathcal{C}$ plays the role of CD by following the transducer $M^{\mathsf{CD}} \xleftarrow{\mathbf{D}^{\mathsf{CD}}} \mathcal{M}^{\mathsf{CD}}$. In this way $\mathcal{C}$ obtains info and the voter credentials $\mathsf{cr}_1, ..., \mathsf{cr}_n$. . If the CD refuses to distribute the credentials to the voters, then the game terminates.

- $\mathcal{A}$ and $\mathcal{C}$ engage in an interaction where $\mathcal{A}$ schedules the **Cast** ceremonies of all voters. For each voter V_ℓ, $\mathcal{A}$ can either completely control the voter or allow $\mathcal{C}$ operate on their behalf. In the latter case. $\mathcal{A}$ provides a option selection $\mathcal{U}_\ell$ to $\mathcal{C}$ which samples a transducer $M_{i_\ell} \xleftarrow{\mathbf{D}_\ell} \mathcal{M}^V$ and engages with the adversary $\mathcal{A}$ in the **Cast** ceremony so that $\mathcal{A}$ plays the role of VSD_ℓ and EA and $\mathcal{C}$ plays the role of V_ℓ according to transducer M_{i_ℓ} on input $(\mathsf{cr}_\ell, \mathcal{U}_\ell)$ and its associated ASD_ℓ. Provided the ceremony terminates successfully, $\mathcal{C}$ obtains the individual audit information audit_ℓ produced by M_{i_ℓ}, on behalf of V_ℓ.

- Finally, $\mathcal{A}$ posts the election transcript τ to the BB.

We define the following subsets of honest voters (i.e., those controlled by $\mathcal{C}$):

- $\mathcal{V}_{\mathsf{succ}}$ is the set of honest voters that terminated successfully.
- $\mathcal{V}_{\mathsf{comp}}$ is the set of honest voters s.t. the special symbol 'Complain' is written on the output tape of the corresponding transducer.
- $\mathcal{V}_{\mathsf{audit}}$ is the set of honest voters s.t. the special symbol 'Audit' is written on the output tape of the corresponding transducer.

The game returns a bit which is 1 if and only if the following conditions hold true:

1. $|\mathcal{V}_{\mathsf{succ}}| \geq \theta$,
2. $|\mathcal{V}_{\mathsf{comp}}| \leq \phi$, (i.e., at most ϕ honest voters complain).
3. $\forall \ell \in [n]$: if $V_\ell \in \mathcal{V}_{\mathsf{audit}}$, then **Verify**$(\tau, \mathsf{audit}_\ell) = 1$.

and either one of the following two conditions:

4. (a) If $\bot \neq \langle \mathcal{U}_\ell \rangle_{V_\ell \in \mathcal{V} \setminus \mathcal{V}_{\mathsf{succ}}} \leftarrow \mathcal{E}(\tau, \{\mathsf{audit}_\ell\}_{V_\ell \in \mathcal{V}_{\mathsf{succ}}})$, then

$$\boxed{\mathrm{d}_1\left(\mathbf{Result}(\tau), f(\langle \mathcal{U}_1, ..., \mathcal{U}_n \rangle)\right) \geq \delta}$$.

(b) $\bot \leftarrow \mathcal{E}(\tau, \{\mathsf{audit}_\ell\}_{V_\ell \in \mathcal{V}_{\mathsf{succ}}})$.

Fig. 2. The E2E verifiability ceremony game between the challenger $\mathcal{C}$ and the adversary $\mathcal{A}$ w.r.t. the vote extractor $\mathcal{E}$ and the vector of transducer distributions $\mathcal{D} = \langle \mathbf{D}_1, ..., \mathbf{D}_n, \mathbf{D}_1^T, ..., \mathbf{D}_k^T, \mathbf{D}^{\mathsf{CD}} \rangle$.

2.4   Threat Model for Voter Privacy

The threat model of privacy concerns the actions that may be taken by the adversary to figure out the choices of the honest voters. We specify the goal of the adversary in a very general way. In particular, for an attack against privacy to succeed, we ask that there is an election result, for which the adversary is capable of distinguishing how people vote while it has access to (i) the actual individual audit information that the voters obtain after ballot-casting as well as (ii) a set of ceremony views that are consistent with all the honest voters' views in the **Cast** ceremony instances they participate.

Observe that any system that is secure against such a threat scenario possesses also "passive coercion resistance", i.e., voters cannot prove how they voted by showing the individual audit information ceremony or even presenting the view they obtain from the **Cast**. Given that in the threat model we allow the adversary to observe the view of the voter in the **Cast** ceremony, we need to allow the voter to be able to lie about her view (otherwise an attack could be trivially mounted). We stress that the simulated view of the voter in the **Cast** ceremony does not contain the view of the internals of the VSD. This means that, with respect to privacy, the adversary may not look into the internals of the VSD for the honest voters. The above is consistent, for instance, with the scenario that the voter can give to the VSD her option choice to be encoded. While the adversary will be allowed to observe a simulated view of the voter during the **Cast** ceremony, it will be denied access to the internals of the VSD during the **Cast** execution. This increases the opportunities where the voter can lie about how she executes the **Cast** ceremony.

The Voter Privacy Game. Following the same logic as in the E2E Verifiability game, we specify a vector of transducer distributions over the collection of voter transducers $\mathcal{M}^V$, trustee transducers $\mathcal{M}^T$ and CD transducers $\mathcal{M}^{CD}$ denoted by $\mathcal{D} = \langle \mathbf{D}_1, \ldots, \mathbf{D}_n, \mathbf{D}_1^T, \ldots, \mathbf{D}_k^T, \mathbf{D}^{CD} \rangle$. We then express the threat model as a *Voter Privacy game*, denoted by $G_{t\text{-priv}}^{\mathcal{A},\mathcal{S},\mathcal{D}}$, that is played between an adversary $\mathcal{A}$ and a challenger $\mathcal{C}$, that takes as input the security parameter λ, the number of voters n, the number of options m, and the number of trustees k as described in Fig. 3 and returns 1 or 0 depending on whether the adversary wins. An important feature of the voter privacy game is the existence of an *efficient simulator* $\mathcal{S}$ that provides a simulated view of the voter in the **Cast** ceremony. Note that the simulator is not responsible to provide the view of the voter's supporting device (VSD). Intuitively, this simulator captures the way the voter can lie about her choice in the **Cast** ceremony in case she is coerced to present her view after she completes the ballot-casting procedure.

The attack game is parameterised by t, v. The adversary starts by selecting the voter, option and trustee identities for given parameters n, m, k and determines the allowed ways to vote. The challenger subsequently flips a coin b (that will change its behaviour during the course of the game) and will perform the **Setup** ceremony with the adversary playing the role of the EA, the CD and up to t trustees along with their associated TSDs and ASDs.

Voter Privacy Game $G_{\text{priv}}^{\mathcal{A},\mathcal{S},\mathcal{D},t,v}(1^\lambda, n, m, k)$

- $\mathcal{A}$ on input $1^\lambda, n, m, k$, chooses a list of options $\mathcal{O} = \{\text{opt}_1, ..., \text{opt}_m\}$, a set of voters $\mathcal{V} = \{V_1, ..., V_n\}$, a set of trustees $\mathcal{T} = \{T_1, ..., T_k\}$ a trustee $T_h \in \mathcal{T}$ and the set of allowed option selections $\mathcal{U}$. It provides $\mathcal{C}$ with the sets $\mathcal{O}, \mathcal{V}, \mathcal{U}$ as well as the set of corrupted trustees $\mathcal{T}_{\text{corr}}$.
- $\mathcal{C}$ flips a coin $b \in \{0, 1\}$ and performs the **Setup** ceremony on input $(1^\lambda, \mathcal{O}, \mathcal{V}, \mathcal{U}, \mathcal{T})$ with the adversary playing the role of the EA, CD and all trustees in $\mathcal{T}_{\text{corr}}$, while $\mathcal{C}$ plays the role of all the honest trustees. The role of every honest trustee $T_h \in \mathcal{T} \setminus \mathcal{T}_{\text{corr}}$ is played by $\mathcal{C}$ following the transducers $M^{T_h} \xleftarrow{\mathbf{D}^{T_h}} \mathcal{M}^T$.
- The adversary $\mathcal{A}$ and the challenger $\mathcal{C}$ engage in an interaction where $\mathcal{A}$ corrupts the EA and schedules the **Cast** ceremonies of all voters which may run concurrently. $\mathcal{A}$ also controls the ASDs of all voters. At the onset of each voter ceremony, $\mathcal{A}$ chooses whether voter V_ℓ, $\ell = 1, ..., n$ and its associated VSD is corrupted or not.
  - If V_ℓ and its associated VSD are corrupted, then no specific action is taken by the challenger, as the execution is internal to adversary.
  - If V_ℓ and its associated VSD are not corrupted, then $\mathcal{A}$ provides $\mathcal{C}$ with two option selections $\langle \mathcal{U}_\ell^0, \mathcal{U}_\ell^1 \rangle$. The challenger samples $M_{i_\ell} \xleftarrow{\mathbf{D}_\ell} \mathcal{M}^V$ and sets V_ℓ's input to $(\text{cr}_\ell, \mathcal{U}_\ell^b)$, where cr_ℓ is the credential provided by the adversarially controlled CD. Then, $\mathcal{C}$ and $\mathcal{A}$ engage in the **Cast** ceremony with $\mathcal{C}$ controlling V_ℓ (that behaves according to M_{i_ℓ}) and her VSD, while the adversary $\mathcal{A}$ observes the network interaction. When the **Cast** ceremony terminates, the challenger $\mathcal{C}$ provides to $\mathcal{A}$: (i) the individual audit information audit_ℓ that V_ℓ obtains from the ceremony, and (ii) <u>if $b = 0$</u>, the current view of the internal state of the voter V_ℓ that the challenger obtains from the **Cast** execution, or <u>if $b = 1$</u>, a simulated view of the internal state of V_ℓ produced by $\mathcal{S}(\text{view}_\mathcal{C})$, where $\text{view}_\mathcal{C}$ is the current view of the challenger.
- $\mathcal{A}$ and $\mathcal{C}$ engage in the **Tally** ceremony with the adversary playing the role of the EA, CD and all trustees in $\mathcal{T}_{\text{corr}}$, while $\mathcal{C}$ plays the role of all the honest trustees.
- Finally, $\mathcal{A}$ terminates returning a bit b^*.

Denote the set of corrupted voters as $\mathcal{V}_{\text{corr}}$. The game returns a bit which is 1 if and only if the following hold true:

1. $b = b^*$ (i.e., the adversary guesses b correctly).
2. $|\mathcal{T}_{\text{corr}}| \leq t$ (i.e., the number of corrupted trustees is bounded by t).
3. $|\mathcal{V}_{\text{corr}}| \leq v$ (i.e., the number of corrupted voters is bounded by v).
4. $f(\langle \mathcal{U}_\ell^0 \rangle_{V_\ell \in \mathcal{V} \setminus \mathcal{V}_{\text{corr}}}) = f(\langle \mathcal{U}_\ell^1 \rangle_{V_\ell \in \mathcal{V} \setminus \mathcal{V}_{\text{corr}}})$ (i.e., the election result w.r.t. the set of non-corrupted voters does not leak b).

Fig. 3. The voter privacy game between the challenger $\mathcal{C}$ and the adversary $\mathcal{A}$ w.r.t. the view simulator $\mathcal{S}$ and the vector of transducer distributions $\mathcal{D} = \langle \mathbf{D}_1, ..., \mathbf{D}_n, \mathbf{D}_1^T, ..., \mathbf{D}_k^T, \mathbf{D}^{\text{CD}} \rangle$.

The honest trustees' behaviours will be determined by transducers selected at random by the challenger from $\mathcal{M}^T$ according to the corresponding distribution. Subsequently, the adversary will schedule all **Cast** ceremonies selecting which voters it prefers to corrupt and which ones it prefers to allow to vote honestly. The adversary is allowed to corrupt at most v voters and their VSDs. In addition, $\mathcal{A}$ is allowed to corrupt the ASDs of all voters. The voters that remain uncorrupted are operated by the challenger and they are given two option selections to vote. For each uncorrupted voter V_ℓ, the challenger first samples a transducer $M_{i_\ell} \leftarrow \mathbf{D}_\ell$ and then executes the **Cast** ceremony according to M_{i_ℓ}'s description to vote one of its two option selections based on b.

The adversary will also receive the individual audit information that is obtained by each voter as well as either (i) the actual view (if $b = 0$) or (ii) a *simulated* view, generated by $\mathcal{S}$ (if $b = 1$), of each voter during the **Cast** ceremony (this addresses the individual audit information-freeness aspect of the attack game). Upon completion of ballot-casting, the adversary will execute with the challenger the **Tally** ceremony and subsequently the adversary will attempt to guess b. The attack is successful provided that the election result is the same with respect to the two alternatives provided for each honest voter by the adversary and the adversary manages to guess the challenger's bit b correctly. The game is presented in detail in Fig. 3.

Definition 2. *Let $m, n, k, t, v \in \mathbb{N}$ with $t \leq k$ and $v \leq n$. Let $\mathcal{VC}$ be an e-voting ceremony with m options, n voters and k trustees w.r.t. the evaluation election unction f. We say that $\mathcal{VC}$ achieves* voter privacy *with error ϵ for transducer distribution vector $\mathcal{D}$, at most t corrupted trustees and v corrupted voters, if there is an efficient simulator $\mathcal{S}$ such that for any PPT adversary $\mathcal{A}$:*

$$\left| \Pr[G_{\text{priv}}^{\mathcal{A},\mathcal{S},\mathcal{D},t,v}(1^\lambda, n, m, k) = 1] - \frac{1}{2} \right| \leq \epsilon \,,$$

Threat Model Alternatives. The framework presented in this section is a first attempt to model human behaviour in the cryptographic e-voting analysis, therefore various approaches or extensions could be considered. In the full version of this paper [33, Sect. 2.5], we discuss on some selected possible alternatives on this subject.

3   Syntax of Helios Ceremony

In this section, we present a formal description of Helios ceremony according to the syntax provided in Subsect. 2.2. For simplicity, we consider the case of *1-out-of-m elections*, where the set of allowed selections $\mathcal{U}$ is the collection of singletons, $\{\{\mathsf{opt}_1\}, \ldots, \{\mathsf{opt}_m\}\}$, from the set of options $\mathcal{O}$. Our syntax does not reflect the current implemented version of Helios, as it adapts necessary minimum modifications to make Helios secure. For instance, we ensure that each voter is given a *unique identifier* to prevent Helios from the clash attacks introduced in [39]. In addition, we consider a hash function $H(\cdot)$ that all parties have oracle access to, used for committing to election information and ballot generation, as well as the *Fiat-Shamir transformations* [24] in the NIZK proofs that the system requires. As we state below, in the generation of the NIZK proofs for ballot correctness, the unique identifier is included in the hash to prevent replaying attacks presented in [17]. Moreover, we apply strong Fiat-Shamir transformations, where the statement of the NIZK should also be included in the hash. As shown in [8], strong Fiat-Shamir based NIZKs are *simulation sound extractable*, while weak Fiat-Shamir based NIZKs make the Helios vulnerable.

Finally, we stress that we model trustees' behaviour by considering the event that the trustee will or will not the verify the correct posting of its partial public key. This is done so that we capture the possible privacy vulnerability in Helios's implementation architecure studied in [35]; that is, in the case where no honest trustee performs such verification then a malicious EA may act as man-in-the-middle and replace the trustees' partial public keys with ones it adversarially generates, thus resulting to a total break of voters' privacy.

The Helios's transducers: We define the collections of transducers $\mathcal{M}^V, \mathcal{M}^T$, $\mathcal{M}^{CD}$ that reflect the admissible behaviours of voters, trustees and CD respectively.

The set of admissible voter transducers is denoted by $\mathcal{M}^V :=$ $\{M_{i,c,a}\}_{i \in [0,q]}^{c,a \in \{0,1\}}$, where $q \in \mathbb{N}$; The transducer $M_{i,c,a}$ audits the ballot created by the VSD exactly i times (using its ASD) and then submits the $(i+1)$-th ballot created by the VSD; Upon successful termination, it outputs a individual audit information audit obtained from the VSD; If the termination is not successful and $c = 1$, $M_{i,c,a}$ outputs a special symbol 'Complain' to complain about its failed engagement in the **Cast** ceremony. In any case of termination, when $a = 1$, $M_{i,c,a}$ also outputs a special symbol 'Audit' and sends audit to the ASD. To guarantee termination, we limit the maximum number of ballot audits by threshold q.

The admissible trustee transducers are two and labelled as M_0^T, M_1^T (so that $\mathcal{M}^T = \{M_0^T, M_1^T\}$). At a high level, both M_0^T and M_1^T will utilise the TSD to generate a partial public/secret key pair in the **Setup** ceremony. However, only M_1^T will verify the correct posting of its partial public key in the BB, whereas M_0^T will have no other interaction with the election.

The CD is required to check the validity of the credentials $cr_1, \ldots, cr_n$ generated by the potentially malicious EA before distributing them. In Helios, we define the credential $cr_i := (ID_i, t_i)$, where ID_i is a unique voter identity and t_i is an authentication token. The credential distributor first checks for all $i, j \in [n]$: if $i \neq j$ then $ID_i \neq ID_j$, and halts if the verification fails. Upon success, it randomly sends each voter V_ℓ a credential though some human channels. Hence, we define the set of CD transducers as $\mathcal{M}^{CD} := \{M_\sigma^{CD}\}_{\sigma \in S_n}$, where S_n stands for all possible permutations $[n] \mapsto [n]$.

We define the Helios ceremony quintuple $\langle$**Setup, Cast, Tally, Result, Verify**$\rangle$, using the hash function $H(\cdot)$ as follows:

The **Setup**$(1^\lambda, \mathcal{O}, \mathcal{V}, \mathcal{U}, \mathcal{T})$ *Ceremony*: Each trustee transducer $M_{b_i}^{T_i} \in \{M_0^T, M_1^T\}$, $i = 1, \ldots, k$ sends signal to its TSD. The TSD generates a pair of threshold ElGamal partial keys $(\mathsf{pk}_i, \mathsf{sk}_i)$ and sends pk_i together with a Schnorr (strong Fiat-Shamir) NIZK proof of knowledge of sk_i to the EA. In addition, the TSD returns a trustee secret $\bar{s}_i := (H(\mathsf{pk}_i), \mathsf{sk}_i)$ to $M_{b_i}^{T_i}$. If there is a proof that EA does not verify, then EA aborts the protocol. Next, EA computes the election public key $\mathsf{pk} = \prod_{i \in [k]} \mathsf{pk}_i$. The public parameters, info, which include pk and the partial public keys $\mathsf{pk}_1, \ldots, \mathsf{pk}_k$ as well as the related NIZK proofs of knowledge are posted in the BB by the EA.

Trustee Auditing Step [35]: for $i = 1, \ldots, k$, if $b_i = 1$, then $M_{b_i}^{T_i}$ sends $H(\mathsf{pk}_i)$ to its ASD, and the ASD will fetch info from the BB to verify if there exists a partial public key pk_* such that its hash matches $H(\mathsf{pk}_i)$. In case this verification fails, T_i sends a message 'Invalid public key' to all the voters via the human communication channels shown in Fig. 1.

Finally, the EA generates the voter credentials $\mathsf{cr}_1, \ldots, \mathsf{cr}_n$, where $\mathsf{cr}_i := (\mathsf{ID}_i, t_i)$, and t_i is a random authentication code. Then, forwards the credentials to the CD transducer M^{CD}. The CD transducer M_σ^{CD} checks the uniqueness of each ID_i and distributes them to the voter transducers $M_{i_\ell, c_\ell, a_\ell}$ for $\ell \in [n]$, according to the permutation σ over $[n]$ that specifies its behaviour.

The **Cast** *Ceremony*: For each voter V_ℓ, the corresponding transducer $M_{i_\ell, c_\ell, a_\ell}$ has a pre-defined number of i_ℓ ballot auditing steps, where $i_\ell \in [0, q]$. The input of $M_{i_\ell, c_\ell, a_\ell}$ is $(\mathsf{cr}_\ell, \mathcal{U}_\ell)$. If V_ℓ has received an 'Invalid public key' from at least one trustee, then it aborts the ceremony. If no such message was sent, then for $u \in [i_\ell]$, the following steps are executed:

1. $M_{i_\ell, c_\ell, a_\ell}$ sends $(\mathsf{ID}_\ell, \mathcal{U}_\ell)$ to its VSD, labelled as VSD_ℓ. Let opt_{j_ℓ} be the option selection of V_ℓ, i.e. $\mathcal{U}_\ell = \{\mathsf{opt}_{j_\ell}\}$.
2. For $j = 1, \ldots, m$, VSD_ℓ creates a ciphertext, $C_{\ell,j}$, that is a lifted ElGamal encryption under pk of 1, if $j = j_\ell$ (the selected option position), or 0 otherwise. In addition, it attaches a NIZK proof $\pi_{\ell,j}$ showing that $C_{\ell,j}$ is an encryption of 1 or 0. Finally, an overall NIZK proof π_ℓ is generated, showing that exactly one of these ciphertexts is an encryption of 1. These proofs are strong Fiat-Shamir transformations of *disjunctive Chaum-Pedersen (CP)* proofs [13]. To generate the CP proofs, the unique identifier ID_ℓ is included in the hash. The ballot generated is $\psi_{\ell,u} = \langle \psi_{\ell,u}^0, \psi_{\ell,u}^1 \rangle$, where $\psi_{\ell,u}^0 = \langle (C_{\ell,1}, \pi_{\ell,1}), \ldots, (C_{\ell,m}, \pi_{\ell,m}), \pi_\ell \rangle$ and $\psi_{\ell,u}^1 = H(\psi_{\ell,u}^0)$. The VSD responds to $M_{i_\ell, c_\ell, a_\ell}$ with the ballot $\psi_{\ell,u}$.
3. Then, $M_{i_\ell, c_\ell, a_\ell}$ sends a *Benaloh audit request* to VSD_ℓ. In turn, VSD_ℓ returns the randomness $r_{\ell,u}$ that was used to create the ballot $\psi_{\ell,u}$. The $M_{i_\ell, c_\ell, a_\ell}$ sends $(\mathsf{ID}_\ell, \psi_{\ell,u}, r_{\ell,u})$ to its ASD, which will audit the validity of the ballot. If the verification fails, $M_{i_\ell, c_\ell, a_\ell}$ halts. If the latter happens and $c_\ell = 1$, $M_{i_\ell, c_\ell, a_\ell}$ outputs a special symbol 'Complain', otherwise it returns no output.

After the i_ℓ-th successfully Benaloh audit, $M_{i_\ell, c_\ell, a_\ell}$ invokes VSD_ℓ to produce a new ballot ψ_ℓ as described in step 2 above; however, upon receiving ψ_ℓ, $M_{i_\ell, c_\ell, a_\ell}$

now sends cr_ℓ to VSD_ℓ, indicating it to submit the ballot to the EA. The M_{i_ℓ,c_ℓ,a_ℓ} then outputs $audit_\ell := (ID_\ell, \psi_\ell^1)$. If $a_\ell = 1$, M_{i_ℓ,c_ℓ,a_ℓ} also outputs a special symbol 'Audit' which indicates that it will send $audit_\ell$ to ASD_ℓ which will audit the BB afterwards, as specified in the **Verify** algorithm below.

When EA receives a cast vote (cr_ℓ, ψ_ℓ) from VSD_ℓ, it checks the validity of the credential cr_ℓ and that ψ_ℓ is a well-formed ballot by verifying the NIZK proofs. If the check fails, then it aborts the protocol. After voting ends, EA updates its state with the pairs $\{(\psi_\ell, ID_\ell)\}_{V_\ell \in \mathcal{V}_{\text{succ}}}$ of cast votes and the associated identifiers, where $\mathcal{V}_{\text{succ}}$ is the set of voters that voted successfully.

The **Tally** *Ceremony*: In the **Tally** ceremony, EA sends $\{\psi_\ell\}_{V_\ell \in \mathcal{V}_{\text{succ}}}$ to all trustee transducers $M_{b_i}^{T_i}$'s TSD, $i = 1, \ldots, k$. Next, the TSD of each $M_{b_i}^{T_i}$, $i = 1, \ldots, k$, performs the following computation: it constructs the product ciphertext $\mathbf{C}_j = \prod_{V_\ell \in \mathcal{V}_{\text{succ}}} C_{\ell,j}$ for $j = 1, \ldots, m$. By the additive homomorphic property of (lifted) ElGamal, each $\mathbf{C}_j$ is a valid encryption of the number of votes that the option opt_j received. Then, the TSD uses sk_i to produce the partial decryption of all C_j, denoted by x_j^i, and sends it to the EA along with NIZK proofs of correct partial decryption. The latter are Fiat-Shamir transformations of CP proofs. If there is a proof that EA does not verify, then it aborts the protocol. After all trustees finish their computation, EA updates τ with $\{(x_1^i, \ldots, x_m^i)\}_{i \in [k]}$ and the NIZK proofs.

The **Result**(τ) *Algorithm*: For each option opt_j, the **Result** algorithm computes the number of votes, x_j, that opt_j has received using the partial decryptions $x_j^1, \ldots, x_j^k$. The output of the algorithm is the vector $\langle x_1, \ldots, x_m \rangle$.

The **Verify**$(\tau, audit_\ell)$ *Algorithm*: The algorithm **Verify**$(\tau, audit_\ell)$ outputs 1 if the following conditions hold:

1. The structure of τ and all election information is correct (using info).
2. There exists a ballot in τ, indexed by ID_ℓ, that contains the hash value ψ_ℓ^1.
3. The NIZK proofs for the correctness of all ballots in τ verify.
4. The NIZK proofs for the correctness of all trustees' partial decryptions verify.
5. For $j = 1, \ldots, m$, x_j is a decryption of $\mathbf{C}_j'$, where $\mathbf{C}_j'$ is the homomorphic ciphertext created by multiplying the respective ciphertexts in the ballots published on the BB (in an honest execution, $\mathbf{C}_j'$ should be equal to $\mathbf{C}_j$).

4   E2E Verifiability of Helios E-Voting Ceremony

In a Helios e-voting ceremony, an auditor can check the correct construction of the ballots and the valid decryption of the homomorphic tally by verifying the NIZK proofs. In our analysis, it is sufficient to require that all NIZK proofs have negligible soundness error $\epsilon(\cdot)$ in the RO model. Note that in Sect. 3, we explicitly modify Helios to associate ballots with the voters' identities, otherwise a clash attack [39] would break verifiability. For simplicity in presentation, we assume that the identifiers are created by the adversary, i.e. the set $\{ID_\ell\}_{\ell \in [n]}$ matches the set of voters $\mathcal{V}$.

Throughout our analysis, we assume the honesty of the CD and thus the distribution of the credentials is considered to be an arbitrary permutation over $[n]$. Since there are only two admissible trustee transducers M_0^T, M_1^T, the distribution of trustee transducers $\mathbf{D}_p^T$ is set as the p-biased coin-flip below:

$$\Pr_{\mathbf{D}_p^T}[M] = \begin{cases} p, & \text{if } M = M_1^T \\ 1 - p, & \text{if } M = M_0^T \end{cases} \tag{1}$$

Moreover, in the **Cast** ceremony, the ballots and individual audit information are produced before the voters show their credentials to the system. Since the CD is honest, the adversary is oblivious the the maps between the credentials to the voter transducers. The credentials are only required when the voters want to submit their ballots, hence, according to the discussion in Remark 1, we will consider only a universal voter transducer distribution $\mathbf{D}$ in the case study of Helios. Namely, $\mathbf{D}_1 = \cdots = \mathbf{D}_n = \mathbf{D}$.

4.1   Attacks on Verifiability

As mentioned earlier, we have modified Helios to prevent the system from clash attacks [39]. For simplicity, we exclude all the trivial attacks that the adversary may follow, i.e. the ones that will be detected with certainty (e.g. malformed or unreadable voting interface and public information). Therefore, the meaningful (non-trivial) types of attack that an adversary may launch are the following:

■ **Collision attack**: the adversary computes two votes which hash to the same value. The collision resistance of the hash function $H(\cdot)$, prevents from these attacks except from some negligible probability ϵ'^5.

■ **Invalid vote attack**: the adversary creates a vote for some invalid plaintext, i.e. a vector that does not encode a candidate selection (e.g., multiple votes for some specific candidate). This attack can be prevented by the soundness of the NIZK proofs, except from the negligible soundness error ϵ. The NIZK verification is done via the voter's ASD.

■ **VSD attack**: the adversary creates a vote which is valid, but corresponds to different selection than the one that the voter intended. A Benaloh audit at the **Cast** ceremony step can detect such an attack with certainty, as the randomness provided by the VSD perfectly binds the plaintext with the audited ElGamal ciphertext.

■ **Replacement attack**: the adversary deletes/inserts an honest vote from/to the BB, or replaces it with some other vote of its choice, after voting has ended. Assuming no hash collisions, any such modification will be detected if the voter chooses to audit the BB via her ASD.

■ **Invalid tally decryption attack**: the adversary provides a decryption which is not the plaintext that the homomorphic tally vector encrypts. The NIZK proofs of correct decryption prevent this attack, except for a negligible soundness error ϵ.

---

[5] This requires that $H(\cdot)$ has resistance to second preimage attacks.

Remark 2 (Completeness of the attack list). It can be easily shown that the above list exhausts all possible non-trivial attack strategies against Helios in our threat model. Namely, in an environment with no clash, collision and invalid encryption attacks, the set of votes is in the correct (yet unknown) one-to-one correspondence with the set of voters, and all votes reflect a valid candidate selection of the unique corresponding voter. As a result, a suitably designed vote extractor will decrypt (in super-polynomial time) and output the actual votes from the non-honest-and-successful voters, up to permutation. Consequently, if no honest vote has been modified during and after voting, and the homomorphic tally of the votes is correctly computed and decrypted, then the perfect binding of the plaintexts and ciphertexts of ElGamal implies that the decryption of the tally matches the *intended election result*.

4.2   Attacking the Verifiability of Helios E-Voting Ceremony

As explained in the previous subsection, any attempt of collision, invalid vote and invalid tally decryption attacks has negligible probability of success for the adversary due to the collision resistance of the hash function and the soundness of the ZK proofs. Therefore, in a setting where no clash attacks are possible, the adversary's chances to break verifiability rely on combinations of VSD and Replacement attacks. The probability of these attacks being detected depends on the voter transducer distribution **D** which expresses their auditing behaviour during and after voting. In the following theorem, we prove that the verifiability of Helios is susceptible to VSD or/and Replacement attacks, when the voters sample from a class of assailable voter transducer distributions.

Theorem 1 (*Vulnerability of Helios ceremony*). *Assume an election run of Helios with n voters, m candidates and k trustees. Let $q, \delta, \theta, \phi \in \mathbb{N}$, where $0 < \theta, \phi \le n$ and q is the maximum number of Benaloh audits. Let **D** be a (universal) voter transducer distribution s.t. for some $\kappa_1, \kappa_2, \kappa_3, \mu_1, \mu_2 \in [0,1)$ at least one of the two following conditions holds:*

(i) There is an $i^* \in \{0, \ldots, q\}$ that determines "vulnerable VSD auditing behaviour". Namely, (i.a) the probability that a voter executes at least i^* Benaloh audits is $1 - \kappa_1$ AND (i.b) the probability that a voter, given that she has executed at least i^* Benaloh audits, will cast her vote after exactly i^* Benaloh audits is $1 - \kappa_2$ AND (i.c) the probability that a voter, given that she will execute exactly i^* Benaloh audits, will not complain in case of unsuccessful audit is κ_3.

(ii) There is a subset $\mathcal{J}^* \subseteq \{0, \ldots, q\}$ that determines "vulnerable BB auditing behaviour". Namely, (ii.a) the probability that a voter executes j Benaloh audits for some $j \in \mathcal{J}^*$ is $1 - \mu_1$ AND (ii.b) for every $j \in \mathcal{J}^*$, the probability that a voter, given she has executed j Benaloh audits, will not audit the BB is at least $1 - \mu_2$.

Let $\mathcal{D} = \langle \mathbf{D}, \ldots, \mathbf{D}, \mathbf{D}^{T_1}, \ldots, \mathbf{D}^{T_k}, \mathbf{D}^{\mathsf{CD}} \rangle$ be a transducer distribution vector where $\mathbf{D}^{T_i} = \mathbf{D}^T_{p_i}$, $i = 1, \ldots, k$, is the p_i-biased coin-flip trustee transducer distribution in Eq. (1) for arbitrary $p_i \in [0,1]$ and $\mathbf{D}^{\mathsf{CD}}$ is an arbitrary CD transducer *distribution. Then, there is a PPT adversary $\mathcal{A}$ that wins the E2E verifiability ceremony game $G_{\mathrm{E2E}}^{\mathcal{A},\mathcal{E},\mathcal{D},\delta,\theta,\phi}(1^\lambda, n, m, k)$ in Fig. 2 for any vote extractor $\mathcal{E}$, any $\Delta \in [0, 1)$ as follows:*

▶ *under condition (i), provided the parameters δ, θ, ϕ satisfy:*

$$\delta \le (1 - \Delta)^2 (1 - \kappa_2)(1 - \kappa_1)n$$
$$\theta \le n - (1 + \Delta)(\kappa_2 + \Delta - \Delta\kappa_2)(1 - \kappa_1)n$$
$$\phi \ge (1 + \Delta)^2 \kappa_3 (\kappa_2 + \Delta - \Delta\kappa_2)(1 - \kappa_1)n$$

with probability of success at least $\boxed{1 - 5e^{-\kappa_3\beta_2\beta_1\frac{\Delta^2}{3}}}$ *where $\beta_1 = (1 - \Delta)(1 - \kappa_1)n$ and $\beta_2 = (\kappa_2 - \Delta + \Delta\kappa_2)(1 - \kappa_2)$.*

▶ *under condition (ii), provided the parameter δ satisfies $\delta \le (1-\Delta)(1-\mu_1)n$ with probability of success at least* $\boxed{(1 - e^{-(1-\mu_1)n\frac{\Delta^2}{2}})(1 - \mu_2)^\delta}$.

Proof. We prove the Theorem in the full version [33, Theorem 1].

4.3 End-to-End Verifiability Theorem Helios E-Voting Ceremony

In this subsection, we prove the E2E verifiability of Helios e-voting ceremony in the RO model, when the voter transducer distribution satisfies two conditions. As we will explain at length in the next subsection, these conditions are logically complementary to the ones stated in Theorem 1, as long as the complaining behaviour of the voters is balanced (i.e. the voters have $1/2$ probability of complaining in case of unsuccessful termination).

Theorem 2 (*Verifiability of Helios ceremony*). *Assume an election run of Helios with n voters, m candidates and k trustees. Assume that the hash function $H(\cdot)$ considered in Sect. 3 is a random oracle. Let $q, \delta, \theta, \phi \in \mathbb{N}$, where $0 < \theta, \phi \le n$ and q is the maximum number of Benaloh audits. Let $\mathbf{D}$ be a (universal) transducer distribution and some $\kappa_1, \kappa_2, \kappa_3, \mu_1, \mu_2 \in [0, 1)$ s.t. the two following conditions hold:*

(i) *There is an $i^* \in \{0, \dots, q + 1\}$ that guarantees "resistance against VSD attacks". Namely, (i.a) the probability that a voter executes at least i^* Benaloh audits is κ_1 and (i.b) for every $i \in \{0, \dots, q\}$, if $i < i^*$, then the probability that a voter, given that she will execute at least i Benaloh audits, will cast her vote after exactly i Benaloh audits, is no more than κ_2 AND the probability that a voter, given that she will execute exactly i Benaloh audits, will complain in case of unsuccessful audit is at least $1 - \kappa_3$.*

(ii) *There is a subset $\mathcal{J}^* \subseteq \{0, \dots, q\}$ that guarantees "resistance against Replacement attacks". Namely, (ii.a) the probability that a voter executes j Benaloh audits for some $j \in \mathcal{J}^*$ is $1 - \mu_1$ AND (ii.b) for every $j \in \mathcal{J}^*$, the probability that a voter, given she has executed j Benaloh audits, will audit the BB is at least $1 - \mu_2$.*

Let $\mathcal{D} = \langle \mathbf{D}, \ldots, \mathbf{D}, \mathbf{D}^{T_1}, \ldots, \mathbf{D}^{T_k}, \mathbf{D}^{CD} \rangle$ be a transducer distribution vector where $\mathbf{D}^{T_i} = \mathbf{D}^T_{p_i}$, $i = 1, \ldots, k$, is the p_i-biased coin-flip trustee transducer distribution in Eq. (1) for arbitrary $p_i \in [0, 1]$ and $\mathbf{D}^{CD}$ is an arbitrary CD transducer distribution. Then, for any $\Delta \in [0, 1)$ for any δ, θ, and under the constraint

$$\phi \leq (1 - \Delta)(1 - \kappa_3)\left(\frac{1}{(1 + \Delta)\kappa_2} - 1\right)\left(\frac{\delta}{2} - (1 + \Delta)\kappa_1 n\right),$$

the Helios e-voting ceremony achieves E2E verifiability for $\mathcal{D}$, a number of θ honest successful voters, a number of ϕ honest complaining voters and tally deviation δ with error

$$e^{-\min\left\{\kappa_1 n \frac{\Delta^2}{3}, \, \mu_1 n \frac{\Delta^2}{3}, \, \gamma(\frac{\delta}{2} - (1 + \Delta)\kappa_1 n)\frac{\Delta^2}{3}, \, \ln\left(\frac{1}{\mu_2}\right)(\frac{\delta}{2} - (1 + \Delta)\mu_1 n)\right\}} +$$

$$+ (\mu_1 + \mu_2 - \mu_1 \mu_2)^{\theta} + \mathsf{negl}(\lambda),$$

where $\gamma = \min\left\{\kappa_2, \frac{3}{2}(1 - \kappa_3)\left(\frac{1}{(1 + \Delta)\kappa_2} - 1\right)\right\}$.

Proof. We prove the Theorem in the full version [33, Theorem 2].

4.4   Illustrating Theorems 1 and 2

In order to provide intuition, we provide examples of assailable and resistant voter transducer distributions, in the full version [33, Subsects. 4.2.1 and 4.3.1]. For every case, we illustrate our analysis via comprehensive graphs. Among other remarks, we study the role of Δ as trade off factor between (a) optimising the bounds stated in Theorems 1 and 2, and (b) the corresponding "effectiveness zone" determined by the parameters δ, θ, ϕ (normalised by the electorate size n).

4.5   On the tightness of the conditions of Theorems 1 and 2

The conditions stated in Theorems 1 and 2 determine two classes of voter transducer distributions that correspond to vulnerable and insusceptible settings, respectively. We observe that weakening the condition (i) of Theorem 1 (resp. (i) of Theorem 2) cannot imply vulnerability (resp. security). Namely, in condition (i) of Theorem 1, if one of (1.a), (1.b) or (1.c) does not hold, then the adversary cannot be certain that it will achieve a sufficiently large deviation from VSD attacks without increasing rapidly the number of complaints. On the other hand, if condition (i.a) of Theorem 2 does not hold, then E2E verifiability cannot be preserved when (1.b) becomes a disjunction, since a high complaint rate alone is meaningless if the adversary has high success rate of VSD attacks.

Consequently, it is not possible to achieve logical (i.e. probability thresholds are considered either sufficiently **high** or sufficiently **low**) tightness for interesting sets of parameters δ, θ, ϕ only by negating the conditions of each of the two theorems. However, this is possible if we assume that the voter's complaining behaviour is *balanced* by setting $\kappa_3 = 1 - \kappa_3 = 1/2$. Namely, the voters flip coins in order to decide whether they will complain in case of unsuccessful termination. Given that $\kappa_3 = 1/2$ is a "neutral" value, we have that

Condition (i) of Theorem 1 does not hold, iff condition (i) of Theorem 2 holds.
Condition (ii) of Theorem 1 does not hold, iff condition (ii) of Theorem 2 holds.

The above statement is argued in detail in the full version [33, Subsect. 4.4].

5   Voter Privacy of Helios E-Voting Ceremony

In this section, we prove the voter privacy of the Helios e-voting ceremony. The proof is carried out via a reduction. Namely, we show that unless no honest trustee verifies the correct posting of their public data, if there exists a PPT adversary $\mathcal{A}$ that wins the voter privacy/PCR game for Helios with nonnegligible distinguishing advantage, then there exists a PPT adversary $\mathcal{B}$ that breaks the IND-CPA security of the ElGamal encryption scheme with blackbox access to $\mathcal{A}$. Throughout the proof, we view $H(\cdot)$ as a RO.

Theorem 3 (*Voter Privacy of Helios ceremony*). *Assume an election run of Helios with n voters, m candidates and k trustees. Assume that the hash function $H(\cdot)$ considered in Sect. 3 is a random oracle and the underlying ElGamal encryption scheme is IND-CPA secure. Let $t, v \in \mathbb{N}$, where $t < k$ and $v < n$.*

Let $\mathcal{D} = \langle \mathbf{D}, \ldots, \mathbf{D}, \mathbf{D}^{T_1}, \ldots, \mathbf{D}^{T_k}, \mathbf{D}^{\mathsf{CD}} \rangle$ be a transducer distribution vector where $\mathbf{D}^{T_i} = \mathbf{D}_{p_i}^T$, $i = 1, \ldots, k$, is the p_i-biased coin-flip trustee transducer distribution in Eq. (1) for arbitrary $p_i \in [0, 1]$ and $\mathbf{D}^{\mathsf{CD}}$ is an arbitrary CD transducer distribution.

Assume that $p_1, \ldots, p_k$ are sorted in increasing order as $p_{i_1} \leq \cdots \leq p_{i_k}$. Then, Helios e-voting ceremony achieves voter privacy for $\mathcal{D}$, at most t corrupted trustees and v corrupted voters with error

$$\frac{1}{2} \cdot \prod_{x=1}^{k-t} (1 - p_{i_x}) + \mathsf{negl}(\lambda) \, .$$

Proof. We prove the Theorem in the full version [33, Theorem 3].

6   Evaluating the E2E Verifiability of an E-Voting Ceremony

In this section, we evaluate our results for the E2E verifiability of Helios, by instantiating the bounds in Theorems 1 and 2 for various voter transducer distributions. Our evaluations are separated into two categories: (i) evaluations that are based on actual human data that derive from elections using Helios and (ii) evaluations that are based on simulated data for various sets of parameters.

6.1   Evaluations Based on Human Data

Our human data are sampled from two independent surveys: the first sample is from the member elections of the Board of Directors of the International Association for Cryptographic Research (IACR); the second is a non-binding poll among the students of the Department of Informatics and Telecommunications (DI&T) of the University of Athens.

Due to space limitations, we present at length the methodology for both our surveys in the full version [33, Subsect. 6.1.1]. Here, we provide the computed parameters $\kappa_1, \kappa_2, \kappa_3, \mu_1, \mu_2$ of Theorem 1 for the IACR and the DI&T surveys in Table 1. For both surveys, no complaints or audit failures were reported. Hence, due to lack of data, we choose a "neutral" value for κ_3 equal to 0.5 (see also Subsect. 4.5). Note that our analysis will hold for any other value of κ_3 *not close to 0*. The case of $\kappa_3 = 0$, i.e., when the voter always complains to the authority when a Benaloh audit goes wrong, would make VSD attacks unattractive in the case that ϕ is small and would suggest that the attacker will opt for Replacement attacks, if such attacks are feasible.

The parameters $\kappa_1, \kappa_2, \kappa_3, \mu_1, \mu_2$ used in Theorem 1 express the vulnerability of Helios ceremony against verifiability attacks w.r.t. a specific voter transducer distribution. Namely, parameters $\kappa_1, \kappa_3, \mu_1$ determine the *size* of the subsets of vulnerable voters, while κ_2, μ_2 can be seen as measures of the *quality* of the VSD and Replacement attacks.

Table 1. Instantiated parameters $\kappa_1, \kappa_2, \kappa_3, \mu_1, \mu_2$ of Theorem 1 for the IACR and the DI&T surveys.

Survey	i^*	$\mathcal{J}^*$	Parameters				
			κ_1	κ_2	κ_3	μ_1	μ_2
IACR elections	0	$\{0\}$	0	0.315	0.5	0.315	0.084
DI&T poll	1	—	0.408	0.069	0.5	—	—

Analysis of the IACR Survey: From the first row of Table 1, we read that $\mu_2 = 0.084$ which is a very small value as opposed to $\kappa_2 = 0.315$. Thus, we expect that elections where the electorate follows the voter transducer distribution of IACR elections are much more vulnerable to Replacement attacks rather than VSD attacks. Indeed, this is consistent with the analysis that we describe below.

We computed the percentage of *tally deviation/No. of voters* that the adversary can achieve when the success probability is lower bounded by 25%, 10%, 5% and 1% for various electorate scales. Specifically, we observed that the success probability bounds stated in Theorem 1 express more accurately the effectiveness of the adversarial strategy for (i) medium to large scale elections when the adversary attacks via the VSD and (ii) for small to medium scale elections when the adversary attacks via the BB. As a consequence, we present our analysis for $n = 100, 500, 1000, 2500$ and 5000 voters w.r.t. Replacement attack effectiveness and for $n = 5000, 10000$ and 50000 voters w.r.t. VSD attack effectiveness.

The data in Table 2 illustrate the power of Replacement attacks against compact bodies of voters (e.g. organizations, unions, board elections, etc.) where BB auditing is rare. We can see that in the order of hundreds, more than 5% of the votes could be swapped with significant probability of no detection. This power deteriorates rapidly as we enter the order of thousands, yet the election result could still be undermined, as deviation between 1%–2%, is possible, without the risk of *any* complaint due to unsuccessful engagement in the **Cast** ceremony (i.e. $\theta = n, \phi = 0$). Therefore, even in a setting of high complaint rate (κ_3 is close to 0), the adversary may turn into a Replacement attack strategy and still be able to alter radically the election result, as marginal differences are common in all types of elections. We stress that from published data we are aware of, there have been elections for the IACR board where the votes for winning candidates were closer than 3% to the votes of candidates that lost in the election. Therefore, if the voter distribution had been as the one derived by Table 1, and 500 members had voted, the result could have been overturned with success probability 25% even if a single complaint was considered a "stop election event" (since $\phi = 0$).

To provide more context, in Table 3, we provide the cutoff between elected and non-elected candidates for the last 11 years of IACR elections for the Board of Directors, followed by the exact success probability of a hypothetical Replacement attack strategy to overturn the election result given the actual number of cast ballots per year. We observe that the attacker success probability for many of the elections is considerable (2011, 2014, 2015, 2016), or even unacceptable (2006, 2008, 2009, 2013), at least in our estimation.

On the other hand, the effectiveness of a VSD attack strategy against an election that follows the voter distribution in IACR elections would not have a great impact unless an unnatural number of complaints could be tolerated. Indeed, from our evaluation, it appears even for the scale of 5000, 10000 and 50000 that voters, the rate of complaints that is ignored must be close to 24%, 21% and 17% respectively, which is rather unacceptable in a real world setting. Such number of complaints would most definitely lead to a stop election event.

We conclude that the IACR voter behaviour is susceptible to Replacement attacks with significant probability of success but not VSD attacks unless there is high tolerance in voter complaints.

Table 2. Percentage of *tally deviation/No. of voters* achieved in elections under Replacement attack strategies against electorates following the voter transducer distribution of IACR elections. The attack succeeds even when $\theta = n$ and $\phi = 0$.

Voters	Success probability %			
	≥ 25	≥ 10	≥ 5	≥ 1
100	15.92	26.4	34.42	51.42
500	3.18	5.28	6.87	10.56
1000	1.59	2.64	3.42	5.28
2500	0.636	1.05	1.37	2.11
5000	0.31	0.52	0.68	1.05

Table 3. Success probability of a hypothetical Replacement attack strategy against the IACR elections for the Board of Directors per election year. The success probability is computed given the number of participants and the cutoff between the last elected director and the first candidate that was not elected. The dashed line denotes the actual start of Helios use for IACR elections. Regarding the year 2007, no data were recorded in https://www.iacr.org/elections/.

Year	Participants	Cutoff %	Success probability %
2016	522	6.13	6.03
2015	437	6.87	7.35
2014	575	5.57	6.17
2013	637	2.99	19.14
2012	518	11.59	0.5
2011	621	4.03	11.35
2010	475	8.64	2.82
2009	325	4.93	24.8
2008	312	0.33	91.66
2007	–	–	–
2006	324	4.33	29.57

Analysis of the DI&T Poll: Due to space limitations, we present the analysis of the DI&T poll in the full version [33, Subsect. 6.1.3]. In few words, from the second row of Table 1, we read that $\kappa_2 = 0.069$ which is a very small value leading to significant VSD vulnerability.

6.2   Evaluations Based on Simulated Data

Our human data analysis is obtained by real bodies of voters that have an imperfect voting behaviour. To understand what would be the security level of a Helios e-voting ceremony when executed by an "ideally trained" electorate, we evaluated the security of simulated elections. Namely, we computed the *detection probability* that Theorem 2 can guarantee defined as $(1 - \epsilon) \cdot 100\%$, where ϵ is the error stated in Theorem 2.

The voter distributions we considered were chosen from $\{\mathbf{D}_{p,q}\}_{p\in[0,1],q\in\mathbb{N}}$, a collection of distributions defined as follows: when behaving according to distribution $\mathbf{D}_{p,q}$, the voter flips a coin b with bias p to perform Benaloh audits when $b = 1$, up to a maximum number of q audits. In any case of termination, she flips a coin b' with bias p to perform BB audit when $b' = 1$.

By the above description, we select as VSD resistance index $i^* = q$ and BB resistance set $\mathcal{J}^* = \{0,\ldots,q\}$. For these $i^*, \mathcal{J}^*$ we compute the parameters $\kappa_1 = \mu_1 = p^q$ and $\kappa_2 = \mu_2 = 1-p$, while we also set κ_3 to the balanced parameter $1/2$. Intuitively, this type of voter behaviour should result in a sufficient level of resistance against of VSD and Replacement attacks, if the values $1 - p$ and p^q are small enough.

As an instance of our search, we present our findings for $n = 250000$ voters for distributions $\mathbf{D}_{p,q}$, where $p = 0.25, 0.5, 0.75$ and $q = 3, 5, 8, 10$ in Table 4. In particular, we present the deviation cutoff that can be guaranteed with detection probability 90%, 99% and 99.9%, in an election where the ratio of complaining voters is no more than 0.1%. For a more detailed description of our methodology, we refer the reader to the full version [33, Sect. 6.2].

Table 4. Security w.r.t. detection probability $90\%, 99\%$ and $99, 9\%$ of $\delta/n \cdot \% := (tally$ $deviation)/(No.\ of\ voters)$ percentage for elections with $n = 250000$ voters and $\phi/n \leq$ $0, 1\%$ for distributions $\mathbf{D}_{p,q}$, where $p = 0.25, 0.5, 0.75$ and $q = 3, 5, 8, 10$. The detection probability is defined as $(1 - \epsilon) \cdot 100\%$, where ϵ is the error stated in Theorem 2.

Distribution	Detection probability		
	90%	99%	99.9%
	$\delta/n\%$	$\delta/n\%$	$\delta/n\%$
$\mathbf{D}_{0.25,3}$	6.1	7.31	8.71
$\mathbf{D}_{0.25,5}$	3.63	7.05	17.6
$\mathbf{D}_{0.5,3}$	28.99	30.17	31.12
$\mathbf{D}_{0.5,5}$	7.7	8.06	8.34
$\mathbf{D}_{0.5,8}$	1.5	1.62	1.69
$\mathbf{D}_{0.5,10}$	0.9	1.09	1.28
$\mathbf{D}_{0.75,8}$	26.2	27.71	28.35
$\mathbf{D}_{0.75,10}$	14.79	15.76	16.47

By reading the data in Table 4, we observe that the security guarantee is optimised for the fair coin flipping case $p = 0.5$. Nevertheless, even for this case, acceptable levels of security (e.g., (tally deviation)/(No. of voters) $\leq 3\%$ or error probability $\leq 1\%$) can be achieved only for relatively high values of $q \geq 8$. Besides, recall that these values are reached in the setting where a very small rate ($\leq 0.1\%$) of complaining voters is allowed. As a result, the auditing behaviour of the voters and the complaint tolerance must be almost ideal in order for a high level of security to be achieved.

7   Conclusion

We have introduced the concept of ceremonies to the setting of e-voting systems. Our framework enables the modelling of all human participants to an e-voting protocol as nodes in the protocol execution. Human nodes are modelled as random variables over a set of admissible protocol behaviours which are described by (finite state) transducers. Our analysis enables the exploration of feasibility and infeasibility results regarding the verifiability of the Helios system (suitably modified to be a ceremony) conditioning on general classes of possible voter behaviours. The results from our characterization are essentially tight in the sense that behaviours excluded from our security theorem are too weak/predictable to offer a reasonable level of verifiability.

Our results are only an initial step in the direction of fully incorporating human behavior and interaction within cryptographic modeling. There are many ways to extend the way human nodes are affected by the environment (e.g., taking into account the timing of other nodes) or being manipulated to perform the protocol steps in a wrong order (cf. [29]). Still, even with our limited analysis, we demonstrated that current election procedures, even those performed by cryptographers, are extremely prone to manipulation. Our positive results, albeit also modest, show that there exist behaviors that if uniformly regimented they can provide a reasonable level of e-voting security. Designing e-voting protocols for which this set of behaviors can be efficiently learnable by humans is a further interesting direction motivated by our work.

References

1. Adida, B.: Helios: web-based open-audit voting. In: USENIX Security Symposium (2008)
2. Alwen, J., Ostrovsky, R., Zhou, H.-S., Zikas, V.: Incoercible multi-party computation and universally composable receipt-free voting. In: Gennaro, R., Robshaw, M. (eds.) CRYPTO 2015. LNCS, vol. 9216, pp. 763–780. Springer, Heidelberg (2015). doi:10.1007/978-3-662-48000-7_37
3. Bella, G., Coles-Kemp, L.: Layered analysis of security ceremonies. In: Gritzalis, D., Furnell, S., Theoharidou, M. (eds.) SEC 2012. IAICT, vol. 376, pp. 273–286. Springer, Heidelberg (2012). doi:10.1007/978-3-642-30436-1_23
4. Benaloh, J.: Verifiable secret-ballot elections. Ph.D. thesis YALEU/DCS/TR-561. Yale University, New Haven (1987)
5. Benaloh, J.: Simple verifiable elections. In: Wallach, D.S., Rivest, R.L. (eds.) EVT. USENIX Association (2006)
6. Benaloh, J.C., Tuinstra, D.: Receipt-free secret-ballot elections (extended abstract). In: STOC (1994)
7. Bernhard, D., Cortier, V., Pereira, O., Smyth, B., Warinschi, B.: Adapting helios for provable ballot privacy. In: Atluri, V., Diaz, C. (eds.) ESORICS 2011. LNCS, vol. 6879, pp. 335–354. Springer, Heidelberg (2011). doi:10.1007/978-3-642-23822-2_19
8. Bernhard, D., Pereira, O., Warinschi, B.: How not to prove yourself: pitfalls of the fiat-shamir heuristic and applications to helios. In: Wang, X., Sako, K. (eds.) ASIACRYPT 2012. LNCS, vol. 7658, pp. 626–643. Springer, Heidelberg (2012). doi:10.1007/978-3-642-34961-4_38
9. Carlos, M.C., Martina, J.E., Price, G., Custódio, R.F.: An updated threat model for security ceremonies. In: Proceedings of ACM SAC, pp. 1836–1843. ACM (2013)
10. Carlos, M., Price, G.: Understanding the weaknesses of human-protocol interaction. In: Blyth, J., Dietrich, S., Camp, L.J. (eds.) FC 2012. LNCS, vol. 7398, pp. 13–26. Springer, Heidelberg (2012). doi:10.1007/978-3-642-34638-5_2
11. Chaum, D.: Untraceable electronic mail, return addresses, and digital pseudonyms. Commun. ACM 24(2), 84–88 (1981)
12. Chaum, D.: Secret-ballot receipts: true voter-verifiable elections. IEEE Secur. Priv. 2(1), 38–47 (2004)

13. Chaum, D., Pedersen, T.P.: Wallet databases with observers. In: Brickell, E.F. (ed.) CRYPTO 1992. LNCS, vol. 740, pp. 89–105. Springer, Heidelberg (1993). doi:10.1007/3-540-48071-4_7

14. Chevallier-Mames, B., Fouque, P.-A., Pointcheval, D., Stern, J., Traoré, J.: On some incompatible properties of voting schemes. In: Chaum, D., Jakobsson, M., Rivest, R.L., Ryan, P.Y.A., Benaloh, J., Kutylowski, M., Adida, B. (eds.) Towards Trustworthy Elections. LNCS, vol. 6000, pp. 191–199. Springer, Heidelberg (2010). doi:10.1007/978-3-642-12980-3_11

15. Cohen, J.D., Fischer, M.J.: A robust and verifiable cryptographically secure election scheme (extended abstract). In: FOCS (1985)

16. United States Election Assistance Commission. Voluntary voting systems guidelines (2005)

17. Cortier, V., Smyth, B.: Attacking and fixing Helios: an analysis of ballot secrecy. ePrint Archive, 2010:625 (2010)

18. Cramer, R., Franklin, M., Schoenmakers, B., Yung, M.: Multi-authority secret-ballot elections with linear work. In: Maurer, U. (ed.) EUROCRYPT 1996. LNCS, vol. 1070, pp. 72–83. Springer, Heidelberg (1996). doi:10.1007/3-540-68339-9_7

19. Cramer, R., Gennaro, R., Schoenmakers, B.: A secure and optimally efficient multi-authority election scheme. In: Fumy, W. (ed.) EUROCRYPT 1997. LNCS, vol. 1233, pp. 103–118. Springer, Heidelberg (1997). doi:10.1007/3-540-69053-0_9

20. Damgård, I., Groth, J., Salomonsen, G.: The theory and implementation of an electronic voting system. In: Gritzalis, D. (ed.) Secure Electronic Voting. Advances in Information Security, vol. 7, pp. 77–98. Springer, Heidelberg (2003)

21. Delaune, S., Kremer, S., Ryan, M.: Verifying privacy-type properties of electronic voting protocols. J. Comput. Secur. 17(4), 435–487 (2009)

22. Delis, A., Gavatha, K., Kiayias, A., Koutalakis, C., Nikolakopoulos, E., Roussopoulou, M., Sotirellis, G., Stathopoulos, P., Paschos, L., Vasilopoulos, P., Zacharias, T., Zhang, B.: Pressing the button for European elections 2014: public attitudes towards verifiable e-voting in Greece. In: EVOTE (2014)

23. Ellison, C.M.: Ceremony design and analysis. IACR Cryptology ePrint Archive, 2007:399 (2007)

24. Fiat, A., Shamir, A.: How to prove yourself: practical solutions to identification and signature problems. In: Odlyzko, A.M. (ed.) CRYPTO 1986. LNCS, vol. 263, pp. 186–194. Springer, Heidelberg (1987). doi:10.1007/3-540-47721-7_12

25. Groth, J.: Evaluating security of voting schemes in the universal composability framework. In: Jakobsson, M., Yung, M., Zhou, J. (eds.) ACNS 2004. LNCS, vol. 3089, pp. 46–60. Springer, Heidelberg (2004). doi:10.1007/978-3-540-24852-1_4

26. Hatunic-Webster, E., Mtenzi, F., O'Shea, B.: Model for analysing anti-phishing authentication ceremonies. In: ICITST, pp. 144–150 (2014)

27. Johansen, C., Jøsang, A.: Probabilistic modelling of humans in security ceremonies. In: Garcia-Alfaro, J., Herrera-Joancomartí, J., Lupu, E., Posegga, J., Aldini, A., Martinelli, F., Suri, N. (eds.) DPM/QASA/SETOP -2014. LNCS, vol. 8872, pp. 277–292. Springer, Heidelberg (2015). doi:10.1007/978-3-319-17016-9_18

28. Juels, A., Catalano, D., Jakobsson, M.: Coercion-resistant electronic elections. IACR Cryptology ePrint Archive, 2002:165 (2002)

29. Karlof, C., Sastry, N., Wagner, D.: Cryptographic voting protocols: a systems perspective. In: USENIX (2005)

30. Karlof, C., Tygar, J.D., Wagner, D.: Conditioned-safe ceremonies and a user study of an application to web authentication. In: SOUPS, ACM International Conference Proceeding Series. ACM (2009)

31. Karlof, C., Tygar, J.D., Wagner, D.: Conditioned-safe ceremonies and a user study of an application to web authentication. In: NDSS (2009)
32. Kiayias, A., Korman, M., Walluck, D.: An internet voting system supporting user privacy. In: ACSAC, pp. 165–174. IEEE Computer Society (2006)
33. Kiayias, A., Zacharias, T., Zhang, B.: Ceremonies for end-to-end verifiable elections. IACR Cryptology ePrint Archive, 2015:1166 (2015)
34. Kiayias, A., Zacharias, T., Zhang, B.: End-to-end verifiable elections in the standard model. In: Oswald, E., Fischlin, M. (eds.) EUROCRYPT 2015. LNCS, vol. 9057, pp. 468–498. Springer, Heidelberg (2015). doi:10.1007/978-3-662-46803-6_16
35. Kiayias, A., Zacharias, T., Zhang, B.: On the necessity of auditing for election privacy in e-voting Systems. In: Katsikas, S.K., Sideridis, A.B. (eds.) e-Democracy 2015. CCIS, vol. 570, pp. 3–17. Springer, Heidelberg (2015). doi:10.1007/978-3-319-27164-4_1
36. Kremer, S., Ryan, M., Smyth, B.: Election verifiability in electronic voting protocols. In: Gritzalis, D., Preneel, B., Theoharidou, M. (eds.) ESORICS 2010. LNCS, vol. 6345, pp. 389–404. Springer, Heidelberg (2010). doi:10.1007/978-3-642-15497-3_24
37. Küsters, R., Truderung, T., Vogt, A.: Accountability: definition and relationship to verifiability. IACR Cryptology ePrint Archive, 2010:236 (2010)
38. Küsters, R., Truderung, T., Vogt, A.: Verifiability, privacy, and coercion-resistance: new insights from a case study. In: IEEE Symposium on Security and Privacy, pp. 538–553. IEEE Computer Society (2011)
39. Küsters, R., Truderung, T., Vogt, A.: Clash attacks on the verifiability of e-voting systems. In: IEEE Symposium on Security and Privacy, pp. 395–409. IEEE Computer Society (2012)
40. Martina, J.E., dos Santos, E., Carlos, M.C., Price, G., Custódio, R.F.: An adaptive threat model for security ceremonies. Int. J. Inf. Secur. **14**(2), 103–121 (2015)
41. Moran, T., Naor, M.: Receipt-free universally-verifiable voting with everlasting privacy. In: Dwork, C. (ed.) CRYPTO 2006. LNCS, vol. 4117, pp. 373–392. Springer, Heidelberg (2006). doi:10.1007/11818175_22
42. Neff, C.A.: Practical high certainty intent verification for encrypted votes. Votehere, Inc. Whitepaper (2004)
43. Olembo, M.M., Bartsch, S., Volkamer, M.: Mental models of verifiability in voting. In: Heather, J., Schneider, S., Teague, V. (eds.) Vote-ID 2013. LNCS, vol. 7985, pp. 142–155. Springer, Heidelberg (2013). doi:10.1007/978-3-642-39185-9_9
44. Radke, K., Boyd, C., Gonzalez Nieto, J., Brereton, M.: Ceremony analysis: strengths and weaknesses. In: Camenisch, J., Fischer-Hübner, S., Murayama, Y., Portmann, A., Rieder, C. (eds.) SEC 2011. IAICT, vol. 354, pp. 104–115. Springer, Heidelberg (2011). doi:10.1007/978-3-642-21424-0_9
45. Sako, K., Kilian, J.: Receipt-free mix-type voting scheme. In: Guillou, L.C., Quisquater, J.-J. (eds.) EUROCRYPT 1995. LNCS, vol. 921, pp. 393–403. Springer, Heidelberg (1995). doi:10.1007/3-540-49264-X_32
46. Smyth, B., Frink, S., Clarkson, M.R.: Computational election verifiability: definitions and an analysis of Helios and JCJ. Technical report
47. Tsoukalas, G., Papadimitriou, K., Louridas, P., Tsanakas, P.: From Helios to Zeus. In: EVT/WOTE (2013)
48. Zagórski, F., Carback, R.T., Chaum, D., Clark, J., Essex, A., Vora, P.L.: Remotegrity: design and use of an end-to-end verifiable remote voting system. In: Jacobson, M., Locasto, M., Mohassel, P., Safavi-Naini, R. (eds.) ACNS 2013. LNCS, vol. 7954, pp. 441–457. Springer, Heidelberg (2013). doi:10.1007/978-3-642-38980-1_28

A Modular Security Analysis of EAP and IEEE 802.11

Chris Brzuska[1] and Håkon Jacobsen[2]([✉])

[1] Hamburg University of Technology, Hamburg, Germany
brzuska@tuhh.de
[2] Norwegian University of Science and Technology, Trondheim, Norway
hakoja@item.ntnu.no

Abstract. We conduct a reduction-based security analysis of the Extensible Authentication Protocol (EAP), a widely used three-party authentication framework. We show that the main EAP construction, considered as a 3P-AKE protocol, achieves a security notion which we call AKE^w under the assumption that the EAP method employs channel binding. The AKE^w notion resembles two-pass variant of the eCK model. Our analysis is modular and reflects the compositional nature of EAP. Furthermore, we show that the security of EAP can easily be upgraded by adding an additional key-confirmation step. This key-confirmation step is often carried out in practice in the form of a link-layer specific AKE protocol that uses EAP for bootstrapping its authentication. A concrete example of this is the extremely common IEEE 802.11 4-Way-Handshake protocol used in WLANs. Building on our modular results for EAP, we get as our second major result the first provable security result for IEEE 802.11 with upper-layer authentication.

1 Introduction

The Extensible Authentication Protocol (EAP), specified in RFC 3748 [4], is a widely used authentication framework for network access control. It is particularly common in wireless networks, being used by protocols like IEEE 802.11 (Wi-Fi), IEEE 802.16 (WiMAX) and various 3G/4G mobile networks. The typical use case of EAP is in settings where a *client* seeks to gain access to a network controlled by an *authenticator*, but where the client and authenticator do not share any common credentials. EAP allows the client and authenticator to authenticate each other based on a mutually trusted *server*. Technically, EAP is not a specific authentication mechanism on its own, but rather specifies a certain generic three-party construction that composes other concrete authentication protocols into a unified framework. This provides applications of EAP the freedom to choose whatever concrete instantiation is suitable for their own specific setting. The success of this approach is apparent by the huge and diverse set of real-life deployments using the EAP framework.

Håkon Jacobsen was supported by a STSM Grant from COST Action IC1306.

S. Fehr (Ed.): PKC 2017, Part II, LNCS 10175, pp. 335–365, 2017.
DOI: 10.1007/978-3-662-54388-7_12

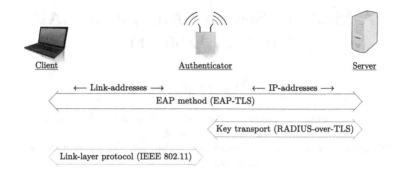

Fig. 1. The three-party EAP architecture. Example protocols shown in parenthesis.

Surprisingly then, given its prevalence and importance, there has been no formal reduction-based provable security analysis of EAP. One reason for this might be due to the general nature of EAP itself. As mentioned above, EAP is not a single protocol on its own, but relies on other sub-protocols to instantiate it. As such, many things in the EAP specification are left unspecified or considered out of scope. However, in order to conduct a formal security analysis of EAP, these details matter and require a careful treatment. Generally, the need to make assumptions on protocols outside of EAP makes analysis harder (see also [15]), because now it is not sufficient to consider a single protocol in isolation, but rather it has to be considered it in tandem with other protocols.

Another reason for the lack of provable security analyses of EAP might be the fact that it is a three-party protocol. As pointed out by Schwenk in his recent work on Kerberos [28], apart from a few papers like [3,5,8,24,28] relatively little work has been done on three-party protocols[1] in the computational setting compared to the huge literature on two-party protocols.

In this paper we aim to remedy this state-of-affairs by providing a formal reductionist analysis of EAP. We then build on our result to obtain a result for the extremely common IEEE 802.11 wireless standard *with* upper-layer authentication. Current results on IEEE 802.11 have so far only focused on the much simpler pre-shared key setting, while we can now provide an analysis of the full protocol. Below we will further expand upon our results, but first we provide a brief description of the EAP architecture and how IEEE 802.11 relates to it.

Review of EAP and IEEE 802.11. The general EAP architecture is shown in Fig. 1. The exchange begins with the client and trusted server authenticating each other using some concrete authentication protocol, like TLS. However, the whole TLS exchange is wrapped within a generic set of EAP messages, known as Request/Response messages. The combination of a concrete authentication protocol together with the EAP encapsulation is called an *EAP method*. Numerous EAP methods have been defined, with EAP-TLS being one of the most

---

[1] Considered distinct from *group-key exchange* protocols.

widely supported. Besides authenticating each other, the EAP-method usually also results in the client and server agreeing upon a shared key. The server will forward this key to the authenticator over some separately established channel. The EAP standard does not specify which protocol to use here, but in practice the de-facto standard is RADIUS [26].[2] Once the key is transported from the server to the authenticator—which so far has only operated in pass-through mode between the client and the server—the EAP exchange is technically complete. However, the client and authenticator now typically use the key distributed by EAP to authenticate each other using some link-layer specific protocol. If the link-layer media is a wireless link provided by the IEEE 802.11 protocol [2], then this entire exchange is usually referred to as "802.11 with upper-layer authentication".

On the Difficulty of Modeling EAP. In this paper we consider the provable security of both EAP and 802.11 with upper-layer authentication in the game-based setting. We do this in a modular way: first considering the security properties provided by EAP and 802.11 in isolation, then using a composition theorem to link them together. However, since EAP inherently depends on other protocols, assessing the exact security guarantees it provides is in a sense harder than for "standalone" protocols like TLS, IKE and SSH. While the EAP specification defines the security requirements of each EAP method [4, Sect. 7], this only covers the communication between the client and the trusted server. Still, as pointed out in the beginning, it is more accurate to think of EAP as a three-party protocol. But RFC 3748 leaves unspecified how, for example, the derived key should be transferred from the server to the authenticator. Hence, solely using the security claims from RFC 3748 is not sufficient to decide the security of EAP considered as a three-party protocol. In fact, without making further assumptions on the various protocols that make up EAP, it is impossible to talk about "the" EAP and its security. Consequently, in order to be able to analyze EAP, we will have to make some assumptions on these protocols.

Firstly, in this paper we are going to assume that the communication between the authenticator and the trusted server takes place over a secure channel. Specifically, we model the link as a two-party authenticated channel establishment protocol (2P-ACCE) based on symmetric long-term pre-shared keys[3] (see Sect. 2.3 for a formal definition). Since most key-transport protocols used between the server and the authenticator support to be run over a secure channel (see e.g. RADIUS-over-TLS [30]), this assumption seems reasonable.

Second, a well-known issue with the EAP architecture is the so-called "lying authenticator problem". Namely, a malicious authenticator may present false

---

[2] Within the EAP standard lingo, the protocol run between the server and authenticator is generally referred to as an *Authentication, Authorization and Accounting (AAA)* protocol.

[3] There is nothing fundamental about our assumption on symmetric PSKs here. We made the choice simply because the trust-relationship between the server and authenticator is commonly based on symmetric PSKs in practice. Our results work just as well for certificate-based authentication.

identity information to the client and the trusted server. Unless the EAP method provides a feature known as *channel binding* [14], there is no way for the client and server to verify that they are in fact talking to the same authenticator (see [14, Sect. 3] for examples of attacks that this may enable). Hence, in this paper we are generally going to assume that EAP provides channel binding, although we will also briefly explore the security guarantees provided by EAP without channel binding in Sect. 4.3. While there are a couple of ways to achieve channel binding in EAP (see [14, Sect. 4.1]), here we are only going to focus on the cryptographically simplest one, described in RFC draft `draft-ohba-eap-channel-binding-02` [25]. In this approach, the client and authenticator identities are being input to the key-derivation step of EAP, cryptographically binding the session key to the right pair of identities (see Sect. 4.2 for details).

Our Contributions. The main contributions of this paper are the following.

- We provide the first reductionist-based provable security result for three-party EAP with channel binding.
- We show how the security guarantees of EAP can be upgraded by adding an additional key-confirmation step (modeled as a 2P-AKE). This corresponds to a common usage pattern where EAP is first used to bootstrap the establishment of a common key among the client and authenticator, then some lower-layer specific 2P-AKE is run between the client and authenticator to mutually prove possession of that key (in addition to establishing session keys for the lower-layer link).
- We provide the first game-based provable security result for the IEEE 802.11 4-way-handshake protocol in the pre-shared key setting. This corresponds to the setting typically found in home WLANs.
- More importantly however, the results above combine to provide the first reductionist-based provable-security result for the full IEEE 802.11 protocol with upper-layer authentication. This corresponds to the setting usually found in enterprise and university WLANs. For instance, the *eduroam* network, which is used to provide wireless roaming services to university and research institutions, uses IEEE 802.11 with upper-layer authentication.
- Our technical means for obtaining the above results are two modular composition theorems which may be of separate interest. Namely, the two theorems consider a fairly generic way of constructing a 3P-AKE protocol, using generic 2P-AKEs and secure channels as building blocks. For instance, both Kerberos and the AKA protocol used within the UMTS and LTE mobile networks, fit the description of our 3P-AKE construction. In particular, for the latter protocol, our theorems might enable a more general and modular analysis than the one recently provided by Alt et al. [5].

Technical Overview of Our Results. The main technical contributions of this paper are two fairly generic composition theorems which correspond to the "cryptographic core" of EAP and IEEE 802.11 with upper-layer authentication, respectively. To obtain these theorems, however, we have to provide an appropriate security model. Our starting point is the original 3P-AKE model of Bellare and Rogaway [8], but which we update to accommodate our needs. Most importantly, EAP and IEEE 802.11—both when considered separately and when combined—can achieve different levels of security. In order to capture these differences we have to define *three* different corruption models of differing strengths. These definitions are based on the eCK model[4] [21], and are primarily concerned with the level of adaptivity afforded to the adversary with respect to corruption queries. Preempting our own results a bit, we show that standalone EAP can achieve a restricted variant of forward secrecy, while IEEE 802.11 *without* upper-layer authentication achieves no forward secrecy (this is natural since it relies on symmetric primitives exclusively). However, when EAP and 802.11 are *combined*, the security is upgraded to achieve forward secrecy in our strongest corruption model. Briefly, the difference between the strongest security model and the intermediate one depends on what happens if the test-session does not have partner. When the test-session does not have a partner in the strongest model, the adversary is still allowed to learn all the long-term keys of the parties involved, as long as this happens after the test-session accepted. On the other hand, if the test-session does not have a partner in the intermediate model, then the adversary is forbidden from learning any of these long-term keys. If the test-session *does* have a partner, then there is no difference between the two models: the adversary is allowed to learn any long-term key at any time. The formal definitions of these models are provided in Sect. 2.2.

Intuitively, the reason why EAP on its own cannot achieve security in our strongest model is because it does not provide explicit entity authentication. Specifically, the client has no guarantee that the key-transport protocol between the server and authenticator actually took place without running some lower-link protocol to confirm. Suppose an adversary could learn the long-term key shared between the server and the authenticator *after* the client accepted, but *before* the key transport took place. Then it could simply impersonate the authenticator towards the server and have it send over the session key it previously established with the client. According to our strongest security model this adversary would be valid (since the exposure of the PSK happened after the client accepted this is allowed), whereas in the intermediate one it would not (since the client session does have a partner, the PSK cannot be exposed at all). Essentially, the purpose of the lower-layer protocol is to provide key-confirmation to the standalone EAP protocol, which ensures that the client will always have a partner before it accepts.

Besides the introduction of the three different corruption models, we only provide a few other changes to the original 3P-AKE model of Bellare and Rogaway [8]. For example, we support both asymmetric and symmetric long-term keys, and dispense with the explicit SendS query to the trusted server (now modeled simply as a regular Send query).

One thing we *do* keep from [8] however, is the concept of *partner functions*. Interestingly, the use of partner functions has seen rather limited adoption when

---

[4] However, we do not consider ephemeral key leakage in this paper.

compared to partnering based on matching conversations [7] or abstract session identifiers (SIDs) [6]. However, when modeling EAP, we are in the peculiar situation that the parties that we need to partner (the client and the authenticator) do not have any messages in common! Naturally, this makes partnering based on matching conversations more difficult, but it also severely limits our choice of SIDs: we are essentially forced to pick their session keys as the SID. While using the session key as the SID is reasonable in many settings (cf. [17]), it does not guarantee *public* partnering (see [11]). This is important for modular composition proofs like our own. While partnering functions have been criticized for being non-intuitive and hard to work with (even by Rogaway himself [27, Sect. 6]), they generalize more naturally to the three-party setting than SIDs. Essentially, this is because partner functions can take global transcript information into consideration rather than only the local views of the two partners. In a companion manuscript [10] we explore partner functions in more detail, showing their soundness as a partnering tool for analyzing key exchange protocols.

After proving the two composition results in Sect. 3 for generic protocols, we show how to apply them to EAP with and without upper-layer authentication in Sects. 4 and 5, respectively.

2   Formal Models

2.1   A Unified Execution Model

Protocol Participants. An AKE protocol is carried out by a set of *parties* $U \in \mathcal{P}$, where U either takes on the role of *initiator*, *responder* or *server*, i.e., $\mathcal{P}$ is partitioned into three disjoint sets $\mathcal{I}$, $\mathcal{R}$ and $\mathcal{S}$, consisting of the initiators, responders and servers, respectively. In this paper we assume that all initiators and servers are in possession of a long-term asymmetric key-pair (sk_U, pk_U), while all responders and servers share a symmetric pre-shared key K. For every party holding a public key, we assume that the other parties have an authenticated copy of it.

Syntax. A *protocol* is a tuple $\Pi = (\mathsf{KG}, \Sigma)$ of probabilistic polynomial-time algorithms, where KG specifies how long-term keys are generated for each party, and Σ specifies how (honest) parties behave. Each party $U \in \mathcal{P}$ can take part in multiple executions of the protocol, both concurrently and subsequently, called a *session*. We use an administrative label π_U^i to refer to the ith session at user U. This will sometimes also be simplified to π. Associated to each session π_U^i, there is a collection of variables that embodies the (local) state of π_U^i during the protocol.

- sk_U, pk_U – the long-term private/public key of party U,
- peers – a list of the identities of the intended communication peers of π_U^i,
- peerPK – a list of the public keys of the parties in π_U^i.peers,
- peerPSK – a list of the long-term PSKs shared between U and π_U^i.peers,
- $\vec{\alpha} = (\alpha_1, \ldots, \alpha_n)$ – a vector of *accept states* $\alpha_i \in \{\mathsf{running}, \mathsf{accepted}, \mathsf{rejected}\}$,
- $k \in \{0,1\}^\lambda \cup \{\bot\}$ – the symmetric session-key derived by π_U^i.

$\mathsf{Exp}_{\Pi,\mathcal{Q},\mathcal{A}}(\lambda)$:
1: **for all** $U \in \mathcal{I} \cup \mathcal{S}$ **do**
2:     $(sk_U, pk_U) \leftarrow_\$ \mathsf{KG}(1^\lambda)$
3: **for all** $(U, V) \in \mathcal{R} \times \mathcal{S}$ **do**
4:     $K_{UV} = K_{VU} \leftarrow_\$ \{0,1\}^\lambda$
5: $\mathsf{pks} \leftarrow \{(U, pk_U) \mid U \in \mathcal{I} \cup \mathcal{S}\}$
6: $out \leftarrow_\$ \mathcal{A}^{\mathcal{Q}}(1^\lambda, \mathsf{pks})$

Fig. 2. Generic security experiment for a three-party protocol where all initiators and servers are in possession of a public key, and all responders and servers share a symmetric PSK.

Only initiators and responders accepts sessions keys, i.e., if $S \in \mathcal{S}$, then we always have $\pi_S^i.k = \bot$. Note that this is pure formalism; we certainly except many protocols in which the trusted server might be in possession of the session key—in fact, the trusted server might be the one that choses and distributes it—we simply do no not associate it with the variable k.

Remark 1. We use a *list* of acceptance states $\vec{\alpha}$ in order to model protocols that are logically built out of sub-protocols. The individual acceptance states α_i provides a convenient way to signal to the adversary that a session has accepted in some intermediate sub-protocol Π_i of the full protocol Π. By convention, we will let α_n represent the running-state of the full protocol, and use $\alpha_F \stackrel{\text{def}}{=} \alpha_n$ to denote this state. Specifically, α_F has the same role as the *single* running-state variable α which is typically used by most other formal protocol models. Saying that π is *running*, or that it has *accepted* or *rejected*, refers to the value of α_F.

We require the following semantics of the variables $\vec{\alpha} = (\alpha_1, \ldots, \alpha_n)$ and k:

$$\alpha_i = \mathsf{accepted} \implies \alpha_{i-1} = \mathsf{accepted}, \tag{1}$$

$$\alpha_i = \mathsf{rejected} \implies \alpha_{i+1} = \mathsf{rejected}, \tag{2}$$

$$\pi.\alpha_n = \mathsf{accepted} \implies \pi.k \neq \bot. \tag{3}$$

By convention, whenever we set $\alpha_i = \mathsf{rejected}$, we also automatically set $\alpha_j = \mathsf{rejected}$ for all $i < j$, in accordance with (2). Moreover, we assume that the session key $\pi.k$ is set only once.

A Unified Security Experiment. To define the security goals of both AKE and ACCE protocols we use the unified experiment shown in Fig. 2. Experiment $\mathsf{Exp}_{\Pi,\mathcal{Q},\mathcal{A}}(\lambda)$ is parameterized on the protocol Π, a *query set* $\mathcal{Q}$, and the adversary $\mathcal{A}$. While the query sets used to define AKE and ACCE security will be different, they will both contain the following "base" query set $\mathcal{Q}_{base}$:

- NewSession$(U, [V, W])$: This query creates a new session π_U^i at party U, optionally specifying its intended communication peers V and W. The state variables are initiated as follows: $\pi_U^i.k = \bot$, $\pi_U^i.\vec{\alpha} = \{\mathsf{running}, \ldots, \mathsf{running}\}$, if V

and/or W are specified as U's peers, then $\pi_U^i.\mathsf{peers} = \{V, W\}$, $\pi_U^i.sk = sk_U$, $\pi_U^i.pk = pk_U$, $\pi.\mathsf{peerPK} = \{pk_V, pk_W\}^5$ and $\pi.\mathsf{peerPSK} = \{K_{UV}, K_{UW}\}$ (See footnote 5). It is required that U, V and W all have different roles. Finally, if $U \in \mathcal{I}$, then π_U^i also produces its first message m according to specification of protocol Π. Both the administrative label π_U^i and m are returned to $\mathcal{A}$.

- Send(π, m): If $\pi.\alpha_F \neq \mathsf{running}$, return $\bot$. Otherwise, π creates a response message m^* according to the specification Σ. This depends on π's role and current internal state. Both m^* and $\pi.\vec{\alpha}$ are returned to $\mathcal{A}$.
- Reveal(π_U^i): If $\pi.\alpha_F \neq \mathsf{accepted}$ or $U \in \mathcal{S}$, return $\bot$. Else, return $\pi_U^i.k$. From this point on π_U^i is said to be *revealed*. Note that π_U^i is *not* considered revealed if the Reveal query was made before π accepted.
- LongTermKeyReveal$(U, [V])$: Depending on the second input parameter, this query returns a certain long-term key of party U.
  - LongTermKeyReveal(U): If U has an associated private-public key-pair (sk_U, pk_U), return the private key sk_U.
  - LongTermKeyReveal(U, V): If U and V share a symmetric long-term key K_{UV}, return K_{UV}.

After a long-term key is leaked we say that it is *exposed* and the corresponding party *corrupted*.

Note that we are working in the post-specified peer model [13], meaning that the identities of a session's peers might not necessarily be known by the session at the onset of the protocol, but are instead learned as the protocol progresses.

Protocol Correctness. It is required that a protocol satisfies the following correctness requirement. In an honest execution of the protocol between an initiator π_A^i, a responder π_B^j and a trusted server π_S^k—meaning that all messages are faithfully transmitted between them according the protocol description—then all sessions end up accepting, and π_A^i and π_B^j both hold the same session key $k \neq \bot$.

Remark 2. Note that experiment $\mathsf{Exp}_{\Pi, \mathcal{Q}, \mathcal{A}}(\lambda)$ does not provide any output and does not define any "winning condition" for $\mathcal{A}$. Instead, it provides a single execution experiment on which we can define many different winning conditions. This is convenient when we later want to define AKE-security and ACCE-security.

Transcripts and Partner Functions. Consider a run of experiment $\mathsf{Exp}_{\Pi, \mathcal{Q}, \mathcal{A}}(\lambda)$, where $\mathcal{Q}_{base} \subseteq \mathcal{Q}$. Let T be the ordered transcript consisting of all the Send and NewSession queries made by $\mathcal{A}$, together with their responses. A transcript T is a *prefix* of T', written $T \subseteq T'$, if the first $|T|$ entries of T' are identical to T. We let $\mathcal{T}$ denote the set of all possible transcripts generated from running experiment $\mathsf{Exp}_{\Pi, \mathcal{Q}, \mathcal{A}}(\lambda)$. To define partnering in our security analysis we use the concept of partner functions as introduced by Bellare and Rogaway [8].

---

^{5} In case V or W does not hold a public key, or if U does not a share a PSK with V or W, then these values are set to $\bot$.

Definition 1 (Partner functions). *A partner function is a polynomial-time function $f\colon \mathcal{T} \times (\mathcal{P} \setminus \mathcal{S}) \times \mathbb{N} \to ((\mathcal{P} \setminus \mathcal{S}) \times \mathbb{N}) \cup \{\bot\}$, subject to the following requirement*

$$f(T,U,i) = (V,j) \implies f(T',U,i) = (V,j) \text{ for all } T \subseteq T'. \qquad (4)$$

Instead of $f(T,U,i) = (V,j)$, we also write $f_T(\pi^i_U) = \pi^j_V$, or even just $f_T(\pi) = \pi'$ if the exact identities of the sessions are irrelevant.

Definition 2 (Partnering). *Let f be a partner function. A session π' is a partner to π if $f_T(\pi) = \pi'$.*

Remark 3. Partnering is only defined between initiators and responders. Servers are not considered partners to any session.

Partnering Soundness. For a security analysis based on partner functions to be meaningful, the partner function needs to satisfy certain soundness properties. Briefly, soundness demands that partners should: (1) end up with the same session key, (2) agree upon who they are talking to, (3) have compatible roles, and (4) be unique. These requirements are essentially the same as those demanded for SIDs through the "Match-security" notion introduced by Brzuska et al. [11].

Definition 3 (Partnering soundness predicate). *Consider a run of experiment $\mathsf{Exp}_{\Pi,\mathcal{Q},\mathcal{A}}(\lambda)$, and let T be the corresponding transcript. Predicate* Sound *is true if and only if the following holds for all $T' \subseteq T$. If sessions π^i_U and π^j_V have both accepted and $f_{T'}(\pi^i_U) = \pi^j_V$, then*

1. $\pi^i_U.k = \pi^j_V.k \neq \bot$,
2. $\pi^i_U.\mathsf{peers} = \{V,W\}$, $\pi^j_V.\mathsf{peers} = \{U,W\}$, and $W \in \mathcal{S}$,
3. $U \in \mathcal{I} \wedge V \in \mathcal{R}$ *or* $U \in \mathcal{R} \wedge V \in \mathcal{I}$,
4. *there is no $\pi' \neq \pi^i_U$ such that $f_{T'}(\pi') = f_{T'}(\pi^i_U)$.*

We let $\mathsf{Exp}^{\mathsf{Sound}}_{\Pi,\mathcal{Q},\mathcal{A}}(\lambda) \Rightarrow 1$ denote the event that predicate Sound evaluated to true.

Remark 4. Note that predicate Sound depends on the partner function f.

Remark 5. The use of partner functions to analyze key exchange protocols is rare in the literature. To the best of our knowledge, besides the original paper by Bellare and Rogaway [8], it has only been used in one other paper by Shoup and Rubin [29].

2.2 2P-AKE and 3P-AKE

Syntax. A *2P/3P-AKE protocol* has the same syntax as the general protocol defined in Sect. 2.1. Moreover, in our framework, there is no syntactical difference between a 2P-AKE protocol and a 3P-AKE protocol. However, in a 2P-AKE protocol there is no trusted server session $S \in \mathcal{S}$, and the session variables $\pi.\mathsf{peers}$, $\pi.\mathsf{peerPK}$ and $\pi.\mathsf{peerPSK}$ contain at most a single entry.

Fresh$_{\mathsf{AKE}^*}(\pi_U^i)$:

1: $\{V, W\} \leftarrow \pi_U^i.\mathsf{peers}$
2: LTKeys $\leftarrow \{sk_V, sk_W, K_{UV}, K_{UW}, K_{VW}\}$
3: if $\pi_U^i.\alpha_F = \mathsf{accepted}$
4:    $\wedge\, \pi_U^i$ and $f_T(\pi_U^i)$ not revealed
5:    $\wedge$ LTKeysLeaked* = false:
6:    return true
7: else
8:    return false

Fresh$_{\mathsf{ACCE}}(\pi_U^i)$:

1: $\{V, W\} \leftarrow \pi_U^i.\mathsf{peers}$
2: LTKeys $\leftarrow \{sk_V, sk_W, K_{UV}, K_{UW}, K_{VW}\}$
3: if $\pi_U^i.\alpha_F = \mathsf{accepted}$
4:    $\wedge\, \pi_U^i$ and $f_T(\pi_U^i)$ not revealed
5:    $\wedge$ LTKeysLeaked = false:
6:    return true
7: else
8:    return false

- LTKeysLeaked = true $\iff f_T(\pi_U^i) = \perp \wedge$ a key in LTKeys were exposed before π_U^i accepted.
- LTKeysLeaked^w = true $\iff f_T(\pi_U^i) = \perp \wedge$ a key in LTKeys is exposed.
- LTKeysLeaked^{static} = true $\iff$ a key in LTKeys is exposed.

Fig. 3. Freshness predicates for security models AKE$^* \in \{\mathrm{AKE}, \mathrm{AKE}^w, \mathrm{AKE}^{\mathsf{static}}\}$ and ACCE. The list LTKeys only contains actually existing long-term keys, e.g., if V is a responder party, then there is no corresponding private key sk_V.

AKE Security. Besides soundness, a secure AKE protocol is supposed to provide secrecy of the distributed session keys. To capture this, the base query set $\mathcal{Q}_{base}$ is extended with the following query.

- Test(π_U^i): If $\pi_U^i.\alpha_F \neq \mathsf{accepted}$ or $U \in \mathcal{S}$, return $\perp$. Otherwise, draw a random bit b, and return π_U^i's session key if $b = 0$, or a random key if $b = 1$. We call π_U^i the *test-session* and the returned key the *challenge-key*. The Test query can only be made once.

Let $\mathcal{Q} = \mathcal{Q}_{base} \cup \{\mathsf{Test}\}$. Experiment $\mathsf{Exp}_{\Pi, \mathcal{Q}, \mathcal{A}}(\lambda)$ stops when $\mathcal{A}$ outputs a bit b'. The goal of the adversary is to correctly guess the secret bit b used to answer the Test query. However, $\mathcal{A}$ is only given "credit" if the chosen test-session was *fresh*. A session is fresh if the adversary did not learn its session by trivial means, for example by revealing it or by impersonating its peers after having obtained their long-term keys etc. Formally, in Fig. 3, we specify three *freshness predicates* Fresh$_{\mathsf{AKE}}$, Fresh$_{\mathsf{AKE}^w}$, and Fresh$_{\mathsf{AKE}^{\mathsf{static}}}$, of various permissiveness with respect to long-term key leakage. Each freshness predicate also give rise to a corresponding security notion AKE, AKE^w and AKE^{static}.

The AKE model is our "partner function analogue" of the standard eCK model (as defined in the updated version [21] of the original paper [22]), with the main difference being that we do not consider leakage of ephemeral values. In particular, the AKE model captures both key-compromise impersonation (KCI) attacks and forward secrecy. KCI attacks are captured since the test-session's own long-term private key can always be exposed by the adversary. Forward secrecy is captured since the adversary can, under certain conditions, learn the long-term keys of the peers of the test-session too. Specifically, the forward secrecy guarantees provided by the AKE model are rather strong: if a session has a partner, then the adversary is allowed to expose *any* long-term key it wants, while if the session does not have a partner, then the adversary must wait until after the session accepted before it can expose the relevant keys. Note that partnering is used to model *passiveness* by the adversary in the test-session. Intuitively, even if the adversary knew all the long-term keys before the test-session started, if the test-session ends up with a partner, then the adversary cannot actually have exploited its knowledge of the keys.

Compared to the AKE model, the AKE^w model is more restrictive with respect to forward secrecy: if the test-session does not have partner, then the adversary is disallowed from exposing any of the relevant long-term keys. The AKE^w model is similar to the two-pass variant of the eCK model (see [21, Definition 3]). As mentioned in the introduction, standalone EAP does not achieve security in the AKE model, but we will show that it *is* secure in the AKE^w model.

Finally, the $\mathsf{AKE}^{\mathsf{static}}$ model targets protocols that do not provide any forward secrecy, hence it disallows the adversary from exposing the long-term keys altogether (of course, the adversary is allowed to expose long-term keys unrelated to the test-session and its peers).

Definition 4 (Key-indistinguishability predicate). *Suppose π was the test-session chosen by $\mathcal{A}$ in a run of experiment $\mathsf{Exp}_{\Pi,\mathcal{Q},\mathcal{A}}(\lambda)$, b was the random bit used in answering the* Test *query, and suppose b' was the final output of $\mathcal{A}$. Define predicate* $\mathsf{AKE}^* \in \{\mathsf{AKE}, \mathsf{AKE}^w, \mathsf{AKE}^{\mathsf{static}}\}$ *as follows:*

$$\mathsf{AKE}^* \stackrel{\text{def}}{=} \begin{cases} b = b', & \text{if } \mathsf{Fresh}^*_{\mathsf{AKE}}(\pi) = \mathtt{true} \\ \mathtt{true} \text{ with probability } 1/2, & \text{if } \mathsf{Fresh}^*_{\mathsf{AKE}}(\pi) = \mathtt{false}. \end{cases} \tag{5}$$

Let $\mathsf{Exp}^{\mathsf{AKE}^*}_{\Pi,\mathcal{Q},\mathcal{A}}(\lambda) \Rightarrow 1$ denote the event that AKE^* evaluated to true.

Definition 5 (AKE security). *A protocol Π is AKE^*-secure, if there exists a partnering function f, such that for all PPT adversaries $\mathcal{A}$,*

- $\mathsf{Adv}^{\mathsf{Sound}}_{\Pi,\mathcal{A},f}(\lambda) \stackrel{\text{def}}{=} 1 - \Pr[\mathsf{Exp}^{\mathsf{Sound}}_{\Pi,\mathcal{Q},\mathcal{A}}(\lambda) \Rightarrow 1]$ *is negligible in security parameter λ, and*
- $\mathsf{Adv}^{\mathsf{AKE}^*}_{\Pi,\mathcal{A},f}(\lambda) \stackrel{\text{def}}{=} |2 \cdot \Pr[\mathsf{Exp}^{\mathsf{AKE}^*}_{\Pi,\mathcal{Q},\mathcal{A}}(\lambda) \Rightarrow 1] - 1|$ *is negligible in security parameter λ,*

where $\mathsf{AKE}^* \in \{\mathsf{AKE}, \mathsf{AKE}^w, \mathsf{AKE}^{\mathsf{static}}\}$.

2.3   (2P)-ACCE

Syntax. A (2P)-ACCE protocol is a two-party protocol as defined in Sect. 2.1, together with an associated *stateful authenticated encryption scheme (stAE)* $\mathsf{stE} = (\mathsf{st.Gen}, \mathsf{stE.Init}, \mathsf{stE.Enc}, \mathsf{stE.Dec})$ (following [20][6]). Intuitively, an ACCE

---

[6] For simplicity, we omit the properties of *length-hiding* and *associated data* in our treatment of ACCE. This omission is immaterial for the results established in this paper.

Encrypt(π, m_0, m_1):	Decrypt(π, C):
1: **if** $\pi.\alpha_F \neq$ accepted $\vee \ |m_0| \neq |m_1|$:	1: **if** $\pi.\alpha_F \neq$ accepted:
2: **return** $\perp$	2: **return** $\perp$
3: $u \leftarrow u + 1$	3: $\pi' \leftarrow f_T(\pi)$
4: $(C^0, st_E^0) \leftarrow$ stE.Enc(k, m_0, st_E)	4: $v \leftarrow v + 1$;
5: $(C^1, st_E^1) \leftarrow$ stE.Enc(k, m_1, st_E)	5: $(m, st_D) \leftarrow$ stE.Dec(k, C, st_D)
6: $(\vec{C}[u], st_E) \leftarrow (C^b, H, st_E^b)$	6: **if** $\pi' = \perp \vee v > \pi'.u \vee C \neq \pi'.\vec{C}[v]$:
7: **return** $\vec{C}[u]$	7: in-sync $\leftarrow$ false
	8: **if** in-sync $=$ false:
	9: **return** m
	10: **return** $\perp$

Fig. 4. The Encrypt and Decrypt queries for the ACCE security experiments. The variables $k, b, st_D, st_D, \vec{C}, u, v$ and in-sync all belong to the internal state of π. At the creation of every session π, a bit b is drawn uniformly at random from $\{0, 1\}$, st_E and st_D and are initialized by stE.Gen, the list $\vec{C}$ is initialized to $\emptyset$, the counters u and v are set to 0, and in-sync is set to **true**.

protocol is an amalgamation of an ordinary 2P-AKE protocol and a secure channel based on symmetric keys, where the session keys of the 2P-AKE protocol are used to key the secure channel.

Correctness of the stAE scheme demands that if the *deterministic* algorithm st.Init produced initial states st_E^0, st_D^0; and the ACCE session key k was used to produce a sequence of ciphertext/state pairs $(C_i, st_E^{i+1}) \leftarrow$ stE.Enc(k, m_i, st_E^i) such that $C_i \neq \perp$ for all $i \geq 0$; then one must have, for all $i \geq 0$, that $m_i' = m_i$ in the sequence of decryptions $(m_i', st_D^{i+1}) \leftarrow$ stE.Dec(k, C_i, st_D^i).

ACCE Security. To define security of an ACCE protocol, we extend the base query set $\mathcal{Q}_{base}$ with two additional queries, Encrypt and Decrypt, that allow the adversary to interact with the channels established in the protocol. The two queries are specified in Fig. 4.

Let $\mathcal{Q} = \mathcal{Q}_{base} \cup \{$Encrypt, Decrypt$\}$. Experiment $\text{Exp}_{\Pi, \mathcal{Q}, \mathcal{A}}(\lambda)$ stops when $\mathcal{A}$ outputs a pair (π, b'), consisting of a session π and a bit b'. The goal of the adversary, formally captured in the following predicate, is to break either the confidentiality or integrity of one of the channels established by a fresh session.

Definition 6 (ACCE predicates). *Consider a run of experiment* $\text{Exp}_{\Pi, \mathcal{Q}, \mathcal{A}}$ (λ), *and let* T *be the corresponding transcript. Suppose* (π, b') *was the final output by* $\mathcal{A}$.

- *Predicate* ACCE-int *is true if and only if, sometime during* $\text{Exp}_{\Pi, \mathcal{Q}, \mathcal{A}}(\lambda)$, $\mathcal{A}$ *made a* Decrypt *query that output something other than* $\perp$ *for a fresh session* π.
- *Predicate* ACCE-priv *is defined as follows:*

$$\text{ACCE-priv} \overset{\text{def}}{=} \begin{cases} \pi.b = b', & \text{if Fresh}(\pi) = \text{true} \\ \text{true with probability } 1/2, & \text{if Fresh}(\pi) = \text{false}. \end{cases} \quad (6)$$

Let $\text{Exp}_{\Pi, \mathcal{Q}, \mathcal{A}}^{\text{ACCE-int}}(\lambda) \Rightarrow 1$ *(resp.* $\text{Exp}_{\Pi, \mathcal{Q}, \mathcal{A}}^{\text{ACCE-priv}}(\lambda) \Rightarrow 1$) *denote the event that* ACCE-int *(resp.* ACCE-priv*) evaluated to true.*

Definition 7 (ACCE security). *A protocol* Π *is* ACCE-secure, *if there exists a partnering function* f, *such that for all PPT adversaries* $\mathcal{A}$, *the following are all negligible in the security parameter* λ,

- $\mathsf{Adv}_{\Pi,\mathcal{A},f}^{\mathsf{Sound}}(\lambda) \stackrel{\text{def}}{=} \Pr[\mathsf{Exp}_{\Pi,\mathcal{Q},\mathcal{A}}^{\mathsf{Sound}}(\lambda) \Rightarrow 1]$,
- $\mathsf{Adv}_{\Pi,\mathcal{A},f}^{\mathsf{ACCE\text{-}int}}(\lambda) \stackrel{\text{def}}{=} \Pr[\mathsf{Exp}_{\Pi,\mathcal{Q},\mathcal{A}}^{\mathsf{ACCE\text{-}int}}(\lambda) \Rightarrow 1]$,
- $\mathsf{Adv}_{\Pi,\mathcal{A},f}^{\mathsf{ACCE\text{-}priv}}(\lambda) \stackrel{\text{def}}{=} |2 \cdot \Pr[\mathsf{Exp}_{\Pi,\mathcal{Q},\mathcal{A}}^{\mathsf{ACCE\text{-}priv}}(\lambda) \Rightarrow 1] - 1|$.

Remark 6. Our definition of ACCE security is slightly different from the standard one introduced by Jager et al. [16]. Specifically, in the standard formulation of ACCE, the Decrypt oracle is *conditional*, meaning that if $\pi.b = 0$, then Decrypt always returns $\perp$ irregardless of whether the supplied ciphertext was a valid forgery or not. This is done in order to encode both the channel privacy and the channel integrity goal as a single distinguishing game. However, this makes proofs relying on ACCE security more cumbersome since the Decrypt query does not actually provide a proper decryption oracle. By casting ACCE channel security as two separate security goals, the Decrypt query becomes a proper decryption oracle. In the full version we prove that our definition of ACCE is equivalent with the standard one.

2.4 Explicit Entity Authentication

Explicit entity authentication is frequently considered one of the required security properties of a protocol. However, in this paper we will only prove/assume it for *some* protocols, because some of the protocols we consider simply cannot achieve it. The need for AKE protocols to provide explicit entity authentication has actually been somewhat disputed in the literature (see e.g. [8, Sect. 1.6], [27, Sect. 6] or [19, Sect. 1.2]). On the other hand, explicit entity authentication has always been part of the requirements of ACCE security [16,18,20]. Since the definition of entity authentication is formulated identically for both AKE and ACCE protocols, we give a merged definition here. Let $\mathcal{Q}_{\mathsf{AKE}}$ denote the query set of the AKE experiment, and let $\mathcal{Q}_{\mathsf{ACCE}}$ denote the query set of the ACCE experiment.

Definition 8 (Entity authentication predicate). *Let* T *be the transcript of experiment* $\mathsf{Exp}_{\Pi,\mathcal{A},\mathcal{Q}_{\mathsf{x}}}(\lambda)$. *Predicate* Auth *is true if and only if the following holds for all* $T' \subseteq T$. *For all fresh sessions* π *in* T':

$$\pi.\alpha = \mathsf{accepted} \implies \exists \pi' \; such that \; f_{T'}(\pi) = \pi'. \tag{7}$$

Let $\mathsf{Exp}_{\Pi,\mathcal{Q}_{\mathsf{x}},\mathcal{A}}^{\mathsf{X\text{-}Auth}}(\lambda) \Rightarrow 1$ *denote the event that* Auth *is true, where* $\mathsf{X} \in \{\mathsf{AKE}, \mathsf{ACCE}\}$.

Definition 9 (Explicit entity authentication). *A protocol* Π *provides* explicit entity authentication *if there exists partner function* f, *such that for all PPT adversaries* $\mathcal{A}$, *it holds that*

1. Π *is* X-*secure, and*

2. $\mathsf{Adv}_{\Pi,\mathcal{A},\mathcal{Q}}^{\mathsf{X\text{-}EA}}(\lambda) \overset{\mathrm{def}}{=} 1 - \Pr[\mathsf{Exp}_{\Pi,\mathcal{A},f}^{\mathsf{X\text{-}Auth}}(\lambda) \Rightarrow 1]$ *is negligible in security parameter* λ,

where $\mathsf{X} \in \{\mathsf{AKE}, \mathsf{AKE}^w, \mathsf{AKE}^{\mathsf{static}}, \mathsf{ACCE}\}$.

Remark 7. Note that the explicit entity authentication of an AKE (resp. ACCE) scheme needs to hold with the *same* partner function as used to prove its AKE (resp. ACCE) security.

3   Generic Composition Results

In this section we prove two composition theorems for two fairly generic constructions of 3P-AKE protocols. The first construction, shown as protocol Π_3 in Fig. 5, resembles the standalone EAP. It uses as building blocks any secure 2P-AKE protocol (in the strongest AKE model), any secure 2P-ACCE protocol, and a pseudorandom function for channel binding. The second construction, shown as protocol Π_5 in Fig. 5, resembles the EAP combined with a subsequent key-confirmation step, modeled here as a 2P-AKE protocol secure in the weakest $\mathsf{AKE}^{\mathsf{static}}$ model. We emphasize that the 3P-AKE protocol used as the underlying building block by protocol Π_5, does not necessarily have to be based on the Π_3 construction. Any 3P-AKE protocol secure according to the AKE^w model works. In Sects. 4 and 5, we will see how these generic constructions can be instantiated with EAP and IEEE 802.11 with upper-layer authentication, respectively.

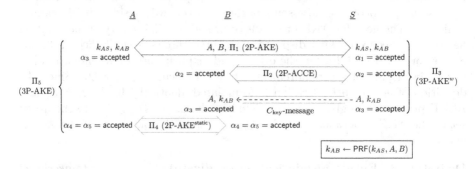

Fig. 5. (Right) Construction of a 3P-AKE^w-secure protocol Π_3, using as building blocks a 2P-AKE-secure protocol Π_1, an ACCE-secure protocol Π_2, and a pseudorandom function PRF. (Left) Construction of a 3P-AKE secure protocol Π_5, using as building blocks a 3P-AKE^w secure protocol Π_3 and a 2P-$\mathsf{AKE}^{\mathsf{static}}$-secure protocol Π_4.

3.1   2P-AKE + 2P-ACCE + Channel Binding $\Longrightarrow$ 3P-AKE^w

Construction. From a 2P-AKE protocol Π_1 (based on public keys), a 2P-ACCE protocol Π_2 (based on pre-shared symmetric keys), and a pseudorandom function PRF, we construct the 3P-AKE protocol Π_3 shown in Fig. 5. Specifically, protocol

Π_3 works as follows. First, sub-protocol Π_1 is run between the initiator A and the trusted server S to derive an intermediate key k_{AS}. A also communicates the identities A and B to S, where B is the identity of responder that A wants to talk to. Note that A knows both S and B at the beginning of the protocol whereas S learns about B from the identities communicated by A. Technically, this means that a session at A needs to be initialized with the identities of S and B (setting the peers variable accordingly), while a session at S will update its peers variable to include B after receiving this identity from A.

From k_{AS}, both A and S derive the key $k_{AB} \leftarrow \mathsf{PRF}(k_{AS}, A, B)$. This key will be the ultimate session key shared between A and B in protocol Π_3. In order for S to transfer k_{AB} to B they establish a secure channel using sub-protocol Π_2. Once established, S sends the session key k_{AB} over the channel to B. Alongside k_{AB}, the server S also sends the identity of A to B (causing the receiving B to update its peers variable). For simplicity, we assume that the transfer of A and k_{AB} is done using a *single* channel message, which we call the C_{key} *message*. Note that the initiator A accepts in protocol Π_3 when it has derived k_{AB}, while the responder B accepts once it has received—and properly decrypted—the C_{key} message, finally obtaining k_{AB}.

Result. Our first composition result shows that protocol Π_3 is 3P-AKE^w-secure if sub-protocol Π_1 is 2P-AKE-secure, sub-protocol Π_2 is 2P-ACCE-secure, and PRF is a pseudorandom function. Note that since Π_3 does not provide explicit entity authentication—in fact, no initiator session A will have a partner at the time it accepts—it cannot achieve security in the strongest AKE model due to the attack mentioned for standalone EAP in the introduction.

Roughly, the proof of the first composition theorem works as follows. The 2P-AKE-security of sub-protocol Π_1 allows us to swap out the intermediate keys k_{AS} with random ones. The PRF-security of the function PRF then allows us to replace the derived session keys k_{AB} with random ones. Finally, the ACCE channel-privacy of sub-protocol Π_2 ensures that the adversary learns nothing about the session keys transfered in the C_{key} messages.

However, in order to make our proof work, we have to make one technical assumption on the partner function of sub-protocol Π_2. Namely, we have to assume that it is *symmetric*, meaning that $f_2(\pi) = \pi'$ implies $f_2(\pi') = \pi$. Note that this requirement is straightforwardly met by partner functions based on SIDs.

Theorem 1. *Let Π_3 be the protocol described in Sect. 3.1. If protocol Π_1 is 2P-AKE-secure, Π_2 is ACCE-secure using a symmetric partner function, and PRF is a secure PRF, then there exists a partner function f_3, such that protocol Π_3 is 3P-AKE^w-secure.*

Concretely, if Π_1 is AKE-secure with the partner function f_1, and Π_2 is ACCE-secure with the symmetric partner function f_2, then we can create a partner function f_3, and adversaries $\mathcal{B}_1, \ldots, \mathcal{B}_4$ and $\mathcal{D}$, such that

$$\mathsf{Adv}^{\mathsf{3P\text{-}AKE}^w}_{\Pi_3, \mathcal{A}, f_3}(\lambda) \leq \mathsf{Adv}^{\mathsf{ACCE\text{-}EA}}_{\Pi_2, \mathcal{B}_1, f_2}(\lambda) + \mathsf{Adv}^{\mathsf{ACCE\text{-}int}}_{\Pi_2, \mathcal{B}_2, f_2}(\lambda)$$
$$+ (n_\pi + 1)^2 \cdot |\mathcal{I} \cup \mathcal{R}|^2 \cdot \left(\mathsf{Adv}^{\mathsf{ACCE\text{-}priv}}_{\Pi_2, \mathcal{B}_3, f_2}(\lambda) + \mathsf{Adv}^{\mathsf{2P\text{-}AKE}}_{\Pi_1, \mathcal{B}_4, f_1}(\lambda) + \mathsf{Adv}^{\mathsf{PRF}}_{\mathsf{PRF}, \mathcal{D}}(\lambda) \right),$$
$$\tag{8}$$

where n_π is an upper bound on the number of sessions at each party.

Proof. We begin by defining the partner function f_3 using the partner functions for sub-protocols Π_1 and Π_2.

Defining the Partner Function for Π_3. Intuitively, f_3 is constructed by "composing" the two partner functions f_1 and f_2 assumed to exist for sub-protocols Π_1 and Π_2. For example, if π_A^i is an initiator session, then $f_3(\pi_A^i) = \pi_B^j$ if there exists a trusted server session π_S^k, such that $f_1(\pi_A^i) = \pi_S^k$ and $f_2(\pi_S^k) = \pi_B^j$. That is, π_B^j is π_A^i's f_3-partner if there exists a server session π_S^k that acts as the connection between them in the two sub-protocols Π_1 and Π_2.[7]

More detailed, when π_A^i is an initiator session having intended peers B (responder) and S (server), then:

- $f_{3,T_3}(\pi_A^i) = \pi_B^j$ if,
    1. $f_{1,T_1}(\pi_A^i) = \pi_S^k$ and $f_{2,T_2}(\pi_S^k) = \pi_B^j$,
    2. $\pi_B^j.\mathsf{peers} = \{A, S\}$,
    3. $\pi_S^k.\mathsf{peers} = \{A, B\}$ (in particular, this means that π_S^k received the same identities that π_A^i sent on the A-S link Fig. 5),
- $f_{3,T_3}(\pi_A^i) = \bot$, otherwise.

When π_B^j is a responder session having intended peers A and S, then f_3 is defined similarly by "reversing" the order of f_1 and f_2:

- $f_{3,T_3}(\pi_B^j) = \pi_A^i$ if,
    1. $f_{2,T_2}(\pi_B^j) = \pi_S^k$ and $f_{1,T_1}(\pi_S^k) = \pi_A^i$;
    2. $\pi_A^i.\mathsf{peers} = \{B, S\}$,
    3. $\pi_S^k.\mathsf{peers} = \{A, B\}$,
- $f_{3,T_3}(\pi_B^j) = \bot$, otherwise.

Soundness. The soundness of f_3 follows from the soundness of f_1 and f_2, the ACCE-security of protocol Π_2 (specifically, its channel integrity), together with the fact that PRF is deterministic. The proof is given in the full version.

AKE^w-Security. The proof of AKE^w-security of protocol Π_3 is structured as a sequence of games. In the following, when we say that a certain game *aborts*, we mean that the challenger stops the execution of the experiment and outputs a random bit on $\mathcal{A}$'s behalf.

---

[7] Technically, to make this formally precise, one needs to extract from the 3P-AKE transcript T two transcripts T_1 and T_2, containing the queries pertaining to the two-party sub-protocols Π_1 and Π_2, respectively, so that running f_1 and f_2 on them is well-defined. The details are provided in the full paper.

Game 0: This is the real 3P-AKE^w security game, hence

$$\mathsf{Adv}^{G_0}_{\Pi_3,\mathcal{A},f_3}(\lambda) = \mathsf{Adv}^{3P\text{-}AKE^w}_{\Pi_3,\mathcal{A},f_3}(\lambda).$$

Game 1: This game proceeds as the previous one, but aborts if a fresh responder or trusted server session *accepts maliciously* in sub-protocol Π_2, meaning that it accepted without a partner in Π_2 according to f_2.

Lemma 1. $\mathsf{Adv}^{G_0}_{\Pi_3,\mathcal{A},f_3}(\lambda) \leq \mathsf{Adv}^{G_1}_{\Pi_3,\mathcal{A},f_3}(\lambda) + \mathsf{Adv}^{ACCE\text{-}EA}_{\Pi_2,\mathcal{B}_1,f_2}(\lambda).$

Proof (Sketch). Reduction $\mathcal{B}_1$ begins by creating all the long-term keys for sub-protocol Π_1 and selecting a random bit b. Essentially, $\mathcal{B}_1$ will simulate the Π_1 part of Π_3 itself, while forwarding all messages pertaining to Π_2 to its 2P-ACCE challenger. In particular, $\mathcal{B}_1$ creates all the intermediate keys k_{AS} itself, and from them derive the session keys k_{AB}. In order to create the C_{key} message of some trusted server session π, $\mathcal{B}_1$ issues an $\mathsf{Encrypt}(\pi, k_{AB}, k_{AB})$ query to its own ACCE experiment. Moreover, when $\mathcal{A}$ issues a Test query, then depending on bit b, $\mathcal{B}_1$ returns the real session key or a random key. When $\mathcal{A}$ terminates, then $\mathcal{B}_1$ terminates too (in this case no malicious accept has occurred).

To analyze $\mathcal{B}_1$'s winning probability, we only have to observe that $\mathcal{B}_1$ provides a perfect simulation of Π_3 for $\mathcal{A}$. This means that if a malicious accept occurs in sub-protocol Π_2, then a malicious accept also occurs in $\mathcal{B}_1$'s ACCE experiment. □

Remark 8. Note that the abort condition in Game 1 does not mean that every session in protocol Π_3 will have a partner (according to f_3). In fact, all the initiator sessions in protocol Π_3 will accept without a partner.

Game 2: This game proceeds as the previous one, but it aborts if a fresh responder session accepts on receiving a C_{key} message that was not legitimately produced by its partner in Π_2.

Lemma 2. $\mathsf{Adv}^{G_1}_{\Pi_3,\mathcal{A},f_3}(\lambda) \leq \mathsf{Adv}^{G_2}_{\Pi_3,\mathcal{A},f_3}(\lambda) + \mathsf{Adv}^{ACCE\text{-}int}_{\Pi_2,\mathcal{B}_2,f_2}(\lambda).$

Proof (Sketch). $\mathcal{B}_2$ works exactly like algorithm $\mathcal{B}_1$ in the previous proof, but it also simulates the abort on malicious accept. This simulation is possible because the partnering function f_2 is based on the *public* transcript T_2. It only remains to argue that the new abort event of Game 2 implies a forgery in $\mathcal{B}_2$'s ACCE experiment. This amounts to showing that if a session in Π_3 is fresh according to Fresh_{AKE^w}, then the corresponding session in Π_2 is fresh according to Fresh_{ACCE}. But this is true because the Fresh_{AKE^w} predicate is more restrictive than the Fresh_{ACCE} predicate. □

Game 3: In this game the challenger tries to guess the test-session chosen by $\mathcal{A}$, together with its eventual partner (if any). If the guess is wrong, or if $\mathcal{A}$ violates the freshness of the guessed test-session, the challenger aborts with a random output. Technically, the challenger proceeds as follows.

For $m \leq n$, let $[m, n] \overset{\text{def}}{=} \{m, m + 1, \ldots n\}$. First, the challenger randomly guesses the test-session $(U, i) \leftarrow\!\$\, (\mathcal{I} \cup \mathcal{R}) \times [1, n_\pi]$, where n_π is an upper bound on the number of sessions at each party. Then, depending on the role of U, the challenger either guess $(V, j) \leftarrow\!\$\, \mathcal{I} \times [0, n_\pi]$ or $(V, j) \leftarrow\!\$\, \mathcal{R} \times [0, n_\pi]$ as the expected partner of (U, i), where a pick of $j = 0$ means that (U, i) is not expected to get any partner session at its peer V. Finally, the challenger aborts by outputting a random bit if either of the following bad event occurs:

(i) (U, i) was not selected as the test-session by $\mathcal{A}$.
(ii) (U, i) was guessed to be without a partner, but gets one.
(iii) (U, i) was guessed to have a partner, but either gets none or someone different from (V, j).
(iv) $\mathcal{A}$ makes a Reveal or Corrupt query that would make (U, i) unfresh.

Lemma 3.

$$\mathsf{Adv}^{G_2}_{\Pi_3, \mathcal{A}, f_3}(\lambda) \leq (n_\pi + 1)^2 \cdot |\mathcal{I} \cup \mathcal{R}|^2 \cdot \mathsf{Adv}^{G_3}_{\Pi_3, \mathcal{A}, f_3}(\lambda). \qquad (9)$$

Proof. The occurrence of the bad events is independent from $\mathcal{A}$'s view up to the moment of where the bad event occurs. When none of the bad events occurs, then $\mathcal{A}$'s success probability is the same in G_2 and G_3, and the challenger guesses the right (pair of) session(s) with probability at least $1/\left((n_\pi + 1) \cdot |\mathcal{I} \cup \mathcal{R}|\right)^2$. And if a bad event occurs, then $\mathcal{A}$ wins G_3 with probability at least $1/2$. $\qquad \square$

In the remaining games, let $\pi^* = \pi^i_U$ denote the guessed test-session, and let $\pi' = \pi^j_V$ denote its expected partner. Define the *co-partner* of π^* to be the trusted server session being involved in the protocol run between π^* and π'. Specifically, if π^* is an initiator, then its co-partner is defined to be $f_{1,T_1}(\pi^*)$; while if π^* is a responder, then its co-partner is defined to be $f_{2,T_2}(\pi^*)$.

Game 4: This game proceeds as the previous one, except that it swaps out the intermediate key k_{AS} derived in sub-protocol Π_1 with a random key for the guessed initiator session (either π^* or π') and its co-partner (if any).

Lemma 4. $\mathsf{Adv}^{G_3}_{\Pi_3, \mathcal{A}, f_3}(\lambda) \leq \mathsf{Adv}^{G_4}_{\Pi_3, \mathcal{A}, f_3}(\lambda) + \mathsf{Adv}^{\text{2P-AKE}}_{\Pi_1, \mathcal{B}_3, f_1}(\lambda).$

Proof (Sketch). Reduction $\mathcal{B}_3$ begins by drawing a random bit b and creates all the long-term PSKs for sub-protocol Π_2. It also guesses the sessions π^* and π' as in Game 3. $\mathcal{B}_3$ then runs $\mathcal{A}$ and forwards all of its queries pertaining to sub-protocol Π_1 to its own AKE experiment, while all queries pertaining to sub-protocol Π_2 reduction $\mathcal{B}_3$ answers itself using the PSKs it created. It also implements all the abort conditions of the previous games. To answer $\mathcal{A}$'s Test(π^*) query, $\mathcal{B}_3$ does the following. If $b = 1$ then it responds with a random key as normal. If $b = 0$ and π^* is an initiator session, then $\mathcal{B}_3$ forwards $\mathcal{A}$'s Test(π^*) query to its own AKE game to obtain π^*'s intermediate key k_{AS} in sub-protocol Π_1. $\mathcal{B}_3$ then uses k_{AS} to derive the session key k_{AB} which it returns to $\mathcal{A}$. If $b = 0$ and π^* is a responder session, then by our abort conditions, π^* must have a co-partner π_S^k by Game 1. To obtain the intermediate key k_{AS} needed to derive k_{AB}, $\mathcal{B}_3$ queries $\mathsf{Test}(\pi_S^k)$ to its own AKE experiment and returns k_{AB} to $\mathcal{A}$. When $\mathcal{A}$ outputs its guess b', then $\mathcal{B}_3$ stops and outputs 0 if $b = b'$, and 1 otherwise.

Note that if the test-query in $\mathcal{B}_3$'s own AKE experiment returns real keys k_{AS}, then $\mathcal{B}_4$ perfectly simulates Game 3, while if it returns random keys then $\mathcal{B}_3$ simulates Game 4. However, we still need to argue that the test-session chosen in $\mathcal{B}_3$'s experiment is fresh. If π^* is an initiator session then $\mathcal{B}_3$ also uses π^* as the test-session in its own AKE experiment, hence it is fresh since the predicate $\mathsf{Fresh}_{\mathsf{AKE}^w}$ is more restrictive than $\mathsf{Fresh}_{\mathsf{AKE}}$. If π^* is a responder session, then the test-session chosen by $\mathcal{B}_3$ is π^*'s co-partner π_S^k, so we need to argue that π_S^k is fresh in $\mathcal{B}_3$'s AKE experiment. There are two cases to consider: either π^* has an f_3-partner or it does not. If π^* does have a partner (which by Game 3 must be π'), then $\mathcal{A}$ cannot have made any $\mathsf{Reveal}(\pi')$ queries since this would violate the AKE^w-freshness of π^*. Moreover, since f_3 is constructed from f_1 and f_2, π' must be π_S^k's f_1-partner. Thus, $\mathcal{B}_3$ is also allowed to forward any $\mathsf{Corrupt}$ query to either A or S without violating the freshness of π_S^k according to $\mathsf{Fresh}_{\mathsf{AKE}}$. If π^* does not have an f_3-partner, then $\mathcal{A}$ cannot have made any $\mathsf{Corrupt}$ query to A or S (since this would violate AKE^w-freshness), and thus neither has $\mathcal{B}_3$. Moreover, if π^* does not have an f_3-partner then in particular its co-partner π_S^k cannot have an f_1-partner. Thus, $\mathcal{B}_3$ can safely forward all of $\mathcal{A}$'s Reveal queries without violating the AKE-freshness of π_S^k. □

Game 5: This game proceeds as the previous one, except that when deriving the session key k_{AB} for the guessed initiator session (either π^* or π') and its co-partner (if it exists), the challenger uses a random function $\$(\cdot, \cdot)$ rather than $\mathsf{PRF}(k_{AS}, \cdot, \cdot)$.

Lemma 5. $\mathsf{Adv}_{\Pi_3, \mathcal{A}, f_3}^{G4}(\lambda) \leq \mathsf{Adv}_{\Pi_3, \mathcal{A}, f_3}^{G5}(\lambda) + \mathsf{Adv}_{\mathsf{PRF}}^{\mathsf{PRF}}(\mathcal{D})$.

Proof Algorithm $\mathcal{D}$ has access to an oracle $\mathcal{O}$ which either implements the function $\mathsf{PRF}(\tilde{k}, \cdot, \cdot)$ with an independent and uniformly distributed key $\tilde{k}$, or a random function $\$(\cdot, \cdot)$. $\mathcal{D}$ begins by drawing a random bit b and creates all the long-term keys for sub-protocols Π_1 and Π_2. Next, it runs $\mathcal{A}$ and answers all its queries according to Game 4 by using the keys it created, except that it answers $\mathcal{A}$'s $\mathsf{Test}(\pi^*)$ query as follows. If $b = 1$, then $\mathcal{D}$ returns a random key. If $b = 1$, then $\mathcal{D}$ answers as follows. If π^* is an initiator session, then $\mathcal{D}$ answers with $\mathcal{O}(U, V)$ (recall that $\pi^* = \pi_U^i$ and $\pi' = \pi_V^j$). If π^* is a responder session, then $\mathcal{D}$ answers with $\mathcal{O}(V', U')$, where V' and U' were the identities that the co-partner of π^* received over the initiator-server link in Fig. 5 (recall that if π^* is a responder session it is guaranteed to have a co-partner by Game 1). When $\mathcal{A}$ outputs its guess b', then $\mathcal{D}$ stops and outputs 0 if $b = b'$, and 1 otherwise.

When $\mathcal{D}$'s oracle $\mathcal{O}$ implements PRF, then $\mathcal{D}$ perfectly simulates Game 4, while if $\mathcal{O}$ implements a random function $\$(\cdot, \cdot)$, then $\mathcal{D}$ perfectly simulates Game 5. Thus, the advantage difference of $\mathcal{A}$ winning in Game 4 and Game 5 corresponds exactly to the probability difference that $\mathcal{D}$ outputs 1 when interacting with PRF or a random function $\$(\cdot, \cdot)$ as its oracle $\mathcal{O}$. □

Note that by the change in Game 5, the session key of π^* and π' is derived using a random function rather then the pseudorandom function PRF. In the following, let $\widetilde{k_{AB}}$ denote the session key derived in this manner at the co-partner of π^* (if it exists).

Game 6: This game proceeds as the previous one, but when creating the C_{key} message of the co-partner of π^*, the challenger encrypts the "dummy" string 0^λ instead of the session key $\widetilde{k_{AB}}$. If this C_{key} message is eventually delivered to the intended responder session (either π^* or π'), then its session key is still set to $\widetilde{k_{AB}}$ however.

Lemma 6 $\mathsf{Adv}^{\mathsf{G_5}}_{\Pi_3,\mathcal{A},f_3}(\lambda) \leq \mathsf{Adv}^{\mathsf{G_6}}_{\Pi_3,\mathcal{A},f_3}(\lambda) + \mathsf{Adv}^{\mathsf{ACCE\text{-}priv}}_{\Pi_2,\mathcal{B}_4,f_2}(\lambda).$

Proof (Sketch). Reduction $\mathcal{B}_4$ begins by drawing a random bit b and creates all the long-term keys for sub-protocol Π_1. It also guesses the sessions π^* and π' as in Game 3, and implements all of the abort conditions introduced so far. All of $\mathcal{A}$'s queries pertaining to sub-protocol Π_1 $\mathcal{B}_4$ answers itself using the long-term keys it created, while queries pertaining to sub-protocol Π_2 $\mathcal{B}_4$ forwards to its own ACCE experiment. In particular, $\mathcal{B}_4$ creates the C_{key} message of a server session π_S^k as follows.

If π_S^k is not the co-partner of the test-session π^*, then $\mathcal{B}_4$ makes the query $\mathsf{Encrypt}(\pi_S^k, A\|k_{AB}, A\|k_{AB})$ to its ACCE experiment, where "A" is the identity of the initiator that π received on the A-S link in Fig. 5, and k_{AB} is the session key $\mathcal{B}_4$ derived from π's intermediate key k_{AS} in sub-protocol Π_1. The returned ciphertext is used as the C_{key} message of π_S^k. If π *is* the co-partner of π^*, then $\mathcal{B}_4$ instead makes the query $\mathsf{Encrypt}(\pi_S^k, A\|k_{AB}, A\|0^\lambda)$ to create C_{key}.

Finally, when $\mathcal{A}$ outputs its guess b', then $\mathcal{B}_4$ outputs the following to its ACCE experiment. If the test-session π^* has a co-partner π_S^k, then $\mathcal{B}_4$ outputs $(\pi_S^k, 0)$ if $b = b'$ and $(\pi_S^k, 1)$ otherwise. If the test-session does not have a co-partner, then $\mathcal{B}_4$ simply outputs an arbitrary session together with a random bit.

Note that if the test-session does not have a co-partner then there is no difference between Game 5 and Game 6, and $\mathcal{B}_4$ perfectly simulates it. If the test-session has a co-partner π_S^k, and $\pi_S^k.b = 0$ in $\mathcal{B}_4$'s ACCE experiment, then $\mathcal{B}_4$ perfectly simulates Game 5 (since the C_{key} message of π_S^k is an encryption of the actual session key k_{AB}). On the other hand, if $\pi_S^k.b = 1$ then $\mathcal{B}_4$ perfectly simulates Game 6 (since the C_{key} message of π_S^k is an encryption of 0^λ). What remains to show that π_S^k is fresh in $\mathcal{B}_4$'s ACCE experiment, i.e., that π_S^k is fresh according to predicate $\mathsf{Fresh}_{\mathsf{ACCE}}$.

Suppose first that the test-session π^* is a responder. This is where we will use the assumption that the partner function f_2 for sub-protocol Π_2 is symmetric. By Game 1 π^* has a co-partner $f_2(\pi^*) = \pi_S^k$, and by the symmetry of f_2 we also have $f_2(\pi_S^k) = \pi^*$. It follows that π_S^k is fresh according to $\mathsf{Fresh}_{\mathsf{ACCE}}$ (note that since $\mathcal{B}_4$ makes no Reveal query to π_S^k in its ACCE experiment, we only have to consider the exposure of its PSK).

Now suppose the test-session is an initiator. There are two cases to consider: either π^* has an f_3-partner or it does not have an f_3-partner. If π^* has an f_3-partner π', then by the construction of f_3 from f_1 and f_2, we have in particular that $f_2(\pi_S^k) = \pi'$. Again, this implies that π_S^k is fresh according to $\mathsf{Fresh_{ACCE}}$. Conversely, if π^* does not have an f_3-partner, then none of the long-term keys and PSKs of its peers can be exposed if π^* is to be fresh according to $\mathsf{Fresh_{AKE^w}}$. In particular, this means that the long-term PSK of π_S^k must be unexposed. Thus, π_S^k is fresh according to $\mathsf{Fresh_{ACCE}}$ (this is regardless of whether it has an f_2-partner or not).   □

Concluding the Proof of Theorem 1. We argue that $\mathsf{Adv}_{\Pi_3, \mathcal{A}, f_3}^{G_6}(\lambda) = 0$. By the change in Game 5, the session key of the test-session π^* is derived using a random function $\$(A, B)$, where "$A$" and "$B$" are the identities of the initiator and responder that π^* believes took part in this protocol run. We claim that the only other session that holds a session key derived from $\$(\cdot, \cdot)$ using the same identities "A" and "B", is π^*'s partner π' (if it exists).

First, note that the random function is evaluated for at most two sessions: one initiator session and one server session. Second, the session key derived by the server session is delivered to at most one responder session. Finally, the identities used to evaluate $\$(\cdot, \cdot)$ at the initiator and server might be different since the adversary can modify the communicated identities at the A-S link in Fig. 5.

However, if the adversary modifies these identities, then the initiator and server derive independent keys, which ultimately means that the initiator and responder will have independent keys too. Moreover, the initiator and responder sessions will not be partners since the communicated identities at the S-B link in Fig. 5 will be different too (recall that f_3-partnering includes the sessions' recorded peers, and by Game 2 the adversary is unable to change the C_{key} message). On the other hand, if the identities were the same, then the initiator and responder session would necessarily be f_3-partners. This follows because the initiator has the server session as its co-partner (in sub-protocol Π_1), and the server session's C_{key} message is only delivered to *its* co-partner (in sub-protocol Π_2). Combined with their agreement on their peers, this means that they would be partners by the definition of f_3.

Altogether, since the session key of the test-session is derived using an independent random function, and since the corresponding C_{key} message leaks nothing about the session key by Game 6, the adversary has zero advantage in Game 6 as claimed. Combining all the lemmas yields the theorem.   □

Note that the conclusion above only holds because of the channel binding. In particular, if the identities of A and B did not go into to the evaluation of the pseudorandom function PRF, then Π_3 would be vulnerable to a simple UKS attack: just change the responder identity sent over the (unauthenticated) A-S link from B to B'. Without channel binding, A and B' obtain the same session key but disagree on their intended peers.

3.2 3P-AKE^w + 2P-AKE $\implies$ 3P-AKE

Construction. From a 3P-AKE protocol Π_3 and a 2P-AKE protocol Π_4, we construct the 3P-AKE protocol Π_5 shown in Fig. 5. Specifically, protocol Π_5 works as follows. First, sub-protocol Π_3 is run between A, B and S in order to establish an intermediate "session key" K_{Π_3}. Then, sub-protocol Π_4 is run between A and B using K_{Π_3} as the their shared "long-term key". The session key derived in Π_4 becomes A and B's final session key in Π_5.

Result. Our second composition result shows that protocol Π_5 is 3P-AKE-secure if sub-protocol Π_3 is 3P-AKE^w-secure and sub-protocol Π_4 is 2P-AKE^{static}-secure with explicit entity authentication. We remark that the last requirement is necessary in order for our proof to go through. In fact, Π_5 inherits the property of explicit entity authentication from sub-protocol Π_4. On the other hand, while Π_4 does not achieve forward secrecy on its own, protocol Π_5 does. The reason is that within Π_5, sub-protocol Π_4 is merely used to upgrade the security of Π_3, which does provide forward secrecy (albeit limited).

Theorem 2 *Let Π_5 be the protocol described in Sect. 3.2. If protocol Π_3 is 3P-AKE^w-secure and protocol Π_4 is 2P-AKE ^{static}-secure with explicit entity authentication, then there exists a partner function f_5 such that protocol Π_5 is 3P-AKE-secure.*

Concretely, for partner functions f_3 and f_4, we can create a partner function f_5, and adversaries $\mathcal{B}_1$, $\mathcal{B}_2$ and $\mathcal{B}_3$, such that

$$
\mathsf{Adv}^{\mathsf{3P\text{-}AKE}}_{\Pi_5,\mathcal{A},f_5}(\lambda) \leq (n_\pi + 1)^2 \cdot |\mathcal{I} \cup \mathcal{R}|^2 \cdot \left(2 \cdot \mathsf{Adv}^{\mathsf{3P\text{-}AKE}^w}_{\Pi_3,\mathcal{B}_1,f_3}(\lambda) + \mathsf{Adv}^{\mathsf{2P\text{-}AKE}^{static}}_{\Pi_4,\mathcal{B}_2,f_4}(\lambda) \right)
$$
$$
+ (n_\pi + 1)^2 \cdot |\mathcal{I} \cup \mathcal{R}|^2 \cdot \mathsf{Adv}^{\mathsf{2P\text{-}AKE}^{static}\text{-}EA}_{\Pi_4,\mathcal{B}_3,f_4}(\lambda)
$$

(10)

where n_π is an upper bound on the number of sessions at each party.

The proof of Theorem 2 is very similar to that of Theorem 1 and is provided in the full version.

4   Security of EAP

4.1   EAP with Channel Binding

In this section we explore the security guarantees provided by EAP. As mentioned in the introduction, there is no single definitive version of EAP which we can use for this purpose, because the specification itself (RFC 3748 [4]) leaves many of its components undefined. Thus, any analysis of EAP will have to make assumptions on these components.

In Theorem 1, let us identify sub-protocol Π_1 with the EAP method run between the client and the trusted server. Let sub-protocol Π_2 be the key-transport protocol run between the server and the authenticator. Finally, suppose that EAP employs the channel binding mechanism defined in [25]. Then we immediately get the following result for EAP.

Theorem 3 (3P-AKE^w security of EAP). *If the chosen EAP method used within EAP is 2P-AKE-secure, the key-transport protocol is 2P-ACCE-secure, and the employed key derivation function is a secure PRF that provides channel binding on the client's and authenticator's identities, then EAP is 3P-AKE^w-secure.*

To be even more concrete, we can also instantiate sub-protocols Π_1 and Π_2 with some actual protocols. For example, Brzuska et al. [12] recently showed that the EAP-TLS method constitutes a secure 2P-AKE protocol, thus satisfying the requirements on sub-protocol Π_1. For sub-protocol Π_2 we take RADIUS-over-TLS [30], which then reduces to the security of TLS. Multiple papers [9,16,18, 20,23] have shown TLS to be a secure 2P-ACCE protocol. Hence, RADIUS-over-TLS fulfills the requirement on sub-protocol Π_2.

4.2 Channel-Binding Scope

In Theorems 1, and 3, we assumed that the channel binding mechanism included the identity of the client and the authenticator in order to bind the identities cryptographically to the session key. Implicitly, this also assumes that all identities are globally unique and belong to the same namespace. This is a standard assumption when doing cryptographic modeling. However, in reality, the various links in EAP take place over different types of communication media with different types of identities and addressing schemes. For instance, in IEEE 802.11 with upper-layer authentication, the communication between the client and the access point is based on link-layer addresses, the communication between the client and the server is typically based on usernames (client) and domain names (server), while the communication between the server and the access point might be based solely on IP addresses. Mapping between these identifiers is not always straightforward (see [15]). In fact, some of the identifiers might not even be available to all the protocol participants. Specifically, since the communication between the client and the access point happens at the link-layer, the IP addresses used by the access point towards the server might not be available to the client unless the access point broadcasts it. In practice, most link-layer protocols have facilities for providing this kind of information to the client[8], but there is no guarantee that the authenticator will actually provide it.

Moreover, in some settings this information may not even be relevant. For example, in a WLAN supported by many access points, the client might not care about *which* specific access point it connects to, as long as it connects to a legitimate access point of that WLAN. Thus, in this case the granularity of the channel-binding should not be at the individual access point level, but rather at the WLAN level, defined by all the access points broadcasting the same network identifier (SSID). However, in this case the security guarantees provided by the channel-binding will be weaker. Specifically, when channel-binding occurs at the individual level, then the corruption of a single access point will not influence clients connecting to access points having a *different* identity. On the other hand, when channel-binding occurs at the network level, then a single corrupted access point will affect *all* connections within that network. In this case, the channel binding only protects connections occurring in networks having a different SSID.

---

[8] For instance, the Identity type field in EAP Request messages are often "piggy-backed" by layer 2 protocols (like EAPOL/802.1X [1]) to include this information.

More generally, the information included in the channel-binding defines the scope of the protection it provides, and can include more than just identities. For instance, physical media types, data rates, cost-information, channel frequencies, etc., can all be used as input to the channel-binding. The specifications for channel-binding within EAP [14, 25] leaves open exactly the kind of information that should go into the binding, because the amount of information that will be available to both the client and the server can vary.

4.3   EAP Without Channel Binding

Without channel binding, it suffices to compromise a single access point in order to compromise an entire network. As access points are typically not highly protected devices, this is a substantial attack vector on enterprise networks. Even if the channel binding only included the network name, it would clearly be an upgrade over EAP without channel binding, and comes at essentially no cost. The situation in the AKA protocol used in the UMTS and LTE mobile networks is similar. The AKA protocol is similarly structured as the EAP protocol[9], where a mobile client that wants to connect to a base station first has to authenticate to its home operator. So-called *authentication vectors*, which in particular includes a session key, are then forwarded from the operator to the base station in much the same way as the server forwards the session key to the authenticator in EAP. Moreover, similar to many EAP methods, the AKA protocol too lacks channel-binding for its authentication vectors. In their recent analysis of the AKA protocol, Alt et al. [5] noted (Sect. 5) this lack of channel-binding, and suggested a fix identical to the key-derivation approach analyzed in this paper.

5   Security of IEEE 802.11

5.1   Description of the IEEE 802.11 Protocol

IEEE 802.11 [2] is the most widely used standard for creating WLANs. It supports three modes of operation depending on the network topology: infrastructure mode, ad-hoc mode, and mesh network mode. In ad-hoc mode and mesh-networking mode there is no central infrastructure, and the wireless *clients* talk directly to each other. On the other hand, in infrastructure mode the clients only communicate through an *access point (AP)*, which provides connectivity to a larger WAN. In this paper we only cover IEEE 802.11 in infrastructure mode, which is by far the most common mode.

The IEEE 802.11 protocol is a layer 2 protocol, aiming to secure the wireless link between the client and the AP. It defines two main security protocols: the *4-Way-Handshake (4WHS)*, used to authenticate and establish session keys between the client and the AP; and the *Counter Mode CBC-MAC protocol (CCMP)*, used to secure the actual application data. We will only cover the 4WHS in this paper.

---

[9] In fact, EAP is widely used within mobile networks.

The 4WHS is based on a symmetric *Pairwise Master Key* (PMK), shared between the client and the AP. The analysis of IEEE 802.11 will therefore crucially depend on how this PMK is obtained. In Sect. 5.2 we will analyze the 4WHS when the PMK is simply taken for granted, i.e., the PMK is a pre-shared key. This is already quite significant on its own because it corresponds to the setting found in virtually every wireless home-network. Still, in most enterprise and university environments, the PMK is not a pre-shared key, but is rather distributed to the client and AP through some upper-level authentication mechanism involving a mutually trusted server. While technically outside the scope of the IEEE 802.11 standard, the de-facto protocol for this is EAP. The analysis of IEEE 802.11 with upper-level authentication is the topic of Sect. 5.3.

5.2 Analyzing the 4-Way-Handshake

The 4WHS is shown in Fig. 6. It depends on a pseudorandom function PRF and a MAC scheme $\Sigma = (\mathsf{kg}, \mathsf{MAC}, \mathsf{Vrfy})$. Identities are based on the parties' 48-bit link-layer addresses. This makes it possible to compare the parties' identities based on their corresponding numerical values. Particularly, the functions $\max\{A, B\}$ and $\min\{A, B\}$ returns, respectively, the largest and the smallest of two link-layer addresses A and B. We use the notation $[x]_k \overset{\text{def}}{=} x \| \sigma$ to denote a message x together with its MAC tag σ, computed with $\Sigma.\mathsf{MAC}$ and key k.

The 4WHS begins with the AP sending the message $m_1 = \eta_{AP} \| p_1$ to the client C, where η_{AP} is a nonce and p_1 is some auxiliary information included in the IEEE 802.11 packet.

On receiving m_1, C generates its own nonce η_C and derives a key PTK $= k_\mu \| k_\alpha \leftarrow \mathsf{PRF}_K(P \| \eta)$ using the pseudorandom function PRF and the long-term key it shares with AP. Here $P \| \eta = \min\{AP, C\} \| \max\{AP, C\} \| \min\{\eta_{AP}, \eta_C\} \| \max\{\eta_{AP}, \eta_C\}$. The sub-key k_α will be the session key output by the 4WHS, while k_μ will be used by the MAC scheme Σ to protect the handshake messages. After deriving PTK, C creates and sends the next protocol message $m_2 = [\eta_C \| p_2]_{k_\mu}$.

On receiving $m_2 = [\eta_C \| p_2]_{k_\mu}$, AP uses the containing nonce η_C to derive the keys PTK $= k_\mu \| k_\alpha \leftarrow \mathsf{PRF}_K(P \| \eta)$. Using k_μ as the key, it verifies the integrity of m_2 with the MAC scheme $\Sigma.\mathsf{Vrfy}$. If the verification goes through, AP creates and send the third protocol message $m_3 = [\eta_{AP} \| p_3]_{k_\mu}$.

On receiving m_3, C first verifies it using the MAC key k_μ. If the check goes through, it sends out the final handshake message $m_4 = [p_4]_{k_\mu}$. Additionally, it sets its own acceptance state to $\alpha = \mathsf{accepted}$. Once AP receives and verifies m_4, it sets its acceptance status to $\alpha = \mathsf{accepted}$ too.

Remark 9. The fourth handshake message m_4 serves no cryptographic purpose and could safely have been omitted. However, to stay true to the actual 4WHS, we leave it in.

In the following analysis, let $\mathcal{P}_{AP} = \mathcal{I}$ and $\mathcal{P}_C = \mathcal{R}$, i.e., in the 4WHS protocol APs are the initiators and the clients are the responders.

$$\underline{C} \hspace{8cm} \underline{AP}$$

$$
\begin{array}{ccc}
& m_1 = (\eta_{AP}, p_1) & \eta_{AP} \leftarrow \{0,1\}^\lambda \\
\eta_C \leftarrow \{0,1\}^\lambda & \xleftarrow{\hspace{2cm}} & \\
k_\mu \| k_\alpha \leftarrow \mathsf{PRF}_K(P\|\eta) & \xrightarrow{\hspace{1cm} m_2 = [\eta_C, p_2]_{k_\mu} \hspace{1cm}} & \left\{ \begin{array}{l} k_\mu \| k_\alpha \leftarrow \mathsf{PRF}_K(P\|\eta) \\ \text{if } \Sigma.\mathsf{Vrfy}(k_\mu, m_2) = 1: \\ \hspace{0.5cm} \text{continue} \end{array} \right. \\
\text{if } \Sigma.\mathsf{Vrfy}(k_\mu, m_3) = 1: & \xleftarrow{\hspace{1cm} m_3 = [\eta_{AP}, p_3]_{k_\mu} \hspace{1cm}} & \\
\hspace{0.5cm} \alpha = \text{accept} & & \\
& \xrightarrow{\hspace{1cm} m_4 = [p_4]_{k_\mu} \hspace{1cm}} & \alpha = \text{accepted}
\end{array}
$$

Fig. 6. The IEEE 802.11 4-Way-Handshake protocol. The client C and the access point AP share a symmetric key PMK $= K$, $P\|\eta = \min\{AP, C\}\| \max\{AP, C\}\| \min\{\eta_{AP}, \eta_C\}\| \max\{\eta_{AP}, \eta_C\}$, and $\Sigma = (\mathsf{kg}, \mathsf{MAC}, \mathsf{Vrfy})$ is MAC scheme.

Theorem 4. *The 4WHS protocol is AKE* ^{static}*-secure. In particular, for any PPT adversary $\mathcal{A}$, there exists a partner function f and algorithm $\mathcal{D}$, such that*

$$\mathsf{Adv}^{\text{2P-AKE}^{\text{static}}}_{\text{4WHS}, \mathcal{A}, f}(\lambda) \leq |\mathcal{P}_C| \cdot |\mathcal{P}_{AP}| \cdot \mathsf{Adv}^{\text{prf}}_{\mathsf{PRF}}(\mathcal{D}) + \frac{(n_P n_\pi)^2}{2^{\lambda+1}}, \tag{11}$$

where n_π is the number of sessions at each party, and $n_P = |\mathcal{P}_C| + |\mathcal{P}_{AP}|$.

For this protocol it is natural to use SIDs as our partnering mechanism. However, because our paper is phrased in terms of partnering functions, we "synthetically" encode the SID as a partnering function by saying that the partner session is the *first* other session that gets the same SID $P\|\eta$. Taking the *first* one is important because a partner function is a function and not a relation.

Proof. Suppose $P\|\eta = \min\{U, V\}\| \max\{U, V\}\| \min\{\eta_U, \eta_V\}\| \max\{\eta_U, \eta_V\}$ was the string that π^i_U input to its pseudorandom function PRF. Then $f_T(\pi^i_U)$ is defined to be the *first* session at V that input the same string $P\|\eta$ to its PRF. Note that this can be computed based on publicly available transcript information.

Soundness. The soundness of f is immediate from its definition and PRF being deterministic.

AKE ^{static}*-Security.*

Game 0: This is the real 2P-AKE security game, hence

$$\mathsf{Adv}^{G_0}_{\text{4WHS}, \mathcal{A}, f}(\lambda) = \mathsf{Adv}^{\text{2P-AKE}^{\text{static}}}_{\text{4WHS}, \mathcal{A}, f}(\lambda).$$

Game 1: This game proceeds as the previous one, but aborts if not all the nonces in the game are distinct, hence

$$\mathsf{Adv}^{G_0}_{\text{4WHS}, \mathcal{A}, f}(\lambda) \leq \mathsf{Adv}^{G_1}_{\text{4WHS}, \mathcal{A}, f}(\lambda) + \frac{(n_P n_\pi)^2}{2^{\lambda+1}}. \tag{12}$$

Game 2: In this game the challenger guesses the pre-shared key that will be used by the test-session and aborts if that guess was wrong, hence

$$\mathsf{Adv}^{G_1}_{4\mathsf{WHS},\mathcal{A},f}(\lambda) \leq |\mathcal{P}_{AP}| \cdot |\mathcal{P}_C| \cdot \mathsf{Adv}^{G_2}_{4\mathsf{WHS},\mathcal{A},f}(\lambda). \tag{13}$$

Let PMK^* denote the guessed pre-shared key. Note that by the $\mathsf{Fresh}_{\mathsf{AKE}^{\mathsf{static}}}$ requirement (Fig. 3), PMK^* cannot be exposed.

Game 3: In this game the challenger replaces the pseudorandom function PRF with a random function $\$(\cdot)$ in all evaluations using the guessed pre-shared key PMK^*. That is, calls of the form $\mathsf{PRF}(\mathrm{PMK}^*, \cdot)$ are instead answered by $\$(\cdot)$.

Lemma 7. $\mathsf{Adv}^{G_2}_{4\mathsf{WHS},\mathcal{A},f}(\lambda) \leq \mathsf{Adv}^{G_3}_{4\mathsf{WHS},\mathcal{A},f}(\lambda) + \mathsf{Adv}^{\mathsf{prf}}_{\mathsf{PRF},\mathcal{D}}(\lambda).$

Proof. Algorithm $\mathcal{D}$ has access to an oracle $\mathcal{O}$, which either implements the function $\Pi.\mathsf{PRF}(\widetilde{\mathrm{PMK}}, \cdot)$ for some independently and uniformly distributed key $\widetilde{\mathrm{PMK}}$, or it implements a truly random function $\$(\cdot)$. $\mathcal{D}$ begins by choosing a random bit b and guessing a client-AP pair (C, AP). All computations that would normally involve the pre-shared key of C and AP, algorithm $\mathcal{D}$ will instead forward to its oracle $\mathcal{O}$. For all other client-AP pairs, $\mathcal{D}$ creates their the pre-shared keys itself, allowing it to simulate them perfectly. If $\mathcal{A}$ outputs b', then $\mathcal{D}$ outputs 1 if $b = b'$, and 0 otherwise.

When $\mathcal{O} = \Pi.\mathsf{PRF}(\widetilde{\mathrm{PMK}}, \cdot)$, then $\mathcal{D}$ perfectly simulates Game 2 since the PMKs are chosen independently and uniformly at random; while when $\mathcal{O} = \$(\cdot)$, then $\mathcal{D}$ perfectly simulates Game 3. □

Concluding the Proof of Theorem 4. Suppose the test-session in Game 3 accepted with the "SID" $P\|\eta$. By Game 1 we know that the only sessions that evaluated the pseudorandom function on this SID was the test-session and possibly its partner. However, by Game 3 the PRF is now a truly random function unavailable to the adversary (since we are in the static corruption model). In particular, this means that the PTK derived by the test-session (and possibly its partner) is a truly random string $\widetilde{\mathrm{PTK}} = \widetilde{k_\mu}\|\widetilde{k_\alpha} \leftarrow \{0,1\}^{2\lambda}$, and where $\widetilde{k_\alpha}$ is independent of all other values. Thus, $\mathsf{Adv}^{G_3}_{4\mathsf{WHS},\mathcal{A},f}(\lambda) = 0$, and Theorem 4 follows. □

We now turn to proving explicit entity authentication for the 4WHS.

Theorem 5. *The 4WHS provides explicit entity authentication. In particular, for any PPT adversary $\mathcal{A}$, there exists algorithms $\mathcal{D}$ and $\mathcal{F}$, such that*

$$\mathsf{Adv}^{\mathsf{2P\text{-}AKE}^{\mathsf{static}}\text{-}\mathsf{EA}}_{4\mathsf{WHS},\mathcal{A},f}(\lambda) \leq |\mathcal{P}_C| \cdot |\mathcal{P}_{AP}| \cdot \left(\mathsf{Adv}^{\mathsf{prf}}_{\mathsf{PRF},\mathcal{D}}(\lambda) + \frac{(n_P n_\pi)^2}{2^{\lambda+1}} + 2n_\pi \cdot \mathsf{Adv}^{\mathsf{UF\text{-}CMA}}_{\Sigma,\mathcal{F}}(\lambda) \right),$$

$$\tag{14}$$

where f, n_π, and n_P are the same as in Theorem 4.

Proof. This proof uses the exact same three game hops as in the proof of Theorem 4, differing only in its interpretation of the guessed pre-shared key PMK^*: instead of hoping that PMK^* belongs to the test-session, we now hope that it belongs to the first session that accepts maliciously. To recap, in Game 3 the challenger aborts if any nonces collide, or the first session that accepts maliciously uses a different pre-shared key then PMK^*. Moreover, all evaluations of $PRF(PMK^*, \cdot)$ are replaced with a truly random function $\$(\cdot)$. Since all the game hops are the same, we only have the analyze the probability that a session accepts maliciously in Game 3.

Lemma 8. $\mathsf{Adv}_{4WHS, f, \mathcal{A}}^{G_3\text{-}EA}(\lambda) \leq 2n_\pi \cdot \mathsf{Adv}_{\Sigma, \mathcal{F}}^{UF\text{-}CMA}(\lambda).$

Proof. The forger $\mathcal{F}$ has access to two oracles $\mathcal{O}^{MAC}$ and $\mathcal{O}^{Vrfy}$, which implements the MAC and Vrfy algorithms of the MAC scheme Σ for some independent random key $\widetilde{k_\mu}$. Among all the sessions that use PMK^*, $\mathcal{F}$ will guess a random session π^* and embed the oracles $\mathcal{O}^{MAC}$ and $\mathcal{O}^{Vrfy}$ into it. Let V^* denote the intended communication partner of π^*. We consider two cases based on whether π^* is a client or an AP.

Case $U^* \in \mathcal{P}_{AP}$. $\mathcal{F}$ will simulate Game 3 by creating all the pre-shared keys and implementing the random function $\$(\cdot)$ by lazy-sampling. However, when creating and verifying the handshake messages of π^*, it will use the oracles $\mathcal{O}^{MAC}$ and $\mathcal{O}^{Vrfy}$. Specifically, when receiving the handshake message m_2, π^* will accept only if $\mathcal{O}^{Vrfy}(m_2) = 1$. Moreover, if any session accepts maliciously before π^*, then $\mathcal{F}$ aborts. Additionally, $\mathcal{F}$ also aborts if the nonce η_C contained in m_2 was created by a session at V^* that received the correct nonce η_{AP} from π^*. Note that this event simply means that $\mathcal{F}$'s guess of π^* was wrong, because if π^* were to accept on receiving this m_2 message, it could not have accepted maliciously by the definition of f, since the session creating η_C would be its partner (here we are also using that all the nonces are unique).

By the uniqueness of nonces, and the assumptions above, no session will evaluate $\$(\cdot)$ on the same input as π^*. Hence, embedding the oracles $\mathcal{O}^{MAC}$, $\mathcal{O}^{Vrfy}$ into π^* provides a perfect simulation of Game 3. But this means that π^* accepts maliciously iff $\mathcal{O}^{Vrfy}(m_2) = 1$, with m_2 being a valid forgery.

Case $U^* \in \mathcal{P}_C$. Similar to the previous case, $\mathcal{F}$ embeds $\mathcal{O}^{MAC}$, $\mathcal{O}^{Vrfy}$ into π^*, and aborts if the guess was wrong. This again provides a perfect simulation of Game 3, and π^* accepts maliciously iff the call to $\mathcal{O}^{Vrfy}$ is a valid forgery.

Since in both cases malicious acceptance by π^* implies a forgery for Σ, the lemma follows. □

5.3   Security of IEEE 802.11 with Upper-Layer Authentication

In enterprise and university networks it is both inconvenient and less secure for every user to share a common PMK when accessing the WLAN. In these environments, user authentication is instead handled by a central authentication server, which is then accessed via some EAP variant. While the IEEE 802.11 standard technically allows for upper-level authentication mechanisms other than EAP, the de-facto standard is EAP. Since we have already proved that certain variants of EAP satisfies the 3P-AKE^w notion (Theorem 3), and that the 4WHS is a secure 2P-AKE protocol with static corruption (Theorems 4 and 5); the security of IEEE 802.11 with upper-level authentication now follows directly by applying our second composition theorem (Theorem 2) with $\Pi_3 =$ EAP and $\Pi_4 =$ 4WHS.

Theorem 6 (3P-AKE security of IEEE 802.11 w/upper-layer authentication). *If the PMK for the 4WHS is derived using a variant of EAP that is 3P-AKE^w-secure, then the IEEE 802.11 protocol with upper-layer authentication is 3P-AKE-secure.*

Acknowledgments. We would like to thank Colin Boyd, Britta Hale and Cas Cremers for helpful comments and discussions. Chris Brzuska is grateful to NXP for supporting his chair for IT Security Analysis.

References

1. IEEE standard for local and metropolitan area networks - port-based network access control. IEEE Std 802.1X-2010 (Revision of IEEE Std 802.1X-2004), pp. C1–205, February 2010
2. IEEE standard for information technology-telecommunications and information exchange between systems local and metropolitan area networks-specific requirements part 11: wireless LAN medium access control (MAC) and physical layer (PHY) specifications. IEEE Std 802.11-2012, pp. 1–2793, March 2012
3. Abdalla, M., Fouque, P.-A., Pointcheval, D.: Password-based authenticated key exchange in the three-party setting. In: Vaudenay, S. (ed.) PKC 2005. LNCS, vol. 3386, pp. 65–84. Springer, Heidelberg (2005). doi:10.1007/978-3-540-30580-4_6
4. Aboba, B., Blunk, L.J., Vollbrecht, J.R., Carlson, J., Levkowetz, H.: Extensible Authentication Protocol. RFC 3748, RFC Editor, June 2004. https://tools.ietf.org/html/rfc3748
5. Alt, S., Fouque, P.-A., Macario-rat, G., Onete, C., Richard, B.: A cryptographic analysis of UMTS/LTE AKA. In: Manulis, M., Sadeghi, A.-R., Schneider, S. (eds.) ACNS 2016. LNCS, vol. 9696, pp. 18–35. Springer, Heidelberg (2016). doi:10.1007/978-3-319-39555-5_2
6. Bellare, M., Pointcheval, D., Rogaway, P.: Authenticated key exchange secure against dictionary attacks. In: Preneel, B. (ed.) EUROCRYPT 2000. LNCS, vol. 1807, pp. 139–155. Springer, Heidelberg (2000). doi:10.1007/3-540-45539-6_11
7. Bellare, M., Rogaway, P.: Entity authentication and key distribution. In: Stinson, D.R. (ed.) CRYPTO 1993. LNCS, vol. 773, pp. 232–249. Springer, Heidelberg (1994). doi:10.1007/3-540-48329-2_21
8. Bellare, M., Rogaway, P.: Provably secure session key distribution: the three party case. In: 27th ACM STOC, pp. 57–66. ACM Press, May/June 1995
9. Bhargavan, K., Fournet, C., Kohlweiss, M., Pironti, A., Strub, P.-Y., Zanella-Béguelin, S.: Proving the TLS handshake secure (as It Is). In: Garay, J.A., Gennaro, R. (eds.) CRYPTO 2014. LNCS, vol. 8617, pp. 235–255. Springer, Heidelberg (2014). doi:10.1007/978-3-662-44381-1_14
10. Brzuska, C., Cremers, C., Jacobsen, H., Kohbrok, K., Warinschi, B.: Partner mechanisms in key exchange protocols (2017, unpublished manuscript)

11. Brzuska, C., Fischlin, M., Warinschi, B., Williams, S.C.: Composability of Bellare-Rogaway key exchange protocols. In: Chen, Y., Danezis, G., Shmatikov, V. (eds.) ACM CCS 11. pp. 51–62. ACM Press, October 2011

12. Brzuska, C., Jacobsen, H., Stebila, D.: Safely exporting keys from secure channels. In: Fischlin, M., Coron, J.-S. (eds.) EUROCRYPT 2016. LNCS, vol. 9665, pp. 670–698. Springer, Heidelberg (2016). doi:10.1007/978-3-662-49890-3_26

13. Canetti, R., Krawczyk, H.: Security analysis of IKE's signature-based key-exchange protocol. In: Yung, M. (ed.) CRYPTO 2002. LNCS, vol. 2442, pp. 143–161. Springer, Heidelberg (2002). doi:10.1007/3-540-45708-9_10. http://eprint.iacr.org/2002/120/

14. Hartman, S., Clancy, T.C., Hoeper, K.: Channel-Binding Support for Extensible Authentication Protocol (EAP) Methods. RFC 6677, RFC Editor, July 2012. https://tools.ietf.org/html/rfc6677

15. Hoeper, K., Chen, L.: Where EAP security claims fail. In: QSHINE, p. 46. ACM (2007)

16. Jager, T., Kohlar, F., Schäge, S., Schwenk, J.: On the security of TLS-DHE in the standard model. In: Safavi-Naini, R., Canetti, R. (eds.) CRYPTO 2012. LNCS, vol. 7417, pp. 273–293. Springer, Heidelberg (2012). doi:10.1007/978-3-642-32009-5_17

17. Kobara, K., Shin, S., Strefler, M.: Partnership in key exchange protocols. In: Li, W., Susilo, W., Tupakula, U.K., Safavi-Naini, R., Varadharajan, V. (eds.) ASIACCS 09, pp. 161–170. ACM Press, New York (2009)

18. Kohlar, F., Schäge, S., Schwenk, J.: On the security of TLS-DH and TLS-RSA in the standard model. Cryptology ePrint Archive, report 2013/367 (2013). http://eprint.iacr.org/2013/367

19. Krawczyk, H.: HMQV: A high-performance secure Diffie-Hellman protocol. In: Shoup, V. (ed.) CRYPTO 2005. LNCS, vol. 3621, pp. 546–566. Springer, Heidelberg (2005). doi:10.1007/11535218_33

20. Krawczyk, H., Paterson, K.G., Wee, H.: On the security of the TLS protocol: a systematic analysis. In: Canetti, R., Garay, J.A. (eds.) CRYPTO 2013. LNCS, vol. 8042, pp. 429–448. Springer, Heidelberg (2013). doi:10.1007/978-3-642-40041-4_24

21. LaMacchia, B., Lauter, K., Mityagin, A.: Stronger security of authenticated key exchange. Cryptology ePrint Archive, report 2006/073 (2006). http://eprint.iacr.org/2006/073

22. LaMacchia, B., Lauter, K., Mityagin, A.: Stronger security of authenticated key exchange. In: Susilo, W., Liu, J.K., Mu, Y. (eds.) ProvSec 2007. LNCS, vol. 4784, pp. 1–16. Springer, Heidelberg (2007). doi:10.1007/978-3-540-75670-5_1

23. Li, Y., Schäge, S., Yang, Z., Kohlar, F., Schwenk, J.: On the security of the pre-shared key ciphersuites of TLS. In: Krawczyk, H. (ed.) PKC 2014. LNCS, vol. 8383, pp. 669–684. Springer, Heidelberg (2014). doi:10.1007/978-3-642-54631-0_38

24. Nam, J., Choo, K.K.R., Paik, J., Won, D.: Two-round password-only authenticated key exchange in the three-party setting. Cryptology ePrint Archive, report 2014/017 (2014). http://eprint.iacr.org/2014/017

25. Ohba, Y., Parthasarathy, M., Yanagiya, M.: Channel Binding Mechanism based on Parameter Binding in Key Derivation. RFC (Informational), RFC Editor, December 2006. https://tools.ietf.org/html/draft-ohba-eap-channel-binding-02

26. Rigney, C., Willens, S., Rubens, A., Simpson, W.: Remote Authentication Dial in User Service (RADIUS). RFC 2865, RFC Editor, June 2000. https://tools.ietf.org/html/rfc2865

27. Rogaway, P.: On the role definitions in and beyond cryptography. In: Maher, M.J. (ed.) ASIAN 2004. LNCS, vol. 3321, pp. 13–32. Springer, Heidelberg (2004). doi:10.1007/978-3-540-30502-6_2

28. Schwenk, J.: Nonce-based kerberos is a secure delegated AKE protocol. Cryptology ePrint Archive, report 2016/219 (2016). http://eprint.iacr.org/2016/219
29. Shoup, V., Rubin, A.: Session key distribution using smart cards. In: Maurer, U. (ed.) EUROCRYPT 1996. LNCS, vol. 1070, pp. 321–331. Springer, Heidelberg (1996). doi:10.1007/3-540-68339-9_28
30. Winter, S., McCauley, M., Venaas, S., Wierenga, K.: Transport Layer Security (TLS) encryption for RADIUS. RFC 6614 (Experimental), RFC Editor, May 2012. https://tools.ietf.org/html/rfc6614

Multiparty Computation

On the Computational Overhead of MPC
with Dishonest Majority

Jesper Buus Nielsen[1] and Samuel Ranellucci[2,3(✉)]

[1] Department of Computer Science, Aarhus University, Aarhus, Denmark
jbn@cs.au.dk
[2] Department of Computer Science, George Mason University,
Virginia, USA
[3] Department of Computer Science, University of Maryland,
Maryland, USA
samuel@umd.edu

Abstract. We consider the situation where a large number n of players
want to securely compute a large function f with security against an
adaptive, malicious adversary which might corrupt $t < cn$ of the parties
for some given $c \in [0,1)$. In other words, only some arbitrarily small
constant fraction of the parties are assumed to be honest. For any fixed
c, we consider the asymptotic complexity as n and the size of f grows.
We are in particular interested in the computational overhead, defined
as the total computational complexity of all parties divided by the size of
f. We show that it is possible to achieve poly-logarithmic computational
overhead for all $c < 1$. Prior to our result it was only known how to get
poly-logarithmic overhead for $c < \frac{1}{2}$. We therefore significantly extend
the area where we can do secure multiparty computation with poly-
logarithmic overhead. Since we allow that more than half the parties are
corrupted, we can only get security with abort, i.e., the adversary might
make the protocol abort before all parties learn their outputs. We can,
however, for all c make a protocol for which there exists $d > 0$ such that
if at most dn parties are actually corrupted in a given execution, then
the protocol will not abort. Our result is solely of theoretical interest. In
its current form, it has not practical implications whatsoever.

1   Introduction

We consider the situation where a large number n of players want to securely
compute a large function f with security against an adaptive, malicious adversary which might corrupt $t < cn$ of the parties for some given constant $c \in [0,1)$.
In other words, only some arbitrarily small constant fraction of parties are
assumed to be honest. We also require that there exists $d > 0$ such that if
at most dn parties are actually corrupted in a given execution, then the protocol will not abort. We call this the setting with constant honesty and constant
termination guarantee.

For any fixed c, we consider the asymptotic complexity as n and the size of
f grows. We are in particular interested in the computational overhead, defined

© International Association for Cryptologic Research 2017
S. Fehr (Ed.): PKC 2017, Part II, LNCS 10175, pp. 369–395, 2017.
DOI: 10.1007/978-3-662-54388-7_13

by summing the total computational complexity of all parties and dividing by the size of f. We show that it is possible to achieve poly-logarithmic computational overhead for all $c < 1$. Prior to our result, it was only known how to get poly-logarithmic overhead for settings with constant honesty and constant termination guarantee for $c < \frac{1}{2}$ (cf. [DIK+08, CDD+15, BSFO12, BCP15, CDI+13]). We therefore significantly extend the area where we can do secure multiparty computation with poly-logarithmic overhead. Let us state up front that our result is only meant as an asymptotic feasibility result. The constants hidden by the asymptotic analysis are so huge that the protocol has no practical implications.

Our protocol is based on standard assumptions. It can be built in a white-box manner from essentially any multiparty computation protocol secure against any number of corrupted parties and a secure multiparty computation protocol which has poly-logarithmic overhead and which is secure when at most a quarter of parties are corrupt. Both protocols should be secure against a malicious, adaptive adversary. We give an information-theoretic secure protocol in the hybrid model with oblivious transfer and a small number of initial broadcasts. We also give a computationally secure protocol in the hybrid model with a CRS and a PKI.

We note that approaches based on selecting a small committees and having the committee run the computation are doomed to failure in our model. This is because any small committee can be corrupted by the adaptive adversary. The protocol from [CPS14] is insecure in our model precisely for this reason. We also note that our protocol, in contrast to the low overhead protocols of [DPSZ12, DZ13, DKL+13], does not rely on pre-processing. The IPS compiler [IPS08] is also a generic protocol with low computational overhead, but it has a quadratic overhead in the number of players, so it does not have a low computational overhead in the sense that we consider here. Finally, notice that an approach based on fully homomorphic encryption, where the n parties send their encrypted inputs to one party and lets this party do the computation can have a poly-logarithmic computational overhead. However, it does not have constant termination guarantee. To ensure this, it seems one would still need some constant fraction of the parties to do all the computation, suffering a blow up in the overhead of a factor $\Theta(n)$.

2   Technical Overview

Our protocol follows the same high level approach as [DIK+08] which is based on the work of [Bra87]. Our protocol is also inspired by the IPS compiler from [IPS08] and the player virtualization technique from [HM00]. The main idea is that we will run an honest majority protocol with poly-logarithmic overhead. Following [IPS08], we call this the outer protocol. Each of the parties P_i in the outer protocol will be emulated by a constant number of the parties running a protocol with security against any number of corrupted parties. The set of parties that run P_i is called committee number i. The protocol that committees run is called the inner protocol.

We use an expander graph to set up the committees so that except with negligible probability, a vast majority of committees will contain at least one honest player as long as at most cn of the real parties are corrupted. We call a committee consisting of only honest parties an honest committee. We call a committee containing at least one honest party and at least one corrupted party a crashable committee. We call a committee consisting of only corrupted parties a corrupted committee. Since the inner protocol is secure against any number of corrupted parties, an honest committee corresponds to an honest party in the outer protocol and a corrupted committee corresponds to a corrupted party in the outer protocol. Since the inner protocol only guarantees termination when all parties in the committee are honest, a crashable committee corresponds to a party in the outer protocol which is running correctly and which has a private state, but which might crash—if a corrupted committee member makes the inner protocol abort.

We need the outer protocol to tolerate a large constant fraction of malicious corruptions (one quarter) along with any number of fail-stop errors. At the same time, we need it to guarantee termination if there is a large enough fraction of honest parties. On top of that the protocol needs to have poly-logarithmic overhead. Prior to our work, there is no such protocol in the literature. We show how to build such a protocol in a white-box manner from off-the-shelf protocols with poly-logarithmic overhead.

There are many additional complications along the way. Most honest majority protocols rely on private and authenticated channels. Since an adversary can corrupt players so that all committees contain a corrupted member,[1] we need a way to allow the inner protocols emulated by different sets of parties to communicate securely while hiding the messages from the committee members. We should also prevent corrupted committee members from attacking the delivery or authentication of the transmitted messages. In addition, when a user sends his input to an emulated party of the outer protocol emulated by a committee that may only have a single honest party, we should still be able guarantee that he can securely send a message to the inner protocol. This is necessary to ensure that an honest party cannot be prevented from giving input. To prevent this, we employ a multitude of new techniques described in the following technical sections which includes player elimination and the use of a tamper-resilient secret-sharing scheme.

Although the basic approach is the same, there are important technical differences between this work and [DIK+08]. In the following, we describe the most important ones. The work of [DIK+08] employs Verifiable Secret Sharing (VSS) to solve the problem of secure message transmission between parties. It also uses VSS to allow real parties to provide their inputs to the emulated parties of the outer protocol. The work of [DIK+08] can employ VSS because it can set up committees so that it is guaranteed that most committees have an honest majority. In contrast, since it could be that a majority of players are corrupt, we cannot ensure that any committee has an honest majority and therefore we cannot employ VSS. Another difference is that we need an explicit bipartite

---

[1] If we for instance start out with a setting where 99 out of every 100 parties are corrupted and we start forming random committees, of course we should expect all or essentially all committees to get a corrupted member.

expander graph with constant left degree and constant right degree. Since we could not find such a construction in the literature, we constructed such an expander using standard techniques.

3   Setting the Stage

We use λ to denote the *security parameter*. We consider a setting with n *players* $P_1, \ldots, P_n$. Here P_i is just a distinct name for each of the participating players. We use $\mathcal{P} = \{P_1, \ldots, P_n\}$ to denote the *set of players*. We assume that all players agree on $\mathcal{P}$. We assume that n is a function of λ and that $n(\lambda) \geq \lambda$. We often write n instead of $n(\lambda)$.

We also assume that the parties agree on a circuit C to be computed. We assume that all parties have a fixed size input in C. We use $s = \text{size}_{\text{BOOL}}(C)$ to denote the size of C.

By a protocol π, we mean a generic protocol which has an instantiation $\pi(C, \lambda, n)$ for each circuit C, value of the security parameter λ and number n of parties. We assume that there exists a uniform poly-time Turing machine which produces circuits computing $\pi(f, \lambda, n)$ given input $(C, 1^\lambda, 1^n)$. We do not consider the production of $\pi(C, \lambda, n)$ as part of the complexity of π. We use $\text{comp}(\pi(C, n, \lambda))$ to denote the expected total work done by all parties in $\pi(C, n, \lambda)$, where the work is measured as local *computation*, counting the sending and receiving of one bit as 1 towards the work. Note that $\text{comp}(\pi(C, n, \lambda))$ in particular is an upper bound on the *communication* of the protocol.

We are interested in the complexity of MPC as the size of C and the number of parties grow. We are in particular interested in the *overhead* of the computation, defined as the complexity of the protocol divided by the size of C. As usual, we are also interested in how the complexity grows with the security parameter λ and the number of parties n. In defining the computational overhead, we follow [DIK10]. Let OH be a function $\text{OH} : \mathbb{N} \times \mathbb{N} \times \mathbb{N} \to \mathbb{R}$. We say that π has computational overhead OH if there exists a polynomial $p : \mathbb{N} \times \mathbb{N} \times \mathbb{N} \to \mathbb{N}$ such that for all C, n and λ it holds that

$$\text{comp}(\pi(C, n, \lambda)) \leq \text{size}(C) \cdot \text{OH}(n, \lambda, \text{size}(f)) + p(n, \lambda, \log \text{size}(f)).$$

Let NC be Nick's class, i.e., the set of functions that can be computed by circuits of poly-logarithmic depth. We want to securely evaluate f in a distributed manner without much overhead. Current techniques even for honest majority only achieve this if the computation of f can be parallelised. This is why we consider NC. Previous protocols essentially have the same restriction. For instance, the protocol in [DIK10] has a complexity of the form $s \log(s) + d^2 \cdot \text{poly}(n, \log(s))$, where s is the size of the circuit computing f and d is the depth of the circuit. That means that if d is not polylog(s), then the overhead will not be polylog(s).

We prove security in the UC model assuming a synchronous model, point-to-point channels and broadcast. The UC model is originally best geared towards modeling asynchronous computation, but it can be adapted to model synchronous computation.

3.1   UC and Synchronous Computation

Our study is cast in the synchronous model. Still, we would like to prove security in the UC model which by design considers asynchronous computation. The reason why we would like to use the UC model is to give modular proofs. We need to consider reactive secure computations for which the UC model is the *de facto* standard. One can cast synchronous computation in the UC model by using the techniques of [KMTZ13]. The model from [KMTZ13] is, however, much more refined and detailed than what we need, so we have decided to go for a simpler model that we present below.

We are going to assume that synchrony is ensured by the environment giving the parties P_i special inputs TICK modeling that the time has increased by one tick for P_i. The parties can then simply count what time it is. We then simply require that the environment keeps the clocks of two honest parties at most one tick apart. To make sure that all parts of a composed protocol and all ideal functionalities know what time it is, we require that all parties which receive an input TICK passes it on to all its sub-protocols and ideal functionalities.

In a bit more detail, synchrony is defined via a *synchrony contract* that all entities must follow for as long as all other entities do so. We describe the contract now for the different entities of the UC framework. In doing so, we describe the behaviour that the entity must show, assuming that all other parties followed the contract until that point. If an entity A observes another entity B breaking the contract, then A is allowed to exhibit arbitrary behaviour after that point.

Synchronous Environment. A round is defined by all parties having received the input TICK from the environment. The environment might in each round give additional input x_i to a party P_i by inputting (TICK, x_i). In most of our we use r_i to denote the round in which P_i is. We say that party P_i is in round r_i, if it has received the input TICK exactly r_i times from the environment. The environment must ensure that $r_i \leq r_j + 1$ for all honest parties P_i and P_j. Furthermore, when the environment sends TICK to an honest party, it cannot send another TICK to that party until it has received an output from P_i.

Synchronous Parties. If a party P_i gets input TICK from its environment it must after this input, send TICK exactly once to each of its ideal functionalities. Note that the caller might be a super-protocol instead of an environment and that P_i might be calling a sub-protocol instead of an ideal functionality. This is transparent to P_i and we will use *environment* to denote the entity calling P_i and *ideal functionality* to denote the entity being called by P_i. When an honest party received back an output from all the sub-entities to which it input TICK, it must deliver an output to its environment as the next thing.

Notice that if we compose a synchronous environment with a synchronous protocol to get a new environment, then we again have a synchronous environment, which is the main observation needed to lift the UC composition theorem to the synchronous setting.

In the following we will ignore the inputs TICK as they are only used to define which round we are in. We will say that P_i gets input x_i in round r_i if it gets input (TICK, x_i) in that round. We will say that P_i gets no input in round r_i if it gets input (TICK) in that round.

A *synchronous ideal functionality* is given by a transition function Tr which in each evaluation takes the state from the previous evaluation, an input from each other party and computes a new state and one output for each of the other parties. Each evaluation is started by the honest parties, each giving an input. For simplicity we require that these inputs are all given in the same round. We also assume that each evaluation has a fixed round complexity, given by a round function R. Evaluation number e will take $R(e)$ rounds. If a corrupted party does not give an input, a default value is used. For a given transition function Tr and round function R the corresponding synchronous ideal functionality $\mathcal{F}_{\mathsf{Tr},\mathsf{R}}^{\mathrm{SYNC}}$ is given in Fig. 1.

Initialize Let $e = 0$; This is a counter of how many evaluations were done so far. Throughout, let C denote the current set of corrupted parties and let H denote the current set of honest parties. Let $\sigma = 1^\lambda$; This is the initial internal state. Let State $\leftarrow$ INPUTTING.

Honest Input If in some round all parties $P_i \in H$ give an input x_i and State = INPUTTING, then set $x_j = \bot$ for $P_j \in C$, store $(x_1, \ldots, x_n)$, let $e \leftarrow e+1$ and let State $\leftarrow$ COMPUTING. (If in some round some honest party P_i gives an input x_i and some honest party P_j does not give an input or State $\neq$ INPUTTING, then do a complete breakdown.)

Corrupt Input On input (P_i, x) for $P_i \in C$ while State = COMPUTING, update $x_i \leftarrow x$. Then turn over the activation to the adversary.

Compute During the next $R(e)$ rounds after setting State $\leftarrow$ COMPUTING all honest parties just output TICK.

Eval If the adversary inputs (EVAL) and State = COMPUTING, then compute $(\sigma_e, y_1, \ldots, y_n) \leftarrow \mathsf{Tr}(\sigma_{e-1}, x_1, \ldots, x_n)$. Set State $\leftarrow$ EVALUATED. Output $\{(i, y_i)\}_{P_i \in C}$ to the adversary.

Output In round $R(e) + 1$, after setting State $\leftarrow$ COMPUTING, output y_i to P_i for $P_i \in H$ and let the adversary decide the order of delivery.

Abort The ideal functionality can be parametrized by an abort threshold a. If a is not specified, it is assumed that $a = n$. If the adversary inputs (ABORT) and $|C| > a$, then output ABORT to all honest parties and terminate.

Total Breakdown Doing a total breakdown in a given round means that the ideal functionality outputs the current and all previous σ_i to the adversary along with all previous inputs and then switches to a mode where it is the adversary that determines which messages are sent by the ideal functionality.

Fig. 1. Synchronous ideal functionality $\mathcal{F}_{\mathsf{Tr}}^{\mathrm{SYNC}}$ for transition function Tr and round function R

We will be using an ideal functionality for synchronous communication. In each evaluation, party P_i has input $(x_{i,1}, \ldots, x_{i,n})$ and receives the output

$(x_{1,i}, \ldots, x_{n,i})$, i.e., in each round each party can send a message to each other party. We will not write this ideal functionality explicitly in our formal statements. We consider it the ground model of communication, i.e., it is present in all our (hybrid) models. The round complexity of each evaluation is 1.

We will be using an ideal functionality for broadcast between a set of parties $P_1, \ldots, P_n$. In each evaluation each party has input x_i and receives the output $(x_1, \ldots, x_n)$. The round complexity is the same in all rounds but might depend on the number of parties. For n parties, we use $R_{\text{BROADCAST}}(n)$ to denote the round complexity of each round of broadcast among n parties.

3.2 Broadcast

For our protocols, we require a synchronous broadcast channel. A broadcast channel is a primitive that allows a player to broadcast a message to a subset of the players. When a player receives a broadcasted message, he is assured that each other player received the same message.

The ideal functionality is for one sender S and r receivers $R_1, \ldots, R_r$.

Broadcast On input m from S and input BEGIN from all honest receivers R_i in the same round, wait for $R_{\text{BROADCAST}}$ rounds and then output m to all receivers, letting the adversary determine the order of delivery.

Corrupt sender If S is corrupt and does not provide an input, then let $m = \bot$. Furthermore, if S is corrupt and the adversary inputs (REPLACE INPUT, m') before an output was delivered to the first honest party, then let $m \leftarrow m'$.

Fig. 2. The broadcast functionality $\mathcal{F}_{\text{BROADCAST}}$

4 The Outer Protocol

The *outer protocol* π_{OUT} involves n users $U_1, \ldots, U_n$ and m servers $S_1, \ldots, S_m$. Only the users have inputs and outputs. The protocol computes an n-party function $f : D^n \to E^n$ given by circuit C. We assume that $D = \{0,1\}^k$ and that $E = D \cup \{\bot\}$, but the protocol obviously generalises to differently structured inputs and outputs. We use $\bot$ to signal that a user did not get an output.

We assume that f is fixed and that the protocol runs in some fixed number of rounds, which we denote by R_{OUT}.

We assume that the only interactions involving users is in the first round where all users send a message to all servers (we call these the input messages) and in some given round R_{OUT} all servers send a message to all users (we call these the output messages). We use In_{OUT} to denote the randomized function used to compute input messages from an input and we use Out_{OUT} to denote the deterministic function used to compute the output from output messages.

We assume that in each round r, each server S_j sends one message $y^r_{j,k}$ to each of the other servers S_k. We use $y^r_{j,j}$ to denote the state of S_i after round r and at the start of round $r + 1$. We use $\mathsf{Tr}_{\mathrm{OUT}}$ to denote the transition function of the servers: the function applied in each round to compute a new state and the messages to be sent in the given round.

Inputs

For $i = 1, \ldots, n$ user U_i has input x_i and has random tape t_i. For $j = 1, \ldots, m$ server S_j has no input and has random tape r_j.

Server initialization

For $j, k = 1, \ldots, m$ server S_j lets $y^0_{k,j}$ be the empty string.

Generation of input shares

For $i = 1, \ldots, n$ user U_i samples $(x_{i,1}, \ldots, x_{i,m}) \leftarrow \mathsf{In}_{\mathrm{OUT}}(x_i; t_i)$.

Distribution of input shares

For $i = 1, \ldots, n$ and $j = 1, \ldots, m$ user U_i sends $x_{i,j}$ to server S_j.

Embedding of input shares

For $j = 1, \ldots, m$ server S_j sets $y^0_{j,j} \leftarrow (x_{1,j}, \ldots, x_{n,j}, r_j)$.

Evaluation rounds

For $r = 1, \ldots, \mathsf{R}_{\mathrm{OUT}}$ round r runs as follows:

Transition

For $j = 1, \ldots, m$ server S_j computes $(y^r_{j,1}, \ldots, y^r_{j,m}) \leftarrow \mathsf{Tr}_{\mathrm{OUT}}(r, y^{r-1}_{1,j}, \ldots, y^{r-1}_{m,j})$.

Communication

For $j, k = 1, \ldots, m$ server S_j sends $y^r_{j,k}$ to server S_k.

Generation of output shares

For $j = 1, \ldots, m$ server S_j computes $(z_{j,1}, \ldots, z_{j,n}) \leftarrow \mathsf{Tr}_{\mathrm{OUT}}(\mathsf{R}_{\mathrm{OUT}} + 1, y^{\mathsf{R}_{\mathrm{OUT}}}_{1,j}, \ldots, y^{\mathsf{R}_{\mathrm{OUT}}}_{m,j})$

Distribution of output shares

For $j = 1, \ldots, m$ and $i = 1, \ldots, n$ server S_j sends $z_{j,i}$ to user U_i.

Output reconstruction

For $i = 1, \ldots, n$ user U_i computes $z_i \leftarrow \mathsf{Out}_{\mathrm{OUT}}(z_{1,i}, \ldots, z_{n,i})$.

Fig. 3. Running an outer protocol $\pi_{\mathrm{OUT}} = (\mathsf{R}_{\mathrm{OUT}}, \mathsf{In}_{\mathrm{OUT}}, \mathsf{Tr}_{\mathrm{OUT}}, \mathsf{Out}_{\mathrm{OUT}})$ for f

We assume that users can be actively corrupted. To actively corrupt U_i the adversary will input (ACTIVE-CORRUPT) to U_i. In response to this U_i sends its internal state to the adversary, will forward all incoming messages to the adversary, and from now on, it is the adversary that determines what U_i sends. After an active corruption, a user is called malicious. A user is called correct if it is not malicious. We assume that a server S_j can be actively corrupted or crash-stop corrupted. Active corruption is handled as usual. To crash-stop corrupt S_j the adversary will input (CRASH-STOP-CORRUPT) to S_j. In response to this S_j, sends CRASHED to all other servers and stops giving any outputs and stops sending any messages. After this we say that S_j is crashed. The adversary might actively corrupt a crashed server. A server is called correct if it is not malicious nor crashed. We work with two thresholds $t^{\mathrm{MAL}}_{\mathrm{OUT}}$ $t^{\mathrm{TERM}}_{\mathrm{OUT}}$ which are values between and 0 and 1 that represent proportions of servers. We assume that at most a t_{OUT}^{MAL} proportion of servers are actively corrupted. We will allow any number of malicious users and we will allow any number of crashed servers. However, we will only guarantee termination if less than a t_{OUT}^{TERM} proportion of servers are incorrect (Fig 4).

The ideal functionality is for n users $U_1, \ldots, U_n$ and m servers $S_1, \ldots, S_m$ and a function f.

Input If in some round all correct users U_i give an input x_i and in the same round all correct servers get an input **begin**, then set $x_i = \perp$ for all actively corrupted users. In the first round where a correct user or correct server gets an input not of the above form, do a total break down.

Compute During the next R_{OUT} rounds, output nothing. We call this the *computation period*.

Eval If during the computation period the adversary inputs **eval** or if R_{OUT} rounds have passed without such an input from the adversary, then compute $(z_1, \ldots, z_n) \leftarrow f(x_1, \ldots, x_n)$. After this we say that the *evaluation has taken place*. Now for all U_i which are passively or actively corrupted, output (i, z_i) to the adversary.

Replace inputs If the evaluation has not yet taken place and the adversary inputs (**replace input**, i, x_i') and U_i is actively corrupted, then set $x_i \leftarrow x_i'$.

Replace outputs If the evaluation has taken place and outputs have not yet been delivered and the adversary inputs (**replace output**, i) and there are more than t_{OUT}^{TERM} incorrect servers, then set $z_i = \perp$.

Output After $R_{OUT} + 1$ rounds have passed output z_i to U_i. After this we say that *outputs have been delivered*.

Fig. 4. The ideal functionality $\mathcal{F}_{OUT}^{t_{OUT}^{TERM}}$ corresponding to an outer protocol for f

Definition 1. *We say that π_{OUT} is a $(t_{OUT}^{MAL}, t_{OUT}^{TERM})$-suitable outer protocol if it UC realises the corresponding $\mathcal{F}_{OUT}^{t_{OUT}^{TERM}}$ against a proportion t_{OUT}^{MAL} of adaptive, active corruptions and any number of adaptive crash-stop corruptions.*

Theorem 1. *There exists a suitable outer protocol π for all $C \in \mathsf{NC}$ with OH $=$ polylog(n) · log(size(C)).*

Proof (sketch). We only sketch a proof of the theorem as the desired protocol can be built in a fairly straightforward manner from off-the-shelf techniques.

Starting from [DIK10] we get a protocol π for m servers and a circuit C which is perfectly secure against $m/4$ adaptive, active corruptions. We can extend this to the client-server setting by having each U_i secret share its input among $S_1, \ldots, S_m$ and then computing the function f' which first reconstructs the secret sharings, computes f, and outputs secret sharings of the results. We denote the resulting protocol by π_f'. It runs the protocol $\pi_{f'}$, i.e., the protocol π from [DIK10] for the function f'.

The secret-sharing scheme used for the inputs and outputs should have the following properties. First, that given m shares of which at most $\frac{1}{4}m$ are incorrect, one can efficiently reconstruct the message. Furthermore, the secret-sharing scheme should also have the property that given at most $m/4$ shares, one gets no information on the secret. Finally, when secret sharing a message x, the secret-sharing scheme should produce a secret sharing of size $O(|x| + m)$ and it should be possible to share and reconstruct in time $O(|x| + m)$. The secret sharing scheme from [CDD+15] meets these criteria.

We now do a generic, white-box transformation of the protocol π into a protocol π'_f which can tolerate crash errors. Each server S_j will run exactly as in π except that it keeps a counter c_j which is initialized to 0 and which is increased whenever S_j sees a party sent CRASHED. There is a threshold $t = m/8$ and when $c_j \geq t$, server S_j will crash itself, i.e., it sends CRASHED to all parties and stops sending messages. If at the end of the computation of f', a server is not crashed, it sends its share of the output of U_i to U_i.

The intuition behind π'_f is that we try to keep the number malicious servers plus the number of crashed servers within the threshold $m/4$ of π. We will use $m/8$ of the budget for crashes and have $m/8$ left for tolerating some additional malicious corruptions. If we see too many crashed servers, then all servers will shut down the execution of π by self-crashes. We say that π was *shut down* if all correct servers did a self-crash.

We are going to reduce the security of π'_f to that of π by considering all parties which deviate from π'_f as actively corrupted. Notice that in π'_f there are three types of parties which deviate from the underlying protocol $\pi_{f'}$. (1) The servers S_j which are actively corrupted in π'_f. (2) The servers S_j which are crash-stop corrupted in π'_f. (3) The correct servers S_j which did a self-crash and hence stopped running $\pi_{f'}$. At any point in the execution, let d_i denote the number of servers which deviated from π and are of type i and let $d = d_1 + d_2 + d_3$. We are going to show that at any point before the shut-down point, it holds that $d < m/4$. This means that up to the shut-down point, we can perfectly emulate an attack on π'_f by an attack on $\pi_{f'}$ using $< m/4$ active corruption. This also holds after the shut-down point since all honest parties have self-crashed and therefore there is no more communication from honest parties to simulate.

What remains is to show that if $d \geq m/4$, then the shut-down point has been reached. Assume that $d \geq m/4$. If in a given round there are (d_1, d_2, d_3) deviators of the various types, then at the beginning of the next round all correct servers have seen $d_2 + d_3$ messages CRASHED as both crashed and self-crashed parties sent out CRASHED to all parties. Hence before the next round begins it will hold for all correct S_j that $c_j \geq d_2 + d_3 = d - d_1 \geq m/4 - d_1 \geq m/4 - m/8 = m/8 = t$. Hence the shut-down point has been reached.

We then show that if any party gets an output then all honest users have their inputs considered correctly and all honest parties who get an output get the correct output. If the shut-down point is reached, then clearly no party gets an output, so assume that the shut-down point was not reached. Then the attack can be emulated given $m/4$ active corruptions. This means that at most $m/4$ of the shares of the honest parties are missing or modified. Therefore each honest U_i will correctly reconstruct z_i.

This ends the proof that the protocol is secure. We now address when the protocol is guaranteed to terminate.

It is clear that as long as $d_1 + d_2 < t$, we will have that $d_3 = 0$ as all $c_j \le d_1 + d_2$ until the first self-crash. This shows that as long as $d_1 + d_2 < t$ we will have $d < t = m/8$ and therefore we will have guaranteed termination of π'_f. Furthermore, if $d_1 + d_2 < m/8$ then at least $m - d \ge \frac{7}{8}m$ shares of the secret shared inputs are correct and at most $d_1 + d_2 \le m/8$ are incorrect. Hence, all honest parties will have their inputs x_i reconstructed inside f'. It will similarly be guaranteed that each U_j receives at least $m - d \ge \frac{7}{8}m$ shares of the secret shared output and that at most $m/8$ of these are incorrect. Hence U_i can compute the correct z_i.

We then address the complexity of the functions. By the assumptions on the secret sharing scheme and on the size of f, we have that $|f'| = O(|f| + n \cdot m)$. Assuming that $m = O(n)$, this is of the form $|f'| = O(|f|) + \text{poly}(n)$, so for the sake of computing the overhead, we can assume that $|f'| = O(|f|)$. When $f \in \mathsf{NC}$, then the protocol from [DIK10] has $\text{OH} = \text{polylog}(n) \cdot \log(|f'|)$.

5   The Inner Protocol

The *inner protocol* π_{OUT} involves c parties $U_1, \ldots, U_c$. It must securely realize reactive secure computation, i.e., there are several stages of inputs and outputs and a secure state is kept between the stages. Each stage is computed via a transition function Tr_{IN}. We need that the round complexity of each stage is known before the protocol is run. The round complexity of stage Stage is denoted by $R_{\text{IN}}(\text{Stage})$.

Definition 2. *We say that π_{IN} is a* suitable inner protocol *for $(\mathsf{Tr}_{\text{IN}}, R_{\text{IN}})$ if it UC realises $\mathcal{F}_{\text{IN}}^{\mathsf{Tr}_{\text{IN}}, R_{\text{IN}}}$ against adaptive, active corruption of any number of parties.*

Theorem 2. *For for all c and poly-sized Tr_{IN} there exists R_{IN} and π_{IN} such that π_{IN} is a suitable inner protocol for $(\mathsf{Tr}_{\text{IN}}, R_{\text{IN}})$ in the OT-hybrid model with statistical security and complexity $O(\text{poly}(c)|\mathsf{Tr}_{\text{IN}}|)$, where in the complexity the calls to the OT functionality are counted as the size of the inputs and outputs.*

Proof. One can use the protocol from [IPS08]. One can in particular note that once the circuit to be computed is fixed, [IPS08] has a fixed round complexity.

Theorem 3. *For all c and poly-sized Tr_{IN} there exists R_{IN} and π_{IN} such that π_{IN} is a suitable inner protocol for $(\mathsf{Tr}_{\text{IN}}, R_{\text{IN}})$ in the CRS model with computational complexity $O(\text{poly}(c)|\mathsf{Tr}_{\text{IN}}|\lambda)$.*

Proof. Replace the ideal OTs in Theorem 2 by the adaptive secure OT from [GWZ09].

The ideal functionality is for c parties $\mathsf{P}_1, \ldots, \mathsf{P}_c$, transition function $\mathsf{Tr}_{\mathrm{IN}}$ and round complexity function R_{IN}.

Init Initialize a stage counter $\mathsf{Stage} \leftarrow 1$ and initialize a state variable $\mathsf{State} \leftarrow$ INPUTTING.

Input If in some round all correct parties U_i give an input x_i and $\mathsf{State} =$ INPUTTING, then set $x_i = \perp$ for all actively corrupted parties. Set $\mathsf{State} \leftarrow$ COMPUTING. If in some round some honest party gives an input and ($\mathsf{State} \neq$ INPUTTING or some honest party does not give an input), then do a complete breakdown.

Compute During the $\mathsf{R}_{\mathrm{IN}}(\mathsf{Stage})$ rounds which follow State being set to COMPUTING, output TICK to all parties.

Replace inputs If $\mathsf{State} =$ COMPUTING and the adversary inputs (REPLACE INPUT, i, x_i') and P_i is actively corrupted, then set $x_i \leftarrow x_i'$.

Eval If $\mathsf{State} =$ COMPUTING and the adversary inputs EVAL or if $\mathsf{R}_{\mathrm{IN}}(\mathsf{Stage})$ rounds have passed since State was set to COMPUTING without such an input from the adversary, then compute $(\sigma_{\mathsf{Stage}+1}, y_1, \ldots, y_c) \leftarrow \mathsf{Tr}_{\mathrm{IN}}(\sigma_{\mathsf{Stage}}, x_1, \ldots, x_c)$ and for all corrupted P_i, output (i, y_i) to the adversary. Set $\mathsf{State} \leftarrow$ EVALUATED.

Replace outputs If $\mathsf{State} =$ EVALUATED and the adversary inputs (REPLACE OUTPUT, i) and P_i is honest, then set $y_i = \perp$.

Output Exactly $\mathsf{R}_{\mathrm{IN}}(\mathsf{Stage})$ rounds after State was set to COMPUTING, output y_i to P_i and let the adversary specify the order of delivery. Set $\mathsf{State} \leftarrow$ INPUTTING. If any honest P_i receives $\perp$, then do a crash (see below).

Crash Set $\mathsf{State} \leftarrow$ CRASH, output CRASH to all parties, ignore all future input, and in all future rounds output TICK to all parties.

Crashing If all honest parties input CRASH in the same round, then do a crash as above. If some corrupted party inputs CRASH then do a crash as above. If in some round, some honest party inputs CRASH and some honest party does not input CRASH, then do a complete breakdown.

Fig. 5. The ideal functionality $\mathcal{F}_{\mathrm{IN}}$ for the inner protocol

6 Combining the Inner Protocol and the Outer Protocol

In this section, we describe how to combine the inner and outer protocol into the protocol that we call the combined protocol. This is a new instance of a black-box protocol transformation defined by [IKP+16]. First, we will describe tools that we will need. The first tool is called an expander graph. The second tool called authentic secret sharing is a secret sharing scheme that allows an honest party that receives shares to detect tampering. Our third tool is called Authenticated One-Time Encryption which is an information-theoretic authenticated encryption scheme. It is analogous to the one-time pad. Finally, we will describe how to run the combined protocol. We will describe what to do when an emulated server crashes, how emulated servers can exchange keys with other parties even when its committee only has a single honest party and then how the servers can then use those keys to securely communicate. We will then describe our final protocol and prove that it has poly-log overhead and some termination guarantees.

6.1 More Tools

Threshold Bipartite Expander Graph. A threshold bipartite expander graph is a bipartite graph with n left nodes and m right nodes which guarantees that that for any set of left nodes that has size greater or equal to αn, the size of the neighborhood of that set is greater or equal to βm. Recall that given a graph $G = (V, E)$ and some subset $S \subseteq V$, the neighbourhood of S denoted by $N(S)$ is the set of nodes that are adjacent to a node in S, i.e., $N(S) := \{v \in V \mid \exists\, u \in S : (u, v) \in E\}$. As usual a bipartite graph is a graph $G = (L \cup R, E)$ where $L \cap R = \emptyset$, $N(L) \subseteq R$ and $N(R) \subseteq L$. The left (right) degree is the maximal degree of a node in L (R).

Definition 3. *A (n, m, α, β)-threshold bipartite expander is a bipartite graph $G = (L \cup R, E)$ with $|L| = n$, $|R| = m$ such that if $S \subseteq L$ and $|S| \geq \alpha n$ then $N(S) \geq \beta m$.*

We show that for all constant $0 < \alpha < 1$ and $0 < \beta < 1$ there exists $m = O(n)$ and an (n, m, α, β)-threshold bipartite expander where the left degree is $O(1)$ and the right degree is $O(1)$.

We describe a simple construction of a bipartite threshold expander graph. It is inspired by [SS96]. We will show that for any $\alpha > 0$, that there exists a degree d such that for every n, β there exists an explicit way of constructing graphs such that the resulting graph is (n, n, α, β)-threshold bipartite expander graph except with probability negligible in n. In addition, the degree of the graph is at most d and each right node has at least one edge. We denote the binary entropy function as $\mathbb{H}$.

The construction is rather simple. First, we sample at random a set of d permutations.

$$\Pi \leftarrow \{\pi_1, \ldots, \pi_d : [n] \rightarrow [n]\}$$

We denote $L = \{1, \ldots, n\}$ as the set of left edges and $R = \{n+1, \ldots, 2n\}$ as the set of right edges. We select the graph as follows:

$$E \leftarrow \bigcup_{\pi \in \Pi} \{(1, n + \pi(1)), \ldots, (n, n + \pi(n))\} \tag{1}$$

$$G \leftarrow (L \cup R, E) \tag{2}$$

Theorem 4. *For any $0 < \alpha, \beta < 1$, let $d = \left\lceil -\frac{\mathbb{H}(\alpha) + \mathbb{H}(\beta)}{\alpha \log \beta} \right\rceil + 1$ then for any $n \in N$ the previous construction results in a bipartite (n, n, α, β)-threshold expander except with probability smaller than $2^{\alpha n \log \beta}$*

We note that the number of left sets of size αn is equal to $\binom{n}{\alpha n}$. We note that the number of right sets of size $(1 - \beta)n$ is equal to $\binom{n}{\beta n} = \binom{n}{(1-\beta)n}$.

We will now upper bound the probability that the neighborhood of αn left nodes does not intersect a set of $(1 - \beta)n$ right nodes. We can see that for each permutation, for each element in the left set, the probability that the element is not mapped to an element in the right set is less than or equal to β. Therefore we have that the probability is upper bounded $\beta^{\alpha nd}$.

By the union bound, we know that the probability that there exists such sets is less than $\beta^{\alpha nd} \binom{n}{\alpha n} \binom{n}{\beta n}$. By applying Stirling's approximation, we get that this probability is upper bounded by

$$2^{n \mathbb{H}(\alpha) + n \mathbb{H}(\beta) + \alpha nd \log(\beta)} = 2^{n(\mathbb{H}(\alpha) + \mathbb{H}(\beta) + \alpha d \log(\beta))}$$

Finally, by setting $d = \left\lceil -\frac{\mathbb{H}(\alpha) + \mathbb{H}(\beta)}{\alpha \log \beta} \right\rceil + 1$

$$2^{n(\mathbb{H}(\alpha) + \mathbb{H}(\beta) + \alpha d \log(\beta))} \leq 2^{\alpha n \log \beta}$$

Lemma 1. *For the construction above, the degree of the graph is at most d.*

This follows since there are d permutations in Π and each node gains at most one edge per permutation.

Lemma 2. *For the construction above, each right node has at least one edge.*

This follows since each permutation assigns each right node to a left node.

Authentic Secret Sharing. Let $\mathbb{F}$ be a finite field and n be an integer. A secret sharing scheme consists of two algorithms share and rec. For every $s \in \mathbb{F}$, share(s) outputs a randomized set of shares $(s_1, \ldots, s_n)$. We use share(s) to denote the distribution on $(s_1, \ldots, s_n)$ when the input is s. The algorithm rec takes as input $(s'_1, \ldots, s'_n)$ and gives an output in $\mathbb{F} \cup \{\perp\}$ where $\perp$ signals error.

For any $i \in [n]$ we let $(s_1, \ldots, s_n)_{-i} = (s_1, \ldots, s_{i-1}, s_{i+1}, \ldots, s_n)$. For any $(s_1, \ldots, s_n)_{-i}$ and any s we let $((s_1, \ldots, s_n)_{-i}, s) = (s_1, \ldots, s_{i-1}, s, s_{i+1}, \ldots, s_n)$. For all i and all $s \in \mathbb{F}$ and all unbounded adversaries A taking as input $(s_1, \ldots, s_n)_{-i}$ and giving outputs $(s'_1, \ldots, s'_n)_{-i}$ consider the game where we sample $(s_1, \ldots, s_n) \leftarrow$ share(s) and compute $s' = \text{rec}(A((s_1, \ldots, s_n)_{-i}), s_i)$. Note that it might be the case that $s' = \perp$. We use $A_{-i}(s)$ to denote the distribution of s', i.e., the result of reconstructing with the $n-1$ possibly modified shares. Let $\delta(\perp) = \perp$ and $\delta(x) = \top$ for $x \neq \perp$. We use $\hat{A}_{-i}(s)$ to denote $(\delta(s'), (s_1, \ldots, s_n)_{-i})$, i.e., the shares seen by the adversary plus the information whether reconstructing with the wrong shares gave an error or not.

Definition 4 (authentic secret sharing). *Let* (share, rec) *be a secret sharing scheme. We call* (share, rec) *an authentic secret sharing scheme if the following conditions hold.*

Reconstruction. *For all $s \in \mathbb{F}$ it holds that $\Pr[\text{rec}(\text{share}(s)) = s] = 1$.*
Sound. *For all $s \in \mathbb{F}$ and all $i \in [n]$ and all unbounded adversaries A it holds that $\Pr[A_{-i}(s) \in \{s, \perp\}] = 1$.*
Privacy. *For all $s, \bar{s} \in \mathbb{F}$ and all $i \in [n]$ and all unbounded adversaries A it holds that $\hat{A}_{-i}(s)$ and $\hat{A}_{-i}(\bar{s})$ are statistically close.*

Authenticated One-Time Encryption. An Authenticated One-Time Encryption scheme is given by a key space, encryption algorithm and decryption algorithm $(\mathcal{K}, \mathsf{Enc}, \mathsf{Dec})$. For each message length m and value λ of the security parameter we have a key space $\mathcal{K}_{m,\lambda}$. Given $K \in \mathcal{K}_{m,\lambda}$, λ and message $x \in \{0,1\}^m$ the encryption algorithm outputs a ciphertext $A = \mathsf{Enc}_{K,\lambda}(x)$. Given $K \in \mathcal{K}_{m,\lambda}$, λ, m and ciphertext A the decryption algorithm outputs message $x = \mathsf{Dec}_{K,\lambda,m}(A)$.

Correctness. For all m and all $x \in \{0,1\}^m$ it holds with probability 1 for a random key $K \leftarrow \mathcal{K}_{m,\lambda}$ that $\mathsf{Dec}_{K,\lambda,m}(\mathsf{Enc}_{K,\lambda}(x)) = x$.

Security. Let $\mathcal{A}$ be a computationally unbounded algorithm. Input λ to $\mathcal{A}$ and run it to get m and $x_0, x_1 \in \{0,1\}^m$. Sample a uniformly random bit $b \leftarrow \{0,1\}$. Sample $K \leftarrow \mathcal{K}_{m,\lambda}$ and $A \leftarrow \mathsf{Enc}_{K,\lambda}(x_b)$. Let $\mathcal{O}_{m,K,A}(B)$ be the oracle which on input $B \neq A$ returns $\mathsf{Dec}_{K,\lambda,m}(B)$. Compute $g \leftarrow \mathcal{A}^{\mathcal{O}_{m,K,A}(B)}(A)$ for $g \in \{0,1\}$. The advantage of $\mathcal{A}$ is given by $\mathsf{Adv}_{\mathcal{A}}(\lambda) = |\Pr[g = b] - \frac{1}{2}|$. We say that $(\mathcal{K}, \mathsf{Enc}, \mathsf{Dec})$ is secure if $\mathsf{Adv}_{\mathcal{A}}(\lambda) \in \mathsf{negl}(\lambda)$ for all $\mathcal{A}$ which makes at most a polynomial number of queries to its oracle.

Authenticity. Let $\mathcal{A}$ be a computationally unbounded algorithm. Input λ to $\mathcal{A}$ and run it to get m. Sample $K \leftarrow \mathcal{K}_{m,\lambda}$. Let $\mathcal{O}_{m,K}(B)$ be the oracle which on input B returns $\mathsf{Dec}_{K,\lambda,m}(B)$. Compute $c \leftarrow \mathcal{A}^{\mathcal{O}_{m,K,A}(B)}()$. We say that $(\mathcal{K}, \mathsf{Enc}, \mathsf{Dec})$ has authenticity if $\Pr[\mathsf{Dec}_{K,\lambda,m}(c) \neq \perp] \in \mathsf{negl}(\lambda)$ for all $\mathcal{A}$ which makes at most a polynomial number of queries to its oracle.

We say that an Authenticated One-Time Encryption scheme has overhead $O(1)$ if it holds for all messages x and all $K \in \mathcal{K}_{|x|,\lambda}$ that $|K| + |\mathsf{Enc}_K(x)| \in O(|x| + \mathsf{poly}(\lambda))$ for a polynomial independent of $|x|$ and if we can encrypt and decrypt in time $O(|K| + |\mathsf{Enc}_K(x)| + |x|)$. This means that for large enough x we have that $|K| + |\mathsf{Enc}_K(x)| \in O(|x|)$ and that we can encrypt and decrypt in time $O(|x|)$. We can construct such a scheme off-the-shelf. Let MAC be an information-theoretic MAC which can handle message of length $O(\lambda)$ using keys of length $O(\lambda)$ and which can be computed in time $\mathsf{poly}(\lambda)$. Such a scheme is described for instance in [WC81]. Let $\mathcal{H}$ be a family of almost universal hash-functions which can be computed in linear time, see for instance [IKOS07]. For messages of length m, the key for the encryption scheme will consist of (L, H, P), where L is a random key for the MAC, $H \leftarrow \mathcal{H}$ is a random hash function from the family and P is uniformly random in $\{0,1\}^m$. To encrypt, compute $C = x \oplus P$, $M = H(C)$ and $A = \mathsf{MAC}_L(M)$ and send (C, A). To decrypt, if $|C| \neq m$, output $\perp$. Otherwise, compute $M = H(C)$ and $A' = \mathsf{MAC}_L(M)$. If $A' \neq A$, output $\perp$. Otherwise, output $C \oplus P$. The complexity is as claimed and the security follows from [WC81].

6.2 The Combined Protocol

For the combined protocol we have n parties $\mathsf{P}_1, \ldots, \mathsf{P}_n$ of which at most $n \cdot \mathsf{t}_{\mathrm{MAL,COMB}}$ are corrupted. We want to compute a function f. The parties are going to run one execution of the outer protocol to compute f. In the outer protocol we have n users $\mathsf{U}_1, \ldots, \mathsf{U}_n$ and m servers $\mathsf{S}_1, \ldots, \mathsf{S}_m$ of which we need that at most $\mathsf{t}_{\mathrm{MAL,OUT}} \cdot m$ are corrupted. Party P_i is going to run the code of U_i. Each server S_j is going to be emulated by a small subset of the parties. The inner protocol will be used to emulate servers. We set $\alpha = 1 - \mathsf{t}_{\mathrm{MAL,COMB}}$ and set $\beta = 1 - \mathsf{t}_{\mathrm{MAL,OUT}}$. We use a (n, m, α, β)-threshold expander graph $G = (V, E)$ to form the committees. For $j = 1, \ldots, m$ we let

$$\mathcal{C}_j = \{\mathsf{P}_i \mid (i, j) \in V\}$$

We call $\mathcal{C}_j$ *committee* j. Using the graph from Sect. 6.1, the size of committees is constant and except with negligible probability all sets of αn parties have members in at least βm committees.

We will present our result in a hybrid model with ideal functionalities for the inner protocol. We call this the *inner-hybrid model*. For each $i = 1, \ldots, m$, we are going to have an ideal functionality $\mathcal{F}_j$ of the form given in Fig. 5 with $c = |\mathcal{C}_j|$ and the parties being $\mathcal{C}_j$. We call $\mathcal{F}_j$ virtual server j and we specify later the behaviour of $\mathcal{F}_j$.

We set up some notation. Let $\mathcal{P} = \{\mathsf{P}_1, \ldots, \mathsf{P}_n\}$. At any point in the execution, $\mathcal{P}_{\mathrm{HONEST}} \subset \mathcal{P}$ denotes the set of parties which are honest in the combined protocol and we let $\mathcal{P}_{\mathrm{MAL}}$ be the set of maliciously corrupted parties.

We use $\mathcal{S} = \{1, \ldots, m\}$ to denote the identities of the virtual servers. We define three disjoint subsets as follows

$$\mathcal{S}_{\mathrm{HONEST}} = \{j \in \mathcal{S} \mid \mathcal{C}_j \subseteq \mathcal{P}_{\mathrm{HONEST}}\}$$
$$\mathcal{S}_{\mathrm{MAL}} = \{j \in \mathcal{S} \mid \mathcal{C}_j \subseteq \mathcal{P}_{\mathrm{MAL}}\}$$
$$\mathcal{S}_{\mathrm{CRASHABLE}} = \mathcal{S} \setminus (\mathcal{S}_{\mathrm{HONEST}} \cup \mathcal{S}_{\mathrm{MAL}})$$

If $j \in \mathcal{S}_{\mathrm{HONEST}}$, then all parties in committee j are honest. Therefore, $\mathcal{F}_j$ is secure and also has guaranteed output delivery. This will correspond to S_j being secure in the outer protocol. If $j \in \mathcal{S}_{\mathrm{MAL}}$, then all parties in committee j are malicious. Therefore, $\mathcal{F}_j$ provides no security. This will correspond to S_j being malicious in the outer protocol. If $j \in \mathcal{S}_{\mathrm{CRASHABLE}}$, then at least one party in committee j is honest and at least one party is malicious. Therefore $\mathcal{F}_j$ provides privacy and correctness, but some or all honest parties might not learn the output. If at some point a party in committee j does not get an output, then $\mathcal{F}_j$ will abort. This corresponds to S_j crashing in the outer protocol. We will let the honest party in $\mathcal{C}_j$ which received output $\perp$ inform all other parties that $\mathcal{F}_j$ has aborted. Overall, this will correspond to a crash-stop corruption of S_j in the outer protocol.

By the way we have set the parameters of the threshold expander graph it follows that if $|\mathcal{P}_{\mathrm{MAL}}| \leq n \cdot \mathsf{t}_{\mathrm{MAL,COMB}}$ then $|\mathcal{S}_{\mathrm{MAL}}| \leq m \cdot \mathsf{t}_{\mathrm{MAL,OUT}}$. We have therefore almost perfectly emulated the entities $\mathsf{U}_1, \ldots, \mathsf{U}_n, \mathsf{S}_1, \ldots, \mathsf{S}_m$ of the outer protocol with the needed adversary structure as long as $|\mathcal{P}_{\mathrm{MAL}}| \leq n \cdot \mathsf{t}_{\mathrm{MAL,COMB}}$. The only significant difference between $\mathsf{U}_1, \ldots, \mathsf{U}_n, \mathsf{S}_1, \ldots, \mathsf{S}_m$ and $\mathsf{P}_1, \ldots, \mathsf{P}_n, \mathcal{F}_1, \ldots, \mathcal{F}_m$ is the fact that in the outer protocol, the entities $\mathsf{U}_1, \ldots, \mathsf{U}_n, \mathsf{S}_1, \ldots, \mathsf{S}_m$ can send private messages to each other, whereas most of the entities $\mathsf{P}_1, \ldots, \mathsf{P}_n$, $\mathcal{F}_1, \ldots, \mathcal{F}_m$ cannot send private messages to each other. This is going to give us the so-called *secret communication problems* when we emulate the protocol in Fig. 3.

Distribution of Input Shares. To give inputs, each U_i sends a share to S_j. In the emulated outer protocol this corresponds to P_i inputting a message to $\mathcal{F}_j$. If $P_i \notin \mathcal{C}_j$, this is not allowed.

Server Communication. As part of the evaluation, each S_j sends a message to S_k. In the emulated outer protocol, this corresponds to $\mathcal{F}_j$ sending a message to $\mathcal{F}_k$. This is not allowed since ideal functionalities cannot communicate.

Distribution of Output Shares. To give outputs, S_j sends a share to U_i. In the emulated outer protocol this corresponds to $\mathcal{F}_j$ outputting a message to P_i. If $P_i \notin \mathcal{C}_j$, this is not allowed.

Another problem is that in the outer protocol, if a server S_i crashes, it will by definition notify the other servers. However, now the code of S_i is "trapped" inside $\mathcal{F}_i$ so S_i must notify S_j via the parties $\mathcal{C}_i$ and $\mathcal{C}_j$ and there might be corrupted parties among $\mathcal{C}_i \cup \mathcal{C}_j$. We call this the *abort propagation problem*. Handling of the abort propagation problem is described in Fig. 6.

The parties run a copy of the outer protocol. The code and state for S_i will be inside $\mathcal{F}_i$. If S_i crashes inside $\mathcal{F}_i$, then $\mathcal{F}_i$ will also crash, i.e., it will enter a state with State = CRASH and will output CRASH to all parties. As we will describe later, there will be other events which can trigger $\mathcal{F}_i$ to crash. In all those cases, we want that all other $\mathcal{F}_j$ learn that $\mathcal{F}_i$ has crashed. This is handled as follows:

Define Crashing We say that $\mathcal{F}_i$ is crashed if it enters a state where State = CRASH. If this happens, it outputs CRASH to all $P \in \mathcal{C}_i$

Crash Alerting If at any point during the execution a party $P \in \mathcal{C}_i$ sees $\mathcal{F}_i$ output CRASH, then for $j = 1 \ldots m$, P broadcasts (CRASH, i) to all parties in $\mathcal{C}_i \cup \mathcal{C}_j$.

Crash Recording A crash alert is received as follows.
- If at any point during the execution, a party $P_k \in \mathcal{C}_j$ receives a broadcast (CRASH, i) from a party in $\mathcal{C}_i$ to $\mathcal{C}_i \cup \mathcal{C}_j$ then P_k inputs (CRASH, i) to $\mathcal{F}_j$.
- If $\mathcal{F}_j$ receives input (CRASH, i) from all parties in $\mathcal{C}_j$ then it inputs (CRASH, i) to S_j as if coming from S_i in a run of the outer protocol. If $\mathcal{F}_j$ receives input (CRASH, i) from all honest parties but some corrupted party did not give input (CRASH, i) then $\mathcal{F}_j$ does a crash. [a] If $\mathcal{F}_j$ receives input (CRASH, i) from some honest parties but some other honest party did not input (CRASH, i), then $\mathcal{F}_j$ does a complete break down.

---
[a] Recall that in the UC model ideal functionalities know which parties are corrupt.

Fig. 6. Crash handling part of π_{COMB}

We handle all three secret communication problems by letting the entities that need to communicate share a secret key which is used to encrypt the given message using an Authenticated One-Time Encryption scheme. Then the authenticated ciphertext c can be sent in cleartext between the two involved entities. This solves the problem as an ideal functionality $\mathcal{F}_j$ for instance can output c to all members of $\mathcal{C}_j$ which can then all send c to all the members of $\mathcal{C}_k$ who will input it to $\mathcal{F}_k$. Our way to solve the secret communication problems is significantly more complicated than the approach in [IPS08] and other player emulation protocols. The reason is that previous techniques incur an overhead of at least n. For instance, in [IPS08] each message is secret shared among all parties, which means that messages will become a factor n longer. We need constant overhead. This is not an issue for [IPS08] as they consider n to be a constant. Also, the technique in [IPS08] do not guarantee termination if there is just one corrupted party.

To have servers and players share keys, we use a subprotocol to do so. This introduces another problem. It is possible that all committees contain at least one corrupt player. When a player is generating a key with a committee, a problem may arise. This can occur because either the player is corrupt or the committee contains at least one dishonest member. It is imperative that a server with at least one honest member must get the key from each honest user or abort. Otherwise, the corrupt parties can prevent honest parties from giving inputs. We employ player elimination techniques [HMP00] to solve this problem.

Distribution of Input Shares. When U_i needs to send a message m to S_j and they are both honest there will exist a random secret key K_j^i which is held by P_i and which is inside $\mathcal{F}_j$. Then P_i computes $c = \mathsf{Enc}_{K_j^i}(m)$ and sends it to each $\mathsf{P}_k \in \mathcal{C}_j$. Then each P_k inputs c to $\mathcal{F}_j$. Let c_k denote the value input by P_k. Then the virtual server $\mathcal{F}_j$ computes $m_k = \mathsf{Dec}_{K_j^i}(c)$. If $|\{m_k\}_{k \in \mathcal{C}_j} \setminus \{\bot\}| = 1$, then let m be the unique value in $\{m_k\}_{k \in \mathcal{C}_j} \setminus \{\bot\}$. Otherwise, let $m = \bot$. Notice that if P_i is honest and there is at least one honest $\mathsf{P}_k \in \mathcal{C}_j$, then the correct ciphertext will be input to the virtual server and therefore $m \in \{m_k\}_{k \in \mathcal{C}_j}$. Furthermore, no corrupted committee member can input another valid ciphertext. In particular, when the correct message is not received, either P_i is corrupted or $j \in \mathcal{S}_{\mathrm{MAL}}$.

Server Communication. When S_i needs to send a message m to S_j and they are both honest there will exist a random secret key $K_{i,j}$ which is inside $\mathcal{F}_i$ and $\mathcal{F}_j$. Then $\mathcal{F}_i$ computes $c = \mathsf{Enc}_{K_{i,j}}(m)$ and outputs it to all $\mathsf{P}_k \in \mathcal{F}_i$. Then all $\mathsf{P}_k \in \mathcal{F}_i$ sends c to all $\mathsf{P}_l \in \mathcal{C}_j$ and they all input all the ciphertexts they received. The virtual server decrypts all ciphertexts and sets m to be the unique message different from $\bot$ if it exists and $\bot$ otherwise. If $\mathcal{C}_i$ crashes the message is also set to $\bot$. Assume that $\mathcal{C}_i$ is not crashed and $\mathcal{C}_j$ is not corrupted. Then all the honest parties $\mathsf{P}_k \in \mathcal{C}_i$ sent the correct ciphertext and no party knows the secret key, so the only correct ciphertext input to the virtual server is the correct one. Hence m arrives correctly. Assume then that that $\mathcal{C}_i$ is crashed and $\mathcal{C}_j$ is not corrupt. Then the message is set to $\bot$ as it should be.

Distribution of Output Shares. When S_j needs to send a message m to U_i and they are both honest there will exist a random secret key K_j^i which is held by P_i and which is inside $\mathcal{F}_j$. Then $\mathcal{F}_j$ computes $c = \mathsf{Enc}_{K_j^i}(m)$ and outputs it to all parties $\mathsf{P}_k \in \mathcal{C}_j$, who all forward it to P_i. The party decrypts all ciphertexts and sets m as above. Assume that $\mathcal{C}_j$ is not crashed or corrupted and that P_i is honest. Then all the honest parties $\mathsf{P}_k \in \mathcal{C}_j$ sent the correct ciphertext and no party knows the secret key, so the only correct ciphertext sent to P_i is the correct one. Hence m arrives correctly. Assume then that C_j is crashed and that P_i is honest. Then the message is set to $\bot$ as it should be. Assume that C_j is corrupted and that P_i is honest. Then any message might arrive, but this is allowed as it correspond to S_j being corrupted. Similarly if P_i is corrupted.

It should be clear that the above emulation of the outer protocol should work as long as the security of the encryption scheme is not broken. We are, however, still left with the problem of getting the keys in place. We describe the key distribution protocols below.

Generating Input Keys. The basic idea behind generating the key K_i^j is to let P_i generate it and distribute an authentic secret sharing $\{K_{i,k}^j\}_{k \in C_j} \leftarrow$ share($K_{i,k}^j$) among the parties $P_k \in C_j$ who will input the shares to $\mathcal{F}_j$ which will in turn compute $K_i^j \leftarrow \text{rec}(\{K_{i,k}^j\}_{k \in C_j})$ and store it for later use. The main problem arises when the reconstruction fails. This will prevent P_i from giving (secure) inputs to $\mathcal{F}_j$. Unfortunately the error can arise either due to P_i being corrupted or some $P_k \in C_j$ being corrupted. In the later case C_j is crashable but might not be crashed, in which case P_i must be able to give secure inputs, as an honest U_i can give secure inputs to an honest S_j in the outer protocol.

We describe how to handle the case when reconstruction fails. First $\mathcal{F}_j$ will output to all parties in C_j all the shares $\{\hat{K}_{i,k}^j\}_{k \in C_j}$ that was input. If this does not crash C_j then all parties $P_k \in C_j$ will broadcast $\{\hat{K}_{i,k}^j\}_{k \in C_j}$ to $C_j \cup \{P_i\}$. If all parties $P_k \in C_j$ do not broadcast the same values, then all honest parties $P_k \in C_j$ will crash C_j by sending CRASH to all parties and $\mathcal{F}_j$. Otherwise, P_i will identify the indices k such that $\hat{K}_{i,k}^j \neq K_{i,k}^j$ and will broadcast the indices to $C_j \cup \{P_i\}$. If P_i does not do so, then P_i is corrupted and the parties in C_j will ignore all future messages from P_i. If parties were excluded, then the above procedure is repeated, but now P_i secret shares only among the committee members that were not excluded. Notice that only corrupted parties are excluded. Therefore, if C_j is not corrupted, the procedure will terminate before all committee members were excluded, at which point K_i^j was added to $\mathcal{F}_j$. If eventually all committee members were excluded, P_i will consider C_j corrupted (Fig 7).

Generating Committee Keys. The basic idea behind generating $K_{i,j}$ is to let $\mathcal{F}_i$ generate $K_{i,j}$ and sample an authentic secret sharing $\{K_{i,j,k}\}_{k \in C_i} \leftarrow$ share($K_{i,j}$) and output $K_{i,j,k}$ to P_k. Then P_k inputs $K_{i,j,k}$ to C_j using the method for when U_k gives input to $\mathcal{F}_j$. Recall that when U_k gives input to $\mathcal{F}_j$ it will succeed unless $\mathcal{F}_j$ crashes or C_j detects U_k as being corrupted. If $\mathcal{F}_j$ crashes there is no need to generate a key. If C_j detects P_k as corrupted, they all broadcast this to $C_i \cup C_j$ and P_k. Notice that if this happens, then either P_k is corrupted, and it is secure to excluded it, or C_j is corrupt, which corresponds to S_j being corrupt, and hence there is no reason to keep the key secret, so again it is secure

Key Generation We use a key generation protocol $\mathsf{KeyGeneration}_{i,j}^{U \leftrightarrow S}$ run between P_i and the parties in $\mathcal{C}_j$. It is invoked by all parties in the same round by giving the input (KEY, kid, m), where kid is a fresh key id and m is the length of the message that will later be encrypted. It proceeds as follows:

1. Let $C = \mathcal{C}_j$;
2. If $C = \emptyset$, then P_i terminates the protocol. Otherwise it proceeds as follows.
3. P_i samples $K_j^i \leftarrow \mathcal{K}_{m,\lambda}$;
4. P_i samples an authenticated secret sharing $\{K_{j,k}^i\}_{k \in C} \leftarrow \mathsf{share}(K_j^i)$ among the parties C.
5. For $k \in C$, party P_i sends $K_{j,k}^i$ to P_k and P_k inputs $K_{j,k}^i$ to $\mathcal{F}_j$.
6. Let $\hat{K}_{j,k}^i$ be the value of $K_{j,k}^i$ received by $\mathcal{F}_j$;
7. $\mathcal{F}_j$ computes $\hat{K}_j^i \leftarrow \mathsf{rec}(\{\hat{K}_{j,k}^i\}_{k \in C})$;
8. If $\hat{K}_j^i \neq \perp$, then $\mathcal{F}_j$ outputs SUCCESS to all parties in $\mathcal{C}_j$ and stores $(kid, m, \hat{K}_j^i)$. All parties terminate the protocol.
9. If $\hat{K}_j^i = \perp$, then $\mathcal{F}_j$ outputs $\{\hat{K}_{j,k}^i\}_{k \in C}$ to all parties in $\mathcal{C}_j$;
10. Each party $\mathsf{P}_k \in \mathcal{C}_j$ broadcasts $\{\hat{K}_{j,k}^i\}_{k \in C}$ to $\mathcal{C}_j \cup \{\mathsf{P}_i\}$.
11. If $\mathsf{P}_k \in \mathcal{C}_j$ sees that not all parties from $\mathcal{C}_j$ broadcast the same values, then P_k inputs CRASH to $\mathcal{F}_j$ and waits for two rounds to let the crash propagate.
12. If $\mathcal{F}_j$ crashed during the above, then each $\mathsf{P}_k \in \mathcal{C}_j$ broadcasts CRASH to $\mathcal{C}_j \cup \{\mathsf{P}_i\}$;
13. If $\mathcal{F}_j$ did not crash during the above but still some $\mathsf{P}_k \in \mathcal{C}_j$ broadcast CRASH, then all honest $\mathsf{P}_k \in \mathcal{C}_j$ inputs CRASH to $\mathcal{F}_j$;
14. If P_i did not see any $\mathsf{P}_k \in \mathcal{C}_j$ broadcast CRASH, then P_i received $\{\hat{K}_{j,k}^i\}_{k \in C}$ from all parties. It then finds k such that $\hat{K}_{j,k}^i \neq K_{j,k}^i$ and broadcasts k to $\mathcal{C}_j$;
15. If P_i does not broadcast $k \in C$ then P_i is corrupt and the protocol terminates with the output being some dummy key.
16. If P_i does broadcast $k \in C$, then each $\mathsf{P} \in \mathcal{C}_j$ sets $C \leftarrow C \setminus \{k\}$ and inputs k to $\mathcal{F}_j$;
17. Unless all $\mathsf{P} \in \mathcal{C}_j$ input the same k, $\mathcal{F}_j$ will crash. Otherwise it sets $C \leftarrow C \setminus \{k\}$;
18. P_i and all parties in $\mathcal{C}_j$ go to Step 2.

Fig. 7. User-Server key-generation communication part of π_{COMB}

to exclude P_k. Let $\mathcal{C}_i' \subseteq \mathcal{C}_i$ be the parties that were not excluded. If any parties were excluded, then $\mathcal{F}_i$ generates a new key $K_{i,j}$ and samples an authentic secret sharing $\{K_{i,j,k}\}_{k \in \mathcal{C}_i'} \leftarrow \mathsf{share}(K_{i,j})$ and outputs $K_{i,j,k}$ to P_k. The procedure is repeated until $\mathcal{C}_i' = \emptyset$ or $\mathcal{C}_i$ crashed or $\mathcal{C}_j$ crashed or in some attempt all keys $\{K_{i,j,k}\}_{k \in \mathcal{C}_i'}$ were successfully input to $\mathcal{F}_j$. In the three first cases, either $\mathcal{C}_i$ or $\mathcal{C}_j$ is corrupted and there is no need for a key. In the last case, $\mathcal{F}_j$ computes $K_{i,j} \leftarrow \mathsf{rec}(\{K_{i,j,k}\}_{k \in \mathcal{C}_i'})$. If $K_{i,j} \neq \perp$, then the key is the same as generated by $\mathcal{F}_i$ unless the security of the secret sharing scheme was broken. Assume then $K_{i,j} = \perp$. Since we are in a situation which might correspond to both S_i and S_j being honest (if for instance $\mathcal{C}_i$ and $\mathcal{C}_j$ are crashable but not crashed) we have

---

User-Server communication We use a communication protocol $\mathsf{Send}_{i,j}^{U \to S}$ run between P_i and the parties in $\mathcal{C}_j$. It is invoked by all parties in the same round by giving the input (SEND, kid), where some (kid, K, m) is stored. In addition P_i inputs $x \in \{0,1\}^m$. It proceeds as follows.

1. Delete (kid, K, m).
2. If $x \in \{0,1\}^m$ then P_i computes $c = \mathsf{Enc}_{\lambda, K}(x)$ and sends c to all parties $\mathsf{P}_k \in \mathcal{C}_j$.
3. Each P_k inputs the received c to $\mathcal{F}_j$. Let c_k be the value received from P_k.
4. For $k \in \mathcal{C}_j$ the ideal functionality computes $x_k = \mathsf{Dec}_{\lambda, m, K}(c_k)$.
5. If there exists $x \in \{0,1\}^m$ such that $\{x\} = \{x_k\}_{k \in \mathcal{C}_j} \setminus \{\bot\}$, then store $(\mathrm{MESSAGE}, kid, x)$. Otherwise, store $(\mathrm{MESSAGE}, kid, \bot)$.

Server-User communication We use a communication protocol $\mathsf{Send}_{j,i}^{S \to U}$ run between P_i and the parties in $\mathcal{C}_j$. It is invoked by all parties in the same round by giving the input (SEND, kid), where some (kid, K, m) is stored. It proceeds as follows.

1. $\mathcal{F}_j$ deletes (kid, K, m).
2. $\mathcal{F}_j$ computes $c = \mathsf{Enc}_{\lambda, K}(x)$ and sends c to all parties $\mathsf{P}_k \in \mathcal{C}_j$.
3. Each $\mathsf{P}_k \in \mathcal{C}_j$, awaits c from $\mathcal{F}_j$.
4. Each $\mathsf{P}_k \in \mathcal{C}_j$, sends c to P_i. Let c_k be the value received from P_k.
5. For $k \in \mathcal{C}_j$, P_i computes $x_k = \mathsf{Dec}_{\lambda, m, K}(c_k)$.
6. If there exists $x \in \{0,1\}^m$ such that $\{x\} = \{x_k\}_{k \in \mathcal{C}_j} \setminus \{\bot\}$, then store $(\mathrm{MESSAGE}, kid, x)$. Otherwise, store $(\mathrm{MESSAGE}, kid, \bot)$.

Fig. 8. User-server communication

to handle $K_{i,j} = \bot$ by trying again. When $K_{i,j} = \bot$ the virtual server $\mathcal{F}_j$ will output this to $\mathcal{C}_j$ along with $\{K_{i,j,k}\}_{k \in \mathcal{C}_i'}$ which will all broadcast the shares to $\mathcal{C}_i \cup \mathcal{C}_j$. If they do not all broadcast the same value, then the honest parties in $\mathcal{C}_j$ will crash $\mathcal{C}_j$ which is safe as there must be a corrupted party in $\mathcal{C}_j$. If they all broadcast the same value, denote this value by $\{K_{i,j,k}\}_{k \in \mathcal{C}_i'}$. Then all parties in $\mathcal{C}_i$ will give these values to $\mathcal{F}_i$. Again, if they do not all give the same values, the $\mathcal{F}_i$ will crash. Otherwise $\mathcal{F}_i$ will find the indices k for which the wrong shares arrived at $\mathcal{F}_j$. This only happens if P_k is corrupted, so it is not safe to remove P_k from the set of parties among which the secret sharing is done and try again. The code is given in Figs. 9 and 10.

Putting the Pieces Together. We now describe how to put the pieces together. The combined protocol is given in Fig. 11. Since the tools we use are information-theoretically secure, the information theoretic security of π_{COMB} is fairly straight forward to argue, using the arguments we gave above for the security of the individual sub-protocols.

Termination. To analyze termination, we use that each party is in at most $d = O(1)$ committees and that $n = O(m)$. Let $\delta = m/(8nd)$. If less than δn parties are corrupted, there will be at most $d\delta n = m/8$ committees which even

---

Key Generation We use a key generation protocol KeyGeneration$_{i,j}^{S \leftrightarrow S}$ run between the parties in $C_i \cup C_j$. It is invoked by all parties in the same round by giving the input (KEY, kid, m), where kid is a fresh key id and m is the length of the message that will later be encrypted. It proceeds as follows:

1. All parties in $C_i \cup C_j$ set $C = C_i$;
2. If $C = \emptyset$, then terminate and use a dummy key. Otherwise proceed as follows.
3. $\mathcal{F}_i$ samples $K_{i,j} \leftarrow \mathcal{K}_{m,\lambda}$;
4. $\mathcal{F}_i$ samples an authenticated secret sharing $\{K_{i,j,k}\}_{k \in C} \leftarrow$ share(K_j^i) among the parties C.
5. For $k \in C$, the functionality $\mathcal{F}_i$ outputs $K_{i,j,k}$ to P_k.
6. For $k \in C$, party P_k uses the code in Fig. 8 to send $K_{i,j,k}$ to $\mathcal{F}_j$.
7. Let $\hat{K}_{i,j,k}$ be the value of $K_{i,j,k}$ received by $\mathcal{F}_j$ (if the transmission fails, then $\hat{K}_{i,j,k} = \bot$ which will trigger a reconstruction error which is handled below);
8. $\mathcal{F}_j$ computes $\hat{K}_{i,j} \leftarrow$ rec($\{\hat{K}_{i,j,k}\}_{k \in C}$);
9. If $\hat{K}_{i,j} \neq \bot$, then $\mathcal{F}_j$ outputs SUCCESS to all parties in C_j and stores (KEY, $kid, i, j, m, \hat{K}_{i,j}$). All parties terminate the protocol.
10. If $\hat{K}_{i,j} = \bot$, then $\mathcal{F}_j$ outputs $\{\hat{K}_{i,j,k}\}_{k \in C}$ to all parties in C_j.
11. Each party $\mathsf{P}_k \in C_j$ broadcasts $\{\hat{K}_{j,k}^i\}_{k \in C}$ to $C_i \cup C_j$.
12. If $\mathsf{P}_k \in C_j$ sees that not all parties from C_j broadcasts the same values, then P_k inputs CRASH to $\mathcal{F}_j$ and waits for two rounds to make the crash propagate. In this case no key is needed.
13. If $\mathcal{F}_i$ does not consider $\mathcal{F}_j$ crashed during the above, then all $\mathsf{P}_k \in C_i$ inputs $\{\hat{K}_{j,k}^i\}_{k \in C}$ to $\mathcal{F}_i$. If they do not all input the same value, $\mathcal{F}_i$ will crash.
14. If $\mathcal{F}_i$ did not crash it will find k such that $K_{i,j,k} \neq \hat{K}_{i,j,k}$ and outputs k to all parties in C_i. Following the usual patterns, they will all broadcast k to $C_i \cup C_j$, crash $\mathcal{F}_i$ if there is not agreement and otherwise let all parties input k to $\mathcal{F}_j$ which will crash if there is not agreement.
15. If neither $\mathcal{F}_i$ nor $\mathcal{F}_j$ is crashed, then set $C \leftarrow C \setminus \{k\}$ and go to Step 2.

Fig. 9. Server-server communication part of π_{COMB} (Key Generation)

contain a corrupted member. Therefore the total number of corrupted committees plus crashable committees will be at most $m/8$. Since the outer protocol is secure (including termination guarantee) against $m/8$ malicious corruptions, it follows that the combined protocol guarantees termination against δn malicious corruptions.

Complexity. We now address the complexity of the combined protocol when run in inner-hybrid model. We count one computational step by some $\mathcal{F}_j$ as 1 towards the complexity. We count one computational step by some P_i as 1 towards the complexity. We count the sending of a message x by some P_i as $|x|$ towards the complexity. We count the broadcast of one bit to $\log(n)$ parties as polylog(n). Notice that throughout the protocol, we ever only broadcast to sets of parties of constant size, as all committees have constant size. Let c denote

---

Communication Defines a procedure $\mathsf{Send}_{i,j}^{S \to S}$. It is invoked by all parties in the same round by giving the input (SEND, kid), where some (KEY, i, j, kid, K, m) is stored inside $\mathcal{F}_i$ and some (MESSAGE, $i, j, kid, x \in \{0, 1\}^m$) is stored inside $\mathcal{F}_i$. It proceeds as follows:

1. $\mathcal{F}_i$ deletes (KEY, i, j, kid, K, m);
2. $\mathcal{F}_i$ computes $c = \mathsf{Enc}_{\lambda, K}(x)$ and outputs c to all parties $\mathsf{P}_k \in \mathcal{C}_i$.
3. Each $\mathsf{P}_k \in \mathcal{C}_i$ sends c to all parties $\mathsf{P}_l \in \mathcal{C}_j$. The parties P_l might receive conflicting values, in which case they keep them all.
4. For $l \in \mathcal{C}_j$ each P_l inputs all the values c received from parties $\mathsf{P}_k \in \mathcal{C}_i$ to $\mathcal{F}_j$. The functionality accepts at most $|\mathcal{C}_i|$ values from each party.
5. Let $\mathcal{A}$ denote the set of ciphertexts c received by $\mathcal{F}_j$. There might be up to $|\mathcal{C}_i| \cdot |\mathcal{C}_j|$ such values.
6. If there exist $x \in \{0, 1\}^m$ such that $\{x\} = \{\mathsf{Dec}_{\lambda, K, m}(c)\}_{c \in \mathcal{A}} \setminus \{\bot\}$, then store (MESSAGE, i, j, kid, x). Otherwise, store (MESSAGE, $i, j, kid, \bot$).

Fig. 10. Server-Server communication part of π_{COMB} (communication)

the complexity of running the outer protocol as a plain protocol. We want to compute the complexity of running the combined protocol and show that it is of the form $O(c \cdot \mathrm{polylog}(n)) + \mathrm{poly}(n, \lambda)$. This would show that the overhead of the outer protocol is $\mathrm{OH} = \mathrm{polylog}(n)$. The emulation of the computation of the outer protocol clearly introduces no other overhead than the abort handling, key generation and the encryption of messages. It is clear that crash handling sends at most $O(n^2)$ messages of constant size. This can be swallowed by the $\mathrm{poly}(n, \lambda)$ term. It is clear that one attempt of a key generation of a key of length k will have complexity $O(k)$, as secret sharing is done among a constant number of parties and secret sharing and reconstruction is linear and we broadcast a constant number of messages in one attempt. Since C initially has constant size and each attempt of generating a key sees the size of C go down by at least 1 and the procedure stops when $C = \emptyset$, it follows that key generation has complexity $O(k)$. By assumption the overall complexity of key generation and sending a message is therefore $O(k) + \mathrm{poly}(\lambda)$. There are in the order of $2n + m^2 \mathrm{R}_{\mathrm{OUT}}$ messages, so the total complexity of sending the encrypted messages of total length M will be $O(M) + (2n + m^2) \cdot \mathrm{poly}(\lambda)$. The total length M of the messages is already counted as part of the complexity c and can therefore be swallowed by the $O(c \cdot \mathrm{polylog}(n))$ terms. The remaining $(2n + m^2) \cdot \mathrm{poly}(\lambda)$ can be swallowed by $\mathrm{poly}(n, \lambda)$ as $m = O(n)$.

Theorem 5. *For all $c \in [0, 1)$ there exists a protocol π for the inner-hybrid model for all $f \in \mathsf{NC}$ secure against malicious, adaptive corruption of up to cn parties and with termination guarantee against a non-zero constant fraction of corruptions with $\mathrm{OH} = \mathrm{polylog}(n) \cdot \log(\mathrm{size}(f))$.*

We can use the UC theorem to replace each $\mathcal{F}_j$ by a suitable inner protocol. Using the fact that all $\mathcal{C}_j$ have constant size along with Theorem 2, this gives a combined protocol for the model with OT and a broadcast between sets of parties of constant size with an overhead of $\mathrm{OH} = \mathrm{polylog}(n) \cdot \log(\mathrm{size}(f))$.

Formation For $j = 1, \ldots, m$ initialize $\mathcal{F}_j$ with committee $\mathcal{C}_j$ as defined above. The code of $\mathcal{F}_j$ is describe in the figures above . Below, we describe further behaviour of $\mathcal{F}_j$.

Crash Handling Start running the sub protocols in Fig. 6. If $\mathcal{F}_j$ learns that $\mathcal{F}_i$ is crashed as part of the crash handling, then this is added to the current state $y_{i,j}^r$ of S_j below as in a run of the outer protocol.

Key Generation For all U_i and S_j and messages x of length m and with id kid to be sent from U_i to S_j or S_j to U_i, run $\mathsf{KeyGeneration}_{i,j}^{U \leftrightarrow S}(kid, m)$. For all S_i and S_j and messages x of length m and with id kid to be sent from S_i to S_j in the outer protocol, run $\mathsf{KeyGeneration}_{i,j}^{S \leftrightarrow S}(kid, m)$. All parties wait a number of rounds which upper bounds the worst case running time of all the sub protocols to stay synchronized.

Computation Now emulate the outer protocol π_{OUT} as follows.

    Inputs For $i = 1, \ldots, n$ party P_i has input x_i.

    Server initialization For $j, k = 1, \ldots, m$ functionality $\mathcal{F}_j$ initializes S_j by letting $y_{k,j}^0$ be the empty string.

    Generation of input shares For $i = 1, \ldots, n$ user P_i samples $(x_{i,1}, \ldots, x_{i,m}) \leftarrow \mathsf{In}_{\mathrm{OUT}}(x_i; t_i)$ for a random tape t_i.

    Distribution of input shares For $i = 1, \ldots, n$ and $j = 1, \ldots, m$ user P_i sends $x_{i,j}$ to server $\mathcal{F}_j$ using $\mathsf{Send}_{i,j}^{U \to S}$.

    Embedding of input shares For $j = 1, \ldots, m$ functionality $\mathcal{F}_j$ sets $y_{j,j}^0 \leftarrow (x_{1,j}, \ldots, x_{n,j}, r_j)$ for a random tape r_j.

    Evaluation rounds For $r = 1, \ldots, \mathsf{R}_{\mathrm{OUT}}$ round r is emulated as follows:

        Transition

            For $j = 1, \ldots, m$ functionality $\mathcal{F}_j$ computes $(y_{j,1}^r, \ldots, y_{j,m}^r) \leftarrow \mathsf{Tr}_{\mathrm{OUT}}(r, y_{1,j}^{r-1}, \ldots, y_{m,j}^{r-1})$.

        Communication

            For $j, k = 1, \ldots, m$ functionality $\mathcal{F}_j$ sends $y_{j,k}^r$ to functionality $\mathcal{F}_k$ using $\mathsf{Send}_{j,k}^{S \to S}$

    Generation of output shares For $j = 1, \ldots, m$ functionality S_j computes $(z_{j,1}, \ldots, z_{j,n}) \leftarrow \mathsf{Tr}_{\mathrm{OUT}}(\mathsf{R}_{\mathrm{OUT}} + 1, y_{1,j}^{\mathsf{R}_{\mathrm{OUT}}}, \ldots, y_{m,j}^{\mathsf{R}_{\mathrm{OUT}}})$

    Distribution of output shares For $j = 1, \ldots, m$ and $i = 1, \ldots, n$ server S_j sends $z_{j,i}$ to party P_i using $\mathsf{Send}_{j,i}^{S \to U}$.

    Output reconstruction For $i = 1, \ldots, n$ party P_i computes $z_i \leftarrow \mathsf{Out}_{\mathrm{OUT}}(z_{1,i}, \ldots, z_{n,i})$.

Fig. 11. The combined protocol π_{COMB}

When we want to tolerate that more than half the parties are corrupted, there is no way to implement the broadcast from scratch. We can, however, weaken the assumption on broadcast to only having access to poly(n) broadcasts which are all performed prior to the protocol being run. They might even be performed prior to knowing f. The broadcasts can either be used to set up a public-key infrastructure and then rely on signatures. They can also be used to run the setup phase of the protocol from [PW92] which can then be used to implement an unbounded of number of broadcasts in the online phase.

The protocol from [PW92] has information theoretic security. To broadcast between c parties the protocol from [PW92] has complexity poly$(c) \cdot \lambda$ to broadcast one bit. Since we broadcast $poly(n, \lambda)$ bits among log-size sets this will all in all contribute with a complexity of $poly(n, \lambda)$, which does not affect the overhead.

Corollary 1. *For all $c \in [0, 1)$ there exists an information-theoretically secure protocol π secure against adaptive, malicious corruption of up to cn parties and with termination guarantee against a non-zero constant fraction of corruptions for the hybrid model with initial broadcast and oblivious transfer for all $f \in$ NC with $OH = polylog(n) \cdot \log(size(f))$.*

We can similarly use Theorem 3 to get a protocol for the CRS model and initial broadcast between log-size sets of parties. In this case we will only get computational security, and we might therefore as well go for the weaker model where we assume a PKI instead of initial broadcasts. Given a PKI we can implement the broadcasts using for instance the protocol in [DS83].

Corollary 2. *For all $c \in [0, 1)$ there exists a protocol π secure against adaptive, malicious corruption of up to cn parties and with termination guarantee against a non-zero constant fraction of corruptions for the (PKI, CRS)-hybrid model for all $f \in$ NC with $OH_{\text{ARITH}} = \lambda \cdot polylog(n) \cdot \log(size(f))$.*

Acknowledgments. This work is supported by European Research Council Starting Grant 279447. Samuel Ranellucci is supported by NSF grants #1564088 and #1563722. This work is partially supported by the H2020-LEIT-ICT project SODA, project number 731583. The authors would also like to thank the anonymous reviewers for their valuable comments and suggestions. Any opinions, findings, and conclusions or recommendations expressed in this material are those of the authors and do not necessarily reflect the views of the National Science Foundation.

References

[BCP15] Boyle, E., Chung, K.-M., Pass, R.: Large-scale secure computation: multi-party computation for (Parallel) RAM programs. In: Gennaro, R., Robshaw, M. (eds.) CRYPTO 2015. LNCS, vol. 9216, pp. 742–762. Springer, Heidelberg (2015). doi:10.1007/978-3-662-48000-7_36

[Bra87] Bracha, G.: An o (log n) expected rounds randomized byzantine generals protocol. J. ACM (JACM) **34**(4), 910–920 (1987)

[BSFO12] Ben-Sasson, E., Fehr, S., Ostrovsky, R.: Near-linear unconditionally-secure multiparty computation with a dishonest minority. In: Safavi-Naini, R., Canetti, R. (eds.) CRYPTO 2012. LNCS, vol. 7417, pp. 663–680. Springer, Heidelberg (2012). doi:10.1007/978-3-642-32009-5_39

[CDD+15] Cramer, R., Damgård, I.B., Döttling, N., Fehr, S., Spini, G.: Linear secret sharing schemes from error correcting codes and universal hash functions. In: Oswald, E., Fischlin, M. (eds.) EUROCRYPT 2015. LNCS, vol. 9057, pp. 313–336. Springer, Heidelberg (2015). doi:10.1007/978-3-662-46803-6_11

[CDI+13] Cohen, G., Damgård, I.B., Ishai, Y., Kölker, J., Miltersen, P.B., Raz, R., Rothblum, R.D.: Efficient multiparty protocols via log-depth threshold formulae. In: Canetti, R., Garay, J.A. (eds.) CRYPTO 2013. LNCS, vol. 8043, pp. 185–202. Springer, Heidelberg (2013). doi:10.1007/978-3-642-40084-1_11

[CPS14] Choudhury, A., Patra, A., Smart, N.P.: Reducing the overhead of MPC over a large population. In: Abdalla, M., Prisco, R. (eds.) SCN 2014. LNCS, vol. 8642, pp. 197–217. Springer, Heidelberg (2014). doi:10.1007/978-3-319-10879-7_12

[DIK+08] Damgård, I., Ishai, Y., Krøigaard, M., Nielsen, J.B., Smith, A.: Scalable multiparty computation with nearly optimal work and resilience. In: Wagner, D. (ed.) CRYPTO 2008. LNCS, vol. 5157, pp. 241–261. Springer, Heidelberg (2008). doi:10.1007/978-3-540-85174-5_14

[DIK10] Damgård, I., Ishai, Y., Krøigaard, M.: Perfectly secure multiparty computation and the computational overhead of cryptography. In: Gilbert, H. (ed.) EUROCRYPT 2010. LNCS, vol. 6110, pp. 445–465. Springer, Heidelberg (2010). doi:10.1007/978-3-642-13190-5_23

[DKL+13] Damgård, I., Keller, M., Larraia, E., Pastro, V., Scholl, P., Smart, N.P.: Practical covertly secure MPC for dishonest majority–or: breaking the SPDZ limits. In: Crampton, J., Jajodia, S., Mayes, K. (eds.) ESORICS 2013. LNCS, vol. 8134, pp. 1–18. Springer, Heidelberg (2013). doi:10.1007/978-3-642-40203-6_1

[DPSZ12] Damgård, I., Pastro, V., Smart, N., Zakarias, S.: Multiparty computation from somewhat homomorphic encryption. In: Safavi-Naini, R., Canetti, R. (eds.) CRYPTO 2012. LNCS, vol. 7417, pp. 643–662. Springer, Heidelberg (2012). doi:10.1007/978-3-642-32009-5_38

[DS83] Dolev, D., Strong, H.R.: Authenticated algorithms for byzantine agreement. SIAM J. Comput. 12(4), 656–666 (1983)

[DZ13] Damgård, I., Zakarias, S.: Constant-overhead secure computation of boolean circuits using preprocessing. In: Sahai, A. (ed.) TCC 2013. LNCS, vol. 7785, pp. 621–641. Springer, Heidelberg (2013). doi:10.1007/978-3-642-36594-2_35

[GWZ09] Garay, J.A., Wichs, D., Zhou, H.-S.: Somewhat non-committing encryption and efficient adaptively secure oblivious transfer. In: Halevi, S. (ed.) CRYPTO 2009. LNCS, vol. 5677, pp. 505–523. Springer, Heidelberg (2009). doi:10.1007/978-3-642-03356-8_30

[HM00] Hirt, M., Maurer, U.: Player simulation and general adversary structures in perfect multiparty computation. J. Cryptol. 13(1), 31–60 (2000)

[HMP00] Hirt, M., Maurer, U., Przydatek, B.: Efficient secure multi-party computation. In: Okamoto, T. (ed.) ASIACRYPT 2000. LNCS, vol. 1976, pp. 143–161. Springer, Heidelberg (2000). doi:10.1007/3-540-44448-3_12

[IKOS07] Ishai, Y., Kushilevitz, E., Ostrovsky, R., Sahai, A.: Zero-knowledge from secure multiparty computation. In: Johnson, D.S., Feige, U. (eds.) Proceedings of the 39th Annual ACM Symposium on Theory of Computing, San Diego, California, USA, 11–13 June, pp. 21–30. ACM (2007)

[IKP+16] Ishai, Y., Kushilevitz, E., Prabhakaran, M., Sahai, A., Yu, C.-H.: Secure protocol transformations. In: Robshaw, M., Katz, J. (eds.) CRYPTO 2016. LNCS, vol. 9815, pp. 430–458. Springer, Heidelberg (2016). doi:10.1007/978-3-662-53008-5_15

[IPS08] Ishai, Y., Prabhakaran, M., Sahai, A.: Founding cryptography on oblivious transfer – efficiently. In: Wagner, D. (ed.) CRYPTO 2008. LNCS, vol. 5157, pp. 572–591. Springer, Heidelberg (2008). doi:10.1007/978-3-540-85174-5_32

[KMTZ13] Katz, J., Maurer, U., Tackmann, B., Zikas, V.: Universally composable synchronous computation. In: Sahai, A. (ed.) TCC 2013. LNCS, vol. 7785, pp. 477–498. Springer, Heidelberg (2013). doi:10.1007/978-3-642-36594-2_27

[PW92] Pfitzmann, B., Waidner, M.: Unconditional byzantine agreement for any number of faulty processors. In: Finkel, A., Jantzen, M. (eds.) STACS 1992. LNCS, vol. 577, pp. 337–350. Springer, Heidelberg (1992). doi:10.1007/3-540-55210-3_195

[SS96] Sipser, M., Spielman, D.A.: Expander codes. IEEE Trans. Inf. Theory 42(6), 1710–1722 (1996)

[WC81] Wegman, M.N., Carter, L.: New hash functions and their use in authentication and set equality. J. Comput. Syst. Sci. 22(3), 265–279 (1981)

Better Two-Round Adaptive Multi-party Computation

Ran Canetti[1,2], Oxana Poburinnaya[1(✉)],
and Muthuramakrishnan Venkitasubramaniam[3]

[1] Boston University, Boston, USA
{canetti,oxanapob}@bu.edu
[2] Tel Aviv University and CPIIS, Tel Aviv, Israel
[3] University of Rochester, Rochester, USA
muthu@cs.rochester.edu

Abstract. The only known two-round multi-party computation protocol that withstands adaptive corruption of all parties is the ingenious
protocol of Garg and Polychroniadou [TCC 15]. We present protocols
that improve on the GP protocol in a number of ways. First, concentrat-
ing on the semi-honest case and taking a different approach than GP, we
show a two-round, adaptively secure protocol where:

- Only a global (i.e., non-programmable) reference string is needed. In
  contrast, in GP the reference string is programmable, even in the
  semi-honest case.
- Only *polynomially-secure* indistinguishability obfuscation for circuits and injective one way functions are assumed. In GP, sub-
  exponentially secure IO is assumed.

Second, we show how to make the GP protocol have only RAM complexity, even for Byzantine corruptions. For this we construct the first
statistically-sound non-interactive Zero-Knowledge scheme with RAM
complexity.

1 Introduction

Adaptive security of protocols, namely security against an adversary that decides
whom to corrupt adaptively during the execution of the protocol, has been an
ongoing focus in cryptography. Indeed, adaptive security better captures real life
adversaries, which can often make adaptive corruption choices.

Two cases which are of particular importance in this setting are (a) the
case where no data erasures are possible, hence the adversary gets to see all
the past internal states of a corrupted party, and (b) the case where all parties are eventually corrupted. Indeed, while for static corruptions the case of
all parties being corrupted is uninteresting, for adaptive corruptions the case
of all parties being eventually corrupted is of central interest. For one, in the
case of protocols for computing randomized functions, it allows requiring that

Research supported by the NSF MACS Frontier project, ISF grant 1523/14, Google
Faculty Research Grant and NSF Awards CNS-1526377/1618884.

S. Fehr (Ed.): PKC 2017, Part II, LNCS 10175, pp. 396–427, 2017.
DOI: 10.1007/978-3-662-54388-7_14

the internal randomness of the function remains hidden even when the entire state of the system is exposed. It also allows arguing about the security of other, uncorrupted parties in a larger system which uses our protocol. Furthermore, the combination of these properties allows demonstrating leakage tolerance properties even when all parties may leak some side-channel information on their local computations [BCH12]. We call protocols that are secure in this setting *fully adaptive*.

Constructing fully adaptive protocols is a significant challenge. The difficulty here is that the adversary eventually sees all the inputs and random choices of the parties, and yet security of the output and the computational process should be maintained. Indeed, such protocols with constant number of rounds appeared only recently [CGP15, DKR14, GP14]; among these protocols, only [GP14] is a *multiparty* protocol with *two* rounds (which is the minimum possible).

We construct better two-round, fully adaptive protocols for general multiparty computation. Our improvements span a number of security, functionality, and efficiency aspects. We start by presenting and discussing some of these aspects.

Randomness-Hiding Functionalities. Consider a set S of parties that want to run a secure function evaluation protocol in order to jointly generate an obfuscated program, where the program is to be used in some other protocol that involves additional parties. Security of the obfuscated program should be preserved even when everybody in the set S is corrupted (which could be important for the remaining honest parties in the other protocol). Note that this program-obfuscating functionality is randomized, and security of the overall system requires that the randomness of this function remains secret even when all parties in S are corrupted. Another example of such a task is to instruct parties to joinly sample an RSA public key $N = pq$ without knowing the actual factorization p, q, even when the secret information of all parties is pooled together. We call protocols that hide the actual randomness which was used to compute the function even when everybody is corrupted *randomness-hiding*.

We note that the standard methodology of evaluating a randomized functionality via secure evaluation of a circuit, where some of the input values to the circuit are the result of xor-ing the local random inputs of all parties, results in a protocol that is inherently not randomness-hiding[1]. With this approach the adversary corrupting everybody learns the randomness of each and every party, and therefore the internal randomness of the function (e.g. random coins of obfuscation); thus no security is left.

Randomness hiding is also useful in another, perhaps less obvious, scenario. Adaptive security is often used to argue leakage tolerance [BCH12]: assume parties are computing a randomized functionality, and the adversary decides to leak 1 bit of each party's randomness. If the protocol looses security when everybody is corrupted, the simulator from [BCH12] cannot simulate such leakage,

---

[1] For instance, parties can choose randomness r_i, make it part of their input, and evaluate the functionality $F((x_1, r_1), \ldots, (x_n, r_n)) = f(x_1, \ldots, x_n; \bigoplus r_i)$.

since the argument from [BCH12] requires that the simulator should be able to potentially simulate *the full randomness of each party whose internal state was leaked,* even though the adversary actually sees only a single bit of randomness of each party.[2] In contrast, if the protocol supports randomness-hiding functionalities, then the simulator can simulate randomness of all parties, and therefore the protocol remains leakage-tolerant even if the adversary decides to leak from everybody.

Global Common Reference String. In the common reference string (CRS) model, all parties have access to a string, generated in advance by a trusted entity (which doesn't need to participate in the protocol). In a *local* (sometimes called *programmable*) CRS model, which is most often used, the simulator has the power to generate the CRS itself. This makes the task of designing protocols easier, since the simulator can generate the CRS in such a way that it knows corresponding trapdoors and therefore has more power than the adversary. The major drawback of a local CRS is that when two different protocols use the same CRS, *there is no guarantee of security whatsoever,* even if each of them separately is secure. Thus, to preserve security of a protocol that was proven secure in the *local* CRS model within a larger system, one has to make sure that no other protocol in the system will ever use that same CRS, either inadvertently or via malicious protocol design. See e.g. [CDPW07] for more discussion.

To overcome these issues with composability, the *global* CRS model was introduced. In this model the simulator doesn't have the power to generate the CRS; instead, it has to work with a given CRS. The global CRS model makes significantly weaker trust assumptions on the reference string and its generation process. In particular, a global CRS can be known globally and used by all protocols in the system without any prior coordination; in this sence composition-wise *the global CRS model is very close to the plain model*: once we proved that the protocol is secure with a global CRS, we don't need to take this CRS into account anymore, since it can be used by any other protocol without the risk of compromising security.

On the Need of the Common Reference String. Our protocol works in a common reference string (CRS) model. While there is no evidence that computing randomness-hiding functionalities require a CRS[3], it is not known how to compute general randomness-hiding functionalities in the plain model. In fact, this is an interesting open problem, and solving it would allow to remove the CRS requirement from many works (including this work), where the CRS is an obfuscated program whose keys and randomness should remain hidden.

---

[2] To be more precise, [BCH12] require that there exist a translation function which maps ideal world internal state into real world internal state.

[3] Indeed, some simple functions can be computed in a randomness-hiding way even in the plain model; for instance, the function $f(r) = g^r$, where g is a group generator and r is randomness, can be simply computed by choosing a random element in a group; in this case randomness r remains unknown.

As discussed in [IKOS10], adaptively secure protocols for randomized functionalities are tightly connected to extractable one way functions (EOWF). Namely, this work shows that the existence of such a protocol for general functionalities *in the plain model* implies that EOWFs with uniform auxiliary input don't exist, since one-wayness of the function can be broken by first using the simulator to obtain random coins for a given output and then by running the extractor on these random coins to extract the actual input of the EOWF.

We also stress that the CRS appears to be essential, even in the semi-honest setting. Recall that in the case of non-adaptive semi-honest security, CRS is not needed; indeed, instead of having a CRS, parties can generate the CRS by themselves, in the plain model, in the beginning of the protocol, at the cost of one more round. However, this is not true in the case of adaptive security. The reason is that our CRS contains secrets (e.g. randomness of the obfuscation, PRF keys) which shouldn't be known to anybody, including parties running the protocol. Working in the plain model would require parties to generate this CRS in a way that even all parties together do not know corresponding secrets. As discussed in the previous paragraph, this is an open problem.

Computation and Communication Complexity. The majority of existing protocols assume that the function is represented as a circuit. This means that the work of parties and, in some cases, the length of communication both depend on the size of a circuit to be computed. Given that Turing machines and RAM machines may have significantly more efficient parameters than circuits, building MPC protocols which use the advantage of more efficient models of computation is an important task. (In particular, in the case of RAM computation that does not necessarily need to access all the input, the gap could be exponential.)

Although we cannot take advantage of a potentially sublinear RAM computations (indeed, unlike, say, the persistent garbled RAM setting where database garbling phase could be long, but the actual computations are very short, the MPC setting requires the computation to touch every input), multiparty computation can still benefit from the RAM model in several ways. As one example, consider the case where parties are willing to trade some security for efficiency; in this case they can obtain efficiency close to the input-specific running time (rather than worst-case running time)[4]. For instance, let's say there is a database with medical data, and a group of researchers is interested in average age of persons satisfying some sparse property P (say, having rare medical condition). If these researches don't care about hiding P, then they can compute the average fairly efficiently, with running time comparable to the number of entries satisfying P. However, if P cannot be made public, then need to run a protocol with P being their secret input; this immediately makes their running time worst-case

---

[4] Recall that the security of MPC requires that no information about inputs of parties is leaked. Running time of a program M on input x could potentially leak information about x. Therefore if full security is needed then programs should necessarily work as long as their worst-case running time, even if computation on this particular input is short.

(for all possible P), which is comparable to the size of the database. If these researchers are willing to sacrifice some security to gain efficiency (for instance, if others are allowed to learn that P is a rare disease, but cannot learn which one), then they can perform very efficient computation (like in the first case), while still having meaningful security guarantees.

On the Limitations of the [IK02, AIK06] *Approach in the Fully Adaptive Setting.* A natural approach to obtaining protocols with RAM efficiency is to use ideas of [IK02, AIK06]: Instead of directly evaluating the desired function, have the parties jointly evaluate a garbling (or, randomized encoding) of the function and input. Then each party locally computes the output. Plugging-in a RAM-efficient garbling scheme [CHJV15, CH16] results in RAM-efficient protocols. However, this approach has a caveat in our fully adaptive setting: note that the functionality which needs to be computed (i.e. garbling) is randomized. If we want to achieve full adaptive security, the randomness used in the garbling should remain hidden even when everybody is corrupted; in other words, for the whole construction to be secure, the underlying protocol should be randomness-hiding. However, the only two-round protocol with full adaptive security we know (that of [GP14]) is not randomness-hiding, and therefore to use this approach we need to come up with adaptively secure randomness-hiding protocol first.

1.1   Our Results: Semi-honest Setting

Our main result is the first two-round MPC protocol with *global* (non-programmable) CRS, which is secure against adaptive semi-honest corruption of all parties. Besides globality, our protocol has other features: First, the protocol allows to securely compute even randomness-hiding functionalities, and furthermore, it guarantees leakage tolerance even when every party can be leaked from (for the discussion on why this is usually not the case, see the paragraph about randomness-hiding functionalities in the first part of the introduction). Second, the protocol is RAM-friendly, i.e. the amount of communication in our protocol only depends on the RAM size of a function, not on its circuit size, and the work of each party which obtains the output is proportional to RAM complexity of the function. Third, we assume only polynomially secure IO and injective OWFs.

Theorem 1. *Assuming injective one way functions and indistinguishability obfuscation for circuits, there exists a two-round multiparty protocol with global CRS for computing any randomized functionalities, even randomness-hiding ones. The protocol is adaptively secure against honest-but-curious corruptions of possibly all parties, with oblivious simulation. Its communication complexity depends on $\lambda, \{|x_i|\}_{i=1}^n, y, |f|_{\mathsf{RAM}}$ (logarithmic parameters omitted), and time and space of every party depends on $\lambda, \{|x_i|\}_{i=1}^n, y, |f|_{\mathsf{RAM}}$, and time or space needed to evaluate RAM $f(x_1, \ldots, x_n)$ in the worst case.*

Our result improves the state of the art in a number of ways. In particular, this is:

- The first 2-round fully adaptive semi-honest MPC with global setup[5];
- The first 2-round fully adaptive semi-honest MPC which doesn't require subexponential security of iO;
- The first 2-round fully adaptive semi-honest MPC which supports all (even randomness-hiding) functionalities, and which therefore is fully leakage tolerant.

Making this Protocol Secure Against Malicious Adversaries. The common techniques [CLOS02] can be applied to compile this protocol into its malicious version. The resulting protocol needs 4 rounds - two rounds should be added in the beginning to do a malicious coin toss by first committing to inputs and randomness and then partially opening randomness. We observe however that the first round of the semi-honest protocol is a commitment round as well, and thus in the malicious version we can use CLOS commitments as if they were round-1 messages of the semi-honest protocol. Thus, then protocol requires only three rounds (round 1 for commitments, round 2 for partial opening randomness, and round 3 for round 2 of the semi-honest protocol). The resulting protocol preserves all properties of the semi-honest version (in particular, it remains randomness-hiding as long as there is at least one uncorrupted party during round 2, which could be corrupted later). The only property that is lost is globality of the CRS, which is inherent in the malicious setting). The resulting protocol outperforms the protocol by Dachman-Soled et al. [DKR14], which is a 4-round protocol against semi-honest adversaries.

1.2 Our Results: Malicious Setting

As an additional result, we show how to make the protocol of [GP14] RAM-efficient: namely, we construct the first RAM-efficient statistically-sound non-interactive zero-knowledge proofs, and then plug this NIZK into the protocol of [GP14]. Compared to the malicious version of our first protocol, this protocol needs only two rounds (instead of three), however, it requires subexponentially-secure iO, and is not randomness-hiding.

Theorem 2 [GP14]. *Assuming the existence of RAM-efficient statistically sound NIZK, subexponentially secure iO for circuits, and one way functions, there exists a two-round multiparty protocol with local CRS adaptively secure against malicious corruptions of possibly all parties. Its communication complexity depends on $\lambda, \{|x_i|\}_{i=1}^n, y, |f|_{\mathsf{RAM}}$ (logarithmic parameters omitted), and time and space of every party depends on $\lambda, \{|x_i|\}_{i=1}^n, y, |f|_{\mathsf{RAM}}$, and time or space needed to evaluate RAM $f(x_1, \ldots, x_n)$ in the worst case.*

RAM-Efficient Statistically Sound NIZK. We construct the first RAM-efficient NIZK with statistical soundness, assuming statistically-sound NIZK for circuits (which can be obtained from trapdoor permutations) and a RAM-efficient garbling scheme (which can be built from iO and OWFs [CH16]):

---

[5] We underline that the approach of [GP14] requires a local CRS even in the honest-but-curious setting.

Theorem 3. *(Informal) Assuming statistically sound non-interactive zero knowledge (NIZK) for circuits and a succinct garbling scheme for* RAM*, there exists a NIZK for* RAM*, where the work of the prover and the size of the proof depends on* $|R|_{\mathsf{RAM}}$*, and the work of the verifier depends on the* RAM *complexity of* R *(where* $R(x, w)$ *is a relation which defines the language for the proof).*

We note that our succinct NIZK is useful also in other settings. For instance, in the two-round protocol of Garg et al. [GGHR14] the parties exchange obfuscated programs which compute next message functions (of some underlying many-round protocol) together with a proof that the computation was done correctly. If the underlying protocol has number of rounds proportional to the RAM complexity of the function (say, the protocol by Damgard et al. [DMN11]), plugging our RAM-efficient NIZK makes [GGHR14] protocol RAM-efficient.

1.3   Related Work

Fully Adaptively Secure Protocols. Until now, only three constant-round fully adaptively secure protocols were known. [CGP15] is a two-round protocol for two-party computation; [DKR14] is an MPC protocol, but requires 4 rounds; both protocols have global CRS and allow to compute randomness-hiding functionalities. [GP14] is a two-round MPC protocol secure against malicious adversaries; thus their reference string is necessarily local[6]. Their protocol doesn't support randomness-hiding functionalities.

All three protocols require the function to be represented as a circuit: namely, the core part in both [CGP15, DKR14] are Yao garbled circuits[7]. The protocol of [GP14] requires a statistically-sound NIZK for the statement $f(x_1, \ldots, x_n) = y$, and prior to our work such proofs required verification time proportional to the size of the circuit.

In addition, [CGP15, GP14] require subexponentially-secure iO.

RAM-Efficient Protocols. Existing protocols for (even static) RAM MPC follow one of the two approaches. The work of Boyle et al. [BCP15] shares a paradigm of Damgard et al. [DMN11] which instructs parties to jointly evaluate steps of a RAM CPU; this approach results in number of rounds proportional to the number of CPU steps needed to compute a function.

The other approach, introduced by Ishai and Kushilevitz [IK02, AIK06], requires parties to jointly evaluate a randomized encoding of the function and input and then locally compute the output of this randomized encoding. Thus,

---

[6] We note however that merely using their protocol in the semi-honest case doesn't allow for a local CRS: their approach requires proving statements to an obfuscated program, which requires NIZK (and therefore a local CRS) even in the honest-but-curious case.

[7] Which cannot be easily switched to the garbling scheme for RAM. For instance, in both protocols the underlying garbling scheme should support bit-by-bit garbling of an input. [DKR14] makes even further use of the actual construction of garbled circuits.

plugging a RAM-efficient garbling scheme [CHJV15, CH16] into known constructions results in statically-secure RAM-efficient protocols. However, in order to achieve adaptive security, the underlying protocol must support randomness-hiding functionalities. Prior to our work, no fully adaptive, two round protocol with randomness hiding was known.

Constant Round Adaptively Secure RAM-efficient Protocols. Combining several existing techniques, it is possible to construct adaptively secure protocols for RAM. Namely, following the Ishai-Kushilevitz approach outlined above, we can plug the succinct garbling schemes for RAM into constant-round adaptively secure MPC (such as [DKR14, GP14]). The first protocol yields a fully adaptive MPC for RAM with 4 rounds; we refer to this protocol as "augmented [DKR14]".

The second construction, however, loses full security, since evaluating a garbling is a randomized functionality, and since their protocol doesn't guarantee secrecy of randomness of the function when everybody is corrupted. Namely, the simulator of the composed scheme will not be able to simulate the random coins of each party, since it needs to simulate generation randomness of the garbling scheme, consistent with simulated garbled values. This can be circumvented by using a garbling scheme where the simulator can also simulate random coins of the garbling, i.e. "adaptively secure" garbling[8] It is possible to construct such a garbling scheme by putting a mechanism allowing deniability (like in deniable encryption of [SW14]) on top of a garbling algorithm of RAM-efficient garbling scheme, say, [CH16], and obfuscating the whole circuit. This obfuscated circuit is a CRS of an adaptive garbling scheme[9]. Such a construction seems to give a RAM-efficient MPC protocol, which even allows to compute randomness-hiding functionalities (roughly, because the deniability mechanism of [SW14] generates random coins which are hidden from everybody). Still, this approach, which we call "augmented [GP14]", requires subexponentially-secure iO, and, since they use NIZK even in the semi-honest case, a local CRS.

In the table below we compare our result with existing work on constant round fully adaptive MPC [DKR14, GP14], as well as with augmented versions of these protocols described above. All parameters are for the semi-honest setting.

	Rounds	Supports RAM	Global CRS	Randomness hiding	Assumptions
[DKR14]	4	−	+	+	iO+OWF
[GP14]	2	−	−	−	subexp. iO+OWF
augmented [DKR14]	4	+	+	+	iO+OWF
augmented [GP14]	2	+	−	+	subexp. iO+OWF
our result	2	+	+	+	iO+OWF

---

[8] Note that usually the term "adaptive security" in the context of garbling is used to denote a different property: that the adversary can choose new inputs and functions after seeing garbled values.

[9] With this approach the environment has to fix inputs *before* seeing the CRS, i.e. this garbling scheme is only selectively secure. However, this is good enough for the protocol of [GP14], since they anyway use complexity leveraging and subexponentially-secure iO.

Succinct NIZK Proofs. The only approach for building NIZK proof systems where the length of the proof is independent of a circuit is based on encrypting satisfying assignment via FHE and making the verifier homomorphically evaluate the SAT circuit. This includes the work of [Gen09], who proposed the approach, and [Gro11], who shows how to bring the size of the proof down from $|w| \cdot \mathsf{poly}(\lambda)$ to $|w| + \mathsf{poly}(\lambda)$ (where w is the witness and λ is a security parameter); thus, the question of communication complexity of NIZK is resolved. However, in both schemes the verifier needs to do the work proportional to the circuit complexity of the function. Up to now we didn't know any fully succinct NIZK proof system (i.e. NIZK where both communication complexity and work of both parties is smaller than the circuit size).

1.4 Our Techniques: Semi-honest Case

Our MPC protocol takes a different approach than either of [GP14, DKR14, CGP15]. We present and motivate the approach.

First Attempt. A natural idea for building MPC protocols is to use an obfuscated program to emulate a trusted party. That is, the CRS contains an obfuscated program which collects all inputs, does the computation, and outputs the result.

More precisely, the CRS should contain an encryption program Enc, which takes an input x_i and outputs its encryption c_i, and a decryption/evaluation program Eval, which takes $c_1, \ldots, c_n$, decrypts them, computes $y = f(x_1, \ldots, x_n)$ and outputs y. The parties can compute $f(x_1, \ldots, x_n)$ by encrypting $c_i = \mathsf{Enc}(x_i)$, broadcasting c_i, and computing $y \leftarrow \mathsf{Eval}(c_1, \ldots, c_n)$. However, such a protocol is clearly insecure: each party (say, P_1) can compute many different $y' = f(x'_1, x_2, \ldots, x_n)$ for any desired x'_1 by generating $c'_1 = \mathsf{Enc}(x'_1)$ and running $\mathsf{Eval}(c'_1, c_2, \ldots, c_n)$.

A natural way to mitigate such an attack is to make the parties commit to their input first, and only then exchange ciphertexts and do the computation. Therefore we now have two rounds: in the first round parties exchange their commitments a_i, and in the second round they exchange ciphertexts c_i. To make sure that no party can run Eval on a different input than the one he committed to, Eval should check that x_i in c_i is consistent with the commitment a_i in the previous round. To achieve this, we need to put into c_i not only x_i, but also a_i together with its opening. Note however that this still allows a curious party to generate a different c'_i encrypting a different x'_i and a different, but valid commitment a'_i to x'_i, and then run Eval; thus we have to include *all* first-round commitments $a_1, \ldots, a_n$ within each c_i (together with an opening for a_i), so that a curious party couldn't modify its own a_i without being noticed.

At this point the protocol looks like this:

1. **The CRS:** Programs Enc and Eval, a CRS for a commitment scheme μ_{bind}
2. **Round 1:** Each party broadcasts $a_i \leftarrow \mathsf{Commit}(x_i)$, and keeps decommitment information r_i;
3. **Round 2:** Each party broadcasts $c_i \leftarrow \mathsf{Enc}(x_i; r_i; a_1, \ldots, a_n)$

4. **Evaluation:** Each party computes $y \leftarrow \mathsf{Eval}(c_1, \ldots, c_n)$.

Here Eval decrypts each c_i and performs two checks: first, it checks that the set of $(a_1, \ldots, a_n)$ is the same in each c_i. Second, it checks that for all i r_i is a correct opening of a_i to x_i. If all checks pass, it outputs $f(x_1, \ldots, x_n)$.

While this idea works in general, the exact implementation becomes a challenge. Our goal is to show that a real execution is indistinguishable from a simulated one, where the simulated execution (and in particular, programs and communication) is generated by a simulator who doesn't know inputs of parties. One difficulty is to be able to switch the ciphertext from real (encrypting x_i) to simulated, and at the same time be able to generate Eval with the secret key of encryption inside. Several ways to accomplish this are known. One approach is to use a "double encryption + NIZK" paradigm [NY90]; this method is chosen by [GP14] and it leads to a protocol secure against malicious adversaries. However, one disadvantage of this approach is that the CRS is necessarily local, even in the semi honest case.

The approach we take in order to switch c_i from real to simulated in the presence of the secret key is the "punctured key" technique, which guarantees that real and dummy ciphertexts are indistinguishable, even in the presence of "almost all" key - i.e. the key which decrypts everything except for this ciphertext. This allows us to first indistinguishably modify Eval such that it needs only a punctured key, and then switch a ciphertext (which the punctured secret key cannot decrypt) to a dummy ciphertext.

However, this approach has two shortcomings, which are not obvious from this discussion, but which would appear if we went deeper into the simulation and proofs. First, the technique requires hardwiring input-dependent values (such as x_i and c_i) into the program in the proof. This means that the inputs have to be fixed *before* the adversary sees Eval (and therefore the whole CRS), giving only *selective* security. Second, with this approach the programs in the simulated CRS have to contain simulated ciphertexts, and therefore we can only hope to get *local*, or *programmable*, CRS.

Second Attempt. To solve both issues, we exploit an indirection technique similar to the one used in [KSW14, CPR16]: namely, we generate Enc and Eval during the runtime instead of fixing them in the CRS. Note that Enc is needed only in round 2 (and Eval is needed even later). Therefore we can let parties agree on generation randomness r_{Gen} in round 1, and then, after round 1 is complete, each party can run a special generation program Gen (which is now in the CRS instead of Enc and Eval) to produce a fresh pair of Enc and Eval, which are then used as before. In addition, we add to the CRS a special program $\mathsf{Explain}$, which inverts Gen, i.e. for any given output it produces consistent randomness r_{Gen}; this is used by the simulator only.

Therefore the protocol now looks like this:

- **The global CRS:** programs Gen, $\mathsf{Explain}$, a CRS for a commitment scheme μ_{bind}

- **Round 1**: parties broadcast commitments $a_i = \mathsf{Commit}(x_i; r_i)$ together with randomness $r_{\mathsf{Gen},i}$;
- **After round 1**: each party sets generation randomness $r_{\mathsf{Gen}} \leftarrow \bigoplus r_{\mathsf{Gen},i}$ and obtains $\mathsf{Enc}, \mathsf{Eval} \leftarrow \mathsf{Gen}(r_{\mathsf{Gen}})$;
- **Round 2**: each party broadcasts $c_i \leftarrow \mathsf{Enc}(x_i; r_i; a_1, \ldots, a_n)$;
- **Evaluation**: each party computes $y \leftarrow \mathsf{Eval}(c_1, \ldots, c_n)$.

The simulator works as follows. First it generates programs $\mathsf{Enc}', \mathsf{Eval}'$ (which, as we said earlier, are different from real world programs). Next it uses $\mathsf{Explain}$ to generate randomness r_{Gen} on which Gen outputs these simulated $\mathsf{Enc}', \mathsf{Eval}'$. It generates all $r_{\mathsf{Gen},i}$ such that they xor to r_{Gen}, and sets a_i and c_i to be a dummy commitment and a dummy ciphertext. $(r_{\mathsf{Gen},i}, a_i, c_i)$ constitute simulated communications. To handle corruption of a party, the simulator equivocates the commitment; also the simulator needs to show the randomness for encryption, which it can do as long as underlying encryption is non-committing or deniable. Note that the the only reason why the simulator needs to generate the CRS is a commitment scheme.

Third Attempt. So far our CRS is still local due to a commitment scheme. However, it turns out that we don't need the full power of the commitments; for the proof of security our commitment scheme should be statistically binding *only at round-1 commitments*, not everywhere. Since we are in the semi-honest setting, it is enough to have a commitment scheme that is statistically binding only on honestly generated commitments. We call this primitive honest-but-curious (HBC) commitments.

Such a primitive can be easily constructed from one way functions: consider a length-doubling prg mapping $\{0,1\}^l$ to $\{0,1\}^{2l}$. For random $s \in \{0,1\}^l, r \in \{0,1\}^{2l}$, let $(\mathsf{prg}(s), r)$ be a commitment to 0 and $(r, \mathsf{prg}(s))$ be a commitment to 1. To open the commitment, show s. As long as a commitment was generated honestly, i.e. r was truly random, it doesn't have a valid prg preimage and therefore this commitment is statistically binding. The simulator can simulate the commitment by generating $\mathsf{prg}(s_0), \mathsf{prg}(s_1)$ and later open it to any bit. (Note that dishonest sender could cheat in the same way, and therefore binding holds only for honestly generated commitments. But it suffices for our MPC protocol, since we need a statistical binding property only for round 1 commitments a_i, which are generated by honest parties.)

Note that HBC commitments don't require a CRS, and therefore the CRS of the overall scheme is now global.

The Choice of Encryption Scheme for the MPC Protocol. As we said earlier, perhaps the most challenging part of the proof is to switch ciphertexts from real to simulated, while keeping the decryption key inside Eval. For this we take a punctured programming approach, and therefore we need an encryption scheme where it is possible to give a partial key, called a punctured key, which doesn't reveal anything about the challenge ciphertext. Our goal is the following: first we want to modify Eval so that it uses a punctured key instead of a real one;

this should be done without changing the functionality of Eval, since we want to base security on iO. Importantly, *modified* Eval *should not contain* x_i, *or any input-dependent values*, since Eval should be generated by a simulator during the protocol execution, when the simulator might not know inputs of the parties yet. Next we want to use security of the punctured key and switch the ciphertext from real to simulated.

The puncturable deterministic encryption [Wat15], which is commonly used in this scenario, doesn't help us: if we were using this scheme, the punctured program would depend on inputs, making the simulation impossible. We therefore use a different encryption scheme, which we call a puncturable randomized encryption (PRE)[10]. In addition, this primitive may be viewed as a simulation-secure variant of PDE, and might be of independent interest.

Puncturable Randomized Encryption (PRE). In a definition of a semantically secure encryption scheme a real ciphertext is indistinguishable from a simulated one, even in the presence of a public key. A much stronger CCA security requires that ciphertexts are still indistinguishable even given access to a decryption oracle, i.e. to the functionality of a secret key everywhere except the challenge ciphertext. One can consider an ultimate version of CCA security and require that ciphertexts are indistinguishable even when *the secret key itself* is given in the clear (of course, for this to be meaningful, the secret key shouldn't be able to decrypt the challenge ciphertext, just like in case of standard definition of CCA-security). This is exactly what our puncturable randomized encryption achieves. In other words, a PRE scheme is a symmetric key encryption scheme secure under simulation security definition, where the simulator needs to simulate a punctured key as well: that is, we require that a real-world punctured key and a ciphertext $(k\{c\}, c)$ are indistinguishable from simulated $(k\{c\}, c)$.

We build a secret key version of this primitive using puncturable PRFs and an injective public key encryption scheme (injective means that there doesn't exist a tuple (x, r, x', r') such that $(x, r) \neq (x', r')$ and $\mathsf{Enc}_{pk}(x; r) = \mathsf{Enc}_{pk}(x'; r')$). The secret key of a PRE consists of a public key of encryption scheme pk and a PRF key k. To encrypt a message m with randomness r, compute $T \leftarrow \mathsf{Enc}_{pk}(m; r)$, $C \leftarrow F_k(T) \oplus (m, r)$, and set the ciphertext to be (T, C). To decrypt (T, C), compute $(m, r) \leftarrow C \oplus F_k(T)$ and verify that $T = \mathsf{Enc}_{pk}(m; r)$.

To puncture a key at a ciphertext $(T^*, C^*) = \mathsf{PRE.Enc}(m; r)$, output $(pk, k\{T^*\})$, i.e. puncture PRF key k at T^*. This punctured PRE key doesn't give any information about plaintext of the ciphertext (T^*, C^*): intuitively, C^* looks uniformly random since k is punctured at T^*, and T^* itself doesn't reveal m since it is a ciphertext of a public key encryption. On the other hand, the punctured key still allows to encrypt all other plaintexts-randomness pairs and decrypt all other ciphertexts: note that for a given T there is only a single C which makes (T, C) a valid encryption; therefore puncturing out $k\{T^*\}$ affects exactly one valid ciphertext, i.e. (T^*, C^*).

---

[10] Note that merely randomizing the PDE plaintext doesn't yield a PRE.

The simulator can generate a dummy ciphertext (T^*, C^*) by setting $T^* \leftarrow$ $\mathsf{Enc}_{pk}(0; r)$ and choosing C^* at random. It can also generate a corresponding punctured key as $(pk, k\{T^*\})$. This simulated ciphertext and punctured key $(T^*, C^*), (pk, k\{T^*\})$ can be shown to be indistinguishable from real ones by invoking security of a punctured PRF and an encryption scheme.

Computing Randomness-Hiding Functionalities. So far we described a protocol for deterministic functionalities. Here we describe how we handle randomized functionalities in a randomness-hiding way, i.e. the actual randomness used to compute the function should remain hidden even when all parties are corrupted and all their randomness is learned by the adversary.

It might seem first that to achieve randomness hiding we can use ideas of [SW14] and let the encryption program internally choose randomness by applying an extractor to the random input provided by a party - the technique used in both [CGP15, DKR14] to achieve randomness hiding. Namely, let the encryption program B generate a ciphertext containing not only input x_i of a party, but also randomness r_i derived internally by the program without help of the party. Later Eval can decrypt ciphertexts, learn all x_i and r_i and compute the function as $f(x_1, \ldots, x_n; \bigoplus r_i)$. However, this approach is bound to fail in our case: for our proof of security to go through, we crucially need the fact that *round-1 messages (i.e. commitments) completely determine the computation*, and therefore parties would have to commit to r_i in round 1. This means that parties have to know r_i themselves, and therefore the randomness of the computation will be revealed upon corruption.

Another idea to let our protocol compute randomized functionalities while hiding the randomness is to randomize program Eval in a natural way, i.e. let Eval apply a PRF on its inputs, and use the resulting randomness for computing the function. Hopefully, security of a PRF will guarantee that this randomness remains hidden. However, this idea still doesn't work in of itself: it again violates our crucial property that round-1 messages should determine the computation. Namely, if randomness was derived as a PRF of inputs to Eval (recall that Eval takes round-2 ciphertexts as inputs), this property would be violated, since for a given set of round-1 messages there may be many corresponding round-2 ciphertexts, and thus many possible randomness of the computation.

Our actual solution modifies the previous attempt so that the crucial computation-fixing property is not violated. For this, we let program Eval decrypt ciphertexts, compute a PRF *on round-1 commitments* and evaluate a randomized functionality with resulting randomness. Intuitively, security of a PRF (and obfuscation on top of it) guarantees that this value remains hidden. The simulator can generate simulated Eval where this PRF is punctured and the result of the computation is hardcoded. For this idea to work it is important that Eval is generated during the runtime; if it was fixed in the CRS, we would have to hardwire outputs for every execution and therefore the CRS would have to grow with the number of executions.

Achieving RAM Efficiency. There are two ways to use our construction in order to achieve an efficient protocol. One way is to use iO for RAM in all programs involved. However, iO for RAM requires sub-exponential security of underlying iO for circuits. The other way, which only needs polynomially-secure iO for circuits, is to use the protocol to evaluate a functionality which takes parties' inputs and a function and outputs garbled function and garbled inputs; then parties can evaluate garbling themselves locally. If a RAM-efficient garbling scheme is used [CH16], then the whole protocol becomes RAM-efficient. Note that it is enough to use *statically secure* garbling scheme, since our base protocol supports randomness-hiding functionalities, i.e. doesn't reveal randomness of the computation even when everybody is corrupted[11]. The composed scheme also supports randomized randomness-hiding functionalities: to evaluate such a functionality $f(x_1, \ldots, x_n; r)$, parties should use basic protocol to evaluate a randomized function $F(x_1, \ldots, x_n; (r_1, r_2))$ which uses r_1 as randomness to garble function f and inputs $x_1, \ldots, x_n, r_2$ (r_2 being random input of f).

1.5   Our Techniques: Malicious Case

To obtain a two-round RAM efficient protocol in a malicious setting, we observe that the protocol of [GP14] becomes RAM-efficient, as long as statistically-sound NIZK they use is RAM-efficient. Let us briefly describe their protocol. Very roughly, in their protocol parties exchange commitments in round 1, and in round 2 they broadcast their input encrypted twice together with a NIZK proof that plaintexts are the same (the actual statement for the proof is more complicated, as discussed below). The CRS contains an obfuscated program which expects to see commitments from round 1, together with ciphertexts from round 2 and corresponding proofs. This program checks NIZKs and uses a hardwired decryption key of a double encryption to decrypt the ciphertexts and evaluate the function. Each party can feed its transcript to this program and obtain the output.

So far the protocol seems to work in any model of computation: indeed, if we use iO for RAM to obfuscate the evaluation program in the CRS, then the work of each party becomes proportional to RAM complexity of a function. However, the problem is that the NIZK statement is more complicated than described above: it also requires proving that $y = f(x_1, \ldots, x_n)$, which is needed for the security proof to go through. As usual in "iO + NIZK" techniques, the NIZK has to be *statistically sound*. For all known NIZKs, this means that the verifier

---

[11] If the protocol revealed randomness of the computation, then the garbling scheme would have to be adaptively secure, i.e. the simulator of the garbling scheme would have to first simulate it and then, once it learned inputs, provide consistent generation randomness of the garbling scheme (note that the term "adaptive security" is ambiguous: in the context of garbling it usually denotes a different property, saying that simulation is possible even if inputs or functions are chosen adaptively after seeing some garbled values. Here by adaptive security we mean that random coins can be generated by the simulator).

(in our case, the obfuscated evaluation program) has to do work proportional to the circuit complexity of f, even if the program is obfuscated with iO for RAM.

Therefore to make this protocol RAM-efficient, it suffices to build RAM-efficient statistically sound NIZK.

RAM-Efficient Statistically Sound NIZK for NP. Let a language L be specified by a relation $R(x, w)$. We build a statistically sound NIZK where, roughly, the work of the prover and NIZK length depends on $|R|_{\mathsf{RAM}}$, and the work of the verifier depends on worst-case RAM complexity of R.

Our main idea is the following: to prove that $x^* \in L$, the prover should send to a verifier a garbled program $\mathsf{GProg}(R(x, w))$, a garbled input $\mathsf{GInp}(x^*, w^*)$, and a NIZK proof (for circuits) that the garbling was done correctly: i.e. that the prover followed the garbling algorithm, and that it garbled correct function R and input x. The verifier should accept the proof if the NIZK proof verifies, and if the evaluation of a garbled program on a garbled input results in 1.

However, there are two issues. First, since we assume that we only have a NIZK for circuits, we need to make sure that the statement which we prove (i.e. that garbling was done correctly) is independent of the circuit complexity of R (in particular, we need a garbling scheme where the size of circuits which generate garbling, i.e. the size of $\mathsf{GInp}, \mathsf{GProg}$, only depend on a size of RAM description of a program to be garbled).

Second, note that this scheme guarantees that the garbler follows the garbling instructions (because of the NIZK), but there is no way to guarantee that the prover uses truly random coins to garble. This might introduce problems. Consider a garbling scheme which is not perfectly correct: say, for some choice of parameters the garbled program always outputs 1, no matter what the underlying program does[12]. In this case a malicious and unbounded prover could choose these bad parameters and therefore convince the verifier in wrong statements, since the evaluation of a garbled program results in 1 no matter whether $R(x, w)$ holds or not. Thus, we need a garbling scheme where the evaluation can never result in the wrong answer, i.e. where the computation *always* results in either a correct result or $\perp$. We call this property *perfect correctness with abort*.

We observe that the garbling scheme of Canetti and Holmgren ([CH16]) already has both properties; see full version [CPV16] for details. Thus, our scheme yeilds a NIZK system when instantiated with the garbling scheme by [CH16].

Organization. Section 2 contains definitions and constructions of building blocks for our protocol, namely, of an honest-but-curious commitment and a puncturable randomized encryption. The protocol itself is given in Sect. 3, together with an overview of hybrids. The full proof of security and our NIZK is presented in the full version [CPV16]. The description of the malicious version of our main protocol is given in Appendix B.

---

[12] Note that the proof of garbling done correctly doesn't save us, since the garbler followed the garbling algorithm; it's just the scheme itself allows for wrong garbling.

2 Building Blocks

In this section we define and build *puncturable randomized encryption (PRE)* and *an honest-but-curious commitment* - primitives used in our MPC protocol (Sect. 3).

2.1 Puncturable Randomized Encryption

Puncturable randomized encryption (PRE) is a randomized, symmetric key encryption. Besides standard algorithms Gen, Enc, Dec, there is additional procedure Puncture(k, c^*) which takes as input a key k and a ciphertext $c^* = $ Enc($m^*; r^*$) and outputs a partial, or *punctured*, key $k\{c^*\}$. Such a key has two properties. First, it doesn't reveal any information about the plaintext of c^*; this is captured by requiring that a simulator should simulate a ciphertext and a punctured key without knowing a plaintext. Second, the key should still have the same functionality in all other points: namely, it should correctly decrypt all other $c \neq c^*$, and it should correctly encrypt all other $(m, r) \neq (m^*, r^*)$.

PRE can be viewed as a randomized, simulation-secure analog of a puncturable deterministic encryption (PDE) [SW14].

Definition 1. *Puncturable randomized encryption (PRE) is a tuple of algorithms* (Gen, Enc, Dec, Puncture, Sim)*, which satisfy the following properties:*

- **Statistical correctness:** *With overwhelming probability over the choice of the key $k \leftarrow$ Gen(1^λ), for any message m and randomness r* Dec$_k$(Enc$_k$($m; r$)) $= m$.
- **Statistical correctness of the punctured key:** *With overwhelming probability over the choice of the key $k \leftarrow$ Gen(1^λ), for any message m^* and randomness r^*, let $c^* \leftarrow$ Enc$_k$($m^*; r^*$), and $k\{c^*\} \leftarrow$ Puncture(k, c^*). Then:*
  - *for any (m, r) such that $(m, r) \neq (m^*, r^*)$,* Enc$_k$($m; r$) $=$ Enc$_{k\{c^*\}}$($m; r$)*;*
  - *for any $c \neq c^*$* Dec$_k$(c) $=$ Dec$_{k\{c^*\}}$(c) *(in particular, both decryptions should output $\perp$ on the same set of ciphertexts, except c^*).*
- **Simulation security with the punctured key:** *For any PPT adversary A and for any message m^*, consider the following experiment: $k \leftarrow$ Gen(1^λ), r^* is chosen at random, $c^* \leftarrow$ Enc$_k$($m^*; r^*$), $k\{c^*\} \leftarrow$ Puncture(k, c^*), and* $(c_{\mathsf{Sim}}, k\{c_{\mathsf{Sim}}\}) \leftarrow$ Sim()*. Then* Pr$[A(k\{c^*\}, m^*, c^*) = 1] -$ Pr$[A(k\{c_{\mathsf{Sim}}\}, m^*, c_{\mathsf{Sim}}) = 1] <$ negl(λ)*.*

Simulation security says that even if an adversary has almost all key, it cannot tell whether it sees an encryption of a known message m^* or a simulated encryption (as long as randomness of encryption remains hidden). Note that simulation security with the punctured key implies normal security of PRE as a secret-key encryption, since with $k\{c^*\}$ the adversary can answer encryption-decryption queries itself.

Our Construction in a Nutshell. The key of a PRE consists of a key K of a puncturable PRF and a public key pk of an injective encryption scheme. To encrypt message m under randomness r, the sender computes $T \leftarrow \mathsf{Enc}_{\mathsf{pk}}(m;r)$, $C \leftarrow F_K(T) \oplus (m,r)$, and sets its ciphertext to be (T,C). To decrypt, the receiver computes $(m,r) \leftarrow F_K(T) \oplus C$ and checks whether $T = \mathsf{Enc}_{\mathsf{pk}}(m;r)$. To puncture the key at a ciphertext (T,C), output $(pk, K\{T\})$, where $K\{T\}$ is a PRF key punctured at T.

In this construction the encryption scheme should be injective for both message and randomness. We observe that the encryption scheme by [SW14], where the ciphertext is $(\mathsf{prg}(r), F_k(\mathsf{prg}(r)) \oplus m)$, satisfies this property, as long as the underlying prg is injective. In turn, (the family of) injective prgs exists assuming iO and injective OWFs: indeed, the fact that iO(PRF) is a hardcore function [BST14] immediately implies that this is also a prg family; this prg can be made injective by putting an injective PRF [SW14] inside. Note that injective PRF doesn't require injective OWFs; instead, the existence of injective OFWs is required for the proof of [BST14] (that iO(PRF) is a hardcore function) to go through.

Therefore we obtain PRE assuming iO and injective OWFs.

More Detailed Description. We construct PRE from puncturable PRFs and a public key encryption which is injective with respect to both message and randomness (i.e. it should hold that $\mathsf{Enc}_{\mathsf{pk}}(m_1;r_1) = \mathsf{Enc}_{\mathsf{pk}}(m_2;r_2)$ implies $(m_1, r_1) = (m_2, r_2)$).

Lemma 1. [SW14,BST14] *Assuming indistinguishability obfuscation for circuits and injective one way functions, there exists a public key encryption which is statistically injective with respect to both message and randomness.*

Proof. In short, the work of [BST14] essentially builds an injective prg, which can be plugged into encryption scheme of [SW14] to obtain injective PKE. We briefly present all constructions here for completeness.

Overall Encryption Scheme. Recall that in the PKE scheme of [SW14] the public key is an obfuscated program which takes (m,r) as input, computes $t = \mathsf{prg}(r)$, and outputs $(t, F_k(t) \oplus m)$ as a ciphertext. Note that this scheme is only injective for messages, but not for randomness, since underlying prg could map two different randomness to the same output. Thus for this encryption to be injective, we need an injective prg. In addition, note that for this construction it is enough to have *a family* of prgs (which is statistically injective): the prg could be chosen from the family during the process of the key generation for the encryption scheme.

Injective PRG Family. We note that the work of Bellare *et al.* [BST14], which proves that iO(PRF) is a hardcore function for any injective OWF[13], also implies

---

[13] In fact, for them it is enough that OWF is poly-to-one. Thus we can relax our assumptions for MPC protocol from injective OWF to poly-to-one OWF.

that iO(PRF) is a prg family, as long as there exist injective OWFs. Indeed, in their work they show that $H = \text{iO(PRF)}$ is a hardcore function for any injective OWF f, i.e. that for random r $(f, H, f(r), H(r)) \approx_c (f, H, f(r), U_{|H(r)|})$. This implies the following: as long as there exists an injective OWF f, it holds that $(f, H, f(r), H(r)) \approx_c (f, H, f(r), U_{|H(r)|})$ and therefore it also holds that $(H, H(r)) \approx_c (H, U_{|H(r)|})$, which means that this is a prg family.

This prg family is statistically injective, as long as the underlying PRF is statistically injective.

Injective PRF Family. Sahai and Waters [SW14] build a statistically injective puncturable PRF family from a PRF family $\{F_k(x)\}$ (which in turn can be built from OWFs) and a 2-universal hash function $h(x)$ (which exists unconditionally) as $F_k(x) \oplus h(x)$, as long as the output of a PRF is large enough. Namely, they show that as long as $m(\lambda) > 2n(\lambda) + e(\lambda)$, there exists such a statistically injective PRF family which maps $n(\lambda)$ bits to $m(\lambda)$ bits and has a failure probability $2^{-e(\lambda)}$ (i.e. with probability $2^{-e(\lambda)}$ over the choice of the PRF key the PRF is not injective).

This concludes the proof that a statistically injective PKE exists assuming iO and injective OWFs. We underline that this PKE is only statistically injective, since underlying PRFs might be non-injective with some negligible probability.

From Injective PKE to PRE. Our PRE is constructed as follows (see Fig. 1 for a more concise description):

- **Key generation:** $\text{PRE.Gen}(1^\lambda, r_{\text{Gen}})$ uses r_{Gen} to sample a PRF key K and generate (pk, sk)-pair of a public key encryption scheme which is statistically injective for messages and randomness. It sets $\text{PRE}.k \leftarrow (K, \text{pk})$.
- **Encryption:** $\text{PRE.Enc}_{\text{PRE}.k}(m; r)$ sets $T \leftarrow \text{Enc}_{\text{pk}}(m; r)$ and $C \leftarrow F_K(T) \oplus (m, r)$ (if the key K is punctured at point T, encryption outputs $\perp$). It outputs the ciphertext $c = (T, C)$.
- **Decryption:** $\text{PRE.Dec}_{\text{PRE}.k}(c)$ parses c as (T, C) and sets $(m, r) \leftarrow F_K(T) \oplus C$ (if the key K is punctured at point T, decryption outputs $\perp$). Next it verifies that $\text{Enc}_{\text{pk}}(m; r) = T$; if this check passes, it outputs m, otherwise it outputs $\perp$.
- **Puncture:** $\text{PRE.Puncture}(\text{PRE}.k, c)$ parses c as (T, C) and punctures the PRF key at T; it outputs the PRE punctured key $(\text{pk}, K\{T\})$.
- **Simulation:** $\text{PRE.Sim}()$ first chooses the key $\text{PRE}.k$ by sampling a PRF key K and generating (pk, sk)-pair of a public key encryption scheme. Next it generates $T = \text{Enc}_{\text{pk}}(0; r)$ for random r and sets C to be a random string. It sets the simulated ciphertext c_{Sim} to be (T, C) and outputs it. Next, it punctures the PRF key K at T and sets the simulated punctured key $k\{c_{\text{Sim}}\}$ to be $(\text{pk}, K\{T\})$.

Theorem 4. *Assuming that PKE is a public key encryption scheme, injective for both messages and randomness, and assuming one way functions, the construction presented on Fig. 1 is a puncturable randomized encryption.*

Construction of a PRE

PRE.Gen($1^\lambda, r_{\text{Gen}}$):

1. Sample PRF.K and (PKE.pk, PKE.sk);
2. Output (PRF.K, PKE.pk)

PRE.Enc$_{\text{PRE}.k}(m; r)$:

1. $T \leftarrow \text{Enc}_{\text{pk}}(m; r)$
2. If K is punctured at T, output $\perp$ and halt;
3. $C \leftarrow F_K(T) \oplus (m, r)$.
4. outputs (T, C).

PRE.Dec$_{\text{PRE}.k}(T, C)$:

1. If K is punctured at T, output $\perp$ and halt;
2. $(m, r) \leftarrow F_K(T) \oplus C$
3. If $\text{Enc}_{\text{pk}}(m; r) = T$ then output m, else $\perp$.

PRE.Puncture(PRE.$k, c = (T, C)$):

1. Output PRE.$k\{c\} = (pk, K\{T\})$

PRE.Sim():

1. PRE.$k \leftarrow$ PRE.Gen(r_{Gen}) for random r_{Gen};
2. $T = \text{Enc}_{\text{pk}}(0; r)$ for random r;
3. $C \leftarrow$ random ;
4. output $c = (T, C)$, PRE.$k\{c\} = (pk, K\{T\})$;

Fig. 1. Construction of a PRE from a puncturable PRF and injective PKE.

Proof. Before showing correctness and security, we note the following useful property of our encryption:

First Part of a Ciphertext Determines the Second. For a given T^*, there exists at most one C^* such that (T^*, C^*) is a valid (i.e. decrypted to non-$\perp$) ciphertext. Indeed, due to injectivity of underlying PKE, there exists at most one (m^*, r^*) pair such that $T^* = \text{PKE.Enc}_{\text{pk}}(m^*; r^*)$. Therefore the check in the decryption algorithm will only pass for $C^* = F_K(T^*) \oplus (m^*, r^*)$.

Correctness. This scheme is statistically correct, as immediately follows from correctness of encryption $C = F_K(T) \oplus (m, r)$ and the fact that the check $T = \text{Enc}_{\text{pk}}(m; r)$ passes for honestly generated ciphertext.

Next, correctness of the punctured key also holds, as long as underlying PKE is injective: indeed, there is only a single (m, r)-pair which results in $T = T^*$, and therefore puncturing out T^* in k only affects encryption of m^* with r^*. On a decryption side, since only (T^*, C^*) is a valid ciphertext with $T = T^*$, puncturing k only affects the decryption of (T^*, C^*). Indeed, ciphertexts of the form $(T \neq T^*, C)$ are decrypted in the same way regardless of which key is used, the full key or the punctured one. On the other hand, ciphertexts of the form $(T^*, C \neq C^*)$ are rejected by decryption with both real and punctured keys: indeed, decryption with the full key rejects it since the ciphertext is invalid, and decryption with the punctured key rejects it since decryption tries to evaluate the PRF at the punctured point T^*, so the check in line 1 of decryption fails.

Security. To show security, we need to show that the punctured key, the message, and the ciphertext, i.e. $((K\{T^*\}, pk), m^*, (T^*, C^*))$, is indistinguishable in the two cases: in one case $T^* = \mathsf{Enc}_{pk}(m^*; r^*)$, $C^* = F_K(T^*) \oplus (m^*, r^*)$, and in the other case $T^* = \mathsf{Enc}_{pk}(0)$ and C^* is randomly chosen. We do this by considering a middle distribution where T^* is real, i.e. $T^* = \mathsf{Enc}_{pk}(m^*; r^*)$, but C^* is random. The middle and the real distribution are indistinguishable due to the property of a punctured PRF: $F_K(T^*)$ is indistinguishable from random, therefore so is $F_K(T^*) \oplus (m^*, r^*)$. Middle and simulated distributions are indistinguishable by security of a PKE.

2.2 Honest-but-Curious Equivocal Commitments

Motivated by the fact that standard non-interactive commitments are unnecessary strong for our protocol (i.e. support malicious behavior of the sender) and at the same time make the CRS local, we consider a weaker semi-honest commitment which doesn't have this disadvantage.

Namely, an honest-but-curious commitment scheme $(\mathsf{HBCCommit}, \mathsf{Verify})$ can be used to commit to a value x with randomness r using $c \leftarrow \mathsf{HBCCommit}(x; r)$, which later can be opened to convince the verifier that it was x that was committed to. The difference between this primitive and the standard commitment is in the security guarantee. Here we only require that an *honestly* generated commitment cannot be opened in a different way, even by an unbounded adversary. The other way to state this property is to say that for overwhelming fraction of randomness, commitments are statistically binding; this means that a semi-honest sender will generate a statistically binding commitment. (Still, there can be a negligible fraction of commitments which can be easily opened in both ways).

In addition, we require the commitment scheme to be equivocal, or adaptively secure, i.e. the simulator should be able to provide randomness consistent with the simulated commitment.

Unlike its stronger counterpart, honest-but-curious commitment can be constructed in a plain model, in a fairly simple way.

Definition 2. *An honest-but-curious commitment scheme for a message space M is a pair of PPT algorithms $(\mathsf{HBCCommit}(x; r), \mathsf{Verify}(x, r, c))$, such that the following properties hold:*

- **Correctness:** *For any x, r $\mathsf{Verify}(x, r, \mathsf{HBCCommit}(x; r)) = 1$;*
- **Most commitments are statistically binding:** *For any $x \in M$*
  $\Pr_r[\exists r', x' \ s.t. \ x' \neq x \land \mathsf{Verify}(x', r', \mathsf{HBCCommit}(x; r)) = 1] < \mathsf{negl}(\lambda)$.

– **Computational hiding and equivocation:** *There exist a PPT simulator* Sim *such that for any* $x \in M$ *it holds that*

$$\{(r,x,c) : c \leftarrow \mathsf{HBCCommit}(x;r), r \leftarrow \{0,1\}^{|r|}\} \approx_c$$
$$\{(r,x,c) : (c,\mathsf{state}) \leftarrow \mathsf{Sim}(), r \leftarrow \mathsf{Sim}(x,\mathsf{state})\}.$$

Construction. We build a semi-honest commitment scheme for message space $M = \{0,1\}$. Consider a prg with exponentially sparse range (say, length-doubling prg, mapping λ bits to 2λ bits). To commit to 0, output $(\mathsf{prg}(s), r)$, and to commit to 1, output $(r, \mathsf{prg}(s))$, where s is a random value of size λ, and r is a random value of size 2λ. To open the commitment, show (s,r).

Since honestly generated (i.e. random) r is outside the image of the prg with overwhelming probability, there is no s such that $\mathsf{prg}(s) = r$, and therefore for honestly generated commitment there doesn't exist the wrong opening. On the other hand, the simulator can generate its commitment as $(\mathsf{prg}(s_0), \mathsf{prg}(s_1))$ and later open it to any bit b, showing s_b and claiming that the other value is randomly chosen. Thus we proved the following statement:

Theorem 5. *Assuming the existence of one way functions, the above scheme is an honest-but-curious commitment scheme for the message space $M = \{0,1\}$.*

3   Our MPC Protocol Against Semi-honest Adversaries

In this section we present our two-round, RAM-efficient, semi-honest protocol with global CRS.

Our protocol is described in Fig. 2 and corresponding programs are given in Figs. 3 and 4. The CRS consists of two programs, Gen and ExplainGen. Gen is a generation algorithm which produces "encryption" program B, "decryption-and-evaluation" program Eval and program ExplainB. Both ExplainGen and ExplainB are not used in the protocol execution; they are used in the simulation only in order to provide consistent randomness for Gen and B.

The protocol

CRS: programs Gen and ExplainGen
inputs: x_i; randomness: $r_{\mathsf{com},i}, r_{B,i}, r_{\mathsf{Gen},i}$

1. **Round 1:** Each party P_i computes $a_i \leftarrow \mathsf{HBCCommit}(i, x_i; r_{\mathsf{com},i})$ and broadcasts $(a_i, r_{\mathsf{Gen},i})$;
2. Each party sets $r_{\mathsf{Gen}} \leftarrow \bigoplus r_{\mathsf{Gen},i}$ and runs $\{\mathsf{B}, \mathsf{Eval}, \mathsf{ExplainB}\} \leftarrow \mathsf{Gen}(r_{\mathsf{Gen}})$;
3. **Round 2:** Each party broadcasts $b_i \leftarrow \mathsf{B}(i, x_i, r_{\mathsf{com},i}, a_1, \ldots, a_n; r_{B,i})$;
4. Each party sets its output to be $y \leftarrow \mathsf{Eval}(b_1, \ldots, b_n)$.

Fig. 2. MPC protocol.

In the first round everybody uses the semi-honest commitment scheme (defined and constructed in Sect. 2.2) to "commit" to (i, x_i) with randomness r_{com}, i. In addition, parties exchange randomness $r_{Gen,i}$ and everybody sets (the same) $r_{Gen} \leftarrow \bigoplus r_{Gen,i}$. Everybody runs $\mathsf{Gen}(r_{Gen})$ to obtain the same programs $\mathsf{B}, \mathsf{Eval}, \mathsf{ExplainB}$.

In round 2 everybody runs $b_i \leftarrow \mathsf{B}(i, x_i, r_{com}, i, a_1, \ldots, a_n; r_{B,i})$ (which essentially encrypts all round 1 messages together with a party's own opening of a commitment, under some randomness $r_{B,i}$) and sends out b_i. Then everybody computes $y \leftarrow \mathsf{Eval}(b_1, \ldots, b_n)$. Eval decrypts every ciphertext, validates each commitment using opening provided in corresponding ciphertext, and in addition checks that all ciphertexts agree on the set of round-one commitments. If these checks pass, Eval does the computation (computing randomness as a PRF of commitments, if the function is randomized) and outputs y.

The central encryption scheme used by program B to encrypt and by Eval to decrypt is a puncturable randomized encryption (PRE), which we built in Sect. 2.1) from iO and injective OWFs. In addition, both Gen and B have a trapdoor branch which helps the simulator to generate consistent randomness with the help of programs $\mathsf{ExplainGen}, \mathsf{ExplainB}$. Essentially helper programs $\mathsf{ExplainGen}, \mathsf{ExplainB}$ use a special encryption scheme (puncturable deterministic encryption, PDE, [Wat15]), in order to encode an instruction "output *output** and halt" into a random-looking value, which pretends to be true randomness of a party. Gen and B try to decrypt this value in a trapdoor branch and follow the instruction encoded. In addition, this technique requires to use a special PRF, called extracting PRF, F_{Ext} [SW14] We don't elaborate on this mechanism further since it closely follows the original idea of [SW14], [DKR14].

Theorem 6. *Assuming injective one way functions[14] and indistinguishability obfuscation for circuits, the presented protocol is a two-round multiparty protocol with global CRS adaptively secure against honest-but-curious corruptions of possibly all parties. The protocol allows to compute any randomized functionalities, even randomness-hiding ones. Its communication complexity depends on* $\lambda, \{|x_i|\}_{i=1}^n, y, |f|_{RAM}$ *(logarithmic parameters omitted), and time and space of every party depends on* $\lambda, \{|x_i|\}_{i=1}^n, y, |f|_{RAM}$, *and time or space needed to evaluate RAM* $f(x_1, \ldots, x_n)$ *in the worst case.*

On Achieving RAM Efficiency. There are two ways to use our construction in order to achieve an efficient protocol. One way is to use iO for RAM in all programs involved (in particular, the program Gen, which obfuscates three programs, should use an obfuscator for RAM). The other way is to use the protocol to evaluate a functionality which takes parties' inputs and a function and outputs garbled function and garbled inputs; then parties can evaluate garbling

---

[14] In fact, this requirement can be relaxed down to one way functions with at most polynomial-size preimage, since such OWF suffices to prove that the construction of [BST14] is secure; and therefore the PRE scheme (Sect. 2.1) exists under this assumption and iO.

Programs in the CRS:

Program $\mathsf{Gen}(r_{\mathsf{Gen}})$
Constants: an extracting PRF key $\mathsf{Ext}_{\mathsf{Gen}}$, faking PDE key f_{Gen}

- **Trapdoor branch:**
  1. set $(\mathsf{Prog1}, \mathsf{Prog2}, \mathsf{Prog3}, \tilde{\rho}) \leftarrow \mathsf{PDE.Dec}_{f_{\mathsf{Gen}}}(r_{\mathsf{Gen}})$. If decryption returns $\perp$ then goto normal branch;
  2. output $\mathsf{Prog1}, \mathsf{Prog2}, \mathsf{Prog3}$ and halt;
- **Normal branch:**
  1. $u_{\mathsf{Gen}} \leftarrow F_{\mathsf{Ext}_{\mathsf{Gen}}}(r_{\mathsf{Gen}})$;
  2. use u_{Gen} to sample extracting PRF key $\mathsf{Ext}_{\mathsf{B}}$, PRE key K, PRF key k, faking PDE key f_{B} and obfuscation randomness for B, Eval, ExplainB;
  3. output obfuscated programs $\mathsf{B}[\mathsf{Ext}_{\mathsf{B}}, f_{\mathsf{B}}, K]$, $\mathsf{Eval}[K, k]$, $\mathsf{ExplainB}[f_{\mathsf{B}}]$.

Program $\mathsf{ExplainGen}(\mathsf{Prog1}, \mathsf{Prog2}, \mathsf{Prog3}; \rho)$
Constants: faking PDE key f_{Gen}

  1. Set $M = ((\mathsf{Prog1}, \mathsf{Prog2}, \mathsf{Prog3}), \mathsf{prg}(\rho))$;
  2. Set $r_{\mathsf{Gen}} \leftarrow \mathsf{PDE.Enc}_{f_{\mathsf{Gen}}}(M)$;
  3. output r_{Gen}.

Fig. 3. Programs in the CRS of our protocol. Program Gen chooses keys and outputs obfuscated programs B, Eval, ExplainB, defined in Fig. 4. Program ExplainGen is only used by the simulator in order to generate consistent random coins for Gen.

themselves locally. If a RAM-efficient garbling scheme is used [CH16], then it suffices to use iO for circuits to make the whole protocol RAM-efficient. Note that it is enough to use statically secure garbling scheme, since our base protocol supports randomness-hiding functionalities, i.e. doesn't reveal randomness of the computation even when everybody is corrupted[15]. The composed scheme also supports randomized randomness-hiding functionalities: to evaluate such a functionality $f(x_1, \ldots, x_n; r)$, parties should use basic protocol to evaluate a randomized function $F(x_1, \ldots, x_n; (r_1, r_2))$ which uses r_1 as randomness to garble function f and inputs $x_1, \ldots, x_n, r_2$ (r_2 being random part of input).

Unlike the first approach, the second approach doesn't require subexponentially-secure iO (which is an assumption currently required for iO for RAM).

---

[15] If the protocol revealed randomness of the computation, then the garbling scheme would have to be adaptively secure, i.e. the simulator of the garbling scheme would have to first simulate it and then, once it learned inputs, provide consistent generation randomness of the garbling scheme (note that the term "adaptive security" is ambiguous: in the context of garbling it usually denotes a different property, saying that simulation is possible even if inputs or functions are chosen adaptively after seeing some garbled values. Here by adaptive security we mean that random coins can be generated by the simulator).

Programs produced by the CRS:

Program $B(i, x_i, r_{\mathsf{com},i}, a_1, \ldots, a_n; r_{B,i})$
Constants: an extracting PRF key Ext_B, faking PDE key f_B, PRE key K

- **Trapdoor branch:**
  1. set $(i', x', r'_{\mathsf{com},i}, a'_1, \ldots, a'_n, b', \bar{\rho}) \leftarrow \mathsf{PDE.Dec}_{f_B}(r_{B,i})$. If decryption returns $\perp$ then goto normal branch;
  2. if $(i', x', r'_{\mathsf{com},i}, a'_1, \ldots, a'_n) \neq (i, x_i, r_{\mathsf{com},i}, a_1, \ldots, a_n)$ then goto normal branch;
  3. output b' and halt;
- **Normal branch:**
  1. Set $M = (i, x_i, r_{\mathsf{com},i}, a_1, \ldots, a_n)$
  2. $u_{B,i} \leftarrow F_{\mathsf{Ext}_B}(M, r_{B,i})$
  3. Set $b \leftarrow \mathsf{PRE.Enc}_K(M; \mathsf{prg}(u_{B,i}))$
  4. Output b

Program $\mathsf{Eval}(b_1, \ldots, b_n)$
Constants: PRE key K, key k of a PRF G

1. For every i decrypt:
   (a) Set $M_i \leftarrow \mathsf{PRE.Dec}_K(b_i)$;
   (b) Parse M_i as $(i, x_i, r_{\mathsf{com},i}, a_1, \ldots, a_n)$. If the format is wrong (in particular, if i is wrong), output $\perp$.
2. For every i check consistency:
   (a) Verify that the set $(a_1, \ldots, a_n)$ is the same in all $M_1, \ldots, M_n$;
   (b) Verify that $a_i = \mathsf{HBCCommit}(i, x_i; r_{\mathsf{com},i})$
3. Set $R \leftarrow G_k(a_1, \ldots, a_n)$.
4. Output $y \leftarrow f(x_1, \ldots, x_n; R)$. (If f is deterministic, ignore R).

Program $\mathsf{ExplainB}(i, x, r_{\mathsf{com},i}, a_1, \ldots, a_n; b; \rho)$
Constants: PDE key f_B

1. Set $M = ((i, x, r_{\mathsf{com},i}, a_1, \ldots, a_n), b, \mathsf{prg}(\rho))$
2. Set $r_{B,i} \leftarrow \mathsf{PDE.Enc}_{f_B}(M)$
3. output $r_{B,i}$

Fig. 4. Programs used in the protocol.

In both cases, we assume that the simulator gets all necessary information about the computation (such as worst-case running time, space, etc.) from the ideal functionality. As discussed in the introduction, setting a lower (than the worst-case) bound on the running time/space of the computation might be useful if parties agree to sacrifice some security for efficiency.

Correctness. Correctness of the scheme can be immediately verified. Note that in case of randomized functionalities the randomness for the computation is obtained via a PRF G, and therefore the distribution of the output is only computationally close to the ideal distribution.

Simulation. The simulator works as follows:

CRS: The simulator generates the CRS honestly.

Round 1: Each a_i^* is simulated by a simulator of a semi-honest commitment scheme. Each b_i^* is simulated by PRE.Sim, together with a punctured key $K\{\{b_i^*\}_{i=1}^n\}$. Eval1, B1 are generated as in Fig. 5 (using punctured keys $K\{\{b_i^*\}_{i=1}^n\}$ and $k\{(a_1^*, \ldots, a_n^*)\}$), and ExplainB is generated as in Fig. 3. r_{Gen}^* is set to explain these B1, Eval1, ExplainB (i.e. it is generated as $r_{\mathsf{Gen}}^* \leftarrow$ ExplainGen(Eval1, B1, ExplainB; ρ) for random ρ). Each $r_{\mathsf{Gen},i}^*$ is set to sum up to r_{Gen}^*. $(a_i^*, r_{\mathsf{Gen},i}^*)$ is a simulated first message of each party.

Round 2: b_i^* (generated in round 1) is a simulated second message of each party.

Simulating internal state: $r_{\mathsf{com}, i}^* \leftarrow$ HBCCommit.Sim(a_i^*, x_i) is generated, and $r_{B,i}^*$ is set to explain b_i^* on input $(i, x_i^*, r_{\mathsf{com}}^*, i, a_1^*, \ldots, a_n^*)$ (i.e. it is generated as $r_{B,i}^* \leftarrow$ ExplainB$((i, x_i^*, r_{\mathsf{com}}^*, i, a_1^*, \ldots, a_n^*), b_i^*; \rho_i))$ for some random ρ_i. $(r_{\mathsf{com}, i}^*, r_{B,i}^*)$ is internal state of each party.

Simulator's Knowledge of the Output. Note that the simulator is required to hardwire the output y^* into Eval1 (Fig. 5); Eval1 has to be generated at the end of round 1, since r_{Gen}^* (which is determined right after round 1 ends) depends on it. It could be that at that moment nobody is corrupted, and the simulator, formally speaking, doesn't know the output y^*.

However, we can always assume that it knows y^* as soon as the simulation starts. The idea is similar to the idea allowing parties to compute different outputs: they should evaluate a different function $f'((x_1, r_1), \ldots, (x_n, r_n)) = f_1(x_1, \ldots, x_n) \oplus r_1 || \ldots || f_n(x_1, \ldots, x_n) \oplus r_n$, where r_i is randomness chosen by party i. In this new protocol the simulator can set the output to be a random value z (which can be chosen even before the protocol starts), and as soon as party i is corrupted and the simulator learns y_i, it can set $r_i \leftarrow z_i \oplus y_i$ (where z_i is the i-th block of z corresponding to the output of party i).

Leakage Resilience. For an adaptively secure protocol to be leakage resilient, the simulator has to be *corruption oblivious*, i.e. when simulating leakage from a party, the simulator can only use ideal-world leakage from *this party*; even if some information was leaked from other parties before (and therefore the simulator knows the information and simulated leakage), it cannot be used in simulation of leakage of the current party.

A convenient way to think about this is to imagine that the simulator S should have special subroutines $S_1, \ldots, S_n$ (each S_i handles leakage from party i), such that the only possible information flow between them all is $S \rightarrow S_i$. In other words, S_i gets as input ideal leakage together with necessary information from S (e.g. trapdoors, but not leakage from other parties, since S doesn't know it) and simulates leakage based on this information. S itself doesn't see anything S_i learns from the ideal functionality or simulates. For a more formal treatment, see [BCH12].

Our simulation is corruption oblivious. Each internal state of the party (i.e. $r_{\mathsf{com}, i}^*, r_{B,i}^*$) can be simulated by a subroutine S_i which gets from S a trapdoor to open HBC commitment, the program ExplainB, and communication $a_1^*, \ldots, a_n^*$, b_i^*. S_i can first set $r_{\mathsf{com},\ i}^*$ by opening the commitment appropriately, and then it can generate $r_{B,i}^* \leftarrow \mathsf{ExplainB}((i, x_i, r_{\mathsf{com},\ i}, a_1^*, \ldots, a_n^*); b_i^*; \rho)$ for random ρ.

3.1 An Overview of the Hybrids

Here we present an overview of the hybrids. The full proof with security reductions is in the full version [CPV16].

We start with a real execution, where $r_{\mathsf{com},\ i}^*, r_{B,i}^*, r_{\mathsf{Gen}}^*$ are randomly chosen, each a_i^* is set to $\mathsf{HBCCommit}(i, x_i^*; r_{\mathsf{com},\ i}^*)$, $(\mathsf{B}, \mathsf{Eval}) \leftarrow \mathsf{Gen}(r_{\mathsf{Gen}}^*)$, $b_i^* \leftarrow \mathsf{B}(i, x_i^*, r_{\mathsf{com},\ i}^*, a_1^* \ldots, a_n^*; r_{B,i}^*)$, $y^* \leftarrow G_k(a_1^*, \ldots, a_n^*)$.

Hybrid 1: We make challenge programs B, Eval, and ExplainB independent of Gen: Namely, we choose internal keys of B, Eval, ExplainB, as well as their obfuscation randomness, at random (instead of generating these values by running Gen). In addition, r_{Gen}^* is now a simulated randomness such that $\mathsf{Gen}(r_{\mathsf{Gen}}^*)$ outputs B, Eval via the trapdoor branch (instead of r_{Gen}^* being randomly chosen). Indistinguishability holds by selective indistinguishability of source and explanation for program Gen (Sect. A).

Hybrid 2: We make randomness for challenge ciphertexts b_i^* independent of B: Namely, we use randomness $\mathsf{prg}(u_i^*)$, where u_i^* is chosen at random (instead of u_i^* being computed according to B). In addition, $r_{B,i}^*$ is now a simulated randomness such that $\mathsf{B}(i, x_i^*, r_{\mathsf{com},\ i}^*, a_1^*, \ldots, a_n^*; r_{B,i}^*)$ outputs b_i^* via the trapdoor branch (instead of $r_{B,i}^*$ being randomly chosen). Indistinguishability holds by selective indistinguishability of source and explanation for program B (Sect. A).

This modification is done for every party.

Hybrid 3: For every party i we switch randomness used to generate challenge b_i^* from $\mathsf{prg}(u_{B,i}^*)$ to truly random $\tilde{u}_{B,i}^*$, by security of a prg.

Hybrid 4: We modify programs B, Eval so that they only use a punctured version of a PRE key $K\{\{b_i^*\}_{i=1}^n\}$ and a PRF key $k\{(a_1^*, \ldots, a_n^*)\}$ (see Fig. 5. Note that K is punctured at several points, while k is punctured at a single point $(a_1^*, \ldots, a_n^*)$). We don't change functionality of these programs and rely on security of iO.

In program B we can puncture the key K directly (since challenge ciphertexts use truly random $\tilde{u}_{B,i}^*$ as randomness for encryption, and since B always computes randomness as $\mathsf{prg}(u_i^*)$, the program never tries to compute a ciphertext with challenge randomness $\tilde{u}_{B,i}^*$; by correctness of a punctured PRE key, this key correctly computes ciphertexts with randomness different from randomness used for puncturing, i.e. $\tilde{u}_{B,i}^*$).

Eval is modified as follows: if it gets as input the challenge set $(b_1^*, \ldots, b_n^*)$, then it just outputs hardwired y^*. If none of the input ciphertext is a challenge ciphertext, then it just uses a punctured key $K\{\{b_i^*\}_{i=1}^n\}$ to do its normal computation (by correctness of a PRE punctured key, these ciphertexts are decrypted correctly). The only difference is that it uses punctured PRF key $k\{(a_1^*, \ldots, a_n^*)\}$ to compute randomness R for the computation. (If it happened that b's decrypted

---

Programs used in the proof and the simulation

Program $B1(i, x_i, r_{\mathsf{com},i}, a_1, \ldots, a_n; r_{B,i})$
Constants: an extracting PRF key $\mathsf{Ext_B}$, faking PDE key f_{B}, punctured PRE key $K\{\{b_i^*\}_{i=1}^n\}$

- **Trapdoor branch:**
    1. set $(i', x', r'_{\mathsf{com},i}, a_1', \ldots, a_n', b', \tilde{\rho}) \leftarrow \mathsf{PDE.Dec}_{f_{\mathsf{B}}}(r_{B,i})$. If decryption returns $\perp$ then goto normal branch;
    2. if $(i', x', r'_{\mathsf{com},i}, a_1', \ldots, a_n') \neq (i, x_i, r_{\mathsf{com},i}, a_1, \ldots, a_n)$ then goto normal branch;
    3. output b' and halt;
- **Normal branch:**
    1. Set $M = (i, x_i, r_{\mathsf{com},i}, a_1, \ldots, a_n)$
    2. $u_{B,i} \leftarrow F_{\mathsf{Ext_B}}(M, r_{B,i})$
    3. Set $b \leftarrow \mathsf{PRE.Enc}_{K\{\{b_i^*\}_{i=1}^n\}}(M; \mathsf{prg}(u_{B,i}))$
    4. Output b

Program $\mathsf{Eval}1(b_1, \ldots, b_n)$
Constants: punctured PRE key $K\{\{b_i^*\}_{i=1}^n\}$, punctured PRF key $k\{(a_1^*, \ldots, a_n^*)\}, a_1^*, \ldots, a_n^*$, $b_1^*, \ldots, b_n^*, y^*$
Case 0: If there is $i \neq j$ such that $b_i = b_j^*$, output $\perp$.
Case 1: If for all i $b_i = b_i^*$, then output y^* and halt.
Case 2: If for some i $b_i = b_i^*$ (denote such set as $\mathcal{I}$), then:

1. For every $i \notin \mathcal{I}$ decrypt:
    (a) Set $M_i \leftarrow \mathsf{PRE.Dec}_{K\{\{b_i^*\}_{i=1}^n\}}(b_i)$;
    (b) Parse M_i as $(i, x_i, r_{\mathsf{com},i}, a_1, \ldots, a_n)$
2. For every $i \notin I$ check consistency:
    (a) Verify that the set $(a_1, \ldots, a_n)$ is the same as $(a_1^*, \ldots, a_n^*)$
    (b) Verify that $a_i = \mathsf{HBCCommit}(i, x_i; r_{\mathsf{com},i})$
3. Output y^*.

Case 3: If for all i $b_i \neq b_i^*$, then:

1. For every i decrypt:
    (a) Set $M_i \leftarrow \mathsf{PRE.Dec}_{K\{\{b_i^*\}_{i=1}^n\}}(b_i)$;
    (b) Parse M_i as $(i, x_i, r_{\mathsf{com},i}, a_1, \ldots, a_n)$
2. For every i check consistency:
    (a) Verify that the set $(a_1, \ldots, a_n)$ is the same in all $M_1, \ldots, M_n$;
    (b) Verify that $a_i = \mathsf{HBCCommit}(i, x_i; r_{\mathsf{com},i})$
3. If $(a_1, \ldots, a_n) = (a_1^*, \ldots, a_n^*)$ then output y^*
4. Set $R \leftarrow G_{k\{(a_1^*, \ldots, a_n^*)\}}(a_1, \ldots, a_n)$.
5. Output $y \leftarrow f(x_1, \ldots, x_n; R)$.

Fig. 5. Programs used in the proof and the simulation.

to the challenge set $a_1^*, \ldots, a_n^*$, then the program outputs hardwired y^*, if consistency checks pass. Recall that honestly generated $\{a_i^*\}_{i=1}^n$ completely define all inputs and randomness of the computation, therefore y^* is the only non-$\perp$ output in this case). Thus the evaluation of both punctured keys on punctured inputs is avoided.

The question is what to do in Eval when some inputs are challenge ciphertexts and some are not. We claim that in this case the program should output either y^* or $\perp$ (but cannot output a different $y' \neq y^*$): indeed, since at least one of the ciphertexts is a challenge ciphertext, it contains challenge $a_1^*, \ldots, a_n^*$, and by statistical binding of an honest-but-curious commitment, each a_i^* can be verified only for x_i^*. R is completely determined by $(a_1, \ldots, a_n)$ too; thus Eval can only output $y^* = f(x_1^*, \ldots, x_n^*; R^*)$ or $\perp$. Therefore we modify the program as follows: we decrypt only non-challenge ciphertexts, and compare their $a_1, \ldots, a_n$ with challenge $a_1^*, \ldots, a_n^*$. In addition, we check that their openings of commitments are correct. If these checks pass, we output hardwired y^*, otherwise $\perp$.

Hybrid 5: We switch each ciphertext b_i^* from a real ciphertext encrypting $(i, x_i^*, r_{\mathsf{com},\ i}^*, a_1^*, \ldots, a_n^*)$ to a simulated one. At the same time we switch the PRE key from the real punctured key to the simulated punctured key. Indistinguishability holds by the simulation security of a PRE with the punctured key.

Hybrid 6: We exploit the computational hiding property of an equivocal honest-but-curious commitment scheme and switch commitments a_i^* to simulated, together with commitment randomness $r_{\mathsf{com},\ i}^*$, for each party.

Hybrid 7: Finally, using security of a PRF G with punctured key $k\{(a_1^*, \ldots, a_n^*)\}$, we switch randomness R^* from $G_k(a_1^*, \ldots, a_n^*)$ to truly random value, thus making the output $y^* = f(x_1^*, \ldots, x_n^*; R^*)$ independent of our programs.

At this point the transcript can be simulated by a simulator who might not know inputs during the execution of the protocol (and only gets them upon corruption of a party), but knows the output, as explained in the beginning of the proof. Namely, commitments a_i^* and ciphertexts b_i^* are simulated; Eval, B, ExplainB are programs generated by the simulator using the PRE key $K\{\{b_i^*\}_{i=1}^n\}$, PRF key $k\{(a_1^*, \ldots, a_n^*)\}$. Hardwired variables inside programs B, Eval are $\{a_i^*\}_{i=1}^n$, $\{b_i^*\}_{i=1}^n$, y^*, which are all known to the simulator at the end of round 1; thus, Eval, B, ExplainB, and therefore r_{Gen}^* and each $r_{\mathsf{Gen},i}^*$, can be simulated. Internal state of the party can be generated by opening the commitment and by running ExplainB to get randomness consistent with simulated Eval, B, ExplainB.

Acknowledgments. We thank Justin Holmgren for pointing out that our MPC protocol can be used to compute a garbling scheme in [IK02] manner, which allows us to avoid the use of subexponentially-secure iO even in the RAM setting.

A   Explainability Compiler

The original construction of a deniable encryption by Sahai and Waters [SW14] gives a way to make a single algorithm "adaptively secure": i.e. it transforms a randomized program $\mathsf{Alg}(x;r)$ into a different one $\widetilde{\mathsf{Alg}}(x;r)$ (by adding a trapdoor branch and rerandomizing the program) so that is possible to generate fake randomness consistent with a given input and output.

The important property which we use in our proofs is *indistinguishability of source and explanation*. Roughly speaking, indistinguishability of source says that for random r $\mathsf{Alg}(x;r)$ and $\widetilde{\mathsf{Alg}}(x;r)$ are indistinguishable. Indistinguishability of explanations says that real randomness r is indistinguishable from fake randomness r which results in the same output $a = \widetilde{\mathsf{Alg}}(x;r)$. These properties combined together state that random r and the output $a = \widetilde{\mathsf{Alg}}(x;r)$ are indistinguishable from the output of original program $a = \mathsf{Alg}(x;u)$ on some random u, together with fake randomness r which makes compiled $\widetilde{\mathsf{Alg}}(x;r)$ output a. This holds even when the program to generate fake randomness is publicly available.

The way to think about indistinguishability of source and explanation is the following: it is possible to move from "a real world" (random r, $a \leftarrow \widetilde{\mathsf{Alg}}(x;r)$) to a "hybrid" where $a \leftarrow \mathsf{Alg}(x;u)$, and r is fake, but pretending to be real randomness. Essentially this step allows to "detach" a from a complicated $\widetilde{\mathsf{Alg}}$ and make it the result of a simpler Alg. Because of this detaching, in the next hybrid we could use security of the primitive realized by Alg while still being able to generate internal state r: say, if Alg is an encryption scheme, then in the next hybrid we could switch it to encryption of a different value.

We also note that this indistinguishability is only selective, i.e. the input x has to be known before the indistinguishability game can be played. This imposes some restrictions on the constructions and proofs (in particular, this is one of the reasons why we need nested programs).

Since this technique became standard in the world of adaptive security, we only briefly outlined it here. For formal definitions, constructions, and proofs, we refer the reader to the paper of Dachman-Soled et al. [DKR14] who formalized the technique under the name of explainability compiler.

B   Three Round MPC Against Malicious Adversaries

In this section we present our three-round, RAM-efficient, maliciously secure protocol with local CRS. Our protocol is described in Fig. 6. The CRS consists of two programs, Gen and ExplainGen. The CRS will also contain a CRS σ_{CLOS} corresponding to the adaptively secure commitment scheme of [CLOS02] and a CRS σ_{NIZK} corresponding to a NIZK argument system that is simulation sound and secure against adaptive adversaries [GOS06].[16] We will denote

---

[16] We remark that the [GOS06] do not explicitly claim simulation soundness. It is easy to obtain a simulation-sound argument by sampling an independent CRS for every pair of parties.

by $\mathsf{adCom}_x(msg; r)$ the procedure to commit using the commitment scheme of [CLOS02] where x is the common reference string for the commitment, msg is the message and r is the randomness required. We will rely exactly on the same programs for Gen and ExplainGen from the semi-honest protocols described in Figs. 3 and 4. Recall that Gen is a generation algorithm which produces "encryption" program B, "decryption-and-evaluation" program Eval and program ExplainB.

The protocol

CRS: σ_{CLOS}, σ_{NIZK} and programs Gen and ExplainGen,
inputs: x_i; randomness: $r^1_{\mathsf{com},i}, r^2_{\mathsf{com},i}, r^3_{\mathsf{com},i}, \{r_{B,i,j}\}_{j=1,\ldots,n}, r_{\mathsf{Gen},i}$

1. **Round 1:** Each party P_i computes $a_i \leftarrow \mathsf{adCom}_{\sigma_{\mathsf{CLOS}}}(i, x_i; r^1_{\mathsf{com},i})$, $\widetilde{r}_{\mathsf{Gen},i} \leftarrow \mathsf{adCom}_{\sigma_{\mathsf{CLOS}}}(r_{\mathsf{Gen},i}; r^2_{\mathsf{com},i})$, $\widetilde{r}_{B,i,j} \leftarrow \mathsf{adCom}_{\sigma_{\mathsf{CLOS}}}(r_{B,i,j}; r^3_{\mathsf{com},i})$ and broadcasts $(a_i, \widetilde{r}_{\mathsf{Gen},i}, \widetilde{r}_{B,i,j})$;
2. **Round 2:** Each party P_i broadcasts $r_{\mathsf{Gen},i}, \{r_{B,i,j}\}_{j\neq i}$ and proof Π_i of the statement S_i using an NIZK proof with CRS σ_{NIZK};
3. Each party sets $r_{\mathsf{Gen}} \leftarrow \bigoplus r_{\mathsf{Gen},i}$ and runs $\{B, \mathsf{Eval}, \mathsf{ExplainB}\} \leftarrow \mathsf{Gen}(r_{\mathsf{Gen}})$;
4. **Round 3:** Each party broadcasts $b_i \leftarrow \mathsf{B}(i, x_i, r_{\mathsf{com},i}, a_1, \ldots, a_n; r_{B,i})$ where $r_{B,i} = \bigoplus_j r_{B,j,i}$;
5. Each party sets its output to be $y \leftarrow \mathsf{Eval}(b_1, \ldots, b_n)$.

Language S_i used in the protocol:

$S_i := ((\widetilde{r}_{\mathsf{Gen},i}, r_{\mathsf{Gen},i}, \widetilde{r}_{B,i,j}, r_{B,i,j}) : \exists r^2_{\mathsf{com},i}, r^3_{\mathsf{com},i},$ such that
$\widetilde{r}_{\mathsf{Gen},i} = \mathsf{adCom}_{\sigma_{\mathsf{CLOS}}}(r_{\mathsf{Gen},i}; r^2_{\mathsf{com},i})$ and $\widetilde{r}_{B,i,j} = \mathsf{adCom}_{\sigma_{\mathsf{CLOS}}}(r_{B,i,j}; r^3_{\mathsf{com},i}))$

Fig. 6. Malicious MPC protocol.

In the first round everybody uses the commitment scheme of [CLOS02] to separately commit to (i, x_i), $\{r_{B,i,j}\}_{j=1,\ldots,n}$ (to be used as a coin toss for encryption randomness) and $r_{\mathsf{Gen},i}$ (to be used as a coin toss for generation randomness).

In the second round, all parties reveal $r_{\mathsf{Gen},i}$ and $\{r_{B,i,j}\}_{j\neq i}$ and prove using an NIZK proof that this is indeed the string committed to in the first round. More formally, party P_i proves the following NP-statement:

$S_i := ((\widetilde{r}_{\mathsf{Gen},i}, r_{\mathsf{Gen},i}, \widetilde{r}_{B,i,j}, r_{B,i,j}) : \exists r^2_{\mathsf{com},\,i}, r^3_{\mathsf{com},\,i},$ such that
$\widetilde{r}_{\mathsf{Gen},i} = \mathsf{adCom}_{\sigma_{\mathsf{CLOS}}}(r_{\mathsf{Gen},i}; r^2_{\mathsf{com},\,i})$ and $\widetilde{r}_{B,i,j} = \mathsf{adCom}_{\sigma_{\mathsf{CLOS}}}(r_{B,i,j}; r^3_{\mathsf{com},\,i}))$,

where $\widetilde{r}_{\mathsf{Gen},i}$ is defined in round 1 of the protocol and $r_{\mathsf{Gen},i}$ is the message revealed by party P_i in round 2. Then everybody sets (the same) $r_{\mathsf{Gen}} \leftarrow \bigoplus r_{\mathsf{Gen},i}$. Everybody runs $\mathsf{Gen}(r_{\mathsf{Gen}})$ to obtain the same programs B, Eval, ExplainB.

In the third round, all parties perform exactly the same instructions as they executed in round 2 of the semi-honest protocol. Namely, everybody runs the program B as: $b_i \leftarrow \mathsf{B}(i, x_i, r_{\mathsf{com},\,i}, a_1, \ldots, a_n; r_{B,i})$ (using randomness $r_{B,i} = \bigoplus_j r_{B,j,i}$) and broadcasts b_i. Then everybody computes $y \leftarrow \mathsf{Eval}(b_1, \ldots, b_n)$.

Theorem 7. *The protocol described above UC-securely implements* $\mathcal{F}_{\mathsf{multi-f}}$ *for any functionality f in the presence of malicious adaptive adversaries.*

We present a formal proof of the Theorem in the full version [CPV16].

References

[AIK06] Applebaum, B., Ishai, Y., Kushilevitz, E.: Computationally private randomizing polynomials and their applications. Comput. Complex. **15**(2), 115–162 (2006)

[BCH12] Bitansky, N., Canetti, R., Halevi, S.: Leakage-tolerant interactive protocols. In: Cramer, R. (ed.) TCC 2012. LNCS, vol. 7194, pp. 266–284. Springer, Heidelberg (2012). doi:10.1007/978-3-642-28914-9_15

[BCP15] Boyle, E., Chung, K.-M., Pass, R.: Large-scale secure computation: multi-party computation for (Parallel) RAM programs. In: Gennaro, R., Robshaw, M. (eds.) CRYPTO 2015. LNCS, vol. 9216, pp. 742–762. Springer, Heidelberg (2015). doi:10.1007/978-3-662-48000-7_36

[BST14] Bellare, M., Stepanovs, I., Tessaro, S.: Poly-many hardcore bits for any one-way function and a framework for differing-inputs obfuscation. In: Sarkar, P., Iwata, T. (eds.) ASIACRYPT 2014. LNCS, vol. 8874, pp. 102–121. Springer, Heidelberg (2014). doi:10.1007/978-3-662-45608-8_6

[CDPW07] Canetti, R., Dodis, Y., Pass, R., Walfish, S.: Universally composable security with global setup. In: Vadhan, S.P. (ed.) TCC 2007. LNCS, vol. 4392, pp. 61–85. Springer, Heidelberg (2007). doi:10.1007/978-3-540-70936-7_4

[CGP15] Canetti, R., Goldwasser, S., Poburinnaya, O.: Adaptively Secure Two-Party Computation from Indistinguishability Obfuscation. In: Dodis, Y., Nielsen, J.B. (eds.) TCC 2015. LNCS, vol. 9015, pp. 557–585. Springer, Heidelberg (2015). doi:10.1007/978-3-662-46497-7_22

[CH16] Canetti, R., Holmgren, J.: Fully succinct garbled RAM. In: Proceedings of the ACM Conference on Innovations in Theoretical Computer Science. Cambridge, MA, USA, 14–16 January, pp. 169–178 (2016)

[CHJV15] Canetti, R., Holmgren, J., Jain, A., Vaikuntanathan, V.: Succinct garbling and indistinguishability obfuscation for RAM programs. In: Proceedings of the Forty-Seventh Annual ACM on Symposium on Theory of Computing, STOC. Portland, OR, USA, 14–17 June, pp. 429–437 (2015)

[CLOS02] Canetti, R., Lindell, Y., Ostrovsky, R., Sahai, A.: Universally composable two-party and multi-party secure computation. In Proceedings on 34th Annual ACM Symposium on Theory of Computing, 19–21 May. Montréal, Québec, Canada, pp. 494–503 (2002)

[CPR16] Canetti, R., Poburinnaya, O., Raykova, M.: Optimal-rate non-committing encryption in a CRS model. IACR Cryptology ePrint Archive 2016:511 (2016)

[CPV16] Canetti, R., Poburinnaya, O., Venkitasubramaniam, M.: Better two-round adaptive multiparty computation. In: Cryptology ePrint Archive, Report 2016/614 (2016). http://eprint.iacr.org/2016/614

[DKR14] Dachman-Soled, D., Katz, J., Rao, V.: Adaptively secure, universally composable, multi-party computation in constant rounds. IACR Cryptology ePrint Archive 2014, 858 (2014)

[DMN11] Damgård, I., Meldgaard, S., Nielsen, J.B.: Perfectly secure oblivious RAM without random oracles. In: Ishai, Y. (ed.) TCC 2011. LNCS, vol. 6597, pp. 144–163. Springer, Heidelberg (2011). doi:10.1007/978-3-642-19571-6_10

[Gen09] Gentry, C.: A Fully Homomorphic Encryption Scheme. Ph.D. thesis. Stanford, CA, USA, AAI3382729 (2009)

[GGHR14] Garg, S., Gentry, C., Halevi, S., Raykova, M.: Two-round secure MPC from indistinguishability obfuscation. In: Lindell, Y. (ed.) TCC 2014. LNCS, vol. 8349, pp. 74–94. Springer, Heidelberg (2014). doi:10.1007/978-3-642-54242-8_4

[GOS06] Groth, J., Ostrovsky, R., Sahai, A.: Perfect non-interactive zero knowledge for NP. In: Vaudenay, S. (ed.) EUROCRYPT 2006. LNCS, vol. 4004, pp. 339–358. Springer, Heidelberg (2006). doi:10.1007/11761679_21

[GP14] Garg, S., Polychroniadou, A.: Two-round adaptively secure MPC from indistinguishability obfuscation. IACR Cryptology ePrint Archive 2014:844 (2014)

[Gro11] Groth, J.: Minimizing non-interactive zero-knowledge proofs using fully homomorphic encryption. IACR Cryptology ePrint Archive 2011:12 (2011)

[IK02] Ishai, Y., Kushilevitz, E.: Perfect constant-round secure computation via perfect randomizing polynomials. In: Widmayer, P., Eidenbenz, S., Triguero, F., Morales, R., Conejo, R., Hennessy, M. (eds.) ICALP 2002. LNCS, vol. 2380, pp. 244–256. Springer, Heidelberg (2002). doi:10.1007/3-540-45465-9_22

[IKOS10] Ishai, Y., Kumarasubramanian, A., Orlandi, C., Sahai, A.: Proceedings on invertible sampling and adaptive security. In: Abe, M. (ed.) ASIACRYPT 2010. LNCS, vol. 6477, pp. 466–482. Springer, Heidelberg (2010). doi:10.1007/978-3-642-17373-8_27

[KSW14] Khurana, D., Sahai, A., Waters, B.: How to generate and use universal parameters. IACR Cryptology ePrint Archive 2014:507 (2014)

[NY90] Naor, M., Yung, M.: Public-key cryptosystems provably secure against chosen ciphertext attacks. In: Proceedings of the 22nd Annual ACM Symposium on Theory of Computing. Baltimore, Maryland, USA, 13–17 May, pp. 427–437 (1990)

[SW14] Sahai, A., Waters, B.: How to use indistinguishability obfuscation: deniable encryption, and more. In: Symposium on Theory of Computing, STOC 2014, New York, NY, USA, 31 May-03 June, pp. 475–484 (2014)

[Wat15] Waters, B.: A punctured programming approach to adaptively secure functional encryption. In: Gennaro, R., Robshaw, M. (eds.) CRYPTO 2015. LNCS, vol. 9216, pp. 678–697. Springer, Heidelberg (2015). doi:10.1007/978-3-662-48000-7_33

Constant Round Adaptively Secure Protocols in the Tamper-Proof Hardware Model

Carmit Hazay[1]($^{\boxtimes}$), Antigoni Polychroniadou[2],
and Muthuramakrishnan Venkitasubramaniam[3]

[1] Bar-Ilan University, Ramat Gan, Israel
carmit.hazay@gmail.com
[2] Aarhus University, Aarhus, Denmark
[3] University of Rochester, Rochester, NY, USA

Abstract. Achieving constant-round adaptively secure protocols (where all parties can be corrupted) in the plain model is a notoriously hard problem. Very recently, three works published in TCC 2015 (Dachman-Soled et al., Garg and Polychroniadou, Canetti et al.), solved the problem in the Common Reference String (CRS) model. In this work, we present a constant-round adaptive UC-secure computation protocol for all well-formed functionalities in the tamper-proof hardware model using stateless tokens from *only* one-way functions. In contrast, all prior works in the CRS model require very strong assumptions, in particular, the existence of indistinguishability obfuscation.

As a corollary to our techniques, we present the first adaptively secure protocols in the Random Oracle Model (ROM) with round complexity proportional to the depth of circuit implementing the functionality. Our protocols are secure in the Global Random Oracle Model introduced recently by Canetti, Jain and Scafuro in CCS 2014 that provides strong compositional guarantees. More precisely, we obtain an adaptively secure UC-commitment scheme in the global ROM assuming only one-way functions. In comparison, the protocol of Canetti, Jain and Scafuro achieves only static security and relies on the specific assumption of Discrete Diffie-Hellman assumption (DDH).

1 Introduction

Background. Secure multi-party computation enables a set of parties to mutually run a protocol that computes some function f on their private inputs, while guaranteeing maximal privacy of the inputs. It is by now well known how to securely compute any efficient functionality [3,5,30,47,56] in various models and under the stringent simulation-based definitions. However, these results were originally investigated in the *stand-alone setting*, where a single instance of the protocol is run in isolation. A stronger notion is that of *concurrent security*, which guarantees security even when many different protocol executions are carried out concurrently. The strongest (as well as most realistic) model of concurrent security is universally-composable (UC) security [5] which guarantees security even

© International Association for Cryptologic Research 2017
S. Fehr (Ed.): PKC 2017, Part II, LNCS 10175, pp. 428–460, 2017.
DOI: 10.1007/978-3-662-54388-7_15

when an unbounded number of different protocol executions are run concurrently in an arbitrary uncontrolled environment. Unfortunately, UC-security cannot be achieved for general functions, unless trusted setup is assumed [9,12,42]. Previous works overcome this barrier either by using some trusted setup infrastructure [1,7,9,14,15,39,41], or by relaxing the definition of security [2,13,27,37,52,54].

Typical protocols, including results mentioned above only consider benign models of *static corruption* in which the adversary is required to pick which parties it corrupts *before* the execution (which may include many concurrent protocol sessions) begins. In practice, this is a highly restrictive model. A more realistic model known as the *adaptive corruption model*, introduced by Canetti et al., considers an adversary that can hijack a host *any time* during the course of the computation [8]. This models "hacking" attacks where an external attacker breaks into parties' machines in the midst of a protocol execution and it captures additional threats. In general, security against static corruptions does not guarantee security against adaptive corruptions [6]. Furthermore, adaptive security has been a notoriously difficult notion to achieve.

Adaptive Security Requires Stronger (General) Computational Assumptions. Lindell and Zarosim showed that there exists no black-box construction of an adaptively secure oblivious transfer (OT) protocol from enhanced trapdoor-permutations [45]. In practice, the constructions we know, actually require much stronger assumptions. The smallest general assumption to construct adaptively secure OT in the plain model is trapdoor simulatable public-key encryption [17]. In the UC-setting, the work of [20,55] showed how to achieve adaptive UC-security in various models (including trusted setups and relaxed security notions) assuming the existence of simulatable public-key encryption [21]. In the Common Reference String model (CRS) model,[1] the construction was improved to rely on the weaker assumption of trapdoor simulatable public-key encryption [36]. In the tamper-proof model, where the parties are assumed to have the capability of creating "tamper-proof hardware tokens", the work of Goyal et al. [33] shows how to realize unconditional (and hence, adaptive) UC-security in the tamper-proof model assuming stateful tokens. Yet, when we consider the weaker and more realistic model of stateless tokens, there is no known construction of adaptively secure protocols.

Adaptive Security Requires Higher Round Complexity. At present, we have no constant-round adaptively secure protocols for general functionalities in the plain model, where all parties can be corrupted. If we further restrict the constructions to rely on black-box simulation techniques, the work of Garg and Sahai [29] shows that a linear number of rounds are required (in the multi-party setting). A notable exception here, is the work of [22,38] who provide constant-round adaptively secure protocols under a restricted class of adversaries that

---

[1] In the CRS model, all parties receive as common input in an initial setup phase, a string sampled from an a priori fixed distribution (from some trusted authority).

is allowed to corrupt at most $n - 1$ parties among n parties. [38] also presents constant-round adaptively secure protocols secure against arbitrary corruptions assuming the stronger model of erasures. However, in standard models, where all parties can be corrupted the round-complexity of the best protocol is proportional to the depth of the circuit computing the function [6,14,38]. In fact, even in the UC-setting, the round complexity suffers the depth of circuit barrier [14,20,55]. Only very recently, and under very strong assumptions, namely existence of (subexponentially-hard) indistinguishability obfuscation (iO) of circuits, the works of [10,19,28] provided the first constant-round adaptively secure protocols in the CRS model.[2]

As such, the best known adaptively secure protocols require very strong assumptions and often higher round complexity. Given the state of affairs, in this work, we are motivated by the following natural question concerning adaptive security:

- *Can we construct adaptive UC-secure constant-round protocols under standard polynomial-time assumptions from minimal setup?*

As mentioned before, concurrent security cannot be achieved without assuming some form of trusted setup [9,12,42]. However, in many scenarios, it is impossible to agree on a *trusted entity*. Specifically, protocols in the literature that rely on a trusted setup are rendered completely insecure if the setup is compromised. In the absence of setup, concurrently secure protocols have to rely on relaxed notions of security. The most popular notion in this line of work is security with super-polynomial simulators (SPS) [2,41,52,54] which is a relaxation of the traditional simulation-based notion, that allows the simulator to run in super-polynomial time. All these constructions require super-polynomial security of the underlying cryptographic primitives. Breakthrough work by Canetti, Lin and Pass showed how to obtain SPS security from standard polynomial time assumptions [13]. In the adaptive setting, the works of [2,20,55] show how to obtain adaptive UC-secure protocols with SPS under super-polynomial time assumptions. More recently, the work of [37] shows how to obtain a $O(n^\epsilon)$ (for any constant $0 < \epsilon < 1$) round adaptive UC-secure protocol with SPS under standard polynomial time assumptions.

Motivated by designing practical protocols in the concurrent setting, another approach taken by Canetti et al. [11] considers the Random Oracle Model of Bellare and Rogaway [4]. In order to provide strong compositional guarantees, they introduce the Global Random Oracle Model and show how to obtain UC-secure protocols in the static setting. Their construction is based on the Decisional Diffie-Hellman assumption (DDH). In this line of work, we are interested in addressing the following questions that remain open:

Can we construct UC-secure protocols in the Global Random Oracle Model from minimal general assumptions?, and
Can we construct adaptive UC-secure protocols in the Global Random Oracle Model?

---

[2] The work of [19] assumes only polynomially-hard indistinguishability obfuscation.

Our Results. We answer all our questions in the affirmative. Furthermore, all our results will be presented in the stronger global-UC (GUC) setting of [7] that provide strong(-er) compositional guarantees. We will rely on the recent work [34] who model tokens for the GUC-setting. In order to incorporate adaptive corruptions we will have to determine the precise capabilities of the adversary when it can also corrupt the creator of the token post-execution and know the actual code embedded in the token. This is discussed in the next section and we argue that the $\mathcal{F}_{\mathrm{gWRAP}}$-functionality introduced in the work [34] will be sufficient to capture the adversary's capabilities.

Our first result shows how to construct constant-round adaptive GUC-secure protocols in the *tamper-proof hardware* model assuming *only* stateless tokens and the existence of one-way functions. More precisely, we obtain the following theorem.

Theorem 1 (Informal). *Assuming the existence of one-way functions, there exists a constant-round GUC-secure protocol for the commitment functionality in the presence of adaptive, malicious adversaries in the $\mathcal{F}_{\mathrm{gWRAP}}$-hybrid.*

Next, we extend the ideas in this protocol to obtain an adaptive GUC-secure protocol for the oblivious-transfer functionality from one-way functions.

Theorem 2 (Informal). *Assuming the existence of one-way functions, there exists a constant-round GUC-secure protocol for the oblivious-transfer functionality in the presence of adaptive, malicious adversaries in the $\mathcal{F}_{\mathrm{gWRAP}}$-hybrid.*

Combining this protocol with the adaptive UC-secure protocol in the OT-hybrid of Ishai et al. [38], we can obtain as a corollary an adaptive GUC-secure protocol in the $\mathcal{F}_{\mathrm{gWRAP}}$-hybrid assuming only one-way functions. However, this protocol will require $O(d)$ rounds where d is the depth of the circuit computing the function. Our main contribution in this work is to reduce the round complexity and show how to realize any well-formed functionality in $O(1)$-rounds independent of the complexity of the function. Below, we state this main theorem.

Theorem 3 (Informal). *Assuming the existence of one-way functions, there exists a constant-round GUC-secure two-party protocol to realize any well-formed functionality in the presence of malicious adaptive adversaries in the $\mathcal{F}_{\mathrm{gWRAP}}$-hybrid.*

As noted in [34], the $\mathcal{F}_{\mathrm{gWRAP}}$-functionality closely follows the approach taken by Canetti et al. [11] where they capture the global non-programmable random oracle using the $\mathcal{F}_{\mathrm{gRO}}$-functionality described in [35]. In this work we show that a variant of our GUC-commitment protocol directly yields a GUC-commitment scheme in the $\mathcal{F}_{\mathrm{gRO}}$-hybrid. More precisely, we obtain the following theorem.

Theorem 4 (Informal). *Assuming the existence of one-way functions, there exists a constant-round GUC-secure protocol for the commitment functionality in the presence of adaptive, malicious adversaries in the global, non-programmable random oracle model, i.e. $\mathcal{F}_{\mathrm{gRO}}$-hybrid.*

This commitment scheme can be combined with the protocol of [17], to obtain a malicious adaptive GUC-oblivious transfer protocol assuming the existence of UC-secure semi-honest adaptive oblivious-transfer protocol. This oblivious-transfer can be further combined with the work of [38] to realize any functionality in the $\mathcal{F}_{\mathrm{gRO}}$-hybrid with adaptive security. More formally, we obtain the following corollary.

Corollary 1. *Assuming the existence of semi-honest UC-secure adaptive oblivious-transfer protocol, there exists a malicious adaptive $O(d_{\mathcal{F}})$-round GUC-secure protocol to securely realize any (well-formed) functionality in the $\mathcal{F}_{\mathrm{gRO}}$-hybrid where $d_{\mathcal{F}}$ is the depth of the circuit that implements $\mathcal{F}_{\mathrm{gRO}}$.*

If we instead combine the commitment scheme with the protocol of Hazay and Venkitasubramaniam [36], we obtain a GUC-secure protocol in the *static* setting assuming stand-alone semi-honest oblivious-transfer.

Corollary 2. *Assuming the existence of semi-honest oblivious-transfer protocol, there exists a constant-round static and malicious GUC-secure protocol to securely realize any (well-formed) functionality in the $\mathcal{F}_{\mathrm{gRO}}$-hybrid.*

We remark that the round complexity of our adaptively secure protocol in Corollary 1 is proportional to the depth of the circuit implementing the functionality, while the protocol in Corollary 2 in the static setting requires only constant number of rounds. These corollaries improve the result of [11] in two ways. First, we show that under the minimal assumption of one-way functions, we can get a GUC-commitment that is adaptively secure. In contrast, the result of [11], obtains a GUC-commitment secure in the static setting assuming DDH. Second, we obtain static and adaptive GUC-secure computation of general functionalities under minimal assumptions, namely, semi-honest OT in the static setting and GUC-secure semi-honest adaptive OT in the adaptive setting.

Related Work. The work of Goldreich and Ostrovsky [31] first considered the use of hardware tokens in the context of *software obfuscation* via Oblivious RAMs. A decade later, Katz in [40] demonstrated the feasibility of achieving UC-secure protocols for arbitrary functionalities assuming tamper-proof tokens under static corruptions. In his formulation, the parties can create a token that computes arbitrary functionalities such that any adversary that is given access to the token can *only* observe the input/output behavior of the token. In the UC framework, Katz described an ideal functionality $\mathcal{F}_{\mathrm{WRAP}}$ that captures this model. Note that tokens can either be stateful or stateless, depending on whether the tokens are allowed to maintain some state between invocations (where stateless tokens are easier to implement). Following [40], Goldwasser et al. [32] investigated the use of *one-time programs*, that allow a semi-honest sender to create simple stateful tokens where a potentially malicious receiver executes them exactly once (or a bounded number of times). Their work considered concrete applications such as zero-knowledge proofs and focused on minimizing the number of required tokens.

The construction of [40] relied on stateful tokens based on the DDH assumption, and was later improved by Lin et al. [41] to rely on the minimal assumption of one-way functions. Goyal et al. [33] resolved the power of stateful tokens and showed how to obtain unconditionally secure protocols using stateful tokens. The work of Chandran et al. [16] was the first to achieve UC-security using only stateless tokens. Choi et al. [18] gave the first constant-round UC-secure protocols using stateless tokens assuming collision-resistant hash-functions. The works of [46,50] consider a GUC-like formulation of the tokens for the two-party setting where the parties have fixed roles. The focus in [46,50] was to obtain a formulation that accommodates reusability of a single token for several independent protocols in the UC-setting for the specific two-party case. In contrast to the work of [34], [46,50] does not explicitly model or discuss adversarial transferability of the tokens. Finally, the work of Hazay et al. [34] resolved the question of identifying the minimal assumptions to construct UC-secure protocols under static corruptions with stateless tokens, namely, they show how to realize constant-round two-party and multi-party UC-secure protocols assuming only the existence of one-way functions. Besides these works, there have been several works in the tamper-proof token model [16,18,20,24–26,33,41,48] addressing various efficiency parameters. In the adaptive setting, the works of [20,55] and [33] construct adaptive UC-secure protocols in the tamper-proof model using stateful tokens with round-complexity proportional to the depth of the circuit. While the works of [20,55] rely on simulatable public-key encryption schemes, Goyal et al. in [33] provide unconditionally secure protocols (which in particular imply adaptive UC-security). As such, none of the previous works have addressed the feasibility of adaptive security using stateless tokens, and our work is the first to address this question.

2 Modelling Tamper Proof Model with Adaptive Corruptions

We begin with a brief overview of the tamper-proof hardware model and point out some subtleties that arise when considering adaptive adversaries.

In recent work [34], it was shown that the standard (and most popular) formalization of the tamper proof hardware tokens (namely the $\mathcal{F}_{\text{WRAP}}$-functionality due to Katz [40],) does not fully capture the power of the adversary in a concurrent setting. In particular, the formulation in [40] does not capture a man-in-the-middle attack where an adversary can transfer the tokens received from one session to another. In [34], a new formulation of tamper-proof hardware in the Global Universal Composable (GUC) framework was introduced that addressed these shortcomings. A side effect of this formulation is that this functionality denies the ability of the simulator to "program" the token.[3] In the same work [34], they provide

---

[3] In contrast, in many previous constructions that relied on tamper-proof hardware, the simulator emulated the token for the adversary. In such a simulation, it would be possible for a simulator to program the responses to the queries made by the adversary.

constant-round constructions of two party and multi-party secure protocols in the GUC-setting tolerating static adversaries. Our approach is to extend this framework to incorporate adaptive adversaries. First, we explain a subtlety that arises when considering adaptive adversaries. Consider a protocol where one party P_1 creates a token $\mathcal{T}$ and sends it to party P_2. Suppose an adversary corrupts P_2 at the beginning of the protocol and P_1 at the end of the execution. This adversary can gain access to the token received by P_2 during the protocol and the code of the program P installed in the token at the end of the execution after corrupting P_1. In such a scenario, one needs to determine the extent to which an adversary can verify that program P was installed in token $\mathcal{T}$. There are two possible ways to model this:

First Model: In this model, if the receiver of a token is corrupted the adversary has input/output access to the token. If in addition the adversary corrupts the creator of the token, it will obtain the code of the program, i.e. a circuit layout, and it will be able to completely verify that the token precisely contains this circuit.

Second Model: In this model, if the receiver of a token is corrupted the adversary has input/output access to the token. If in addition the adversary corrupts the creator of the token, it will obtain the code of the program (by concluding it from the randomness provided by the simulator), however, it will continue to have only input/output access to the physical token. In essence, it will be able to verify the "functionality" on a arbitrary (but bounded) number of points of the function.

It is clear that the first model is stronger as it guarantees that the functionality of the token is exactly the code provided by the creator. In the second model, the adversary will only be able to verify in a polynomial number of points of the function. We argue that the second model is realistic as it is reasonable to assume that the integrity of a physical token remains intact even for an adversary with some auxiliary digital information, such as the code or circuit embedded in the token. In essence, we require that a tamper-proof token remain "tamper-proof" always and restrict the adversary to only input/output access.

All our results will be in the second model with the exception of our adaptive GUC-commitment which will be secure even in the first model. As mentioned before we will rely on the $\mathcal{F}_{\text{gWRAP}}$-functionality to capture tokens. In order to incorporate the second model, we can use the $\mathcal{F}_{\text{gWRAP}}$-functionality without modification. If the creator is corrupted, the creator simply provides the token to the adversary together with the creator's secret input and randomness, which induce the program code as would have embedded by the honest creator. The $\mathcal{F}_{\text{gWRAP}}$-functionality will continue to provide only input/output access to the functionality in the token throughout the lifetime of the execution. We remark however that if one wanted to capture the first model, the $\mathcal{F}_{\text{gWRAP}}$-functionality would have to be modified so that when the creator of a token is corrupted, the functionality directly provides the code embedded in the token to the adversary. As we will be considering only the second model, we do not formalize the first model in this work.

3   Our Techniques

We begin with our approach for our main theorem where we construct a constant-round adaptively secure protocol in the $\mathcal{F}_{\text{gWRAP}}$-hybrid.

Constant-Round Secure Computation. Recently, the works of [10,19,28] show how to get constant-round malicious adaptive UC-secure protocols in the CRS model assuming indistinguishability obfuscation. A first attempt here would be to replace the obfuscated programs with tokens. Several problems arise with this intuition:

- The main advantage of the CRS model with obfuscation is that it can provide publicly available (concealed) code that is correct by simply placing an obfuscated code in the CRS. In contrast with tokens, one of the parties need to generate the tokens and it could be malicious.
- Second and more importantly in the case of adaptive corruption, the creator of the token can be corrupted at which point the code embedded in the token needs to be revealed. In contrast, in the CRS model, no adversary can get the random coins used to generate the CRS model.

We instead pursue a different approach. Let us begin with the following simple (yet, incorrect) approach. On a high-level the idea is to use tokens to enable evaluation of the garbled circuit in Yao's garbling technique [56]. That basic intuition here is that we view the garbling technique as system of labels where evaluation can be performed by "multiplexer" tokens (MPLX) where for each gate given labels corresponding to the inputs, the MPLX picks the corresponding output label for a gate. This basic idea can be made to work in the static setting to construct a secure computation protocol. However, in the adaptive setting things get problematic. The simulator in the garbling technique relies on a "fake" garbled circuit where only the "active keys" are correctly embedded in the garbled tables for the evaluator.[4] In the adaptive setting, if the garbled circuit evaluator is corrupted at the beginning and the generator is corrupted at the end of the execution the simulator needs to reveal the fake garbling as a real garbling. This is not possible in the $\mathcal{F}_{\text{gWRAP}}$ modelling of the tokens as the simulator is not allowed to "program" the token after creation.[5]

Instead, we solve this problem differently. We will not alter the honest generator's strategy. We modify the simulation strategy as follows:

- We embed a key K to a symmetric encryption scheme in each gate token.
- The token will be hardwired with three labels, $\ell_{\omega_1}, \ell_{\omega_2}$ and ℓ_{ω_3} which will be the active labels for this gate and a random string r.

---

[4] Using the terminology of [44], active keys are observed by the evaluator while evaluating the garbled circuit, while inactive labels are the labels that remain hidden during the evaluation.

[5] In the $\mathcal{F}_{\text{gWRAP}}$-hybrid programmability is explicitly removed so as to provide stronger compositional guarantees.

- On input ℓ_1, ℓ_2, the token will behave as follows: If $\ell_1 = \ell_{\omega_1}$ and $\ell_2 = \ell_{\omega_2}$ it will output ℓ_{ω_3}. This corresponds to what the evaluator can obtain prior to corrupting the generator.
- If either ℓ_1 or ℓ_2 is different from the hardwired labels, it attempts to do the following. It decrypts the label that is different using the key K to obtain a string z that it reads as (x, y). The token then evaluates the circuit assuming the generator's input is x and the evaluator's input is y to obtain the actual values in the wires ω_1 and ω_2 that are the inputs to this gate, say b_1 and b_2. With this information, the token internally assigns the bit b_1 to label ℓ_{ω_1} and b_2 to label ℓ_{ω_2} and $G(b_1, b_2)$ to ℓ_{ω_3} where $G \in \{\text{AND}, \text{XOR}\}$ is the gate function. Next, it outputs based on the following strategy:
  1. If $\ell_1 = \ell_{\omega_1}$ and $\ell_2 \neq \ell_{\omega_2}$ output ℓ_{ω_3} if $G(b_1, 1-b_2) = G(b_1, b_2)$, and output $\text{Enc}(K, (x, y); r)$ otherwise.
  2. If $\ell_1 \neq \ell_{\omega_1}$ and $\ell_2 = \ell_{\omega_2}$ output ℓ_{ω_3} if $G(1-b_1, b_2) = G(b_1, b_2)$, and output $\text{Enc}(K, (x, y); r)$ otherwise.
  3. If $\ell_1 \neq \ell_{\omega_1}$ and $\ell_2 \neq \ell_{\omega_2}$ output ℓ_{ω_3} if $G(1 - b_1, 1 - b_2) = G(b_1, b_2)$, and output $\text{Enc}(K, (x, y); r)$ otherwise.

In essence, this strategy figures out what bits the active labels should be associated with, and outputs the labels correctly. Furthermore, the information required to figure out the association is passed along. While this high-level idea allows to "equivocate" the circuit, we need the encryption to satisfy some additional properties such as non-malleability and evasiveness. Note that the above strategy does provide a fake code to be embedded in the token, but once the sender is corrupted post-execution the simulator reveals an honest looking code to the adversary which does not include any information about the fake code e.g., the secret key K.

We formally described our protocol and argue correctness in Sect. 6. Then we show how to adopt the cut-and-choose compilation of Lindell and Pinkas [43] in conjunction with our adaptive GUC-commitment protocol and adaptive GUC-OT protocol that we explain next to obtain a protocol that is secure against malicious adaptive adversaries in Sect. 6.1.

Commitments. Recall that an adaptive GUC-commitment is a commitment scheme between a sender and a receiver that can be (straight-line) equivocated and also allows both parties to be corrupted at the end of the execution. Moreover, as we rely on the $\mathcal{F}_{\text{gWRAP}}$-functionality to model tokens we need a simulator that is only allowed to observe queries to the tokens made by the adversary but not program them.

Our starting point is the static GUC-commitment scheme from [34] which in turn rely on the work of [33]. Roughly speaking, in order to extract the sender's input, the receiver chooses a function F from a pseudorandom function family that maps $\{0, 1\}^m$ to $\{0, 1\}^n$ bits where $m \gg n$, and incorporates it into a token which is transferred to the sender. Next, the sender commits to its input message b by first querying the PRF token on a random string $u \in \{0, 1\}^m$ to obtain v. Then, it sends $\text{com}_b = (\text{Ext}(u; r) \oplus b, r, v)$ where $\text{Ext}(\cdot, \cdot)$ is a (strong) randomness extractor. Now, since the PRF is highly compressing, it holds with high probability that conditioned on v, u has high min-entropy and therefore $\mathsf{Ext}(u; r) \oplus b, r$ statistically hides b. Furthermore, since the simulator monitors the queries made by the sender to the PRF token, by observing which query yielded the response v and with the knowledge of this query u it extracts the message b. The commitment is statistically binding since it is computationally infeasible for an adversarial receiver to obtain two values u, u' that map to v. This commitment scheme allows for extraction but not equivocation. To make this protocol equivocal, [34] use the Pass-Wee look-ahead commitment scheme [53] that allows for transforming an extractable commitment to one that also admits equivocation.

If we consider the same protocol under adaptive corruption, we need a simulator that will be able to equivocate. Unfortunately, the previous protocol fails to be secure when the receiver is corrupted first and the sender is corrupted post-execution. This is because, in the Pass-Wee scheme, several commitments are made using the extractable commitment scheme and only a subset of them are revealed during the commitment and decommitment phase. If additionally, the sender is corrupted at the end of the execution, the simulator will have to open the remaining commitments. The simulator will not be able to do this since they will not contain messages generated according to the honest sender's strategy and given a commitment to some message b, $\mathsf{com}_b = (\mathsf{Ext}(u; r) \oplus b, r, v)$, the simulator cannot equivocate the message since the value v binds u. This is because given a PRF it is infeasible for a simulator to find $u \neq u'$ such that $\mathsf{PRF}(u) = \mathsf{PRF}(u')$ (even if the key of the PRF is revealed).

As such this approach does not help us with adaptive corruption. We instead follow a different approach, starting from the work of [36]. More precisely, in this work, the authors show how to construct an adaptive UC-commitment scheme in the CRS model starting from a public-key encryption scheme which additionally has the property that ciphertexts can be obliviously generated and any valid ciphertext can be later revealed as obliviously generated. The high-level idea is that such an encryption scheme provides a mechanism to construct a straight-line extractable commitment scheme which additionally has an oblivious generation property (i.e., analogous to the property for ciphertexts just specified above). Then given such a primitive, it is shown how to compile it into a commitment scheme that is adaptively secure. We will first directly construct a primitive that has this extractability property in the $\mathcal{F}_{\mathsf{gWRAP}}$-hybrid and then use their compilation to get a full-fledged adaptive GUC-commitment.

To obtain an extractable commitment with oblivious generation, our first attempt is to modify the static extractable commitment from [34] as follows: Instead of sending $\mathsf{com}_b = (\mathsf{Ext}(u; r) \oplus b, r, v)$ as the message, suppose that the sender sent $(\mathsf{Ext}(u; r) \oplus b, r, \mathsf{Com}(v))$ where Com is any non-interactive commitment scheme with pseudorandom commitments.[6] This commitment scheme has an oblivious generation property where the sender can simply send a

---

[6] In our protocol, we only need a statistically binding commitment scheme and we will rely on the construction of Naor [49] based on one-way functions.

random string. However, it loses its extractability property as the simulator will no longer be able to identify the right "u" query that leads to v, as it only sees $\mathsf{Com}(v)$ rather than v.

To regain extractability, we use unique unforgeable signatures. More precisely, the receiver generates a $(\mathsf{sk}, \mathsf{vk})$-pair of a signature scheme and sends vk to the sender. The sender commits to its query u using the scheme Com and obtains a signature σ on the commitment from the receiver. Then we modify the PRF token, to reply with $\mathsf{PRF}(u)$ only if it can provide (c, d, σ) such that c is a commitment to u with decommitment information d and σ is a valid signature of c using sk. We also modify the decommitment phase, were in addition to u, we require the sender to provide a decommitment of u to c. This will allow to regain extractability as this protocol will force the sender to use only the commitment that it used to obtain a signature from the receiver to obtain a response from the PRF token. More precisely, let c be the message that the sender sends in the first step to receive a signature σ from the receiver. Then, the simulator will monitor the queries made by the sender to the PRF token and wait until the sender makes a valid query of the form (c, d, σ) and use d (i.e., a decommitment of c to u) to extract u.

The binding property of this scheme will follow from the binding property of the Com scheme and the unforgeability of the signature scheme. Given this extractable commitment scheme with oblivious generation property we compile using the protocol of [36] to obtain a full-fledged adaptive GUC-commitment. We describe and prove correctness of our extractable commitment scheme in Sect. 4.1 and full-fledged GUC-commitment in the full version [35].

Oblivious Transfer. Our oblivious transfer protocol will closely follow the static GUC-secure OT protocol in [34]. On a high-level, the idea here is that the receiver commits to its input bit b and the sender sends a token that contains s_0, s_1 and reveals s_b only if the receiver provides a valid decommitment to b. We refer to such a token as an OT-type token. This basic protocol is vulnerable to input-dependent attacks and we rely on standard mechanisms to design a combiner to address this. In particular, following an approach analogous to [34], we will adapt the combiner of [51]. While our protocol structure remains the same as [34], certain subtleties arise that we list below and briefly mention how we address them.

- The protocol in [34] involves the sender sending several OT-type tokens and along with it commitments to all the entries in these tokens via a GUC-commitment. Furthermore, the OT-type tokens in addition to revealing one of the entries in the token given the receiver's bit b, also reveals a decommitment of that entry for the GUC-commitment scheme. A main issue that arises here is that we require a token to reveal a decommitment of a GUC-commitment scheme and this is infeasible if the GUC-commitments were made in a $\mathcal{F}_{\mathrm{COM}}$-hybrid since there is no notion of a decommitment besides a message communicated from $\mathcal{F}_{\mathrm{COM}}$. Previous works in this area [14] rely on a Commit-and-Prove functionality to address this issue. We instead construct an OT protocol directly in the $\mathcal{F}_{\text{gWRAP}}$-hybrid instead of constructing it in the $(\mathcal{F}_{\text{COM}}, \mathcal{F}_{\text{gWRAP}})$-hybrid. More precisely, we first describe an (adaptively secure) commitment scheme Π_{COM} in the $\mathcal{F}_{\text{gWRAP}}$-hybrid that comes with an NP-relation for verifying decommitments and is straight-line extractable and equivocable. We then use this as a sub-protocol in our OT-protocol. The formal properties and realization of our commitment scheme, as well as our OT protocol and its security proof can be found in the full version [35].

– Since we need to deal with adaptive corruptions, in the case of a malicious receiver where the adversary also corrupts the sender post-execution we have the following subtle issue. Here the simulator can extract the receiver's input b and obtain s_b from the $\mathcal{F}_{\text{OT}}$ functionality. However, the simulator needs to provide the OT-type tokens in the protocol without having complete knowledge of the sender's real inputs. This is because in the $\mathcal{F}_{\text{gWRAP}}$-hybrid the simulator is not allowed to program the tokens and needs to provide an actual code to the $\mathcal{F}_{\text{gWRAP}}$-hybrid whenever the adversary expects to receive a token. Furthermore, when the sender is corrupted at the end of the execution and the simulator learns the real inputs of the sender, it needs to provide the code incorporated in the tokens (that looks like something the honest sender strategy generated). We handle this issue by providing a strategy for the simulator to provide a fake code to be embedded in the token but later reveal an honest looking code to the adversary. Indistinguishability of the real and ideal world will then follow by establishing that it would be computationally infeasible for the adversary to find the query that distinguishes the alleged code revealed by the simulator and the actual code embedded in the token.

Note that a reader can first read our two-party protocol in Sect. 6 since the OT (Sect. 5) and commitment (Sect. 4) protocols are treated in a black box way.

4   Adaptive GUC-Commitments from OWF Using Tokens

In this section we construct adaptively secure GUC-commitment schemes using tokens. In the heart of our construction lies the observation that the adaptive UC-commitment scheme from [36] can be realized using extractable commitment schemes with some additional feature. Loosely speaking, extractable commitment scheme is a weaker primitive than UC-commitment in the sense that it does not require equivocality. Namely, the simulator is not required to commit to one message and then later convince the receiver that it committed to a different value. In the following section we consider extractable commitment schemes with oblivious generation, for which the committer can obliviously generate a commitment without knowing the committed message. This property is analogue to public key encryption scheme with oblivious sampling of ciphertexts (where the plaintext is not known), and allows to use this primitive as a building block in our adaptively secure GUC-commitments. Moreover, any commitment made to a message can later be revealed as a commitment that was obliviously generated. In Sect. 4.1 we define our new notion of security for extractable commitment schemes with oblivious generation of commitments and present our extractable commitment scheme. In [35] we discuss how to realize UC-commitment schemes based on the construction from [36] and our new notion of extractable commitments with oblivious generation.

4.1   Extractable Commitments with Oblivious Generation

We begin with our definition of extractable commitment schemes. A commitment scheme is a protocol between a sender S with input a message m and a receiver R. The protocol is marked by two distinct phases: a commitment phase and a decommitment phase. We will consider our definition in the $\mathcal{F}_{\mathrm{gWRAP}}$-hybrid, i.e. both the sender and the receiver will have access to the ideal $\mathcal{F}_{\mathrm{gWRAP}}$-functionality. Since, this protocol will eventually be incorporated into a protocol in the GUC-setting, the parties will have as common input a session identifier sid. All the commitment schemes presented in this work will have a non-interactive decommitment phase that can be verified via a NP-relation $\mathcal{R}_{\mathrm{decom}}$ with the statement being the transcript of the commitment phase. This relation will be referred to as the decommitment relation. While our definitions can be generalized, for simplicity of exposition, we will restrict our definition to such protocols in this work. We call this property stand-alone verifiability and define it formally below.

Definition 1. *We say that a commitment scheme $\langle S, R \rangle$ in the $\mathcal{F}_{\mathrm{gWRAP}}$-hybrid is stand-alone verifiable with NP-relation $\mathcal{R}$ if in the decommitment phase the sender sends a single decommitment message (m, d) and the receiver outputs 1 if and only if $\mathcal{R}(\tau, (m, d)) = 1$ where τ is the transcript of the interaction between S and R in the commitment phase (excluding the communication between the parties and the $\mathcal{F}_{\mathrm{gWRAP}}$-functionality).*

Definition 2. *A commitment scheme $(\langle S, R \rangle, \mathcal{R}_{\mathrm{decom}})$ with stand-alone verifiability is said to be an extractable with oblivious generation if the following properties hold.*

Straightline Extractability: *For every malicious sender S*, there exists a strategy Ext that, after the completion of commitment phase in an interaction between S* and the honest receiver R with common input $(1^\kappa, \mathrm{sid})$ in the $\mathcal{F}_{\mathrm{gWRAP}}$-hybrid can do the following: On input the transcript of the commitment phase τ and the queries made by S* to all tokens it receives via $\mathcal{F}_{\mathrm{gWRAP}}$ for the current session sid can output m such that, the probability that S* outputs (m', d') with $m' \neq m$ and $\mathcal{R}_{\mathrm{decom}}(\tau, (m', d')) = 1$ is negligible.*

Oblivious Generation: *There is a PPT algorithm $\widehat{S}$ and polynomial-time computable function Adapt such that for any message m and any malicious receiver R*, it can produce random coins for $\widehat{S}$ which "explains" a (possibly partial) transcript generated in an interaction using $\langle S, R \rangle$ with R* where S's input is m. More formally, for every PPT machine R*, it holds that, the following ensembles are computationally indistinguishable.*

- $\{(\tau, v) \leftarrow \mathsf{sta}^{\mathrm{R}^*}_{\langle \widehat{\mathrm{S}}, \mathrm{R} \rangle}(1^\kappa, \mathsf{sid}, r, m, z) : (v, r)\}$
- $\{(\tau, v) \leftarrow \mathsf{sta}^{\mathrm{R}^*}_{\langle \mathrm{S}, \mathrm{R} \rangle}(1^\kappa, \mathsf{sid}, r', z) : (v, \mathsf{Adapt}(\tau))\}$

where $\kappa \in \mathbb{N}, m \in \{0,1\}^\kappa, r \in \{0,1\}^{p(n)}, r' \in \{0,1\}^{q(n)}, z \in \{0,1\}^*$ *and where* $\mathsf{sta}^{\mathrm{R}^*}_{\langle \mathrm{S}, \mathrm{R} \rangle}(1^\kappa, \mathsf{sid}, r, m, z)$ *and* $\mathsf{sta}^{\mathrm{R}^*}_{\langle \widehat{\mathrm{S}}, \mathrm{R} \rangle}(1^\kappa, \mathsf{sid}, r', z)$ *denote the random variables describing the (possibly partial) transcript of the interaction and output of* $\mathrm{R}^*(z)$ *upon interacting with the sender* S *on input* m *randomness* r *and* $\widehat{\mathrm{S}}$ *on randomness* r', *respectively.*

Next, we construct a commitment scheme that satisfies these properties. We present our protocol in Fig. 1. Informally speaking, our construction follows by having the sender commit using a PRF token, where extraction is carried out by monitoring the sender's queries to this token. In order to force the sender to use the token only once, the receiver signs on a commitment of the PRF query, where the token verifies the validity of both the decommitment and the signature. A similar approach was pursued in the work of [18] where digital signatures, which require an additional property of *unique* signatures, are employed. Recall first that a signature scheme (GenSig, Sig, Ver) is said to be unique if for every verification key vk and every message m, there exists only one signature σ for which $\mathsf{Ver}_{\mathsf{vk}}(m, \sigma) = 1$. Such signature schemes can be constructed based on specific number theoretic assumptions [23]. In [34] a different approach was taken using one-time signatures based on statistically binding commitment schemes that can be based on one-way functions. Their scheme ensures uniqueness in the sense of [18]. We follow their approach in this paper as well.

Lemma 1. *Assume the exitance of one-way functions. Then protocol* $\Pi_{\mathrm{OBL-EXT}}$ *presented in Fig. 1 is an extractable commitment scheme with oblivious generation in the global* $\mathcal{F}_{\mathrm{gWRAP}}$-*hybrid in the presence of adaptive malicious adversaries.*

Proof. We prove that the protocol $\Pi_{\mathrm{OBL-EXT}}$ satisfies both straight-line extractability and the oblivious generation property:

Straightline Extractability: We need to define the Ext algorithm. Recall that Ext receives the transcript τ and the queries that S^* makes to the token it receives from R, namely the PRF token. This can be obtained from the $\mathcal{F}_{\mathrm{gWRAP}}$ functionality by issuing the query (retreive, sid, mid). In the list of queries, Ext finds a tuple (c, u, σ, r) where c is the first message sent by the sender and σ is the signature the receiver returned. Then, it checks if the randomness r correctly decommits c to u. If no valid query is made or the decommitment is incorrect, the extracted value is set to $\bot$. Otherwise, it retrieves the message by computing $m = m' + \mathsf{H}(u)$ where (m', c') is the second message sent by the sender in the commit phase. If there are multiple valid queries then it sets the extracted value to $\bot$.

Correctness of extraction follows from the unforgeability of the signature scheme and the statistically-binding property of the commitment scheme Com. More formally, we show that the probability that Ext fails to retrieve the

---

Protocol $\Pi_{\mathrm{OBL-EXT}}$

The commitment scheme ExtCom is run between sender S and receiver R and relation $\mathcal{R}_{\mathsf{decom}}$. Let (1) Com denote the Naor commitment scheme [50] which is statistically binding and has pseudorandom commitments (2) (GenSig, Sig, Ver) denote a one-time signature scheme with unique signatures (3) $\mathsf{PRF}_k : \{0,1\}^{5\kappa} \to \{0,1\}^{\kappa}$ is a PRF and (4) $\mathsf{H} : \{0,1\}^{\kappa} \mapsto \{0,1\}$ denote a hardcore predicate.

Input: S holds a message $m \in \{0,1\}$. Common inputs are 1^{κ} and session identifier sid.

Commit Phase:

R → S: R generates $(\mathsf{sk}, \mathsf{vk}) \leftarrow \mathsf{GenSig}(1^{\kappa})$ of a unique (or one-time) signature scheme Π_{SIG} and sends vk to S.

S → R: S samples $u \leftarrow \{0,1\}^{5\kappa}$ and sends $c = \mathsf{Com}(u; r)$ to R.

R → S: R computes $\sigma \leftarrow \mathsf{Sig}(\mathsf{sk}, c)$ and forwards σ to S. R also sends a PRF token $\mathsf{TK}_{\mathsf{R}}^{\mathsf{PRF}}$ by sending $(\mathsf{Create}, \mathsf{sid}, \mathsf{S}, \mathsf{R}, \mathsf{mid}, M_1)$ to $\mathcal{F}_{\mathrm{gWRAP}}$ where M_1 is the functionality that on input $(\mathsf{sid}^*, (c, \sigma, u, r))$ proceeds as follows:
  - If $\mathsf{sid}^* \neq \mathsf{sid}$ return $\perp$.
  - Otherwise, if $c = \mathsf{Com}(u; r)$ and $\mathsf{Ver}(\mathsf{vk}, c, \sigma) = 1$ return $v = \mathsf{PRF}_k(u)$.

S obtains $(\mathsf{Create}, \mathsf{sid}, \mathsf{R}, \mathsf{S}, \mathsf{mid}, M_1)$ from the functionality $\mathcal{F}_{\mathrm{gWRAP}}$.

S → R: S sends $(\mathsf{Run}, \mathsf{sid}, \mathsf{S}, \mathsf{mid}, (c, \sigma, u, r))$ and obtains v. It then sends (m', c') to R where $m' = \mathsf{H}(u) + m$ and $c' = \mathsf{Com}(v; r')$.

Decommit Phase:

S reveals (m, u, r, r') and R checks if the relation $\mathcal{R}_{\mathsf{decom}}(\tau, (m, (u, r, r')))$ is satisfied where the transcript $\tau = (\mathsf{vk}, c, m', c')$ and

$$\mathcal{R}_{\mathsf{decom}}((\mathsf{vk}, c, m', c'), (m, (u, r, r'))) = 1 \text{ iff}$$
$$c = \mathsf{Com}(u; r) \wedge \mathsf{PRF}_k(u) = v \wedge m' = \mathsf{H}(u) + m \wedge c' = \mathsf{Com}(v; r'))$$

Fig. 1. Extractable commitments with oblivious generation.

correct message is negligible. First, we claim that the sender will be able to run the PRF token only on one input, namely (c, u, σ, r) for which σ is a valid signature for c and c is a valid commitment to u that was computed using randomness r. This is because for any other valid query, the sender is able to produce a valid signature for message other than c or produce two decommitments of c to Com. Now, since Ext receives all queries from the $\mathcal{F}_{\mathrm{gWRAP}}$, given any adversarial sender S* that is able to give a valid query (c', u', σ', r') where $c' \neq c$ or $u' \neq u$, we can construct an adversary that respectively breaks the unforgeability of the signature scheme or the binding property of Com.

Oblivious Generation: The oblivious sender algorithm $\widehat{\mathsf{S}}$ simply sends random strings of appropriate length in the first and second messages. Namely, in the first message it picks a random string of length C and in the second message it sends $|m| + C$ where $|m| = 1$ is the length of the message and C is the length of the commitment message using Com. Given a partial transcript, the Adapt algorithm simply reconstructs the random tape of S by observing the messages sent in the transcript by the honest sender S and placing that message in the random tape.

The indistinguishability property of the randomness output by the Adapt algorithm follows essentially from the pseudorandomness of the Naor's commitment scheme Com [49] and the statistically hiding property of $H(u)$ given v for any length compressing PRF. More formally, we consider a sequence of hybrids executions, starting from an execution of a commitment to a message m and obtaining an oblivious generated commitment.

- **Hybrid H_1:** The output of this hybrid is the view of R^* when it is interacting with a simulator that follows the honest sender's strategy S with input m.
- **Hybrid H_2:** In this hybrid, the simulator follows the honest strategy with the exception that in the fourth message instead of committing to v, it sends a random string. The indistinguishability of Hybrids H_1 and H_2 follows from the pseudorandomness of the commitment made using Com.
- **Hybrid H_3:** In this hybrid, the simulator follows the strategy as in H_2 with the exception that instead of sending $H(u)+m$ as part of the fourth message, it sends a random bit. Indistinguishability follows from the hiding property of the Com scheme. More formally, consider any adversary R^* such that the outputs of Hybrid H_2 and H_3 can be distinguished. Using R^* we construct an adversary $\mathcal{A}$, that on input a commitment c made using Com, can extract the committed value by internally emulating H_2 (or H_3), by feeding c as part of the first message and then using the Goldreich-Levin theorem to extract u. In this reduction, $\mathcal{A}$ cannot obtain the value $v = PRF(u)$ since it cannot produce a decommitment of c. Yet, since in hybrid H_2 we already replaced the commitment to v in the fourth message to a random string, $\mathcal{A}$ can still complete the execution without knowing the value v. This adversary $\mathcal{A}$ violates the hiding property of Com.
- **Hybrid H_4:** In this hybrid, the simulator follows the strategy $\widehat{S}$. Observe that this strategy is the same strategy as in H_3 with the exception that instead of sending a commitment to randomly sampled u in the second message, it sends a random string. The indistinguishability of Hybrids H_3 and H_4 follows from the pseudorandomness of the commitment made using Com.

We further address here an adaptive corruption of the sender as we use our protocol as a sub-protocol in order to construct a GUC commitment scheme that maintains adaptive security. In case of such corruption the adversary demands the sender's actual randomness or the randomness according to oblivious generation. The only case we will need to address in our proof is explaining a valid commitment as an obliviously generated one, for which our Adapt algorithm takes care even on partial transcripts.

4.2 Obtaining GUC-Commitments in the gRO Model

An implication of the above extractable commitment scheme is that we can further realize $\mathcal{F}_{COM}$ in the global random oracle model [11]. Specifically, our commitment, shown in the full version [35], calls an extractable commitment which is implemented, in turn, using PRF tokens (for which the simulator exploits in order to extract the committed message). A similar construction can be shown using a global random oracle that is used instead of the PRF tokens. Namely, instead of using signature schemes and pseudorandom commitment schemes in order to enforce a single usage of the PRF token, the sender directly calls the random oracle on some random value u, obtaining the value v, and then masking the committed message by sending $(u + m, v)$. Consequently, we obtain the first GUC-commitment construction in the global random oracle model from OWF with adaptive security. In contrast, the scheme in [11] only achieves security against static corruptions and relies on concrete number theoretic assumptions. We remark here that while the construction of an extractable commitment scheme with oblivious generation is easy to construct in the gRO model following our construction from the previous section, obtaining this corollary relies on the compilation of such a commitment to a full-fledged adaptively secure commitment that we present in the full version [35].

More formally, we claim the following.

Corollary 3. *Assume the existence of one-way functions. Then the protocol specified above is an extractable commitment scheme with oblivious generation in the $\mathcal{F}_{\mathrm{gRO}}$-hybrid in the presence of adaptive malicious adversaries.*

Intuitively, this scheme is extractable since the simulator can monitor the sender's queries to the random oracle. That is, the simulator obtains from $\mathcal{F}_{\mathrm{gRO}}$ the query list made by the adversary and search a pair (u, v) that is consistent with the commitment (m', v). If so, it outputs the message $m = m' + u$. Else, it sets the extracted message to $\perp$. Finally, oblivious sampling holds trivially as well due to the fact that the random oracle behaves like a truly random function and given an honestly generated commitment $(u + m, v)$ the message is indistinguishable from a truly random string and therefore can be revealed as something that is obliviously generated.

In [17], they show how to obtain adaptive UC-secure computation of arbitrary functionalities assuming UC-secure adaptive semi-honest oblivious-transfer in the $\mathcal{F}_{\mathsf{Com}}$-hybrid (See Theorem 1). Combining this result with Corollary 3, we obtain the following corollary.

Corollary 4. *Assume the existence of UC-secure adaptive semi-honest oblivious transfer. Then for any well-formed functionlaity $\mathcal{F}$, there exists a $O(d_{\mathcal{F}})$-round protocol that securely realizes $\mathcal{F}$ in the GUC-setting in the presence of adaptive malicious adversaries, where $d_{\mathcal{F}}$ is the depth of the circuit that implements $\mathcal{F}$.*

In [36], they provide a compiler that takes any extractable commitment scheme (even without oblivious generation) and constructs a UC-secure protocols for general functionalities in the static setting assuming semi-honest (static) oblivious transfer. Combining this result with Corollary 3, we obtain the following result:

Corollary 5. *Assume the existence of (static) semi-honest oblivious-transfer. Then for any well-formed functionality $\mathcal{F}$, there exists a $O(1)$-round protocol that securely realizes $\mathcal{F}$ in the GUC-setting in the presence of malicious adversaries.*

This result improves the result of Canetti, Jain and Sahai that relies on the specific DDH assumption for their construction.

5   Adaptive OT from OWF Using Tokens

In this section we present our GUC OT protocol. On a high-level, our protocol is identical to the OT protocol from [34] with the exception that the parties apply the adaptive commitment scheme from Sect. 4. In contrast, [34] relies on a UC-commitment scheme in the token model that is secure only against static corruptions. Namely, we describe our protocol Π_{OT} in the $\mathcal{F}_{\mathrm{gWRAP}}$-hybrid model with sender S and receiver R using the following building blocks: let (1) Com be a non-interactive perfectly binding commitment scheme, (2) let $\mathcal{SS} = (\mathsf{Share}, \mathsf{Recon})$ be a $(\kappa+1)$-out-of-2κ Shamir secret-sharing scheme over $\mathbb{Z}_p$, together with a linear map $\phi : \mathbb{Z}_p^{2\kappa} \to \mathbb{Z}_p^{\kappa-1}$ such that $\phi(v) = 0$ iff v is a valid sharing of some secret, (3) F, F' be two families of pseudorandom functions that map $\{0,1\}^{5\kappa} \to \{0,1\}^\kappa$ and $\{0,1\}^\kappa \to \{0,1\}^{p(\kappa)}$, respectively (4) H denote a hardcore bit function and (5) $\mathsf{Ext} : \{0,1\}^{5\kappa} \times \{0,1\}^d \to \{0,1\}$ denote a randomness extractor where the source has length 5κ and the seed has length d. Our protocol is presented in Fig. 2 and involves using our GUC-commitment scheme.

Theorem 5. *Assume the existence of one-way functions. Then protocol Π_{OT} presented in Fig. 2 GUC realizes $\mathcal{F}_{\mathrm{OT}}$ in the $\mathcal{F}_{\mathrm{gWRAP}}$-hybrid model in the presence of adaptive malicious adversaries.*

Proof Overview. On a high-level, our proof follows analogously to the proof in [34] (which in turn relies on the simulation strategy of [51]). Crucially, we need to address the issue of adaptive corruptions in our proof of *both* parties. In case of a receiver corruption we need to be able to generate a view for the receiver corresponding to its input and output. As part of the protocol, the receiver commits to its input before receiving the tokens and uses the decommitment as input to the tokens. We further note that the simulation strategy in [34] for a corrupted sender relies on following the honest receiver's strategy and extracting the sender's input by monitoring the sender's queries to the tokens. While this strategy is appropriate to handle static corruptions, it requires handling new subtleties in case of adaptive corruption. Specifically, it is still possible to rely on the honest receiver's strategy, however, upon post corrupting the receiver the simulator must be able to produce random coins for the receiver that demonstrates consistency with its real input. To achieve this, we make the receiver commit its input using a GUC-commitment scheme secure against adaptive corruptions. Such a scheme is described in our previous section. This enables us to equivocate the receiver's input. Next, in case of sender corruption we again need to be able to equivocate the sender's OT inputs. In fact, we need to be able to equivocate

---

Protocol Π_{OT}

Input: S holds two strings $s_0, s_1 \in \{0,1\}^\kappa$ and R holds a bit b.

The Protocol:

R $\leftrightarrow$ S:

1. R selects a random subset $T_{1-b} \subseteq [2\kappa]$ of size $\kappa/2$. Define $T_b = [2\kappa]/T_{1-b}$. For every $j \in [2\kappa]$, R sets $b_j = \beta$ if $j \in T_\beta$.
2. R samples uniformly at random $c_1, \ldots, c_\kappa \leftarrow \{0,1\}$.
3. Finally, R and S engage in 3κ instances of protocol Π_{COM}, described in the full version [36], where upon completing the commitment phase S holds transcripts of the commitment phase $(\{\mathsf{com}_{b_j}\}_{j\in[2\kappa]}, \{\mathsf{com}_{c_i}\}_{i\in[\kappa]})$ to values $(\{b_j\}_{j\in[2\kappa]}, \{c_i\}_{i\in[\kappa]})$, respectively.

S $\leftrightarrow$ R:

1. S picks two random strings $x_0, x_1 \leftarrow \mathbb{Z}_p$ and secret shares them using $\mathcal{SS}$. In particular, S computes $[x_b] = (x_b^1, \ldots, x_b^{2\kappa}) \leftarrow \mathsf{Share}(x_b)$ for $b \in \{0,1\}$.
2. S commits to the shares $[x_0], [x_1]$ as follows. It picks random matrices $A_0, B_0 \leftarrow \mathbb{Z}_p^{\kappa \times 2\kappa}$ and $A_1, B_1 \leftarrow \mathbb{Z}_p^{\kappa \times 2\kappa}$ such that $\forall i \in [\kappa]$:

$$A_0[i, \cdot] + B_0[i, \cdot] = [x_0], \quad A_1[i, \cdot] + B_1[i, \cdot] = [x_1].$$

S computes two matrices $Z_0, Z_1 \in \mathbb{Z}_p^{\kappa \times \kappa - 1}$ and sends them in the clear such that:

$$Z_0[i, \cdot] = \phi(A_0[i, \cdot]), Z_1[i, \cdot] = \phi(A_1[i, \cdot]).$$

3. S and R engage in $8\kappa^2$ instances of protocol Π_{COM}, described in the full version [36], where upon completing the commitment phase R holds the transcripts of the commitment phase $(\mathsf{com}_{A_0}, \mathsf{com}_{B_0}, \mathsf{com}_{A_1}, \mathsf{com}_{B_1})$ to matrices A_0, B_0, A_1, B_1, respectively.
4. S sends $C_0 = s_0 \oplus x_0$ and $C_1 = s_1 \oplus x_1$ to R.
5. For all $j \in [2\kappa]$, S creates a token TK_j by sending $(\mathsf{Create}, \mathsf{sid}, \mathsf{R}, \mathsf{S}, \mathsf{mid}_{3\kappa+j}, M_3)$ to $\mathcal{F}_{\mathrm{gWRAP}}$ where M_3 is the functionality that on input $(b_j, \mathsf{decom}_{b_j})$, aborts if decom_{b_j} is not a valid decommitment of the commitment in the first round to b_j. Otherwise it outputs $(A_{b_j}[\cdot, j], \mathsf{decom}_{A_{b_j}[\cdot, j]}, B_{b_j}[\cdot, j], \mathsf{decom}_{B_{b_j}[\cdot, j]})$.
6. For all $i \in [\kappa]$, S creates a token $\widehat{\mathsf{TK}}_i$ by sending $(\mathsf{Create}, \mathsf{sid}, \mathsf{R}, \mathsf{S}, \mathsf{mid}_{5\kappa+i}, M_4)$ to $\mathcal{F}_{\mathrm{gWRAP}}$ where M_4 is the functionality that on input $(c_i, \mathsf{decom}_{c_i})$ aborts if decom_{c_i} is not verified correctly. Otherwise it outputs,

$$(A_0[i, \cdot], \mathsf{decom}_{A_0[i, \cdot]}, A_1[i, \cdot], \mathsf{decom}_{A_1[i, \cdot]}), \text{ if } c = 0$$
$$(B_0[i, \cdot], \mathsf{decom}_{B_0[i, \cdot]}, B_1[i, \cdot], \mathsf{decom}_{B_1[i, \cdot]}), \text{ if } c = 1$$

Output Phase: See Figure 3.

Fig. 2. GUC OT with tokens.

s_{1-b} among (s_0, s_1) of the sender's inputs where b is the receiver's input. In the protocol, the sender commits to the secret-sharing of two random strings x_0 and x_1 and masks the real inputs with them. The tokens allow the receiver to extract the shares of x_b and obtain s_b. The main argument in [34] is that the receiver will not be able to receive sufficiently many shares of x_{1-b} and hence s_{1-b} remains hidden. In our protocol we first rely on an adaptive GUC-commitment, and thus able to equivocate the sender's commitments. However, the tokens reveal the values stored in the commitments (by producing the decommitments) and these values need to be changed corresponding to x_{1-b} for equivocation.

In more details, for sender corruption, our simulation proceeds analogously to the simulation from [51] where the simulator generates the view of the malicious sender by following the honest receiver's strategy to simulate messages and then extracting all the values committed to by the sender. In [51] they rely on extractable commitments and extract the sender's inputs via rewinding, we here directly extract its inputs by monitoring the queries made by the malicious sender to the tokens embedded within our GUC-commitment protocol Π_{COM}. The proof of correctness follows analogously. More explicitly, the share consistency check ensures that for any particular column that the receiver obtains, if the sum of the values agree on the same bit, then the receiver extracts the correct share of $[x_b]$ with high probability. Note that it suffices for the receiver to obtain $\kappa + 1$ good columns for its input b to extract enough shares to reconstruct x_b since the shares can be checked for validity. Namely, the receiver chooses $\kappa/2$ indices T_b and sets its input for these OT executions as b. For the rest of the OT executions, the receiver sets its input as $1 - b$. Denote this set of indices by T_{1-b}. Then, upon receiving the sender's response to its challenge and the OT responses, the receiver first performs the shares consistency check. If this check passes, it performs the shares validity check for all columns, both with indices in T_{1-b} and for the indices in a random subset of size $\kappa/2$ within T_b. If one of these checks do not pass, the receiver aborts. If both checks pass, it holds with high probability that the decommitment information for $b = 0$ and $b = 1$ are correct in all but $s \in \omega(\log n)$ indices. Therefore, the receiver will extract $[x_b]$ successfully both when its input $b = 0$ and $b = 1$. Furthermore, it is ensured that if the two checks performed by the receiver pass, then a simulator can extract both x_0 and x_1 correctly by simply extracting the sender's input to the OT protocol and following the receiver's strategy to extract.

On the other hand, when the receiver is corrupted, our simulation proceeds analogous to the simulation in [51] where the simulator generates the view of the malicious receiver by first extracting the receiver's input b and then obtaining s_b from the ideal functionality. It then completes the execution by following the honest sender's code with (s_0, s_1), where s_{1-b} is set to random. Moreover, while in [51] the authors rely on a special type of interactive commitment that allows the extraction of the receiver's input via rewinding, we instead extract this input directly by monitoring the queries made by the malicious receiver to the tokens embedded within protocol Π_{COM}. The proof of correctness follows analogously. Informally, the idea is to show that the receiver can learn $\kappa + 1$ or more shares for either x_0 or x_1 but not both. In other words there exists a bit b for which a corrupted receiver can learn at most κ shares relative to s_{1-b}.

Output Phase for Π_{OT}

Output Phase:
1. For all $j \in [2\kappa]$, R sends $(\mathsf{Run}, \mathsf{sid}, \mathsf{S}, \mathsf{mid}_{3\kappa+j}, (b_j, \mathsf{decom}_{b_j}))$ receiving back $(A_{b_j}[\cdot, j], \mathsf{decom}_{A_{b_j}[\cdot, j]}, B_{b_j}[\cdot, j], \mathsf{decom}_{B_{b_j}[\cdot, j]})$.
2. For all $i \in [\kappa]$, R sends $(\mathsf{Run}, \mathsf{sid}, \mathsf{S}, \mathsf{mid}_{5\kappa+i}, (c_i, \mathsf{decom}_{c_i}))$ receiving back $(A_0[\cdot, i], A_1[\cdot, i])$ or $(B_0[\cdot, i], B_1[\cdot, i])$.

Combiner:

Shares Validity Check Phase: For all $i \in [\kappa]$, if $c_i = 0$ check that $Z_0[i, \cdot] = \phi(A_0[i, \cdot])$ and $Z_1[i, \cdot] = \phi(A_1[i, \cdot])$. Otherwise, if $c_i = 1$ check that $\phi(B_0[i, \cdot]) + Z_0[i, \cdot] = 0$ and $\phi(B_1[i, \cdot]) + Z_1[i, \cdot] = 0$. If the tokens do not abort and all the checks pass, the receiver proceeds to the next phase.

Shares Consistency Check Phase: For each $b \in \{0, 1\}$, R randomly chooses a set T_b for which $b_j = b$ of $\kappa/2$ coordinates. For each $j \in T_b$, R checks that there exists a unique x_b^j such that $A_b[i, j] + B_b[i, j] = x_b^j$ for all $i \in [\kappa]$. If so, x_b^j is marked as consistent. If the tokens do not abort and all the shares obtained in this phase are consistent, R proceeds to the reconstruction phase. Else it abort.

Reconstruction Phase: For $j \in [2\kappa]/T_{1-b}$, if there exists a unique x_b^j such that $A_b[i, j] + B_b[i, j] = x_b^j$, mark share j as a good column. If R obtains less than $\kappa + 1$ good shares, it aborts. Otherwise, let $x_b^{j_1}, \ldots, x_b^{j_{\kappa+1}}$ be any set of $\kappa + 1$ consistent shares. R computes $x_b \leftarrow \mathsf{Recon}(x_b^{j_1}, \ldots, x_b^{j_{\kappa+1}})$ and outputs $s_b = C_b \oplus x_b$.

Fig. 3. Output phase for Π_{OT}.

Thus, by replacing s_{1-b} with a random string, it follows from the secret-sharing property that obtaining at most κ shares keeps s_{1-b} information theoretically hidden. The proof can be found in the full version [35] (Fig. 3).

6 Adaptively Secure Two-Party Computation

In this section we demonstrate the feasibility of *constant-round* adaptively secure two-party computation in the token model. Loosely speaking, the idea is to associate a token with each gabled gate where the gabled table is embedded within the token, where the token mimics the circuit's evaluator in the sense that it returns the output label that corresponds to the pair of the input labels of this gate entered by the receiver (if such a key exists). This allows to implement each garbled gate in a form of OT rather than providing a set of four ciphertexts. We further make use of notions such as active/inactive labels as defined in [44], where active labels are the labels that observed by the receiver while evaluating the garbled circuit, while inactive labels are the labels that remain hidden during the evaluation.

In more detail, the basic tokens that we will use in our protocol will intuitively implement the functionality of a garbled gate in Yao's construction. Given a function f, let C be the boolean circuit (with the conventions made in [44]) such that for every $x, y \in \{0, 1\}^n$, $\mathrm{C}(x, y) = f(x, y)$ where $f : \{0, 1\}^n \times \{0, 1\}^n \rightarrow \{0, 1\}^n$. The sender will follow typical garbled circuit constructions and first create labels for each wire in the circuit. Next, instead of garbling a gate by using the labels as keys to an encryption scheme, we will incorporate in a token the functionality that on input, labels of the incoming wires, will output the corresponding label of the output wire. In essence, the token behaves as 1-out-of-4 OT token. More precisely, for every wire identified by index ω in the circuit, we pick two random strings $\mathsf{lab}_\omega^0, \mathsf{lab}_\omega^1 \in \{0, 1\}^\kappa$. Then corresponding to gate Gate_c, the sender S creates a token that on input (ℓ_1, ℓ_2) finds α and β such that $\ell_1 = \mathsf{lab}_{\omega_1}^\alpha$ and $\ell_1 = \mathsf{lab}_{\omega_2}^\beta$ and outputs $\mathsf{lab}_{\omega_3}^{\mathsf{Gate}_c(\alpha,\beta)}$ where ω_1, ω_2 are the incoming wire identifiers, ω_3 is the identifier of the output wire to gate c and $\mathsf{Gate}_c \in \{\mathrm{AND}, \mathrm{XOR}\}$ is the corresponding boolean function of the gate c.

Furthermore, assume that the oblivious transfer protocol that realizes $\mathcal{F}_{\mathrm{OT}}$ is simulatable in the presence of malicious receivers and semi-honest senders, then the combined protocol is secure with these security guarantees. We note that the main challenge in achieving security for protocols that are based on garbled circuits, is proving the case where the sender is corrupted after the garbled circuit has been sent, whereas the receiver is statically corrupted. This is due to the fact that the corrupted receiver observes active labels that are determined by an arbitrary input for the sender. Then, upon corrupting the sender, the simulator must provide randomness that is consistent with the sender's real input which is a difficult task. Our idea follows by having the simulator define a different set of tokens in the simulation that are embedded with the active labels and a symmetric key K, where the inactive labels are determined on the fly using key K upon corrupting the sender and obtaining its input x. The complete proof follows.

Theorem 6. *Let f be a well-formed functionality. Then, protocol Π from Fig. 4 GUC realizes f in the presence of malicious receivers and semi-honest senders in the $\{\mathcal{F}_{\mathrm{gWRAP}}, \mathcal{F}_{\mathrm{OT}}\}$-hybrid.*

Proof. Let $\mathcal{A}$ be a malicious PPT real adversary attacking protocol Π from Fig. 4 in the $\{\mathcal{F}_{\mathrm{gWRAP}}, \mathcal{F}_{\mathrm{OT}}\}$-hybrid model. We construct an ideal adversary $\mathcal{S}$ with access to $\mathcal{F}_f$ which simulates a real execution of Π with $\mathcal{A}$ such that no environment $\mathcal{Z}$ can distinguish the ideal process with $\mathcal{S}$ and $\mathcal{F}_f$ from a hybrid execution of Π with $\mathcal{A}$. $\mathcal{S}$ starts by invoking a copy of $\mathcal{A}$ and running a simulated interaction of $\mathcal{A}$ with environment $\mathcal{Z}$, emulating the honest party. We describe the actions of $\mathcal{S}$ for every corruption case.

Simulating the Communication with $\mathcal{Z}$: Every message that $\mathcal{S}$ receives from $\mathcal{Z}$ is internally fed to $\mathcal{A}$ and every output written by $\mathcal{A}$ is relayed back to $\mathcal{Z}$.

The hardest adaptive corruption case to argue here is if the receiver is corrupted at the begining of the execution and the sender is corrupted at the end.

Simulating Static Corruption of the Receiver and Adaptive Corruption of the Sender Post-execution. We begin by describing our simulation:

Adaptively secure 2PC Π in the presence of malicious receivers

Protocol Π is presented in the $(\mathcal{F}_{\text{gWRAP}}, \mathcal{F}_{\text{OT}})$-hybrid model with sender S and receiver R.

Auxiliary Input: A boolean circuit C such that for every $x, y \in \{0,1\}^n$, $C(x, y) = f(x, y)$ where $f : \{0,1\}^n \times \{0,1\}^n \rightarrow \{0,1\}^n$.

Inputs: S holds $x \in \{0,1\}^n$ and R holds $y \in \{0,1\}^n$. Let $x = x_1, \ldots, x_n$ and $y = y_1, \ldots, y_n$.

The Protocol: Let $(\text{lab}_1^0, \text{lab}_1^1), \ldots, (\text{lab}_n^0, \text{lab}_n^1)$ be the circuit-input labels corresponding to input wires $\omega_1, \ldots, \omega_n$, and let $(\text{lab}_{n+1}^0, \text{lab}_{n+1}^1), \ldots, (\text{lab}_{2n}^0, \text{lab}_{2n}^1)$ be the circuit-input labels corresponding to input wires $\omega_{n+1}, \ldots, \omega_{2n}$. Then,

1. For every $i \in [n]$, the parties call the $\mathcal{F}_{\text{OT}}$ functionality in which S sends the message $(\text{S}, \text{sid}, \text{lab}_{n+i}^0, \text{lab}_{n+i}^1)$ and R sends $(\text{R}, \text{sid}, y_i)$. Then, R receives $(\text{sid}, \text{lab}_{n+i}^{y_i})$.

2. S sends the labels $\text{lab}_1^{x_1}, \ldots, \text{lab}_n^{x_n}$ and the decoding information d to R.

3. Next, the sender creates tokens for machines M_c for every gate c and sends them to the R via $\mathcal{F}_{\text{gWRAP}}$. More precisely, for every intermediate wire identified by index ω in the circuit, S chooses two random strings $\text{lab}_\omega^0, \text{lab}_\omega^1 \in \{0,1\}^\kappa$. Then corresponding to gate Gate_c, S creates a token $\text{TK}_\text{S}^{\text{Gate}_c}$ by sending $(\text{Create}, \text{sid}, \text{R}, \text{S}, \text{mid}_c, M_c)$ to $\mathcal{F}_{\text{gWRAP}}$, where M_c is the functionality that on input $(\text{sid}^*, (\ell_1, \ell_2))$ proceeds as follows:
   - If $\text{sid}^* \neq \text{sid}$, then return $\perp$.
   - Otherwise, if $\ell_1 = \text{lab}_{\omega_1}^\alpha$ and $\ell_2 = \text{lab}_{\omega_2}^\beta$ output $\text{lab}_{\omega_3}^{\text{Gate}_c(\alpha, \beta)}$.

   Where ω_1, ω_2 are the incoming wire identifiers, ω_3 is the identifier of the output wire to gate Gate_c and $\text{Gate}_c \in \{\text{AND}, \text{XOR}\}$ is the corresponding boolean function of this gate.

Circuit Evaluation: Upon receiving the labels $\text{lab}_1^{x_1}, \ldots, \text{lab}_n^{x_n}$ and $\text{lab}_{n+1}^{y_1}, \ldots, \text{lab}_{2n}^{y_n}$, R evaluates the circuit, obtaining the output $f(x, y)$ as follows.

1. For every gate $\text{Gate}_c \in C$, let ω_c^1, ω_c^2 (resp., ω_c^3) denote the input (resp., output) wires of gate Gate_c, then R sends $(\text{Run}, \text{sid}, \text{S}, \text{mid}_c, (\text{lab}_{\omega_c^1}^\alpha, \text{lab}_{\omega_c^2}^\beta))$ and obtains $\text{lab}_{\omega_c^3}^{\text{Gate}_c(\alpha, \beta)}$.

2. R runs the algorithm $z \leftarrow \text{De}(d, \tilde{z})$ and outputs z, where $\tilde{z}$ is the encoding of the output wires.

Fig. 4. Adaptively secure 2PC in the presence of malicious receivers

1. Upon corrupting R the simulator $\mathcal{S}$ generates first the codes to be emulated in the tokens. Towards this it first samples a single label for each wire ω, i.e. $\widetilde{\text{lab}}_\omega \leftarrow \{0,1\}^\kappa$. For each gate c, it sends $(\text{Create}, \text{sid}, \text{S}, \text{R}, \text{mid}_c, M_c)$ to $\mathcal{F}_{\text{gWRAP}}$ for all $\text{Gate}_c \in C$ where the code M_c is defined as follows: Let $\widetilde{\text{lab}}_{\omega_c^1}, \widetilde{\text{lab}}_{\omega_c^2}, \widetilde{\text{lab}}_{\omega_c^3}$, a secret key K for a non-malleable symmetric encryption $\Pi_{\text{ENC}} = (\text{Gen}, \text{Enc}, \text{Dec})$ with pseudorandom ciphertext, and randomness r be hardwired in the token where ω_c^1, ω_c^2 are the input wire identifiers and ω_c^3 is

the output wire identifier.[7] Upon receiving the input (ℓ_1, ℓ_2), M_c proceeds in one of the following four cases:

Case 1: Both labels are active key labels. If $\ell_1 = \widetilde{\mathsf{lab}}_{\omega_c^1}$ and $\ell_2 = \widetilde{\mathsf{lab}}_{\omega_c^2}$ of this gate then output $\widetilde{\mathsf{lab}}_{\omega_c^3}$.

Case 2: One of them is active and the other is not. If $\ell_1 \neq \widetilde{\mathsf{lab}}_{\omega_c^1}^{\alpha}$ and $\ell_2 = \widetilde{\mathsf{lab}}_{\omega_c^2}^{\beta}$ then perform the following actions:

(a) Compute $\tau_c = \mathsf{Dec}_K(\ell_1)$. Check if τ_c is of the form (x, y, ω_c^1) where $x, y \in \{0, 1\}^n$, and abort if it is not of that form.

(b) Next determine inputs α, β and output γ to gate c assuming S's input is x and R's input is y by running $C(x, y)$.

(c) Set $\mathsf{lab}_{\omega_c^1}^{\alpha} = \widetilde{\mathsf{lab}}_{\omega_c^1}$ and $\mathsf{lab}_{\omega_c^2}^{\beta} = \widetilde{\mathsf{lab}}_{\omega_c^1}$ and $\mathsf{lab}_{\omega_c^3}^{\gamma} = \widetilde{\mathsf{lab}}_{\omega_c^3}$. Let $\mathsf{lab}_{\omega_c^3}^{1-\gamma} = \mathsf{Enc}_K(x, y, \omega_c^3; r)$ where r is the randomness hardwired in the token.

(d) Output $\mathsf{lab}_{\omega_c^3}^{\mathsf{Gate}_c(1-\alpha, \beta)}$.

If $\ell_1 = \widetilde{\mathsf{lab}}_{\omega_c^1}^{\alpha}$ and $\ell_2 \neq \widetilde{\mathsf{lab}}_{\omega_c^2}^{\beta}$, we first compute $\tau_c = \mathsf{Dec}_K(\ell_2)$ and checking if τ_c is of the form (x, y, ω_c^2). Next, we perform the same steps (c) and (d) as above to determine α, β and γ and make label associations. Finally, instead of the last step (e), we output $\mathsf{lab}_{\omega_c^3}^{\mathsf{Gate}_c(\alpha, 1-\beta)}$.

Case 3: Neither of them is active. If $\ell_1 \neq \widetilde{\mathsf{lab}}_{\omega_c^1}^{\alpha}$ and $\ell_2 \neq \widetilde{\mathsf{lab}}_{\omega_c^2}^{\beta}$, we first compute $\tau_c = \mathsf{Dec}_K(\ell_1)$ and $\widetilde{\tau}_c = \mathsf{Dec}_K(\ell_2)$. Next we check if τ_c is of the form (x, y, ω_c^1) and $\widetilde{\tau}_c$ is of the form (x, y, ω_c^2) for the same x and y. If so, we perform the same steps (c) and (d) as above to determine α, β and γ and make label associations. Finally, instead of the last step (e), we output $\mathsf{lab}_{\omega_c^3}^{\mathsf{Gate}_c(1-\alpha, 1-\beta)}$. Else, if the plaintexts are of incorrect format the token aborts.

Making the Size of Tokens Proportional to the Width of the Evaluated Circuit. We consider a levelled circuit with fan-in two. A levelled circuit is a circuit in which the incoming edges to the gates of depth i comes only from the gates of depth $i - 1$ or from the inputs. That said, edges only exist between adjacent levels of the circuit. Furthermore, the width of a levelled circuit is the maximum size of any level. We define the evaluated circuit as a sequence of circuits $C = C_1 || ... || C_d$ where C_i denotes the circuit in level i for $i \in [d]$. The high-level idea is to evaluate the circuit level by level where each level will receive the labels of the previous level and will output the output labels for the next level. In particular, each token will run $C_d(x_d, y_d)$ instead of $C(x, y)$ where x_d denotes the input of S in level d and y_d denotes the input of R in level d. In addition, the underlying encryption scheme will encrypt plaintexts of the form $(x_d, y_d, \cdot)$. Therefore, each token performs a computation proportional to the width of the circuit rather than the entire circuit.

---

[7] Looking ahead, these input labels are the (respective inputs/output) active labels observed by the evaluator. Moreover, the input labels for each gate equal the output labels of the gates connected to it.

2. $\mathcal{S}$ emulates the OT executions by playing the role of $\mathcal{F}_{\mathrm{OT}}$ and extracting the receiver's inputs $y = y_1, \ldots, y_n$ to these executions. The simulator sends y to the trusted party computing f, receiving back $f(x, y)$. $\mathcal{S}$ completes the $\mathcal{F}_{\mathrm{OT}}$ executions by sending the receiver the active labels that it picked for the receiver's input wires.

3. When the sender is corrupted post execution, it receives the sender's real input x. In this case the simulator needs to explain the sender's view, i.e. it needs to explain the sender's input to the OT queries and the code for M_c supplied to the $\mathcal{F}_{\mathrm{gWRAP}}$. Towards this, the sender first generates labels for the inactive label for all gates. For any input wire ω, the inactive label is set as $\mathsf{Enc}_K(x, y, \omega)$ where the randomness is chosen uniformly and for any intermediate wire it is set to $\mathsf{Enc}_K(x, y, \omega; r)$ where r is the randomness hardwired in the gate for which ω is the output wire. It supplies all the labels to the adversary.

4. $\mathcal{S}$ outputs whatever $\mathcal{A}$ does.

Note that the receiver's view is composed of the set of input labels it obtains from the OT executions and the tokens evaluations. Indistinguishability of real and simulated cases, assuming that the receiver cannot invoke any of the tokens on an inactive label, boils down to the ability of generating a fresh valid ciphertext that encrypts the parties' inputs and the corresponding identifiers under the key K that is hardwired inside the tokens. Intuitively, this event occurs with negligible probability due to the evasiveness property of the encryption scheme. More formally, we prove indistinguishability of the real and simulated executions via the following sequence of hybrid games.

Hybrid$_1$: The hybrid is the real execution as defined in Protocol Π in Fig. 4.

Hybrid$_2$: In this hybrid game we consider a simulator $\mathcal{S}_2$ that knows the sender's real input and generates the tokens just like honest sender. This game produces an identical distribution as the real execution.

Hybrid$_3$: In this game simulator $\mathcal{S}_3$ generates all active labels uniformly at random, but the inactive labels are generated using random encryptions of $z_c = (x, y, \mathsf{id}_c)$. To prove that this game is indistinguishable from the previous hybrid game, we consider a sequence of sub-hybrids **Hybrid$_2^i$** for $i \in [m]$ the total number of inactive labels. Specifically, in **Hybrid$_2^i$** the first i inactive labels are encryptions of (x, y, ω_j) whereas the rest of the inactive labels are picked uniformly as random. Note that **Hybrid$_2^0$** is identically distributed to hybrid **Hybrid$_2$**, whereas **Hybrid$_2^m$** is identically distributed to hybrid **Hybrid$_3$**. The indistinguishability of **Hybrid$_2^{i-1}$** and **Hybrid$_2^i$** directly follows from the pseudorandomness of the ciphertexts. More formally, assume by contradiction the existence of an adversary $\mathcal{A}$, a distinguisher D and a polynomial $q(\cdot)$ such that $\big| \Pr[D(\mathbf{Hybrid_2}) = 1] - \Pr[D(\mathbf{Hybrid_3}) = 1] \big| \geq 1/q(\kappa)$ for infinitely many κ's, where D obtains the malicious receiver's view in the corresponding hybrid execution. Then we claim that there exists an index $i \in [m]$ such that

$$\big| \Pr[D(\mathbf{Hybrid_2^{i-1}}) = 1] - \Pr[D(\mathbf{Hybrid_2^i}) = 1] \big| \geq 1/(q(\kappa) \cdot m).$$

We define an adversary $\mathcal{A}_{\text{ENC}}$ that breaks the pseudorandom property of the underlying symmetric encryption scheme as follows. Upon receiving access to the encryption oracle, $\mathcal{A}_{\text{ENC}}$ uses its oracle to generate the first $i-1$ inactive labels as required in the simulation. For the rest of the inactive labels, namely those with indices in $\{(i+1), \ldots, m\}$ the adversary picks random strings. Finally, for the ith inactive label, the adversary provides the message (x, y, ω_i) to the challenger. The challenger either returns a uniform random string or an encryption of (x, y, ω_i). The adversary feeds whatever the challenger provides in the pseudorandomness security game internally, as the label for the ith inactive label. It follows from our construction that depending on the challenger's message, the view of the receiver is distributed according to $\textbf{Hybrid}_2^{i-1}$ or $\textbf{Hybrid}_2^i$ and thus, this adversary breaks the pseudorandomness property of the ciphertexts. In addition, we would like to claim that the adversary, who corrupts the sender after the generation of the garble circuit and the tokens, cannot produce a ciphertext for a valid input which will allow it to query the token on $\text{Enc}_K(g_1(x), g_2(y), \cdot)$ where g_1, g_2 are arbitrary functions that produce related plaintexts. As such an attack will allow the adversary to learn some additional information about the receiver's input breaking its privacy or learning a new, in addition to an output he may already learns. We claim that the probability of this event to occur is negligible due to the non-malleability of the encryptions scheme. Specifically, the simulator may monitor the adversary's queries to the token and observe if such an event occurs.

$\textbf{Hybrid}_4$: In this game simulator $\mathcal{S}_4$ generates all the tokens as in the simulation. To prove that this game is indistinguishable from the previous hybrid game, we will rely on the evasiveness of the underlying encryption scheme. First, we observe that the distribution of the labels provided by the real simulator before and after the sender is corrupted are identically distributed in both hybrids. This is because the active labels are uniformly generated in both hybrids and the inactive labels are encryptions of (x, y, ω_i) for the different wires in the circuit. Next, we observe that the only way an adversary can distinguish $\textbf{Hybrid}_4$ from $\textbf{Hybrid}_3$ is if it feeds any of the tokens a fresh valid ciphertext of a message that is different from all the labels provided by the simulator after the sender is corrupted. By the evasiveness of the underlying encryption scheme the probability that an adversary can generate such ciphertexts is negligible. Therefore, the view of the adversary in $\textbf{Hybrid}_3$ and $\textbf{Hybrid}_4$ is statistically close.

$\textbf{Hybrid}_5$: The last hybrid game is the simulation which is identical to hybrid $\textbf{Hybrid}_4$.

Simulating Static Corruption of the Sender. We begin by describing our simulation:

1. Upon corrupting S the simulator receives the adversary's input x and proceeds as follows.
2. S first communicates with the functionality $\mathcal{F}_{\text{gWRAP}}$, that upon receiving the messages for creating the tokens $\{(\text{Create}, \text{sid}, \text{R}, \text{S}, \text{mid}_c, M_c)\}_{\text{Gate}_c \in C}$ from $\mathcal{A}$ stores the codes of these tokens.

3. $\mathcal{S}$ obtains the inputs labels from $\mathcal{A}$ and then plays the role of $\mathcal{F}_{\mathrm{OT}}$, receiving from the adversary n pairs of input labels.
4. $\mathcal{S}$ outputs whatever $\mathcal{A}$ does.

Security for this case is proven in a straightforward manner as the adversary does not receive any message from the receiver in the hybrid model.

- In case no party is corrupted yet, the simulator generates the active labels for the entire set of wires and simulates the message from the sender to the receiver that includes the sender's input labels and the decoding information.

Simulating the Adaptive Corruption of the Receiver After Corrupting the Sender.

– Upon corrupting the sender, the simulator receives the adversary's input x and proceeds as follows.
  1. $\mathcal{S}$ emulates the tokens transfer phase as the honest sender would do. Namely, $\mathcal{S}$ creates the tokens honestly and provides the corrupted sender with the randomness that is used to generate the garbled gates.
  2. Next, $\mathcal{S}$ provides the sender's queries made to $\mathcal{F}_{\mathrm{OT}}$ where the input to the ith OT query is the pair of the random labels $((\mathsf{lab}_{n+1}^0, \mathsf{lab}_{n+1}^1), \ldots, (\mathsf{lab}_{2n}^0, \mathsf{lab}_{2n}^1))$ that correspond to the receiver's input labels. $\mathcal{S}$ further explains the message that includes the sender's input labels and the decoding information.
– Upon corrupting the receiver second, the simulator receives the adversary's input y and output $f(x, y))$ and proceeds as follows.
  1. In this case the simulator needs to explain the receiver's internal state condition on the sender's view. This implies that the simulator needs only to explain the OT queries and the messages to $\mathcal{F}_{\mathrm{OT}}$ and $\mathcal{F}_{\mathrm{gWRAP}}$. Specifically, the description of the garbled circuit is already determined upon corrupting the sender, whereas the sender's active input labels are already fixed in the protocol communication. The receiver's OT queries/responses can be explained accordingly to $y_1, \ldots, y_n$ and the active input labels of the receiver, respectively. Note that the simulator knows the active input labels of the receiver as it generated the garbled circuit.
  2. Finally, the communication with $\mathcal{F}_{\mathrm{gWRAP}}$ can be explained by mimicking the flow of the garbled circuit evaluation as determined by the simulator. Simulation here follows honestly as the simulator generated the tokens honestly.
  3. $\mathcal{S}$ outputs whatever $\mathcal{A}$ does.

Indistinguishability for this case follows directly as the parties observe the same messages as in the real execution. Specifically, the simulator generates the tokens honestly and the receiver obtains the correct input labels in the OT and thus, the correct labels for the entire evaluation.

6.1   Adaptively Secure Malicious Two-Party Computation

We recall that the protocol presented in Fig. 4 obtains security in the presence of malicious receiver and semi-honest sender. In the following, we briefly discuss how to transform this protocol into fully secure in the presence of malicious senders as well by adopting the protocol from [43]. Loosely speaking the main tool for achieving correctness of garbling is by applying the cut-and-choose technique, where the sender generates s garbled circuits and the receiver asks to open half of them at random. One immediate issue that emerges when considering tokens, is what does it mean to open a garbled circuit that is implemented using tokens and how can the token's functionality be verified for correctness. Our approach considers asking the sender to commit to any pair of labels through the garbling (that is, the labels associated with each wire). Then, upon receiving an opening request for a garbled circuit, the sender further decommit these commitments for which the receiver can invoke the token on each pair of labels and verify whether the correct output label has been obtained.

We give a high-level description of our protocol based on the [43] protocol with the modifications required for embedding the tokens.

- **Auxiliary Input:** A boolean circuit C such that for every $x, y \in \{0,1\}^n$, $C(x,y) = f(x,y)$ where $f : \{0,1\}^n \times \{0,1\}^n \to \{0,1\}^n$ and a statistical parameter s.
- **Inputs:** S holds $x \in \{0,1\}^n$ and R holds $y \in \{0,1\}^n$. Let $x = x_1, \ldots, x_n$ and $y = y_1, \ldots, y_n$.
- **The protocol:**
    0. **Circuit Construction.** The parties decide on a circuit computing f. They then change the circuit by replacing each input wire of R by a gate whose input consists of s new input wires of R and whose output is the exclusive-or of these wires (such an s-bit exclusive-or gate can be implemented using $s - 1$ two-bit exclusive-or gates).
    1. **Tokens and Commitments Constructions.** Next, the sender constructs s independent copies of a garbled circuit of C, where for each such garbled circuit it creates a set of tokens as in Protocol Π from Fig. 4. More precisely, for every intermediate wire identified by index ω in the circuit, let the two random strings $\mathsf{lab}_\omega^0, \mathsf{lab}_\omega^1 \in \{0,1\}^\kappa$ denote the labels associated with this wire. Then corresponding to gate Gate_c, S creates a token $\mathsf{TK}_S^{\mathsf{Gate}_c}$ by sending $(\mathsf{Create}, \mathsf{sid}, \mathsf{R}, \mathsf{S}, \mathsf{mid}_c, M_c)$ to $\mathcal{F}_{\mathsf{gWRAP}}$, where M_c is the functionality that on input ℓ_1, ℓ_2 proceeds as follows:
        - If $\ell_1 = \mathsf{lab}_{\omega_1}^\alpha$ and $\ell_2 = \mathsf{lab}_{\omega_2}^\beta$ output $\mathsf{lab}_{\omega_3}^{\mathsf{Gate}_c(\alpha,\beta)}$.
        Where ω_1, ω_2 are the incoming wire identifiers, ω_3 is the identifier of the output wire to gate Gate_c and $\mathsf{Gate}_c \in \{\mathrm{AND}, \mathrm{XOR}\}$ is the corresponding boolean function of this gate.
        S commits to the garbled values of the wires corresponding to R's input to each circuit by running n instances of Π_{COM}. Moreover, S executes additional $s \times n$ instances of Π_{COM} for the garbled values corresponding to the input wires of the circuits. These commitments-sets are constructed in a special way in order to enable consistency checks (here we follow the same method of [43]). Finally, S commits to the labels associated with each internal wire in each garbled circuit (we note that these commitments instances are not part of the [43] protocol and are required to verify the tokens' functionality).

2. **Oblivious Transfers.** For every $i \in [n]$, the parties call the $\mathcal{F}_{\text{OT}}$ functionality in which R receives the garbled values for the wires that correspond to its input bit (in every circuit). This phase is carried out exactly as in [43].

3. **Send Tokens and Commitments.** S sends R all the commitments of Step 1 and forwards the tokens generated in that step to $\mathcal{F}_{\text{gWRAP}}$.

4. **Coin Tossing.** S and R run a coin-tossing protocol in order to choose a random string that defines which commitments and garbled circuits will be opened.

5. **Decommitment Phase for Check Circuits.** S opens the garbled circuits and committed input values that were chosen in the previous step. R verifies the correctness of the opened circuits and runs consistency checks based on the decommitted input values and internal wires while verifying the tokens functionality.

   More specifically, the check phase is computed as in [43] with the following additional phase. Upon opening some garbling and obtaining the labels that are associated with all wires, the receiver first verifies that the output label of each garbled gate is consistent with the corresponding committed label from Step 1. Next, the receiver invokes each token on each possible pair of input labels and verifies that the output label is consistent with the committed wires. Meaning, the receiver checks that the token indeed implements a lookup table of size four and that the entries of the table correspond to a valid garbled gate.

6. **Send Input Labels.** S sends R the garbled values corresponding to S's input wires in the unopened circuits as well as the decoding information.

7. **Circuits Evaluations.** Assuming that all of the checks pass, R evaluates the unopened circuits and takes the majority value as its output. Namely, upon receiving the labels $\mathsf{lab}_{1,j}^{x_1}, \ldots, \mathsf{lab}_{n,j}^{x_n}$ and $\mathsf{lab}_{n+1,j}^{y_1}, \ldots, \mathsf{lab}_{2n,j}^{y_n}$ for the jth unopened circuit, R evaluates the circuit, obtaining the output $\tilde{f}(x, y)$ as follows.

   (a) For every gate $\mathsf{Gate}_c \in C$, let ω_c^1, ω_c^2 (resp., ω_c^3) denote the input (resp., output) wires of gate Gate_c, then R sends $(\mathsf{Run}, \mathsf{sid}, \mathsf{S}, \mathsf{mid}_c, (\mathsf{lab}_{\omega_c^1,j}^{\alpha}, \mathsf{lab}_{\omega_c^2,j}^{\beta}))$ and obtains $\mathsf{lab}_{\omega_c^3,j}^{\mathsf{Gate}_c(\alpha,\beta)}$.

   (b) R runs the algorithm $z \leftarrow \mathsf{De}(d, \tilde{z})$ and outputs z, where $\tilde{z}$ is the encoding of the output wires.

Theorem 7. *Let f be a well-formed functionality. Then, the above two-party protocol GUC realizes f in the presence of malicious adversaries in the $\{\mathcal{F}_{\text{gWRAP}}, \mathcal{F}_{\text{OT}}\}$-hybrid.*

The proof for a corrupted receiver remains almost identical to the proof of Theorem 6 and the proof from [43], where input extraction is carried out via the OT executions and the original simulation for a single set of tokens is repeated s times with the exception that the simulator prepares $s/2$ valid garbled circuits and then biases the coin tossing outcome so that the valid garbled circuits are the check circuits.

The main difference is with respect to the security proof of the sender. Loosely speaking, we apply the same standard cut-and-choose analysis from [43], where a corrupted sender cannot cheat in the garbling constructions and the input labels it provides for the evaluations. Yet, when using tokens the prime challenge is to ensure that the tokens' functionality is correct. We recall that in our protocol the tokens functionality is a lookup table of four rows that corresponds to the garbling of some gate. Then, by enforcing the sender to commit to all wire labels, the receiver can be convinced that the tokens were generated correctly with very high probability. Namely, with all but negligible probability, the tokens' functionality (for the evaluation circuits) are consistent with the committed labels. We stress that this does not imply that the token cannot be maliciously designed, encoded with some internal state, yet the cut-and-choose argument ensures that with high probability the tokens are encoded with a valid lookup table for their corresponding gates.

Acknowledgements. The first author acknowledges support from the Israel Ministry of Science and Technology (grant No. 3-10883) and support by the BIU Center for Research in Applied Cryptography and Cyber Security in conjunction with the Israel National Cyber Bureau in the Prime Minister's Office. The second author acknowledges support from the Danish National Research Foundation and the National Science Foundation of China (under the grant 61061130540) for the Sino-Danish Center for the Theory of Interactive Computation and from the Center for Research in Foundations of Electronic Markets (CFEM), supported by the Danish Strategic Research Council. In addition, this work was done in part while visiting the Simons Institute for the Theory of Computing, supported by the Simons Foundation and by the DIMACS/Simons Collaboration in Cryptography through NSF grant CNS-1523467. The third author is supported by Google Faculty Research Grant and NSF Awards CNS-1526377/1618884.

References

1. Barak, B., Canetti, R., Nielsen, J.B., Pass, R.: Universally composable protocols with relaxed set-up assumptions. In: FOCS, pp. 186–195 (2004)
2. Barak, B., Sahai, A.: How to play almost any mental game over the net - concurrent composition via super-polynomial simulation. In: FOCS, pp. 543–552 (2005)
3. Beaver, D.: Foundations of secure interactive computing. In: Feigenbaum, J. (ed.) CRYPTO 1991. LNCS, vol. 576, pp. 377–391. Springer, Heidelberg (1992). doi:10.1007/3-540-46766-1_31
4. Bellare, M., Rogaway, P.: Random oracles are practical: a paradigm for designing efficient protocols. In: CCS, pp. 62–73 (1993)
5. Canetti, R.: Universally composable security: a new paradigm for cryptographic protocols. In: FOCS, pp. 136–145 (2001)
6. Canetti, R., Damgård, I., Dziembowski, S., Ishai, Y., Malkin, T.: Adaptive versus non-adaptive security of multi-party protocols. J. Cryptol. 17(3), 153–207 (2004)
7. Canetti, R., Dodis, Y., Pass, R., Walfish, S.: Universally composable security with global setup. In: Vadhan, S.P. (ed.) TCC 2007. LNCS, vol. 4392, pp. 61–85. Springer, Heidelberg (2007). doi:10.1007/978-3-540-70936-7_4
8. Canetti, R., Feige, U., Goldreich, O., Naor, M.: Adaptively secure multi-party computation. In: STOC, pp. 639–648 (1996)
9. Canetti, R., Fischlin, M.: Universally composable commitments. In: Kilian, J. (ed.) CRYPTO 2001. LNCS, vol. 2139, pp. 19–40. Springer, Heidelberg (2001). doi:10.1007/3-540-44647-8_2

10. Canetti, R., Goldwasser, S., Poburinnaya, O.: Adaptively secure two-party computation from indistinguishability obfuscation. In: Dodis, Y., Nielsen, J.B. (eds.) TCC 2015. LNCS, vol. 9015, pp. 557–585. Springer, Heidelberg (2015). doi:10.1007/978-3-662-46497-7_22

11. Canetti, R., Jain, A., Scafuro, A.: Practical UC security with a global random oracle. In: CCS, pp. 597–608 (2014)

12. Canetti, R., Kushilevitz, E., Lindell, Y.: On the limitations of universally composable two-party computation without set-up assumptions. J. Cryptol. 19(2), 135–167 (2006)

13. Canetti, R., Lin, H., Pass, R.: Adaptive hardness and composable security in the plain model from standard assumptions. In: FOCS, pp. 541–550 (2010)

14. Canetti, R., Lindell, Y., Ostrovsky, R., Sahai, A.: Universally composable two-party and multi-party secure computation. In: STOC (2002)

15. Canetti, R., Pass, R., Shelat, A.: Cryptography from sunspots: how to use an imperfect reference string. In: FOCS, pp. 249–259 (2007)

16. Chandran, N., Goyal, V., Sahai, A.: New constructions for UC secure computation using tamper-proof hardware. In: Smart, N. (ed.) EUROCRYPT 2008. LNCS, vol. 4965, pp. 545–562. Springer, Heidelberg (2008). doi:10.1007/978-3-540-78967-3_31

17. Choi, S.G., Dachman-Soled, D., Malkin, T., Wee, H.: Simple, black-box constructions of adaptively secure protocols. In: Reingold, O. (ed.) TCC 2009. LNCS, vol. 5444, pp. 387–402. Springer, Heidelberg (2009). doi:10.1007/978-3-642-00457-5_23

18. Choi, S.G., Katz, J., Schröder, D., Yerukhimovich, A., Zhou, H.-S.: (Efficient) universally composable oblivious transfer using a minimal number of stateless tokens. In: Lindell, Y. (ed.) TCC 2014. LNCS, vol. 8349, pp. 638–662. Springer, Heidelberg (2014). doi:10.1007/978-3-642-54242-8_27

19. Dachman-Soled, D., Katz, J., Rao, V.: Adaptively secure, universally composable, multiparty computation in constant rounds. In: Dodis, Y., Nielsen, J.B. (eds.) TCC 2015. LNCS, vol. 9015, pp. 586–613. Springer, Heidelberg (2015). doi:10.1007/978-3-662-46497-7_23

20. Dachman-Soled, D., Malkin, T., Raykova, M., Venkitasubramaniam, M.: Adaptive and concurrent secure computation from new adaptive, non-malleable commitments. In: Sako, K., Sarkar, P. (eds.) ASIACRYPT 2013. LNCS, vol. 8269, pp. 316–336. Springer, Heidelberg (2013). doi:10.1007/978-3-642-42033-7_17

21. Damgård, I., Nielsen, J.B.: Improved non-committing encryption schemes based on a general complexity assumption. In: Bellare, M. (ed.) CRYPTO 2000. LNCS, vol. 1880, pp. 432–450. Springer, Heidelberg (2000). doi:10.1007/3-540-44598-6_27

22. Damgård, I., Polychroniadou, A., Rao, V.: Adaptively secure multi-party computation from LWE (via equivocal FHE). In: Cheng, C.-M., Chung, K.-M., Persiano, G., Yang, B.-Y. (eds.) PKC 2016. LNCS, vol. 9615, pp. 208–233. Springer, Heidelberg (2016). doi:10.1007/978-3-662-49387-8_9

23. Dodis, Y., Yampolskiy, A.: A verifiable random function with short proofs and keys. In: Vaudenay, S. (ed.) PKC 2005. LNCS, vol. 3386, pp. 416–431. Springer, Heidelberg (2005). doi:10.1007/978-3-540-30580-4_28

24. Döttling, N., Kraschewski, D., Müller-Quade, J.: Unconditional and composable security using a single stateful tamper-proof hardware token. In: Ishai, Y. (ed.) TCC 2011. LNCS, vol. 6597, pp. 164–181. Springer, Heidelberg (2011). doi:10.1007/978-3-642-19571-6_11

25. Döttling, N., Kraschewski, D., Müller-Quade, J., Nilges, T.: General statistically secure computation with bounded-resettable hardware tokens. In: Dodis, Y., Nielsen, J.B. (eds.) TCC 2015. LNCS, vol. 9014, pp. 319–344. Springer, Heidelberg (2015). doi:10.1007/978-3-662-46494-6_14

26. Döttling, N., Mie, T., Müller-Quade, J., Nilges, T.: Implementing resettable UC-functionalities with untrusted tamper-proof hardware-tokens. In: Sahai, A. (ed.) TCC 2013. LNCS, vol. 7785, pp. 642–661. Springer, Heidelberg (2013). doi:10. 1007/978-3-642-36594-2_36
27. Garg, S., Goyal, V., Jain, A., Sahai, A.: Concurrently secure computation in constant rounds. In: Pointcheval, D., Johansson, T. (eds.) EUROCRYPT 2012. LNCS, vol. 7237, pp. 99–116. Springer, Heidelberg (2012). doi:10.1007/ 978-3-642-29011-4_8
28. Garg, S., Polychroniadou, A.: Two-round adaptively secure MPC from indistinguishability obfuscation. In: Dodis, Y., Nielsen, J.B. (eds.) TCC 2015. LNCS, vol. 9015, pp. 614–637. Springer, Heidelberg (2015). doi:10.1007/978-3-662-46497-7_24
29. Garg, S., Sahai, A.: Adaptively secure multi-party computation with dishonest majority. In: Safavi-Naini, R., Canetti, R. (eds.) CRYPTO 2012. LNCS, vol. 7417, pp. 105–123. Springer, Heidelberg (2012). doi:10.1007/978-3-642-32009-5_8
30. Goldreich, O., Micali, S., Wigderson, A.: How to play any mental game or a completeness theorem for protocols with honest majority. In STOC, pp. 218–229 (1987)
31. Goldreich, O., Ostrovsky, R.: Software protection and simulation on oblivious rams. J. ACM 43(3), 431–473 (1996)
32. Goldwasser, S., Kalai, Y.T., Rothblum, G.N.: One-time programs. In: Wagner, D. (ed.) CRYPTO 2008. LNCS, vol. 5157, pp. 39–56. Springer, Heidelberg (2008). doi:10.1007/978-3-540-85174-5_3
33. Goyal, V., Ishai, Y., Sahai, A., Venkatesan, R., Wadia, A.: Founding cryptography on tamper-proof hardware tokens. In: Micciancio, D. (ed.) TCC 2010. LNCS, vol. 5978, pp. 308–326. Springer, Heidelberg (2010). doi:10.1007/978-3-642-11799-2_19
34. Hazay, C., Polychroniadou, A., Venkitasubramaniam, M.: Composable security in the tamper-proof hardware model under minimal complexity. In: Hirt, M., Smith, A. (eds.) TCC 2016. LNCS, vol. 9985, pp. 367–399. Springer, Heidelberg (2016). doi:10.1007/978-3-662-53641-4_15
35. Hazay, C., Polychroniadou, A., Venkitasubramaniam, M.: Constant round adaptively secure protocols in the tamper-proof hardware model. Manuscript (2016)
36. Hazay, C., Venkitasubramaniam, M.: On black-box complexity of universally composable security in the CRS model. In: Iwata, T., Cheon, J.H. (eds.) ASIACRYPT 2015. LNCS, vol. 9453, pp. 183–209. Springer, Heidelberg (2015). doi:10.1007/ 978-3-662-48800-3_8
37. Hazay, C., Venkitasubramaniam, M.: Composable adaptive secure protocols without setup under polytime assumptions. In: Hirt, M., Smith, A. (eds.) TCC 2016. LNCS, vol. 9985, pp. 400–432. Springer, Heidelberg (2016). doi:10.1007/ 978-3-662-53641-4_16
38. Ishai, Y., Prabhakaran, M., Sahai, A.: Founding cryptography on oblivious transfer–efficiently. In: Wagner, D. (ed.) CRYPTO 2008. LNCS, vol. 5157, pp. 572–591. Springer, Heidelberg (2008). doi:10.1007/978-3-540-85174-5_32
39. Kalai, Y.T., Lindell, Y., Prabhakaran, M.: Concurrent composition of secure protocols in the timing model. J. Cryptol. 20(4), 431–492 (2007)
40. Katz, J.: Universally Composable multi-party computation using tamper-proof hardware. In: Naor, M. (ed.) EUROCRYPT 2007. LNCS, vol. 4515, pp. 115–128. Springer, Heidelberg (2007). doi:10.1007/978-3-540-72540-4_7
41. Lin, H., Pass, R., Venkitasubramaniam, M.: A unified framework for concurrent security: universal composability from stand-alone non-malleability. In: STOC, pp. 179–188 (2009)
42. Lindell, Y.: General composition and universal composability in secure multi-party computation. In: FOCS, pp. 394–403 (2003)

43. Lindell, Y., Pinkas, B.: An efficient protocol for secure two-party computation in the presence of malicious adversaries. In: Naor, M. (ed.) EUROCRYPT 2007. LNCS, vol. 4515, pp. 52–78. Springer, Heidelberg (2007). doi:10.1007/978-3-540-72540-4_4

44. Lindell, Y., Pinkas, B.: A proof of security of Yao's protocol for two-party computation. J. Cryptol. **22**(2), 161–188 (2009)

45. Lindell, Y., Zarosim, H.: Adaptive zero-knowledge proofs and adaptively secure oblivious transfer. J. Cryptol. **24**(4), 761–799 (2011)

46. Mechler, J., Müller-Quade, J., Nilges, T.: Universally composable (non-interactive) two-party computation from untrusted reusable hardware tokens. IACR Cryptology ePrint Archive 2016:615 (2016)

47. Micali, S., Rogaway, P.: Secure computation. In: Feigenbaum, J. (ed.) CRYPTO 1991. LNCS, vol. 576, pp. 392–404. Springer, Heidelberg (1992). doi:10.1007/3-540-46766-1_32

48. Moran, T., Segev, G.: David and Goliath commitments: UC computation for asymmetric parties using tamper-proof hardware. In: Smart, N. (ed.) EUROCRYPT 2008. LNCS, vol. 4965, pp. 527–544. Springer, Heidelberg (2008). doi:10.1007/978-3-540-78967-3_30

49. Naor, M.: Bit commitment using pseudorandomness. J. Cryptol. **4**(2), 151–158 (1991)

50. Nilges, T.: The cryptographic strength of tamper-proof hardware. Ph.D. thesis, Karlsruhe Institute of Technology (2015)

51. Ostrovsky, R., Richelson, S., Scafuro, A.: Round-optimal black-box two-party computation. In: Gennaro, R., Robshaw, M. (eds.) CRYPTO 2015. LNCS, vol. 9216, pp. 339–358. Springer, Heidelberg (2015). doi:10.1007/978-3-662-48000-7_17

52. Pass, R.: Simulation in quasi-polynomial time, and its application to protocol composition. In: Biham, E. (ed.) EUROCRYPT 2003. LNCS, vol. 2656, pp. 160–176. Springer, Heidelberg (2003). doi:10.1007/3-540-39200-9_10

53. Pass, R., Wee, H.: Black-box constructions of two-party protocols from one-way functions. In: Reingold, O. (ed.) TCC 2009. LNCS, vol. 5444, pp. 403–418. Springer, Heidelberg (2009). doi:10.1007/978-3-642-00457-5_24

54. Prabhakaran, M., Sahai, A.: New notions of security: achieving universal composability without trusted setup. In: STOC, pp. 242–251 (2004)

55. Venkitasubramaniam, M.: On adaptively secure protocols. In: Abdalla, M., Prisco, R. (eds.) SCN 2014. LNCS, vol. 8642, pp. 455–475. Springer, Heidelberg (2014). doi:10.1007/978-3-319-10879-7_26

56. Yao, A.C.C.: How to generate and exchange secrets (extended abstract). In: FCOS, pp. 162–167 (1986)

Primitives

Constrained Pseudorandom Functions for Unconstrained Inputs Revisited: Achieving Verifiability and Key Delegation

Pratish Datta[✉], Ratna Dutta, and Sourav Mukhopadhyay

Department of Mathematics, Indian Institute of Technology Kharagpur,
Kharagpur 721302, India
{pratishdatta,ratna,sourav}@maths.iitkgp.ernet.in

Abstract. In EUROCRYPT 2016, Deshpande et al. presented a construction of *constrained pseudorandom function* (CPRF) supporting inputs of *unconstrained* polynomial length based on indistinguishability obfuscation and injective pseudorandom generators. Their construction was claimed to be selectively secure. We demonstrate in this paper that their CPRF construction can actually be proven secure not in the selective model, rather in a *significantly weaker* security model where the adversary is forbidden to query constrained keys adaptively. We also show how to allow *adaptive* constrained key queries in their construction by innovating new technical ideas. We suitably redesign the security proof. We emphasize that our modification does not involve any additional heavy duty cryptographic tool. Our improved CPRF is further enhanced to present the *first* constructions of *constrained verifiable pseudorandom function* (CVPRF) and *delegatable constrained pseudorandom function* (DCPRF) supporting inputs of *unconstrained* polynomial length, employing only standard public key encryption (PKE).

Keywords: Constrained pseudorandom functions · Verifiable constrained pseudorandom function · Key delegation · Indistinguishability obfuscation

1 Introduction

Constrained Pseudorandom Functions: *Constrained pseudorandom functions* (CPRF), concurrently introduced by Boneh and Waters [6], Boyle et al. [7], as well as Kiayias et al. [19], are promising extension of the notion of standard *pseudorandom functions* (PRF) [15]. PRF is a fundamental primitive in modern cryptography. A PRF is a deterministic keyed function with the following property: Given a key, the function can be computed in polynomial time at all points of its input domain. But, without the key it is computationally hard to distinguish the PRF output at any arbitrary input from a uniformly random value, even after seeing the PRF evaluations on a polynomial number of inputs. A CPRF is an augmentation of a PRF with an additional *constrain algorithm*

© International Association for Cryptologic Research 2017
S. Fehr (Ed.): PKC 2017, Part II, LNCS 10175, pp. 463–493, 2017.
DOI: 10.1007/978-3-662-54388-7_16

which enables a party holding a master PRF key to derive constrained keys that allow the evaluation of the PRF over certain subsets of the input domain. However, PRF evaluations on the rest of the inputs still remain computationally indistinguishable from random.

Since their inception, CPRF's have found countless applications in various branches of cryptography ranging from broadcast encryption, attribute-based encryption to policy-based key distribution, multi-party on-interactive key exchange. Even the simplest class of CPRF's, known as *puncturable pseudorandom functions* (PPRF) [23], have turned out to be a powerful tool in conjunction with indistinguishability obfuscation [14]. In fact, the combination of these two primitives have led to solutions of longstanding open problems including deniable encryption, full domain hash, adaptively secure functional encryption for general functionalities, and functional encryption for randomized functionalities through the classic punctured programming technique introduced in [23].

Over the last few years there has been a significant progress in the field of CPRF's. In terms of expressiveness of the constraint predicates, starting with the most basic type of constraints such as prefix constraints [6,7,19] (which also encompass puncturing constraints) and bit fixing constraints [6,13], CPRF's have been constructed for highly rich constraint families such as circuit constraints [4,6,8,16] employing diverse cryptographic tools and based on various complexity assumptions. In terms of security, most of the existing CPRF constructions are only *selectively* secure. The stronger and more realistic notion of *adaptive* security seems to be rather challenging to achieve without complexity leveraging. In fact, the best known results so far on adaptive security of CPRF's require super-polynomial security loss [13], or work for very restricted form of constraints [17], or attain the security in non-collusion mode [8], or accomplish security in the random oracle model [16].

Constrained Verifiable Pseudorandom Functions: An interesting enhancement of the usual CPRF's is *verifiability*. A *verifiable constrained pseudorandom function* (CVPRF), independently introduced by Fuchsbauer [12] and Chandran et al. [9], is the unification of the notions of a *verifiable random function* (VRF) [21] and a standard CPRF. In a CVPRF system, a public verification key is set similar to a traditional VRF, along with the master PRF key. Besides enabling the evaluation of the PRF, the master PRF key can be utilized to generate a non-interactive proof of correctness of the evaluation. This proof can be verified by any party using only the public verification key. On the other hand, as in the case of a CPRF, here also the master PRF key holder can give out constrained keys for specific constraint predicates. A constrained key corresponding to some constraint predicate p allows the evaluation of the PRF together with the generation of a non-interactive proof of correct evaluation for only those inputs x for which $p(x) = 1$. In essence, CVPRF's resolve the issue of trust on a CPRF evaluator for the correctness of the received PRF output. In [9,12], the authors have shown that the CPRF constructions of [6] for the bit fixing and circuit constraints can be augmented with the verifiability feature without incurring any significant additional cost.

Delegatable Constrained Pseudorandom Functions: *Key delegation* is another interesting enrichment of standard CPRF's. This feature empowers the holder of a constrained key, corresponding to some constraint predicate $p \in \mathbb{P}$ with the ability to distribute further restricted keys corresponding to the joint predicates $p \wedge \widetilde{p}$, for constraints $\widetilde{p} \in \mathbb{P}$, where $\mathbb{P}$ is certain constraint family over the input domain of the PRF. Such a delegated key can be utilized to evaluate the PRF on only those inputs x for which $[p(x) = 1] \wedge [\widetilde{p}(x) = 1]$, whereas, the PRF outputs on the rest of the inputs are computationally indistinguishable from random values. The concept of key delegation in the context of CPRF's has been recently introduced by Chandran et al. [9], who have shown how to extend the bit fixing and circuit-based CPRF constructions of [6] to support key delegation.

CPRF's for Unconstrained Inputs: Until recently, the research on CPRF's has been confined to inputs of apriori bounded length. In fact, all the CPRF constructions mentioned above could handle only bounded length inputs. Abusalah et al. [2] have taken a first step forward towards overcoming the barrier of bounded input length. They have also demonstrated highly motivating applications of CPRF's supporting apriori unconstrained length inputs such as broadcast encryption with an unbounded number of recipients and multi-party identity-based non-interactive key exchange with no pre-determined bound on the number of parties. They presented a selectively secure CPRF for unconstrained length inputs by viewing the constraint predicates as *Turing machines* (TM) that can handle inputs of arbitrary polynomial length. In a more recent work, Abusalah and Fuchsbauer [1] have made progress towards efficiency improvements by constructing TM-based CPRF's with much shorter constrained keys compared to the CPRF construction of [2].

However, both the aforementioned CPRF constructions rely on the existence of public-coin differing-input obfuscators and succinct non-interactive arguments of knowledge, which are believed to be risky assumptions due to their inherent extractability nature. In EUROCRYPT 2016, Deshpande et al. [10] presented a CPRF for TM constraints, supporting inputs of unconstrained polynomial length, which they claimed to be selectively secure. Their CPRF construction utilizes indistinguishability obfuscators (IO) for circuits and injective pseudorandom generators. Currently, there is no known impossibility or implausibility result on IO and, moreover, in the last few years, there has been a significant progress towards constructing IO based on standard complexity assumptions.

Our Contributions: Unfortunately, the CPRF construction of [10] can not be proven secure in the selective model, as will be shown in this paper, rather the construction actually derives its security in a *significantly weaker* model. Further, as per as we know, there is no existing construction of CVPRF's or delegatable CPRF's (DCPRF) supporting inputs of unconstrained length. Our work in this paper is two-fold:

- Firstly, we identify a flaw in the security argument of the CPRF construction of [10], by a thorough analysis of the construction and its security proof. Selective security is a security notion for CPRF's where the adversary is bound to declare

upfront the challenge input, on which it wishes to distinguish the PRF output from random, but is allowed to query the legitimate constrained keys and PRF values *adaptively*. We observe that the CPRF construction of [10] can be proven secure only if the adversary is not just forced to declare the challenge input, but also is bound to make all the constrained key queries *prior to setting up the system*. To address the security limitation of the CPRF construction of [10], we carefully modify their construction by innovating new technical ideas, which might be useful elsewhere, and suitably redesign the security proof. For building our improved CPRF system, we additionally use a somewhat statistically binding (SSB) hash function [18,22] beyond the cryptographic tools used in [10]. Currently, efficient constructions of SSB hash based on standard number theoretic assumptions exist [22]. In effect, our modified CPRF stands out to be the *first* IO-based provably selectively secure CPRF for TM constraints that can handle inputs of arbitrary polynomial length.
- Secondly, we enhance our construction of CPRF with verifiability and key delegation features, thereby, developing the *first* IO-based selectively secure constructions of CVPRF and DCPRF supporting inputs of *unconstrained* polynomial length. Towards achieving these two augmentations of our CPRF, we only assume the existence of a perfectly correct and chosen plaintext attack (CPA) secure public key encryption scheme, which is evidently a minimal assumption. Finally, we note that following [9,12], our CVPRF construction would imply the *first* selectively unforgeable *policy-based signature* (PBS) scheme [5] where policies are represented as Turing machines.

2   Preliminaries

Here we give the necessary background on various cryptographic primitives we will be using throughout this paper. Let $\lambda \in \mathbb{N}$ denotes the security parameter. For $n \in \mathbb{N}$ and $a, b \in \mathbb{N} \cup \{0\}$ (with $a < b$), we let $[n] = \{1, \ldots, n\}$ and $[a, b] = \{a, \ldots, b\}$. For any set S, $v \xleftarrow{\$} S$ represents the uniform random variable on S. For a randomized algorithm $\mathcal{R}$, we denote by $\psi = \mathcal{R}(v; \rho)$ the random variable defined by the output of $\mathcal{R}$ on input v and randomness ρ, while $\psi \xleftarrow{\$} \mathcal{R}(v)$ has the same meaning with the randomness suppressed. Also, if $\mathcal{R}$ is a deterministic algorithm $\psi = \mathcal{R}(v)$ denotes the output of $\mathcal{R}$ on input v. We will use the alternative notation $\mathcal{R}(v) \to \psi$ as well to represent the output of the algorithm $\mathcal{R}$, whether randomized or deterministic, on input v. For any string $s \in \{0,1\}^*$, $|s|$ represents the length of the string s. For any two strings $s, s' \in \{0,1\}^*$, $s\|s'$ represents the concatenation of s and s'.

2.1   Turing Machines

A Turing machine (TM) M is a 7-tuple $M = \langle Q, \Sigma_{\text{INP}}, \Sigma_{\text{TAPE}}, \delta, q_0, q_{\text{AC}}, q_{\text{REJ}} \rangle$ with the following semantics:

- Q: The finite set of possible states of M.
- Σ_{INP}: The finite set of input symbols.

- Σ_{TAPE}: The finite set of tape symbols such that $\Sigma_{\text{INP}} \subset \Sigma_{\text{TAPE}}$ and there exists a special blank symbol '$\_$' $\in \Sigma_{\text{TAPE}} \backslash \Sigma_{\text{INP}}$.
- $\delta : Q \times \Sigma_{\text{TAPE}} \to Q \times \Sigma_{\text{TAPE}} \times \{+1, -1\}$: The transition function of M.
- $q_0 \in Q$: The designated start state.
- $q_{\text{AC}} \in Q$: The designated accept state.
- $q_{\text{REJ}}(\neq q_{\text{AC}}) \in Q$: The distinguished reject state.

For any $t \in [T = 2^\lambda]$, we define the following variables for M, while running on some input (without the explicit mention of the input in the notations):

- $\text{POS}_{M,t}$: An integer which denotes the position of the header of M after the tth step. Initially, $\text{POS}_{M,0} = 0$.
- $\text{SYM}_{M,t} \in \Sigma_{\text{TAPE}}$: The symbol stored on the tape at the $\text{POS}_{M,t}{}^{\text{th}}$ location.
- $\text{SYM}_{M,t}^{(\text{WRITE})} \in \Sigma_{\text{TAPE}}$: The symbol to be written at the $\text{POS}_{M,t-1}{}^{\text{th}}$ location during the tth step.
- $\text{ST}_{M,t} \in Q$: The state of M after the tth step. Initially, $\text{ST}_{M,0} = q_0$.

At each time step, theTM M reads the tape at the header position and based on the current state, computes what needs to be written on the tape at the current header location, the next state, and whether the header must move left or right. More formally, let $(q, \zeta, \beta \in \{+1, -1\}) = \delta(\text{ST}_{M,t-1}, \text{SYM}_{M,t-1})$. Then, $\text{ST}_{M,t} = q$, $\text{SYM}_{M,t}^{(\text{WRITE})} = \zeta$, and $\text{POS}_{M,t} = \text{POS}_{M,t-1} + \beta$. M accepts at time t if $\text{ST}_{M,t} = q_{\text{AC}}$. In this paper we consider $\Sigma_{\text{INP}} = \{0,1\}$ and $\Sigma_{\text{TAPE}} = \{0,1,\_\}$. Given any TM M and string $x \in \{0,1\}^*$, we define $M(x) = 1$, if M accepts x within T steps, and 0, otherwise.

2.2 Indistinguishability Obfuscation

Definition 2.1 (Indistinguishability Obfuscation: IO [14]). An indistinguishability obfuscator (IO) $\mathcal{IO}$ for a certain circuit class $\{\mathbb{C}_\lambda\}_\lambda$ is a probabilistic polynomial-time (PPT) uniform algorithm satisfying the following conditions:

▶ **Correctness:** $\mathcal{IO}(1^\lambda, C)$ preserves the functionality of the input circuit C, i.e., for any $C \in \mathbb{C}_\lambda$, if we compute $C' = \mathcal{IO}(1^\lambda, C)$, then $C'(v) = C(v)$ for all inputs v.

▶ **Indistinguishability:** For any security parameter λ and any two circuits $C_0, C_1 \in \mathbb{C}_\lambda$ with same functionality, the circuits $\mathcal{IO}(1^\lambda, C_0)$ and $\mathcal{IO}(1^\lambda, C_1)$ are computationally indistinguishable. More precisely, for all (not necessarily uniform) PPT adversaries $\mathcal{D} = (\mathcal{D}_1, \mathcal{D}_2)$, there exists a negligible function negl such that, if

$$\Pr\big[(C_0, C_1, \xi) \xleftarrow{\$} \mathcal{D}_1(1^\lambda) \ : \ \forall v, C_0(v) = C_1(v)\big] \geq 1 - \mathsf{negl}(\lambda),$$

then $\big|\Pr\big[\mathcal{D}_2(\xi, \mathcal{IO}(1^\lambda, C_0)) = 1\big] - \Pr\big[\mathcal{D}_2(\xi, \mathcal{IO}(1^\lambda, C_1)) = 1\big]\big| \leq \mathsf{negl}(\lambda).$

When clear from the context, we will drop 1^λ as an input to $\mathcal{IO}$ and λ as a subscript of $\mathbb{C}$.

2.3   IO-Compatible Cryptographic Primitives

In this section, we present the syntax and correctness requirement of certain IO-friendly cryptographic tools which we will be using in the sequel. The security properties of these primitives can be found in the full version of this paper or in the references provided in the respective subsections below.

2.3.1   Puncturable Pseudorandom Function

Definition 2.2 (Puncturable Pseudorandom Function: PPRF [23]**).** A puncturable pseudorandom function (PPRF) $\mathcal{F} : \mathcal{K}_{\mathrm{PPRF}} \times \mathcal{X}_{\mathrm{PPRF}} \to \mathcal{Y}_{\mathrm{PPRF}}$ consists of an additional punctured key space $\mathcal{K}_{\mathrm{PPRF\text{-}PUNC}}$ other than the usual key space $\mathcal{K}_{\mathrm{PPRF}}$ and PPT algorithms ($\mathcal{F}$.Setup, $\mathcal{F}$.Eval, $\mathcal{F}$.Puncture, $\mathcal{F}$.Eval-Punctured) described below. Here, $\mathcal{X}_{\mathrm{PPRF}} = \{0,1\}^{\ell_{\mathrm{PPRF\text{-}INP}}}$ and $\mathcal{Y}_{\mathrm{PPRF}} = \{0,1\}^{\ell_{\mathrm{PPRF\text{-}OUT}}}$, where $\ell_{\mathrm{PPRF\text{-}INP}}$ and $\ell_{\mathrm{PPRF\text{-}OUT}}$ are polynomials in the security parameter λ,

$\mathcal{F}$.Setup(1^λ) $\to K$: The setup authority takes as input the security parameter 1^λ and uniformly samples a PPRF key $K \in \mathcal{K}_{\mathrm{PPRF}}$.

$\mathcal{F}$.Eval(K, x) $\to r$: The setup authority takes as input a PPRF key $K \in \mathcal{K}_{\mathrm{PPRF}}$ along with an input $x \in \mathcal{X}_{\mathrm{PPRF}}$. It outputs the PPRF value $r \in \mathcal{Y}_{\mathrm{PPRF}}$ on x. For simplicity, we will represent by $\mathcal{F}(K, x)$ the output of this algorithm.

$\mathcal{F}$.Puncture(K, x) $\to K\{x\}$: Taking as input a PPRF key $K \in \mathcal{K}_{\mathrm{PPRF}}$ along with an element $x \in \mathcal{X}_{\mathrm{PPRF}}$, the setup authority outputs a punctured key $K\{x\} \in \mathcal{K}_{\mathrm{PPRF\text{-}PUNC}}$.

$\mathcal{F}$.Eval-Puncured($K\{x\}, x'$) $\to r$ or $\perp$: An evaluator takes as input a punctured key $K\{x\} \in \mathcal{K}_{\mathrm{PPRF\text{-}PUNC}}$ along with an input $x' \in \mathcal{X}_{\mathrm{PPRF}}$. It outputs either a value $r \in \mathcal{Y}_{\mathrm{PPRF}}$ or a distinguished symbol $\perp$ indicating failure. For simplicity, we will represent by $\mathcal{F}(K\{x\}, x')$ the output of this algorithm.

The algorithms $\mathcal{F}$.Setup and $\mathcal{F}$.Puncture are randomized, whereas, the algorithms $\mathcal{F}$.Eval and $\mathcal{F}$.Eval-Punctured are deterministic.

▶ **Correctness Under Puncturing:** Consider any security parameter λ, $K \in \mathcal{K}_{\mathrm{PPRF}}$, $x \in \mathcal{X}_{\mathrm{PPRF}}$, and $K\{x\} \xleftarrow{\$} \mathcal{F}$.Puncture($K, x$). Then it must hold that

$$\mathcal{F}(K\{x\}, x') = \begin{cases} \mathcal{F}(K, x'), & \text{if } x' \neq x \\ \perp, & \text{otherwise} \end{cases}$$

2.3.2   Somewhere Statistically Binding Hash Function

Definition 2.3 (Somewhere Statistically Binding Hash Function: SSB [18,22]**).** A somewhere statistically binding (SSB) hash consists of PPT algorithms (SSB.Gen, $\mathcal{H}$, SSB.Open, SSB.Verify) along with a block alphabet $\Sigma_{\mathrm{SSB\text{-}BLK}} = \{0,1\}^{\ell_{\mathrm{SSB\text{-}BLK}}}$, output size $\ell_{\mathrm{SSB\text{-}HASH}}$, and opening space $\Pi_{\mathrm{SSB}} = \{0,1\}^{\ell_{\mathrm{SSB\text{-}OPEN}}}$, where $\ell_{\mathrm{SSB\text{-}BLK}}, \ell_{\mathrm{SSB\text{-}HASH}}, \ell_{\mathrm{SSB\text{-}OPEN}}$ are some polynomials in the security parameter λ. The algorithms have the following syntax:

SSB.Gen($1^\lambda, n_{\mathrm{SSB\text{-}BLK}}, i^*$) $\to \mathrm{HK}$: The setup authority takes as input the security parameter 1^λ, an integer $n_{\mathrm{SSB\text{-}BLK}} \leq 2^\lambda$ representing the maximum number of blocks that can be hashed, and an index $i^* \in [0, n_{\mathrm{SSB\text{-}BLK}} - 1]$ and publishes a public hashing key HK.

$\mathcal{H}_{\text{HK}} : x \in \Sigma_{\text{SSB-BLK}}^{n_{\text{SSB-BLK}}} \to h \in \{0,1\}^{\ell_{\text{SSB-HASH}}}$: This is a deterministic function that has the hash key HK hardwired. A user runs this function on input $x = x_0\| \ldots \|x_{n_{\text{SSB-BLK}}-1} \in \Sigma_{\text{SSB-BLK}}^{n_{\text{SSB-BLK}}}$ to obtain as output $h = \mathcal{H}_{\text{HK}}(x) \in \{0,1\}^{\ell_{\text{SSB-HASH}}}$.

SSB.Open(HK, x, i) $\to \pi_{\text{SSB}}$: Taking as input the hash key HK, input $x \in \Sigma_{\text{SSB-BLK}}^{n_{\text{SSB-BLK}}}$, and an index $i \in [0, n_{\text{SSB-BLK}} - 1]$, a user creates an opening $\pi_{\text{SSB}} \in \Pi_{\text{SSB}}$.

SSB.Verify(HK, $h, i, u, \pi_{\text{SSB}}$) $\to \hat{\beta} \in \{0,1\}$: On input a hash key HK, a hash value $h \in \{0,1\}^{\ell_{\text{SSB-HASH}}}$, an index $i \in [0, n_{\text{SSB-BLK}} - 1]$, a value $u \in \Sigma_{\text{SSB-BLK}}$, and an opening $\pi_{\text{SSB}} \in \Pi_{\text{SSB}}$, a verifier outputs a bit $\hat{\beta} \in \{0,1\}$.

The algorithms SSB.Gen and SSB.Open are randomized, while the algorithm SSB.Verify is deterministic.

▶ **Correctness:** For any security parameter λ, integer $n_{\text{SSB-BLK}} \leq 2^\lambda$, $i, i^* \in [0, n_{\text{SSB-BLK}} - 1]$, HK $\xleftarrow{\$}$ SSB.Gen($1^\lambda, n_{\text{SSB-BLK}}, i^*$), $x \in \Sigma_{\text{SSB-BLK}}^{n_{\text{SSB-BLK}}}$, and $\pi_{\text{SSB}} \xleftarrow{\$}$ SSB.Open(HK, x, i), we have SSB.Verify(HK, $\mathcal{H}_{\text{HK}}(x), i, x_i, \pi_{\text{SSB}}$) = 1.

2.3.3   Positional Accumulator

Definition 2.4 (Positional Accumulator [20,22]). A positional accumulator consists of PPT algorithms (ACC.Setup, ACC.Setup-Enforce-Read, ACC.Setup-Enforce-Write, ACC.Prep-Read, ACC.Prep-Write, ACC.Verify-Read, ACC.Write-Store, ACC.Update) along with a block alphabet $\Sigma_{\text{ACC-BLK}} = \{0,1\}^{\ell_{\text{ACC-BLK}}}$, accumulator size $\ell_{\text{ACC-ACCUMULATE}}$, proof space $\Pi_{\text{ACC}} = \{0,1\}^{\ell_{\text{ACC-PROOF}}}$ where $\ell_{\text{ACC-BLK}}$, $\ell_{\text{ACC-ACCUMULATE}}$, $\ell_{\text{ACC-PROOF}}$ are some polynomials in the security parameter λ. The algorithms have the following syntax:

ACC.Setup($1^\lambda, n_{\text{ACC-BLK}}$) $\to$ (PP$_{\text{ACC}}, w_0, $ STORE$_0$) : The setup authority takes as input the security parameter 1^λ and an integer $n_{\text{ACC-BLK}} \leq 2^\lambda$ representing the maximum number of blocks that can be accumulated. It outputs the public parameters PP$_{\text{ACC}}$, an initial accumulator value w_0, and an initial storage value STORE$_0$.

ACC.Setup-Enforce-Read($1^\lambda, n_{\text{ACC-BLK}}, ((x_1, i_1), \ldots, (x_\kappa, i_\kappa)), i^*$) $\to$ (PP$_{\text{ACC}}, w_0,$ STORE$_0$) : Taking as input the security parameter 1^λ, an integer $n_{\text{ACC-BLK}} \leq 2^\lambda$ representing the maximum number of blocks that can be accumulated, a sequence of symbol-index pairs $((x_1, i_1), \ldots, (x_\kappa, i_\kappa)) \in (\Sigma_{\text{ACC-BLK}} \times [0, n_{\text{ACC-BLK}} - 1])^\kappa$, and an additional index $i^* \in [0, n_{\text{ACC-BLK}} - 1]$, the setup authority publishes the public parameters PP$_{\text{ACC}}$, an initial accumulator value w_0, together with an initial storage value STORE$_0$.

ACC.Setup-Enforce-Write($1^\lambda, n_{\text{ACC-BLK}}, ((x_1, i_1), \ldots, x_\kappa, i_\kappa)))$ $\to$ (PP$_{\text{ACC}}, w_0,$ STORE$_0$) : On input the security parameter 1^λ, an integer $n_{\text{ACC-BLK}} \leq 2^\lambda$ denoting the maximum number of blocks that can be accumulated, and a sequence of symbol-index pairs $((x_1, i_1), \ldots, (x_\kappa, i_\kappa)) \in (\Sigma_{\text{ACC-BLK}} \times [0, n_{\text{ACC-BLK}} - 1])^\kappa$, the setup authority publishes the public parameters PP$_{\text{ACC}}$, an initial accumulator value w_0, as well as, an initial storage value STORE$_0$.

ACC.Prep-Read(PP$_{\text{ACC}}$, STORE$_{\text{IN}}, i_{\text{IN}}$) $\to (x_{\text{OUT}}, \pi_{\text{ACC}})$: A storage-maintaining party takes as input the public parameter PP$_{\text{ACC}}$, a storage value STORE$_{\text{IN}}$, and an index $i_{\text{IN}} \in [0, n_{\text{ACC-BLK}} - 1]$. It outputs a symbol $x_{\text{OUT}} \in \Sigma_{\text{ACC-BLK}} \cup \{\epsilon\}$ (ϵ being the empty string) and a proof $\pi_{\text{ACC}} \in \Pi_{\text{ACC}}$.

ACC.Prep-Write$(\mathrm{PP_{ACC}, STORE_{IN}}, i_{\mathrm{IN}}) \to \mathrm{AUX}$: Taking as input the public parameter $\mathrm{PP_{ACC}}$, a storage value $\mathrm{STORE_{IN}}$, together with an index $i_{\mathrm{IN}} \in [0, n_{\mathrm{ACC\text{-}BLK}} - 1]$, a storage-maintaining party outputs an auxiliary value AUX.

ACC.Verify-Read$(\mathrm{PP_{ACC}}, w_{\mathrm{IN}}, x_{\mathrm{IN}}, i_{\mathrm{IN}}, \pi_{\mathrm{ACC}}) \to \hat{\beta} \in \{0,1\}$: A verifier takes as input the public parameter $\mathrm{PP_{ACC}}$, an accumulator value $w_{\mathrm{IN}} \in \{0,1\}^{\ell_{\mathrm{ACC\text{-}ACCUMULATE}}}$, a symbol $x_{\mathrm{IN}} \in \Sigma_{\mathrm{ACC\text{-}BLK}} \cup \{\epsilon\}$, an index $i_{\mathrm{IN}} \in [0, n_{\mathrm{ACC\text{-}BLK}} - 1]$, and a proof $\pi_{\mathrm{ACC}} \in \Pi_{\mathrm{ACC}}$. It outputs a bit $\hat{\beta} \in \{0,1\}$.

ACC.Write-Store$(\mathrm{PP_{ACC}, STORE_{IN}}, i_{\mathrm{IN}}, x_{\mathrm{IN}}) \to \mathrm{STORE_{OUT}}$: On input the public parameters $\mathrm{PP_{ACC}}$, a storage value $\mathrm{STORE_{IN}}$, an index $i_{\mathrm{IN}} \in [0, n_{\mathrm{ACC\text{-}BLK}} - 1]$, and a symbol $x_{\mathrm{IN}} \in \Sigma_{\mathrm{ACC\text{-}BLK}}$, a storage-maintaining party computes a new storage value $\mathrm{STORE_{OUT}}$.

ACC.Update$(\mathrm{PP_{ACC}}, w_{\mathrm{IN}}, x_{\mathrm{IN}}, i_{\mathrm{IN}}, \mathrm{AUX}) \to w_{\mathrm{OUT}}$ or $\perp$: An accumulator-updating party takes as input the public parameters $\mathrm{PP_{ACC}}$, an accumulator value $w_{\mathrm{IN}} \in \{0,1\}^{\ell_{\mathrm{ACC\text{-}ACCUMULATE}}}$, a symbol $x_{\mathrm{IN}} \in \Sigma_{\mathrm{ACC\text{-}BLK}}$, an index $i_{\mathrm{IN}} \in [0, n_{\mathrm{ACC\text{-}BLK}} - 1]$, and an auxiliary value AUX. It outputs the updated accumulator value $w_{\mathrm{OUT}} \in \{0,1\}^{\ell_{\mathrm{ACC\text{-}ACCUMULATE}}}$ or the designated reject string $\perp$.

Following [10,20], in this paper we will consider the algorithms ACC.Setup, ACC.Setup-Enforce-Read, and ACC.Setup-Enforce-Write as randomized while all other algorithms as deterministic.

▶ **Correctness:** Consider any symbol-index pair sequence $((x_1, i_1), \ldots, (x_\kappa, i_\kappa))$ $\in (\Sigma_{\mathrm{ACC\text{-}BLK}} \times [0, n_{\mathrm{ACC\text{-}BLK}} - 1])^\kappa$. Fix any $(\mathrm{PP_{ACC}}, w_0, \mathrm{STORE_0}) \xleftarrow{\$} \mathrm{ACC.Setup}(1^\lambda, n_{\mathrm{ACC\text{-}BLK}})$. For $j = 1, \ldots, \kappa$, iteratively define the following:

- $\mathrm{STORE}_j = \mathrm{ACC.Write\text{-}Store}(\mathrm{PP_{ACC}}, \mathrm{STORE}_{j-1}, i_j, x_j)$
- $\mathrm{AUX}_j = \mathrm{ACC.Prep\text{-}Write}(\mathrm{PP_{ACC}}, \mathrm{STORE}_{j-1}, i_j)$
- $w_j = \mathrm{ACC.Update}(\mathrm{PP_{ACC}}, w_{j-1}, x_j, i_j, \mathrm{AUX}_j)$

The following correctness properties are required to be satisfied:

(i) For any security parameter λ, $n_{\mathrm{ACC\text{-}BLK}} \leq 2^\lambda$, index $i^* \in [0, n_{\mathrm{ACC\text{-}BLK}} - 1]$, sequence of symbol-index pairs $((x_1, i_1), \ldots, (x_\kappa, i_\kappa)) \in (\Sigma_{\mathrm{ACC\text{-}BLK}} \times [0, n_{\mathrm{ACC\text{-}BLK}} - 1])^\kappa$, and $(\mathrm{PP_{ACC}}, w_0, \mathrm{STORE_0}) \xleftarrow{\$} \mathrm{ACC.Setup}(1^\lambda, n_{\mathrm{ACC\text{-}BLK}})$, if STORE_κ is computed as above, then ACC.Prep-Read$(\mathrm{PP_{ACC}}, \mathrm{STORE}_\kappa, i^*)$ returns $(x_j, \pi_{\mathrm{ACC}})$ where j is the largest value in $[\kappa]$ such that $i_j = i^*$.

(ii) For any security parameter λ, $n_{\mathrm{ACC\text{-}BLK}} \leq 2^\lambda$, sequence of symbol-index pairs $((x_1, i_1), \ldots, (x_\kappa, i_\kappa)) \in (\Sigma_{\mathrm{ACC\text{-}BLK}} \times [0, n_{\mathrm{ACC\text{-}BLK}} - 1])^\kappa$, $i^* \in [0, n_{\mathrm{ACC\text{-}BLK}} - 1]$, and $(\mathrm{PP_{ACC}}, w_0, \mathrm{STORE_0}) \xleftarrow{\$} \mathrm{ACC.Setup}(1^\lambda, n_{\mathrm{ACC\text{-}BLK}})$, if STORE_κ and w_κ are computed as above and $(x_{\mathrm{OUT}}, \pi_{\mathrm{ACC}}) = \mathrm{ACC.Prep\text{-}Read}(\mathrm{PP_{ACC}}, \mathrm{STORE}_\kappa, i^*)$, then ACC.Verify-Read$(\mathrm{PP_{ACC}}, w_\kappa, x_{\mathrm{OUT}}, i^*, \pi_{\mathrm{ACC}}) = 1$

2.3.4 Iterator

Definition 2.5 (Iterator [20]). A cryptographic iterator consists of PPT algorithms (ITR.Setup, ITR.Set-Enforce, ITR.Iterate) along with a message space $\mathcal{M}_{\mathrm{ITR}} = \{0,1\}^{\ell_{\mathrm{ITR\text{-}MSG}}}$ and iterator state size $\ell_{\mathrm{ITR\text{-}ST}}$, where $\ell_{\mathrm{ITR\text{-}MSG}}, \ell_{\mathrm{ITR\text{-}ST}}$ are some polynomials in the security parameter λ. Algorithms have the following syntax:

ITR.Setup($1^\lambda, n_{\text{ITR}}$) $\rightarrow$ ($\text{PP}_{\text{ITR}}, v_0$) : The setup authority takes as input the security parameter 1^λ along with an integer bound $n_{\text{ITR}} \leq 2^\lambda$ on the number of iterations. It outputs the public parameters PP_{ITR} and an initial state $v_0 \in \{0,1\}^{\ell_{\text{ITR-ST}}}$.

ITR.Setup-Enforce($1^\lambda, n_{\text{ITR}}, (\mu_1, \ldots, \mu_\kappa)$) $\rightarrow$ ($\text{PP}_{\text{ITR}}, v_0$) : Taking as input the security parameter 1^λ, an integer bound $n_{\text{ITR}} \leq 2^\lambda$, together with a sequence of κ messages $(\mu_1, \ldots, \mu_\kappa) \in \mathcal{M}_{\text{ITR}}^\kappa$, where $\kappa \leq n_{\text{ITR}}$, the setup authority publishes the public parameters PP_{ITR} and an initial state $v_0 \in \{0,1\}^{\ell_{\text{ITR-ST}}}$.

ITR.Iterate($\text{PP}_{\text{ITR}}, v_{\text{IN}} \in \{0,1\}^{\ell_{\text{ITR-ST}}}, \mu$) $\rightarrow$ v_{OUT} : On input the public parameters PP_{ITR}, a state v_{IN}, and a message $\mu \in \mathcal{M}_{\text{ITR}}$, an iterator outputs an updated state $v_{\text{OUT}} \in \{0,1\}^{\ell_{\text{ITR-ST}}}$. For any integer $\kappa \leq n_{\text{ITR}}$, we will write ITR.Iterate$^\kappa$(PP_{ITR}, $v_0, (\mu_1, \ldots, \mu_\kappa)$) to denote ITR.Iterate($\text{PP}_{\text{ITR}}, v_{\kappa-1}, \mu_\kappa$), where v_j is defined iteratively as $v_j = $ ITR.Iterate($\text{PP}_{\text{ITR}}, v_{j-1}, \mu_j$) for all $j = 1, \ldots, \kappa - 1$.

The algorithm ITR.Iterate is deterministic, while the other two are randomized.

2.3.5 Splittable Signature

Definition 2.6 (Splittable Signature: SPS [20]**).** A splittable signature scheme (SPS) for message space $\mathcal{M}_{\text{SPS}} = \{0,1\}^{\ell_{\text{SPS-MSG}}}$ and signature space $\mathcal{S}_{\text{SPS}} = \{0,1\}^{\ell_{\text{SPS-SIG}}}$, where $\ell_{\text{SPS-MSG}}, \ell_{\text{SPS-SIG}}$ are some polynomials in the security parameter λ, consists of PPT algorithms (SPS.Setup, SPS.Sign, SPS.Verify, SPS.Split, SPS.Sign-ABO) which are described below:

SPS.Setup(1^λ) $\rightarrow$ ($\text{SK}_{\text{SPS}}, \text{VK}_{\text{SPS}}, \text{VK}_{\text{SPS-REJ}}$) : The setup authority takes as input the security parameter 1^λ and generates a signing key SK_{SPS}, a verification key VK_{SPS}, together with a reject verification key $\text{VK}_{\text{SPS-REJ}}$.

SPS.Sign($\text{SK}_{\text{SPS}}, m$) $\rightarrow$ σ_{SPS} : A signer given a signing key SK_{SPS} along with a message $m \in \mathcal{M}_{\text{SPS}}$, produces a signature $\sigma_{\text{SPS}} \in \mathcal{S}_{\text{SPS}}$.

SPS.Verify($\text{VK}_{\text{SPS}}, m, \sigma_{\text{SPS}}$) $\rightarrow$ $\hat{\beta} \in \{0,1\}$: A verifier takes as input a verification key VK_{SPS}, a message $m \in \mathcal{M}_{\text{SPS}}$, and a signature $\sigma_{\text{SPS}} \in \mathcal{S}_{\text{SPS}}$. It outputs a bit $\hat{\beta} \in \{0,1\}$.

SPS.Split($\text{SK}_{\text{SPS}}, m^*$) $\rightarrow$ ($\sigma_{\text{SPS-ONE},m^*}, \text{VK}_{\text{SPS-ONE}}, \text{SK}_{\text{SPS-ABO}}, \text{VK}_{\text{SPS-ABO}}$) : On input a signing key SK_{SPS} along with a message $m^* \in \mathcal{M}_{\text{SPS}}$, the setup authority generates a signature $\sigma_{\text{SPS-ONE},m^*} = $ SPS.Sign($\text{SK}_{\text{SPS}}, m^*$), a one-message verification key $\text{VK}_{\text{SPS-ONE}}$, and all-but-one signing-verification key pair ($\text{SK}_{\text{SPS-ABO}}, \text{VK}_{\text{SPS-ABO}}$).

SPS.Sign-ABO($\text{SK}_{\text{SPS-ABO}}, m$) $\rightarrow$ σ_{SPS} or $\perp$: An all-but-one signer given an all-but-one signing key $\text{SK}_{\text{SPS-ABO}}$ and a message $m \in \mathcal{M}_{\text{SPS}}$, outputs a signature $\sigma_{\text{SPS}} \in \mathcal{S}_{\text{SPS}}$ or a distinguished string $\perp$ to indicate failure. For simplicity of notation, we will often use SPS.Sign($\text{SK}_{\text{SPS-ABO}}, m$) to represent the output of this algorithm.

We note that among the algorithms described above, SPS.Setup and SPS.Split are randomized while all the others are deterministic.

▶ **Correctness:** For any security parameter λ, message $m^* \in \mathcal{M}_{\mathrm{SPS}}$, $(\mathrm{SK}_{\mathrm{SPS}}, \mathrm{VK}_{\mathrm{SPS}},$ $\mathrm{VK}_{\mathrm{SPS\text{-}REJ}}) \xleftarrow{\$} \mathsf{SPS.Setup}(1^\lambda)$, and $(\sigma_{\mathrm{SPS\text{-}ONE},m^*}, \mathrm{VK}_{\mathrm{SPS\text{-}ONE}}, \mathrm{SK}_{\mathrm{SPS\text{-}ABO}}, \mathrm{VK}_{\mathrm{SPS\text{-}ABO}}) \xleftarrow{\$}$ $\mathsf{SPS.Split}(\mathrm{SK}_{\mathrm{SPS}}, m^*)$ the following correctness conditions hold:

(i) $\forall m \in \mathcal{M}_{\mathrm{SPS}}, \mathsf{SPS.Verify}(\mathrm{VK}_{\mathrm{SPS}}, m, \mathsf{SPS.Sign}(\mathrm{SK}_{\mathrm{SPS}}, m)) = 1.$

(ii) $\forall m \neq m^* \in \mathcal{M}_{\mathrm{SPS}}, \mathsf{SPS.Sign}(\mathrm{SK}_{\mathrm{SPS}}, m) = \mathsf{SPS.Sign\text{-}ABO}(\mathrm{SK}_{\mathrm{SPS\text{-}ABO}}, m).$

(iii) $\forall \sigma_{\mathrm{SPS}} \in \mathcal{S}_{\mathrm{SPS}}, \mathsf{SPS.Verify}(\mathrm{VK}_{\mathrm{SPS\text{-}ONE}}, m^*, \sigma_{\mathrm{SPS}}) = \mathsf{SPS.Verify}(\mathrm{VK}_{\mathrm{SPS}}, m^*, \sigma_{\mathrm{SPS}}).$

(iv) $\forall m \neq m^* \in \mathcal{M}_{\mathrm{SPS}}, \sigma_{\mathrm{SPS}} \in \mathcal{S}_{\mathrm{SPS}}, \mathsf{SPS.Verify}(\mathrm{VK}_{\mathrm{SPS\text{-}ABO}}, m, \sigma_{\mathrm{SPS}}) = \mathsf{SPS.Verify}(\mathrm{VK}_{\mathrm{SPS}}, m, \sigma_{\mathrm{SPS}}).$

(v) $\forall m \neq m^* \in \mathcal{M}_{\mathrm{SPS}}, \sigma_{\mathrm{SPS}} \in \mathcal{S}_{\mathrm{SPS}}, \mathsf{SPS.Verify}(\mathrm{VK}_{\mathrm{SPS\text{-}ONE}}, m, \sigma_{\mathrm{SPS}}) = 0.$

(vi) $\forall \sigma_{\mathrm{SPS}} \in \mathcal{S}_{\mathrm{SPS}}, \mathsf{SPS.Verify}(\mathrm{VK}_{\mathrm{SPS\text{-}ABO}}, m^*, \sigma_{\mathrm{SPS}}) = 0.$

(vii) $\forall m \in \mathcal{M}_{\mathrm{SPS}}, \sigma_{\mathrm{SPS}} \in \mathcal{S}_{\mathrm{SPS}}, \mathsf{SPS.Verify}(\mathrm{VK}_{\mathrm{SPS\text{-}REJ}}, m, \sigma_{\mathrm{SPS}}) = 0.$

3 Our **CPRF** for Turing Machines

3.1 Notion

Definition 3.1 (Constrained Pseudorandom Function for Turing Machines: CPRF [10]). Let $\mathbb{M}_\lambda$ be a family of TM's with (worst case) running time bounded by $T = 2^\lambda$. A constrained pseudorandom function (CPRF) with key space $\mathcal{K}_{\mathrm{CPRF}}$, input domain $\mathcal{X}_{\mathrm{CPRF}} \subset \{0,1\}^*$, and output space $\mathcal{Y}_{\mathrm{CPRF}} \subset \{0,1\}^*$ for the TM family $\mathbb{M}_\lambda$ consists of an additional key space $\mathcal{K}_{\mathrm{CPRF\text{-}CONST}}$ and PPT algorithms $(\mathsf{CPRF.Setup}, \mathsf{CPRF.Eval}, \mathsf{CPRF.Constrain}, \mathsf{CPRF.Eval\text{-}Constrained})$ described as follows:

$\mathsf{CPRF.Setup}(1^\lambda) \rightarrow \mathrm{SK}_{\mathrm{CPRF}}$: The setup authority takes as input the security parameter 1^λ and generates the master CPRF key $\mathrm{SK}_{\mathrm{CPRF}} \in \mathcal{K}_{\mathrm{CPRF}}$.

$\mathsf{CPRF.Eval}(\mathrm{SK}_{\mathrm{CPRF}}, x) \rightarrow y$: On input the master CPRF key $\mathrm{SK}_{\mathrm{CPRF}}$ along with an input $x \in \mathcal{X}_{\mathrm{CPRF}}$, the setup authority computes the value of the CPRF $y \in \mathcal{Y}_{\mathrm{CPRF}}$. For simplicity of notation, we will use $\mathsf{CPRF}(\mathrm{SK}_{\mathrm{CPRF}}, x)$ to indicate the output of this algorithm.

$\mathsf{CPRF.Constrain}(\mathrm{SK}_{\mathrm{CPRF}}, M) \rightarrow \mathrm{SK}_{\mathrm{CPRF}}\{M\}$: Taking as input the master CPRF key $\mathrm{SK}_{\mathrm{CPRF}}$ and a TM $M \in \mathbb{M}_\lambda$, the setup authority provides a constrained key $\mathrm{SK}_{\mathrm{CPRF}}\{M\} \in \mathcal{K}_{\mathrm{CPRF\text{-}CONST}}$ to a legitimate user.

$\mathsf{CPRF.Eval\text{-}Constrained}(\mathrm{SK}_{\mathrm{CPRF}}\{M\}, x) \rightarrow y$ or $\bot$: A user takes as input a constrained key $\mathrm{SK}_{\mathrm{CPRF}}\{M\} \in \mathcal{K}_{\mathrm{CPRF\text{-}CONST}}$, corresponding to a legitimate TM $M \in \mathbb{M}_\lambda$, along with an input $x \in \mathcal{X}_{\mathrm{CPRF}}$. It outputs either a value $y \in \mathcal{Y}_{\mathrm{CPRF}}$ or $\bot$ indicating failure.

The algorithms $\mathsf{CPRF.Setup}$ and $\mathsf{CPRF.Constrain}$ are randomized, whereas, the other two are deterministic.

▶ **Correctness Under Constraining:** Consider any security parameter λ, $\mathrm{SK}_{\mathrm{CPRF}} \in \mathcal{K}_{\mathrm{CPRF}}$, $M \in \mathbb{M}_\lambda$, and $\mathrm{SK}_{\mathrm{CPRF}}\{M\} \xleftarrow{\$} \mathsf{CPRF.Constrain}(\mathrm{SK}_{\mathrm{CPRF}}, M)$. The following must hold:

$$\mathsf{CPRF.Eval\text{-}Constrained}(\mathrm{SK}_{\mathrm{CPRF}}\{M\}, x) = \begin{cases} \mathsf{CPRF}(\mathrm{SK}_{\mathrm{CPRF}}, x), & \text{if } M(x) = 1 \\ \bot, & \text{otherwise} \end{cases}$$

▶ **Selective Pseudorandomness:** This property of a CPRF is defined through the following experiment between an adversary $\mathcal{A}$ and a challenger $\mathcal{B}$:

- $\mathcal{A}$ submits a challenge input $x^* \in \mathcal{X}_{\text{CPRF}}$ to $\mathcal{B}$.
- $\mathcal{B}$ generates a master CPRF key $\text{SK}_{\text{CPRF}} \xleftarrow{\$} \text{CPRF.Setup}(1^\lambda)$. Next it selects a random bit $b \xleftarrow{\$} \{0,1\}$. If $b = 0$, it computes $y^* = \text{CPRF}(\text{SK}_{\text{CPRF}}, x^*)$. Otherwise, it chooses a random $y^* \xleftarrow{\$} \mathcal{Y}_{\text{CPRF}}$. It returns y^* to $\mathcal{A}$.
- $\mathcal{A}$ may adaptively make a polynomial number of queries of the following kinds to $\mathcal{B}$:
  - **Evaluation query:** $\mathcal{A}$ queries the CPRF value at some input $x \in \mathcal{X}_{\text{CPRF}}$ such that $x \neq x^*$. $\mathcal{B}$ provides the CPRF value $\text{CPRF}(\text{SK}_{\text{CPRF}}, x)$ to $\mathcal{A}$.
  - **Key query:** $\mathcal{A}$ queries a constrained key corresponding to TM $M \in \mathbb{M}_\lambda$ subject to the constraint that $M(x^*) = 0$. $\mathcal{B}$ gives the constrained key $\text{SK}_{\text{CPRF}}\{M\} \xleftarrow{\$} \text{CPRF.Constrain}(\text{SK}_{\text{CPRF}}, M)$ to $\mathcal{A}$
- $\mathcal{A}$ eventually outputs a guess bit $b' \in \{0,1\}$.

The CPRF is said to be selectively pseudorandom if for any PPT adversary $\mathcal{A}$, for any security parameter λ,

$$\text{Adv}_{\mathcal{A}}^{\text{CPRF,SEL-PR}}(\lambda) = |\Pr[b = b'] - 1/2| \leq \text{negl}(\lambda)$$

for some negligible function negl.

Remark 3.1. As pointed out in [9,16], note that in the above selective pseudorandomness experiment, without loss of generality we may assume that the adversary $\mathcal{A}$ only makes constrained key queries and no evaluation query. This is because any evaluation query at input $x \in \mathcal{X}_{\text{CPRF}}$ can be replaced by constrained key query for a TM $M_x \in \mathbb{M}_\lambda$ that accepts only x. Since, the restriction on the evaluation queries is that $x \neq x^*$, $M_x(x^*) = 0$, and thus M_x is a valid constrained key query. We will use this simplification in our proof.

3.2   The CPRF Construction of Deshpande et al.

In EUROCRYPT 2016, Deshpande et al. [10] presented a CPRF construction supporting inputs of unconstrained polynomial length based on indistinguishability obfuscation and injective pseudorandom generators, which they claimed to be selectively secure. Unfortunately, their security argument has a flaw. In this section, we give an informal description of their CPRF construction and point out the flaw in their security argument.

Overview of the CPRF Construction of [10]: The principle ideas behind the CPRF construction of [10] are as follows: To produce the CPRF output their construction uses a PPRF $\mathcal{F}$ and a positional accumulator. A master CPRF key consists of a key K for the PPRF $\mathcal{F}$ and a set of public parameters PP_{ACC} of the positional accumulator. The CPRF evaluation on some input $x = x_0 \ldots x_{\ell_x - 1} \in$

$\mathcal{X}_{\text{CPRF}} \subset \{0,1\}^*$ is simply $\mathcal{F}(K, w_{\text{INP}})$, where w_{INP} is the accumulation of the bits of x using PP_{ACC}.

A constrained key of the CPRF, corresponding to some TM M, comprises of PP_{ACC} along with two programs $\mathcal{P}_1$ and $\mathcal{P}_{\text{CPRF}}$, which are obfuscated using IO. The first program $\mathcal{P}_1$, also known as the *initial signing program*, takes as input an accumulator value and outputs a signature on it together with the initial state and header position of the TM M. The second program $\mathcal{P}_{\text{CPRF}}$, also called the *next step program*, takes as input a state and header position of M along with an input symbol and an accumulator value. It essentially computes the next step function of M on the input state-symbol pair, and eventually outputs the proper PRF value, if M reaches the accepting state. The program $\mathcal{P}_{\text{CPRF}}$ also performs certain authenticity checks before computing the next step function of M in order to prevent illegal inputs. For this purpose, $\mathcal{P}_{\text{CPRF}}$ additionally takes as input a signature on the input state, header position, and accumulator value, together with a proof for the positional accumulator. The program $\mathcal{P}_{\text{CPRF}}$ verifies the signature as well as checks the accumulator proof to get convinced that the input symbol is indeed the one placed at the input header position of the underlying storage of the input accumulator value. If all these verifications pass, then $\mathcal{P}_{\text{CPRF}}$ determines the next state and header position of M, as well as, the new symbol that needs to be written to the input header position. The program $\mathcal{P}_{\text{CPRF}}$ then updates the accumulator value by placing the new symbol at the input header position as well as signs the updated accumulator value along with the computed next state and header position of M. The signature scheme used by the two programs is a splittable signature. In order to deal with the positional accumulator related verifications and updations, the program $\mathcal{P}_{\text{CPRF}}$ has PP_{ACC} hardwired.

Evaluating the CPRF on some input x using a constrained key, corresponding to some TM M, consists of two steps. In the first step, the evaluator computes the accumulation w_{INP} of the bits of x using PP_{ACC}, which are also included in the constrained key, and then obtains a signature on w_{INP} together with the initial state and header position of M by running the program $\mathcal{P}_1$. The second step is to repeatedly run the program $\mathcal{P}_{\text{CPRF}}$, each time on input the current accumulator value, current state and header position of M, along with the signature on them. Additionally, in each iteration the evaluator also feeds w_{INP} to $\mathcal{P}_{\text{CPRF}}$. The iteration is continued until the program $\mathcal{P}_{\text{CPRF}}$ either outputs the PRF evaluation or the designated null string $\bot$ indicating failure.

The Flaw: In order to prove selective pseudorandomness of the above CPRF construction, the authors of [10] extends the techniques introduced in [20] in the context of proving security of message-hiding encoding scheme for TM's. More precisely, the authors of [10] proceed as follows: During the course of the proof, the authors aim to modify the constrained keys given to the adversary $\mathcal{A}$ in the selective pseudorandomness experiment, discussed in Sect. 3.1, to embed the punctured PPRF key $K\{w_{\text{INP}}^*\}$ punctured at w_{INP}^* instead of the full PPRF key K, which is part of the master CPRF key sampled by the challenger $\mathcal{B}$. Here, w_{INP}^* is the accumulation of the bits of the challenge input x^*, submitted by the adversary $\mathcal{A}$, using PP_{ACC}, included within the master CPRF key generated by the challenger $\mathcal{B}$. In order to make this substitution, it is to be ensured that the obfuscated next step programs included in the constrained keys never outputs the PRF evaluation for inputs corresponding to w_{INP}^* even if reaching the accepting state. The proof transforms the constrained keys one at a time through multiple hybrid steps. Suppose that the total number of constrained keys queried by $\mathcal{A}$ be $\hat{q}$. Consider the transformation of the νth constrained key $(1 \leq \nu \leq \hat{q})$ corresponding to the TM $M^{(\nu)}$ that runs on the challenge input x^* for $t^{*(\nu)}$ steps and reaches the rejecting state. In the course of transformation, the obfuscated next step program $\mathcal{P}_{\text{CPRF}}^{(\nu)}$ of the νth constrained key is first altered to one that never outputs the PRF evaluation for inputs corresponding to w_{INP}^* within the first $t^{*(\nu)}$ steps. Towards accomplishing this transition, the challenger $\mathcal{B}$ at various stages needs to generate PP_{ACC} in read/write enforcing mode where the enforcing property should be tailored to the steps of execution of the specific TM $M^{(\nu)}$ on x^*. For instance, at some point of transformation of the νth constrained key, PP_{ACC} needs to be set in the read enforcing mode by $\mathcal{B}$ on input (i) the entire sequence of symbol-position pairs arising from iteratively running $M^{(\nu)}$ on x^* upto the tth step and (ii) the enforcing index corresponding to the header position of $M^{(\nu)}$ at the tth step while running on x^*, where $1 < t \leq t^{*(\nu)}$. Evidently, if $\mathcal{A}$ makes the constrained key queries adaptively, which it is allowed to do in the selective pseudorandomness experiment, then $\mathcal{B}$ can determine those symbol-position pairs *only after receiving* the νth queried TM $M^{(\nu)}$ from $\mathcal{A}$. However, $\mathcal{B}$ would also require PP_{ACC} while creating the constrained keys queried by $\mathcal{A}$ before making the νth constrained key query and even possibly for preparing the challenge value for $\mathcal{A}$. Thus, it is immediate that $\mathcal{B}$ must generate PP_{ACC} *prior to receiving* the νth query from $\mathcal{A}$. This is *impossible* as setting PP_{ACC} in read enforcing mode requires the knowledge of the TM $M^{(\nu)}$, which is *not available* before the νth constrained key query of $\mathcal{A}$. A similar conflict also arises when $\mathcal{B}$ attempts to setup PP_{ACC} in the write enforcing mode tailored to $M^{(\nu)}$. This serious flaw renders the proof of selective pseudorandomness of the CPRF construction of [10] invalid. Ofcourse, this problem would clearly not arise if the pseudorandomness of the CPRF construction of [10] is analysed in a weaker model in which the adversary $\mathcal{A}$ is forced to submit all the constrained key queries along with the challenge input at the beginning of the experiment, i.e., before the challenger $\mathcal{B}$ performs the setup. However, this weaker model is rather unrealistic as it renders the adversary $\mathcal{A}$ completely static.

3.3   Our Techniques to Fix the Flaw of [10]

Observe that a set of public parameters of the positional accumulator must be included within each constrained key. This is mandatory due to the required updatability feature of positional accumulator, which is indispensable to keep track of the current situation while running the obfuscated next step program $\mathcal{P}_{\text{CPRF}}$ iteratively in the course of evaluating the CPRF on some input. The root cause of the problem in the selective security argument of [10] is the use of a single set of public parameters PP_{ACC} of the positional accumulator throughout the system. Therefore, as a first step, we attempt to assign a fresh set of public parameters of the positional accumulator to each constrained key. However, for compressing the PRF input to a fixed length, on which $\mathcal{F}$ can be applied producing the PRF output, we need a system-wide compressing tool. We employ SSB hash for this purpose. The idea is that while evaluating the CPRF on some input x using a constrained key, corresponding to some TM M, the evaluator first computes the hash value h by hashing x using the system wide SSB hash key, which is part of the master key. The evaluator also computes the accumulator value w_{INP} by accumulating the bits of x using the public parameters of positional accumulator included in the constrained key. Then, using the obfuscated initial signing program $\mathcal{P}_1$, included in the constrained key, the evaluator will obtain a signature on w_{INP} along with the initial state and header position of M. Finally, the evaluator will repeatedly run the obfuscated next step program $\mathcal{P}_{\text{CPRF}}$, included in the constrained key, each time giving as input all the quantities as in the evaluation algorithm of [10], except that it now feeds the SSB hash value h in place of w_{INP} in each iteration. This is because, in case $\mathcal{P}_{\text{CPRF}}$ reaches the accepting state, it would require h to apply $\mathcal{F}$ for producing the PRF output.

However, this approach is not completely sound yet. Observe that, a possibly malicious evaluator can compute the SSB hash value h on the input x, on which it wishes to evaluate the CPRF although M does not accepts it, and initiates the evaluation by accumulating the bits of only a substring of x or some entirely different input, which is accepted by M. To prevent such malicious behavior, we include another IO-obfuscated program $\mathcal{P}_2$ within the constrained key, known as the *accumulating program*, whose purpose is to *restrict* the evaluator from accumulating the bits of a different input rather than the hashed one. The program $\mathcal{P}_2$ takes as input an SSB hash value h, an index i, a symbol, an accumulator value, a signature on the input accumulator value (along with the initial state and header position of M), and an opening value for SSB. The program $\mathcal{P}_2$ verifies the signature and also checks whether the input symbol is indeed present at the index i of the string that has been hashed to form h, using the input opening value. If all of these verifications pass, then $\mathcal{P}_2$ updates the input accumulator value by writing the input symbol at the ith position of the accumulator storage. We also modify the obfuscated initial signing program $\mathcal{P}_1$, included in the constrained key, to take as input a hash value and output a signature on the accumulator value corresponding to the empty accumulator storage, along with the initial state and header position of M.

Moreover, for forbidding the evaluator from performing the evaluation by accumulating an M-accepted substring of the hashed input, we define our PRF output as the evaluation of $\mathcal{F}$ on the pair (hash value, length) of the input instead of just the hash value of the input. Note that, without loss of generality, we can set the upper bound of the length of PRF inputs to be 2^{λ}, where λ is the underlying security parameter in view of the fact that by suitably choosing λ we can accommodate inputs of any polynomial length. This setting of upper bound on the input length is implicitly considered in [10]. Now, as the input length is bounded by 2^{λ}, the input length can be expressed as a bit strings of length λ.

Thus, the PRF input length can be safely fed along with the SSB hash value of PRF input to $\mathcal{F}$, which can handle only inputs of apriori bounded length. Hence, the obfuscated next step programs $\mathcal{P}_{\mathrm{CPRF}}$ included in our constrained keys must also take as input the length of the PRF input for producing the PRF value if reaching to the accepting state.

Therefore, to evaluate the CPRF on some input using a constrained key, corresponding to some TM M, an evaluator first hash the PRF input. The evaluator also obtains a signature on the empty accumulator value included in the constrained key, by running the obfuscated initial signing program $\mathcal{P}_1$ on input the computed hash value. Next, it repeatedly runs the obfuscated accumulating program $\mathcal{P}_2$ to accumulate the bits of the PRF input. Finally, it runs the obfuscated next step program $\mathcal{P}_{\mathrm{CPRF}}$ iteratively on the current accumulator value along with other legitimate inputs until it obtains either the PRF output or $\perp$.

Regarding the proof of security, notice that the problem with enforcing the public parameters of the positional accumulator while transforming the queried constrained keys will not appear in our case as we have assigned a separate set of public parameters of positional accumulator to each constrained key. However, our actual security proof involves many subtleties that are difficult to describe with this high level description and is provided in full details in the sequel. We would only like to mention here that to cope up with certain issues in the proof we further include another IO-obfuscated program $\mathcal{P}_3$ in the constrained keys, known as the *signature changing program*, that changes the signature on the accumulation of the bits of the PRF input before starting the iterative computation with the obfuscated next step program $\mathcal{P}_{\mathrm{CPRF}}$.

We follow the same novel technique introduced in [10] for handling the tail hybrids in the final stage of transformation of the constrained keys. Note that as in [10], we are also considering TM's which run for at most $T = 2^{\lambda}$ steps on any input. Unlike [20], the authors of [10] have devised a beautiful approach to obtain an end to end polynomial reduction to the security of IO for the tail hybrids by means of an injective pseudorandom generator (PRG). We directly adopt that technique to deal with the tail hybrids in our security proof. A high level overview of the approach is sketched below. Let us call the time step 2^{τ} as the τth landmark and the interval $[2^{\tau}, 2^{\tau+1} - 1]$ as the τth interval. Like [10], our obfuscated next step programs $\mathcal{P}_{\mathrm{CPRF}}$ included within the constrained keys take an additional PRG seed as input at each time step, and perform some additional checks on the input PRG seed. At time steps just before a landmark, the programs output a new pseudorandomly generated PRG seed, which is then used in the next interval. Using standard IO techniques, it can be shown that for inputs corresponding to (h^*, ℓ^*), if the program $\mathcal{P}_{\mathrm{CPRF}}$ outputs $\perp$, for all time steps upto the one just before a landmark, then we can alter the program indistinguishably so that it outputs $\perp$ at all time steps in the next interval. Here h^* and ℓ^* are respectively the SSB hash value and length of the challenge input x^* submitted by the adversary $\mathcal{A}$ in the selective pseudorandomness experiment. Employing this technique, we can move across an exponential number of time steps at a single switch of the next step program $\mathcal{P}_{\mathrm{CPRF}}$.

3.4   Formal Description of Our CPRF

Now we will formally present our CPRF construction where the constrained keys are associated with TM's. Let λ be the underlying security parameter. Consider the family $\mathbb{M}_\lambda$ of TM's, the members of which have (worst-case) running time bounded by $T = 2^\lambda$, input alphabet $\Sigma_{\mathrm{INP}} = \{0,1\}$, and tape alphabet $\Sigma_{\mathrm{TAPE}} = \{0,1,\_\}$. Our CPRF construction utilizes the following cryptographic building blocks:

(i) $\mathcal{IO}$: An indistinguishability obfuscator for general polynomial-size circuits.
(ii) SSB $=$ (SSB.Gen, $\mathcal{H}$, SSB.Open, SSB.Verify): A somewhere statistically binding hash function with $\Sigma_{\mathrm{SSB\text{-}BLK}} = \{0,1\}$.
(iii) ACC $=$ (ACC.Setup, ACC.Setup-Enforce-Read, ACC.Setup-Enforce-Write, ACC.Prep-Read, ACC.Prep-Write, ACC.Verify-Read, ACC.Write-Store, ACC.Update): A positional accumulator with $\Sigma_{\mathrm{ACC\text{-}BLK}} = \{0,1,\_\}$.
(iv) ITR = (ITR.Setup, ITR.Setup-Enforce, ITR.Iterate): A cryptographic iterator with an appropriate message space $\mathcal{M}_{\mathrm{ITR}}$.
(v) SPS $=$ (SPS.Setup, SPS.Sign, SPS.Verify, SPS.Split, SPS.Sign-ABO): A splittable signature scheme with an appropriate message space $\mathcal{M}_{\mathrm{SPS}}$.
(vi) PRG : $\{0,1\}^\lambda \to \{0,1\}^{2\lambda}$: A length-doubling pseudorandom generator.
(vii) $\mathcal{F} = (\mathcal{F}.\mathsf{Setup}, \mathcal{F}.\mathsf{Puncture}, \mathcal{F}.\mathsf{Eval})$: A puncturable pseudorandom function whose domain and range are chosen appropriately. For simplicity, we assume that $\mathcal{F}$ has inputs and outputs of bounded length instead of fixed length inputs and outputs. This assumption can be easily removed by using different PPRF's for different input and output lengths.

Our CPRF construction is described below:

CPRF.Setup(1^λ) $\to$ $\mathrm{SK}_{\mathrm{CPRF}} = (K, \mathrm{HK})$: The setup authority takes as input the security parameter 1^λ and proceeds as follows:
1. It first chooses a PPRF key $K \xleftarrow{\$} \mathcal{F}.\mathsf{Setup}(1^\lambda)$.
2. Next it generates $\mathrm{HK} \xleftarrow{\$} \mathsf{SSB.Gen}(1^\lambda, n_{\mathrm{SSB\text{-}BLK}} = 2^\lambda, i^* = 0)$.
3. It sets the master CPRF key as $\mathrm{SK}_{\mathrm{CPRF}} = (K, \mathrm{HK})$.
CPRF.Eval($\mathrm{SK}_{\mathrm{CPRF}}, x$) $\to$ $y = \mathcal{F}(K, (h, \ell_x))$: Taking as input the master CPRF key $\mathrm{SK}_{\mathrm{CPRF}} = (K, \mathrm{HK})$ along with an input $x = x_0 \ldots x_{\ell_x-1} \in \mathcal{X}_{\mathrm{CPRF}}$, where $|x| = \ell_x$, the setup authority executes the following steps:
1. It computes $h = \mathcal{H}_{\mathrm{HK}}(x)$.
2. It outputs the CPRF value on input x to be $y = \mathcal{F}(K, (h, \ell_x))$.
CPRF.Constrain($\mathrm{SK}_{\mathrm{CPRF}}, M$) $\to$ $\mathrm{SK}_{\mathrm{CPRF}}\{M\} = (\mathrm{HK}, \mathrm{PP}_{\mathrm{ACC}}, w_0, \mathrm{STORE}_0, \mathrm{PP}_{\mathrm{ITR}}, v_0, \mathcal{P}_1, \mathcal{P}_2, \mathcal{P}_3, \mathcal{P}_{\mathrm{CPRF}})$: On input the master CPRF key $\mathrm{SK}_{\mathrm{CPRF}} = (K, \mathrm{HK})$ and a TM $M = \langle Q, \Sigma_{\mathrm{INP}}, \Sigma_{\mathrm{TAPE}}, \delta, q_0, q_{\mathrm{AC}}, q_{\mathrm{REJ}} \rangle \in \mathbb{M}_\lambda$, the setup authority performs the following steps:
1. At first, it selects PPRF keys $K_1, \ldots, K_\lambda, K_{\mathrm{SPS},A}, K_{\mathrm{SPS},E} \xleftarrow{\$} \mathcal{F}.\mathsf{Setup}(1^\lambda)$.
2. Next, it generates $(\mathrm{PP}_{\mathrm{ACC}}, w_0, \mathrm{STORE}_0) \xleftarrow{\$} \mathsf{ACC.Setup}(1^\lambda, n_{\mathrm{ACC\text{-}BLK}} = 2^\lambda)$ and $(\mathrm{PP}_{\mathrm{ITR}}, v_0) \xleftarrow{\$} \mathsf{ITR.Setup}(1^\lambda, n_{\mathrm{ITR}} = 2^\lambda)$.

3. Then, it constructs the following obfuscated programs:
   - $\mathcal{P}_1 = \mathcal{IO}(\text{Init-SPS.Prog}[q_0, w_0, v_0, K_{\text{SPS},E}])$,
   - $\mathcal{P}_2 = \mathcal{IO}(\text{Accumulate.Prog}[n_{\text{SSB-BLK}} = 2^\lambda, \text{HK}, \text{PP}_{\text{ACC}}, \text{PP}_{\text{ITR}}, K_{\text{SPS},E}])$,
   - $\mathcal{P}_3 = \mathcal{IO}(\text{Change-SPS.Prog}[K_{\text{SPS},A}, K_{\text{SPS},E}])$,
   - $\mathcal{P}_{\text{CPRF}} = \mathcal{IO}(\text{Constrained-Key.Prog}_{\text{CPRF}}[M, \ T = 2^\lambda, \ \text{PP}_{\text{ACC}}, \ \text{PP}_{\text{ITR}}, \ K,$
     $K_1, \ldots, K_\lambda, K_{\text{SPS},A}])$,

where the programs Init-SPS.Prog, Accumulate.Prog, Change-SPS.Prog, and Constrained-Key.Prog$_{\text{CPRF}}$ are depicted respectively in Figs. 1, 2, 3 and 4.

4. It Provides the constrained key $\text{SK}_{\text{CPRF}}\{M\} = (\text{HK}, \text{PP}_{\text{ACC}}, w_0, \text{STORE}_0,$
$\text{PP}_{\text{ITR}}, v_0, \mathcal{P}_1, \mathcal{P}_2, \mathcal{P}_3, \mathcal{P}_{\text{CPRF}}) \in \mathcal{K}_{\text{CPRF-CONST}}$ to a legitimate user.

CPRF.Eval-Constrained$(\text{SK}_{\text{CPRF}}\{M\}, x) \to y = \mathcal{F}(K, (h, \ell_x))$ or $\bot$: A user takes
as input its constrained key $\text{SK}_{\text{CPRF}}\{M\} = (\text{HK}, \text{PP}_{\text{ACC}}, w_0, \text{STORE}_0, \text{PP}_{\text{ITR}}, v_0,$

Constants: Initial TM state q_0, Accumulator value w_0, Iterator value v_0, PPRF key
$K_{\text{SPS},E}$

   Input: SSB hash value h

   Output: Signature $\sigma_{\text{SPS,OUT}}$

1. Compute $r_{\text{SPS},E} = \mathcal{F}(K_{\text{SPS},E}, (h, 0))$ and $(\text{SK}_{\text{SPS},E}, \text{VK}_{\text{SPS},E}, \text{VK}_{\text{SPS-REJ},E}) = \text{SPS.Setup}(1^\lambda; r_{\text{SPS},E})$.
2. Output $\sigma_{\text{SPS,OUT}} = \text{SPS.Sign}(\text{SK}_{\text{SPS},E}, (v_0, q_0, w_0, 0))$.

Fig. 1. Init-SPS.Prog

Constants: Maximum number of blocks for SSB hash $n_{\text{SSB-BLK}} = 2^\lambda$, SSB hash
key HK, Public parameters for positional accumulator PP$_{\text{ACC}}$, Public
parameters for iterator PP$_{\text{ITR}}$, PPRF key $K_{\text{SPS},E}$

   Inputs: Index i, Symbol SYM$_{\text{IN}}$, TM state ST, Accumulator value w_{IN}, Auxiliary
value AUX, Iterator value v_{IN}, Signature $\sigma_{\text{SPS,IN}}$, SSB hash value h, SSB
opening value π_{SSB}

   Output: (Accumulator value w_{OUT}, Iterator value v_{OUT}, Signature $\sigma_{\text{SPS-OUT}}$), or $\bot$

1.(a) Compute $r_{\text{SPS},E} = \mathcal{F}(K_{\text{SPS},E}, (h, i))$ and $(\text{SK}_{\text{SPS},E}, \text{VK}_{\text{SPS},E}, \text{VK}_{\text{SPS-REJ},E}) = \text{SPS.Setup}(1^\lambda; r_{\text{SPS},E})$.
  (b) Set $m_{\text{IN}} = (v_{\text{IN}}, \text{ST}, w_{\text{IN}}, 0)$. If $\text{SPS.Verify}(\text{VK}_{\text{SPS},E}, m_{\text{IN}}, \sigma_{\text{SPS,IN}}) = 0$, output $\bot$.
2. If $\text{SSB.Verify}(\text{HK}, h, i, \text{SYM}_{\text{IN}}, \pi_{\text{SSB}}) = 0$, output $\bot$.
3.(a) Compute $w_{\text{OUT}} = \text{ACC.Update}(\text{PP}_{\text{ACC}}, w_{\text{IN}}, \text{SYM}_{\text{IN}}, i, \text{AUX})$. If $w_{\text{OUT}} = \bot$, output $\bot$.
  (b) Compute $v_{\text{OUT}} = \text{ITR.Iterate}(\text{PP}_{\text{ITR}}, v_{\text{IN}}, (\text{ST}, w_{\text{IN}}, 0))$.
4.(a) Compute $r'_{\text{SPS},E} = \mathcal{F}(K_{\text{SPS},E}, (h, i + 1))$ and $(\text{SK}'_{\text{SPS},E}, \text{VK}'_{\text{SPS},E}, \text{VK}'_{\text{SPS-REJ},E}) = \text{SPS.Setup}(1^\lambda; r'_{\text{SPS},E})$.
  (b) Set $m_{\text{OUT}} = (v_{\text{OUT}}, \text{ST}, w_{\text{OUT}}, 0)$. Compute $\sigma_{\text{SPS,OUT}} = \text{SPS.Sign}(\text{SK}'_{\text{SPS},E}, m_{\text{OUT}})$.
5. Output $(w_{\text{OUT}}, v_{\text{OUT}}, \sigma_{\text{SPS,OUT}})$.

Fig. 2. Accumulate.Prog

Constants: PPRF keys $K_{\text{SPS},A}, K_{\text{SPS},E}$

   Inputs: TM state ST, Accumulator value w, Iterator value v, SSB hash value h, Length ℓ_{INP}, Signature $\sigma_{\text{SPS,IN}}$

   Output: Signature $\sigma_{\text{SPS,OUT}}$, or $\perp$

1.(a) Compute $r_{\text{SPS},E} = \mathcal{F}(K_{\text{SPS},E}, (h, \ell_{\text{INP}}))$ and $(\text{SK}_{\text{SPS},E}, \text{VK}_{\text{SPS},E}, \text{VK}_{\text{SPS-REJ},E}) = \text{SPS.Setup}(1^\lambda; r_{\text{SPS},E})$.

  (b) Set $m = (v, \text{ST}, w, 0)$. If $\text{SPS.Verify}(\text{VK}_{\text{SPS},E}, m, \sigma_{\text{SPS,IN}}) = 0$, output $\perp$.

2.(a) Compute $r_{\text{SPS},A} = \mathcal{F}(K_{\text{SPS},A}, (h, \ell_{\text{INP}}, 0))$ and $(\text{SK}_{\text{SPS},A}, \text{VK}_{\text{SPS},A}, \text{VK}_{\text{SPS-REJ},A}) = \text{SPS.Setup}(1^\lambda; r_{\text{SPS},A})$.

  (b) Output $\sigma_{\text{SPS,OUT}} = \text{SPS.Sign}(\text{SK}_{\text{SPS},A}, m)$.

Fig. 3. Change-SPS.Prog

Constants: TM $M = \langle Q, \Sigma_{\text{INP}}, \Sigma_{\text{TAPE}}, \delta, q_0, q_{\text{AC}}, q_{\text{REJ}} \rangle$, Time bound $T = 2^\lambda$, Public parameters for positional accumulator PP_{ACC}, Public parameters for iterator PP_{ITR}, PPRF keys $K, K_1, \ldots, K_\lambda, K_{\text{SPS},A}$

   Inputs: Time t, String SEED$_{\text{IN}}$, Header position POS$_{\text{IN}}$, Symbol SYM$_{\text{IN}}$, TM state ST$_{\text{IN}}$, Accumulator value w_{IN}, Accumulator proof π_{ACC}, Auxiliary value AUX, Iterator value v_{IN}, SSB hash value h, length ℓ_{INP}, Signature $\sigma_{\text{SPS,IN}}$

   Output: CPRF evaluation $\mathcal{F}(K, (h, \ell_{\text{INP}}))$, or Header Position (POS$_{\text{OUT}}$, Symbol SYM$_{\text{OUT}}$, TM state ST$_{\text{OUT}}$, Accumulator value w_{OUT}, Iterator value v_{OUT}, Signature $\sigma_{\text{SPS,OUT}}$, String SEED$_{\text{OUT}}$), or $\perp$

1. Identify an integer τ such that $2^\tau \leq t < 2^{\tau+1}$. If $[\text{PRG}(\text{SEED}_{\text{IN}}) \neq \text{PRG}(\mathcal{F}(K_\tau, (h, \ell_{\text{INP}})))] \wedge [t > 1]$, output $\perp$.

2. If $\text{ACC.Verify-Read}(\text{PP}_{\text{ACC}}, w_{\text{IN}}, \text{SYM}_{\text{IN}}, \text{POS}_{\text{IN}}, \pi_{\text{ACC}}) = 0$, output $\perp$.

3.(a) Compute $r_{\text{SPS},A} = \mathcal{F}(K_{\text{SPS},A}, (h, \ell_{\text{INP}}, t - 1))$ and $(\text{SK}_{\text{SPS},A}, \text{VK}_{\text{SPS},A}, \text{VK}_{\text{SPS-REJ},A}) = \text{SPS.Setup}(1^\lambda; r_{\text{SPS},A})$.

  (b) Set $m_{\text{IN}} = (v_{\text{IN}}, \text{ST}_{\text{IN}}, w_{\text{IN}}, \text{POS}_{\text{IN}})$. If $\text{SPS.Verify}(\text{VK}_{\text{SPS},A}, m_{\text{IN}}, \sigma_{\text{SPS,IN}}) = 0$, output $\perp$.

4.(a) Compute $(\text{ST}_{\text{OUT}}, \text{SYM}_{\text{OUT}}, \beta) = \delta(\text{ST}_{\text{IN}}, \text{SYM}_{\text{IN}})$ and $\text{POS}_{\text{OUT}} = \text{POS}_{\text{IN}} + \beta$.

  (b) If $\text{ST}_{\text{OUT}} = q_{\text{REJ}}$, output $\perp$.
     Else if $\text{ST}_{\text{OUT}} = q_{\text{AC}}$, output $\mathcal{F}(K, (h, \ell_{\text{INP}}))$.

5.(a) Compute $w_{\text{OUT}} = \text{ACC.Update}(\text{PP}_{\text{ACC}}, w_{\text{IN}}, \text{SYM}_{\text{OUT}}, \text{POS}_{\text{IN}}, \text{AUX})$. If $w_{\text{OUT}} = \perp$, output $\perp$.

  (b) Compute $v_{\text{OUT}} = \text{ITR.Iterate}(\text{PP}_{\text{ITR}}, v_{\text{IN}}, (\text{ST}_{\text{IN}}, w_{\text{IN}}, \text{POS}_{\text{IN}}))$.

6.(a) Compute $r'_{\text{SPS},A} = \mathcal{F}(K_{\text{SPS},A}, (h, \ell_{\text{INP}}, t))$ and $(\text{SK}'_{\text{SPS},A}, \text{VK}'_{\text{SPS},A}, \text{VK}'_{\text{SPS-REJ},A}) = \text{SPS.Setup}(1^\lambda; r'_{\text{SPS},A})$.

  (b) Set $m_{\text{OUT}} = (v_{\text{OUT}}, \text{ST}_{\text{OUT}}, w_{\text{OUT}}, \text{POS}_{\text{OUT}})$.
     Compute $\sigma_{\text{SPS,OUT}} = \text{SPS.Sign}(\text{SK}'_{\text{SPS},A}, m_{\text{OUT}})$.

7. If $t + 1 = 2^{\tau'}$, set $\text{SEED}_{\text{OUT}} = \mathcal{F}(K_{\tau'}, (h, \ell_{\text{INP}}))$.
  Else, set $\text{SEED}_{\text{OUT}} = \epsilon$.

8. Output $(\text{POS}_{\text{OUT}}, \text{SYM}_{\text{OUT}}, \text{ST}_{\text{OUT}}, w_{\text{OUT}}, v_{\text{OUT}}, \sigma_{\text{SPS,OUT}}, \text{SEED}_{\text{OUT}})$.

Fig. 4. Constrained-Key.Prog$_{\text{CPRF}}$

$\mathcal{P}_1, \mathcal{P}_2, \mathcal{P}_3, \mathcal{P}_{\mathrm{CPRF}}) \in \mathcal{K}_{\mathrm{CPRF\text{-}CONST}}$ corresponding to some legitimate TM $M = \langle Q, \Sigma_{\mathrm{INP}}, \Sigma_{\mathrm{TAPE}}, \delta, q_0, q_{\mathrm{AC}}, q_{\mathrm{REJ}} \rangle$ and an input $x = x_0 \ldots x_{\ell_x - 1} \in \mathcal{X}_{\mathrm{CPRF}}$ with $|x| = \ell_x$. It proceeds as follows:

1. It first computes $h = \mathcal{H}_{\mathrm{HK}}(x)$.
2. Next, it computes $\breve{\sigma}_{\mathrm{SPS},0} = \mathcal{P}_1(h)$.
3. Then for $j = 1, \ldots, \ell_x$, it iteratively performs the following:
   (a) It computes $\pi_{\mathrm{SSB},j-1} \xleftarrow{\$} \mathrm{SSB.Open}(\mathrm{HK}, x, j-1)$.
   (b) It computes $\mathrm{AUX}_j = \mathrm{ACC.Prep\text{-}Write}(\mathrm{PP}_{\mathrm{ACC}}, \mathrm{STORE}_{j-1}, j-1)$.
   (c) It computes $\mathrm{OUT} = \mathcal{P}_2(j-1, x_{j-1}, q_0, w_{j-1}, \mathrm{AUX}_j, v_{j-1}, \breve{\sigma}_{\mathrm{SPS},j-1}, h, \pi_{\mathrm{SSB},j-1})$.
   (d) If $\mathrm{OUT} = \bot$, it outputs OUT. Else, it parses OUT as $\mathrm{OUT} = (w_j, v_j, \breve{\sigma}_{\mathrm{SPS},j})$.
   (e) It computes $\mathrm{STORE}_j = \mathrm{ACC.Write\text{-}Store}(\mathrm{PP}_{\mathrm{ACC}}, \mathrm{STORE}_{j-1}, j-1, x_{j-1})$.
4. It computes $\sigma_{\mathrm{SPS},0} = \mathcal{P}_3(q_0, w_{\ell_x}, v_{\ell_x}, h, \ell_x, \breve{\sigma}_{\mathrm{SPS},\ell_x})$.
5. It sets $\mathrm{POS}_{M,0} = 0$ and $\mathrm{SEED}_0 = \epsilon$.
6. Suppose, M runs for t_x steps on input x. For $t = 1, \ldots, t_x$, it iteratively performs the following steps:
   (a) It computes $(\mathrm{SYM}_{M,t-1}, \pi_{\mathrm{ACC},t-1}) = \mathrm{ACC.Prep\text{-}Read}(\mathrm{PP}_{\mathrm{ACC}}, \mathrm{STORE}_{\ell_x + t - 1}, \mathrm{POS}_{M,t-1})$.
   (b) It computes $\mathrm{AUX}_{\ell_x + t} = \mathrm{ACC.Prep\text{-}Write}(\mathrm{PP}_{\mathrm{ACC}}, \mathrm{STORE}_{\ell_x + t - 1}, \mathrm{POS}_{M,t-1})$.
   (c) It computes $\mathrm{OUT} = \mathcal{P}_{\mathrm{CPRF}}(t, \mathrm{SEED}_{t-1}, \mathrm{POS}_{M,t-1}, \mathrm{SYM}_{M,t-1}, \mathrm{ST}_{M,t-1}, w_{\ell_x + t - 1}, \pi_{\mathrm{ACC},t-1}, \mathrm{AUX}_{\ell_x + t}, v_{\ell_x + t - 1}, h, \ell_x, \sigma_{\mathrm{SPS},t-1})$.
   (d) If $t = t_x$, it outputs OUT. Otherwise, it parses OUT as $\mathrm{OUT} = (\mathrm{POS}_{M,t}, \mathrm{SYM}_{M,t}^{(\mathrm{WRITE})}, \mathrm{ST}_{M,t}, w_{\ell_x + t}, v_{\ell_x + t}, \sigma_{\mathrm{SPS},t}, \mathrm{SEED}_t)$.
   (e) It computes $\mathrm{STORE}_{\ell_x + t} = \mathrm{ACC.Write\text{-}Store}(\mathrm{PP}_{\mathrm{ACC}}, \mathrm{STORE}_{\ell_x + t - 1}, \mathrm{POS}_{M,t-1}, \mathrm{SYM}_{M,t}^{(\mathrm{WRITE})})$.

Theorem 3.1. *Assuming $\mathcal{IO}$ is a secure indistinguishability obfuscator for P/poly, $\mathcal{F}$ is a secure puncturable pseudorandom function, SSB is a somewhere statistically binding hash function, ACC is a secure positional accumulator, ITR is a secure cryptographic iterator, SPS is a secure splittable signature scheme, and PRG is a secure injective pseudorandom generator, our CPRF construction satisfies correctness under constraining and selective pseudorandomness properties.*

The proof of Theorem 3.1 is provided in the full version of this paper.

Remark 3.2. We note that concurrently and independently of our work, Deshpande et al. [11] have recently provided an alternative fix to the flaw in [10] discussed in Sect. 3.2, by replacing the standard positional accumulators used in the CPRF construction of [10] with an advanced variant of positional accumulators, namely, history-less positional accumulators [3]. Unlike standard positional accumulators, in case of history-less positional accumulators, setting up the public parameters in read/write enforcing mode does not require any history of symbol-index pairs as input. Consequently, the problem in the simulation of [10] discussed in Sect. 3.2, resulting from the use of standard positional accumulators, would clearly not arise if history-less positional accumulators are utilized in the CPRF construction of [10] instead. However, we emphasize that our approach towards resolving the flaw of [10] brings about some new subtle technical ideas which might be useful elsewhere as well.

4   Our CVPRF for Turing Machines

4.1   Notion

Definition 4.1 (Constrained Verifiable Pseudorandom Function for Turing Machines: CVPRF). Let $\mathbb{M}_\lambda$ be a family of TM's with (worst-case) running time bounded by $T = 2^\lambda$. A constrained verifiable pseudorandom function (CVPRF) for $\mathbb{M}_\lambda$ with key space $\mathcal{K}_{\mathrm{CVPRF}}$, input domain $\mathcal{X}_{\mathrm{CVPRF}} \subset \{0,1\}^*$, and output space $\mathcal{Y}_{\mathrm{CVPRF}} \subset \{0,1\}^*$ consists of a constrained key space $\mathcal{K}_{\mathrm{CVPRF\text{-}CONST}}$, a proof space Π_{CVPRF}, along with PPT algorithms (CVPRF.Setup, CVPRF.Eval, CVPRF.Prove, CVPRF.Constrain, CVPRF.Prove-Constrained, CVPRF.Verify) which are described below:

CVPRF.Setup(1^λ) $\rightarrow$ ($\mathrm{SK}_{\mathrm{CVPRF}}, \mathrm{VK}_{\mathrm{CVPRF}}$) : The setup authority takes as input the security parameter 1^λ and generates a master CVPRF key $\mathrm{SK}_{\mathrm{CVPRF}}$ along with a public verification key $\mathrm{VK}_{\mathrm{CVPRF}}$.

CVPRF.Eval($\mathrm{SK}_{\mathrm{CVPRF}}, x$) $\rightarrow y$: Taking as input the master CVPRF key $\mathrm{SK}_{\mathrm{CVPRF}}$ and an input $x \in \mathcal{X}_{\mathrm{CVPRF}}$, the trusted authority outputs the value of the function $y \in \mathcal{Y}_{\mathrm{CVPRF}}$. For simplicity of notation, we will denote by $\mathrm{CVPRF}(\mathrm{SK}_{\mathrm{CVPRF}}, x)$ the output of this algorithm.

CVPRF.Prove($\mathrm{SK}_{\mathrm{CVPRF}}, x$) $\rightarrow \pi_{\mathrm{CVPRF}}$: Taking as input the master CVPRF key $\mathrm{SK}_{\mathrm{CVPRF}}$ and an input $x \in \mathcal{X}_{\mathrm{CVPRF}}$, the trusted authority outputs a proof $\pi_{\mathrm{CVPRF}} \in \Pi_{\mathrm{CVPRF}}$.

CVPRF.Constrain($\mathrm{SK}_{\mathrm{CVPRF}}, M$) $\rightarrow \mathrm{SK}_{\mathrm{CVPRF}}\{M\}$: On input the master CVPRF key $\mathrm{SK}_{\mathrm{CVPRF}}$ and a TM $M \in \mathbb{M}_\lambda$, the setup authority provides a constrained key $\mathrm{SK}_{\mathrm{CVPRF}}\{M\}$ to a legitimate user.

CVPRF.Prove-Constrained($\mathrm{SK}_{\mathrm{CVPRF}}\{M\}, x$) $\rightarrow (y, \pi_{\mathrm{CVPRF}})$ or $\bot$: A user takes as input its constrained key $\mathrm{SK}_{\mathrm{CVPRF}}\{M\}$ corresponding to a legitimate TM $M \in \mathbb{M}_\lambda$ and an input $x \in \mathcal{X}_{\mathrm{CVPRF}}$. It outputs either a value-proof pair $(y, \pi_{\mathrm{CVPRF}}) \in \mathcal{Y}_{\mathrm{CVPRF}} \times \Pi_{\mathrm{CVPRF}}$ or $(\bot, \bot)$ indicating failure.

CVPRF.Verify($\mathrm{VK}_{\mathrm{CVPRF}}, x, y, \pi_{\mathrm{CVPRF}}$) $\rightarrow \hat{\beta} \in \{0,1\}$: A verifier takes as input the public verification key $\mathrm{VK}_{\mathrm{CVPRF}}$, an input $x \in \mathcal{X}_{\mathrm{CVPRF}}$, a value $y \in \mathcal{Y}_{\mathrm{CVPRF}}$, together with a proof $\pi_{\mathrm{CVPRF}} \in \Pi_{\mathrm{CVPRF}}$. It outputs a bit $\hat{beta} \in \{0,1\}$.

The algorithms CVPRF.Setup, CVPRF.Prove, CVPRF.Constrain and CVPRF. Prove-Constrained are randomized, while the other two algorithms are deterministic.

▶ **Provability**: For any security parameter λ, $(\mathrm{SK}_{\mathrm{CVPRF}}, \mathrm{VK}_{\mathrm{CVPRF}}) \xleftarrow{\$} \mathrm{CVPRF}.$ Setup(1^λ), $M \in \mathbb{M}_\lambda$, $\mathrm{SK}_{\mathrm{CVPRF}}\{M\} \xleftarrow{\$} \mathrm{CVPRF}.\mathrm{Constrain}(\mathrm{SK}_{\mathrm{CVPRF}}, M)$, $x \in \mathcal{X}_{\mathrm{CVPRF}}$, and $(y, \pi_{\mathrm{CVPRF}}) \xleftarrow{\$} \mathrm{CVPRF}.\mathrm{Prove\text{-}Constrained}(\mathrm{SK}_{\mathrm{CVPRF}}\{M\}, x)$, the following holds:

- If $M(x) = 1$, then $y = \mathsf{CVPRF}(\mathsf{SK}_{\mathsf{CVPRF}}, x)$ and $\mathsf{CVPRF.Verify}(\mathsf{VK}_{\mathsf{CVPRF}}, x, y, \pi_{\mathsf{CVPRF}}) = 1$.
- If $M(x) = 0$, then $(y, \pi_{\mathsf{CVPRF}}) = (\perp, \perp)$.

The security requirements of a CVPRF are formally defined in the full version of this paper.

4.2   Techniques Adapted in Our CVPRF Construction

Let us now sketch our technical ideas to extend our CPRF construction to incorporate the verifiability feature. The additional tool that we use for this enhancement is a public key encryption (PKE) scheme which is perfectly correct and chosen plaintext attack (CPA) secure. Besides the PPRF key K, used to generate the PRF output, and the SSB hash key, we include within the master key another PPRF key K_{PKE} to generate randomness for the setup and encryption algorithms of PKE. As earlier, the PRF output on some input x is $\mathcal{F}(K, (h, \ell_x))$, where h and ℓ_x are respectively the SSB hash value and length of x. The non-interactive proof of correctness consists of a PKE public key $\mathsf{PK}_{\mathsf{PKE}}$ together with a pseudorandom string $r_{\mathsf{PKE},2}$. The randomness $r_{\mathsf{PKE},1}$ for setting up the PKE public key $\mathsf{PK}_{\mathsf{PKE}}$ along with the pseudorandom string $r_{\mathsf{PKE},2}$ are formed as $r_{\mathsf{PKE},1} \| r_{\mathsf{PKE},2} = \mathcal{F}(K_{\mathsf{PKE}}, (h, \ell_x))$.

The public verification key comprises of the same SSB hash key as included in the master PRF key, together with an IO-obfuscated program $\mathcal{V}_{\mathsf{CVPRF}}$, known as the *verifying program*. The verifying program $\mathcal{V}_{\mathsf{CVPRF}}$ has the PPRF keys K and K_{PKE} hardwired in it. It takes as input an SSB hash value h and PRF input length ℓ_{INP}. It first computes the concatenated pseudorandom strings $\hat{r}_{\mathsf{PKE},1} \| \hat{r}_{\mathsf{PKE},2} = \mathcal{F}(K_{\mathsf{PKE}}, (h, \ell_{\mathsf{INP}}))$. Next, it runs the PKE setup algorithm using the generated randomness $\hat{r}_{\mathsf{PKE},1}$ and creates a PKE public key $\widehat{\mathsf{PK}}_{\mathsf{PKE}}$. The program outputs $\widehat{\mathsf{PK}}_{\mathsf{PKE}}$ together with the ciphertext $\widehat{\mathsf{CT}}_{\mathsf{PKE}}$ encrypting the PRF value $\mathcal{F}(K, (h, \ell_{\mathsf{INP}}))$ under $\widehat{\mathsf{PK}}_{\mathsf{PKE}}$ utilizing the randomness $\hat{r}_{\mathsf{PKE},2}$.

To verify a purported PRF value-proof pair $(y, \pi_{\mathsf{CVPRF}} = (\mathsf{PK}_{\mathsf{PKE}}, r))$ for some input x using the public verification key, a verifier first hashes x using the SSB hash key and then obtains a PKE public key-ciphertext pair $(\widehat{\mathsf{PK}}_{\mathsf{PKE}}, \widehat{\mathsf{CT}}_{\mathsf{PKE}})$ by running the obfuscated verifying program $\mathcal{V}_{\mathsf{CVPRF}}$ on input the computed hash value and length of the input x. The verifier accepts the proof if $\widehat{\mathsf{PK}}_{\mathsf{PKE}}$ matches with $\mathsf{PK}_{\mathsf{PKE}}$, as well as $\widehat{\mathsf{CT}}_{\mathsf{PKE}}$ matches with the ciphertext formed by encrypting the purported PRF value y under $\mathsf{PK}_{\mathsf{PKE}}$ using the string r included within the proof. Observe that the soundness of verification follows directly from the perfect correctness property of the underlying PKE scheme. Specifically, due to the perfect correctness of PKE, it is guaranteed that two different values cannot map to the same ciphertext under the same public key.

Finally, to enable the generation of the proof along with the PRF value using a constrained key, we modify the obfuscated next step program, which we denote as $\mathcal{P}_{\mathsf{CVPRF}}$, included in the constrained key to output the proof together with the PRF value when it reaches the accepting state.

4.3   Formal Description of Our CVPRF

Here we will provide our CVPRF for TM's. This construction is obtained by extending our CPRF construction described in Sect. 3.4. Let λ be the underlying security parameter. Let $\mathbb{M}_\lambda$ be a class of TM's, the members of which have (worst-case) running time bounded by $T = 2^\lambda$, input alphabet $\Sigma_{\text{INP}} = \{0,1\}$, and tape alphabet $\Sigma_{\text{TAPE}} = \{0,1,\_\}$. Our CVPRF construction for TM family $\mathbb{M}_\lambda$ will employ all the building blocks utilized in our CPRF construction. Additionally, we will use a perfectly correct and chosen plaintext attack (CPA) secure public key encryption scheme PKE = (PKE.Setup, PKE.Encrypt, PKE.Decrypt) with an appropriate message space. The formal description of our CVPRF construction follows:

CVPRF.Setup(1^λ) $\rightarrow$ (SK$_{\text{CVPRF}}$ = $(K, K_{\text{PKE}}, \text{HK})$, VK$_{\text{CVPRF}}$ = (HK, $\mathcal{V}_{\text{CVPRF}}$)): The setup authority takes as input the security parameter 1^λ and proceeds as follows:
1. It first chooses PPRF keys $K, K_{\text{PKE}} \xleftarrow{\$} \mathcal{F}.\text{Setup}(1^\lambda)$.
2. Next it generates HK $\xleftarrow{\$}$ SSB.Gen($1^\lambda, n_{\text{SSB-BLK}} = 2^\lambda, i^* = 0$).
3. Then, it creates the obfuscated program $\mathcal{V}_{\text{CVPRF}} = \mathcal{IO}(\text{Verify.Prog}_{\text{CVPRF}}[K, K_{\text{PKE}}])$, where the program Verify.Prog$_{\text{CVPRF}}$ is described in Fig. 5.
4. It sets the master CVPRF key as SK$_{\text{CVPRF}}$ = $(K, K_{\text{PKE}}, \text{HK})$ and publishes the public verification key VK$_{\text{CVPRF}}$ = (HK, $\mathcal{V}_{\text{CVPRF}}$).

Constants: PPRF keys K, K_{PKE}
   Inputs: SSB hash value h, Length ℓ_{INP}
   Output: (PKE public key $\widehat{\text{PK}}_{\text{PKE}}$, Encryption of CVPRF value $\widehat{\text{CT}}_{\text{PKE}}$)

1. Compute $\hat{r}_{\text{PKE},1} \| \hat{r}_{\text{PKE},2} = \mathcal{F}(K_{\text{PKE}}, (h, \ell_{\text{INP}}))$, $(\widehat{\text{PK}}_{\text{PKE}}, \widehat{\text{SK}}_{\text{PKE}}) = \text{PKE.Setup}(1^\lambda; \hat{r}_{\text{PKE},1})$.
2. Compute $\widehat{\text{CT}}_{\text{PKE}} = \text{PKE.Encrypt}(\widehat{\text{PK}}_{\text{PKE}}, \mathcal{F}(K, (h, \ell_{\text{INP}})); \hat{r}_{\text{PKE},2})$.
3. Output $(\widehat{\text{PK}}_{\text{PKE}}, \widehat{\text{CT}}_{\text{PKE}})$.

Fig. 5. Verify.Prog$_{\text{CVPRF}}$

CVPRF.Eval(SK$_{\text{CVPRF}}, x$) $\rightarrow y = \mathcal{F}(K, (h, \ell_x))$: Taking as input the master CVPRF key SK$_{\text{CVPRF}}$ = $(K, K_{\text{PKE}}, \text{HK})$ along with an input $x = x_0 \ldots x_{\ell_x - 1} \in \mathcal{X}_{\text{CVPRF}}$, where $|x| = \ell_x$, the setup authority proceeds in an identical fashion to CPRF.Eval(SK$_{\text{CPRF}}, x$) described in Sect. 3.4.

CVPRF.Prove(SK$_{\text{CVPRF}}, x$) $\rightarrow \pi_{\text{CVPRF}}$ = (PK$_{\text{PKE}}, r_{\text{PKE},2}$): The setup authority takes as input the master CVPRF key SK$_{\text{CVPRF}}$ = $(K, K_{\text{PKE}}, \text{HK})$ along with an input $x = x_0 \ldots x_{\ell_x - 1} \in \mathcal{X}_{\text{CVPRF}}$, where $|x| = \ell_x$. It proceeds as follows:
1. At first, it computes $h = \mathcal{H}_{\text{HK}}(x)$.
2. Then, it computes $r_{\text{PKE},1} \| r_{\text{PKE},2} = \mathcal{F}(K_{\text{PKE}}, (h, \ell_x))$, (PK$_{\text{PKE}}$, SK$_{\text{PKE}}$) = PKE.Setup($1^\lambda; r_{\text{PKE},1}$).
3. It outputs π_{CVPRF} = (PK$_{\text{PKE}}, r_{\text{PKE},2}$).

Constants: PPRF key K_{PKE} along with everything hardwired within the program Constrained-Key.Prog$_{\text{CPRF}}$ (Fig. 3.4)

Inputs: Same as those to the program Constrained-Key.Prog$_{\text{CPRF}}$ (Fig. 3.4)

Output: (CVPRF evaluation $\mathcal{F}(K, (h, \ell_{\text{INP}}))$, CVPRF proof $\pi_{\text{CVPRF}} = (\text{PK}_{\text{PKE}}, r_{\text{PKE},2})$) or Header Position ($\text{POS}_{\text{OUT}}$, Symbol SYM_{OUT}, TM state ST_{OUT}, Accumulator value w_{OUT}, Iterator value v_{OUT}, Signature $\sigma_{\text{SPS,OUT}}$, String SEED_{OUT}), or $\perp$

The functionality of this program is exactly the same as that of the program Constrained-Key.Prog$_{\text{CPRF}}$ (Fig. 3.4) except that Step 4.(b) is replaced with the following:

4.(b) If $\text{ST}_{\text{OUT}} = q_{\text{REJ}}$, output $\perp$.
    Else if $\text{ST}_{\text{OUT}} = q_{\text{AC}}$, perform the following:
    (I) Compute $r_{\text{PKE},1} \| r_{\text{PKE},2} = \mathcal{F}(K_{\text{PKE}}(h, \ell_{\text{INP}}))$ and $(\text{PK}_{\text{PKE}}, \text{SK}_{\text{PKE}}) = \text{PKE.Setup}(1^\lambda; r_{\text{PKE},1})$.
    (II) Output $(\mathcal{F}(k, (h, \ell_{\text{INP}})), \pi_{\text{CVPRF}} = (\text{PK}_{\text{PKE}}, r_{\text{PKE},2}))$.

Fig. 6. Constrained-Key.Prog$_{\text{CVPRF}}$

CVPRF.Constrain$(\text{SK}_{\text{CVPRF}}, M) \rightarrow \text{SK}_{\text{CVPRF}}\{M\} = (\text{HK}, \text{PP}_{\text{ACC}}, w_0, \text{STORE}_0, \text{PP}_{\text{ITR}}, v_0, \mathcal{P}_1, \mathcal{P}_2, \mathcal{P}_3, \mathcal{P}_{\text{CVPRF}})$: On input the master CVPRF key $\text{SK}_{\text{CVPRF}} = (K, K_{\text{PKE}}, \text{HK})$ and a TM $M = \langle Q, \Sigma_{\text{INP}}, \Sigma_{\text{TAPE}}, \delta, q_0, q_{\text{AC}}, q_{\text{REJ}} \rangle \in \mathbb{M}_\lambda$, the setup authority proceeds identically to CPRF.Constrain$(\text{SK}_{\text{CPRF}}, M)$ with the only difference that in place of $\mathcal{P}_{\text{CPRF}}$ it includes $\mathcal{P}_{\text{CVPRF}} = \mathcal{IO}(\text{Constrained-Key.Prog}_{\text{CVPRF}}[M, T = 2^\lambda, \text{PP}_{\text{ACC}}, \text{PP}_{\text{ITR}}, K, K_{\text{PKE}}, K_1, \ldots, K_\lambda, K_{\text{SPS},A}])$ within the constrained key $\text{SK}_{\text{CVPRF}}\{M\}$, where the program Constrained-Key.Prog$_{\text{CVPRF}}$ is depicted in Fig. 6.

CVPRF.Prove-Constrained$(\text{SK}_{\text{CVPRF}}\{M\}, x) \rightarrow (y = \mathcal{F}(K, (h, \ell_x)), \pi_{\text{CVPRF}} = (\text{PK}_{\text{PKE}}, r_{\text{PKE},2}))$ or $\perp$: A user takes as input its constrained key $\text{SK}_{\text{CVPRF}}\{M\} = (\text{HK}, \text{PP}_{\text{ACC}}, w_0, \text{STORE}_0, \text{PP}_{\text{ITR}}, v_0, \mathcal{P}_1, \mathcal{P}_2, \mathcal{P}_3, \mathcal{P}_{\text{CVPRF}})$ corresponding to some legitimate TM $M = \langle Q, \Sigma_{\text{INP}}, \Sigma_{\text{TAPE}}, \delta, q_0, q_{\text{AC}}, q_{\text{REJ}} \rangle$ and an input $x = x_0 \ldots x_{\ell_x-1} \in \mathcal{X}_{\text{CVPRF}}$ with $|x| = \ell_x$. It proceeds in the exact same manner as the algorithm CPRF.Eval-Constrained$(\text{SK}_{\text{CPRF}}\{M\}, x)$ described in Sect. 3.4. However, note that now the constrained key $\text{SK}_{\text{CVPRF}}\{M\}$ of the user contains the obfuscated program $\mathcal{P}_{\text{CVPRF}}$ instead of $\mathcal{P}_{\text{CPRF}}$. Thus, it utilizes the program $\mathcal{P}_{\text{CVPRF}}$ in place of $\mathcal{P}_{\text{CPRF}}$ in the course of execution.

CVPRF.Verify$(\text{VK}_{\text{CVPRF}}, x, y, \pi_{\text{CVPRF}}) \rightarrow \hat{\beta} \in \{0, 1\}$: A verifier takes as input the public verification key $\text{VK}_{\text{CVPRF}} = (\text{HK}, \mathcal{V}_{\text{CVPRF}})$, an input $x = x_0 \ldots x_{\ell_x-1} \in \mathcal{X}_{\text{CVPRF}}$, where $|x| = \ell_x$, a value $y \in \mathcal{Y}_{\text{CVPRF}}$, and a proof $\pi_{\text{CVPRF}} = (\text{PK}_{\text{PKE}}, r) \in \Pi_{\text{CVPRF}}$. It executes the following:

1. It first computes $h = \mathcal{H}_{\text{HK}}(x)$.
2. Next, it computes $(\widehat{\text{PK}}_{\text{PKE}}, \widehat{\text{CT}}_{\text{PKE}}) = \mathcal{V}_{\text{CVPRF}}(h, \ell_x)$.
3. If $[\text{PK}_{\text{PKE}} = \widehat{\text{PK}}_{\text{PKE}}] \wedge [\text{PKE.Encrypt}(\text{PK}_{\text{PKE}}, y; r) = \widehat{\text{CT}}_{\text{PKE}}]$, it outputs 1. Otherwise, it outputs 0.

Theorem 4.1. *Assuming* $\mathcal{IO}$ *is a secure indistinguishability obfuscator for* P/poly, $\mathcal{F}$ *is a secure puncturable pseudorandom function,* SSB *is a somewhere statistically binding hash function,* ACC *is a secure positional accumulator,* ITR *is a secure cryptographic iterator,* SPS *is a secure splittable signature scheme,* PRG *is a secure injective pseudorandom generator, and* PKE *is a perfectly correct* CPA *secure public key encryption scheme, our* CVPRF *construction satisfies all the properties of a secure* CVPRF.

The proof of Theorem 4.1 is given in the full version of this paper.

5 Our **DCPRF** for Turing Machines

5.1 Notion

Definition 5.1. (Delegatable Constrained Pseudorandom Function for Turing Machines: DCPRF). Let $\mathbb{M}_\lambda$ be a family of TM's with (worst-case) running time bounded by $T = 2^\lambda$. A delegatable constrained pseudorandom function (DCPRF) with key space $\mathcal{K}_{\text{DCPRF}}$, input domain $\mathcal{X}_{\text{DCPRF}} \subset \{0,1\}^*$, and output space $\mathcal{Y}_{\text{DCPRF}} \subset \{0,1\}^*$ for the TM family $\mathbb{M}_\lambda$ consists of an additional key space $\mathcal{K}_{\text{DCPRF-CONST}}$ and PPT algorithms (DCPRF.Setup, DCPRF.Eval, DCPRF.Constrain, DCPRF.Delegate, DCPRF.Eval-Constrained) described as follows:

DCPRF.Setup$(1^\lambda) \to \text{SK}_{\text{DCPRF}}$: The setup authority takes as input the security parameter 1^λ and generates the master DCPRF key $\text{SK}_{\text{DCPRF}} \in \mathcal{K}_{\text{DCPRF}}$.

DCPRF.Eval$(\text{SK}_{\text{DCPRF}}, x) \to y$: On input the master DCPRF key SK_{DCPRF} along with an input $x \in \mathcal{X}_{\text{DCPRF}}$, the setup authority computes the value of the DCPRF $y \in \mathcal{Y}_{\text{DCPRF}}$. For simplicity of notation, we will use DCPRF$(\text{SK}_{\text{DCPRF}}, x)$ to indicate the output of this algorithm.

DCPRF.Constrain$(\text{SK}_{\text{DCPRF}}, M) \to \text{SK}_{\text{DCPRF}}\{M\}$: Taking as input the master DCPRF key $\text{SK}_{\text{DCPRF}} \in \mathcal{K}_{\text{DCPRF}}$ and a TM $M \in \mathbb{M}_\lambda$, the setup authority provides a constrained key $\text{SK}_{\text{DCPRF}}\{M\} \in \mathcal{K}_{\text{DCPRF-CONST}}$ to a legitimate user.

DCPRF.Delegate$(\text{SK}_{\text{DCPRF}}\{M\}, \widetilde{M}) \to \text{SK}_{\text{DCPRF}}\{M \wedge \widetilde{M}\}$: Taking as input a constrained key $\text{SK}_{\text{DCPRF}}\{M\} \in \mathcal{K}_{\text{DCPRF-CONST}}$ corresponding to a legitimate TM $M \in \mathbb{M}_\lambda$ along with another TM $\widetilde{M} \in \mathbb{M}_\lambda$, a user gives a delegated constrained key $\text{SK}_{\text{DCPRF}}\{M \wedge \widetilde{M}\} \in \mathcal{K}_{\text{DCPRF-CONST}}$ to a legitimate delegate.

DCPRF.Eval-Constrained$(\text{SK}_{\text{DCPRF}}\{M\}/\text{SK}_{\text{DCPRF}}\{M \wedge \widetilde{M}\}, x) \to y$ or $\perp$: A user takes as input a constrained key $\text{SK}_{\text{DCPRF}}\{M\} \in \mathcal{K}_{\text{DCPRF-CONST}}$ obtained from the setup authority, corresponding to TM $M \in \mathbb{M}_\lambda$, or a delegated constrained key $\text{SK}_{\text{DCPRF}}\{M \wedge \widetilde{M}\} \in \mathcal{K}_{\text{DCPRF-CONST}}$ delegated by a constrained key holder holding the constrained key $\text{SK}_{\text{DCPRF}}\{M\} \in \mathcal{K}_{\text{DCPRF-CONST}}$, corresponding to TM $\widetilde{M} \in \mathbb{M}_\lambda$, along with an input $x \in \mathcal{X}_{\text{DCPRF}}$. It outputs either a value $y \in \mathcal{Y}_{\text{DCPRF}}$ or $\perp$ indicating failure.

The algorithms DCPRF.Eval and DCPRF.Eval-Constrained are deterministic, while, all the others are randomized.

▶ **Correctness under Constraining/Delegation**: Let us consider any security parameter λ, $x \in \mathcal{X}_{\mathrm{DCPRF}}$, $\mathrm{SK}_{\mathrm{DCPRF}} \xleftarrow{\$} \mathrm{DCPRF.Setup}(1^{\lambda})$, $M, \widetilde{M} \in \mathbb{M}_{\lambda}$, $\mathrm{SK}_{\mathrm{DCPRF}}\{M\} \xleftarrow{\$} \mathrm{DCPRF.Constrain}(\mathrm{SK}_{\mathrm{DCPRF}}, M)$ and $\mathrm{SK}_{\mathrm{DCPRF}}\{M \wedge \widetilde{M}\} \xleftarrow{\$} \mathrm{DCPRF.Delegate}(\mathrm{SK}_{\mathrm{DCPRF}}\{M\}, \widetilde{M})$. The following must hold:

$$\mathrm{DCPRF.Eval\text{-}Constrained}(\mathrm{SK}_{\mathrm{DCPRF}}\{M\}/\mathrm{SK}_{\mathrm{DCPRF}}\{M \wedge \widetilde{M}\}, x) =$$
$$\begin{cases} \mathrm{DCPRF}(\mathrm{SK}_{\mathrm{DCPRF}}, x), & \text{if } M(x) = 1/[M(x) = 1] \wedge [\widetilde{M}(x) = 1] \\ \bot, & \text{otherwise} \end{cases}$$

The security notion of a DCPRF, namely, the pseudorandomness property is formally defined in the full version of this paper.

5.2 Techniques Adapted in Our DCPRF Construction

Here again our starting point is our CPRF construction. We again use a perfectly correct and CPA secure PKE scheme for accomplishing key delegation. Precisely, while generating a constrained key corresponding to some TM M, we create a PPRF key K' specific to that constrained key. We then modify the output of the next step program, which we refer to as $\mathcal{P}_{\mathrm{DCPRF}}$, when it reaches the accepting state. In stead of outputting the PRF value, the program $\mathcal{P}_{\mathrm{DCPRF}}$ outputs an encryption of the PRF value. For performing this encryption it generates a PKE public key $\mathrm{PK}_{\mathrm{PKE}}$. The program computes the randomness $r_{\mathrm{PKE},1}$ for generating the PKE public key $\mathrm{PK}_{\mathrm{PKE}}$ as well as the randomness $r_{\mathrm{PKE},2}$ for the encryption as $r_{\mathrm{PKE},1} \| r_{\mathrm{PKE},2} = \mathcal{F}(K', (h, \ell_{\mathrm{INP}}))$, where h and ℓ_{INP} denote respectively the SSB hash value and length of the PRF input. We also include the PPRF key K' in the clear within the constrained key. Thus, while evaluating the PRF on some input using the constrained key, the evaluator will be able to recompute the pseudorandom string $r_{\mathrm{PKE},1}$ using K' and then can generate the necessary PKE secret key $\mathrm{SK}_{\mathrm{PKE}}$ by running the setup algorithm using the randomness $r_{\mathrm{PKE},1}$ on its own. Once the secret key $\mathrm{SK}_{\mathrm{PKE}}$ is obtained, the evaluator can simply decrypt the ciphertext obtained from the next step program $\mathcal{P}_{\mathrm{DCPRF}}$ to uncover the PRF value. However, if a party does not have the key K' or the randomness that would have to be used for creating the required PKE secret key, then it cannot derive the PRF value from the ciphertext obtained from the next step program $\mathcal{P}_{\mathrm{DCPRF}}$. We encash this idea to design the key delegation functionality.

The structure of our delegated key is as follows: Suppose a party holding a constrained key, corresponding to some TM M, wishes to construct a delegated key for $M \wedge \widetilde{M}$, where $\widetilde{M}$ is some other TM. The party generates all the components and obfuscated programs as those formed while constructing a constrained key for $\widetilde{M}$ with the only exception that it embeds the PPRF key K', included in its constrained key, inside the obfuscated next step program for $\widetilde{M}$ in place of the PPRF key K, which is part of the master PRF key and provides the PRF output. In fact, since the party only has a constrained key and not the master key, it does not possess the key K in the clear and hence cannot embed it within the obfuscated programs that it generates. The delegated key, corresponding to $M \wedge \widetilde{M}$ consists of all the generated components and obfuscated programs for $\widetilde{M}$ together with all the components and obfuscated programs included in the constrained key for M possessed by the delegator except the PPRF key K'.

The idea is that, while evaluating the PRF on some input x using the delegated key for $M \wedge \widetilde{M}$, the evaluator proceeds in three steps. In the first step, provided $\widetilde{M}(x) = 1$, the evaluator computes the output of $\mathcal{F}$ with key K' on the SSB hash value and length of x by making use of the delegated key components pertaining to $\widetilde{M}$. Next, using the obtained PPRF output, the evaluator runs the PKE setup algorithm to obtain the necessary PKE secret key. In the second step, utilizing the delegated key components associated to M, the evaluator obtains a ciphertext encrypting the PRF output on x, provided $M(x) = 1$. Finally, the evaluator decrypts the ciphertext using the computed PKE secret key to reveal the PRF output.

5.3   Formal Description of Our DCPRF

In this section, we will present our DCPRF for TM's. The construction presented here considers only one level of delegation, however, it can readily be generalized to support multiple delegation levels. Let λ be the underlying security parameter. Consider the class $\mathbb{M}_\lambda$ of TM's, the members of which have (worst-case) running time bounded by $T = 2^\lambda$, input alphabet $\Sigma_{\text{INP}} = \{0, 1\}$, and tape alphabet $\Sigma_{\text{TAPE}} = \{0, 1, \_\}$. Our DCPRF construction is an augmentation of our CPRF construction with a delegation functionality and employs all the cryptographic building blocks utilized by our CPRF construction. In addition, we use a perfectly correct and CPA secure public key encryption scheme PKE = (PKE.Setup, PKE.Encrypt, PKE.Decrypt) with an appropriate message space. The formal description of our DCPRF follows:

DCPRF.Setup(1^λ) $\rightarrow$ $\text{SK}_{\text{DCPRF}} = (K, \text{HK})$: The setup authority takes as input the security parameter 1^λ and proceeds the same way as CPRF.Setup(1^λ) described in Sect. 3.4.

DCPRF.Eval($\text{SK}_{\text{DCPRF}}, x$) $\rightarrow$ $y = \mathcal{F}(K, (h, \ell_x))$: Taking as input the master DCPRF key $\text{SK}_{\text{DCPRF}} = (K, \text{HK})$ and an input $x = x_0 \ldots x_{\ell_x - 1} \in \mathcal{X}_{\text{DCPRF}}$, where $|x| = \ell_x$, the setup authority executes identical steps as CPRF.Eval($\text{SK}_{\text{CPRF}}, x$) described in Sect. 3.4.

DCPRF.Constrain($\text{SK}_{\text{DCPRF}}, M$) $\rightarrow$ $\text{SK}_{\text{DCPRF}}\{M\} = (K', \text{HK}, \text{PP}_{\text{ACC}}, w_0, \text{STORE}_0,$ $\text{PP}_{\text{ITR}}, v_0, \mathcal{P}_1, \mathcal{P}_2, \mathcal{P}_3, \mathcal{P}_{\text{DCPRF}})$: On input the master DCPRF key $\text{SK}_{\text{DCPRF}} = (K, \text{HK})$ and a TM $M = \langle Q, \Sigma_{\text{INP}}, \Sigma_{\text{TAPE}}, \delta, q_0, q_{\text{AC}}, q_{\text{REJ}} \rangle \in \mathbb{M}_\lambda$, the setup authority performs the following steps:

1. At first, it selects PPRF keys $K', K_1, \ldots, K_\lambda, K_{\text{SPS},A}, K_{\text{SPS},E} \xleftarrow{\$} \mathcal{F}.\text{Setup}(1^\lambda)$.

2. Next, it generates $(\text{PP}_{\text{ACC}}, w_0, \text{STORE}_0) \xleftarrow{\$} \text{ACC.Setup}(1^\lambda, n_{\text{ACC-BLK}} = 2^\lambda)$ and $(\text{PP}_{\text{ITR}}, v_0) \xleftarrow{\$} \text{ITR.Setup}(1^\lambda, n_{\text{ITR}} = 2^\lambda)$.

3. Then, it constructs the obfuscated programs

Constants: PPRF key K' along with everything hardwired within the program Constrained-Key.Prog$_{\text{CPRF}}$ (Fig. 3.4)

    Inputs: Same as those to the program Constrained-Key.Prog$_{\text{CPRF}}$ (Fig. 3.4)

   Output: Encryption of DCPRF value CT$_{\text{PKE}}$, or Header Position (POS$_{\text{OUT}}$, Symbol SYM$_{\text{OUT}}$, TM state ST$_{\text{OUT}}$, Accumulator value w_{OUT}, Iterator value v_{OUT}, Signature $\sigma_{\text{SPS,OUT}}$, String SEED$_{\text{OUT}}$), or $\perp$

This program functions in the same fashion as the program Constrained-Key.Prog$_{\text{CPRF}}$ (Fig. 3.4) except that Step 4.(b) is replaced with the following:

4.(b) If ST$_{\text{OUT}} = q_{\text{REJ}}$, output $\perp$.
     Else if ST$_{\text{OUT}} = q_{\text{AC}}$, perform the following steps:
      (I) Compute $r_{\text{PKE},1} \| r_{\text{PKE},2} = \mathcal{F}(K', (h, \ell_{\text{INP}}))$ and $(\text{PK}_{\text{PKE}}, \text{SK}_{\text{PKE}}) = \text{PKE.Setup}(1^\lambda; r_{\text{PKE},1})$.
      (II) Output CT$_{\text{PKE}} = \text{PKE.Encrypt}(\text{PK}_{\text{PKE}}, \mathcal{F}(K, (h, \ell_{\text{INP}})); r_{\text{PKE},2})$.

Fig. 7. Constrained-Key.Prog$_{\text{DCPRF}}$

- $\mathcal{P}_1 = \mathcal{IO}(\text{Init-SPS.Prog}[q_0, w_0, v_0, K_{\text{SPS},E}])$,
- $\mathcal{P}_2 = \mathcal{IO}(\text{Accumulate.Prog}[n_{\text{SSB-BLK}} = 2^\lambda, \text{HK}, \text{PP}_{\text{ACC}}, \text{PP}_{\text{ITR}}, K_{\text{SPS},E}])$,
- $\mathcal{P}_3 = \mathcal{IO}(\text{Change-SPS.Prog}[K_{\text{SPS},A}, K_{\text{SPS},E}])$,
- $\mathcal{P}_{\text{DCPRF}} = \mathcal{IO}(\text{Constrained-Key.Prog}_{\text{DCPRF}}[M, T = 2^\lambda, \text{PP}_{\text{ACC}}, \text{PP}_{\text{ITR}}, K, K',$
   $K_1, \ldots, K_\lambda, K_{\text{SPS},A}])$,

where the programs Init-SPS.Prog, Accumulate.Prog, and Change-SPS.Prog are depicted respectively in Figs. 1, 2 and 3 in Sect. 3.4, while the program Constrained-Key.Prog$_{\text{DCPRF}}$ is described in Fig. 7.
4. It provides the constrained key SK$_{\text{DCPRF}}\{M\} = (K', \text{HK}, \text{PP}_{\text{ACC}}, w_0, \text{STORE}_0,$ $\text{PP}_{\text{ITR}}, v_0, \mathcal{P}_1, \mathcal{P}_2, \mathcal{P}_3, \mathcal{P}_{\text{DCPRF}})$ to a legitimate user.

DCPRF.Delegate(SK$_{\text{DCPRF}}\{M\}, \widetilde{M}) \rightarrow \text{SK}_{\text{DCPRF}}\{M \wedge \widetilde{M}\} = (\widetilde{K}', \text{HK}, \text{PP}_{\text{ACC}}, \widetilde{\text{PP}}_{\text{ACC}},$ $w_0, \widetilde{w}_0, \text{STORE}_0, \widetilde{\text{STORE}}_0, \text{PP}_{\text{ITR}}, \widetilde{\text{PP}}_{\text{ITR}}, v_0, \widetilde{v}_0, \mathcal{P}_1, \widetilde{\mathcal{P}}_1, \mathcal{P}_2, \widetilde{\mathcal{P}}_2, \mathcal{P}_3, \widetilde{\mathcal{P}}_3,$ $\mathcal{P}_{\text{DCPRF}}, \widetilde{\mathcal{P}}_{\text{DCPRF}})$: A user takes as input a constrained key SK$_{\text{DCPRF}}\{M\} = (K',$ $\text{HK}, \text{PP}_{\text{ACC}}, w_0, \text{STORE}_0, \text{PP}_{\text{ITR}}, v_0, \mathcal{P}_1, \mathcal{P}_2, \mathcal{P}_3, \mathcal{P}_{\text{DCPRF}})$, corresponding to a legitimate TM $M \in \mathbb{M}_\lambda$ and another TM $\widetilde{M} = \langle \widetilde{Q}, \Sigma_{\text{INP}}, \Sigma_{\text{TAPE}}, \widetilde{\delta}, \widetilde{q}_0, \widetilde{q}_{\text{AC}}, \widetilde{q}_{\text{REJ}} \rangle \in \mathbb{M}_\lambda$. It proceeds as follows:

1. It first picks fresh PPRF keys $\widetilde{K}', \widetilde{K}_1, \ldots, \widetilde{K}_\lambda, \widetilde{K}_{\text{SPS},A}, \widetilde{K}_{\text{SPS},E} \xleftarrow{\$} \mathcal{F}.\text{Setup}(1^\lambda)$.

2. Next it generates $(\widetilde{\text{PP}}_{\text{ACC}}, \widetilde{w}_0, \widetilde{\text{STORE}}_0) \xleftarrow{\$} \text{ACC.Setup}(1^\lambda, n_{\text{ACC-BLK}} = 2^\lambda)$ and $(\widetilde{\text{PP}}_{\text{ITR}}, \widetilde{v}_0) \xleftarrow{\$} \text{ITR.Setup}(1^\lambda, n_{\text{ITR}} = 2^\lambda)$ afresh.

3. Then, it constructs the obfuscated programs
   - $\widetilde{\mathcal{P}}_1 = \mathcal{IO}(\text{Init-SPS.Prog}[\widetilde{q}_0, \widetilde{w}_0, \widetilde{v}_0, \widetilde{K}_{\text{SPS},E}])$,
   - $\widetilde{\mathcal{P}}_2 = \mathcal{IO}(\text{Accumulate.Prog}[n_{\text{SSB-BLK}} = 2^\lambda, \text{HK}, \widetilde{\text{PP}}_{\text{ACC}}, \widetilde{\text{PP}}_{\text{ITR}}, \widetilde{K}_{\text{SPS},E}])$,
   - $\widetilde{\mathcal{P}}_3 = \mathcal{IO}(\text{Change-SPS.Prog}[\widetilde{K}_{\text{SPS},A}, \widetilde{K}_{\text{SPS},E}])$,

- $\widetilde{\mathcal{P}}_{\mathrm{DCPRF}} = \mathcal{IO}(\text{Constrained-Key.Prog}_{\mathrm{DCPRF}}[\widetilde{M}, T = 2^{\lambda}, \widetilde{\mathrm{PP}}_{\mathrm{ACC}}, \widetilde{\mathrm{PP}}_{\mathrm{ITR}}, K',$
  $\widetilde{K}', \widetilde{K}_1, \ldots, \widetilde{K}_{\lambda}, \widetilde{K}_{\mathrm{SPS}, A}]),$

where the programs Init-SPS.Prog, Accumulate.Prog, and Change-SPS.Prog are depicted respectively in Figs. 1, 2 and 3 in Sect. 3.4, while the program Constrained-Key.Prog$_{\mathrm{DCPRF}}$ is described in Fig. 7.

4. It gives the delegated key $\mathrm{SK}_{\mathrm{DCPRF}}\{M \wedge \widetilde{M}\} = (\widetilde{K}', \mathrm{HK}, \mathrm{PP}_{\mathrm{ACC}}, \widetilde{\mathrm{PP}}_{\mathrm{ACC}},$
   $w_0, \widetilde{w}_0, \mathrm{STORE}_0, \widetilde{\mathrm{STORE}}_0, \mathrm{PP}_{\mathrm{ITR}}, \widetilde{\mathrm{PP}}_{\mathrm{ITR}}, v_0, \widetilde{v}_0, \mathcal{P}_1, \widetilde{\mathcal{P}}_1, \mathcal{P}_2, \widetilde{\mathcal{P}}_2, \mathcal{P}_3, \widetilde{\mathcal{P}}_3, \mathcal{P}_{\mathrm{DCPRF}},$
   $\widetilde{\mathcal{P}}_{\mathrm{DCPRF}})$ to a legitimate delegate.

DCPRF.Eval-Constrained($\mathrm{SK}_{\mathrm{DCPRF}}\{M\}/\mathrm{SK}_{\mathrm{DCPRF}}\{M \wedge \widetilde{M}\}, x) \to y = \mathcal{F}(K, (h,$
$\ell_x))$ or $\perp$: A user takes as input a constrained key $\mathrm{SK}_{\mathrm{DCPRF}}\{M\}$
$= (K', \mathrm{HK}, \mathrm{PP}_{\mathrm{ACC}}, w_0, \mathrm{STORE}_0, \mathrm{PP}_{\mathrm{ITR}}, v_0, \mathcal{P}_1, \mathcal{P}_2, \mathcal{P}_3, \mathcal{P}_{\mathrm{DCPRF}})$ obtained from the setup authority, corresponding to some legitimate TM $M = \langle Q, \Sigma_{\mathrm{INP}}, \Sigma_{\mathrm{TAPE}},$
$\delta, q_0, q_{\mathrm{AC}}, q_{\mathrm{REJ}} \rangle \in \mathbb{M}_{\lambda}$, or a delegated key $\mathrm{SK}_{\mathrm{DCPRF}}\{M \wedge \widetilde{M}\} = (\widetilde{K}', \mathrm{HK},$
$\mathrm{PP}_{\mathrm{ACC}}, \widetilde{\mathrm{PP}}_{\mathrm{ACC}}, w_0, \widetilde{w}_0, \mathrm{STORE}_0, \widetilde{\mathrm{STORE}}_0, \mathrm{PP}_{\mathrm{ITR}}, \widetilde{\mathrm{PP}}_{\mathrm{ITR}}, v_0, \widetilde{v}_0, \mathcal{P}_1, \widetilde{\mathcal{P}}_1, \mathcal{P}_2, \widetilde{\mathcal{P}}_2, \mathcal{P}_3,$
$\widetilde{\mathcal{P}}_3, \mathcal{P}_{\mathrm{DCPRF}}, \widetilde{\mathcal{P}}_{\mathrm{DCPRF}})$ obtained from the holder of the constrained key
$\mathrm{SK}_{\mathrm{DCPRF}}\{M\}$, corresponding to TM $\widetilde{M} = \langle \widetilde{Q}, \Sigma_{\mathrm{INP}}, \Sigma_{\mathrm{TAPE}}, \widetilde{\delta}, \widetilde{q}_0, \widetilde{q}_{\mathrm{AC}}, \widetilde{q}_{\mathrm{REJ}} \rangle \in \mathbb{M}_{\lambda}$,
along with an input $x = x_0 \ldots x_{\ell_x - 1} \in \mathcal{X}_{\mathrm{DCPRF}}$ with $|x| = \ell_x$. It proceeds as follows:

(A) If $M(x) = 0$, it outputs $\perp$. Otherwise, it performs the following steps:
   1. It first computes $h = \mathcal{H}_{\mathrm{HK}}(x)$.
   2. Next, it computes $\breve{\sigma}_{\mathrm{SPS},0} = \mathcal{P}_1(h)$.
   3. Then for $j = 1, \ldots, \ell_x$, it iteratively performs the following:
      (a) It computes $\pi_{\mathrm{SSB}, j-1} \xleftarrow{\$} \mathrm{SSB.Open}(\mathrm{HK}, x, j - 1)$.
      (b) It computes $\mathrm{AUX}_j = \mathrm{ACC.Prep\text{-}Write}(\mathrm{PP}_{\mathrm{ACC}}, \mathrm{STORE}_{j-1}, j - 1)$.
      (c) It computes $\mathrm{OUT} = \mathcal{P}_2(j - 1, x_{j-1}, q_0, w_{j-1}, \mathrm{AUX}_j, v_{j-1}, \breve{\sigma}_{\mathrm{SPS}, j-1}, h,$
          $\pi_{\mathrm{SSB}, j-1})$.
      (d) If $\mathrm{OUT} = \perp$, it outputs OUT. Else, it parses OUT as $\mathrm{OUT} = (w_j, v_j,$
          $\breve{\sigma}_{\mathrm{SPS}, j})$.
      (e) It computes $\mathrm{STORE}_j = \mathrm{ACC.Write\text{-}Store}(\mathrm{PP}_{\mathrm{ACC}}, \mathrm{STORE}_{j-1}, j - 1,$
          $x_{j-1})$.
   4. It computes $\sigma_{\mathrm{SPS},0} = \mathcal{P}_3(q_0, w_{\ell_x}, v_{\ell_x}, h, \ell_x, \breve{\sigma}_{\mathrm{SPS}, \ell_x})$.
   5. It sets $\mathrm{POS}_{M,0} = 0$ and $\mathrm{SEED}_0 = \epsilon$.
   6. Suppose, M accepts x in t_x steps. For $t = 1, \ldots, t_x$, it iteratively performs the following steps:
      (a) It computes $(\mathrm{SYM}_{M,t-1}, \pi_{\mathrm{ACC},t-1}) = \mathrm{ACC.Prep\text{-}Read}(\mathrm{PP}_{\mathrm{ACC}},$
          $\mathrm{STORE}_{\ell_x + t - 1}, \mathrm{POS}_{M, t-1})$.
      (b) It computes $\mathrm{AUX}_{\ell_x + t} = \mathrm{ACC.Prep\text{-}Write}(\mathrm{PP}_{\mathrm{ACC}}, \mathrm{STORE}_{\ell_x + t - 1},$
          $\mathrm{POS}_{M, t-1})$.
      (c) It computes $\mathrm{OUT} = \mathcal{P}_{\mathrm{DCPRF}}(t, \mathrm{SEED}_{t-1}, \mathrm{POS}_{M, t-1}, \mathrm{SYM}_{M, t-1},$
          $\mathrm{ST}_{M, t-1}, w_{\ell_x + t - 1}, \pi_{\mathrm{ACC}, t-1}, \mathrm{AUX}_{\ell_x + t}, v_{\ell_x + t - 1}, h, \ell_x, \sigma_{\mathrm{SPS}, t-1})$.
      (d) If $t = t_x$, it sets $\mathrm{CT}_{\mathrm{PKE}} = \mathrm{OUT}$. Otherwise, it parses OUT as $\mathrm{OUT} = (\mathrm{POS}_{M,t}, \mathrm{SYM}_{M,t}^{(\mathrm{WRITE})}, \mathrm{ST}_{M,t}, w_{\ell_x + t}, v_{\ell_x + t}, \sigma_{\mathrm{SPS}, t}, \mathrm{SEED}_t)$.
      (e) It computes $\mathrm{STORE}_{\ell_x + t} = \mathrm{ACC.Write\text{-}Store}(\mathrm{PP}_{\mathrm{ACC}}, \mathrm{STORE}_{\ell_x + t - 1},$
          $\mathrm{POS}_{M, t-1}, \mathrm{SYM}_{M,t}^{(\mathrm{WRITE})})$.

(B) If the user is using the constrained key $\text{SK}_{\text{DCPRF}}\{M\}$, then it computes $r_{\text{PKE},1}\|r_{\text{PKE},2} = \mathcal{F}(K',(h,\ell_x))$, $(\text{PK}_{\text{PKE}},\text{SK}_{\text{PKE}}) = \text{PKE.Setup}(1^\lambda;\ r_{\text{PKE},1})$, and outputs $\text{PKE.Decrypt}(\text{SK}_{\text{PKE}},\text{CT}_{\text{PKE}})$. On the other hand, if the user is using the delegated key $\text{SK}_{\text{DCPRF}}\{M \wedge \widetilde{M}\}$ and $\widetilde{M}(x) = 0$, then it outputs $\bot$, while if $\widetilde{M}(x) = 1$, it further executes the following steps:

1. It computes $\widetilde{\check{\sigma}}_{\text{SPS},0} = \widetilde{\mathcal{P}}_1(h)$.
2. Then for $j = 1,\ldots,\ell_x$, it iteratively performs the following:
    (a) It computes $\widetilde{\pi}_{\text{SSB},j-1} \xleftarrow{\$} \text{SSB.Open}(\text{HK},x,j-1)$.
    (b) It computes $\widetilde{\text{AUX}}_j = \text{ACC.Prep-Write}(\widetilde{\text{PP}}_{\text{ACC}},\widetilde{\text{STORE}}_{j-1},j-1)$.
    (c) It computes $\widetilde{\text{OUT}} = \widetilde{\mathcal{P}}_2(j-1,x_{j-1},\widetilde{q}_0,\widetilde{w}_{j-1},\widetilde{\text{AUX}}_j,\widetilde{v}_{j-1},\widetilde{\check{\sigma}}_{\text{SPS},j-1},h,$ $\widetilde{\pi}_{\text{SSB},j-1})$.
    (d) If $\widetilde{\text{OUT}} = \bot$, it outputs $\widetilde{\text{OUT}}$. Else, it parses $\widetilde{\text{OUT}}$ as $\widetilde{\text{OUT}} = (\widetilde{w}_j,\widetilde{v}_j,$ $\widetilde{\check{\sigma}}_{\text{SPS},j})$.
    (e) It computes $\widetilde{\text{STORE}}_j = \text{ACC.Write-Store}(\widetilde{\text{PP}}_{\text{ACC}},\widetilde{\text{STORE}}_{j-1},j-1,$ $x_{j-1})$.
3. It computes $\widetilde{\sigma}_{\text{SPS},0} = \widetilde{\mathcal{P}}_3(\widetilde{q}_0,\widetilde{w}_{\ell_x},\widetilde{v}_{\ell_x},h,\ell_x,\widetilde{\check{\sigma}}_{\text{SPS},\ell_x})$.
4. It sets $\text{POS}_{\widetilde{M},0} = 0$ and $\widetilde{\text{SEED}}_0 = \epsilon$.
5. Suppose, $\widetilde{M}$ accepts x in $\widetilde{t}_x$ steps. For $t = 1,\ldots,\widetilde{t}_x$, it iteratively performs the following steps:
    (a) It computes $(\text{SYM}_{\widetilde{M},t-1},\widetilde{\pi}_{\text{ACC},t-1}) = \text{ACC.Prep-Read}(\widetilde{\text{PP}}_{\text{ACC}},$ $\widetilde{\text{STORE}}_{\ell_x+t-1},\text{POS}_{\widetilde{M},t-1})$.
    (b) It computes $\widetilde{\text{AUX}}_{\ell_x+t} = \text{ACC.Prep-Write}(\widetilde{\text{PP}}_{\text{ACC}},\widetilde{\text{STORE}}_{\ell_x+t-1},$ $\text{POS}_{\widetilde{M},t-1})$.
    (c) It computes $\widetilde{\text{OUT}} = \widetilde{\mathcal{P}}_{\text{DCPRF}}(t,\widetilde{\text{SEED}}_{t-1},\text{POS}_{\widetilde{M},t-1},\text{SYM}_{\widetilde{M},t-1},$ $\text{ST}_{\widetilde{M},t-1},\widetilde{w}_{\ell_x+t-1},\widetilde{\pi}_{\text{ACC},t-1},\widetilde{\text{AUX}}_{\ell_x+t},\widetilde{v}_{\ell_x+t-1},h,\ell_x,\widetilde{\sigma}_{\text{SPS},t-1})$.
    (d) If $t = \widetilde{t}_x$, it sets $\widetilde{\text{CT}}_{\text{PKE}} = \widetilde{\text{OUT}}$. Otherwise, it parses $\widetilde{\text{OUT}}$ as $\widetilde{\text{OUT}} = (\text{POS}_{\widetilde{M},t},\text{SYM}_{\widetilde{M},t}^{(\text{WRITE})},\text{ST}_{\widetilde{M},t},\widetilde{w}_{\ell_x+t},\widetilde{v}_{\ell_x+t},\widetilde{\sigma}_{\text{SPS},t},\widetilde{\text{SEED}}_t)$.
    (e) It computes $\widetilde{\text{STORE}}_{\ell_x+t} = \text{ACC.Write-Store}(\widetilde{\text{PP}}_{\text{ACC}},\widetilde{\text{STORE}}_{\ell_x+t-1},$ $\text{POS}_{\widetilde{M},t-1},\text{SYM}_{\widetilde{M},t}^{(\text{WRITE})})$.

(C) Finally, it computes
 - $\widetilde{r}_{\text{PKE},1}\|\widetilde{r}_{\text{PKE},2} = \mathcal{F}(\widetilde{K}',(h,\ell_x))$,
 - $(\widetilde{\text{PK}}_{\text{PKE}},\widetilde{\text{SK}}_{\text{PKE}}) = \text{PKE.Setup}(1^\lambda;\ \widetilde{r}_{\text{PKE},1})$,
 - $r_{\text{PKE},1}\|r_{\text{PKE},2} = \text{PKE.Decrypt}(\widetilde{\text{SK}}_{\text{PKE}},\widetilde{\text{CT}}_{\text{PKE}})$,
 - $(\text{PK}_{\text{PKE}},\text{SK}_{\text{PKE}}) = \text{PKE.Setup}(1^\lambda;\ r_{\text{PKE},1})$,

and outputs $\text{PKE.Decrypt}(\text{SK}_{\text{PKE}},\text{CT}_{\text{PKE}})$.

Theorem 5.1. *Assuming $\mathcal{IO}$ is a secure indistinguishability obfuscator for P/poly, $\mathcal{F}$ is a secure puncturable pseudorandom function, SSB is a somewhere statistically binding hash function, ACC is a secure positional accumulator, ITR is a secure cryptographic iterator, SPS is a secure splittable signature scheme, PRG is a secure injective pseudorandom generator, and PKE is CPA secure, our DCPRF construction satisfies the correctness and selective pseudorandomness properties.*

The proof of Theorem 5.1 is given in the full version of this paper.

References

1. Abusalah, H., Fuchsbauer, G.: Constrained PRFs for unbounded inputs with short keys. In: Manulis, M., Sadeghi, A.-R., Schneider, S. (eds.) ACNS 2016. LNCS, vol. 9696, pp. 445–463. Springer, Heidelberg (2016). doi:10.1007/978-3-319-39555-5_24
2. Abusalah, H., Fuchsbauer, G., Pietrzak, K.: Constrained PRFs for unbounded inputs. In: Sako, K. (ed.) CT-RSA 2016. LNCS, vol. 9610, pp. 413–428. Springer, Heidelberg (2016). doi:10.1007/978-3-319-29485-8_24
3. Ananth, P., Chen, Y.-C., Chung, K.-M., Lin, H., Lin, W.-K.: Delegating RAM computations with adaptive soundness and privacy. In: Hirt, M., Smith, A. (eds.) TCC 2016. LNCS, vol. 9986, pp. 3–30. Springer, Heidelberg (2016). doi:10.1007/978-3-662-53644-5_1
4. Banerjee, A., Fuchsbauer, G., Peikert, C., Pietrzak, K., Stevens, S.: Key-homomorphic constrained pseudorandom functions. In: Dodis, Y., Nielsen, J.B. (eds.) TCC 2015. LNCS, vol. 9015, pp. 31–60. Springer, Heidelberg (2015). doi:10.1007/978-3-662-46497-7_2
5. Bellare, M., Fuchsbauer, G.: Policy-based signatures. In: Krawczyk, H. (ed.) PKC 2014. LNCS, vol. 8383, pp. 520–537. Springer, Heidelberg (2014). doi:10.1007/978-3-642-54631-0_30
6. Boneh, D., Waters, B.: Constrained pseudorandom functions and their applications. In: Sako, K., Sarkar, P. (eds.) ASIACRYPT 2013. LNCS, vol. 8270, pp. 280–300. Springer, Heidelberg (2013). doi:10.1007/978-3-642-42045-0_15
7. Boyle, E., Goldwasser, S., Ivan, I.: Functional signatures and pseudorandom functions. In: Krawczyk, H. (ed.) PKC 2014. LNCS, vol. 8383, pp. 501–519. Springer, Heidelberg (2014). doi:10.1007/978-3-642-54631-0_29
8. Brakerski, Z., Vaikuntanathan, V.: Constrained key-homomorphic PRFs from standard lattice assumptions. In: Dodis, Y., Nielsen, J.B. (eds.) TCC 2015. LNCS, vol. 9015, pp. 1–30. Springer, Heidelberg (2015). doi:10.1007/978-3-662-46497-7_1
9. Chandran, N., Raghuraman, S., Vinayagamurthy, D.: Constrained pseudorandom functions: verifiable and delegatable. Cryptology ePrint Archive, Report 2014/522 (2014)
10. Deshpande, A., Koppula, V., Waters, B.: Constrained pseudorandom functions for unconstrained inputs. In: Fischlin, M., Coron, J.-S. (eds.) EUROCRYPT 2016. LNCS, vol. 9666, pp. 124–153. Springer, Heidelberg (2016). doi:10.1007/978-3-662-49896-5_5
11. Deshpande, A., Koppula, V., Waters, B.: Constrained pseudorandom functions for unconstrained inputs. Cryptology ePrint Archive, Report 2016/301, Version 20160819:153952 (2016)
12. Fuchsbauer, G.: Constrained verifiable random functions. In: Abdalla, M., Prisco, R. (eds.) SCN 2014. LNCS, vol. 8642, pp. 95–114. Springer, Heidelberg (2014). doi:10.1007/978-3-319-10879-7_7
13. Fuchsbauer, G., Konstantinov, M., Pietrzak, K., Rao, V.: Adaptive security of constrained PRFs. In: Sarkar, P., Iwata, T. (eds.) ASIACRYPT 2014. LNCS, vol. 8874, pp. 82–101. Springer, Heidelberg (2014). doi:10.1007/978-3-662-45608-8_5
14. Garg, S., Gentry, C., Halevi, S., Raykova, M., Sahai, A., Waters, B.: Candidate indistinguishability obfuscation and functional encryption for all circuits. In: 2013 IEEE 54th Annual Symposium on Foundations of Computer Science (FOCS), pp. 40–49. IEEE (2013)

15. Goldreich, O., Goldwasser, S., Micali, S.: How to construct random functions. J. ACM (JACM) **33**(4), 792–807 (1986)
16. Hofheinz, D., Kamath, A., Koppula, V., Waters, B.: Adaptively secure constrained pseudorandom functions. Cryptology ePrint Archive, Report 2014/720 (2014)
17. Hohenberger, S., Koppula, V., Waters, B.: Adaptively secure puncturable pseudorandom functions in the standard model. In: Iwata, T., Cheon, J.H. (eds.) ASIACRYPT 2015. LNCS, vol. 9452, pp. 79–102. Springer, Heidelberg (2015). doi:10.1007/978-3-662-48797-6_4
18. Hubacek, P., Wichs, D.: On the communication complexity of secure function evaluation with long output. In: The 2015 Conference on Innovations in Theoretical Computer Science, pp. 163–172. ACM (2015)
19. Kiayias, A., Papadopoulos, S., Triandopoulos, N., Zacharias, T.: Delegatable pseudorandom functions and applications. In: The 2013 ACM SIGSAC Conference on Computer Communications Security, pp. 669–684. ACM (2013)
20. Koppula, V., Lewko, A.B., Waters, B.: Indistinguishability obfuscation for turing machines with unbounded memory. In: The 47th Annual ACM on Symposium on Theory of Computing, pp. 419–428. ACM (2015)
21. Micali, S., Rabin, M., Vadhan, S.: Verifiable random functions. In: 40th Annual Symposium on Foundations of Computer Science, pp. 120–130. IEEE (1999)
22. Okamoto, T., Pietrzak, K., Waters, B., Wichs, D.: New realizations of somewhere statistically binding hashing and positional accumulators. In: Iwata, T., Cheon, J.H. (eds.) ASIACRYPT 2015. LNCS, vol. 9452, pp. 121–145. Springer, Heidelberg (2015). doi:10.1007/978-3-662-48797-6_6
23. Sahai, A., Waters, B.: How to use indistinguishability obfuscation: deniable encryption, and more. In: The 46th Annual ACM Symposium on Theory of Computing, pp. 475–484. ACM (2014)

Constraining Pseudorandom Functions Privately

Dan Boneh, Kevin Lewi, and David J. Wu[✉]

Stanford University, Stanford, USA
{dabo,klewi,dwu4}@cs.stanford.edu

Abstract. In a constrained pseudorandom function (PRF), the master secret key can be used to derive constrained keys, where each constrained key k is constrained with respect to some Boolean circuit C. A constrained key k can be used to evaluate the PRF on all inputs x for which $C(x) = 1$. In almost all existing constrained PRF constructions, the constrained key k reveals its constraint C.

In this paper we introduce the concept of *private* constrained PRFs, which are constrained PRFs with the additional property that a constrained key does not reveal its constraint. Our main notion of privacy captures the intuition that an adversary, given a constrained key k for one of two circuits C_0 and C_1, is unable to tell which circuit is associated with the key k. We show that constrained PRFs have natural applications to searchable symmetric encryption, cryptographic watermarking, and much more.

To construct private constrained PRFs we first demonstrate that our strongest notions of privacy and functionality can be achieved using indistinguishability obfuscation. Then, for our main constructions, we build private constrained PRFs for bit-fixing constraints and for puncturing constraints from concrete algebraic assumptions.

1 Introduction

A pseudorandom function (PRF) [41] is a (keyed) function $F : \mathcal{K} \times \mathcal{X} \to \mathcal{Y}$ with the property that, for a randomly chosen key $\mathsf{msk} \in \mathcal{K}$, the outputs of $F(\mathsf{msk}, \cdot)$ look indistinguishable from the outputs of a truly random function from $\mathcal{X}$ to $\mathcal{Y}$. Constrained PRFs[1], proposed independently by Boneh and Waters [12], Boyle et al. [16], and Kiayias et al. [47], behave just like standard PRFs, except that the holder of the (master) secret key $\mathsf{msk} \in \mathcal{K}$ for the PRF is also able to produce a constrained key sk_C for a Boolean circuit C. This constrained key sk_C can be used to evaluate the PRF $F(\mathsf{msk}, \cdot)$ on all inputs $x \in \mathcal{X}$ where $C(x) = 1$, but sk_C reveals nothing about $F(\mathsf{msk}, x)$ when $C(x) = 0$. Constrained PRFs have found many applications, for example, in broadcast encryption [12] and in the "punctured programming" techniques of Sahai and Waters [54].

The Goldreich-Goldwasser-Micali (GGM) PRF [41] is a *puncturable* PRF, that is, a constrained PRF for the special class of puncturing constraints. In a

---

The full version of this paper is available at http://eprint.iacr.org/2015/1167.pdf.

[1] They have also been called *functional* PRFs [16] and *delegatable* PRFs [47].

© International Association for Cryptologic Research 2017
S. Fehr (Ed.): PKC 2017, Part II, LNCS 10175, pp. 494–524, 2017.
DOI: 10.1007/978-3-662-54388-7_17

puncturable PRF, each constrained key k is associated with an input $x_0 \in \mathcal{X}$, and the constrained key enables the evaluation at all points $x \neq x_0$ while revealing no information about $F(\mathsf{msk}, x_0)$. It is not difficult to see that the constrained key k completely reveals the point x_0.

Boneh and Waters [12] show how to use multilinear maps [28, 29, 33, 36] to construct constrained PRFs for more expressive classes of constraints, including bit-fixing constraints as well as general circuit constraints (of a priori bounded depth). Subsequent works in this area have focused on achieving adaptive notions of security [43, 44], developing schemes with additional properties such as verifiability [19], and constructing (single-key) circuit-constrained PRFs from standard lattice-based assumptions [17].

Constraining Privately. In this work, we initiate the study of *private* constrained PRFs, which are a natural extension of constrained PRFs with the additional property that the constrained keys should not reveal their constraints.

Our definition of privacy requires that an adversary, given a single constrained key sk for one of two possible circuits C_0 and C_1, cannot tell which circuit was used as the constraint for sk. We also generalize this definition to the setting where the adversary obtains multiple constrained keys. Since the adversary can compare the outputs from multiple constrained keys, some information is necessarily leaked about the underlying constraints. In this setting, our privacy property ensures that the adversary learns the minimum possible. We formally define our privacy notion in Sect. 2.

For the special case of a puncturable PRF (where the adversary only has access to a single constrained key), the privacy requirement is that for any two adversarially-chosen points $x_0, x_1 \in \mathcal{X}$, the adversary cannot distinguish a secret key punctured at x_0 from one punctured at x_1. In particular, this means that using a secret key punctured at the input x to evaluate the PRF on x must return a value that is *unpredictable* to the adversary, as opposed to a fixed constant value or $\perp$ as is done in existing (non-private) constrained PRF constructions.

While privacy is a very simple requirement to impose on constrained PRFs, it is not clear how to adapt existing schemes to satisfy this property, even just for puncturing. As a first attempt to constructing private puncturable PRFs, let the PRF input space $\mathcal{X}$ be $\{0, 1\}^n$, and consider the GGM tree-based PRF [41], where the outputs are computed as the leaf nodes of a binary tree with the PRF secret key occupying the root node. To puncture the GGM PRF at an input x, the puncturing algorithm reveals the secret keys of all internal nodes that are adjacent[2] to the path from the root to the leaf node corresponding with x. Certainly then, the GGM construction is not private—given the punctured key, an adversary can easily reconstruct the path from the root to the punctured leaf node, and hence, recover the input x.

However, the GGM PRF is a private constrained PRF for the class of length-ℓ prefix constraints, for an integer $\ell \leq n$. This class refers to the family of constraints described by a prefix $s \in \{0, 1\}^\ell$, where an input satisfies the constraint

---

[2] Here, an internal node is "adjacent" to a path if it does not lie on the path but its parent does.

if its first ℓ bits match s. To constrain the GGM PRF on a prefix s, the constrain algorithm reveals the secret key for the internal node associated with s in the GGM tree. Then, to evaluate an input x using the constrained key, the evaluator discards the first ℓ bits of x and, beginning with the node associated with the constrained key, uses the remaining bits of x to traverse down the GGM tree, outputting the value associated with the resulting leaf node. Privacy follows from the fact that, without the original root of the GGM tree, the secret key for the internal node for s appears to be distributed uniformly and independently of s.

While the GGM PRF provides an efficient solution to privately constraining PRFs under fixed-length prefix constraints, this is insufficient for the applications we have in mind. Instead, we construct private constrained PRFs for more general classes of constraints: puncturing and general circuit constraints.

1.1   Applications of Private Constrained PRFs

To illustrate the power of private constrained PRFs we first describe a few natural applications, including private constrained MACs, watermarkable PRFs, and searchable encryption. In Sect. 6.2, we also describe an application to symmetric deniable encryption.

Private Constrained MACs. Constrained MACs are the secret-key variant of constrained signatures, which were first introduced by Boyle et al. [16]. In a constrained MAC, the holder of the master secret key can issue constrained secret keys to users. Given a constrained key, a user can only generate MACs for messages that conform to some pre-specified constraint. Here, we consider private constrained MACs, where the constraint is also hidden from the user. Just as a secure PRF implies a secure MAC, a private constrained PRF yields a private constrained MAC.

As a concrete example, suppose a company would like to enforce spending limits on its employees. For business reasons, they do not want employees to be able to learn their precise spending limit, which might reveal confidential information about their position and rank within the company. For example, an employee Alice might only be allowed to create spending requests for at most $500. In this case, Alice's company could issue a constrained key to Alice that restricts her to only being able to compute MACs for messages which contain her name and whose spending requests do not exceed $500. If Alice attempts to create a MAC for a spending request that either exceeds $500 or is not bound to her name, then the computed MAC will not pass verification. Moreover, privacy of the constrained key ensures that Alice cannot tell if the MAC she constructed is valid or not with respect to the master verification key. Hence, without interacting with the verifier, Alice learns nothing about her exact spending limit. A key advantage in this scenario is that the verifier, who is issued a constrained key[3] from the offline key distributor, is able to verify Alice's requests without knowing or learning anything about her spending limits.

---

[3] The verifier's constrained key is chosen so that the constraint is always satisfied. Note that this is not the same as giving out the master verification key, which may allow the verifier to learn Alice's spending limits.

Watermarking PRFs. A watermarking scheme for programs [5,24,25,45,51] consists of a marking algorithm, which takes as input a program and embeds a "mark" in it, and a verification algorithm that takes an arbitrary program and determines whether it has been marked. The requirement is that a marked program should preserve the functionality of the original program on almost all inputs, but still be difficult for an adversary to remove the watermark without destroying the functionality. As discussed in [5,24,45], the marking algorithm can be extended to embed a string into the program; correspondingly, the verification algorithm would extract the embedded string when run on a watermarked program. We say such schemes are message-embedding [24].

Hopper et al. [45] first introduced the formal notion of a secretly-verifiable watermarking scheme, which was then discussed and adapted to the setting of watermarking cryptographic programs in Barak et al. [5]. In a secretly-verifiable scheme, only the holder of a secret key can test if a program is watermarked. More recently, Cohen et al. [24] showed how to construct publicly-verifiable watermarking for puncturable PRFs from indistinguishability obfuscation. In the publicly-verifiable setting, anyone with the public parameters is able to test whether a program is watermarked or not. Moreover, Cohen et al. noted that watermarkable PRFs have applications in challenge-response authentication and traitor tracing. We survey more related work in Sect. 6.1.

In our work, we show that starting with a private *programmable* PRF, we obtain a watermarkable family of PRFs, where the associated watermarking scheme is secretly-verifiable and supports message embedding. Intuitively, a programmable PRF is a puncturable PRF, except with the property that the holder of the master secret key can additionally specify the value the constrained key evaluates to at the punctured point. The privacy requirement stipulates that a programmed key hides the point which was "reprogrammed." We give the formal definitions of this concept and a concrete construction based on indistinguishability obfuscation in the full version of this paper [10].

We now give an overview of our construction of a watermarkable PRF. For simplicity, we describe our construction without message embedding. To mark a key msk for a private programmable PRF F, the marking algorithm first evaluates $F(\mathsf{msk}, \cdot)$ at several (secret) points $z_1, \ldots, z_d \in \mathcal{X}$ to obtain values $t_1, \ldots, t_d$. The marking algorithm then derives a pseudorandom pair (x, y) from the values $t_1, \ldots, t_d$, and outputs a programmed key for msk with the value at x replaced by y. To test whether a circuit C is marked or not, the verification algorithm applies the same procedure as the marking algorithm to obtain a test point (x', y'). The test algorithm then outputs "marked" if $C(x') = y'$ and "unmarked" otherwise. Privacy is crucial here because if the adversary knew the "reprogrammed" point x, it can trivially remove the watermark by producing a circuit that simply changes the value at x. We show in Sect. 6.1 that this simple construction not only satisfies our notion of secretly-verifiable watermarking, but can also be easily extended to support embedding arbitrary messages as the watermark.

Although our current constructions of private programmable PRFs rely on indistinguishability obfuscation, we stress that advances in constructing private programmable PRFs from weaker assumptions or with improved efficiency would have implications in constructing watermarkable PRFs as well.

Searchable Encryption. In searchable symmetric encryption (SSE) [6,20,30, 40,55], a server holds a set of encrypted documents and a client wants to retrieve all documents that match its query. For simplicity, suppose each document is tagged, and the client wants to retrieve all documents with a particular tag. One of the simplest SSE approaches is to compute and store an encrypted index on the server. Specifically, fix a PRF F and a key msk. For each tag t, the encrypted index maps the token $F(\mathsf{msk}, t)$ onto an encrypted list of document indices that match the tag. To search for a tag t, a user who holds the PRF key msk can issue a query $F(\mathsf{msk}, t)$. The server returns the encrypted list of matching documents.

We consider a new notion called restrictable SSE, where multiple parties can search the database, and the database owner wants to prevent some users from searching for certain tags. For example, suppose a company hosts all of its documents in a central database and tags each document with the name of its associated project. Moreover, suppose the company is developing a top-secret project and wants to restrict access so that only employees working on the project are able to search for documents related to the project. Using restrictable SSE, the company can issue restricted search keys to all employees not working on the project. Security of the constrained PRF ensures that an employee is unable to search for documents pertaining to the secret project. If we moreover assume that the tags are drawn from a small (polynomially-sized) domain (e.g., the English dictionary), privacy ensures that an employee cannot tell if a search came back empty because she was not allowed to search for a particular tag, or if there are actually no documents that match the tag. Privacy also ensures that unauthorized employees cannot infer the name of the secret project from their search keys.

By instantiating F with a private constrained PRF, we easily obtain a restrictable SSE system. The construction is collusion resistant: if several employees who individually cannot search for the tag t combine their search keys, they still cannot search for t. However, it does become possible for them to test whether a certain tag is in the intersection of their restricted sets.

Online/Offline 2-Server Private Keyword Search. In private keyword search [23,32,53], a server holds a database $D = \{w_1, \ldots, w_n\}$ of keywords, and a client wants to determine whether a specific keyword is in the database without revealing the keyword to the server. This setting differs from searchable encryption in that the server learns nothing about the client's query, whereas in the searchable encryption framework, information about the client's query (such as whether or not there are any matching results) could be leaked.

In the 2-server variant of this problem [15,39], the database is shared among two servers. The client can send queries to each server independently, and then combine the results of the queries to obtain the answer. We assume moreover that the two servers are non-colluding. Recently, Boyle, Gilboa and Ishai [15, 39] gave a secure solution for the 2-server variant of the problem that is more efficient than the solutions for 1-server private keyword search, and relies on weaker cryptographic assumptions.

Using a private puncturable PRF, we can construct an online/offline version of the 2-server keyword-search protocol. In an online/offline 2-server private keyword search protocol, there is an "offline" server and an "online" server. The offline server can process the search query before the client has decided its query (for instance, the offline computation can be preformed in a separate setup phase). When the client issues a search query, it only communicates with the online server. The client then combines the response from both servers to learn the result of the query. Our protocol can be seen as a hybrid between the 1-server and 2-server protocols. In the 1-server setting, there is no offline setup component in the protocol, while in the 2-server setting, we require both servers to be online during the query phase.

To implement online/offline 2-server private keyword search using private puncturable PRFs, during the offline (setup) phase, the client generates a master secret key msk for the private puncturable PRF, and sends msk to the offline server. Let $\{0,1\}^m$ be the range of the PRF. For each word $w_i \in D$, the offline server computes $s_i = F(\mathsf{msk}, w_i)$, and returns $s = \bigoplus_{i=1}^{n} s_i$ to the client. Note that all computation in the offline phase is *independent* of the client's search query. In the online phase, after the client has determined its search query w^*, she sends a key sk_{w^*} punctured at w^* to the online server. For each word $w_i \in D$, the online server evaluates sk_{w^*} on w_i to obtain a value t_i. Finally, the online server returns the value $t = \bigoplus_{i=1}^{n} t_i$. To learn the result of the keyword search, the client tests whether $z = s \oplus t$ is the all-zeros string 0^m or not. If $z = 0^m$, then the client concludes $w^* \notin D$; otherwise, the client concludes that $w^* \in D$. To see why, consider the case where $w^* \notin D$, so $w^* \neq w_i$ for all i. By correctness of the punctured PRF, $s_i = t_i$ for all i, in which case $z = 0^m$. Conversely, if $w^* = w_{i^*}$ for some i^*, then for all $i \neq i^*$, $s_i = t_i$. Moreover, security of the PRF implies that $s_{i^*} \neq t_{i^*}$ with high probability, and so $z \neq 0^m$.

For the security parameter λ and a dictionary of n keywords, the size of the search tokens sent to the online and offline servers is $O(\lambda \log N)$. The size of the responses from each server is $O(\lambda)$ bits. For single-server private keyword search, Ostrovsky and Skeith [53] show how to construct a private keyword search protocol, using homomorphic encryption and a private information retrieval (PIR) protocol. Instantiating the PIR protocol with the scheme of Gentry and Ramzan [38] results in a 1-server private keyword search with $O(\lambda + \log N)$ communication, which is optimal. We remark that although our current constructions do not result in a more efficient private keyword search protocol, improved constructions of private puncturable PRFs would have direct implications for the online/offline 2-server variant of private keyword search.

1.2   Constructing Private Constrained PRFs

We formally define our notion of privacy in Sect. 2. In this section, we briefly outline our constructions of private constrained PRFs. As a warmup, we begin with a construction from indistinguishability obfuscation, and then we give an overview of our two constructions from concrete assumptions on multilinear maps for bit-fixing constraints and puncturing constraints.

A Construction from Indistinguishability Obfuscation. Indistinguishability obfuscation (iO) [3–5,34,37,54,56] is a powerful primitive that has enabled a number of new constructions in cryptography [14,34,54]. Informally, an indistinguishability obfuscator is a machine that takes as input a program and outputs a second program with the identical functionality, but at the same time, hides some details on how the original program works.

We first show how indistinguishability obfuscation can be used to construct a private constrained PRF for general circuit constraints. Suppose $F : \mathcal{K} \times \mathcal{X} \to \mathcal{Y}$ is a PRF with master secret key $\mathsf{msk} \in \mathcal{K}$. We use F in conjunction with iO to construct a private circuit-constrained PRF. We describe the constrain algorithm. On input a circuit C, the constrain algorithm samples another secret key $\mathsf{sk} \in \mathcal{K}$ and outputs the obfuscation of the following program P:

"On input x, if $C(x) = 1$, output $F(\mathsf{msk}, x)$. Otherwise, output $F(\mathsf{sk}, x)$."

In the above program, note that C, msk, and sk are all hard-coded into the program. Let $\hat{P}$ be the obfuscated program. Evaluation of the PRF using the constrained key corresponds to evaluating the program $\hat{P}(x)$. We see that on all inputs x where $C(x) = 1$, $\hat{P}(x) = F(\mathsf{msk}, x)$, so correctness is immediate.

At a high level, the constrain algorithm generates a "fake" PRF key sk, and the constrained key is just a program that either evaluates the "real" PRF or the fake PRF, depending on the value of $C(x)$. Since the adversary cannot distinguish between the outputs under the real PRF key from those under the fake PRF key, the adversary cannot simply use the input-output behavior of the obfuscated program to learn anything about C. Moreover, in Sect. 3, we show that if the underlying PRF F is puncturable (not necessarily privately), the indistinguishability obfuscation of the program does in fact hide the constraining circuit C. We note though that for general circuits, our security reduction requires subexponential hardness of iO (and one-way functions). For restricted classes of circuits, such as puncturing, however, we can obtain security from polynomially-hard iO (and one-way functions).

Multilinear Maps. Although our construction from indistinguishability obfuscation is clean and simple, we treat it primarily as a proof-of-feasibility for private constrained PRFs. For our two main constructions, we build private constrained PRFs for more restrictive classes of constraints based on concrete assumptions over multilinear maps.

Multilinear maps [11,28,29,33,36] have been successfully applied to many problems in cryptography, most notably in constructing indistinguishability obfuscation [2–4,34,37,56]. Unfortunately, a number of recent attacks [13,21, 22,26,27,46] have invalidated many of the basic assumptions on multilinear maps. However, indistinguishability obfuscation is an example of a setting where the adversary often does not have the necessary information to carry out these attacks, and so some of the existing constructions are not known to be broken [31,35]. In our first construction from multilinear maps, we rely on the Multilinear Diffie-Hellman (MDH) assumption [11,33] over prime-order multilinear maps. In our second construction, we rely on the Subgroup Decision assumption [9,33] as well as a generalization which we call the Multilinear Diffie-Hellman Subgroup Decision (MDHSD) assumption over composite-order multilinear maps.[4] Our assumptions plausibly hold in existing multilinear map candidates, notably the Garg et al. construction in the prime-order setting [33], and the Coron et al. construction for the composite-order setting [28]. We also note that starting from iO, it is also possible to construct multilinear maps where the MDH assumption holds [1].

Two Constructions from Multilinear Maps. Using multilinear maps, we give two constructions of private constrained PRFs: one for the class of bit-fixing constraints, and the other for puncturing. A bit-fixing constraint is described by a pattern $s \in \{0, 1, ?\}^n$. An input $x \in \{0, 1\}^n$ satisfies the constraint if it matches the pattern—that is, for each coordinate i, either $s_i = ?$ or $s_i = x_i$. Our private bit-fixing PRF builds off of the Boneh-Waters bit-fixing PRF [12] based on prime-order multilinear maps [11,33]. We give the full construction in Sect. 4. In Sect. 5, we give the full construction of our privately puncturable PRF from composite-order multilinear maps. Here, security and privacy are based on the n-MDHSD and Subgroup Decision assumptions.

1.3 Related Work

Kiayias et al. [47] introduced a notion of policy privacy for delegatable PRFs. In a delegatable PRF, a proxy can evaluate the PRF on a subset of its domain by using a trapdoor derived from the master secret key, where the trapdoor (constrained key) is constructed based on a policy predicate (circuit constraint) which determines which values in the domain the proxy is able to compute the PRF on. Here, policy privacy refers to the security property that the trapdoor does not reveal the underlying policy predicate. The notion of policy privacy is conceptually similar to our notion of privacy for constrained PRFs, except that the delegatable PRFs which they construct are for policy predicates that describe a consecutive range of PRF inputs. Moreover, this restriction is reflected in their definition of policy privacy, and hence, their notion of privacy is incomparable to ours. However, we note that their delegatable PRF constructions are GGM-based and, thus, more efficient than our PRF constructions.

---

[4] In the full version [10], we show this assumption holds in a generic multilinear map model.

As discussed earlier, Boyle et al. [16] introduced the notion of constrained signatures (which they call functional signatures). Here, in addition to the master signing key, there are secondary signing keys for functions f which restrict the signer to only being able to construct valid signatures for a range of messages determined by f. They also proposed the notion of function privacy, which intuitively states that a signature constructed from a secondary signing key should not reveal the function associated with the signing key, nor the message that the function was applied to. However, critically, this notion of privacy does not prevent the secondary signing key itself from revealing the function it corresponds to; in this respect, their notion of function privacy is incomparable to our notion of privacy for constrained PRFs.

In Sect. 6.1, we also survey the related work on cryptographic watermarking.

Private Puncturing and Distributed Point Functions. Recently, Boyle, Gilboa and Ishai introduced the notion of a distributed point function (DPF) [15, 39], which are closely related to private puncturable PRFs. In a DPF, there are two functions Gen and Eval. The function Gen takes as input a pair $x, y \in \{0, 1\}^*$ and outputs two keys k_0 and k_1, and Eval is defined such that $\mathsf{Eval}(k_0, x') \oplus \mathsf{Eval}(k_1, x') = 0^{|y|}$ if $x' \neq x$, and $\mathsf{Eval}(k_0, x) \oplus \mathsf{Eval}(k_1, x) = y$. The security of the DPF stipulates that each of the keys individually appear to be distributed independently of x and y. A DPF is similar to a private puncturable PRF in that we can view k_0 as the master secret key for a PRF and k_1 as a constrained key punctured at x. However, there are two significant differences: first, the keys k_0 and k_1 need not be PRF keys (in the sense that $\mathsf{Eval}(k_0, \cdot)$ and $\mathsf{Eval}(k_1, \cdot)$ need not be pseudorandom),[5] and second, the keys k_0 and k_1 are generated *together* depending on x, whereas in a punctured PRF, the master secret key is generated *independently* of x. We note though that a private puncturable PRF can be used directly to construct a DPF: we simply let k_0 be the master secret key of the PRF and k_1 be a key punctured at x.

2   Private Constrained PRFs

In this section, we first review some notational conventions that we use throughout the work, along with the definition of a pseudorandom function (PRF). Then, we define constrained PRFs and the notion of privacy.

2.1   Conventions

For an integer n, we write $[n]$ to denote the set $\{1, \ldots, n\}$. For a finite set S, we write $x \xleftarrow{\mathrm{R}} S$ to denote that x is drawn uniformly at random from S. For two finite sets S and T, we write $\mathsf{Funs}(S, T)$ to denote the set of all (well-defined) functions $f : S \to T$. Hence, if $f \xleftarrow{\mathrm{R}} \mathsf{Funs}(S, T)$, then for every distinct input $a \in S$, the

---

[5] Though this property is not explicitly required by a DPF, in existing constructions [15,39], the functions $\mathsf{Eval}(k_0, \cdot)$ and $\mathsf{Eval}(k_1, \cdot)$ are individually pseudorandom.

value $f(a)$ is distributed uniformly and independently in T. We say a function $f(\lambda)$ is negligible in the parameter λ, denoted as $\mathrm{negl}(\lambda)$, if $f(\lambda) = o(1/\lambda^c)$ for all $c \in \mathbb{N}$. We say an algorithm is efficient if it runs in probabilistic polynomial time in the length of its input. For two families of distributions $\mathcal{D}_1$ and $\mathcal{D}_2$, we write $\mathcal{D}_1 \equiv \mathcal{D}_2$ if the two distributions are identical. We write $\mathcal{D}_1 \stackrel{c}{\approx} \mathcal{D}_2$ if the two distributions are computationally indistinguishable, that is, no efficient algorithm can distinguish $\mathcal{D}_1$ from $\mathcal{D}_2$, except perhaps with negligible probability.

2.2 Pseudorandom Functions

We first review the definition of a pseudorandom function (PRF) [41]. Unless otherwise noted, we will specialize the domain of our PRFs to $\{0,1\}^n$ and the range to $\{0,1\}^m$.

Definition 2.1 (Pseudorandom Function [41]). *Fix the security parameter* λ. *A PRF* $F : \mathcal{K} \times \{0,1\}^n \rightarrow \{0,1\}^m$ *with key space* $\mathcal{K}$, *domain* $\{0,1\}^n$, *and range* $\{0,1\}^m$ *is secure if for all efficient algorithms* $\mathcal{A}$,

$$\left| \Pr\left[k \xleftarrow{\text{R}} \mathcal{K} : \mathcal{A}^{F(k,\cdot)}(1^\lambda) = 1 \right] - \right.$$
$$\left. \Pr\left[f \xleftarrow{\text{R}} \mathsf{Funs}(\{0,1\}^n, \{0,1\}^m) : \mathcal{A}^{f(\cdot)}(1^\lambda) = 1 \right] \right| = \mathrm{negl}(\lambda).$$

We also review the definition of a constrained PRF [12,16,47]. Consider a PRF $F : \mathcal{K} \times \{0,1\}^n \rightarrow \{0,1\}^m$, and let msk be the master secret key for F. In a constrained PRF, the holder of msk can derive keys sk for some circuit $C : \{0,1\}^n \rightarrow \{0,1\}$, such that given sk, the evaluator can compute the PRF on all inputs $x \in \{0,1\}^n$ where $C(x) = 1$. More precisely, we have the following definition.

Definition 2.2 (Constrained PRF [12,16,47]). *A constrained PRF for a circuit class* $\mathcal{C}$ *is a tuple of algorithms* $\Pi = (\mathsf{cPRF.Setup}, \mathsf{cPRF.Constrain}, \mathsf{cPRF.ConstrainEval}, \mathsf{cPRF.Eval})$ *over the input space* $\{0,1\}^n$ *and output space* $\{0,1\}^m$, *with the following properties:*

- $\mathsf{cPRF.Setup}(1^\lambda) \rightarrow \mathsf{msk}$. *On input the security parameter* λ, *the setup algorithm* $\mathsf{cPRF.Setup}$ *outputs the master secret key* msk.
- $\mathsf{cPRF.Constrain}(\mathsf{msk}, C) \rightarrow \mathsf{sk}$. *On input the master secret key* msk *and a circuit* $C \in \mathcal{C}$, *the constrain algorithm* $\mathsf{cPRF.Constrain}$ *outputs a secret key* sk *for the circuit* C.
- $\mathsf{cPRF.ConstrainEval}(\mathsf{sk}, x) \rightarrow y$. *On input a secret key* sk, *and an input* $x \in \{0,1\}^n$, *the constrained evaluation algorithm* $\mathsf{cPRF.ConstrainEval}$ *outputs an element* $y \in \{0,1\}^m$.
- $\mathsf{cPRF.Eval}(\mathsf{msk}, x) \rightarrow y$. *On input the master secret key* msk *and an input* $x \in \{0,1\}^n$, *the evaluation algorithm* $\mathsf{cPRF.Eval}$ *outputs an element* $y \in \{0,1\}^m$.

Correctness. A constrained PRF is correct for a circuit class C if msk $\leftarrow$ cPRF.Setup(1^λ), for every circuit $C \in \mathcal{C}$ and input $x \in \{0,1\}^n$ such that $C(x) = 1$, it is the case that

$$\mathsf{cPRF.ConstrainEval(cPRF.Constrain(msk}, C), x) = \mathsf{cPRF.Eval(msk}, x).$$

Security. We now describe two security properties for a constrained PRF. The first property is the basic security notion for a constrained PRF and is adapted from the definitions of Boneh and Waters [12]. This notion captures the property that given several constrained keys as well as PRF evaluations at points of the adversary's choosing, the output of the PRF on points the adversary cannot compute itself looks random. The second property, which we call privacy, captures the notion that a constrained key does not reveal the associated constraining function. Each security definition is accompanied by an experiment between a challenger and an adversary, along with admissibility restrictions on the power of the adversary.

Definition 2.3 (Experiment $\mathsf{Expt}_b^{\mathsf{cPRF}}$). *For the security parameter $\lambda \in \mathbb{N}$, a family of circuits $\mathcal{C}$, and a bit $b \in \{0,1\}$, we define the experiment $\mathsf{Expt}_b^{\mathsf{cPRF}}$ between a challenger and an adversary $\mathcal{A}$, which can make oracle queries of the following types: constrain, evaluation, and challenge. First, the challenger sets $\mathsf{msk} \leftarrow \mathsf{cPRF.Setup}(1^\lambda)$ and samples a function $f \xleftarrow{\text{R}} \mathsf{Funs}(\{0,1\}^n, \{0,1\}^m)$ uniformly at random. For $b \in \{0,1\}$, the challenger responds to each oracle query made by $\mathcal{A}$ in the following manner.*

- **Constrain oracle.** *On input a circuit $C \in \mathcal{C}$, the challenger returns a constrained key $\mathsf{sk} \leftarrow \mathsf{cPRF.Constrain(msk}, C)$ to $\mathcal{A}$.*
- **Evaluation oracle.** *On input $x \in \{0,1\}^n$, the challenger returns $y \leftarrow \mathsf{cPRF.Eval(msk}, x)$.*
- **Challenge oracle.** *On input $x \in \{0,1\}^n$, the challenger returns $y \leftarrow \mathsf{cPRF.Eval(msk}, x)$ to $\mathcal{A}$ if $b = 0$, and $y \leftarrow f(x)$ if $b = 1$.*

Eventually, $\mathcal{A}$ outputs a bit $b' \in \{0,1\}$, which is also output by $\mathsf{Expt}_b^{\mathsf{cPRF}}$. Let $\Pr[\mathsf{Expt}_b^{\mathsf{cPRF}}(\mathcal{A}) = 1]$ denote the probability that $\mathsf{Expt}_b^{\mathsf{cPRF}}$ outputs 1 with $\mathcal{A}$.

At a high level, we say that a constrained PRF is secure if no efficient adversaries can distinguish $\mathsf{Expt}_0^{\mathsf{cPRF}}$ from $\mathsf{Expt}_1^{\mathsf{cPRF}}$. However, we must first restrict the set of allowable adversaries. For example, an adversary that makes a constrain query for a circuit $C \in \mathcal{C}$ and a challenge query for a point $x \in \{0,1\}^n$ where $C(x) = 1$ can trivially distinguish the two experiments. Hence, we first define an admissibility criterion that precludes such adversaries.

Definition 2.4 (Admissible Constraining). *We say an adversary is admissible if the following conditions hold:*

- *For each constrain query $C \in \mathcal{C}$ and each challenge query $y \in \{0,1\}^n$, $C(y) = 0$.*

– *For each evaluation query $x \in \{0,1\}^n$ and each challenge query $y \in \{0,1\}^n$, $x \neq y$.*

Definition 2.5 (Constrained Security). *A constrained PRF Π is secure if for all efficient and admissible adversaries $\mathcal{A}$, the following quantity is negligible:*

$$\mathsf{Adv}^{\mathsf{cPRF}}[\Pi, \mathcal{A}] \stackrel{\text{def}}{=} \left| \Pr[\mathsf{Expt}_0^{\mathsf{cPRF}}(\mathcal{A}) = 1] - \Pr[\mathsf{Expt}_1^{\mathsf{cPRF}}(\mathcal{A}) = 1] \right|.$$

Remark 2.6 (Multiple Challenge Queries). In our constructions of constrained PRFs, it will be convenient to restrict the adversary's power and assume that the adversary makes at most one challenge query. As was noted by Boneh and Waters [12], a standard hybrid argument shows that any constrained PRF secure against adversaries that make a single challenge oracle query is also secure against adversaries that make Q challenge oracle queries while only incurring a $1/Q$ loss in advantage. Thus, this restricted definition is equivalent to Definition 2.5.

Remark 2.7 (Adaptive Security). We say that a constrained PRF Π is *selectively* secure if for all efficient adversaries $\mathcal{A}$, the same quantity $\mathsf{Adv}^{\mathsf{cPRF}}[\Pi, \mathcal{A}]$ is negligible, but in the security game, the adversary first commits to its challenge query $x \in \{0,1\}^n$ at the start of the experiment. If we do not require the adversary to first commit to its challenge query, then we say that the scheme is *adaptively* (or *fully*) secure. A selectively-secure scheme can be shown to be fully secure using a standard technique called complexity leveraging [7] (at the expense of a super-polynomial loss in the security reduction).

Privacy. In the privacy game, the adversary is allowed to submit two circuits C_0, C_1 to the challenger. On each such query, it receives a PRF key constrained to C_b for some fixed $b \in \{0,1\}$. The adversary can also query the PRF at points of its choosing, and its goal is to guess the bit b. We now give the formal definitions.

Definition 2.8 (Experiment $\mathsf{Expt}_b^{\mathsf{cpriv}}$). *For the security parameter $\lambda \in \mathbb{N}$, a family of circuits $\mathcal{C}$, and a bit $b \in \{0,1\}$, we define the experiment $\mathsf{Expt}_b^{\mathsf{cpriv}}$ between a challenger and an adversary $\mathcal{A}$, which can make evaluation and challenge queries. First, the challenger obtains $\mathsf{msk} \leftarrow \mathsf{cPRF.Setup}(1^\lambda)$. For $b \in \{0,1\}$, the challenger responds to each oracle query type made by $\mathcal{A}$ in the following manner.*

– *Evaluation oracle. On input $x \in \{0,1\}^n$, the challenger returns $y \leftarrow \mathsf{cPRF.Eval}(\mathsf{msk}, x)$.*
– *Challenge oracle. On input a pair of circuits $C_0, C_1 \in \mathcal{C}$, the challenger returns $\mathsf{sk} \leftarrow \mathsf{cPRF.Constrain}(\mathsf{msk}, C_b)$.*

Eventually, $\mathcal{A}$ outputs a bit $b' \in \{0,1\}$, which is also output by $\mathsf{Expt}_b^{\mathsf{cPRF}}$. Let $\Pr[\mathsf{Expt}_b^{\mathsf{cpriv}}(\mathcal{A}) = 1]$ denote the probability that $\mathsf{Expt}_b^{\mathsf{cpriv}}$ outputs 1.

Roughly speaking, we say that a constrained PRF is private if no efficient adversary can distinguish $\mathsf{Expt}_0^{\mathsf{cpriv}}$ from $\mathsf{Expt}_1^{\mathsf{cpriv}}$. As was the case with constraining security, when formulating the exact definition, we must preclude adversaries that can trivially distinguish the two experiments.

Definition 2.9 (Admissible Privacy). *Let $C_0^{(i)}, C_1^{(i)} \in \mathcal{C}$ be the pair of circuits submitted by the adversary on the ith challenge oracle query, and let d be the total number of challenge oracle queries made by the adversary. For a circuit $C \in \mathcal{C}$, define $S(C) \subseteq \{0,1\}^n$ where $S(C) = \{x \in \{0,1\}^n : C(x) = 1\}$. Then, an adversary is* **admissible** *if:*

1. *For each evaluation oracle query with input x, and for each $i \in [d]$, it is the case that $C_0^{(i)}(x) = C_1^{(i)}(x)$.*
2. *For every pair of distinct indices $i, j \in [d]$,*

$$S\left(C_0^{(i)}\right) \cap S\left(C_0^{(j)}\right) = S\left(C_1^{(i)}\right) \cap S\left(C_1^{(j)}\right). \tag{2.1}$$

Definition 2.10 (d-Key Privacy). *A constrained PRF Π is (adaptively)* **d-key private** *if for all efficient and admissible adversaries $\mathcal{A}$ that make d challenge oracle queries, the following quantity is negligible:*

$$\mathsf{Adv}^{\mathsf{cpriv}}[\Pi, \mathcal{A}] \stackrel{\mathsf{def}}{=} \left| \Pr[\mathsf{Expt}_0^{\mathsf{cpriv}}(\mathcal{A}) = 1] - \Pr[\mathsf{Expt}_1^{\mathsf{cpriv}}(\mathcal{A}) = 1] \right|.$$

Furthermore, we say a constrained PRF is **multi-key** *private if it is d-key private for all $d \in \mathbb{N}$.*

Remark 2.11 (Admissibility Requirement). We remark that any non-admissible adversary (Definition 2.9) can trivially win the privacy game if the constrained PRF is secure (Definition 2.5). Thus, Definition 2.9 gives the minimal requirements for a satisfiable notion of multi-key privacy for constrained PRFs. To see this, take an adversary $\mathcal{A}$ that makes two challenge queries $(C_0^{(1)}, C_1^{(1)})$ and $(C_0^{(2)}, C_1^{(2)})$. Suppose that for some x, $C_0^{(1)}(x) = 1 = C_0^{(2)}(x)$, but $C_1^{(1)}(x) = 1$ and $C_1^{(2)}(x) = 0$. Let sk_1 and sk_2 be the keys $\mathcal{A}$ receives from the challenger in $\mathsf{Expt}_b^{\mathsf{cpriv}}$. For $i \in \{1,2\}$, the adversary computes $z_i = \mathsf{cPRF.ConstrainEval}(\mathsf{sk}_i, x)$. When $b = 0$, correctness implies that $z_1 = z_2$. When $b = 1$, security of the constrained PRF implies that $z_2 \neq z_1$ with overwhelming probability. The claim follows.

Remark 2.12 (Weaker Notions of Privacy). In some cases, we also consider a weaker notion of privacy where the adversary is not given access to an evaluation oracle in experiment $\mathsf{Expt}_b^{\mathsf{cpriv}}$. While this can be a weaker notion of privacy (for instance, in the case of d-key privacy for bounded d), in all of our candidate applications, a scheme that satisfies this weaker notion suffices.

Puncturable PRFs. A *puncturable* PRF [12,16,47,54] is a special case of a constrained PRF, where the constraining circuit describes a point function, that is, each constraining circuit C_{x^*} is associated with a point $x^* \in \{0,1\}^n$, and $C_{x^*}(x) = 1$ if and only if $x \neq x^*$. More concretely, a puncturable PRF is specified by a tuple of algorithms $\Pi = (\mathsf{cPRF.Setup}, \mathsf{cPRF.Puncture}, \mathsf{cPRF.ConstrainEval}, \mathsf{cPRF.Eval})$, which is identical to the syntax of a constrained PRF with the exception that the algorithm $\mathsf{cPRF.Constrain}$ is replaced with the algorithm $\mathsf{cPRF.Puncture}$.

- $\mathsf{cPRF.Puncture}(\mathsf{msk}, x) \to \mathsf{sk}$. On input the master secret key msk and an input $x \in \{0,1\}^n$, the puncture algorithm $\mathsf{cPRF.Puncture}$ outputs a secret key sk.

The correctness and security definitions (for constrained security and privacy) are analogous to those for private constrained PRFs.

3   Private Circuit Constrained PRFs from Obfuscation

In this section, we show how multi-key private circuit-constrained PRFs follow straightforwardly from indistinguishability obfuscation and puncturable PRFs (implied by one-way functions [12,16,41,47]). First, we review the notion of indistinguishability obfuscation introduced by Barak et al. [5].

Definition 3.1 (Indistinguishability Obfuscation(iO) [5,34]). *An indistinguishability obfuscator* iO *for a circuit class* $\{\mathcal{C}_\lambda\}$ *is a uniform and efficient algorithm satisfying the following requirements:*

- **Correctness.** *For all security parameters* $\lambda \in \mathbb{N}$, *all circuits* $C \in \mathcal{C}_\lambda$, *and all inputs* x, *we have that*

$$\Pr[C' \leftarrow \mathsf{iO}(C) : C'(x) = C(x)] = 1.$$

- **Indistinguishability.** *For all security parameters* λ, *and any two circuits* $C_0, C_1 \in \mathcal{C}_\lambda$, *if* $C_0(x) = C_1(x)$ *for all inputs* x, *then for all efficient adversaries* $\mathcal{A}$, *we have that the distinguishing advantage* $\mathsf{Adv}_{\mathsf{iO},\mathcal{A}}(\lambda)$ *is negligible:*

$$\mathsf{Adv}_{\mathsf{iO},\mathcal{A}}(\lambda) = |\Pr[\mathcal{A}(\mathsf{iO}(C_0)) = 1] - \Pr[\mathcal{A}(\mathsf{iO}(C_1)) = 1]| = \mathsf{negl}(\lambda).$$

For general circuit constraints, our construction will require the stronger assumption that the indistinguishability obfuscator and puncturable PRF be secure against subexponential-time adversaries. However, for more restrictive circuit families, such as puncturing, our construction can be shown to be secure assuming the more standard polynomial hardness of iO and the puncturable PRF We provide a more detailed discussion of this in the full version [10]. Also in the full version, we define the notion of a private *programmable* PRF and show how to adapt our private circuit-constrained PRF to also obtain a private programmable PRF from (polynomially-hard) iO and one-way functions.

Construction Overview. Our starting point is the circuit-constrained PRF by Boneh and Zhandry [14, Construction 9.1]. In the Boneh-Zhandry construction, the master secret key msk is a key for a puncturable PRF, and a constrained key for a circuit $C : \{0,1\}^n \to \{0,1\}$ is an obfuscation of the program that outputs cPRF.Eval(msk, x) if $C(x) = 1$ and $\perp$ otherwise. Because the program outputs $\perp$ on inputs x where $C(x) = 0$, simply evaluating the PRF at different points x reveals information about the underlying constraint. In our construction, we structure the program so that on an input x where $C(x) = 0$, the program's output is the output of a different PRF. Intuitively, just by looking at the outputs of the program, it is difficult to distinguish between the output of the real PRF and the output of the other PRF. In Theorem 3.3, we formalize this intuition by showing that our construction provides multi-key privacy.

Construction. We now describe our construction of a multi-key private circuit-constrained PRF. Let iO be an indistinguishability obfuscator, and let $\Pi_F = $ (F.Setup, F.Puncture, F.ConstrainEval, F.Eval) be any puncturable (but not necessarily private) PRF. Our multi-key private circuit-constrained PRF $\Pi_{ioPRF} = $ (cPRF.Setup, cPRF.Constrain, cPRF.ConstrainEval, cPRF.Eval) is given as follows:

- cPRF.Setup(1^λ). The setup algorithm outputs msk $\leftarrow$ F.Setup(1^λ).
- cPRF.Constrain(msk, C). First, the constrain algorithm computes msk' $\leftarrow$ F.Setup(1^λ). Then, it outputs an obfuscated program iO $\left(P_1 \left[C, \text{msk}', \text{msk}\right]\right)$, where $P_1 \left[C, \text{msk}', \text{msk}\right]$ is the program shown in (Fig. 1).[6]
- cPRF.ConstrainEval(sk, x). The constrained evaluation algorithm outputs the evaluation of the obfuscated program sk on x.
- cPRF.Eval(msk, x). The evaluation algorithm outputs F.Eval(msk, x).

Constants: a circuit $C : \{0,1\}^n \to \{0,1\}$, and master secret keys msk_0, msk_1 for the puncturable PRF $\Pi_F = $ (F.Setup, F.Puncture, F.ConstrainEval, F.Eval).

On input $x \in \{0,1\}^n$:

1. Let $b = C(x)$. Output F.Eval(msk_b, x).

Fig. 1. The program $P_1 [C, \text{msk}_0, \text{msk}_1]$

Correctness. By definition, the program $P_1[C, \text{msk}', \text{msk}]$ outputs F.Eval (msk, x) on all $x \in \{0,1\}^n$ where $C(x) = 1$. Correctness of Π_{ioPRF} immediately follows from correctness of the indistinguishability obfuscator.

Security. We now state our security theorems, but defer their formal proofs to the full version [10].

---

[6] We pad the program $P_1 [C, \text{msk}', \text{msk}]$ to the maximum size of any program that appears in the hybrid experiments in the proofs of Theorem 3.2 and 3.3.

Theorem 3.2. *Suppose* iO *is an indistinguishability obfuscator and* Π_F *is a selectively-secure puncturable PRF. Then,* Π_ioPRF *is selectively secure (Definition 2.5).*

Theorem 3.3. *Suppose* iO *is a indistinguishability obfuscator, and* Π_F *is a selectively-secure puncturable PRF, both secure against subexponential adversaries. Then,* Π_ioPRF *is multi-key private (Definition 2.10).*

We note that Theorem 3.3 only requires subexponentially-secure[7] iO if the set of challenge circuits $\{C_0^{(j)}\}_{j\in[d]}$ and $\{C_1^{(j)}\}_{j\in[d]}$ the adversary submits differs on a super-polynomial number of points. In particular, this implies that Π_ioPRF is a private puncturable PRF assuming only polynomial hardness of iO and selective security of Π_F. We discuss this in greater detail in the full version [10].

4   A Private Bit-Fixing PRF

In this section, we construct a constrained PRF for the class of bit-fixing circuits, a notion first introduced in [12]. First, a bit-fixing string s is an element of $\{0,1,?\}^n$. We say a bit-fixing string s matches $x \in \{0,1\}^n$ if for all $i \in [n]$, either $s_i = x_i$ or $s_i = ?$. We now define the class of bit-fixing circuits.

Definition 4.1 (Bit-Fixing Circuits [12]). *For a circuit* $C : \{0,1\}^n \to \{0,1\}$, *a string* $s \in \{0,1,?\}^n$ *is* **bit-fixing** *for* C *if* $C(x) = 1$ *on precisely the inputs* $x \in \{0,1\}^n$ *that* s *matches. The* **class of bit-fixing circuits** $\mathcal{C}_\mathsf{bf}$ *is the class of all circuits* $C : \{0,1\}^n \to \{0,1\}$ *for which there exists a bit-fixing string for* C.

Our bit-fixing construction uses multilinear maps [11], which are a generalization of bilinear maps [8,48,49]. While constructing ideal multilinear maps remains an open problem, there have been several recent candidates of graded encodings schemes [28,29,33,36], which are often a suitable substitute for ideal multilinear maps. For ease of presentation, we describe our constructions using the simpler abstraction of ideal multilinear maps. However, we note that we can easily map our constructions to the language of graded encodings using the same techniques as in [12, Appendix B]. We begin by defining multilinear maps over prime-order groups. In the full version [10], we also recall the ℓ-Multilinear Diffie-Hellman assumption [11,33] over prime-order multilinear maps.

Definition 4.2 (Prime-Order Multilinear Map [11,28,29,33,36]). *We define a* **prime-order multilinear map** *to consist of a setup algorithm* MMGen *along with a map function* e, *defined as follows.*

- MMGen($1^\lambda, 1^\ell$). *The setup algorithm* MMGen *takes as input the security parameter* λ *and a positive integer* ℓ, *and outputs a sequence of groups* $\overrightarrow{\mathbb{G}} = (\mathbb{G}_1, \ldots, \mathbb{G}_\ell)$ *each of prime order* p *(for a* λ*-bit prime* p). *The algorithm also outputs canonical generators* $g_i \in \mathbb{G}_i$ *for each* $i \in [\ell]$, *and the group order* p.

---

[7] Specifically, we require that for all efficient adversaries $\mathcal{A}$, the distinguishing advantage $\mathsf{Adv}_{\mathsf{iO},\mathcal{A}}(\lambda)$ defined in Definition 3.1 satisfies $2^n \cdot \mathsf{Adv}_{\mathsf{iO},\mathcal{A}}(\lambda) = \mathrm{negl}(\lambda)$.

– $e(g_1^{a_1}, \ldots, g_1^{a_\ell})$. *The map function* $e : (\mathbb{G}_1)^\ell \to \mathbb{G}_\ell$ *takes as input* ℓ *elements from* $\mathbb{G}_1$ *and outputs an element in* $\mathbb{G}_\ell$ *such that, for all* $a_1, \ldots, a_\ell \in \mathbb{Z}_p$,

$$e(g_1^{a_1}, \ldots, g_1^{a_\ell}) = g_\ell^{a_1 a_2 \cdots a_\ell}.$$

Construction Overview. Our starting point is the bit-fixing PRF by Boneh and Waters [12]. The Boneh-Waters bit-fixing PRF uses a symmetric multilinear map. To provide context, we give a brief description of the Boneh-Waters construction. Let $\{0,1\}^n$ be the domain of the PRF, and let $\overrightarrow{\mathbb{G}} = (\mathbb{G}_1, \ldots, \mathbb{G}_{n+1})$ be a sequence of leveled multilinear groups of prime order p. For each $i \in [n+1]$, let g_i be a canonical generator of $\mathbb{G}_i$; for notational convenience, we will often write $g = g_1$. In the Boneh-Waters construction, they define the multilinear map in terms of a collection of bilinear maps $e_{i,j} : \mathbb{G}_i \times \mathbb{G}_j \to \mathbb{G}_{i+j}$ for each $i, j \in [n]$ where $i + j \leq n + 1$. The master secret key in the Boneh-Waters PRF consists of exponents $\alpha, \{d_{i,0}, d_{i,1}\}_{i \in [n]} \in \mathbb{Z}_p$. For an input $x \in \{0,1\}^n$, the value of the PRF at x is $g_{n+1}^{\alpha \prod_{i \in [n]} d_{i,x_i}}$. A constrained key for a pattern $s \in \{0, 1, ?\}^n$ consists of a "pre-multiplied" element $g_{1+|S|}^{\alpha \prod_{i \in S} d_{i,s_i}}$, where $S \subseteq [n]$ is the subset of indices where $s_i \neq ?$, along with components $g_1^{d_{i,b}}$ for $i \notin S$ and $b \in \{0,1\}$. While this construction is selectively secure [12], it does not satisfy our notion of privacy. By simply inspecting the constrained key and seeing which elements $g_1^{d_{i,b}}$ are given out, an adversary can determine the indices s_i in the pattern s where $s_i = ?$.

A first attempt to make the Boneh-Waters construction private is to publish g^α along with a complete set of group elements $\{g^{d_{i,0}^*}, g^{d_{i,1}^*}\}_{i \in [n]}$ where $d_{i,b}^* = d_{i,b}$ if $s_i = ?$ or $s_i = b$, and otherwise, set $d_{i,b}^* \xleftarrow{\text{R}} \mathbb{Z}_p$. By construction, this only permits evaluation of the PRF at the points x that match s. However, this does not yield a secure constrained PRF, since an adversary that sees more than one constrained key can mix and match components from different keys, and learn the value of the PRF at points it could not directly evaluate given any of the individual keys. To prevent mixing and matching attacks in our construction, we rerandomize the elements in the constrained key. We give our construction below.

Construction. For simplicity, we describe the algorithm cPRF.Constrain as taking as input the master secret key msk and a bit-fixing string $s \in \{0, 1, ?\}^n$ rather than a circuit $C \in \mathcal{C}$. We define $\Pi_{\text{bfPRF}} = (\text{cPRF.Setup}, \text{cPRF.Constrain}, \text{cPRF.ConstrainEval}, \text{cPRF.Eval})$ as follows.

– cPRF.Setup(1^λ). The setup algorithm runs MMGen($1^\lambda, 1^{n+1}$) and outputs a sequence of groups $\overrightarrow{\mathbb{G}} = (\mathbb{G}_1, \ldots, \mathbb{G}_{n+1})$ each of prime order p, along with generators $g_i \in \mathbb{G}_i$ for all $i \in [n+1]$. As usual, we set $g = g_1$. Next, for $i \in [n]$, it samples $(d_{i,0}, d_{i,1}) \xleftarrow{\text{R}} \mathbb{Z}_p^2$, along with a random $\alpha \xleftarrow{\text{R}} \mathbb{Z}_p$. It outputs

$$\text{msk} = \left(g, g_{n+1}, \alpha, \{d_{i,0}, d_{i,1}\}_{i \in [n]} \right). \tag{4.1}$$

- cPRF.Constrain(msk, s). Let msk be defined as in Eq. (4.1) and $s = s_1 s_2 \cdots s_n$. For $i \in [n]$ and $b \in \{0, 1\}$, the constrain algorithm samples n random elements $\beta_1 \ldots, \beta_n \xleftarrow{\text{R}} \mathbb{Z}_p$ uniformly and independently, along with n random elements $r_1, \ldots, r_n \xleftarrow{\text{R}} \mathbb{Z}_p$. Define $\beta_0 = (\beta_1 \beta_2 \cdots \beta_n)^{-1}$. For each $i \in [n]$, define

$$
(D_{i,0}, D_{i,1}) = \begin{cases} \left(g^{d_{i,0}}, g^{r_i}\right), & \text{if } s_i = 0 \\ \left(g^{r_i}, g^{d_{i,1}}\right), & \text{if } s_i = 1 \ . \\ \left(g^{d_{i,0}}, g^{d_{i,1}}\right), & \text{if } s_i = \ ? \end{cases}
$$

It outputs

$$
\mathsf{sk} = \left((g^\alpha)^{\beta_0}, \left\{ (D_{i,0})^{\beta_i}, (D_{i,1})^{\beta_i} \right\}_{i \in [n]} \right). \tag{4.2}
$$

- cPRF.ConstrainEval(sk, x). Write $\mathsf{sk} = \left(g^\sigma, \{ g^{\mu_{i,0}}, g^{\mu_{i,1}} \}_{i \in [n]} \right)$, and let $x = x_1 x_2 \cdots x_n$. The constrained evaluation algorithm computes and outputs $y = e(g^\sigma, g^{\mu_{1,x_1}}, \ldots, g^{\mu_{n,x_n}})$.
- cPRF.Eval(msk, x). Let msk be defined as in Eq. (4.1), and let $x = x_1 x_2 \cdots x_n$. The evaluation algorithm outputs $y = g_{n+1}^{\alpha \prod_{i \in [n]} d_{i,x_i}}$.

Correctness and Security. We now state the correctness and security theorems for Π_{bfPRF}, but defer the formal proofs to the full version [10].

Theorem 4.3. *The bit-fixing PRF Π_{bfPRF} is correct.*

Theorem 4.4. *Under the $(n+1)$-MDH assumption, the bit-fixing PRF Π_{bfPRF} is selectively secure.*

Theorem 4.5. *The bit-fixing PRF Π_{bfPRF} is (unconditionally) 1-key private in the model where the adversary does not have access to an evaluation oracle.*

5   A Private Puncturable PRF

Recall from Sect. 2 that a puncturable PRF is a special class of constrained PRFs where the constraint can be described by a point function that is 1 everywhere except at a single point $s \in \{0, 1\}^n$. In this section, we give a construction of a private puncturable PRF using multilinear maps over a composite-order ring. We give an adaptation of Definition 4.2 to the composite-order setting. In the full version [10], we review the standard Subgroup Decision assumption [9,33] over composite-order groups, and a new assumption which we call the ℓ-Multilinear Diffie-Hellman Subgroup Decision (MDHSD) assumption. Also in the full version, we show that the ℓ-MDHSD assumption holds in a generic model of composite-order multilinear maps, provided that factoring is hard.

Definition 5.1 (Composite-Order Multilinear Map [11,28,29]). *We define a* **composite-order multilinear map** *to consist of a setup algorithm* CMMGen *along with a map function e, defined as follows:*

- CMMGen($1^\lambda, 1^\ell$). *The setup algorithm* CMMGen *takes as input the security parameter* λ *and a positive integer* ℓ, *and outputs a sequence of groups* $\overrightarrow{\mathbb{G}} = (\mathbb{G}_1, \ldots, \mathbb{G}_\ell)$ *each of composite order* $N = pq$ *(where* p, q *are* λ-*bit primes). For each* $\mathbb{G}_i$, *let* $\mathbb{G}_{p,i}$ *and* $\mathbb{G}_{q,i}$ *denote the order-p and order-q subgroups of* $\mathbb{G}_i$, *respectively. Let* $g_{p,i}$ *be a canonical generator of* $\mathbb{G}_{p,i}$, $g_{q,i}$ *be a canonical generator of* $\mathbb{G}_{q,i}$, *and* $g_i = g_{p,i}g_{q,i}$. *In addition to* $\overrightarrow{\mathbb{G}}$, *the algorithm outputs the generators* $g_{p,1}, \ldots, g_{p,\ell}, g_{q,1}, \ldots, g_{q,\ell}$, *and the primes* p, q.
- $e(g_1^{a_1}, \ldots, g_1^{a_\ell})$. *The map function* $e : (\mathbb{G}_1)^\ell \to \mathbb{G}_\ell$ *takes as input* ℓ *elements from* $\mathbb{G}_1$ *and outputs an element in* $\mathbb{G}_\ell$ *such that, for all* $a_1, \ldots, a_\ell \in \mathbb{Z}_N$,

$$e(g_1^{a_1}, \ldots, g_1^{a_\ell}) = g_\ell^{a_1 a_2 \cdots a_\ell}.$$

Construction Overview. Our construction builds on the Naor-Reingold PRF [50], and uses composite-order multilinear maps of order $N = pq$ (Definition 5.1). In our description, we use the same notation for group generators as in Definition 5.1. The master secret key in our construction is a collection of exponents $\{d_{i,0}, d_{i,1}\}_{i \in [n]}$ where each $d_{i,b}$ for all $i \in [n]$ and $b \in \{0, 1\}$ is random over $\mathbb{Z}_N$. The value of the PRF at a point $x \in \{0, 1\}^n$ is the element $g_{p,n}^{\prod_{i \in [n]} d_{i,x_i}} \in \mathbb{G}_{p,n}$.

Suppose we want to puncture at a point $s = s_1 \cdots s_n \in \{0, 1\}^n$. Our constrained key consists of a collection of points $\{D_{i,0}, D_{i,1}\}_{i \in [n]}$. For $b \neq s_i$, we set $D_{i,b} = g_{p,1}^{d_{i,b}} \in \mathbb{G}_{p,1}$ to be an element in the order-p subgroup, and for $b = s_i$, we set the element $D_{i,b} = g_{p,1}^{d_{i,b}} g_{q,1}^{d_{i,b}} \in \mathbb{G}_1$ to be an element in the full group. To evaluate the PRF at a point $x \in \{0, 1\}^n$ using the constrained key, one applies the multilinear map to the components D_{i,x_i} in the constrained key. By multilinearity and the fact that the order-p and order-q subgroups are orthogonal, if any of the inputs to the multilinear map lie in the $\mathbb{G}_{p,1}$ subgroup, then the output will be an element of the $\mathbb{G}_{p,n}$ subgroup. Thus, as long as there exists some index $i \in [n]$ such that $x_i \neq s_i$, the constrained key will evaluate to the real PRF output. If however $x = s$, then the constrained key on x will evaluate to an element of the full group $\mathbb{G}_n$. We show in Theorem 5.3 that under the n-MDHSD assumption, this element hides the true value of the PRF at x, which gives puncturing security. Moreover, since the constrained key is just a collection of random elements in either $\mathbb{G}_{p,1}$ or in $\mathbb{G}_1$, the scheme is 1-key private under the Subgroup Decision assumption (Theorem 5.4).

Construction. For simplicity in our description, we describe the cPRF.Constrain algorithm as taking as input the master secret key msk and a point $s \in \{0, 1\}$ to puncture rather than a circuit C. We define $\Pi_{\mathsf{puncPRF}} = (\mathsf{cPRF.Setup}, \mathsf{cPRF.Puncture}, \mathsf{cPRF.ConstrainEval}, \mathsf{cPRF.Eval})$ as follows.

- cPRF.Setup(1^λ). The setup algorithm runs CMMGen($1^\lambda, 1^n$) and outputs a sequence of groups $\overrightarrow{\mathbb{G}} = (\mathbb{G}_1, \ldots, \mathbb{G}_n)$, each of composite order $N = pq$, along with the factorization of N, and the generators $g_{p,i}, g_{q,i} \in \mathbb{G}_i$ of the order-p and order-q subgroups of $\mathbb{G}_i$, respectively for all $i \in [n]$. Let $g_1 = g_{p,1}g_{q,1}$ be the canonical generator of $\mathbb{G}_1$. Finally, the setup algorithm samples $2n$ random elements $(d_{1,0}, d_{1,1}), \ldots, (d_{n,0}, d_{n,1}) \xleftarrow{\text{R}} \mathbb{Z}_N^2$, and outputs the following master secret key msk:

$$\mathsf{msk} = \left(p, q, g_1, g_{p,1}, g_{p,n}, \{d_{i,0}, d_{i,1}\}_{i \in [n]} \right) \tag{5.1}$$

- cPRF.Puncture(msk, $s \in \{0,1\}^n$). Write $s = s_1 s_2 \cdots s_n$. Let $g_1 = g_{p,1} g_{q,1}$. For each $i \in [n]$, define

$$(D_{i,0}, D_{i,1}) = \begin{cases} (g_1^{d_{i,0}}, \ g_{p,1}^{d_{i,1}}), & \text{if } s_i = 0 \\ (g_{p,1}^{d_{i,0}}, \ g_1^{d_{i,1}}), & \text{if } s_i = 1 \end{cases}.$$

The algorithm then outputs the constrained key $\mathsf{sk} = \{D_{i,0}, D_{i,1}\}_{i \in [n]}$.
- cPRF.ConstrainEval(sk, x). Write sk as $\{D_{i,0}, D_{i,1}\}_{i \in [n]}$, and $x = x_1 x_2 \cdots x_n$. The constrained evaluation algorithm outputs $y = e(D_{1,x_1}, \ldots, D_{n,x_n})$.
- cPRF.Eval(msk, x). Let msk be defined as in Eq. (5.1), and $x = x_1 x_2 \cdots x_n$. The evaluation algorithm outputs $y = g_{p,n}^{\Pi_{i \in [n]} d_{i,x_i}}$.

Correctness and Security. We now state the correctness and security theorems, but defer the formal analysis to the full version [10].

Theorem 5.2. *The puncturable PRF Π_{puncPRF} is correct.*

Theorem 5.3. *Under the n-MDHSD assumption, the puncturable PRF Π_{puncPRF} is selectively secure.*

Theorem 5.4. *Under the Subgroup Decision assumption, the puncturable PRF Π_{puncPRF} is 1-key private in the model where the adversary does not have access to an evaluation oracle.*

6 Applications

In Sect. 1.1, we outlined several applications of private constrained PRFs. Several of our applications (private constrained MACs, restrictable SSE, and online/offline 2-server private keyword search) follow readily from our definitions of private constrained PRFs, and so we do not elaborate further on them. In this section, we give a more formal treatment of using private constrained PRFs to build secretly-verifiable message-embedding watermarking of PRFs and symmetric deniable encryption.

6.1 Watermarking PRFs

In this section, we show how to construct watermarkable PRFs from private programmable PRFs.[8] The watermarking scheme we give is secretly-verifiable

---

[8] Intuitively, a programmable PRF is the same as a puncturable PRF except that the holder of the master secret key can also program the value at the punctured point. We give a formal definition of programmable PRFs in the full version [10].

and supports message embedding [24], where the marking algorithm can embed a string into the program that can later be extracted by the verification algorithm. We first introduce some definitions for unremovability and unforgeability. The unremovability definitions are adapted from the corresponding definition in [24] while the unforgeability definitions are adapted from that in [25]. We then show how to construct a watermarkable PRF from any private programmable PRF. Finally, we conclude with a survey of related work.

Definition 6.1 (Watermarkable Family of PRFs [24, adapted]). *For the security parameter λ and a message space $\{0,1\}^t$, a secretly-verifiable message-embedding watermarking scheme for a PRF with key-space $\mathcal{K}$ is a tuple of algorithms $\Pi = (\mathsf{WM.Setup}, \mathsf{WM.Mark}, \mathsf{WM.Verify})$ with the following properties.*

- $\mathsf{WM.Setup}(1^\lambda) \to \mathsf{msk}$. *On input the security parameter λ, the setup algorithm outputs the watermarking secret key msk.*
- $\mathsf{WM.Mark}(\mathsf{msk}, m) \to (k, C)$. *On input the watermarking secret key msk and a message $m \in \{0,1\}^t$, the mark algorithm outputs a PRF key $k \in \mathcal{K}$ and a marked circuit C.*
- $\mathsf{WM.Verify}(\mathsf{msk}, C') \to m$. *On input the master secret key msk and an arbitrary circuit C', the verification algorithm outputs a string $m \in \{0,1\}^t \cup \{\bot\}$.*

Definition 6.2 (Circuit Similarity). *Fix a circuit class $\mathcal{C}$ on n-bit inputs. For two circuits $C, C' \in \mathcal{C}$ and for a non-decreasing function $f : \mathbb{N} \to \mathbb{N}$, we write $C \sim_f C'$ to denote that the two circuits agree on all but an $1/f(n)$ fraction of inputs. More formally, we define*

$$C \sim_f C' \qquad \Longleftrightarrow \qquad \Pr_{x \xleftarrow{\text{R}} \{0,1\}^n} [C(x) \neq C'(x)] \leq 1/f(n).$$

We also write $C \not\sim_f C'$ to denote that C and C' differ on at least a $1/f(n)$ fraction of inputs.

Definition 6.3 (Correctness ([24, adapted])). *Fix the security parameter λ. A watermarking scheme for a PRF with key-space $\mathcal{K}$ and domain $\{0,1\}^n$ is **correct** if for all messages $m \in \{0,1\}^t$, $\mathsf{msk} \leftarrow \mathsf{WM.Setup}(1^\lambda)$, $(k, C) \leftarrow \mathsf{WM.Mark}(\mathsf{msk}, m)$, we have that*

- *The key k is uniformly distributed over the key-space $\mathcal{K}$ of the PRF.*
- *$C(\cdot) \sim_f F(k, \cdot)$, where $1/f(n) = \mathrm{negl}(\lambda)$.*
- *$\Pr[\mathsf{WM.Verify}(\mathsf{msk}, C) = m]$ with overwhelming probability.*

Watermarking Security. We define watermarking security in the context of an experiment $\mathsf{Expt}_{\mathsf{wm}}$ between a challenger and an adversary $\mathcal{A}$, which can make marking oracle and challenge oracle queries.

Definition 6.4 (Experiment $\mathsf{Expt}_{\mathsf{wm}}$). *First, the challenger samples $\mathsf{msk} \leftarrow \mathsf{WM.Setup}(1^\lambda)$, and the challenger then responds to each oracle query made by $\mathcal{A}$ in the following manner.*

– **Marking oracle.** On input a message $m \in \{0,1\}^t$, the challenger returns the pair $(k, C) \leftarrow$ WM.Mark(msk, m) to $\mathcal{A}$.
– **Challenge oracle.** On input a message $m \in \{0,1\}^t$, the challenger computes $(k, C) \leftarrow$ WM.Mark(msk, m) but only returns C to $\mathcal{A}$.

Eventually, $\mathcal{A}$ *outputs a circuit* C'*, and the challenger computes and outputs* WM.Verify(msk, C')*, which is also the output of the experiment, denoted as* $\mathsf{Expt}_{\mathsf{wm}}(\mathcal{A})$*.*

Definition 6.5 (Unremoving Admissibility). *An adversary* $\mathcal{A}$ *is* **unremoving admissible** *if* $\mathcal{A}$ *only queries the challenge oracle once, and* $C(\cdot) \sim_f C'(\cdot)$*, where* C *is the output of the challenge oracle query,* C' *is the output of* $\mathcal{A}$*, and* $1/f(n) = \mathrm{negl}(\lambda)$*.*

Definition 6.6 (Unremovability). *A watermarking scheme* Π *is* **unremovable** *if for all efficient and unremoving admissible adversaries* $\mathcal{A}$*, if* $m \in \{0,1\}^t$ *is the message submitted by* $\mathcal{A}$ *to the challenge oracle in* $\mathsf{Expt}_{\mathsf{wm}}$*, the probability* $\Pr[\mathsf{Expt}_{\mathsf{wm}}(\mathcal{A}) \neq m]$ *is negligible.*

Definition 6.7 (δ-Unforging Admissibility). *We say an adversary* $\mathcal{A}$ *is* δ**-unforging admissible** *if* $\mathcal{A}$ *does not make any challenge oracle queries, and for all* $i \in [Q]$*,* $C_i(\cdot) \not\sim_f C'(\cdot)$*, where* Q *is the total number of marking queries the adversary makes,* C_i *is the output of the marking oracle on the* i^{th} *query,* C' *is the circuit output by the adversary, and* $1/f(n) \geq \delta$ *for all* $n \in \mathbb{N}$*.*

Definition 6.8 (δ-Unforgeability). *We say a watermarking scheme* Π *is* δ**-unforgeable** *if for all efficient and* δ*-unforging admissible adversaries* $\mathcal{A}$*, the probability* $\Pr[\mathsf{Expt}_{\mathsf{wm}}(\mathcal{A}) \neq \bot]$ *is negligible.*

Construction. Fix the security parameter λ, positive integers $n, \ell, t \geq \lambda$, and a positive real value $\delta < 1$, such that $d = \lambda/\delta = \mathrm{poly}(\lambda)$. Let $F : \mathcal{K} \times (\{0,1\}^\ell \times \{0,1\}^t)^d \rightarrow \{0,1\}^n \times \{0,1\}^\ell \times \{0,1\}^t$ be a PRF, and let $\Pi_{\mathsf{pprf}} = (\mathsf{pPRF.Setup}, \mathsf{pPRF.Program}, \mathsf{pPRF.ProgramEval}, \mathsf{pPRF.Eval})$ be a programmable PRF with input space $\{0,1\}^n$ and output space $\{0,1\}^\ell \times \{0,1\}^t$. We construct a watermarking scheme $\Pi_{\mathsf{wm}} = (\mathsf{WM.Setup}, \mathsf{WM.Mark}, \mathsf{WM.Verify})$ for the PRF Π_{pprf} as follows:

– WM.Setup(1^λ). The setup algorithm chooses $\mathsf{k} \xleftarrow{\mathrm{R}} \mathcal{K}$ and $(z_1, \ldots, z_d) \xleftarrow{\mathrm{R}} (\{0,1\}^n)^d$ uniformly at random and outputs $\mathsf{msk} = (\mathsf{k}, z_1, \ldots, z_d)$.
– WM.Mark(msk, m). The mark algorithm first parses $\mathsf{msk} = (\mathsf{k}, z_1, \ldots, z_d)$. It generates $k' \leftarrow \mathsf{pPRF.Setup}(1^\lambda)$, and then computes the point $(x, y, \tau) = F(\mathsf{k}, (\mathsf{pPRF.Eval}(k', z_1), \ldots, \mathsf{pPRF.Eval}(k', z_d)))$ and $v = m \oplus \tau$. Then, it computes $\mathsf{sk}_k \leftarrow \mathsf{pPRF.Program}(k', x, (y, v))$ and outputs (k', C), where $C(\cdot) = \mathsf{pPRF.ProgramEval}(\mathsf{sk}_k, \cdot)$.
– WM.Verify(msk, C). The verification algorithm first parses $\mathsf{msk} = (\mathsf{k}, z_1, \ldots, z_d)$ and then computes $(x, y, \tau) = F(\mathsf{k}, (C(z_1), \ldots, C(z_d)))$. It then sets $(y', v) = C(x)$ and outputs $v \oplus \tau$ if $y = y'$, and $\bot$ otherwise.

We state our correctness and security theorems here, but defer their proofs to the full version [10].

Theorem 6.9. *If F is a secure PRF and Π_{pprf} is a programmable PRF, then the watermarking scheme Π_{wm} is correct.*

Theorem 6.10. *If F is a secure PRF and Π_{pprf} is a private programmable PRF, then the watermarking scheme Π_{wm} is unremovable.*

Theorem 6.11. *If F is a secure PRF and Π_{pprf} is a programmable PRF, then for $\delta = 1/\mathrm{poly}(\lambda)$, the watermarking scheme Π_{wm} is δ-unforgeable.*

Related Work. Recently, Cohen et al. [24] showed how to construct publicly-verifiable watermarking for puncturable PRFs from indistinguishability obfuscation. They pursue the notion of approximate functionality-preserving for watermarking, where the watermarked program agrees with the original program on *most* inputs. Previously, Barak et al. [5] showed that assuming iO, perfectly functionality-preserving watermarking is impossible.

Cohen et al. [25] gave a construction from iO which achieves publicly-verifiable watermarking for relaxed notions of unremovability and unforgeability, namely where the adversary can only query the marking oracle before receiving the challenge program in the unremovability game and moreover, is only allowed to query the challenge oracle once (lunchtime unremovability). In addition, the adversary must submit a forged program which differs on the same set of inputs with respect to all programs submitted to the mark oracle in the unforgeability game.

In a concurrent work to [25], Nishimaki and Wichs [51] considered a relaxed notion of watermarking security for message-embedding schemes by considering "selective-message" security, where the adversary must commit to the message to be embedded into the challenge program before interacting with the mark oracle. This limitation is removed in their subsequent work [24].

Comparison to Previous Works. In previous constructions of watermarkable PRFs [24,25,51], the authors show how to watermark any family of puncturable PRFs. In contrast, our construction gives a family of watermarkable PRFs from private programmable PRFs. In our construction, we also consider a slightly weaker version of the mark oracle which takes as input a message and outputs a *random* program that embeds the message. This is a weaker notion of security than providing the adversary access to a marking oracle that take as input an (adversarially-chosen) program and a message and outputs a watermarked program with the embedded message.[9] In addition, we consider secretly-verifiable watermarking constructions while Cohen et al. and Nishimaki and Wichs focus on publically-verifiable constructions. However, despite these limitations, we note

---

[9] The reason for this stems from the fact that we require PRF security in our security reductions, which cannot be guaranteed when the PRF key is chosen adversarially (as opposed to randomly).

that the family of watermarkable PRFs we construct are still sufficient to instantiate the motivating applications for watermarkable PRFs by Cohen et al. [24]. In our model, we are able to achieve full security for unremovability as well as strong unforgeability.

6.2 Symmetric Deniable Encryption

The notion of deniable encryption was first introduced by Canetti et al. [18]. Informally speaking, a deniable encryption scheme allows a sender and receiver, after exchanging encrypted messages, to later on produce either fake randomness (in the public-key setting), or a fake decryption key (in the symmetric-key setting) that opens a ciphertext to another message of their choosing. Of course, the fake randomness or decryption key that is constructed by this "deny" algorithm should look like legitimately-sampled randomness or an honestly-generated decryption key.

Recently, Sahai and Waters [54] used indistinguishability obfuscation [4,5, 34,37,54,56] to give the first construction of public-key deniable encryption that achieves the security notions put forth by Canetti et al.[10] In all prior constructions of deniable encryption, the adversary is able to distinguish real randomness from fake randomness with advantage $1/n$, where n roughly corresponds to the length of a ciphertext in the scheme [18].

Surprisingly, the machinery of private puncturable PRFs provides a direct solution to a variant of symmetric deniable encryption. In the symmetric setting, we assume that an adversary has intercepted a collection of ciphertexts $c_1, \ldots, c_n$ and asks the sender to produce the secret key to decrypt this collection of messages. The deniable encryption scheme that we construct enables the sender to produce a fake secret key sk that looks indistinguishable from an honestly generated encryption key, and yet, will only correctly decrypt all but one of the intercepted ciphertexts.[11] In our particular construction, the sender (or receiver) has a trapdoor that can be used to deny messages. Our framework is similar to the *flexibly* deniable framework where there are separate key-generation and encryption algorithms [18,52] for so-called "honest" encryption and "dishonest" encryption. A second difference in our setting is that we only support denying to a random message rather than an arbitrary message of the sender's choosing. Thus, our scheme is better-suited for scenarios where the messages being encrypted have high entropy (e.g., cryptographic keys).

In this section, we give a formal definition of symmetric deniable encryption adapted from those of Canetti et al. [18]. We then give a construction of our variant of symmetric deniable encryption from private puncturable PRFs. Finally, we conclude with a brief survey of related work in this area.

---

[10] In fact, their construction achieves the stronger notion of publicly deniable encryption where the sender does not have to remember the randomness it used to construct a particular ciphertext when producing fake randomness.

[11] It is important to define our notions with respect to multiple intercepted messages. Otherwise, the one-time-pad is a trivial (one-time) symmetric deniable encryption scheme.

Definition 6.12 (Symmetric Deniable Encryption [18, adapted]). *A symmetric deniable encryption scheme is a tuple of algorithms $\Pi_{DE} = $ (DE.Setup, DE.Encrypt, DE.Decrypt, DE.Deny) defined over a key space $\mathcal{K}$, a message space $\mathcal{M}$ and a ciphertext space $\mathcal{C}$ with the following properties:*

- *DE.Setup(1^λ) → (dk, sk). On input the security parameter λ, the setup algorithm outputs a secret key sk $\in \mathcal{K}$ and a denying key dk.*
- *DE.Encrypt(sk, m) → ct. On input the secret key sk $\in \mathcal{K}$ and a message $m \in \mathcal{M}$, the encryption algorithm outputs a ciphertext ct $\in \mathcal{C}$.*
- *DE.Decrypt(sk, ct) → m. On input a secret key sk $\in \mathcal{K}$ and a ciphertext ct $\in \mathcal{C}$, the decryption algorithm outputs a message $m \in \mathcal{M}$.*
- *DE.Deny(dk, ct) → sk'. On input a denying key dk and a ciphertext ct, the deny algorithm outputs a key sk' $\in \mathcal{K}$.*

The first property we require is that the tuple of algorithms (DE.Setup, DE.Encrypt, DE.Decrypt, DE.Deny) should satisfy the usual correctness and semantic security requirements for symmetric encryption schemes [42].

Definition 6.13 (Correctness). *A symmetric deniable encryption scheme $\Pi_{DE} = $ (DE.Setup, DE.Encrypt, DE.Decrypt, DE.Deny) is correct if for all messages $m \in \mathcal{M}$, with (sk, dk) ← DE.Setup(1^λ), we have that*

$$\Pr\left[\text{DE.Decrypt}(\text{sk}, \text{DE.Encrypt}(\text{sk}, m)) \neq m\right] = \text{negl}(\lambda),$$

where the probability is taken oven the randomness of DE.Setup and DE.Encrypt.

Definition 6.14 (Semantic Security [42, adapted]). *A symmetric deniable encryption scheme $\Pi_{DE} = $ (DE.Setup, DE.Encrypt, DE.Decrypt, DE.Deny) is semantically secure if for all efficient adversaries $\mathcal{A}$ and (sk, dk) ← DE.Setup(1^λ),*

$$\left|\Pr\left[\mathcal{A}^{\mathcal{O}_0(\text{sk},\cdot,\cdot)}(1^\lambda) = 1\right] - \Pr\left[\mathcal{A}^{\mathcal{O}_1(\text{sk},\cdot,\cdot)}(1^\lambda)\right]\right| = \text{negl}(\lambda),$$

where for $b \in \{0,1\}$, $\mathcal{O}_b(\text{sk}, \cdot, \cdot)$ is an encryption oracle that takes as input two messages $m_0, m_1 \in \mathcal{M}$ and outputs the ciphertext DE.Encrypt(sk, m_b).

Finally, we define the notion of deniability for a symmetric deniable encryption scheme. Our notion is similar to that defined in Canetti et al. [18, Definition 4]. Let $m_1, \ldots, m_n$ be a collection of messages, and let $\text{ct}_1, \ldots, \text{ct}_n$ be encryptions of these messages under a symmetric key sk. Suppose without loss of generality that the sender wants to deny to message m_n. Then, the fake secret key sk' output by DE.Deny should be such that the joint distribution $(\text{sk}', \text{ct}_1, \ldots, \text{ct}_n)$ of the fake secret key and the real ciphertexts should look indistinguishable from the joint distribution $(\text{sk}, \text{ct}_1, \ldots, \text{ct}_{n-1}, \text{ct}^*)$ of the real secret key and the real ciphertexts with ct_n substituted for an encryption ct^* of a random message. Our definition captures both the property that the fake secret key looks indistinguishable from a legitimately-generated secret key and that the fake secret key does not reveal any additional information about the denied message m_n beyond what the adversary could already infer. We now proceed with the formal security definition.

Definition 6.15 (Experiment $\mathsf{Expt}_b^{\mathsf{DE}}$). *For the security parameter $\lambda \in \mathbb{N}$, we define the experiment $\mathsf{Expt}_b^{\mathsf{DE}}$ between a challenger and an adversary $\mathcal{A}$ as follows:*

1. *The challenger begins by running $(\mathsf{sk}, \mathsf{dk}) \leftarrow \mathsf{DE.Setup}(1^\lambda)$.*
2. *The adversary $\mathcal{A}$ chooses a tuple of messages $(m_1, \ldots, m_q) \in \mathcal{M}^q$ and an index $i^* \in [q]$. It gives $(m_1, \ldots, m_q)$ and i^* to the challenger.*
3. *For each $i \in [q]$, the challenger computes $\mathsf{ct}_i \leftarrow \mathsf{DE.Encrypt}(\mathsf{sk}, m_i)$. Then, depending on the bit b, the challenger does the following:*
   - *If $b = 0$, the challenger first runs $\mathsf{sk}' \leftarrow \mathsf{DE.Deny}(\mathsf{dk}, \mathsf{ct}_{i^*})$, and then sends $\left(\mathsf{sk}', \{\mathsf{ct}_i\}_{i \in [q]}\right)$ to the adversary.*
   - *If $b = 1$, the challenger chooses a random message $m^* \xleftarrow{\mathsf{R}} \mathcal{M}$, and computes $\mathsf{ct}^* \leftarrow \mathsf{DE.Encrypt}(\mathsf{sk}, m^*)$. It sends $\left(\mathsf{sk}, \{\mathsf{ct}_i\}_{i \neq i^*} \cup \{\mathsf{ct}^*\}\right)$ to the adversary.*
4. *At the end of the experiment, the adversary outputs a bit $b' \in \{0, 1\}$, which is the output of the experiment. Let $\Pr[\mathsf{Expt}_b^{\mathsf{DE}}(\mathcal{A}) = 1]$ denote the probability that adversary $\mathcal{A}$ outputs 1 in experiment $\mathsf{Expt}_b^{\mathsf{DE}}$.*

Definition 6.16. *A symmetric deniable encryption scheme $\Pi_{\mathsf{DE}} = (\mathsf{DE.Setup}, \mathsf{DE.Encrypt}, \mathsf{DE.Decrypt}, \mathsf{DE.Deny})$ is deniable if for all efficient adversaries $\mathcal{A}$,*

$$\left|\Pr[\mathsf{Expt}_0^{\mathsf{DE}}(\mathcal{A}) = 1] - \Pr[\mathsf{Expt}_1^{\mathsf{DE}}(\mathcal{A}) = 1]\right| = \mathrm{negl}(\lambda).$$

Construction. We now describe our construction of a symmetric deniable encryption scheme from a private puncturable PRF (such as the one from Sect. 5). Let $\Pi_{\mathsf{cprf}} = (\mathsf{cPRF.Setup}, \mathsf{cPRF.Puncture}, \mathsf{cPRF.ConstrainEval}, \mathsf{cPRF.Eval})$ be a private puncturable PRF with key space $\mathcal{K}$, domain $\{0, 1\}^n$ and range $\{0, 1\}^\ell$. We use Π_{cprf} to build a symmetric deniable encryption scheme $\Pi_{\mathsf{DE}} = (\mathsf{DE.Setup}, \mathsf{DE.Encrypt}, \mathsf{DE.Decrypt}, \mathsf{DE.Deny})$ with key space $\mathcal{K}$ and message space $\{0, 1\}^\ell$ as follows:

- $\mathsf{DE.Setup}(1^\lambda)$. On input the security parameter λ, run $\mathsf{msk} \leftarrow \mathsf{cPRF.Setup}(1^\lambda)$ to obtain the master secret key for the puncturable PRF. Choose a random point $x \xleftarrow{\mathsf{R}} \{0, 1\}^n$ and run $\mathsf{sk}_x \leftarrow \mathsf{cPRF.Puncture}(\mathsf{msk}, x)$ to obtain a punctured key. Set the symmetric key to $\mathsf{sk} = \mathsf{sk}_x$ and the denying key $\mathsf{dk} = \mathsf{msk}$. Output $(\mathsf{sk}, \mathsf{dk})$.
- $\mathsf{DE.Encrypt}(\mathsf{sk}, m)$. On input the symmetric key sk and a message $m \in \{0, 1\}^\ell$, choose a random value $r \xleftarrow{\mathsf{R}} \{0, 1\}^n$ and output the pair

$$(r, \mathsf{cPRF.ConstrainEval}(\mathsf{sk}, r) \oplus m).$$

- $\mathsf{DE.Decrypt}(\mathsf{sk}, \mathsf{ct})$. On input the symmetric key sk and a ciphertext $\mathsf{ct} = (\mathsf{ct}_0, \mathsf{ct}_1)$, output $\mathsf{cPRF.ConstrainEval}(\mathsf{sk}, \mathsf{ct}_0) \oplus \mathsf{ct}_1$.
- $\mathsf{DE.Deny}(\mathsf{dk}, \mathsf{ct})$. On input the denying key $\mathsf{dk} = \mathsf{msk}$ and a ciphertext $\mathsf{ct} = (\mathsf{ct}_0, \mathsf{ct}_1)$, output $\mathsf{cPRF.Puncture}(\mathsf{msk}, \mathsf{ct}_0)$.

Correctness and Security. We state our correctness and security theorems here, but defer their proofs to the full version [10].

Theorem 6.17. *The deniable encryption scheme Π_{DE} is correct.*

Theorem 6.18. *If Π_{cprf} is a secure PRF, then Π_{DE} is semantically secure.*

Theorem 6.19. *If Π_{cprf} is a 1-key private, selectively-secure PRF, then Π_{DE} is deniable (Definition 6.16).*

Related Work. In their original paper, Canetti et al. also propose a relaxed definition of deniable encryption called *flexibly deniable encryption*. In a flexibly deniable encryption scheme, there are two separate versions of the setup and encryption algorithms: the "honest" version and the "dishonest" version. The guarantee is that if a user encrypts a message m using the dishonest encryption algorithm to obtain a ciphertext ct, it is later able to produce randomness r that makes it look as if ct is an *honest* encryption of some arbitrary message m' under randomness r. Using standard assumptions, Canetti et al. give a construction of a sender-deniable flexibly deniable encryption scheme trapdoor permutations: that is, a scheme that gives the sender the ability to later fake the randomness for a particular ciphertext. O'Neill et al. [52] later extend these ideas to construct a secure flexibly bideniable encryption scheme from lattices. A bideniable encryption scheme is one that allows both the sender and the receiver to fake randomness for a particular message. We note that in a flexibly deniable encryption scheme, only ciphertexts generated via the "dishonest" algorithms can later be opened as honestly-generated ciphertexts of a different message.

Canetti et al. also introduce the notion of deniable encryption with pre-planning. In this setting, the sender can commit ("pre-plan") to deny a message at a later time. The authors show that in the pre-planning model, there are trivial constructions of symmetric deniable encryption schemes if the ciphertext length is allowed to grow with the number of possible openings of a particular message. We note that our construction does not require pre-planning.

There are several differences between our definitions and those of Canetti et al. that we note here. Let c_i be the ciphertext that the sender chooses to deny. First, unlike the definitions proposed in Canetti et al., the sender cannot program the key sk so that c_i decrypts to an arbitrary message of its choosing. Rather, c_i will decrypt to a uniformly random message under the fake key sk′. Thus, our deniable encryption scheme is best suited for scenarios where the messages being encrypted are drawn uniformly from a message space, for instance, when encrypting cryptographic keys. Next, our key generation algorithm outputs a "trapdoor" that the sender (or receiver) uses to generate fake keys. This is similar to the flexibly deniable encryption setting when we have two sets of algorithms for key generation and encryption. However, in our construction, there is only one encryption algorithm, and all ciphertexts output by the encryption algorithm can be denied (provided that the sender or receiver has the denying key).

We note also that the Sahai-Waters construction provides strictly stronger guarantees than those achieved by our construction. However, our primary motivation here is to show how private puncturable PRFs can be directly applied to provide a form of symmetric deniable encryption without relying on obfuscation.

7   Conclusions

In this work, we introduce the notion of privacy for constrained PRFs, and give a number of interesting applications including watermarkable PRFs and searchable encryption. We also give three constructions of private constrained PRFs: one from indistinguishability obfuscation, and two from concrete assumptions on multilinear maps. Our indistinguishability obfuscation result achieves the strongest notion of privacy for general circuit constraints. Our multilinear map constructions yield private bit-fixing PRFs and private puncturable PRFs.

We leave open the question of constructing private constrained PRFs from simpler and more standard assumptions (such as from lattices or pairing-based cryptography). In particular, is it possible to construct a private puncturable PRF from one-way functions? Currently, our best constructions for private puncturable PRFs require multilinear maps.

Acknowledgments. This work was funded by NSF, DARPA, a grant from ONR, the Simons Foundation, and an NSF Graduate Research Fellowship. Opinions, findings and conclusions or recommendations expressed in this material are those of the authors and do not necessarily reflect the views of DARPA.

References

1. Albrecht, M.R., Farshim, P., Hofheinz, D., Larraia, E., Paterson, K.G.: Multilinear maps from obfuscation. In: Kushilevitz, E., Malkin, T. (eds.) TCC 2016. LNCS, vol. 9562, pp. 446–473. Springer, Heidelberg (2016). doi:10.1007/978-3-662-49096-9_19
2. Ananth, P.V., Gupta, D., Ishai, Y., Sahai, A.: Optimizing obfuscation: avoiding barrington's theorem. In: ACM CCS, pp. 646–658 (2014)
3. Applebaum, B., Brakerski, Z.: Obfuscating circuits via composite-order graded encoding. In: Dodis, Y., Nielsen, J.B. (eds.) TCC 2015. LNCS, vol. 9015, pp. 528–556. Springer, Heidelberg (2015). doi:10.1007/978-3-662-46497-7_21
4. Barak, B., Garg, S., Kalai, Y.T., Paneth, O., Sahai, A.: Protecting obfuscation against algebraic attacks. In: Nguyen, P.Q., Oswald, E. (eds.) EUROCRYPT 2014. LNCS, vol. 8441, pp. 221–238. Springer, Heidelberg (2014). doi:10.1007/978-3-642-55220-5_13
5. Barak, B., Goldreich, O., Impagliazzo, R., Rudich, S., Sahai, A., Vadhan, S.P., Yang, K.: On the (im)possibility of obfuscating programs. J. ACM **59**(2), 6 (2012)
6. Boldyreva, A., Chenette, N., Lee, Y., O'Neill, A.: Order-preserving symmetric encryption. In: Joux, A. (ed.) EUROCRYPT 2009. LNCS, vol. 5479, pp. 224–241. Springer, Heidelberg (2009). doi:10.1007/978-3-642-01001-9_13
7. Boneh, D., Boyen, X.: Efficient selective-ID secure identity-based encryption without random oracles. In: Cachin, C., Camenisch, J.L. (eds.) EUROCRYPT 2004. LNCS, vol. 3027, pp. 223–238. Springer, Heidelberg (2004). doi:10.1007/978-3-540-24676-3_14
8. Boneh, D., Franklin, M.: Identity-based encryption from the Weil pairing. In: Kilian, J. (ed.) CRYPTO 2001. LNCS, vol. 2139, pp. 213–229. Springer, Heidelberg (2001). doi:10.1007/3-540-44647-8_13
9. Boneh, D., Goh, E.-J., Nissim, K.: Evaluating 2-DNF formulas on ciphertexts. In: Kilian, J. (ed.) TCC 2005. LNCS, vol. 3378, pp. 325–341. Springer, Heidelberg (2005). doi:10.1007/978-3-540-30576-7_18

10. Boneh, D., Lewi, K., Wu, D.J.: Constraining pseudorandom functions privately. IACR Cryptology ePrint Archive, 2015:1167 (2015)
11. Boneh, D., Silverberg, A.: Applications of multilinear forms to cryptography. Contemp. Math. **324**(1), 71–90 (2003)
12. Boneh, D., Waters, B.: Constrained pseudorandom functions and their applications. In: Sako, K., Sarkar, P. (eds.) ASIACRYPT 2013. LNCS, vol. 8270, pp. 280–300. Springer, Heidelberg (2013). doi:10.1007/978-3-642-42045-0_15
13. Boneh, D., Wu, D.J., Zimmerman, J.: Immunizing multilinear maps against zeroizing attacks. IACR Cryptology ePrint Archive, 2014:930 (2014)
14. Boneh, D., Zhandry, M.: Multiparty key exchange, efficient traitor tracing, and more from indistinguishability obfuscation. In: Garay, J.A., Gennaro, R. (eds.) CRYPTO 2014. LNCS, vol. 8616, pp. 480–499. Springer, Heidelberg (2014). doi:10.1007/978-3-662-44371-2_27
15. Boyle, E., Gilboa, N., Ishai, Y.: Function secret sharing. In: Oswald, E., Fischlin, M. (eds.) EUROCRYPT 2015. LNCS, vol. 9057, pp. 337–367. Springer, Heidelberg (2015). doi:10.1007/978-3-662-46803-6_12
16. Boyle, E., Goldwasser, S., Ivan, I.: Functional signatures and pseudorandom functions. In: Krawczyk, H. (ed.) PKC 2014. LNCS, vol. 8383, pp. 501–519. Springer, Heidelberg (2014). doi:10.1007/978-3-642-54631-0_29
17. Brakerski, Z., Vaikuntanathan, V.: Constrained key-homomorphic PRFs from standard lattice assumptions. In: Dodis, Y., Nielsen, J.B. (eds.) TCC 2015. LNCS, vol. 9015, pp. 1–30. Springer, Heidelberg (2015). doi:10.1007/978-3-662-46497-7_1
18. Canetti, R., Dwork, C., Naor, M., Ostrovsky, R.: Deniable encryption. In: Kaliski, B.S. (ed.) CRYPTO 1997. LNCS, vol. 1294, pp. 90–104. Springer, Heidelberg (1997). doi:10.1007/BFb0052229
19. Chandran, N., Raghuraman, S., Vinayagamurthy, D.: Constrained pseudorandom functions: verifiable and delegatable. IACR Cryptology ePrint Archive, 2014:522 (2014)
20. Chase, M., Kamara, S.: Structured encryption and controlled disclosure. In: Abe, M. (ed.) ASIACRYPT 2010. LNCS, vol. 6477, pp. 577–594. Springer, Heidelberg (2010). doi:10.1007/978-3-642-17373-8_33
21. Cheon, J.H., Fouque, P.-A., Lee, C., Minaud, B., Ryu, H.: Cryptanalysis of the new CLT multilinear map over the integers. In: Fischlin, M., Coron, J.-S. (eds.) EUROCRYPT 2016. LNCS, vol. 9665, pp. 509–536. Springer, Heidelberg (2016). doi:10.1007/978-3-662-49890-3_20
22. Cheon, J.H., Han, K., Lee, C., Ryu, H., Stehlé, D.: Cryptanalysis of the multilinear map over the integers. In: Oswald, E., Fischlin, M. (eds.) EUROCRYPT 2015. LNCS, vol. 9056, pp. 3–12. Springer, Heidelberg (2015). doi:10.1007/978-3-662-46800-5_1
23. Chor, B., Gilboa, N., Naor, M.: Private information retrieval by keywords. IACR Cryptology ePrint Archive, 1998:3 (1998)
24. Cohen, A., Holmgren, J., Nishimaki, R., Vaikuntanathan, V., Wichs, D.: Watermarking cryptographic capabilities. In: STOC, pp. 1115–1127 (2016)
25. Cohen, A., Holmgren, J., Vaikuntanathan, V.: Publicly verifiable software watermarking. IACR Cryptology ePrint Archive, 2015:373 (2015)

26. Coron, J.-S., Gentry, C., Halevi, S., Lepoint, T., Maji, H.K., Miles, E., Raykova, M., Sahai, A., Tibouchi, M.: Zeroizing without low-level zeroes: new MMAP attacks and their limitations. In: Gennaro, R., Robshaw, M. (eds.) CRYPTO 2015. LNCS, vol. 9215, pp. 247–266. Springer, Heidelberg (2015). doi:10. 1007/978-3-662-47989-6_12

27. Coron, J.-S., Lee, M.S., Lepoint, T., Tibouchi, M.: Cryptanalysis of GGH15 multilinear maps. IACR Cryptology ePrint Archive, 2015:1037 (2015)

28. Coron, J.-S., Lepoint, T., Tibouchi, M.: Practical multilinear maps over the integers. In: Canetti, R., Garay, J.A. (eds.) CRYPTO 2013. LNCS, vol. 8042, pp. 476–493. Springer, Heidelberg (2013). doi:10.1007/978-3-642-40041-4_26

29. Coron, J.-S., Lepoint, T., Tibouchi, M.: New multilinear maps over the integers. In: Gennaro, R., Robshaw, M. (eds.) CRYPTO 2015. LNCS, vol. 9215, pp. 267–286. Springer, Heidelberg (2015). doi:10.1007/978-3-662-47989-6_13

30. Curtmola, R., Garay, J.A., Kamara, S., Ostrovsky, R.: Searchable symmetric encryption: improved definitions and efficient constructions. In: ACM CCS, pp. 79–88 (2006)

31. Fernando, R., Rasmussen, P.M.R., Sahai, A.: Preventing CLT zeroing attacks on obfuscation. IACR Cryptology ePrint Archive, 2016:1070 (2016)

32. Freedman, M.J., Ishai, Y., Pinkas, B., Reingold, O.: Keyword search and oblivious pseudorandom functions. In: Kilian, J. (ed.) TCC 2005. LNCS, vol. 3378, pp. 303–324. Springer, Heidelberg (2005). doi:10.1007/978-3-540-30576-7_17

33. Garg, S., Gentry, C., Halevi, S.: Candidate multilinear maps from ideal lattices. In: Johansson, T., Nguyen, P.Q. (eds.) EUROCRYPT 2013. LNCS, vol. 7881, pp. 1–17. Springer, Heidelberg (2013). doi:10.1007/978-3-642-38348-9_1

34. Garg, S., Gentry, C., Halevi, S., Raykova, M., Sahai, A., Waters, B.: Candidate indistinguishability obfuscation and functional encryption for all circuits. In: FOCS, pp. 40–49 (2013)

35. Garg, S., Miles, E., Mukherjee, P., Sahai, A., Srinivasan, A., Zhandry, M.: Secure obfuscation in a weak multilinear map model. In: Hirt, M., Smith, A. (eds.) TCC 2016. LNCS, vol. 9986, pp. 241–268. Springer, Heidelberg (2016). doi:10.1007/ 978-3-662-53644-5_10

36. Gentry, C., Gorbunov, S., Halevi, S.: Graph-induced multilinear maps from lattices. In: Dodis, Y., Nielsen, J.B. (eds.) TCC 2015. LNCS, vol. 9015, pp. 498–527. Springer, Heidelberg (2015). doi:10.1007/978-3-662-46497-7_20

37. Gentry, C., Lewko, A.B., Sahai, A., Waters, B.: Indistinguishability obfuscation from the multilinear subgroup elimination assumption. In: FOCS, pp. 151–170 (2015)

38. Gentry, C., Ramzan, Z.: Single-database private information retrieval with constant communication rate. In: Caires, L., Italiano, G.F., Monteiro, L., Palamidessi, C., Yung, M. (eds.) ICALP 2005. LNCS, vol. 3580, pp. 803–815. Springer, Heidelberg (2005). doi:10.1007/11523468_65

39. Gilboa, N., Ishai, Y.: Distributed point functions and their applications. In: Nguyen, P.Q., Oswald, E. (eds.) EUROCRYPT 2014. LNCS, vol. 8441, pp. 640–658. Springer, Heidelberg (2014). doi:10.1007/978-3-642-55220-5_35

40. Goh, E.-J.: Secure indexes. IACR Cryptology ePrint Archive, 2003:216 (2003)

41. Goldreich, O., Goldwasser, S., Micali, S.: How to construct random functions. J. ACM **33**(4), 792–807 (1986)

42. Goldwasser, S., Micali, S.: Probabilistic encryption and how to play mental poker keeping secret all partial information. In: STOC, pp. 365–377 (1982)

43. Hofheinz, D., Kamath, A., Koppula, V., Waters, B.: Adaptively secure constrained pseudorandom functions. IACR Cryptology ePrint Archive, 2014:720 (2014)

44. Hohenberger, S., Koppula, V., Waters, B.: Adaptively secure puncturable pseudorandom functions in the standard model. In: Iwata, T., Cheon, J.H. (eds.) ASIACRYPT 2015. LNCS, vol. 9452, pp. 79–102. Springer, Heidelberg (2015). doi:10.1007/978-3-662-48797-6_4

45. Hopper, N., Molnar, D., Wagner, D.: From weak to strong watermarking. In: Vadhan, S.P. (ed.) TCC 2007. LNCS, vol. 4392, pp. 362–382. Springer, Heidelberg (2007). doi:10.1007/978-3-540-70936-7_20

46. Hu, Y., Jia, H.: Cryptanalysis of GGH map. In: Fischlin, M., Coron, J.-S. (eds.) EUROCRYPT 2016. LNCS, vol. 9665, pp. 537–565. Springer, Heidelberg (2016). doi:10.1007/978-3-662-49890-3_21

47. Kiayias, A., Papadopoulos, S., Triandopoulos, N., Zacharias, T.: Delegatable pseudorandom functions and applications. In: CCS, pp. 669–684 (2013)

48. Menezes, A., Okamoto, T., Vanstone, S.A.: Reducing elliptic curve logarithms to logarithms in a finite field. IEEE Trans. Inf. Theory 39(5), 1639–1646 (1993)

49. Miller, V.S.: The Weil pairing, and its efficient calculation. J. Cryptol. 17(4), 235–261 (2004)

50. Naor, M., Reingold, O.: Number-theoretic constructions of efficient pseudo-random functions. J. ACM 51(2), 231–262 (2004)

51. Nishimaki, R., Wichs, D.: Watermarking cryptographic programs against arbitrary removal strategies. IACR Cryptology ePrint Archive, 2015:344 (2015)

52. O'Neill, A., Peikert, C., Waters, B.: Bi-deniable public-key encryption. In: Rogaway, P. (ed.) CRYPTO 2011. LNCS, vol. 6841, pp. 525–542. Springer, Heidelberg (2011). doi:10.1007/978-3-642-22792-9_30

53. Ostrovsky, R., Skeith, W.E.: Private searching on streaming data. In: Shoup, V. (ed.) CRYPTO 2005. LNCS, vol. 3621, pp. 223–240. Springer, Heidelberg (2005). doi:10.1007/11535218_14

54. Sahai, A., Waters, B.: How to use indistinguishability obfuscation: deniable encryption, and more. In: STOC, pp. 475–484 (2014)

55. Song, D.X., Wagner, D., Perrig, A.: Practical techniques for searches on encrypted data. In: IEEE Symposium on Security and Privacy, pp. 44–55 (2000)

56. Zimmerman, J.: How to obfuscate programs directly. In: Oswald, E., Fischlin, M. (eds.) EUROCRYPT 2015. LNCS, vol. 9057, pp. 439–467. Springer, Heidelberg (2015). doi:10.1007/978-3-662-46803-6_15

Universal Samplers with Fast Verification

Venkata Koppula[1(✉)], Andrew Poelstra[2], and Brent Waters[1]

[1] University of Texas at Austin, Austin, USA
{kvenkata,bwaters}@cs.utexas.edu
[2] Blockstream, San Francisco, USA
apoelstra@blockstream.com

Abstract. Recently, Hofheinz et al. [9] proposed a new primitive called *universal samplers* that allows oblivious sampling from arbitrary distributions, and showed how to construct universal samplers using indistinguishability obfuscation ($i\mathcal{O}$) in the ROM.

One important limitation for applying universal samplers in practice is that the constructions are built upon indistinguishability obfuscation. The costs of using current $i\mathcal{O}$ constructions is prohibitively large. We ask is whether the cost of a (universal) sampling could be paid by one party and then shared (soundly) with all other users? We address this question by introducing the notion of universal samplers with verification. Our notion follows the general path of [9], but has additional semantics that allows for validation of a sample.

In this work we define and give a construction for universal samplers with verification. Our verification procedure is simple and built upon one-time signatures, making verification of a sample much faster than computing it. Security is proved under the sub exponential hardness of indistinguishability obfuscation, puncturable pseudorandom functions, and one-time signatures.

1 Introduction

The Random Oracle Model (ROM), introduced by Bellare and Rogaway [3], is a widely used heuristic in cryptography. In the random oracle model a hash function H is modeled as an oracle that when sampled with an input x will output a sample of a fresh random string u. This functionality has been applied in numerous cryptographic applications that have leveraged features of the model such programmability and rewinding. However, one significant limitation of the model is that it can only be used to sample from random strings, whereas in many applications we would like the ability of (obliviously) sample from *arbitrary* distributions.[1]

B. Waters—Supported by NSF CNS-1228599 and CNS-1414082, DARPA SafeWare, Microsoft Faculty Fellowship, and Packard Foundation Fellowship.

[1] One could define the random oracle model to provide samples from arbitrary distributions on arbitrary sets. However, such a model no longer heuristically corresponds to real world hash functions.

S. Fehr (Ed.): PKC 2017, Part II, LNCS 10175, pp. 525–554, 2017.
DOI: 10.1007/978-3-662-54388-7_18

Recently, Hofheinz et al. [9], addressed this problem. They proposed a new primitive called *universal samplers* that allows oblivious sampling from arbitrary distributions, and showed how to construct universal samplers using indistinguishability obfuscation ($i\mathcal{O}$) in the ROM.

Hofheinz et al. argued that universal samplers can give way to a powerful notion of universal setup. Several cryptographic schemes require the use of a trusted setup to generate common parameters. For example, in an elliptic curve-based public key scheme we might want to generate a common set of curve parameters for everyone to use. However, each such cryptographic scheme proposed will require its users to agree on some trusted user or process for setting up the parameters for the specific scheme. In practice the cost of executing such a setup for every single instance can be quite onerous and might serve as a barrier to adoption. In particular, the effort to get everyone to agree on an authority or gather an acceptable set of parties together to jointly perform (via multiparty computation) the setup process can be difficult. Such "human overhead" is difficult to measure in terms of traditional computational metrics. Using universal parameters, however, one can service several schemes with one universal trusted setup. Here the trusted setup party (or parties) will create a universal sampler. Then if any particular scheme has a setup algorithm described by circuit d, its users can simply universally sample from the distribution d to get a set of parameters for that particular scheme.

In addition to the application of universal setup described above, Hofheinz et al. provided that several applications of universal samplers, non-interactive key exchange and broadcast encryption. Subsequent works [10,11] used universal parameters to construct universal signature aggregators and constrained pseudorandom functions respectively.

The Costs of Using Universal Samplers. One important limitation for applying universal samplers in practice is that the constructions are built upon indistinguishability obfuscation. The costs of using current $i\mathcal{O}$ constructions is prohibitively large. Even so we might hope that efforts toward moving the performance of $i\mathcal{O}$ to practice [1,2,17] will follow the path of other cryptographic primitives such as multiparty computation and ORAM. Such primitives were once considered way too expensive to even consider, however, sustained algorithmic and engineering efforts (see for example the references in [12]) have gotten reduced the costs by several orders of magnitude and gotten them to the point where many interesting programs or computations can be executed. A central concern though is that even if we assume that the performance costs of obfuscation follow a similar trajectory to other works that the costs will still remain significantly above "traditional" cryptographic primitives such as encryption, signing, etc. that have costs imperceptible to a human.

In the context of universal samplers and a trusted universal setup, it might be acceptable for a well funded party to invest the computation needed to determine a parameter needed for a given scheme, but not acceptable to assume that every single party using the scheme is willing to pay such a high cost.

We ask whether the cost of a (universal) sampling could be paid by one party and then shared (soundly) with all other users. Returning to our elliptic curve example, one could imagine that NIST would run a universal sampler for a particular setup scheme to obtain a set of curve parameters p. Could NIST then share the parameters p with all other users in a manner that convinced them that they were sampled correctly, but where the cost of verification was much smaller than repeating the sampling? We restate this question in terms of universal samplers:

Is it possible to construct a universal sampler that allows for fast verification (that is, verification that uses only traditional cryptography)?

We address this question by introducing the notion of universal samplers with verification. Our notion follows the general path of [9], but has additional semantics that allows for validation of a sample. In our system the Setup outputs a Universal Sampler parameter U as before, but also outputs a verification key VK.[2]

The sampling algorithm Sample as in [9] will maps the sampler parameters U and input circuit $d(\cdot)$ to an element p sampled from d, but also output a certificate σ which can be thought of as a signature on p. Finally, we include an additional algorithm, Check, that takes VK, σ, and the input circuit, and checks whether these are consistent.

We can see now that there are two paths to obtaining a sample from the distribution d. One can call Sample(U, d) and obtain p. Or one can let another party perform this step and receive p, σ and validate this by calling Check(VK, d, p, σ).

We require two security properties. The first is the prior indistinguishability of real world and ideal world given in [9]. The second property we require is that it should be computationally infeasible for any poly-time adversary $\mathcal{A}$ to produce a triple d^*, p^*, σ^* such that Check(VK, $d^*, p^*, \sigma^*) = 1$ and Sample$(U, d^*) \neq p^*$. Intuitively, it should be hard to produce a signature that convokes a third party of the "wrong" output.

The first thing we observe is that any standard universal sampler scheme implies one with verification, but in an uninteresting way. To do this we can simply let VK $= U$ and have the Check algorithm run Sample(U, d) itself. This will clearly result in a secure universal sampler with verification if the base universal sampler is secure, but not result in any of the savings that motivated our discussion above.

For this reason any scheme of interest must have a verification algorithm Check that is significantly more efficient than running Sample. Ideally, the cost will be close to that of "traditional" cryptographic primitives. We choose not to formalize this final requirement.

---

[2] As in [9] there is a single trusted setup process that runs Setup to produces the sampler parameters. It is then expected to erase the random coins it used. Also as noted by [9] one could employ multi-party computation to distribute this initial setup task among multiple parties.

Our Technical Approach. We begin our technical exposition by describing what we call *prefix-restricted signature scheme*. This is specialized signature scheme that will we use to sign samples output from our universal sampler. A *prefix-restricted signature scheme* is over a message space $\mathcal{M}_1 \times \mathcal{M}_2$ and differs from an ordinary signature scheme in the following ways:

- A secret key can either be a "master secret key" or admit a "punctured" form at a message (m_1^*, m_2^*) capable of signing any message (m_1, m_2) such that (a) $m_1 \neq m_1^*$ or (b) $(m_1, m_2) = (m_1^*, m_2^*)$.
- In our security game an attacker selectively gives (m_1^*, m_2^*) and receives back a corresponding punctured signing key. No signing queries are allowed. The attacker should be unable to provide a signature on any message (m_1, m_2) where $m_1 = m_1^*$ and $m_2 \neq m_2^*$.
- The scheme is deterministic, even with respect to the master and punctured keys. Moreover, signatures produced by punctured keys (on messages for which this is possible) must be equal to those produced by unpunctured keys on the same messages.

This notion shares a similar flavor to earlier related concepts such as constrained signature [5]. It is actually the last property of matching signature outputs between all key types that is critical for our use and the most tricky to satisfy. Looking ahead, the reason we will need this is to be able to argue that two programs are equivalent when we switch from using a master key to a punctured key in an experiment.

While achieving some form of signature delegation has been considered in other works and transforming a standard signature scheme to a deterministic one can be done by a straightforward application of a PRF [8], forcing such a constrained signature key to output the same signatures as a master key is somewhat more tricky.

We construct a prefix-restricted signature scheme from a deterministic one-time signature scheme (on arbitrary length messages) and a puncturable pseudo random function [4,6,13,15]. Briefly recall that a puncturable PRF is a PRF when one can create a punctured key that allows a keyed function $F(K, \cdot)$ to be evaluated at all but a small number of points.

Let the length of the first message piece, $\mathcal{M}_1$, be n and let m^i be the i-bit prefix of m and $\overline{m}^i$ be the i-bit prefix of m with bit i flipped. To sign a message $m = (m_1, m_2)$. We will first create a Naor-Yung [14] style certificate tree of length n. To create a signature on m for each $i = 1$ to n we first generate a two verify and signing key pairs (one as the 0 key and the other as the 1 key). We denote the keys output in step i as $(\mathrm{SK}_{m^i}, \mathrm{VK}_{m^i}) \leftarrow \mathsf{KeyGen}_1(1^\lambda; F(K, m^i))$ and $(\mathrm{SK}_{\overline{m}^i}, \mathrm{VK}_{\overline{m}^i}) \leftarrow \mathsf{KeyGen}_1(1^\lambda; F(K, \overline{m}^i))$. Importantly, notice that instead of sampling these keys randomly we replace the setup random coins with the output of $F(K, m^i)$ and $F(K, \overline{m}^i)$. Next we create a signature chain by letting σ_i be the signature on $(\mathrm{VK}_{m^{i-1}|0}, (\mathrm{VK}_{m^{i-1}|1})$ with key SK_{m^i}. Finally, at the bottom of the tree we sign the whole message m using the final key SK_{m^i}. Verification is done by verifying the chain and then the signature on the final message.

A punctured key for (m_1^*, m_2^*) can be created by giving out $(\mathrm{SK}_{\overline{m}^i}$ for $i \in [1, n]$, a puncturable PRF key that is punctured as all prefixes of m_1^*, a signature on (m_1^*, m_2^*), and the signature certificates along the path. The fact that the one-time signatures are deterministic coupled with the deterministic process for generating one-time keys allows for corresponding signatures from the master and punctured keys to be the same.

The Main Construction. Now that we have this tool in place we can get back to our universal sampler construction. As mentioned in the work of [9], when using indistinguishability obfuscation in the random oracle model, the hash function(s) modeled as a random oracle *must* be outside the obfuscated circuit(s). Our approach for doing so is different from that of [9], and a remarkable feature of our scheme is its simplicity. The sampler setup algorithm will first generate a prefix restricted signature scheme verification and signing key pair. Next the universal sampler parameters are created as the obfuscation of a program that takes two inputs x, d and outputs $p = d(r)$, where r is computed using a puncturable PRF on input $x || d$. The program also outputs a signature σ (using the signing key) on $(x || d, p)$ using a prefix-restricted signature scheme. The sampler parameters, U, are the obfuscated program and the verification key VK of the universal sampler is the verification key of the prefix restricted signature.

To sample from a distribution d, one computes $x = H(d)$ and runs the sampler output on inputs x, d. Finally, the verification algorithm is used to check that p was the correct output sample for a circuit d when given a prefix restricted signature σ. The verification algorithm first computes $x = H(d)$. Then, it simply checks that the signature σ verifies on the message $m = (m_1, m_2) = (x || d, p)$.

We can now examine the overhead of verification in our sampler which is simply the prefix restricted signature verification on $(x || d, p)$. The cost of performing this will be ℓ one-time signature verifications where ℓ is the bit length of $x || d$. In our construction the bit length of x will be roughly the size of the output size of samples plus a security parameter and the bit length of d corresponds to the string describing the circuit. While the time to verify these ℓ one time signatures is significantly longer than a standard signature scheme, the verification time will be much shorter than running the obfuscated program. Moreover, we would expect it to remain so even as improvements in obfuscation move towards making it realizable.

Proving Security. The security of our universal sampler with verification is based on subexponential hardness of the underlying building blocks of indistinguishability obfuscation, puncturable pseudorandom functions, and prefix restricted signatures. In addition, the random oracle heuristic is used to prove security.

Let's start by looking at verification security. At a high level our proof proceeds at as a sequence of games. Assume there exists a PPT attacker $\mathcal{A}$ that makes at most q (unique) queries to the random oracle and produces a forgery σ^* of an output p^* on d^*. Our proof starts by guessing both value of d^* and which random oracle query $i \in [q]$ corresponds to d^*. The reduction will abort if the guess is incorrect. It is this complexity leveraging step of guessing over all possible d^* values that requires the use of sub exponential hardness.

Next, suppose that the actual output of the Sample algorithm on input d is out and let $H(d^*) = x^*)$. We change the sampler parameters U to be an obfuscation of a program that uses a restricted key that cannot sign a message ($m_1 = x^*||d^*, m_2$) if $m_2 \neq$ out. This transition is indistinguishable to the attacker by indistinguishability obfuscation. For this proof step to go through it is critical the signatures produced from the master key and punctured keys are deterministic and consistent so that the corresponding programs are equivalent. Finally, the proof can be completed by invoking the hardness of breaking the prefix restricted signature.

We now turn to the proof of proving existing definition from [9] of the indistinguishability of real world and ideal. Our proof proceeds in a similar manner to theirs in that we switch from generating samples from the obfuscated program to receiving them via "delayed backdoor programming" from the random oracle. One important difference is that our main obfuscated program computes the output of samples directly, whereas the main program of Hofheinz et al. produces a one-time sampler program, which is then itself invoked to produce the actual sample.

In doing things directly we benefit from a more direct construction at the expense of applying complexity leveraging. Our proof will proceeds as a hybrid that programs the outputs of the random oracle one at a time. At each step our reduction must guess the input to the random oracle. Thus, if D is the number of possible circuits, we get a loss of $D \cdot q$ in the reduction. (We emphasize that we avoid a loss of D^q which could not be overcome with complexity leveraging.) Again, this loss is balanced out by the use of sub exponential hardness. We also made our proof steps more modular than those in [9]. One tool in doing so is the introduction of a tool we call a puncturable pseudorandom deterministic encryption scheme.

Other Applications of Fast Verification. In addition, to the application of establishing a set of common parameters for a cryptographic scheme [9] give multiple other applications of universal samplers. Here we sketch how some of these can benefit if the sampler has fast verification.

In the Identity-Based Encryption scheme given in [9] a user performs an encryption to an identity Id by first running Sample(U, d_{ID}) where d is a circuit that samples and outputs a fresh public key pk_{ID}. This key is then used to encrypt to the identity. Consider a scenario where more than one party wishes to perform an IBE encryption to the same identity. Using a sampler with fast verification a single party can perform the work of computing pk_{ID} and then share this with all other parties (sparing the rest of them from performing the computation). The other parties will be convinced of the authenticity via the certificate and verification procedure.

Another possibility is that instead of multiple parties wishing to perform the computation, there could be a single party running on a machine that has a untrusted processing environment that is coupled with a trusted, but more expensive environment. Here it would make sense for the untrusted environment to perform the sampling and pass on the answer to the more trusted environment to do the rest of the Identity-Based Encryption.

In general these motivational examples will transcend to other applications of universal samplers ranging from non-interactive key exchange [9] to new constructions of constrained PRFs [10]. In particular, adding the fast verification property helps in any multiparty scenario where multiple (untrusting) parties want to share the output of a call to a sample algorithm. Or where a single party can move the Sample algorithm to an untrusted environment.

1.1 Organization

In Sect. 2, we introduce some notations and preliminaries. Next, we define our primitive - *universal sampler with verification* in Sect. 3. To construct a selectively secure universal sampler with (fast) verification, we require the notion of *prefix-restricted signature schemes* defined in Sect. 4. For the construction, we also require the notion of *puncturable pseudorandom deterministic encryption scheme* defined in Sect. 5. Finally, in Sect. 6, we present our fast verification universal sampler scheme.

2 Preliminaries

2.1 Notations

For integers $\ell_{\text{ckt}}, \ell_{\text{inp}}, \ell_{\text{out}}$, let $C[\ell_{\text{ckt}}, \ell_{\text{inp}}, \ell_{\text{out}}]$ be the set of circuits that have size at most ℓ_{ckt} bits, take ℓ_{inp} bits as input and output ℓ_{out} bits.

2.2 Puncturable Pseudorandom Functions

The notion of constrained PRFs was introduced in the concurrent works of [4,6,13]. Punctured PRFs, first termed by [15] are a special class of constrained PRFs.

A PRF $F : \mathcal{K} \times \mathcal{X} \to \mathcal{Y}$ is a puncturable pseudorandom function if there is an additional key space $\mathcal{K}_p$ and three polynomial time algorithms $F.\text{setup}$, $F.\text{eval}$ and $F.\text{puncture}$ as follows:

- $F.\text{setup}(1^\lambda)$ is a randomized algorithm that takes the security parameter λ as input and outputs a description of the key space $\mathcal{K}$, the punctured key space $\mathcal{K}_p$ and the PRF F.
- $F.\text{puncture}(K, x)$ is a randomized algorithm that takes as input a PRF key $K \in \mathcal{K}$ and $x \in \mathcal{X}$, and outputs a key $K\{x\} \in \mathcal{K}_p$.
- $F.\text{eval}(K\{x\}, x')$ is a deterministic algorithm that takes as input a punctured key $K\{x\} \in \mathcal{K}_p$ and $x' \in \mathcal{X}$. Let $K \in \mathcal{K}, x \in \mathcal{X}$ and $K\{x\} \leftarrow F.\text{puncture}(K, x)$. For correctness, we need the following property:

$$F.\text{eval}(K\{x\}, x') = \begin{cases} F(K, x') & \text{if } x \neq x' \\ \perp & \text{otherwise} \end{cases}$$

We will now recall the selective security game for puncturable PRFs. The following definition is equivalent to the one in [15]. Consider a challenger C and adversary A. The security game between C and A consists of two phases.

Challenge Phase: The adversary A sends its challenge string x^*. The challenger chooses a uniformly random PRF key $K \leftarrow \mathcal{K}$. Next, it chooses a bit $b \in \{0,1\}$ and a uniformly random string $y \leftarrow \mathcal{Y}$. It computes $K\{x^*\} \leftarrow F.\text{puncture}(K, x^*)$. If $b = 0$, the challenger outputs $K\{x^*\}$ and $(F(K, x^*), y)$. Else, the challenger outputs $K\{x^*\}$ and $(y, F(K, x^*))$.

Guess: A outputs a guess b' of b.

A wins the security game if $b = b'$. The advantage of A in the security game against F is defined as $\text{Adv}_A^F = \Pr[b = b'] - 1/2$.

Definition 1. *The PRF F is a selectively secure puncturable PRF if for all probabilistic polynomial time adversaries A $\text{Adv}_A^F(\lambda)$ is negligible in λ.*

Remark 1. Note the difference between this definition and the one in previous works is in the challenge phase. Here, we require that the challenger output a punctured PRF key and a pair $(y_0, y_1) \in \mathcal{Y}^2$. It chooses a bit b. If $b = 0$, then $y_0 = F(K, x^*)$ and y_1 is chosen uniformly at random. Else, y_0 is chosen uniformly at random and $y_1 = F(K, x^*)$.

Remark 2. This definition can be extended to handle multiple points being punctured. More formally, we can define the notion of t-puncturable PRFs, where the PRF key K can be punctured at t points. In the selective security game, the adversary chooses the t puncture points, sends them to the challenger. The challenger outputs a key punctured at the t points, along with t output strings, which are either PRF evaluations at the t points or uniformly random strings.

2.3   Indistinguishability Obfuscation

We recall the definition of indistinguishability obfuscation from [7,15].

Definition 2 (Indistinguishability Obfuscation). *Let $\mathcal{C} = \{\mathcal{C}_\lambda\}_{\lambda \in \mathbb{N}}$ be a family of polynomial-size circuits. Let $i\mathcal{O}$ be a uniform PPT algorithm that takes as input the security parameter λ, a circuit $C \in \mathcal{C}_\lambda$ and outputs a circuit C'. $i\mathcal{O}$ is called an indistinguishability obfuscator for a circuit class $\{\mathcal{C}_\lambda\}$ if it satisfies the following conditions:*

- *(Preserving Functionality) For all security parameters $\lambda \in \mathbb{N}$, for all $C \in \mathcal{C}_\lambda$, for all inputs x, we have that $C'(x) = C(x)$ where $C' \leftarrow i\mathcal{O}(1^\lambda, C)$.*
- *(Indistinguishability of Obfuscation) For any (not necessarily uniform) PPT distinguisher $\mathcal{B} = (Samp, \mathcal{D})$, there exists a negligible function $\text{negl}(\cdot)$ such that the following holds: if for all security parameters $\lambda \in \mathbb{N}$, $\forall x, C_0(x) = C_1(x) : (C_0; C_1; \sigma) \leftarrow Samp(1^\lambda)$, then*

$$| \Pr[\mathcal{D}(\sigma, i\mathcal{O}(1^\lambda, C_0)) = 1 : (C_0; C_1; \sigma) \leftarrow Samp(1^\lambda)] -$$
$$\Pr[\mathcal{D}(\sigma, i\mathcal{O}(1^\lambda, C_1)) = 1 : (C_0; C_1; \sigma) \leftarrow Samp(1^\lambda)]|$$
$$\leq negl(\lambda).$$

In a recent work, [7] showed how indistinguishability obfuscators can be constructed for the circuit class *P/poly*. We remark that $(Samp, \mathcal{D})$ are two algorithms that pass state, which can be viewed equivalently as a single stateful algorithm $\mathcal{B}$. In our proofs we employ the latter approach, although here we state the definition as it appears in prior work.

3   Universal Samplers with Verification

We will now define the syntax and security definitions for universal samplers with verification. In this primitive, as in [9], there is an algorithm Setup which outputs a sampler parameter U as well as a sampling algorithm Sample which maps the sampler parameters and input circuit to an element sampled from the desired distribution. We modify this definition so that Setup also outputs a verification key VK, and Sample also outputs a 'certificate' σ asserting that the sampler output matches the input circuit. An additional algorithm, Check, takes VK, σ, and the input circuit, and checks whether these are consistent.

Syntax. Let ℓ_{ckt}, ℓ_{inp} and ℓ_{out} be polynomials. An $(\ell_{ckt}, \ell_{inp}, \ell_{out})$-universal sampler scheme consists of algorithms Setup, Sample and Check defined below.

- Setup(1^λ) takes as input the security parameter λ and outputs the sampler parameters U and a verification key VK.
- Sample(U, d) takes as input the universal sampler U and a circuit $d \in \mathcal{C}[\ell_{ckt}(\lambda), \ell_{inp}(\lambda), \ell_{out}(\lambda)]$. The output of the function is the induced parameters $p_d \in \{0, 1\}^{\ell_{out}(\lambda)}$ and a certificate σ_d.
- Check(VK, d, p, σ) takes as input the verification key VK, the circuit $d \in \mathcal{C}[\ell_{ckt}(\lambda), \ell_{inp}(\lambda), \ell_{out}(\lambda)], p \in \{0, 1\}^{\ell_{out}(\lambda)}$ and a certificate σ. It outputs either 0 or 1.

For simplicity of notation, we will drop the dependence of $\ell_{ckt}, \ell_{inp}, \ell_{out}$ on λ when the context is clear.

Correctness. For correctness, we require that any honestly generated output and certificate must pass the verification. More formally, for all security parameters λ, $(U, VK) \leftarrow$ Setup(1^λ), circuit $d \in \mathcal{C}[\ell_{ckt}, \ell_{inp}, \ell_{out}]$,

$$\mathsf{Check}(VK, d, \mathsf{Sample}(U, d)) = 1.$$

3.1   Security

For security, we require the primitive to satisfy the real vs ideal world definition from [9]. In addition to that, we also need to ensure that no adversary can output 'fake certificates'. This intuition is captured by the following unforgeability definitions. Informally, we require that any PPT adversary should not be able to output a tuple (d^*, p^*, σ^*) such that $\mathsf{Sample}(U, d^*) \neq p^*$ but $\mathsf{Check}(U, d^*, p^*, \sigma^*) = 1$. For clarity of presentation, we chose to present the [9] definitions for real vs ideal world indistinguishability in Appendix 3.2.

The security definition given here is an adaptive game in the random oracle model. One could consider presenting the definition in the standard model. However, as shown in [9], the simulation security definition must involve the random oracle. As a result, we choose to have a random oracle based definition for unforgeability as well.

Definition 3. *An* $(\ell_{\mathrm{ckt}}, \ell_{\mathrm{inp}}, \ell_{\mathrm{out}})$-*universal sampler scheme* (Setup, Sample, Check) *is said to be a aptively secure against forgeries if every PPT adversary* $\mathcal{A}$, $\Pr[\mathcal{A}$ *wins in* $\mathsf{Expt}] \leq negl(\lambda)$, *where* Expt *is defined as follows.*

1. *The challenger sends* $(U, \mathrm{VK}) \leftarrow \mathsf{Setup}(1^\lambda)$ *to* $\mathcal{A}$.
2. $\mathcal{A}$ *sends random oracle queries* (RO, x). *For each unique query, the challenger chooses a uniformly random string* y *and outputs* y. *It also adds the tuple* (x, y) *to its table.*
3. $\mathcal{A}$ *sends its output* (p^*, σ^*) *to the challenger.*

$\mathcal{A}$ *wins if* $\mathsf{Check}(\mathrm{VK}, d^*, p^*, \sigma^*) = 1$ *and* $\mathsf{Sample}(U, d^*) \neq p^*$.

3.2   Simulation Security - Real vs Ideal World Indistinguishability

In this part, we will recall the adaptive security definition for universal samplers from [9]. As in [9], an *admissible adversary* is an interactive Turing Machine that outputs one bit, with the following input/output behavior:

- $\mathcal{A}$ takes as input security parameter λ and sampler parameters U.
- $\mathcal{A}$ can send a random oracle query (RO, x), and receives the output of the random oracle on input x.
- $\mathcal{A}$ can send a message of the form (params, d) where $d \in \mathcal{C}[\ell_{\mathrm{ckt}}, \ell_{\mathrm{inp}}, \ell_{\mathrm{out}}]$. Upon sending this message, $\mathcal{A}$ is required to honestly compute $p_d = \mathsf{Sample}(U, d)$, making use of any additional random oracle queries, and $\mathcal{A}$ appends (d, p_d) to an auxiliary tape.

Let SimUGen and SimRO be PPT algorithms. Consider the following two experiments:

$\mathsf{Real}^{\mathcal{A}}(1^\lambda)$:

1. The random oracle RO is implemented by assigning random outputs to each unique query made to RO.

2. $U \leftarrow \mathsf{Setup}^{\mathsf{RO}}(1^\lambda)$.
3. $\mathcal{A}(1^\lambda, U)$ is executed, where every message of the form (RO, x) receives the response $\mathsf{RO}(x)$.
4. Upon termination of $\mathcal{A}$, the output of the experiment is the final output of the execution of $\mathcal{A}$.

$\mathsf{Ideal}^{\mathcal{A}}_{\mathsf{SimUGen},\mathsf{SimRO}}(1^\lambda)$:

1. A truly random function F that maps ℓ_{ckt} bits to ℓ_{inp} bits is implemented by assigning random ℓ_{inp}-bit outputs to each unique query made to F. Throughout this experiment, a Samples Oracle O is implemented as follows: On input d, where $d \in \mathcal{C}[\ell_{\mathrm{ckt}}, \ell_{\mathrm{inp}}, \ell_{\mathrm{out}}]$, O outputs $d(F(d))$.
2. $(U, \tau) \leftarrow \mathsf{SimUGen}(1^\lambda)$. Here, $\mathsf{SimUGen}$ can make arbitrary queries to the Samples Oracle O.
3. $\mathcal{A}(1^\lambda, U)$ and $\mathsf{SimRO}(\tau)$ begin simultaneous execution.
   - Whenever $\mathcal{A}$ sends a message of the form (RO, x), this is forwarded to SimRO, which produces a response to be sent back to $\mathcal{A}$.
   - SimRO can make any number of queries to the Samples Oracle O.
   - Finally, after $\mathcal{A}$ sends any message of the form (params, d), the auxiliary tape of $\mathcal{A}$ is examined until an entry of the form (d, p_d) is added to it. At this point, if p_d is not equal to $d(F(d))$, then experiment aborts, resulting in an *Honest Sample Violation*.
4. Upon termination of $\mathcal{A}$, the output of the experiment is the final output of the execution of $\mathcal{A}$.

Definition 4. *A universal sampler scheme* $\mathcal{U} = (\mathsf{Setup}, \mathsf{Sample})$, *parameterized by polynomials* $\ell_{\mathrm{ckt}}, \ell_{\mathrm{inp}}$ *and* ℓ_{out}, *is said to be adaptively secure in the random oracle model if there exist PPT algorithms* $\mathsf{SimUGen}$ *and* SimRO *such that for all PPT adversaries* $\mathcal{A}$, *the following hold:*[3]

$$\Pr[\mathsf{Ideal}^{\mathcal{A}}_{\mathsf{SimUGen},\mathsf{SimRO}}(1^\lambda) aborts] = 0$$

and

$$\left| \Pr[\mathsf{Real}^{\mathcal{A}}(1^\lambda) = 1] - \Pr[\mathsf{Ideal}^{\mathcal{A}}_{\mathsf{SimUGen},\mathsf{SimRO}}(1^\lambda) = 1] \right| \leq negl(\lambda).$$

4 Prefix-Restricted Signatures

In this section we describe a primitive, *prefix-restricted signature schemes*. These are a form of constrained signature [5] which will be used as a building block in the main construction. A prefix-restricted signature schemes is over a message space $\mathcal{M}_1 \times \mathcal{M}_2$ and differs from an ordinary signature scheme in the following ways:

---

[3] The definition in [9] only requires this probability to be negligible in λ. However, the construction actually achieves zero probability of Honest Sample Violation. Hence, for the simplicity of our proof, we will use this definition.

- A secret key can either be a "master secret key" or admit a "punctured" form at a message (m_1^*, m_2^*) capable of signing any message (m_1, m_2) such that (a) $m_1 \neq m_1^*$ or (b) $(m_1, m_2) = (m_1^*, m_2^*)$.
- In our security game an attacker selectively gives (m_1^*, m_2^*) and receives back a corresponding punctured signing key. No signing queries are allowed. The attacker should be unable to provide a signature on any message (m_1, m_2) where $m_1 = m_1^*$ and $m_2 \neq m_2^*$.
  Our security property does not allow the adversary to make signing queries on any message; these are not needed for our purposes.
- The scheme is deterministic, even with respect to punctured keys. That is, signatures produced by punctured keys (on messages for which this is possible) must be equal to those produced by unpunctured keys on the same messages.

This last point is the most important, since this strong determinism is required to obtain the functional equivalence required by indistinguishability obfuscation; it is also the reason that we could not use an existing primitive.

4.1   Definition

Let $\mathcal{M}_1$ and $\mathcal{M}_2$ be two message spaces. We define a prefix-restricted signature scheme for message space $\mathcal{M}_1 \times \mathcal{M}_2$ as a collection of five algorithms:

- Pre.Setup(1^λ) is a randomized algorithm that takes as input the security parameter λ and outputs a master signing key MSK and verification key VK.
- Pre.Sign(MSK, (m_1, m_2)) is a deterministic algorithm that takes a master signing key MSK and message pair (m_1, m_2), and outputs a signature σ.
- Pre.Verify(VK, (m_1, m_2), σ) is deterministic and takes a message pair (m_1, m_2), verification key VK and signature σ, and outputs a bit.
- Pre.Restrict(MSK, (m_1^*, m_2^*)) (possibly randomized) takes a master signing key MSK and message pair (m_1^*, m_2^*), and outputs a restricted key SK$\{m_1^*, m_2^*\}$.
- Pre.ResSign(SK$\{m_1^*, m_2^*\}$, (m_1, m_2)) is deterministic and takes a restricted signing key SK$\{m_1^*, m_2^*\}$, a message pair (m_1, m_2), and outputs a signature σ.

Correctness. We define correctness by the following conditions:

1. For all (MSK, VK) $\leftarrow$ Pre.Setup(1^λ) and message pairs $(m_1, m_2) \in \mathcal{M}_1 \times \mathcal{M}_2$,

$$\text{Pre.Verify}(\text{VK}, (m_1, m_2), \text{Pre.Sign}(\text{MSK}, (m_1, m_2))) = 1.$$

2. For all (MSK, VK) $\leftarrow$ Pre.Setup(1^λ), $(m_1^*, m_2^*) \in \mathcal{M}_1 \times \mathcal{M}_2$, SK$\{m_1^*, m_2^*\} \leftarrow$ Pre.Restrict(MSK, (m_1^*, m_2^*)), and messages $(m_1, m_2) \in \mathcal{M}_1 \times \mathcal{M}_2$ such that either $m_1 \neq m_1^*$ or $(m_1, m_2) = (m_1^*, m_2^*)$,

$$\text{Pre.Sign}(\text{MSK}, (m_1, m_2)) = \text{Pre.ResSign}(\text{SK}\{m_1^*, m_2^*\}, (m_1, m_2)).$$

Security. For security, we require that no polynomial time adversary can output a forgery, even after receiving a restricted signing key.

Definition 5. *A two message signature scheme is selectively secure if every PPT adversary $\mathcal{A}$ has at most negligible advantage in the following security game:*

1. *$\mathcal{A}$ provides a message pair (m_1^*, m_2^*).*
2. *The challenger generates the keys $(\text{MSK}, \text{VK}) \leftarrow \text{Pre.Setup}(1^\lambda)$ and $\text{SK}\{m_1^*, m_2^*\} \leftarrow \text{Pre.Restrict}(\text{MSK}, (m_1^*, m_2^*))$ and sends the tuple $(\text{SK}\{m_1^*, m_2^*\}, \text{VK})$ to $\mathcal{A}$.*
3. *$\mathcal{A}$ replies with a message pair (m_1, m_2) such that $m_1 = m_1^*$ but $m_2 \neq m_2^*$, and signature σ and wins if it verifies; that is, $\text{Pre.Verify}(\text{VK}, (m_1, m_2), \sigma) = 1$.*

We define $\mathcal{A}$'s advantage to be $\Pr[\mathcal{A} \text{ wins}]$.

4.2 Construction

Next, we construct a restricted-prefix signature scheme from a secure puncturable PRF F and secure deterministic one-time signature scheme $(\text{KeyGen}_1, \text{Sign}_1, \text{Verify}_1)$. Deterministic one-time signature schemes can be constructed using one-way functions.

We consider $m = (m_1, m_2)$ to be a single message; let N be the total length $|m| = |m_1| + |m_2|$ and $n = |m_1|$. Our message space is thus $\{0,1\}^N = \{0,1\}^n \times \{0,1\}^{N-n}$. We further define ℓ to be the bit-length of the verification keys produced by KeyGen_1, and require the domain of $F(K, \cdot)$ to be all bitstrings of length at most n. Assume also that the message space of the one-time signature scheme is all bitstrings of length at most $\max\{N, 2\ell+1\}$. Finally, ϵ denotes the empty string.

For any message m and $i \in \{1, \ldots, N\}$ we define

$$m^i = \text{the } i\text{-bit prefix of } m$$
$$\overline{m}^i = \text{the } i\text{-bit prefix of } m \text{ with bit } i \text{ flipped}$$
$$m[i] = \text{the } i\text{th bit of } m$$
$$\overline{m[i]} = \text{the opposite of the } i\text{th bit of } m$$

Notice that with this notation, if $m = (m_1, m_2)$ that $m_1 = m^n$.

Finally, we also define an operator $\text{switch}_b(x, y)$ as follows:

$$\text{switch}_b(x, y) = \begin{cases} (x, y) & \text{if } b = 0. \\ (y, x) & \text{otherwise} \end{cases}$$

Our algorithms are defined as follows:

- $\text{Pre.Setup}(1^\lambda)$ first generates a puncturable PRF key $K \leftarrow F.\text{setup}(1^\lambda)$, then $(\text{SK}_\epsilon, \text{VK}_\epsilon) \leftarrow \text{KeyGen}_1(1^\lambda; F(K, \epsilon))$.
  The verification key is VK_ϵ; the secret key is (K, SK_ϵ).

- Pre.Sign$((K, \mathrm{SK}_\epsilon), m)$ For each i from 1 to n compute

$$(\mathrm{SK}_{m^i}, \mathrm{VK}_{m^i}) = \mathsf{KeyGen}_1(1^\lambda; F(K, m^i))$$
$$(\mathrm{SK}_{\overline{m}^i}, \mathrm{VK}_{\overline{m}^i}) = \mathsf{KeyGen}_1(1^\lambda; F(K, \overline{m}^i))$$
$$(\mathrm{VK}_i, \mathrm{VK}'_i) = \mathsf{switch}_{m[i]}(\mathrm{VK}_{m^i}, \mathrm{VK}_{\overline{m}^i})$$
$$\sigma_i = \mathsf{Sign}(\mathrm{SK}_{m^{i-1}}, (\mathrm{VK}_i, \mathrm{VK}'_i))$$

Finally, compute

$$\sigma^* = \mathsf{Sign}(\mathrm{SK}_{m^n}, m)$$

and output

$$\sigma = \left\{ (\mathrm{VK}_i, \mathrm{VK}'_i, \sigma_i)_{i=1}^n, \sigma^* \right\}$$

- Pre.Verify$(\mathrm{VK}_\epsilon, m, \sigma = \{(\mathrm{VK}_i, \mathrm{VK}'_i, \sigma_i)_{i=1}^n, \sigma^*\})$ checks that for each i from 0 to $(n-1)$, that

$$\mathsf{Verify}_1(\mathrm{VK}_i, \sigma_{i+1}, (\mathrm{VK}_{i+1}, \mathrm{VK}'_{i+1})) = 1$$

Here we consider $\mathrm{VK}_0 = \mathrm{VK}_\epsilon$. We check also that

$$\mathsf{Verify}_1(\mathrm{VK}_n, \sigma^*, m) = 1$$

We output 1 if the above checks passed; otherwise output 0.
- Pre.Restrict$((K, \mathrm{SK}_\epsilon), m)$ computes, for each i from 1 to n,

$$(\mathrm{SK}_{m^i}, \mathrm{VK}_{m^i}) = \mathsf{KeyGen}_1(1^\lambda; F(K, m^i))$$
$$(\mathrm{SK}_{\overline{m}^i}, \mathrm{VK}_{\overline{m}^i}) = \mathsf{KeyGen}_1(1^\lambda; F(K, \overline{m}^i))$$
$$(\mathrm{VK}_i, \mathrm{VK}'_i) = \mathsf{switch}_{m[i]}(\mathrm{VK}_{m^i}, \mathrm{VK}_{\overline{m}^i})$$
$$\sigma_i = \mathsf{Sign}(\mathrm{SK}_{m^{i-1}}, (\mathrm{VK}_i, \mathrm{VK}'_i))$$

as well as

$$\sigma^* = \mathsf{Sign}(\mathrm{SK}_{m^n}, m)$$

It bundles these up into

$$\sigma = \left\{ (\mathrm{VK}_i, \mathrm{VK}'_i, \sigma_i)_{i=1}^n, \sigma^* \right\}$$

Next, it punctures the key K at $\{m^i\}_{i=1}^n \cup \{\epsilon\}$ to obtain a punctured key K'. It outputs the punctured key as

$$\mathrm{SK}\{m\} = \{\sigma, \{\mathrm{SK}_{\overline{m}^i}\}_{i=1}^n, K'\}$$

- Pre.ResSign$(\mathrm{SK}\{m_*\}, m)$ First, expand $\mathrm{SK}\{m_*\}$ as

$$\mathrm{SK}\{m_*\} = \left\{ \sigma = \{(\mathrm{VK}_i, \mathrm{VK}'_i, \sigma_i^*)_{i=1}^n, \sigma^*\}, \{\mathrm{SK}'_i\}_{i=1}^n, K' \right\}$$

We have three cases:
- If $m = m_*$ output σ.
- Otherwise, if $m^n = m_*^n$ but $m \neq m_*$ output $\perp$.

- Otherwise, there is some least bit position i^*, $1 \leq i^* < n$ such that $m[i] \neq m^*[i]$. For $1 \leq i \leq i^*$ set $(\mathrm{VK}_i^{\mathrm{res}}, \mathrm{VK}_i^{\prime\mathrm{res}}, \sigma_i) = (\mathrm{VK}_i, \mathrm{VK}_i', \sigma_i^*)$. For $i^* < i \leq n$ compute

$$(\mathrm{SK}_{m^i}, \mathrm{VK}_{m^i}) = \mathsf{KeyGen}_1(1^\lambda; F(K', m^i))$$
$$(\mathrm{SK}_{\overline{m}^i}, \mathrm{VK}_{\overline{m}^i}) = \mathsf{KeyGen}_1(1^\lambda; F_{K'}(\overline{m}^i))$$
$$(\mathrm{VK}_i^{\mathrm{res}}, \mathrm{VK}_i^{\prime\mathrm{res}}) = \mathsf{switch}_{m[i]}(\mathrm{VK}_{m^i}, \mathrm{VK}_{\overline{m}^i})$$
$$\sigma_i = \mathsf{Sign}(\mathrm{SK}_{m^{i-1}}, (\mathrm{VK}_i^{\mathrm{res}}, \mathrm{VK}_i^{\prime\mathrm{res}}))$$

(Notice that since $m^{i-1} \neq m_*^{i-1}$ for all $i > i^*$, we are not evaluating $F_{K'}$ on any punctured points.) Finally compute $\sigma^* = \mathsf{Sign}(\mathrm{SK}_{m^n}, m)$ and output

$$\sigma = \left\{ (\mathrm{VK}_i^{\mathrm{res}}, \mathrm{VK}_i^{\prime\mathrm{res}}, \sigma_i)_{i=1}^n, \sigma^* \right\}$$

Correctness. For correctness, we need to show that any signature computed using the master signing key verifies, and any signature computed using the restricted key on an unrestricted message is same as the signature computed using the master signing key. The first property is immediate, and follows from the correctness of the one-time deterministic signature scheme.

To prove the second correctness condition, let m be any N bit message, and let $(K, \mathrm{SK}_\epsilon)$ be any master signing key output by $\mathsf{Pre.Setup}$. The restricted key $\mathrm{SK}\{m\}$ consists of a signature $\sigma = \{(\mathrm{VK}_j, \mathrm{VK}_j', \sigma_j)_{j \leq n}, \sigma^*\}$, n secret keys $\{\mathrm{SK}_{\overline{m}^i}\}_{i \leq n}$ and a PRF key K' punctured at $\{\epsilon \cup \{m^i\}\}$. The restricted secret key $\mathrm{SK}\{m\}$ can be used to sign m and any message $\widetilde{m}$ such that $m^n \neq \widetilde{m}^n$. Clearly, $\mathsf{Pre.ResSign}(\mathrm{SK}\{m\}, m) = \mathsf{Pre.Sign}(\mathrm{SK}, m) = \sigma$.

Consider any message $\widetilde{m}$ such that $m^n \neq \widetilde{m}^n$. Let $i \leq n$ be the first index such that $m[i] \neq \widetilde{m}[i]$, and let $\widetilde{\sigma} = \mathsf{Sign}(\mathrm{SK}, \widetilde{m})$, $\widetilde{\sigma^{\mathrm{res}}} = \mathsf{ResSign}(\mathrm{SK}\{m\}, \widetilde{m})$, where $\widetilde{\sigma} = \{(\widetilde{\mathrm{VK}}_j, \widetilde{\mathrm{VK}}_j', \widetilde{\sigma}_j)_{j \leq n}, \widetilde{\sigma^*}\}$ and $\widetilde{\sigma^{\mathrm{res}}} = \{(\widetilde{\mathrm{VK}}_j^{\mathrm{res}}, \widetilde{\mathrm{VK}}_j^{\prime\mathrm{res}}, \widetilde{\sigma_j^{\mathrm{res}}})_{j \leq n}, \widetilde{\sigma^{*\mathrm{res}}}\}$. We need to show that $\widetilde{\sigma} = \widetilde{\sigma^{\mathrm{res}}}$.

From the definition of $\mathsf{Pre.ResSign}$, it follows that for $j \leq i$, $(\widetilde{\mathrm{VK}}_j^{\mathrm{res}}, \widetilde{\mathrm{VK}}_j^{\prime\mathrm{res}}, \widetilde{\sigma_j^{\mathrm{res}}}) = (\widetilde{\mathrm{VK}}_j, \widetilde{\mathrm{VK}}_j', \widetilde{\sigma}_j)$ for all $j \leq i$. Similarly, from the definition of $\mathsf{Pre.Sign}$, it follows that $(\widetilde{\mathrm{VK}}_j, \widetilde{\mathrm{VK}}_j', \widetilde{\sigma}_j) = (\widetilde{\mathrm{VK}}_j, \widetilde{\mathrm{VK}}_j', \widetilde{\sigma}_j)$ for all $j \leq i$ (this is because for $j < i, m^j = \widetilde{m}^j$, and for $j = i$, $(\mathrm{VK}_j, \mathrm{VK}_j') = (\widetilde{\mathrm{VK}}_j, \widetilde{\mathrm{VK}}_j)$).

Finally, for all $j > i$, the punctured PRF key K' can be used to compute the correct secret key/verification key pair, since $\widetilde{m}^j \neq m^j$ for all $j > i$. Therefore, the signature components for $j > i$ are same for both $\widetilde{\sigma}$ and $\widetilde{\sigma^{\mathrm{res}}}$. This concludes our correctness proof.

Security. We prove security of this construction in the following theorem.

Theorem 1. *Assuming F is a selectively secure puncturable PRF and (Setup_1, KeyGen_1, Sign_1, Verify_1) is a secure one time signature scheme, the prefix-restricted signature scheme described above is secure against forgeries as described in Definition 5.*

Proof. To prove this theorem, we will first define a sequence of hybrid experiments.

Hybrid Hyb_0. This is identical to the security game for the prefix-restricted signature scheme.

1. $\mathcal{A}$ sends a message m^* of length N.
2. The challenger chooses a puncturable PRF $K \leftarrow F.\mathsf{setup}(1^\lambda)$.
   Next, it computes $(\mathrm{SK}_\epsilon, \mathrm{VK}_\epsilon) = \mathsf{Setup}_1(1^\lambda; F(K, \epsilon))$.
3. It computes a signature σ for message m^*. Let $\mathrm{SK}_0 = \mathrm{SK}_\epsilon$. For $i = 1$ to n, do the following:
   (a) It computes the keys $(\mathrm{SK}_{m^{*i}}, \mathrm{VK}_{m^{*i}}) = \mathsf{Setup}_1(1^\lambda; F(K, m^{*i}))$, $(\mathrm{SK}_{\overline{m^{*i}}}, \mathrm{VK}_{\overline{m^{*i}}}) = \mathsf{Setup}_1(1^\lambda; F(K, \overline{m^{*i}}))$.
   (b) Next, it computes $(\mathrm{VK}_i, \mathrm{VK}'_i) = \mathsf{switch}_{m^*[i]}(\mathrm{VK}_{m^{*i}}, \mathrm{VK}_{\overline{m^{*i}}})$ and $\sigma_i = \mathsf{Sign}_1(\mathrm{SK}_{m^{*(i-1)}}, (\mathrm{VK}_i, \mathrm{VK}'_i))$ for $1 \le i \le n$.
   (c) Finally, it signs m^* using $\mathrm{SK}_{m^{*n}}$, that is, it computes $\sigma^* = \mathsf{Sign}_1(\mathrm{SK}_{m^{*n}}, m^*)$. It sets $\sigma = \{(\mathrm{VK}_i, \mathrm{VK}'_i, \sigma_i)\}, \sigma^*\}$.
4. It computes a punctured key $K' \leftarrow F.\mathsf{puncture}(K, \{\{m^{*i}\}_{i \le n} \cup \epsilon\})$ and sets $\mathrm{SK}\{m^*\} = \{\sigma, \{\mathrm{SK}_{\overline{m^{*i}}}\}_{i \le n}, K'\}$.
5. Finally, the challenger sends $\mathrm{VK}_\epsilon, \mathrm{SK}\{m^*\}$ to $\mathcal{A}$.
6. $\mathcal{A}$ responds with a forgery $\widetilde{\sigma} = \{\{(\widetilde{\mathrm{VK}_i}, \widetilde{\mathrm{VK}'_i}, \widetilde{\sigma_i})\}, \widetilde{\sigma^*}\}$ and wins if
   (a) For all $1 \le i \le n$, $\mathsf{Verify}_1(\widetilde{\mathrm{VK}_{i-1}}, (\widetilde{\mathrm{VK}_i}, \widetilde{\mathrm{VK}'_i}), \widetilde{\sigma_i}) = 1$, where $\widetilde{\mathrm{VK}_0} = \mathrm{VK}_\epsilon$.
   (b) $\mathsf{Verify}_1(\widetilde{\mathrm{VK}_n}, m^*, \widetilde{\sigma^*}) = 1$.

Hybrid Hyb_1. In this experiment, the challenger chooses $(\mathrm{SK}_{m^{*i}}, \mathrm{VK}_{m^{*i}})$ using true randomness, instead of the pseudorandom string given by $F(K, m^{*i})$.

1. $\mathcal{A}$ sends a message m^* of length N.
2. The challenger chooses a puncturable PRF $K \leftarrow F.\mathsf{setup}(1^\lambda)$.
   Next, it computes $\underline{(\mathrm{SK}_\epsilon, \mathrm{VK}_\epsilon) = \mathsf{Setup}_1(1^\lambda)}$.
3. It computes a signature σ for message m^*. Let $\mathrm{SK}_0 \leftarrow \mathrm{SK}_\epsilon$. For $i = 1$ to n, do the following:
   (a) It computes the keys $\underline{(\mathrm{SK}_{m^{*i}}, \mathrm{VK}_{m^{*i}}) \leftarrow \mathsf{Setup}_1(1^\lambda)}$, $(\mathrm{SK}_{\overline{m^{*i}}}, \mathrm{VK}_{\overline{m^{*i}}}) = \mathsf{Setup}_1(1^\lambda; F(K, \overline{m^{*i}}))$.
   (b) Next, it computes $(\mathrm{VK}_i, \mathrm{VK}'_i) = \mathsf{switch}_{m^*[i]}(\mathrm{VK}_{m^{*i}}, \mathrm{VK}_{\overline{m^{*i}}})$ and $\sigma_i = \mathsf{Sign}_1(\mathrm{SK}_{m^{*(i-1)}}, (\mathrm{VK}_i, \mathrm{VK}'_i))$ for $1 \le i \le n$.
   (c) Finally, it signs m^* using $\mathrm{SK}_{m^{*n}}$, that is, it computes $\sigma^* = \mathsf{Sign}_1(\mathrm{SK}_{m^{*n}}, m^*)$. It sets $\sigma = \{(\mathrm{VK}_i, \mathrm{VK}'_i, \sigma_i)\}, \sigma^*\}$.
4. It computes a punctured key $K' \leftarrow F.\mathsf{puncture}(K, \{\{m^{*i}\}_{i \le n} \cup \epsilon\})$ and sets $\mathrm{SK}\{m^*\} = \{\sigma, \{\mathrm{SK}_{\overline{m^{*i}}}\}_{i \le n}, K'\}$.
5. Finally, the challenger sends $\mathrm{VK}_\epsilon, \mathrm{SK}\{m^*\}$ to $\mathcal{A}$.
6. $\mathcal{A}$ responds with a forgery $\widetilde{\sigma} = \{\{(\widetilde{\mathrm{VK}_i}, \widetilde{\mathrm{VK}'_i}, \widetilde{\sigma_i})\}, \widetilde{\sigma^*}\}$ and wins if
   (a) For all $1 \le i \le n$, $\mathsf{Verify}_1(\widetilde{\mathrm{VK}_{i-1}}, (\widetilde{\mathrm{VK}_i}, \widetilde{\mathrm{VK}'_i}), \widetilde{\sigma_i}) = 1$, where $\widetilde{\mathrm{VK}_0} = \mathrm{VK}_\epsilon$.
   (b) $\mathsf{Verify}_1(\widetilde{\mathrm{VK}_n}, m^*, \widetilde{\sigma^*}) = 1$.

Hybrid Hyb$_2$. In the previous hybrid, the challenger sends VK$_\epsilon$ and n verification keys VK$_{m^{*i}}$ for $1 \leq i \leq n$ as part of the signature σ. In the forgery, the adversary sends n tuples $(\widetilde{\text{VK}}_i, \widetilde{\text{VK}}'_i, \widetilde{\sigma}_i)$. In this game, the challenger guesses the first i such that VK$_{m^{*i}} \neq \widetilde{\text{VK}}_i$. It chooses $i \leftarrow \{1, \ldots, n+1\}$, where $i = n+1$ indicates the guess that VK$_{m^{*i}} = \widetilde{\text{VK}}_i$ for all i. The attacker wins if its forgery verifies and this guess is correct.

1. $\mathcal{A}$ sends a message m^* of length N.
2. The challenger first chooses $i^* \leftarrow \{1, \ldots, n+1\}$.
3. It chooses a puncturable PRF $K \leftarrow F.\text{setup}(1^\lambda)$.
   Next, it computes $(\text{SK}_\epsilon, \text{VK}_\epsilon) = \text{Setup}_1(1^\lambda)$.
4. It computes a signature σ for message m^*. Let SK$_0 \leftarrow$ SK$_\epsilon$. For $i = 1$ to n, do the following:
   (a) It computes the keys $(\text{SK}_{m^{*i}}, \text{VK}_{m^{*i}}) \leftarrow \text{Setup}_1(1^\lambda)$, $(\text{SK}_{\overline{m^{*i}}}, \text{VK}_{\overline{m^{*i}}}) = \text{Setup}_1(1^\lambda; F(K, \overline{m^{*i}}))$.
   (b) Next, it computes $(\text{VK}_i, \text{VK}'_i) = \text{switch}_{m^*[i]}(\text{VK}_{m^{*i}}, \text{VK}_{\overline{m^{*i}}})$ and $\sigma_i = \text{Sign}_1(\text{SK}_{m^{*(i-1)}}, (\text{VK}_i, \text{VK}'_i))$ for $1 \leq i \leq n$.
   (c) Finally, it signs m^* using SK$_{m^{*n}}$, that is, it computes $\sigma^* = \text{Sign}_1(\text{SK}_{m^{*n}}, m^*)$. It sets $\sigma = \{(\text{VK}_i, \text{VK}'_i, \sigma_i)\}, \sigma^*\}$.
5. It computes a punctured key $K' \leftarrow F.\text{puncture}(K, \{\{m^{*i}\}_{i \leq n} \cup \epsilon\})$ and sets $\text{SK}\{m^*\} = \{\sigma, \{\text{SK}_{\overline{m^{*i}}}\}_{i \leq n}, K'\}$.
6. Finally, the challenger sends VK$_\epsilon$, SK$\{m^*\}$ to $\mathcal{A}$.
7. $\mathcal{A}$ responds with a forgery $\widetilde{\sigma} = \{\{(\widetilde{\text{VK}}_i, \widetilde{\text{VK}}'_i, \widetilde{\sigma}_i)\}, \widetilde{\sigma^*}\}$ and wins if
   (a) For all $i < i^*$, VK$_{m^{*i}} = \widetilde{\text{VK}}_i$ and VK$_{m^{*i^*}} \neq \widetilde{\text{VK}}_{i^*}$.
   (b) For all $1 \leq i \leq n$, $\text{Verify}_1(\widetilde{\text{VK}}_{i-1}, (\widetilde{\text{VK}}_i, \widetilde{\text{VK}}'_i), \widetilde{\sigma}_i) = 1$, where $\widetilde{\text{VK}}_0 = \text{VK}_\epsilon$.
   (c) $\text{Verify}_1(\widetilde{\text{VK}}_n, m^*, \widetilde{\sigma^*}) = 1$.

Analysis. We will now analyse the probability of an adversary's success in each of these hybrids. Let $\text{Prob}^i_{\mathcal{A}}$ denote the probability of adversary $\mathcal{A}$ winning in hybrid Hyb$_i$.

Lemma 1. *Assuming F is a selectively secure puncturable pseudorandom function, for any PPT adversary $\mathcal{A}$, $|\text{Prob}^0_{\mathcal{A}} - \text{Prob}^1_{\mathcal{A}}| \leq \text{negl}(\lambda)$.*

Proof. Suppose there exists a PPT adversary $\mathcal{A}$ such that $|\text{Prob}^0_{\mathcal{A}} - \text{Prob}^1_{\mathcal{A}}| = \gamma$. We will construct a PPT algorithm $\mathcal{B}$ that uses $\mathcal{A}$ to break the selective PPRF security of F. $\mathcal{B}$ works as follows.

1. $\mathcal{B}$ receives message m^* from $\mathcal{A}$. $\mathcal{B}$ then requests the PPRF challenger for a key punctured at the set $\{\{m^{*i}\}_{i \leq n} \cup \epsilon\}$ along with the $n + 1$ evaluations at $(\epsilon, m^{*1}, \ldots, m^{*n})$. It receives a punctured key K' and the $n + 1$ strings $(y_0, \ldots, y_n)$, where y_i is either the PRF evaluation at m^{*i} or a uniformly random string.
2. Using K', it computes the PRF evaluations at $\overline{m^{*i}}$ for all $i \leq n$, that is, it sets $\overline{y}_i = F(K', \overline{m^{*i}})$.

3. $\mathcal{B}$ first computes $(\mathrm{SK}_\epsilon, \mathrm{VK}_\epsilon) = \mathsf{KeyGen}_1(1^\lambda; y_0)$.
4. It then computes, for $1 \leq i \leq n$, $(\mathrm{SK}_{m^{*i}}, \mathrm{VK}_{m^{*i}}) = \mathsf{KeyGen}_1(1^\lambda; y_i)$, $(\mathrm{SK}_{\overline{m^{*i}}}, \mathrm{VK}_{\overline{m^{*i}}}) = \mathsf{KeyGen}_1(1^\lambda; \overline{y}_i)$.
5. Next, it computes, for $1 \leq i \leq n$, $(\mathrm{VK}_i, \mathrm{VK}_i') = \mathsf{switch}_{m^*[i]}(\mathrm{VK}_{m^{*i}}, \mathrm{VK}_{\overline{m^{*i}}})$, $\sigma_i = \mathsf{Sign}_1(\mathrm{SK}_{m^{*i}}, (\mathrm{VK}_i, \mathrm{VK}_i'))$ and $\sigma^* = \mathsf{Sign}_1(\mathrm{SK}_{m^{*n}}, m)$. It sets $\sigma = \{(\mathrm{VK}_i, \mathrm{VK}_i', \sigma_i)_{i \leq n}, \sigma^*\}$.
6. $\mathcal{B}$ sets the restricted key $\mathrm{SK}\{m^*\} = \{\sigma, \{\mathrm{SK}_{\overline{m^{*i}}}\}_{i \leq n}, K'\}$ and sends $\mathrm{SK}\{m^*\}, \mathrm{VK}_\epsilon$ to $\mathcal{A}$.
7. Finally, $\mathcal{A}$ sends a forgery. If the forgery verifies, $\mathcal{B}$ sends $b' = 0$, indicating the evaluations $y_0, \ldots, y_n$ were pseudorandom; else it sends $b' = 1$.

To analyse $\mathcal{B}$'s advantage in the PPRF security game, let b denote the bit chosen by challenger. Then $\Pr[b' = 1 | b = 0] = \mathsf{Prob}_\mathcal{A}^0$ and $\Pr[b' = 1 | b = 1] = \mathsf{Prob}_\mathcal{A}^1$. Therefore, if $|\mathsf{Prob}_\mathcal{A}^0 - \mathsf{Prob}_\mathcal{A}^1|$ is non-negligible, then so is $\mathcal{B}$'s advantage in the PPRF security game.

Claim 1. *For any adversary $\mathcal{A}$, $\mathsf{Prob}_\mathcal{A}^2 = \mathsf{Prob}_\mathcal{A}^1 / (q + 1)$.*

Proof. This follows directly from the description of the hybrid experiments Hyb_1 and Hyb_2. The challenger's choice of i^* is independent of $\mathcal{A}$'s view. Therefore, $\Pr[\mathcal{A} \text{ wins in } \mathsf{Hyb}_2] = \Pr[i^* \text{ is correct guess}] \Pr[\mathcal{A} \text{ wins in } \mathsf{Hyb}_1]$.

Lemma 2. *Assuming $\mathcal{S}_1 = (\mathsf{KeyGen}_1, \mathsf{Sign}_1, \mathsf{Verify}_1)$ is a one-time secure deterministic signature scheme, $\mathsf{Prob}_\mathcal{A}^2$ is negligible in λ.*

Proof. We will construct an algorithm $\mathcal{B}$ that breaks the one-time security of $\mathcal{S}_1$ with probability $\mathsf{Prob}_\mathcal{A}^2$. $\mathcal{B}$ is defined as follows.

1. $\mathcal{B}$ chooses $i^* \leftarrow \{1, \ldots, q + 1\}$. It receives verification key VK^* from the $\mathcal{S}_1$ challenger.
2. $\mathcal{A}$ sends the challenge message m^*.
3. For all $i \neq (i^* - 1)$, it chooses $(\mathrm{SK}_{m^{*i}}, \mathrm{VK}_{m^{*i}}) \leftarrow \mathsf{KeyGen}_1(1^\lambda)$ and sets $\mathrm{VK}_{m^{*i^*-1}} = \mathrm{VK}^*$. It also computes $(\mathrm{SK}_{\overline{m^{*i}}}, \mathrm{VK}_{\overline{m^{*i}}}) = \mathsf{KeyGen}_1(1^\lambda; F(K, \overline{m^{*i}}))$.
4. Next, it must compute signatures on the verification key pairs. For all $i \neq i^*$, it computes $\sigma_i = \mathsf{Sign}_1(\mathrm{SK}_{m^{*(i-1)}}, \mathsf{switch}_{m^*[i]}(\mathrm{VK}_{m^{*i}}, \mathrm{VK}_{\overline{m^{*i}}}))$. For $i = i^*$, if $i^* \neq n+1$, it sends as signature query the tuple $\mathsf{switch}_{m^*[i^*]}(\mathrm{VK}_{m^{*i^*}}, \mathrm{VK}_{\overline{m^{*i^*}}})$ to the $\mathcal{S}_1$ challenger; if $i^* = n+1$, it sends m as the signature query. It receives σ^* in response. Therefore, $\mathcal{B}$ can perfectly simulate the signature σ on m^*.
5. To compute the restricted signing key, it computes $K' \leftarrow F.\mathsf{puncture}(K, \{\{m^{*i}\} \cup \epsilon\})$. It has all the required signing keys $\mathrm{SK}_{\overline{m^{*i}}}$. Therefore, it sends VK_ϵ and $\mathrm{SK}\{m^*\} = \{\{\mathrm{SK}_{\overline{m^{*i}}}\}, K', \sigma\}$.
6. $\mathcal{A}$ finally sends a forgery. If $\mathcal{A}$ wins in Hyb_2, then it must send $(\widetilde{\mathrm{VK}_{i^*}}, \widetilde{\mathrm{VK}_{i^*}}) \neq (\mathrm{VK}_{m^{*i^*}}, \mathrm{VK}_{\overline{m^{*i^*}}})$ but $\mathsf{Verify}_1(\mathrm{VK}_{m^{*(i^*-1)}}, (\widetilde{\mathrm{VK}_{i^*}}, \widetilde{\mathrm{VK}_{i^*}})) = 1$. Therefore $\mathcal{B}$ sends $(\widetilde{\mathrm{VK}_{i^*}}, \widetilde{\mathrm{VK}_{i^*}})$ as forgery to $\mathcal{S}_1$ challenger, and wins with the same probability as $\mathcal{A}$.

5   Pseudorandom Puncturable Deterministic Encryption (PPDE)

In this section we describe another primitive, *pseudorandom puncturable deterministic encryption schemes*. This is a variation of puncturable deterministic encryption as put forth by Waters [16].

In this scheme, there is a setup algorithm PPDE.Setup which generates a key K, as well as a deterministic encryption algorithm PPDE.Enc which takes the key K and message m. Since encryption is deterministic, the security property cannot by IND-CPA; instead we introduce a "puncturing algorithm" PPDE.Puncture which inputs a key K and message m and outputs a punctured key $K\{m\}$; the security property is that the encryption of m appears uniformly random to an adversary in possession of $K\{m\}$.

The actual construction uses techniques very similar to the "hidden trigger" mechanism using puncturable PRF's, as described in [15]; this is also used by [16].

5.1   Definition

Let $\mathcal{M}$ be the message space. A *pseudorandom puncturable deterministic encryption scheme* (or *PPDE scheme*) for $\mathcal{M}$ and ciphertext space $\mathcal{CT} \subseteq \{0,1\}^{\ell}$ (for some polynomial ℓ), is defined to be a collection of four algorithms.

- PPDE.Setup(1^{λ}) takes the security parameter and generates a key K in keyspace $\mathcal{K}$. This algorithm is randomized.
- PPDE.Enc(K, m) takes a key $K \in \mathcal{K}$ and message $m \in \mathcal{M}$ and produces a ciphertext ct $\in \mathcal{CT}$. This algorithm is deterministic.
- PPDE.Dec(K, ct) takes a key $K \in \mathcal{K}$ and ciphertext ct $\in \mathcal{CT}$ and outputs $m \in \mathcal{M} \cup \{\perp\}$. This algorithm is deterministic.
- PPDE.Puncture(K, m) takes a key $K \in \mathcal{K}$ and message $m \in \mathcal{M}$ and produces a *punctured key* $K\{m\} \in \mathcal{K}$ and $y \in \{0,1\}^{\ell}$. This algorithm may be randomized.

Correctness. A PPDE scheme is correct if it satisfies the following conditions.

1. **Correct Decryption:** For all messages m and keys $K \leftarrow \mathcal{K}$, we require

$$\text{PPDE.Dec}(K, \text{PPDE.Enc}(K, m)) = m.$$

2. **Correct Decryption Using Punctured Key:** For all distinct messages m, for all keys $K \leftarrow \mathcal{K}$,

$$\Pr\left[\begin{array}{c} \#\{\text{ct} : \text{Decrypt}(K\{m\}, \text{ct}) \neq \text{Decrypt}(K, \text{ct})\} > 1 \Big| \\ (K\{m\}, y) \leftarrow \text{Puncture}(K, m) \end{array} \right]$$

is less than $\text{negl}(\lambda)$, where all probabilities are taken over the coins of PPDE.Puncture.

3. For all messages $m^* \in \mathcal{M}$ and keys $K \leftarrow \mathcal{K}$,

$$\left\{ y \mid (K\{m^*\}, y) \leftarrow \mathsf{PPDE.Puncture}(K, m^*) \right\} \approx U_\ell$$

where U_ℓ denotes the uniform distribution over $\{0,1\}^\ell$.

Definition 6. *A PPDE scheme is selectively secure if no PPT algorithm $\mathcal{A}$ can determine the bit b in the following game except with probability negligibly close to $\frac{1}{2}$:*

1. *$\mathcal{A}$ chooses a message m^* to send to the challenger.*
2. *The challenger chooses $K \leftarrow \mathsf{PPDE.Setup}(1^\lambda)$ and computes $(K\{m^*\}, y) \leftarrow \mathsf{PPDE.Puncture}(K, m^*)$ and $\mathrm{ct} = \mathsf{PPDE.Enc}(K, m^*)$. Next, it chooses $b \leftarrow \{0,1\}$. If $b = 0$, it sends $(K\{m^*\}, (\mathrm{ct}, y))$; otherwise it sends $(K\{m^*\}, (y, \mathrm{ct}))$.*
3. *$\mathcal{A}$ outputs a guess b' for b.*

5.2   Construction

Next, we construct a secure PPDE scheme using a pair F_1, F_2 of selectively secure puncturable PRFs. Here $F_1 : \{0,1\}^m \rightarrow \{0,1\}^n$ and $F_2 : \{0,1\}^n \rightarrow \{0,1\}^m$, where m and n are polynomials in the security parameter λ. Additionally, we require F_1 to be statistically injective.

Our keyspace $\mathcal{K}$ will be the product of the keyspaces of F_1 and F_2; the message space $\mathcal{M} = \{0,1\}^m$ and ciphertext space is $\mathcal{CT} = \{0,1\}^{m+n}$.

Our algorithms are defined as follows:

- $\mathsf{PPDE.Setup}(1^\lambda)$ runs the setup algorithms for F_1 and F_2 to obtain keys K_1, K_2 respectively. It outputs $K = (K_1, K_2)$.
- $\mathsf{PPDE.Enc}((K_1, K_2), m)$ computes $A = F_1(K_1, m)$ and outputs

$$\mathrm{ct} = (A, F_2(K_2, A) \oplus m)$$

- $\mathsf{PPDE.Dec}((K_1, K_2), (\mathrm{ct}_1, \mathrm{ct}_2))$ computes the message $m = F_2(K_2, \mathrm{ct}_1) \oplus \mathrm{ct}_2$. It then checks that $F_1(K_1, m) = \mathrm{ct}_1$; if so it outputs m, otherwise it outputs $\bot$.
- $\mathsf{PPDE.Puncture}((K_1, K_2), m)$ chooses $y = (y_1, y_2) \in \mathcal{CT}$ uniformly randomly. It computes $A = F_1(K_1, m)$, then punctures K_1 at m to obtain $K_1\{m\}$ and K_2 at $\{A, y_1\}$ to produce $K_2\{A, y_1\}$. It outputs

$$K\{m\} = (K_1\{m\}, K_2\{A, y_1\}), y = (y_1, y_2).$$

Correctness. We observe that as long as F_1 is injective (which occurs except with negligible probability in the coins of PPDE.Setup), decryption will be correct on all inputs using the punctured key. Here "correct" means: identical to the behavior at the punctured key on all points except the encryption of the punctured message, where the output is changed to $\bot$. (If F_1 were not injective, the puncturing of K_2 at the output of F_1 may cause other PRF outputs to be changed to $\bot$, violating the requirement that the set of changed outputs have size at most 1.)

Correctness of decryption using non-punctured keys is immediate.

Security. We argue security through a series of hybrids.

Theorem 2. *Suppose that no PPT adversary has advantage greater than ϵ_1 in the selective security game against F_1 or greater than ϵ_2 in the selective security game against F_2. Then no PPT adversary has advantage greater than $\epsilon_1 + \epsilon_2$ in the selective security game as defined in Definition 6.*

Proof. Let $\mathcal{A}$ be an arbitrary PPT adversary. We start by defining a sequence of hybrids.

Hyb_0. This hybrid is identical to the original security game with $b = 0$.

1. $\mathcal{A}$ chooses a message m^* to send to the challenger.
2. The challenger produces $(K_1, K_2) = \mathsf{PPDE.Setup}(1^\lambda)$. He computes the punctured key $(K\{m^*\}, (y_1, y_2)) \leftarrow \mathsf{PPDE.Puncture}((K_1, K_2), m^*)$ and sends $K\{m^*\}$ to $\mathcal{A}$. He also computes $A = F_1(K_1, m^*)$ and sends $\mathsf{ct} = (A, F_2(K_2, A) \oplus m^*)$.

Hyb_1. This hybrid is same as the previous one, except that A is replaced by y_1.

1. $\mathcal{A}$ chooses a message m^* to send to the challenger.
2. The challenger produces $(K_1, K_2) = \mathsf{PPDE.Setup}(1^\lambda)$. He computes the punctured key $(K\{m^*\}, (y_1, y_2)) \leftarrow \mathsf{PPDE.Puncture}((K_1, K_2), m^*)$ and sends $K\{m^*\}$ to $\mathcal{A}$.
   He sends $\underline{\mathsf{ct} = (y_1, F_2(K_2, y_1) \oplus m^*)}$ as the ciphertext.

Hyb_2. This hybrid is the same as the previous one, except that $F_2(K_2, A)$ is replaced by y_2. The ciphertext is now $(y_1, y_2 \oplus m^*)$.

1. $\mathcal{A}$ chooses a message m^* to send to the challenger.
2. The challenger produces $(K_1, K_2) = \mathsf{PPDE.Setup}(1^\lambda)$. He computes the punctured key $(K\{m^*\}, (y_1, y_2)) \leftarrow \mathsf{PPDE.Puncture}((K_1, K_2), m^*)$ and sends $K\{m^*\}$ to $\mathcal{A}$.
   He sends $\underline{\mathsf{ct} = (y_1, y_2 \oplus m^*)}$ as the ciphertext.

We see that Hyb_2 is the original security game with $b = 1$, except for the presence of $y_2 \oplus m^*$ in place of y_2, which does not affect an attacker's advantage. We need only now to argue that these hybrids are indistinguishable.

Hyb_0 to Hyb_1. We claim that an attacker $\mathcal{A}$ which can distinguish between Hyb_0 and Hyb_1 with advantage ϵ can be used by a simulator $\mathcal{B}$ to win the selective security game against F_1 with advantage ϵ.

$\mathcal{B}$ acts as follows:

1. $\mathcal{A}$ sends a message m^* to $\mathcal{B}$, who gives it to the PRF challenger. The challenger replies with a punctured key $K_1(m^*)$ and a challenge pair (x_1, x_2) consisting of $F_1(K_1, m^*)$ and a uniformly random element.

2. $\mathcal{B}$ computes $K_2 = \mathsf{Setup}_{F_2}(1^\lambda)$ and $K_2(x_1, x_2) = \mathsf{Puncture}_{F_2}(K_2, \{x_1, x_2\})$. He sets $K(m^*) = (K_1(m^*), K_2(x_1, x_2))$, ct $= (x_1, F_2(K_2, x_1))$, and sends these to $\mathcal{A}$.
3. $\mathcal{A}$ outputs a guess b that he is in Hyb_b.

We see that if $\mathcal{A}$ is in Hyb_0, this is exactly the case that the PRF challenger set $x_1 = F_1(K_1, m^*)$; Hyb_1 is the case when $x_2 = F_1(K_1, m^*)$. Thus $\mathcal{A}$'s guess can be translated into a guess for which of $\{x_1, x_2\}$ is equal to $F_1(K_1, m^*)$ which is correct exactly when $\mathcal{A}$ is, so that $\mathcal{A}$'s advantage can be at most ϵ_{F_1}.

Hyb_1 to Hyb_2. We claim that an attacker $\mathcal{A}$ which can distinguish between Hyb_1 and Hyb_2 with advantage ϵ can be used by a simulator $\mathcal{B}$ to win the selective security game against F_2 with advantage ϵ.

$\mathcal{B}$ acts as follows:

1. $\mathcal{A}$ sends a message m^* to $\mathcal{B}$. $\mathcal{B}$ computes $K_1 = \mathsf{Setup}_{F_1}(1^\lambda)$ and chooses (y_1, y_2) uniformly at random. It computes $A = F_1(K_1, m^*)$ and submits $\{y_1, A\}$ to the challenger as his selective challenge.
2. The challenger replies with a punctured key $K_2(A, y_1)$ and a pair (x_1, x_2) consisting of both $F_2(K_2, A)$ and a uniformly random element. (In fact, the challenger also provides a pair consisting of $F_2(K_2, y_1)$, but we do not need this and ignore it.)
3. $\mathcal{B}$ sets $K(m^*) = (K_1(m^*), K_2(A, y_1))$ and sends this to $\mathcal{A}$. He also sends ct $= (A, x_1 \oplus m^*)$.
4. $\mathcal{A}$ outputs a guess b that he is in Hyb_{b+1}.

We see that if $\mathcal{A}$ is in Hyb_1, this is exactly the case that the PRF challenger set $x_1 = F_2(K_2, A)$; Hyb_2 is exactly the case that the challenger set $x_2 = F_2(K_2, A)$. We conclude that $\mathcal{A}$'s advantage can be at most ϵ_{F_2}.

Conclusion. Summing the attacker's maximum advantage in distinguishing the hybrids and winning in the game of Hyb_2, we see that the maximum advantage in the selective security game for the PPDE scheme is $\epsilon_{F_1} + \epsilon_{F_2}$.

6   Signed Universal Samplers

In this section, we will describe our construction for a signed universal sampler scheme. We will show that it is both simulation secure (as per Definition 4) and secure against forgeries (as per Definition 3).

A remarkable feature of our scheme is its simplicity. The sampler setup algorithm will first generate a prefix restricted signature scheme verification and signing key pair. Next the universal sampler parameters are created as the obfuscation of a program that takes two inputs x, d and outputs $p = d(r)$, where r is computed using a puncturable PRF on input $x||d$. The program also outputs a signature σ (using the signing key) on $(x||d, p)$ using a prefix-restricted signature scheme. The sampler parameters, U, are the obfuscated program and the verification key VK of the universal sampler is the verification key of the prefix restricted signature.

To sample from a distribution d, one computes $x = H(d)$ and runs the sampler output on inputs x, d. Finally, the verification algorithm is used to check that p was the correct output sample for a circuit d when given a prefix restricted signature σ. The verification algorithm first computes $x = H(d)$. Then, it simply checks that the signature σ verifies on the message $m = (m_1, m_2) = (x||d, p)$.

Our Construction. Let (Pre.Setup, Pre.Sign, Pre.Verify, Restrict, ResSign) be a restructed-prefix signature scheme, F a puncturable PRF with algorithms F.setup, F.puncture and F.eval, PPDE = (PPDE.Setup, PPDE.Enc, PPDE.Dec, PPDE.Puncture) a puncturable deterministic encryption scheme with pseudorandom ciphertexts.

Our $(\ell_{\text{ckt}}, \ell_{\text{rnd}}, \ell_{\text{out}})$-signed universal sampler scheme consists of the following algorithms.

USampler

Inputs $x \in \{0,1\}^{\ell_1}$, $d \in \{0,1\}^{\ell_{\text{ckt}}}$.

Constants Puncturable PRF key K_F, prefix-restricted signing key SK_{pre}.

Compute $r = F(K, (x||d))$.
Compute out $= d(r)$.
Compute $\sigma = \text{Pre.Sign}(\text{SK}_{\text{pre}}, (x||d, \text{out}))$.
Output (out, σ).

Fig. 1. Program USampler

- Setup(1^λ) The setup algorithm first chooses a signing and verification key for the restricted-prefix signature scheme; it computes $(\text{SK}_{\text{pre}}, \text{VK}_{\text{pre}}) \leftarrow$ Pre.Setup(1^λ). Next, it chooses a puncturable PRF key $K_F \leftarrow F$.setup(1^λ) and sets U to be an obfuscation of the program USampler[4] defined in Fig. 1; that is, $U \leftarrow i\mathcal{O}(\text{USampler})$ and $\text{VK} = \text{VK}_{\text{pre}}$. It outputs (U, VK).
- Sample(U, d) The sample generation algorithm computes $x = H(d)$ and $(p_d, \sigma) = U(x, d)$. It outputs (p_d, σ).
- Verify($\text{VK}, d, p_d, \sigma$) The verification algorithm computes $x = H(d)$ and then outputs Pre.Verify($\text{VK}, (x||d, p_d), \sigma$).

6.1   Proof of Unforgeability

We will define a sequence of hybrids to show that the construction satisfies the adaptive unforgeability definition.

Without loss of generality, let us assume the adversary $\mathcal{A}$ makes q unique random oracle queries before submitting the forgery corresponding to one of the queries.

---

[4] Padded to be of the same size as the corresponding programs in the proof.

Proof Intuition. This proof is fairly straightforward. The challenger first guesses the random oracle query which corresponds to the forgery. Let this query be d^*. The challenger then modifies the obfuscated program USampler to use a restricted signing key. Once the program has a restricted signing key, we can use the security of our special signature scheme to argue that the adversary cannot forge a signature corresponding to d^*.

Hybrid Hyb_0. Hyb_0 is the real security game between an adversary $\mathcal{A}$ and challenger.

1. Challenger computes universal samplers. It chooses $K_F \leftarrow F.\mathsf{setup}(1^\lambda)$, $(\mathrm{SK}_{\mathrm{pre}}, \mathrm{VK}_{\mathrm{pre}}) \leftarrow \mathsf{Pre.Setup}(1^\lambda)$ and computes $U \leftarrow i\mathcal{O}(\mathsf{USampler}\{K_F, \mathrm{SK}_{\mathrm{pre}}\})$.
   It sends $(U, \mathrm{VK}_{\mathrm{pre}})$ to $\mathcal{A}$.
2. $\mathcal{A}$ sends q random oracle queries. For i^{th} query d_i, the challenger chooses uniformly random strings $x_i \leftarrow \{0,1\}^{\ell_1}$, sets $H_1(d_i) = x_i$; it sends $H_1(d_i)$ to $\mathcal{A}$.
3. $\mathcal{A}$ finally sends the forgery (d^*, p^*, σ^*) and wins if
   (a) $d^* = d_i$ for some $i \in [q]$,
   (b) $\mathsf{Sample}(U, d^*)_1 \neq p^*$; that is, $x^* = H_1(d^*)$, $(\mathsf{out}, \sigma) = U(x^*, d^*)$ and $\mathsf{out} \neq p^*$,
   (c) $\mathsf{Verify}(\mathrm{VK}_{\mathrm{pre}}, (x^* || d^*, p^*), \sigma^*) = 1$.

Hybrid Hyb_1. In this experiment, the challenger guesses the random oracle query which will correspond to the forgery. If this guess is incorrect, the challenger aborts.

1. Challenger first chooses $i^* \leftarrow [q]$.
2. Challenger computes universal samplers. It chooses $K_F \leftarrow F.\mathsf{setup}(1^\lambda)$, $(\mathrm{SK}_{\mathrm{pre}}, \mathrm{VK}_{\mathrm{pre}}) \leftarrow \mathsf{Pre.Setup}(1^\lambda)$ and computes $U \leftarrow i\mathcal{O}(\mathsf{USampler}\{K_F, \mathrm{SK}_{\mathrm{pre}}\})$.
   It sends $(U, \mathrm{VK}_{\mathrm{pre}})$ to $\mathcal{A}$.
3. $\mathcal{A}$ sends q random oracle queries. For i^{th} query d_i, the challenger chooses uniformly random strings $x_i \leftarrow \{0,1\}^{\ell_1}$, sets $H_1(d_i) = x_i$; it sends $H_1(d_i)$ to $\mathcal{A}$.
4. $\mathcal{A}$ finally sends the forgery (d^*, p^*, σ^*) and wins if
   (a) $\underline{d^* = d_i}$,
   (b) $\mathsf{Sample}(U, d^*)_1 \neq p^*$; that is, $x^* = H_1(d^*)$, $(\mathsf{out}, \sigma) = U(x^*, d^*)$ and $\mathsf{out} \neq p^*$,
   (c) $\mathsf{Verify}(\mathrm{VK}_{\mathrm{pre}}, (x^* || d^*, p^*), \sigma^*) = 1$.

Hybrid Hyb_2. In this experiment, the challenger guesses the circuit sent as the $(i^*)^{th}$ random oracle query. If this guess is incorrect, the challenger aborts.

1. Challenger first chooses $i^* \leftarrow [q]$.
2. Challenger chooses $\underline{d' \leftarrow \{0,1\}^{\ell_{\mathrm{ckt}}}, x' \leftarrow \{0,1\}^{\ell_1}}$ and sets $\underline{H_1(d') = x'}$.

3. Challenger computes universal samplers. It chooses $K_F \leftarrow F.\text{setup}(1^\lambda)$, $(\text{SK}_{\text{pre}}, \text{VK}_{\text{pre}}) \leftarrow \text{Pre.Setup}(1^\lambda)$ and computes $U \leftarrow i\mathcal{O}(\text{USampler} \{K_F, \text{SK}_{\text{pre}}\})$.
   It sends $(U, \text{VK}_{\text{pre}})$ to $\mathcal{A}$.

4. $\mathcal{A}$ sends q random oracle queries. For i^{th} query d_i, if $i \neq i^*$, the challenger chooses uniformly random strings $x_i \leftarrow \{0,1\}^{\ell_1}$, sets $H_1(d_i) = x_i$; it sends $H_1(d_i)$ to $\mathcal{A}$.
   If $i = i^*$ and $d_i = d'$, it sends x' to $\mathcal{A}$, else it aborts.

5. $\mathcal{A}$ finally sends the forgery (d^*, p^*, σ^*) and wins if
   (a) $\underline{d^* = d'}$,
   (b) $(\text{out}, \sigma) = U(x', d')$ and out $\neq p^*$,
   (c) $\text{Verify}(\text{VK}_{\text{pre}}, (x'||d', p^*), \sigma^*) = 1$.

Hybrid Hyb$_3$. In this experiment, the challenger outputs the obfuscation of USampler' (defined in Fig. 2) instead of USampler. The only difference between USampler and USampler' is that USampler' uses a restricted signing key.

USampler'

Inputs $x \in \{0,1\}^{\ell_1}$, $d \in \{0,1\}^{\ell_{\text{ckt}}}$.

Constants Puncturable PRF key K_F, prefix-restricted signing key $\text{SK}\{(x'||d', \text{out}')\}$.

   Compute $r = F(K, (x||d))$.
   Compute out $= d(r)$.
   Compute $\sigma = \text{ResSign}(\text{SK}\{(x'||d', \text{out}')\}, (x||d, \text{out}))$.
   Output (out, σ).

Fig. 2. Program USampler'

---

1. Challenger first chooses $i^* \leftarrow [q]$.
2. Challenger chooses $d' \leftarrow \{0,1\}^{\ell_{\text{ckt}}}$, $x' \leftarrow \{0,1\}^{\ell_1}$ and sets $H_1(d') = x'$.
3. Challenger computes universal samplers. It chooses $K_F \leftarrow F.\text{setup}(1^\lambda)$, $(\text{SK}_{\text{pre}}, \text{VK}_{\text{pre}}) \leftarrow \text{Pre.Setup}(1^\lambda)$.
   It computes $r' = F(K_F, x'||d')$, $\text{out}' = d(r')$.
   It computes $\text{SK}\{(x'||d', \text{out}')\} \leftarrow \text{Restrict}(\text{SK}_{\text{pre}}, (x'||d', \text{out}'))$.
   It sets $U \leftarrow i\mathcal{O}(\text{USampler}'\{K_F, \text{SK}\{x'||d', \text{out}'\}\})$.
   It sends $(U, \text{VK}_{\text{pre}})$ to $\mathcal{A}$.
4. $\mathcal{A}$ sends q random oracle queries. For i^{th} query d_i, if $i \neq i^*$, the challenger chooses uniformly random strings $x_i \leftarrow \{0,1\}^{\ell_1}$, sets $H_1(d_i) = x_i$; it sends $H_1(d_i)$ to $\mathcal{A}$.
   If $i = i^*$ and $d_i = d'$, it sends x' to $\mathcal{A}$, else it aborts.

5. $\mathcal{A}$ finally sends the forgery (d^*, p^*, σ^*) and wins if
   (a) $d^* = d'$,
   (b) $(\mathsf{out}, \sigma) = U(x', d')$ and $\mathsf{out} \neq p^*$,
   (c) $\mathsf{Verify}(\mathrm{VK}_{\mathrm{pre}}, (x'||d', p^*), \sigma^*) = 1$.

Next, we need to analyse the adversary's advantage in each of these games. This analysis is included in the full version of our paper.

6.2   Proof of Simulation Security

Let us assume the adversary $\mathcal{A}$ queries the random oracle by sending a message (RO, d) before sending a message (params, d). Without loss of generality, let q be the number of queries made by $\mathcal{A}$. We will define a sequence of hybrid experiments, and then show that any PPT adversary cannot distinguish between the hybrid experiments with advantage non-negligible in the security parameter λ.

Proof Intuition. First, we give a high level intuition of our proof strategy. The main idea is to gradually change the random oracle query responses from uniformly random strings to more structured strings which will allow simulation. First, the challenger modifies the program USampler in order to allow trapdoors. The program, instead of computing $r = F(K_F, x||d)$ and $p = d(r)$, first decrypts the string x. It also has a string α hardwired. If the decryption is successful, and the output message is $(\tilde{d}, a, m)$ where $d = \tilde{d}$, $\mathrm{PRG}(a) = \alpha$, then the program simply outputs m as the sampled parameter. Due to the security of PRG, we can argue that the adversary cannot notice the difference. Now, the challenger can modify the random oracle queries. For a query corresponding to circuit d, the challenger outputs an encryption of $(d, a, d(t))$ where t is a uniformly random string. This looks like a uniformly random string due to the property of PPDE ciphertexts. However, note that the obfuscated program has the decryption key hardwired. Using the techniques from punctured programming, we show how to transform the random oracle responses from truly random strings to PPDE encryptions.

Experiment Expt_0. This experiment corresponds to the real world. The challenger runs the universal sampler setup honestly to compute U, and sends it to the adversary $\mathcal{A}$. Next, for each random oracle query, it outputs a uniformly random string.

1. Challenger computes universal samplers. It chooses $K_F \leftarrow F.\mathsf{setup}(1^\lambda)$, $(\mathrm{SK}_{\mathrm{pre}}, \mathrm{VK}_{\mathrm{pre}}) \leftarrow \mathsf{Pre.Setup}(1^\lambda)$.
   It computes $U \leftarrow i\mathcal{O}(\mathsf{USampler}\{K_F, \mathrm{SK}_{\mathrm{pre}}\})$.
   It sends $(U, \mathrm{VK}_{\mathrm{pre}})$ to $\mathcal{A}$.
2. $\mathcal{A}$ sends q random oracle queries. For j^{th} query d_j,
   – The challenger chooses uniformly random strings $x_j \leftarrow \{0,1\}^{\ell_1}$, sets $H_1(d_j) = x_j$; it sends $H_1(d_j)$ to $\mathcal{A}$.
3. $\mathcal{A}$ finally sends a bit b.

```
                              USampler-1

    Inputs x ∈ {0,1}^{ℓ₁}, d ∈ {0,1}^{ℓ_ckt}.

    Constants         Puncturable      PRF       key        K_F,
    PPDE key K_PPDE, α ∈ {0,1}^{2λ}, prefix-restricted signing key SK_pre.

        Compute m = PPDE.Dec(K_PPDE, x). If m ≠⊥, let m = (d̃, a, y) ∈
        {0,1}^λ × {0,1}^{ℓ_out}.
        if m ≠⊥ and d̃ = d and α = PRG(a) then
            Set out = y.
        else
            Compute r = F(K, (x||d)).
            Compute out = d(r).
        end if
        Compute σ = Pre.Sign(SK_pre, (x||d, out)).
        Output (out, σ).
```

Fig. 3. Program USampler-1

The output of this experiment is b.

Experiment Expt₁. In this experiment, the challenger outputs an obfuscation of USampler-1 (defined in Fig. 3) as the universal sampler program output during setup. This new program has a PPDE key hardwired, and it uses this key to decrypt the input string. If the decryption is successful (and some additional checks are satisfied), the program outputs the decrypted string. Else, its output is the same as in previous experiment.

1. Challenger computes universal samplers. It chooses $K_F \leftarrow F.\text{setup}(1^\lambda)$, $(\text{SK}_\text{pre}, \text{VK}_\text{pre}) \leftarrow \text{Pre.Setup}(1^\lambda)$.
   It chooses K_PPDE and $\alpha \leftarrow \{0,1\}^{2\lambda}$.
   It computes $U \leftarrow i\mathcal{O}(\text{USampler}\{K_F, \text{SK}_\text{pre}, K_\text{PPDE}, \alpha\})$ and sends $(U, \text{VK}_\text{pre})$ to $\mathcal{A}$.
2. $\mathcal{A}$ sends q random oracle queries. For j^{th} query d_j,
   - The challenger chooses uniformly random strings $x_j \leftarrow \{0,1\}^{\ell_1}$, sets $H_1(d_j) = x_j$; it sends $H_1(d_j)$ to $\mathcal{A}$.
3. $\mathcal{A}$ finally sends a bit b.

Experiment Expt₂. In this experiment, the string α hardwired in the program is a pseudorandom string, computed using PRG.

1. Challenger computes universal samplers. It chooses $K_F \leftarrow F.\text{setup}(1^\lambda)$, $(\text{SK}_\text{pre}, \text{VK}_\text{pre}) \leftarrow \text{Pre.Setup}(1^\lambda)$.
   It chooses a puncturable PPDE key K_PPDE,
   $a \leftarrow \{0,1\}^\lambda$ and sets $\alpha = \text{PRG}(a)$.

It computes $U \leftarrow i\mathcal{O}(\mathsf{USampler}\{K_F, \mathrm{SK}_{\mathrm{pre}}, K_{\mathrm{PPDE}}, \alpha\})$ and sends $(U, \mathrm{VK}_{\mathrm{pre}})$ to $\mathcal{A}$.

2. $\mathcal{A}$ sends q random oracle queries. For j^{th} query d_j,
   - The challenger chooses uniformly random strings $x_j \leftarrow \{0,1\}^{\ell_1}$, sets $H_1(d_j) = x_j$; it sends $H_1(d_j)$ to $\mathcal{A}$.
3. $\mathcal{A}$ finally sends a bit b.

The output of this experiment is b

Next, we will have q hybrid experiments $\mathsf{Expt}_{2,i}$ for $0 \leq i \leq q$. In each hybrid, the challenger changes the response to the random oracle queries. Instead of sending uniformly random strings, it sends encryptions computed using $\mathsf{PPDE.Enc}(\cdot, \cdot)$.

Experiment $\mathsf{Expt}_{2,i}$. In this experiment, the challenger queries the Parameters Oracle to compute the response for the first i random oracle queries. For the remaining queries, it outputs a uniformly random string.

1. Challenger computes universal samplers. It chooses $K_F \leftarrow F.\mathsf{setup}(1^\lambda)$, $(\mathrm{SK}_{\mathrm{pre}}, \mathrm{VK}_{\mathrm{pre}}) \leftarrow \mathsf{Pre.Setup}(1^\lambda)$.
   It chooses a puncturable PPDE key K_{PPDE}, $a \leftarrow \{0,1\}^\lambda$ and sets $\alpha = \mathrm{PRG}(a)$.
   It computes $U \leftarrow i\mathcal{O}(\mathsf{USampler} - 1\{K_F, \mathrm{SK}_{\mathrm{pre}}, K_{\mathrm{PPDE}}, \alpha\})$ and sends $(U, \mathrm{VK}_{\mathrm{pre}})$ to $\mathcal{A}$.
2. $\mathcal{A}$ sends q random oracle queries. For j^{th} query d_j,
   - if $j \leq i$, the challenger queries the Parameter Oracle.
     On input d_j, it receives p_j in response.
     It sets $H_1(d_j) = \mathsf{PPDE.Enc}(K_{\mathrm{PPDE}}, p_j)$ and sends $H_1(d_j)$ to $\mathcal{A}$.
   - if $j > i$, the challenger chooses uniformly random strings $x_j \leftarrow \{0,1\}^{\ell_1}$, sets $H_1(d_j) = x_j$; it sends $H_1(d_j)$ to $\mathcal{A}$.
3. $\mathcal{A}$ finally sends a bit b.

The output of this experiment is b.

Clearly, $\mathsf{Expt}_{2,0}$ is identical to experiment Expt_2, while $\mathsf{Expt}_{2,q}$ corresponds to the ideal world. We now need to show that any PPT adversary has almost identical advantage in each of the experiments described above. Due to space constraints, the detailed analysis is included in the full version. Here, we give an outline of the proof.

In the first hybrid, the challenger replaces the program $\mathsf{USampler}$ with program $\mathsf{USampler}$-1. The only difference between these two programs is that $\mathsf{USampler}$-1 first decrypts the input x using PPDE key. If the decryption is successful and can be parsed as $(\tilde{d}, a, m)$, then the program checks if $d = \tilde{d}$ and $\mathrm{PRG}(a) = \alpha$, where α is a uniformly random string. As a result, this step is never executed, and hence the two programs are identical. Therefore, using security of $i\mathcal{O}$, the hybrids are computationally indistinguishable.

Next, the challenger replaces α with a pseudorandom string. It chooses a string a and sets $\alpha = \text{PRG}(a)$. This step is indistinguishable due to the security of PRG.

Now, the first step of the program is "Decrypt x. If decryption is successful, and outputs $(\tilde{d}, a, m)$ and $d = \tilde{d}$ and $\text{PRG}(a) = \alpha$, then output m". This gives the challenger a 'trapdoor'. Now, the adversary sends encryption of $(d, a, d(t))$ as the response for $\text{RO}(d)$. To prove that the adversary cannot distinguish between the encryptions and random strings, we define q hybrids. In the ith hybrid, the first i responses are encryptions, while the remaining are random strings. We now need to show that the ith and $(i+1)^{th}$ hybrids are indistinguishable. For this, the main idea is to first puncture the PPDE key, and then switch the random RO responses to ciphertexts. However, to puncture the PPDE key, we will need to know the 'puncture point' in advance, resulting in a subexponential security loss. Here, note that the security loss is $q \cdot 2^{\ell_{\text{ckt}}}$, not $2^{q\ell_{\text{ckt}}}$. This allows us to use complexity leveraging with subexponential security for $i\mathcal{O}$, PRG and F.

References

1. Ananth, P.V., Gupta, D., Ishai, Y., Sahai, A.: Optimizing obfuscation: avoiding Barrington's theorem. In: Proceedings of 2014 ACM SIGSAC Conference on Computer and Communications Security, Scottsdale, AZ, USA, 3–7 November 2014, pp. 646–658 (2014)
2. Applebaum, B., Brakerski, Z.: Obfuscating circuits via composite-order graded encoding. In: Dodis, Y., Nielsen, J.B. (eds.) TCC 2015. LNCS, vol. 9015, pp. 528–556. Springer, Heidelberg (2015). doi:10.1007/978-3-662-46497-7_21
3. Bellare, M., Rogaway, P.: Random oracles are practical: a paradigm for designing efficient protocols. In: ACM Conference on Computer and Communications Security, pp. 62–73 (1993)
4. Boneh, D., Waters, B.: Constrained pseudorandom functions and their applications. In: Sako, K., Sarkar, P. (eds.) ASIACRYPT 2013. LNCS, vol. 8270, pp. 280–300. Springer, Heidelberg (2013). doi:10.1007/978-3-642-42045-0_15
5. Boneh, D., Zhandry, M.: Multiparty key exchange, efficient traitor tracing, and more from indistinguishability obfuscation. In: Garay, J.A., Gennaro, R. (eds.) CRYPTO 2014. LNCS, vol. 8616, pp. 480–499. Springer, Heidelberg (2014). doi:10.1007/978-3-662-44371-2_27
6. Boyle, E., Goldwasser, S., Ivan, I.: Functional signatures and pseudorandom functions. In: Krawczyk, H. (ed.) PKC 2014. LNCS, vol. 8383, pp. 501–519. Springer, Heidelberg (2014). doi:10.1007/978-3-642-54631-0_29
7. Garg, S., Gentry, C., Halevi, S., Raykova, M., Sahai, A., Waters, B.: Candidate indistinguishability obfuscation and functional encryption for all circuits. In: FOCS (2013)
8. Goldreich, O.: Two remarks concerning the Goldwasser-Micali-Rivest signature scheme. In: Odlyzko, A.M. (ed.) CRYPTO 1986. LNCS, vol. 263, pp. 104–110. Springer, Heidelberg (1987). doi:10.1007/3-540-47721-7_8
9. Hofheinz, D., Jager, T., Khurana, D., Sahai, A., Waters, B., Zhandry, M.: How to generate and use universal parameters. In: ASIACRYPT (2016)
10. Hofheinz, D., Kamath, A., Koppula, V., Waters, B.: Adaptively secure constrained pseudorandom functions. Cryptology ePrint Archive, Report 2014/720 (2014). http://eprint.iacr.org/

11. Hohenberger, S., Koppula, V., Waters, B.: Universal signature aggregators. In: Advances in Cryptology - EUROCRYPT 2015–34th Annual International Conference on the Theory and Applications of Cryptographic Techniques, Sofia, Bulgaria, 26–30 April 2015, Proceedings, Part II, pp. 3–34 (2015)
12. Huang, Y., Katz, J., Evans, D.: Efficient secure two-party computation using symmetric cut-and-choose. In: Canetti, R., Garay, J.A. (eds.) CRYPTO 2013. LNCS, vol. 8043, pp. 18–35. Springer, Heidelberg (2013). doi:10.1007/978-3-642-40084-1_2
13. Kiayias, A., Papadopoulos, S., Triandopoulos, N., Zacharias, T.: Delegatable pseudorandom functions and applications. In: ACM Conference on Computer and Communications Security, pp. 669–684 (2013)
14. Naor, M., Yung, M.: Universal one-way hash functions and their cryptographic applications. In: Proceedings of 21st Annual ACM Symposium on Theory of Computing, 14–17 May 1989, Seattle, Washigton, USA, pp. 33–43 (1989)
15. Sahai, A., Waters, B.: How to use indistinguishability obfuscation: deniable encryption, and more. In: STOC, pp. 475–484 (2014)
16. Waters, B.: A punctured programming approach to adaptively secure functional encryption. In: Gennaro, R., Robshaw, M. (eds.) CRYPTO 2015. LNCS, vol. 9216, pp. 678–697. Springer, Heidelberg (2015). doi:10.1007/978-3-662-48000-7_33
17. Zimmerman, J.: How to obfuscate programs directly. In: Advances in Cryptology - EUROCRYPT 2015–34th Annual International Conference on the Theory and Applications of Cryptographic Techniques, Sofia, Bulgaria, 26–30 April 2015, Proceedings, Part II, pp. 439–467 (2015)

Author Index

Printed in the United States
By Bookmasters